Street by Street

GLASGOW

AYR, EAST KILBRIDE, GREENOCK, KILMARNOCK, PAISLEY

Clydebank, Coatbridge, Cumbernauld, Hamilton, Helensburgh, Irvine, Lanark, Largs, Motherwell, Shotts

Ist edition May 2001

© Automobile Association Developments Limited 2001

Published by AA Publishing (a trading name of Automobile Association Developments Limited, whose registered office is Norfolk House, Priestley Road, Basingstoke, Hampshire, RG24 9NY. Registered number 1878835).

Mapping produced by the Cartographic Department of The Automobile Association.

A CIP Catalogue record for this book is available from the British Library.

Printed by G. Canale & C. s.p.a., Torino, Italy

The contents of this atlas are believed to be correct at the time of the latest revision. However, the publishers cannot be held responsible for loss occasioned to any person acting or refraining from action as a result of any material in this atlas, nor for any errors, omissions or changes in such material. The publishers would welcome information to correct any errors or omissions and to keep this atlas up to date. Please write to Publishing, The Automobile Association, Fanum House, Basing View, Basingstoke, Hampshire, RG21 4EA.

Ref: MX071

Key to map pages	ii-iii
Key to map symbols	iv-1
Enlarged scale pages	2-19
Street by Street	20-231
Index – towns & villages	232
Index – streets	233-271
Index – featured places	272-277

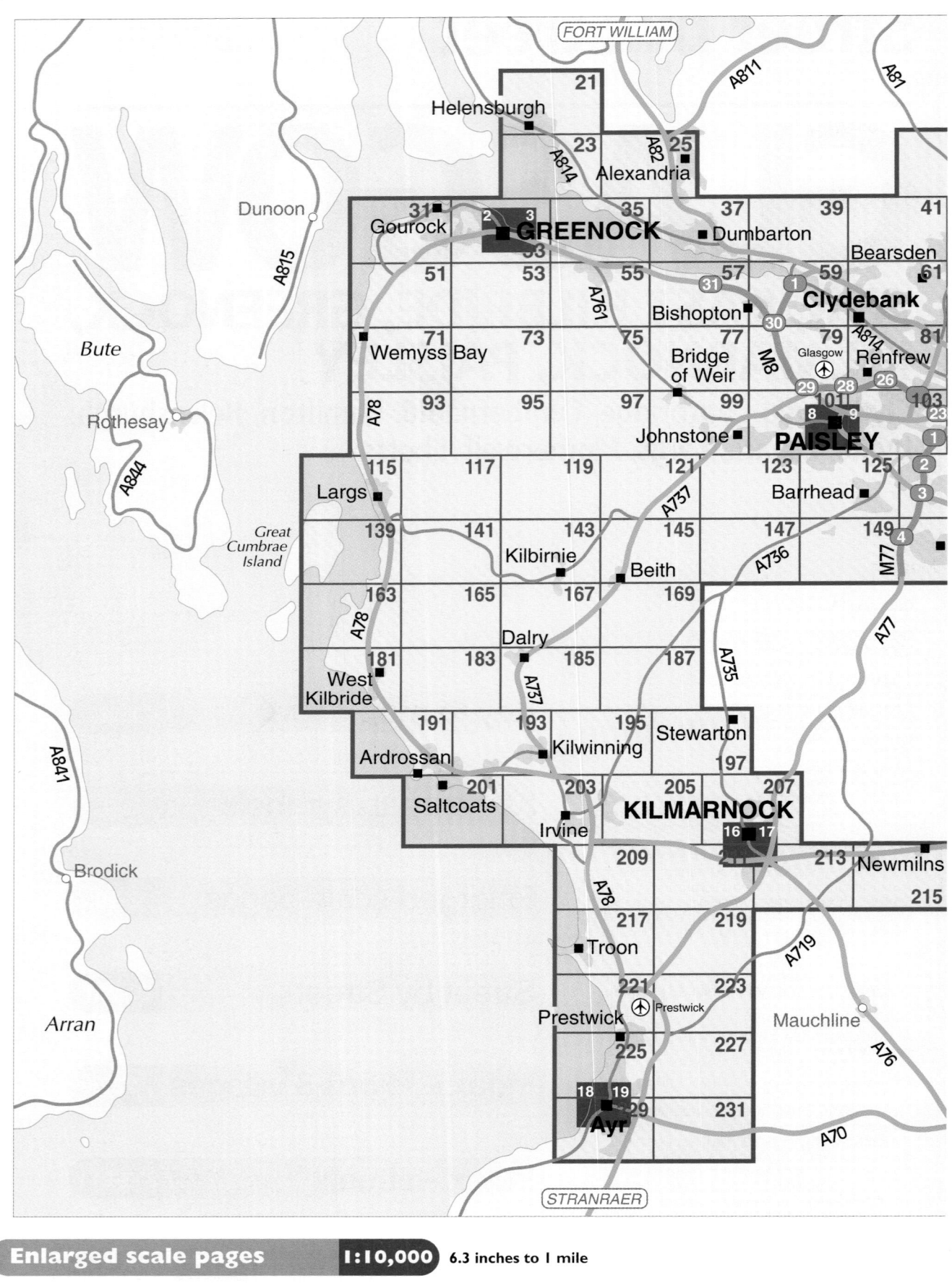

FORT WILLIAM

A811

A81

21

Helensburgh

23

A82

25

A814

Alexandria

Dunoon

A815

31

Gourock

2 **3**

GREENOCK

35

37

Dumbarton

39

41

Bearsden

33

51

53

A761

55

57

31

1

59

61

Bishopton

30

Clydebank

Bute

71

Wemyss Bay

73

75

77

Bridge
of Weir

M8

79

Glasgow

A814

81

Renfrew

Rothesay

A844

93

A78

95

97

99

Johnstone

29

28

26

101

8

9

103

23

PAISLEY

1

Great
Cumbrae
Island

115

Largs

117

119

121

A737

123

125

Barrhead

2

3

139

141

143

Kilbirnie

145

147

A736

149

M77

4

163

A78

165

167

Dalry

169

A735

A77

A841

181

West
Kilbride

183

A737

185

187

191

Ardrossan

193

Kilwinning

195

Stewarton

197

Brodick

201

Saltcoats

203

205

207

KILMARNOCK

16 **17**

213

Newmilns

Irvine

209

A78

211

215

217

Troon

219

A719

221

Prestwick

Prestwick

223

Mauchline

A76

Arran

225

227

18 **19**

29

Ayr

231

A70

STRANRAER

Enlarged scale pages 1:10,000 6.3 inches to 1 mile

0 1/4 miles 1/2 3/4

0 1/4 kilometres 1/2 3/4 1 1 1/4

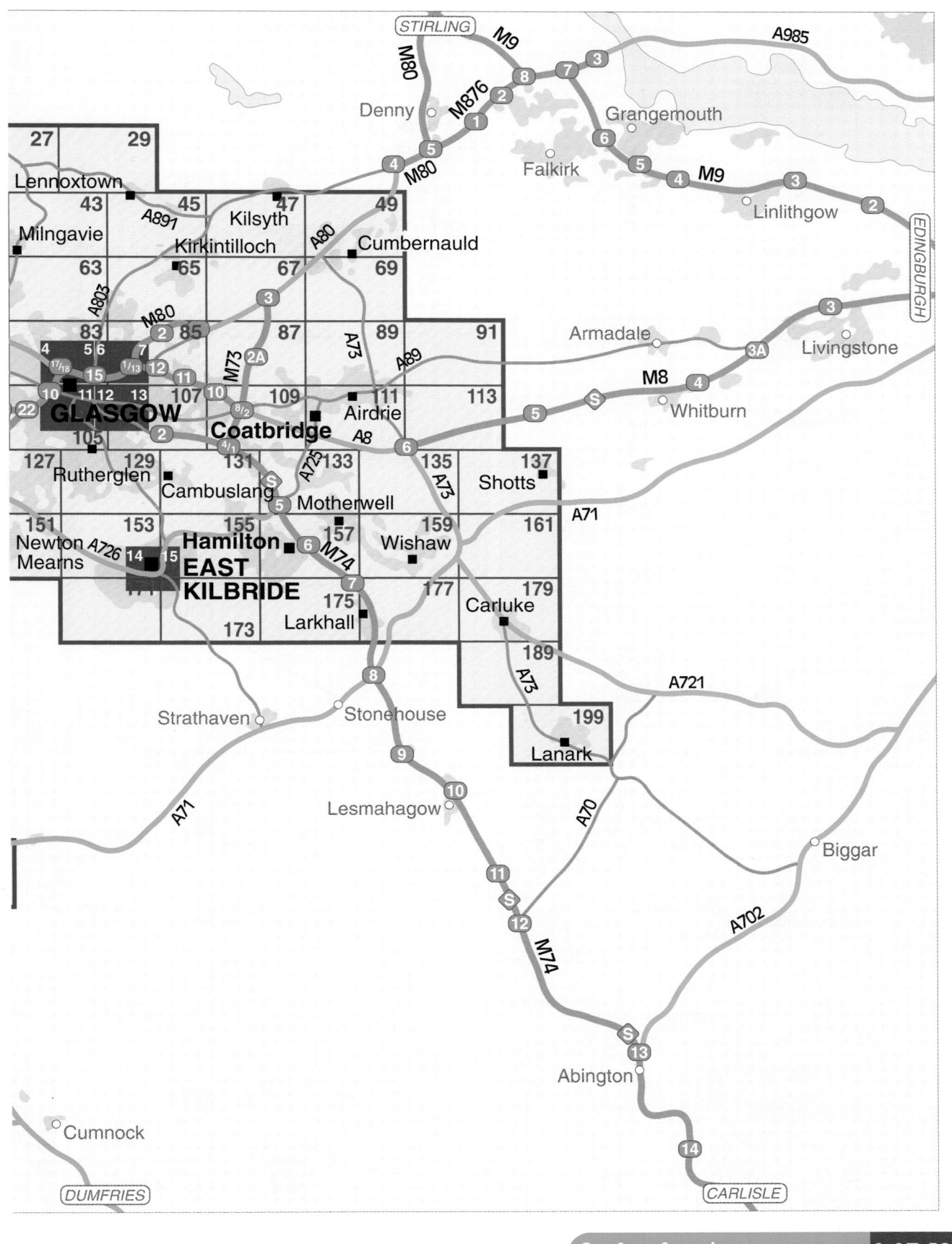

STIRLING

M80

M9

A985

Denny

M876

Grangemouth

M80

Falkirk

M9

Linlithgow

EDINGBURGH

27 | 29

Lennoxtown

43 | 45 | 47 | 49

Milngavie | A891 | Kilsyth | Cumbernauld

Kirkintilloch | A80

63 | 65 | 67 | 69

A803 | M80

Armadale

Livingstone

83 | 85 | 87 | 89 | 91

4 | 5 | 6 | 7 | M73 | 2A | A73 | A89

17/18 | 15 | 1/13 | 12 | 11

M8

10 | 11 | 12 | 13 | 107 | 10 | 109 | 111 | 113

Whitburn

22 | **GLASGOW** | 8/2 | **Coatbridge** | Airdrie

2 | A8

105 | 4/1

127 | 129 | 131 | 133 | 135 | 137

Rutherglen | Cambuslang | A725 | A73 | Shotts

Motherwell

A71

151 | 153 | 155 | 157 | 159 | 161

Newton | A726 | **Hamilton** | M74 | Wishaw

Mearns | 14 | 15 | **EAST**

KILBRIDE | 175 | 177 | 179

171 | 173 | Larkhall | Carluke

189 | A721

A73

Strathaven | Stonehouse | 199

Lanark

Lesmahagow | A70 | Biggar

A71 | A702

Cumnock | M74

Abington

DUMFRIES | CARLISLE

3.6 inches to 1 mile | **Scale of main map pages** | **1:17,500**

0 | 1/2 | miles | 1

0 | 1/2 | 1 | kilometres | 1 1/2 | 2

Junction 9	Motorway & junction
Services	Motorway service area
	Primary road single/dual carriageway
Services	Primary road service area
	A road single/dual carriageway
	B road single/dual carriageway
	Other road single/dual carriageway
	Restricted road
	Private road
←	One way street
	Pedestrian street
	Track/ footpath
	Road under construction
	Road tunnel
P	Parking
P+	Park & Ride
	Bus/coach station
	Railway & main railway station
	Railway & minor railway station
	Underground station
	Light railway & station
	Preserved private railway
LC	Level crossing
	Tramway
	Ferry route
	Airport runway
	Boundaries- borough/ district
	Mounds
93	Page continuation 1:17,500
7	Page continuation to enlarged scale 1:10,000

River/canal lake, pier	Toilet with disabled facilities
Aqueduct lock, weir	Petrol station
465 ▲ Winter Hill — Peak (with height in metres)	Public house
Beach	Post Office
Coniferous woodland	Public library
Broadleaved woodland	Tourist Information Centre
Mixed woodland	Castle
Park	Historic house/ building
Cemetery	Wakehurst Place NT — National Trust property
Built-up area	Museum/ art gallery
Featured building	Church/chapel
City wall	Country park
A&E — Accident & Emergency hospital	Theatre/ performing arts
Toilet	Cinema

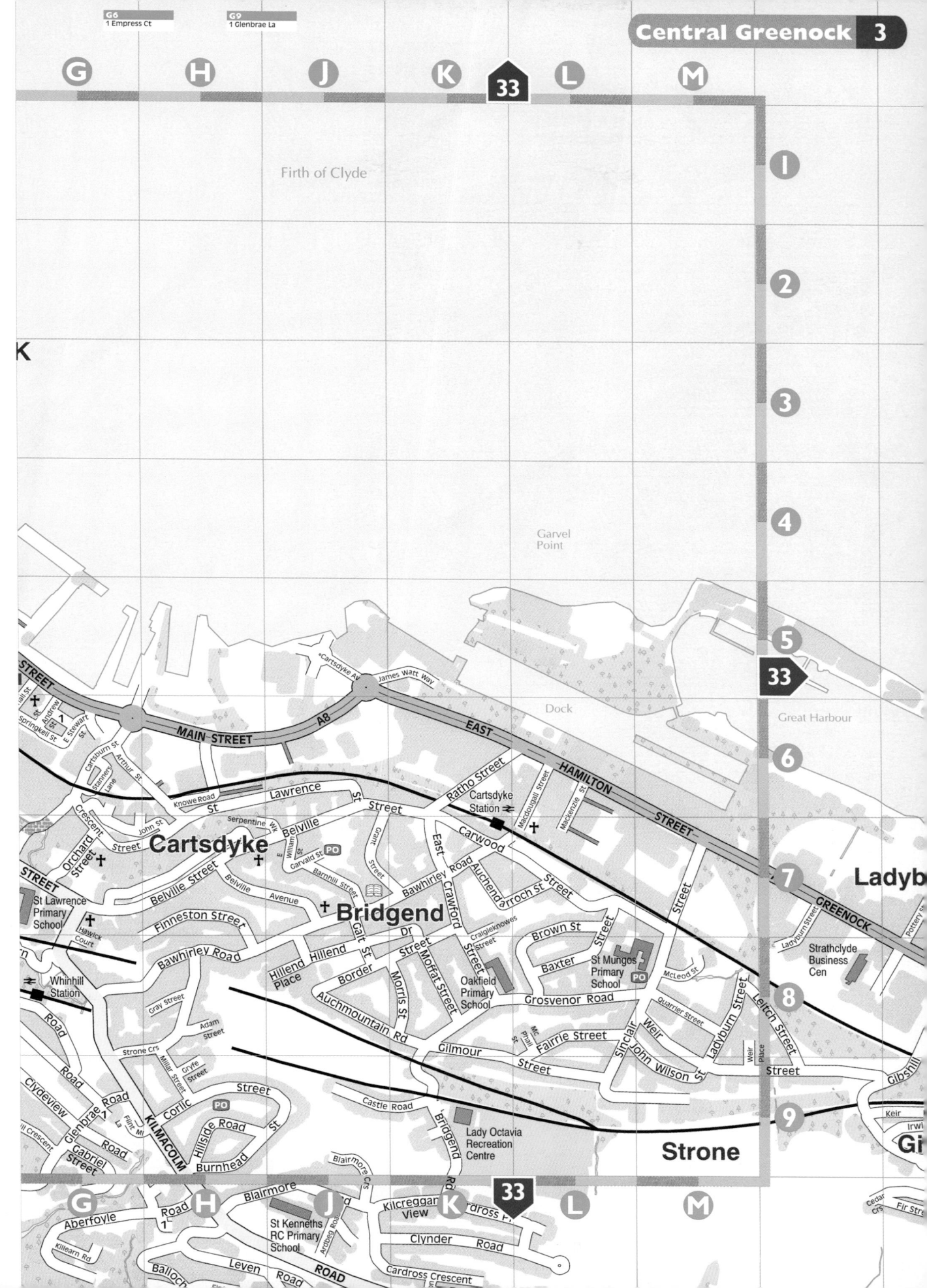

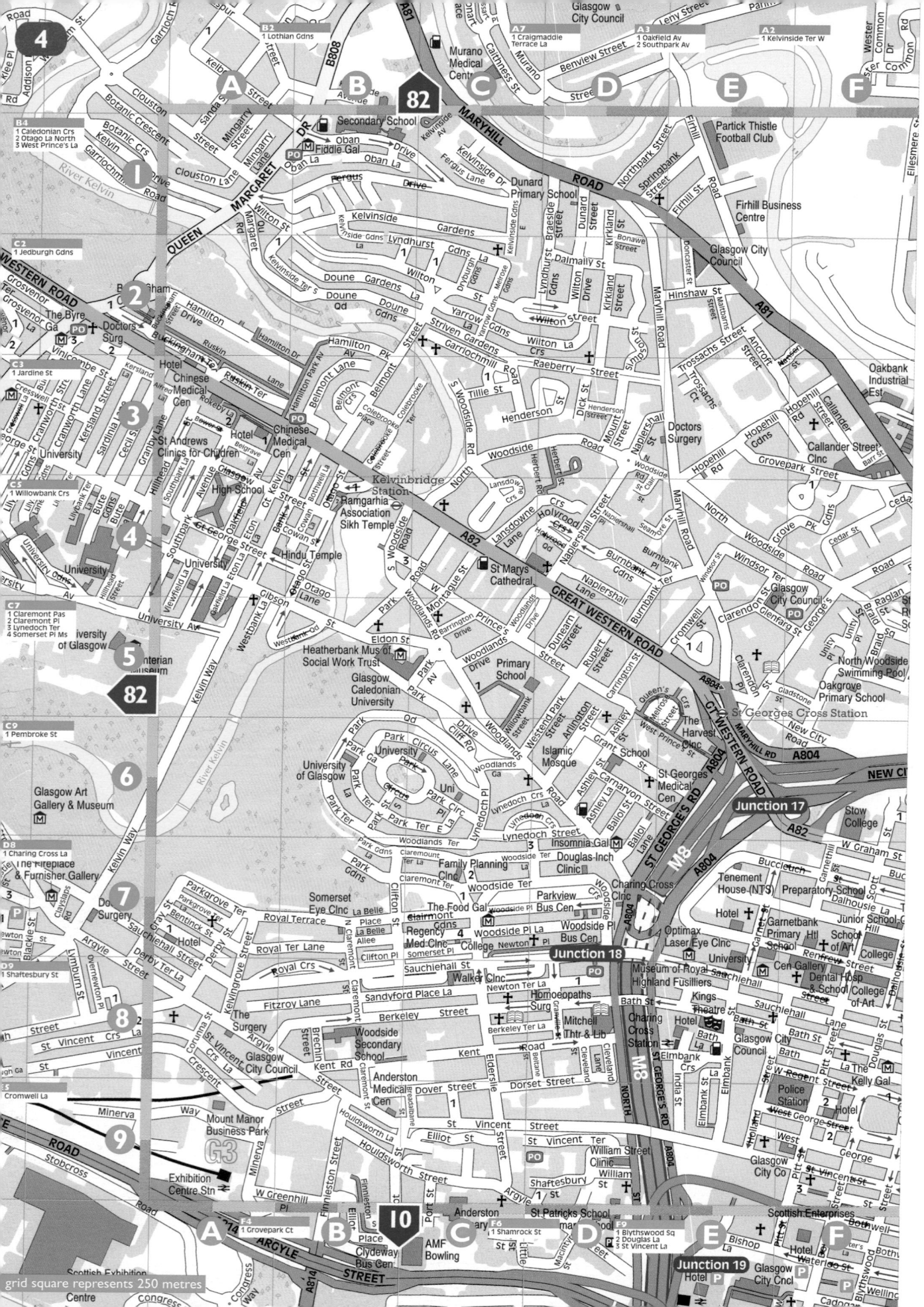

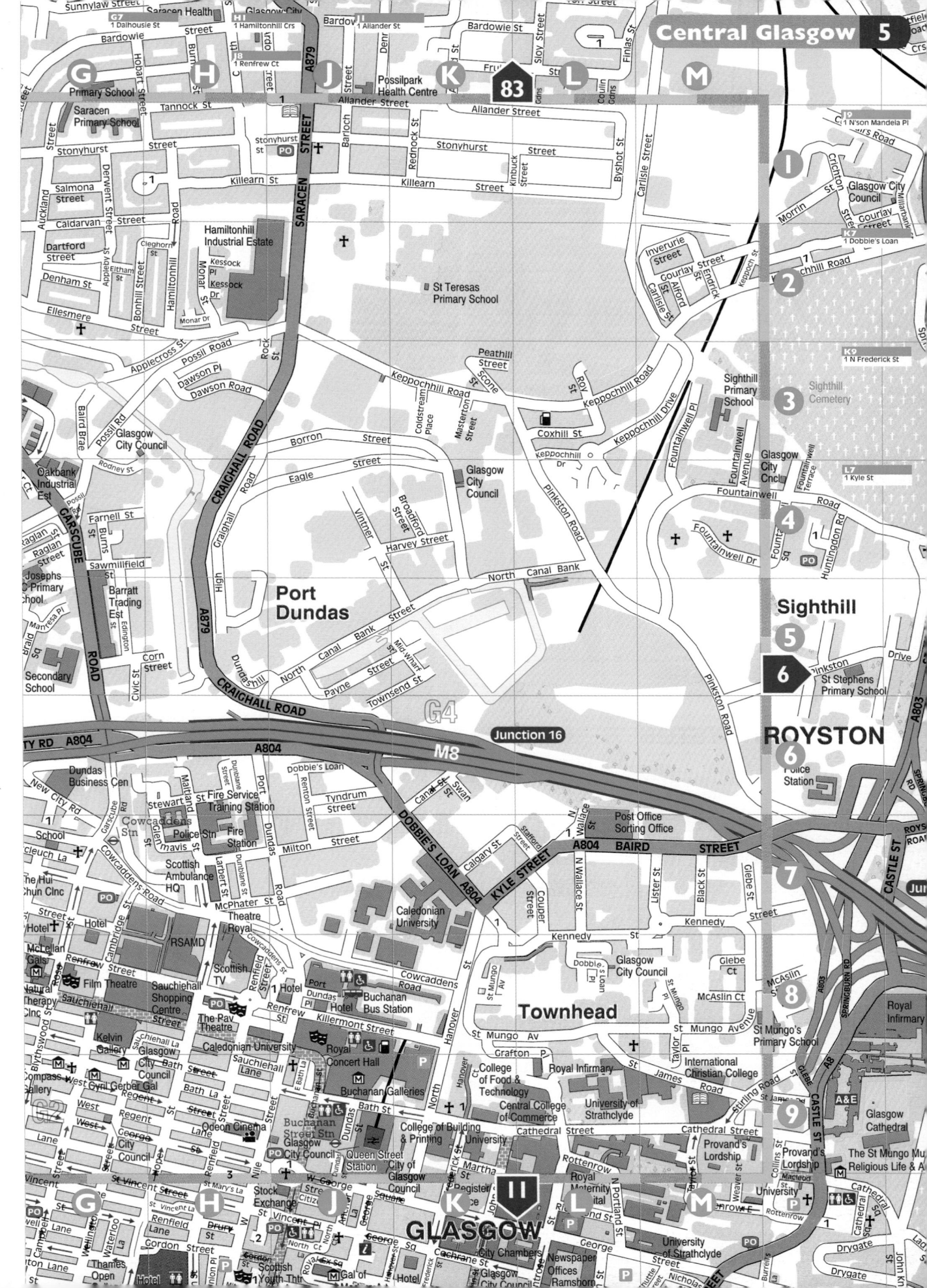

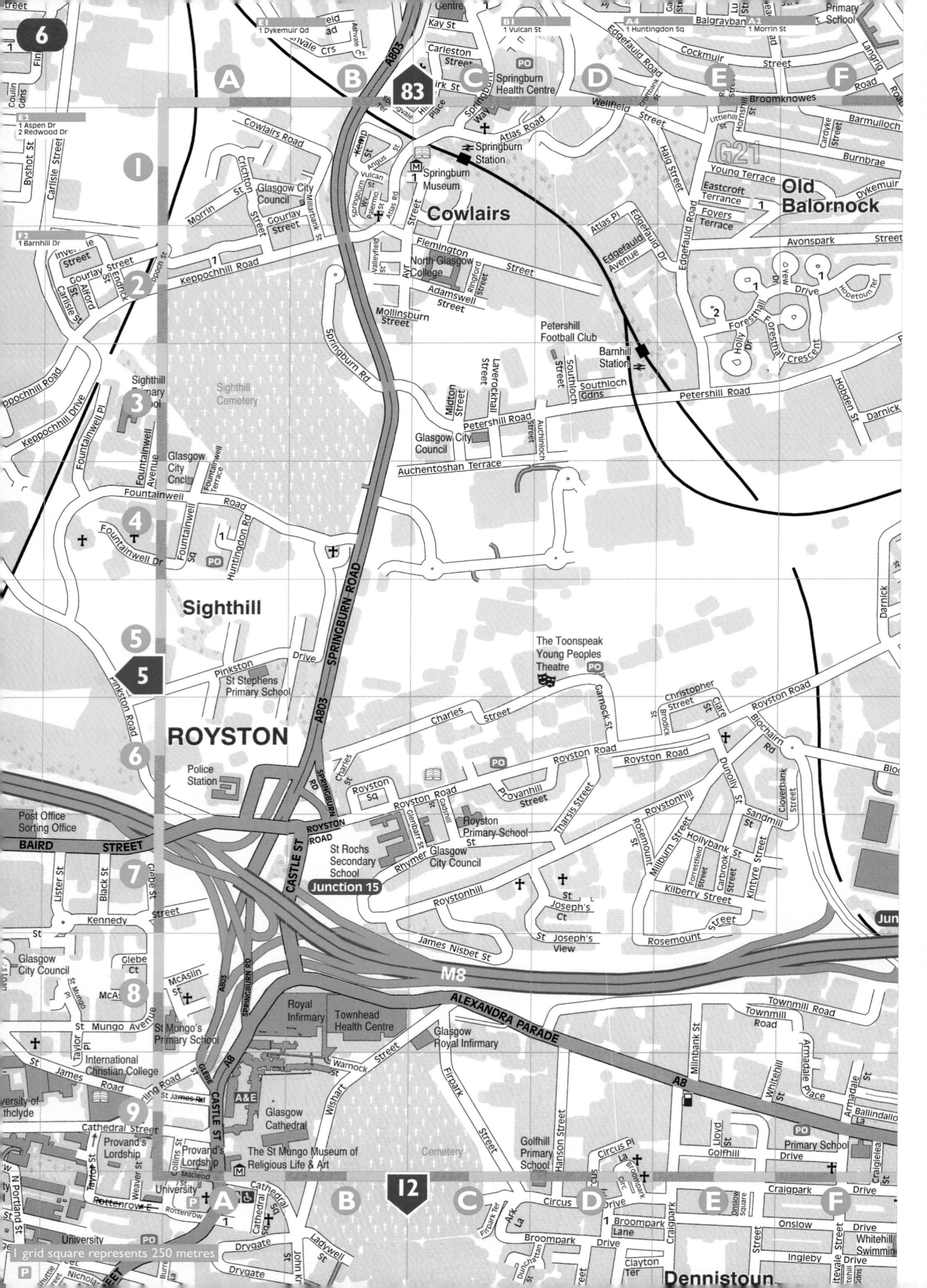

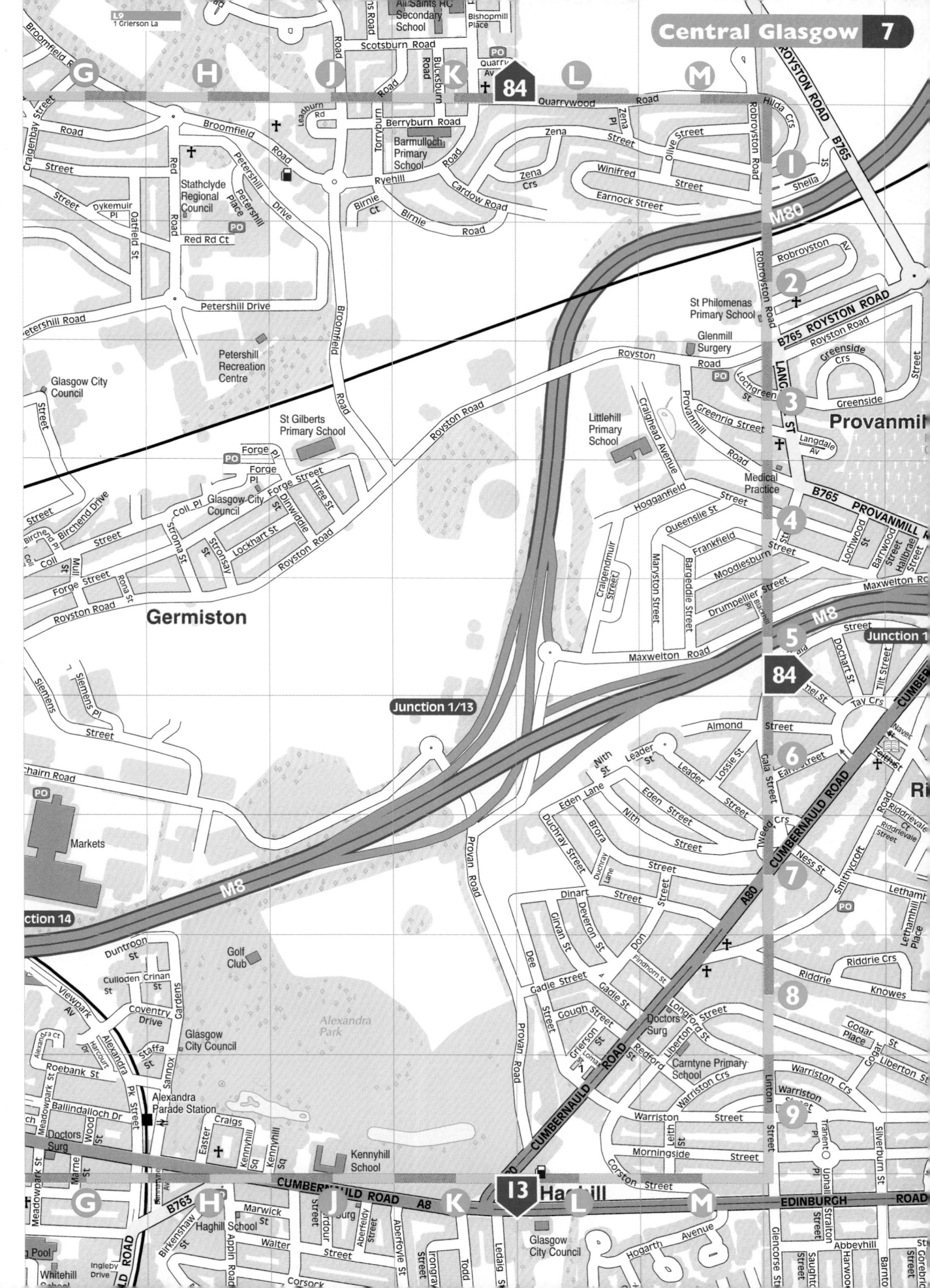

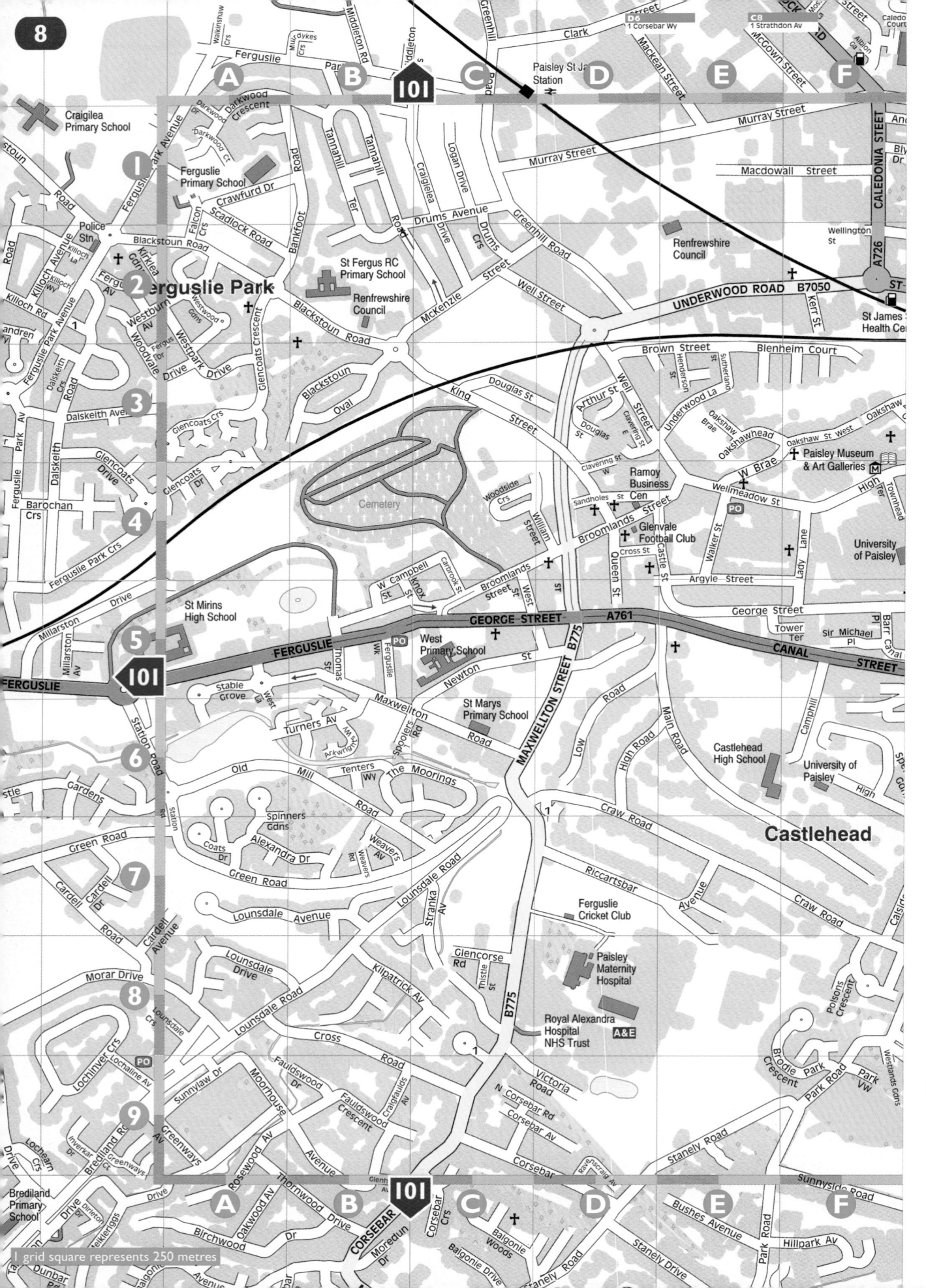

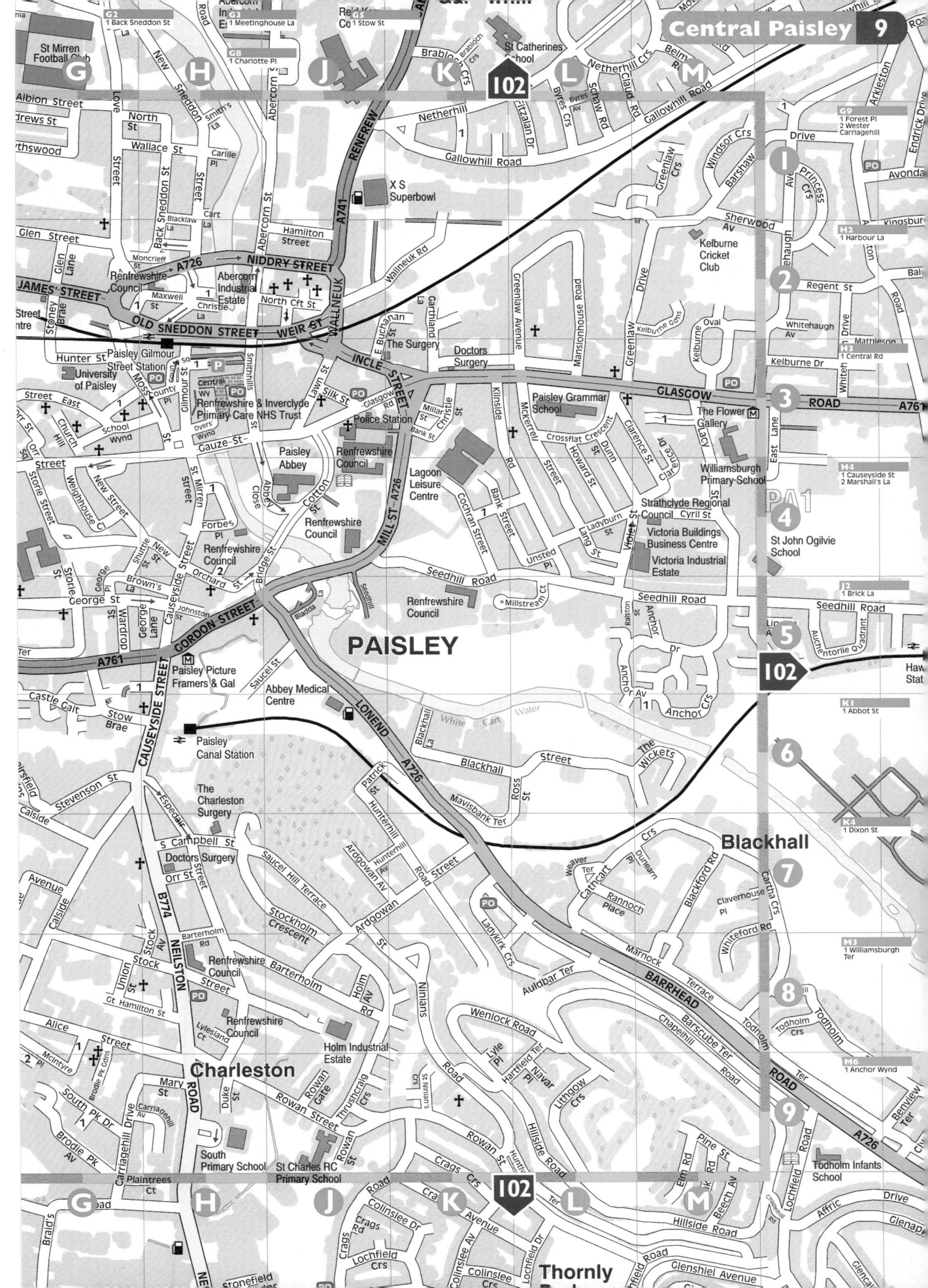

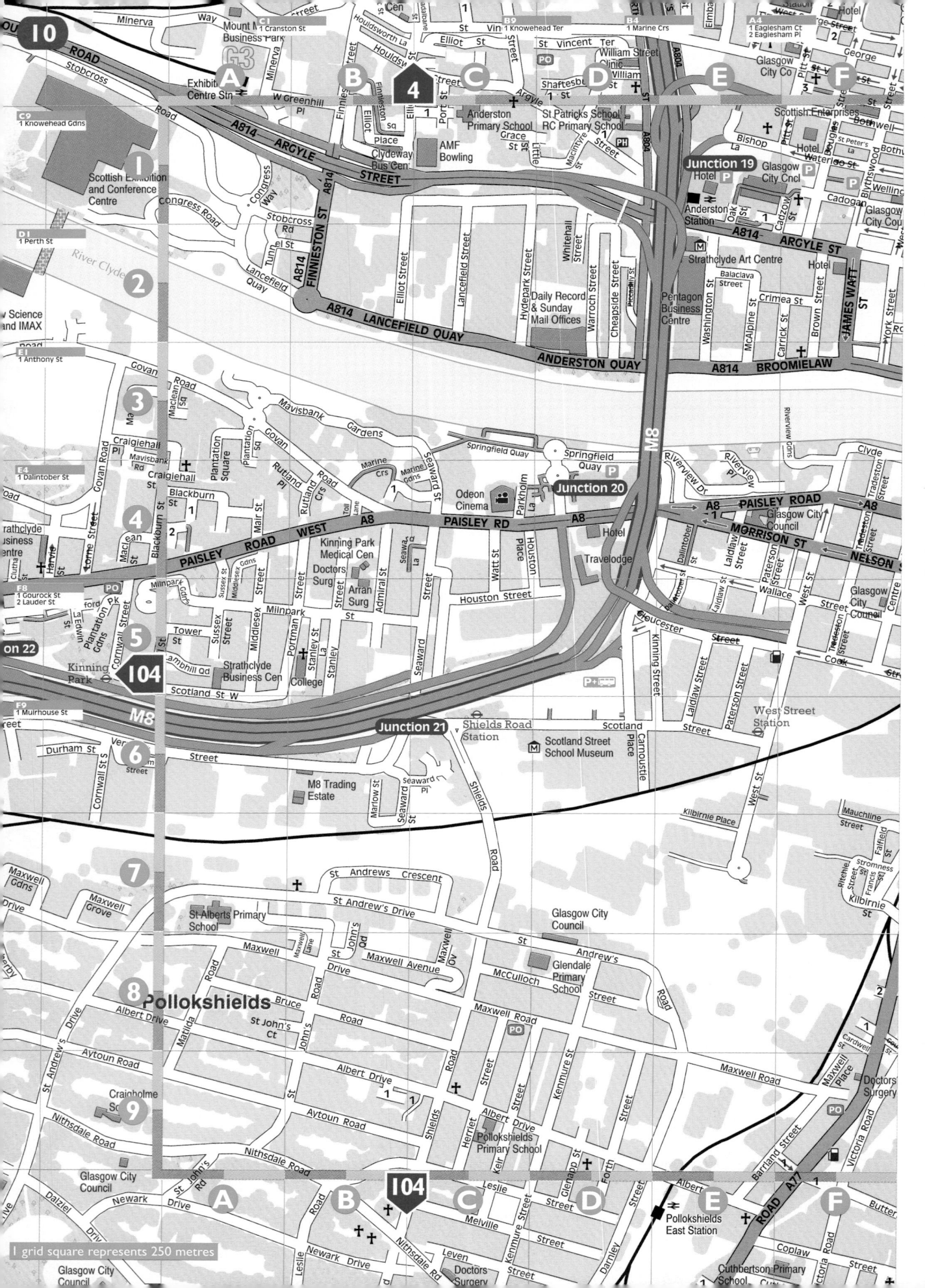

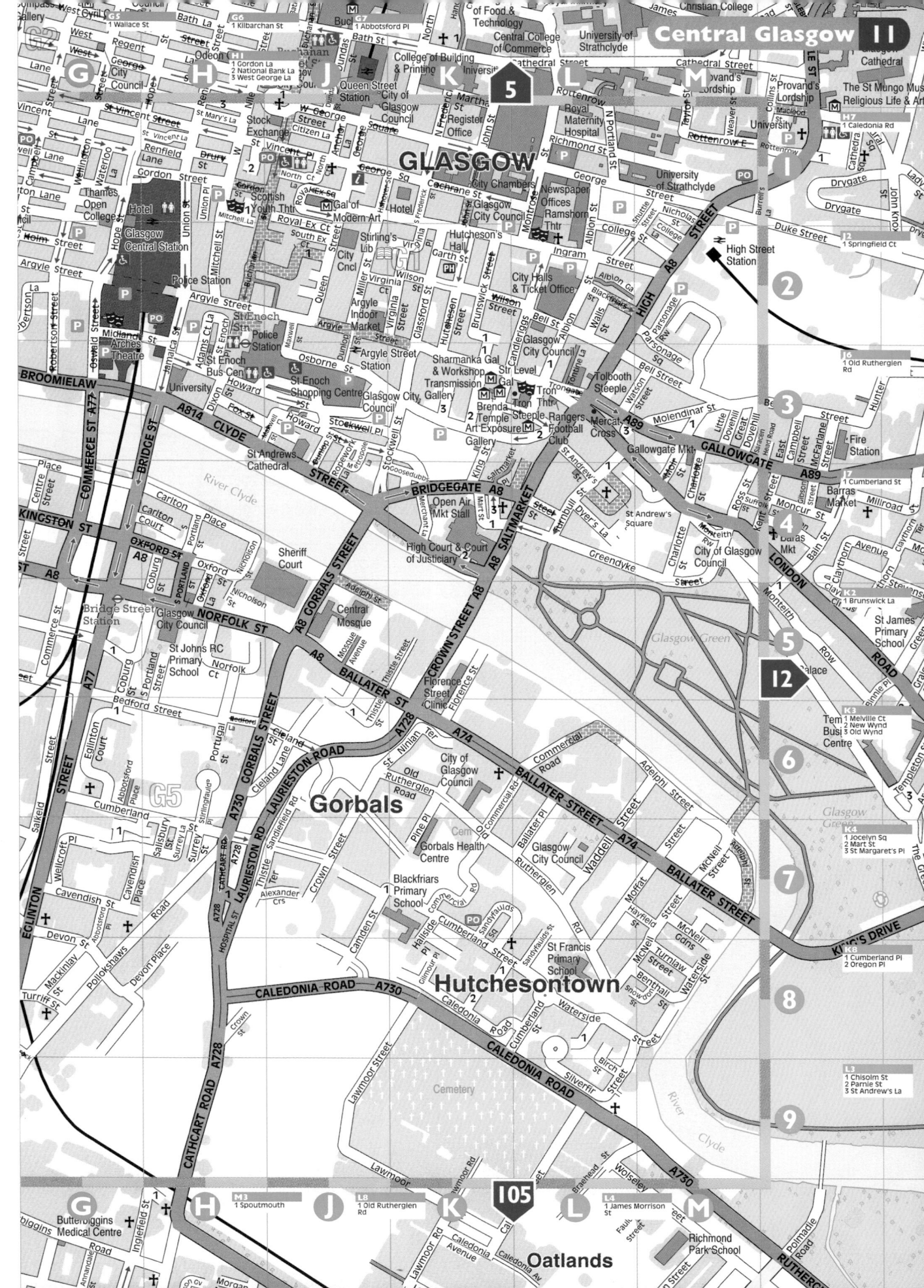

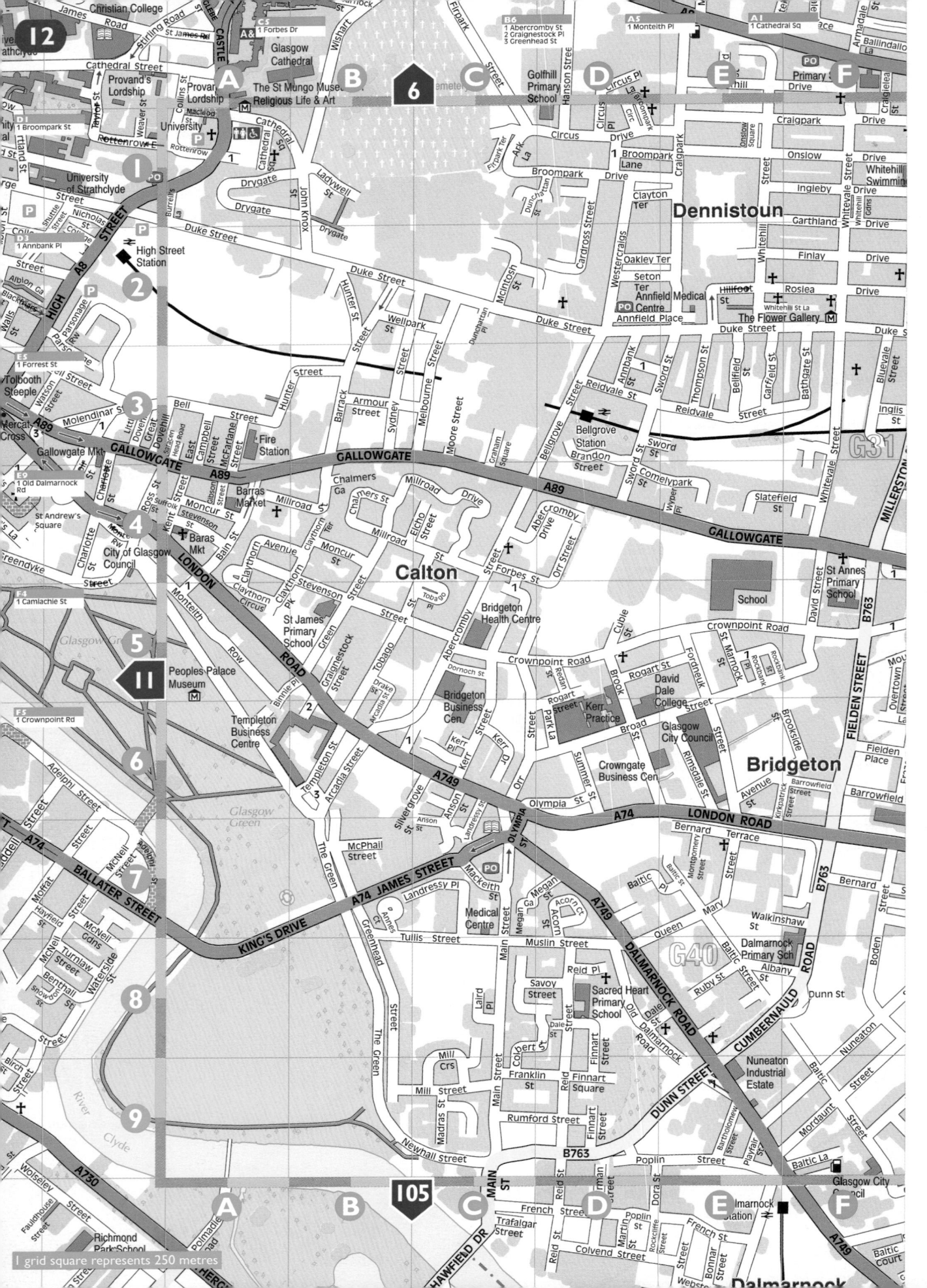

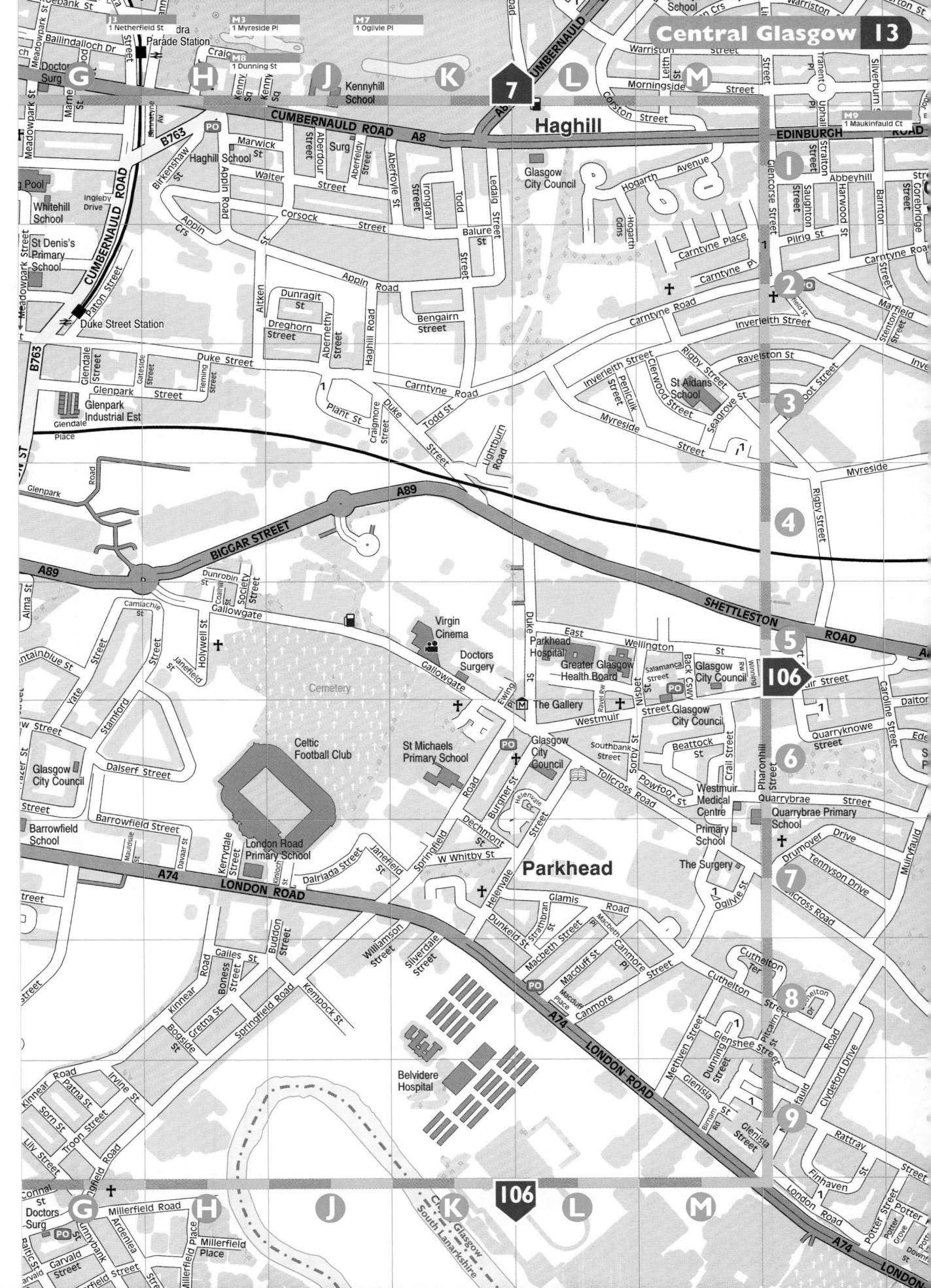

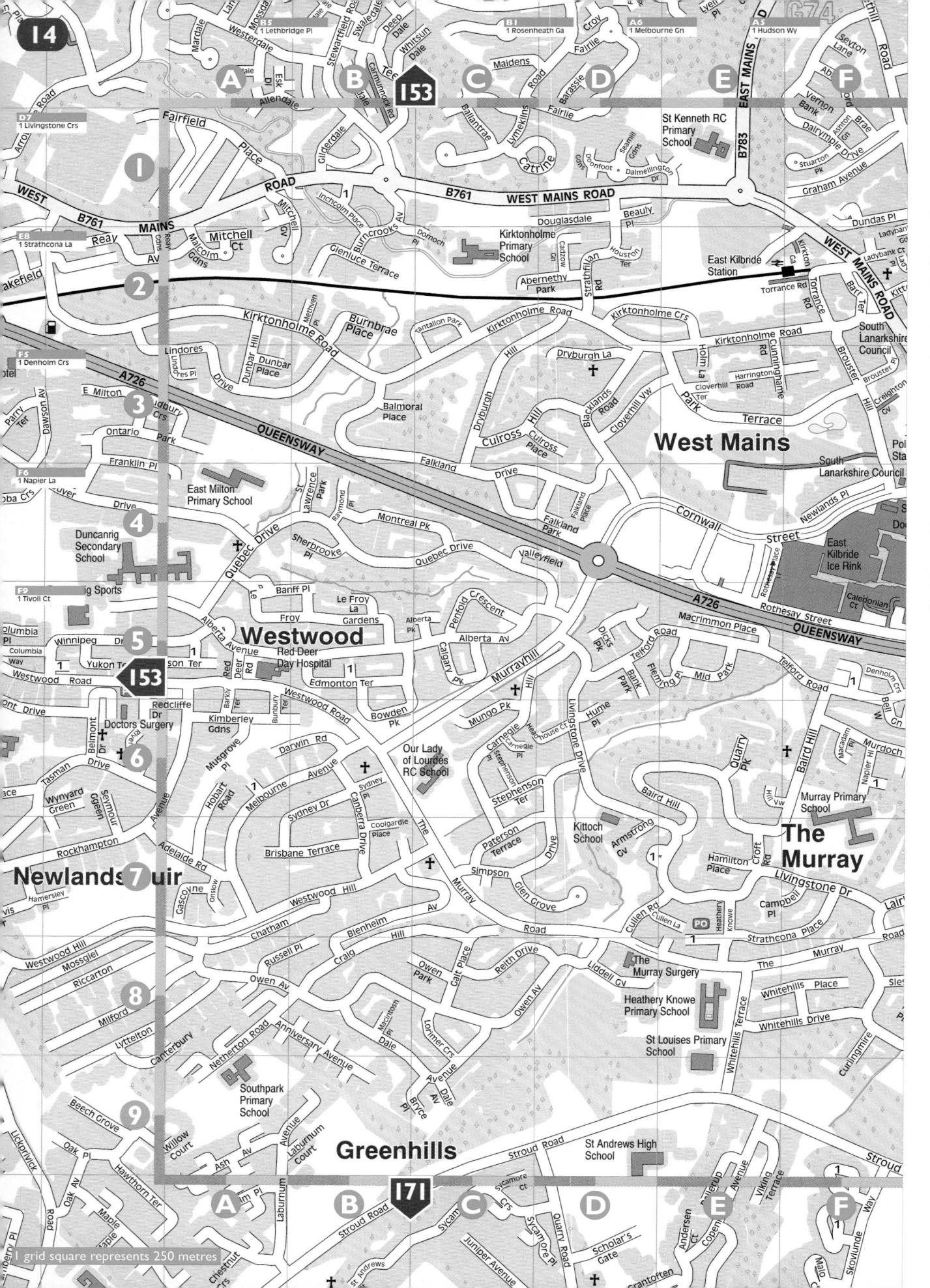

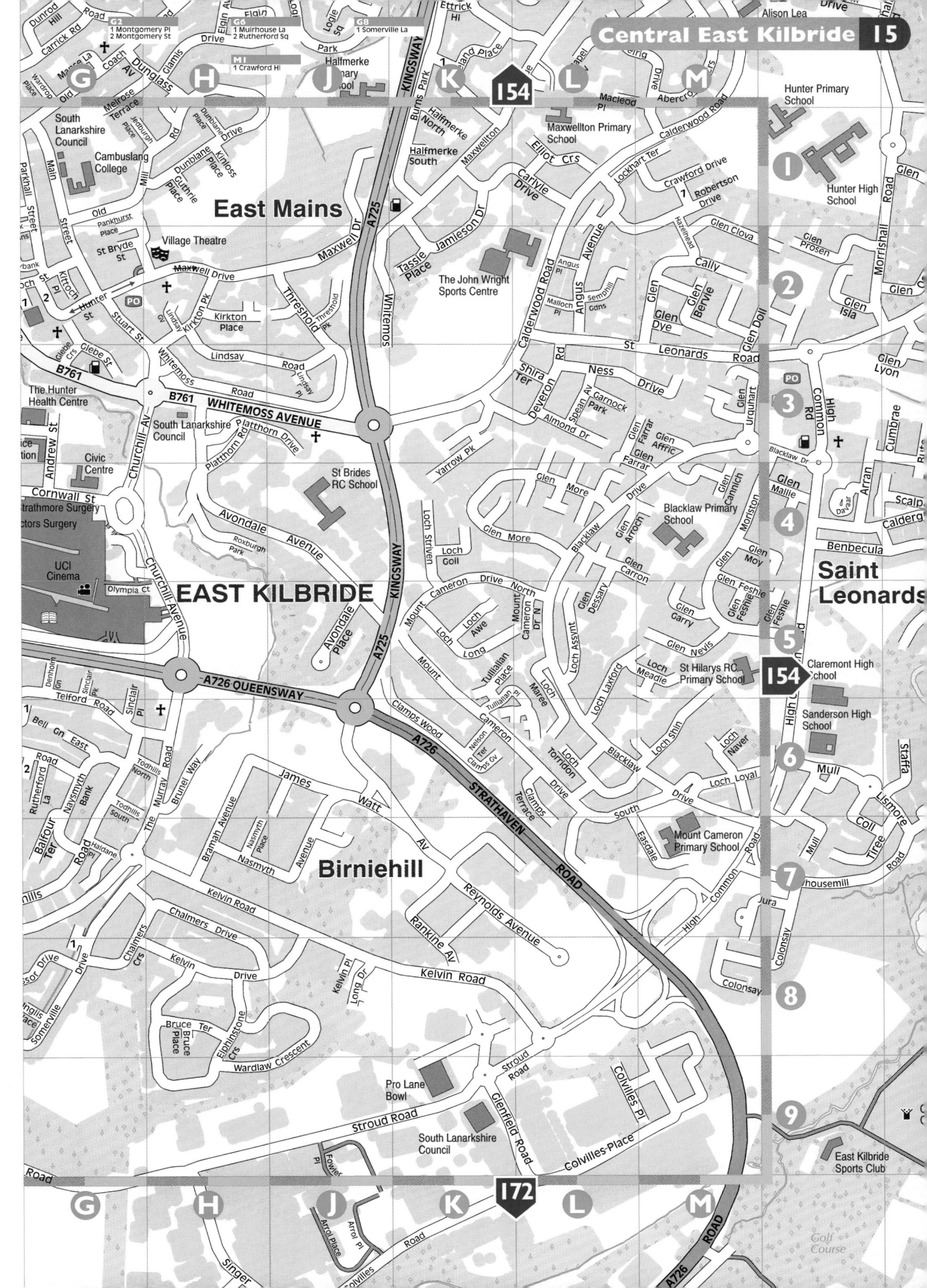

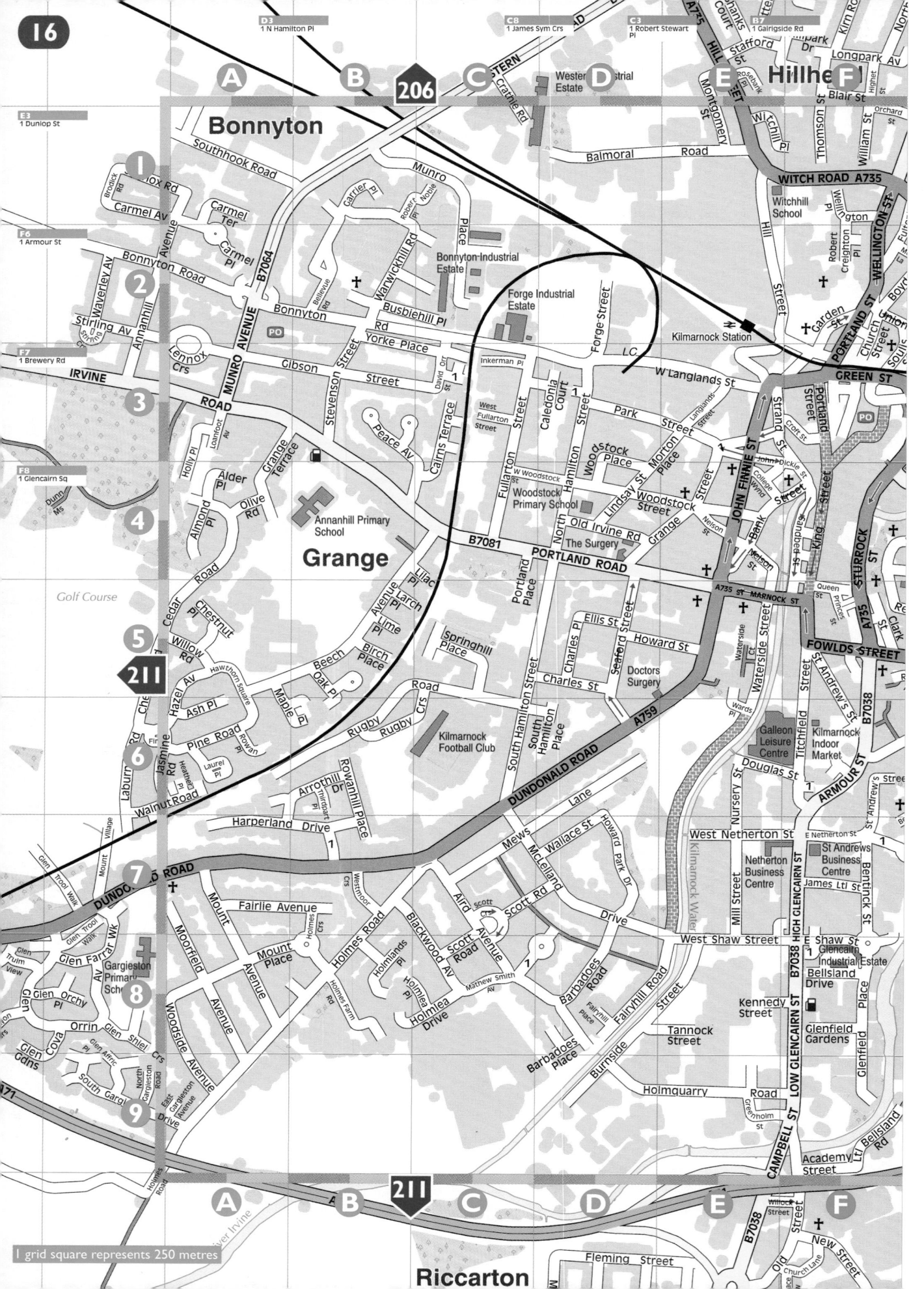

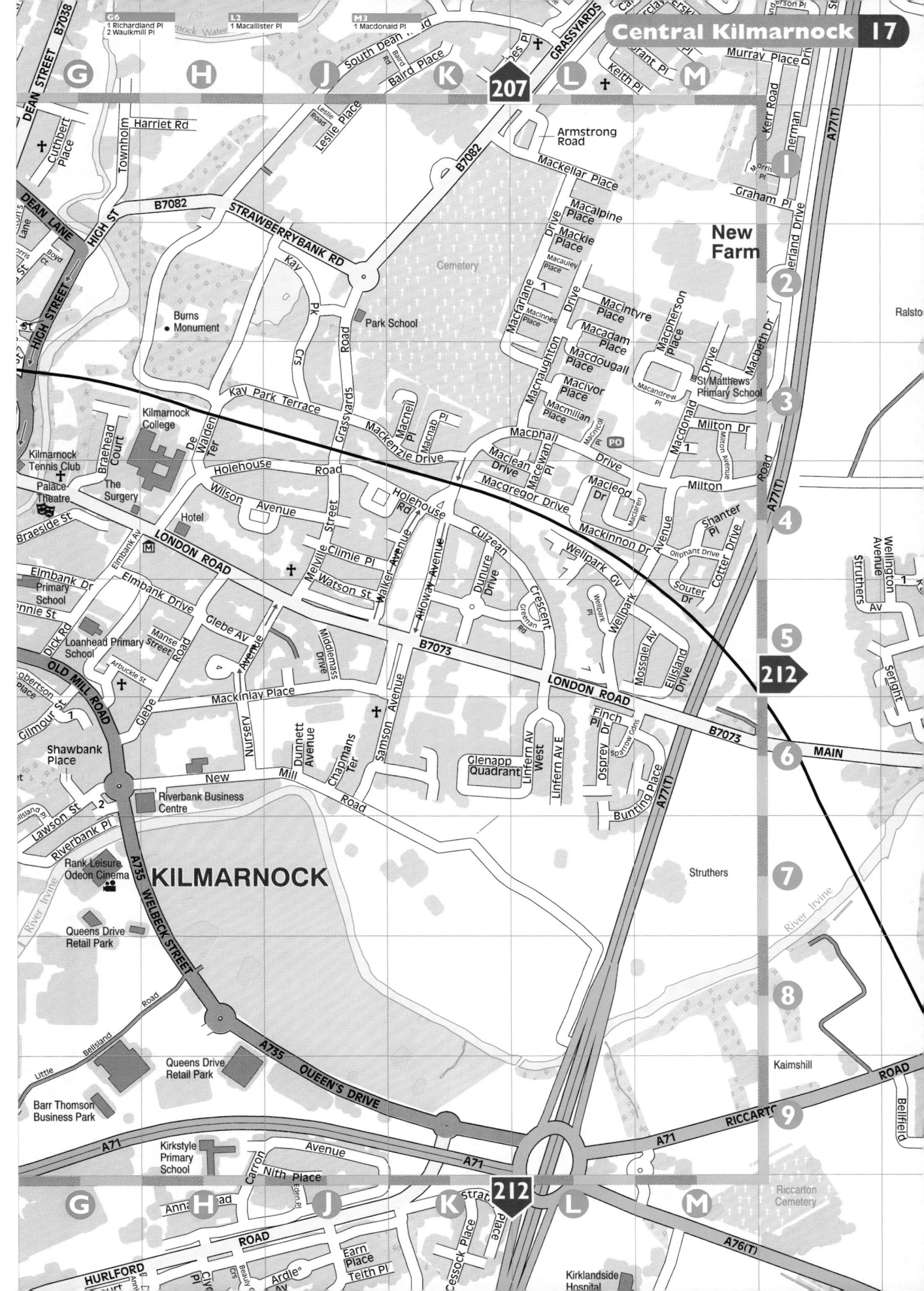

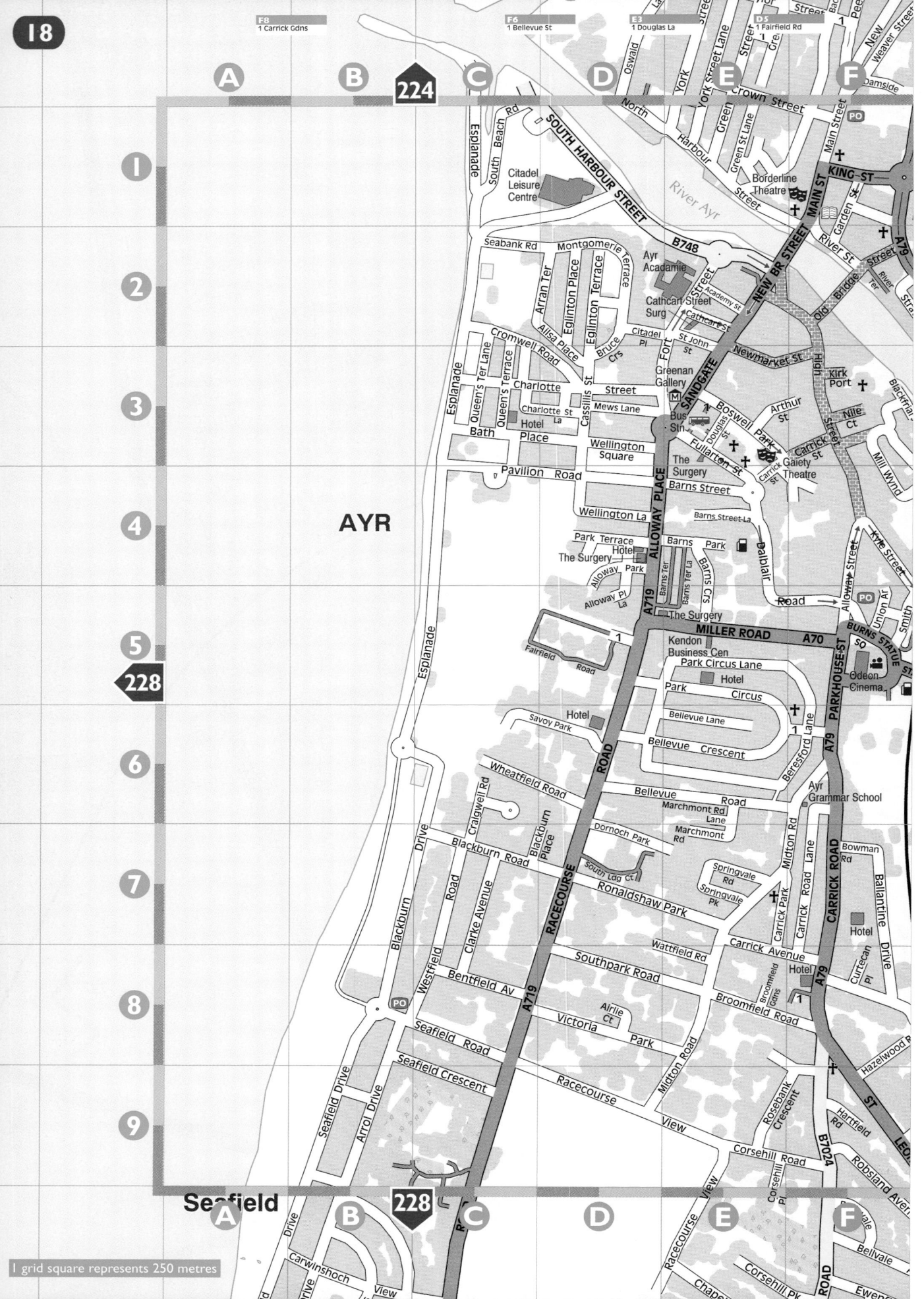

AYR

Seafield

1 grid square represents 250 metres

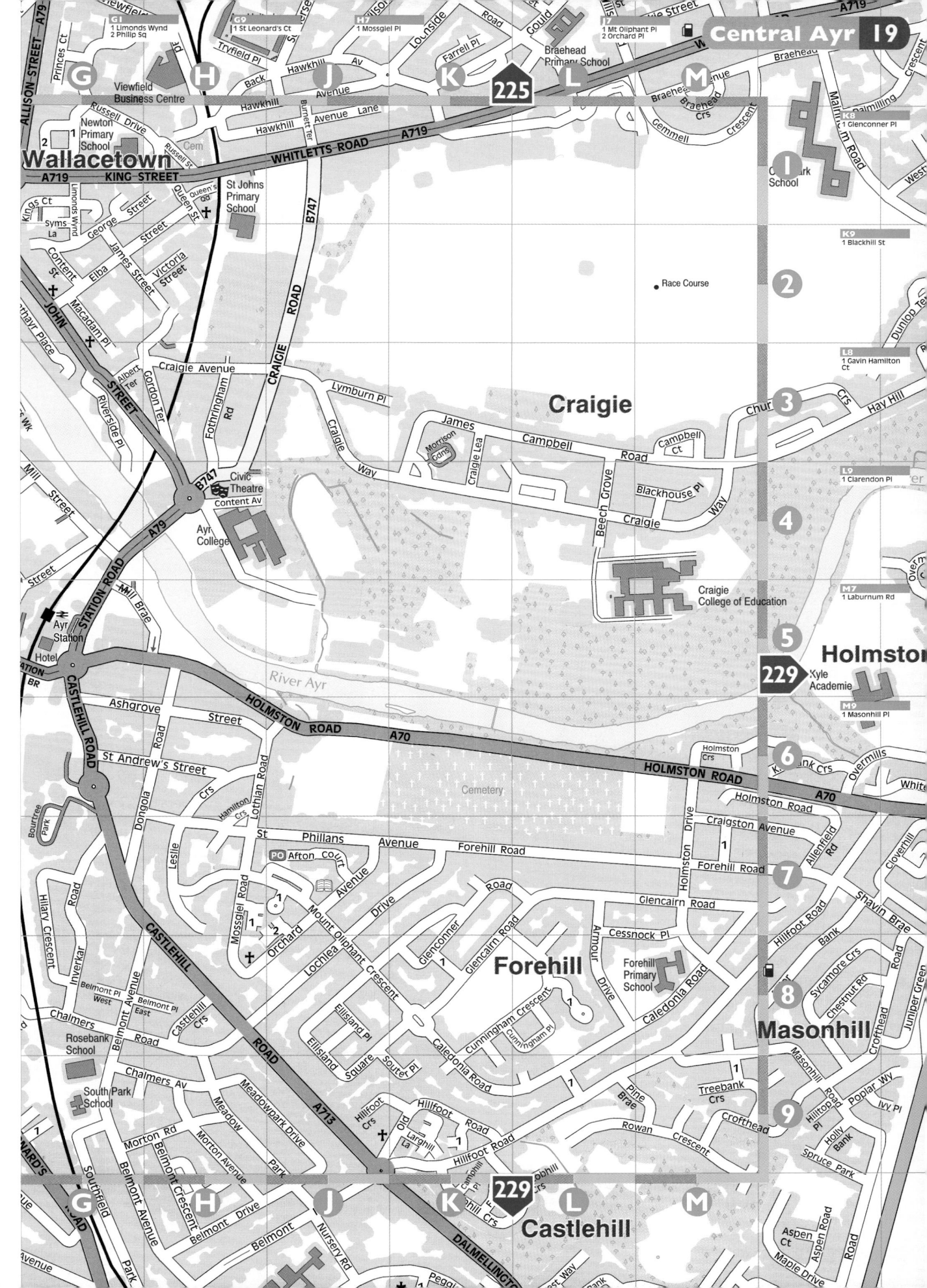

D7
1 Columba St

D8
1 Maitland St

D5
1 Urquhart Pl

D6
1 Abercromby Pl W
2 W Abercromby St

C8
1 Colquhoun Sq

B7
1 Bonar Law Av
2 Camsail Av
3 Cove Pl
4 Roseneath Dr

A7
1 Macaulay Pl
2 Strathclyde Pl

B6
1 Rowallan St
2 Upr Sutherl'nd St

A   B   C   D   E   F

I

2

3

4

Highlandman's Wood

Ardencaple Farm

5

Glenoran Road

Redclyffe Gardens

Kennedy Drive

Hotel

The Hill House (NTS)

B832

SINCLAIR STREET

Blackhill Drive

West Dhuhill Drive

Gillespie Dr

Glen Drive

West Lennox Drive

Upper Colquhoun Street

Douglas Drive

Sinclair Lane

Sinclair Dr

Dhuhill Dr E

Douglas Dr E

Kilbride drive

Douglas Dr

Duncan Road

Crawford Drive

Abercromby Crescent

6

RELOCH ROAD

Helens.. sailing Club

Dalmore Crs

Rhu Road Higher

Cumberland Avenue

Empress Dr

Frazer Av

Main's Av

Duchess Park

Duchess Drive

Macleod Crs

Macleod Drive

Paterson

Edward Drive

Barclay Drive

Queen Street

Millig Street

Upper Sutherland Crs

Lwr Sutherland Crs

West Rossdhu Drive

West Abercromby Street

Helensburgh Upper Station

Munro Dr West

Maclachlan

East Rossdhu Drive

B832

Munro Dr West

Bain Crescent

East Lennox Drive

Eastern Hill Road

Lever Road

St Andrews Wynd

Helensburgh Golf Club

Sannox Place

Machrie

Golfhill Drive

Cairndhu Point

Kathleen Park

Rhu Road

Bannachra Drive

Ardencaple

Ardencaple dr

Cairndhu Avenue

Castle Av

Loch Drive

Kidston Drive

RHU ROAD LOWER

A814

Ferniegair Av

Courtra.. Av

Cairndhu Gdns

Coulport Place

West King Street

Baird Avenue

Sutherland St

West Princes Street

Woodend Street

Stafford St W

West Montrose Street

Glasgow Street

Suffolk Street

Argyle Street West

William Street

John St Lane

John Street

James Street

Campbell Street

Stafford Street

John St

Lomond School

John St Lane

Lomond School

Colquhoun Street

SINCLAIR STREET

Argyle St East

Lorne

Helensburgh Medical Cen.

Hermitage School

Victoria Road

Chapelacre Grove

St Michael Drive

Charlotte

Parklands School

Grant St

Abercromby

Albert Street

Kildonan Drive

Albert Drive

Drumadoon

Lochranza Drive

Havelock

Havelock Place

Montrose

St Josephs School

Primary School

7

8

HELENSBURGH

WEST CLYDE STREET

A814

Scott Ct

Helensburgh Central Station

Princes Street East

Grant St

Lomond Street

George Street

King St East

King St East

Glenfinlas Street

King's Crescent

King Street

George Street

Bell Street

Granville St

Victoria Infirmary

Cemetery

Helensburgh Swimming Pool

PO

Princes Adelaide Street

A814

Henry Street

CLY..

South Kin..

EAST

A814

Craigendoran Avenue

Garralvy Road

Kirkmichael Road

E6
1 Butt Av
2 Dixon Rd
3 Maclachlan Pl
4 Sinclair Dr

A

E8
1 Adelaide St
2 Argyle St East
3 Glenfinlas St

B

F6
1 Boston Dr
2 Brodick Dr
3 Corrie Pl
4 Mcewan Dr

C

22

D

F7
1 Lamlash Pl
2 Mcauslan Pl
3 Pirnmill Pl
4 Shiskine Pl

E

F8
1 Athole St
2 Johnson Ct
3 Millerslea Gdns
4 Mossend Av
5 Rosedale Gdns
6 Upr Adelaide St

F

I grid square represents 500 metres

G6
1 Horton Pl

G7
Street names for
this grid square are
listed at the back of
the index

G8
1 Buchanan Rd

GLEN FRUIN ROAD

GLEN FRUIN ROAD

G H J K L M

I

B832

East
Kilbride

Highfields

2

Inverlauren

Cross
Keys

Du

Drumfad

Callendoun

3

B832

4

Daligan

LUSS ROAD

B832   LUSS   ROAD

5

Bannac
Muir

6

Kent
Drive

Kent Drive

Hardy Hill

Winston

m Place

Malcol

PO

Campardown Court

7

10

6 4

5

11

8 3

Winston

9

Townhead

Road

1

Winston

8

Ben
Bouie
Drive

mson Drive

Colgrain
Primary School

Beech ve
Place

dgauntlet Road Drumfork

uy Mannering

Crescent

Road

Camis Eskan
House

G H J 23 K L M

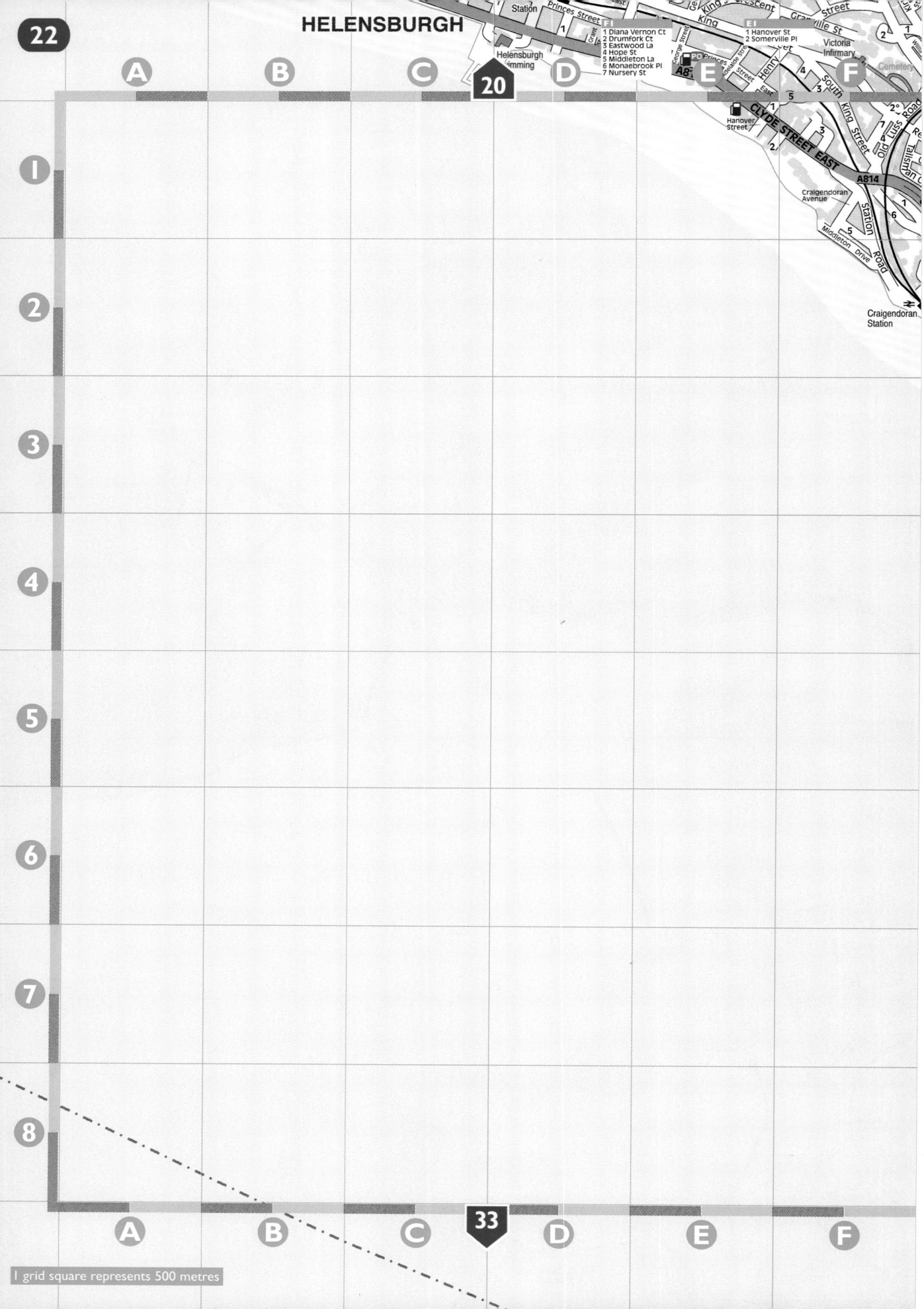

HELENSBURGH

1 Diana Vernon Ct
2 Drumfork Ct
3 Eastwood La
4 Hope St
5 Middleton La
6 Monaebrook Pl
7 Nursery St

1 Hanover St
2 Somerville Pl

20

33

1 grid square represents 500 metres

G1
1 Armstrong Rd
2 Jeanie Deans Dr

G2
1 Moore Dr

H1
1 Aldrin Rd

G H J **21** K L M

Colgr...
Primary School

Ben
Boule
Drive

Beechgrove
Place

Camis Eskan
House

...gauntlet Road Drumfork Road

Ashton
Drive

Collins Road

Kenilworth Avenue

Waverley Avenue

Drumfork Road

Campbell Dr Drive

Craigendoran

CARDROSS ROAD

Marmion Avenue

Lawrence Avenue

Dennistoun Cres C

A814

CARDROSS ROAD

Colgrain

Moss Road

LC

A814

Keppoch
House

Red Road

Lyleston

Badyen
Farm

Drumhead

Lyleston
Farm

Cemetery

LC

Ardmore

Ardardan

Mollandhu

A814 CARDROSS ROAD

Brooks
House

LC

Gellston Burn

Stoneymollan Road

I
2
3
4
24
5
6
7
8

Darleith R...
Mill
Rd
Kirkton

Car
Prir

BARRS CR...

Smithy
Rd

Smithy
Ct

G H J **34** K L M

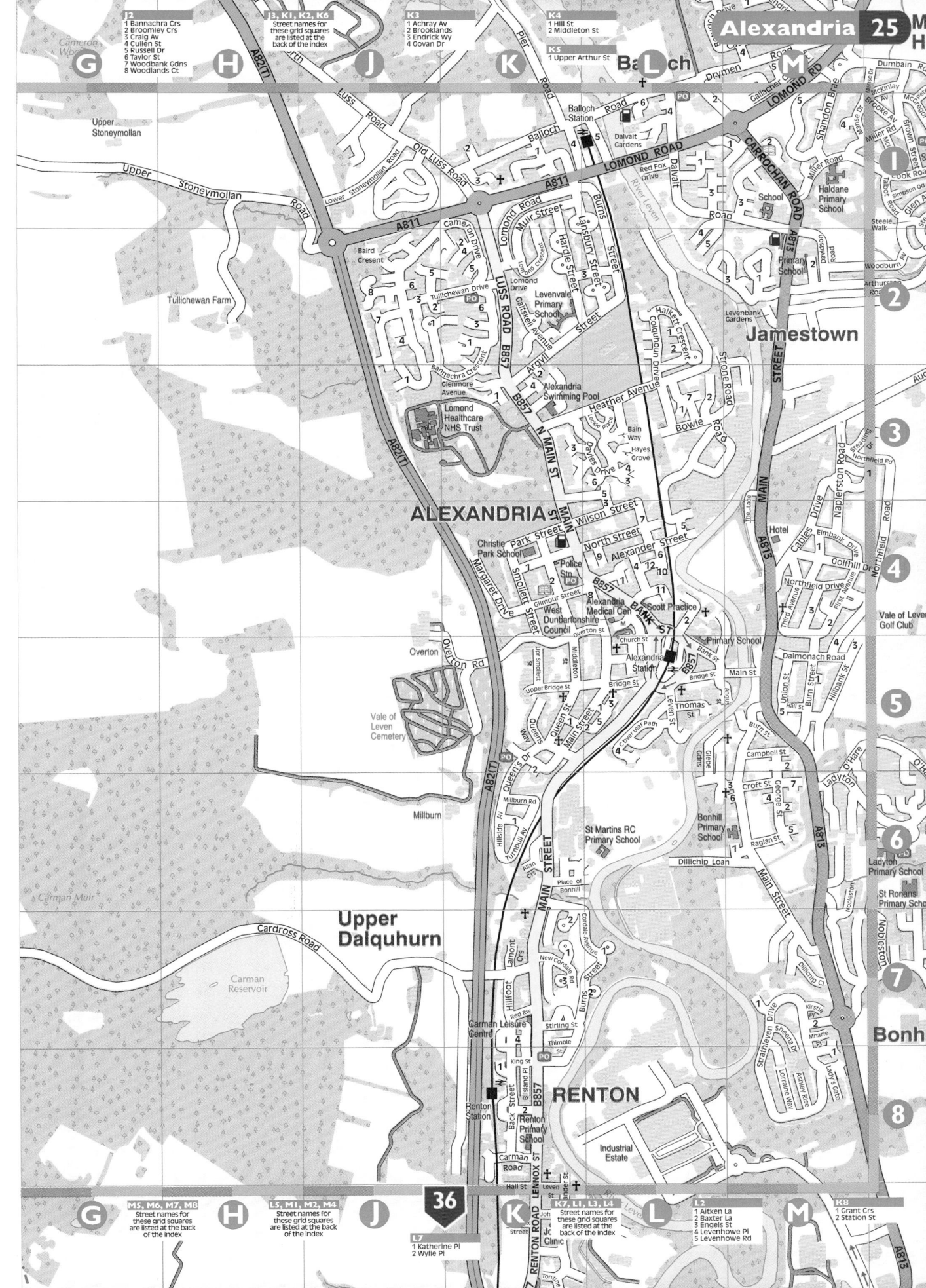

36

I

2

3

4

5

6

7

8

Blairquhosh

A81

Cantywheery

Dumgoyach Farm

Duntreath Castle

Craigbrock

A81

Strath Balne

Middle Ballewan

West Highland Way

West Highland Way

Arlehaven

Ardoch

Aychengillan

Craigmore Cott

STATION ROAD

Craigmore

A809

CUILTS ROAD

B821

BALLACHALAIRY YETT

Carbeth Ho

Easter Carbeth

Cuilt Brae

Carbeth Loch

Boards

West Highland Way

East Dunbartonshire

Stirling

West Highland Way

Craigallian Loch

Visitors Centre

A809

Allander Water

Craigallian

I grid square represents 500 metres

Blane Water

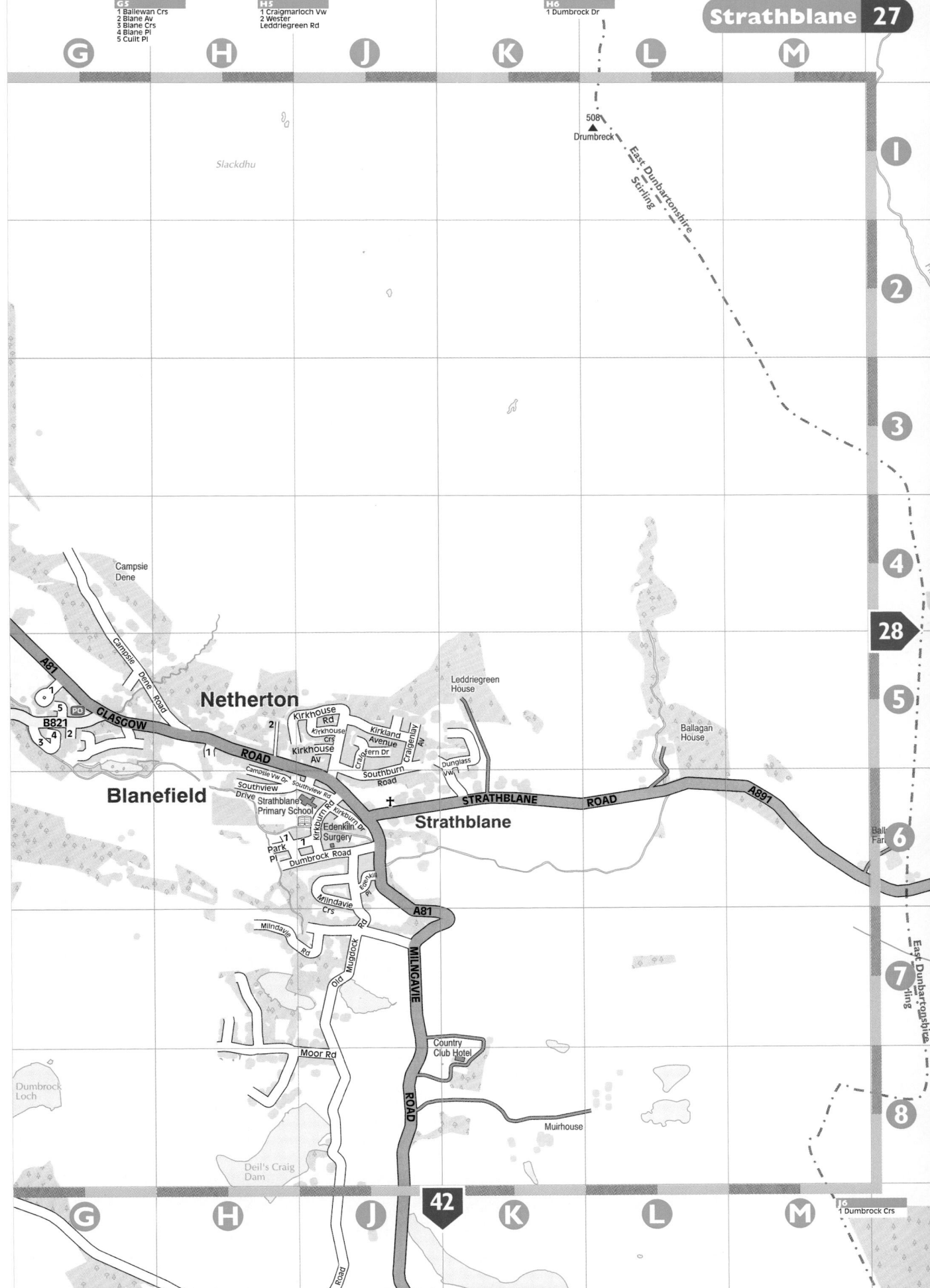

G5
1 Baillewan Crs
2 Blane Av
3 Blane Crs
4 Blane Pl
5 Cuilt Pl

H5
1 Craigmarloch Vw
2 Wester
Leddriegreen Rd

H6
1 Dumbrock Dr

I

2

3

4

28

5

6

7

8

Slackdhu

508
▲
Drumbreck

East Dunbartonshire
Stirling

Fife

Campsie
Dene

Leddriegreen
House

Netherton

Ballagan
House

A81

GLASGOW

B821

Campsie Dene Road

1

ROAD

Kirkhouse
Rd

Kirkhouse
Crs

Kirkland
Avenue

Kirkhouse
AV

Craigenhav Av

Fern Dr

2

Southburn
Road

Dunglass
Vw

Blanefield

Southview
Drive

Campsie Vw Dr

Southview Rd

Strathblane
Primary School

Kirkburn Rd

Kirkburn Dr

+

Strathblane

STRATHBLANE ROAD

A891

Ball
Fan

Edenkiln
Surgery

1

Park
Pl

1

Dumbrock Road

Eden kiln Pl

Milndavie
Crs

Mugdock Rd

A81

MILNGAVIE

Milndavie Rd

Old Mugdock Rd

Dumbrock
Loch

Moor Rd

ROAD

Country
Club Hotel

Muirhouse

Deil's Craig
Dam

J6
1 Dumbrock Crs

G   H   J   K   L   M

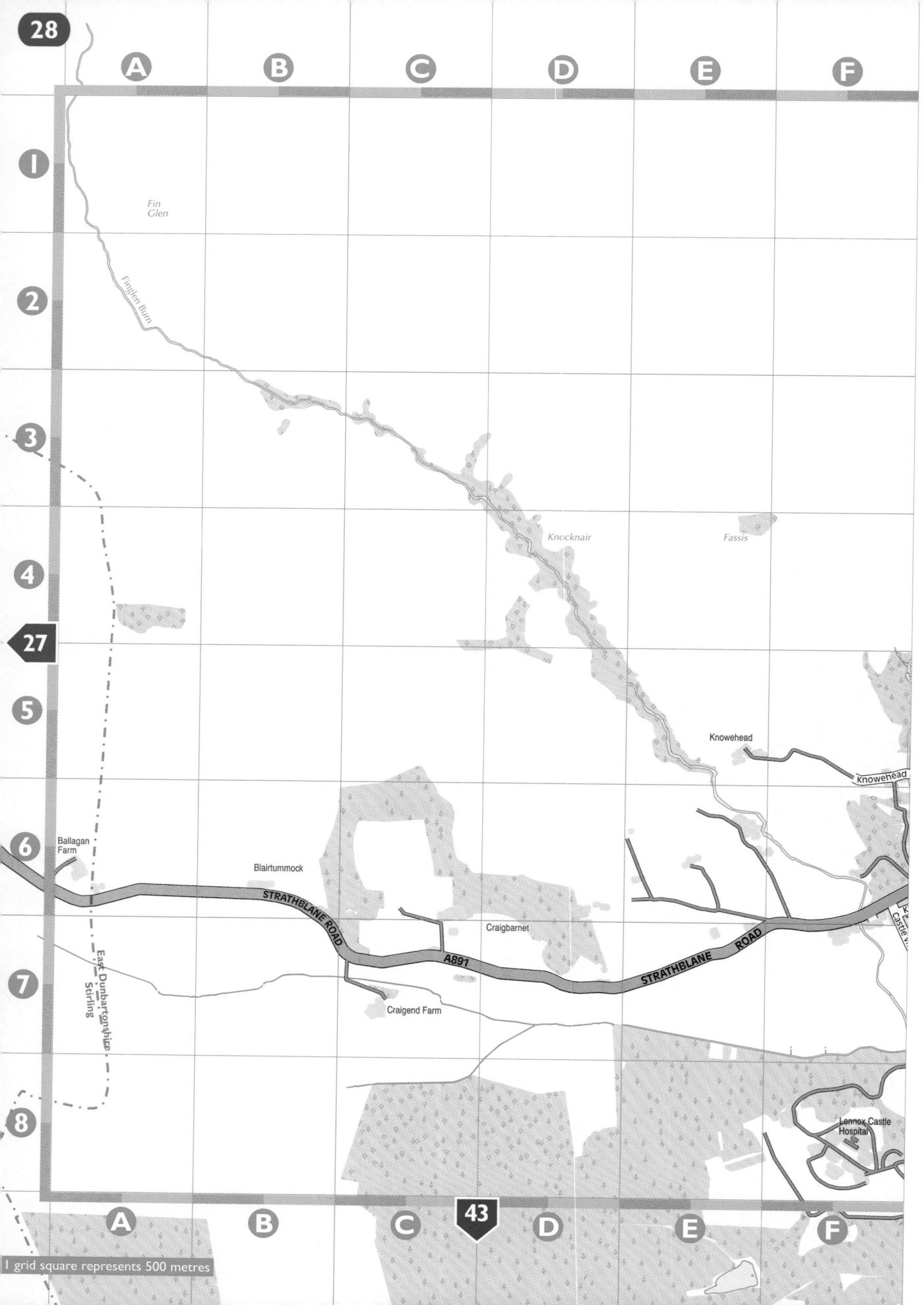

A B C D E F

1

2

3

27

4

5

6

7

8

Fin
Glen

Finglen Burn

Knocknair

Fassis

Knowehead

Knowehead

Ballagan
Farm

Blairtummock

STRATHBLANE ROAD

Craigbarnet

A891

STRATHBLANE ROAD

Craigend Farm

East Dunbartonshire
Stirling

Lennox Castle
Hospital

Castle V...

A B C 43 D E F

I grid square represents 500 metres

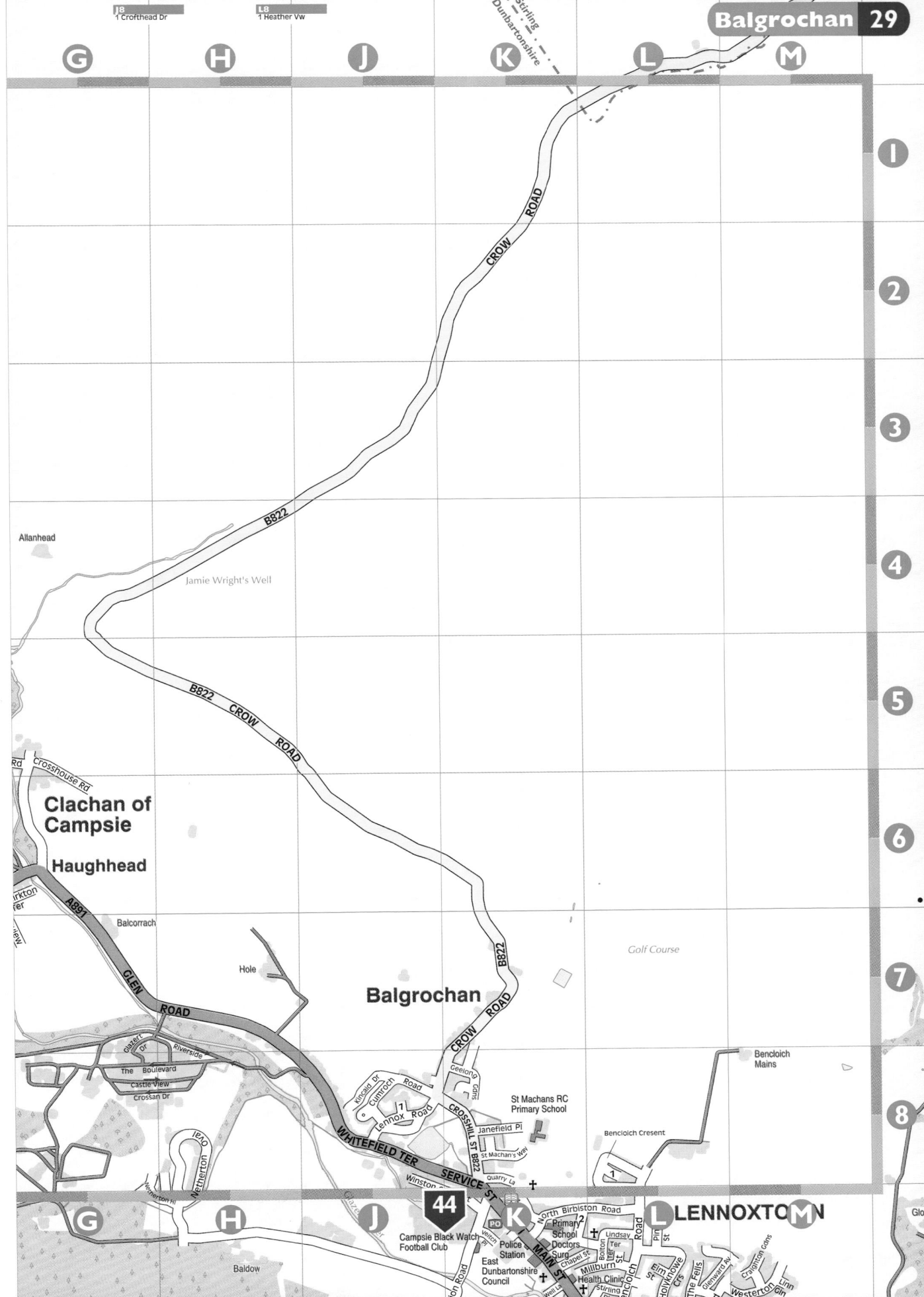

G H J K L M

1
2
3
4
5
6
7
8

CROW ROAD

B822

Allanhead

Jamie Wright's Well

B822 CROW ROAD

Crosshouse Rd

Clachan of Campsie

Haughhead

A891

Balcorrach

GLEN ROAD

Hole

Balgrochan

B822

CROW ROAD

Golf Course

Bencloich Mains

Glazert Dr

Riverside

The Boulevard

Castle View

Crossan Dr

Kincaid Dr

Cumroch Road

Lennox Road

Geelong Gdns

St Machans RC
Primary School

Janefield Pl

Bencloich Cresent

Westerton Hl

Wetherton

Oval

WHITEFIELD TER

CROSHILL ST B822

St Machan's Way

Quarry La

Winston Rd

SERVICE ST

44

G H J K L **LENNOXTOWN** M

Campsie Black Watch
Football Club

PO

Police
Station

East
Dunbartonshire
Council

North Birbiston Road

Primary
School

Doctors
Surg

Chapel St

Lindsay
Ter

Bolton
Ter

Millburn

Stirling Rd

Health Clinic

Bencloich Rd

Elm St

Pin St

Holyknowe

Crs

The Fells

Glenward

Craigton Gdns

Westerton Gdns

Linn Gln

MAIN ST

Baldow

Baldow

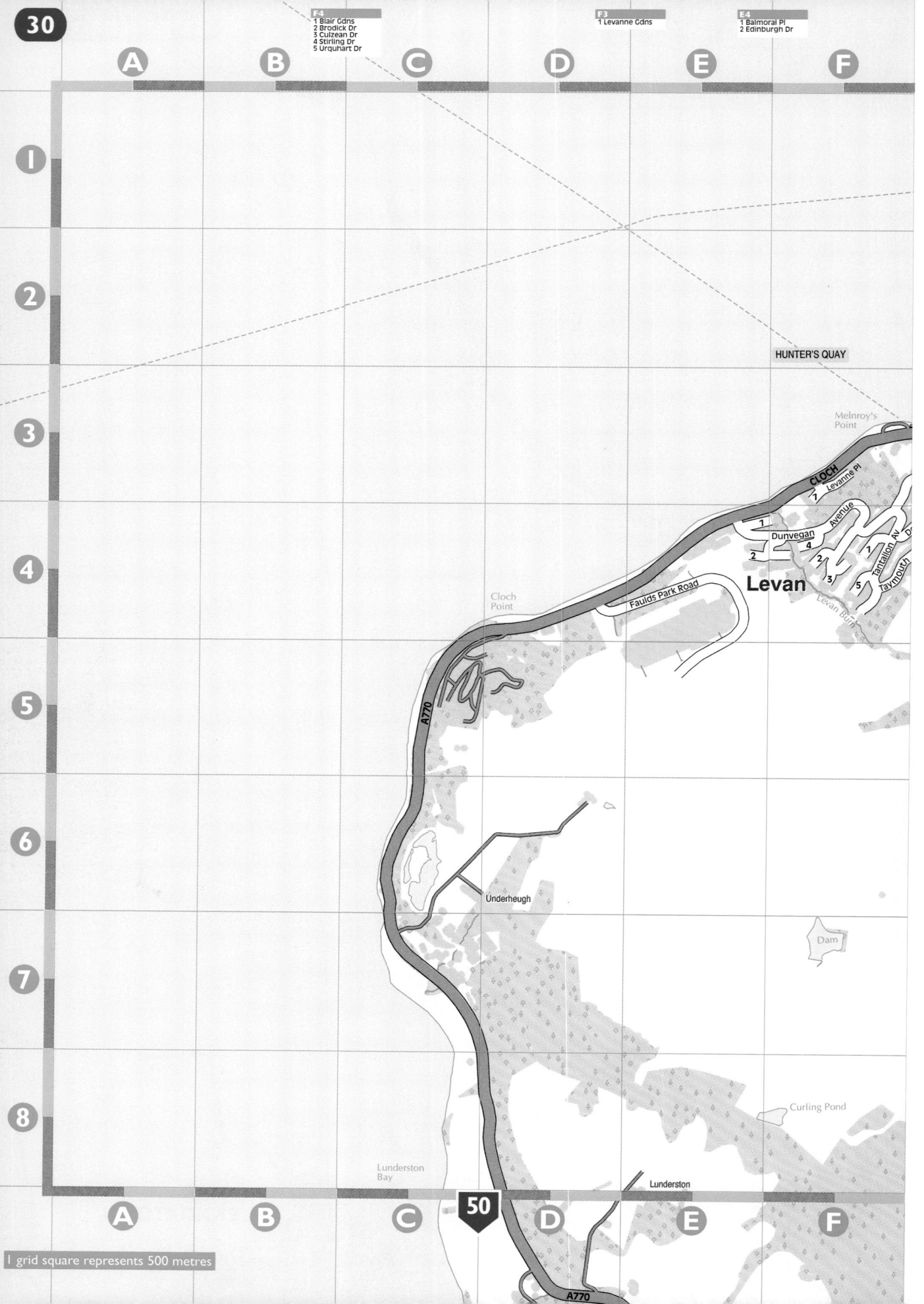

F4
1 Blair Gdns
2 Brodick Dr
3 Culzean Dr
4 Stirling Dr
5 Urquhart Dr

F3
1 Levanne Gdns

E4
1 Balmoral Pl
2 Edinburgh Dr

1
2
3
4
5
6
7
8

HUNTER'S QUAY

Melnroy's
Point

CLOCH

Levanne Pl

Dunvegan

Avenue

Tantallon Av

Taymouth

Levan

Levan Burn

Cloch
Point

Faulds Park Road

A770

Underheugh

Dam

Curling Pond

Lunderston
Bay

50

Lunderston

A770

A   B   C   D   E   F

I grid square represents 500 metres

DUNOON

West Bay

KEMPOCK ST

Ferry Terminal

Gourock Station

Pierhead Clinic

Gourock Health Centre

Bath St

St John's Road

Ferry Terminal

Gourock Bay

Cardwell Bay

ALBERT ROAD

A770

Barnhill

Binnie Street

John Street

Broomberry

PO

Binnie King

Royal Street

St Davidson St

Drive

SHORE STREET

TARBET STREET

A770

Cove Road

CARDWELL RD

Caledonia Crs

Lochview Av

Caled

Manor

Gourock Central Junior School

GOUROCK

Royal Gourock Yacht Club

ASHTON ROAD

Ashton

Victoria

Moorfield Rd

Golf Rd

Road

Gourock High School

PO

Avenue

Fletcher

Drive

Drumshantle

Road

Clyde Rd

Rodney

Argyle Rd

Burnside

Glen Av

Nelson Road

Oxford

Duthie

Cowal Crs

View

Divert Rd

Jacobs Drive

Finnie Ter

Tower

Reservoir Road

Grenville Rd

Avenue

Garvie

Duthie

Ferry Terminal

ROAD

A770

Cloch Brae

Turnberry Av

Cowal

Finnart Cs

Sycamore

Moorfoot

Drive

Alisa Road

Iona Crs

Bute St

Macmillan Dr

Arran Road

Staffa

Street

George Road

Hilltop Rd

Grenville Crescent

Mathie Crs

Hilltop Rd

Coves Reservoir

St Andrews Drive

Belleisle Pl

Gleneagles Dr

Carnoustie

Avenue

Gourock Golf Club

Skye Crs

Kirn

Drive

St Ninians RC Primary School

Larkfield Road

PA19

Moorfoot Primary School

Midton

Cemetery

Darroch Av

Plymouth Av

Weymouth Crs

Falmouth Dr

Larkfield Road

Bournemouth Rd

32

Earnhill Road

Fife Rd

PO

York Road

Chester Rd

Inverclyde Royal Hospital

A&E

Farm Road

Canmore Crs

Fancy

Neil

Sutherland

Gleninver Rd

Earnhill Road

Earnhill

Road

Caithness Road

Nairn

Angus Road

Cambridge Road

Burns Road

Oxford

Devon

Larkfield Primary School

Westmoreland

Cumberland

Sacred Heart Primary School

Stafford Road

Springfield Primary School

Larkfield

Banff

Lothian Rd

Lincoln Rd

Norfolk

PO

Berwick Road

Warwick Rd

Auchmead

Road

Branchton Station

Banks

Jean

Minerva Ter

Armour

Glencairn

Carrick Ter

Ayr Ter

Burns

Road

Kinloch Ter

Ravenscraig Recreation Centre

Primary School

Road

Kirkwall Road

Branchton

Rothesay Road

Branchton

Cupar Dr

Forfar Road

Ravens Hosp

Braeside

Road

Athole Ter

Kintyre Ter

Kylemore Terrace

St Gabriels RC Primary School

INVERKIP

Wellyard Way

Mars Road

Davaar Rd

Dalriada Rd

Braeside Road

Juno Ter

Drumillan Hill

Glenburn School

Alloway

Glenburn

ROAD

Cupar Dr

Leitchland

Flatterton

Greenock High School

Spango

INVERKIP ROAD

A78

Spango Burn

IBM Station

Chrisswell

Reservo

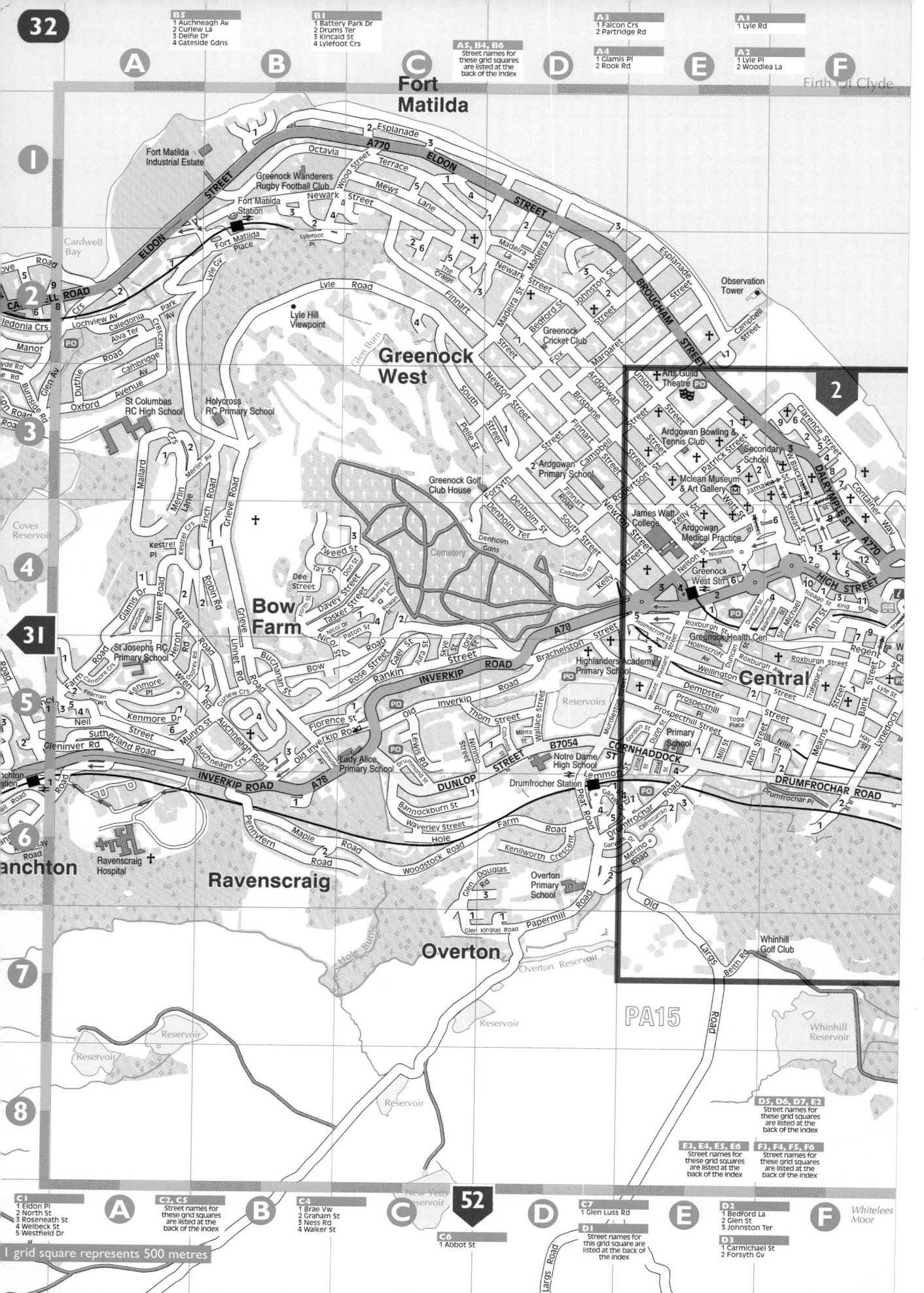

A   B   C   D   E   F

Firth Of Clyde

Fort Matilda

I

Cardwell Bay

Fort Matilda Industrial Estate

Greenock Wanderers Rugby Football Club

Fort Matilda Station

Fort Matilda Place

2

Greenock West

Lyle Hill Viewpoint

St Columbas RC High School

Holycross RC Primary School

3

Greenock Golf Club House

Cemetery

Observation Tower

Arts Guild Theatre

Ardgowan Bowling & Tennis Club

Secondary School

Mclean Museum & Art Gallery

James Watt College

Ardgowan Medical Practice

2

Ardgowan Primary School

4

Bow Farm

Kestrel Pl

St Josephs RC Primary School

31

5

Neil

Highlanders Academy Primary School

Reservoirs

Greenock West Stn

Greenock Health Cen

Central

6

anchton

Ravenscraig Hospital

Lady Alice Primary School

Notre Dame High School

Drumfrocher Station

CORNHADDOCK

Primary School

Ravenscraig

Overton Primary School

Whinhill Golf Club

7

Overton

PA15

Whinhill Reservoir

Reservoir

8

Reservoir

New Yetts

52

Whitelees Moor

1 grid square represents 500 metres

G4, G6, H5, J6
Street names for these grid squares are listed at the back of the index

G5
1 Antigua St
2 Bogie St
3 Dellingburn St
4 Hill St
5 Station Av
6 Virginia St

H6
1 Hawick Ct
2 Kennedy's La

G H J 22 K L M

I
2
3
4
34
5
6
7
8

3

GREENOCK

Argyll and Bute
Inverclyde

Garvel Point

James Watt College
Dalrymple Street
Cathcart St
Bellpark Clinic
Greenock Central Station
Lyle St
Hope St
Dellingburn Street
Scott St
Baker St
Ingleston Street
B7054

Dock Breast
Terrace Road
Chapel St
Bogie St
Rue End Street
Carnock Street
Main Street
A8
James Watt Way
Dock
East Hamilton St
Great Harbour

Arthur St
John Street
Orchard Crescent Street
St Lawrence Street
Crescent Street
Cartsdyke
Belville Street
Finneston St
Belville Av
Bawhirley
Hillend Hillend Drive
Border Street
Morris St
Auchmountain Road
Adam St

Cartsdyke Station
Ratho St
Macdougall
Garvald St
Barnhill
Grant Road
Carwood Street
Brown St
Primary School
Baxter St
Grosvenor Road
Fairlie Street
Gilmour Street
John Wilson st
Weir Street
Mackenzie
McLeod St
Sinclair Street
Quarriers La
Leitch St
Weir St

Ladyburn Business Park
Strathclyde Business Cen
Pottery St
Ladyburn
Cibshill Road
Greenock Road
Fullerton La
Port Glasgow Rd
Ardgowan Street
Bogston Station
A8
Kingston Business

Kilmun Road
Riverside Road
Whinhill Station
Lomond Road
Katrine
Darnaart Rd
Crawberry Road
Clydeview
Whinhill Crs
Glenbrae Gabriel Road
Kilmacolm Street
Hillside Rd
Burnhead Street
Blairmo
Crs
Bridgend Rd
Castle Road
Lady Octavia Recreation Centre

Strone Crescent
Gray St
Gryfe
Corlic St
Miller St

Strone Farm

Strone

Aberfoyle Road
Blairmore Road
Primary School
Leven Road
Fintry Rd
Torrance Rd
Balloch Road
Endrick Rd
Balmore road
Renton
Luss Avenue
Luss Pl
Ardtrea Rd
Kilcreggan
VW
Cardross Pl
Clynder Road
Cardross Crs
Ardmore Rd
Dalmoak Road
Argen Rd

Kings Glen Primary School
Knocknairshill Cemetery

B788
Auchmountain Rd
Lady Burn
B788

Keir Hardie Street
Gibshill
Smillie Gibson St
Cedar Crs
Fir Street
Bell Street
Cobham St
Lansbury St
Dalmally St
Mitchell Street

Shankland Road
Thomas Muir Street
Whitelees Rd
Lilybank Road
Lilybank Sch
East Street
Poplar Street
Mackie Avenue
Devol Avenue
Broadstone Av
Farquhar Road

Lilybank

Deval Burn

Burnhead Moor

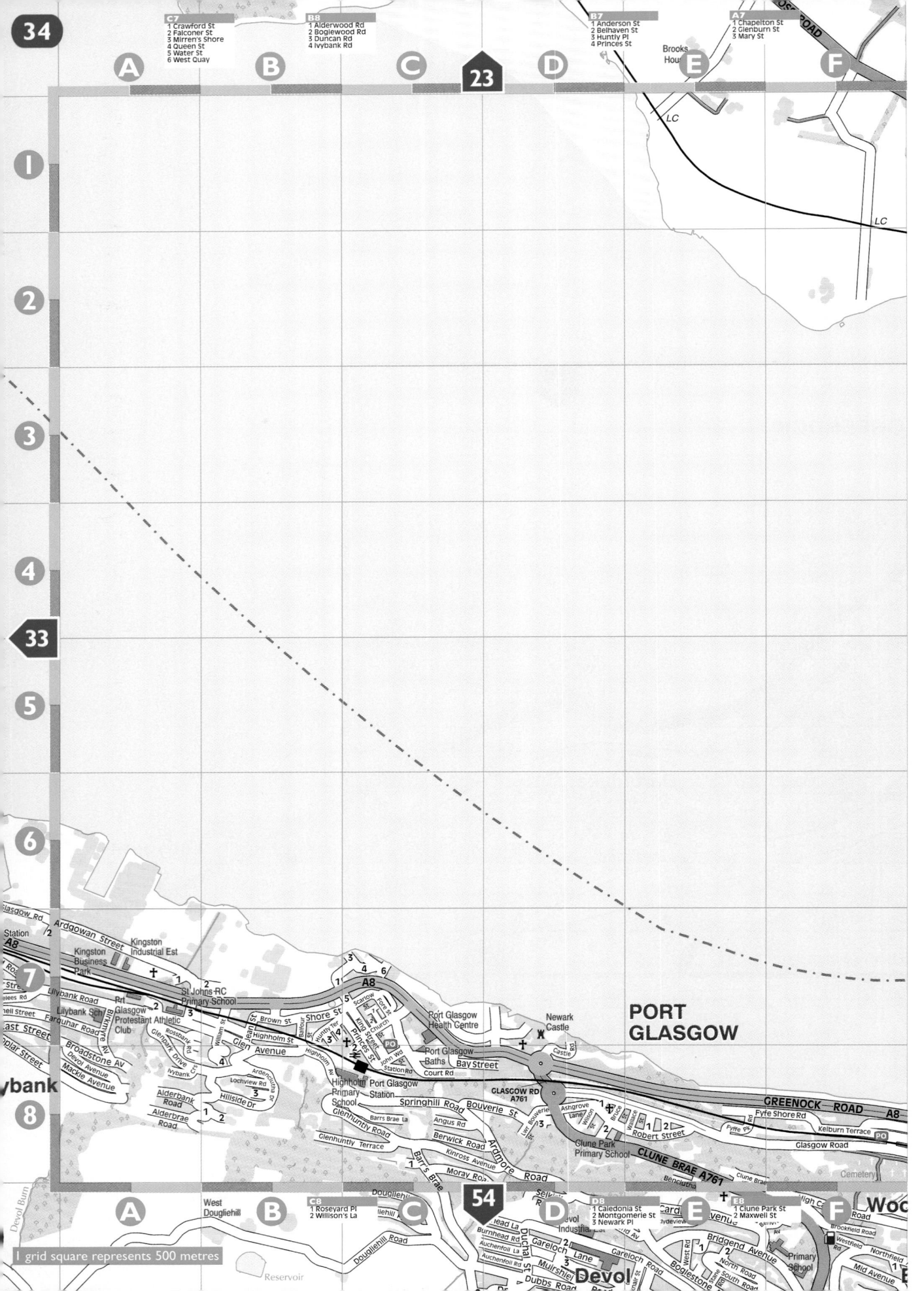

23

33

54

C7
1 Crawford St
2 Falconer St
3 Mirren's Shore
4 Queen St
5 Water St
6 West Quay

B8
1 Alderwood Rd
2 Bogiewood Rd
3 Duncan Rd
4 Ivybank Rd

B7
1 Anderson St
2 Belhaven St
3 Huntly Pl
4 Princes St

A7
1 Chapelton St
2 Glenburn St
3 Mary St

A   B   C   D   E   F

1
2
3
4
5
6
7
8

Brooks House

LC

LC

Glasgow Rd
Ardgowan Street
Kingston Industrial Est
Kingston Business Park
Station
A8
Lilybank Road
Prt Glasgow Protestant Athletic Club
St Johns RC Primary School
A8
Shore St
Scarlow St
Fox St
Brown St
Dean St
Balfour St
Highholm St
William St
Huntly Ter
King Street
Princes St
Church St
Port Glasgow Health Centre
PO
Port Glasgow Baths
Station Rd
Newark Castle
Castle Rd
Bay Street

PORT GLASGOW

Farquhar Road
Birkmyre Av
Broadstone Av
Glenbrae Drive
Rosshall Rd
Glen Avenue
Ardencraig Dr
Lochview Rd
Highholm Av
Port Glasgow Primary School
Station
Court Rd
GLASGOW RD A761
Springhill Road
Bouverie St
Ashgrove Lane
Nelson St
Bruce St
Wallace St
Lwr Bouverie St
Robert street
Clune Park Primary School
CLUNE BRAE A761
Benclutha
Clune Brae
GREENOCK ROAD A8
Fyfe Shore Rd
Fyffe Pk
Kelburn Terrace
Glasgow Road
PO
Cemetery

Devol Avenue
Mackie Avenue
Ivybank
Alderbank Road
Alderbrae Road
Hillside Dr
Barrs Brae La
Glenhuntly Road
Glenhuntly Terrace
Berwick Road
Angus Rd
Kinross Avenue
Ardmore Road
Barr's Brae
Moray Rd
Selvie

Woo

West Dougliehill
Dougliehill Road
Dubbs Road

B8
1 Roseyard Pl
2 Willison's La

C8

D8
1 Caledonia St
2 Montgomerie St
3 Newark Pl

E8
1 Clune Park St
2 Maxwell St

Burnhead La
Head La
Devol Industria
Garelock Lane
Garelock Road
Auchenfoil Rd
Muirshiel Road
Devol
North Road
South Road
Boglestone
Cardwell
Bridgend Avenue
West Rd
Clydeview
Westfield
Primary School
Brookfield Road
Northfield
Mid Avenue
High Co
Road

Reservoir

Devol Burn

1 grid square represents 500 metres

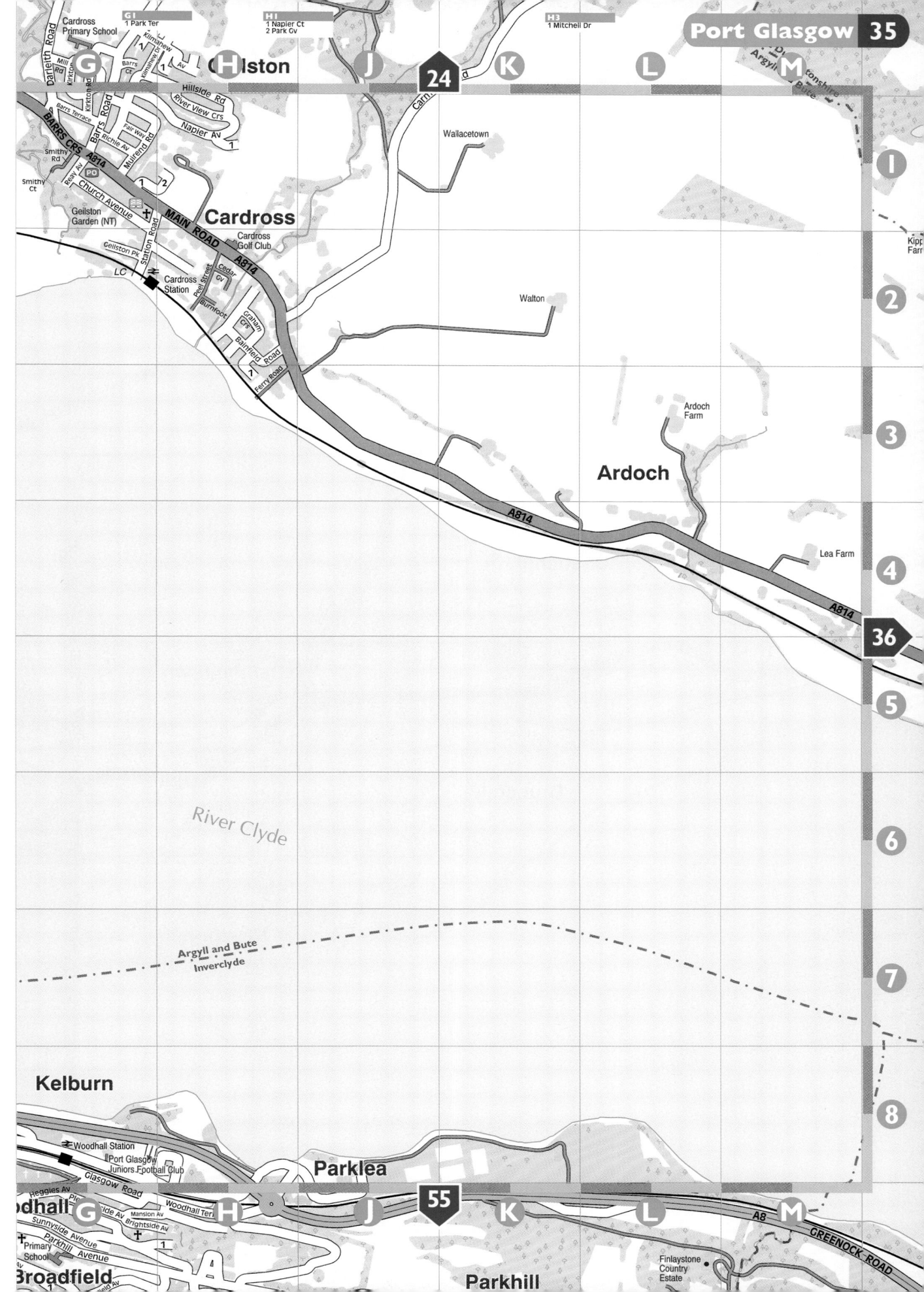

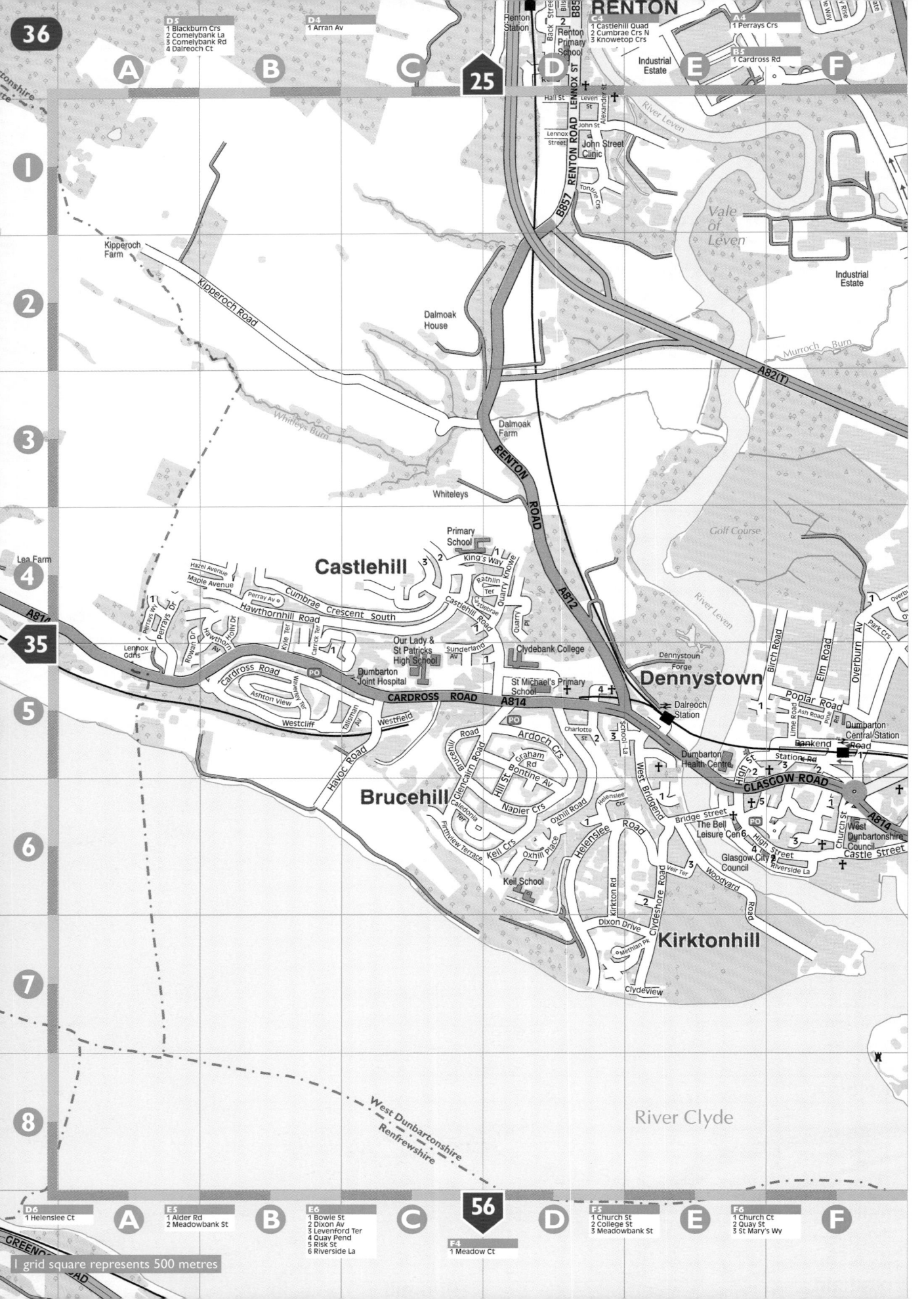

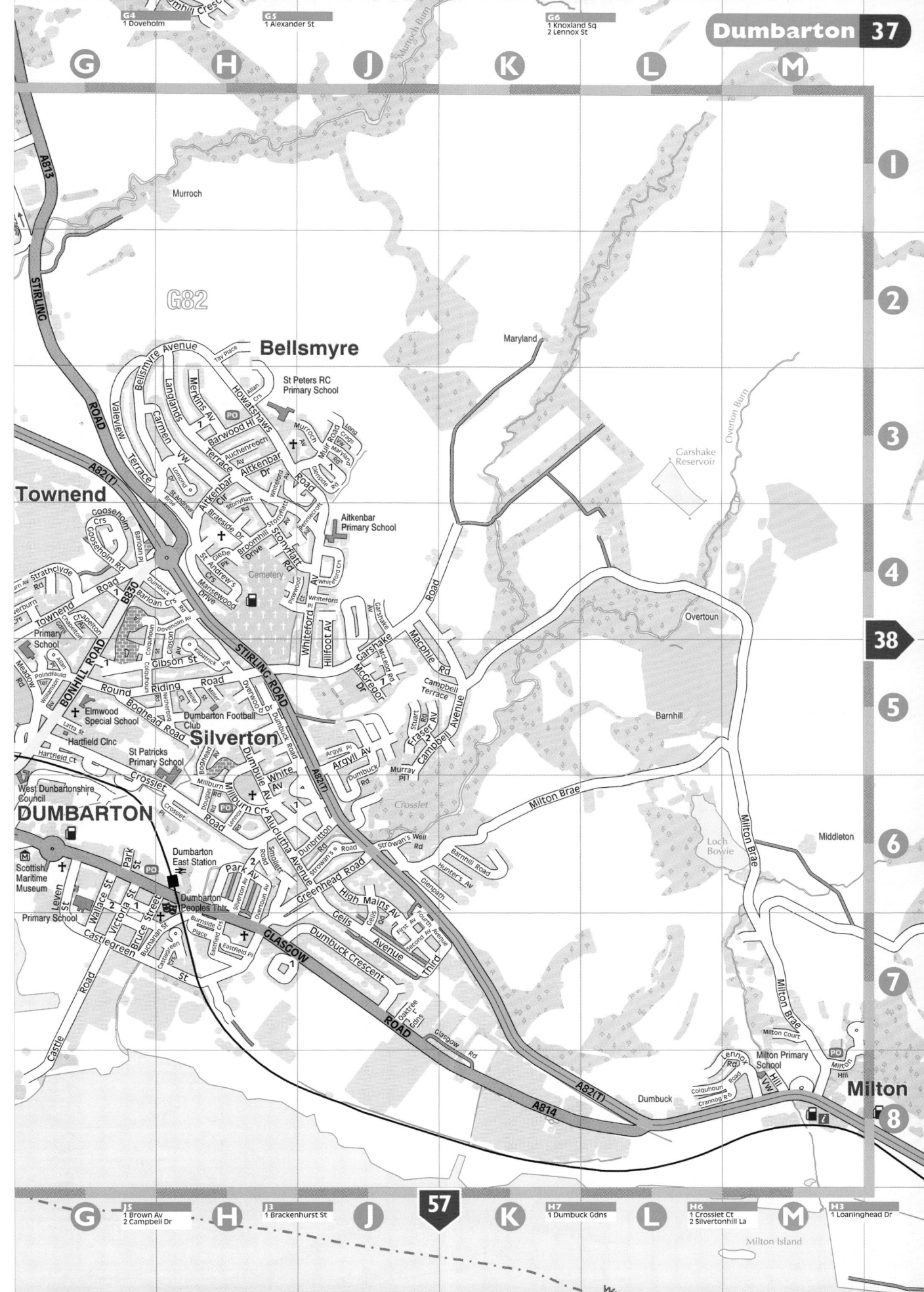

G4
1 Doveholm

G5
1 Alexander St

G6
1 Knoxland Sq
2 Lennox St

G H J K L M

1
2
3
4
38
5
6
7
8

Murroch

G82

Bellsmyre

Maryland

St Peters RC
Primary School

Garshake
Reservoir

Overton Burn

Townend

Aitkenbar
Primary School

Cemetery

Overtoun

Townend
Primary
School

Dumbarton Football
Club

Barnhill

Elmwood
Special School

Silverton

Hartfield Clnc

St Patricks
Primary School

Campbell
Terrace

West Dunbartonshire
Council

DUMBARTON

Crosslet

Loch
Bowie

Middleton

Milton Brae

Scottish
Maritime
Museum

Dumbarton
East Station

Milton Brae

Primary School

Dumbarton
Peoples Thtr

Greenhead Road

High Mains Av

Strowan's Well
Rd

Barnhill Road

Hunter's Av

Glenpath

Milton Court

Milton Primary
School

Milton

Dumbuck

Dumbuck Crescent

GLASGOW

ROAD

A814

A82(T)

G H J K L M

J5
1 Brown Av
2 Campbell Dr

J3
1 Brackenhurst St

H7
1 Dumbuck Gdns

H6
1 Crosslet Ct
2 Silvertonhill La

H3
1 Loaninghead Dr

Milton Island

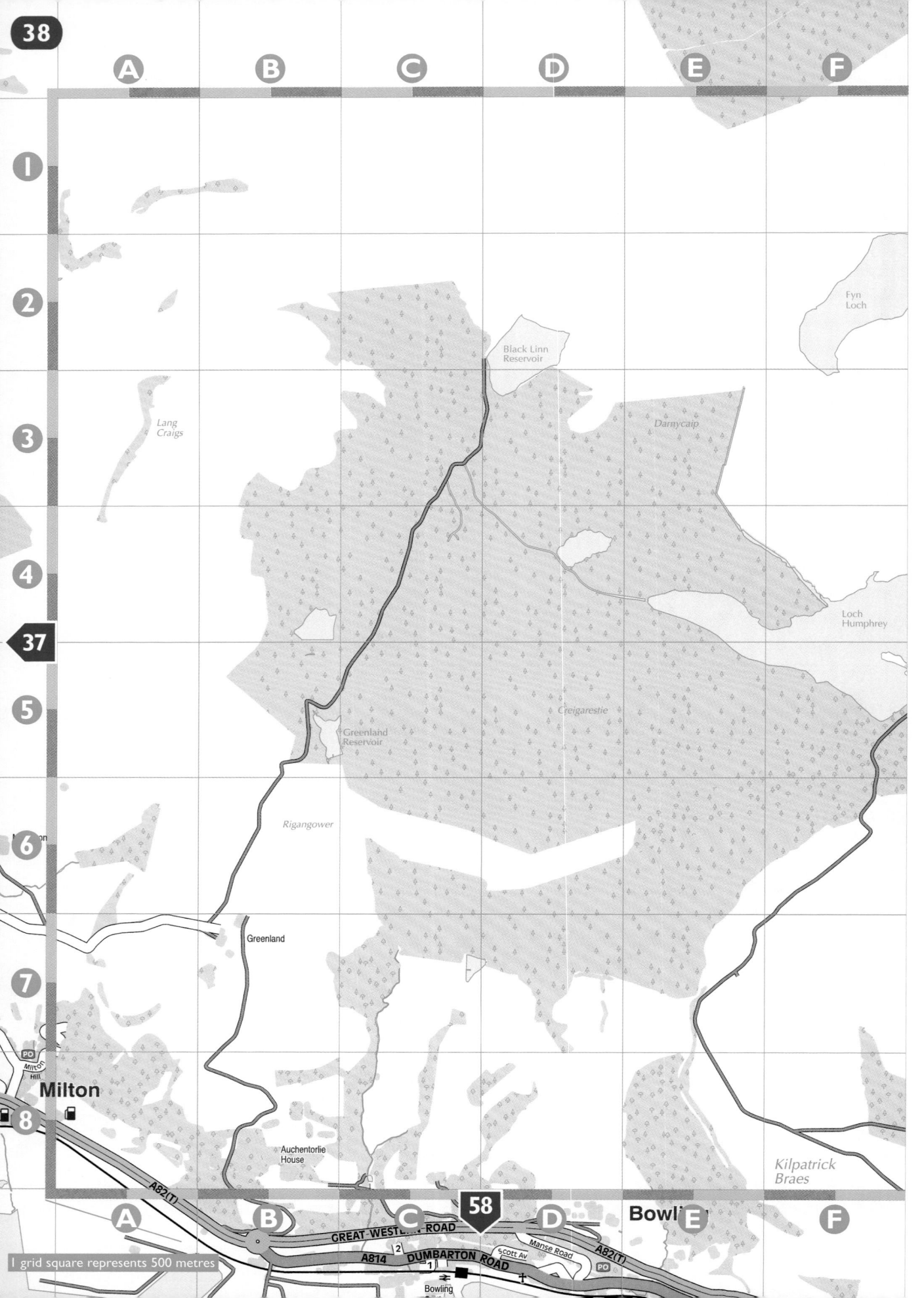

A B C D E F

I

2

3

4

37

5

6

7

8

Fyn Loch

Black Linn Reservoir

Lang Craigs

Darnycaip

Loch Humphrey

Creigarestie

Greenland Reservoir

Rigangower

Greenland

Milton

Auchentorlie House

Kilpatrick Braes

GREAT WESTERN ROAD

A814 DUMBARTON ROAD

Scott Av

Manse Road

A82(T)

Bowling

PO

I grid square represents 500 metres

G   H   J   K   L   M

Saughen
Braes

Lily
Loch

Duncolm

Craighirst

Greenside
Reservoir

Boglairoch

Loch Humphrey Burn

Wester
Cochno

I

2

3

4

40

5

6

7

8

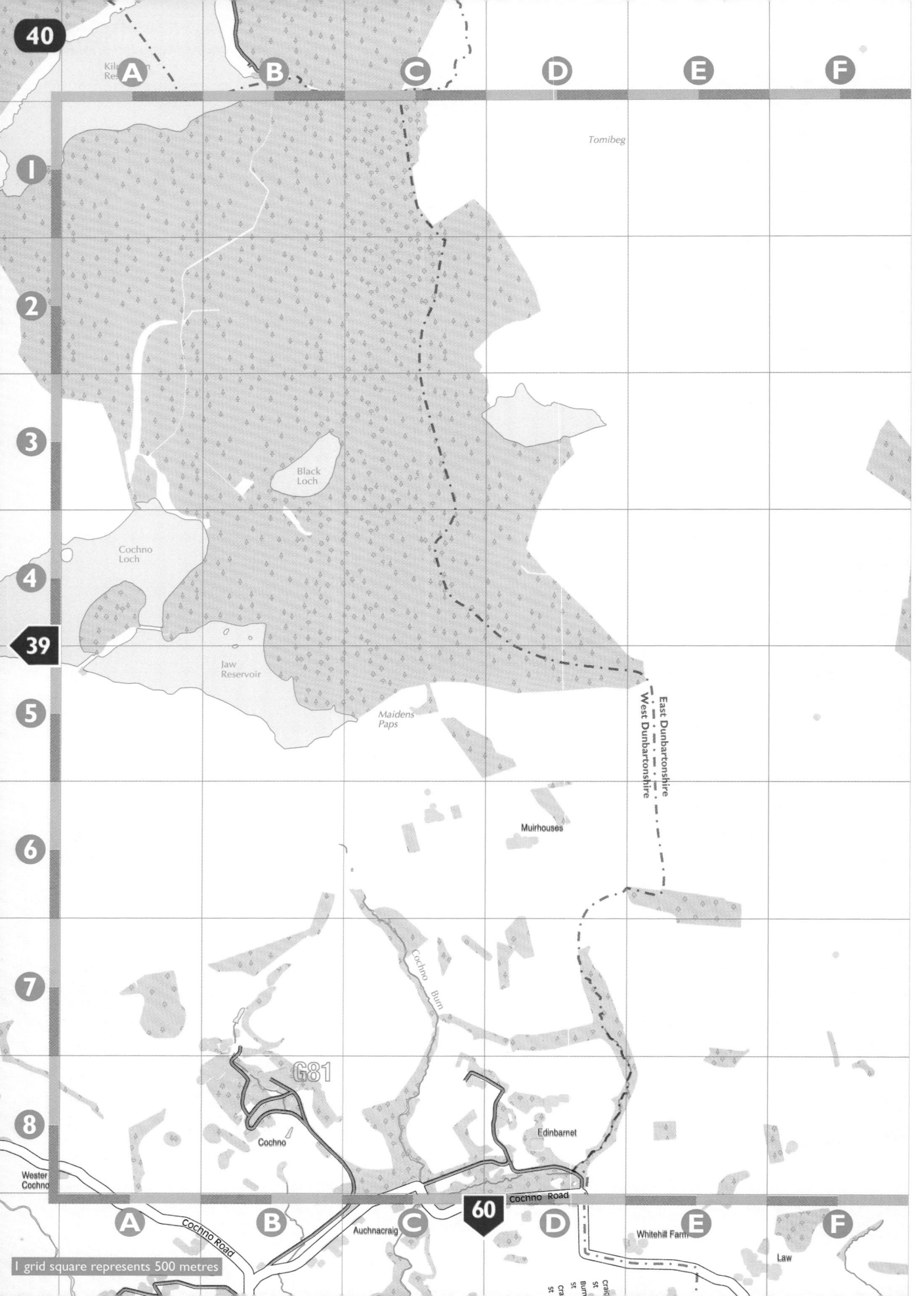

A   B   C   D   E   F

1

2

3

Black
Loch

Cochno
Loch

4

Jaw
Reservoir

Maidens
Paps

5

Tomibeg

East Dunbartonshire
West Dunbartonshire

Muirhouses

6

Cochno Burn

7

G81

8

Cochno

Wester
Cochno

Auchnacraig

Edinbarnet

Whitehill Farm

Law

Cochno Road

Cochno Road

A   B   C   D   E   F

1 grid square represents 500 metres

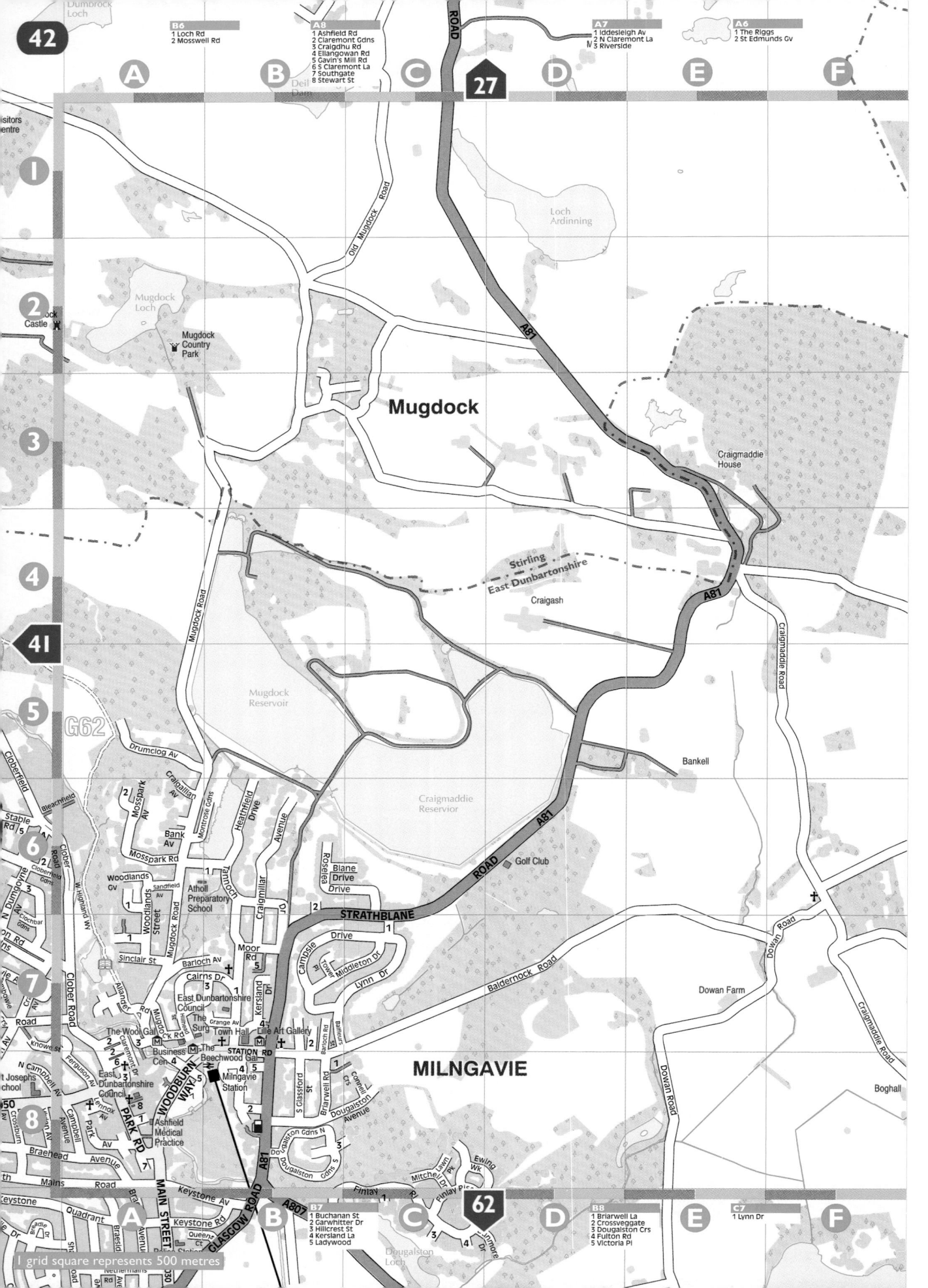

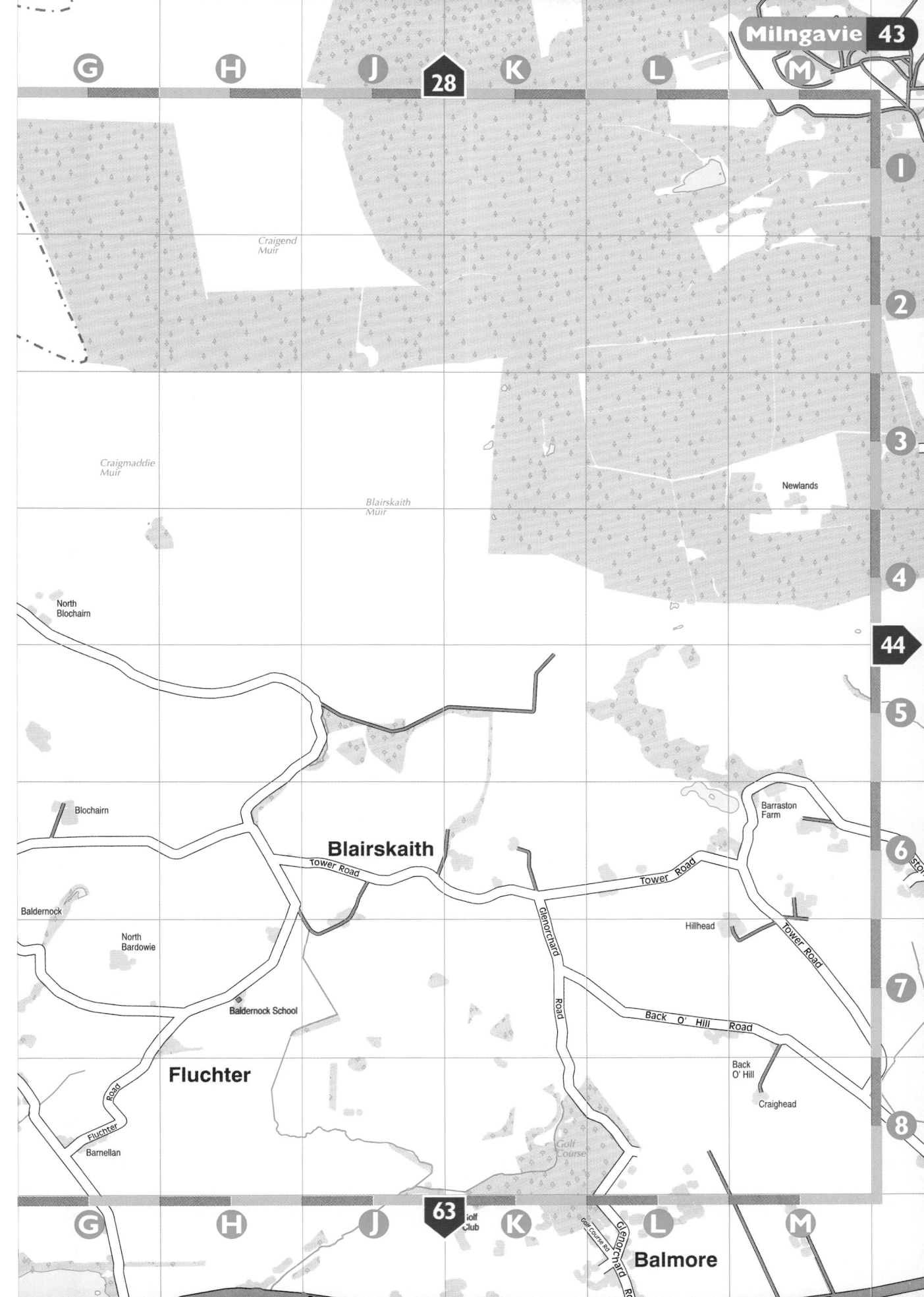

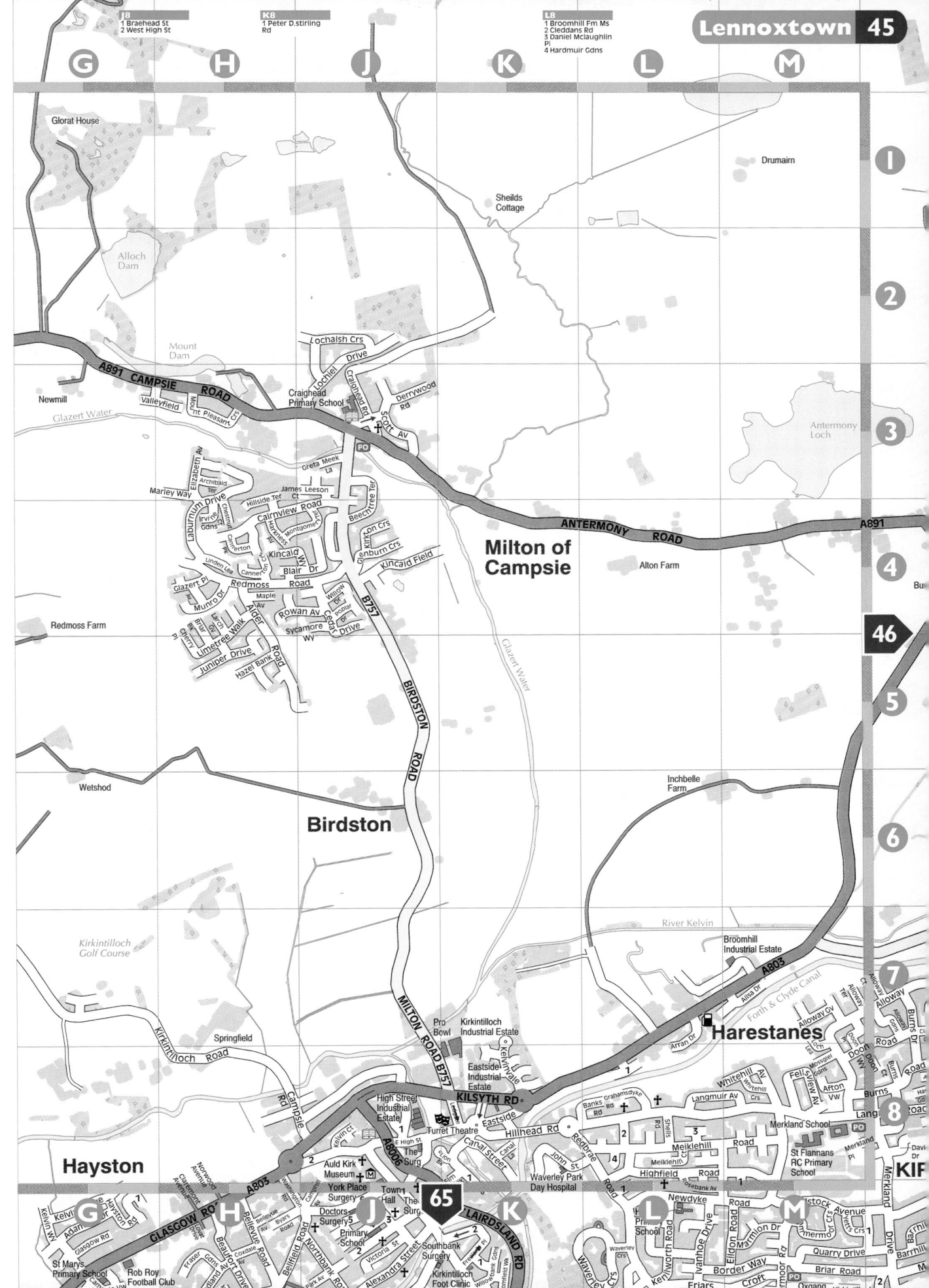

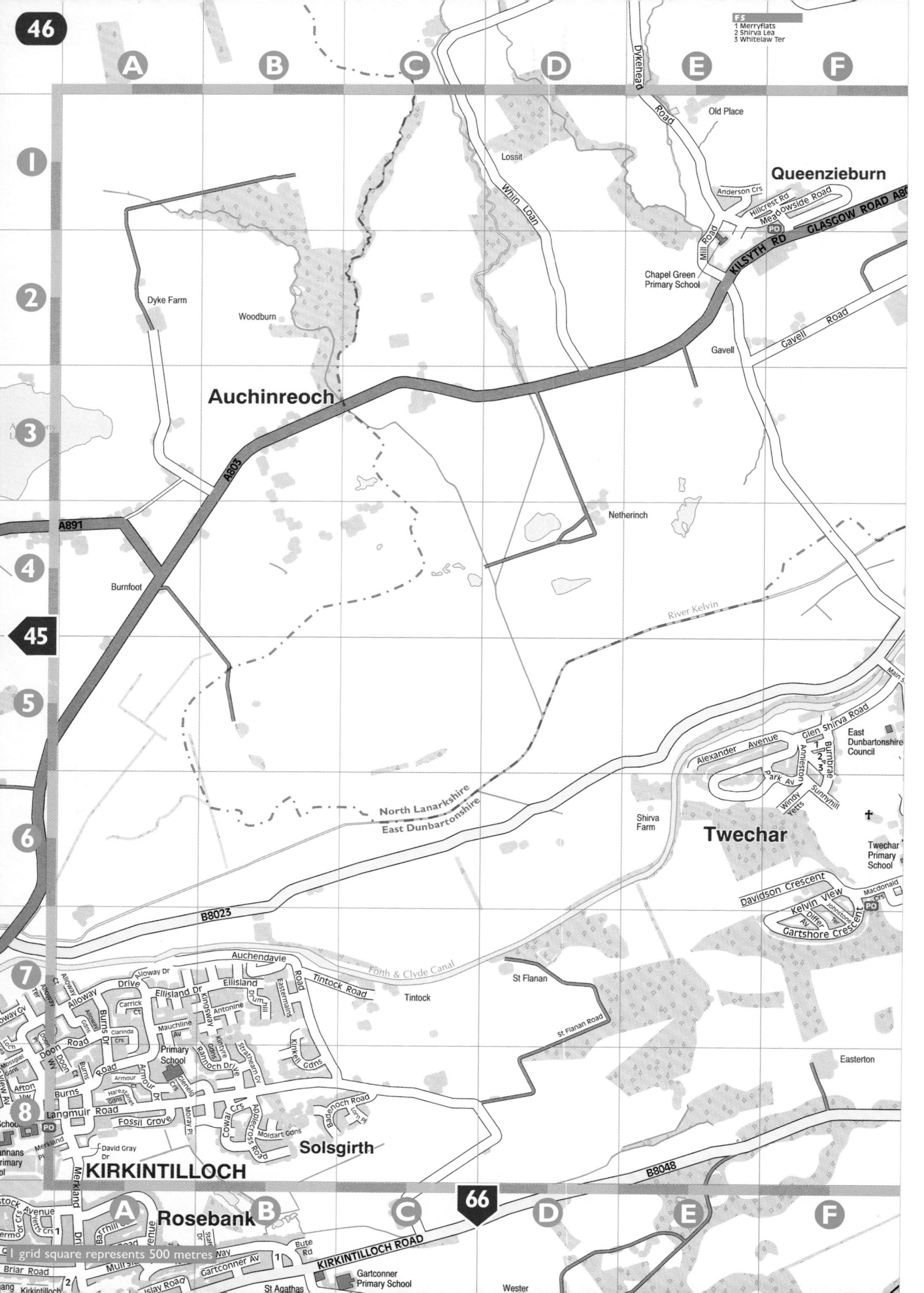

A B C D E F

I

Old Place

Lossit

Queenzieburn

Anderson Crs

Hillcrest Rd

Meadowside Road

PO

KILSYTH RD   GLASGOW ROAD A8

2

Dyke Farm

Woodburn

Chapel Green
Primary School

Gavell

Gavell   Road

A803

Auchinreoch

3

A891

Netherinch

4

Burnfoot

River Kelvin

5

Glen Shirva Road

Alexander   Avenue

Burnbrae

Anniesland

Sunnyhill

East
Dunbartonshire
Council

Park Av

Windy
Yetts

6

North Lanarkshire
East Dunbartonshire

Shirva
Farm

Twechar

Twechar
Primary
School

Davidson Crescent

Kelvin View

Macdonald
Crs

B8023

Johnstone

Differ
Av

PO

Gartshore Crescent

Auchendavie

Tintock Road

Forth & Clyde Canal

St Flanan

7

Alloway Dr

Drive

Ellisland Dr

Ellisland

Eastermains

Drumhill

St Flanan

Tintock

Alloway
Gdns

Carrick
Ct

Kingsway

Antonine

Road

Mauchline
Av

Kintyre   Gdns

St Flanan Road

Alloway Gv

Burns

Road

Ciarinda
Crs

Kintyre
Ct

Strathearn Gv

Doon Dr

Primary
School

Rannoch Drive

Kinkell Gdns

Easterton

Doon W

Burns

Road

Armour   Dr

Armour

Clarinda
Crs

Cowal Crs

Applecross Road

Barenoch Road

Afton

Hare Street
Gdns

Moray Pl

Moidart Gdns

8

Langmuir   Road

Fossil Grove

Solsgirth

PO

David Gray
Dr

Merkland

KIRKINTILLOCH

B8048

A B C D E F

Rosebank

Bute
Rd

KIRKINTILLOCH ROAD

Gartconner Av

St Agathas

Gartconner
Primary School

Wester

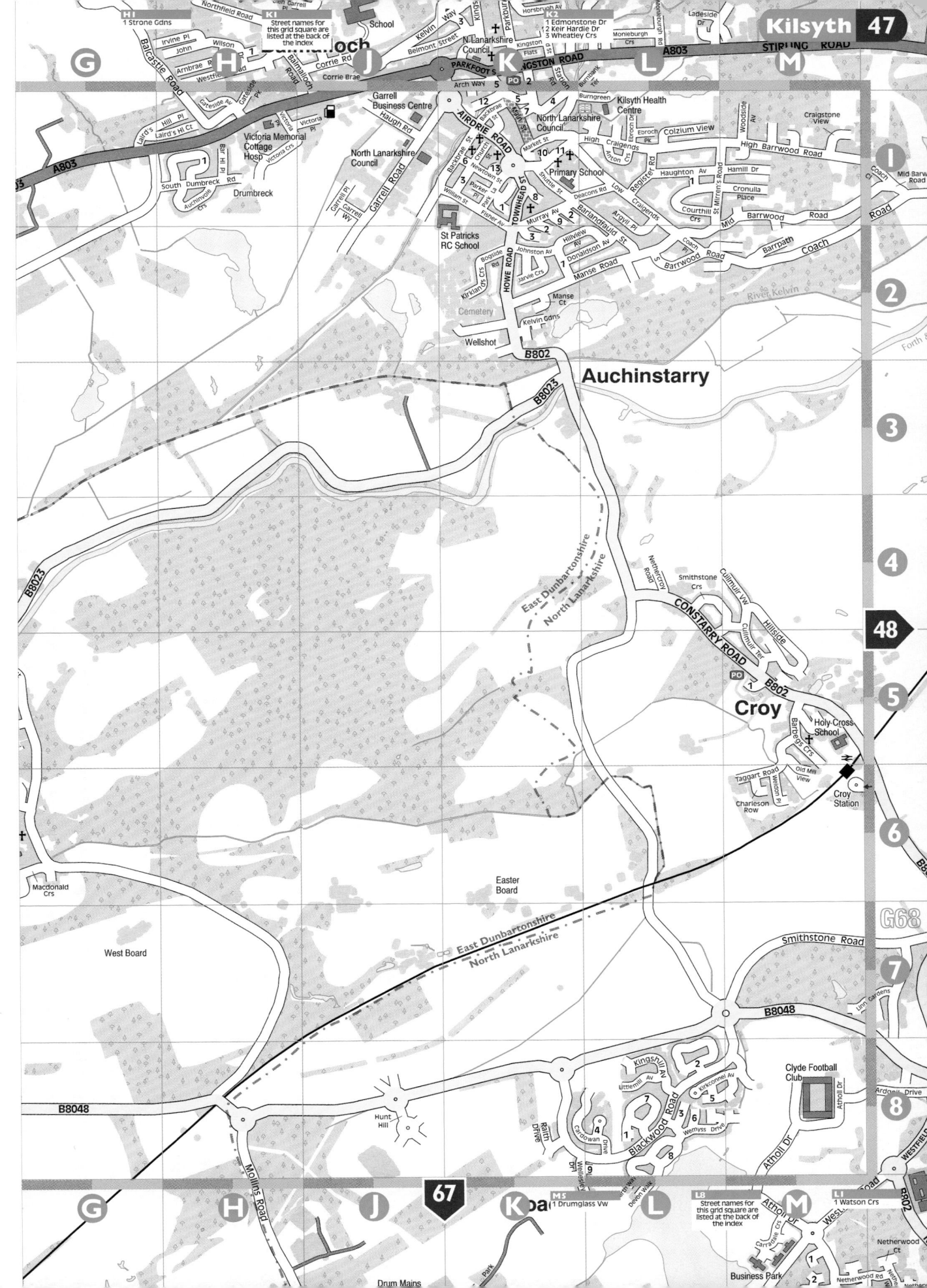

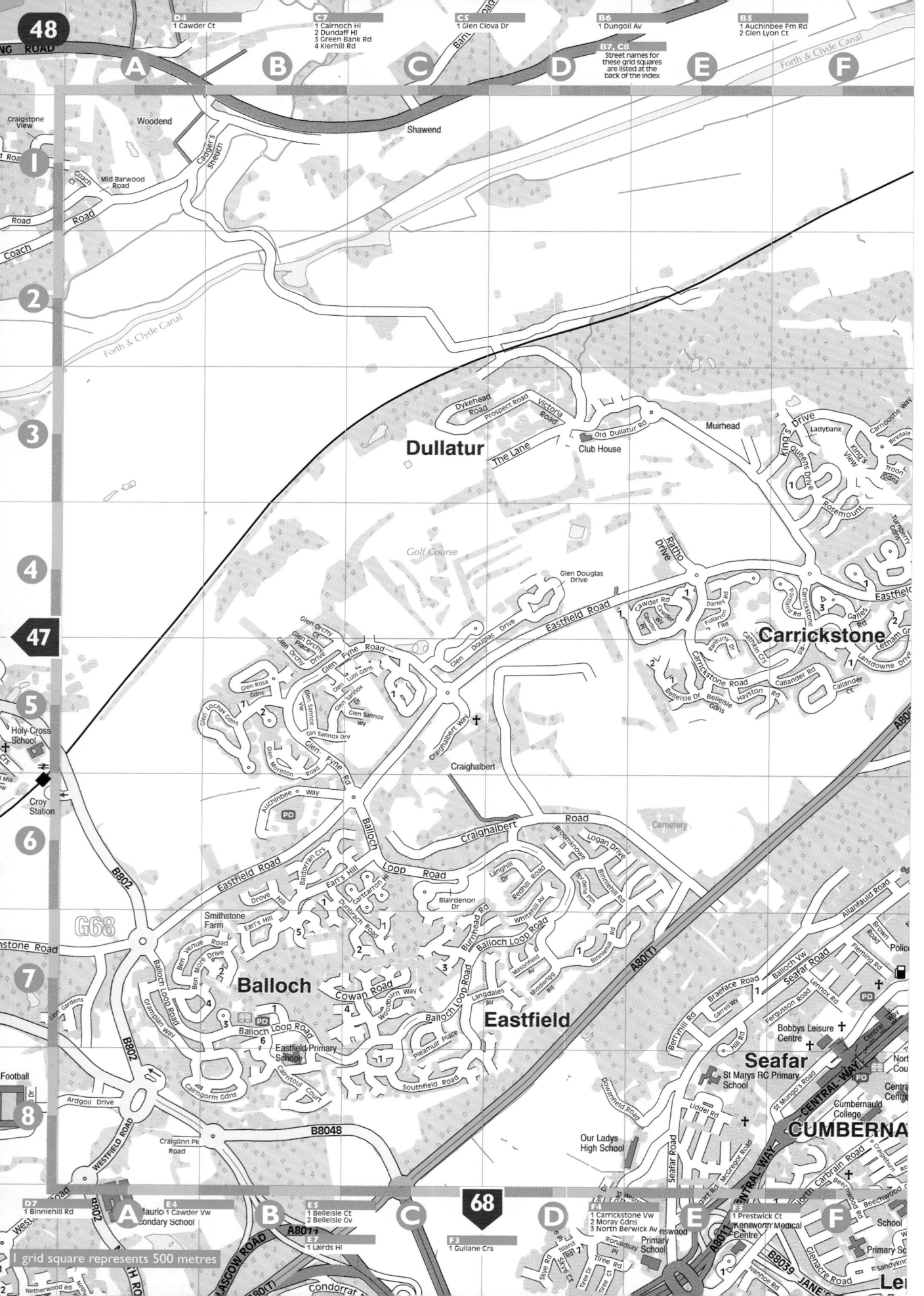

I grid square represents 500 metres

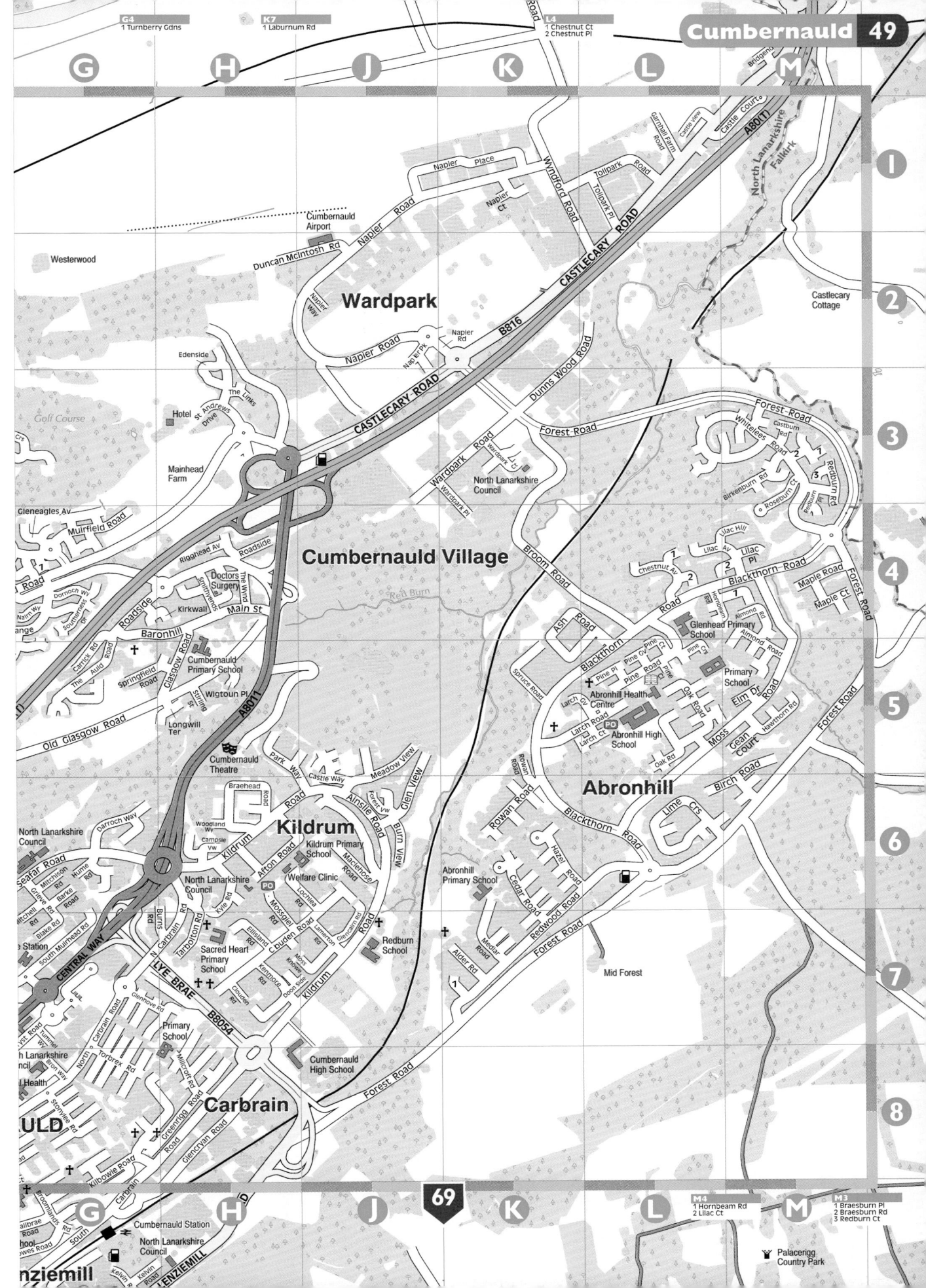

G4
1 Turnberry Gdns
K7
1 Laburnum Rd
L4
1 Chestnut Ct
2 Chestnut Pl

G   H   J   K   L   M

I
2
3
4
5
6
7
8

Westerwood

Cumbernauld Airport

Duncan McIntosh Rd

Wardpark

Napier Road

Napier Place

Napier Ct

Napier Way

Napier Rd

Napier Road

Nap Rd Pk

Tollpark Road

Tollpark Pl

Gunnall Farm Road

Castle View

Castle Courts

A80(T)

CASTLECARY ROAD

B816

North Lanarkshire
Falkirk

Castlecary Cottage

Edenside

The Links

St Andrews Drive

Hotel

Mainhead Farm

Golf Course

Gleneagles Av

Muirfield Road

Dornoch Wy

Southernes Pl

Nairn Wy

Range

Road

Carrick Rd

The Auld Road

Rigghead Av

Roadside

Smithyends

Doctors Surgery

The Wynd

Kirkwall

Main St

Baronhill

Glasgow Road

Springfield Road

Cumbernauld Primary School

Wigtoun Pl

Stirling St

Longwill Ter

Old Glasgow Road

A8011

Cumbernauld Theatre

Braehead

Castle Way

Park Way

Castle Way

Meadow View

Ainslie Road

Glen View

Burn View

Forev Vw

Woodland Wy

Campsie Vw

Darroch Wy

Kildrum

Kildrum Primary School

Afton Road

Maclenose Road

Welfare Clinic

Lochlea

Mossdjel Road

PO

North Lanarkshire Council

Kyle Rd

Tarbolton Rd

Burns Rd

Carbrain Rd

Lamerton Road

Kildrum Road

Glencairn Rd

Redburn School

Ellisand

C Duglen Road

Kenmore Rd

Moss Knowes

Clouden Rd

Doon Side

Sacred Heart Primary School

LYE BRAE

B8054

Glenove Road

Millcroft Road

Primary School

Torbrex Rd

Tunnel Rd

CENTRAL WAY

South Muirhead Rd

Seafar Road

Mitchison Rd

Crowe Rd

Barke Road

Blake Rd

Mitchell

e Station

North Lanarkshire Council

Hume Rd

Carbrain Road

Greenrigg Road

Kilbowie Road

Glencryan Road

Carbrain

ULD

Kilbowie Road

Carbrain Road

h Lanarkshire
ncil
l Health

llibrae
Road

Roadside

Cumbernauld Village

Red Burn

Wyndford Road

Forest Road

Forest Road

Dunns Wood Road

Wardpark Road

Wardpark Pl

Wardpark Ct

North Lanarkshire Council

Broom Road

CASTLECARY ROAD

Forest-Road

Whitelees Road

Castburn Rd

Birkenburn Rd

Roseburn Rd

Redburn Rd

Lilac Hill

Lilac Av

Lilac Pl

Chestnut Av

Blackthorn-Road

Maple Road

Maple Ct

Forest Road

Ash Road

Blackthorn Road

Pine Pl

Pine Gv

Pine Road

Hornbeam Rd

Almond Rd

Almond Road

Glenhead Primary School

Primary School

Elm Dr

Larch Gv

Larch Road

Larch Ct

Abronhill Health Centre

PO

Oak Road

Moss

Gean Court

Hawthorn Rd

Abronhill High School

Oak Rd

Spruce Road

Rowan Road

Abronhill

Rowan Road

Blackthorn Road

Hazel Road

Lime Crs

Birch Road

Forest Road

Abronhill Primary School

Cedar Road

Redwood Road

Alder Rd

Medlar Rd

Forest Road

Mid Forest

Forest Road

Cumbernauld High School

G   H   J   K   L   M

M4
1 Hornbeam Rd
2 Lilac Ct

M3
1 Braesburn Pl
2 Braesburn Rd
3 Redburn Ct

Cumbernauld Station

North Lanarkshire Council

nziemill

Kelvin

Kelvin

TENZIEMILL

Palacerigg Country Park

E4
1 Alison Ct
2 Glebe Rd
3 Langhouse Pl
4 Primrose Pl

D5
1 Ardgowan Crs
2 Finnockbog Dr
3 Hill Rd
4 Willow Pl

D4
1 Station Rd

A8
1 Broom Rd

Curling Pond

A B C 30 D E F

I

A770

2

Bankfoot

Lunderston
Bay

Kip Water

Ardgowan

✝

3

Ardgowan
Point

ROAD

Bridgend

Inverkip

Magpie

Swallow Brae

SWIR

Millhouse
Road

Millhouse
Road

Marina

INVERKIP

Primrose
Crs
Primrose AV

Bogside

4

Street

Langhouse

Cemetery

3

2

Langhouse Road

4

Langhill

Daff AV

✝

Inverkip
Primary
School

PO

Glen Crs

7

Main

1

7

Station AV

4

Finnockbog Road

2

Beatock
Pl

Beatock Burn

Langhouse

5

Commoncraig
Pl

3

Kip AV

Inverkip
Station
⇌

Inverkip
Bay

Daff Burn

Berfern

6

Hill

Everton

Finnock Bog Farm

7

Innellan
Rd

Wilding
Road

Kirn Dr

McChattan
Pl

Brueacre Burn

Toward
Rd

Ascog Pl

Stuart
Road

Leven
Rd

Ardgowan

Brueacre Rd

Mt

8

Castle Road

Carron Rd

1

Wemyss Bay
Primary School

Sunart
Rd

Linnhe Rd

Etive
Road

Melfort Rd

Undercliffe

4

Lomond
Road

Striven
Rd

Ryan Road

Katrine
Road

A B 70 C D E F

PA18

myss

✝

Terrace

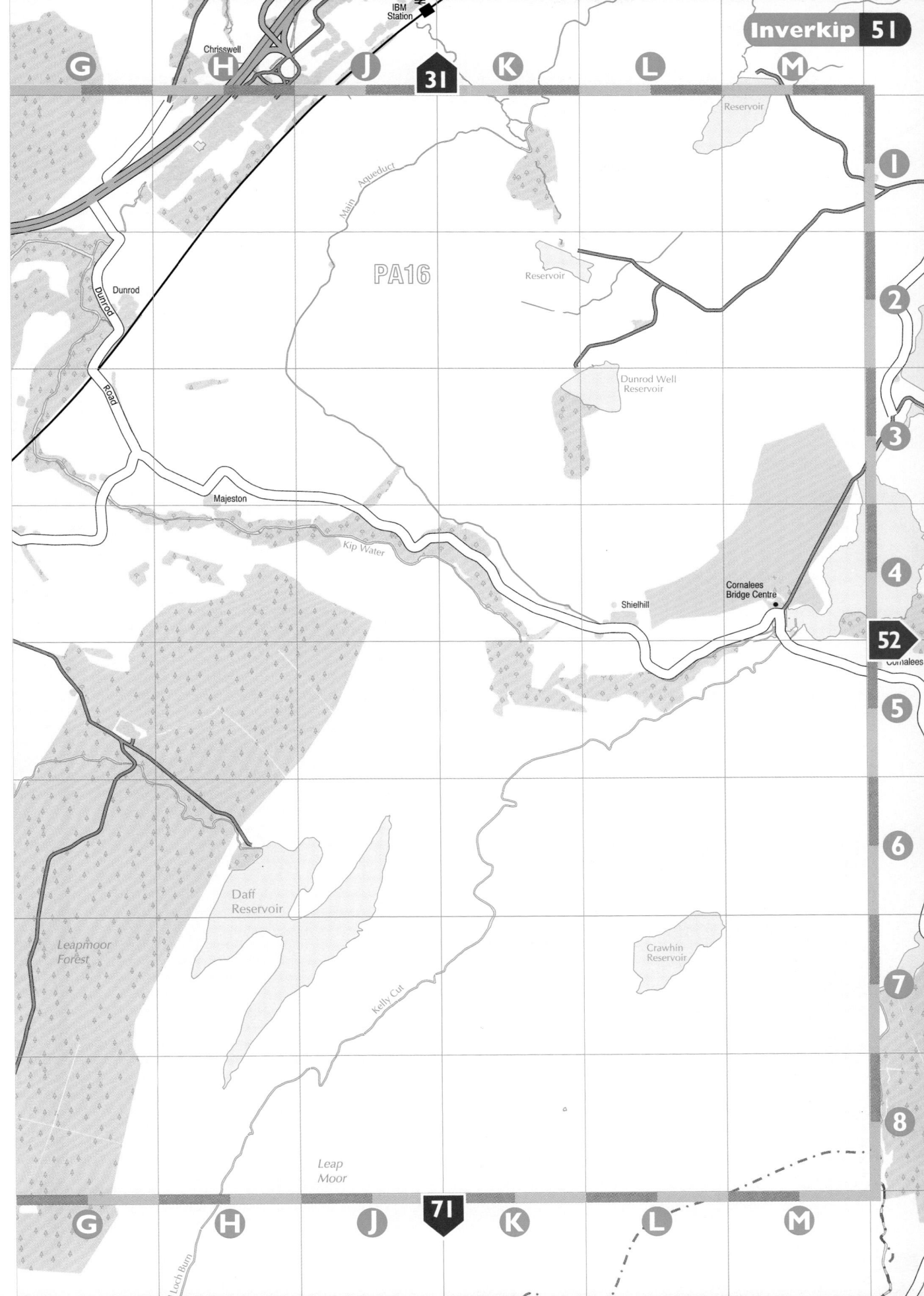

G　H　J　31　K　L　M

IBM
Station

I

2

3

Reservoir

PA16

Reservoir

Dunrod Well
Reservoir

Main Aqueduct

Dunrod

Dunrod

Road

Majeston

Kip Water

Shielhill

Cornalees
Bridge Centre

4

52

Cornalees

5

Daff
Reservoir

Crawhin
Reservoir

6

Leapmoor
Forest

7

Kelly Cut

8

Leap
Moor

Loch Burn

G　H　J　71　K　L　M

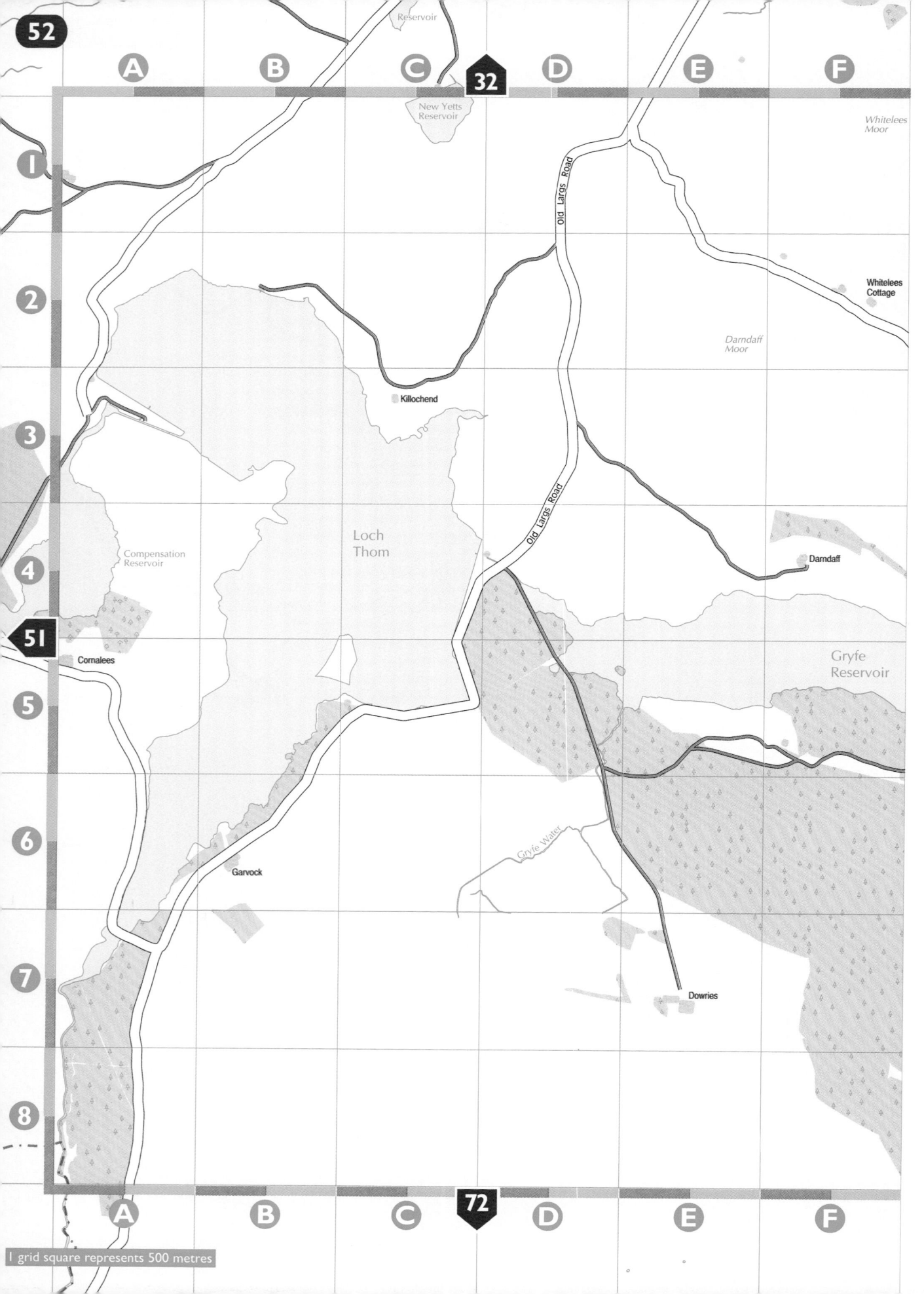

Reservoir

New Yetts
Reservoir

Whitelees
Moor

Old Largs Road

Whitelees
Cottage

Darndaff
Moor

Killochend

Old Largs Road

Compensation
Reservoir

Loch
Thom

Darndaff

Cornalees

Gryfe
Reservoir

Garvock

Gryfe Water

Dowries

1 grid square represents 500 metres

G   H   J   33   K   L   M

Lilybank

ROCHMOUNTAIN RD

Luss Avenue
Luss Pl
Kenton Road
Dalmoak Road
Arden Rd
Lady L
Craigieknowe

B788

Devol Burn

Lurg
Moor

Burnhead
Moor

Knocknair's
Hill
Reservoir

AUCHENFOIL

Burnhead

ROAD

B788

Hare

Gryfe
Reservoir

54

Garshangan

GarshanganBurn

Mansfield

Dykefoot

Hillside

Green Water

G   H   J   73   K   L   M

I
2
3
4
5
6
7
8

I grid square represents 500 metres

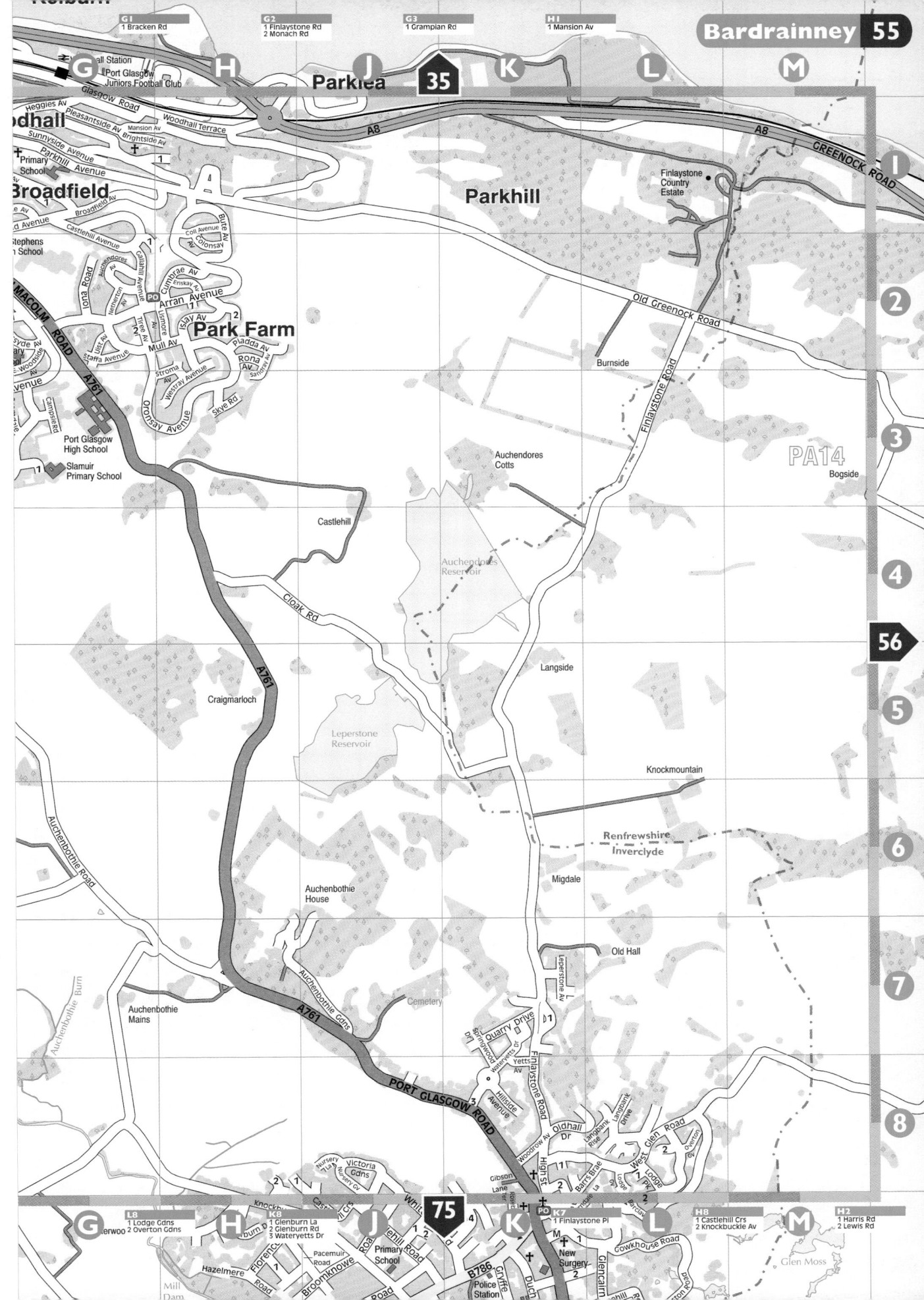

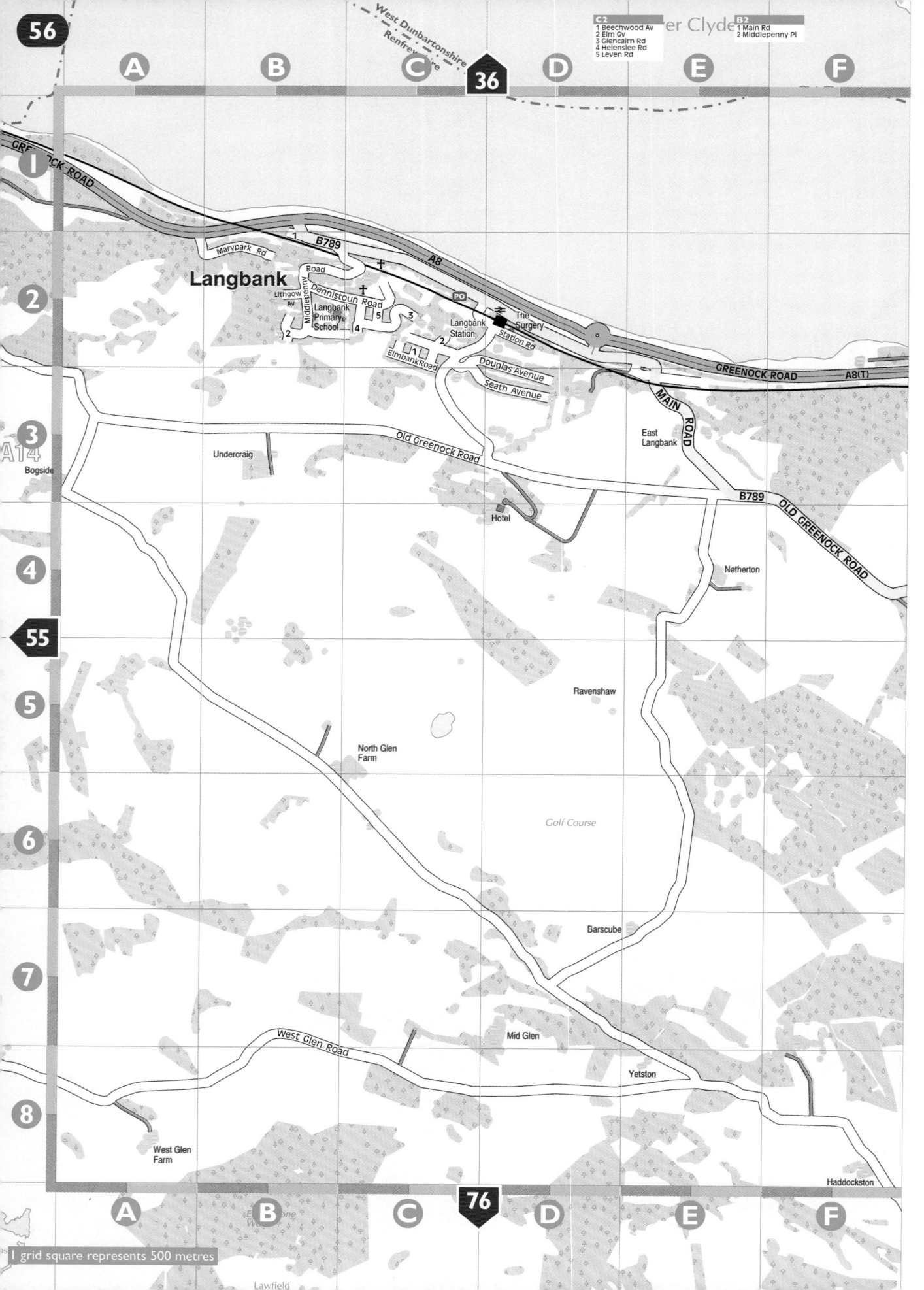

A   B   C   36   D   E   F

C2
1 Beechwood Av
2 Elm Gv
3 Glencairn Rd
4 Helenslee Rd
5 Leven Rd

B2
1 Main Rd
2 Middlepenny Pl

er Clyde

West Dunbartonshire
Renfrewshire

GREENOCK ROAD

1

Marypark Rd   B789   1   A8

Langbank   Road   †

Dennistoun Road   †   PO   The Surgery

Lithgow Av   5   3   Langbank Station   Station Rd

Middlepenny   Langbank Primary School   4   2

2   Elmbank Road   1   Langbank Station   2   Douglas Avenue

Seath Avenue

MAIN ROAD   GREENOCK ROAD   A8(T)

A14   Old Greenock Road   East Langbank

Bogside

Undercraig   B789   OLD GREENOCK ROAD

Hotel   Netherton

55

Ravenshaw

North Glen Farm

Golf Course

Barscube

West Glen Road   Mid Glen

Yetston

West Glen Farm

Haddockston

A   B   C   76   D   E   F

1 grid square represents 500 metres

Lawfield

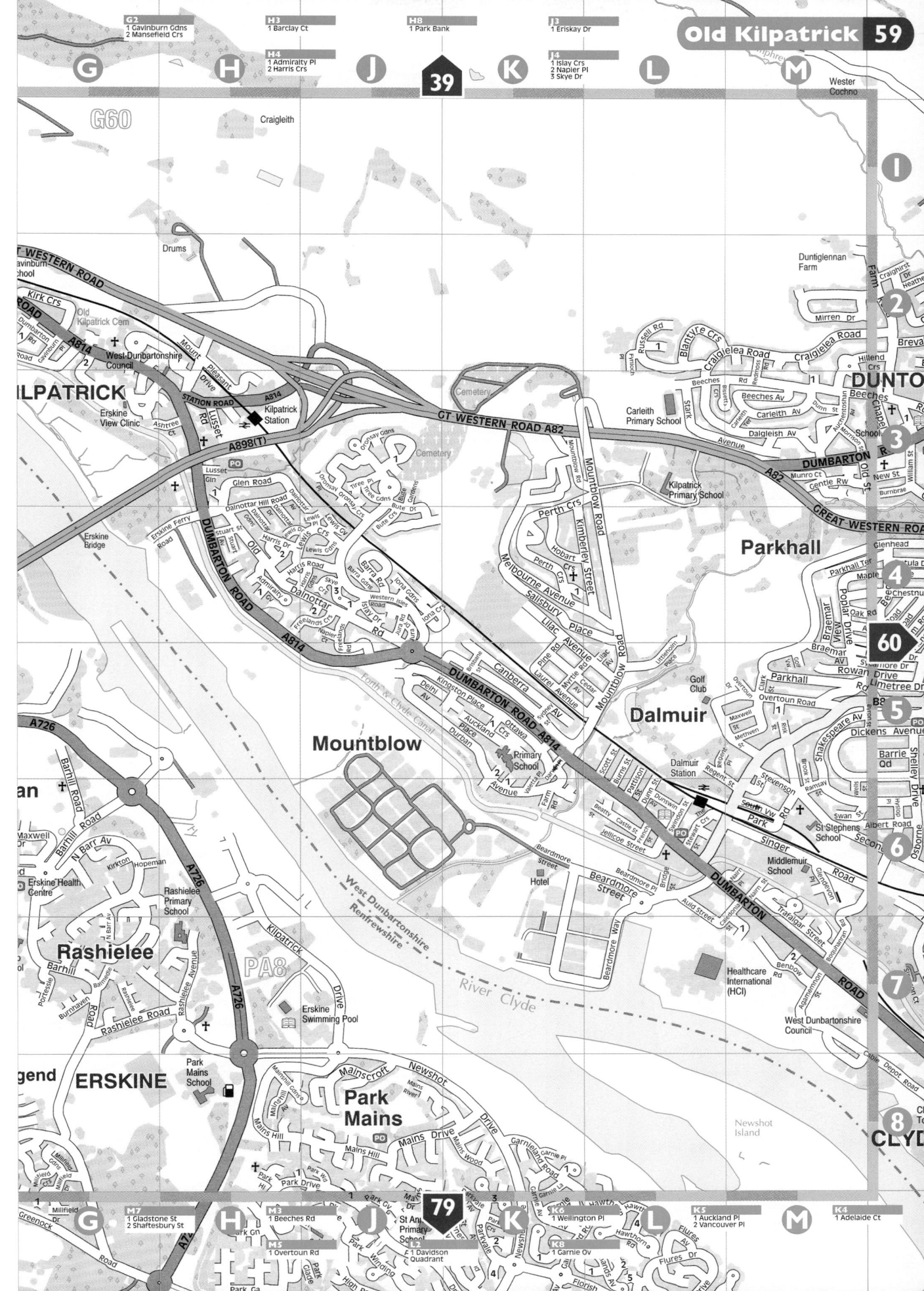

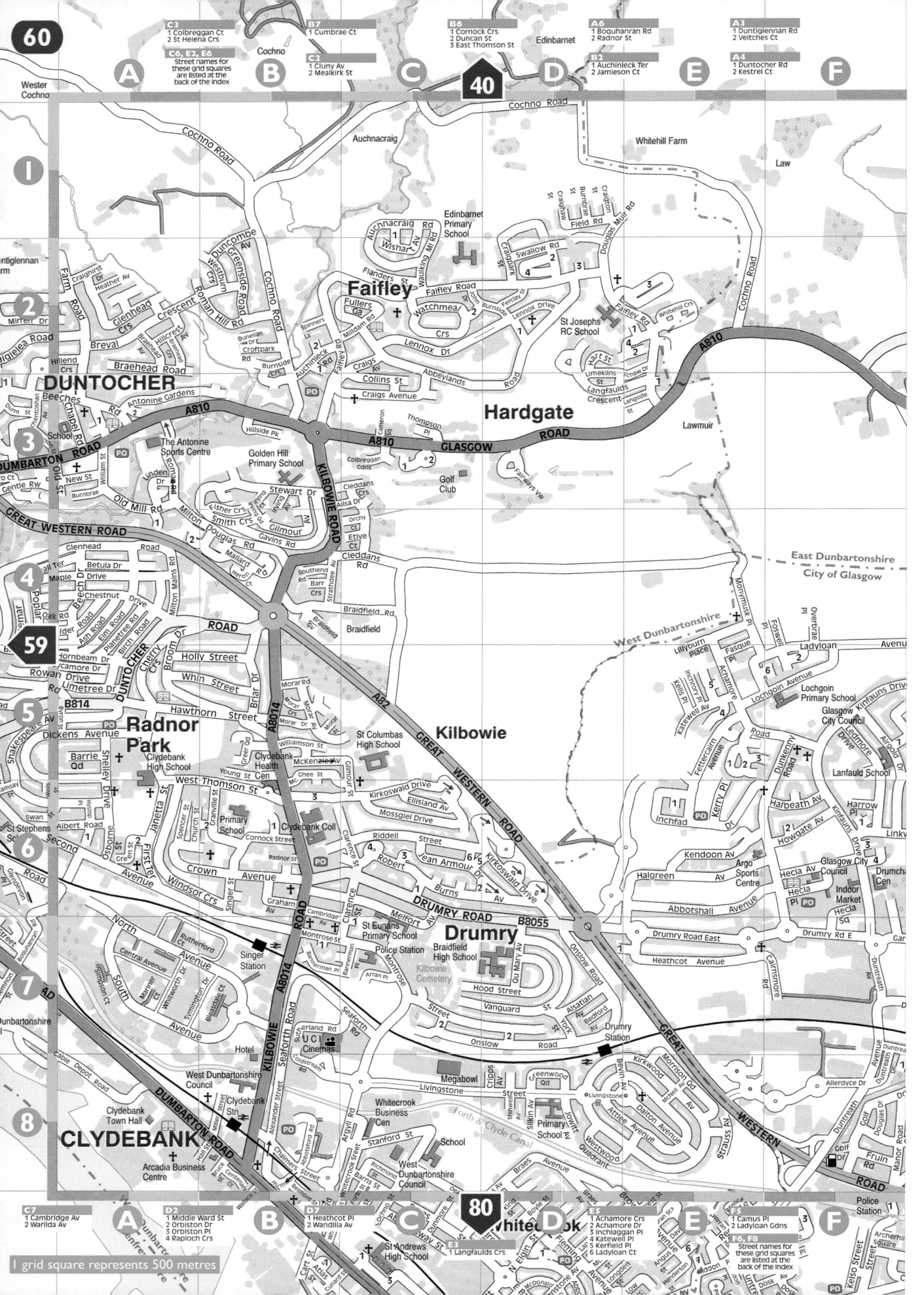

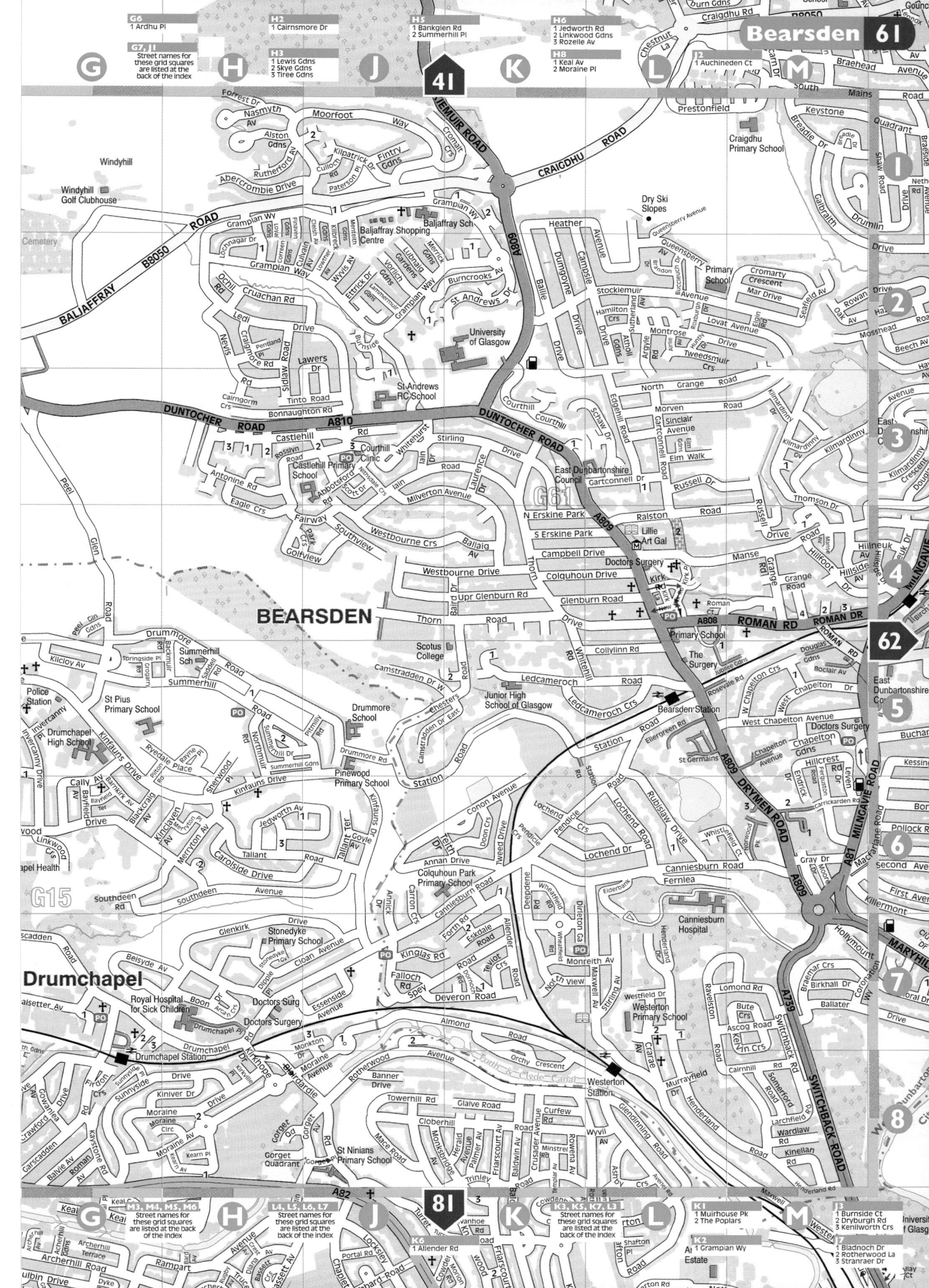

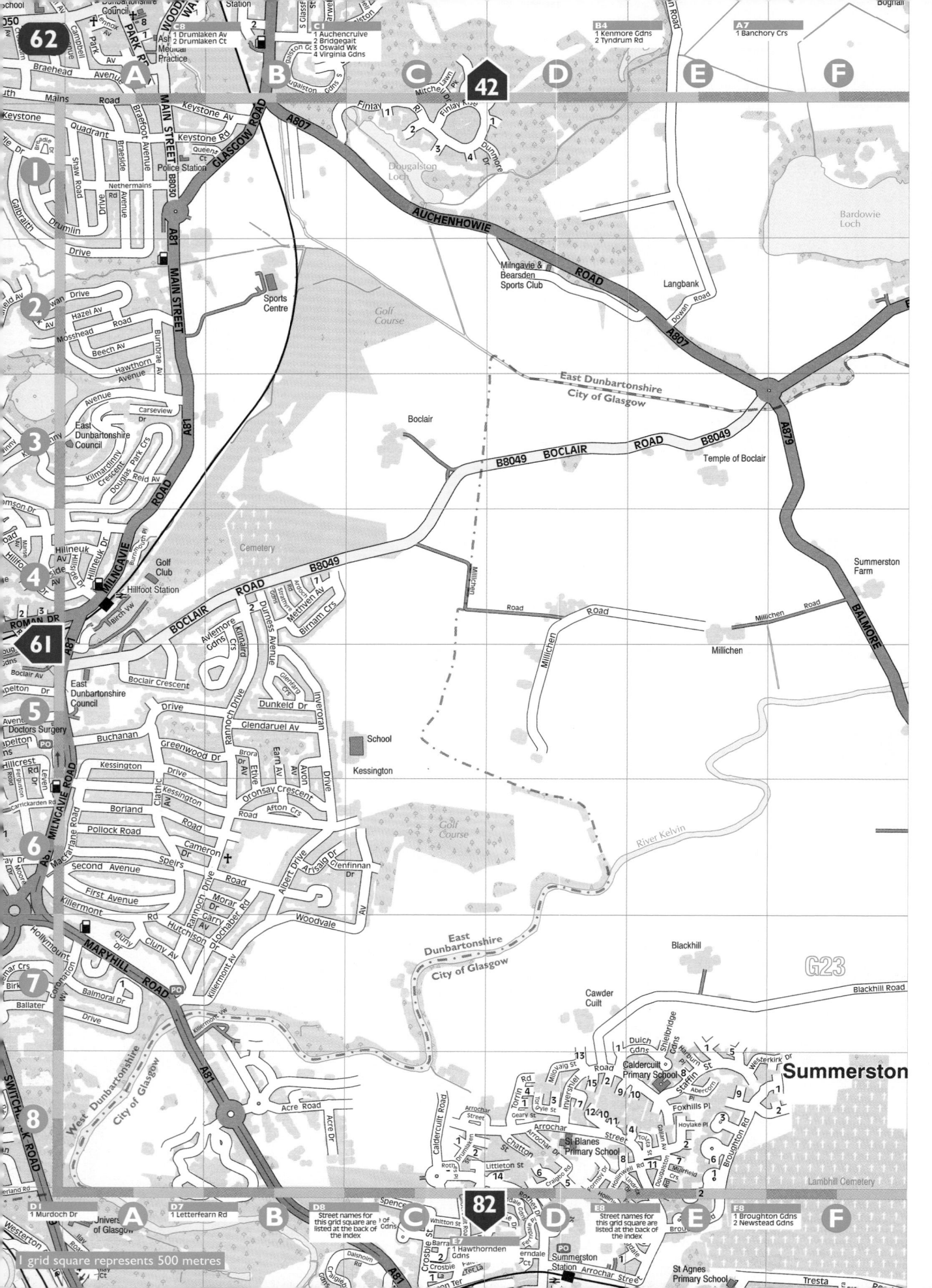

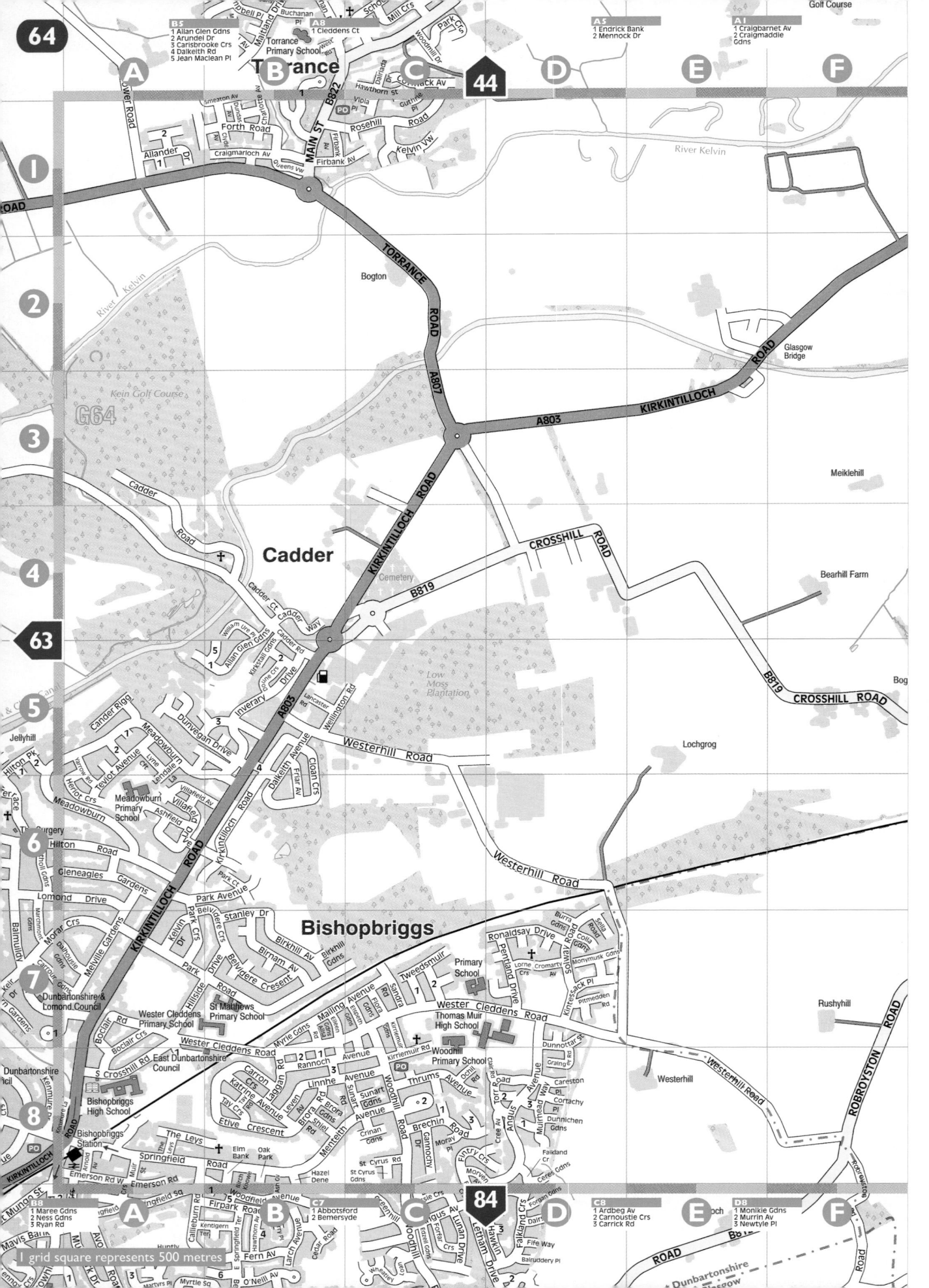

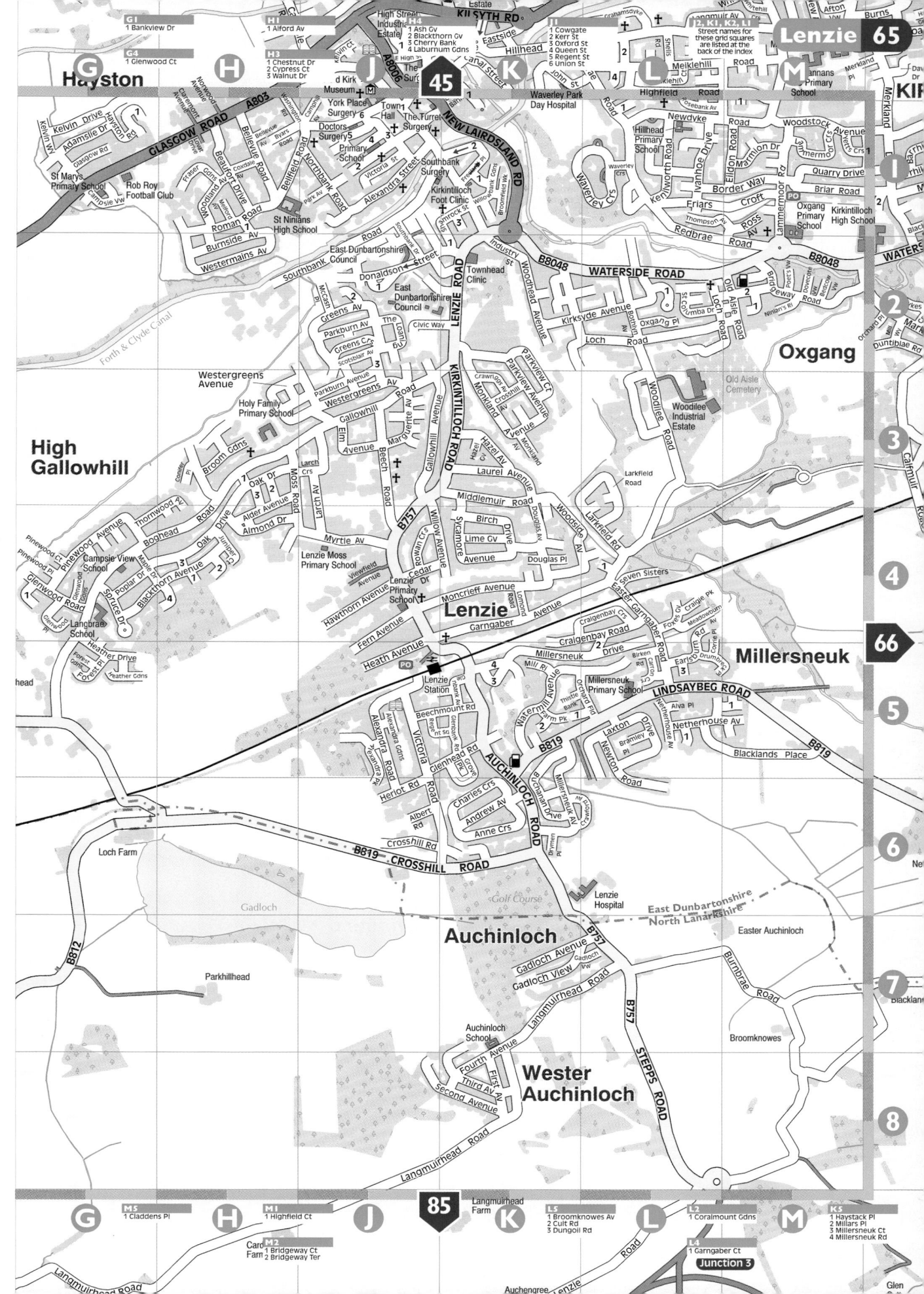

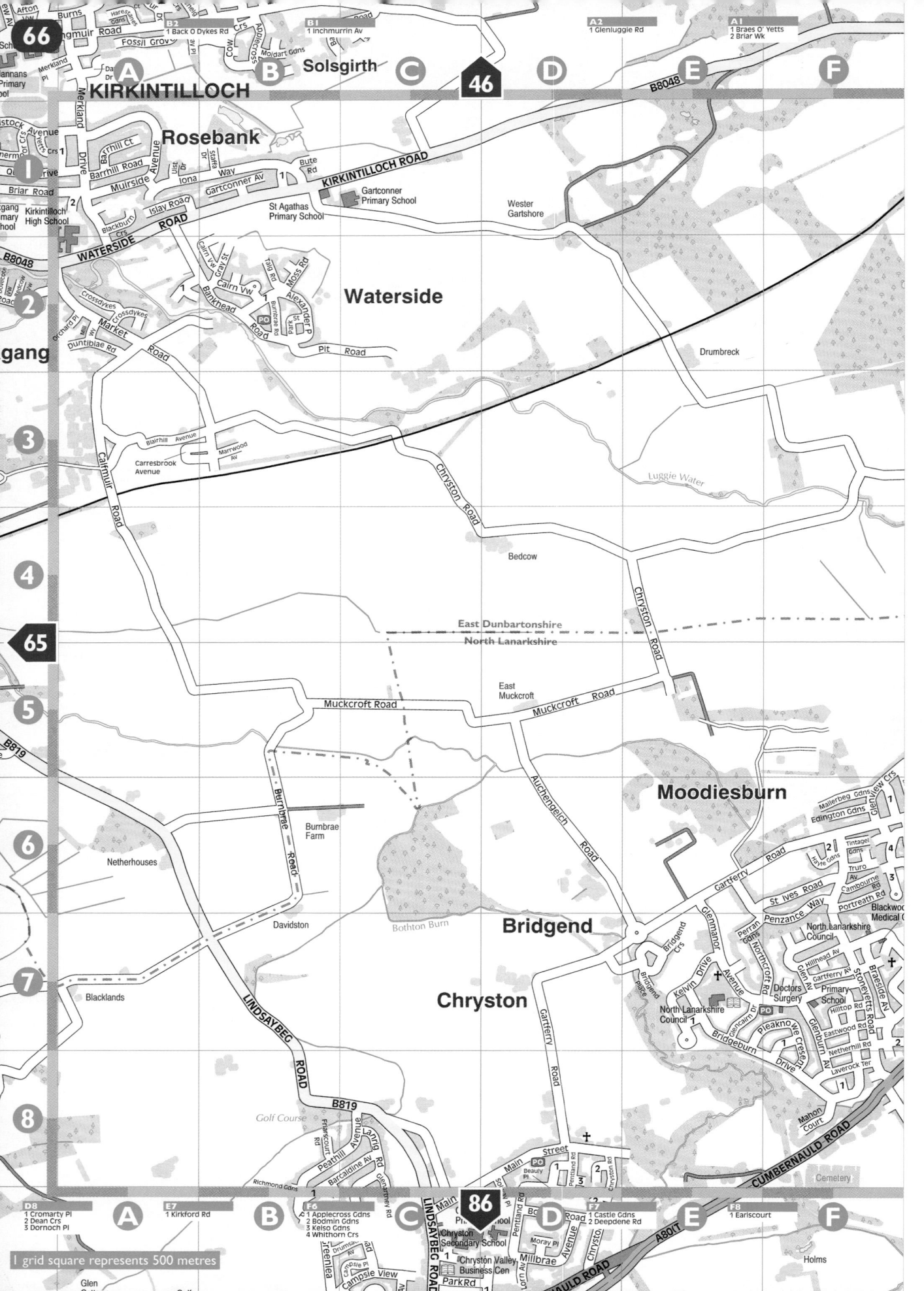

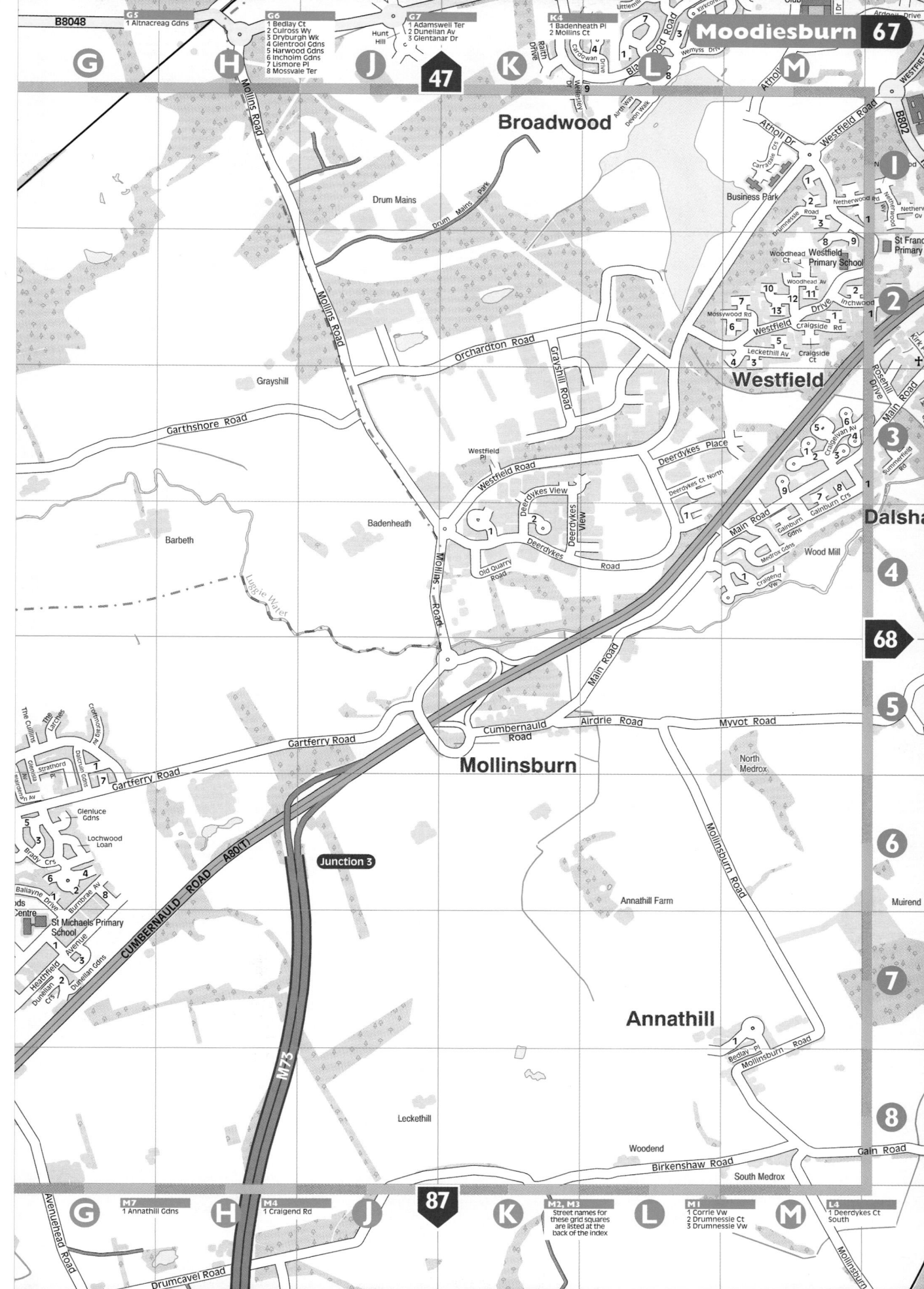

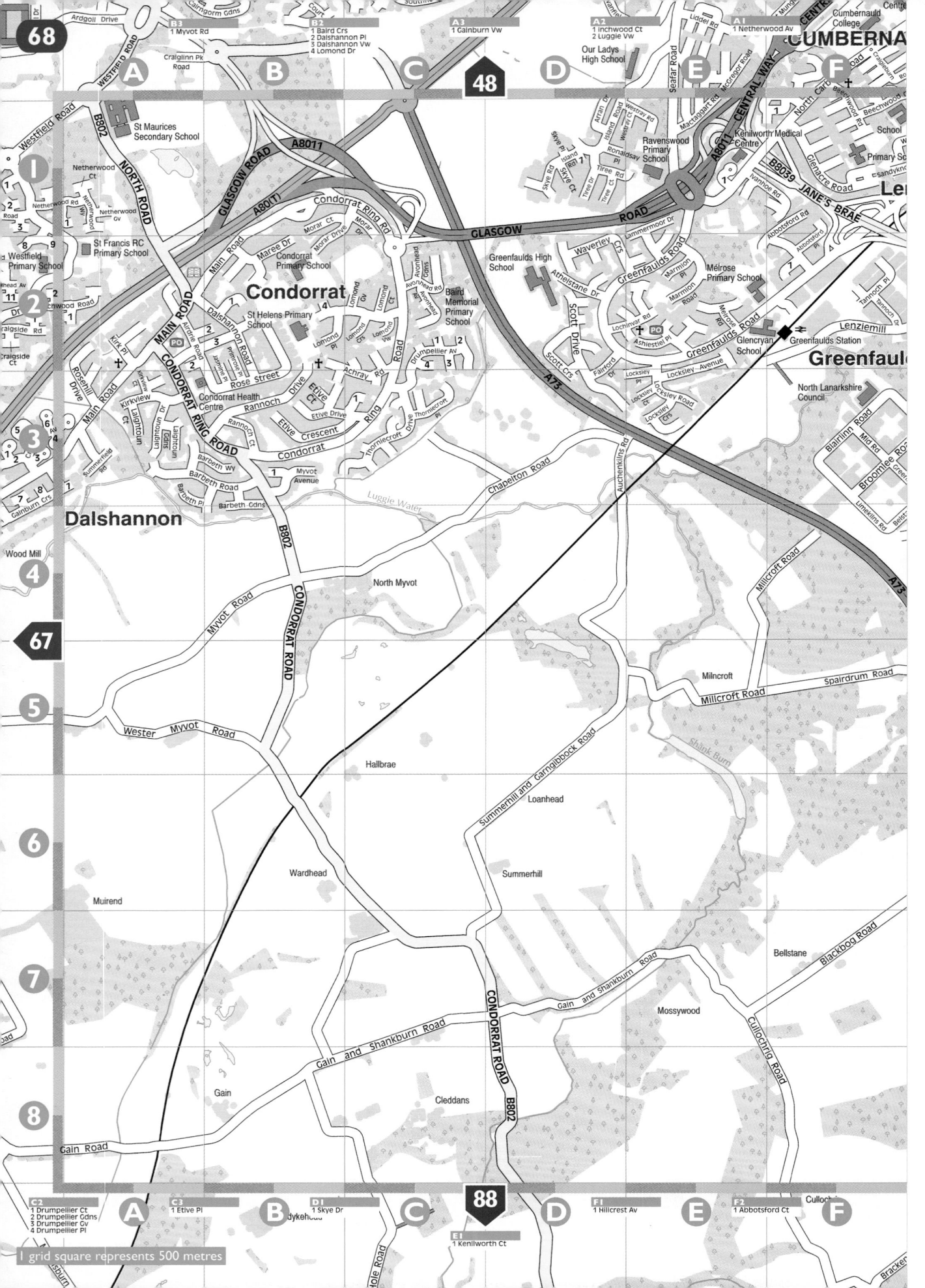

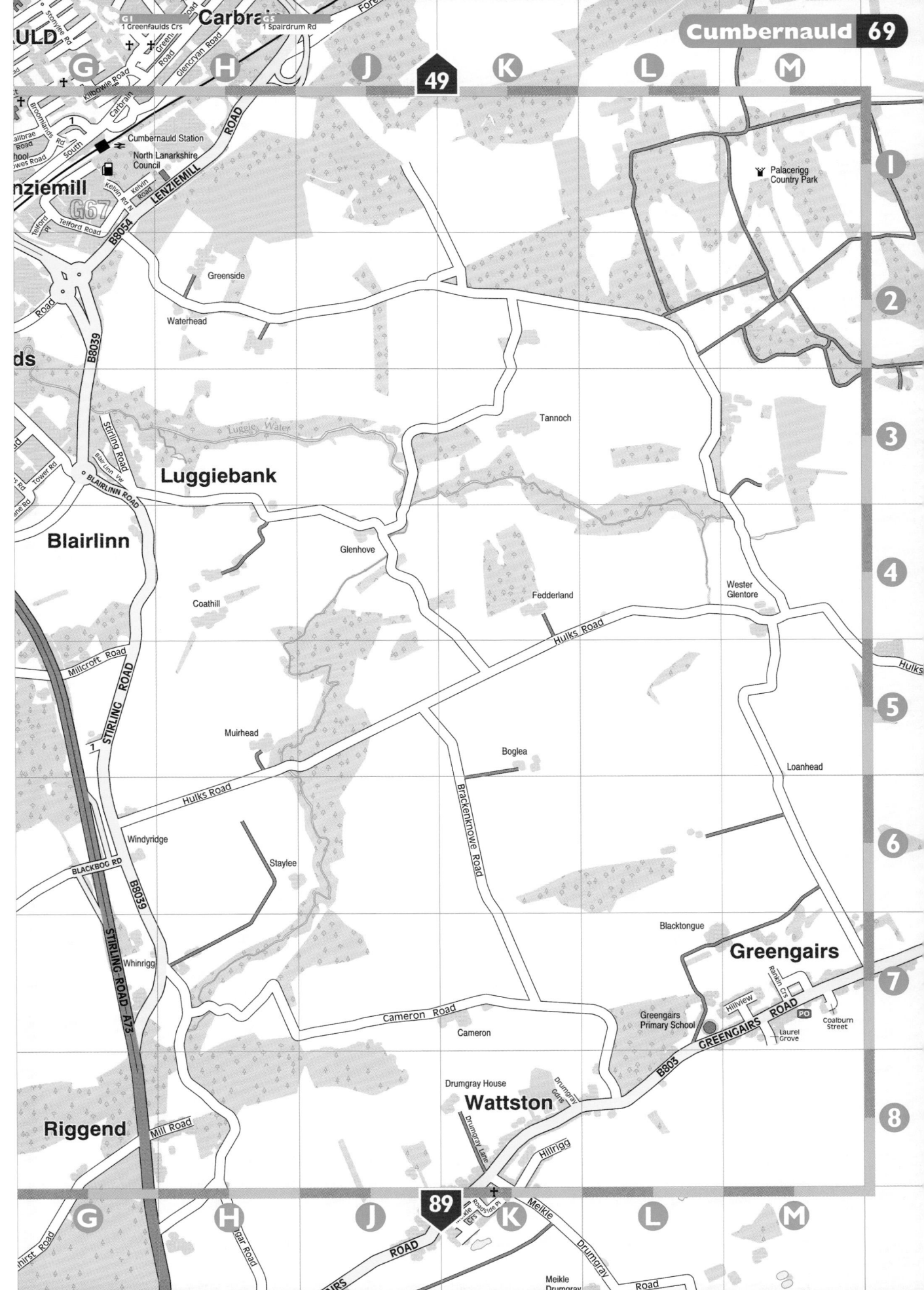

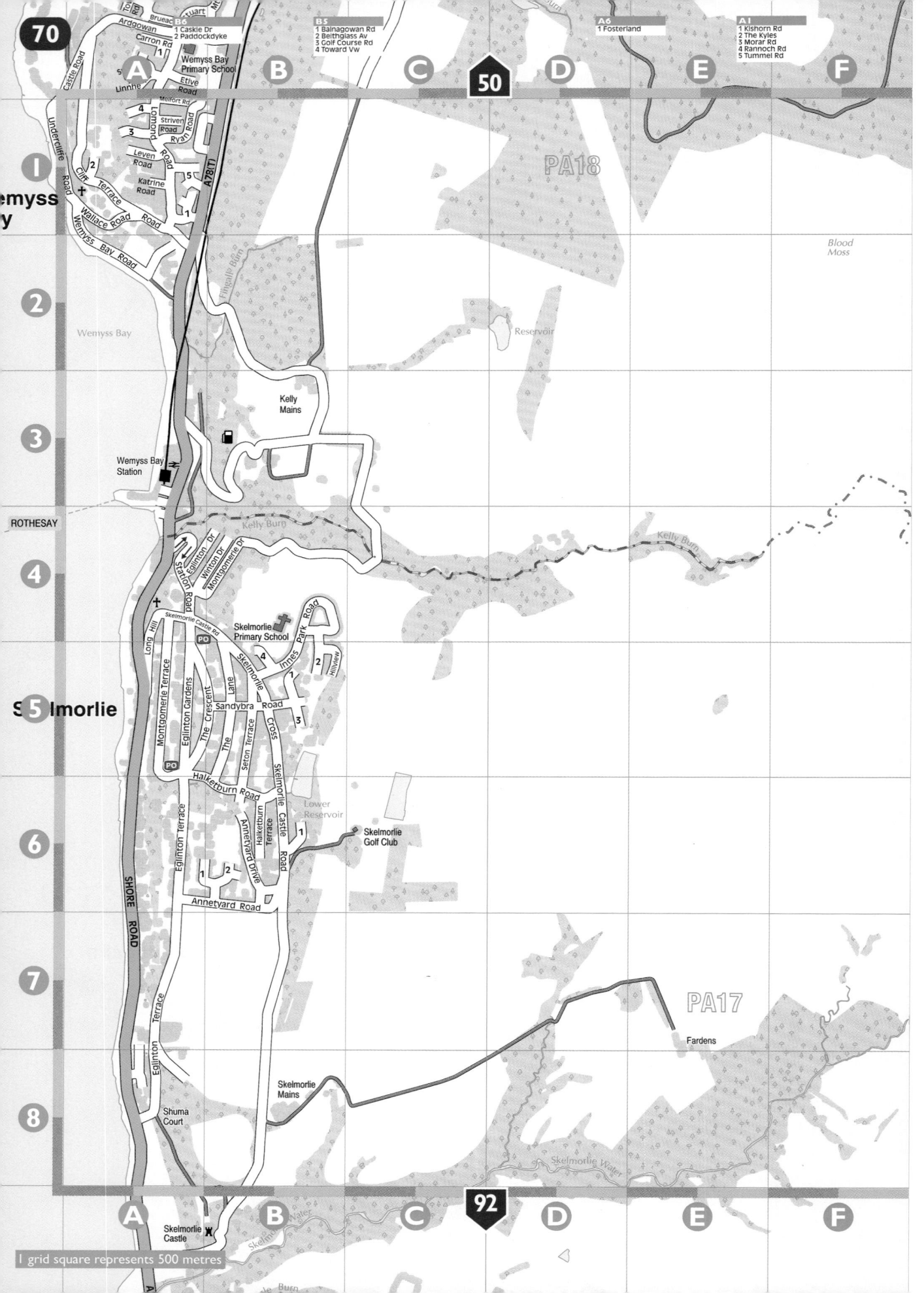

I grid square represents 500 metres

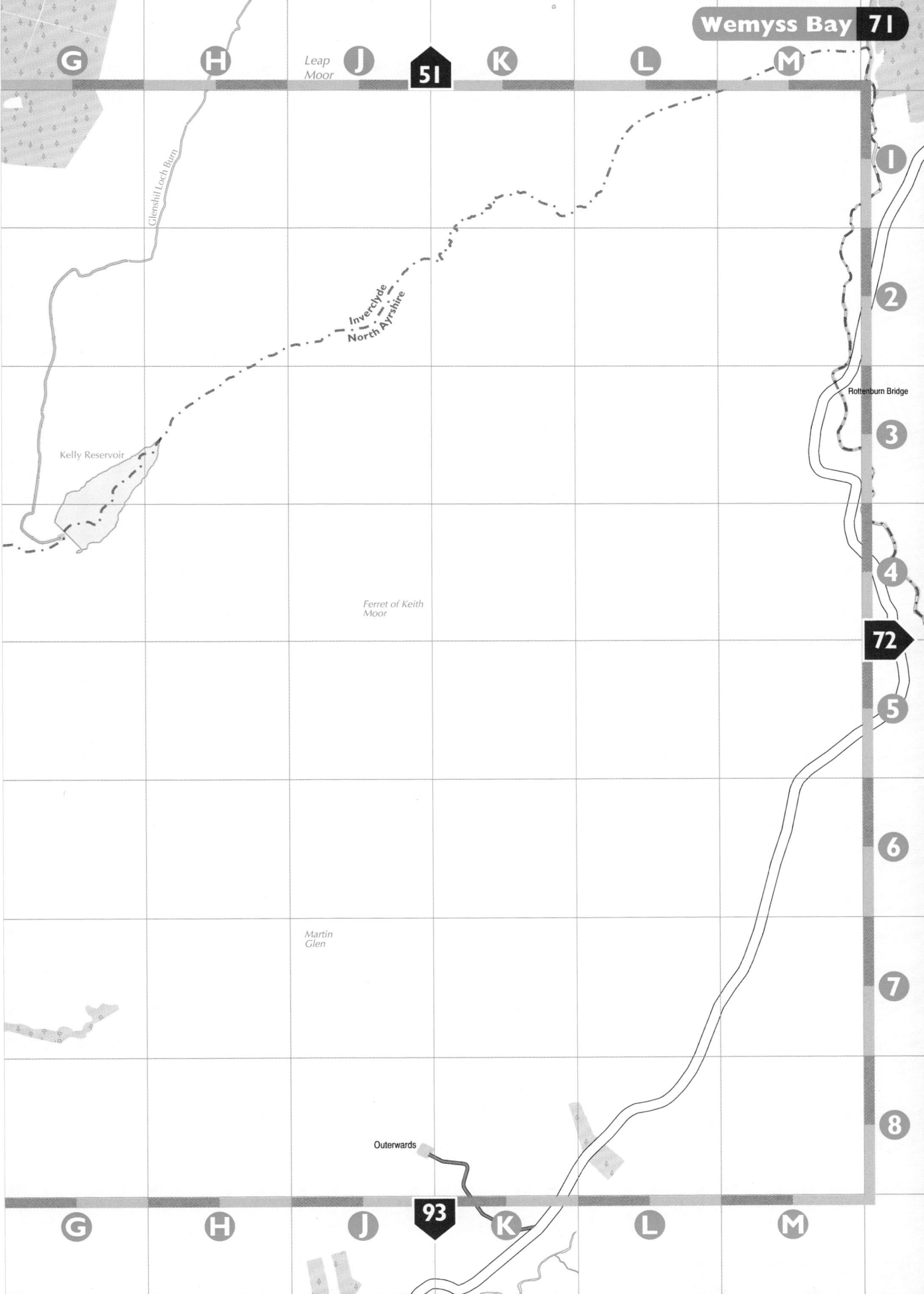

Leap
Moor

51

Glenshil Loch Burn

Inverclyde
North Ayrshire

Kelly Reservoir

Rottenburn Bridge

Ferret of Keith
Moor

72

Martin
Glen

Outerwards

93

G H J K L M
I
2
3
4
5
6
7
8

G H J K L M

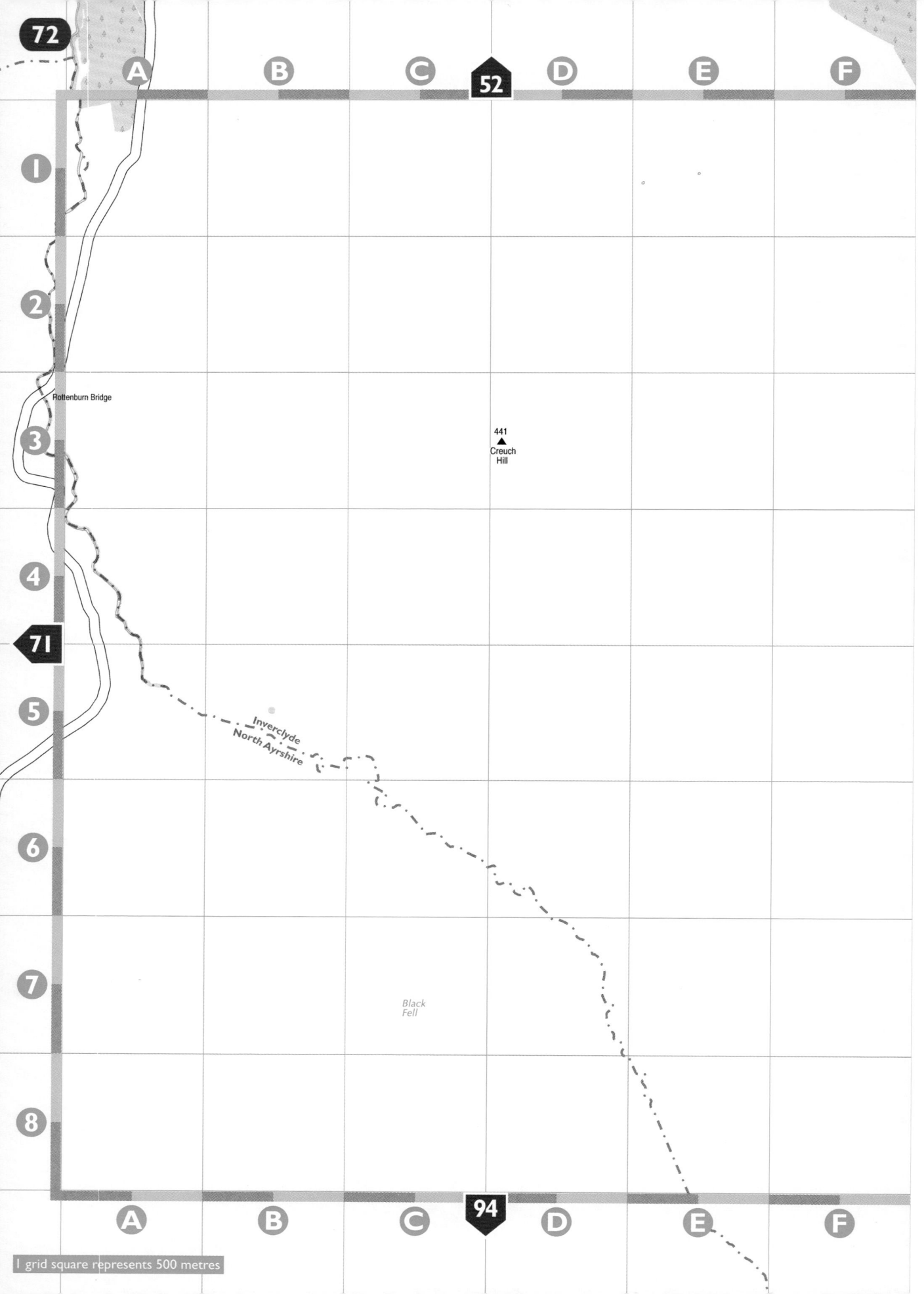

A B C 52 D E F

I

2

Rottenburn Bridge

441
▲
Creuch
Hill

3

4

71

5

Inverclyde
North Ayrshire

6

7

Black
Fell

8

A B C 94 D E F

1 grid square represents 500 metres

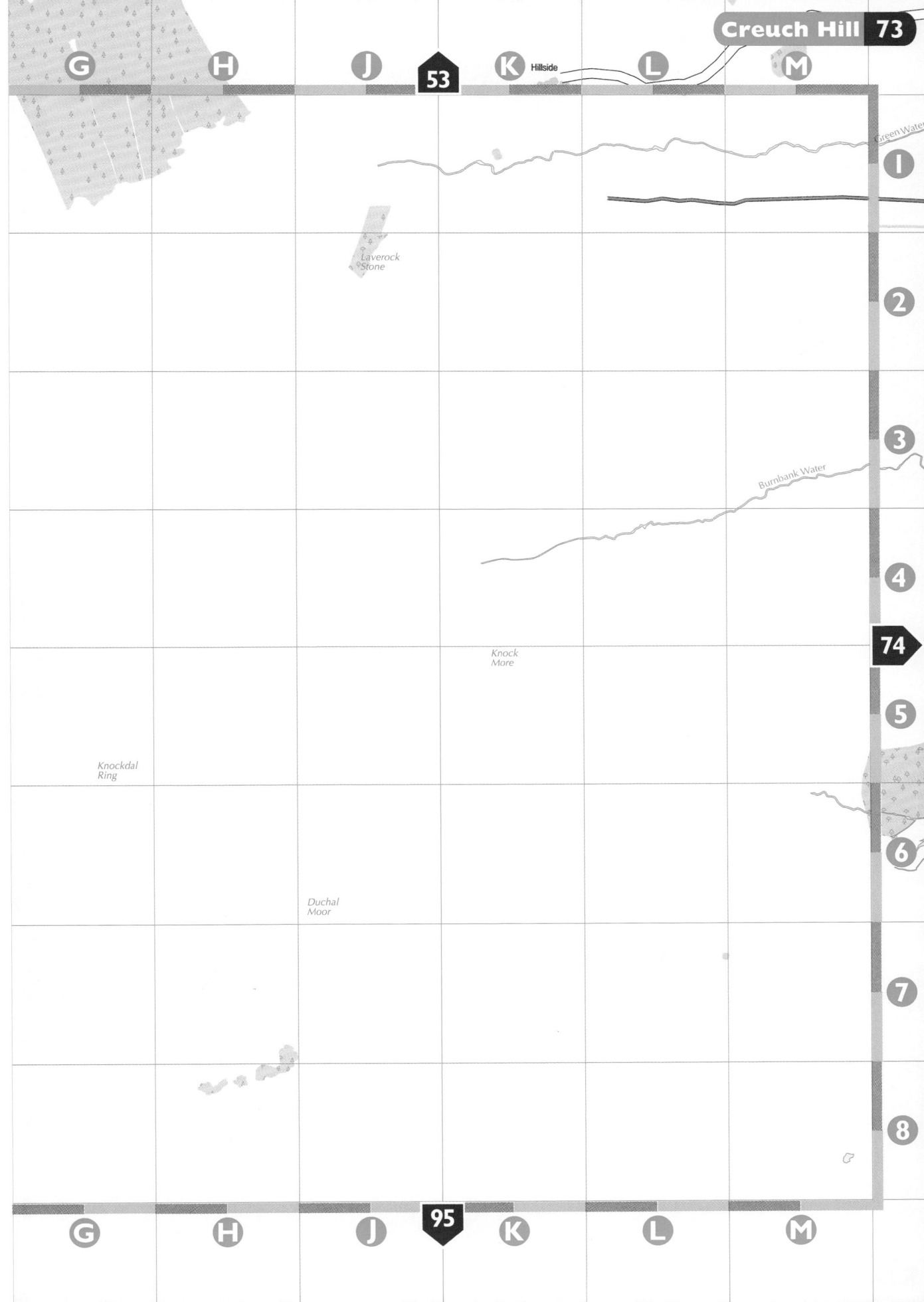

G   H   J   **53**   K   Hillside   L   M

I

Green Water

Laverock
Stone

2

3

Burnbank Water

4

74

Knock
More

5

Knockdal
Ring

6

Duchal
Moor

7

8

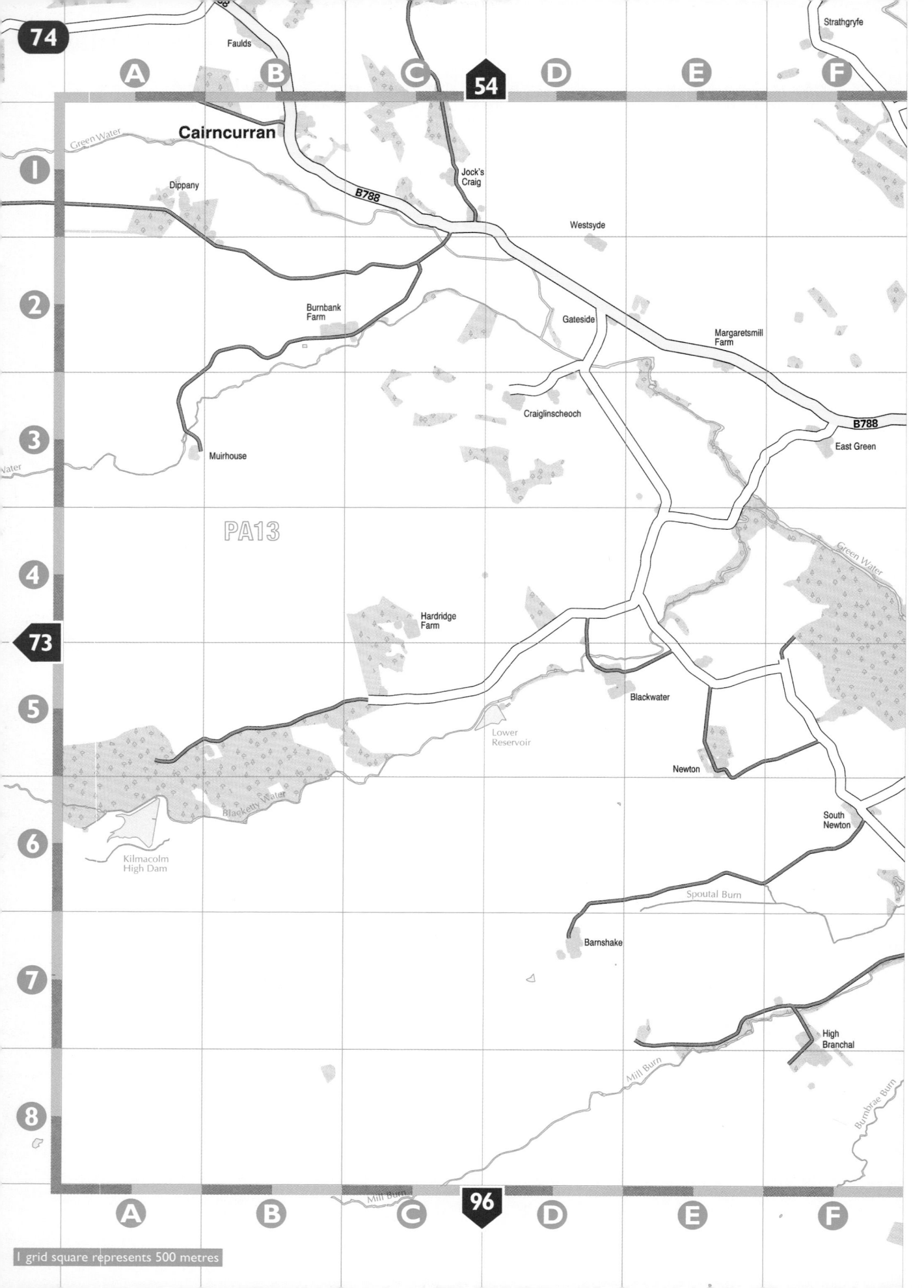

I grid square represents 500 metres

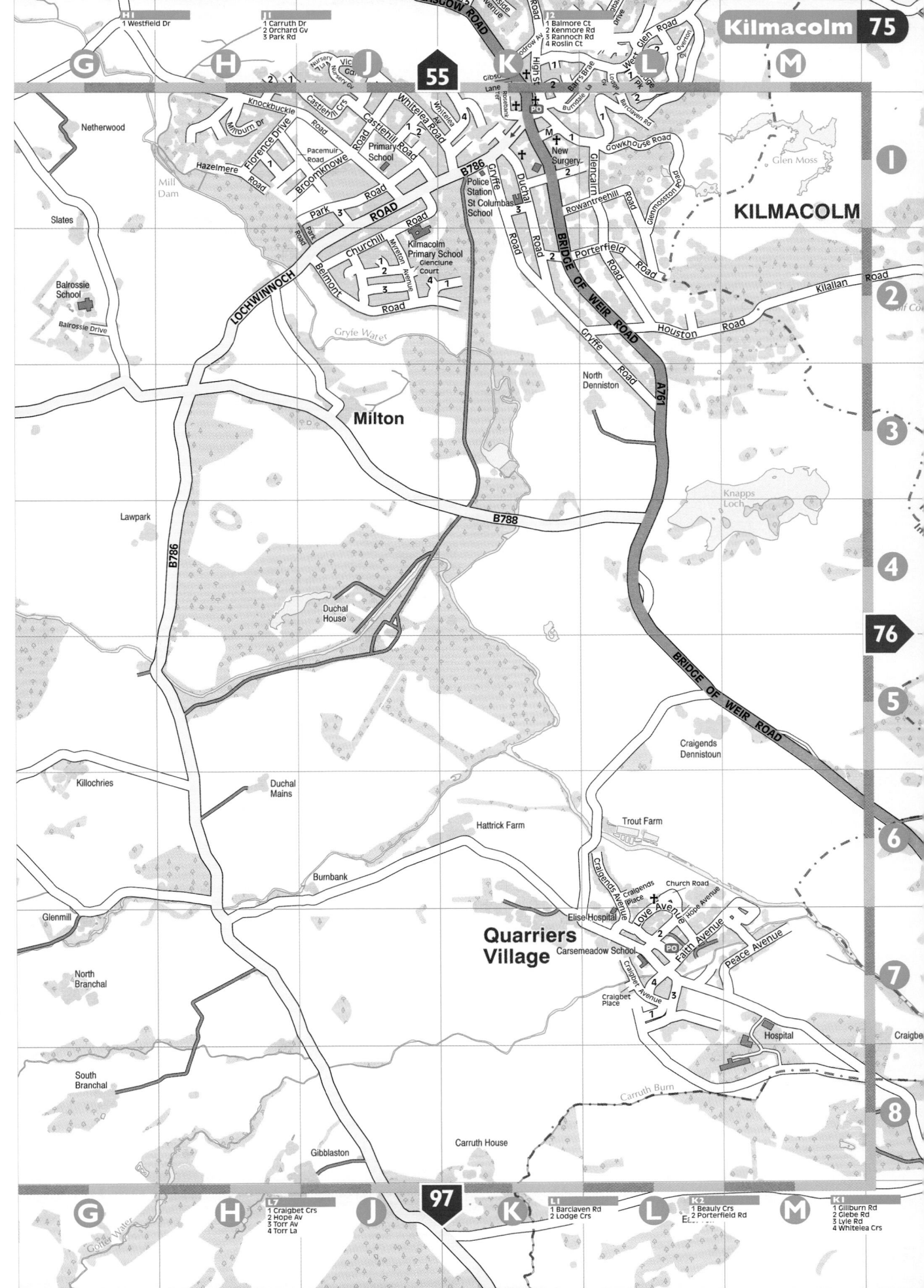

G H J K L M

KILMACOLM

Netherwood

Mill Dam

Slates

Balrossie School

Balrossie Drive

Knockbuckle Road

Milburn Dr

Florence Drive

Hazelmere

Castlehill Crs

Castlehill Road

Pacemuir Road

Broomknowe Road

Park ROAD

Churchill

Belmont Road

LOCHWINNOCH

Primary School

Whitelea Road

Nursery Gr

Vic Gdns

Gryfe Water

Myreton Avenue

Kilmacolm Primary School

Glenclune Court

B786

Gryfe Road

Police Station

St Columbas School

Duchal Road

New Surgery

Glencairn Road

Rowantreehill Road

Cowkhouse Road

Porterfield Road

Glenmosston Road

BRIDGE OF WEIR ROAD

A761

Houston Road

Kilallan Road

Golf Co

Glen Moss

Barrs Brae

High St

PO

West Glen Road

Gibson Avenue

Lodge

Barclaven Rd

Milton

Gryfe Water

North Denniston

Knapps Loch

Lawpark

B786

B788

Duchal House

Killochries

Duchal Mains

Burnbank

Glenmill

North Branchal

Hattrick Farm

Elise Hospital

Craigends Dennistoun

Trout Farm

Craigends Avenue

Craigends Place

Church Road

Love Avenue

Hope Avenue

Faith Avenue

Peace Avenue

Quarriers Village

Carsemeadow School

PO

Craigbet Avenue

Craigbet Place

Hospital

Craigbe

South Branchal

Gibblaston

Carruth House

Carruth Burn

Gotter Water

`55`

`76`

`97`

H1 1 Westfield Dr

J1 1 Carruth Dr 2 Orchard Gv 3 Park Rd

J2 1 Balmore Ct 2 Kenmore Rd 3 Rannoch Rd 4 Roslin Ct

L7 1 Craigbet Crs 2 Hope Av 3 Torr Av 4 Torr La

L1 1 Barclaven Rd 2 Lodge Crs

K2 1 Beauly Crs 2 Porterfield Rd

K1 1 Gilliburn Rd 2 Glebe Rd 3 Lyle Rd 4 Whitelea Crs

I 2 3 4 5 6 7 8

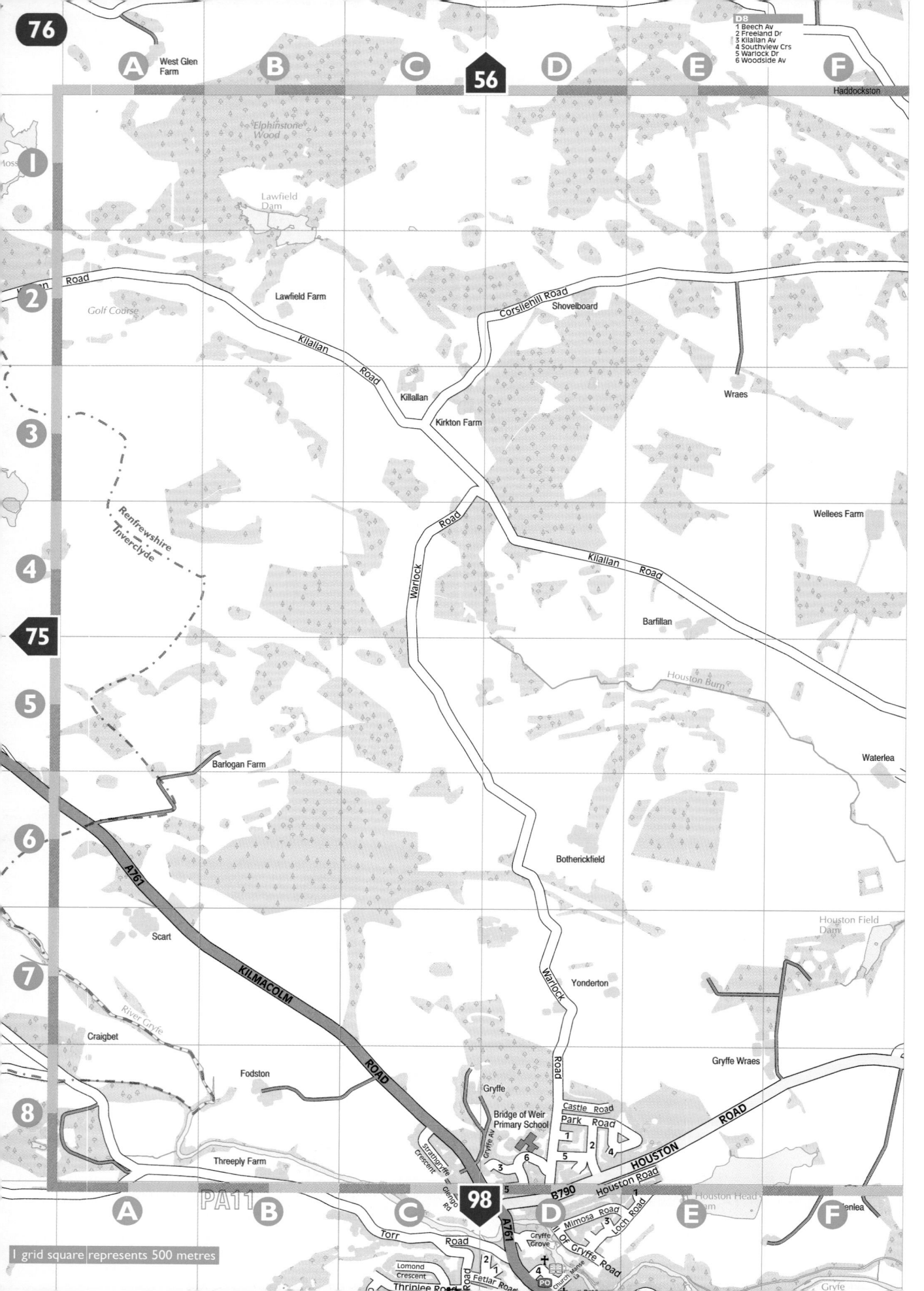

A   West Glen Farm
B
C   56
D   PO
E
F   Haddockston

D8
1 Beech Av
2 Freeland Dr
3 Kilallan Av
4 Southview Crs
5 Warlock Dr
6 Woodside Av

Moss

1

Elphinstone Wood

Lawfield Dam

Road   Lawfield Farm

2   Golf Course

Kilallan   Road

Corsliehill Road   Shovelboard

Killallan

Wraes

3

Kirkton Farm

Renfrewshire Inverclyde

Wellees Farm

Warlock   Road

4   Kilallan   Road

Barfillan

75

Houston Burn

5

Barlogan Farm

Waterlea

6   A761

Botherickfield

Houston Field Dam

Scart

7   River Gryfe   KILMACOLM

Warlock   Road   Yonderton

Craigbet

Gryfe Wraes

Fodston   ROAD

Gryffe

HOUSTON   ROAD

8   Bridge of Weir Primary School
Castle   Road
Park   Road
1
2   4
5
6
3
Threeply Farm
Gryffe Av
Strathgryffe Crescent
Glengro Rd

Torr   Road
Lomond Crescent
Thriplee Road   Fetlar Road
B790   Houston Road
Mimosa   Road
Loch   Road
1
2
3
4
PO
Church Street
OF Gryffe Road
Gryffe Grove
Houston Head
enlea
Gryfe

56
98

1 grid square represents 500 metres

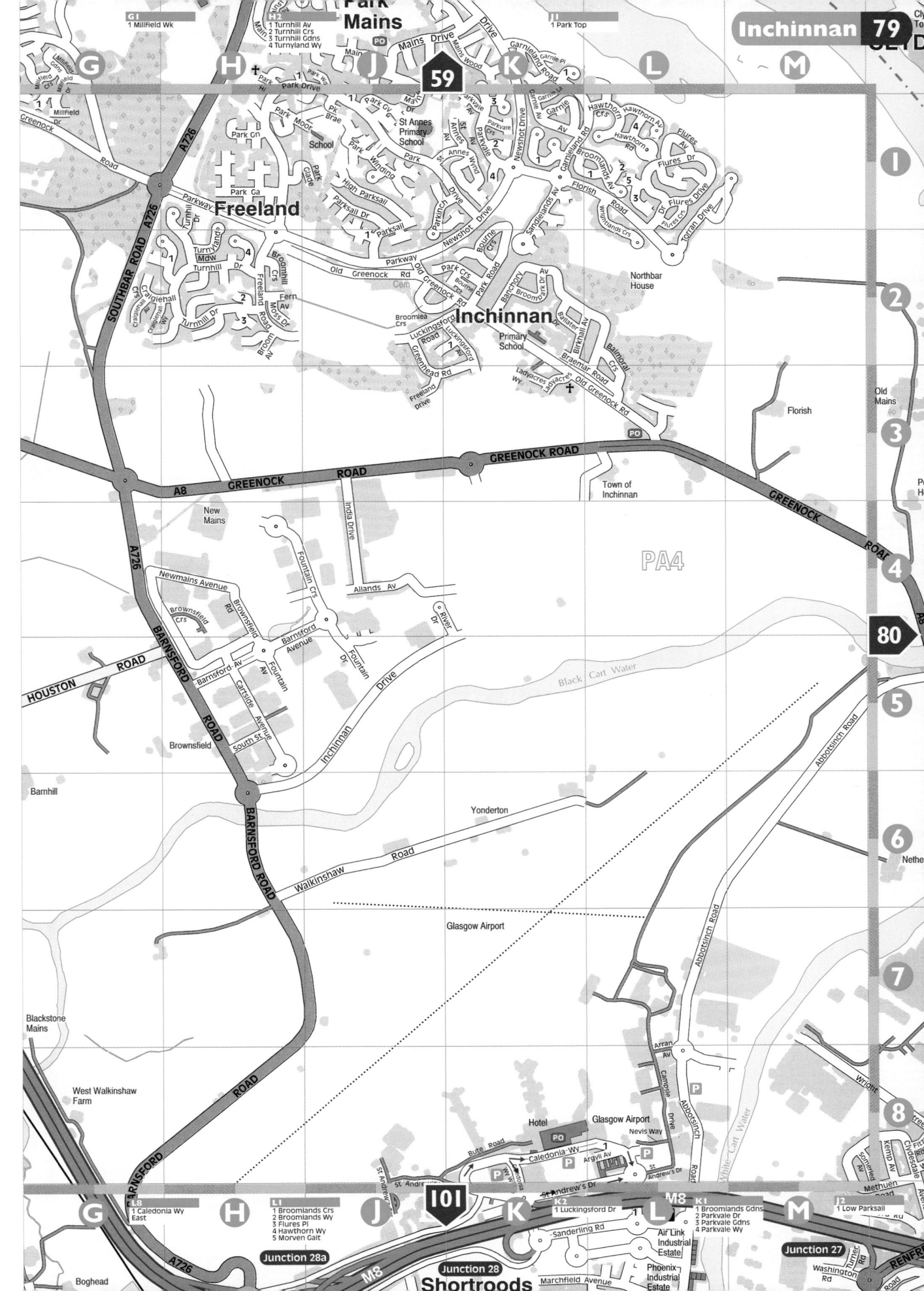

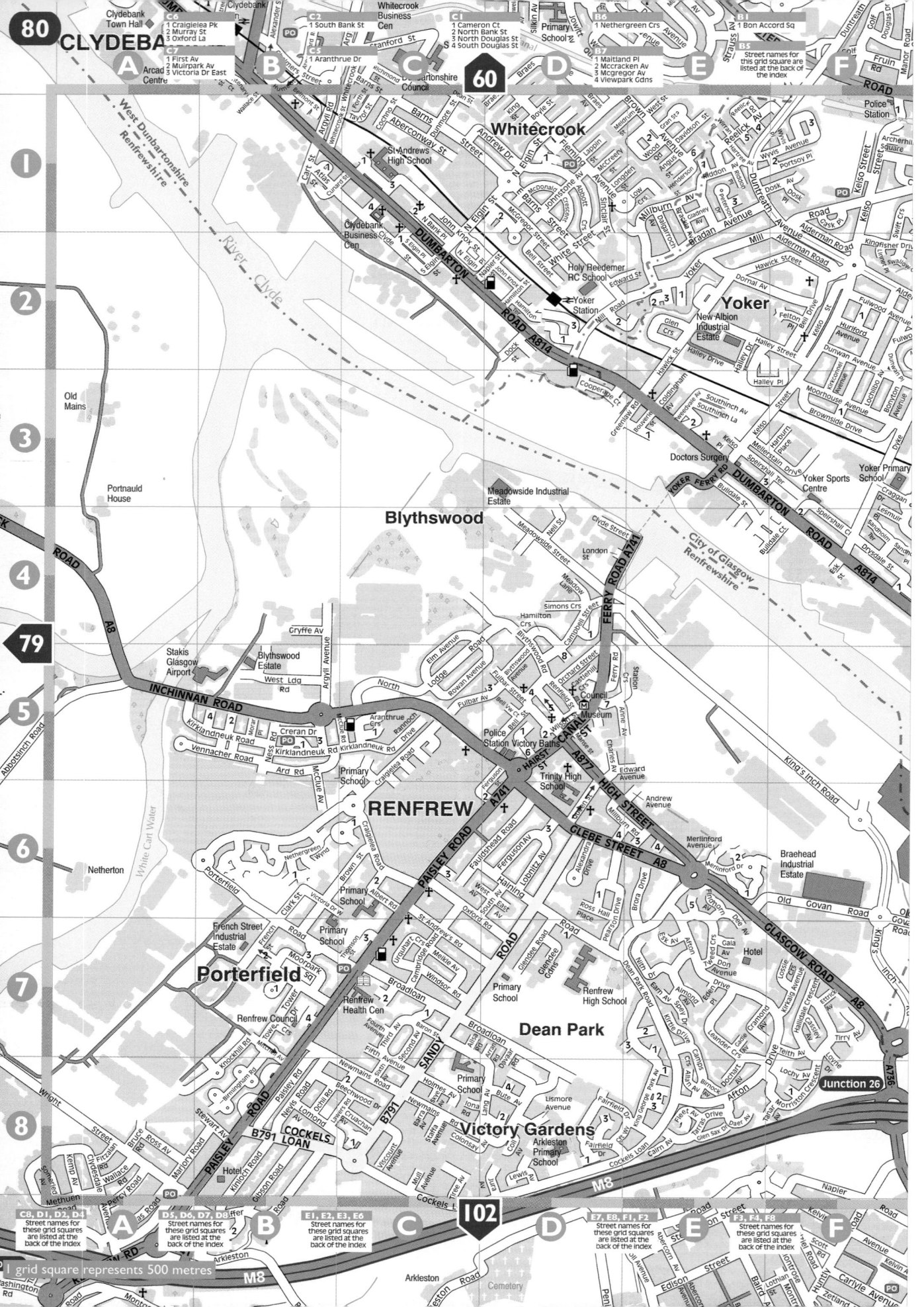

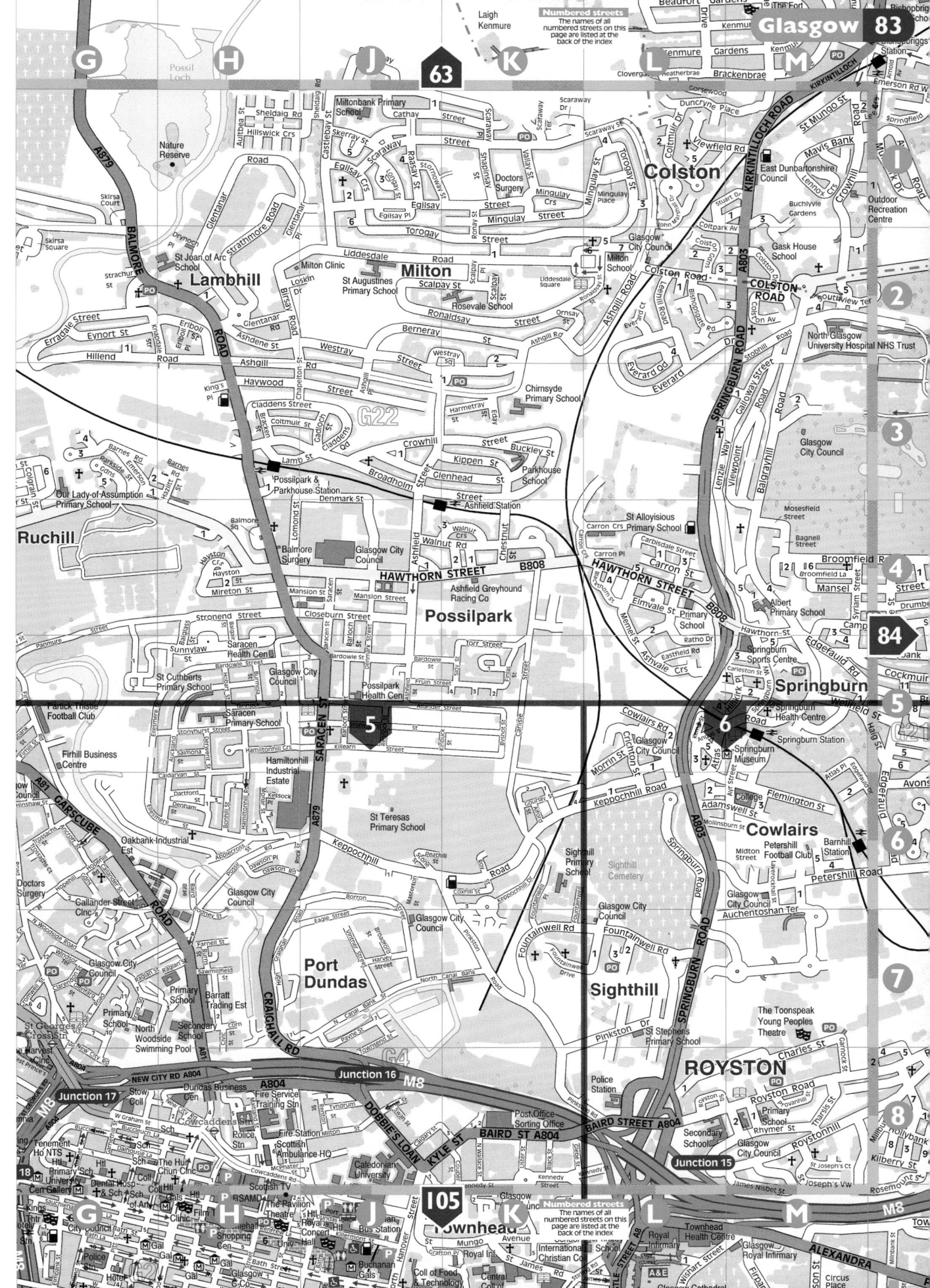

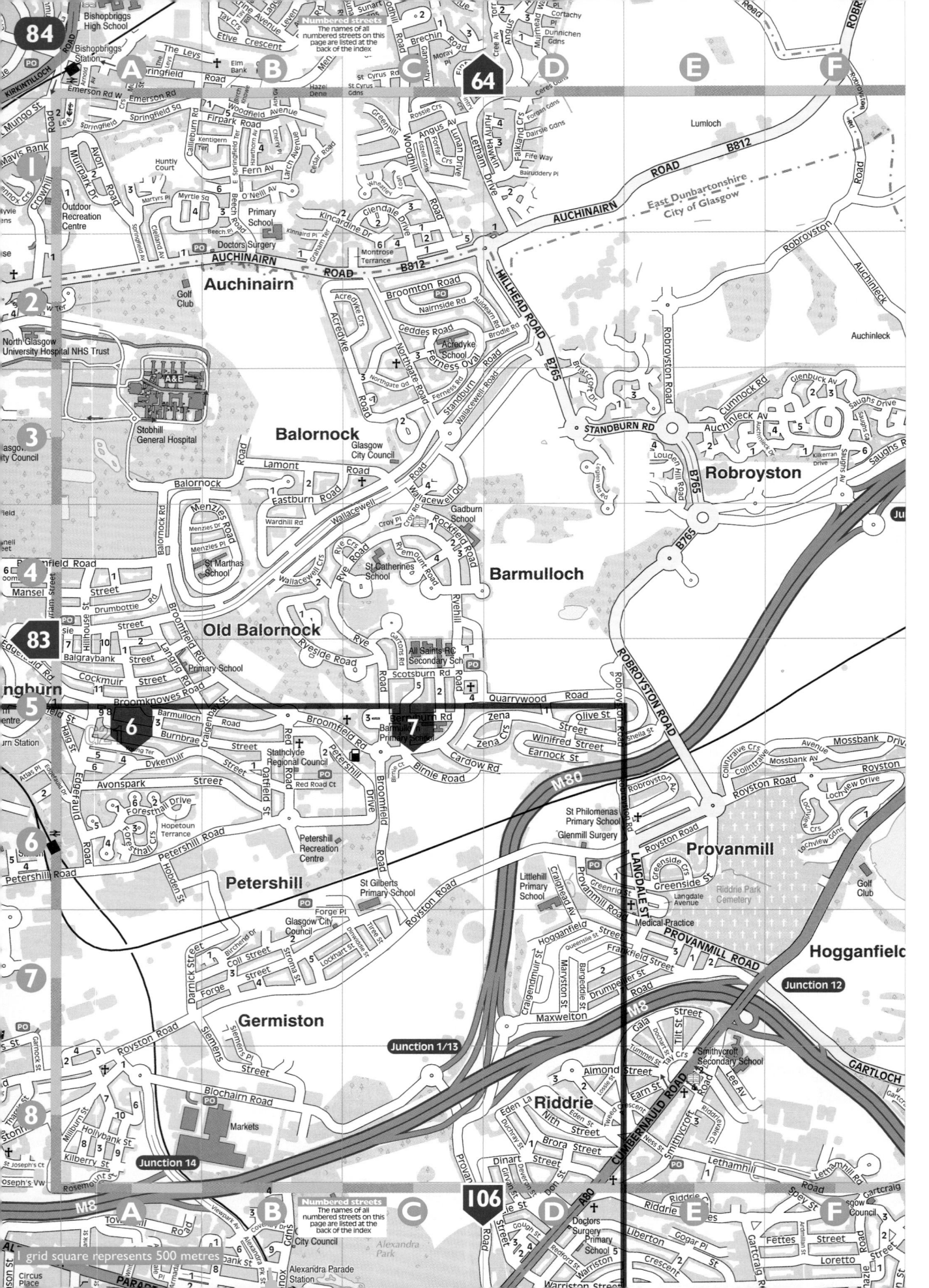

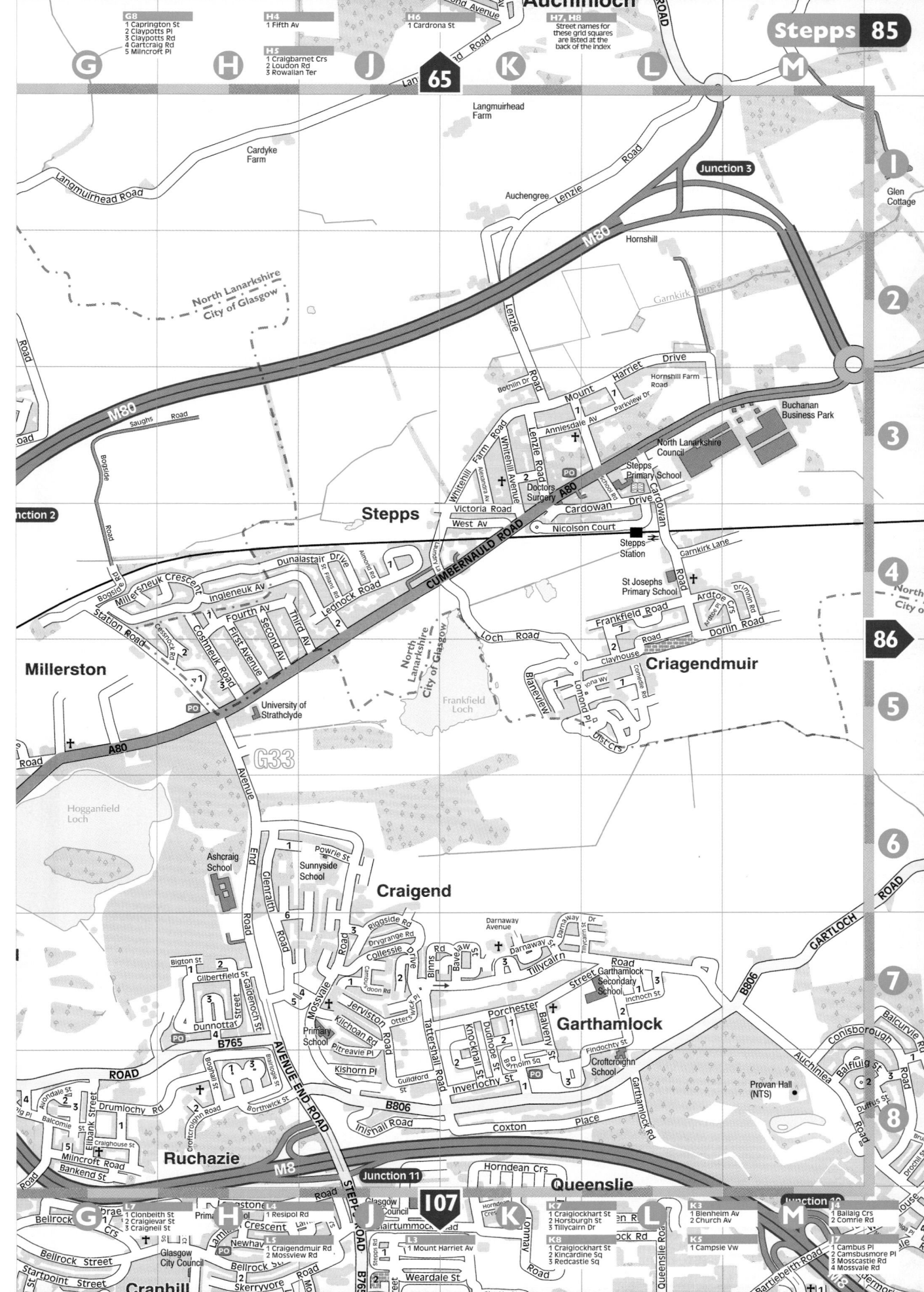

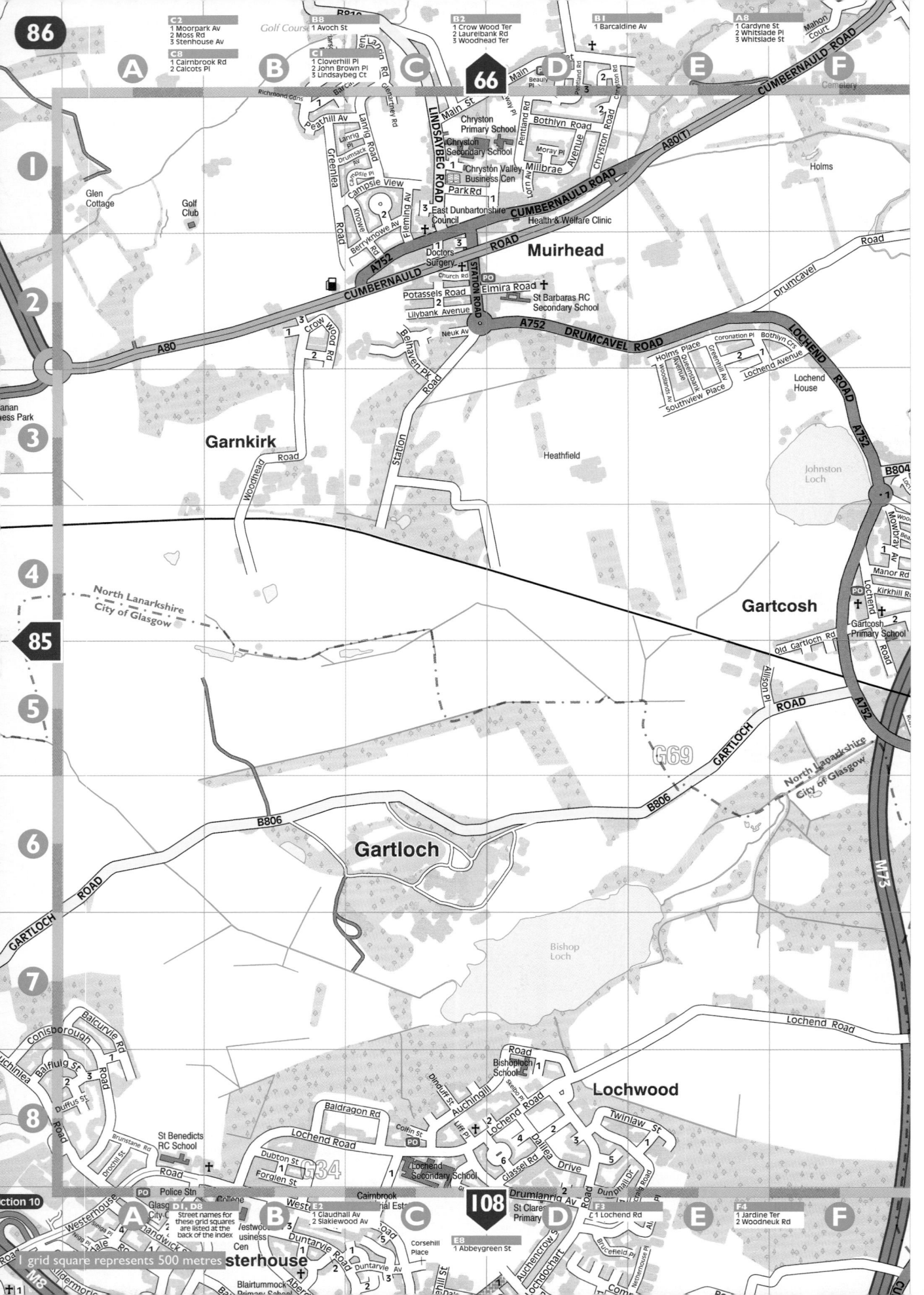

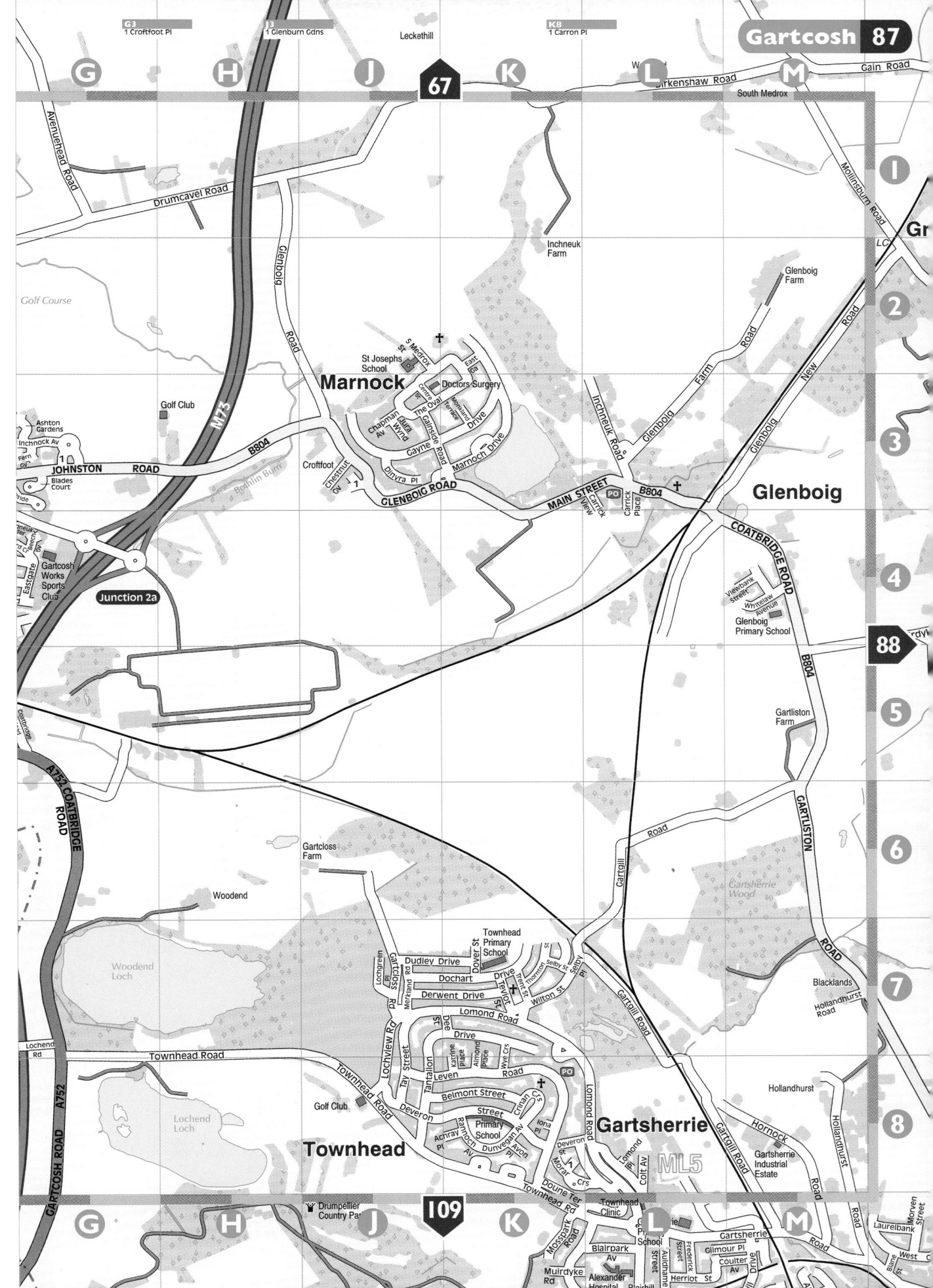

G3
1 Croftfoot Pl

J3
1 Glenburn Gdns

Leckethill

K8
1 Carron Pl

G

H

J

67

K

W

L

Birkenshaw Road

Gain Road

M

South Medrox

1

Gr

Mollinsburn Road

LC

2

Golf Course

Glenboig Farm

Inchneuk Farm

Drumcavel Road

Glenboig Road

3

Glenboig Farm Road

Glenboig New Road

St Medrox St

St Josephs School

Doctors Surgery

Marnock

East St

Inchneuk Road

Golf Club

M73

B804

Ashton Gardens

Inchnock Av

Fern Gr

JOHNSTON ROAD

Blades Court

Croftfoot

Chapman Av

Juno Wynd

Gayne

Centre St

The Oval

Gainside Road

Mountair Terrace

Marnoch Drive

Drive

Glenboig Road

MAIN STREET

PO

B804

Glenboig

Bothlin Burn

Chestnut Gv

Dinyra Pl

GLENBOIG ROAD

Carrick View

Carrick Place

COATBRIDGE ROAD

Gartcosh Works Sports Club

Eastgate

Junction 2a

4

Viewbank Street

Whitelaw Avenue

Glenboig Primary School

88

B804

Gartliston Farm

5

Cartcosh Road

A752 COATBRIDGE ROAD

Gartcloss Farm

Woodend

Cartgill Road

Gartsherrie Wood

Gartliston Road

GARTLISTON ROAD

6

Woodend Loch

Townhead Primary School

Gartcloss Rd

Dudley Drive

Dover St

Dochart

Drive

Thornton St

Selby St

St

Merkland

Lochgreen Rd

Derwent Drive

Teviot

Wilton St

Cartgill Road

Blacklands

Hollandhurst Road

7

Lochend Rd

Townhead Road

Lomond Road

Dee Drive

Lochview Rd

Townhead Road

Tay Street

Kartine Place

Tantallon

Leven

Almond Place

Wye Crs

Road

Cartgill Road

PO

Hollandhurst

Golf Club

Deveron

Belmont Street

Street

Primary School

Crnan Crs

Iona Pl

Lomond Road

Gartsherrie

Hornock

8

Townhead

Achray Pl

Ramsay Av

Dunvegan Av

Avon

Deveron

Lomond

Colt Av

ML5

Gartsherrie Industrial Estate

Drumpellier Country Park

Moar Crs

Doune Ter

Townhead Rd

Townhead Clinic

Townhead

Laurelbank

Morven Street

G

H

J

109

K

Primary School

L

Gartsherrie

Gartsherrie Road

M

GARTCOSH ROAD

Mosspark Road

Blairpark Av

Blairhill

Auldhame Street

Frederick Street

Gilmour Pl

Coulter Av

Blane

West

Muirdyke Rd

Alexander Hospital

Herriot St

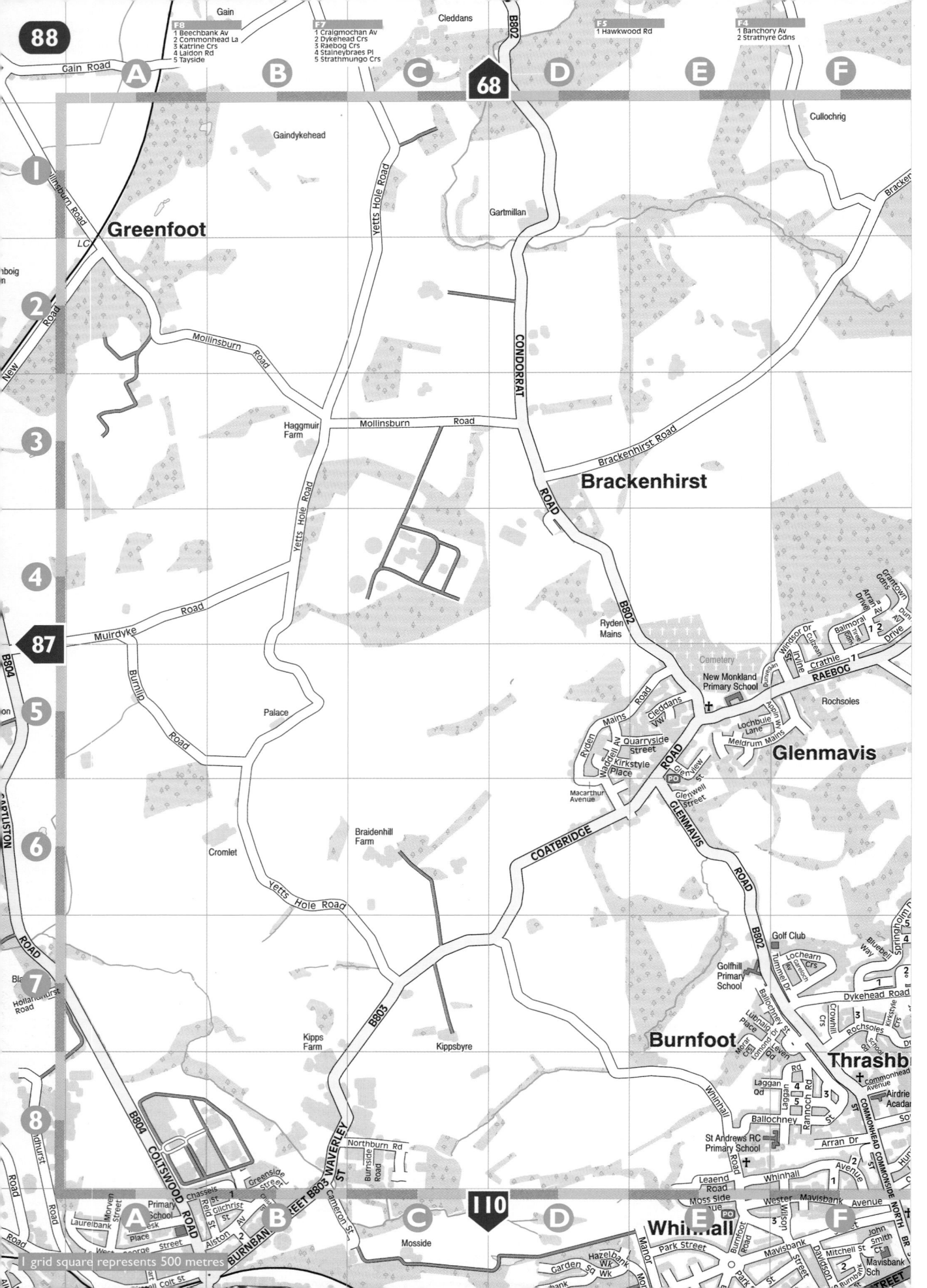

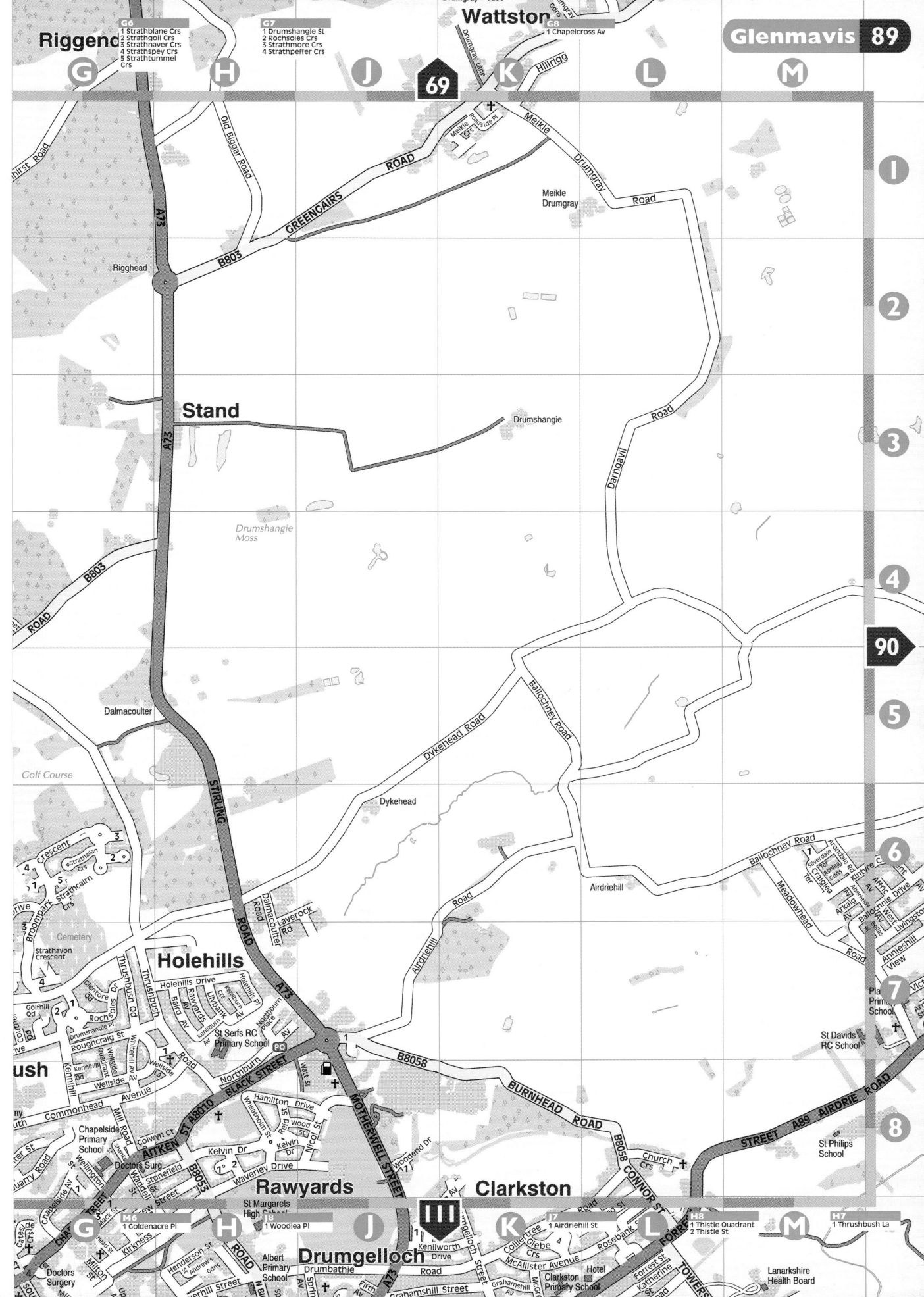

Riggend

Wattston

G H J **69** K L M

I

Old Biggar Road

GREENGAIRS ROAD

B803

A73

Righead

Meikle Road

Meikle Drumgray

Drumgray Road

2

Stand

A73

Drumshangie

Darngavil Road

3

Drumshangie Moss

B803 ROAD

Dalmacoulter

4

90

Golf Course

STIRLING

Dykehead Road

Ballochney Road

5

Dykehead

Airdriehill

Ballochney Road

Silverdale Ter Jonies

Craiglea

Arkalg Av

Kintyre C

Ballochnie WEST

Livingston

Annieshill View

6

Crescent

Strathallan Crs

Strathcairn Crs

Broompark Drive

Strathavon Crescent

Cemetery

Holehills

Holehills Drive

Dalmacoulter Road

Laverock Rd

ROAD

A73

Road

Airdriehill

Pla Primary School

St Davids RC School

Victi

7

Golfhill Qd

Rochs

Roughcraig St

Drumsnangie Pl

Whitenhill Av

Wellside Quadrant

Kennihill Qd

Kennihill

Wellside Av

Wellside

Thrushbush Qd

Thrushbush

Rawyards

Lithbank

Kenilburn Av

Kenilburn Place

Northburn Place

Hollhills Pl

St Serfs RC Primary School

PO

1

B8058

BURNHEAD ROAD

B8058

CONNOR ST

St Philips School

8

ush

Commonhead

Aitken

A8010

BLACK STREET

Mill Road

Colwyn Ct

Chapelside Primary School

Kennihill Qd

Kennihill

ROAD

Wheatholm St

Hamilton Drive

Northmuir

Watt St

MOTHERWELL STREET

Woodend Dr

Church Crs

AIRDRIE ROAD

A89

STREET

Wellington

Kelvin Dr

Kelvin Dr

Stonefield Street

Nicol St

Wood St

Pield St

Wheatholm St

Kelvin Dr

Waverley Drive

Rawyards

Clarkston

St Margarets High School

Albert Primary School

Drumgelloch

Kenilworth Drive

Drumbathie Road

Grahamshill Street

Grahamshill Street

Clarkston Primary School

Hotel

Lanarkshire Health Board

Kirkness

Doctors Surgery

Henderson St

Andrew Gdns

Doctors Surg.

Chapelside Av

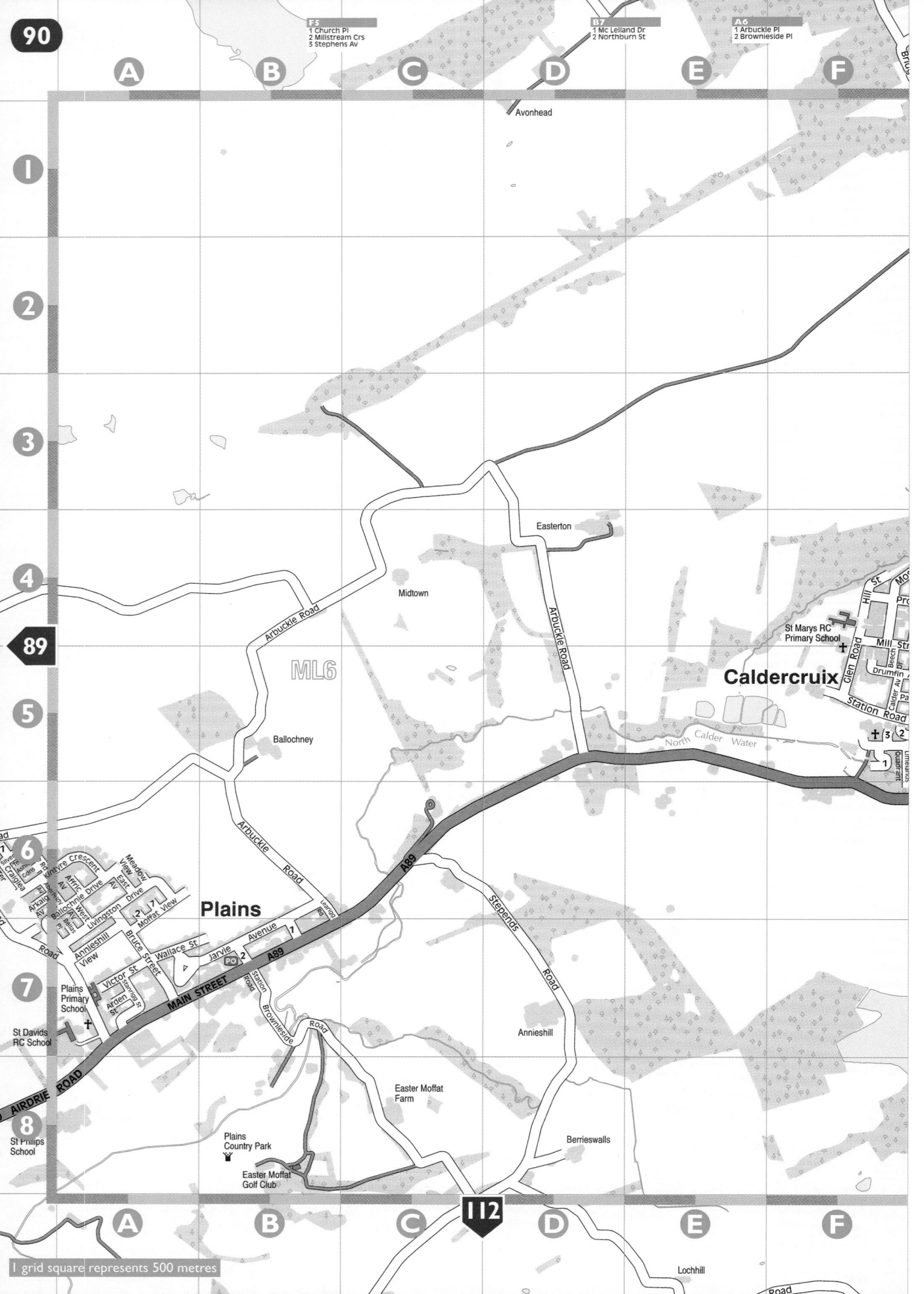

F5
1 Church Pl
2 Millstream Crs
3 Stephens Av

B7
1 Mc Lelland Dr
2 Northburn St

A6
1 Arbuckle Pl
2 Brownieside Pl

Avonhead

Easterton

Arbuckle Road

Midtown

Arbuckle Road

ML6

St Marys RC
Primary School

Caldercruix

Hill St

Glen Road

Mill Str

Drumfin

Beech

Calder Av Pa

Station Road

Limearns
Quadrant

Ballochney

North Calder Water

Arbuckle Road

A89

Stepends Road

Kintyre Crescent

Meadow View

Affric Drive

Livingston Drive

Moffat View

Craigla

Arkald

Ballochnie West

Plains

Jarvie Avenue

Annieshill
View

Bruce Street

Wallace St

Victor St

Arden St

PO

Main Street

A89

Station Road

Brownieside Road

Plains
Primary
School

St Davids
RC School

Airdrie Road

Annieshill

St Phillips
School

Plains
Country Park

Easter Moffat
Farm

Berrieswalls

Easter Moffat
Golf Club

Lochhill

Road

1 grid square represents 500 metres

G H J K L M

Longriggend

Main Street

B825

Telegraph Road

Drumbow

I

CALDERCRUIX ROAD

Forrestfield Road

2

3

Crossrigg

Shields

Eastfield

B825

EASTFIELD ROAD

Avenue

Earl
Av
Princes
St
Liberty
Rd
Dunark
Rd
Loch
Vw

ogress

Drive

Amp
Ave
Dundee
Av
Glengowan

Heather
St
Park
Vw

PO

Street

Avenue

2

Elswick Drive

Glengowan
Road

rk Lea

Glengowan
Primary School

7

Street

Main

Gowan Brae

1

Hillend
Reservoir

Auchengray
House

4

5

6

Hillend

Eastercroft
House

A89

Nether Bracco

7

Lilly Loch

Bracco Road

8

G H J K L M

A B C **70** D E F

I

**Skelmorlie
Mains**

Shuma
Court

Skelmorlie
Castle ⚔

Skelmorlie Water

Meigle Burn

Meigle
Bay

Barr

Meigle

Thirdpart

Ashcraig

Dykes

Auchengarth

Millrig

Auchengarth
Bridge

*Blackhouse
Moor*

Blackhouse Burn

Home Farm

Constablewood

Knock Castle
⚔

Whittlieburn

Knock Farm

Craigton

*Middleton
Reservoir*

Brisbane
Mains

Middleton

Quarter

1
2
3
4
5
6
7
8

A78(T)

A B C **115** D E F

Noddsdale

Routenburn

G   H   J   K   L   M

Outerwards

1

2

3

4

94

5

6

7

8

Outerwards
Reservoir

East
Grassyards

Tourgill

Bessel
Moor

KA30

G   H   J   116   K   L   M

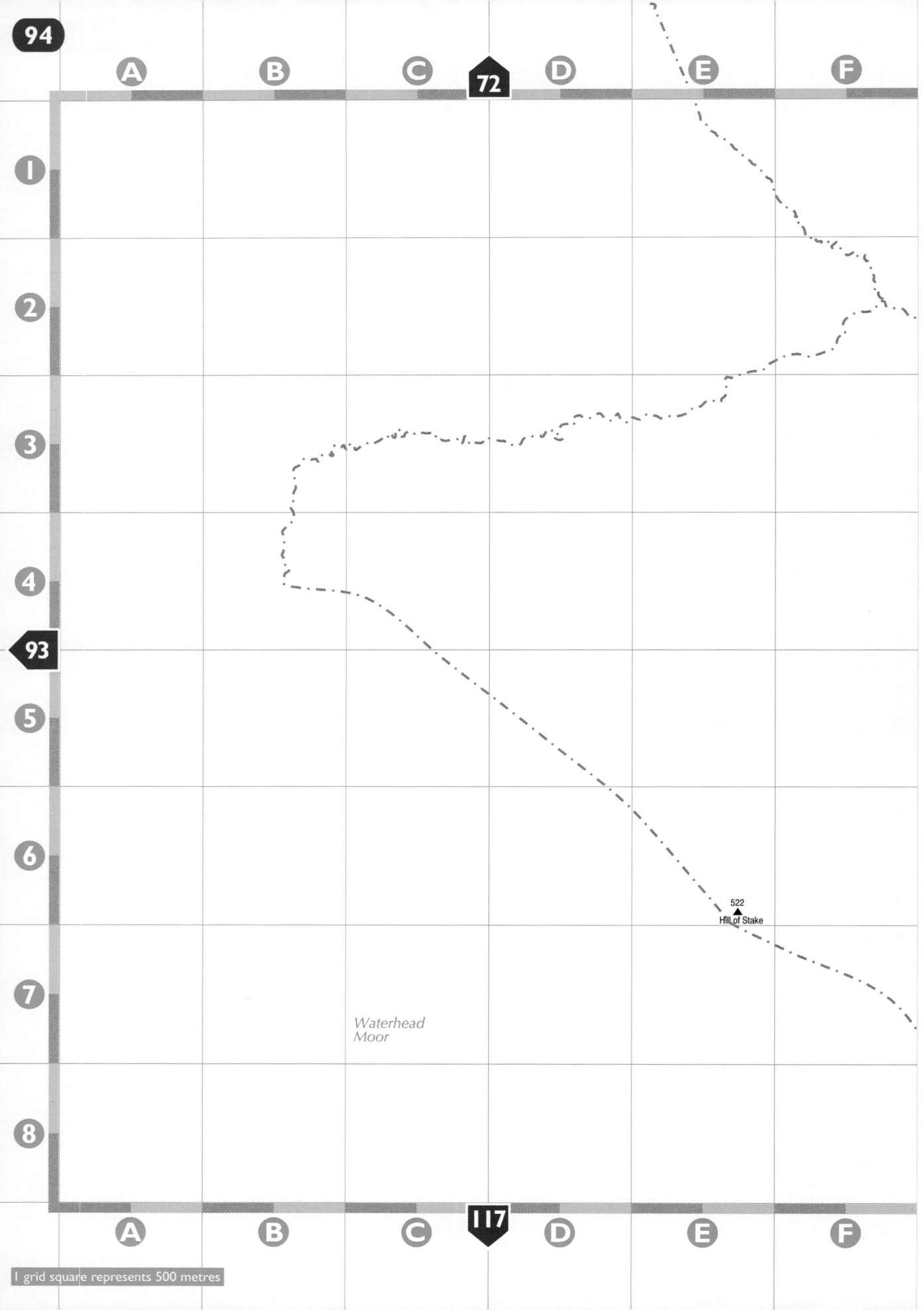

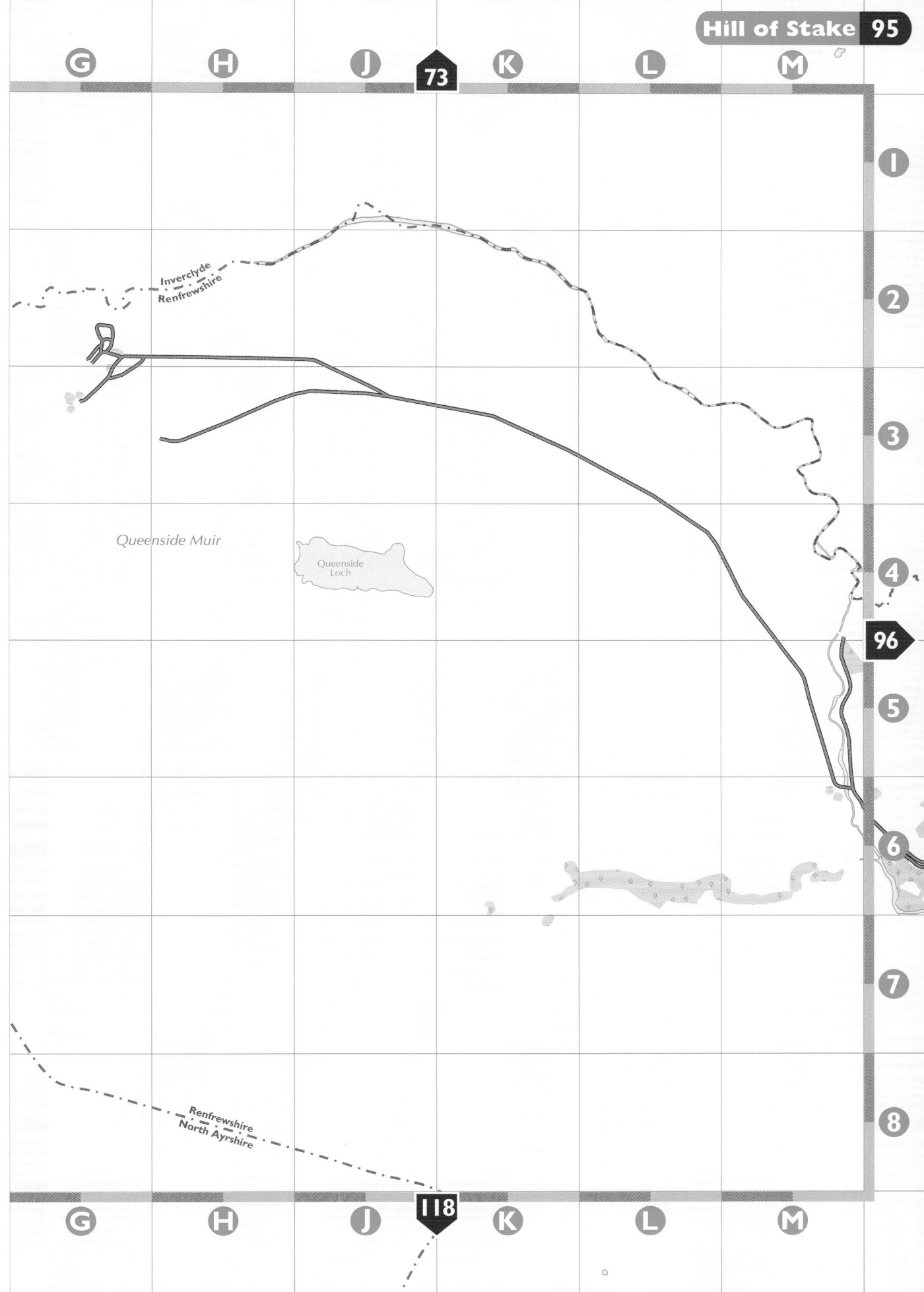

G H J K L M

73

I

2

3

4

96

5

6

7

8

Inverclyde
Renfrewshire

Queenside Muir

Queenside
Loch

Renfrewshire
North Ayrshire

118

G H J K L M

Mill Burn

Craig of
Todholes

Little
Craig
Minnan

Craig
Minnan

Inverclyde
Renfrewshire

Muirshiel
Country
Park

Heathfield

River Calder

Clovenstone

Bumbrae

1 grid square represents 500 metres

G   H   Gibblaston   J   75   Carruth Hous   K   L   M

East Torr

1

Bankbrae

2

B786

Barnbeth

Carruthmuir

3

Ladymuir

4

Locher Bridge

98

Barnbrock Farm

Laigh
Auchencloich

High
Auchencloich

5

Ladymuir
Reservoir

Ward

Gotter Water

Midhouse

Locher Water

Moniabrock

East
Barnaigh

6

Mid Barnaigh

7

Kaim Dam

Weels

8

G   H   J   120   K   L   M

B786

North
Kaim

Greenside

Carruth Burn

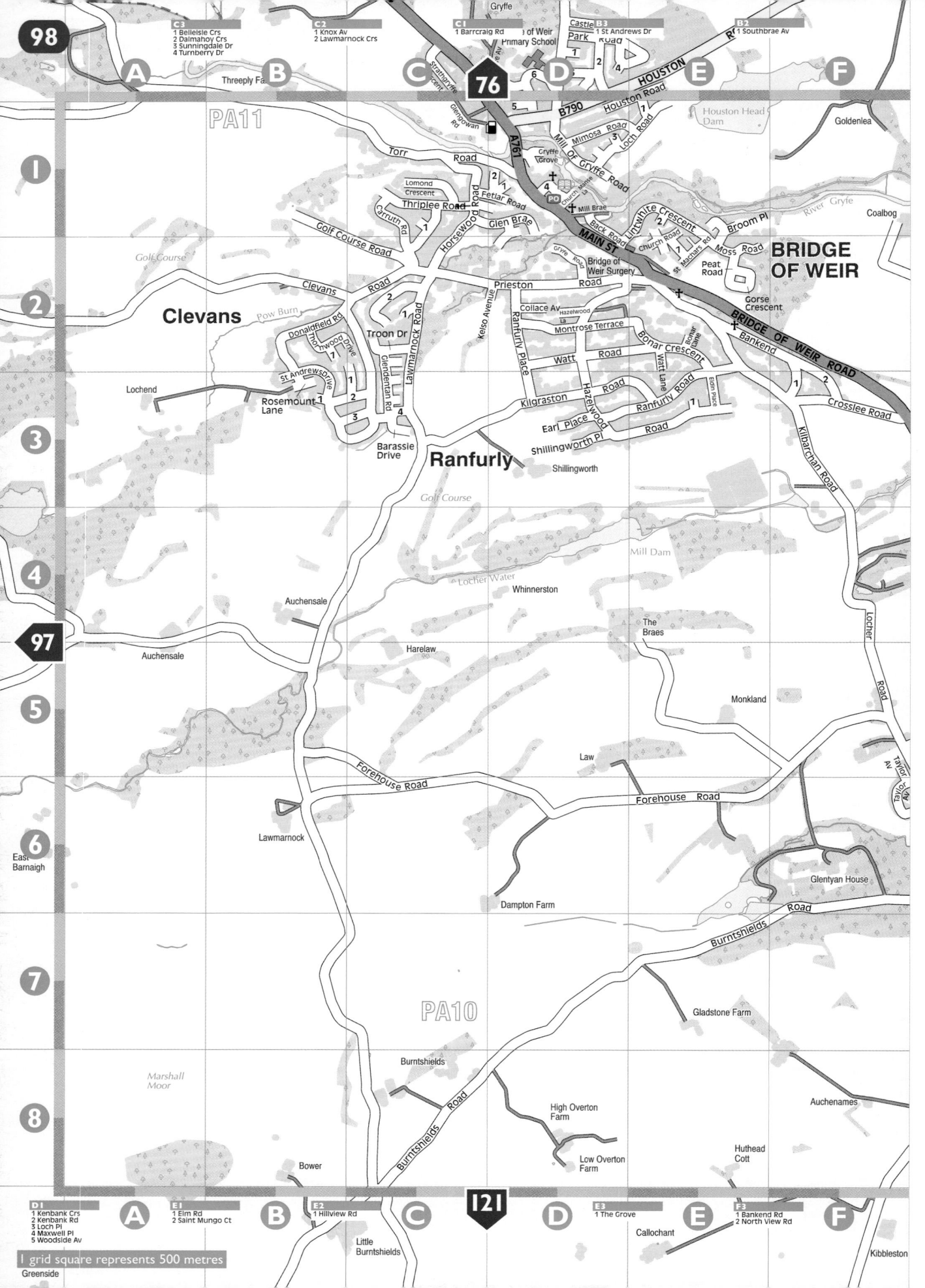

A · B · C · D · E · F

C3
1 Belleisle Crs
2 Dalmahoy Crs
3 Sunningdale Dr
4 Turnberry Dr

C2
1 Knox Av
2 Lawmarnock Crs

C1
1 Barrcraig Rd

B3
1 St Andrews Dr

B2
1 Southbrae Av

Threeply Fa

PA11

Gryffe

e of Weir
Primary School

Castle
Park

Road

76

A761

B790

Houston Road

HOUSTON

Houston Head
Dam

Goldenlea

Torr   Road

Glengowan
Rd

Mill Of Gryffe Road

Gryffe
Grove

Mimosa Road

Loch Road

River Gryfe

Coalbog

Lomond
Crescent

Thriplee Road

Glen Brae

Horsewood Road

Fetlar Road

Back Road

MAIN ST

Lintwhite Crescent

Church Road

Broom Pl

Moss   Road

BRIDGE
OF WEIR

Golf Course

Golf Course Road

Carruth Rd

Clevans   Road

Pow Burn

Clevans

Prieston

Kelso Avenue

Gryfe   Road

Bridge of
Weir Surgery

Road

St Macrae's

Peat
Road

Gorse Crescent

Donaldfield Rd

Thornwood Drive

Troon Dr

Glendentan Rd

Lawmarnock Road

Ranfurly Place

Coilacc Av   Hazelwood
La

Montrose Terrace

Bonar Crescent

Watt Lane

Bankend

BRIDGE OF WEIR ROAD

Lochend

St Andrews Drive

Rosemount
Lane

Watt   Road

Hazelwood

Ranfurly Road

Edin Place

Crosslee Road

Barassie
Drive

Ranfurly

Kilgraston

Earl Place

Shillingworth Pl

Road

Road

Shillingworth

Kilbarchan Road

Golf Course

Locher Water

Whinnerston

Mill Dam

Locher Road

Auchensale

97

Auchensale

Harelaw

The
Braes

Monkland

Taylor Av

Law

Forehouse Road

Forehouse Road

East
Barnaigh

Lawmarnock

PA10

Dampton Farm

Glentyan House

Road

Burntshields

Burntshields   Road

Gladstone Farm

Marshall
Moor

Burntshields

High Overton
Farm

Auchenames

Bower

Low Overton
Farm

Huthead
Cott

A · B · C · D · E · F

D1
1 Kenbank Crs
2 Kenbank Rd
3 Loch Pl
4 Maxwell Pl
5 Woodside Av

E1
1 Elm Rd
2 Saint Mungo Ct

E2
1 Hillview Rd

E3
1 The Grove

F3
1 Bankend Rd
2 North View Rd

Greenside

Little
Burntshields

Callochant

Kibbleston

1 grid square represents 500 metres

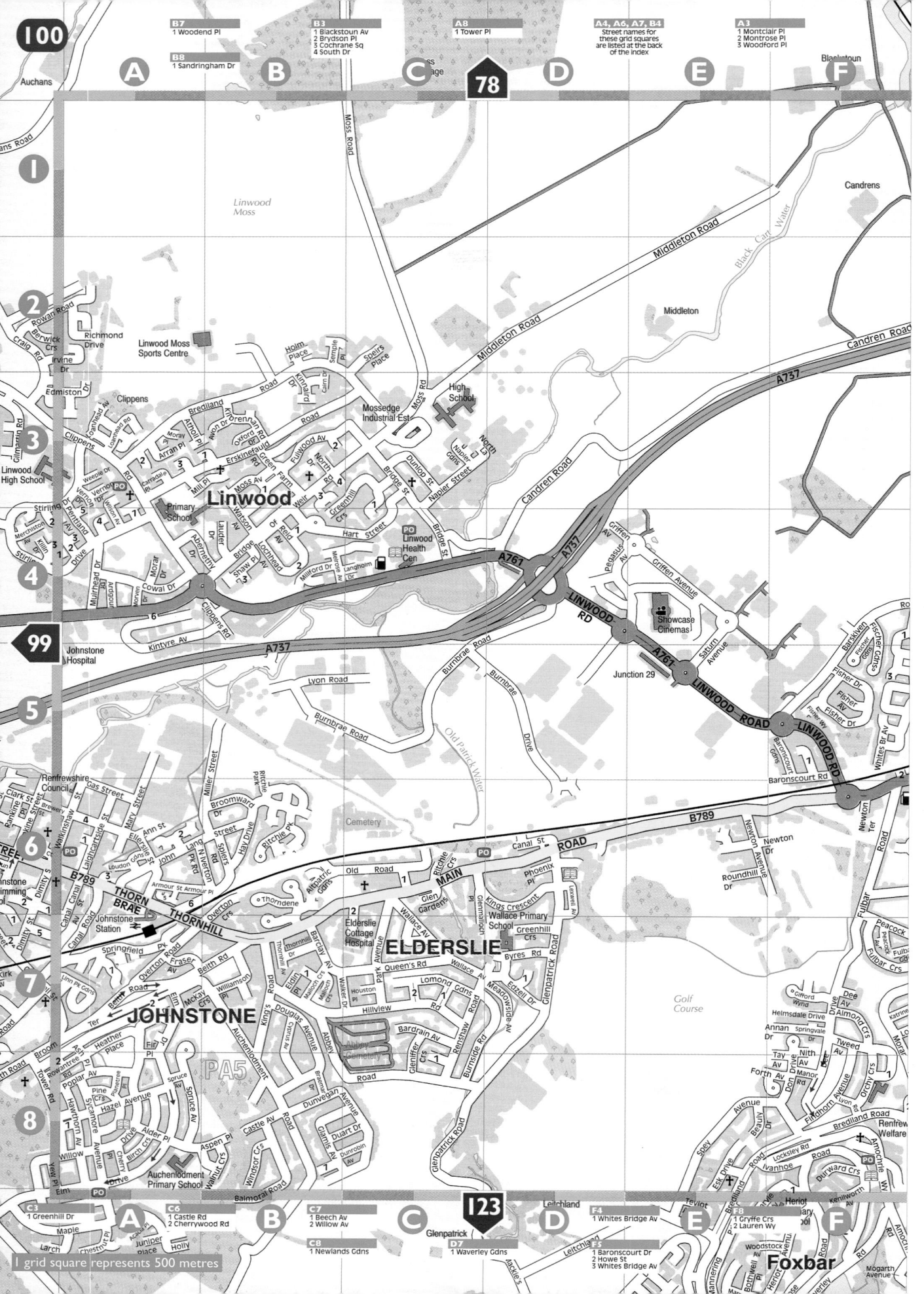

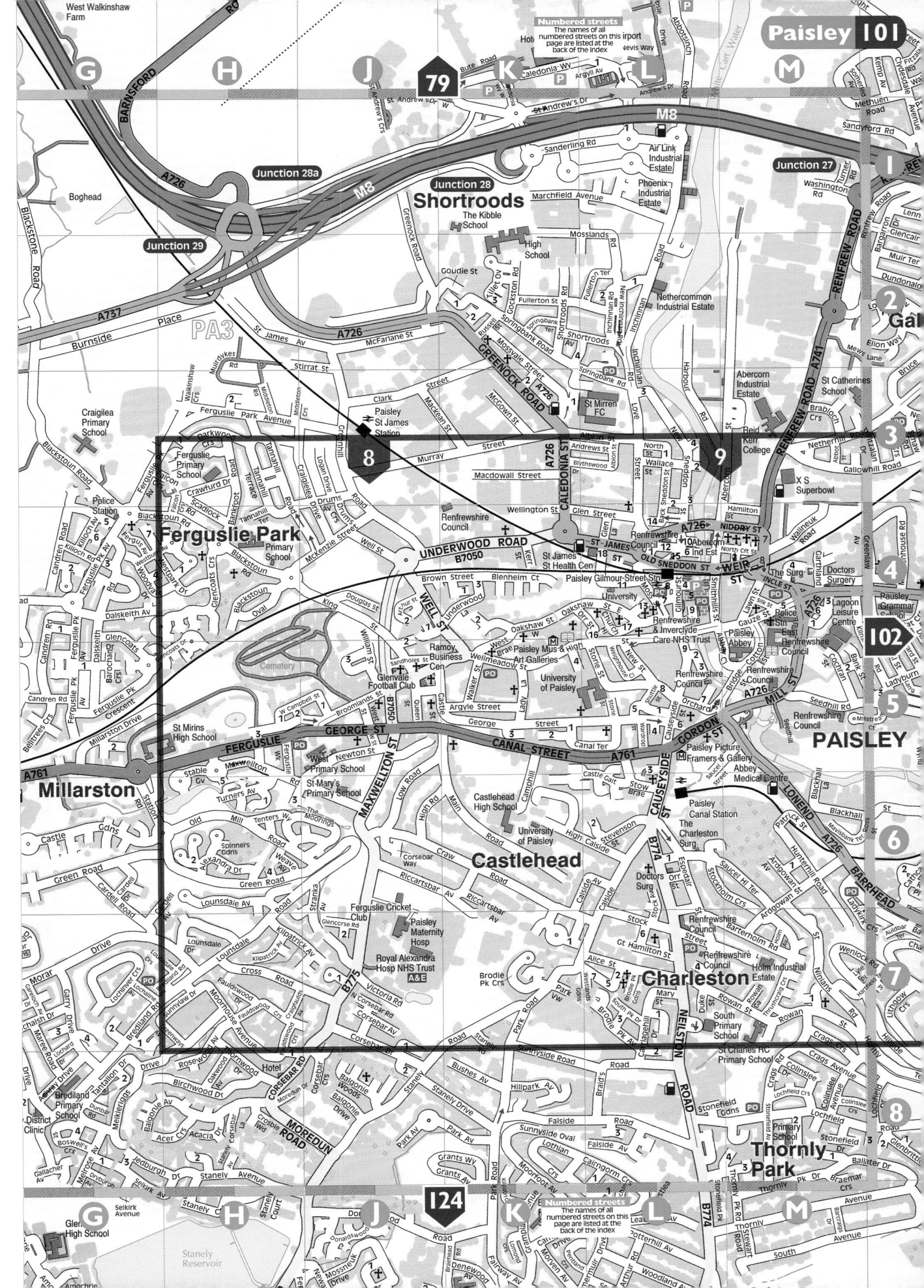

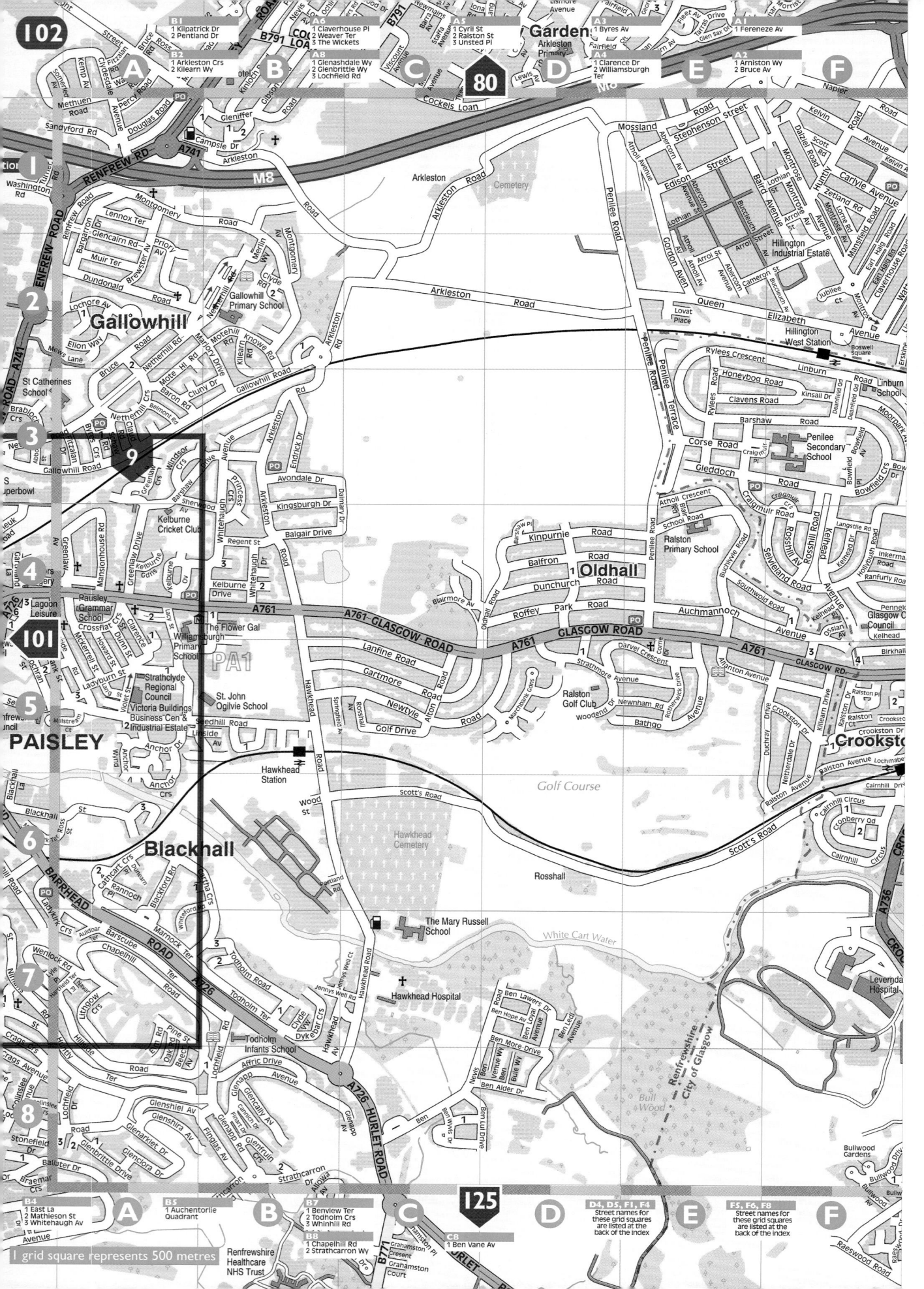

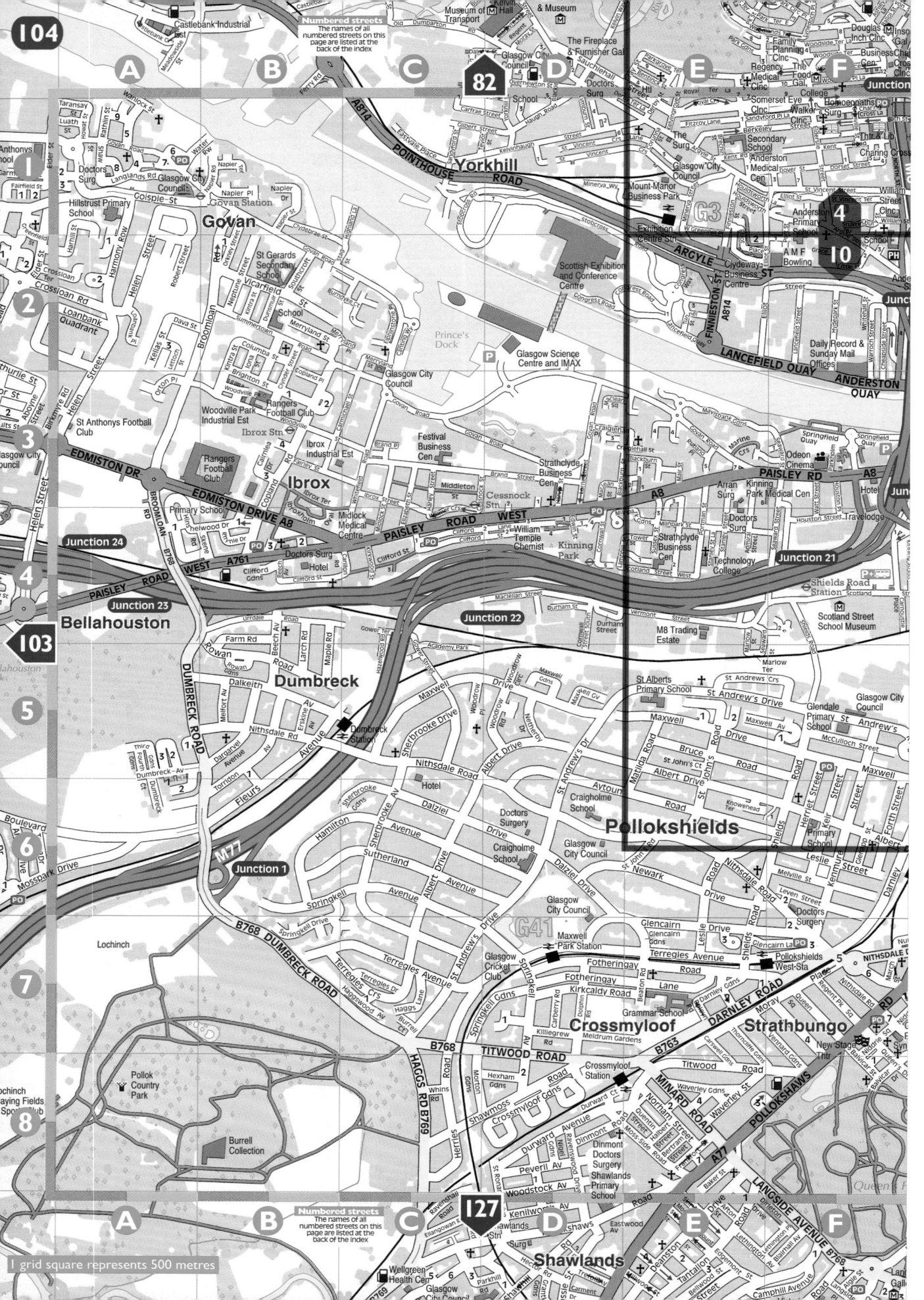

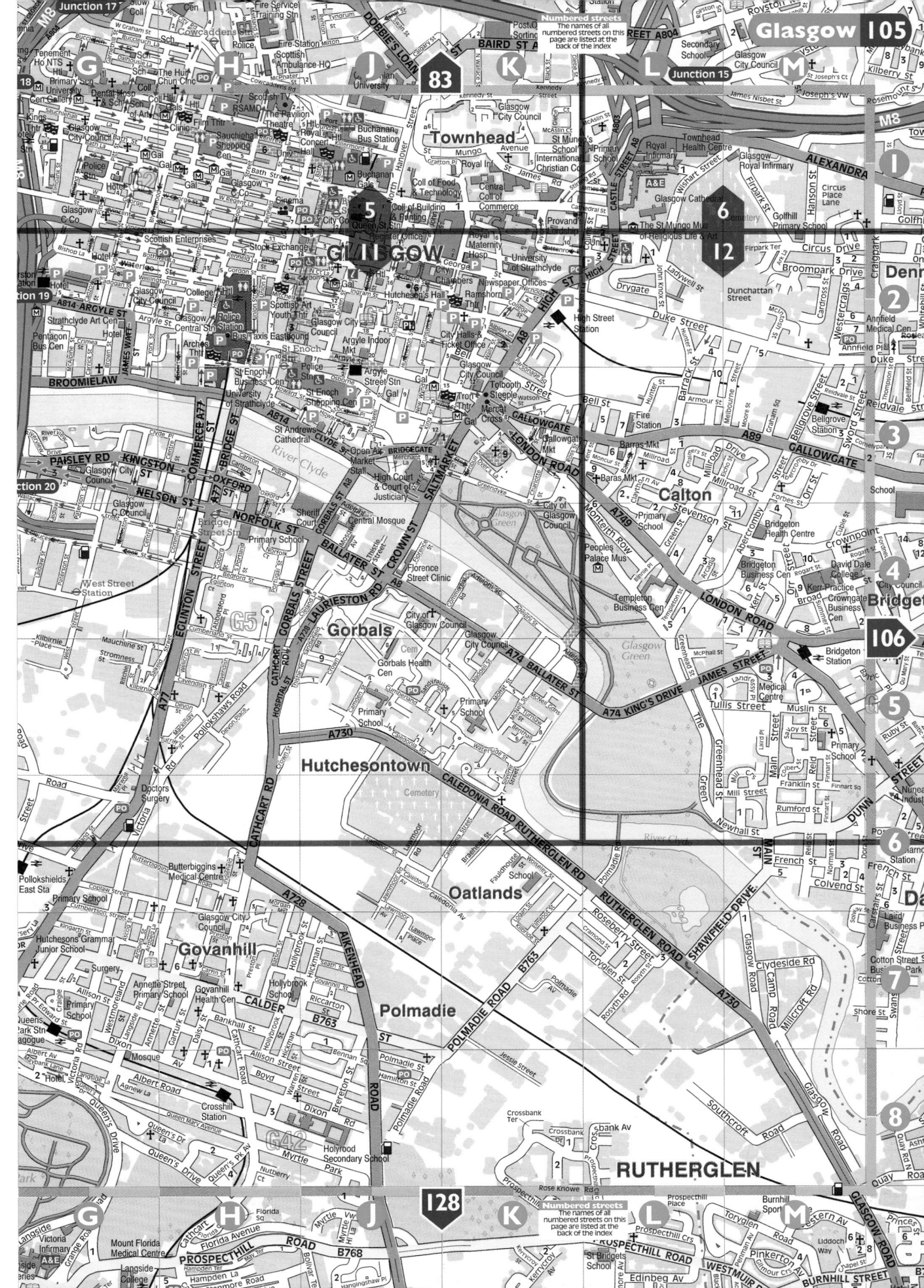

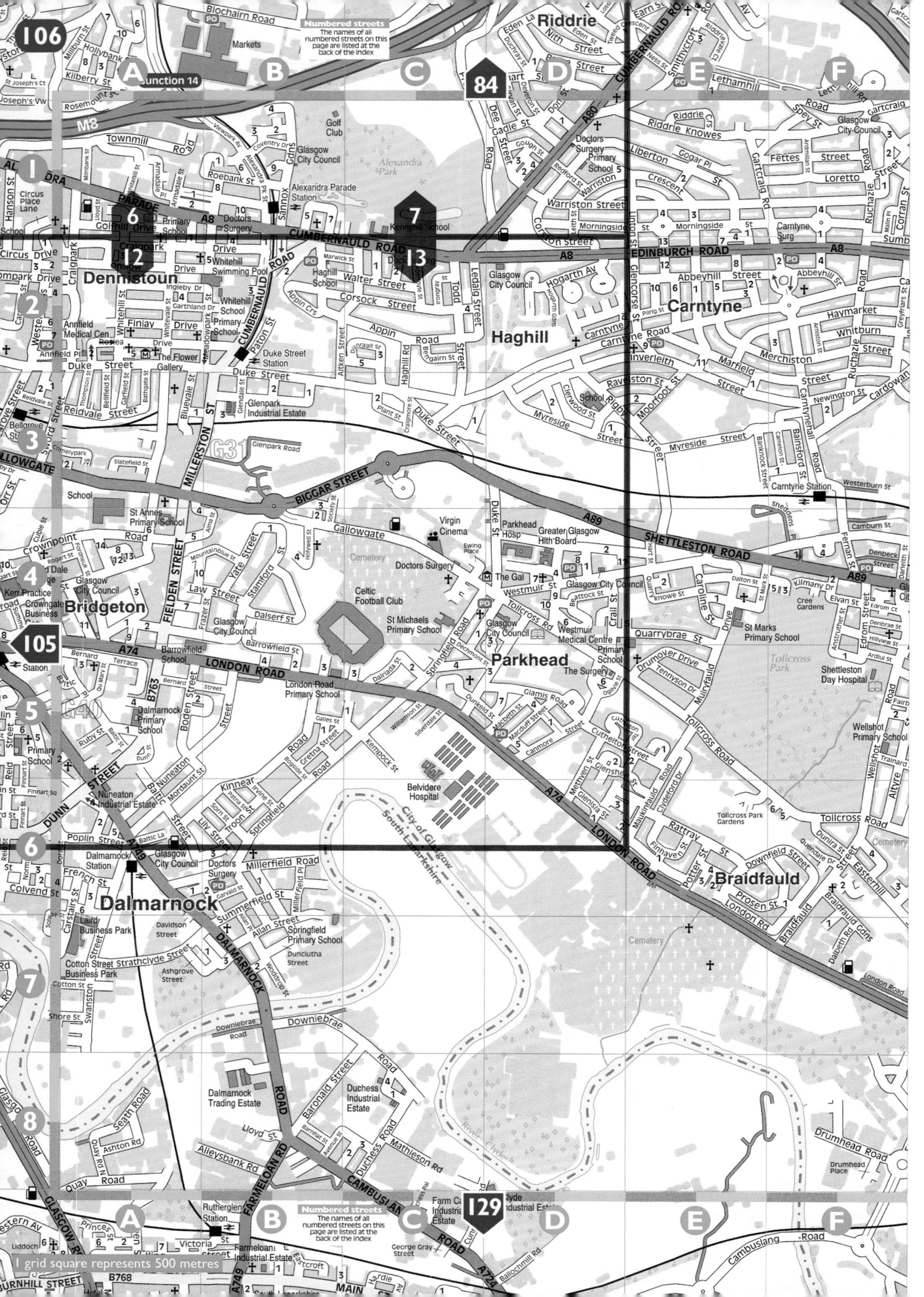

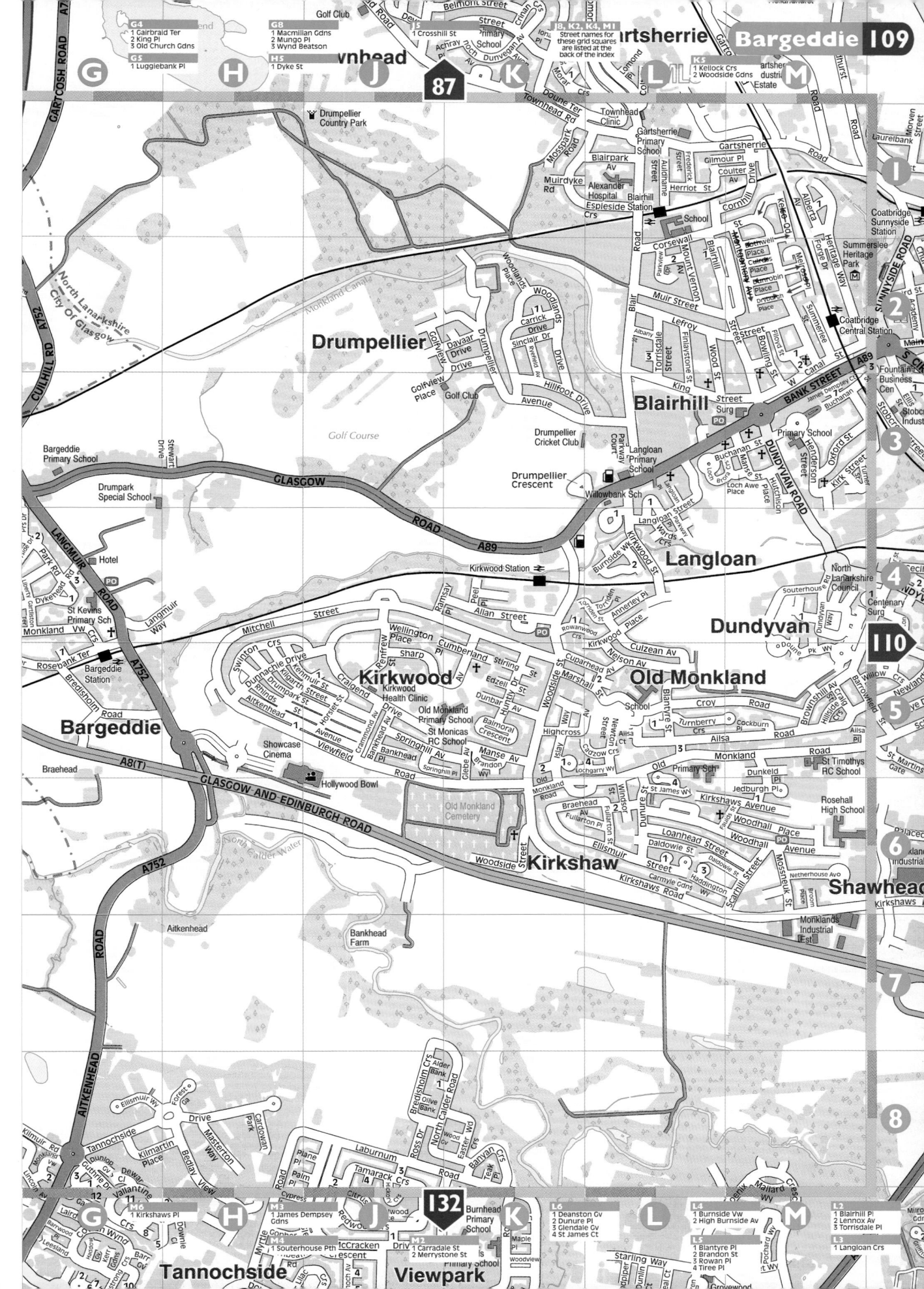

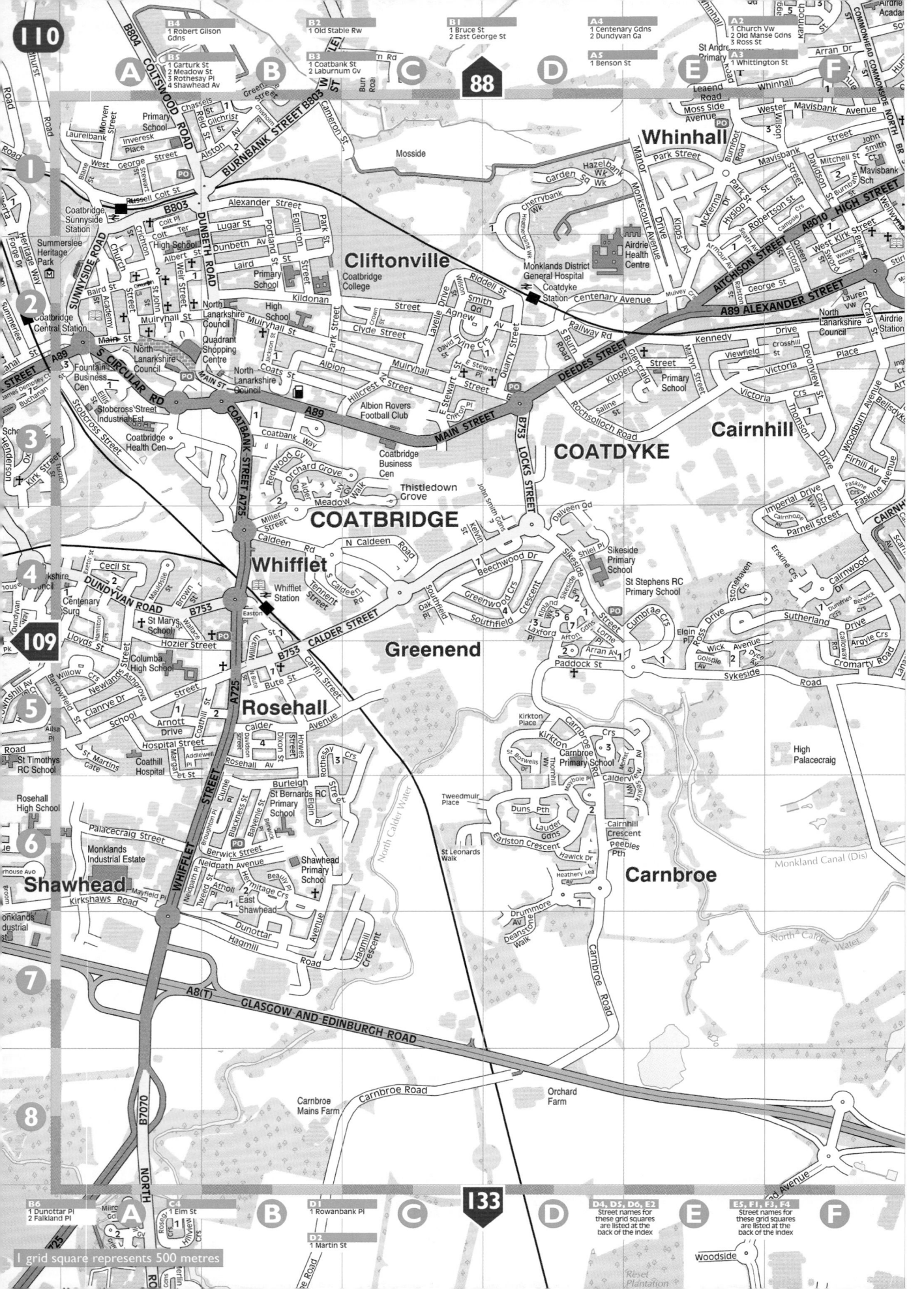

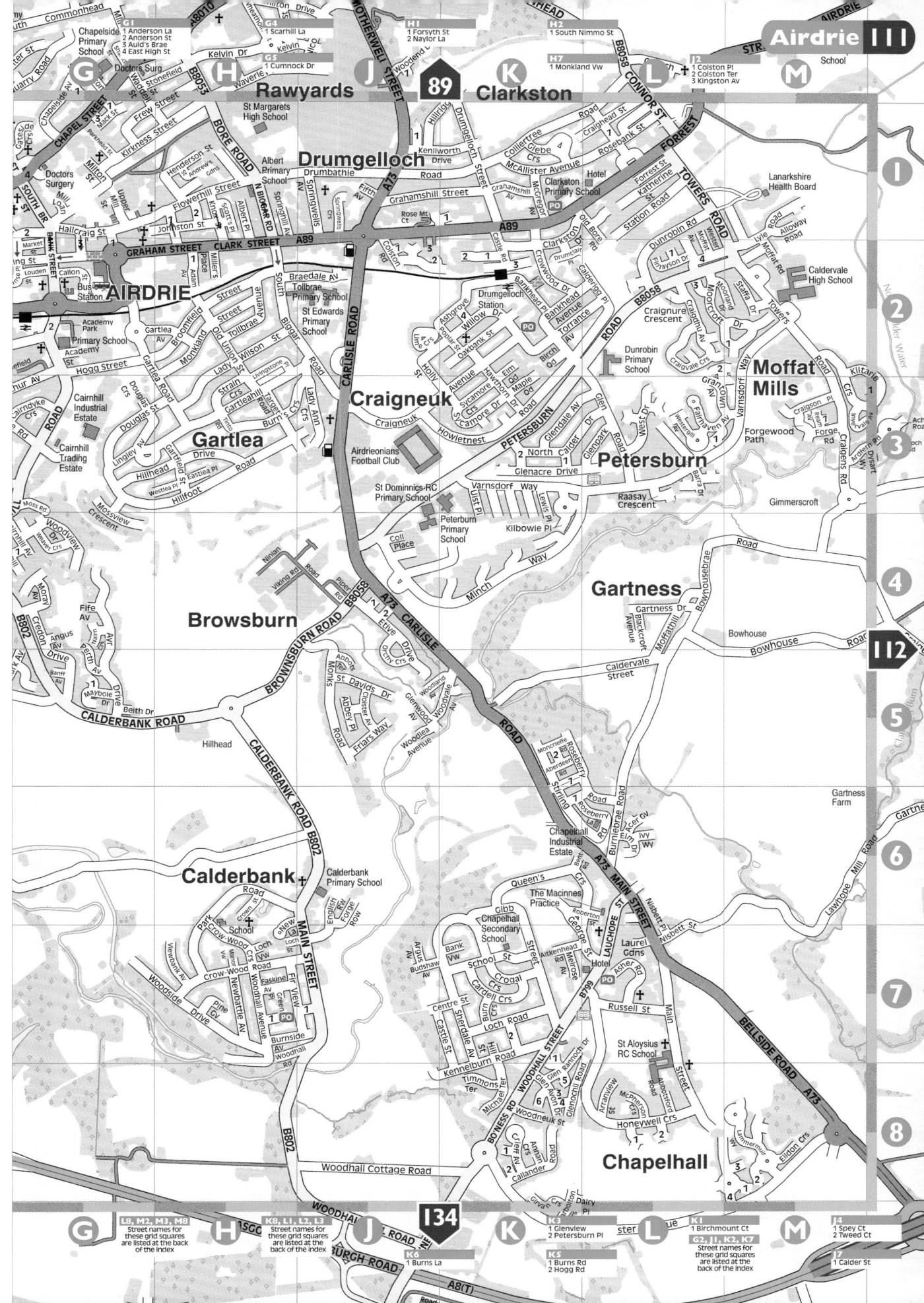

A3
1 Burnwood Dr

AIRDRIE

Sh... School

A   B   C   90   D   E   F

Farm

Plains
Country Park

East... ...nfat
Golf Club

Berrieswalls

1

Lochhill

Duntilland Road

Wester
Bracco

Caldervale
High School

2

North Calder Water

Lady Bell's
Moss

Kiltarie
Crs

Inver... Vale

Achnasheen
Road

Kiltarie
Farm

Stepends Road

Balloch
Road

Ardren Rd   Dysart Wy

Forge

Roughrigg   Road

...roft

3

4

Craigens Road

Clattering Burn

Dunsiston   Road

Easter
Dunsyston

Roughrigg Reservoir

5

Craigends

Gartness
Farm

Lawhope Mill Road

Gartness   Road

Roughrigg Road

Turdees

6

Wester
Dunsyston

Craigens Road

Blackridge
Farm

Langside

7

Bothwellshields Road

Bothwellshields

Craigens Road

M8

Budshaw

Shotts Burn

Peatpots

8

A73

Sandyford

GLASGOW AND EDINBURGH ROAD

M8

A   Junction 6   B   B7066   C   135   D   E   F

North
Linrigg

Linr...

BE... ...DE RO...

1 grid square represents 500 metres

G7
1 Lorne Gdns

H7
1 Bertram Dr
2 David St
3 Gibson St
4 Margaret Av

J7
1 Carvale Av

G H J **91** K L M

1
2 *Papperi*
3
4
5
6 Shot
7
8

Bracco Road

283
▲
Torrance

Mountcow

Duntilland Road

Duntilland Farm

M8

Shottsburn

HIRST ROAD

Kirk of Shotts

School Rd

Manse Road

Newmill and Canthill Road

Bogfoot

Reid Street
Bogfoot Rd
Crosset St
PO

Springfield Road
7

B7066

Muirhall Terrace
3
2
Blackcroft Terrace
Duntilland Av
Sighthill
Kirkview Av
Muirhead Gdns
4
7
Carntyne Rd
Carvale Avenue
7

Salsburgh

Glebe Farm

G H J **136** K L M

Westfield
Manse Road
Road

A   B   C   D   E   F

1

2

3

4

5

6

7

8

A   B   C   D   E   F

Tomont
End

White
Bay

Stinking
Bay

B896

Lady's Bay

Holm Bay

Skate Point

Portrye

Gavin's
Glen

Downcraig
Ferry

B896

Little Skate
Bay

1 grid square represents 500 metres

Great Cumbrae Island

H3
1 Boathouse Av
2 Boathouse Rd
3 Buchanan St
4 Newhaven Gv
5 Northfield Pk
6 Woodbank Gdns

J4
1 Brisbane Crs

J5
1 Cochrane Pl East
2 Gallowgate La

J6
Street names for
this grid square are
listed at the back of
the index

G H J **92** K L M

Brisbane
Mains

Middleton

I
Noddsdale

Routenburn

Holmwood
Court

Bank-Head

2
Harplaw

Danfield
Avenue

Underbank

Hollywood

Netherhall

3
Kilburn
Farm

Routenburn
Golf Club

Kelvin Walk
Kelvin Gardens

Barr Crs

Noddleburn Road

Douglas Place

Laverock Dr

Aubery Crs

Douglas Street

Hutton Pk

Rankin

Burnside Drive

Moorburn Road

Alexander Avenue

4

Brisbane Street

Burnside Road

Mansfield

Beachway

Sinclair Drive

Sinclair Ter

Queens Av

Brisbane
Primary
School

116

Largs
Bay

Glenacre Drive

Haco Street

Kelvin Street

Lindsay Crs

N Middleton Drive

Royal Av

Holehouse Road

Holehouse

5

PO

Nelson Street

Seamore St

Boyd Street

George Street

Middleton

Auchenmaid Drive

Primary
School

Phillips Av

Linn Avenue

Eastern Avenue

Gallowgate St

School St

Allanpark St

Wilson St

Harper Crs

Moorburne

Kelburn
Primary School
Flatt

The Round

Kyles View

Holehouse

Vikingar

Main St

Fife St

Gateside St

Frazer St

Silverdale
Gdns

The Surgery

Waterside

Bellesdale Avenue

Flatt

Largs
Station

Church St

Atten St

10

Stakehill

LARGS

6

Bath Street

Union St

Crawford St

Gogo St

Gogoside

Gogoside Road

Viking Way

Stakehill

Castle
Bay

Burnlea Rd

Mackerston Pl

Charles Street

Lovat St

Scott

Blackdales Av

Bathwood Dr

Silverae Ct

Bankhouse Av

Cunningham

Scott Dr

Scott Crs

Castle Hill
Fort

7

Largs
Sailing
Club

Broomfield Pl

John Street

Hill Street

May Street

Haylie Gdns

Cathcart Rd

Springfields
Gardens

Broomfield Crs

Girtlinghill

Duffield

Cemetery

8

Warrenpark Road

Anthony Road

Acre Av

Warren Pk
Mews

Bowencraig

Walkerston Av

Seabank Av

Largs
Golf Club

139

Dalry Road

A760

Haylie
Reservoir

G

L5
1 Paton Quadrant

H

K8
1 Hutcheson Dr
2 Trigoni Ct
3 Walkerston Av

J

139

K

K6
1 East Castle Av
2 Greenhill
3 Millburn Gdns
4 Park Vw
5 Stakehill

L

K5
1 Scotlaw Dr

M

J7
1 Broomfield

K7
1 Bankhouse Crs
2 Haylie Neuk

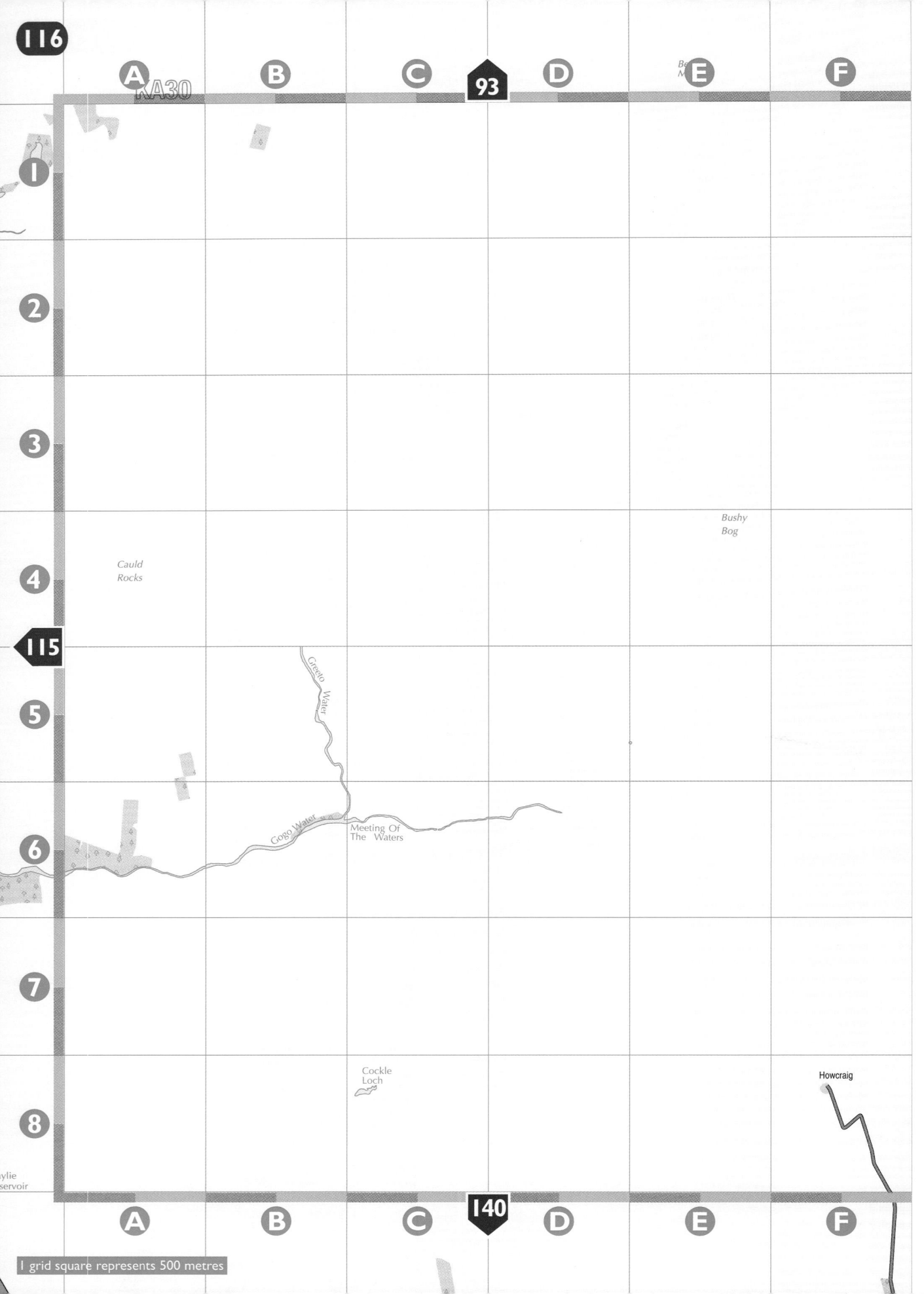

KA30

A   B   C   D   E   F

Ba
M

Bushy
Bog

Cauld
Rocks

115

Creeto Water

Gogo Water   Meeting Of
The Waters

Cockle
Loch

Howcraig

ylie
servoir

A   B   C   D   E   F

1 grid square represents 500 metres

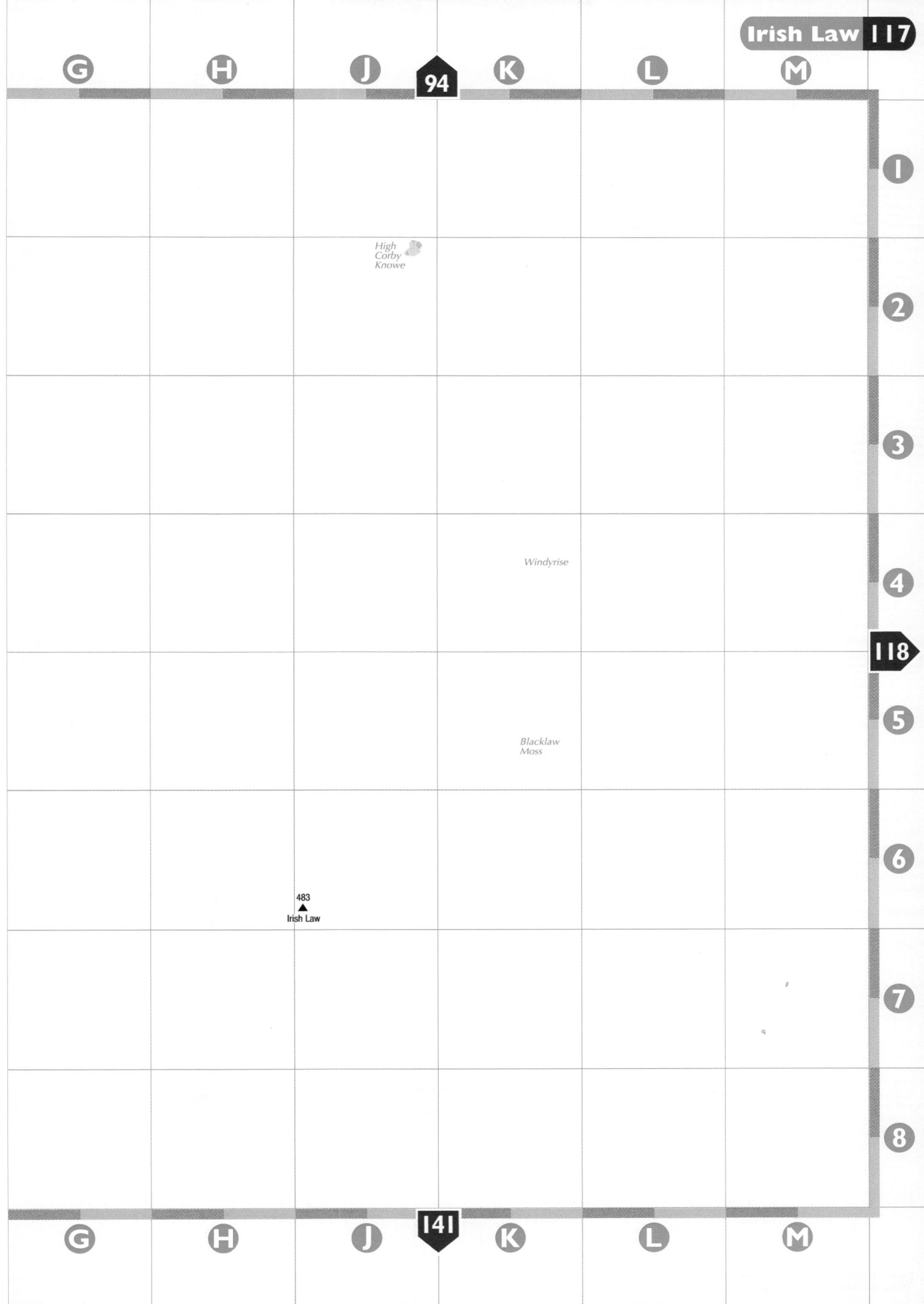

I

High
Corby
Knowe

2

3

Windyrise

4

118

5

Blacklaw
Moss

6

483
▲
Irish Law

7

8

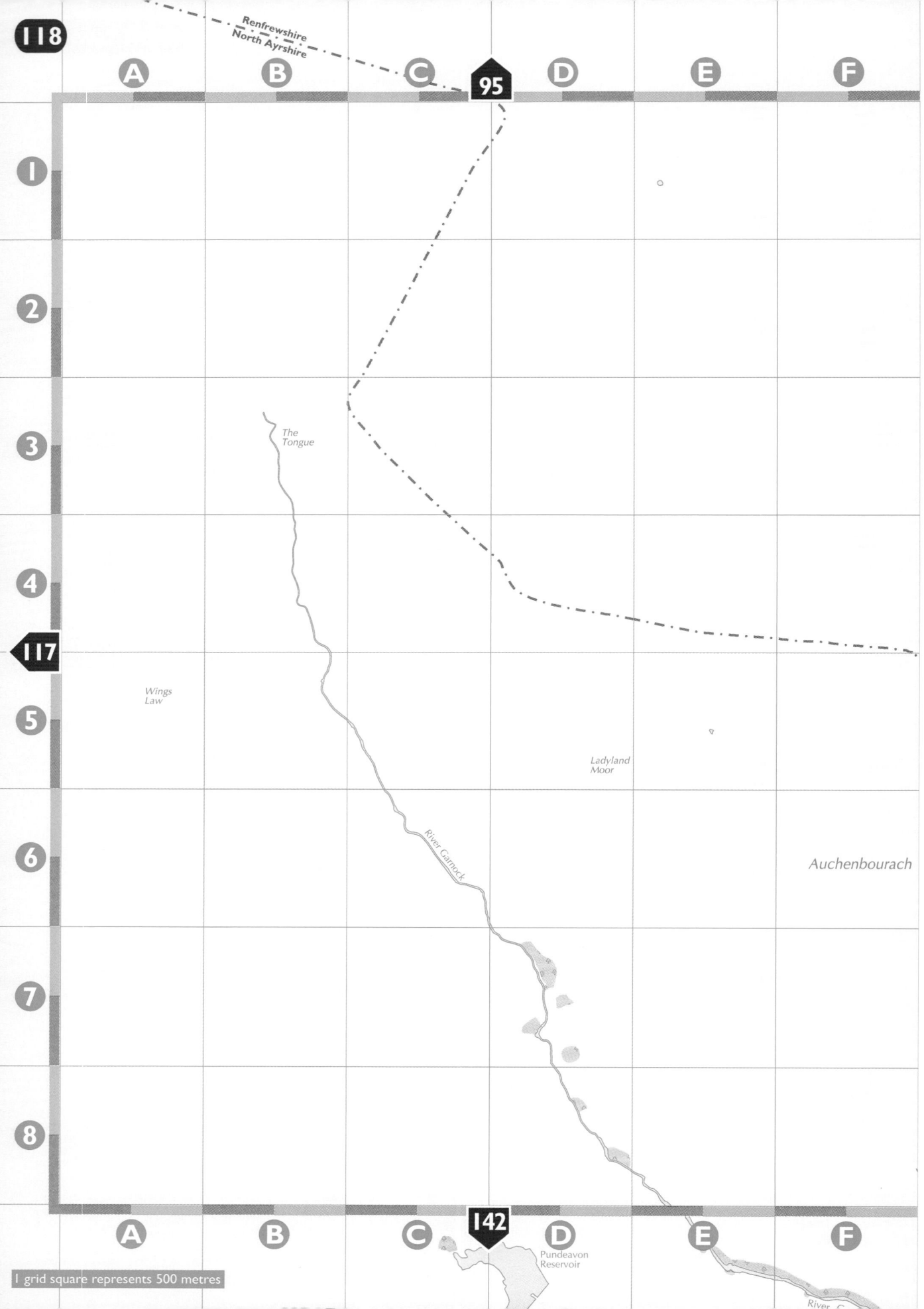

Renfrewshire
North Ayrshire

1

2

3

The
Tongue

4

117

Wings
Law

5

Ladyland
Moor

Auchenbourach

6

River Garnock

7

8

A B C 142 D E F

Pundeavon
Reservoir

River G

1 grid square represents 500 metres

G H J **96** K L M

1

2

3

PA12

4

Clovenstone

River Calder

Tandlemuir

120

Muirfauldhouse

Capel Burn

5

The
Ward

Curling
Pond

6

Gillsyard

Fairhills

Renfrewshire
North Ayrshire

Glenlora

Corsefield Road

7

Easthills

Match Water

Cockston

8

Gavilmoss

Westhills

Lora Burn

G H J **143** K L M

Rashlieyett

Ladyland

Auchenhain

Plantilly

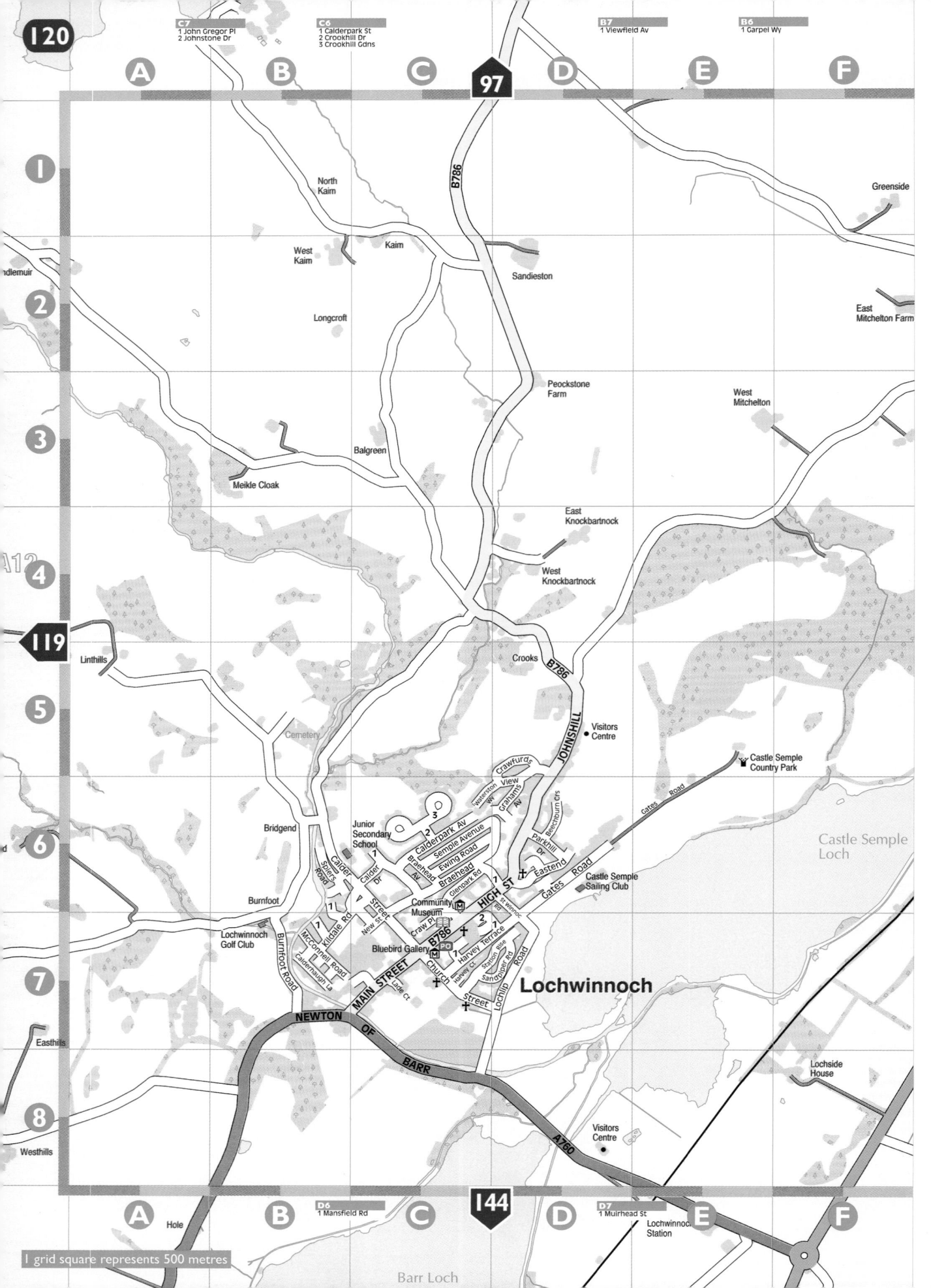

A B C 97 D E F

C7
1 John Gregor Pl
2 Johnstone Dr

C6
1 Calderpark St
2 Crookhill Dr
3 Crookhill Gdns

B7
1 Viewfield Av

B6
1 Garpel Wy

1

Greenside

North
Kaim

2

West
Kaim

Kaim

Sandieston

East
Mitchelton Farm

Longcroft

3

Peockstone
Farm

West
Mitchelton

Balgreen

Meikle Cloak

East
Knockbartnock

4

West
Knockbartnock

119

Linthills

Crooks

B786

5

Cemetery

Visitors
Centre

Castle Semple
Country Park

Castle Semple
Loch

6

Bridgend

Junior
Secondary
School

Crawfurds
View

Grahams
Av

Weavrston Wy

Calderpark Av

Semple Avenue

Ewing Road

Braehead
Av

Braehead

Braehead

Johnshill

Beechburn Crs

Parkhill
Dr

Eastend

Gates Road

Gates Road

Castle Semple
Sailing Club

Burnfoot

Calder
Road

Spiers St

Calder
Dr

New St

Glenpark Rd

Community
Museum

HIGH ST

St winnoc
Rd

2

Lochwinnoch Golf Club

McConnell Road

Kildale Rd

Calderhaugh La

7

Church Street

Bluebird Gallery

Craw Pl

Harvey Terrace

Harvey Ct

Station Rd

Sandpiper Rd

Lochlip Road

PO

B786

7

Lochwinnoch

Easthills

NEWTON

MAIN STREET

Lade Ct

OF

BARR

A760

Lochside
House

8

Westhills

Visitors
Centre

A B C 144 D E F

Barr Loch

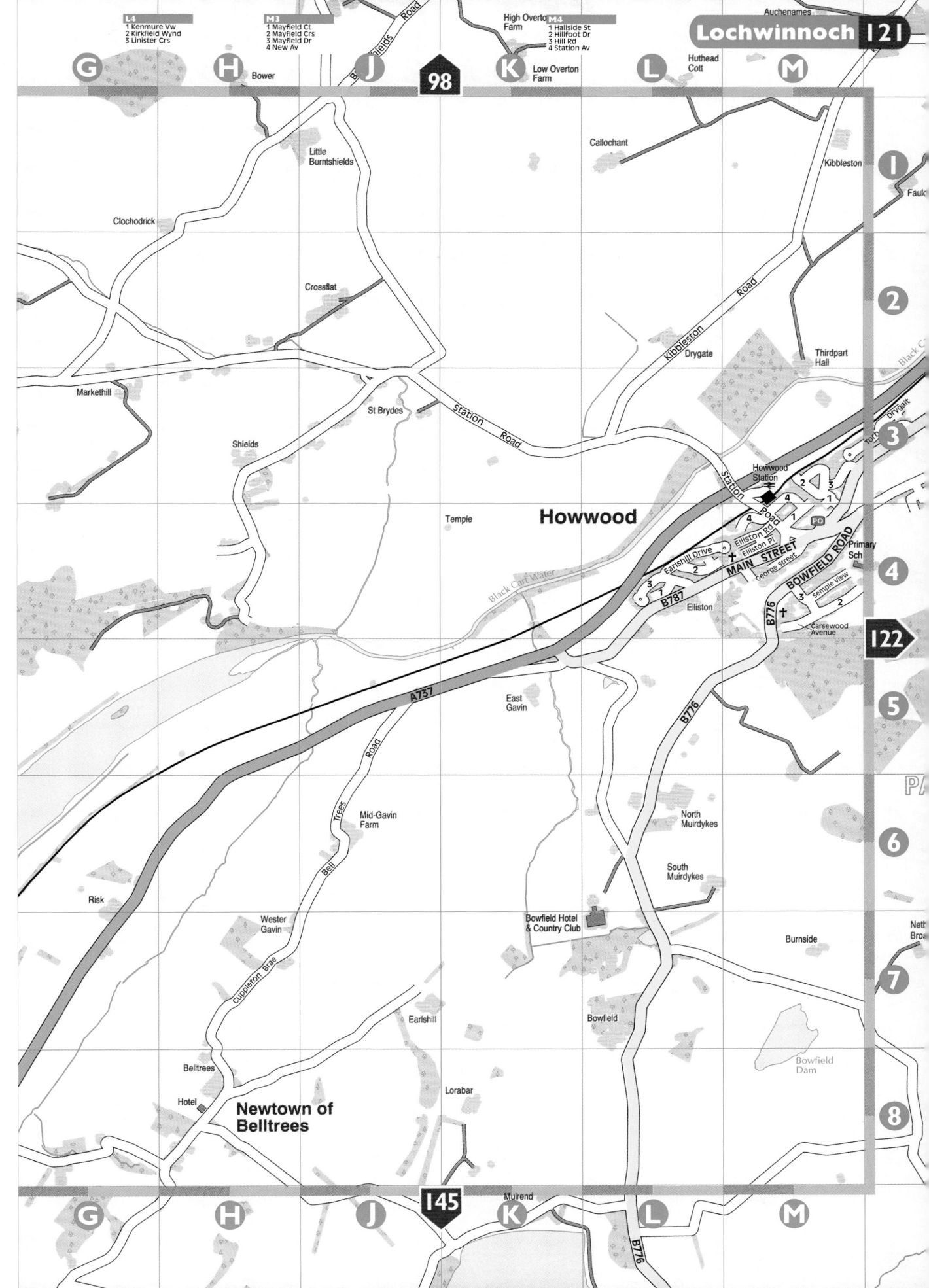

G H J 98 K L M

L4
1 Kenmure Vw
2 Kirkfield Wynd
3 Linister Crs

M3
1 Mayfield Ct
2 Mayfield Crs
3 Mayfield Dr
4 New Av

High Overton
Farm

M4
1 Hallside St
2 Hillfoot Dr
3 Hill Rd
4 Station Av

Bower

Low Overton
Farm

Huthead
Cott

Auchenames

I

Callochant

Kibbleston

Faulk

Little
Burntshields

Kibbleston
Road

Drygate

Thirdpart
Hall

Black C

2

Clochodrick

Crossflat

Markethill

St Brydes

Station
Road

Howwood
Station

Torbi
Drygait

3

Shields

Temple

Howwood

Earlshill Drive

Elliston Rd
Elliston Pl
MAIN STREET
George Street

Primary
Sch

BOWFIELD ROAD

PO

2
3
1
4
4

2

4

Black Cart Water

B787

Elliston

B776

Semple View

3

2

Carsewood
Avenue

122

A737

East
Gavin

B776

North
Muirdykes

P

5

Risk

Trees
Road

Bell

Mid-Gavin
Farm

South
Muirdykes

Nett
Broa

6

Wester
Gavin

Cuppleton Brae

Bowfield Hotel
& Country Club

Burnside

7

Earlshill

Bowfield

Bowfield
Dam

Belltrees

Hotel

**Newtown of
Belltrees**

Lorabar

8

G H J 145 K Muirend L M

B776

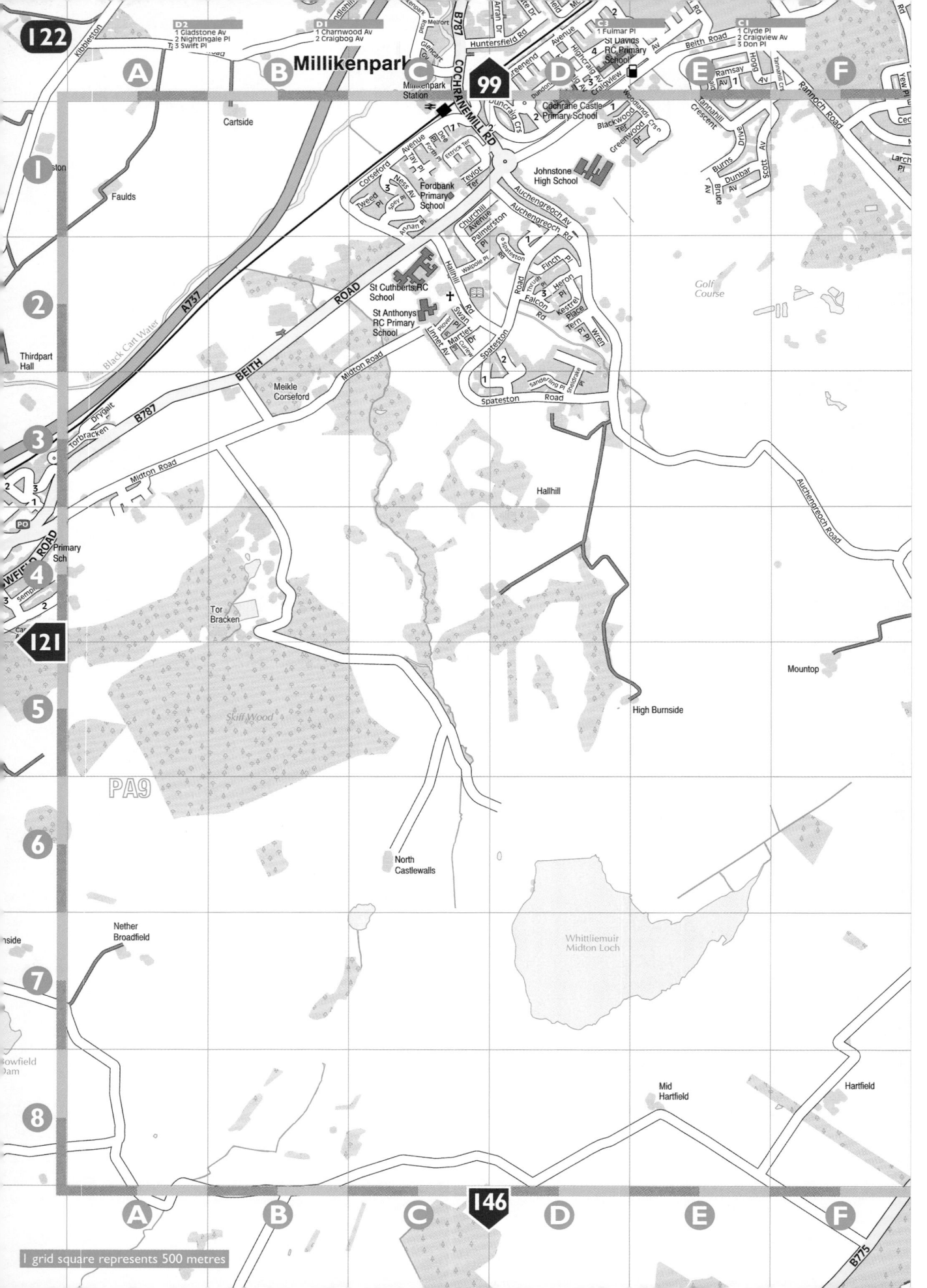

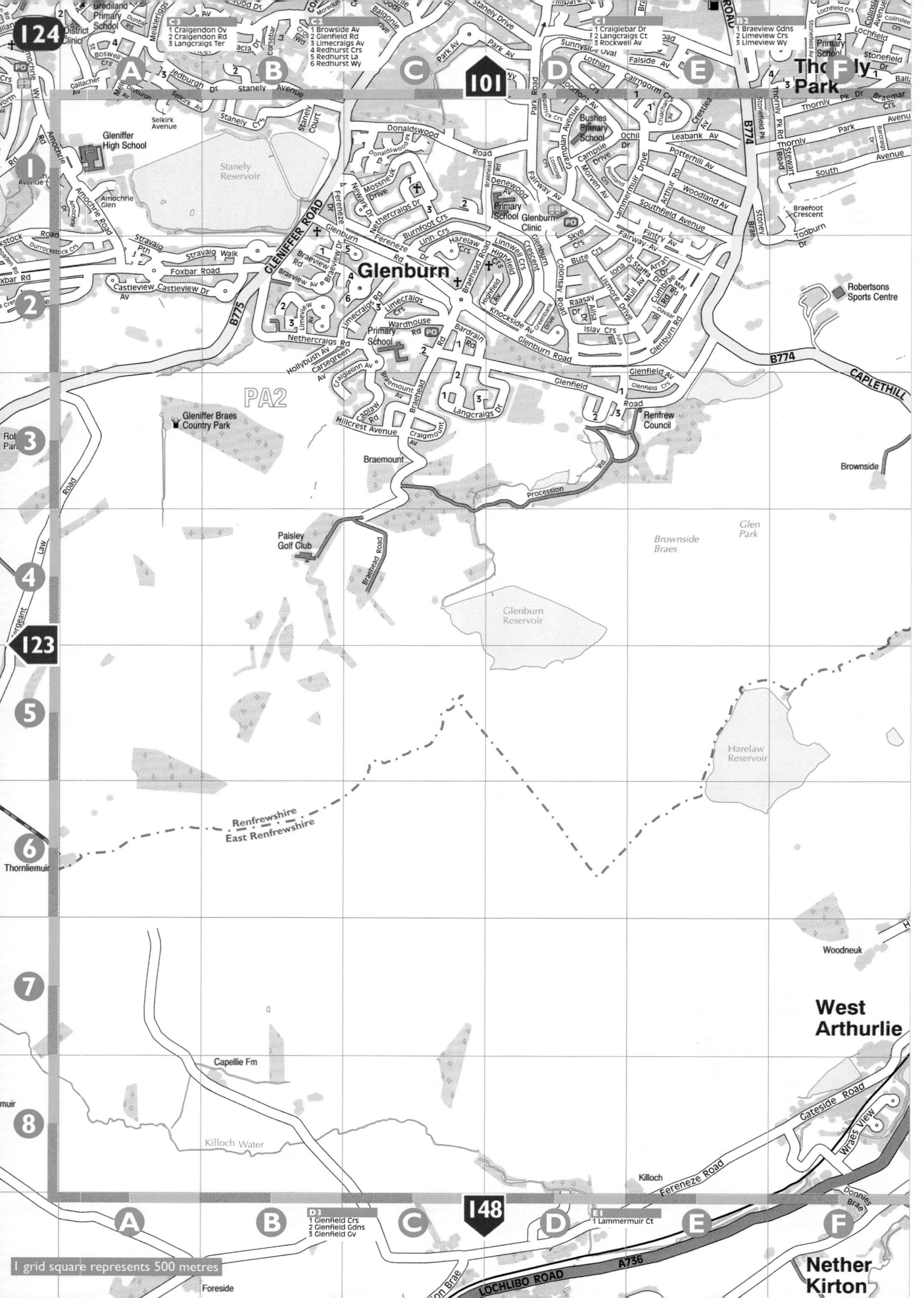

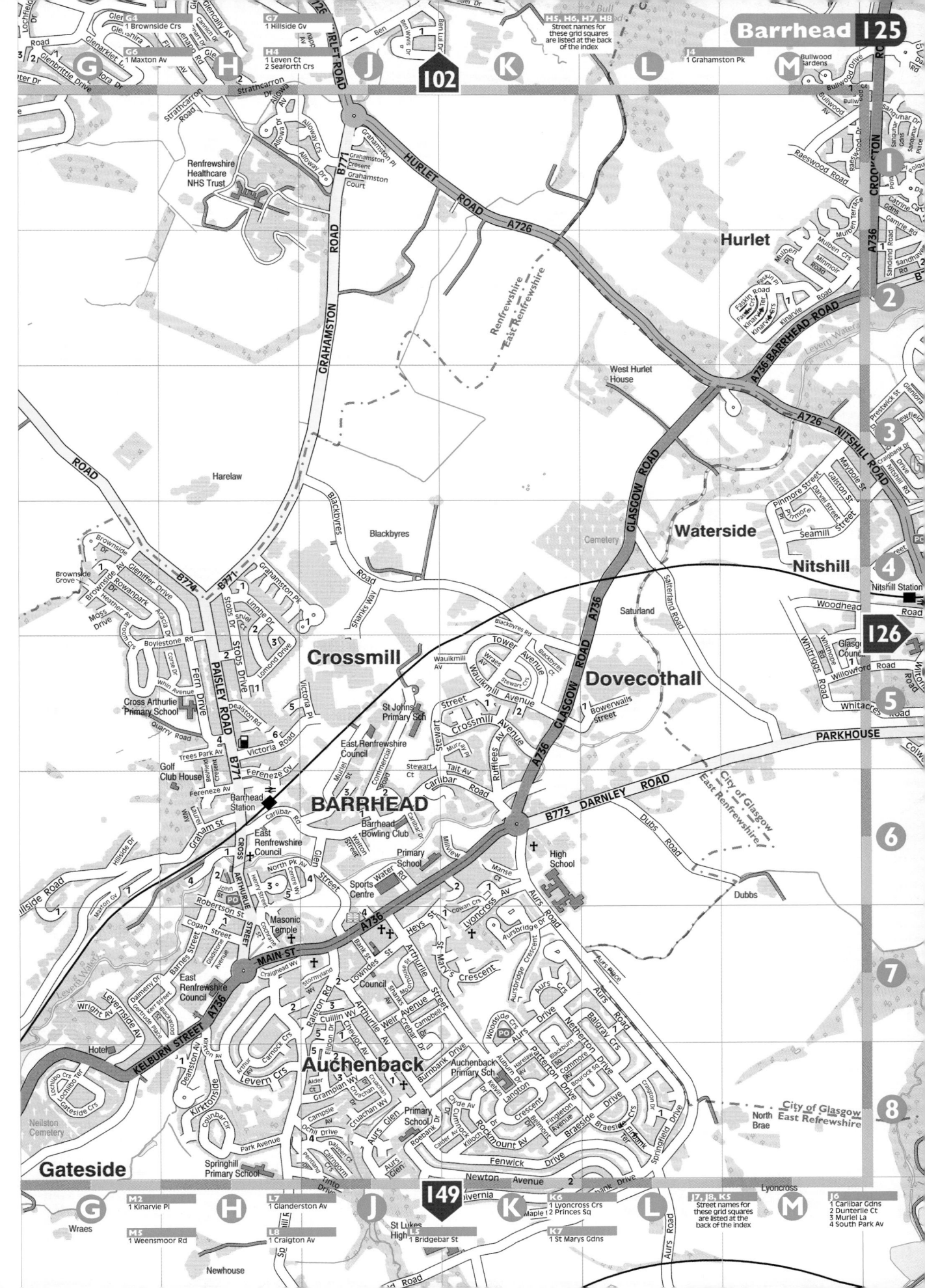

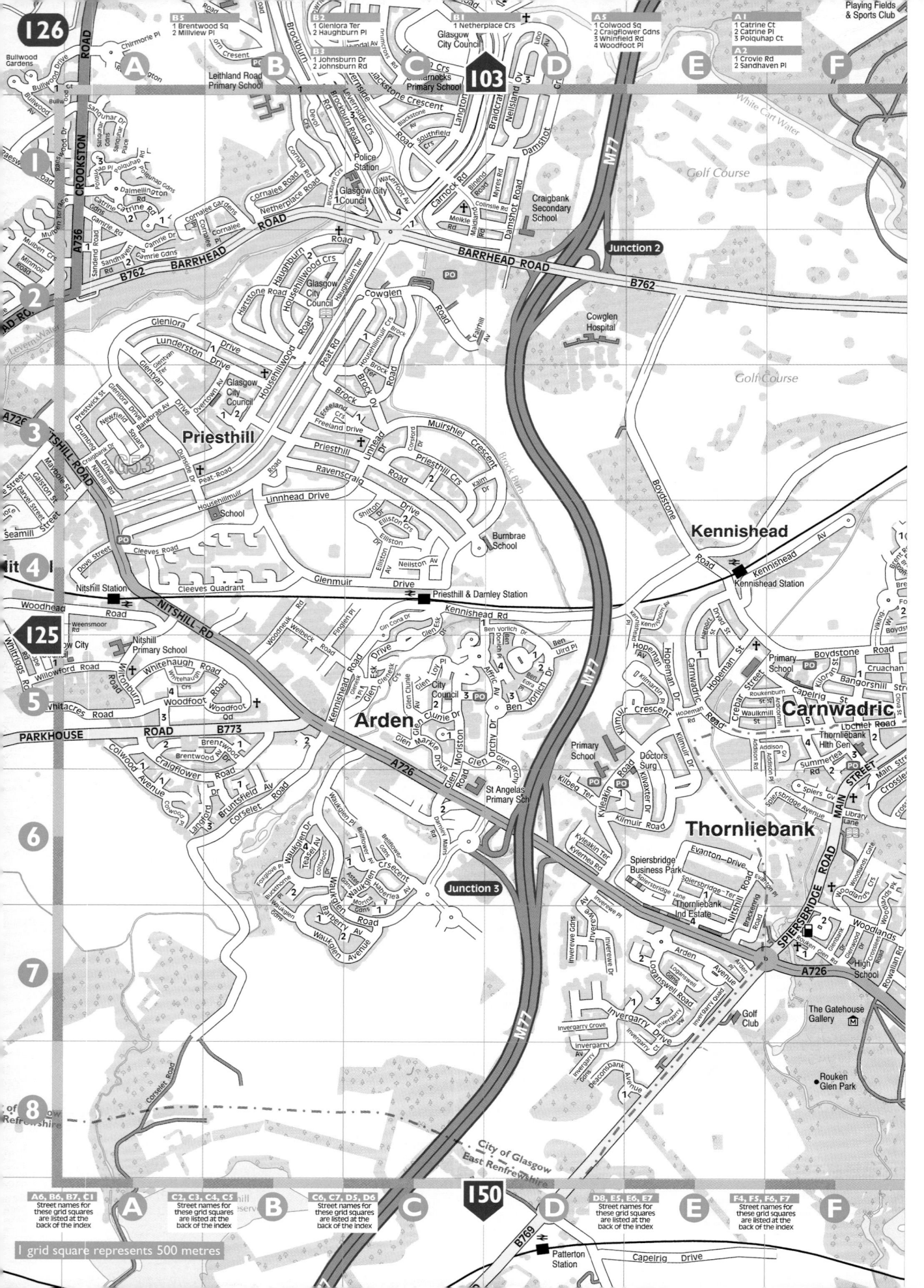

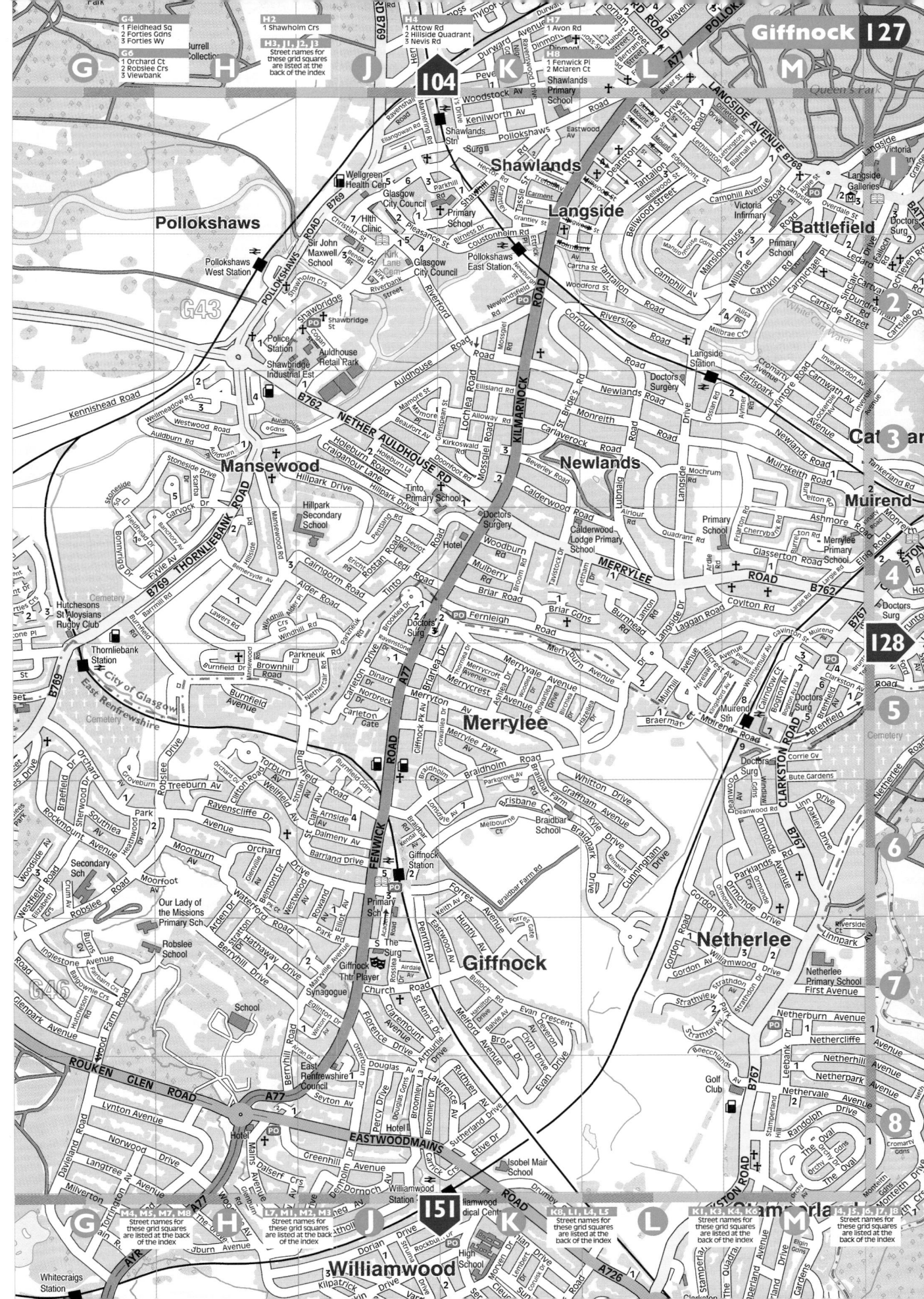

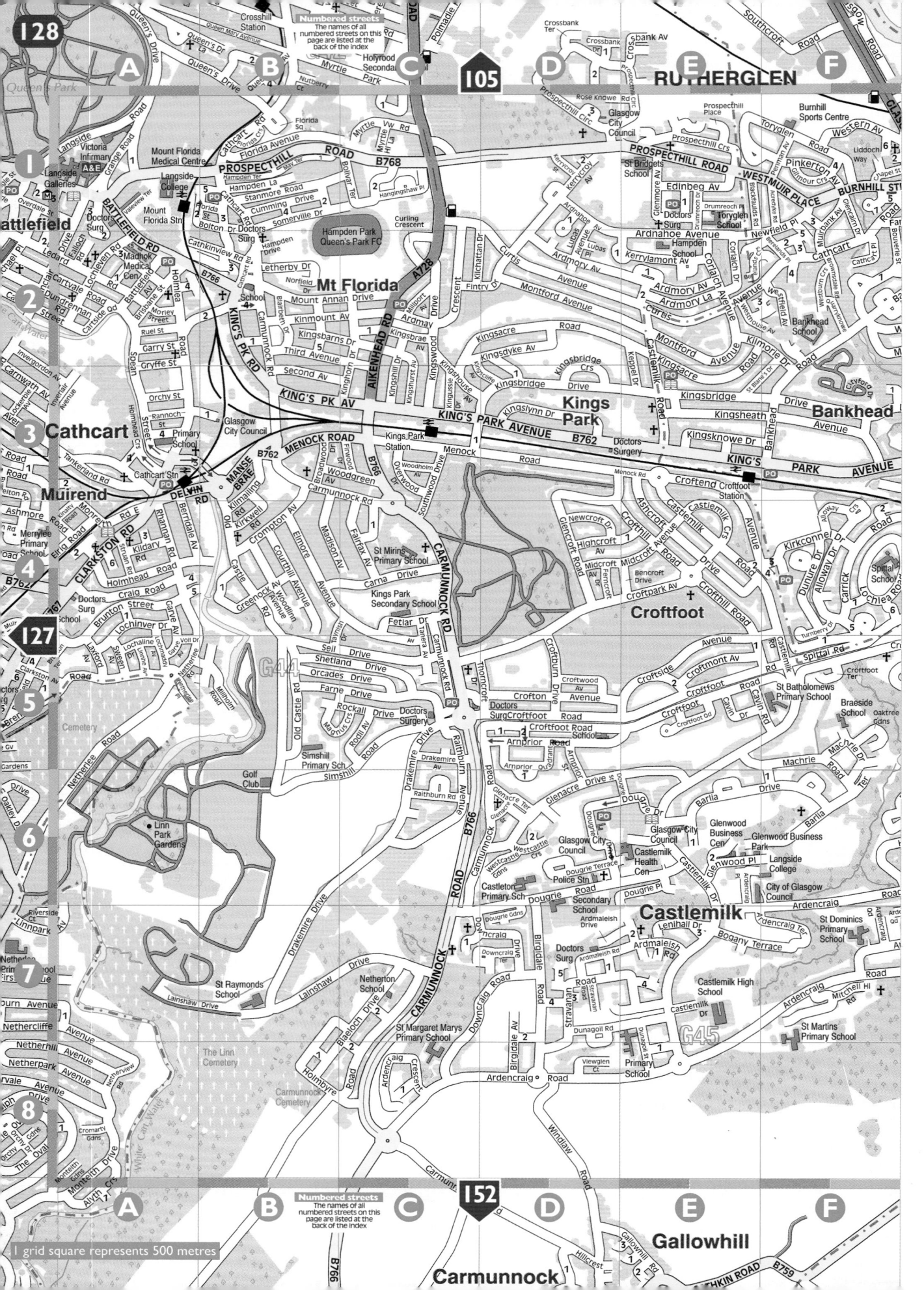

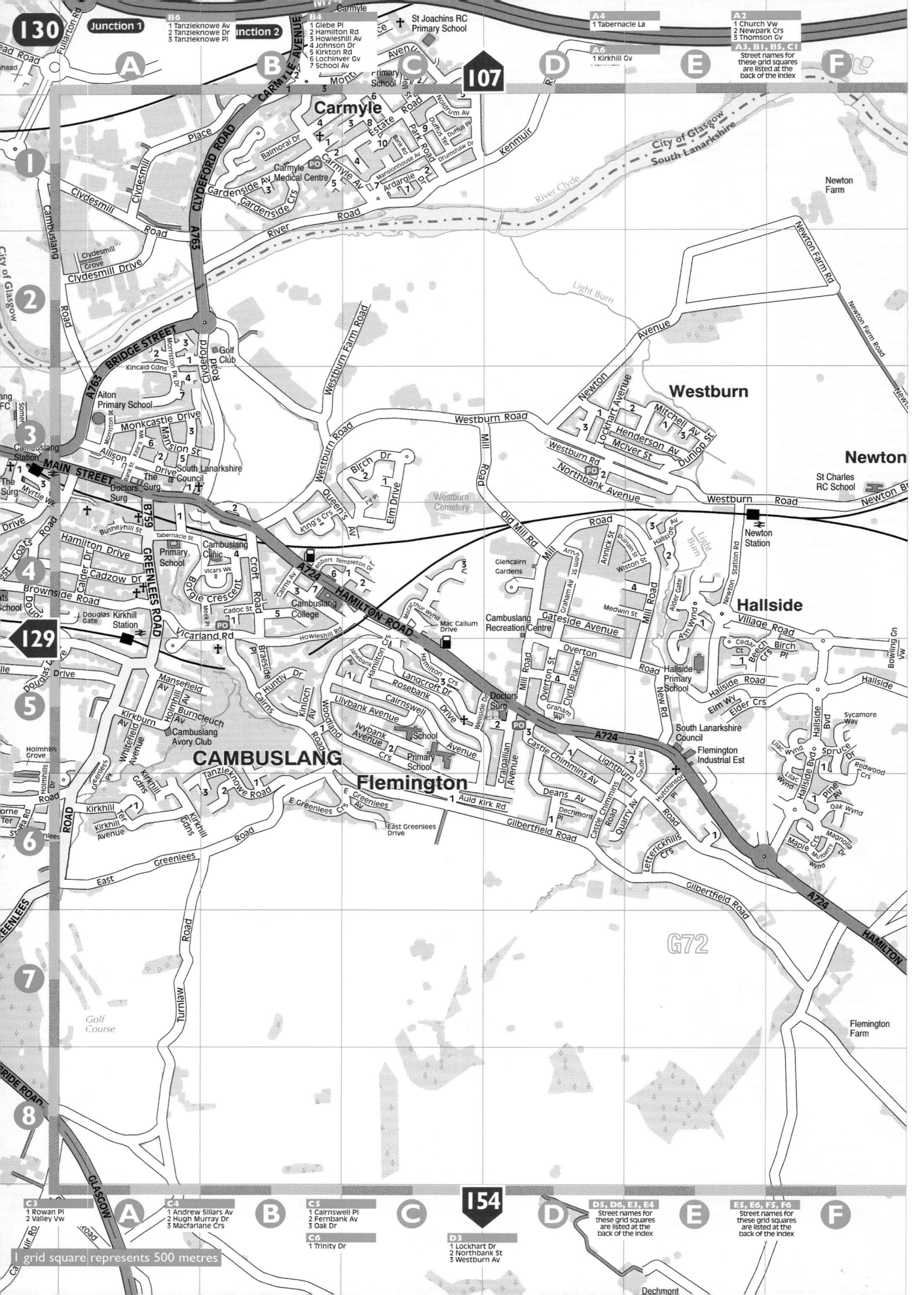

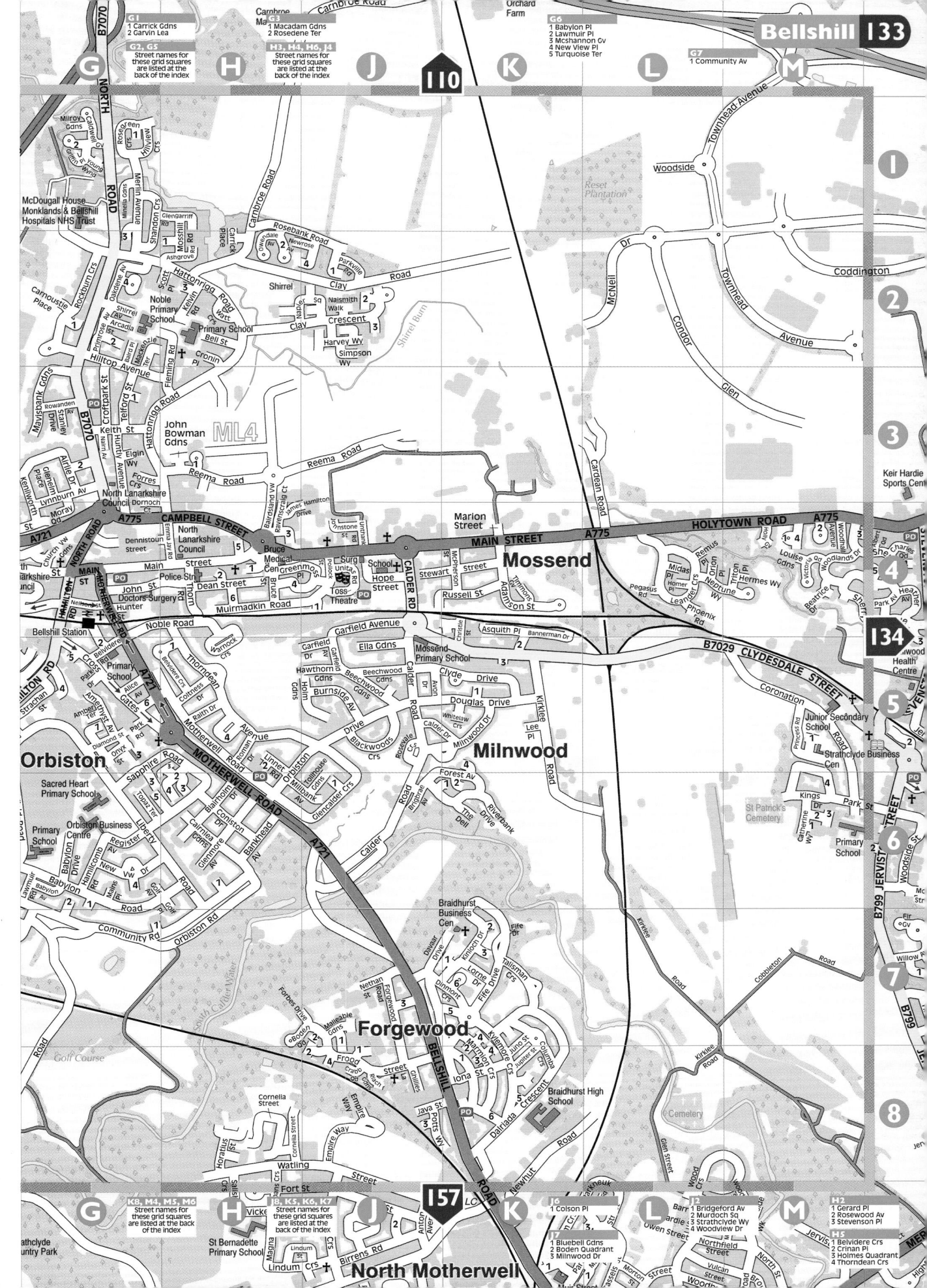

110

McDougall House
Monklands & Bellshill
Hospitals NHS Trust

Noble
Primary
School

Primary School

ML4

John
Bowman
Gdns

North Lanarkshire
Council Dornoch

A775 CAMPBELL STREET

North
Lanarkshire
Council

North
Lanarkshire
Council

Dennistoun
Street

MAIN ST

Bellshill Station

Medical
Cen

Surg
Unitas
Rd

Toss
Theatre

School
Hope
Street

MAIN STREET A775 HOLYTOWN ROAD A775

Mossend

Marion
Street

Keir Hardie
Sports Cen

134

Health
Centre

B7029 CLYDESDALE STREET

Mossend
Primary School

Garfield Avenue

Ella Gdns

Orbiston

Primary
School

Sacred Heart
Primary School

Orbiston Business
Centre

Primary
School

MOTHERWELL ROAD

A721

Milnwood

Douglas Drive

Junior Secondary
School

Strathclyde Business
Cen

St Patrick's
Cemetery

Kings

Primary
School

B799 JERVIST STREET

Forest Av

The
Dell

Community Rd

Orbiston Rd

Golf Course

Braidhurst
Business
Cen

Forgewood

Braidhurst High
School

Cemetery

Cornelia
Street

Watling
Street

157

North Motherwell

A **B** **C** III **D** **E** **F**

1

WOODHALL MILL ROAD

BONESS ROAD

GLASGOW AND EDINBURGH ROAD

Woodrow

McNeil Drive

Crescent

Coddington

A8(T)

B799

Greenside

Road

Howden Avenue

Glasgow   and   Edinburgh   Road

Lancaster Avenue

Biggar Road

A775

2

Lauchope Road

Sandyford Avenue

Mosshall Rd

Sandyford Place

Glen Rd

Sandyford Rd

Rowantree Avenue

Beech Rd

Beech Crs

Kirk Road

Legbrannock

Newhouse Industrial Estate

Bodden Square

Nicklaus Way

A775   EDINBURGH   ROAD

Biggar Road

3

Holytown

Castle Av

O'Wood Avenue

Crantholm Avenue

Plantation Avenue

Stewart Qd

Boness Rd

Cemetery

Legbrannock Road

Legbranock Burn

Legbranock

McPhail Avenue

Manse Vw

A775

4

Keir Hardie Sports Centre

Medical Centre

Main Street

Sunnyside Terrace

Sunnyside Crescent

Melrose Av

Violet Pl

Keir Hardie Av

Crow Av

Birch St

Deveron Rd

Dornoch Rd

Glen Drive

Willow Rd

Maple Rd

Redpath Road

STEVENSTON STREET

Charles Gdns

Glencoe

Howden

Graham St

Windsor Road

Ivy Ter

Rowantree Ter

Dornoch Road

Myrtle Dr

Cuckoo Way

Cedar Rd

Lime Loan

Elm Rd

Poplar Pl

A723

Holytown Primary School

Christ the King Primary School

Manse Vw
Muirhead Dr

B7066

133

Fullwood Health Centre

Shirrel Road

Burn Crs

Dale Dr

East Rd

Clyde Pl

Hamilton Place

Law Dr

Burnside   Road

Brannock Av

Glen St

Kirkhall Road

Kirkoswald Rd

5

Junior Secondary School

Strathclyde Business Cen

STEVENSTON ST

Hall St

Jerviston Street

Quarry Street

Union Street

George St

Macedonian

Cedar Gdns

Hamilton Place

Glenburn Avenue

Little Road

Glenmore Rd

Braeside

Knowe Crs

Benford Knowe

Kirkhall Road

Uchlea Wy

Robert Burns

HIGH   STREET

Mosshall

Mcinnes Doctors Surgery

Newarth

6

B799   JERVISTON STREET

Park St

PO

Thistle Rd

Holytown Station

Laberge Gdns

Atlin Dr

Clarinda Pl

Nith Qd

Martin Rd

Broom Place

Clydeham

Brannock

Hillside

Yett

Keir Hardie Memorial Primary School

Primary School

Loanhead

Silverburn

B7066

Coalhead Crs

Whittagreen

Torrindon

Laughland

Newarthill Primary School

spalehall drive

Cowkhat

Tillanburn Road

7

Taylor High School

Moore Street

Fir Gv

Willow Av

Dunbar La

West Av

Central Av

Buchan Road

Park Road

East Av

Bruce Rd

Beech Av

Hawthorn Dr

B7029

CARFIN STREET

New Stevenston Road

A723

Woodrow Av

Carfin

Hatton Ter

Thornhill Avenue

Hatton Ter

Culzean   Drive

Carroll Crs

Carfin Station

B7066

CARFIN ROAD

Taylor Av

Bernadette Crescent

Our Lady & St Francis Primary School

Beechworth Crs

Whittagreen

Road

ML1

8

B799

JERVISTON ROAD

Hillhead Av

Hillhead Dr

Lloyd Gv

Lloyd St

Loganlea Dr

Linksview Rd

Montalto

Clapperhow Rd

Coalhall Avenue

A723

New Stevenston Road

Glenburn Ter

Byresknowe La

MOTHERWELL ROAD

PO

Manknowe Road

Carfin Mill Rd

B7029   CHAPELKNOWE   ROAD

Morris

Vardon Lea

Hagen Dr

Cotton Crescent

Cleekhimin

A MERRY STREET **B** **C** 158 **D** **E** **F**

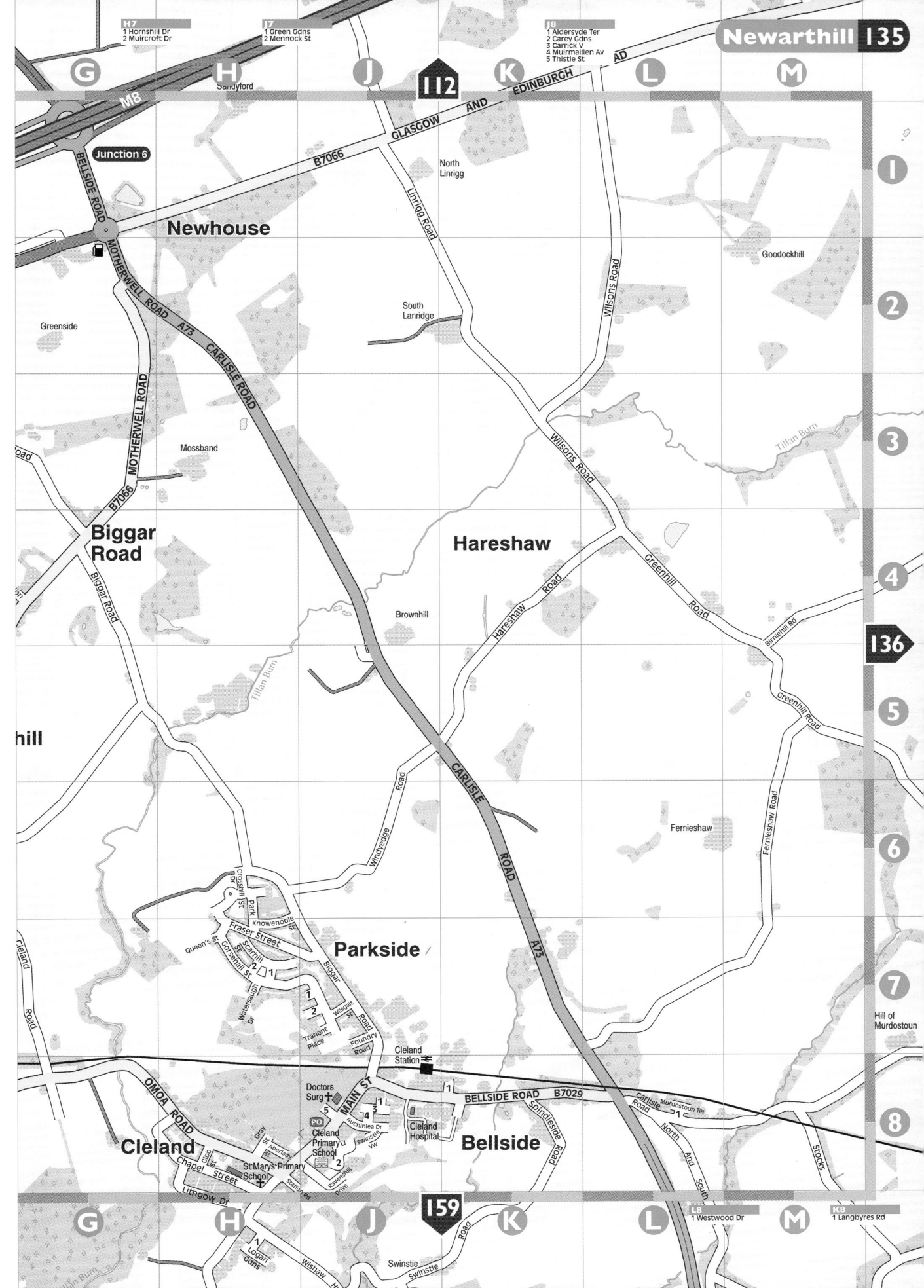

113

135

160

A B C D E F

1
2
3
4
5
6
7
8

Westfield

Manse Road

Roughdike

Muiredge and Jersy Road

Jersay

Muiredge and Jersy Road

Birniehill Road

Burn

Mill Road

Muiredge and Jersy Road

Penty

Hartwood Station

Ashgrove

Home Farm Rd

Newmill Gdns

Canthill

Hartwood Hospital

Hartwood Hospital

Hartwood Gardens

Hartwood Road

Hill of Murdostoun

Shawstonfoot Road

Foulburn Road

Foulburn Road

Castlerigg

Mill Road

E o

Allan

Stocks Road

Calder Rd 1
Coltness
Alliance
Street
Place

1 grid square represents 500 metres

A B C D E F

114

Portrye

Downcraig
Ferry

1 Little Skate
Bay

Bell
Bay

Great Cumbrae Island

Figgatoch

Fairhaven

2 B896

Stinking
Goat

Minnemoor

Ballochmartin

B899

3 Glaid
Stone

Wee
Minnemoor

Sheriff's
Common

KA28

B896

Ballochmartin
Bay

4 Gawk
Stone

Upper
Cumbrae
Reservoir

Ballikillet

Craigengour

Clashfarland
Point

B899

Lower
Cumbrae
Resrvoir

5 Golf
Course

Lady Margaret
Hospital

Butter Lump

Breakough

6 **Millport**

Cumbrae
Primary
School

Lady
Margaret
Hospital

The College
& Cathedral
College

Craig-en-Ros
Road

Copland
Crs

Cumbrae
Dr

Hastie Av

Kames St

College Street

Ferry Road

Balloch Crs

1

Marine Pde

Ninian Brae

Ninian St

Doctors
Surgery

Kelburn Street

Kames Bay

Museum of
The Cumbraes

George

North
Ayrshire
Council

Bute
Terrace

Howard Street

Clifton St

PO

Stuart St

Guildford St

GLASGOW STREET

2

The Lion

7 Cardiff St

Millport
St

Clyde St

2

William St

Crichton St

Newtown
Bay

The
Eileans

Kames
Bay

Museum
& Aquarium

Marine
Station

Keppel
Pier

8 Millport Bay

Luckie's
Bight

Farland
Point

Farland
Bight

B896 MARINE PARADE

162

A B C D E F

K5
1 Bay St
2 Marine Ct

K7
1 Fairlieburne Gdns
2 Kaim Vw
3 Lilybank La
4 Montgomerie Crs

Cemetery

1 Montgomerie Av

Largs
Golf Club

Fairlie
Reservoir

G H J 115 K L M

Rockland Park

Pencil Vw

A760

A78(T)

Kelburn Bridge

Kelburn
Country Centre

Baillie
Rd

Kelburn Avenue

Keppenburn Avenue

Pier Road

140

Bay Street

Castle Pk Gdns

Fife Rd

PO

Jetty Rd

Kelburn Ter

Fife Pl

Castle Pk Gdns

Castle Walk

Castle Park Drive

Bourtrees

Fairlie

Highfield
Terrace

School Brae

The
Cswy

ROAD

MAIN

Glen Rd

Burnfoot Rd

Fairlie Burn

Fairlie
Glen

KA29

Station
Rd

Fairlie
Station

Montgomerie Drive

A78(T)

Southannan
Rd

Miller Av

Semple Crs

G H J 163 K L M

Southannan

I

2

3

4

5

6

7

8

A B C D E F

I

2

Firpark
Plantation

Fechan

Blairpark

3

Kelburn
Country Centre

Fairfieward

4

5

6

Fairlie
Moor

Fairlie

7

8

A B C D E F

1 grid square represents 500 metres

Cock

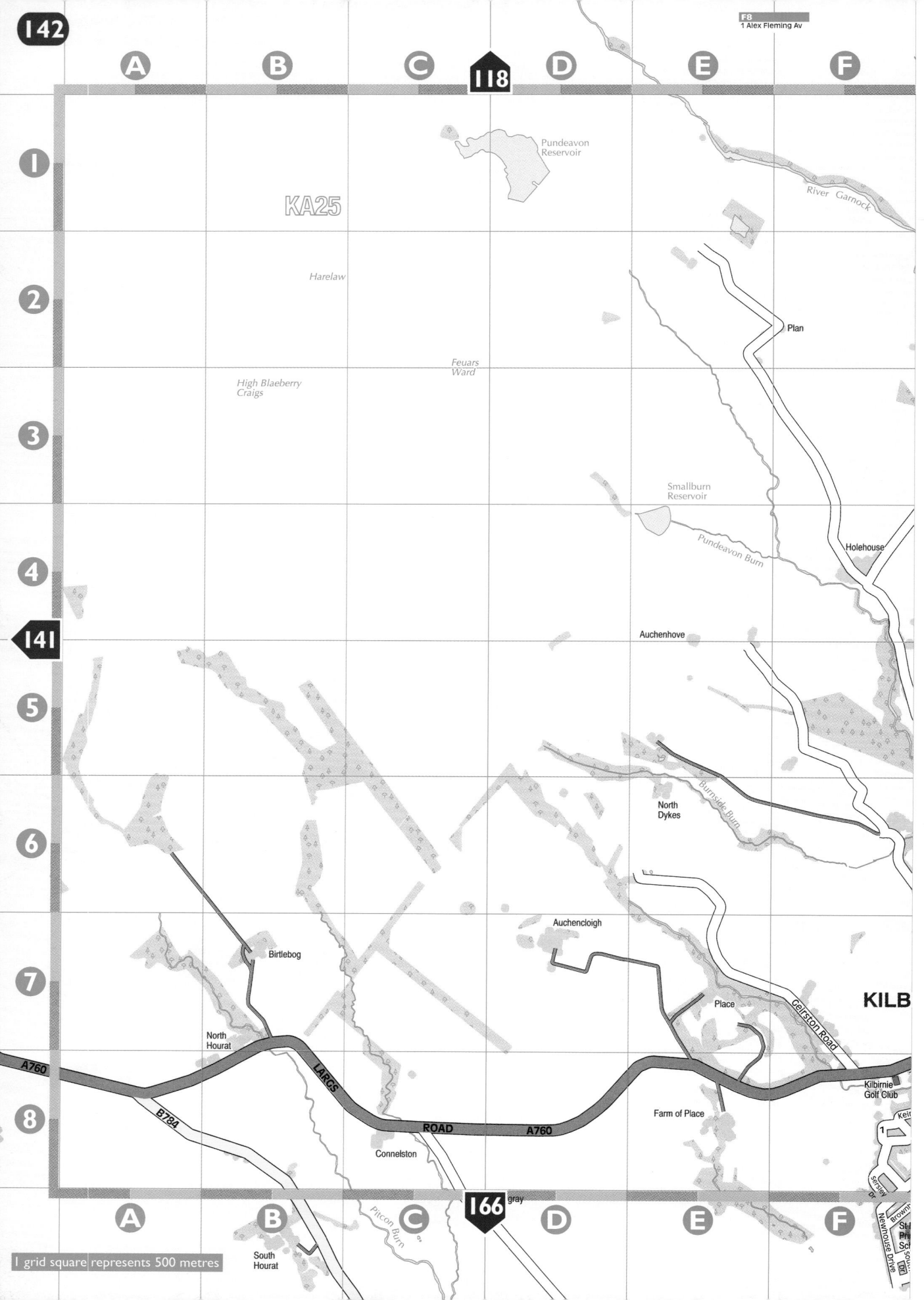

A B C 118 D E F

F8
1 Alex Fleming Av

1

Pundeavon
Reservoir

KA25

River Garnock

2

Harelaw

Plan

Feuars
Ward

High Blaeberry
Craigs

3

Smallburn
Reservoir

Holehouse

Pundeavon Burn

4

Auchenhove

141

5

Burnside Burn

North
Dykes

6

Auchencloigh

Birtlebog

7

Place

Gelrston Road

KILB

North
Hourat

A760

LARGS

Kilbirnie
Golf Club

8

B784

ROAD   A760

Farm of Place

Kei

1

Connelston

A B 166 gray C D E F

South
Hourat

Pitcon Burn

Brown
St
Ph
Sc
Newhouse Drive

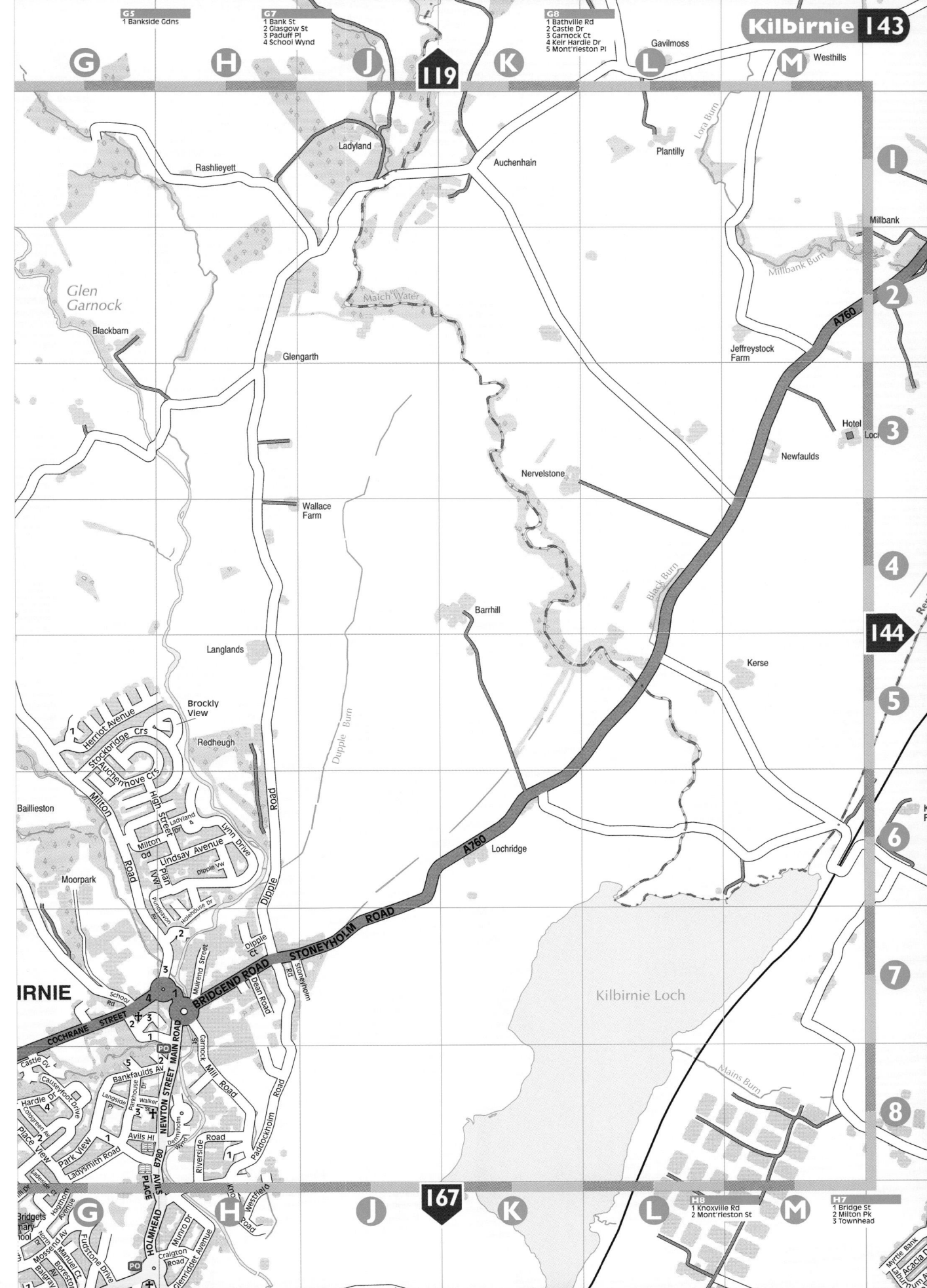

G5
1 Bankside Gdns

G7
1 Bank St
2 Glasgow St
3 Paduff Pl
4 School Wynd

G8
1 Bathville Rd
2 Castle Dr
3 Garnock Ct
4 Keir Hardie Dr
5 Mont'rieston Pl

G H J 119 K L M

Gavilmoss

Westhills

I

Millbank

Rashlieyett

Ladyland

Auchenhain

Plantilly

Millbank Burn

A760

2

Glen Garnock

Blackbarn

Glengarth

Maich Water

Jeffreystock Farm

Hotel
Loch

3

Newfaulds

Wallace Farm

Nervelstone

Black Burn

4

144

Barrhill

Kerse

5

Langlands

Brockly View

Redheugh

Herriot Avenue

Stockbridge Crs

Auchenhove Crs

Baillieston

Milton Road

High Street

Ladyland Pl

Lynn Drive

Dipple Vw

Dipple Burn

Lochridge

A760

6

Moorpark

Milton Rd

Lindsay Avenue

Penderson

Hollenhouse Dr

Dipple Road

Dipple Ct

Stoneyholm Rd

Kilbirnie Loch

7

IRNIE

COCHRANE STREET

School Rd

2 1
3 4 1
2 3
1

BRIDGEND ROAD STONEYHOLM ROAD

Mulrend Street

Dipple Ct

Dean Road

Stoneyholm

Mains Burn

Castle Cv

Causeyfoot Drive

Hardie Dr

PO

Bankfaulds Av

NEWTON STREET MAIN ROAD

Garnock Mill Road

5

Paddockholm Road

8

Langside Pl

Parkhouse Pl

Walker

Avils Hi

B780

Park View

Ladysmith Road

Riverside Road

Knoxville

Westfield

1

Bridgets
nary
ool

G HOLMHEAD

Fudstone Drive

Munro Dr

Knoxville

H Westfield Road J 167 K L M

H8
1 Knoxville Rd
2 Mont'rieston St

H7
1 Bridge St
2 Milton Pk
3 Townhead

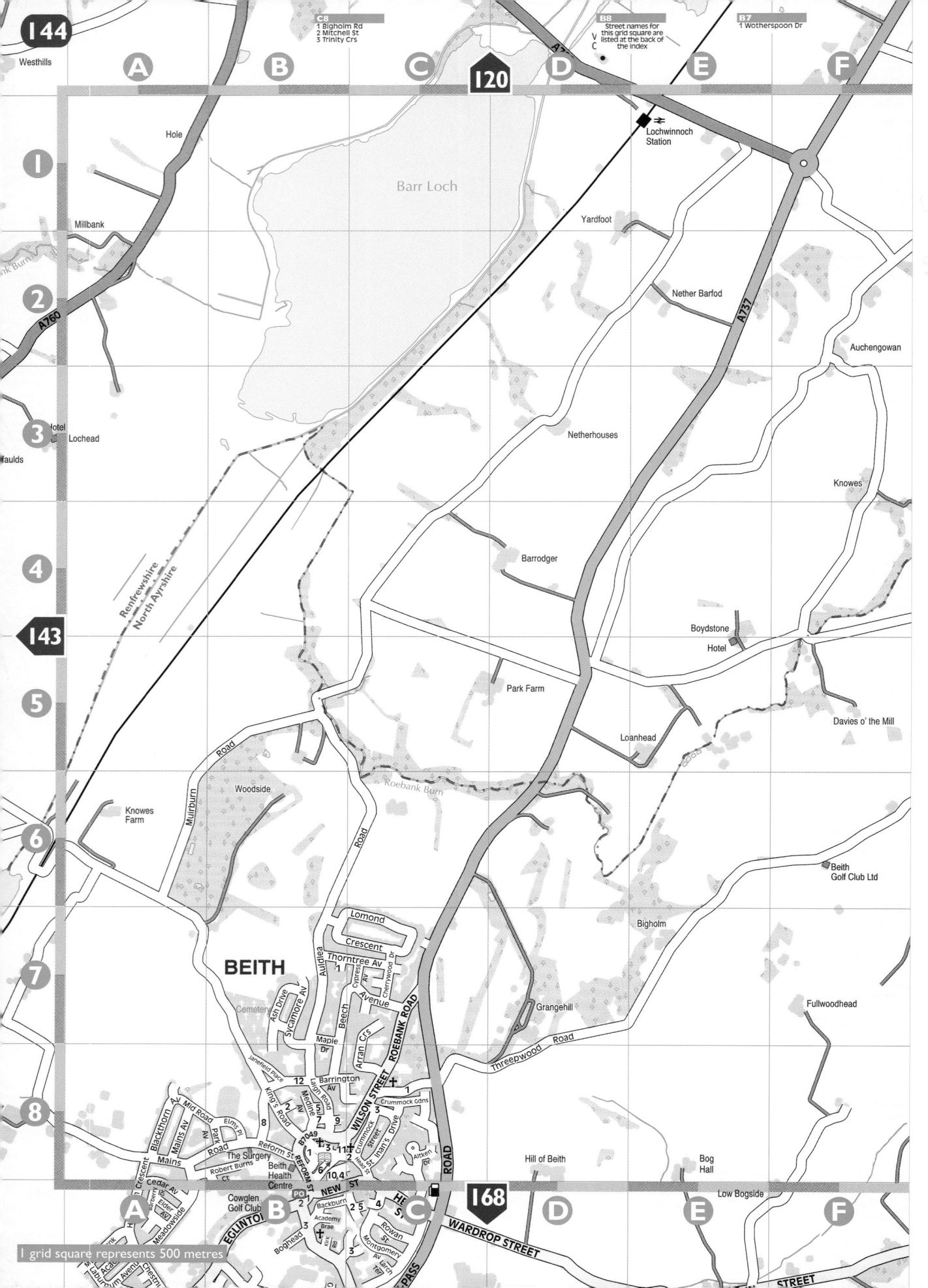

Westhills

C8
1 Bigholm Rd
2 Mitchell St
3 Trinity Crs

B8
Street names for
this grid square are
listed at the back of
the index

B7
1 Wotherspoon Dr

120

Lochwinnoch
Station

Hole

Barr Loch

Yardfoot

Millbank

Nether Barfod

A737

Auchengowan

A760

Netherhouses

Hotel
Lochead

Knowes

faulds

Barrodger

143

Boydstone
Hotel

Park Farm

Davies o' the Mill

Loanhead

Renfrewshire
North Ayrshire

Road

Woodside

Roebank Burn

Muirburn

Knowes
Farm

Beith
Golf Club Ltd

Road

Bigholm

Lomond

Crescent

BEITH

Thorntree Av

Cherrywood Dr

Grangehill

Auldlea

Avenue

ROEBANK ROAD

Cemetery

Sycamore Av

Ash Drive

Beech

Arran Crs

Cypress Av

Fullwoodhead

Maple
Dr

Road

Threepwood   Road

Janefield Place

12

Barrington
Av

WILSON STREET

King's Road

Laigh Road

Crummock Gdns

1

Mid Road

2

Medine
Av

9

3

Mains Av

7

Crummock
Street

Blackthorn

Park
Road

Elms Ct

8

B7049

11

Aitken
Dr

Hill of Beith

Bog
Hall

Reform St

The Surgery

3

1

Crescent

Mains

Cedar Av

Elder St

Robert Burns
Ct

Beith
Health
Centre

6

10,4

Head St

ROAD

168

Low Bogside

EGLINTO

Cowglen
Golf Club

PO

NEW ST

Backburn

2

Meadowside

Chestn

Elm Av

Academy
Brae

2

5

4

Rowan
St

Montgomery

WARDROP STREET

STREET

BYPASS

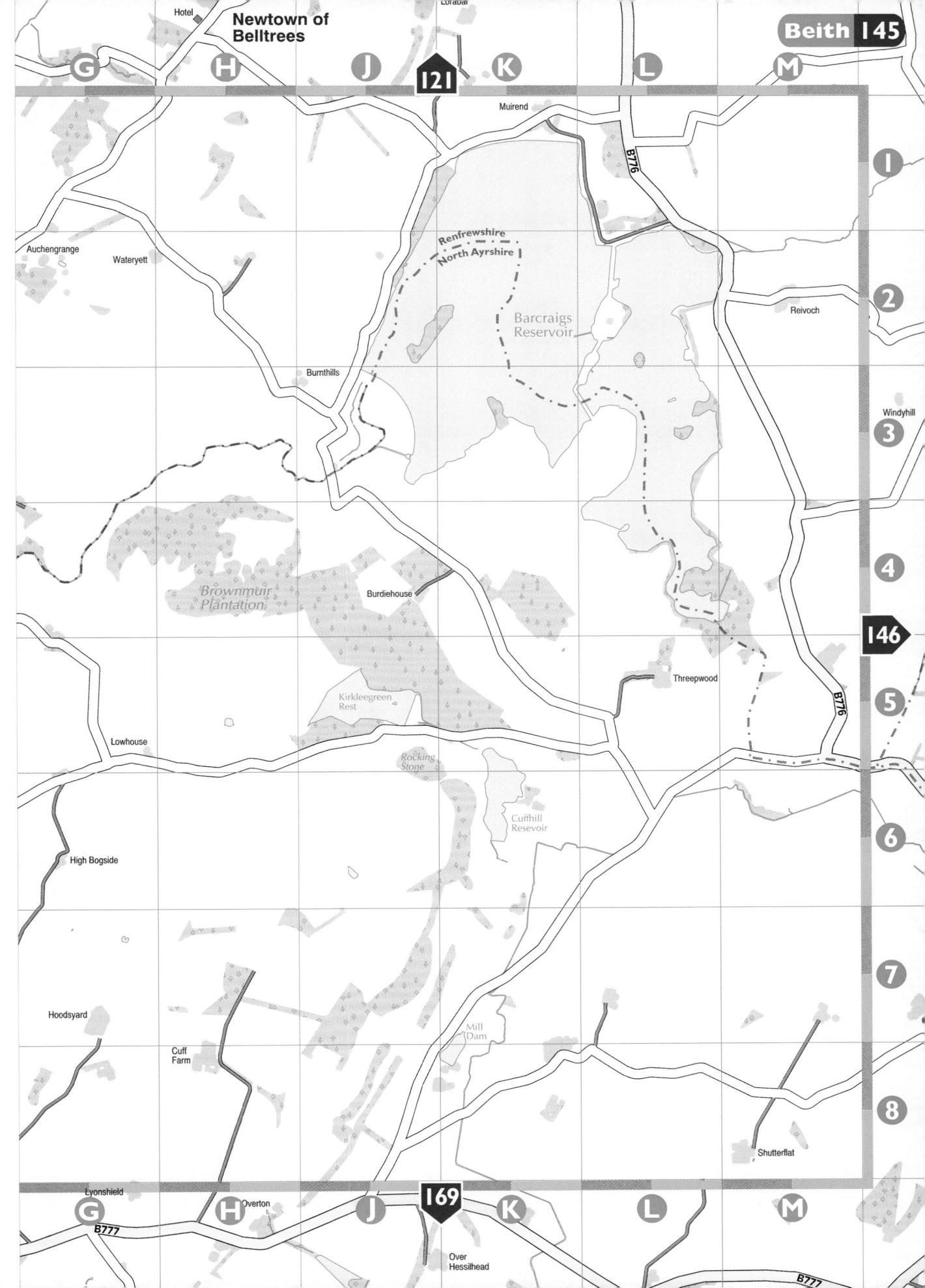

Newtown of
Belltrees

Hotel

Lorabat

Muirend

B776

G H J **121** K L M

1

Auchengrange Wateryett

Renfrewshire
North Ayrshire

Reivoch

2

Barcraigs
Reservoir

Burnthills

Windyhill

3

4

Brownmuir
Plantation

Burdiehouse

146

Threepwood

B776

5

Kirkleegreen
Rest

Lowhouse

Rocking
Stone

Cuffhill
Resevoir

6

High Bogside

Hoodsyard

Mill
Dam

7

Cuff
Farm

Shutterflat

8

Over
Hessilhead

B777

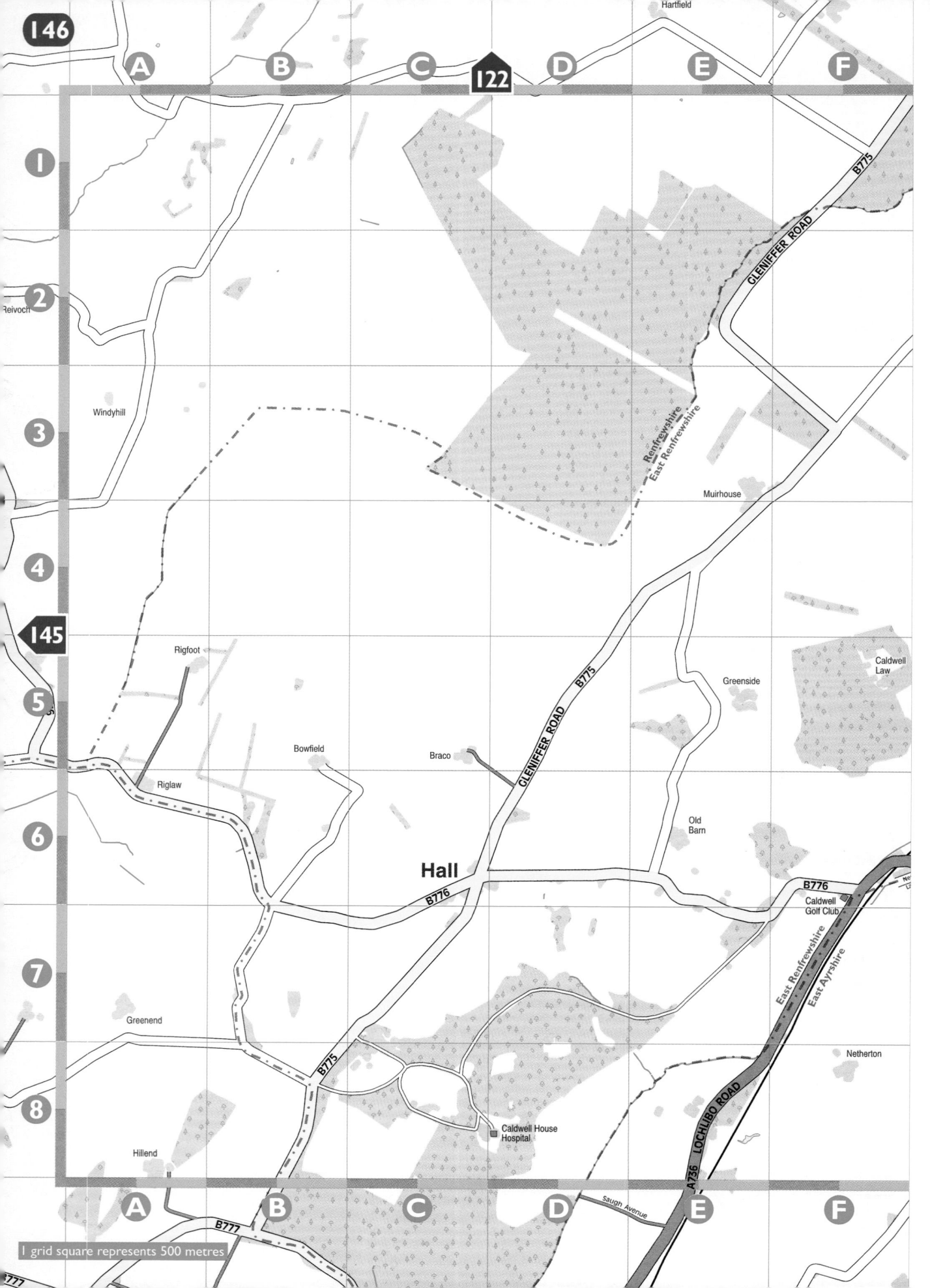

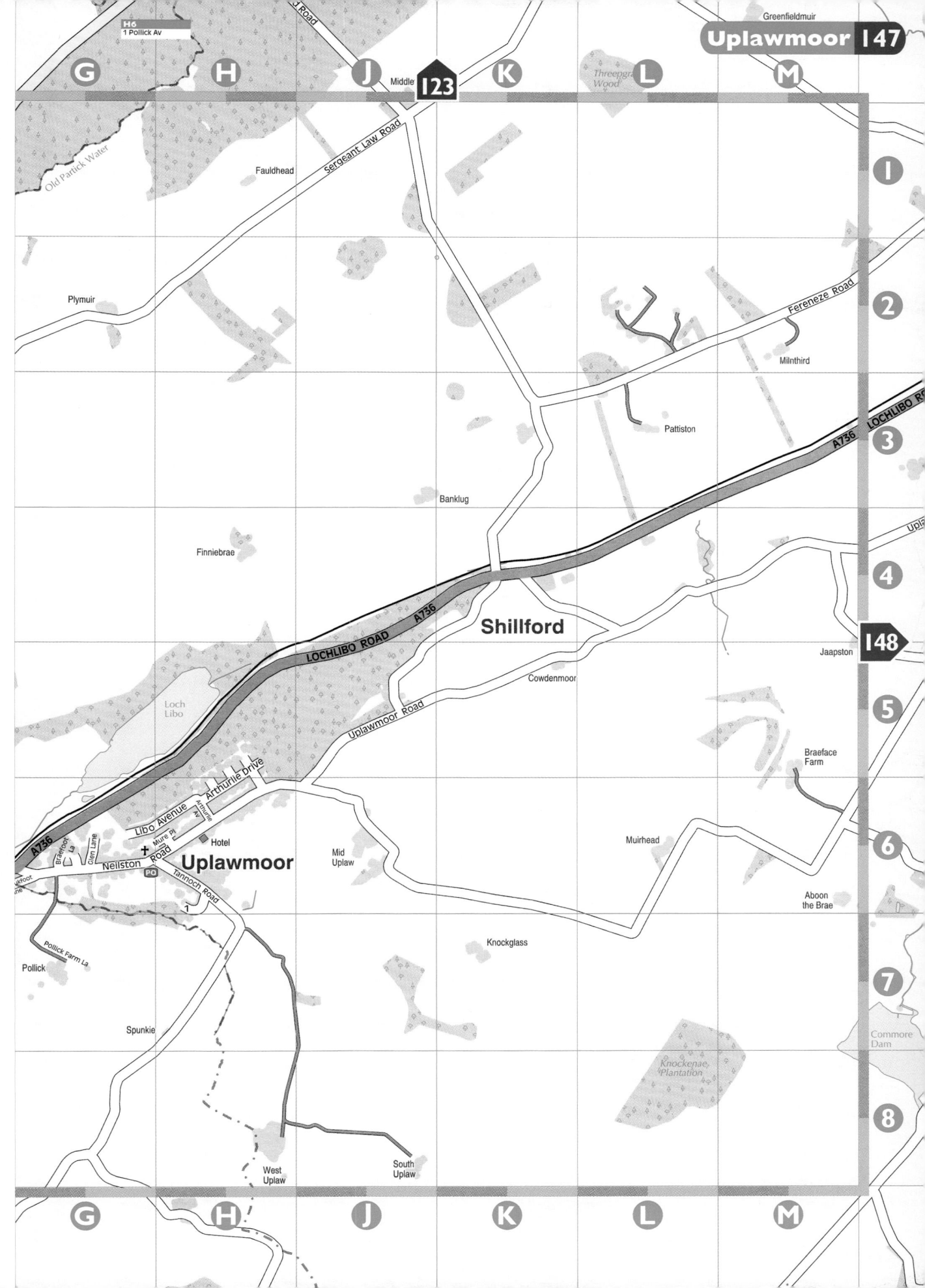

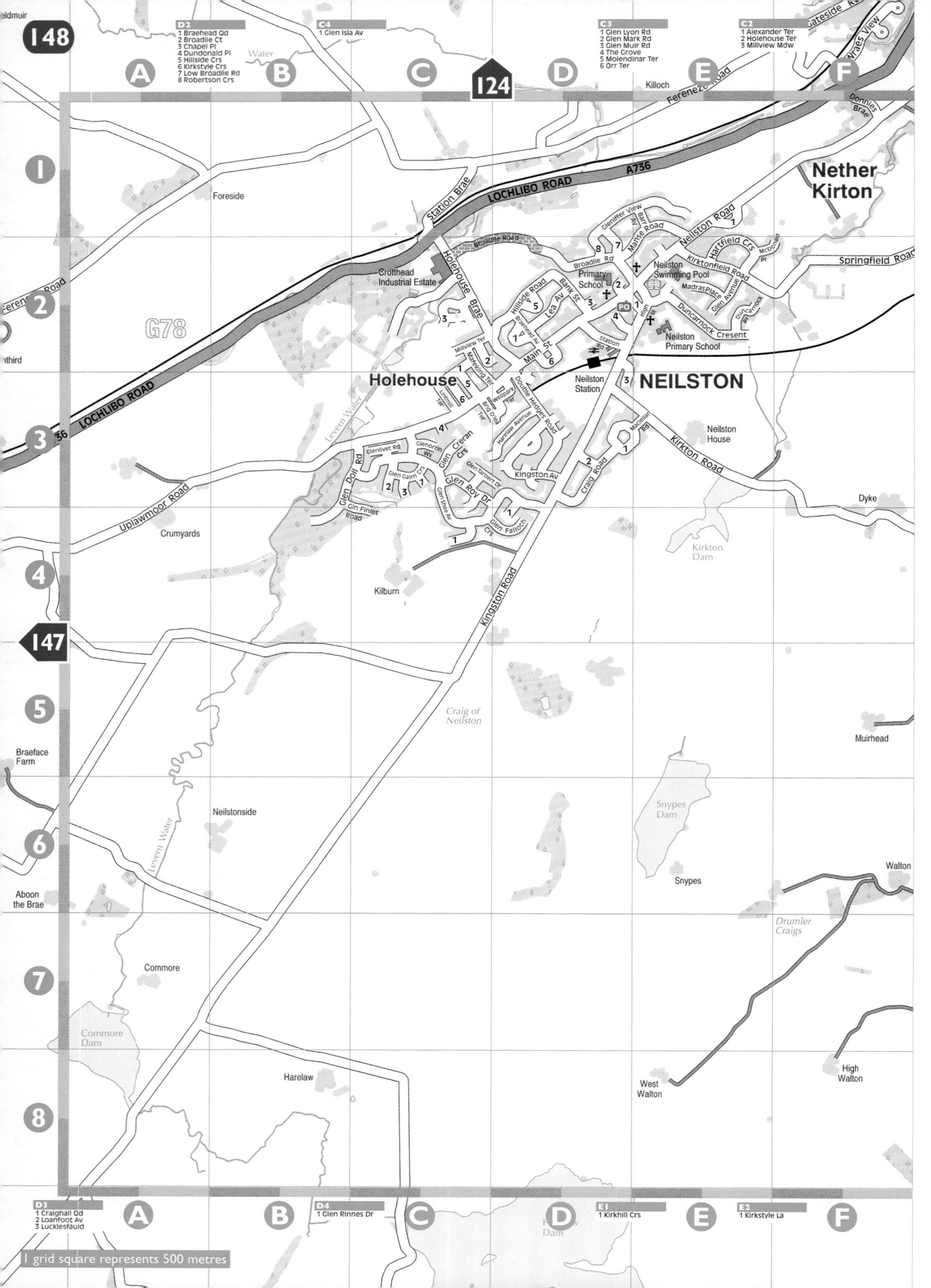

D2
1 Braehead Qd
2 Broadlie Ct
3 Chapel Pl
4 Dundonald Pl
5 Hillside Crs
6 Kirkstyle Crs
7 Low Broadlie Rd
8 Robertson Crs

C4
1 Glen Isla Av

C3
1 Glen Lyon Rd
2 Glen Mark Rd
3 Glen Muir Rd
4 The Grove
5 Molendinar Ter
6 Orr Ter

C2
1 Alexander Ter
2 Holehouse Ter
3 Millview Mdw

A   B   C   124   D   E   F

I

Foreside

Nether
Kirton

Killoch

Ferenaze Road

Springfield Road

2

G78

LOCHLIBO ROAD

A736

Station Brae

Holehouse Brae

Broadlie Road

Crofthead
Industrial Estate

Broadlie Rd

Neilston
Primary
School

Neilston
Swimming Pool

Madras Place

Glenifer View

Manse Road

Neilston Road

Hartfield Crs

Kirktonfield Road

Glen Avenue

Hillside Road

Bank St

Lea Av

Duncarnock Cresent

Neilston
Primary School

3

LOCHLIBO ROAD

Levern Water

Main

PO

Station

Holehouse

Neilston
Station

NEILSTON

Neilston
House

Kirkton Road

Dyke

Uplawmoor Road

Glen Doll Rd

Glenlivet Rd

Glenortin Wy

Glen Gairn Crs

Glen Creran
Crs

Glen Roy Dr

Glen Tarbert Dr

Kingston Av

Craig Road

Macfarlan
Rd

Kirkton
Dam

Crumyards

Gln Finlet
Road

Glen Shiel Av

Glen Falloch
Crs

Kingston Road

4

Kilburn

147

5

Craig of
Neilston

Muirhead

Braeface
Farm

Snypes
Dam

6

Levern Water

Neilstonside

Walton

Aboon
the Brae

Snypes

Drumler
Craigs

7

Commore

Commore
Dam

West
Walton

High
Walton

8

Harelaw

D3
1 Craighall Qd
2 Loanfoot Av
3 Lucklesfauld

D4
1 Glen Rinnes Dr

E1
1 Kirkhill Crs

E2
1 Kirkstyle La

A   B   C   D   E   F

1 grid square represents 500 metres

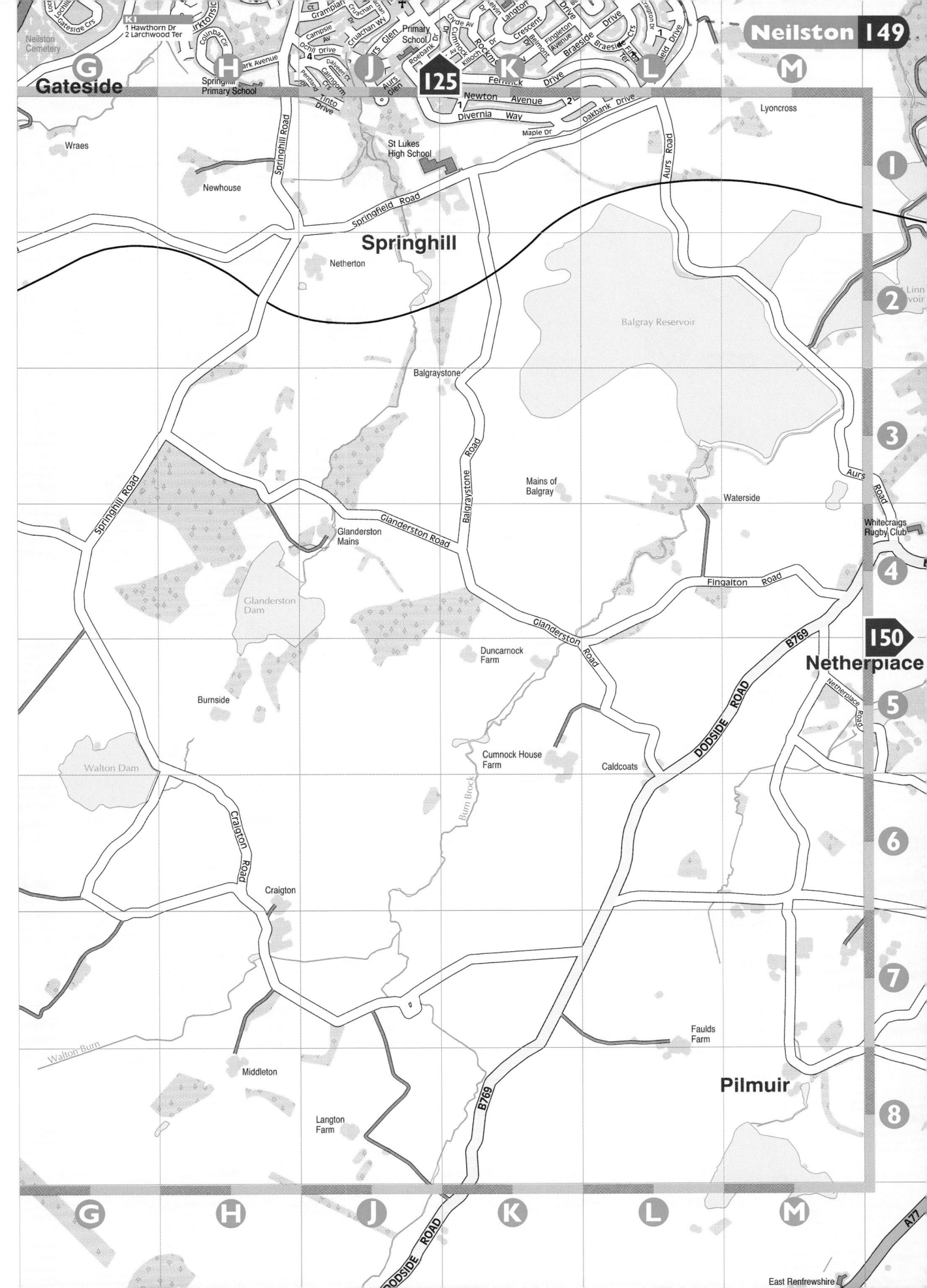

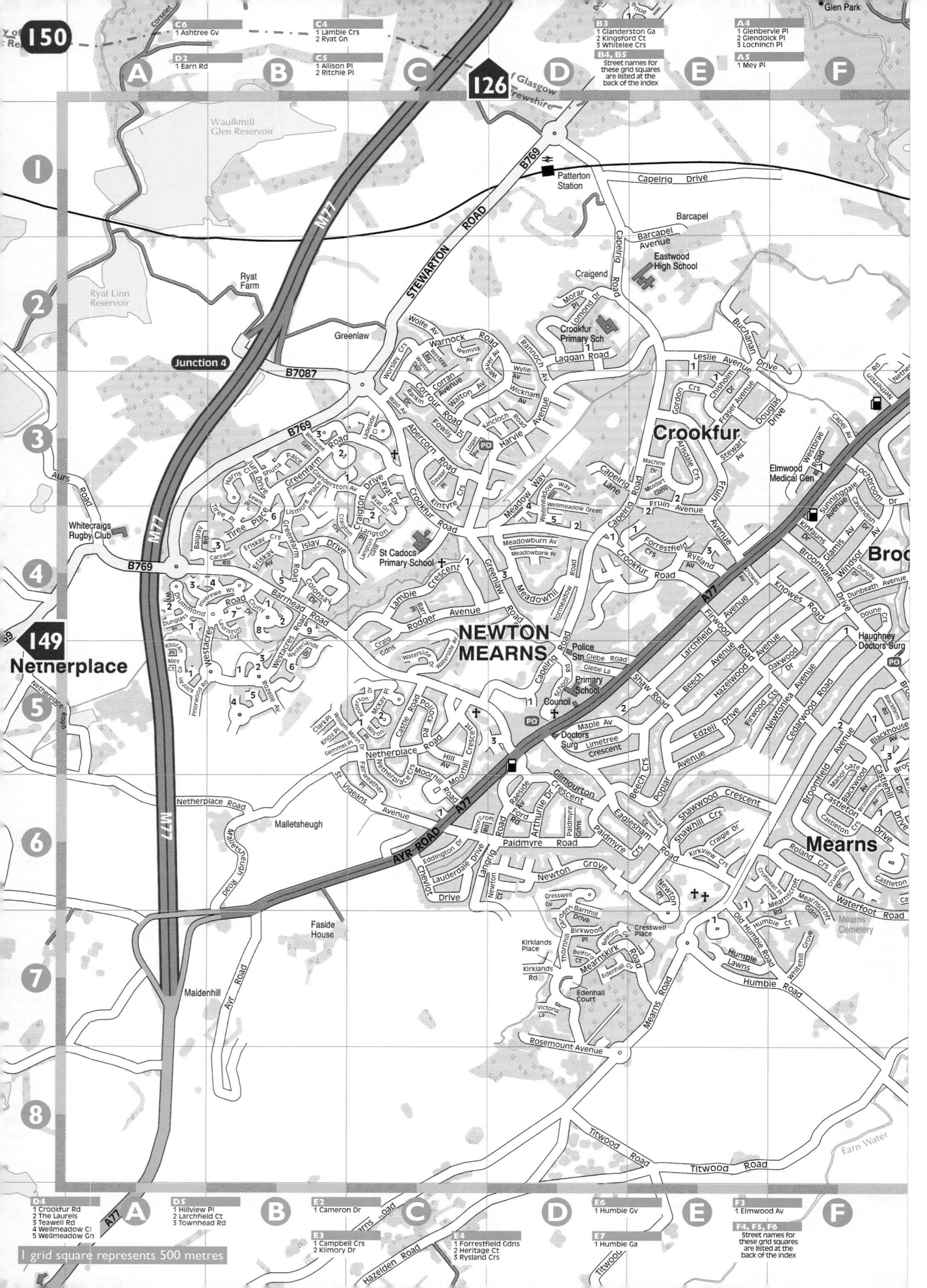

Netnerplace

Waulkmill Glen Reservoir

Ryat Linn Reservoir

Junction 4

Whitecraigs Rugby Club

Patterton Station

Capelrig Drive

Barcapel

Barcapel Avenue

Eastwood High School

Craigend

Crookfur Primary Sch

Crookfur

Elmwood Medical Cen

Broo

Greenlaw

St Cadocs Primary School

NEWTON MEARNS

Police Stn

Primary School

Council

Doctors Surg

Haughney Doctors Surg

Mearns

Malletsheugh

Faside House

Maidenhill

Mearns Cemetery

Earn Water

1 grid square represents 500 metres

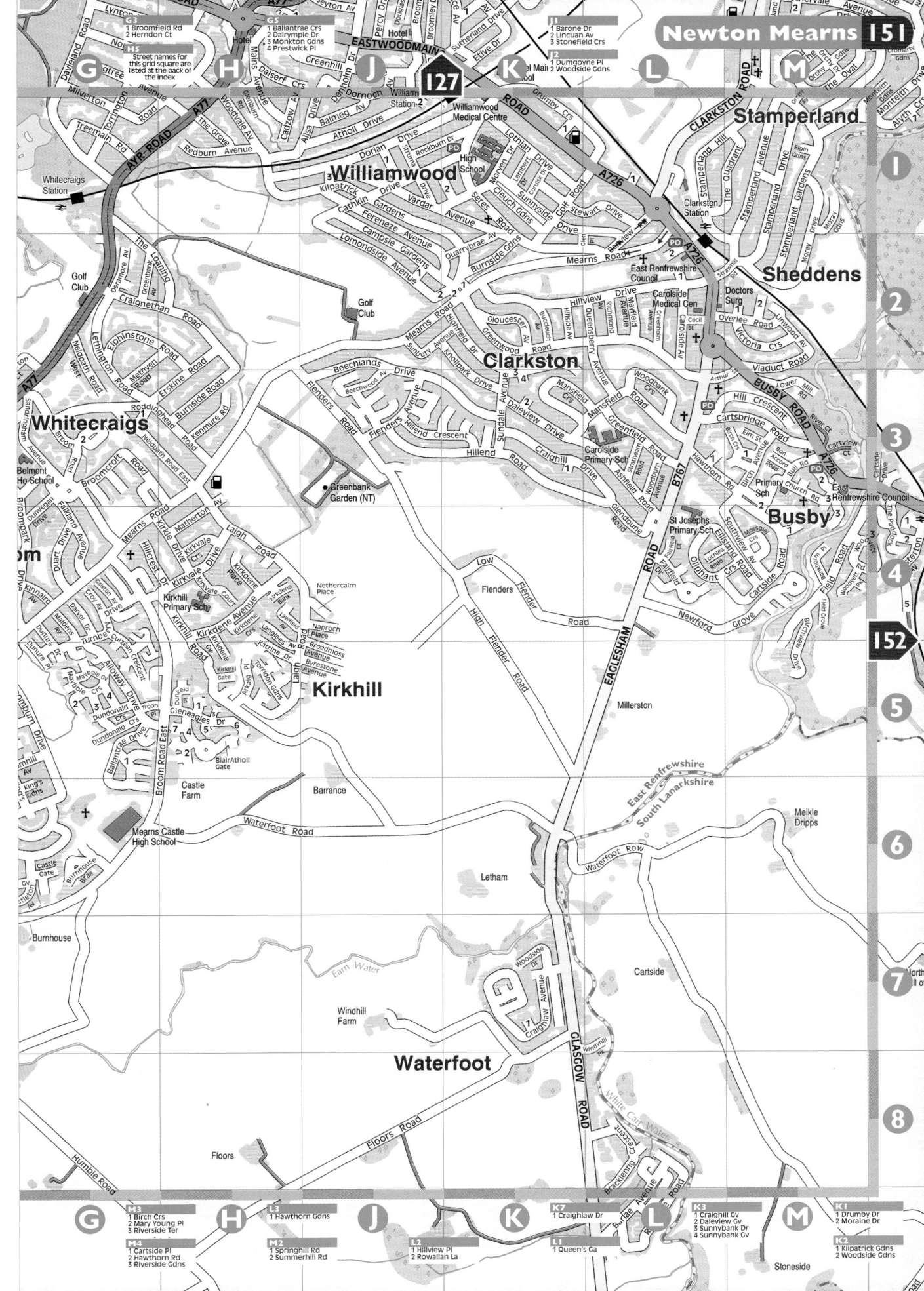

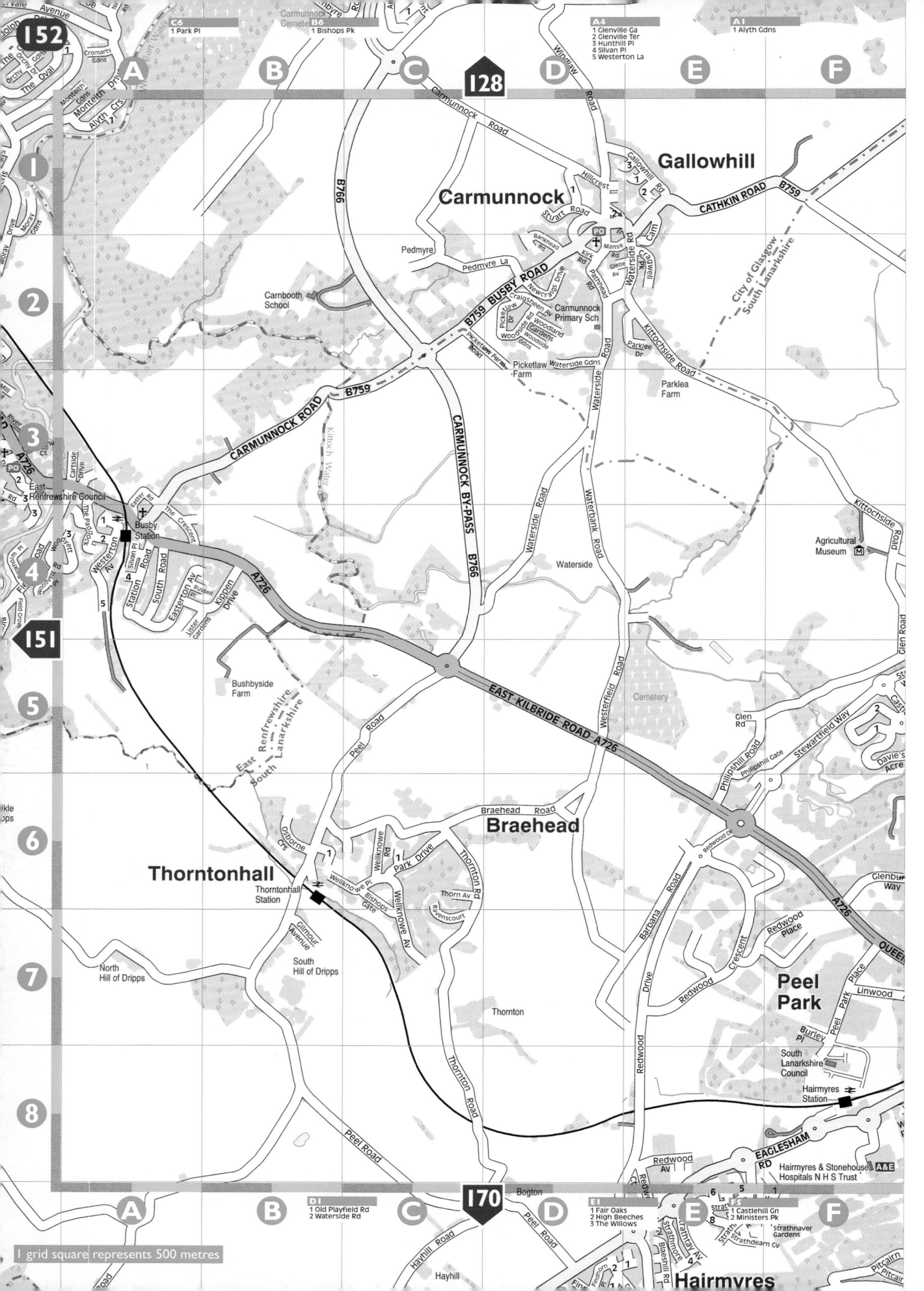

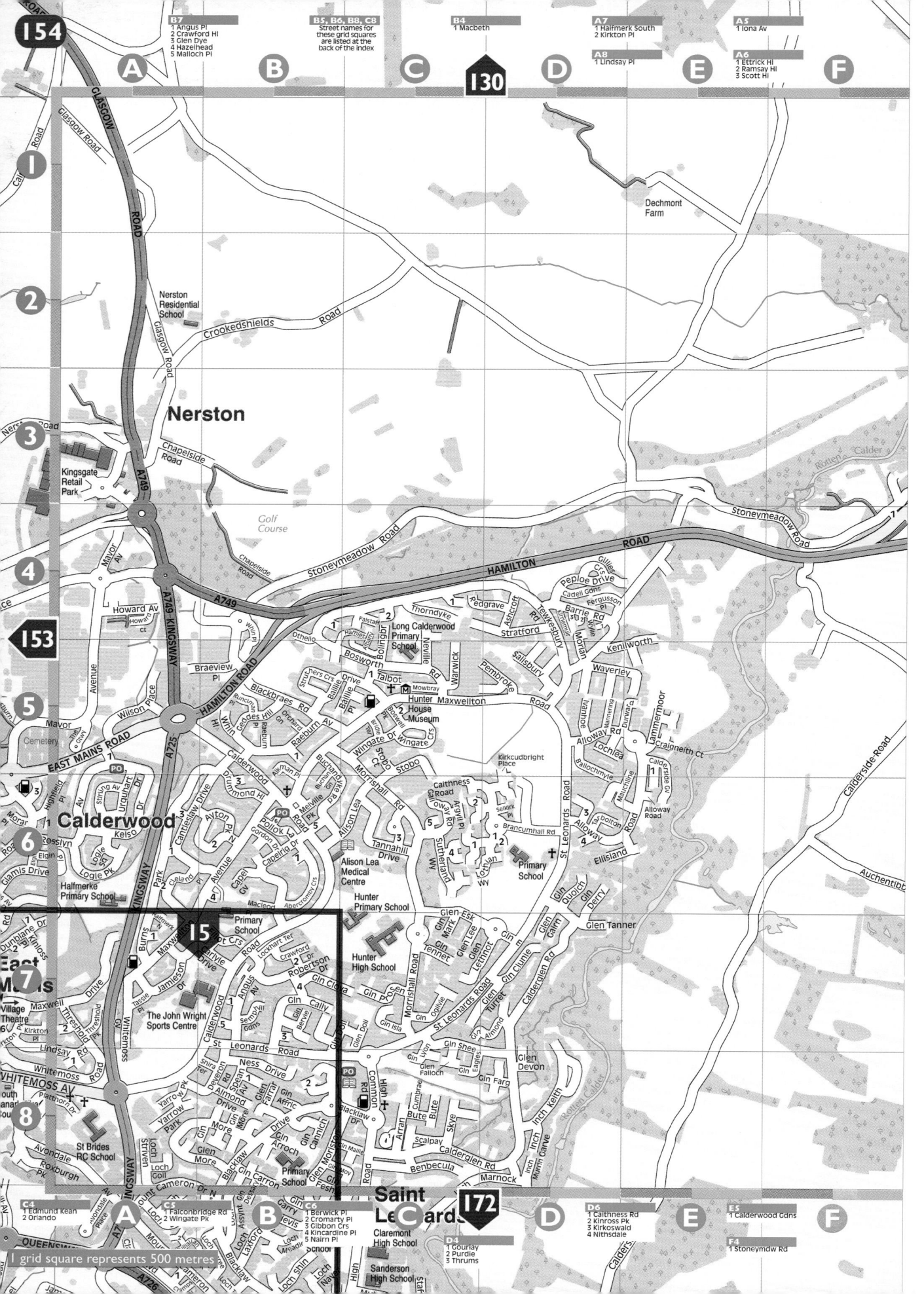

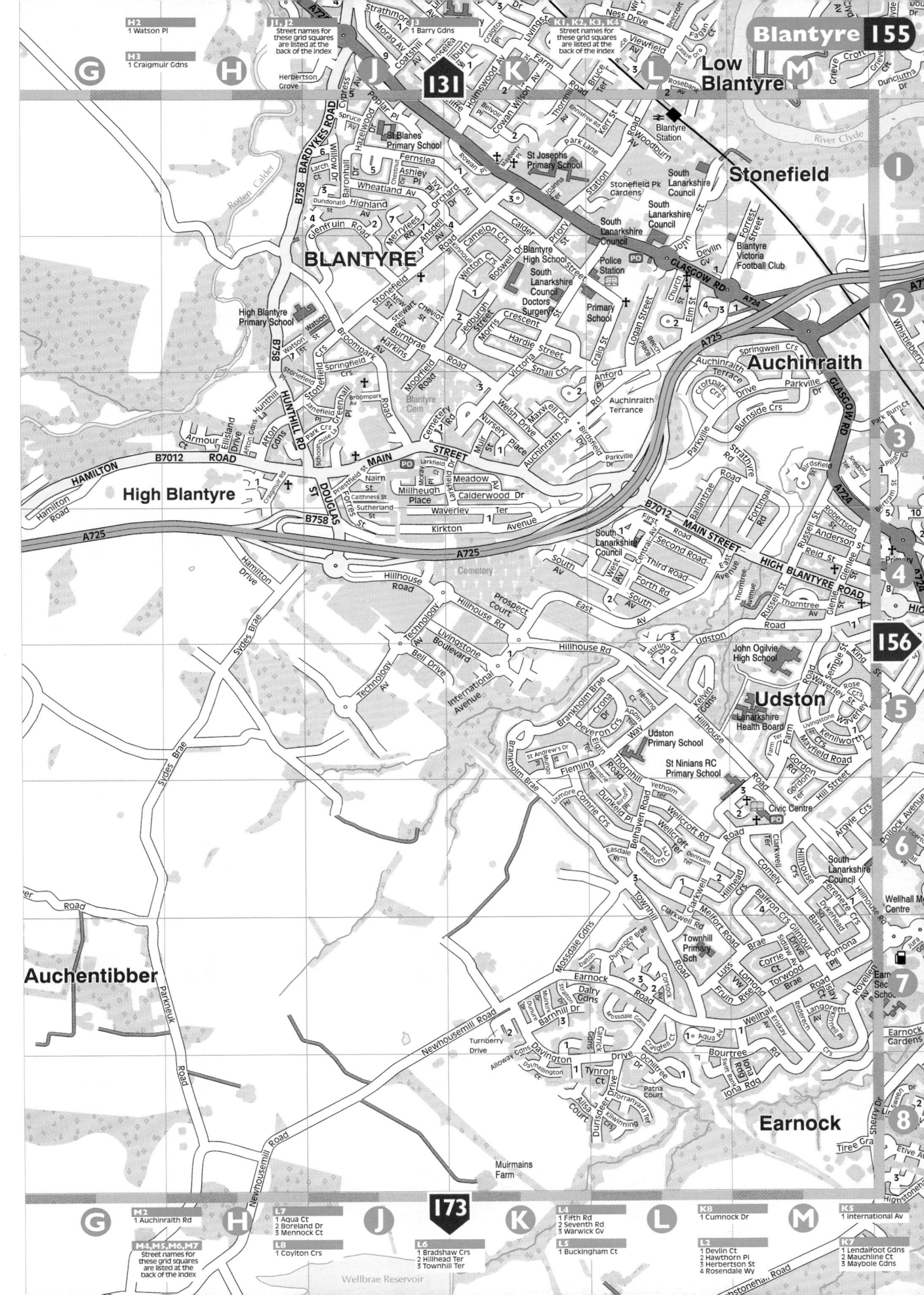

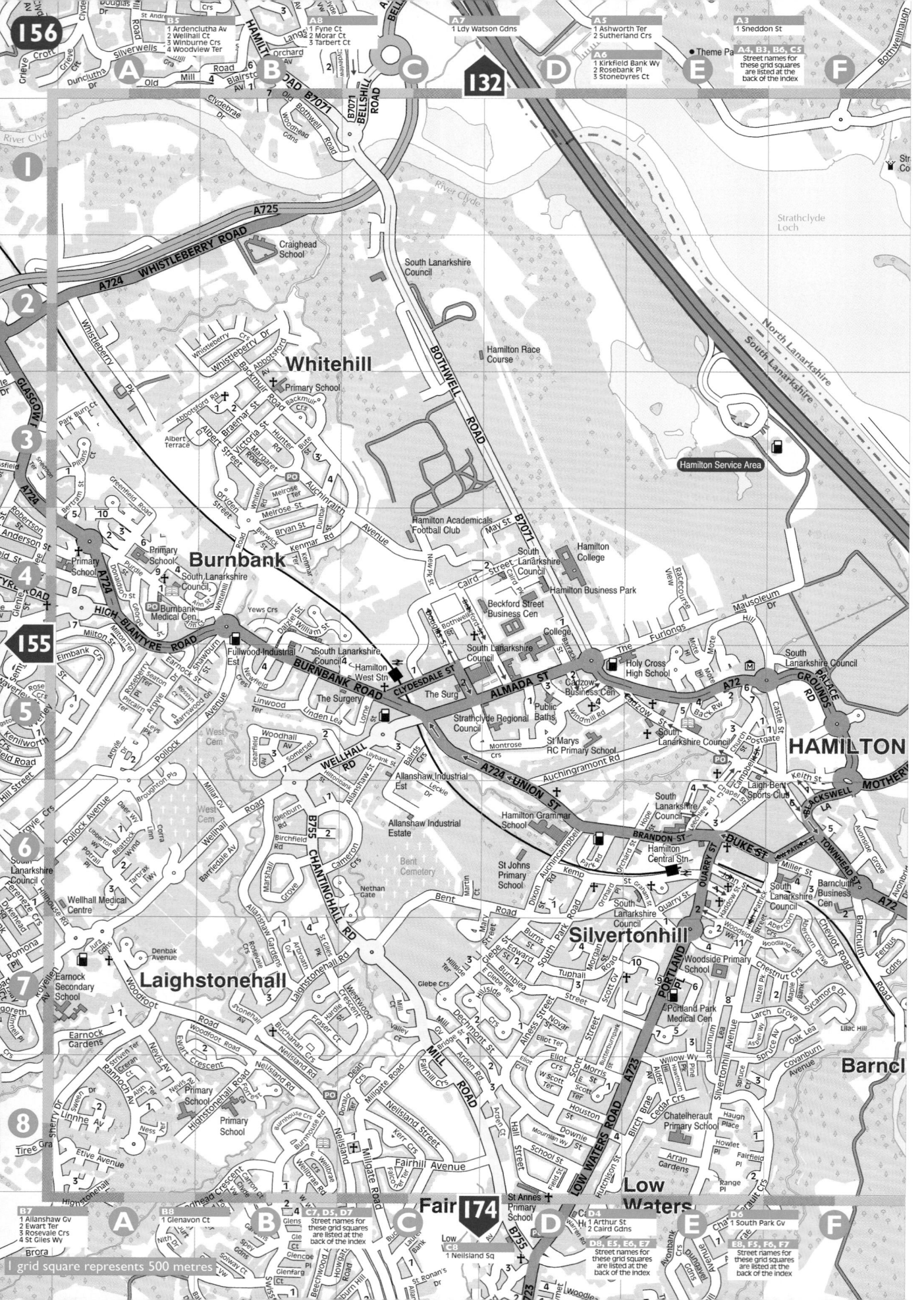

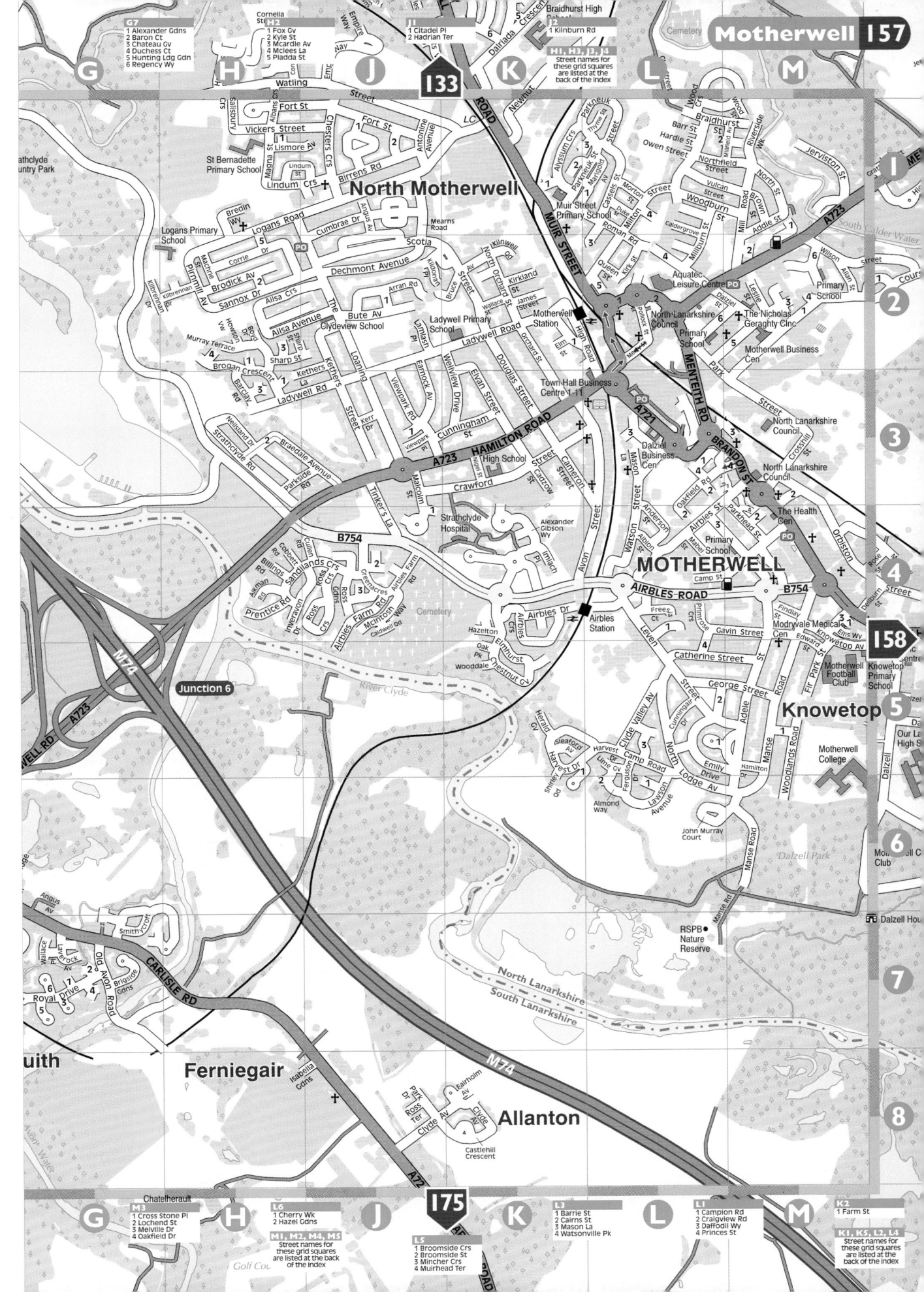

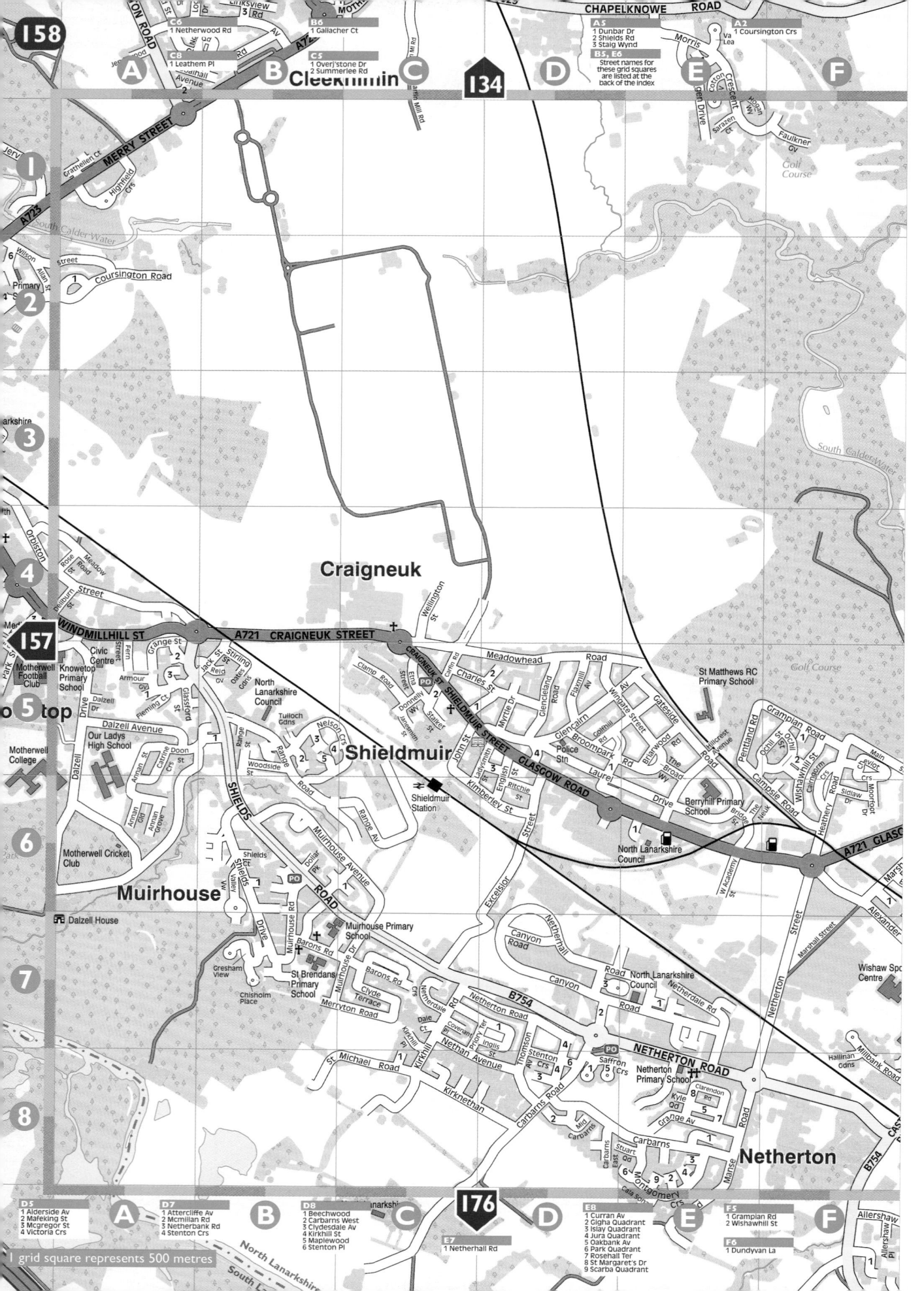

CHAPELKNOWE ROAD

A2
1 Coursington Crs

C6
1 Netherwood Rd
C8
1 Leathem Pl

B6
1 Gallacher Ct
C5
1 Overj'stone Dr
2 Summerlee Rd

Cleekiminin

134

A   B   C   D   E   F

I

6

2

arkshire

3

4

157

Craigneuk

o 5 top

Shieldmuir

6

Muirhouse

7

8

176

MERRY STREET

A723

South Calder Water

Coursington Road

Wellington St

A721 CRAIGNEUK STREET

WINDMILLHILL ST

Civic Centre

Knowetop Primary School

North Lanarkshire Council

CRAIGNEUK ST SHIELDMUIR STREET

GLASGOW ROAD

Meadowhead   Road

Charles St

St Matthews RC Primary School

Golf Course

Golf Course

South Calder Water

Our Ladys High School

Motherwell College

Dalzell Avenue

Shieldmuir Station

Police Stn

Berryhill Primary School

Grampian Road

Motherwell Cricket Club

SHIELDS   ROAD

Shields Valley

Muirhouse Avenue

North Lanarkshire Council

A721 GLASG

Dalzell House

Muirhouse Primary School

Gresham View

St Brendans Primary School

Chisholm Place

Barons Rd

Merryton Road

Clyde Terrace

Netherdale

Netherton Road

B754

Canyon Road

Canyon Road

North Lanarkshire Council

Netherdale Rd

Netherton Street

Wishaw Spo Centre

Michael Road

Nethan Avenue

Kirknethan

Carbarns Road

NETHERTON ROAD

Netherton Primary School

Netherton

Hallinan Gdns

Millbank Road

B754

CAS

Allershaw

A   B   C   D   E   F

1 grid square represents 500 metres

North Lanarkshire

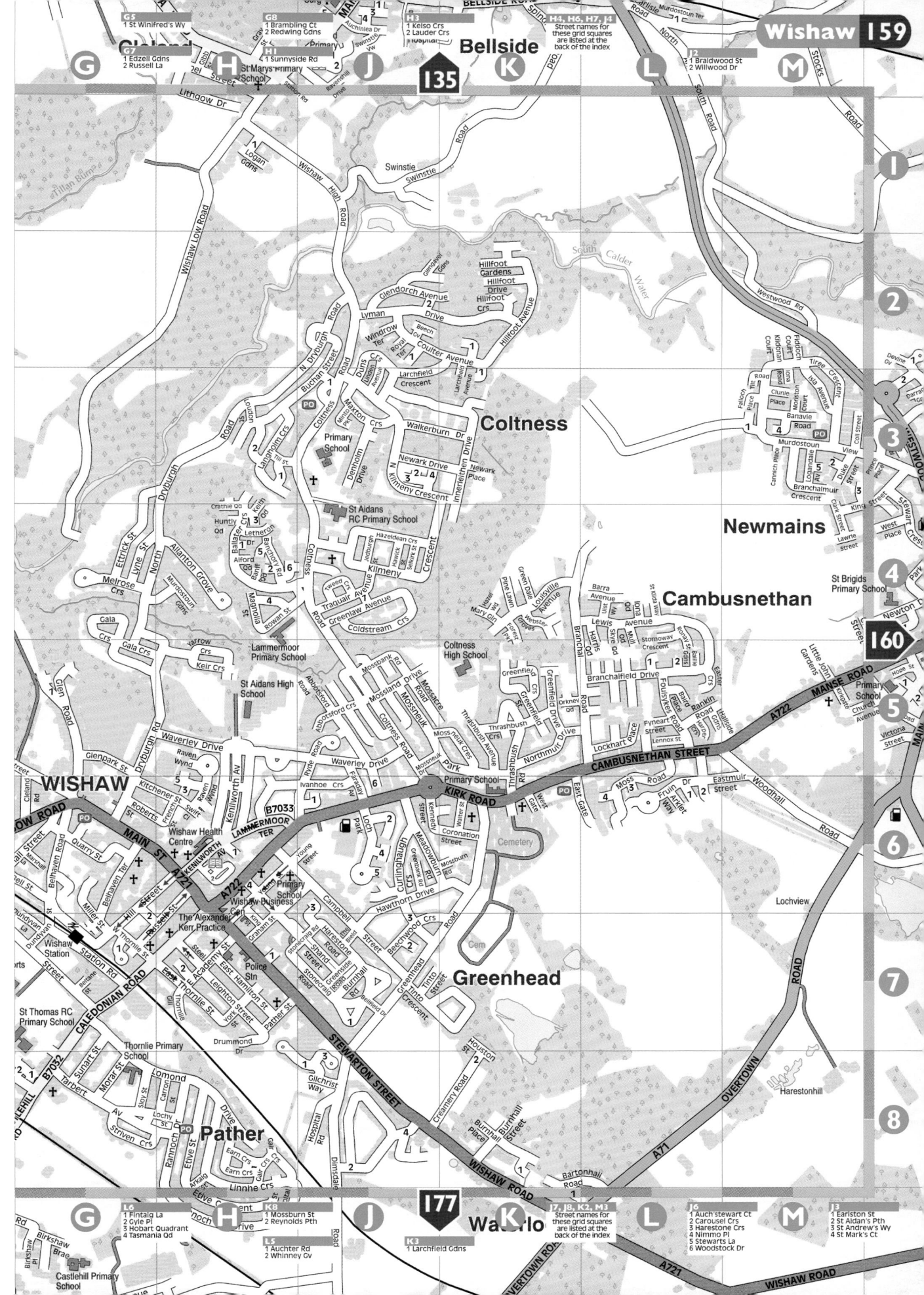

Kepplehill Farm

G H J **137** K L M

Allanton Primary School

Redmire Crescent

Darmeid Place

Hartfield Terrace

Dura Road

Allanton

bank

PO

A71

Kingshill Cr

Houldsworth Cr

Kingshill Rd

Springhead Road

Avenue

1

Hartfield

Netherhall

2

3

Dura Road

4

Kirkhall

5

Daviesdykes

Dura

Brow

6

Dura Road

Summerside

Auchterhead Farm

Auchter Water

7

North Lanarkshire

South Lanarkshire

8

Kingshill Plantation

Millport Bay

Farland
Bight

Luckie's
Bight

Farland
Point **138**

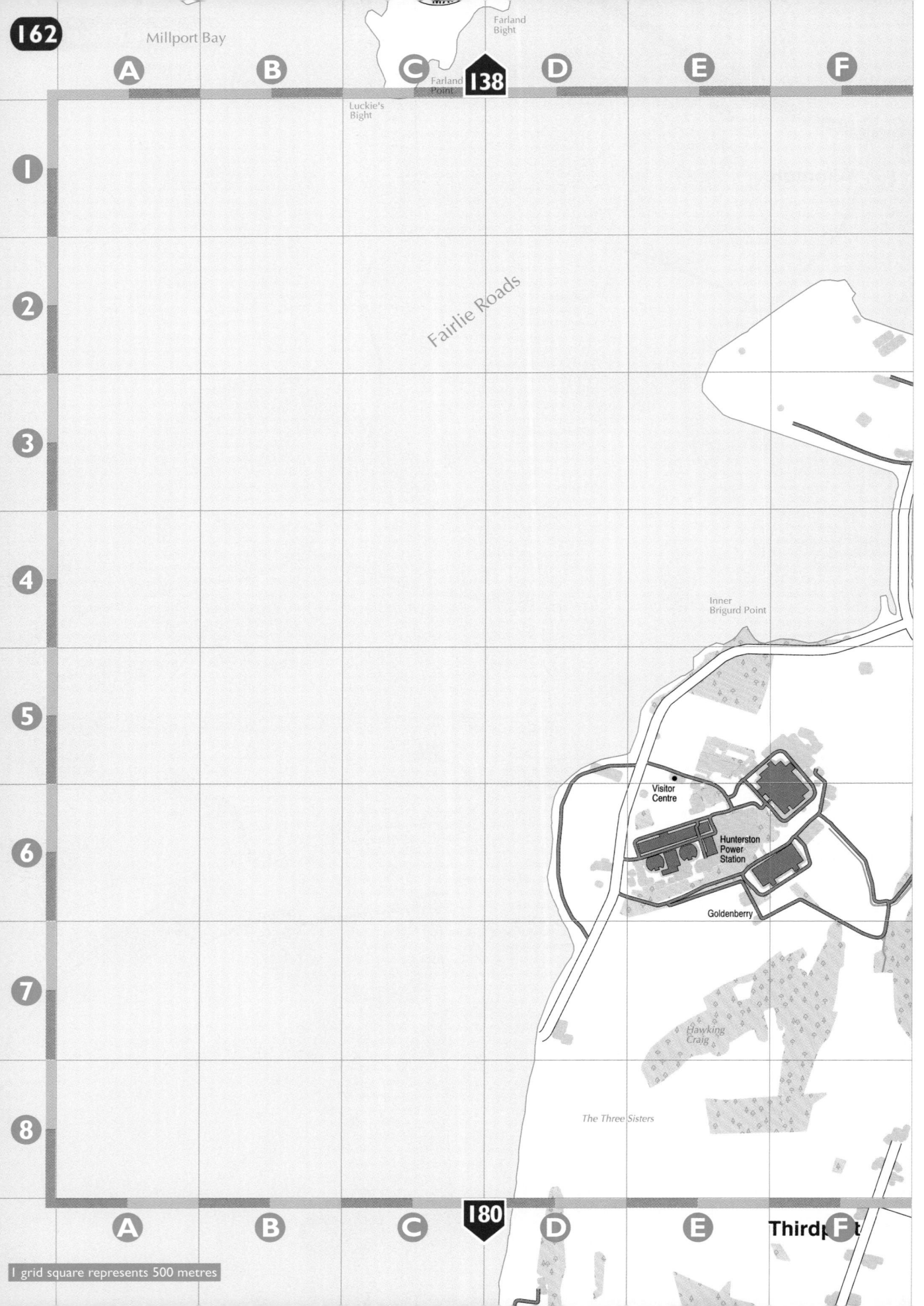

Fairlie Roads

Inner
Brigurd Point

Visitor
Centre

Hunterston
Power
Station

Goldenberry

Hawking
Craig

The Three Sisters

I grid square represents 500 metres

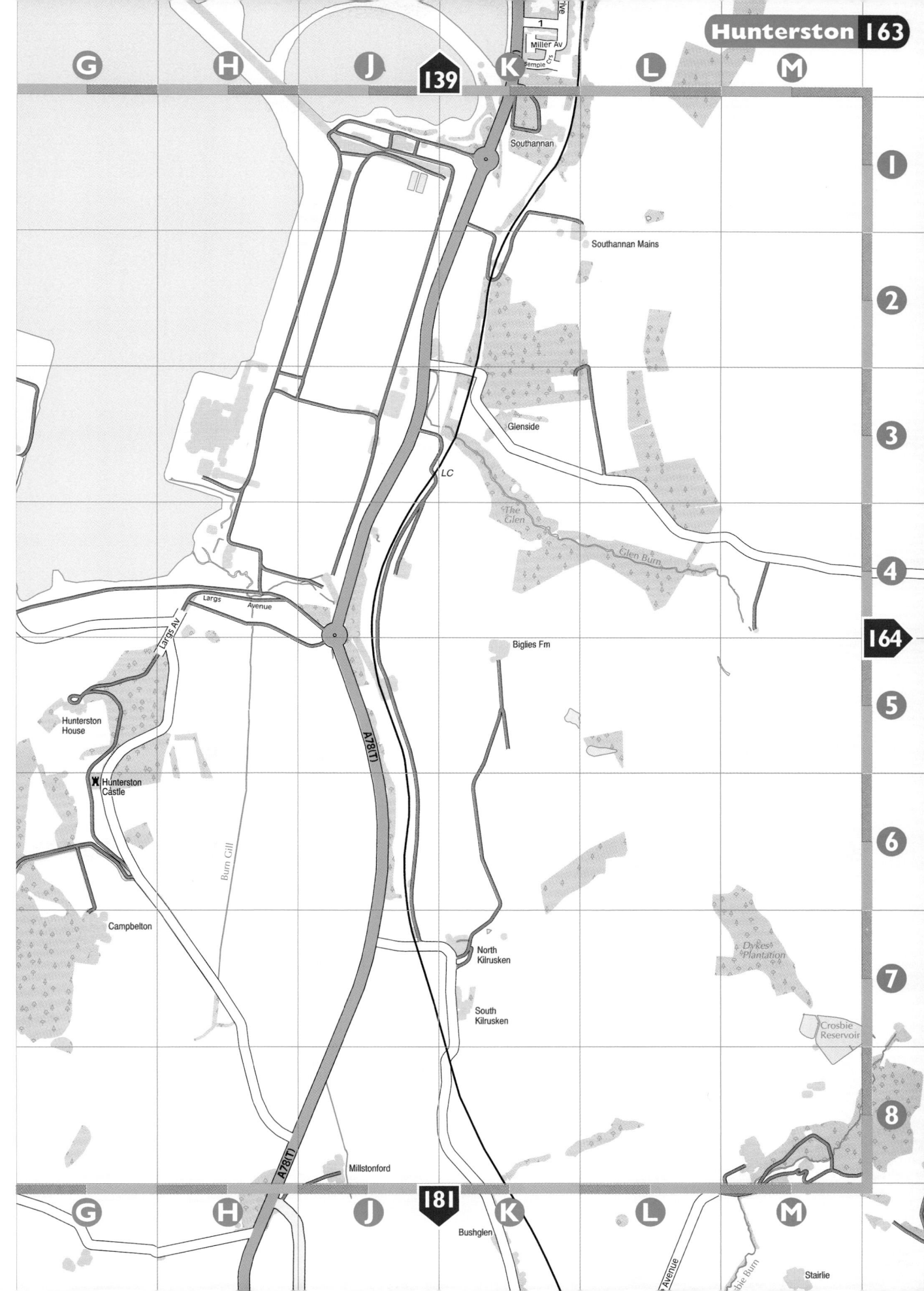

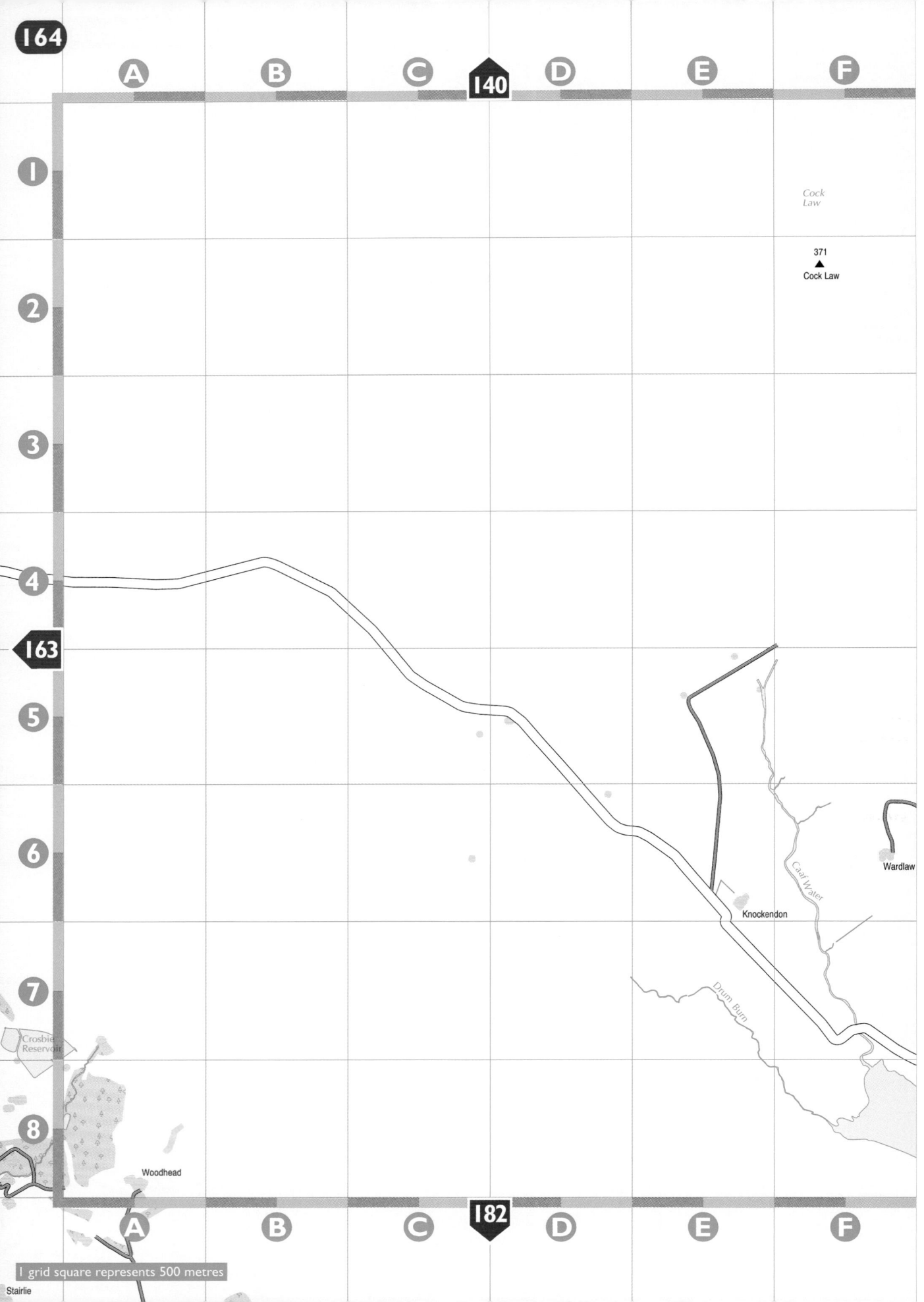

A B C D E F

Cock
Law

371
▲
Cock Law

Caaf Water

Wardlaw

Knockendon

Drum Burn

Crosbie
Reservoir

Woodhead

182

A B C D E F

1 grid square represents 500 metres

Stairlie

G   H   J   **141**   K   L   M

1

Plann

Brodoclea

2

Rye Water

3

Raven's Craig Glen

4

166

Baidlandhill

5

M

Ward Fm

KA24

Whitecraig

6

Windyedge

Cubeside

Thirdpart

7

Auldmuir Reservoir

Burntongues

Caaf Reservoir

8

Compensation Well

Birkhead

G   H   J   **183** muir   K   L   M

Broadlie House

Laigh Baidland

Caaf W

Auldmuir Burn

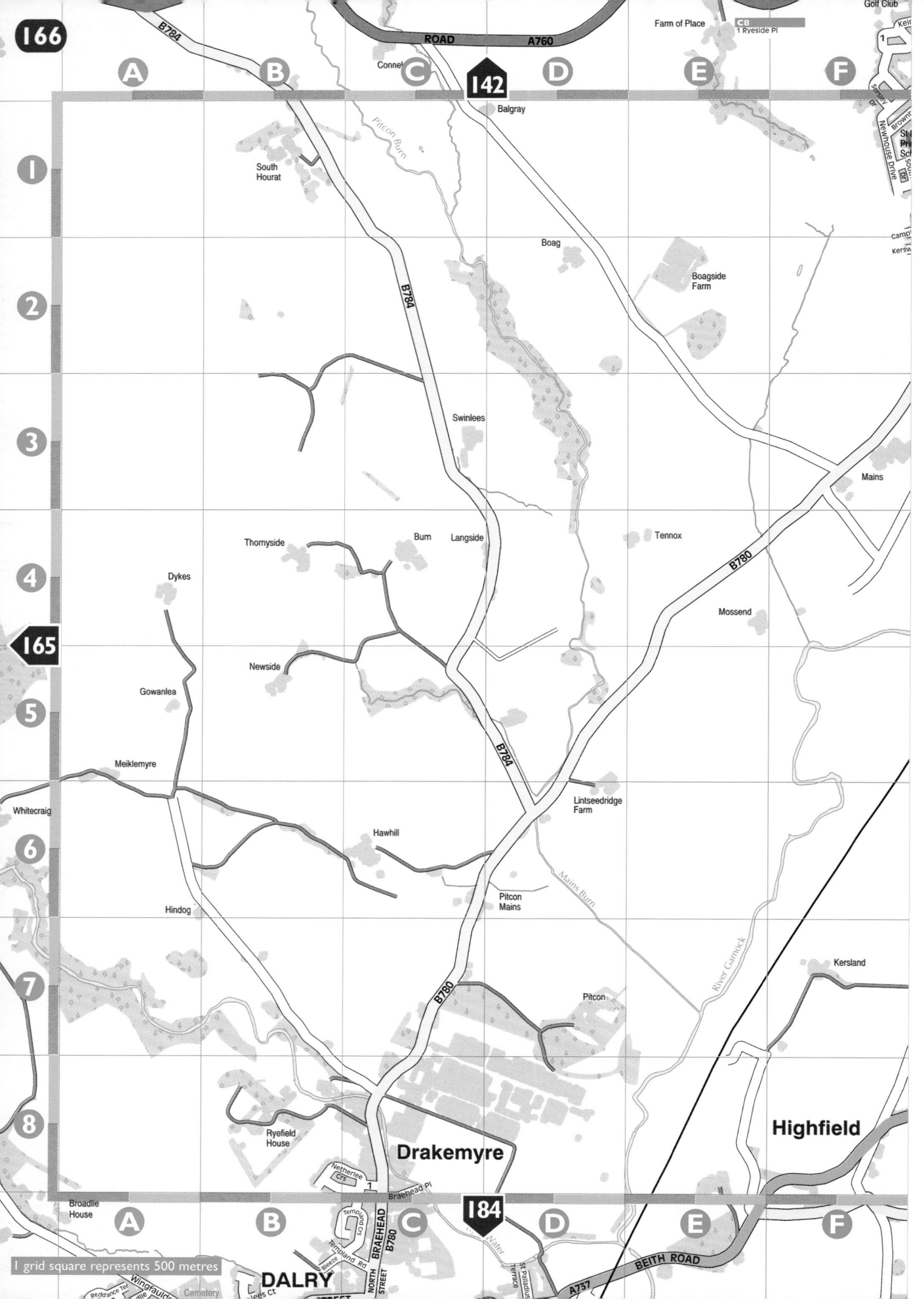

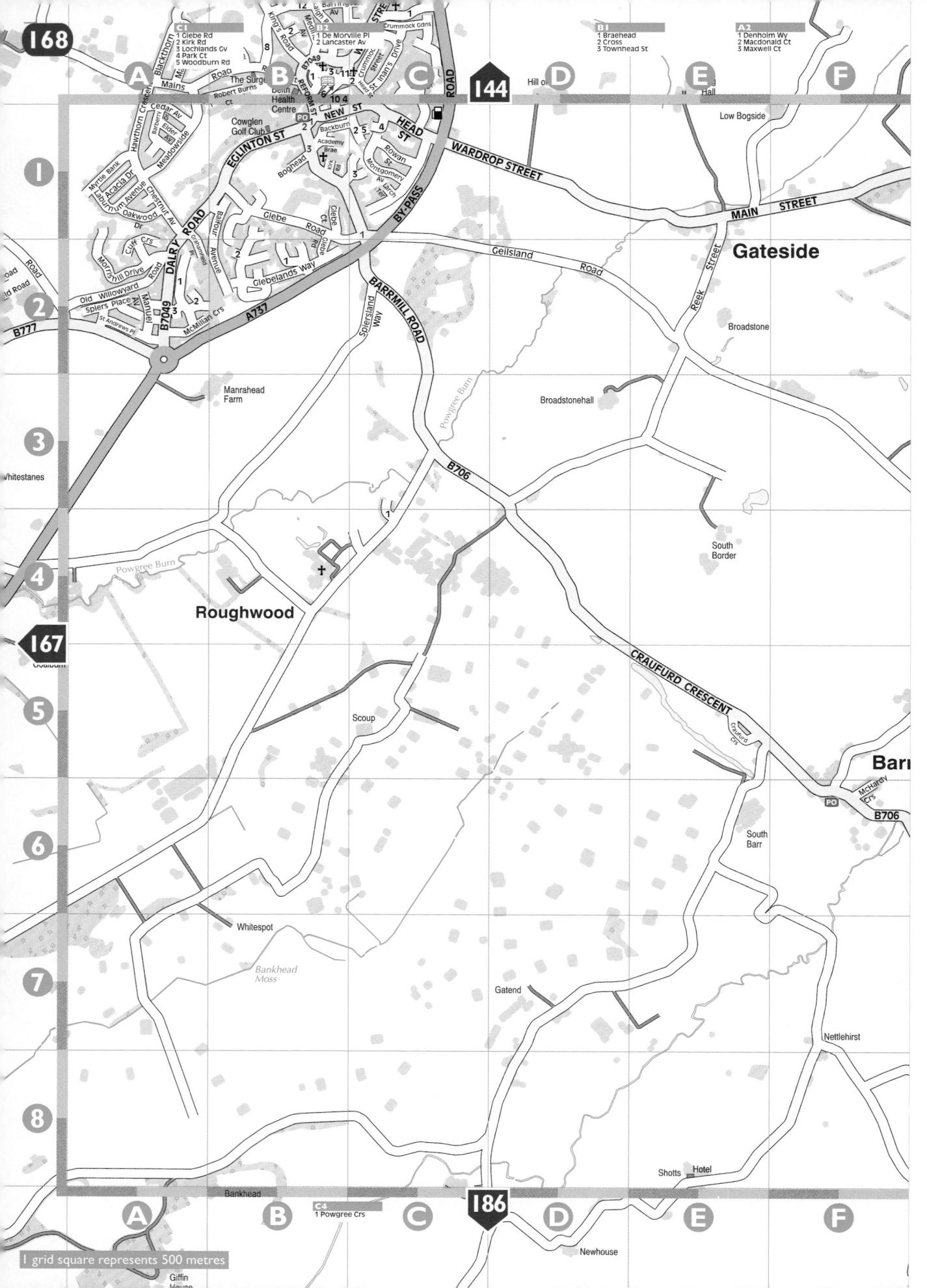

A **B** **C** **D** **E** **F**

C
Blackthorn
1 Glebe Rd
2 Kirk Rd
3 Lochlands Gv
4 Park Ct
5 Woodburn Rd

B1
1 Braehead
2 Cross
3 Townhead St

A2
1 Denholm Wy
2 Macdonald Ct
3 Maxwell Ct

1 De Morville Pl
2 Lancaster Av

Hill of
Low Bogside
Hall

Mains
The Surge
Robert Burns
Ct
Delth
Health
Centre
PO

Myrtle Bank
Hawthorn Crescent
Barberry
Cedar Av
Acacia Dr
Elder
Meadowside
Laburnum Avenue
Oakwood
Chestnut Av
Dr

Cowglen
Golf Club
Boghead

NEW
ST
Academy
Brae
Backburn
Rowan
St
Montgomery
larch
Av

Cliff Crs
Morris Hill Drive
Craufield
Balfour
Avenue
Glebe Road
Glebelands Way
Glebe
Rd
Glebe
Ct

EGLINTON ST
DALRY ROAD
Road

Gateside

WARDROP STREET
MAIN STREET
Reek Street

Geilsland Road

Broadstone

Old   Willowyard
Spiers Place
St Andrews Pl
McMillan Crs
A737
B7049
Manuel

2

B777
Road
Old Road

Manrahead
Farm

BARRMILL ROAD
BY-PASS
Spiersland Way
Powgree Burn

Broadstonehall

3

Whitestanes

B706

South
Border

4

Powgree Burn

Roughwood

Coalburn

CRAUFURD CRESCENT
Craufurd
Crs

Bar

5

Scoup

6

PO
McHardy
Crs
B706

South
Barr

Giffin
House

Whitespot

South
Barr

7

Bankhead
Moss

Gatend

Nettlehirst

8

Shotts   Hotel

A **B** **C** **D** **E** **F**

C4
1 Powgree Crs

Bankhead

Newhouse

1 grid square represents 500 metres

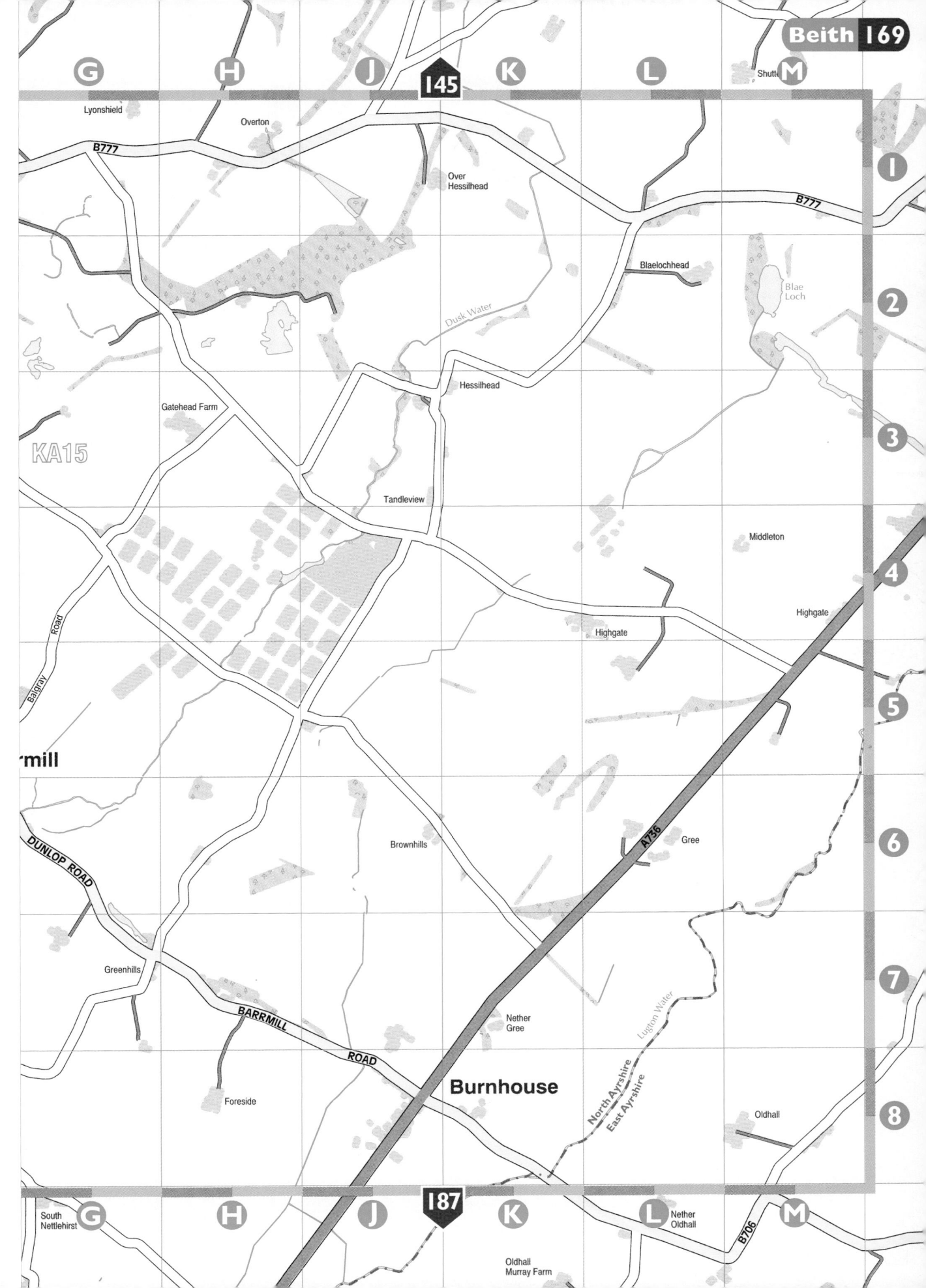

G H J K L M

145

Shutt

B777

Lyonshield

Overton

Over
Hessilhead

B777

Blaelochhead

Blae
Loch

Dusk Water

Hessilhead

Gatehead Farm

KA15

Middleton

Tandleview

Highgate

Highgate

Road

Balgray

Highgate

rmill

DUNLOP ROAD

Brownhills

A736

Gree

Greenhills

BARRMILL

ROAD

Nether
Gree

Lugton Water

Foreside

Burnhouse

North Ayrshire

East Ayrshire

Oldhall

G H J K L M

187

South
Nettlehirst

Nether
Oldhall

B706

Oldhall
Murray Farm

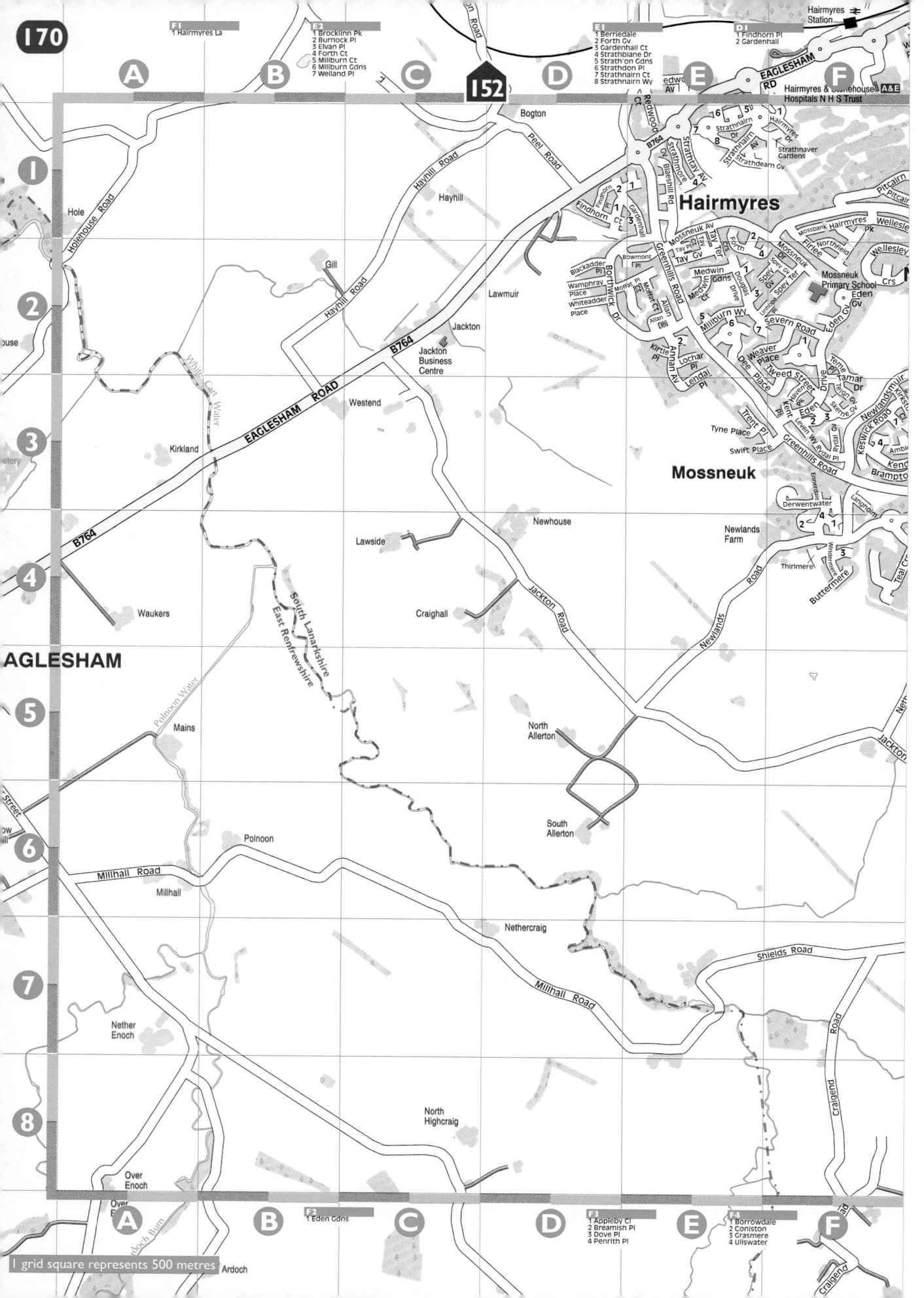

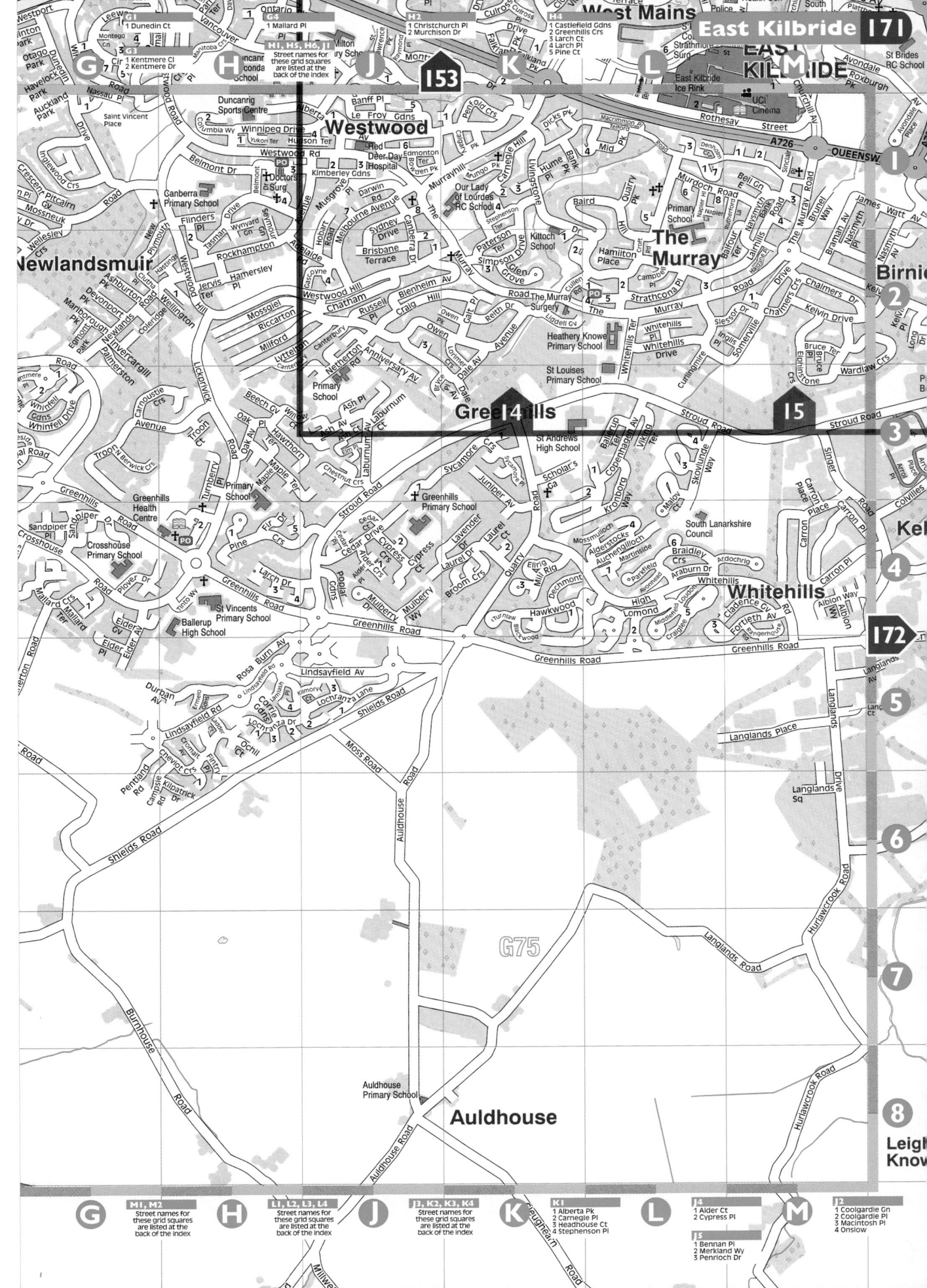

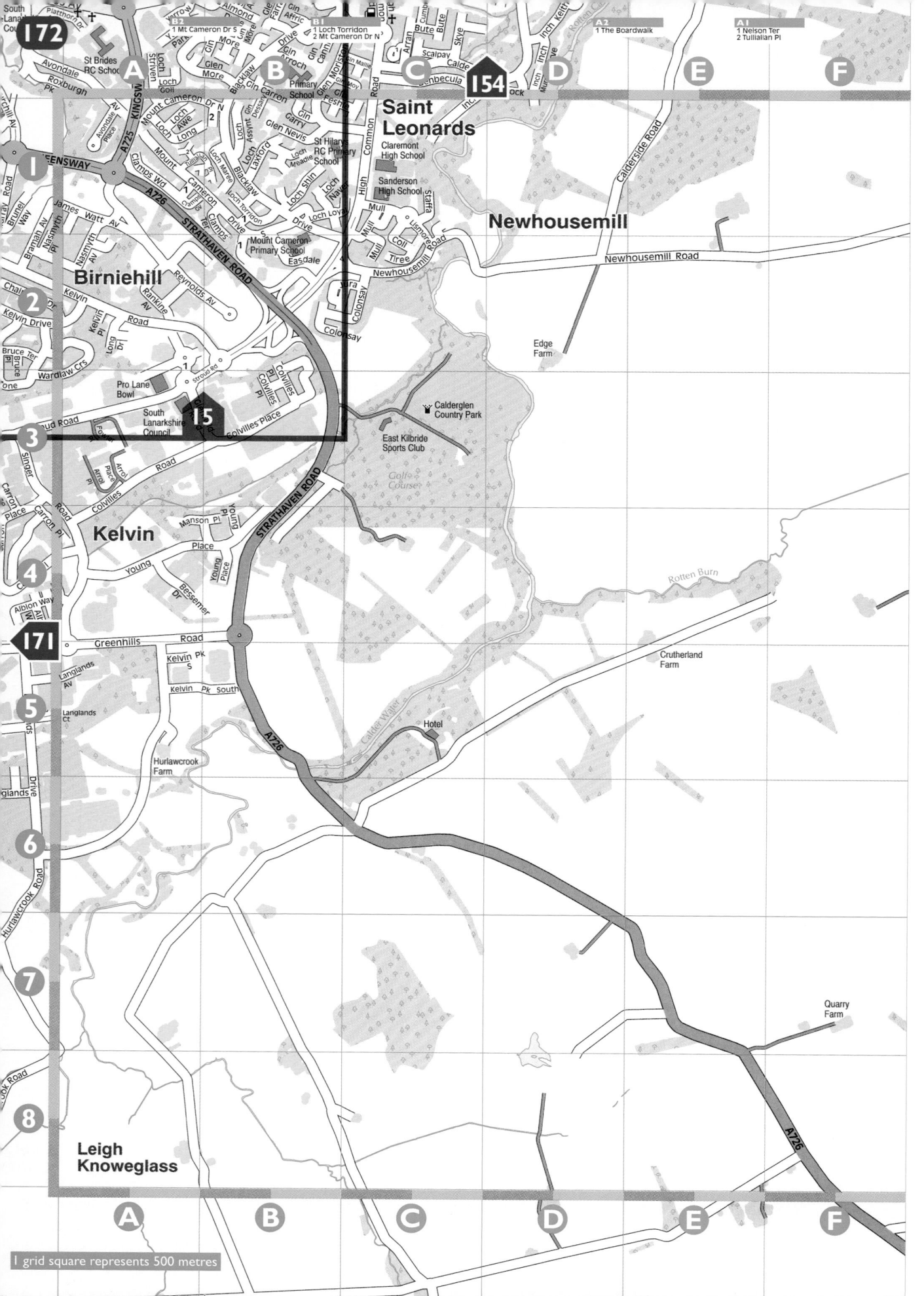

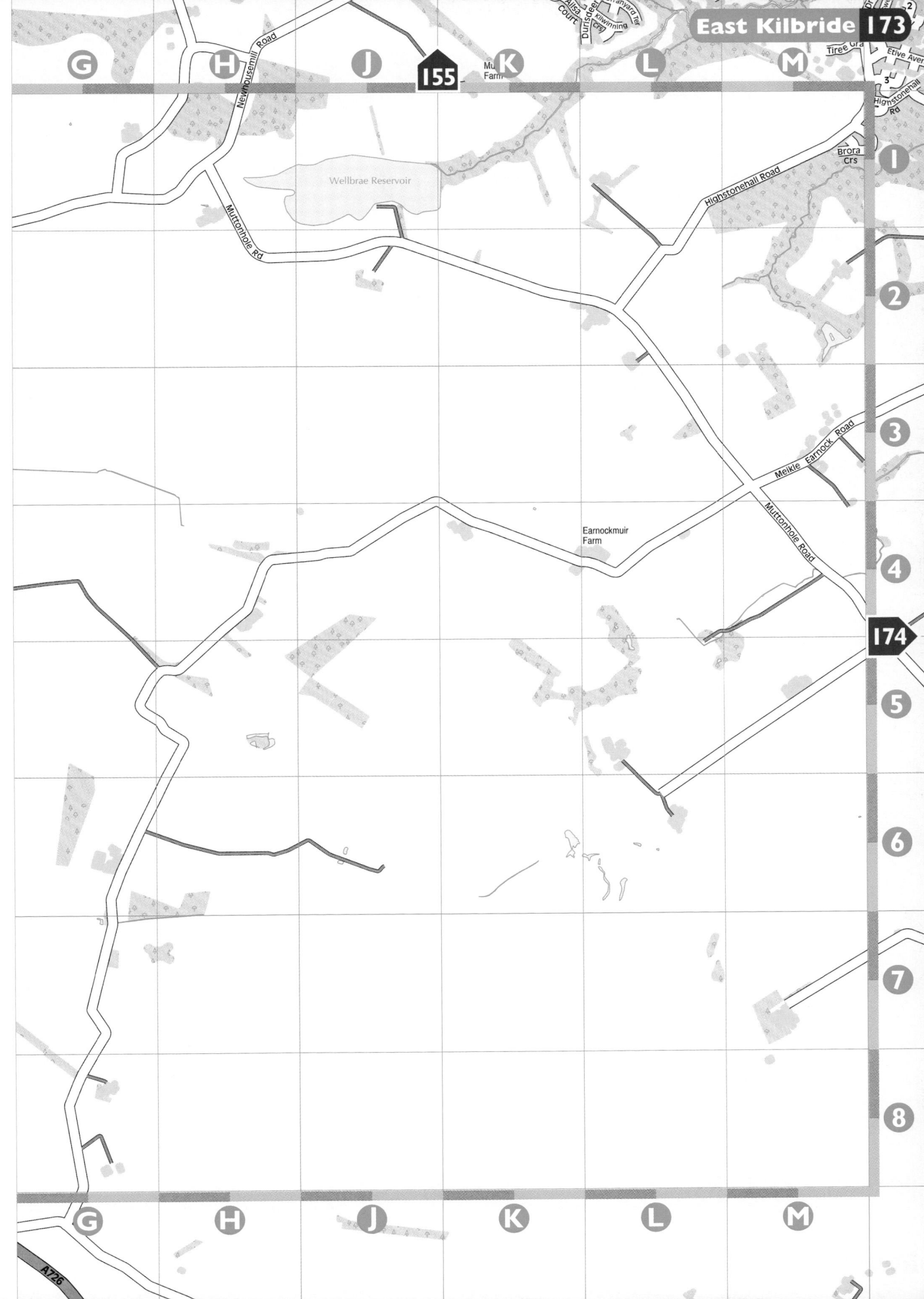

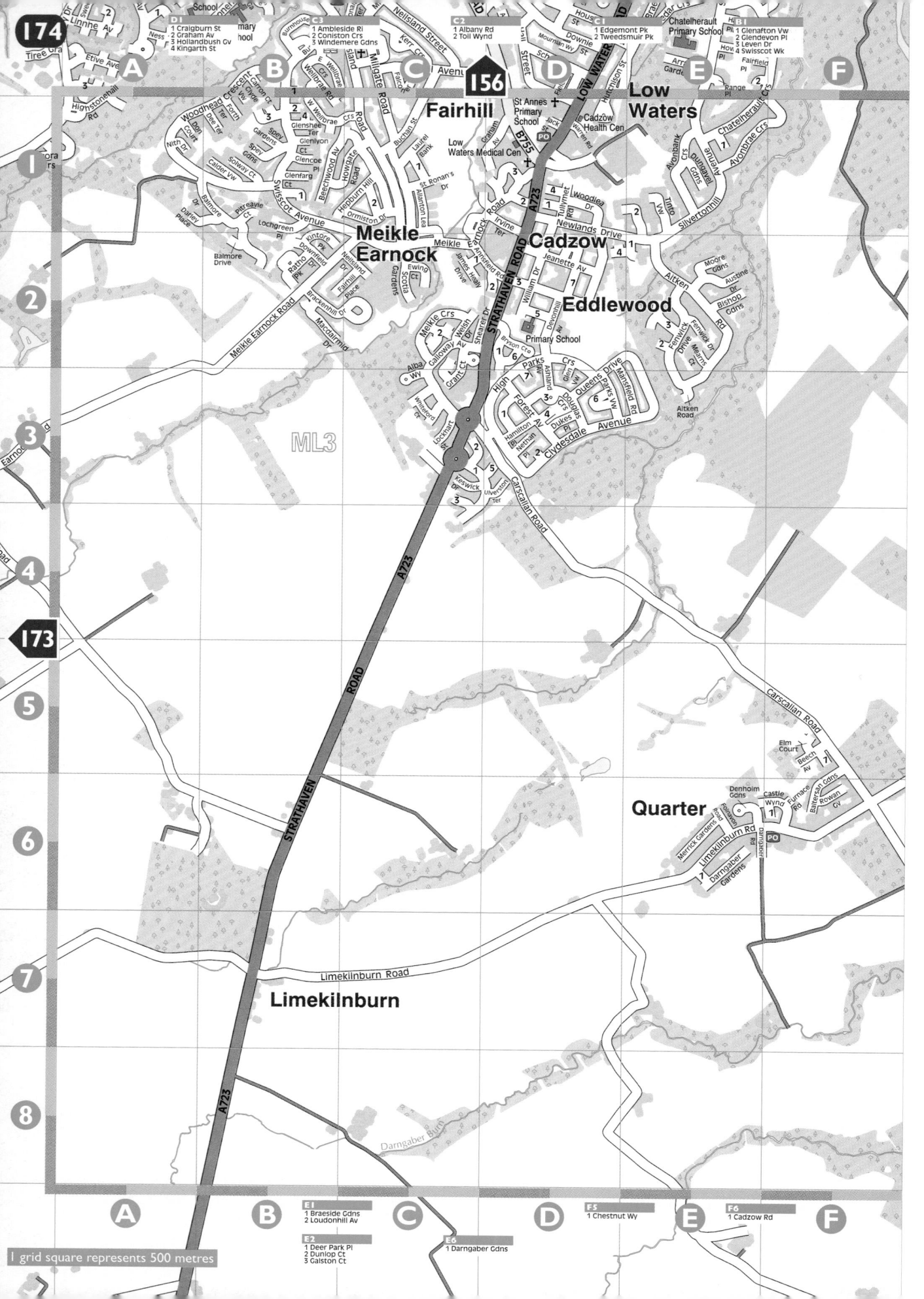

156

Fairhill

Low Waters

Meikle Earnock

Cadzow

Eddlewood

Quarter

173

Limekilnburn

ML3

STRATHAVEN ROAD

A723

Meikle Earnock Road

Swisscot Avenue

Carscallan Road

Limekilnburn Road

Darngaber Burn

A **B** **C** **D** **E** **F**

I **2** **3** **4** **5** **6** **7** **8**

I grid square represents 500 metres

L7
1 Braehead Av

M4
1 Lammermuir Wynd
2 Linnhe Ct

M5
1 High Avon St
2 Sunnyside St

Allan

Castlehill Crescent

157

Chatelherault Visitor Centre

Golf Course

Chatelherault Country Park

CARLISLE ROAD

LANARK ROAD   A72

CARLISLE ROAD

B7078

Avon Water

Merryton Road

Summerlee Road

South Lana Council

Lanarkshire Co Council

Shiel Dr

Fyne Crs

Pentland Crs

HAMILTON RD

GLENVIEW STREET

176

Pentland Crs

W Fairholm

Camtsie St

Merryton St

Beaton St

Fairholm St

Maple

tryt

HA ST

LONDON STREET

Crossgates St

Ian Kenny Gallery

Empire Thr

South Lanarkshire Co

Strathcly Regiona Council

Sunnyside Road

Sunnyside Road

Wee Sunnyside Road

Millheugh

Clove

Powforth Cl

Mill Wynd

Millheugh Brae

Avonbank Rd

Raploch Rd

Broomhill Vw

Avon Street

Watson Street

Ambank St

Raploch St

Burnbrae St

Macneil

Croft Pl

Morgan St

Cherryhill View

Nairn St

Grier Pl

Macmillan St

Primary School

UNIO

Pol Sta Street

Docto Surge

LARKHA

Larkhall Leisure Centre & Baths

7

Carscallan Road

Broomelton Road

Millheugh Road

Avon Water

Robert Smillie Memorial Primary School

Whinnie Knowe

Melrose Pl

Ferndale

8

Plotcock Road

M6
1 Mossblown St
2 Tarbolton Pth
3 Tribboch St

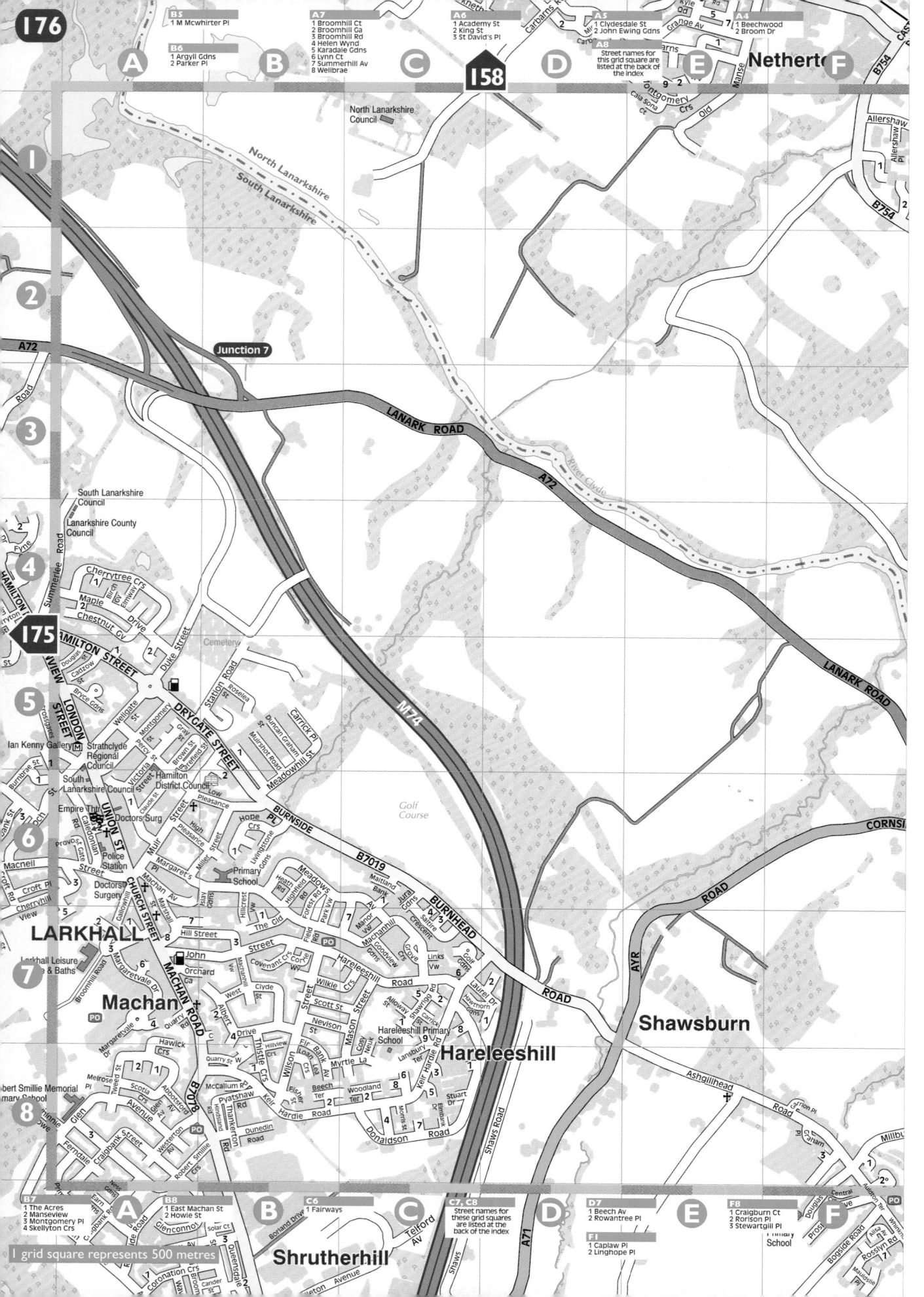

158

175

North Lanarkshire
Council

North Lanarkshire

South Lanarkshire

Junction 7

A72

LANARK ROAD

A72

River Clyde

LANARK ROAD

South Lanarkshire
Council

Lanarkshire County
Council

HAMILTON STREET

Cherrytree Crs

Maple
Chestnut Gv

Drive

Cemetery

Duke Street

Station Road

Roselea

M74

Golf
Course

CORNSI

DRYGATE STREET

LONDON STREET

Ian Kenny Gallery

Strathclyde
Regional
Council

South
Lanarkshire Council

Hamilton
District Council

Empire Thtr

Doctors Surg

BURNSIDE

HOPE PL

B7019

BURNHEAD

AYR ROAD

ROAD

Police
Station

Doctors
Surgery

Primary
School

Meadows

LARKHALL

Larkhall Leisure
Centre & Baths

Hill Street

The Cld
Street

Hareleeshill
Road

Shawsburn

Machan

John
Orchard
Ga

West

Albert

Drive

MACHAN ROAD

Scott St

Wilkie Crs

Mason Street

Hareleeshill Primary
School

Hareleeshill

Hawick
Crs

Quarry St

Thistle Crs

Nevison
St

Fir Bank
Loan
Myrtle La

Ashgillhead
Road

Melrose

Scotia

B7078

McCallum Rd

Pyatshaw
Rd

Keir

Hardie Road

Beech
Ter

Woodland
Ter

Donaldson
Road

Shaws Road

Glen

Avenue

Craigbank

Westerton Rd

Robert Smillie

Dunedin
Road

Albert Smillie Memorial
Primary School

A71

Shrutherhill

Shawsburn

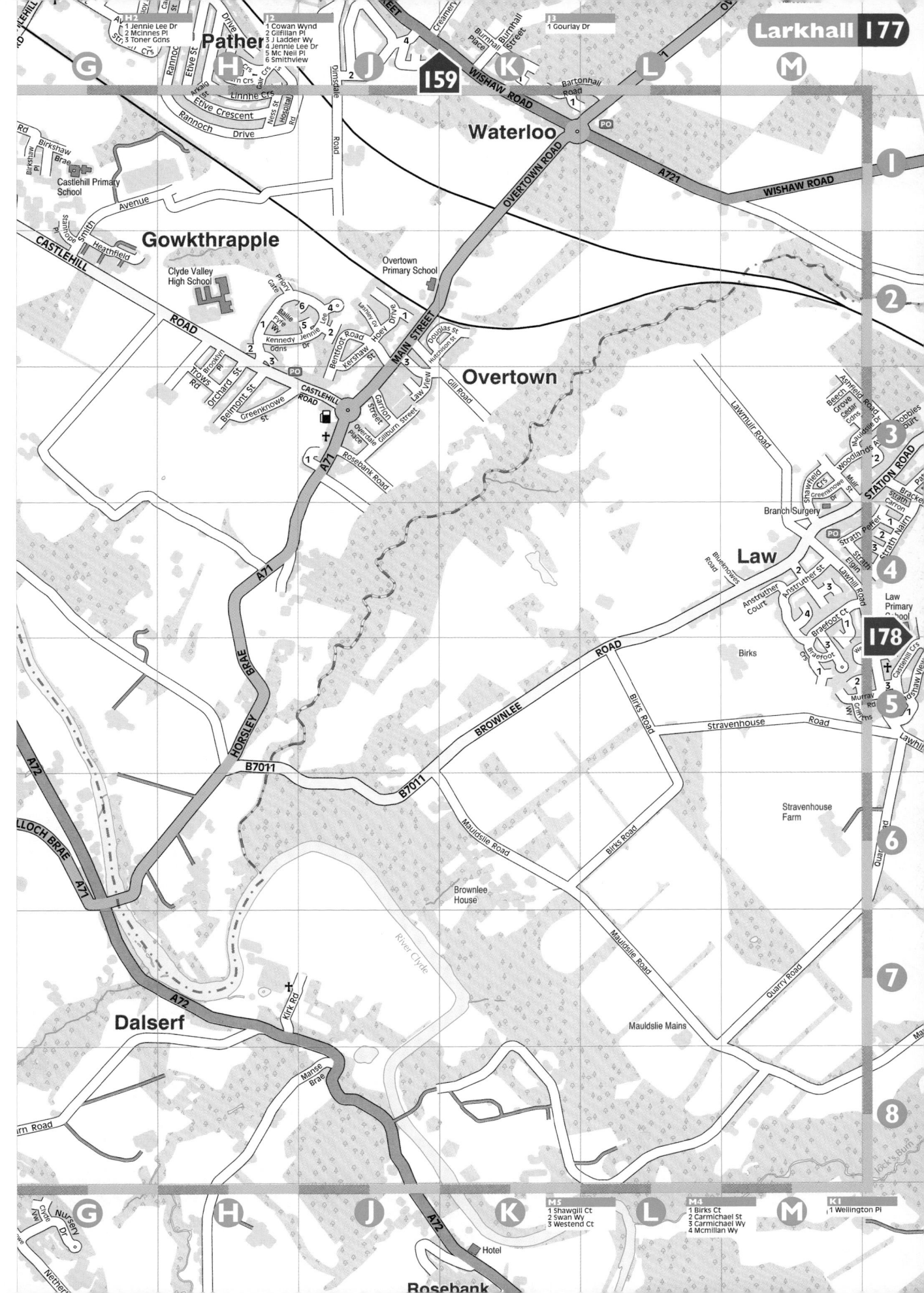

Pather

Waterloo

Gowkthrapple

Overtown

Law

Dalserf

Rosebank

Castlehill Primary School

Clyde Valley High School

Overtown Primary School

Law Primary School

Branch Surgery

Brownlee House

Stravenhouse Farm

Mauldslie Mains

River Clyde

CASTLEHILL ROAD

OVERTOWN ROAD

WISHAW ROAD

MAIN STREET

BROWNLEE ROAD

HORSLEY BRAE

STATION ROAD

A721

A71

A72

B7011

159

178

H2
1 Jennie Lee Dr
2 McInnes Pl
3 Toner Gdns

J2
1 Cowan Wynd
2 Gilfillan Pl
3 J Ladder Wy
4 Jennie Lee Dr
5 Mc Neil Pl
6 Smithview

J3
1 Gourlay Dr

M5
1 Shawgill Ct
2 Swan Wy
3 Westend Ct

M4
1 Birks Ct
2 Carmichael St
3 Carmichael Wy
4 Mcmillan Wy

K1
1 Wellington Pl

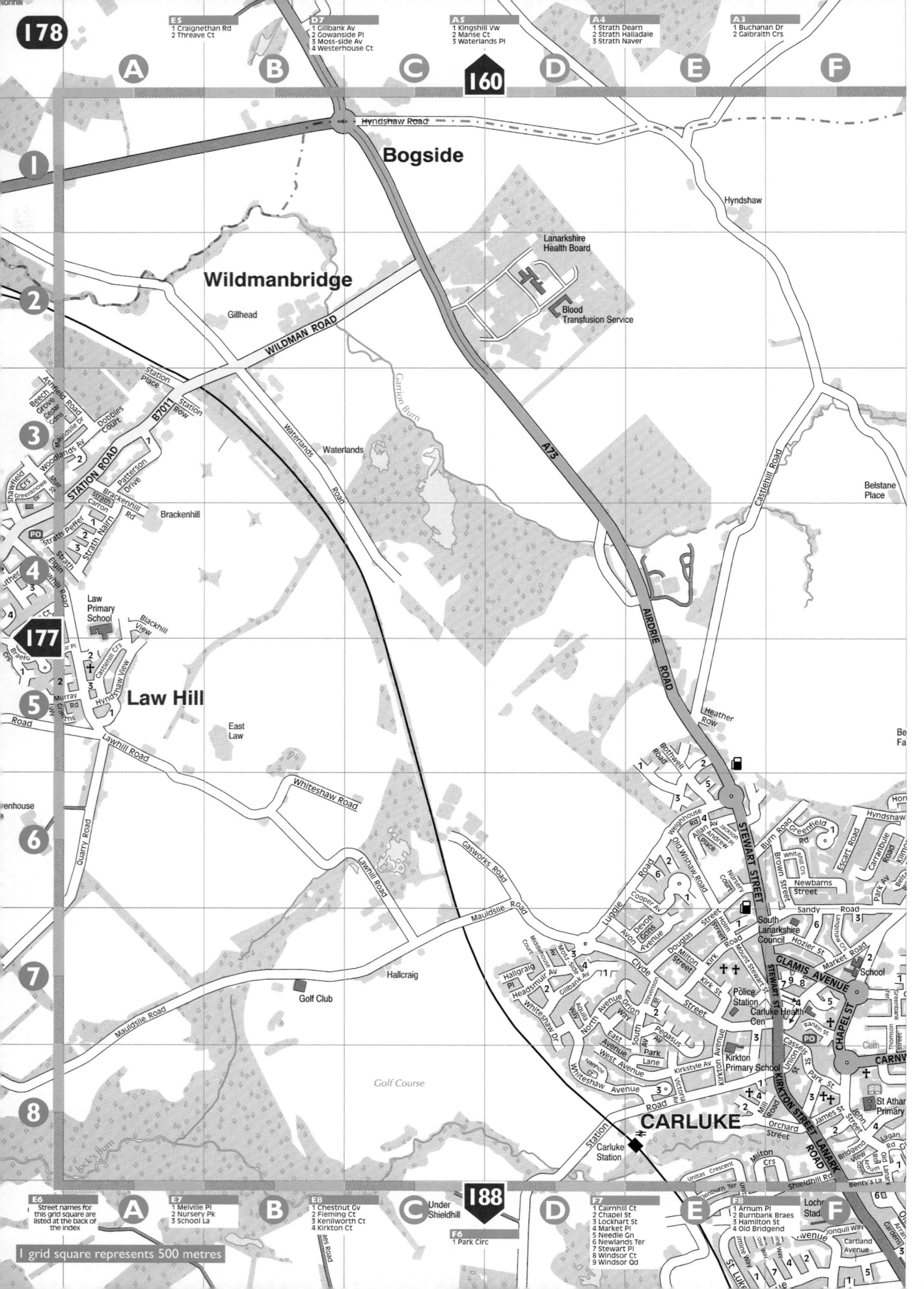

E5
1 Craignethan Rd
2 Threave Ct

D7
1 Gillbank Av
2 Cowanside Pl
3 Moss-side Av
4 Westerhouse Ct

A5
1 Kingshill Vw
2 Manse Ct
3 Waterlands Pl

A4
1 Strath Dearn
2 Strath Halladale
3 Strath Naver

A3
1 Buchanan Dr
2 Galbraith Crs

A   B   C   D   E   F

160

1

Hyndshaw Road

Bogside

Hyndshaw

2

Wildmanbridge

Gillhead

WILDMAN ROAD

Lanarkshire Health Board

Blood Transfusion Service

Carrion Burn

Station Place

B7011

Station Row

3

Beech Grove
Ashfield Road
Cedar Gdns
Dobbies Court
Woodlands Av
Naldslie Dr

Patterson Drive

Waterlands

Waterlands

Waterlands Road

STATION ROAD

Brackenhill Rd

Brackenhill

Belstane Place

Castlehill Road

A73

Shawfield
Greenknowe
Burn St
CFS
PO
Strath Peffer
Carron
Strath Nairn

4

Elgin Road
Strath

Luther
Braefo

177

Law Primary School

Blackhill View

Castlehill Crs

Hyndshaw View

AIRDRIE ROAD

Bothwell Rd

Heather ROW

5

Murray Rd
Glencfns

Law Hill

East Law

Weighhouse Rd
Jackson Pl
Allan Av
Andrew Place

Lawhill Road

Whiteshaw Road

6

Quarry Road

Greenhouse

Luggie Road

Old Wishaw Road

Nursery Court

Stewart Street

Burn Road

White Crs
Greenfield Rd
Hyndshaw

Escart Road
Carrishule

Park Av
Bess
Kim

7

Gasworks Road

Lawhill Road

Mauldslie Road

Hallcraig

Golf Club

Halligraig Pl
Headsmuir Av
Moss-side Rd
Middlehouse Court
Gillbank Av
Clyde Street

Douglas Street
Milton Street
Kirk St
Holm Road
Mount Stewart St

Cooper Av
Devon Gdns
Avon Avenue

Police Station

Carluke Health Cen
PO

South Lanarkshire Council

Hozier St

Sandy Road

Newbarns Street

CLAMIS AVENUE

School

Market Road

Stevenson St
North Avenue
Orion Way
Adam St
Pegasus Av
East Avenue
West Avenue
Park Lane
Kirkstyle Av
Victoria Av

Whiteshaw Dr

Ranfen St

Cassells St
Park St
Union St

CHAPEL ST

Cem

CARN

Mauldslie Road

Golf Course

8

Station Road

Kirkton Primary School

Ivanhoe

Whiteshaw Avenue

Kirkton Avenue

Victoria Road

CARLUKE

Carluke Station

Mill Road

Orchard Street
James St
John St
Kirkton Street
Shieldhill Rd

LANARK ROAD

St Athan Primary

Unitas Crescent
Glenburn Ter
Milton Crs
Bents La

Lagan Rd
Old Bridgend
Jonquil Way
Cartland Avenue

Lochr Stad

Loch's Burn

E6
Street names for this grid square are listed at the back of the index

E7
1 Melville Pl
2 Nursery Pk
3 School La

E8
1 Chestnut Gv
2 Fleming Ct
3 Kenilworth Ct
4 Kirkton Ct

C
Under Shieldhill

188

F6
1 Park Circ

F7
1 Cairnhill Ct
2 Chapel St
3 Lockhart St
4 Market Pl
5 Needle Gn
6 Newlands Ter
7 Stewart Pl
8 Windsor Ct
9 Windsor Gd

F8
1 Arnum Pl
2 Burnbank Braes
3 Hamilton St
4 Old Bridgend

A   B   C   D   E   F

1 grid square represents 500 metres

G6
1 Stonedyke Crs
2 Waterlands Gdns

G7
1 High Mill Rd
2 King's Crs

G8
1 Brookbank Ter
2 Hillfoot Ter
3 Strathlachian Av

North Lanarkshire
South Lanarkshire

161

Gair Reservoirs

Bowridge

Gair

Bogside

Gair Road

King's Law

Under Thorn

Thorn

ulstane Town
rm

eybank Crescent

Road

Gair Crescent

Carluke Primary School

Deeside Drive

Braemar Crs

Stonedyke Road

Moss-side

Thornhome

Hillhead

Moorside Street

Woodend Road

Queens Crescent

Hope Street

Hillhead

Cairneymount Road

Stanistone Rd

Miller Street

Carluke High School

West Quarter

Yieldshields

Equestrian Centre

YIELDSHIELDS ROAD

Croftfoot

VATH ROAD

Glenafeoch

A721

ML8

Blenheim Rd

Ramillies Court

Malplaquet

Corunna Court

Ramage Road

Catteluk Avenue

Charles Crescent

Wilton Road

Kelso Dr

Angus Road

High Meadow

Birkfield

Northflat Pl
Loan

KILNCADZOW ROAD

YIELDSHIELDS ROAD B7085

189

Crawforddyke Primary School

asuis
School

lenmavis
Crs

Glencoe
Rd

Glencoe Road

Lanark Road

Elderslea Road

Wilton

Carradale Gardens

Goremire Road

Hillhouse Gate

Hayward Av

Roadmeeting
spital

Burnhead Farm

West oldstrea

Cemetery

J8
1 Goremire Rd
2 High Meadow
3 Meadow Ct

H8
1 Cameronian Dr
2 Mandora Ct
3 Muirlee Rd
4 Oudenarde Ct

Roadmeetings

G H J K L M

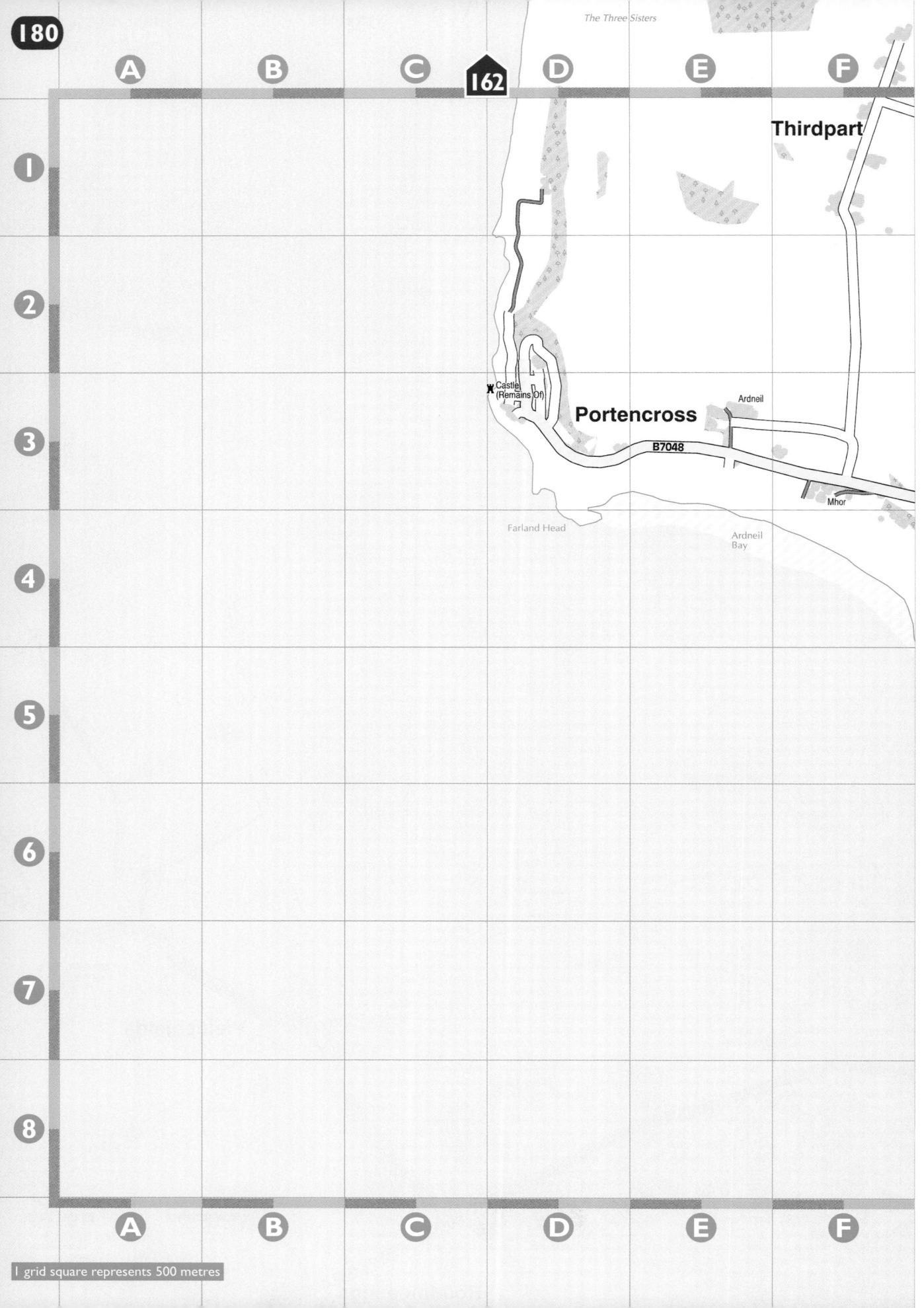

The Three Sisters

Thirdpart

✗ Castle
(Remains Of)

Portencross

Ardneil

B7048

Mhor

Farland Head

Ardneil
Bay

J4
1 Arthur Ct
2 Happyhills
3 Headrigg

J5
1 South Rd

K3
1 Drummilling Av
2 Drummilling Dr

G H J 163 K L M

1

Millstonford

Bushglen

Stairlie

Crosbie Burn

The Avenue

Carlung
Farm

KA23

2

Carlung
House

Kilbride Burn

Lawoodhead

B781

Drummilling

A78(T)

B782

Woodside

Underhill

3

Yonderfield

Cemetery

Faulds
Farm

B7048

Blackshaw
Dr

West
Kilbride
Station

PORTENCROSS ROAD

Avondale Rd

St Bride's Rd

Castle View

GATESIDE STREET

CUBRIESHAW ST

HUNTERSTON RD

Primary
School

The
Surgery

MAIN STREET

B781

Law Brae

4

Corsehill Dr

Corse St

Wellpark

Glen Rd

Halfway St

Arthur St

Well St

RITCHIE ST

The M
Gall

PO

Barony
Glebe

Glenside Crs

Farmfield Ter

Castle Tarbert Av

182

Jack's View

Snowdon Terrace

Overton Dr

Overton

Orchard
Street

North Rd

Alton Street

Glenside Grove

Meadowfoot Road

Nethermilin

Lawfield

Craufurd Av

Lawhill

5

Wildcat
Rd

Summerlea Road

Merriewood
Rd

YERTON BRAE

SNOWDON TER

B781

Bowfield
Road

Weston Ter

Head Rd

Goldenberry Av

Kirkton Av

B7047

Simson Avenue

Ardrossan High Road

Meadowfoot

West Kilbride
Golf Club

Cubrieshaw
Hall

**WEST
KILBRIDE**

Yonderton

Fullerton Drive

A78(T)

Maimhor Rd

Caldwell

Alknut
Road

Fairlands Vw

Cumbrae
Road

Carnung Pl

Kilruskin
Drive

Woodside

6

Gourock Water

PO

Hyndman
Rd

Pantonville
Road

Ardnell Av

Meadowhead

Sandy Road

7

ARDROSSAN

Glenbride
Road

SEAMILL

Chapelton La

ROAD

CHAPELTON ROAD

B7047

Kirkland
Glen

8

Chapelton

South
Inch

Glenhead

L5
1 Simson Av

L4
1 Highthorne Crs

K5
1 Crosbie Dr
2 Cubrieshaw Dr
3 Yonderton Pl

K4
1 Manse Rd
2 Meadowside
3 St Bride's Dr
4 Stairlie Crs

A oodhead
B
C
D
E
F

1 Stairlie

B781

2 Ballees Farm
● Blackshaw Farm
B781

Gill
B781
Munnoch Burn

3 Faulds Farm

4

181

5 Haupland Muir
Knockewart

derton
Busbie Muir

6 Gourock Water

B780

7 Hauplands
Busbie Muir Reservoir
Coalhill

8
B780

A
B
C
D
E
F

Meikle Busbie

1 grid square represents 500 metres

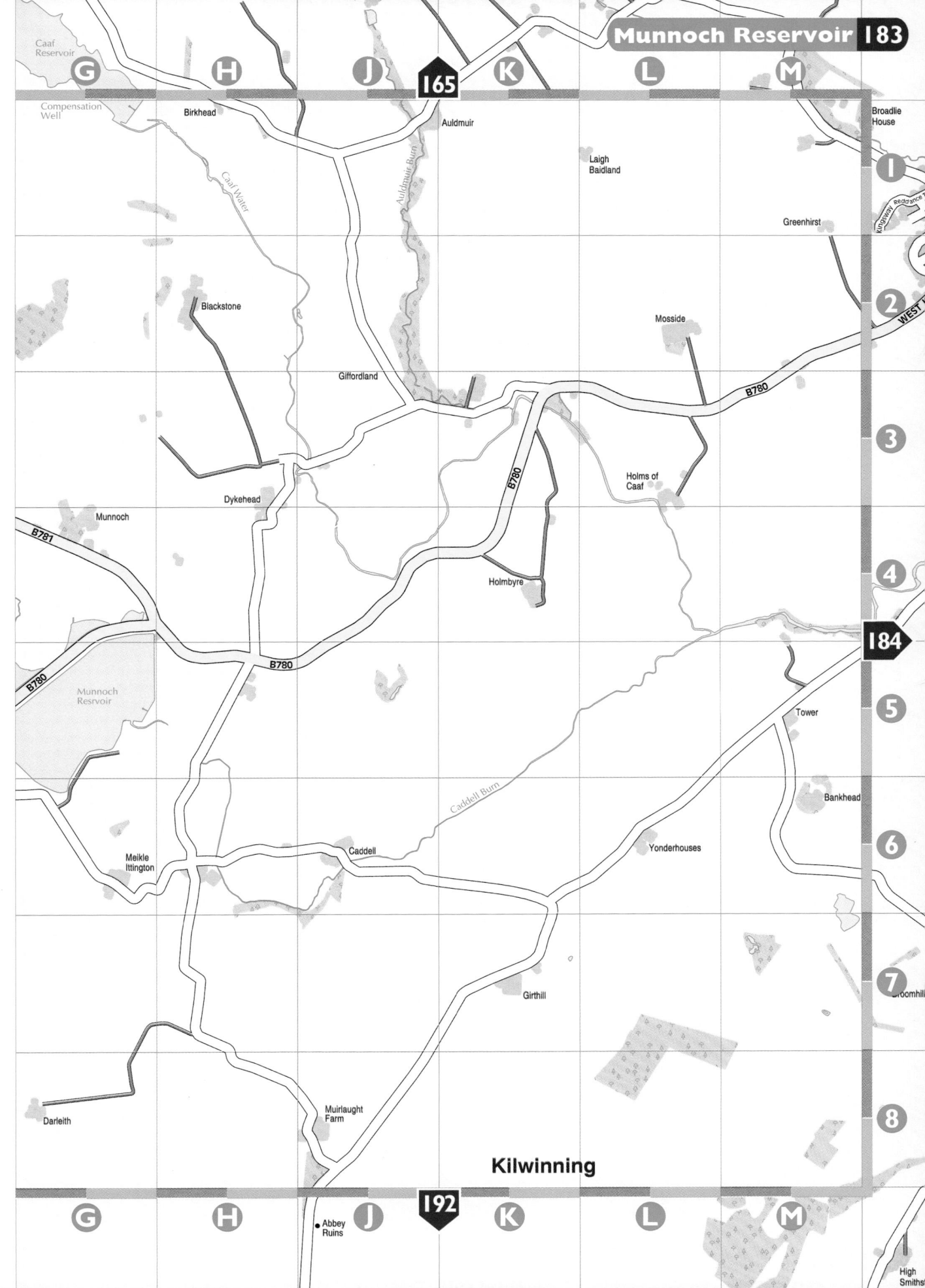

G · H · J · **165** · K · L · M

Caaf
Reservoir

Compensation
Well

Birkhead

Auldmuir

Broadlie
House

I

Laigh
Baidland

Greenhirst

Kingsway · Reddance T

2

WEST

Mosside

B780

Blackstone

Caaf Water

Auldmuir Burn

Giffordland

3

B780

Holms of
Caaf

Dykehead

Munnoch

B781

4

184

B780

Holmbyre

B780

Tower

5

Munnoch
Resrvoir

B780

Bankhead

Caddell Burn

6

Meikle
Ittington

Caddell

Yonderhouses

7

Broomhill

Girthill

8

Darleith

Muirlaught
Farm

Kilwinning

G · H · J · **192** · K · L · M

Abbey
Ruins

High
Smiths

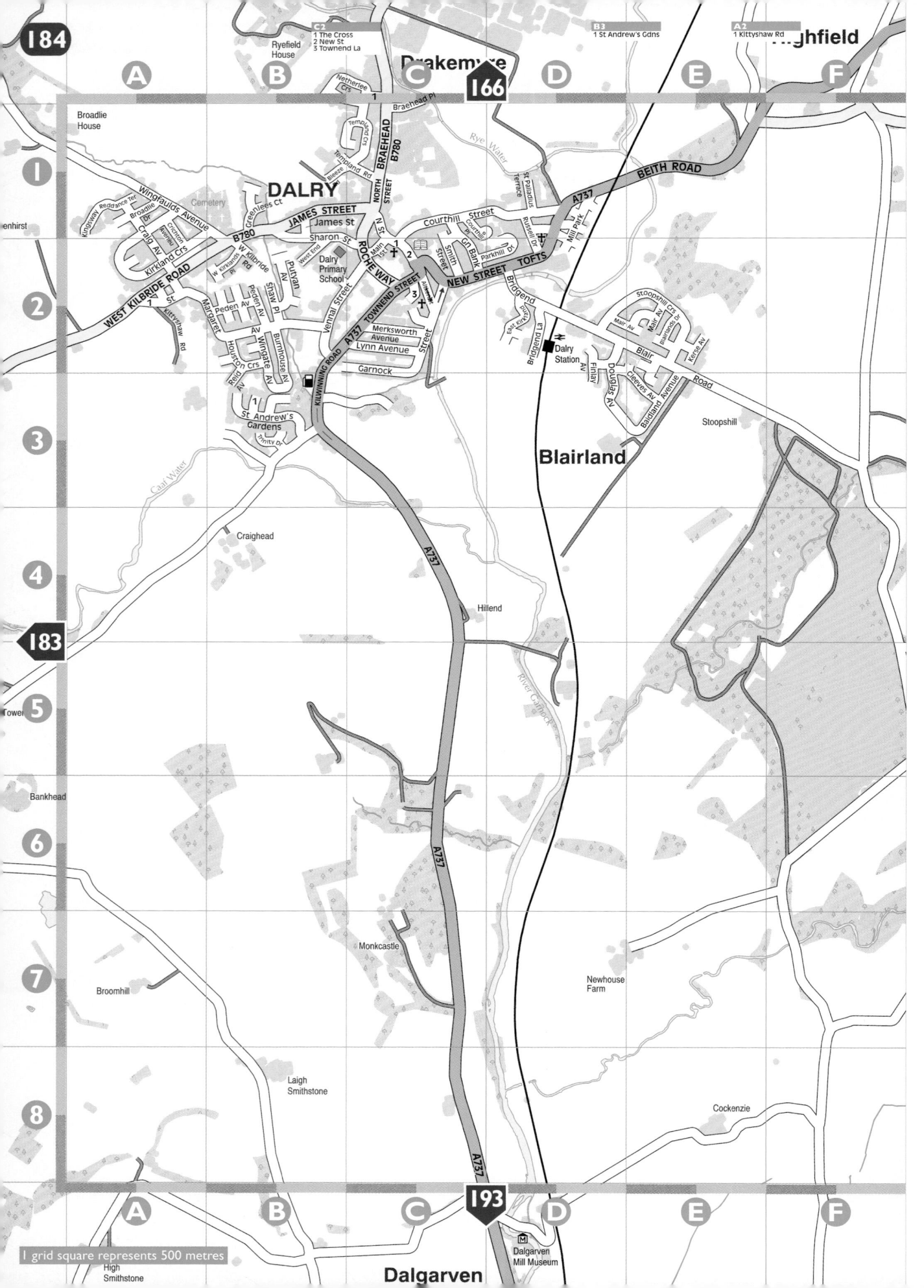

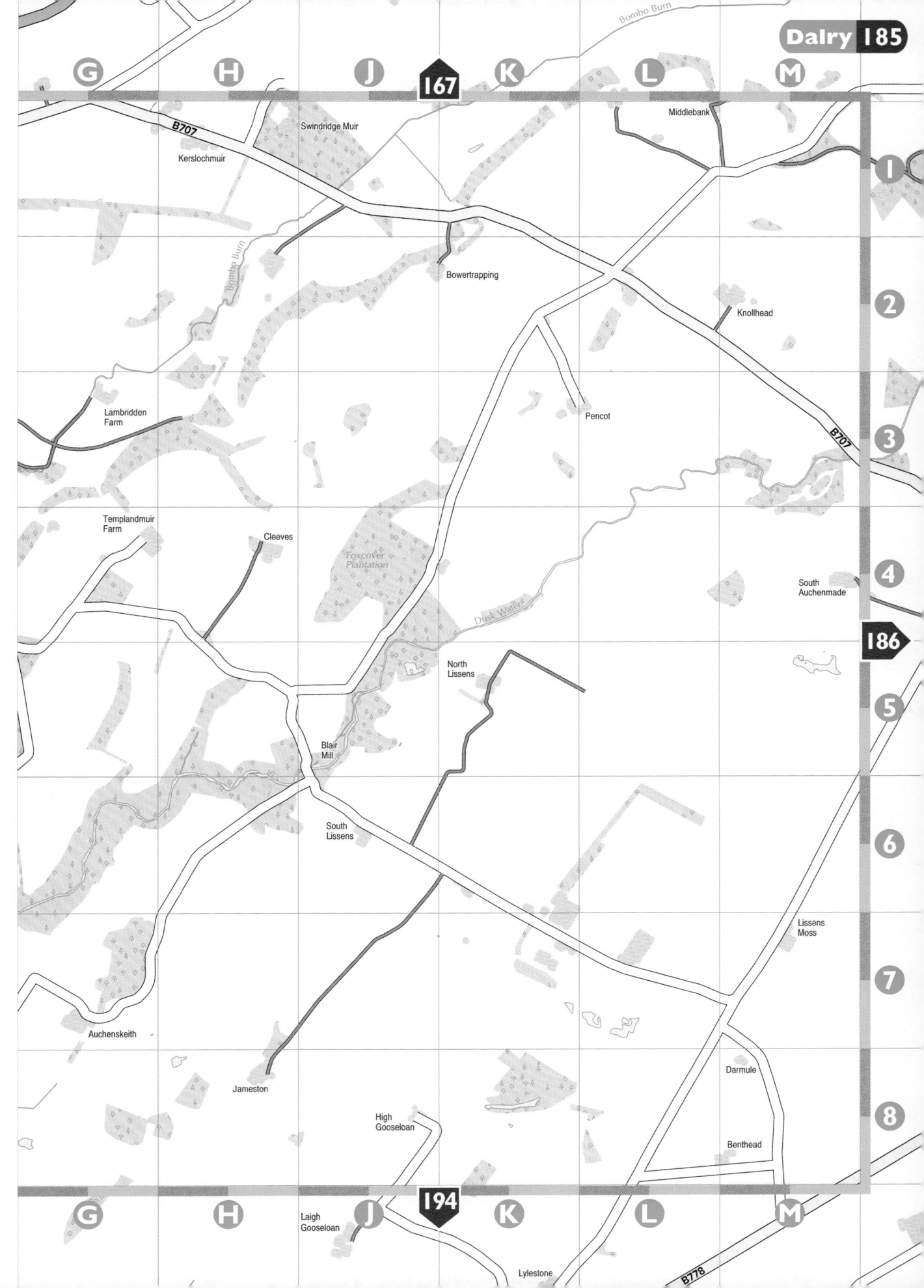

G H J 167 K L M

I

2

3

4

186

5

6

7

8

G H 194 K L M

Bombo Burn

Middlebank

B707

Swindridge Muir

Kerslochmuir

Bowertrapping

Knollhead

B707

Lambridden Farm

Pencot

Templandmuir Farm

Cleeves

Foxcover Plantation

Dusk Waters

South Auchenmade

North Lissens

Blair Mill

South Lissens

Lissens Moss

Auchenskeith

Darmule

Jameston

Benthead

High Gooseloan

Laigh Gooseloan

Lylestone

B778

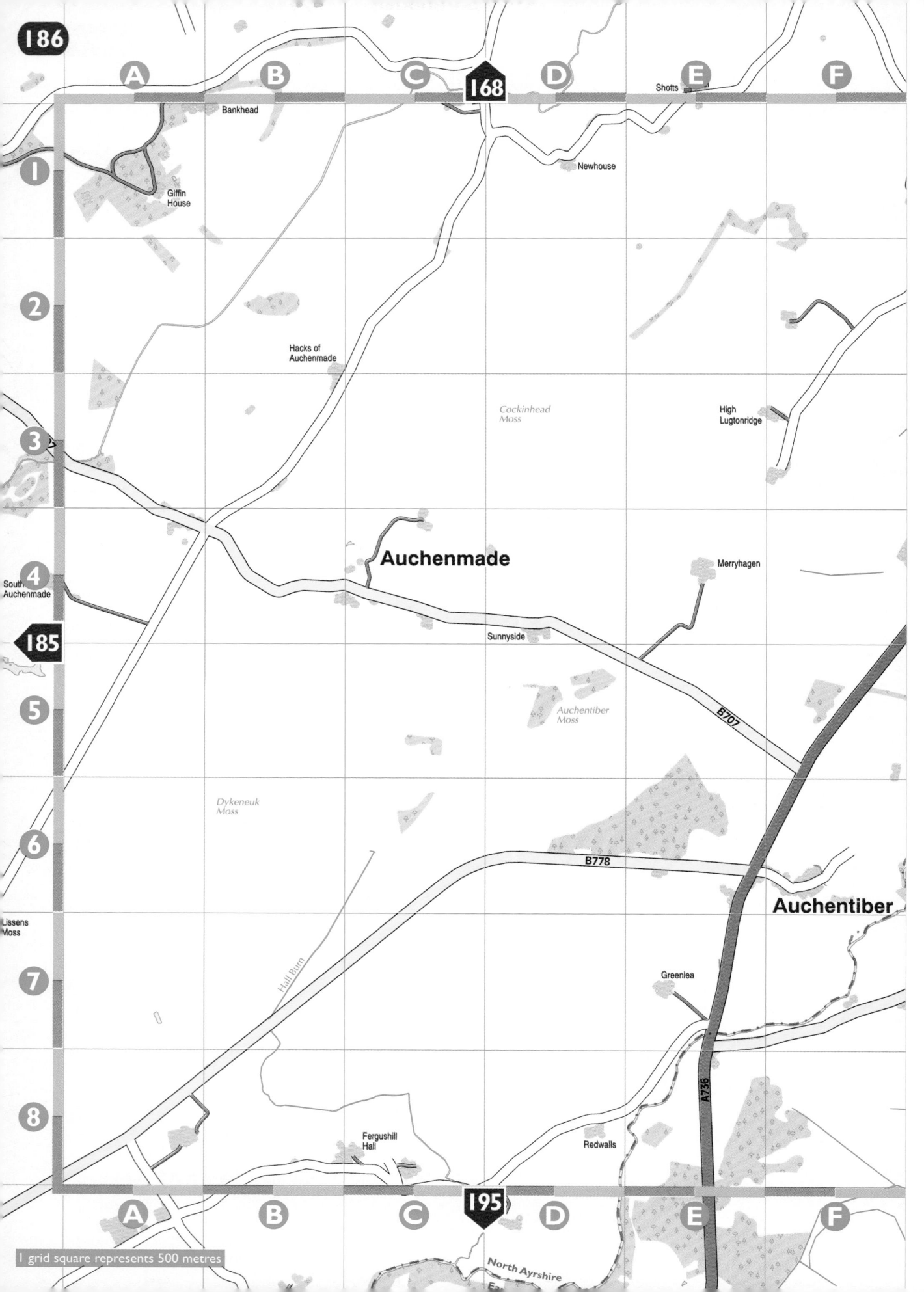

A B C D E F

168

Shotts

Bankhead

1

Giffin
House

Newhouse

2

Hacks of
Auchenmade

Cockinhead
Moss

High
Lugtonridge

3

Auchenmade

South
Auchenmade

Merryhagen

4

185

Sunnyside

B707

5

Auchentiber
Moss

Dykeneuk
Moss

B778

6

Lissens
Moss

Auchentiber

Greenlea

7

Hall Burn

A736

8

Fergushill
Hall

Redwalls

A B C D E F

195

North Ayrshire

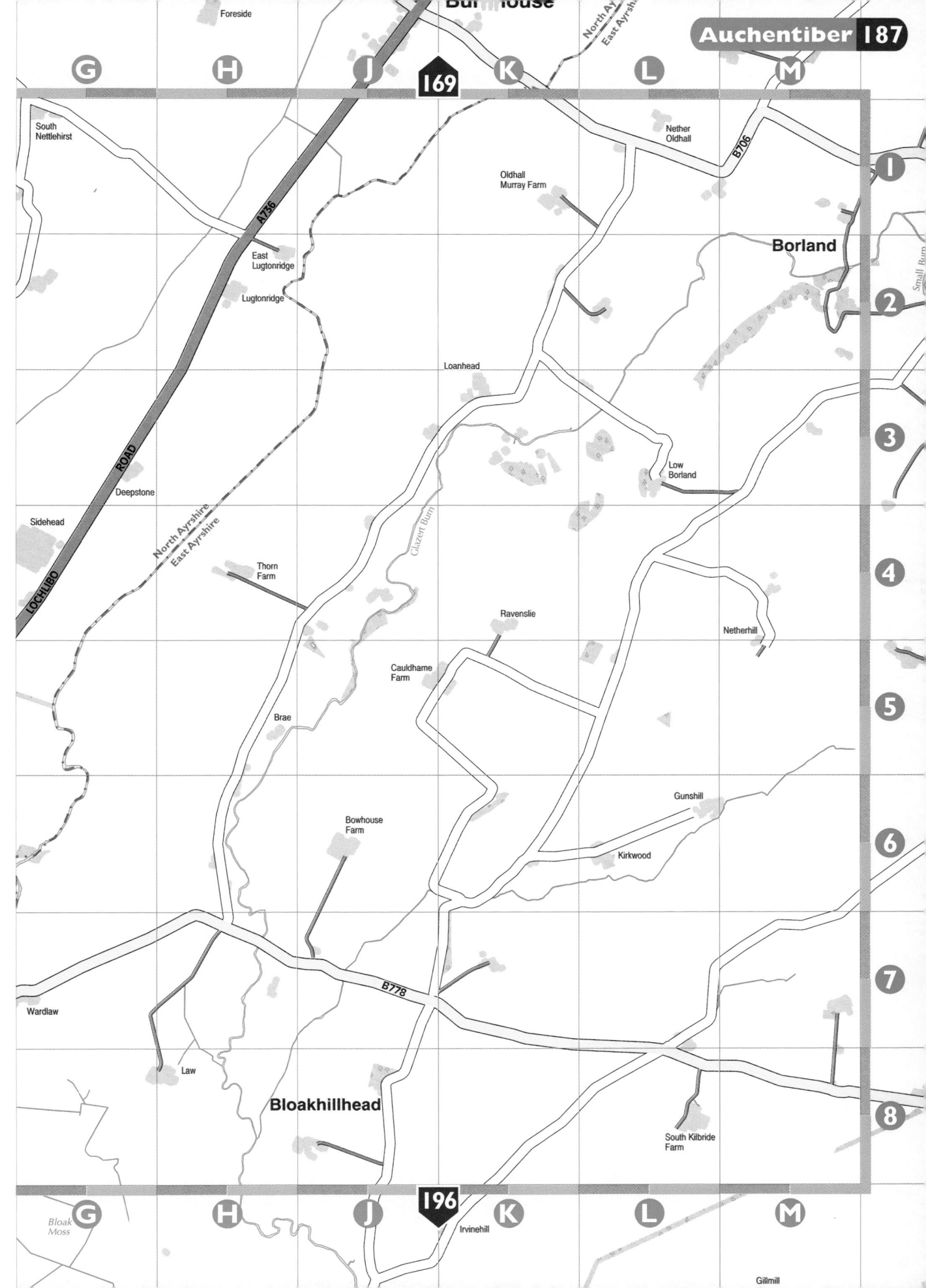

G H J 169 K L M

I
2
3
4
5
6
7
8

South
Nettlehirst

A736

Foreside

North Ay
East Ayrsh

Nether
Oldhall

B706

Borland

Small Burn

East
Lugtonridge

Lugtonridge

Oldhall
Murray Farm

Loanhead

Low
Borland

ROAD

Deepstone

North Ayrshire
East Ayrshire

Sidehead

Thorn
Farm

Glazert Burn

Ravenslie

Netherhill

LOCHLIBO

Cauldhame
Farm

Brae

Gunshill

Bowhouse
Farm

Kirkwood

Wardlaw

B778

Law

Bloakhillhead

South Kilbride
Farm

Bloak
Moss

Irvinehill

Gillmill

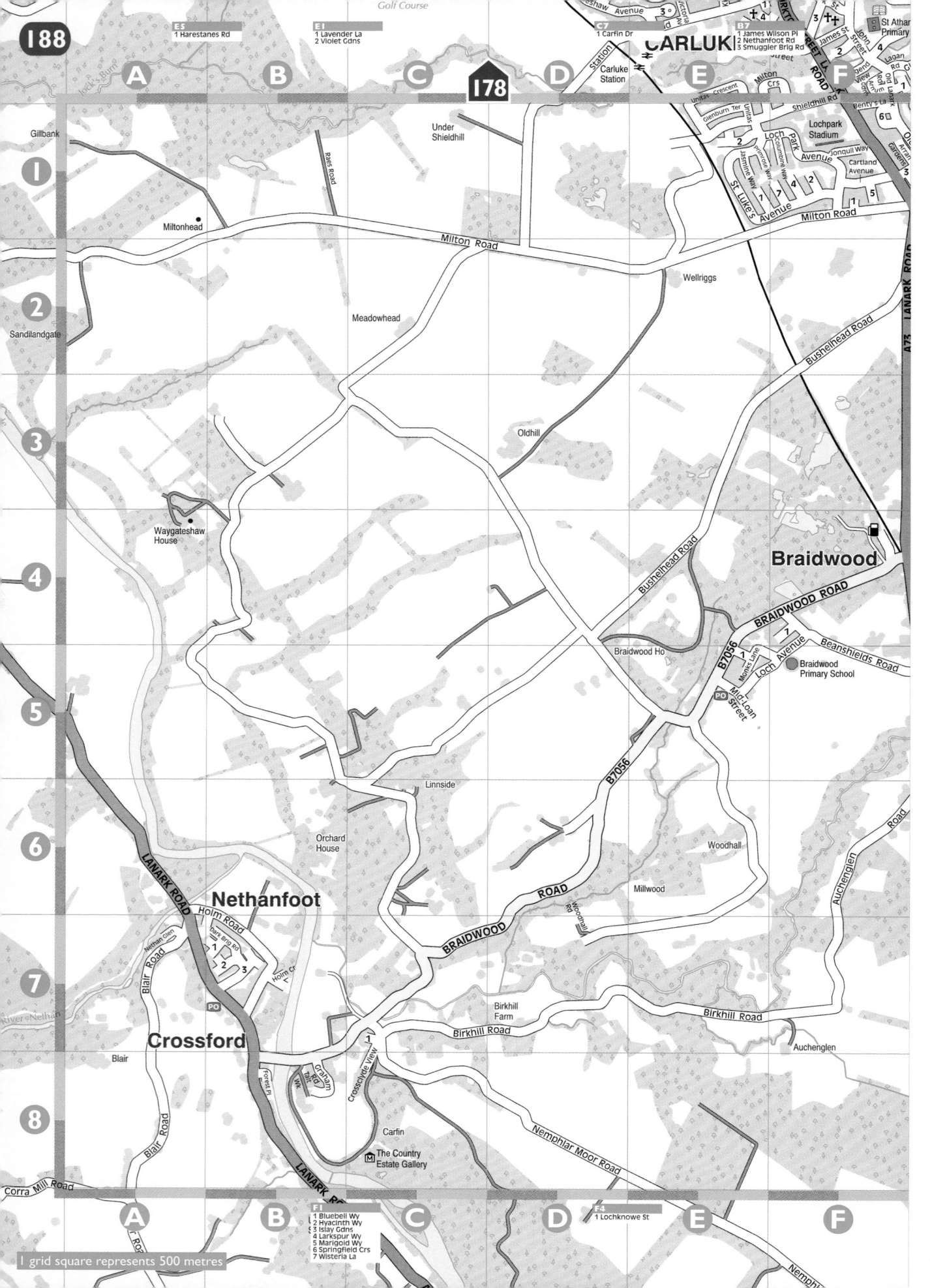

CARLUKE

178

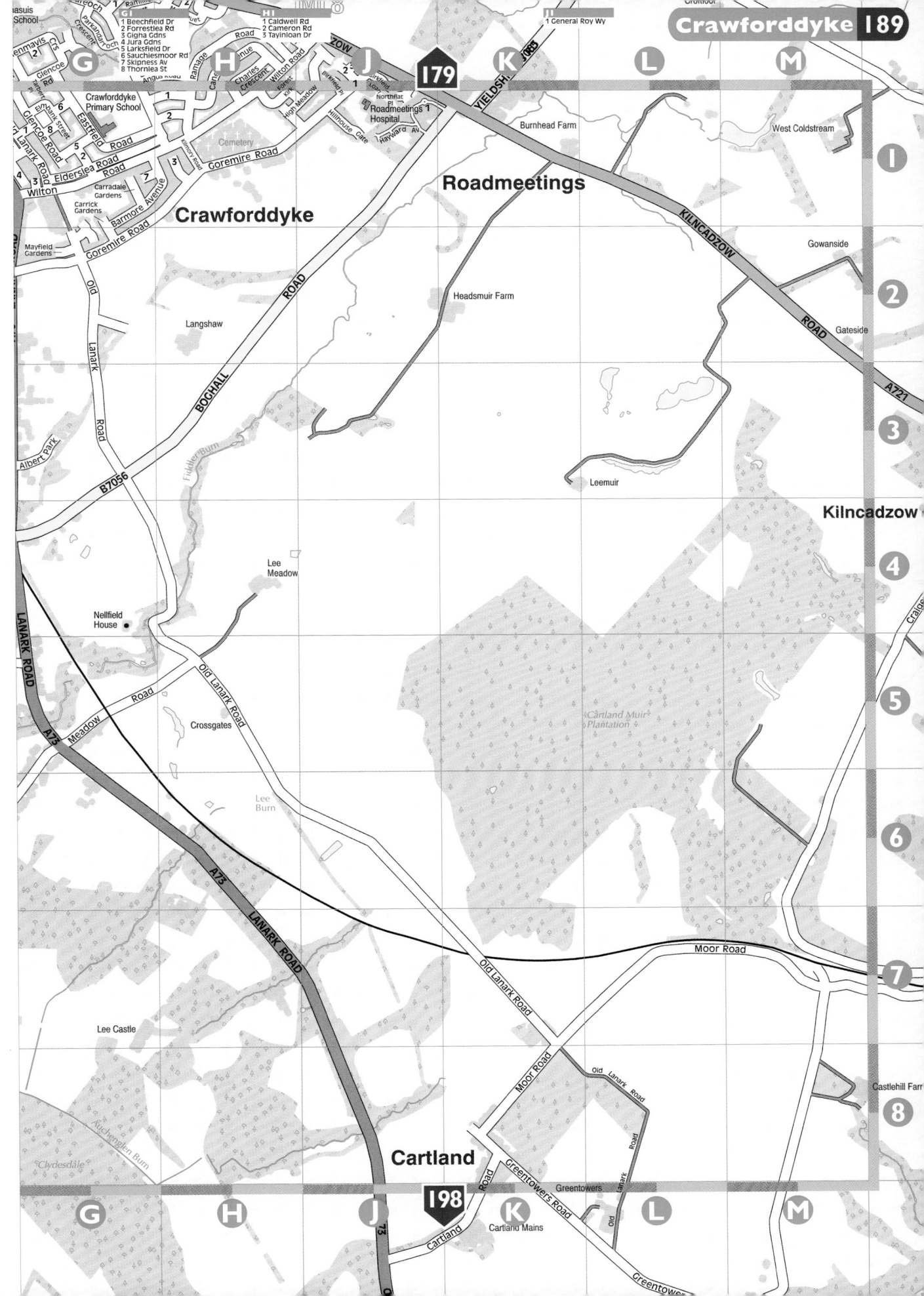

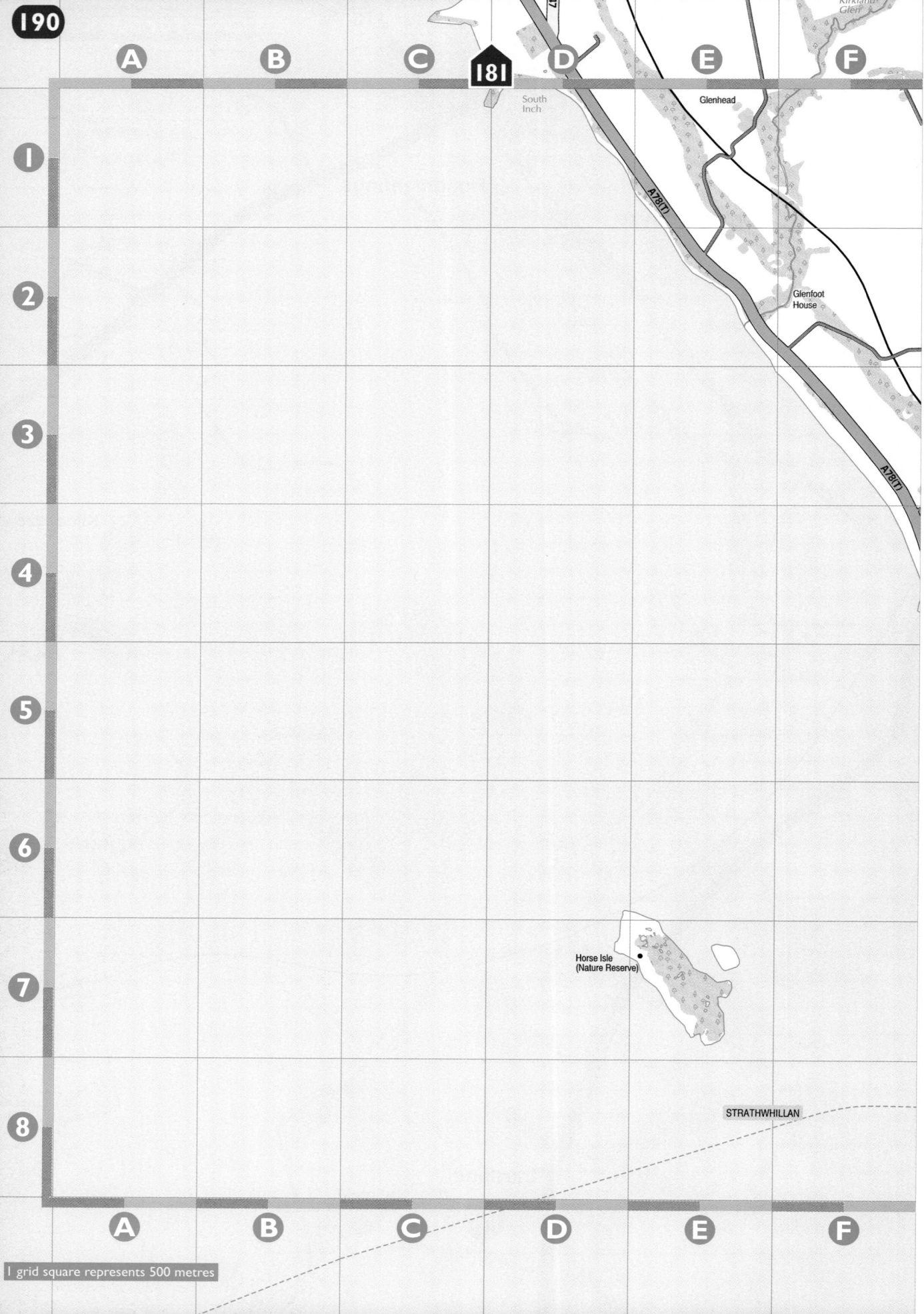

181

A B C D E F

I

2

3

4

5

6

7

8

South
Inch

A78(T)

Glenhead

Glenfoot
House

Kirkland-
Glen

Horse Isle
(Nature Reserve)

STRATHWHILLAN

A B C D E F

I grid square represents 500 metres

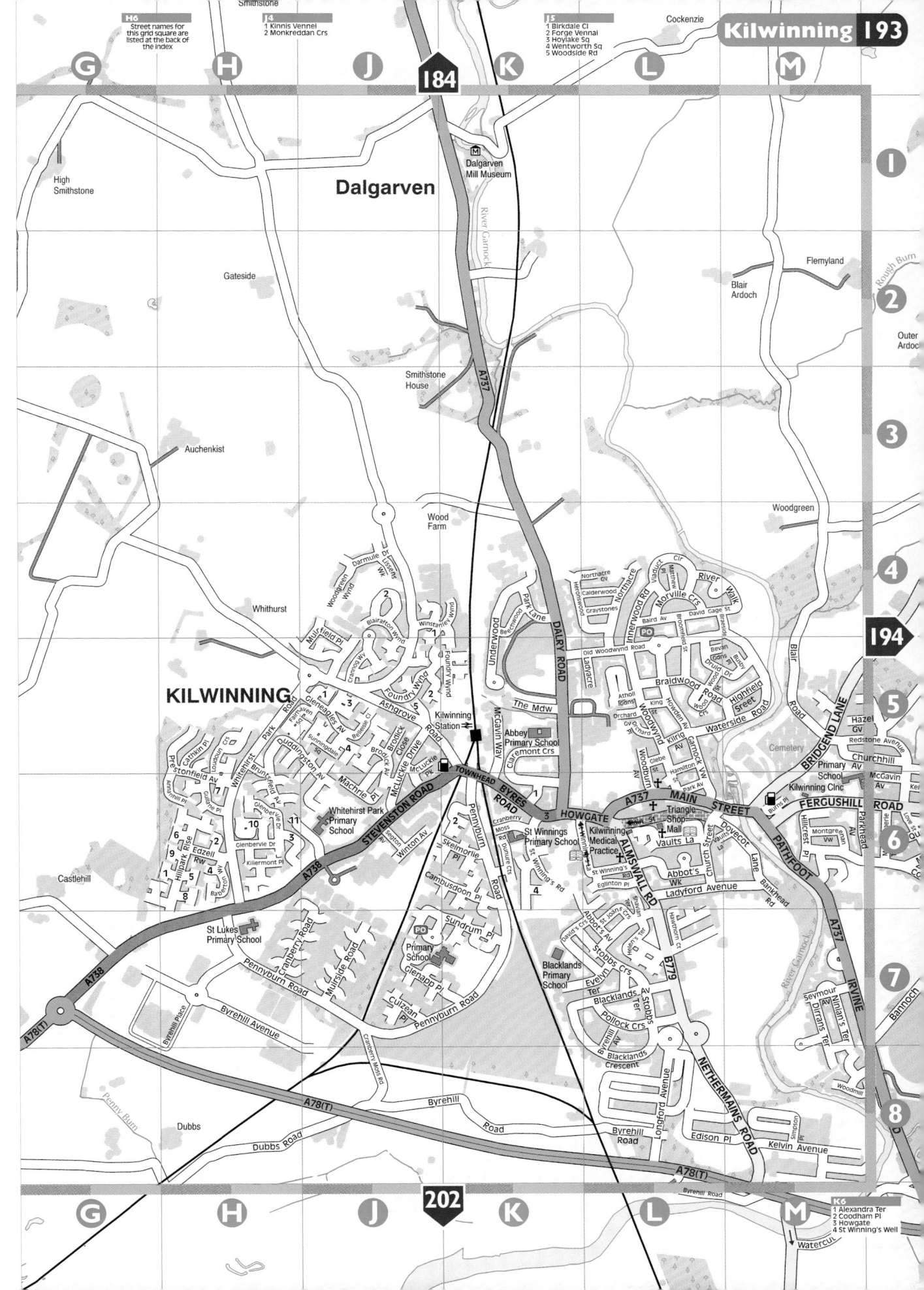

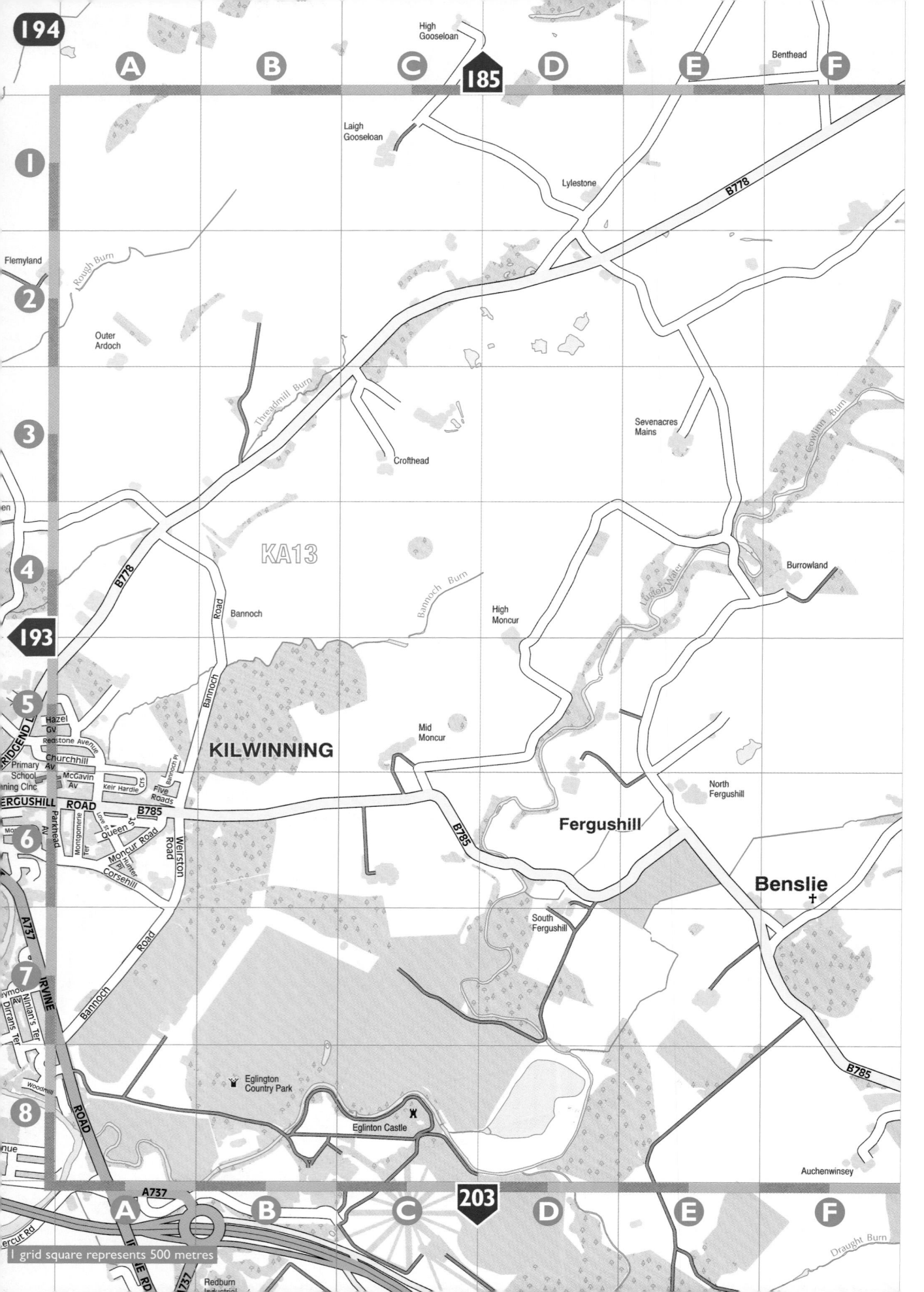

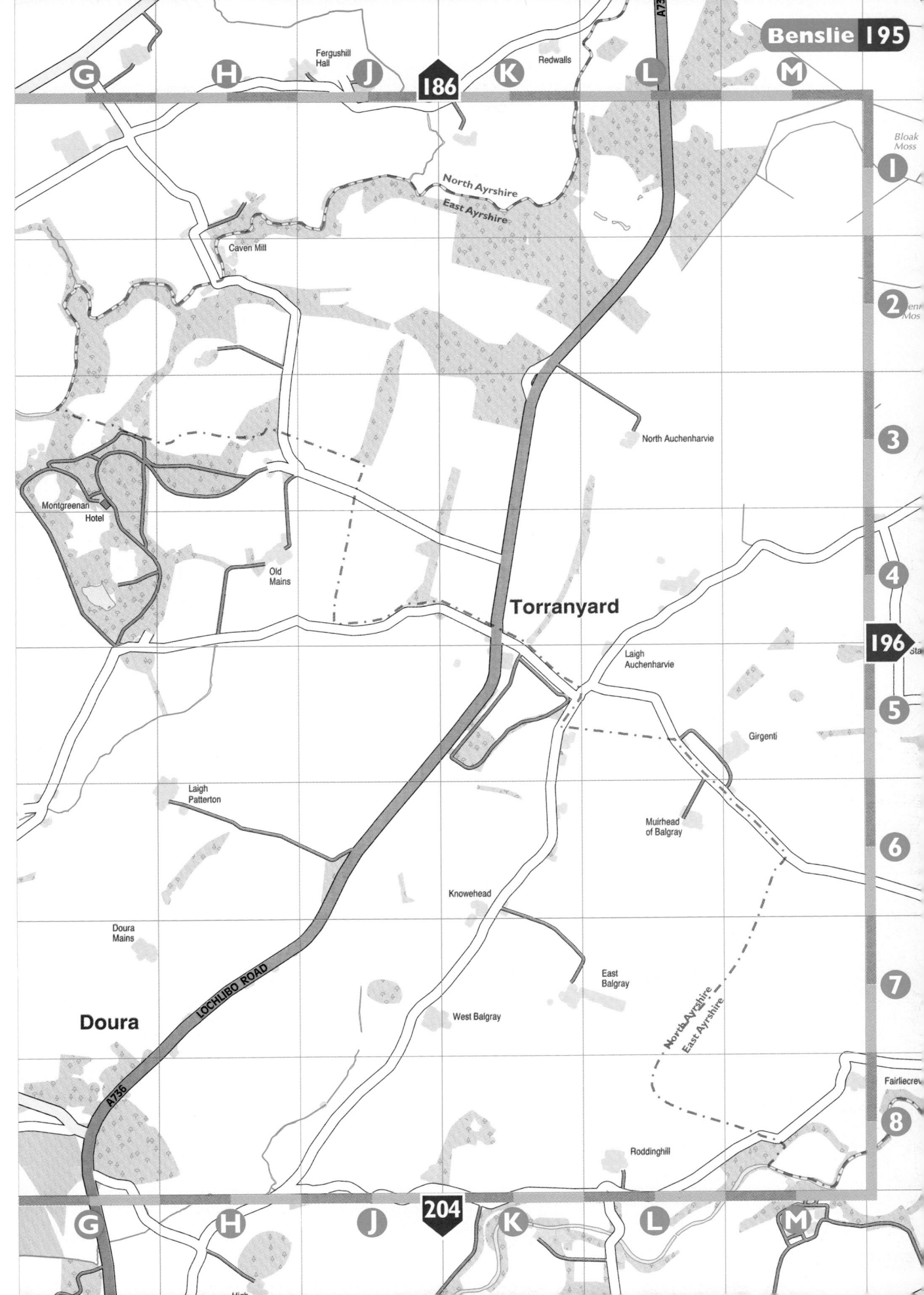

G H J K L M

Fergushill Hall

Redwalls

186

Bloak Moss

I

Glenn Moss

2

North Ayrshire
East Ayrshire

Caven Mill

North Auchenharvie

3

Montgreenan Hotel

Old Mains

4

Torranyard

196

Sta

Laigh Auchenharvie

5

Girgenti

Laigh Patterton

Muirhead of Balgray

6

Knowehead

Doura Mains

7

East Balgray

Doura

LOCHLIBO ROAD

West Balgray

North Ayrshire
East Ayrshire

A736

Fairliecrev

8

Roddinghill

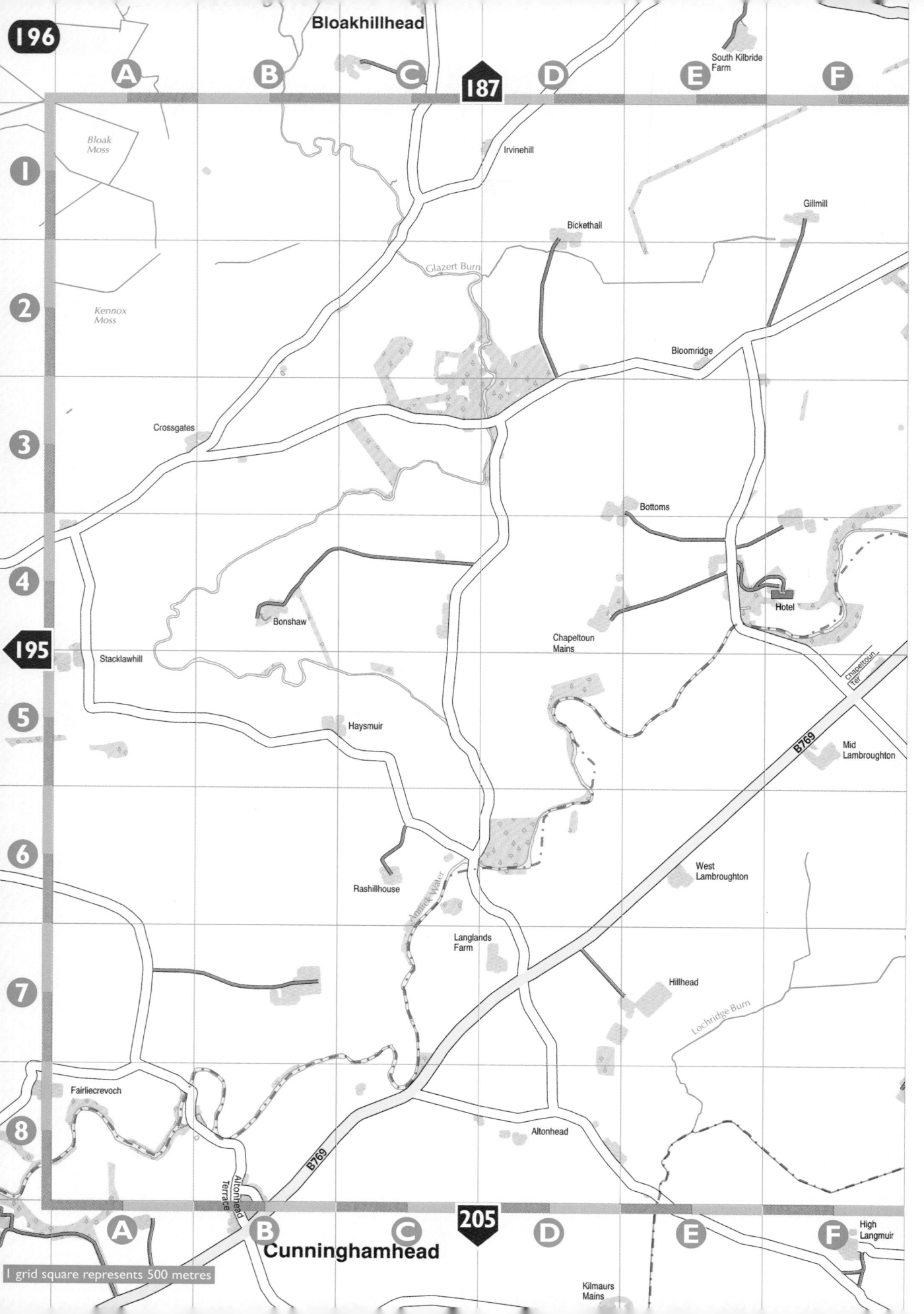

Bloakhillhead

A   B   C   **187**   D   E   F

1

Bloak Moss

Irvinehill

South Kilbride Farm

Gillmill

Bickethall

Glazert Burn

2

Kennox Moss

Bloomridge

3

Crossgates

Bottoms

4

Bonshaw

Hotel

Chapeltoun Mains

Stacklawhill

5

Haysmuir

Mid Lambroughton

Chapeltoun Ter

B769

6

Rashillhouse

West Lambroughton

Annick Water

Langlands Farm

7

Hillhead

Lochridge Burn

Fairliecrevoch

8

Altonhead

B769

Altonhead Terrace

A   B   **205**   C   D   E   F   High Langmuir

Cunninghamhead

Kilmaurs Mains

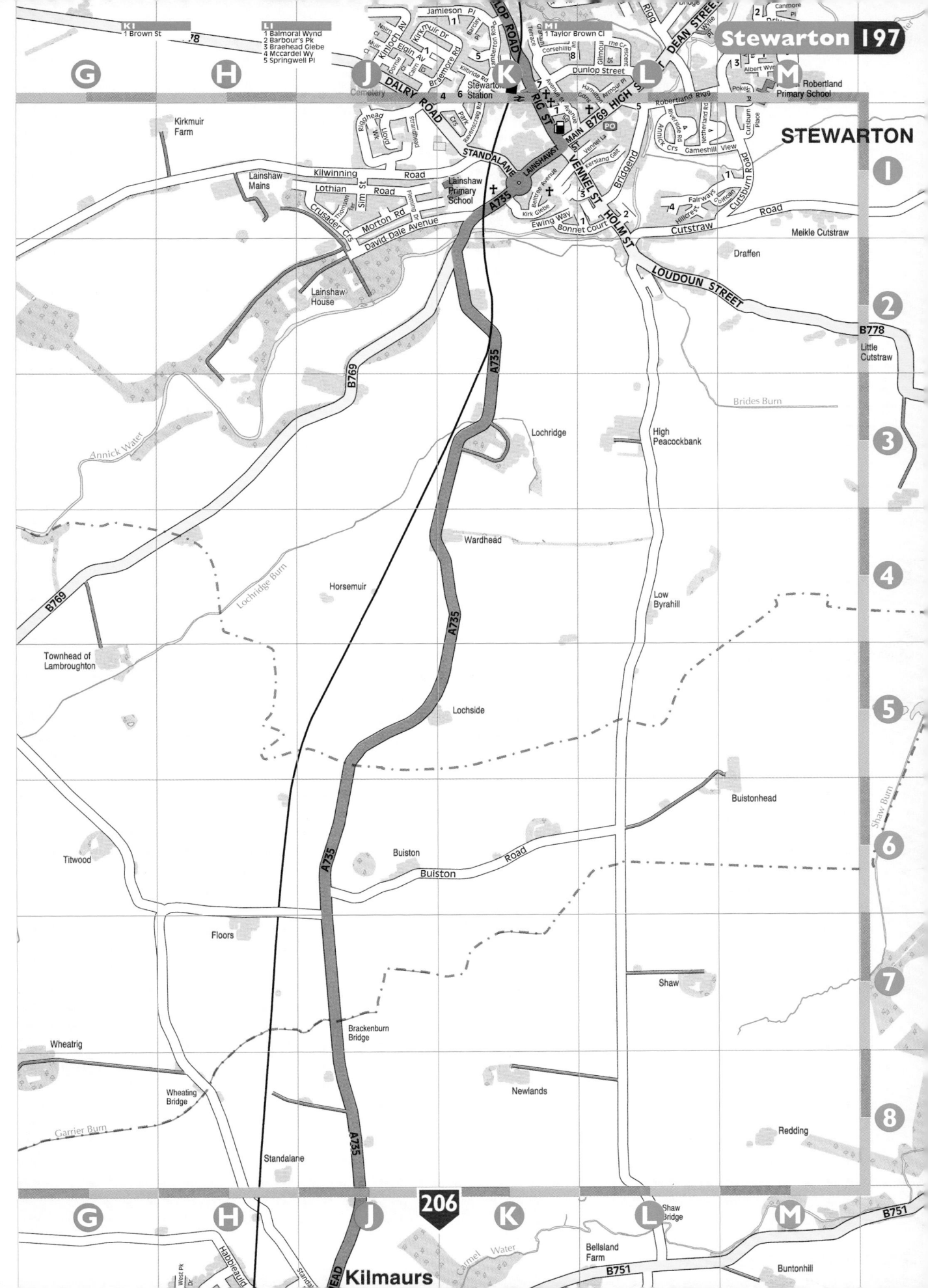

STEWARTON

Kilmaurs

K1
1 Brown St

L1
1 Balmoral Wynd
2 Barbour's Pk
3 Braehead Glebe
4 Mccardel Wy
5 Springwell Pl

M1
1 Taylor Brown Cl

Kirkmuir Farm

Lainshaw Mains

Kilwinning Road

Lothian Road

Crusader Crs

David Dale Avenue

Morton Rd

Lainshaw House

Lainshaw Primary School

DALRY ROAD

STANDALANE

LAINSHAW ST

RIG ST

HOLM ST

VENNEL ST

HIGH ST

MAIN ST

DEAN STREET

Dunlop Street

Bridgend

LOUDOUN STREET

Cutstraw Road

Draffen

Meikle Cutstraw

Little Cutstraw

B778

Brides Burn

High Peacockbank

Lochridge

Robertland Primary School

Annick Water

B769

Lochridge Burn

Wardhead

Horsemuir

Low Byrahill

Townhead of Lambroughton

Lochside

Buistonhead

Shaw Burn

Titwood

Buiston

Buiston Road

Floors

Shaw

Wheatrig

Brackenburn Bridge

Newlands

Wheating Bridge

Garrier Burn

Standalane

Shaw Bridge

Redding

Bellsland Farm

Buntonhill

B751

A735

B769

G H I J K L M

1 2 3 4 5 6 7 8

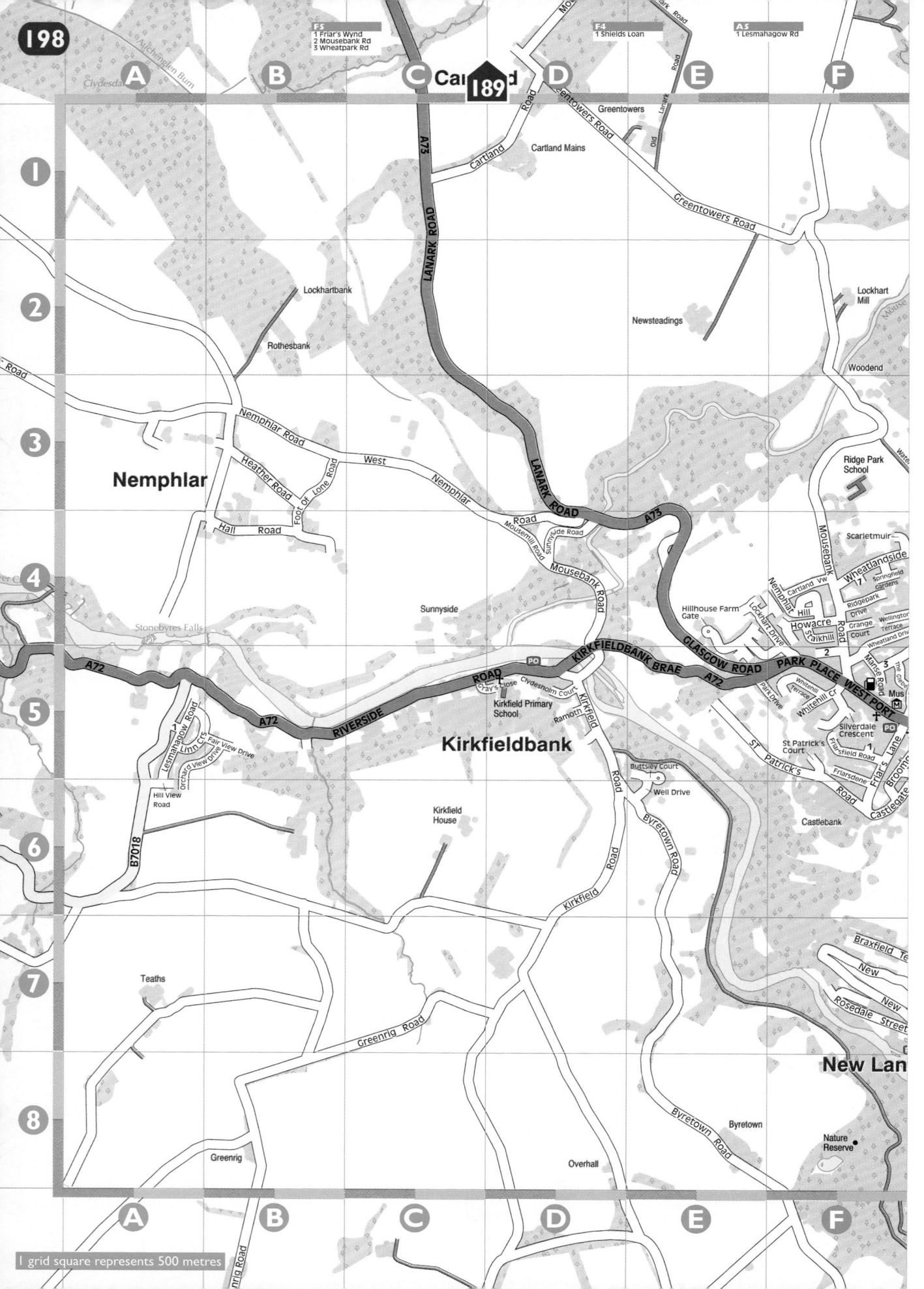

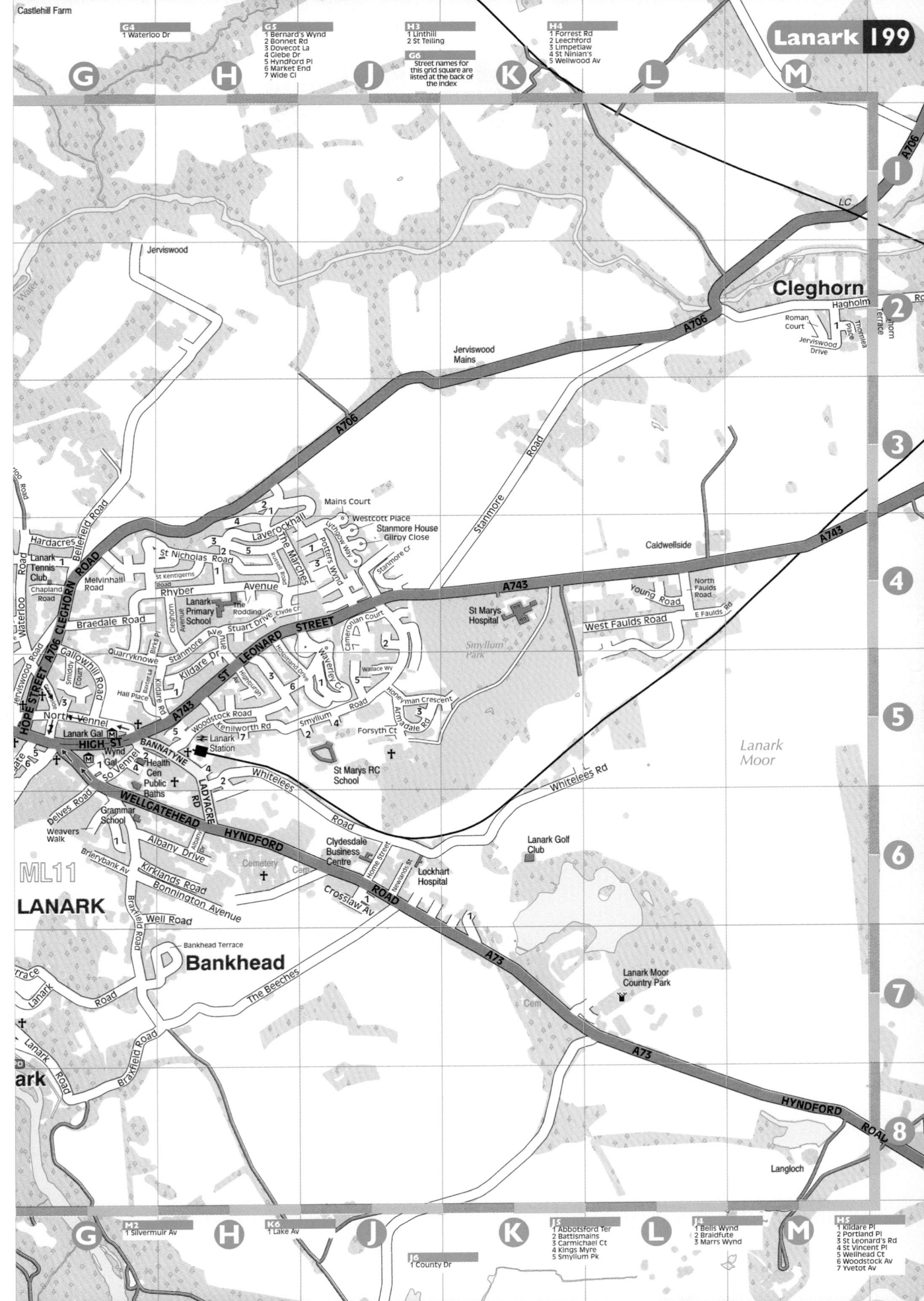

Castlehill Farm

G H J K L M

I

Jerviswood

Cleghorn

Roman
Court

Hagholm

Thorniea
Place

Jerviswood
Drive

Cleghorn
Terrace

LC

RC

2

A706

Jerviswood
Mains

Stanmore Road

3

A706

A743

Caldwellside

4

Hardacres
Bellefield Road

Lanark
Tennis
Club

Chapland
Road

Waterloo
Road

Melvinhall
Road

St Nicholas Road

St Kentigerns
Road

Rhyber

Cleghorn
Avenue

Braedale Road

Mains Court

Laverockhall

The Marches

Westcott Place
Stanmore House
Gilroy Close

Lythgow Way

Potters Wynd

Stanmore Cr

Russell Way

Young Road

West Faulds Road

North
Faulds
Road

E Faulds Rd

St Marys
Hospital

Lanark
Primary
School

The
Rodding

Clyde Cr

Stuart Drive

ST LEONARD STREET

Cameronian Court

Smyllum
Park

Lanark
Moor

5

quarryknowe

Stanmore Av

Kildare Dr

Hogandund Drive

Highburgh Rd

2

Waverley C

Wallace Wy

Honeyman Crescent

Armadale Rd

Kildare
Rd

Hall Place

Smiddy
Court

Gallowhill Road

A706 A743 CLEGHORN ROAD

Jerviswood Rd

Hope Street

North Vennel

Lanark Gal

HIGH ST

BANNATYNE

So Vennel

Gal

Health
Cen
Public
Baths

Woodstock Road

Kenilworth Rd

Smyllum
Road

Smyllum

Forsyth Ct

Lanark
Station

St Marys RC
School

Whitelees Rd

6

Delves Road

Brierybank Av

Braxfield
Road

Weavers
Walk

Grammar
School

Albany Drive

LADYACRE RD

WELLGATEHEAD

HYNDFORD

Whitelees

Road

Home Street

Nethands St

Lanark Golf
Club

ML11

Kirklands Road

Bonnington Avenue

Cemetery

Cem

Clydesdale
Business
Centre

Crosslaw Av

ROAD

Lockhart
Hospital

LANARK

Well Road

Bankhead Terrace

Bankhead

The Beeches

A73

Lanark Moor
Country Park

Cem

7

Lanark
Road

Braxfield Road

Terrace

ark
Road

A73

HYNDFORD
ROAD

8

Langloch

Yvetot Av

G H J K L M

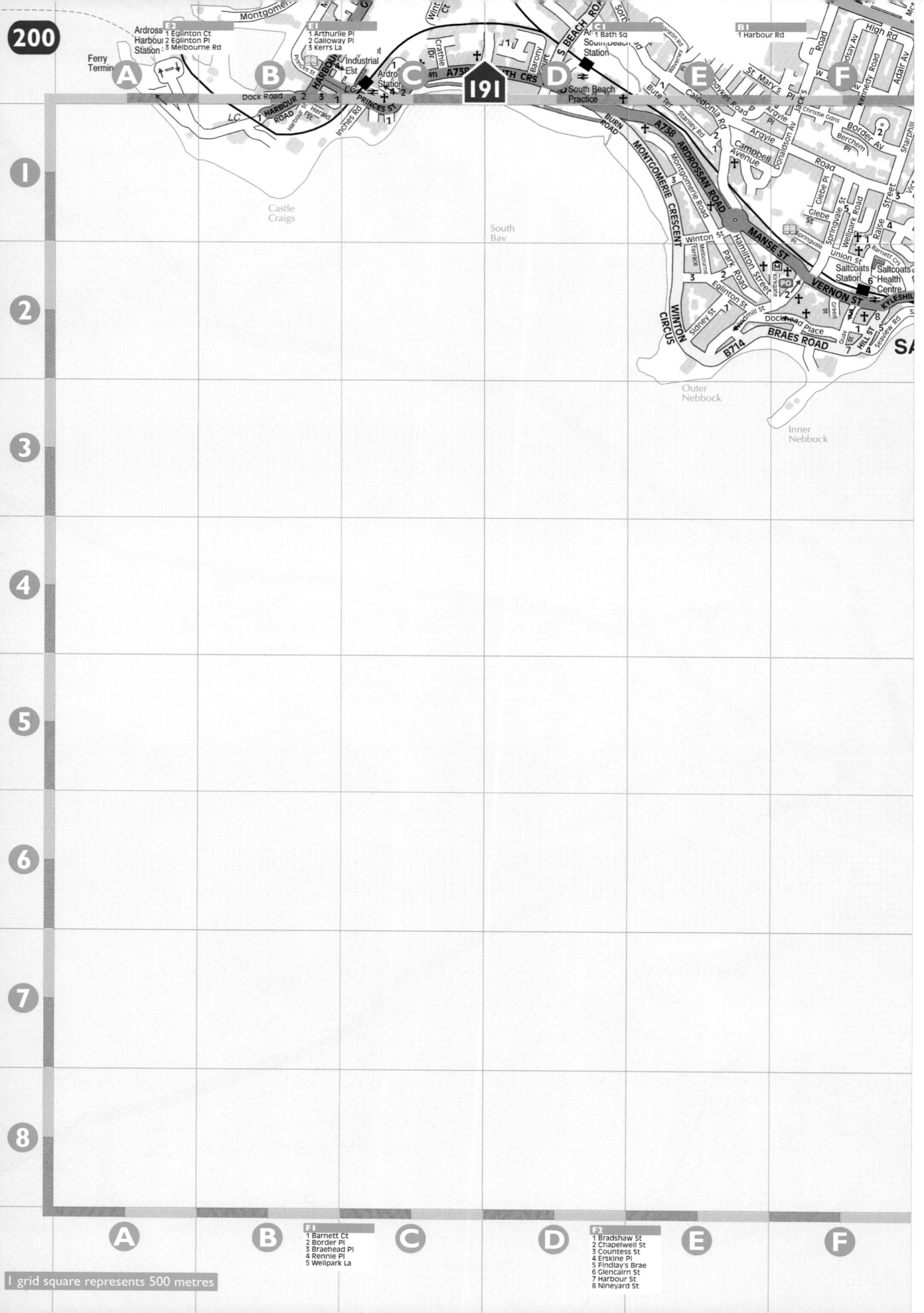

191

Ardross
Harbour
Station
E2
1 Eglinton Ct
2 Eglinton Pl
3 Melbourne Rd

Ferry
Termin

Montgomer

B1
1 Arthurlie Pl
2 Galloway Pl
3 Kerrs La

B1
1 Harbour Rd

Dock Road

Castle
Craigs

South
Bay

Industrial
Est

Princes St

Inches Rd

A73

TH CRS

Baron

S BEACH
RD

South Beach
Practice

A1 Bath Sq
South Beach
Station

St Mary's

Manse St

Montgomerie Rd

BURN
ROAD

ARDROSSAN ROAD

A738

MONTGOMERIE CRESCENT

Campbell
Avenue

Argyle
Av

Border
Av

High Rd

Winton
St

Melbourne
Terrace

Park
Road

Hamilton
Street

Winton St

Glebe Pl

Glebe
St

Union St

Saltcoats
Station

Vernon St

VERNON ST

Saltcoats
Health
Centre

SA

WINTON
CIRCUS

Sidney St

Eglinton St

Dockhead
Place

BRAES ROAD

B714

Outer
Nebbock

Inner
Nebbock

A

B

C

D

E

F

A

B

C

D

E

F

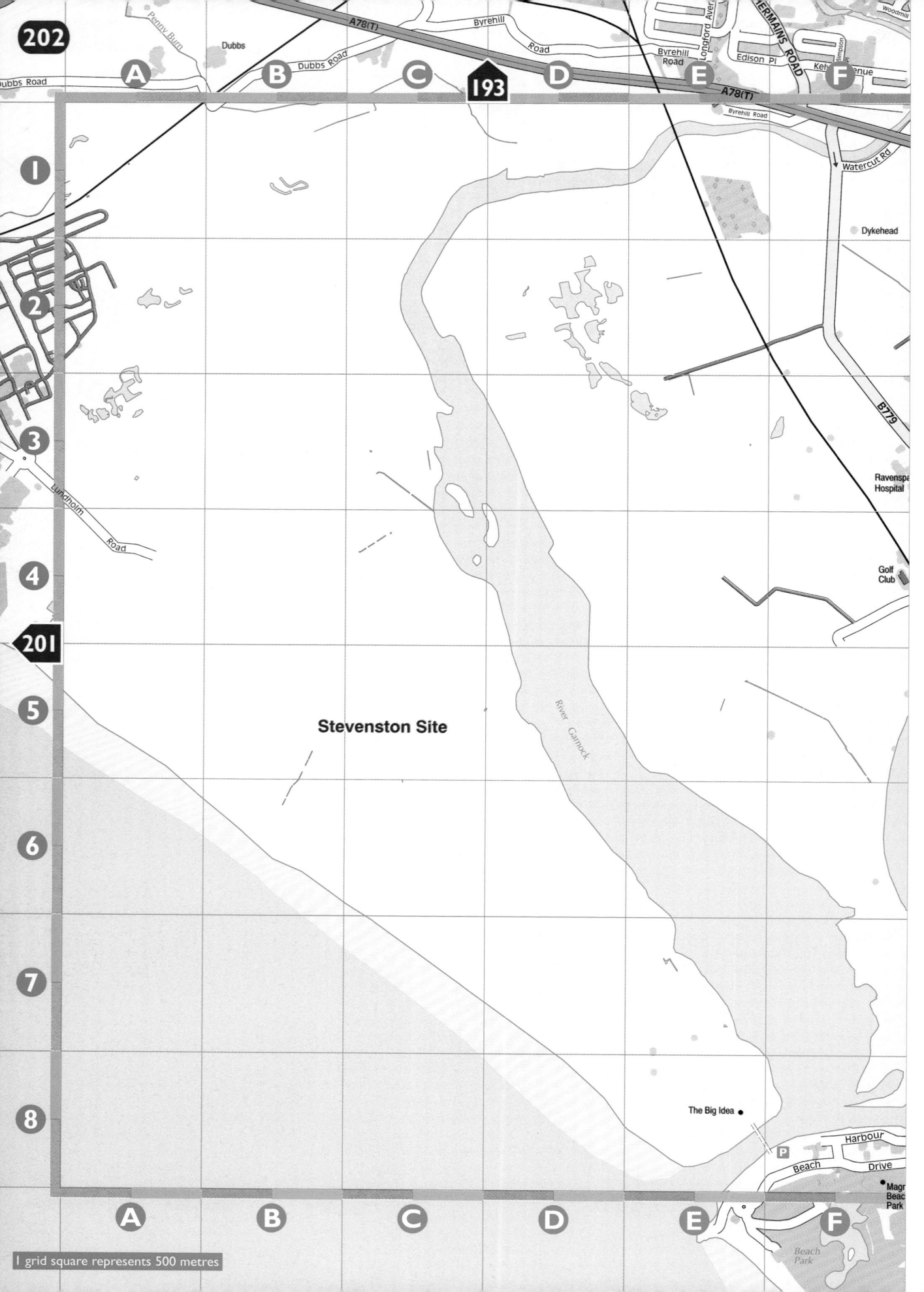

A B C 193 D E A78(T) F

Dubbs Road
Penny Burn
Dubbs
Dubbs Road
Byrehill Road
A78(T)
Byrehill Road
Longford Aver
Edison Pl
Kel
Simpson
enue
MERMAINS ROAD
Woodmill
Byrehill Road

1

Watercut Rd

Dykehead

2

3

Lundholm Road

Ravenspa
Hospital

4

Golf
Club

201

5

Stevenston Site

River Garnock

6

B7779

7

8

The Big Idea

P Harbour

Beach Drive

Magr
Beach
Park

Beach
Park

A B C D E F

1 grid square represents 500 metres

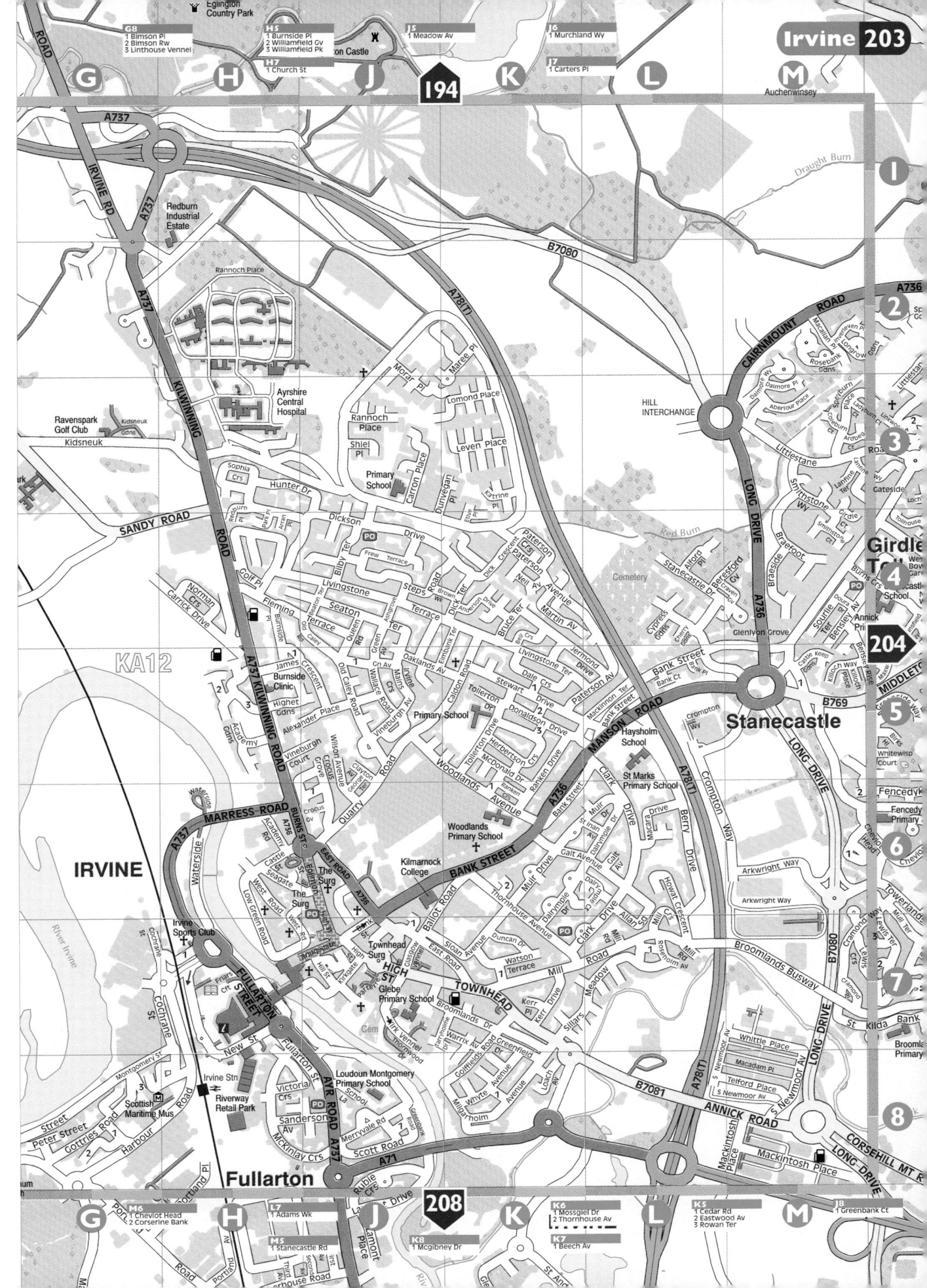

I grid square represents 500 metres

A7
1 Kilpatrick Pl
2 Lewis Ri
3 Lewis Wynd
4 St Kilda Pl

A6
1 Kilsyth Crs
2 Pentland Pl

A5
1 Blaven Head

A3
1 Bowmore Ct
2 Cardow Crs

A   B   C   195   D   E   F

1

2   A736

3

4   203   PO

5

6

7   B7080

8

Sourlie

High Armsheugh

Holehouse

Braehead

Middleton

Overton Farm

Springbank Gdns

Lawthorn

Perceton

Perceton Mains

Cardow Crescent

Ardmore Court

Littlestane

Gateside

Girdle Toll

West Bowhouse Garden

Stanecastle School

Annick Primary Sch

MIDDLETON ROAD

Greenside Way

Whitewisp Court

East Bowhouse Head

Fortacre Place

Cairngorm Court

Ramstane Place

B769

Warwickdale

Drummuir

Fencedyke Way

Fencedyke Primary School

Bourtreehill Health Cen

St John Ogilvie Primary School

Moorfoot

Broomlands

Towerlands Rd

Heatherstane Bank

Primary School

Heatherstane Way

Hillshaw Green

Bourtreehill

Springside Primary School

Towerlands Road

Garrier Road

Station Rd

B7081   MAIN ROAD

Broomlands BusWay

Piadda Av

KA11

Broomlands Primary School

Gigha Ter

Station Brae

Cemetery

MAIN STREET

Dreghorn Primary School

Dreghorn

Corsehill

Greenwood Acadamy

Annick Water

Annick Drive

TOWNFOOT

DUNDONALD RD

Greenwood

LONG DRIVE

Corsehill

CORSEHILL MT ROAD B708

LONG DRIVE

Place

B2
1 Ormiston Pl

B3
1 Strathmore Pk

B6
1 Bencleuch Pl

B8
1 Broomlands Rd
2 Macrobert Av

C7
1 Glenleith Pl
2 Hopetoun Bank
3 Lowther Bank
4 Sidlaw Foot

A   B   209   C   D   E   F

A71

1 Garelet Pl
2 Shalloch Pl

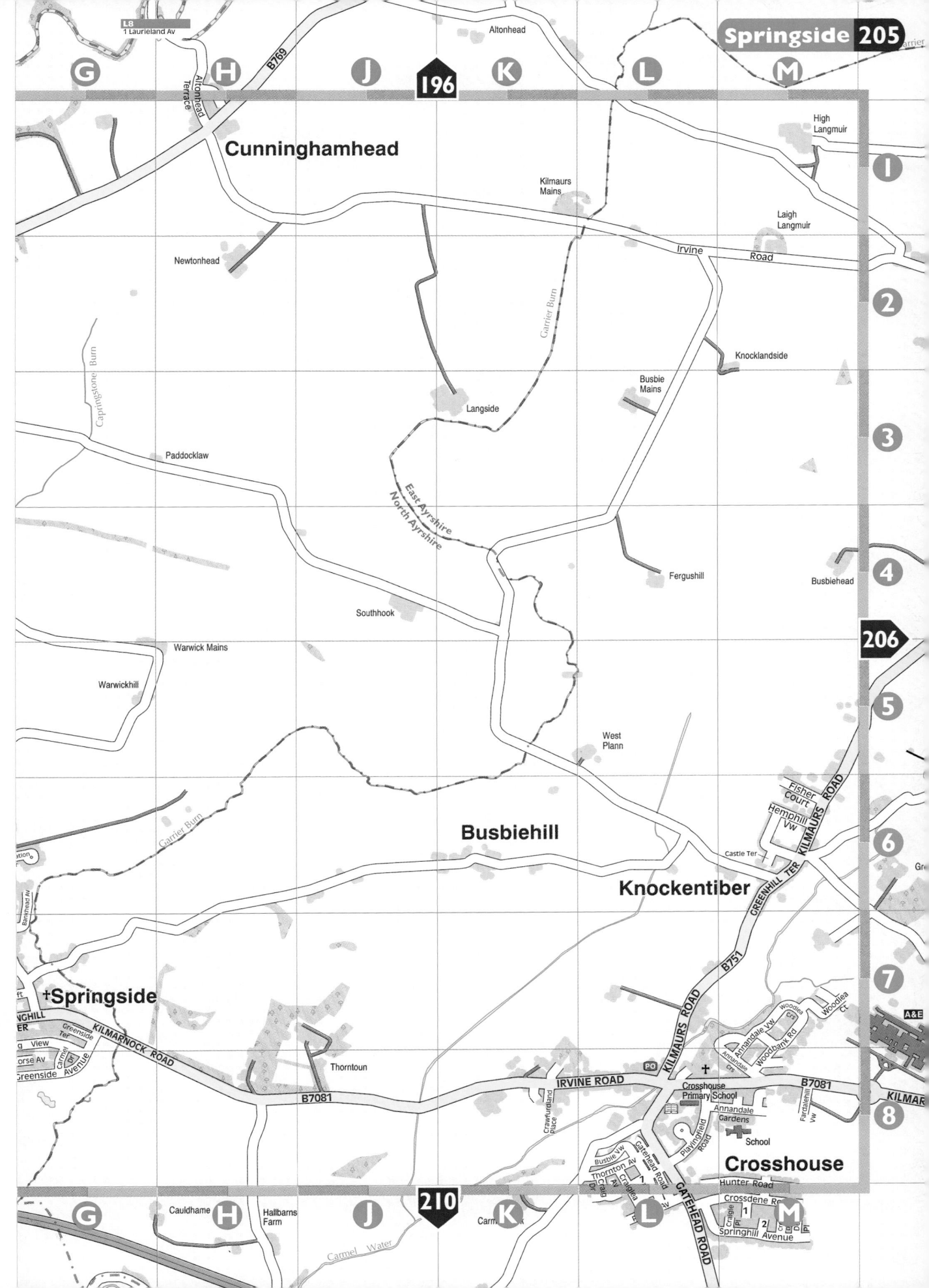

G   H   J   196   K   L   M

I

Altonhead

L8
1 Laurieland Av

Altonhead Terrace

B769

Cunninghamhead

Kilmaurs Mains

High Langmuir

Laigh Langmuir

Irvine Road

2

Newtonhead

Garrier Burn

Capingstone Burn

Knocklandside

Busbie Mains

3

Langside

East Ayrshire
North Ayrshire

Paddocklaw

Fergushill

Busbiehead

4

Southhook

206

Warwick Mains

Warwickhill

West Plann

5

Garrier Burn

Fisher Court

Kilmaurs Road

Hemphill Vw

6

Busbiehill

Castle Ter

Greenhill Ter

Knockentiber

7

A&E

⁺Springside

Woodlea Ct

Woodlea Ct

NGHILL
TER

Greenside
Ter

KILMARNOCK ROAD

Greenside
View

orse Av

Carmel
Dr

Avenue

Greenside

Thorntoun

PO

KILMAURS ROAD

B7751

Annandale Vw

Woodbank Rd

Annandale Crs

Fardalehill Vw

B7081

KILMAR

8

Crawfurdland Place

B7081

IRVINE ROAD

Crosshouse Primary School

Annandale Gardens

School

Busbie Vw

Thornton Av

Craigie Dr

Playingfield Road

GATEHEAD ROAD

Crosshouse

Hunter Road

Crossdene Rd

G   H   J   210   K   L   M

Cauldhame

Hallbarns Farm

Carm

Craigie 1
2

Springhill Avenue

Carmel Water

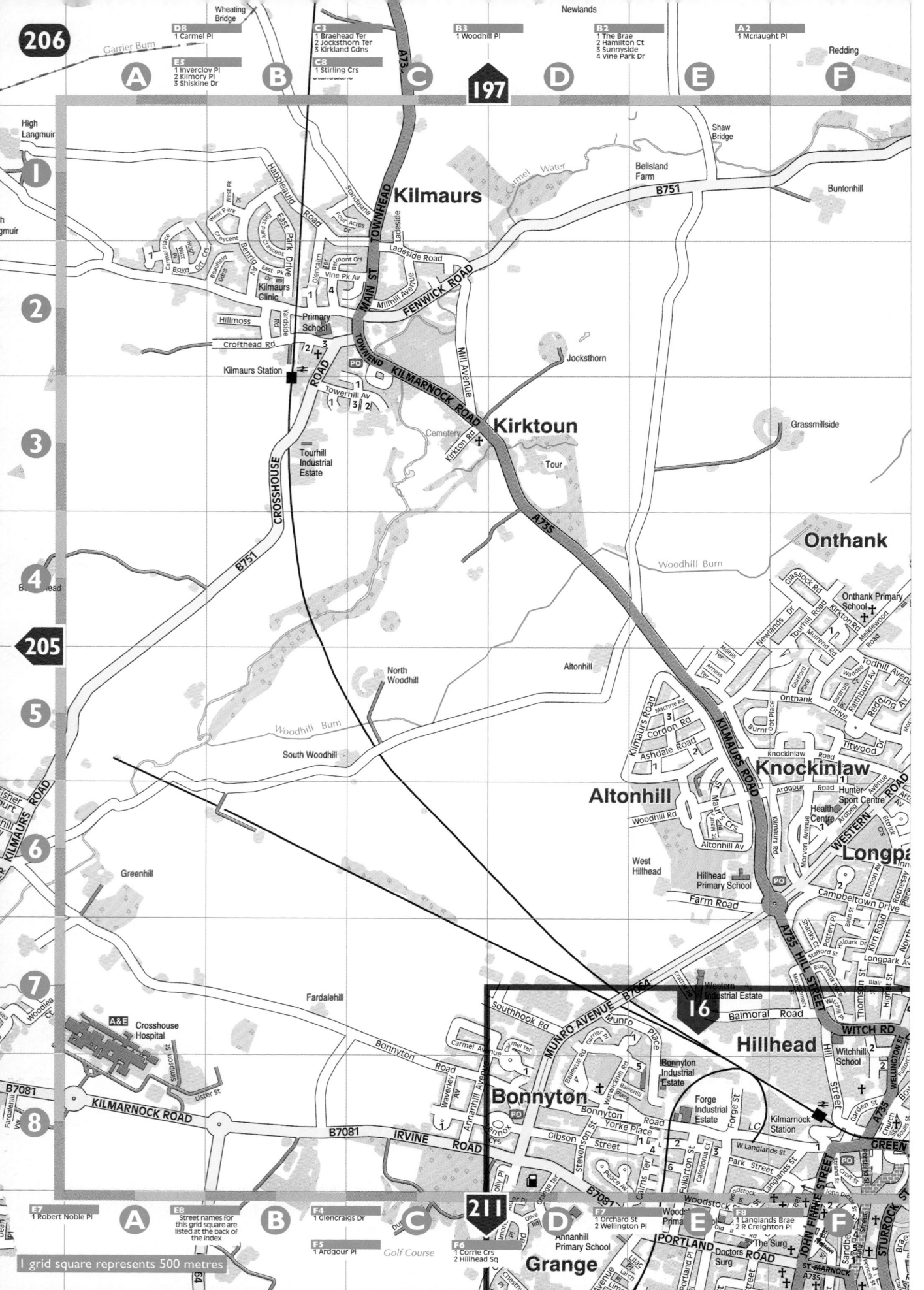

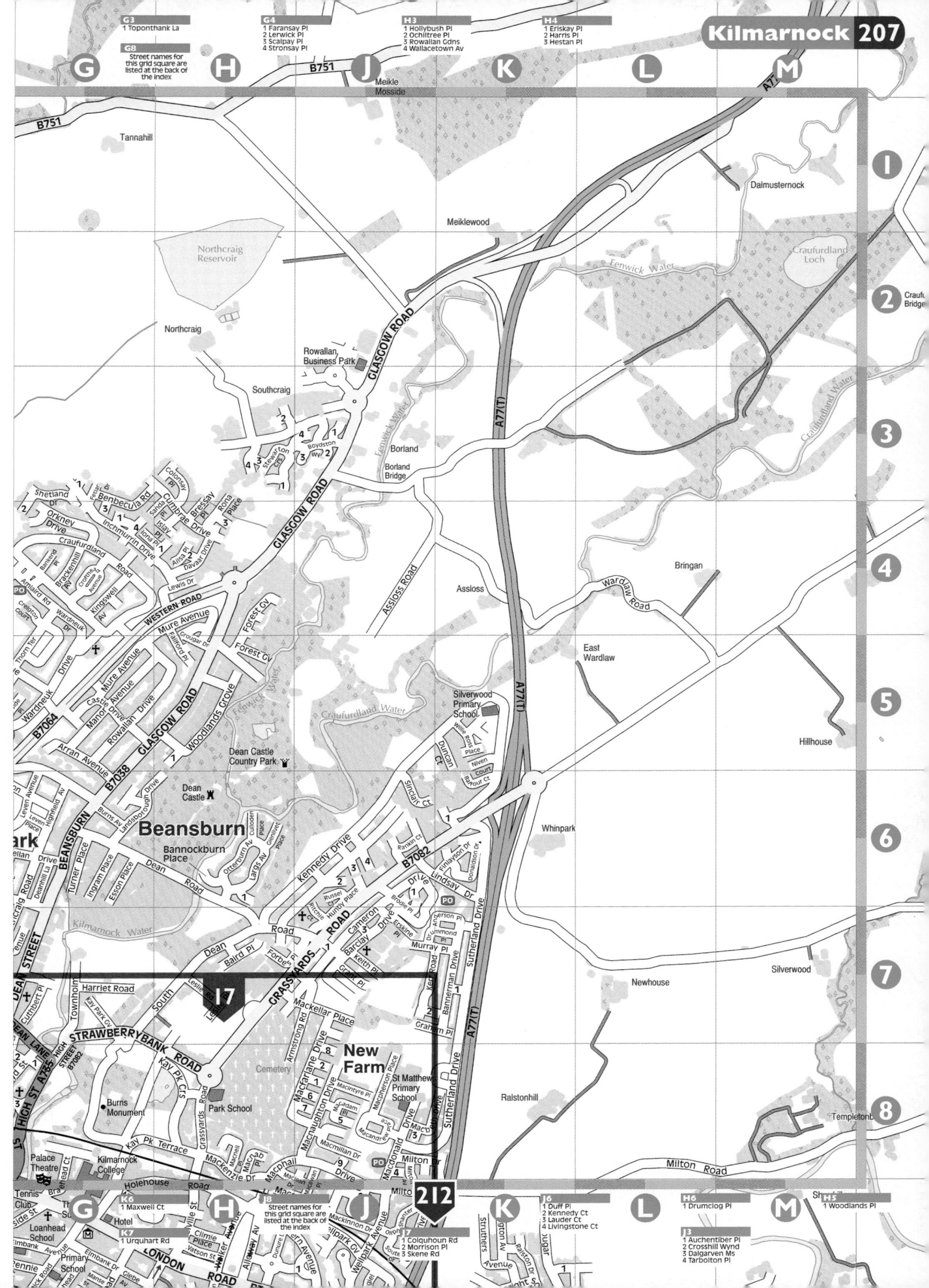

G H J K L M

Tannahill

Meikle
Mosside

Meiklewood

Dalmusternock

Craufurdland
Loch

Crauf
Bridge

Northcraig
Reservoir

Fenwick Water

Craufurdland Water

Northcraig

Rowallan
Business Park

Southcraig

Borland

Borland
Bridge

GLASGOW ROAD

Assloss Road

A77(T)

Assloss

Wardlaw Road

Bringan

Shetland
Dr

Orkney
Drive

Benbecula Rd

Inchmurrin Drive

Cumbrae Drive

Bressay

Rona
Place

Iona Pl

Ailsa Dr

Davar Drive

Stewarton
Cres

Boydston
Wy

Craufurdland
Road

Lewis Dr

Forest Gv

Forest Gv

WESTERN ROAD

Mure Avenue

Crougar Dr

Fairford Pl

East
Wardlaw

Silverwood
Primary
School

Willie Ross
Place

Hillhouse

Mure Avenue

Castle Drive

Manor Drive

Rowallan Drive

GLASGOW ROAD

Woodlands Grove

Fenwick Water

Craufurdland Water

Dean Castle
Country Park

Niven
Court

Arbour Ct

Duncan
Drive

B7064

Arran Avenue

B7038

Lairdsborough Drive

Dean Castle

Beansburn

Bannockburn
Place

Culloden
Place

Otterburn Av

Largs Av

Glenfeet
Place

Kennedy Drive

Sinclair Ct

Rankin Ct

B7082

Whinpark

Leven Avenue

Leven
Highfield

Leven
Place

Burns Av

Dean Road

Ritchie PI

Russel
Gras

Hurdly Place

Finlayson Dr

Donaldson Dr

Lindsay Dr

Brodie Pl

Silverwood

Turner Place

Ingram Place

Esson Place

Cameron
Drive

Anderson Pl

Drummond

Erskine

Murray Rd

Kerr Road

Bannerman Drive

Sutherland Drive

A77(T)

Newhouse

Kilmarnock Water

Dean
Road

Baird Pl

Forbes Pl

GRASSYARDS ROAD

Barclay Dr

Keith Pl

Grant Pl

I7

Harriet Road

STRAWBERRYBANK ROAD

South Townholm

Kay Park Cres

Mackellar Place

Armstrong Rd

Graham Pl

Ralstonhill

Templetonb

STRAWBERRYBANK ROAD

HIGH STREET

B7082

Kay Pk Crs

Cemetery

Macfarlane Drive

Macnaughton Drive

Macintyre Pl

McAdam Pl

Macpherson Place

**New
Farm**

St Matthews
Primary
School

Macanar Row

Burns
Monument

Park School

Kay Pk Terrace

Crossyards Road

Macdonald Drive

Macmillan Dr

Macdonald Drive

Milton Dr

St Matthews
Primary
School

Palace
Theatre

Kilmarnock
College

Holehouse Road

Macphail Drive

Macbeth

Macleod

Macandrew

Milton Road

Tennis
Club

212

LONDON ROAD

I 2 3 4 5 6 7 8

Fullarton

IRVINE

Magnum Beach Park

Scottish Maritime Mus

Riverway Retail Park

203

Heatherhouse Road

Portland Road

Marine Drive

Kyle Road

Ailsa Road

Kyle Road

Cunninghame

Lamont Drive

Lamont Place

Carson Dr

Gray

River Irvine

Glenbervie Wynd

St Andrews Way

Turnberry Wynd

Carnoustie Pl

Warrix

Riverside Way

Shewalton Road

Shewalton Road

Nature Reserve

Symington Pl

Brewster Pl

Murdoch Pl

Metcalfe Pl

Chalmers Place

Cemetery

Glasgow Golf Club

Marine Drive

Gailes

Gailes Rd

MOSS DRIVE B7080

Meadowhead Road

Meadowhead Industrial Estate

Dunlop Place

Meadowhead Av

Western Gailes Golf Club

Meadowhead Road

Irvine Bay

Auchengate Crescent

Dundonald Camp

216

Galles Br

1 grid square represents 500 metres

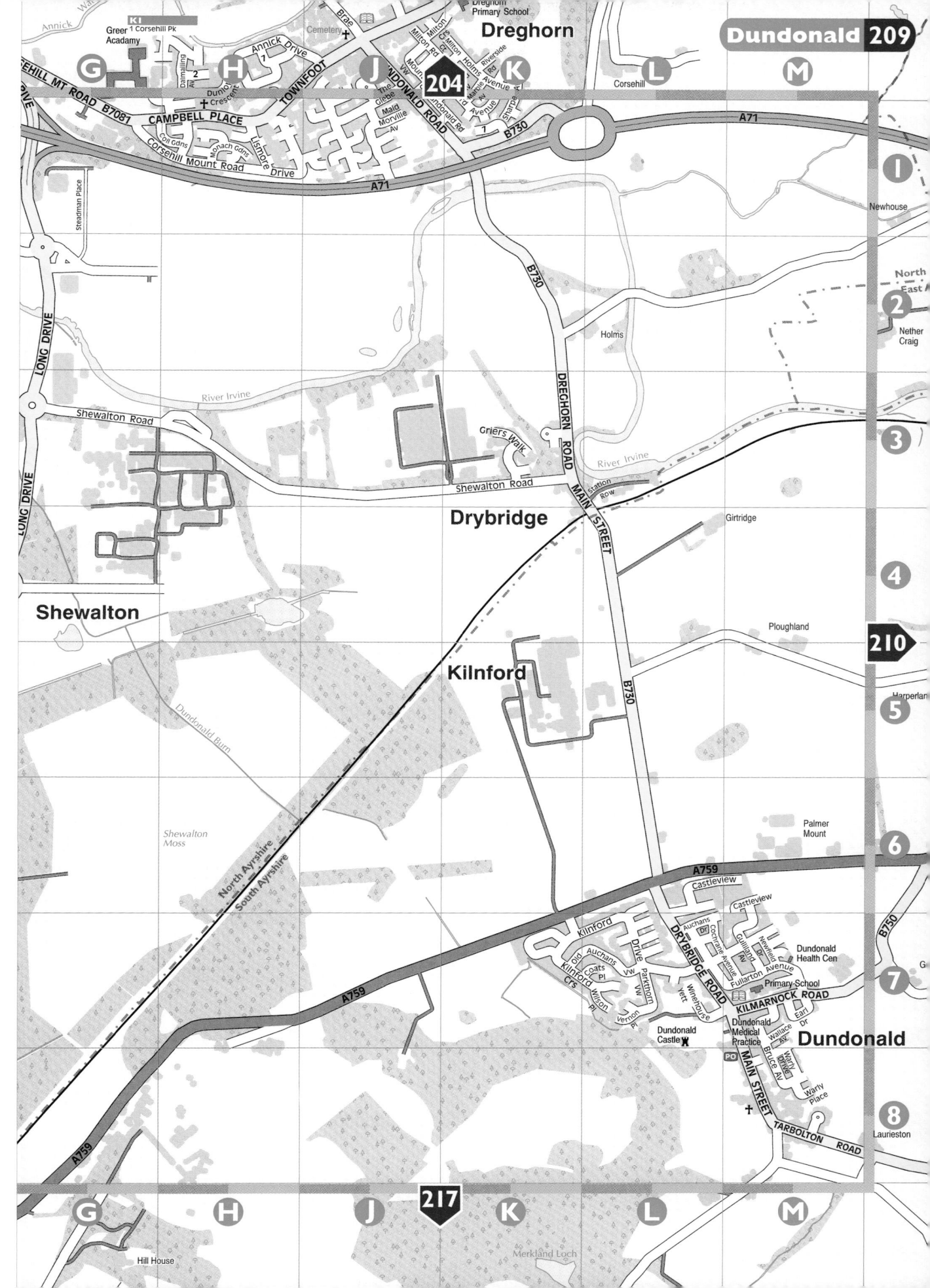

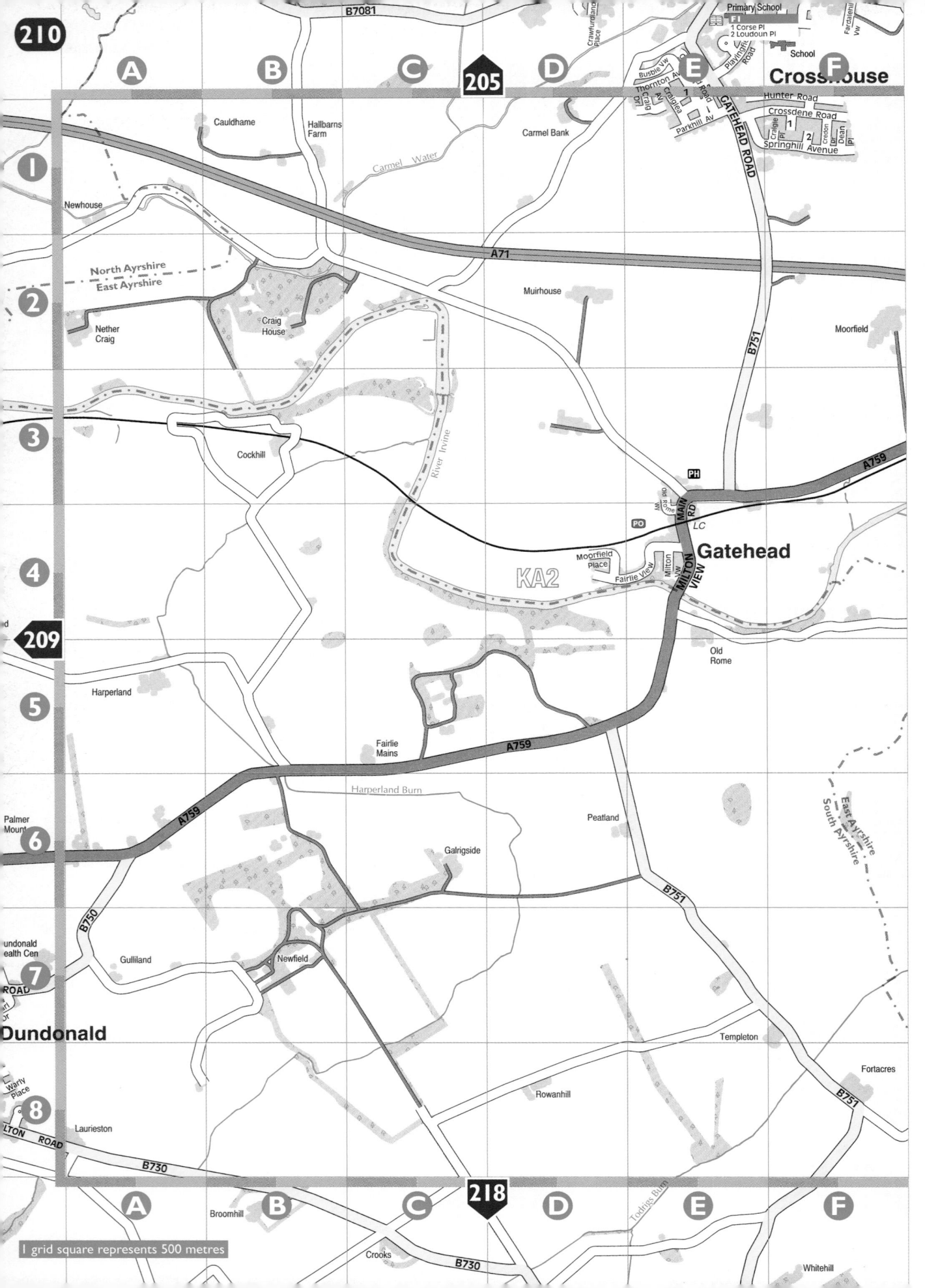

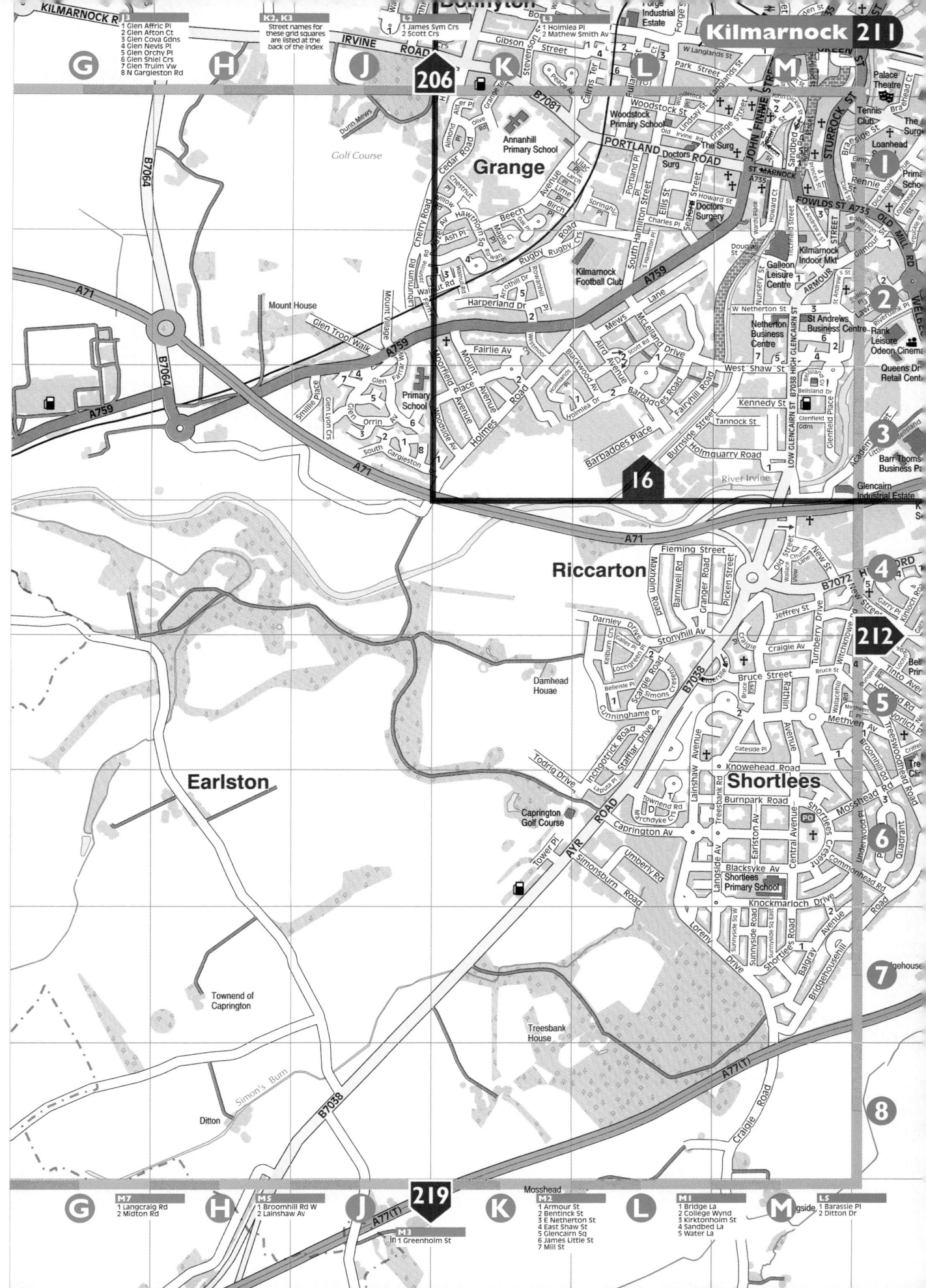

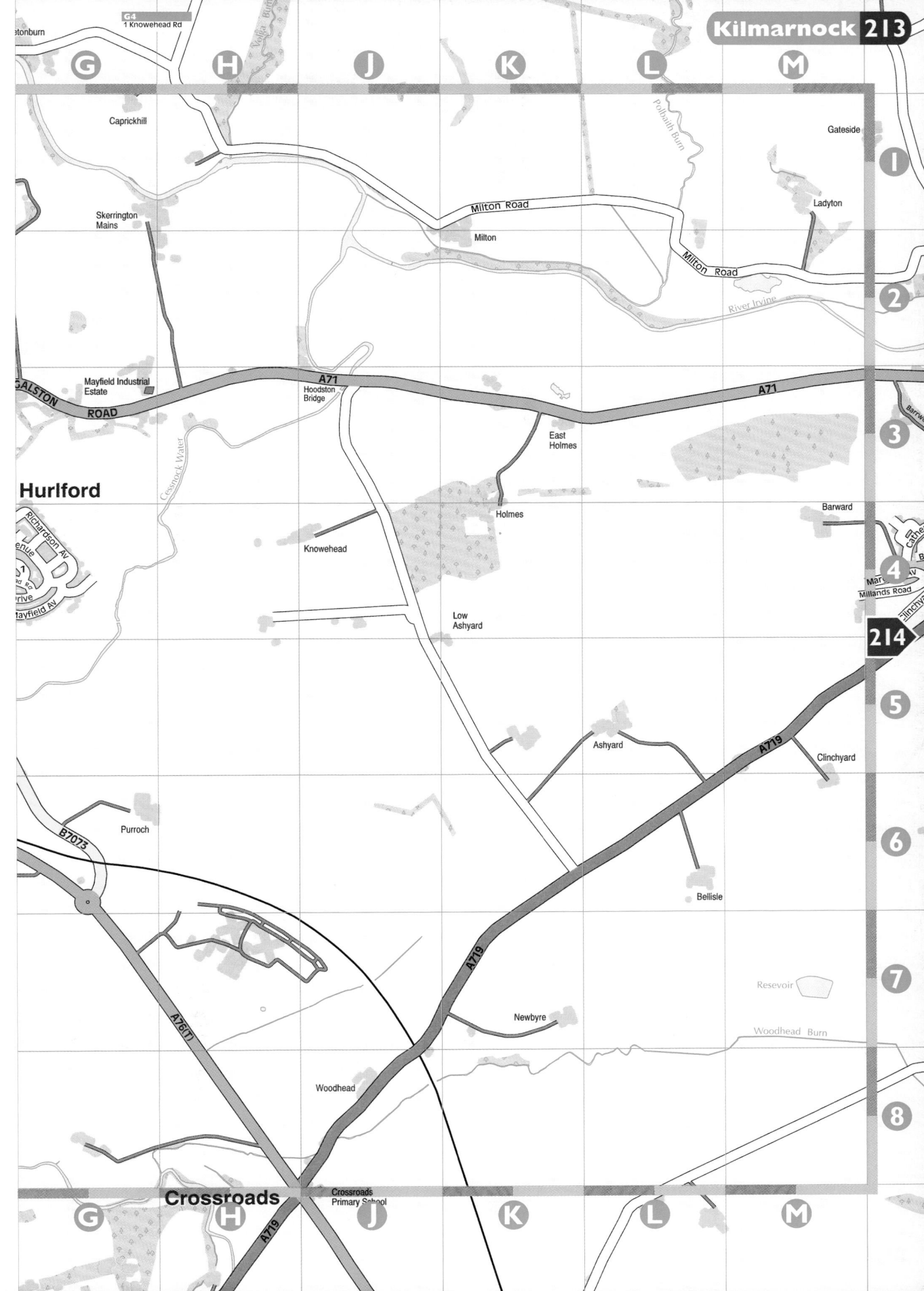

G H J K L M

CapricKhill

Gateside

1 Knowehead Rd
G4

Ladyton

Skerrington
Mains

Milton Road

Milton

Milton Road

River Irvine

Polbaith Burn

Mayfield Industrial
Estate

Hoodston
Bridge

A71

A71

Barrwo

GALSTON

ROAD

East
Holmes

Cessnock Water

Hurlford

Barward

Richardson AV

Knowehead

Holmes

Cathe

B

Mar

Millands Road

Clinchya

Mayfield AV

Drive

Low
Ashyard

214

Ashyard

A719

Clinchyard

B7073

Purroch

Bellisle

A719

A76(T)

Reservoir

Woodhead Burn

Newbyre

Woodhead

Crossroads

Crossroads
Primary School

G H J K L M

A719

I
2
3
4
5
6
7
8

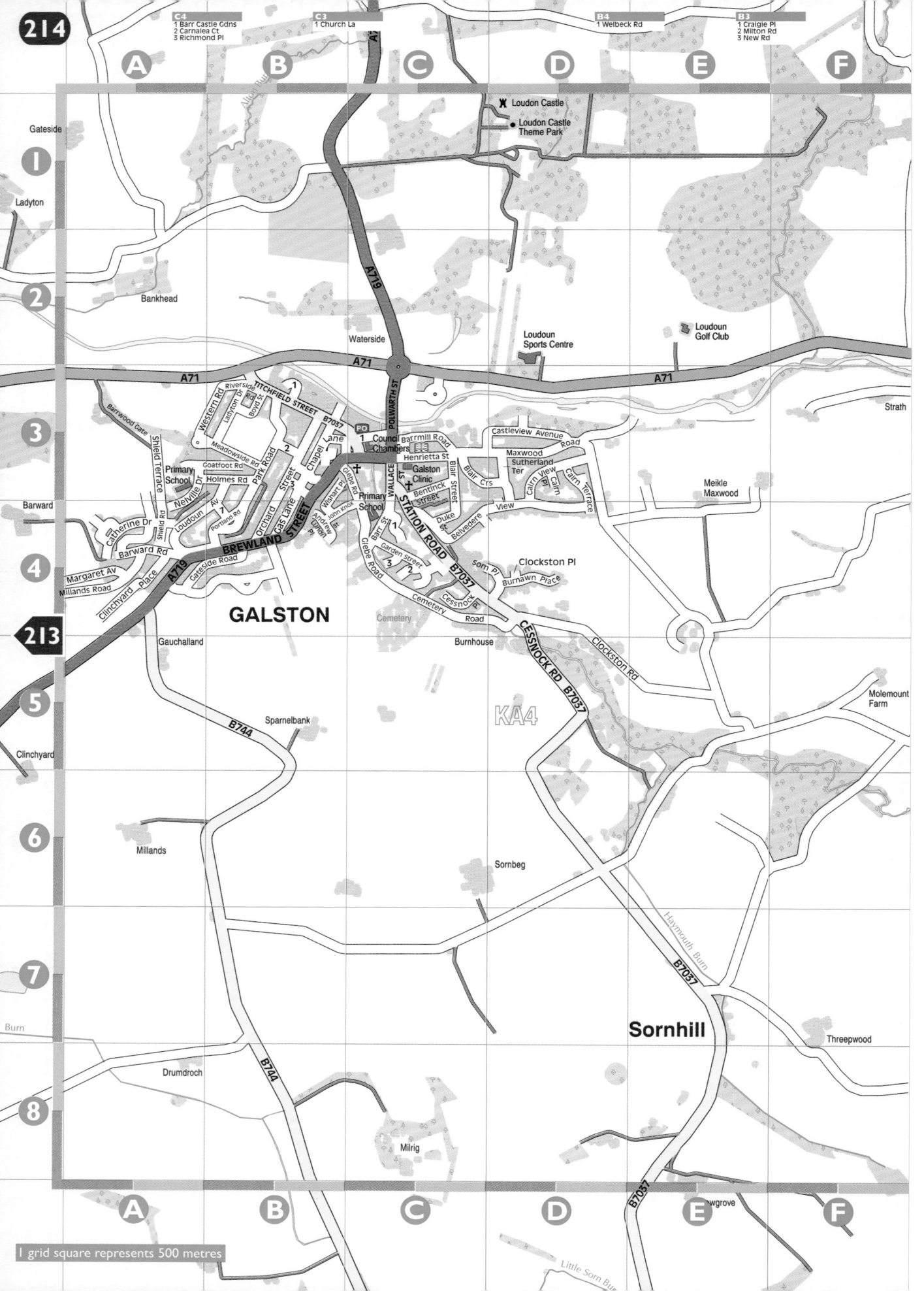

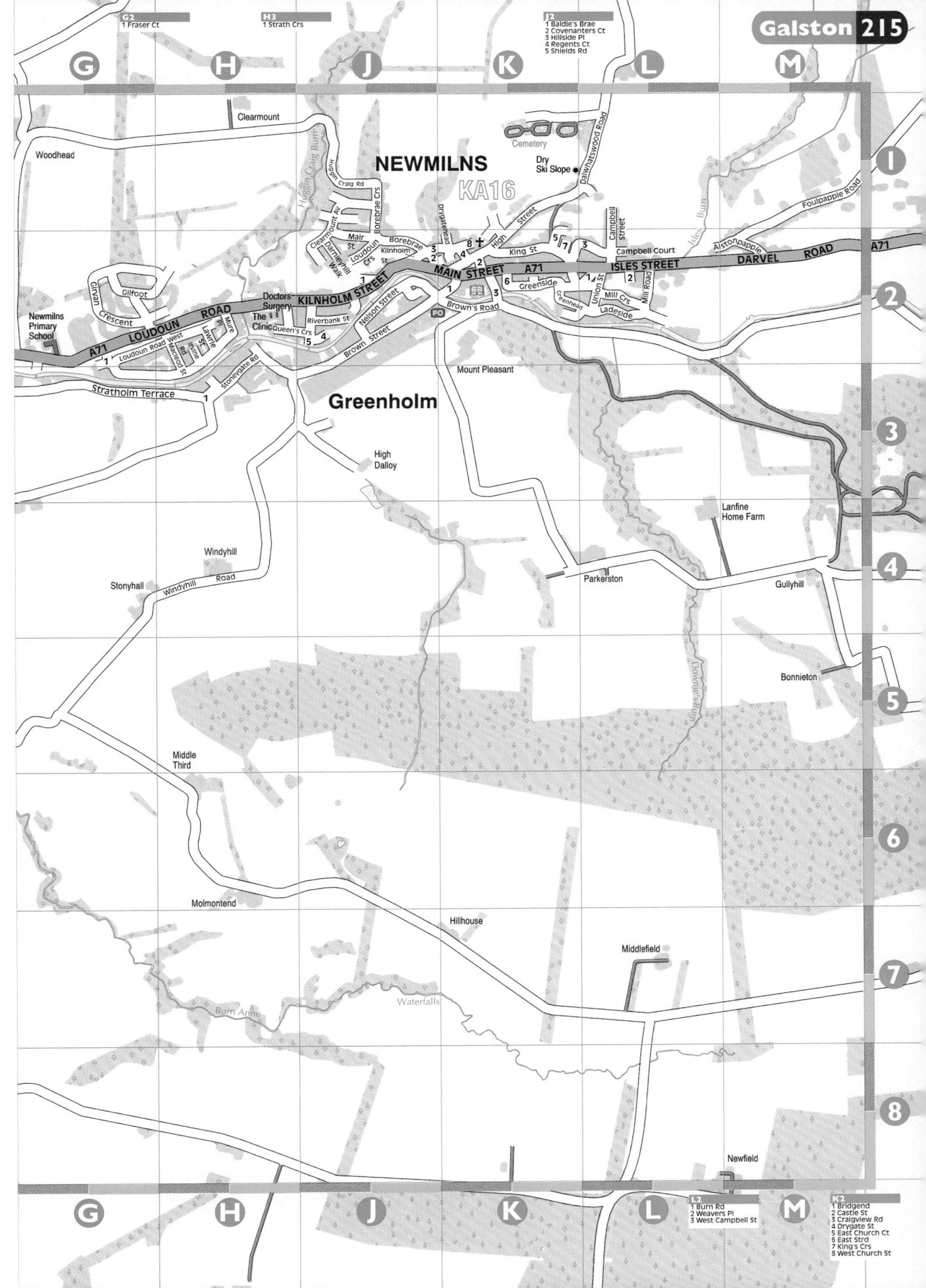

G2
1 Fraser Ct

H3
1 Strath Crs

J2
1 Baldie's Brae
2 Covenanters Ct
3 Hillside Pl
4 Regents Ct
5 Shields Rd

G   **H**   **J**   **K**   **L**   **M**

Clearmount

Woodhead

NEWMILNS

Cemetery

Dry
Ski Slope

KA16

I

Hugon Craig Rd

Craig Rd

Clearmount Av

Mair
St

Loudoun
Crs

Borebrae
Crs

Clearmount

Darnwhill
Walk

Borebrae

Kilnholm
St

Drygatehead

High

Street

King St

Campbell
Street

Campbell Court

Dalwhatswood Road

Isles Burn

Foulpapple Road

Alstonapple

DARVEL   **ROAD**   **A71**

Girvan
Crescent

Gilfoot

Newmilns
Primary
School

A71   **LOUDOUN**   **ROAD**

KILNHOLM STREET

Doctors'
Surgery

The
Clinic

Queen's Crs

Riverbank St

Nelson Street

Brown Street

MAIN STREET   **A71**

Brown's Road

PO

Greenside

Greenhead

Greenside

Union St

Mill Crs

Mill Road

ISLES STREET

Ladeside

2

Loudoun Road West

Lawrie
Pl

Mure
St

Macleod St

Irvine
St

Stratholm Terrace

Stoneygate Rd

Mount Pleasant

Greenholm

High
Dalloy

3

Lanfine
Home Farm

Windyhill

Stonyhall

Windyhill   Road

Parkerston

Gullyhill

4

Bonnieton

5

Middle
Third

Downie Burn

6

Molmontend

Hillhouse

Middlefield

7

Burn Anne

Waterfalls

8

Newfield

G   **H**   **J**   **K**   **L**   **M**

L2
1 Burn Rd
2 Weavers Pl
3 West Campbell St

K2
1 Bridgend
2 Castle St
3 Craigview Rd
4 Drygate St
5 East Church Ct
6 East Strd
7 King's Crs
8 West Church St

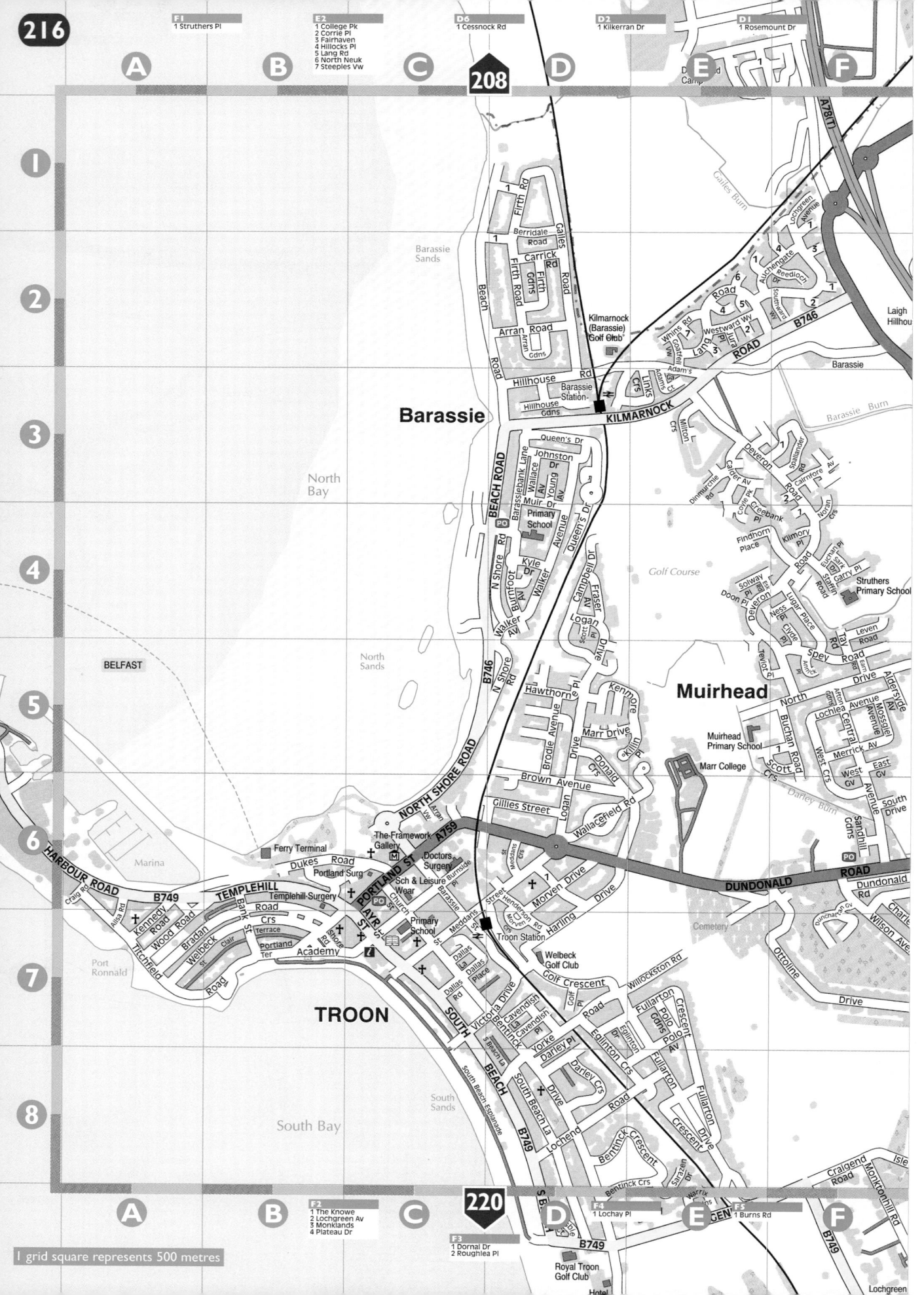

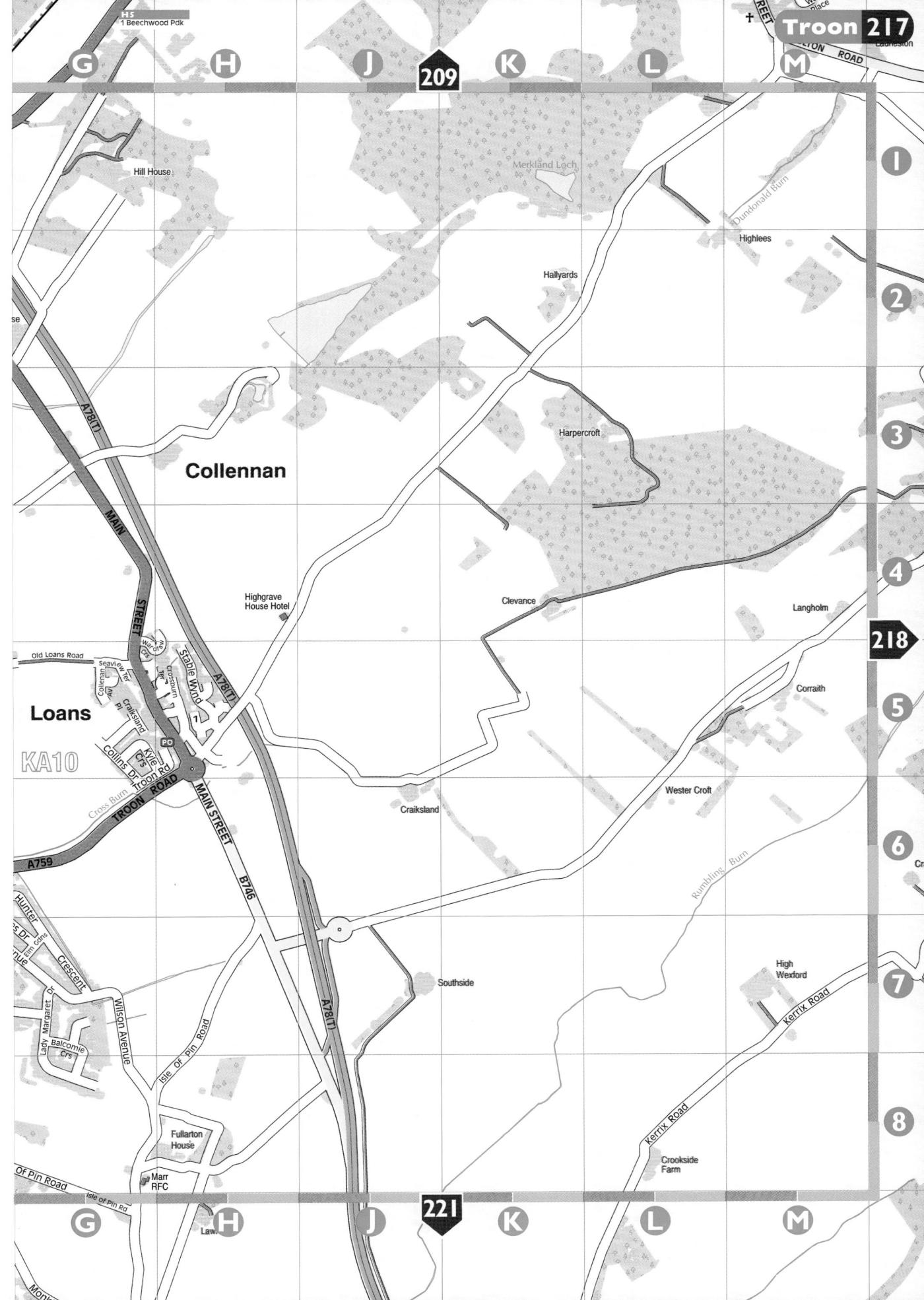

209

G   H   J   K   L   M

1

Hill House

Merkland Loch

Dundonald Burn

Highlees

2

Hallyards

Harpercroft

3

Collennan

Highgrave
House Hotel

Clevance

Langholm

4

218

Old Loans Road

SeaView Ter

Collenan
Ter

Stable Wynd

Crossburn
Ter

Corraith

5

Loans

Craiksland
Pl

War Gdns

KA10

Kyle
Crs

Collins Dr

Craiksland
Rd

PO

Troon Rd

1

Wester Croft

Cross Burn

TROON ROAD

MAIN STREET

Craiksland

6

A759

Rumbling Burn

Cr

Hunter

B746

A78(T)

High
Wexford

7

s Dr

Elm Cons

Balcomie
Crs

Crescent

Wilson Avenue

Southside

Kerrix Road

Of Pin Road

Lady Margaret Dr

Isle Of Pin Road

Kerrix Road

8

Fullarton
House

Crookside
Farm

Marr
RFC

Of Pin Road

Isle of Pin Rd

Law.

221

G   H   J   K   L   M

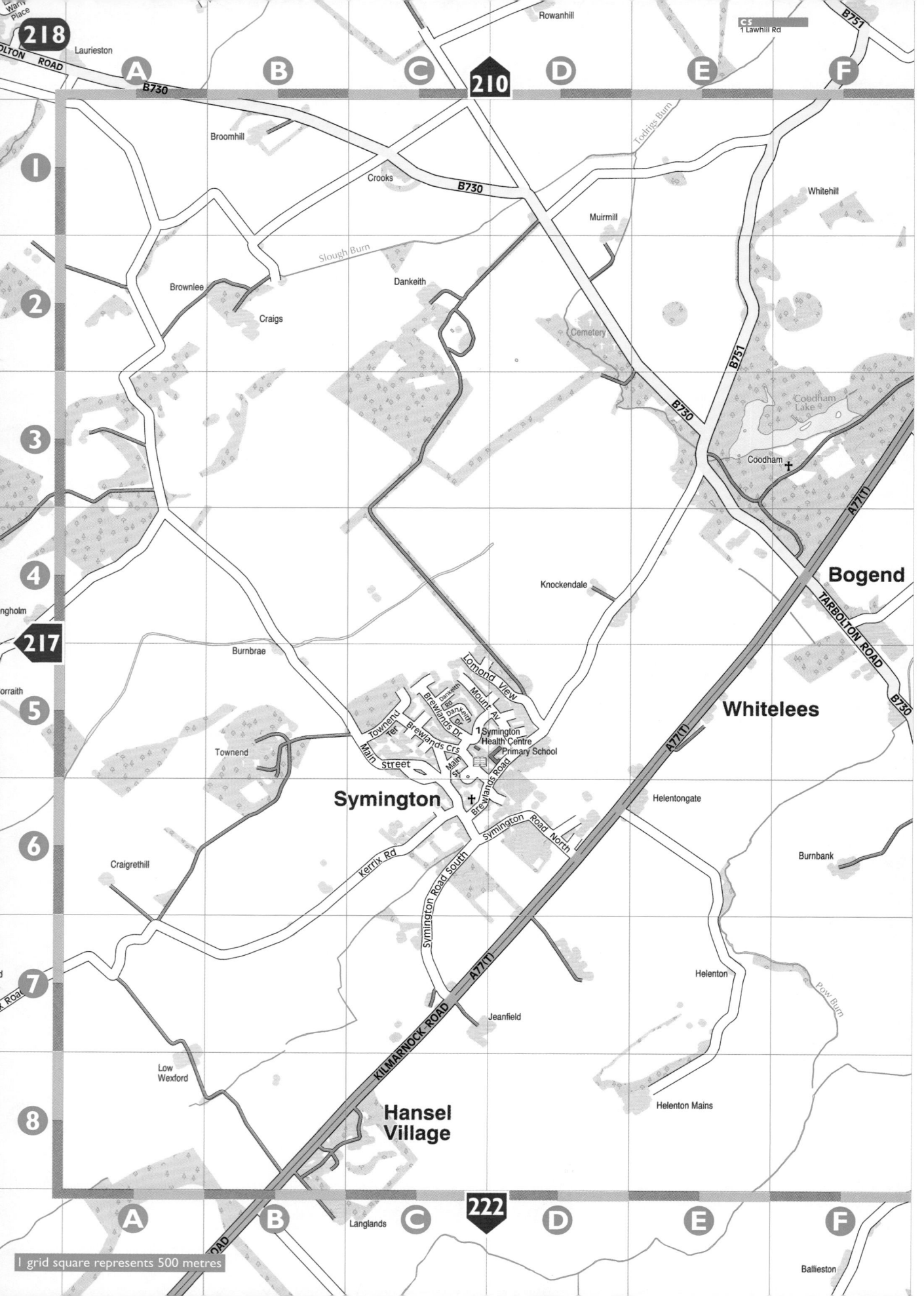

Laurieston

Warn Place

OLTON ROAD

B730

Rowanhill

CS
1 Lawhill Rd

B751

Broomhill

Crooks

B730

Todrigs Burn

Whitehill

1

Muirmill

Slough Burn

Brownlee

Dankeith

Craigs

Cemetery

B730

B751

Coodham Lake

2

3

Coodham

A77(T)

Knockendale

Bogend

4

TARBOLTON ROAD

ngholm

Burnbrae

Lomond View

Whitelees

B730

orraith

5

Townend Ter

Dankeith Rd

Dankeith

Mount Av

Brewlands Dr

Brewlands Crs

1 Symington Health Centre

Symington Primary School

A77(T)

Townend

Main Street

Main St

Brewlands Road

Helentongate

6

Craigrethill

Symington

Kerrix Rd

Symington Road South

Symington Road North

Burnbank

Helenton

7

x Road

A77(T)

Pow Burn

KILMARNOCK ROAD

Jeanfield

Low Wexford

Helenton Mains

8

Hansel Village

Langlands

OAD

Ballieston

1 grid square represents 500 metres

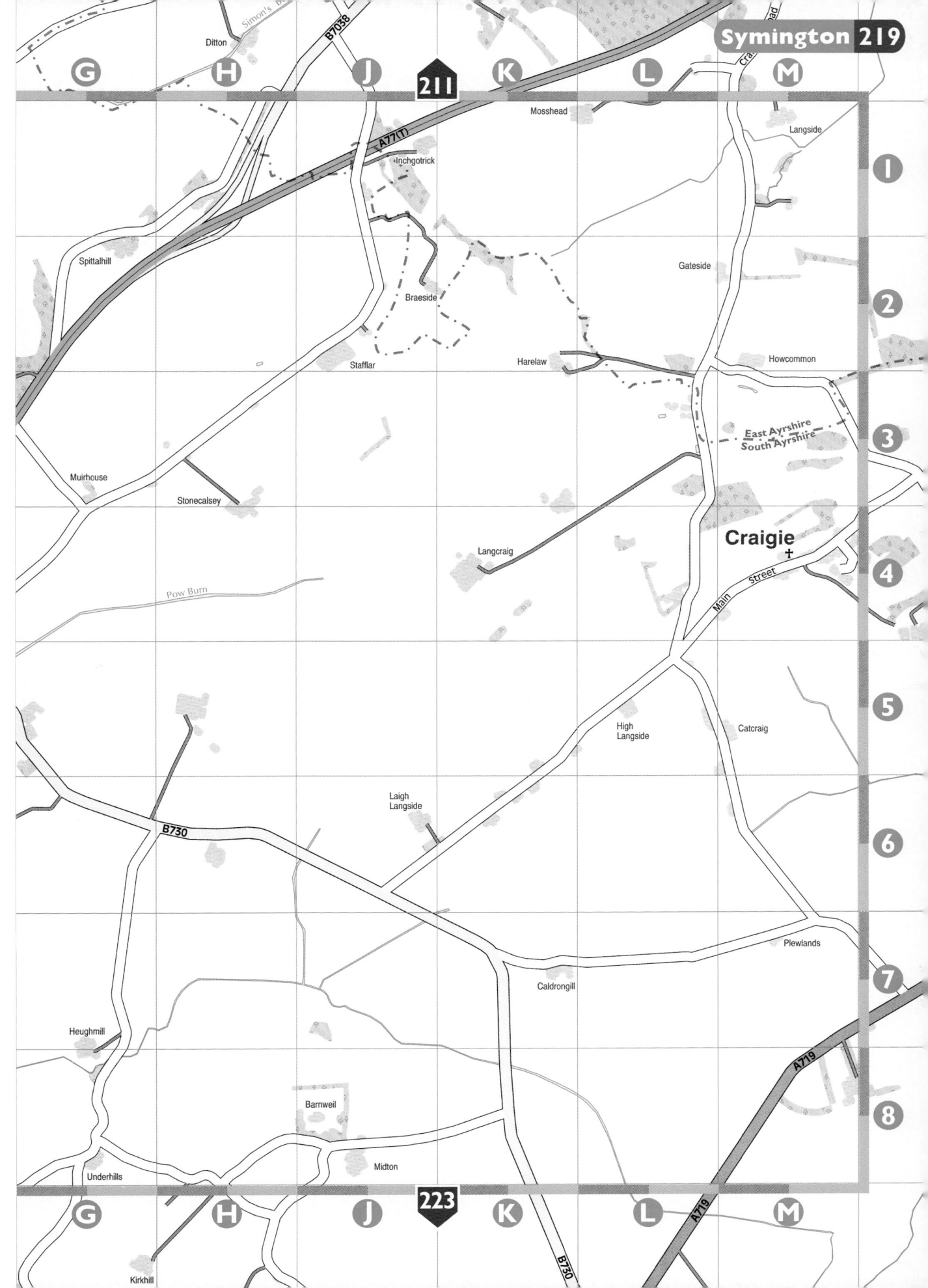

Ditton

G   H   J   K   L   M

B7058

211

A77(T)

Mosshead

Langside

Inchgotrick

Langside

I

Spittalhill

Braeside

Gateside

Harelaw

Howcommon

East Ayrshire
South Ayrshire

Stafflar

Muirhouse

Craigie

Stonecalsey

Langcraig

Pow Burn

Main Street

High
Langside

Catcraig

Laigh
Langside

B730

Plewlands

Caldrongill

Heughmill

A719

Barnweil

Midton

Underhills

Kirkhill

G   H   J   K   L   M

A719

B730

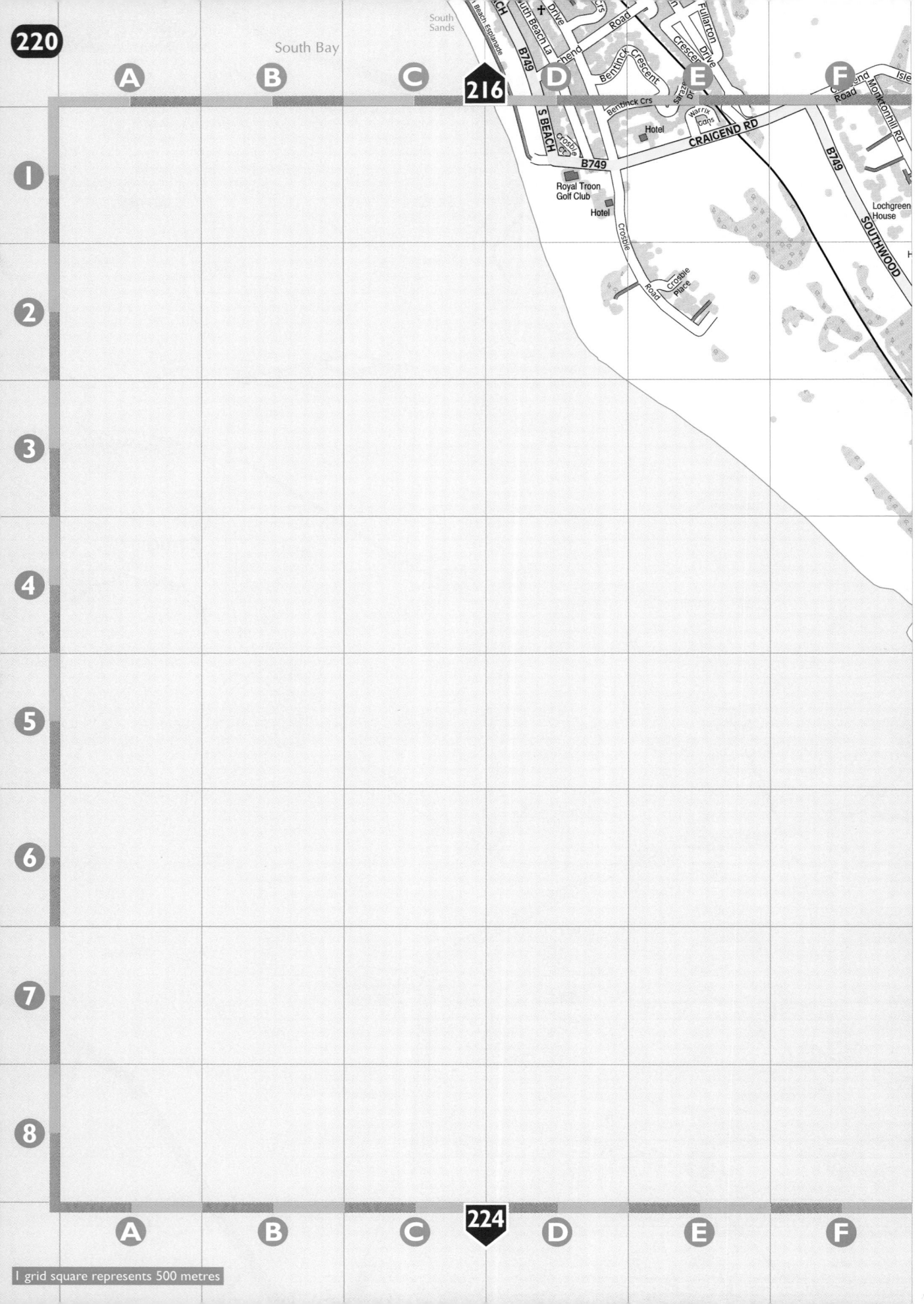

South Bay

South Sands

216

A **B** **C** **D** **E** **F**

1 Beach Esplanade

South Beach La

Drive

hend

B749

S BEACH

B749

Royal Troon
Golf Club

Hotel

Crosbie Crs

Crosbie
Road

Crosbie
Place

Bentinck Crescent

Bentinck Crs

Warrix
Gdns

saraze
or

Hotel

CRAIGEND RD

Fullarton
Drive

Cresce

end
Road

Isle

Monkcnhill Rd

B749

SOUTHWOOD

Lochgreen
House

Lochgreen

1

2

3

4

5

6

7

8

224

A **B** **C** **D** **E** **F**

I grid square represents 500 metres

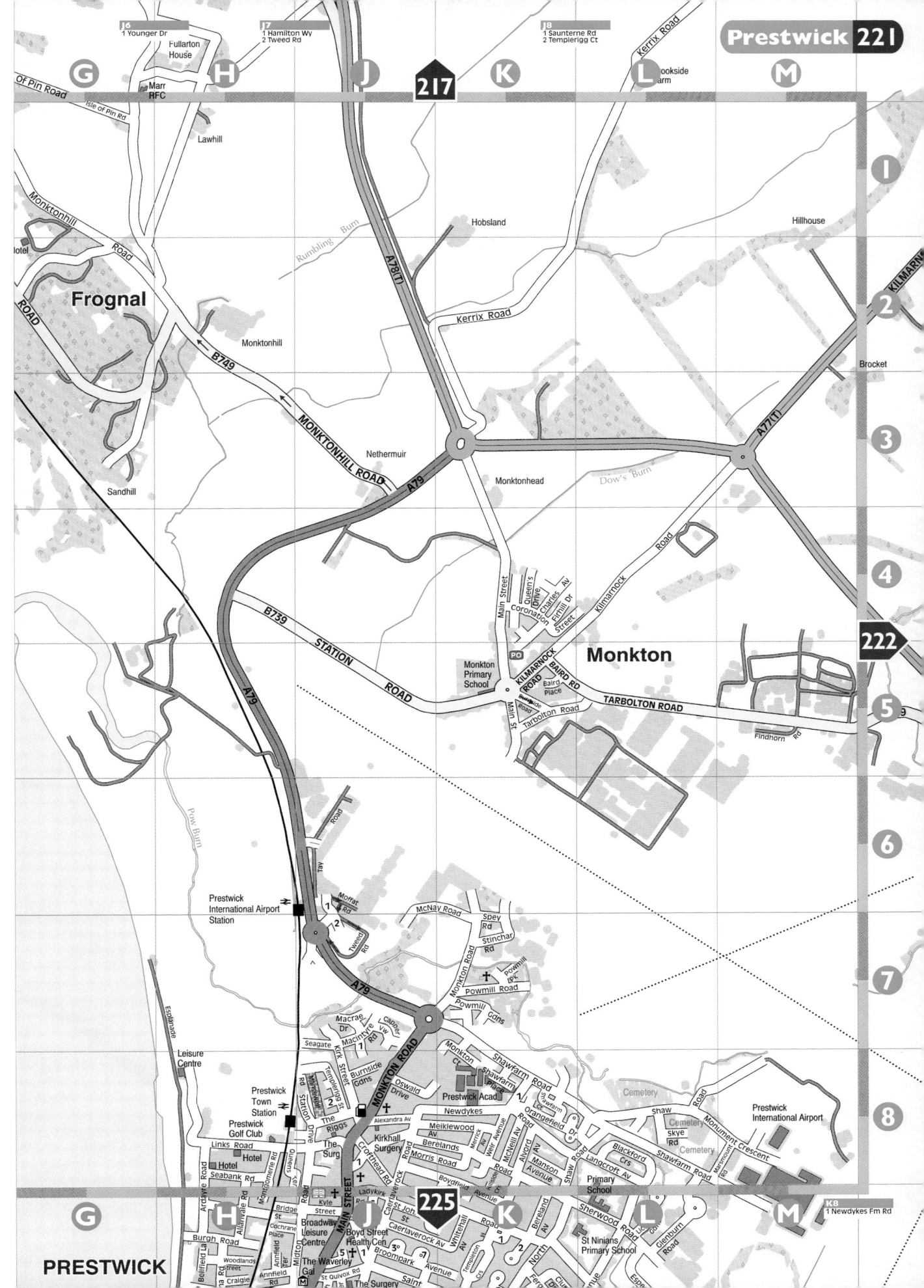

Hansel
Village

A   B   C   D   E   F

Helenton Mains

Langlands

Ballieston

illhouse

KILMARNOCK   ROAD

Brocket

Rosemount

Underwood

Hotel

Underwood Burn

Low
Wardneuk

Adamton
Mains

High
Wardneuk

Pow Burn

Woodside

North
Bogside

B739

A77(T)

Adamton
House

Newlands

Bogside
House

Foulton

Tarshaw

B739

Raith Burn

Ladykirk

B739

Raith

Shawhill
Farm

A719

Ladykirk Burn

Sandyford

Shields

Road

A77(T)

A719

Springbank

A   B   C   D   E   F

1 grid square represents 500 metres

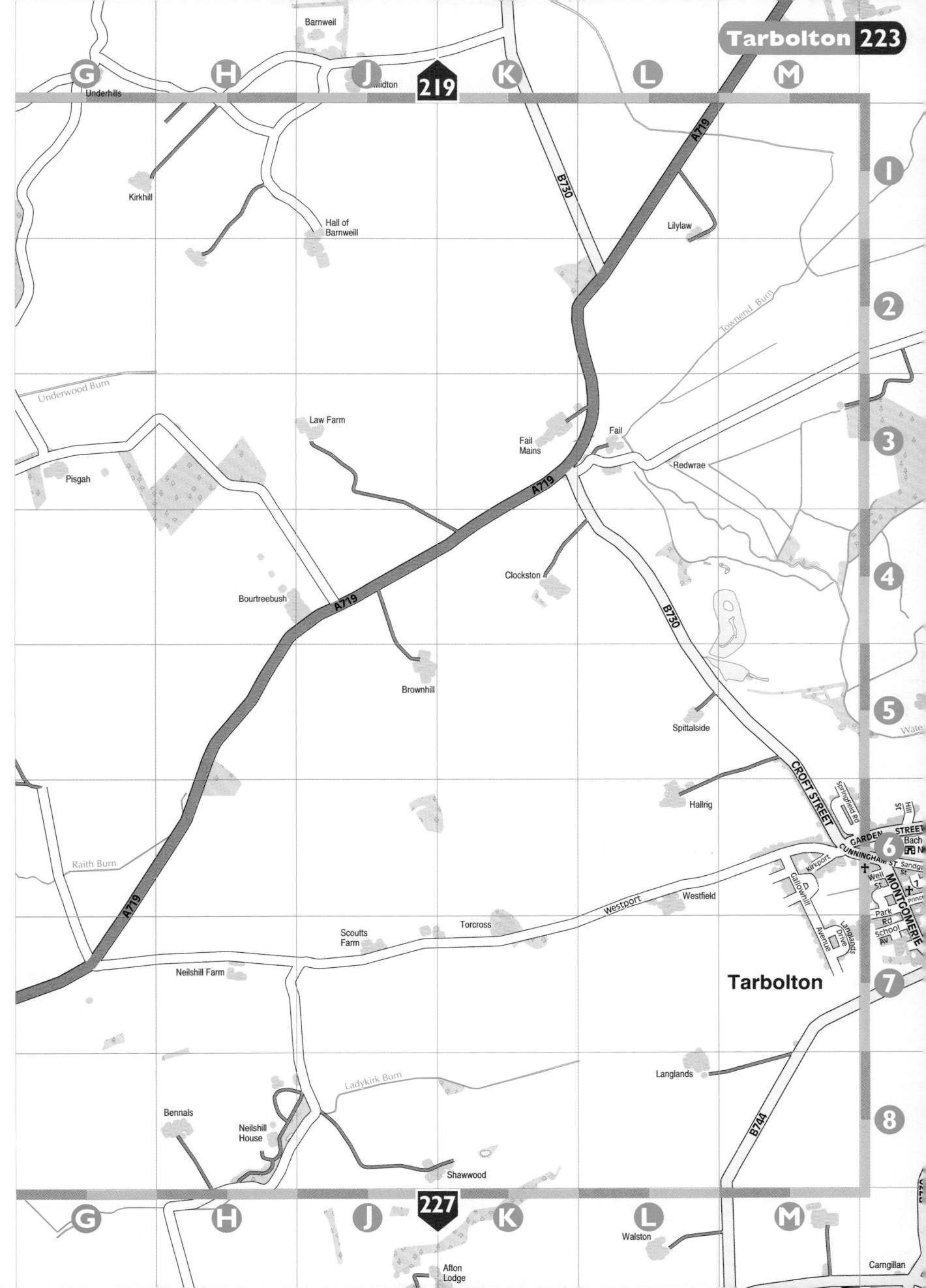

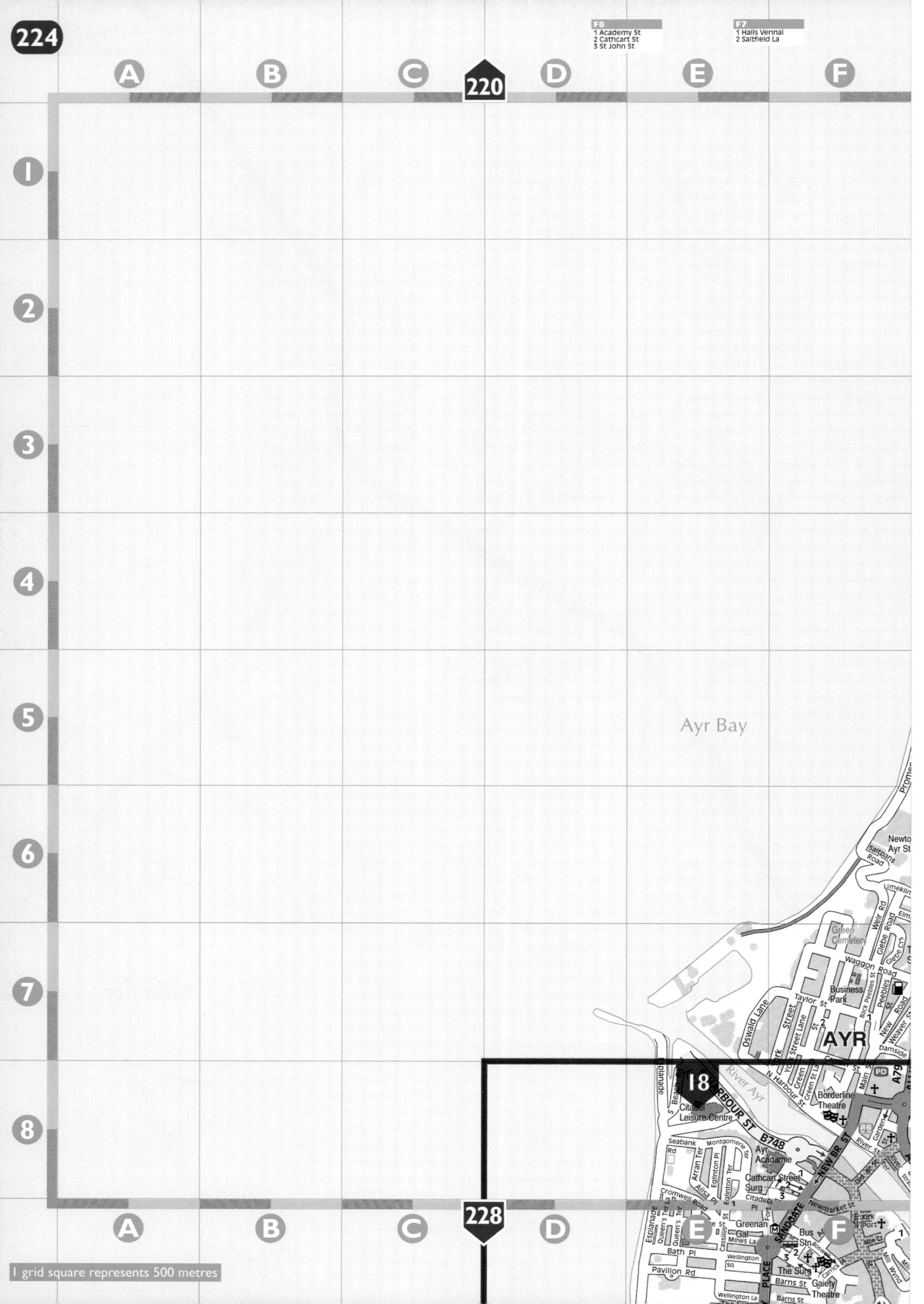

220

Ayr Bay

228

AYR

18

1 grid square represents 500 metres

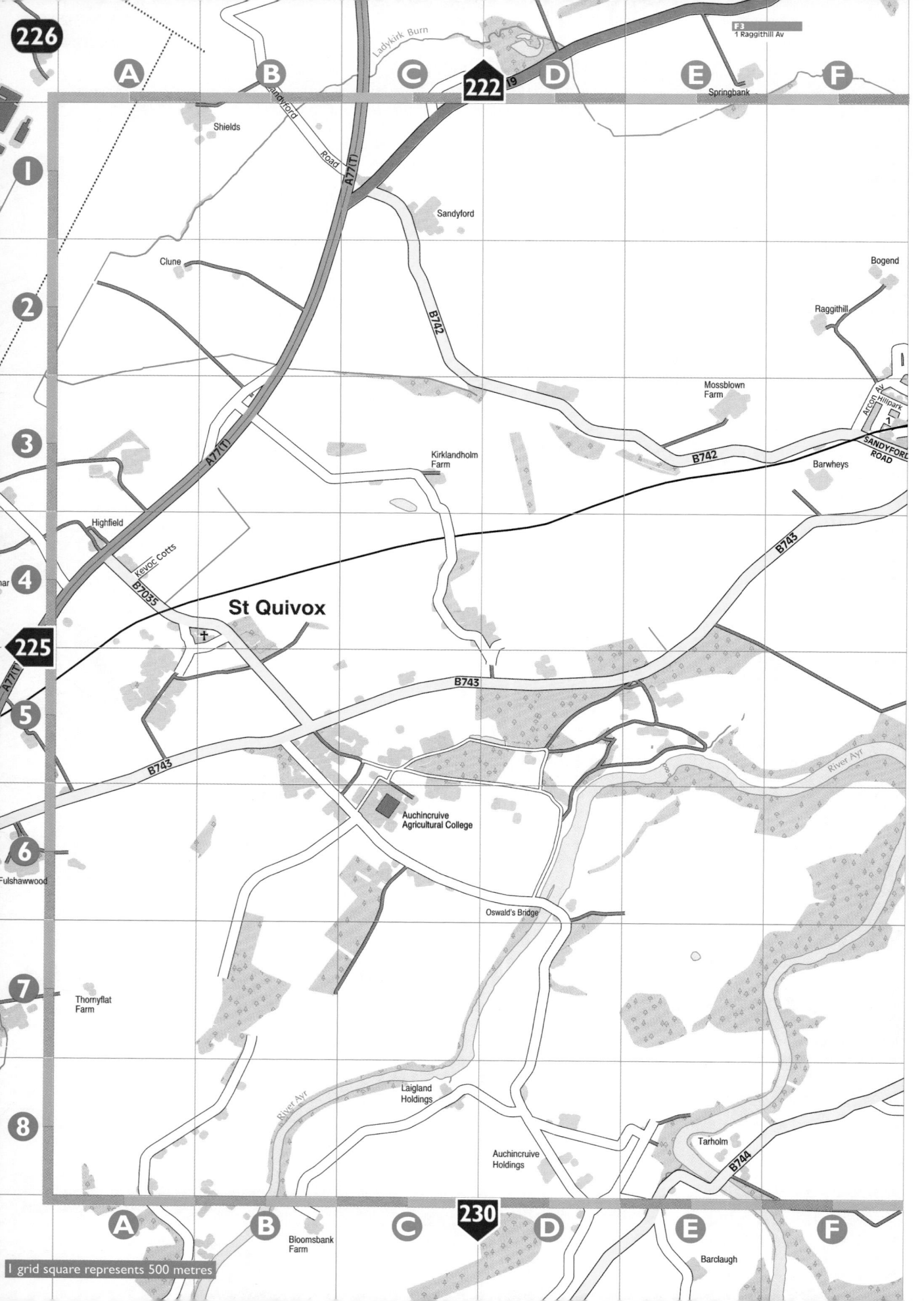

H3
1 Afton Av
2 Mossbank Pl

H7
1 Whitehill Dr

Neilshill House

wwood

Walston

Afton Lodge

B743

Drumley Farm

Townhead

Shacklehill

B744

Drumley House

B743

Roadend

Arcon Av
Arcon Ct
Drumley
Drumley Drive
Av
Hillpark
Miller Pl
MAUCHLINE ROAD
Whiskeyhall
Martin Av
Southside Av
Osbourne Avenue
Johnstone Dr
McEwan Crs
sloan
Gilchrist Pl
2

Dykes

Mossblown

Barwheys Dr
PO
Mossblown Health Centre
Station Rd
Brockiehill Dr
Mossgreen Pl

B743

B742
ANNBANK ROAD
Primary School
1
church Drive
Annbank Cem

Burn Farm

Commonside

B744

Brocklehill

Enterkine

WESTON BRAE

River Ayr

BROWN'S CRS
Brocklehill Av
Brown's Crs
PO

Annbank

WESTON AVENUE
Goodwin Drive

B742

Crawfordston

Knockshoggle

Braefoot

B744
Braeside
Dunlop Avenue
1
Whitehill Crescent

Colvinston

Mill Road

Gadgirth

Broadwood

B742

Carianan

Drumdow

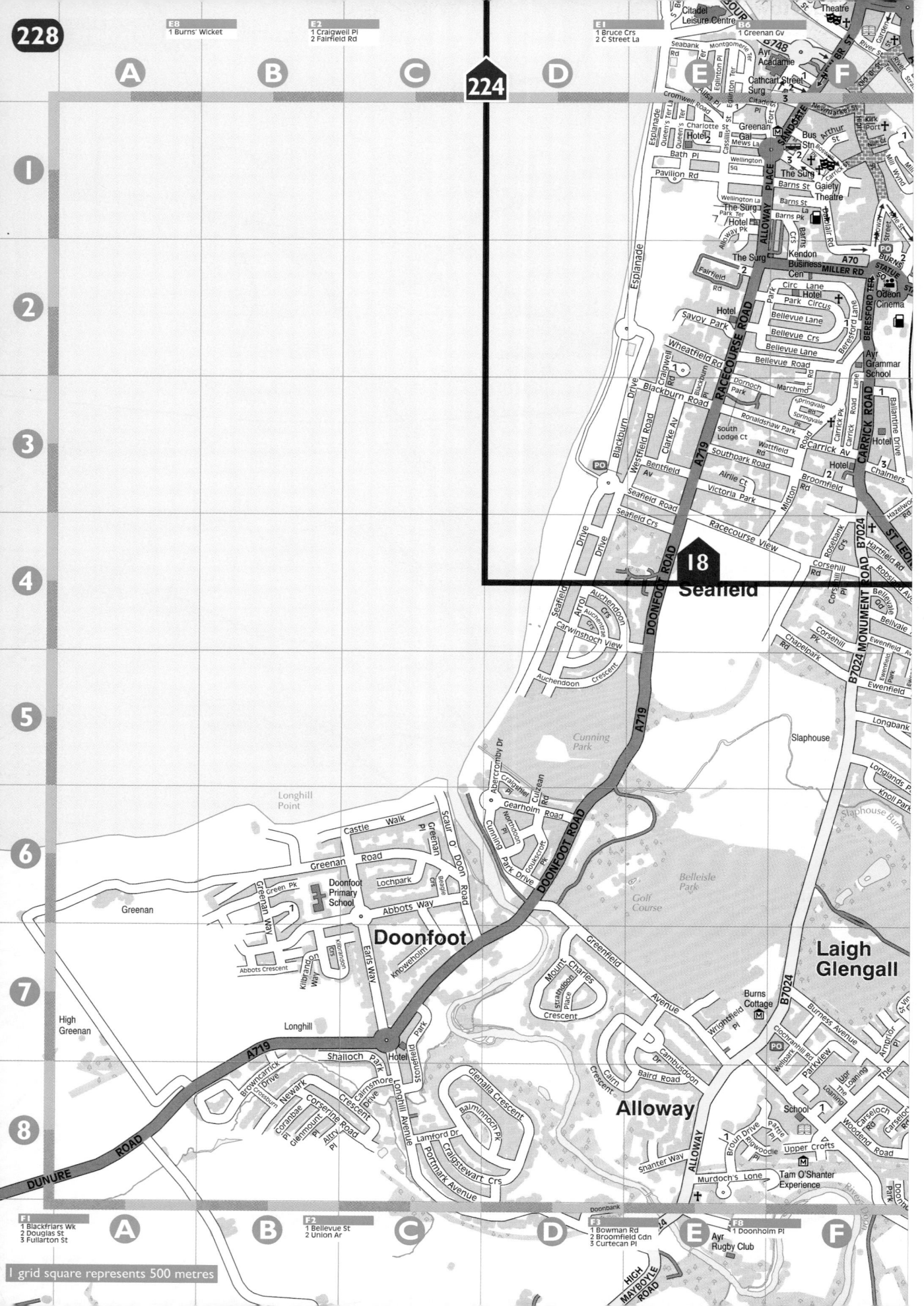

E8
1 Burns' Wicket

E2
1 Craigweil Pl
2 Fairfield Rd

E1
1 Bruce Crs
2 C Street La

B6
1 Greenan Gv

224

A B C D E F

1

2

3

4

18
Seafield

5

6

7

8

Longhill
Point

Castle Walk

Greenan Road

Doonfoot
Primary
School

Abbots Way

Lochpark

Greenan

Green Pk

Abbots Crescent

Doonfoot

Cunning
Park

Belleisle
Park

Golf
Course

Laigh
Glengall

Slaphouse

High
Greenan

Longhill

Shalloch Park

Newark
Crescent

Browncarrick Drive

Corsehine Road

DUNURE ROAD

A719

Alloway

Burns
Cottage

Tam O'Shanter
Experience

Ayr
Rugby
Club

F1
1 Blackfriars Wk
2 Douglas St
3 Fullarton St

A   B

F2
1 Bellevue St
2 Union Ar

C   D

F3
1 Bowman Rd
2 Broomfield Gdn
3 Curtecan Pl

E

F8
1 Doonholm Pl

F

1 grid square represents 500 metres

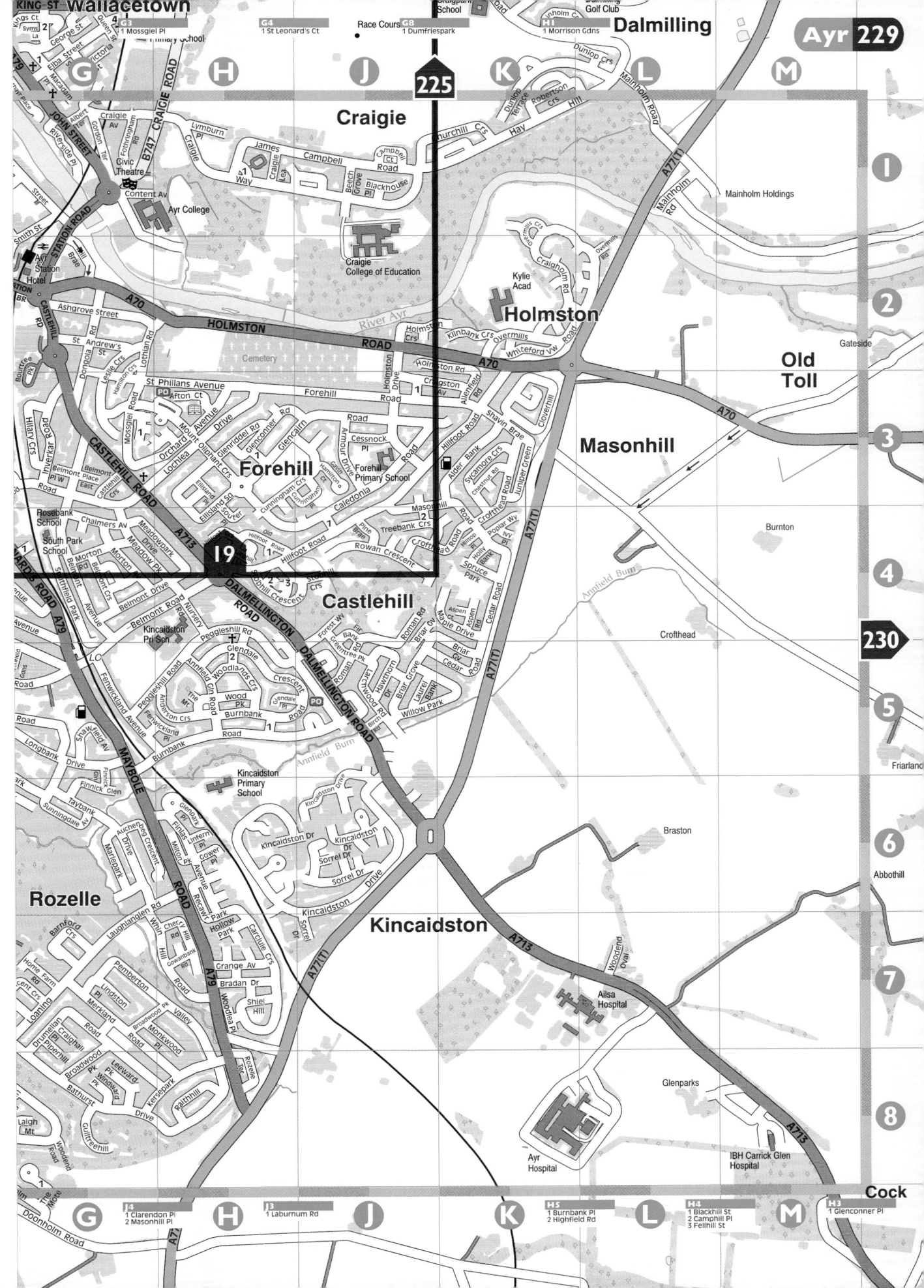

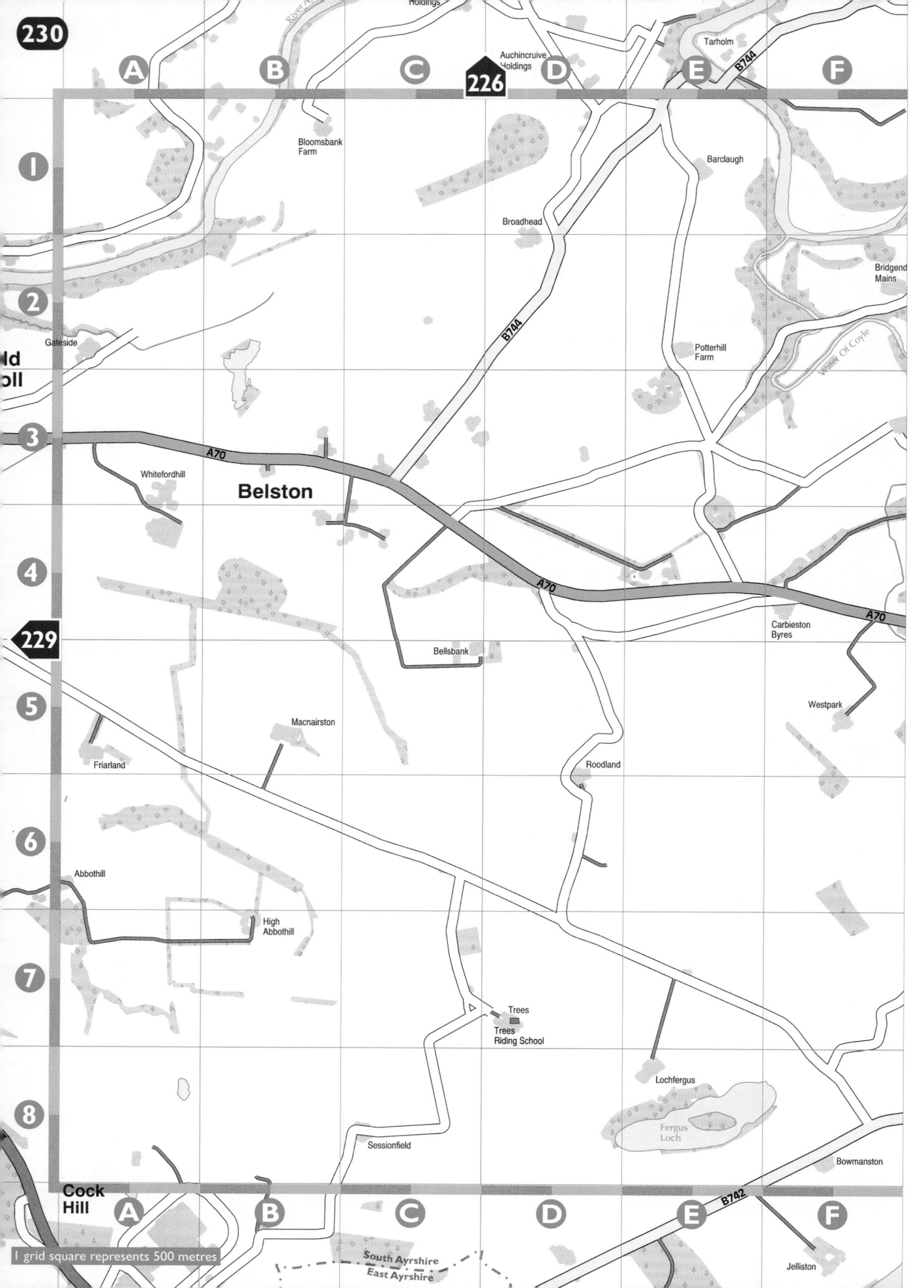

A   B   C   D   E   F

226

B744

Tarholm

Holdings

Auchincruive
Holdings

Bloomsbank
Farm

Barclaugh

1

Broadhead

Bridgend
Mains

2

Potterhill
Farm

Water Of Coyle

Gateside

ld
oll

3   A70   Belston

Whitefordhill

4

Carbieston
Byres

229

Bellsbank

A70

5   Westpark

Macnairston

Friarland

Roodland

6

Abbothill

High
Abbothill

7

Trees

Trees
Riding School

8   Lochfergus

Fergus
Loch

Sessionfield

Bowmanston

Cock
Hill   A   B   C   D   E   F
B742

Jelliston

South Ayrshire
East Ayrshire

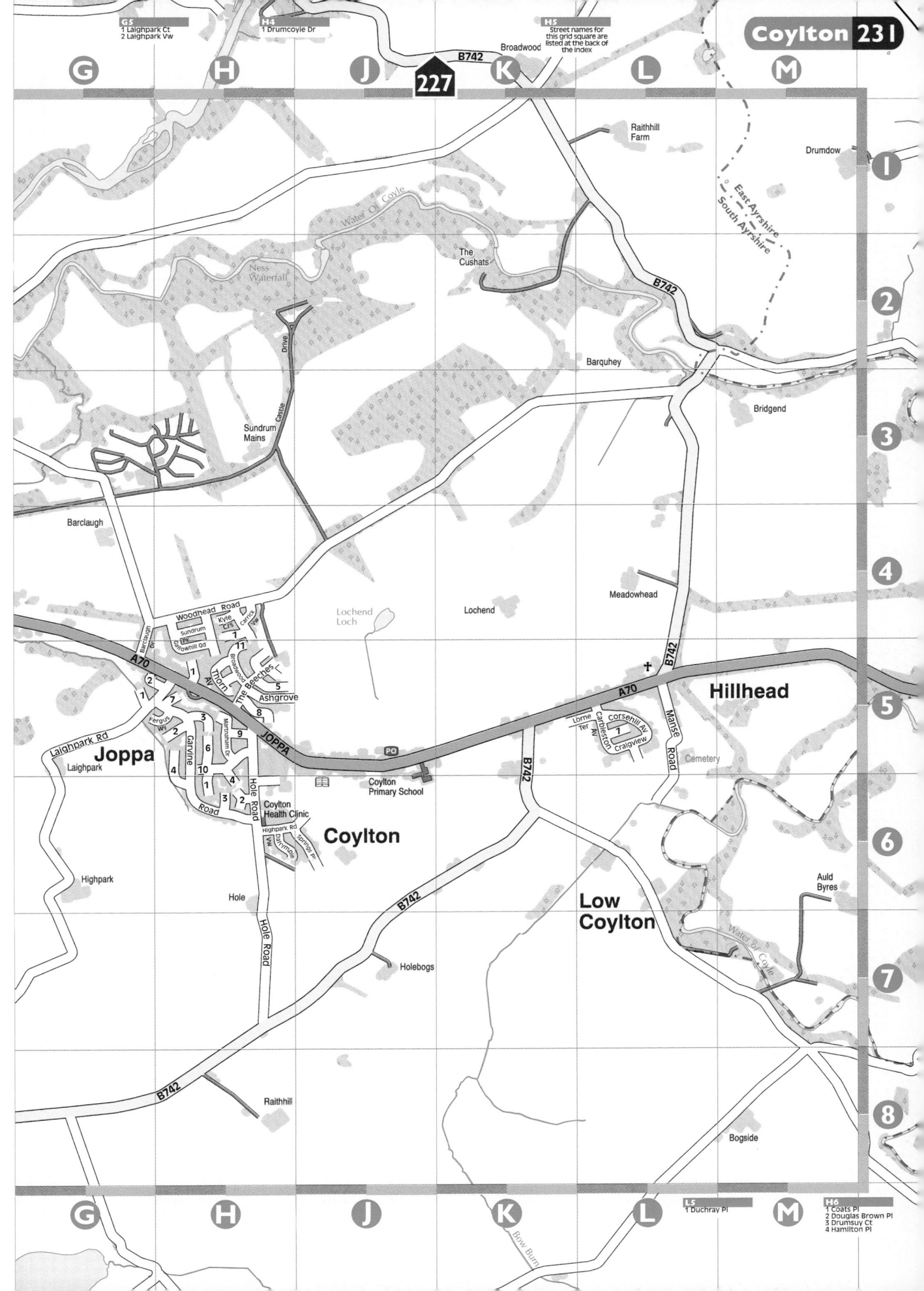

G   H   J   K   L   M

G5
1 Laighpark Ct
2 Laighpark Vw

H4
1 Drumcoyle Dr

H5
Street names for
this grid square are
listed at the back of
the index

227

B742

Broadwood

I

Raithhill
Farm

Drumdow

East Ayrshire
South Ayrshire

Water Of Coyle

2

Ness
Waterfall

The Cushats

B742

Barquhey

3

Bridgend

Sundrum
Mains

Castle Drive

Barclaugh

Lochend
Loch

Lochend

Meadowhead

4

Woodhead   Road

Sundrum
Kyle Crs
Carrick Vw

Barclaugh Dr

11
7

Galrowhill Qd

A70

Broadwood Dr

Thom Av

The Beeches

5
8

Ashgrove

Fergus Wy

Garvine

Marlraham Dr

JOPPA

9

6

10

Laighpark Rd

Laighpark

A70

Lorne
Ter

Carbleston Av

Corsehill Av

7
Craigview

Manse Road

Hillhead

Cemetery

5

Highpark Rd Vw
Dalrymple
Spittos Pl

Coylton
Health Clinic

Highpark

Hole Road

Hole Road

Hole

Coylton
Primary School

PO

B742

Coylton

Joppa

B742

B742

Auld
Byres

Low
Coylton

Water Of Coyle

6

7

Holebogs

Raithhill

Bow Burn

Bogside

8

L5
1 Duchray Pl

H6
1 Coats Pl
2 Douglas Brown Pl
3 Drumsuy Ct
4 Hamilton Pl

Place	Page	Grid
Abronhill	49	L6
Airdrie	111	G2
Alexandria	25	J4
Allanbank	136	F8
Allanton	157	K8
Allanton	161	G1
Alloway	228	D8
Altonhill	206	D6
Annathill	67	L7
Annbank	227	G6
Anniesland	81	K3
Ardeer	201	K3
Arden	126	C5
Ardoch	35	L3
Ardrossan	191	H7
Ashton	31	J2
Auchenback	125	J8
Auchenharvie	201	H1
Auchenmade	186	C4
Auchentibber	155	G7
Auchentiber	186	F6
Auchinairn	84	B2
Auchinloch	65	K7
Auchinraith	155	M2
Auchinreoch	46	B3
Auchinstarry	47	L3
Auldhouse	171	K8
Ayr	18	B4
Baillieston	108	B5
Balgrochan	29	J7
Balloch	48	B7
Balmore	63	L1
Balornock	84	B3
Bankhead	128	F3
Bankhead	199	H7
Barassie	216	C3
Bardowie	63	H2
Bardrainney	54	F2
Bargarran	58	F6
Bargeddie	109	G5
Barlanark	107	L3
Barmulloch	84	D4
Barncluith	156	F8
Barrachnie	107	L4
Barrhead	125	J6
Barrmill	168	F5
Battlefield	127	M1
Beansburn	207	G6
Bearsden	61	H4
Beith	144	B7
Bellahouston	104	A4
Bellfield	212	B5
Bellshill	132	D5
Bellside	135	K8
Bellsmyre	37	H2
Belston	230	B3
Benslie	194	E6
Biggar Road	135	G4
Birdston	45	J6
Birkenshaw	108	E8
Birniehill	15	J7
Bishopbriggs	64	B7
Bishopton	57	M6
Blackhall	9	M7
Blairhill	109	L3
Blairland	184	D3
Blairlinn	69	G4
Blairskaith	43	A4
Blanefield	27	G6
Blantyre	155	J2
Bloakhillhead	187	H8
Blythswood	80	C4
Bogend	218	F4
Bogside	178	C1
Bonkle	160	C3
Bonnyton	16	A1
Borland	187	M2
Bothwell	131	M8
Bourtreehill	204	D7
Bow Farm	32	B4
Bowhousebog or Liquo	136	F7
Bowling	58	E1
Brackenhirst	88	D3
Braehead	152	D6
Braehead	225	J7
Braeside	31	K6
Braidfauld	106	E6
Braidwood	188	F4
Branchton	31	M6
Bridgend	3	J7
Bridgend	66	D7
Bridge of Weir	98	F2
Bridgeton	12	E6
Broadfield	54	F1
Broadwood	67	K1
Brookfield	99	K4
Broom	150	F4
Broomhill	81	M6
Broomhouse	108	A7
Broomlands	204	A7
Browsburn	111	H4
Brucehill	36	C6
Buchley	63	J4
Burnbank	156	A4
Burnfoot	88	E7
Burnhouse	169	K8
Burnside	129	J4
Busbiehill	205	K6
Busby	151	M4
Cadder	64	B4
Cadzow	174	D2
Cairncurran	74	A1
Cairnhill	110	E3
Calderbank	111	H6
Caldercruix	90	E5
Calderwood	153	M6
Calton	12	B4
Cambuslang	130	A5
Cambusnethan	159	L4
Carbrain	49	H8
Cardonald	103	H4
Cardross	35	H1
Carfin	134	B7
Carluke	178	E8
Carmunnock	152	C1
Carmyle	130	B1
Carnbroe	110	E6
Carntyne	106	E2
Carnwadric	126	F5
Cartland	189	J8
Cartsdyke	3	H7
Castlehead	8	E7
Castlehill	36	B4
Castlehill	229	J4
Castlemilk	128	E7
Cathcart	127	M3
Central	2	C5
Chapelhall	111	L8
Charleston	9	H9
Chryston	66	C7
Clachan of Campsie	29	G6
Clarkston	89	K8
Clarkston	151	K2
Cleekhimin	134	B8
Cleghorn	199	M2
Cleland	135	G8
Clevans	98	A2
Cliftonville	110	C2
Clydebank	60	A8
Coatbridge	110	B4
Coatdyke	110	D3
College Milton	153	G6
Collennan	217	H3
Colston	83	L1
Coltness	159	K3
Condorrat	68	B2
Corkerhill	103	L7
Cowlairs	6	C1
Coylton	231	J6
Craigend	58	F8
Craigend	85	J6
Craigendoran	23	H2
Craigends	77	K8
Craigie	19	L3
Craigie	219	M4
Craigneuk	111	J3
Craigneuk	158	B4
Craigton	103	L4
Cranhill	107	G1
Crawforddyke	189	H1
Craigendmuir	85	L5
Crindledyke	160	B4
Croftfoot	128	E4
Crookedholm	212	E2
Crookfur	150	E3
Crookston	102	F5
Crossford	188	A7
Crosshill	108	D4
Crosshouse	205	M8
Crosslee	77	H8
Crossmill	125	J5
Crossmyloof	104	D7
Croy	47	M5
Cumbernauld	48	F8
Cumbernauld Village	49	J4
Cunninghamhead	205	H1
Dalgarven	193	J1
Dalmarnock	106	A6
Dalmilling	225	L8
Dalmuir	59	L5
Dalry	184	B1
Dalserf	177	G7
Dalshannon	68	A4
Dalton	131	G7
Dean Park	80	D7
Dennistoun	12	D1
Dennystown	36	E5
The Den	167	K6
Devol	54	D1
Doonfoot	228	D7
Doura	195	G7
Dovecothall	125	L5
Dowanhill	82	C6
Drakemyre	166	C8
Dreghorn	204	D8
Drumchapel	61	G7
Drumgelloch	111	H1
Drumpellier	109	J2
Drumry	60	C7
Drybridge	209	K4
Dullatur	48	C3
Dumbarton	37	G6
Dumbreck	104	B5
Dundonald	209	M7
Dundyvan	109	L4
Duntocher	59	M3
Dykehead	137	J5
Earlston	211	H6
Earnock	155	M8
Easterhouse	108	A1
Eastfield	48	C7
Eastfield	129	K2
East Kilbride	15	H5
East Mains	15	H1
Eddlewood	174	D7
Elderslie	100	C7
Erskine	59	G8
Faifley	60	C2
Fairhill	174	C1
Fairlie	139	L6
Fallside	132	D2
Fergushill	194	D6
Ferguslie Park	101	G4
Ferniegair	157	H8
Flemington	130	C6
Fluchter	43	H8
Forehill	19	K8
Forgewood	133	J7
Foxbar	123	M1
Freeland	79	H1
Frognal	221	H2
Fullarton	107	G6
Fullarton	203	H8
Gadgirth	227	J7
Gailes	208	C5
Gallowhill	102	A2
Gallowhill	152	E1
Galston	214	B4
Garnkirk	86	B3
Garrowhill	108	A4
Gartcosh	86	E4
Garthamlock	85	K7
Gartlea	111	H3
Gartloch	86	C6
Gartness	111	L4
Gartsherrie	87	L8
Gatehead	210	E4
Gateside	125	G8
Gateside	168	E2
Geilston	24	B8
Germiston	7	G5
Gibshill	33	L7
Giffnock	127	K7
Girdle Toll	204	A4
Glasgow	11	K1
Glenboig	87	L2
Glenburn	124	C1
Glengarnock	167	H3
Glenmavis	88	F5
Gorbals	11	J6
Gourock	31	L2
Govan	104	B1
Govanhill	105	H7
Gowkthrapple	177	G2
Grange	16	B4
Greenend	110	C5
Greenfaulds	68	F2
Greenfield	107	G3
Greenfoot	88	A1
Greengairs	69	M7
Greenhead	159	K7
Greenhills	14	B9
Greenholm	215	J3
Greenock	2	E3
Greenock West	32	C2
Haghill	13	L1
Hairmyres	170	E1
Hall	146	C6
Hallside	130	E4
Hamilton	156	F5
Hansel Village	218	C8
Hardgate	60	D3
Hareleeshill	176	D3
Hareshaw	135	K4
Harestanes	45	M7
Hartwood	137	G6
Haughhead	29	G6
Hayston	45	G8
Heathfield	225	J5
Helensburgh	20	B8
High Blantyre	155	G4
High Crosshill	129	H3
Highfield	166	F8
High Gallowhill	65	G3
Hillend	91	H6
Hillhead	231	L5
Hillington	103	G3
Hogganfield	84	F7
Holehills	89	H7
Holehouse	148	C3
Holmston	229	K2
Holytown	134	A3
Houston	77	H7
Howwood	121	K4
Hurlet	125	M2
Hurlford	213	G3
Hutchesontown	11	K8
Ibrox	104	B3
Inchinnan	79	K2
Inverkip	50	E4
Irvine	203	G6
Jamestown	25	M2
Johnstone	100	A7
Joppa	231	G5
Jordanhill	81	K4
Kelburn	35	G8
Kelvin	172	A4
Kelvindale	82	C3
Kelvinside	82	A4
Kennishead	126	E4
Kilbarchan	99	G6
Kilbirnie	142	F7
Kilbowie	60	C5
Kildrum	49	H6
Kilmacolm	75	M1
Kilmarnock	17	H7
Kilmaurs	206	C1
Kilncadzow	189	M4
Kilnford	209	K5
Kilwinning	183	K8
Kilwinning	193	H5
Kincaidston	229	J7
Kings Park	128	D3
Kirkfieldbank	198	C5
Kirkhill	151	J5
Kirkintilloch	46	A8
Kirk of Shotts	113	K7
Kirkshaw	109	K6
Kirktonhill	36	E7
Kirktoun	206	D3
Kirkwood	109	J5
Knightswood	81	J2
Knockentiber	205	L6
Knockinlaw	206	E5
Knowetop	157	M5
Kylepark	131	K2
Ladyburn	33	M6
Laigh Glengall	228	F7
Laighstonehall	156	A7
Lambhill	83	H2
Lanark	199	G6
Langbank	56	A2
Langloan	109	L4
Langside	127	K1
Largs	115	L6
Larkfield	31	K5
Larkhall	175	M7
Law	177	M4
Law Hill	178	A5
Lawthorn	204	A3
Leigh Knoweglass	172	A8
Lennoxtown	44	E1
Lenzie	65	K4
Lenziemill	68	F1
Levan	30	E4
Lilybank	33	M8
Limekilnburn	174	B7
Linwood	100	B3
Loans	217	G5
Lochside	225	G7
Lochwinnoch	120	D7
Lochwood	86	D8
Longbar	167	K3
Longpark	206	F6
Low Blantyre	131	L8
Low Coylton	231	L6
Low Waters	156	E8
Luggiebank	69	H3
Machan	176	A7
Mansewood	127	H3
Marnock	87	J3
Maryhill	82	B2
Masonhill	19	M8
Meadowfoot	181	L5
Mearns	150	F6
Meigle	92	B2
Meikle Earnock	174	C2
Merrylee	127	K5
Mid Auchinleck	54	D2
Midton	31	K3
Millarston	101	G6
Millersneuk	65	M5
Millerston	85	G5
Millheugh	175	K7
Millikenpark	99	H8
Millport	138	A6
Milngavie	41	K8
Milnwood	133	K5
Milton	37	M8
Milton	75	J3
Milton	83	J2
Milton of Campsie	45	K4
Moffat Mills	111	M2
Mollinsburn	67	K5
Monkton	221	L5
Moodiesburn	66	E6
Morningside	160	C6
Mossblown	227	H3
Mossend	133	K4
Mossneuk	170	E3
Mosspark	103	L6
Motherwell	157	L4
Mountblow	59	J5
Mount Florida	128	B2
Mount Vernon	107	J7
Mugdock	42	C3
Muirend	127	K3
Muirhead	86	D2
Muirhead	107	M6
Muirhead	216	E5
Muirhouse	158	A6
The Murray	14	E7
Neilston	148	E3
Nemphlar	198	A3
Nerston	154	A3
Nethan	188	B6
Netherlee	127	L7
Netherplace	149	M5
Netherton	27	H5
Netherton	158	E8
Newarthill	134	F5
New Farm	17	M2
Newhouse	135	H1
Newhousemill	172	D1
New Lanark	198	F8
Newlands	127	K3
Newlandsmuir	170	F2
Newmains	159	M4
Newmilns	215	J1
New Stevenston	134	B5
Newton	130	F3
Newton Mearns	150	C4
Newton on Ayr	225	H5
Newtown of Belltrees	121	H8
Nitshill	125	M4
North Motherwell	157	J1
Oatlands	105	K6
Old Balornock	6	F1
Oldhall	102	D4
Old Kilpatrick	58	F3
Old Monkland	109	L5
Old Toll	229	M2
Onthank	206	F4
Orbiston	132	F5
Overton	32	C7
Overtown	177	K3
Oxgang	65	M2
Paisley	9	J5
Park Farm	55	H2
Parkhall	59	M4
Parkhead	13	L7
Parkhill	55	K1
Parklea	35	J8
Park Mains	59	J8
Parkside	135	J7
Partick	82	A7
Pather	159	H8
Peel Park	152	F7
Perceton	204	C3
Petersburn	111	L3
Pilmuir	149	L8
Plains	90	B6
Pollok	103	H7
Pollokshaws	127	H1
Pollokshields	104	D6
Polmadie	105	J7
Port Dundas	5	J5
Portencross	180	D3
Porterfield	80	B7
Port Glasgow	34	E7
Possil Park	83	J4
Prestwick	225	G1
Priesthill	126	A3
Provanmill	84	E6
Quarrelton	99	G8
Quarriers Village	75	K7
Quarter	174	E6
Queenslie	107	K1
Queenzieburn	46	F1
Radnor Park	60	A5
Ranfurly	98	C3
Rashielee	59	G3
Ravenscraig	32	B6
Rawyards	89	H8
Renfrew	80	C6
Renton	25	K8
Riccarton	211	K4
Riggend	69	G8
Roadmeetings	189	K1
Robroyston	84	E3
Rogerton	153	K3
Rosebank	66	C4
Rosehall	110	B5
Rossland	58	C7
Roughwood	168	A4
Royston	6	A6
Rozelle	229	G6
Ruchazie	85	H8
Ruchill	83	G4
Rutherglen	105	L8
Rutherglen	128	A1
Saint Leonards	172	C1
St Quivox	226	B4
Salsburgh	113	J8
Saltcoats	200	F2
Scotstoun	81	H4
Seafar	48	E8
Seafield	228	E4
Seamill	181	J7
Shawhead	109	M6
Shawlands	127	K1
Shawsburn	176	E7
Sheddens	151	M2
Sheildmuir	158	C5
Shettleston	107	G4
Shewalton	209	G4
Shieldhall	81	J4
Shillford	147	K4
Shortlees	211	M6
Shortroods	101	J1
Shotts	137	M4
Sighthill	6	A5
Silverton	37	H5
Silvertonhill	156	D7
Solsgirth	46	B8
Sornhill	214	E7
Sourlie	204	A2
Spango	31	K7
Springboig	107	J3
Springburn	83	M5
Springhill	149	J2
Springside	205	G7
Stamperland	151	M1
Stand	89	H3
Stanecastle	203	M5
Stepps	85	J4
Stevenston	201	L1
Stevenston Site	202	B5
Stewartfield	153	J4
Stewarton	197	M1
Stonefield	155	M1
Strathblane	27	J6
Strathbungo	104	E7
Strone	3	M9
Strone Farm	2	E9
Summerston	62	F8
Swinton	108	C3
Symington	218	B6
Tannochside	132	A1
Tarbolton	223	M7
Temple	81	L2
Thirdpart	180	E1
Thornliebank	126	E6
Thornly Park	101	M8
Thorntonhall	152	A6
Thrashbush	88	F8
Torbush	160	B6
Torrance	44	B8
Torranyard	195	K4
Townend	37	G3
Townhead	5	L8
Townhead	87	J8
Troon	216	B7
Twechar	46	E6
Uddingston	131	L6
Udston	155	M5
Uplawmoor	147	H6
Upper Dalguhurn	25	J7
Victory Gardens	80	C7
Viewpark	132	C1
Wallacetown	19	G1
Wardpark	49	J2
Waterfoot	151	J8
Waterloo	177	K1
Waterside	66	C2
Waterside	125	L4
Wattston	69	K8
West Arthurlie	124	F7
Westburn	130	E3
West Drumoyne	103	L2
Wester Auchinloch	65	K8
Westfield	67	M3
West Kilbride	181	K5
West Mains	14	D3
West Porton	58	C5
Westwood	14	A5
Whifflet	110	B4
Whinhall	110	E1
Whitecraigs	151	L3
Whitecrook	80	D1
Whitehill	156	E8
Whitehills	171	M4
Whiteinch	81	K3
Whitelees	218	C5
Whitletts	225	K6
Wildmanbridge	178	A2
Williamwood	151	J1
Wishaw	159	G6
Woodfield	225	G2
Woodhall	54	F1
Yett	134	C6
Yieldshields	179	J7
Yoker	80	E2
Yorkhill	104	C1

USING THE STREET INDEX

Street names are listed alphabetically. Each street name is followed by its postal town or area locality, the Postcode District, the page number, and the reference to the square in which the name is found.

Example: **Abbeygreen St** *ESTRH* G34............... **86** E8 1

Some entries are followed by a number in a blue box. This number indicates the location of the street within the referenced grid square. The full street name is listed at the side of the map page.

GENERAL ABBREVIATIONS

ACC ACCESS
ALY ALLEY
AP APPROACH
AR ARCADE
ASS ASSOCIATION
AV AVENUE
BCH BEACH
BLDS BUILDINGS
BND BEND
BNK BANK
BR BRIDGE
BRK BROOK
BTM BOTTOM
BUS BUSINESS
BVD BOULEVARD
BY BYPASS
CATH CATHEDRAL
CEM CEMETERY
CEN CENTRE
CFT CROFT
CH CHURCH
CHA CHASE
CHYD CHURCHYARD
CIR CIRCLE
CIRC CIRCUS
CL CLOSE
CLFS CLIFFS
CMP CAMP
CNR CORNER
CO COUNTY
COLL COLLEGE
COM COMMON
COMM COMMISSION
CON CONVENT
COT COTTAGE
COTS COTTAGES
CP CAPE
CPS COPSE
CR CREEK
CREM CREMATORIUM
CRS CRESCENT
CSWY CAUSEWAY
CT COURT
CTRL CENTRAL
CTS COURTS
CTYD COURTYARD
CUTT CUTTINGS
CV COVE
CYN CANYON
DEPT DEPARTMENT
DL DALE
DM DAM
DR DRIVE
DRO DROVE
DRY DRIVEWAY
DWGS DWELLINGS
E EAST
EMB EMBANKMENT
EMBY EMBASSY
ESP ESPLANADE
EST ESTATE
EX EXCHANGE
EXPY EXPRESSWAY
EXT EXTENSION
F/O FLYOVER
FC FOOTBALL CLUB
FK FORK
FLD FIELD
FLDS FIELDS
FLS FALLS
FLS FLATS
FM FARM
FT FORT
FWY FREEWAY
FY FERRY
GA GATE
GAL GALLERY
GDN GARDEN
GDNS GARDENS
GLD GLADE
GLN GLEN
GN GREEN
GND GROUND
GRA GRANGE
GRG GARAGE
GT GREAT
GTWY GATEWAY
GV GROVE
HGR HIGHER
HL HILL
HLS HILLS
HO HOUSE
HOL HOLLOW
HOSP HOSPITAL
HRB HARBOUR
HTH HEATH
HTS HEIGHTS
HVN HAVEN
HWY HIGHWAY
IMP IMPERIAL
IN INLET
IND EST INDUSTRIAL ESTATE
INF INFIRMARY
INFO INFORMATION
INT INTERCHANGE
IS ISLAND
JCT JUNCTION
JTY JETTY
KG KING
KNL KNOLL
L LAKE
LA LANE
LDG LODGE
LGT LIGHT
LK LOCK
LKS LAKES
LNDG LANDING
LTL LITTLE
LWR LOWER
MAG MAGISTRATE
MAN MANSIONS
MD MEAD
MDW MEADOWS
MEM MEMORIAL
MKT MARKET
MKTS MARKETS
ML MALL
ML MILL
MNR MANOR
MS MEWS
MSN MISSION
MT MOUNT
MTN MOUNTAIN
MTS MOUNTAINS
MUS MUSEUM
MWY MOTORWAY
N NORTH
NE NORTH EAST
NW NORTH WEST
O/P OVERPASS
OFF OFFICE
ORCH ORCHARD
OV OVAL
PAL PALACE
PAS PASSAGE
PAV PAVILION
PDE PARADE
PH PUBLIC HOUSE
PK PARK
PKWY PARKWAY
PL PLACE
PLN PLAIN
PLNS PLAINS
PLZ PLAZA
POL POLICE STATION
PR PRINCE
PREC PRECINCT
PREP PREPARATORY
PRIM PRIMARY
PROM PROMENADE
PRS PRINCESS
PRT PORT
PT POINT
PTH PATH
PZ PIAZZA
QD QUADRANT
QU QUEEN
QY QUAY
R RIVER
RBT ROUNDABOUT
RD ROAD
RDG RIDGE
REP REPUBLIC
RES RESERVOIR
RFC RUGBY FOOTBALL CLUB
RI RISE
RP RAMP
RW ROW
S SOUTH
SCH SCHOOL
SE SOUTH EAST
SER SERVICE AREA
SH SHORE
SHOP SHOPPING
SKWY SKYWAY
SMT SUMMIT
SOC SOCIETY
SP SPUR
SPR SPRING
SQ SQUARE
ST STREET
STN STATION
STR STREAM
STRD STRAND
SW SOUTH WEST
TDG TRADING
TER TERRACE
THWY THROUGHWAY
TNL TUNNEL
TOLL TOLLWAY
TPK TURNPIKE
TR TRACK
TRL TRAIL
TWR TOWER
U/P UNDERPASS
UNI UNIVERSITY
UPR UPPER
V VALE
VA VALLEY
VIAD VIADUCT
VIL VILLA
VIS VISTA
VLG VILLAGE
VLS VILLAS
VW VIEW
W WEST
WD WOOD
WHF WHARF
WK WALK
WKS WALKS
WLS WELLS
WY WAY
YD YARD
YHA YOUTH HOSTEL

POSTCODE TOWNS AND AREA ABBREVIATIONS

AIRDRIE Airdrie
ALEX/LLW Alexandria/Loch Lomond west
ARD Ardrossan
AYR Ayr
AYRS Ayr south
BAIL/MDB/MHD Baillieston/Moodiesburn/Muirhead
BALLOCH Balloch
BEITH Beith
BLSH Bellshill
BLTYR/CAMB Blantyre/Cambuslang
BNYBR/BNK Bonnybridge/Banknock
BRHD/NEIL Barrhead/Neilston
BRWEIR Bridge of Weir
BSDN Bearsden
BSHPBGS Bishopbriggs
BSHPTN Bishopton
CAR/SHTL Carmyle/Shettleston
CARD/HILL/MSPK Cardonald/Hillington/Mosspark
CARLUKE Carluke
CGLE Central Glasgow east
CGLW Central Glasgow west
CLYDBK Clydebank
CMPF/LLE Campsie Fells/Loch Lomond east
COWCAD Cowcaddens
CRG/CRSL/HOU Craigends/Crosslee/Houston
CRH/DND Crosshouse/Dundonald
CRMNK/CLK/EAG Carmunnock/Clarkston/Eaglesham
CSMK Castlemilk
CTBR Coatbridge
CUMB Cumbernauld
DALRY Dalry
DEN/PKHD Dennistoun/Parkhead
DMBTN Dumbarton
DMNK/BRGTN Dalmarnock/Bridgeton
DRUM Drumchapel
EKILN East Kilbride north
EKILS East Kilbride south
ERSK Erskine
ESTRH Easterhouse
FAIRLIE Fairlie
FLK Falkirk
GBLS Gorbals
GIF/THBK Giffnock/Thornliebank
GLGNK Glengarnock
GLSTN Galston
GOV/IBX Govan/Ibrox
GRK Gourock
GRNK Greenock
GRNKW/INVK Greenock West/Inverkip
GTCI Great Cumbrae Island
GVH/MTFL Govanhill/Mount Florida
HBR/GL Helensburgh/Gare Loch
HMLTN Hamilton
HWWD Howwood
IRV Irvine
IRVSE Irvine south & east
JNSTN Johnstone
KBRN Kilbirnie
KKNTL Kirkintilloch
KLBCH Kilbarchan
KLMCLM Kilmacolm
KLMNK Kilmarnock
KLMNKN/STW Kilmarnock north/Stewarton
KLWNG Kilwinning
KNTSWD Knightswood
KSYTH Kilsyth
KVD/HLHD Kelvindale/Hillhead
KVGV Kelvingrove
LARGS Largs
LNK/LMHG Lanark/Lesmahagow
LNPK/KPK Linn Park/King's Park
LOCHW Lochwinnoch
LRKH Larkhall
MAUCH/CAT Mauchline/Catrine
MLNGV Milngavie
MRYH/FIRH Maryhill/Firhill
MTHW Motherwell
NMLNS Newmilns
NMRNS Newton Mearns
OLDK Old Kilpatrick
PGL Port Glasgow
PLK/PH/NH Pollock/Priesthill/Nitshill
PLKSD/SHW Pollockshields/Shawlands
PLKSW/MSWD Pollockshaws/Mansewood
PPK/MIL Possil Park/Milton
PSLY Paisley
PSLYN/LNWD Paisley north/Linwood
PSLYS Paisley south
PSTWK Prestwick
PTCK Partick
RAYR/DAL Rural Ayr/Dalmellington
RNFRW Renfrew
RUTH Rutherglen
SALT Saltcoats
SCOT Scotstoun
SHOTTS Shotts
SKLM Skelmorlie
SMSTN Summerston
SPRGB/BLRNK Springburn/Balornock
STPS/GTHM/RID Stepps/Garthamlock/Riddrie
STRHV Strathaven
SVSTN Stevenston
TROON Troon
UD/BTH/TAN Uddingston/Bothwell/Tannochside
WISHAW Wishaw
WKIL West Kilbride
WMYSB Wemyss Bay

Index - streets

A

Abbey Cl *PSLY* PA1 **9** J4
Abbeycraig Rd *ESTRH* G34 **108** E1
Abbey Dr *SCOT* G14 **81** L5
Abbeygreen St *ESTRH* G34 **86** E8 1
Abbeyhill St *CAR/SHTL* G32 **106** E2
Abbeylands Rd *CLYDBK* G81 **60** C3
Abbey Pl *AIRDRIE* ML6 **111** J5
Abbey Rd *JNSTN* PA5 **100** B7
Abbot Ct *PSTWK* KA9 **225** K4 1
Abbot's Av *KLWNG* KA13 **193** L7
Abbots Crs *AYRS* KA7 **228** B7
Abbotsford *BSHPBGS* G64 **64** C7 1
Abbotsford Av *HMLTN* ML3 **156** B2
LRKH ML9 **176** A8
RUTH G73 **129** H2
Abbotsford Brae *EKILN* G74 **153** L6
Abbotsford Ct *CUMB* G67 **68** F2 1
Abbotsford Crs *HMLTN* ML3 **156** B3 1
PSLYS PA2 **123** K2
SHOTTS ML7 **137** M4 1
WISHAW ML2 **159** J5
Abbotsford La *BLSH* ML4 **132** F3 1
Abbotsford Pl *CUMB* G67 **68** F2
GBLS G5 **11** G7 1
SALT KA21 **192** A7 1
Abbotsford Rd *AIRDRIE* ML6 **111** L8
BSDN G61 **61** J3
CLYDBK G81 **60** B8
CUMB G67 **68** F2
HMLTN ML3 **156** A3
WISHAW ML2 **159** J5
Abbotsford Ter
LNK/LMHG ML11 **199** J5 1
Abbotshall Av *DRUM* G15 **60** E6
Abbotsinch Rd
PSLYN/LNWD PA3 **79** L7
Abbots Ter *AIRDRIE* ML6 **111** J5
Abbot St *GRNKW/INVK* PA16 **32** C6 1
PLKSD/SHW G41 **104** E8 1
PSLYN/LNWD PA3 **9** K1 1
Abbot's Wk *KLWNG* KA13 **193** L6
Abbots Wy *AYRS* KA7 **228** C6
Abbott Crs *CLYDBK* G81 **80** D1
Aberconway St *CLYDBK* G81 **80** C1
Abercorn Av
CARD/HILL/MSPK G52 **102** E1
Abercorn Crs *HMLTN* ML3 **156** F7
Abercorn Dr *HMLTN* ML3 **156** F6
Abercorn Pl *SMSTN* G23 **62** E8
Abercorn Rd *NMRNS* G77 **150** C3
Abercorn St *CLYDBK* G81 **60** E2 1
PSLYN/LNWD PA3 **9** J2
Abercrombie Crs
BAIL/MDB/MHD G69 **108** F4
Abercrombie Dr *BSDN* G61 **61** H1
Abercromby Crs *EKILN* G74 **154** B6
HBR/GL G84 **20** F6
Abercromby Dr *AYRS* KA7 **228** D6
DMNK/BRGTN G40 **12** C4
Abercromby Pl *EKILN* G74 **154** B6 1
Abercromby Pl West
HBR/GL G84 **20** D6 1
Abercromby St
DMNK/BRGTN G40 **12** B6 1
Abercromby St East
HBR/GL G84 **20** E6
Aberdalgie Rd *ESTRH* G34 **108** B1
Aberdeen Rd *AIRDRIE* ML6 **111** K5
Aberdour St *DEN/PKHD* G31 **13** J1
Aberfeldy Av *AIRDRIE* ML6 **89** M6
Aberfeldy St *DEN/PKHD* G31 **13** J1
Aberfoyle Rd *GRNK* PA15 **33** H7 1
Aberfoyle St *DEN/PKHD* G31 **13** J1
Aberlady Rd *GOV/IBX* G51 **103** L2
Aberlady St *MTHW* ML1 **135** H8
Aberlour Pl *IRVSE* KA11 **203** M3
Abernethy Dr
PSLYN/LNWD PA3 **100** A4
Abernethyn Rd *WISHAW* ML2 **160** A3
Abernethy Pk *EKILN* G74 **14** C2
Abernethy Pl *NMRNS* G77 **151** H5 1
Abernethy St *DEN/PKHD* G31 **13** J3
Aberuthven Dr *CAR/SHTL* G32 **107** H6
Abiegail Pl *BLTYR/CAMB* G72 **131** K8 1
Aboukir St *GOV/IBX* G51 **103** L1
Aboyne Dr *PSLYS* PA2 **101** M8 1
Aboyne St *GOV/IBX* G51 **103** M3
Acacia Dr *BEITH* KA15 **168** A1
BRHD/NEIL G78 **125** G4
PSLYS PA2 **101** H8
Acacia Pl *JNSTN* PA5 **123** G1
Academy Brae *BEITH* KA15 **168** B1
Academy Ct *KLMNK* KA1 **212** E3 1
Academy Gdns *IRV* KA12 **203** H5
Academy Pk *AIRDRIE* ML6 **111** G2
PLKSD/SHW G41 **104** C5
Academy Rd *GIF/THBK* G46 **127** J7
IRV KA12 **203** H6
Academy St *AIRDRIE* ML6 **111** G2
AYRS KA7 **18** E2
CAR/SHTL G32 **107** H5
CTBR ML5 **110** A2
KLMNK KA1 **16** F9
LRKH ML9 **176** A6 1
TROON KA10 **216** B7
Academy Ter *BLSH* ML4 **133** H4 1
Acer Crs *PSLYS* PA2 **101** G8
Acer Gv *AIRDRIE* ML6 **111** L6
Achamore Crs *DRUM* G15 **60** E5 1
Achamore Dr *DRUM* G15 **60** E5 2
Achamore Rd *DRUM* G15 **60** E5
Acherhill Gdns *KNTSWD* G13 **81** G1
Achnasheen Rd *AIRDRIE* ML6 **112** A3
Achray Av *ALEX/LLW* G83 **25** K3 1
Achray Dr *PSLYS* PA2 **101** G8
Achray Pl *CTBR* ML5 **87** J8
MLNGV G62 **41** K6
Achray Rd *CUMB* G67 **68** B3
Acorn Ct *DMNK/BRGTN* G40 **12** D7
Acorn St *DMNK/BRGTN* G40 **12** D7
Acre Av *LARGS* KA30 **115** K7
Acre Dr *MRYH/FIRH* G20 **62** B8
Acredyke Crs *SPRGB/BLRNK* G21 **84** B2
Acredyke Pl
SPRGB/BLRNK G21 **84** C3 1
Acredyke Rd *RUTH* G73 **128** F1
SPRGB/BLRNK G21 **84** B2
Acre Rd *MRYH/FIRH* G20 **62** B8
The Acres *LRKH* ML9 **176** B7 1
Acre Valley Rd *BSHPBGS* G64 **44** B7
Adair Av *SALT* KA21 **191** M8
Adam Av *AIRDRIE* ML6 **111** H2
Adams Av *SALT* KA21 **191** M8
Adams Ct *TROON* KA10 **216** E3
Adams Court La *CGLE* G1 **11** H3
Adam's Ga *TROON* KA10 **216** E3
Adamsliedrive *KKNTL* G66 **65** G1
Adamson St *BLSH* ML4 **133** K4
Adams Pl *KSYTH* G65 **47** K1 1
Adam St *GRK* PA19 **31** M2 1
GRNK PA15 **3** H8
Adams Wk *IRV* KA12 **203** L7 1
Adamswell St *SPRGB/BLRNK* G21 **6** C2
Adamswell Ter
BAIL/MDB/MHD G69 **67** G7 1
Adamton Rd North *PSTWK* KA9 **225** J2
Adamton Rd South *PSTWK* KA9 **225** J3
Adamton Ter *PSTWK* KA9 **225** J2
Addie St *MTHW* ML1 **157** M1
Addiewell Pl *CTBR* ML5 **110** A5
Addiewell St *CAR/SHTL* G32 **107** G2 1
Addison Gv *GIF/THBK* G46 **126** E5
Addison Pl *GIF/THBK* G46 **126** F5
Addison Rd *GIF/THBK* G46 **126** E5
KVD/HLHD G12 **82** D5
Adelaide Ct *CLYDBK* G81 **59** K4 1
Adelaide Rd *EKILS* G75 **171** H2
Adelaide St *GRK* PA19 **31** L1 1
HBR/GL G84 **20** E8 1
Adele St *MTHW* ML1 **157** M5
Adelphi St *GBLS* G5 **11** M6
Admiral St *PLKSD/SHW* G41 **10** B5
Admiralty Gv *OLDK* G60 **59** H4
Admiralty Pl *OLDK* G60 **59** H4 1
Advie Pl *GVH/MTFL* G42 **128** B1 1
Affric Av *AIRDRIE* ML6 **90** A6
GIF/THBK G46 **126** C5
Affric Dr *PSLYS* PA2 **102** B8
Afton Av *KLMNKN/STW* KA3 **206** F6
PSTWK KA9 **225** J4
RAYR/DAL KA6 **227** H3 1
Afton Ct *AYRS* KA7 **19** J7
Afton Crs *BSDN* G61 **62** B6
Afton Dr *RNFRW* PA4 **80** E7
Afton Gdns *BLTYR/CAMB* G72 **155** H3
CTBR ML5 **110** D4
TROON KA10 **216** F5
Afton Pl *ARD* KA22 **191** K5
Afton Rd *CUMB* G67 **49** H6
SVSTN KA20 **192** D8 1
Afton St *LRKH* ML9 **176** C7 1
PLKSD/SHW G41 **127** L1
Afton Vw *KKNTL* G66 **45** M8
Agamemnon St *CLYDBK* G81 **59** M7
Agnew Av *CTBR* ML5 **110** C2
Agnew Gv *UD/BTH/TAN* G71 **132** D4
Agnew La *GVH/MTFL* G42 **105** G8
Aikenhead Rd *GVH/MTFL* G42 **105** J7
LNPK/KPK G44 **128** C3
Aikman Pl *EKILN* G74 **154** B6
Aikman Rd *MTHW* ML1 **157** H4
Aiknut Rd *WKIL* KA23 **181** J5
Ailean Dr *CAR/SHTL* G32 **107** L5
Ailean Gdns *CAR/SHTL* G32 **107** L5 1
Aileymill Gdns
GRNKW/INVK PA16 **31** L6

Aillort Pl *EKILN* G74 .... 153 L6 🅸
Ailort Av *LNPK/KPK* G44 .... 128 A4 🅸
Ailsa Av *MTHW* ML1 .... 157 H2 🅸
Ailsa Ct *CTBR* ML5 .... 109 L5
  HMLTN ML3 .... 155 K8
Ailsa Crs *MTHW* ML1 .... 157 H2 🅸
Ailsa Dr *CLYDBK* G81 .... 60 B3
  GIF/THBK G46 .... 151 J1 🅸
  GVH/MTFL G42 .... 127 M2
  KKNTL G66 .... 45 M7
  PSLYS PA2 .... 124 D2
  RUTH G73 .... 128 F4 🅸
  SVSTN KA20 .... 201 J1
  UD/BTH/TAN G71 .... 132 A5
Ailsa Gdns *ARD* KA22 .... 191 K6
Ailsa Pl *KLMNKN/STW* KA3 .... 207 L4
  AYRS KA7 .... 18 C2
  CTBR ML5 .... 109 M5
Ailsa Rd *BSHPBGS* G64 .... 64 B7
  CTBR ML5 .... 109 L5
  GRK PA19 .... 31 J3
  IRV KA12 .... 208 B2
  RNFRW PA4 .... 80 C7
  SALT KA21 .... 192 A8
  TROON KA10 .... 216 A7
Ailsa St *PSTWK* KA9 .... 225 H1
Ainslie Rd
  CARD/HILL/MSPK G52 .... 103 H2 🅸
  CUMB G67 .... 49 J6
Airbles Crs *MTHW* ML1 .... 157 K4
Airbles Dr *MTHW* ML1 .... 157 K4
Airbles Farm Rd *MTHW* ML1 .... 157 J4
Airbles Rd *MTHW* ML1 .... 157 J4
Airbles St *MTHW* ML1 .... 157 L4
Airdale Av *GIF/THBK* G46 .... 127 J7
Aird Av *KLMNK* KA1 .... 16 C7
Airdriehill Rd *AIRDRIE* ML6 .... 89 J7
Airdriehill St *AIRDRIE* ML6 .... 89 J7 🅸
Airdrie Rd *AIRDRIE* ML6 .... 89 M8
  CARLUKE ML8 .... 178 E4
  CUMB G67 .... 67 L5
  CUMB G67 .... 68 A2
  KSYTH G65 .... 47 K1
Airgold Dr *DRUM* G15 .... 60 F5
Airlie Av *BSDN* G61 .... 61 L2
Airlie Ct *AYRS* KA7 .... 18 D8
Airlie Dr *ML4* .... 133 C3 🅸
Airlie Gdns *RUTH* G73 .... 129 K5
Airlie La *KVD/HLHD* G12 .... 82 B6
Airlie Rd *BAIL/MDB/MHD* G69 ..... 108 A6
Airlie St *KVD/HLHD* G12 .... 82 B6
Airlour Rd *PLKSW/MSWD* G43 ..... 127 L4
Airth Dr *CARD/HILL/MSPK* G52 ..... 103 M6
Airth La
  CARD/HILL/MSPK G52 .... 103 M6 🅸
Airthrey Av *SCOT* G14 .... 81 L5
Airthrey La *SCOT* G14 .... 81 L5 🅸
Airth Wy *BALLOCH* G68 .... 67 L1
Aitchison Ct *AIRDRIE* ML6 .... 110 F1 🅸
Aitchison St *AIRDRIE* ML6 .... 110 E2
Aitkenbar Cir *DMBTN* G82 .... 37 H4
Aitkenbar Dr *DMBTN* G82 .... 37 H3
Aitkenbrae Dr *PSTWK* KA9 .... 225 K1
Aitken Cl *WISHAW* ML2 .... 160 A2 🅸
Aitken Dr *BEITH* KA15 .... 144 C8
Aitkenhead Av *CTBR* ML5 .... 109 H5
Aitkenhead Rd *AIRDRIE* ML6 .... 111 K7
  UD/BTH/TAN G71 .... 109 G8
Aitken La *ALEX/LLW* G83 .... 25 L2 🅸
Aitken Pl *ARD* KA22 .... 191 J6
Aitken Rd *HMLTN* ML3 .... 174 E2
Aitken St *AIRDRIE* ML6 .... 89 G8
  DALRY KA24 .... 184 C2
  DEN/PKHD G31 .... 13 H2
  LARGS KA30 .... 115 J6
Alasdair Ct *BRHD/NEIL* G78 .... 125 J7 🅸
Albans Crs *MTHW* ML1 .... 157 H1
Albany G74 .... 154 C5
Albany Av *CAR/SHTL* G32 .... 107 J5
Albany Dr *LNK/LMHG* ML11 .... 199 G6
  RUTH G73 .... 129 H3
Albany Qd *CAR/SHTL* G32 .... 107 J3
Albany Rd *HMLTN* ML3 .... 174 C2 🅸
Albany St *CTBR* ML5 .... 109 L2
  DMNK/BRGTN G40 .... 12 E8
Albany Ter *BLTYR/CAMB* G72 ...... 129 L6
Alba Wy *HMLTN* ML3 .... 174 C3 🅸
Alberta Av *CTBR* ML5 .... 109 M1
  EKILS G75 .... 14 A5
Alberta Pk *EKILS* G75 .... 14 B5
Albert Av *GVH/MTFL* G42 .... 104 F8
Albert Dr *BSDN* G61 .... 62 B6
  HBR/GL G84 .... 20 E7
  LRKH ML9 .... 176 B7
  RUTH G73 .... 129 H4
Albert Pk *CARLUKE* ML8 .... 189 G3
Albert Pl *AIRDRIE* ML6 .... 111 H1
Albert Qd *MTHW* ML1 .... 134 A4
Albert Rd *CLYDBK* G81 .... 59 M6
  GRK PA19 .... 31 G3
  GRK PA19 .... 31 K2
  GVH/MTFL G42 .... 105 G5
  JNSTN PA5 .... 99 J4
  KKNTL G66 .... 65 J6
  RNFRW PA4 .... 80 C6
Albert St *ALEX/LLW* G83 .... 25 L5 🅸
  CTBR ML5 .... 110 A2
  HBR/GL G84 .... 20 E7
  HMLTN ML3 .... 156 A3
  MTHW ML1 .... 157 M2 🅸
Albert Ter *AYR* KA8 .... 225 L7
  HMLTN ML3 .... 156 A3
Albion Ga *CGLE* G1 .... 11 L6
Albion Rd *BAIL/MDB/MHD* G69 ..... 107 M6
  CGLE G1 .... 11 L2
  CTBR ML5 .... 110 B4
  MTHW ML1 .... 157 L4
  PSLYN/LNWD PA3 .... 9 G1
Albion Wy *EKILS* G75 .... 171 M4
Alcaig Rd *CARD/HILL/MSPK* G52 ... 103 L7
Alcath Rd *WISHAW* ML2 .... 160 B3
Alder Av *HMLTN* ML3 .... 156 E8
  KKNTL G66 .... 65 H4
Alder Bank *AYRS* KA7 .... 229 K3
  UD/BTH/TAN G71 .... 131 J8
Alderbank Rd *PGL* PA14 .... 34 A8
Alderbrae Rd *PGL* PA14 .... 34 A8
Alder Ct *BRHD/NEIL* G78 .... 125 J8

Alder Crs *EKILS* G75 .... 171 J4
Alder Ga *BLTYR/CAMB* G72 .... 130 E4
Alder Gn *IRVSE* KA11 .... 204 A5
Alder Gv *CTBR* ML5 .... 110 B3
Alderman Pl *KNTSWD* G13 .... 81 J3
Alder Pl *EKILS* G75 .... 171 J4
  JNSTN PA5 .... 100 A8
  KLMNK KA1 .... 16 A4
  PLKSW/MSWD G43 .... 127 H4
Alder Rd *CLYDBK* G81 .... 59 M4
  CUMB G67 .... 49 K7
  DMBTN G82 .... 36 E5
  KKNTL G66 .... 45 H4
  PLKSW/MSWD G43 .... 127 J4
Alderside Av *WISHAW* ML2 .... 158 D5
Alderside Gdns
  UD/BTH/TAN G71 .... 131 L2
Alderstocks *EKILS* G75 .... 171 L4
Alderston Av *AYR* KA8 .... 225 G6
Alderston Pl *AYR* KA8 .... 225 G6
  BLSH ML4 .... 132 E5
Aldersyde Av *TROON* KA10 .... 216 F5
Aldersyde Pl
  BLTYR/CAMB G72 .... 131 J8
Aldersyde Ter *MTHW* ML1 .... 135 J8
Alderwood Rd *PGL* PA14 .... 34 B8
Aldrin Rd *HBR/GL* G84 .... 23 H1
Alexander Av *KSYTH* G65 .... 46 C5
  LARGS KA30 .... 115 L4
  SVSTN KA20 .... 192 E7
  UD/BTH/TAN G71 .... 132 C3
Alexander Balfour Gdns
  HMLTN ML3 .... 156 D8 🅸
Alexander Crs *GBLS* G5 .... 11 H7
Alexander Fleming Av
  KBRN KA25 .... 142 F8 🅸
Alexander Gdns *HMLTN* ML3 ..... 157 G7 🅸
Alexander Gibson Wy
  MTHW ML1 .... 157 K4
  KKNTL G66 .... 65 B2
Alexander Pl *IRV* KA12 .... 203 H5
Alexander Rd *SHOTTS* ML7 .... 137 K3
Alexander St *AIRDRIE* ML6 .... 110 E2
  ALEX/LLW G83 .... 25 L4
  CLYDBK G81 .... 60 B8
  CTBR ML5 .... 110 B1
  DMBTN G82 .... 36 D1
  DMBTN G82 .... 37 G5
  WISHAW ML2 .... 158 F6
Alexander Ter
  BRHD/NEIL G78 .... 148 C2 🅸
Alexandra Av *PSTWK* KA9 .... 221 J8
  STPS/GTHM/RID G33 .... 85 K3
Alexandra Ct *DEN/PKHD* G31 ..... 7 G9
Alexandra Dr *PSLY* PA1 .... 8 A7
  RNFRW PA4 .... 80 D6
Alexandra Gdns *KKNTL* G66 ..... 65 J5
Alexandra Pde *DEN/PKHD* G31 ..... 6 C5
Alexandra Pk *KKNTL* G66 .... 65 J3
Alexandra Park St
  DEN/PKHD G31 .... 7 G8
Alexandra Rd *KKNTL* G66 .... 65 J5
Alexandra St *KKNTL* G66 .... 65 J1
Alexandra Ter *AYR* KA8 .... 225 K8
  KLWNG KA13 .... 193 K6
Alexandria Qd *MTHW* ML1 .... 134 A4
Alford Av *KKNTL* G66 .... 65 H1
Alford Pl *IRV* KA12 .... 203 L4
  PSLYN/LNWD PA3 .... 99 J3
Alford Qd *WISHAW* ML2 .... 159 H4
Alford St *SPRGB/BLRNK* G21 .... 5 M2
Algie St *PLKSD/SHW* G41 .... 127 M1
Algoma Pl *EKILS* G75 .... 171 H1
Alice Av *BLSH* ML4 .... 133 G5
Alice St *PSLYS* PA2 .... 9 G8
Aline Ct *BRHD/NEIL* G78 .... 125 H5
Alison Ct *GRNKW/INVK* PA16 ..... 50 E4
Alison Lea *EKILS* G74 .... 154 C6
Allan Av *CARLUKE* ML8 .... 178 E6
  CTBR ML5 .... 88 F6
  RNFRW PA4 .... 80 E8
Allanbank St *SHOTTS* ML7 .... 160 F1
Allan Crs *EKILS* G75 .... 170 E2
Allan Crs *ALEX/LLW* G83 .... 25 K6
  DMBTN G82 .... 37 G5
Allandale Av *MTHW* ML1 .... 134 F4
Allander Av *MLNGV* G62 .... 63 G2
Allander Dr *BSHPBGS* G64 .... 64 A1
Allander Gdns *BSHPBGS* G64 ..... 63 M5
Allander Rd *MLNGV* G62 .... 42 A7
Allander St *PPK/MIL* G22 .... 5 J1
Allands Av *RNFRW* PA4 .... 79 J4
Allanfauld Rd *CUMB* G67 .... 48 F7
Allan Glen Gdns *BSHPBGS* G64 ... 64 B5
Allan Pl *AYR* KA8 .... 225 J6
  DMBTN G82 .... 37 G5
  DMNK/BRGTN G40 .... 106 B6
  EKILS G75 .... 170 E2
Allanshaw Gdns *HMLTN* ML3 ..... 156 B7
Allanshaw Gv *HMLTN* ML3 .... 156 B7
Allanshaw St *HMLTN* ML3 .... 156 C6
Allan Sq *IRV* KA12 .... 203 L7
Allan St *CTBR* ML5 .... 109 K4
  DMNK/BRGTN G40 .... 106 B7
  MTHW ML1 .... 157 M2
Allanton Av *PSLY* PA1 .... 102 C5
Allanton Dr
  CARD/HILL/MSPK G52 .... 103 H4
Allanton Gv *WISHAW* ML2 .... 159 H4
Allanton Lea *HMLTN* ML3 .... 174 C1
Allanton Pl *HMLTN* ML3 .... 156 E8
Allanton Rd *SHOTTS* ML7 .... 137 J8
  WISHAW ML2 .... 160 L1
Allanvale Rd *PSTWK* KA9 .... 225 H1
Allanvale Rd *BLSH* ML4 .... 133 H4
  KSYTH G65 .... 46 E1
Allendale *EKILN* G74 .... 153 J6
Allender Rd *BSDN* G61 .... 61 K6
Allenfield Rd *AYRS* KA7 .... 229 K3
Allen Wy *RNFRW* PA4 .... 80 D8
Allerdyce Dr *DRUM* G15 .... 60 F7
Allershaw Pl *WISHAW* ML2 .... 176 F1
Allershaw Rd *WISHAW* ML2 .... 176 F1
Allerton Gdns *CAR/SHTL* G32 ..... 107 M5
Alleysbank Rd *RUTH* G73 .... 106 A8
Allison Av *ERSK* PA8 .... 58 F7
Allison Dr *BLTYR/CAMB* G72 ..... 130 A3

Allison Pl *BAIL/MDB/MHD* G69 ..... 86 E5
  NMRNS G77 .... 150 C5
Allison St *AYR* KA8 .... 19 G1
  GVH/MTFL G42 .... 105 G7
Allinach Pl *ESTRH* G34 .... 108 L1
Alloa Av *AYRS* KA7 .... 228 E8
Alloway Av *KLMNKN/STW* KA3 ..... 17 K5
  PSLYS PA2 .... 125 H1
Alloway Crs *PSLYS* PA2 .... 125 J1
  RUTH G73 .... 128 F4
Alloway Dr *CLYDBK* G81 .... 60 C6
  KKNTL G66 .... 46 A7
  NMRNS G77 .... 151 G5
  PSLYS PA2 .... 125 H1
  RUTH G73 .... 128 F4
Alloway Gdns *HMLTN* ML3 .... 155 K8
  KKNTL G66 .... 46 A7
Alloway Gv *KKNTL* G66 .... 45 M7
Alloway Pk *AYRS* KA7 .... 18 D5
Alloway Pl *ARD* KA22 .... 191 J5
  AYRS KA7 .... 18 D4
Alloway Place La *AYRS* KA7 .... 18 D5
  EKILN G74 .... 154 D6
  PLKSW/MSWD G43 .... 127 K3
Alloway St *AYRS* KA7 .... 18 F5
  LRKH ML9 .... 176 C7
Alloway Ter *KKNTL* G66 .... 45 M7
Almada La *HMLTN* ML3 .... 156 D5
Almada St *HMLTN* ML3 .... 156 D5
Alma St *DEN/PKHD* G31 .... 13 G5
Almond Av *RNFRW* PA4 .... 80 E7
Almond Crs *PSLYS* PA2 .... 100 F7
Almond Dr *BSHPTN* PA7 .... 58 B7
  EKILN G74 .... 15 L3
  KKNTL G66 .... 65 H4
Almond Pl *CTBR* ML5 .... 87 K8
  KLMNK KA1 .... 16 A4
Almond Rd *BSDN* G61 .... 61 J7
  CUMB G67 .... 49 M4
  STPS/GTHM/RID G33 .... 85 J4
Almond St *STPS/GTHM/RID* G33 ... 7 M6
Almond V *UD/BTH/TAN* G71 .... 132 A2
Almond Wy *MTHW* ML1 .... 157 L6
Almswall Rd *KLWNG* KA13 .... 193 L6
Alness Crs
  CARD/HILL/MSPK G52 .... 103 K6
Alness St *HMLTN* ML3 .... 156 D7
Alness Ter *HMLTN* ML3 .... 156 D7
Alpine Gv *UD/BTH/TAN* G71 .... 131 M2
Alsatian Av *CLYDBK* G81 .... 60 D7
Alsh Ter *HMLTN* ML3 .... 156 A8
Alston Av *CTBR* ML5 .... 110 B1
Alston Gdns *BSDN* G61 .... 61 H1
Alstonpapple *NMLNS* KA16 .... 215 L2
Altnacreag Gdns
  BAIL/MDB/MHD G69 .... 67 G5
Altonhead Ter
  KLMNKN/STW KA3 .... 196 B8
Altonhill Av *KLMNKN/STW* KA3 ..... 206 E6
Alton Rd *PSLY* PA1 .... 102 C5
Alton St *WKIL* KA23 .... 181 J4
Altpatrick Gdns *JNSTN* PA5 ..... 100 B6
Altry Pl *AYRS* KA7 .... 228 B8
Altyre St *CAR/SHTL* G32 .... 106 F6
Aluclutha Av *DMBTN* G82 .... 37 H6
Alva Gdns
  CARD/HILL/MSPK G52 .... 103 L6
Alva Ga *CARD/HILL/MSPK* G52 ..... 103 L6
Alva Pl *KKNTL* G66 .... 65 L5
Alva Ter *GRK* PA19 .... 32 A2
Alvord Av *PSTWK* KA9 .... 221 K8
Alwyn Av *CRG/CRSL/HOU* PA6 ..... 99 K1
Alwyn Ct *EKILN* G74 .... 153 L6
Alwyn Dr *EKILN* G74 .... 153 L6
Alyssum Crs *MTHW* ML1 .... 157 K1
Alyth Crs *CRMNK/CLK/EAG* G76 ... 152 A1
Alyth Gdns
  CARD/HILL/MSPK G52 .... 103 L6 🅸
  CRMNK/CLK/EAG G76 .... 152 A1 🅸
Amber Ter *BLSH* ML4 .... 133 G5
Ambleside *EKILS* G75 .... 170 F3
Ambleside Ri *HMLTN* ML3 .... 174 C3 🅸
Amethyst Av *BLSH* ML4 .... 133 G5
Amisfield St *MRYH/FIRH* G20 ..... 82 E4 🅸
Amlaird Rd *KLMNKN/STW* KA3 ..... 207 G4
Amochrie Dr *PSLYS* PA2 .... 124 A1
Amochrie Gln *PSLYS* PA2 .... 124 A1
Amochrie Rd *PSLYS* PA2 .... 123 M1
Amochrie Wy *PSLYS* PA2 .... 100 F8
Amulree Pl *CAR/SHTL* G32 .... 107 G5
Amulree St *CAR/SHTL* G32 .... 107 G6
Ancaster Dr *KNTSWD* G13 .... 81 M3
Ancaster La *KNTSWD* G13 .... 81 M3
Anchor Av *PSLY* PA1 .... 9 L5
Anchor Crs *PSLY* PA1 .... 9 M6
Anchor Dr *PSLY* PA1 .... 9 M5
Anchor La *CGLE* G1 .... 11 J1
Anchor Wynd *PSLY* PA1 .... 9 M6
Ancroft St *MRYH/FIRH* G20 .... 4 E2
Andersen *EKILS* G75 .... 171 J3
Anderside *EKILS* G75 .... 171 L4
Anderson Ct *BLSH* ML4 .... 133 H4
  KSYTH G65 .... 46 E1
Anderson Crs *AYRS* KA7 .... 229 H5
Anderson La *AIRDRIE* ML6 .... 111 G1
Anderson Pl *KLMNKN/STW* KA3 ... 207 K7
Anderson Rd *BSHPTN* PA7 .... 58 A1
Anderson St *AIRDRIE* ML6 .... 111 G1
  HMLTN ML3 .... 155 M4
  MTHW ML1 .... 157 L4
  PGL PA14 .... 34 B7
  PTCK G11 .... 82 B7
Anderson Ter *ARD* KA22 .... 191 J7
Anderston Quay *KVGV* G3 .... 10 D3
Andrew Av *KKNTL* G66 .... 65 K6
  RNFRW PA4 .... 80 E6
Andrew Dr *IRV* KA12 .... 203 K4
  NMRNS G77 .... 150 C5
  RNFRW PA4 .... 80 D5
  SALT KA21 .... 191 M7
Andrew Lundi Pl *GLSTN* KA4 ..... 214 B4
Andrew Pl *CARLUKE* ML8 .... 178 E6
Andrew Sillars Av
  BLTYR/CAMB G72 .... 130 C4

Andrews St *PSLYN/LNWD* PA3 ..... 8 F1
Andrew St *EKILN* G74 .... 15 G4
Anford Pl *BLTYR/CAMB* G72 .... 155 L3
Angela Wy *UD/BTH/TAN* G71 ..... 131 M5
Angle Ga *SCOT* G14 .... 81 K5
Angus Av *AIRDRIE* ML6 .... 111 G4
  BSHPBGS G64 .... 64 D8
  CARD/HILL/MSPK G52 .... 103 J6
  EKILN G74 .... 15 L2
  HMLTN ML3 .... 157 G6
  MTHW ML1 .... 157 J1
  PSTWK KA9 .... 225 K1
Angus Gdns *UD/BTH/TAN* G71 ..... 131 M1
Angus Ov
  CARD/HILL/MSPK G52 .... 103 H5
Angus Pl
  CARD/HILL/MSPK G52 .... 103 H5 🅸
  EKILN G74 .... 15 L2
  GRNKW/INVK PA16 .... 31 K5
  PGL PA14 .... 34 C8
Angus St *ALEX/LLW* G83 .... 25 M5
  CLYDBK G81 .... 80 E1
  SPRGB/BLRNK G21 .... 6 B1
Annan Av *EKILS* G75 .... 170 E2
Annan Crs *AIRDRIE* ML6 .... 111 K8
Annandale Crs *CRH/DND* KA2 ..... 205 M8
Annandale Gdns *CRH/DND* KA2 ... 205 L8
Annandale St *GVH/MTFL* G42 ..... 105 H6 🅸
Annandale Vw *CRH/DND* KA2 ..... 205 M8
Annandale Wy *IRVSE* KA11 .... 204 A4
Annan Dr *BSDN* G61 .... 61 J6
  PSLYS PA2 .... 100 F7
  RUTH G73 .... 129 K2
Annan Gld *MTHW* ML1 .... 158 A6
Annan Gv *MTHW* ML1 .... 158 A6
Annanhill Av *KLMNK* KA1 .... 206 C8
Annanhill Pl *KLWNG* KA13 .... 193 H6
Annan Pl *JNSTN* PA5 .... 122 C1
Annan Rd *KLMNK* KA1 .... 212 A4
Annan St *GVH/MTFL* G42 .... 128 A1
  MTHW ML1 .... 158 A6
Annathill Gdns *CTBR* ML5 .... 67 M7
Annbank Pl *DEN/PKHD* G31 ..... 12 D3
Annbank Rd *RAYR/DAL* KA6 .... 227 G4
Annbank St *DEN/PKHD* G31 ..... 12 D3
  LRKH ML9 .... 175 M6
Ann Ct *HMLTN* ML3 .... 156 A4
Anne Av *RNFRW* PA4 .... 80 D5
Anne Crs *KKNTL* G66 .... 65 K6
Annerley Pl *CTBR* ML5 .... 109 L4
Annes Ct *DMNK/BRGTN* G40 ..... 12 B7
Annette St *GVH/MTFL* G42 .... 105 G7
Annfield Gdns
  BLTYR/CAMB G72 .... 131 J8 🅸
Annfield Glen Rd *AYRS* KA7 ..... 229 H5
Annfield Pl *DEN/PKHD* G31 ..... 12 D2
Annfield Rd *PSTWK* KA9 .... 225 H1
Annfield Ter *PSTWK* KA9 .... 225 H1
Annick Crs *KLMNKN/STW* KA3 ..... 197 L1
Annick Dr *DRUM* G15 .... 61 J6
  IRVSE KA11 .... 204 D6
Annick Pl *KLMNK* KA1 .... 212 A4 🅸
  TROON KA10 .... 216 F5
Annick Rd *IRVSE* KA11 .... 203 L8
Annick St *BLTYR/CAMB* G72 ..... 130 D4
  CAR/SHTL G32 .... 107 H4
Anniesdale Av
  STPS/GTHM/RID G33 .... 85 K3
Annieshill Vw *AIRDRIE* ML6 .... 90 A7
Anniesland Crs *SCOT* G14 .... 81 G4 🅸
Anniesland Rd *KNTSWD* G13 ..... 81 J3
  SCOT G14 .... 81 G4
Annieston *KSYTH* G65 .... 46 F5
Anniversary Av *EKILS* G75 .... 14 A8
Annpit Rd *AYR* KA8 .... 225 H5
Annsfield Rd *HMLTN* ML3 .... 174 C2
Ann St *GRNK* PA15 .... 2 B6
  HMLTN ML3 .... 156 A4
  JNSTN PA5 .... 100 A6
Ansdell Av *BLTYR/CAMB* G72 ..... 155 J2
Anson St *DMNK/BRGTN* G40 ..... 12 C7
Anstruther Ct *CARLUKE* ML8 ..... 177 M4
Anstruther St *CAR/SHTL* G32 ..... 106 F5
  CARLUKE ML8 .... 177 M4
Antermony Rd *KKNTL* G66 .... 45 K4
Anthony Rd *LARGS* KA30 .... 115 K8
Anthony St *CGLW* G2 .... 10 E1
Antigua St *GRNK* PA15 .... 2 E6
Antigua Wy *EKILS* G75 .... 153 G8 🅸
Anton Crs *KSYTH* G65 .... 47 L1
Antonine *KKNTL* G66 .... 46 B7
Antonine Av *MTHW* ML1 .... 157 J1
Antonine Gdns *CLYDBK* G81 ..... 60 A3
Antonine Rd *BSDN* G61 .... 61 H3
Anwoth St *CAR/SHTL* G32 .... 107 G6
Appin Crs *DEN/PKHD* G31 .... 13 H1
Appin Rd *DEN/PKHD* G31 .... 13 H1
Appin Ter *HMLTN* ML3 .... 155 L5
  RUTH G73 .... 129 K5
Appin Wy *AIRDRIE* ML6 .... 88 E5
Appleby Cl *EKILS* G75 .... 170 E5 🅸
Appleby St *PPK/MIL* G22 .... 5 G2
Applecross Gdns
  BAIL/MDB/MHD G69 .... 66 F6
Applecross Qd *WISHAW* ML2 ..... 159 H4 🅸
Applecross St *KKNTL* G66 .... 46 B8
Applecross St *MRYH/FIRH* G20 ... 5 G1
Appledore Crs
  UD/BTH/TAN G71 .... 132 A6
Apsley La *PTCK* G11 .... 82 A7 🅸
Apsley St *PTCK* G11 .... 82 A7
Aqua Av *HMLTN* ML3 .... 155 L7
Aqua Ct *HMLTN* ML3 .... 155 L7 🅸
Aquila Wy *CARLUKE* ML8 .... 178 D7
Araburn Dr *EKILS* G75 .... 171 L4
Aranthrue Crs *RNFRW* PA4 .... 80 C5 🅸
Aranthrue Dr *RNFRW* PA4 .... 80 C5
Aray St *MRYH/FIRH* G20 .... 82 D3 🅸
Arbroath Av
  CARD/HILL/MSPK G52 .... 103 H5
Arbroath Gv *HMLTN* ML3 .... 156 B7 🅸
Arbuckle Pl *AIRDRIE* ML6 .... 90 A6 🅸
Arbuckle Rd *AIRDRIE* ML6 .... 90 A4
Arbuckle St *KLMNK* KA1 .... 17 G5
Arcadia St *BLSH* ML4 .... 133 G4 🅸

  DMNK/BRGTN G40 .... 12 B6
Arcan Crs *DRUM* G15 .... 61 H7
Archerfield Av
  CAR/SHTL G32 .... 107 G7
Archerfield Crs
  CAR/SHTL G32 .... 107 G7 🅸
Archerfield Dr *CAR/SHTL* G32 ... 107 G7
Archerfield Gv
  CAR/SHTL G32 .... 107 G7 🅸
Archerhill Av *KNTSWD* G13 .... 81 G1
Archerhill Crs *KNTSWD* G13 ..... 81 H1
Archerhill Rd *KNTSWD* G13 .... 81 G1
Archerhill Sq *KNTSWD* G13 .... 80 F1
Archerhill Ter *KNTSWD* G13 ..... 81 G1
Archibald Ter *KKNTL* G66 .... 45 H3
Archiebald Pl *BLSH* ML4 .... 133 K5
Arcon Av *RAYR/DAL* KA6 .... 226 F3
Arcon Ct *RAYR/DAL* KA6 .... 227 G2
Ardargie Dr *CAR/SHTL* G32 ..... 130 C1
Ardargie Gv *CAR/SHTL* G32 ..... 130 C1
Ardargie Pl *CAR/SHTL* G32 ..... 130 C1
Ardayre Rd *PSTWK* KA9 .... 225 H1
Ardbeg Av *BSHPBGS* G64 .... 64 C8
  KLMNKN/STW KA3 .... 206 F6
  RUTH G73 .... 129 L6
Ardbeg Ct *IRVSE* KA11 .... 203 M3
Ardbeg La *GVH/MTFL* G42 .... 105 G7
Ardbeg Rd *GRNK* PA15 .... 33 J7
Ardbeg St *GVH/MTFL* G42 .... 105 G7
Ardchoille Dr *SVSTN* KA20 .... 192 C1
Ardchoille La *SVSTN* KA20 .... 192 E7
Ardconnel St *GIF/THBK* G46 ..... 126 F5
Ardeer La *SVSTN* KA20 .... 201 M3
Arden Av *GIF/THBK* G46 .... 126 E7
Ardencaple Dr *HBR/GL* G84 ..... 20 A7
Ardencaple Qd *HBR/GL* G84 ..... 20 A7
Ardenclutha Av *HMLTN* ML3 ..... 156 B5
Ardenclutha Dr *PGL* PA14 .... 34 B8
Arden Ct *HMLTN* ML3 .... 156 D8
Ardencraig Crs *CSMK* G45 .... 128 C8
Ardencraig Dr *CSMK* G45 .... 128 F7
Ardencraig La *CSMK* G45 .... 128 C8
Ardencraig Pl *CSMK* G45 .... 128 E6
Ardencraig Qd *CSMK* G45 .... 128 E6
Ardencraig Rd *CSMK* G45 .... 129 G6
Ardencraig Ter *CSMK* G45 .... 128 E7
Arden Dr *GIF/THBK* G46 .... 127 H7
Ardenlea *UD/BTH/TAN* G71 ..... 131 M2
Ardenlea St
  DMNK/BRGTN G40 .... 106 B6
Arden Pl *GIF/THBK* G46 .... 126 E7
Arden Rd *GRNK* PA15 .... 33 K8
  HMLTN ML3 .... 156 C7
Arden St *AIRDRIE* ML6 .... 90 A7
Arden Ter *HMLTN* ML3 .... 156 C7
  HMLTN ML3 .... 156 D8
Ardery St *PTCK* G11 .... 82 A7
Ardessie Pl *SMSTN* G23 .... 62 D8
Ardfern Rd *AIRDRIE* ML6 .... 111 M3
Ardfern St *CAR/SHTL* G32 .... 107 G6
Ardfin Ct *PSTWK* KA9 .... 225 J3
Ardfin Rd *PSTWK* KA9 .... 225 J4
Ardgay Pl *CAR/SHTL* G32 .... 107 G5
Ardgay St *CAR/SHTL* G32 .... 107 G5
Ardgay Wy *RUTH* G73 .... 129 H6
Ardgoil Dr *BALLOCH* G68 .... 48 B3
Ardgour Dr *PSLYN/LNWD* PA3 ..... 100 A4
Ardgour Pl
  KLMNKN/STW KA3 .... 206 F5 🅸
Ardgour Rd *KLMNKN/STW* KA3 ... 206 F6
Ardgowan Av *PSLYS* PA2 .... 9 J7
Ardgowan Crs
  GRNKW/INVK PA16 .... 50 D5
Ardgowan Dr *UD/BTH/TAN* G71 ... 131 M1
Ardgowan Pl *SHOTTS* ML7 .... 137 L3
Ardgowan Rd *WMYSB* PA18 ..... 50 A8
Ardgowan St *GRNK* PA15 .... 33 M7
  GRNKW/INVK PA16 .... 32 D3
  PSLYS PA2 .... 9 J8
Ardgryfe Crs
  CRG/CRSL/HOU PA6 .... 77 K8
Ardholm St *CAR/SHTL* G32 ..... 107 G6
Ardhu Pl *DRUM* G15 .... 61 G6
Ardlaw St *GOV/IBX* G51 .... 103 M3
Ardle Av *KLMNK* KA1 .... 212 B4 🅸
Ardle Rd *PLKSW/MSWD* G43 ..... 127 L4
Ardlui Rd *AYR* KA8 .... 225 G5
Ardlui St *CAR/SHTL* G32 .... 106 F5
Ardmaleish Crs *CSMK* G45 ..... 128 E3
Ardmaleish Dr *CSMK* G45 .... 128 D7
Ardmaleish Rd *CSMK* G45 .... 128 D7
Ardmaleish St *CSMK* G45 .... 128 D7
Ardmaleish Ter *CSMK* G45 .... 128 E7 🅸
Ardmay Crs *LNPK/KPK* G44 ..... 128 C2
Ardmillan St
  STPS/GTHM/RID G33 .... 106 F1
Ardmore Ct *IRVSE* KA11 .... 204 A3
Ardmore Pl *GRNK* PA15 .... 2 A7
Ardmore Rd *GRNK* PA15 .... 33 J8
  PGL PA14 .... 34 D8
Ardmory Av *GVH/MTFL* G42 ..... 128 D2
Ardmory La *GVH/MTFL* G42 ..... 128 E2
Ardmory Pl *GVH/MTFL* G42 ..... 128 E2 🅸
Ardnahoe Av *GVH/MTFL* G42 ..... 128 D1
Ardnahoe Pl *GVH/MTFL* G42 ..... 128 D1 🅸
Ardneil Av *WKIL* KA23 .... 181 J6
Ardneil Rd *GOV/IBX* G51 .... 103 M3
Ardnish St *GOV/IBX* G51 .... 103 L2 🅸
Ardoch Ct *SVSTN* KA20 .... 201 L3
Ardoch Crs *DMBTN* G82 .... 36 D5
  SVSTN KA20 .... 201 L3
Ardoch Gv *BLTYR/CAMB* G72 ..... 129 M3
Ardoch Rd *BSDN* G61 .... 62 B4
Ardoch St *PPK/MIL* G22 .... 83 H5 🅸
Ardo Gdns *GOV/IBX* G51 .... 104 A4 🅸
Ardressie Pl *MRYH/FIRH* G20 ..... 82 D4 🅸
Ard Rd *RNFRW* PA4 .... 80 B5
Ardrossan High Rd *WKIL* KA23 ... 181 K5
Ardrossan Rd *SALT* KA21 .... 200 E1
  WKIL KA23 .... 181 J6
Ardshiel Rd *GOV/IBX* G51 .... 103 L2
Ardsloy Pl *SCOT* G14 .... 81 G5
Ard St *CAR/SHTL* G32 .... 107 G5 🅸
Ardtoe Crs *STPS/GTHM/RID* G33 ... 85 L4
Ardtoe Pl *STPS/GTHM/RID* G33 ... 85 L4
Arduthie Rd *GOV/IBX* G51 .... 103 L2

Ard - Bal 235

Ardwell Rd
CARD/HILL/MSPK G52 103 L6
Argus Av AIRDRIE ML6 111 J7
Argyle Crs AIRDRIE ML6 110 F5
HMLTN ML3 155 M6
Argyle Dr HMLTN ML3 156 A5
Argyle Gdns KKNTL G66 44 E2 1
Argyle Pl SALT KA21 200 E1
Argyle Rd BSDN G61 61 L2
GRK PA19 31 M3
SALT KA21 200 E1
Argyle St CGLE G1 11 J2
CGLW G2 11 G2
GRNK PA15 2 C3
KVGV G3 4 C9
KVGV G3 82 D8
PSLY PA1 8 E5
Argyle St East HBR/GL G84 20 E8 2
Argyle St West HBR/GL G84 20 C7
Argyll Av DMBTN G82 37 J5
PSLYN/LNWD PA3 79 K8
RNFRW PA4 80 B5
Argyll Gdns LRKH ML9 176 B6 1
Argyll Pl BLSH ML4 132 F6
DMBTN G82 37 J5
EKILN G74 154 C6
KSYTH G65 47 L1
Argyll Rd CLYDBK G81 80 B1
Argyll St ALEX/LLW G83 25 K3
Arisaig Dr BSDN G61 62 B6
CARD/HILL/MSPK G52 103 K6
Arisaig Pl CARD/HILL/MSPK G52 103 L6
Arisdale Crs NMRNS G77 150 E3
Arkaig Av AIRDRIE ML6 89 M6
Arkaig Pl NMRNS G77 151 H5
Arkaig St WISHAW ML2 177 H1
Ark La DEN/PKHD G31 12 C1
Arkleston Crs
PSLYN/LNWD PA3 102 B2 1
Arkleston Rd PSLY PA1 102 B3
PSLYN/LNWD PA3 102 A1
Arkle Ter BLTYR/CAMB G72 129 L6
Arklet Rd GOV/IBX G51 103 L3
Arklet Wy WISHAW ML2 159 L6
Arkwrights Wy PSLY PA1 8 B6
Arkwright Wy IRVSE KA11 203 M6
Arlington St KVGV G3 4 D6
Armadale Pl DEN/PKHD G31 6 F8
GRNK PA15 2 D5
Armadale Rd LNK/LMHG ML11 199 J5
Armadale St DEN/PKHD G31 6 F9
Armour Av AIRDRIE ML6 110 E2
Armour Ct BLTYR/CAMB G72 155 H3
KKNTL G66 46 A8
Armour Dr AYRS KA7 19 L7
KKNTL G66 46 A8
Armour Gv MTHW ML1 158 A5
Armour Pl ARD KA22 191 J5 1
JNSTN PA5 100 A6
Armour St COWCAD G4 12 B3
JNSTN PA5 100 A6
KLMNK KA1 16 F6 1
Armstrong Crs
UD/BTH/TAN G71 132 A1
Armstrong Gv EKILS G75 14 D7
Armstrong Rd HBR/GL G84 23 G1 1
KLMNKN/STW KA3 17 L1
Arness Ter KLMNKN/STW KA3 206 E5
Arngask Rd GOV/IBX G51 103 L2
Arnhall Pl
CARD/HILL/MSPK G52 103 L6
Arnhem St BLTYR/CAMB G72 130 D4
Arnholm Pl
CARD/HILL/MSPK G52 103 L6 2
Arnisdale Pl ESTRH G34 108 A1 1
Arnisdale Rd ESTRH G34 108 A1
Arnisdale Wy RUTH G73 129 H6 1
Arniston St CAR/SHTL G32 106 F2
Arniston Wy
PSLYN/LNWD PA3 102 A2 1
Arnold Av BSHPBGS G64 64 A8
Arnol Pl
STPS/GTHM/RID G33 107 M2 1
Arnott Dr CTBR ML5 110 A5
Arnott Qd MTHW ML1 133 J8 1
Arnott Wy BLTYR/CAMB G72 130 A3 1
Arnprior Crs CSMK G45 128 D6 1
Arnprior Pl AYRS KA7 228 F7
Arnprior Qd CSMK G45 128 D5
Arnprior Rd CSMK G45 128 D5
Arnprior St CSMK G45 128 D5
Arnside Av GIF/THBK G46 127 J6
Arnum Gdns CARLUKE ML8 178 F8
Arnum Pl CARLUKE ML8 178 F8 1
Arnwood Dr KVD/HLHD G12 82 A4 1
Arondale Rd AIRDRIE ML6 89 M6
Aron Ter BLTYR/CAMB G72 129 M6
Aros Dr CARD/HILL/MSPK G52 103 K7
Arran EKILN G74 154 C8
Arran Av CTBR ML5 110 D5
DMBTN G82 36 D4 1
KLMNKN/STW KA3 207 G5
PGL PA14 55 H2
PSLYN/LNWD PA3 79 L8
Arran Crs BEITH KA15 144 C8
Arran Dr AIRDRIE ML6 88 F4
AIRDRIE ML6 88 F8
CARD/HILL/MSPK G52 103 M6
CUMB G67 68 D1
GIF/THBK G46 127 H7
JNSTN PA5 99 K8
KKNTL G66 45 L8
PSLYS PA2 124 E2
Arran Gdns CARLUKE ML8 188 F1
HMLTN ML3 156 E8
TROON KA10 216 D2
Arran La ARD KA22 191 J8 1
Arran Pk PSTWK KA9 225 H4
Arran Pl ARD KA22 191 J8 2
CLYDBK G81 60 C7
CTBR ML5 110 D5 1
IRV KA12 203 H4
PSLYN/LNWD PA3 100 A3
SALT KA21 192 A7
Arran Rd GRK PA19 31 K3
MTHW ML1 157 J2
RNFRW PA4 80 D7
TROON KA10 216 D2
Arran Ter AYRS KA7 18 D2
RUTH G73 128 F4 2
Arran Vw KSYTH G65 47 K1 2
LARGS KA30 115 L5
TROON KA10 216 C6
Arranview St AIRDRIE ML6 111 L8
Arran Wy UD/BTH/TAN G71 131 M7
Arrochar Ct SMSTN G23 82 D1 1
Arrochar Dr SMSTN G23 62 D8
Arrochar St MRYH/FIRH G20 82 D1
SMSTN G23 62 D8
Arrol Dr AYRS KA7 228 D4
Arrol Pl EKILS G75 172 A3
Arrol St CARD/HILL/MSPK G52 102 E2
Arrothill Dr KLMNK KA1 16 B6
Arrotshole Rd EKILN G74 153 H6
Arrowsmith Av KNTSWD G13 81 K1
Arthur Av AIRDRIE ML6 110 F3
BRHD/NEIL G78 125 H8
Arthur Ct WKIL KA23 181 J4 1
Arthur Gdns AIRDRIE ML6 91 H5 1
Arthurlie Av BRHD/NEIL G78 125 J7
BRHD/NEIL G78 147 H6
Arthurlie Dr BRHD/NEIL G78 147 H6
GIF/THBK G46 127 J8
NMRNS G77 150 D6
Arthurlie Pl SALT KA21 200 E1 1
Arthurlie St BRHD/NEIL G78 125 H7
GOV/IBX G51 103 M2
Arthur Rd PSLYS PA2 124 E1
Arthurston Rd ALEX/LLW G83 25 M2
Arthurston Ter
RAYR/DAL KA6 231 H5 1
Arthur St ALEX/LLW G83 25 L5 2
AYRS KA7 18 E3
CRMNK/CLK/EAG G76 151 L3
GRNK PA15 3 G6
HMLTN ML3 156 D4 1
KVGV G3 82 D8 1
PSLY PA1 8 D3
SALT KA21 201 G2 1
SVSTN KA20 201 K1 1
WKIL KA23 181 J4
Arundel Dr BSHPBGS G64 64 B5 2
GVH/MTFL G42 128 A2 1
Ascaig Crs
CARD/HILL/MSPK G52 103 L7
Ascog Pl WMYSB PA18 50 A8
Ascog Rd BSDN G61 61 M7
Ascog St GVH/MTFL G42 105 G7
Ascot Av KVD/HLHD G12 81 M3
Ash Av EKILS G75 14 A9
Ashburn Gdns GRK PA19 31 J2 1
MLNGV G62 41 L8
Ashburn Ga GRK PA19 31 J2 2
Ashburn Rd MLNGV G62 41 L7
Ashburton La KVD/HLHD G12 82 B3
Ashburton Pk EKILS G75 171 G2
Ashburton Rd KVD/HLHD G12 82 A3
Ashby Crs KNTSWD G13 61 L8
Ash Ct EKILS G75 171 J3
Ashcroft EKILN G74 154 D4
Ashcroft Av KKNTL G66 44 E2
Ashcroft Dr LNPK/KPK G44 128 E3
Ashdale Av SALT KA21 191 M7
Ashdale Dr
CARD/HILL/MSPK G52 103 L6
Ashdale Rd KLMNKN/STW KA3 206 E5
Ashdene St PPK/MIL G22 83 H2
Ash Dr BEITH KA15 144 B7
Asher Rd AIRDRIE ML6 111 L7
Ashfield BSHPBGS G64 64 A6
Ashfield Rd CARLUKE ML8 177 M3
CRMNK/CLK/EAG G76 151 L3
MLNGV G62 42 A8 1
Ashfield St PPK/MIL G22 83 J5
Ashgillhead Rd LRKH ML9 176 E8
Ashgill Pl PPK/MIL G22 83 J3
Ashgill Rd PPK/MIL G22 83 H3
Ash Gv BSHPBGS G64 84 B1
KKNTL G66 65 H4 1
UD/BTH/TAN G71 132 B1
Ashgrove AIRDRIE ML6 91 G4
AIRDRIE ML6 111 K2
CTBR ML5 110 A5
IRV KA12 203 J4
RAYR/DAL KA6 231 H5
SHOTTS ML7 136 F6
Ashgrove Av GRK PA19 31 J2 3
SVSTN KA20 192 E7 2
Ashgrove La PGL PA14 34 D8
Ashgrove Rd ARD KA22 191 J5
BLSH ML4 133 H2
KLWNG KA13 193 J5
Ashgrove St AYRS KA7 19 G6
DMNK/BRGTN G40 106 A7
Ashiestiel Pl CUMB G67 68 E2
Ashkirk Dr
CARD/HILL/MSPK G52 103 L6
Ashland Av HMLTN ML3 174 D2
Ashlea Dr GIF/THBK G46 127 K5
Ashlea Gdns AIRDRIE ML6 89 M6
Ashley Dr UD/BTH/TAN G71 132 B4
Ashley La KVGV G3 4 D6
Ashley Pk UD/BTH/TAN G71 132 C3
Ashley Pl BLTYR/CAMB G72 155 J1
Ashley Ri ALEX/LLW G83 25 M8
Ashley St KVGV G3 4 D6
Ashmore Rd
PLKSW/MSWD G43 127 M4
Ash Pl JNSTN PA5 100 A7
KLMNK KA1 16 A6
Ash Rd BAIL/MDB/MHD G69 108 A6
CLYDBK G81 60 A4
CUMB G67 49 K4
DMBTN G82 36 F5
Ashton Dr HBR/GL G84 23 G1
Ashton Gdns
BAIL/MDB/MHD G69 87 G3
Ashton Gn EKILN G74 14 F1
Ashton La KVD/HLHD G12 82 D7 1
Ashton La North
KVD/HLHD G12 82 D7 2
Ashton Pl GRK PA19 31 J2 4
Ashton Rd GRK PA19 31 J2
KVD/HLHD G12 82 D7
RUTH G73 106 A8
Ashton St MTHW ML1 133 K7 1
Ashton Vw DMBTN G82 36 B5
Ashtree Ct OLDK G60 59 G3
Ashtree Gv NMRNS G77 150 C6 1
Ashtree Rd
PLKSW/MSWD G43 127 J2 1
Ashvale Crs SPRGB/BLRNK G21 83 L5
Ashworth Ter HMLTN ML3 156 A5 1
Ash Wynd BLTYR/CAMB G72 130 E5
Aspen Ct AYRS KA7 229 K4
Aspen Dr SPRGB/BLRNK G21 6 E2 1
Aspen Pl BLTYR/CAMB G72 130 E4 1
JNSTN PA5 100 A8
Aspen Rd AYRS KA7 229 K4
Aspen Wy HMLTN ML3 156 E7
Asquith Pl BLSH ML4 133 K4
Assloss Rd KLMNKN/STW KA3 207 J4
Aster Dr CSMK G45 129 G7 1
Aster Gdns MTHW ML1 157 L4 1
PLK/PH/NH G53 126 C6
Athelstane Dr CUMB G67 68 D2
Athelstane Rd KNTSWD G13 81 J2
Athena Wy UD/BTH/TAN G71 132 A2
Athole Gdns KVD/HLHD G12 82 C6 1
Athole La KVD/HLHD G12 82 C6
Athole St HBR/GL G84 20 F8 1
Athole Ter GRNKW/INVK PA16 31 K6
Atholl Av BSHPBGS G64 44 B8
CARD/HILL/MSPK G52 102 E2
Atholl Crs PSLY PA1 102 E4
Atholl Dr BALLOCH G68 47 M8
GIF/THBK G46 151 J1
Atholl Gdns BSDN G61 61 L2
BSHPBGS G64 63 M6
KLWNG KA13 193 L5
RUTH G73 129 L5 1
Atholl Pl CTBR ML5 110 B6
PSLYN/LNWD PA3 100 A3
Atholl St HMLTN ML3 156 B3 2
Atholl Ter UD/BTH/TAN G71 108 F8 1
Atlas Pl SPRGB/BLRNK G21 6 D2
Atlas Rd SPRGB/BLRNK G21 6 B1
Atlas St CLYDBK G81 80 B1
Atlin Dr MTHW ML1 134 B6
Attercliffe Av WISHAW ML2 158 D7 1
Attlee Av CLYDBK G81 60 D8
Attow Rd PLKSW/MSWD G43 127 H4 1
Aubery Crs LARGS KA30 115 J4
Auburn Dr BRHD/NEIL G78 125 K8
Auchans Dr CRH/DND KA2 209 L7
Auchanshangan Dr SALT KA21 191 L6
Auchans Rd CRG/CRSL/HOU PA6 99 M1
Auchenbeg Crs AYRS KA7 229 G6
Auchenbothie Gdns
KLMCLM PA13 55 H7
Auchenbothie Rd PGL PA14 54 F3
Auchencrow St ESTRH G34 108 D1
Auchencruive MLNGV G62 62 C1 1
Auchendarroch St GRNK PA15 3 K7
Auchendavie Rd KKNTL G66 46 B7
Auchendoon Crs AYRS KA7 228 D5
Auchendores Av PGL PA14 55 G2
Auchenfoil La PGL PA14 54 C1
Auchenfoil Rd GRNK PA15 33 L8
KLMCLM PA13 53 M3
PGL PA14 54 C1
Auchengarth Br SKLM PA17 92 B4
Auchengate TROON KA10 216 E2
Auchengate Crs IRVSE KA11 208 E7
Auchengeich Rd
BAIL/MDB/MHD G69 66 D5
Auchengilloch EKILS G75 171 L4
Auchenglen Rd CARLUKE ML8 188 F6
Auchengree Rd GLGNK KA14 167 K4
Auchengreoch Av JNSTN PA5 122 D1
Auchengreoch Rd JNSTN PA5 122 D1
Auchenharvie Pl SVSTN KA20 192 B8
Auchenharvie Rd SALT KA21 201 G1
Auchenhove Crs KBRN KA25 143 G5
Auchenhowie Rd MLNGV G62 62 C1
Auchenkilns Rd CUMB G67 68 D3
Auchenleck La PGL PA14 54 E2
Auchenleck Rd PGL PA14 54 E2
Auchenlodment Rd JNSTN PA5 100 B7
Auchenmaid Dr LARGS KA30 115 K5
Auchenreoch Av DMBTN G82 37 H3
Auchenstewart Ct
WISHAW ML2 159 J6 1
Auchentibber Rd
BLTYR/CAMB G72 154 F6
Auchentiber Pl
KLMNKN/STW KA3 207 J3 1
Auchentorlie Qd PSLY PA1 102 B5 1
Auchentorlie St PTCK G11 81 M7 1
Auchentoshan Av CLYDBK G81 59 M3
Auchentoshan Ter
SPRGB/BLRNK G21 6 B4
Auchentrae Crs AYRS KA7 228 D4
Auchinairn Rd BSHPBGS G64 84 D1
SPRGB/BLRNK G21 84 C2 1
Auchinbee Farm Rd
BALLOCH G68 48 B5 1
Auchinbee Wy BALLOCH G68 48 B6
Auchincampbell Rd
HMLTN ML3 156 D6
Auchincruive Av PSTWK KA9 225 J2
Auchineden Ct BSDN G61 61 J2 1
Auchingill Pl ESTRH G34 86 D8 1
Auchingill Rd ESTRH G34 86 C8
Auchingramont Rd
HMLTN ML3 156 D6
Auchinlea Dr MTHW ML1 135 J8
Auchinlea Rd ESTRH G34 85 M8
Auchinleck Av
STPS/GTHM/RID G33 84 E3
Auchinleck Crs
STPS/GTHM/RID G33 84 E3 1
Auchinleck Dr
STPS/GTHM/RID G33 84 E3
Auchinleck Gdns
STPS/GTHM/RID G33 84 E3 2
Auchinleck Rd CLYDBK G81 60 B3
STPS/GTHM/RID G33 84 F2
Auchinleck Ter CLYDBK G81 60 B2 1
Auchinloch Rd KKNTL G66 65 K5
Auchinloch St SPRGB/BLRNK G21 6 D3
Auchinraith Av HMLTN ML3 156 B3
Auchinraith Rd
BLTYR/CAMB G72 155 M2 1
Auchinraith Ter
BLTYR/CAMB G72 155 L3
Auchinvole Crs KSYTH G65 47 H1
Auchmannoch Av PSLY PA1 102 E4
Auchmead Rd
GRNKW/INVK PA16 31 L6
Auchmountain Rd GRNK PA15 3 J8
Auchnacraig Rd CLYDBK G81 60 C2
Auchneagh Av
GRNKW/INVK PA16 32 B5 1
Auchneagh Crs
GRNKW/INVK PA16 32 A5
Auchneagh Farm Rd
GRNKW/INVK PA16 32 B4 1
Auchneagh Rd
GRNKW/INVK PA16 32 B5
Auchter Av WISHAW ML2 160 C4
Auchterburn Rd SHOTTS ML7 160 F1 1
Auchter Rd WISHAW ML2 159 L5 1
Auckland Pk EKILS G75 171 G1
Auckland Pl CLYDBK G81 59 K5 1
Auckland St PPK/MIL G22 5 G2
Auldbar Rd
CARD/HILL/MSPK G52 103 M6
Auldbar Ter PSLYS PA2 9 L8
Auldburn Pl PLKSW/MSWD G43 127 H3
Auldburn Rd
PLKSW/MSWD G43 127 G3
Auld Clay Rd SALT KA21 192 E2
Auldearn Rd SPRGB/BLRNK G21 84 C2
Auldgirth Rd
CARD/HILL/MSPK G52 103 M6
Auldhame St CTBR ML5 109 L1
Auldhouse Av
PLKSW/MSWD G43 127 H3 1
Auldhouse Gdns
PLKSW/MSWD G43 127 H3
Auldhouse Rd EKILS G75 171 J8
PLKSW/MSWD G43 127 J3
Auldhouse Ter
PLKSW/MSWD G43 127 K3 1
Auld Kirk Rd BLTYR/CAMB G72 130 C6
Auldlea Rd BEITH KA15 144 B7
Auldmurroch Dr MLNGV G62 41 K7 1
The Auld Rd CUMB G67 49 G5
Auld's Brae AIRDRIE ML6 111 G1 3
Auld St CLYDBK G81 59 L6
Auldton Ter LRKH ML9 176 F8
Aultbea St PPK/MIL G22 83 H1
Aultmore Rd
STPS/GTHM/RID G33 107 M2
Aursbridge Crs BRHD/NEIL G78 125 K7
Aursbridge Dr BRHD/NEIL G78 125 K7
Aurs Crs BRHD/NEIL G78 125 K7
Aurs Dr BRHD/NEIL G78 125 K8
Aurs Gln BRHD/NEIL G78 125 J8
Aurs Pl BRHD/NEIL G78 125 L7
Aurs Rd BRHD/NEIL G78 125 K6
NMRNS G77 150 A4
Austen La KNTSWD G13 81 L4 1
Austen Rd KNTSWD G13 81 L4 2
Austine Dr HMLTN ML3 174 E2
Avenel Rd KNTSWD G13 61 L8
Avenue End Rd
STPS/GTHM/RID G33 85 H5
Avenuehead Rd
BAIL/MDB/MHD G69 87 G1
Avenuepark St MRYH/FIRH G20 82 E5
Avenue Sq KLMNKN/STW KA3 197 K1
Avenue St DMNK/BRGTN G40 12 E6
RUTH G73 106 B8
The Avenue WKIL KA23 181 L1
Aviemore Gdns BSDN G61 62 A4
Aviemore Rd
CARD/HILL/MSPK G52 103 L7
Avils Hl KBRN KA25 143 G8
Avils Pl KBRN KA25 143 G8
Avoch St ESTRH G34 86 B8 1
Avon Av BSDN G61 62 B5
CARLUKE ML8 178 D7
Avonbank Crs HMLTN ML3 174 E1
Avonbank Rd LRKH ML9 175 L7
RUTH G73 128 F2 1
Avonbrae Crs HMLTN ML3 174 E1
Avonbridge Dr HMLTN ML3 156 F6
Avondale Av EKILN G74 15 H4
Avondale Dr PSLY PA1 102 B3
Avondale Pl EKILN G74 15 J5
Avondale Rd WKIL KA23 181 J3
Avondale St
STPS/GTHM/RID G33 85 G8
Avon Dr BLSH ML4 133 J5
PSLYN/LNWD PA3 100 B3
Avonhead EKILS G75 171 L4
Avonhead Av CUMB G67 68 C2
Avonhead Gdns CUMB G67 68 C2
Avonhead Rd CUMB G67 68 C2
Avonmouth Pl
GRNKW/INVK PA16 31 M4 1
Avon Pl CTBR ML5 87 K8
KLMNK KA1 212 B4
Avon Rd BSHPBGS G64 84 A1
GIF/THBK G46 127 H7 1
Avonside Gv HMLTN ML3 156 F6
Avonspark St SPRGB/BLRNK G21 6 F2
Avon St HMLTN ML3 156 E6 1
LRKH ML9 175 M6
MTHW ML1 157 K4
Aylmer Rd PLKSW/MSWD G43 127 M3
Ayr Dr AIRDRIE ML6 111 G4
Ayr Rd IRV KA12 203 J8
KLMNK KA1 211 K6
LRKH ML9 176 E7
NMRNS G77 150 C6
PSTWK KA9 225 H3
Ayr St SPRGB/BLRNK G21 6 B2
TROON KA10 216 C7
Ayr Ter GRNKW/INVK PA16 31 L6
Ayton Pk North EKILN G74 154 B6
Ayton Pk South EKILN G74 154 B6 2
Aytoun Dr ERSK PA8 58 F6
Aytoun Rd PLKSD/SHW G41 104 D6

B

Baberton Wy KLWNG KA13 193 H6
Babylon Av BLSH ML4 133 G6
Babylon Dr BLSH ML4 133 G6
Babylon Pl BLSH ML4 133 G6 1
Babylon Rd BLSH ML4 133 G6
Backbrae St KSYTH G65 47 K1
Backburn BEITH KA15 168 B1
Back Cswy DEN/PKHD G31 13 M5
Back Hawkhill Av AYR KA8 225 G7
Backmuir Crs HMLTN ML3 156 B3
Backmuir Pl HMLTN ML3 156 B3 3
Backmuir Rd DRUM G15 61 H5
HMLTN ML3 156 B2
Back O' Barns HMLTN ML3 156 E5 1
Back O'barns HMLTN ML3 156 F5 1
Back O Dykes Rd KKNTL G66 66 B2 1
Back O Hl CRG/CRSL/HOU PA6 77 H8
Back O' Hill Rd BSHPBGS G64 43 L7
Back Peebles St AYR KA8 224 F7
Back Rd BRWEIR PA11 98 D1
Back Rw HMLTN ML3 156 E5
Back Sneddon St PSLY PA1 9 G2 1
PSLYN/LNWD PA3 9 H2
Back St DMBTN G82 25 K8
Badenheath Pl BALLOCH G68 67 K4 1
Badenoch Road. KKNTL G66 46 B8
Bagnell St SPRGB/BLRNK G21 83 M4
Bahamas Wy EKILS G75 153 G8 2
Baidland Av DALRY KA24 184 E3
Bailie Dr BSDN G61 61 K2
Bailie Fyfe Wy WISHAW ML2 177 H2
Baillie Dr EKILN G74 154 B5
UD/BTH/TAN G71 132 A6
Baillie Gdns WISHAW ML2 159 L5
Baillie Pl EKILN G74 154 C5
Baillie Rd FAIRLIE KA29 139 L4
Baillies La AIRDRIE ML6 111 G2 1
Bailliesmuir Pl WISHAW ML2 160 A3 1
Baillieston Av KBRN KA25 167 G1 1
Baillieston Rd CAR/SHTL G32 107 L5 2
UD/BTH/TAN G71 108 B8 1
Baillie Wynd
UD/BTH/TAN G71 132 A2 2
Bain Crs HBR/GL G84 20 E6
Bainfield Rd DMBTN G82 35 H2
Bainsford St CAR/SHTL G32 106 F3
Bain St DMNK/BRGTN G40 12 A4
Bain Wy ALEX/LLW G83 25 L3
Baird Av AIRDRIE ML6 89 H7
CARD/HILL/MSPK G52 102 E1
HBR/GL G84 20 B7
KLWNG KA13 193 L4
Baird Brae MRYH/FIRH G20 5 G3
Baird Crs ALEX/LLW G83 25 J2
CUMB G67 68 B2 1
Baird Dr BSDN G61 61 K4
ERSK PA8 58 F6
Baird Hl EKILS G75 14 D6
Baird Pl BLSH ML4 133 G2
KLMNKN/STW KA3 207 H7
PSTWK KA9 221 K5
WISHAW ML2 159 L5
Baird Rd AYRS KA7 228 E8
PSTWK KA9 221 K5
Bairds Crs HMLTN ML3 156 C5
Bairdsland Vw BLSH ML4 133 H4
Baird St COWCAD G4 5 L7
CTBR ML5 110 A2
Baker St GRNK PA15 2 F6
PLKSD/SHW G41 104 E8
Bakewell Rd
BAIL/MDB/MHD G69 108 A4
Balaclava St KVGV G3 10 E2
Balado Rd STPS/GTHM/RID G33 107 L2
Balbeggie St CAR/SHTL G32 107 J5
Balbeg St GOV/IBX G51 103 L3
Balblair Rd
CARD/HILL/MSPK G52 103 M7 1
Balcarres Av KVD/HLHD G12 82 C4
Balcomie Crs TROON KA10 217 G7
Balcomie St
STPS/GTHM/RID G33 85 G8
Balcurvie Rd ESTRH G34 86 A7
Baldernock Rd MLNGV G62 42 D7
Baldie's Brae NMLNS KA16 215 J2 1
Baldinnie Rd ESTRH G34 108 B1
Baldorran Crs BALLOCH G68 48 B6
Baldovan Crs
STPS/GTHM/RID G33 107 M1
Baldovie Rd
CARD/HILL/MSPK G52 103 J6
Baldragon Rd ESTRH G34 86 B8
Baldric Rd KNTSWD G13 81 J3
Baldwin Av KNTSWD G13 61 K8
Balerno Dr
CARD/HILL/MSPK G52 103 L6
Balfleurs St MLNGV G62 42 B7
Balfluig St ESTRH G34 85 M8
Balfour Av BEITH KA15 168 B2
Balfour Ct KLMNKN/STW KA3 207 K6
Balfour St MRYH/FIRH G20 82 D3
PGL PA14 34 B7
Balfour Ter EKILS G75 15 G7
Balfron Crs HMLTN ML3 155 M6
Balfron Rd GOV/IBX G51 103 L2
GRNK PA15 33 J8 1
PSLY PA1 102 D4
Balgair Dr PSLY PA1 102 B4
Balgair St PPK/MIL G22 83 H4
Balgair Ter CAR/SHTL G32 107 H4 1
Balglass St PPK/MIL G22 83 H5
Balgonie Av PSLYS PA2 101 G8
Balgonie Dr PSLYS PA2 101 J8
Balgonie Rd
CARD/HILL/MSPK G52 103 L5
Balgonie Woods PSLYS PA2 101 J8
Balgownie Crs GIF/THBK G46 127 G7
Balgray Av KBRN KA25 167 G1
KLMNK KA1 211 M7
Balgraybank St
SPRGB/BLRNK G21 84 A5
Balgray Crs BRHD/NEIL G78 125 L7
Balgray Rd BEITH KA15 169 G5
GLGNK KA14 167 H2
NMRNS G77 150 A4
Balgraystone Rd NMRNS G77 149 K4
Balgray Wy IRVSE KA11 204 A3
Balintore St CAR/SHTL G32 107 G4 2
Baliol La KVGV G3 4 D7

Baliol St *KVGV* G3 ... 4 D6
Baljaffray Rd *BSDN* G61 ... 61 G2
Ballachalairy Yett
  CMPF/LLE G63 ... 26 D5
Ballagan Pl *MLNGV* G62 ... 41 K4
Ballaig Av *BSDN* G61 ... 61 K4
Ballaig Crs
  STPS/GTHM/RID G33 ... 85 J4
Ballantay Qd *CSMK* G45 ... 129 G6
Ballantay Rd *CSMK* G45 ... 129 G6
Ballantay Ter *CSMK* G45 ... 129 G6
Ballantine Av
  CARD/HILL/MSPK G52 ... 103 G2
Ballantine Dr *AYRS* KA7 ... 18 F7
Ballantrae *EKILN* G74 ... 153 K6
Ballantrae Crs *NMRNS* G77 ... 151 G5
Ballantrae Dr *NMRNS* G77 ... 151 G5
Ballantrae Rd
  BLTYR/CAMB G72 ... 155 L4
Ballater Crs *WISHAW* ML2 ... 159 H4
Ballater Dr *BSDN* G61 ... 61 M7
  PSLYS PA2 ... 101 M8
  RNFRW PA4 ... 79 K2
Ballater Pl *GBLS* G5 ... 11 L7
Ballater St *GBLS* G5 ... 11 J5
Ballayne Dr *BAIL/MDB/MHD* G69 ... 67 G6
Ballerup Ter *EKILS* G75 ... 171 L3
Ballewan Crs *CMPF/LLE* G63 ... 27 G5
Ballindalloch Dr *DEN/PKHD* G31 ... 7 G9
Ballindalloch La *DEN/PKHD* G31 ... 6 F9
Balloch Crs *GTCI* KA28 ... 138 C6
Balloch Gdns
  CARD/HILL/MSPK G52 ... 103 M6
Balloch Loop Rd *BALLOCH* G68 ... 48 C7
Ballochmill Rd
  BLTYR/CAMB G72 ... 129 K1
Ballochmyle *EKILN* G74 ... 154 D5
Ballochmyle Rd *AIRDRIE* ML6 ... 89 K5
Ballochney St *AIRDRIE* ML6 ... 88 E7
Ballochnie Dr *AIRDRIE* ML6 ... 89 M7
Balloch Rd *AIRDRIE* ML6 ... 112 A3
  ALEX/LLW G83 ... 25 K1
  GRNK PA15 ... 33 H7
  SHOTTS ML7 ... 137 L3
Balloch Vw *CUMB* G67 ... 48 F7
Ballogie Rd *LNPK/KPK* G44 ... 128 B2
Ballot Rd *IRV* KA12 ... 203 J7
Balmartin Rd *SMSTN* G23 ... 62 D8
Balmedie *ERSK* PA8 ... 59 G7
Balmeg Av *GIF/THBK* G46 ... 151 J1
Balminnoch Pk *AYRS* KA7 ... 228 C8
Balmoral Av *AIRDRIE* ML6 ... 88 F4
Balmoral Crs *CTBR* ML5 ... 109 K5
  RNFRW PA4 ... 79 L2
Balmoral Dr *BLTYR/CAMB* G72 ... 129 L4
  BSDN G61 ... 62 A7
  CAR/SHTL G32 ... 130 B1
Balmoral Gdns
  BLTYR/CAMB G72 ... 131 J7
  UD/BTH/TAN G71 ... 108 F8
  GRK PA19 ... 30 E4
Balmoral Pl *EKILN* G74 ... 14 B3
Balmoral Rd *JNSTN* PA5 ... 123 H1
  KLMNKN/STW KA3 ... 16 D1
Balmoral St *SCOT* G14 ... 81 H6
Balmoral Wynd
  KLMNKN/STW KA3 ... 197 L1
Balmore Ct *KLMCLM* PA13 ... 75 J2
Balmore Dr *HMLTN* ML3 ... 174 A1
Balmore Pl *PPK/MIL* G22 ... 83 H3
Balmore Rd *BSHPBGS* G64 ... 63 L2
  GRNK PA15 ... 33 H8
  MLNGV G62 ... 62 F4
  SMSTN G23 ... 62 F4
Balmore Sq *MRYH/FIRH* G20 ... 83 H4
Balmuildy Rd *BSHPBGS* G64 ... 63 L4
  BSHPBGS G64 ... 63 L5
Balnagowan Rd *SKLM* SA17 ... 70 B5
Balornock Rd
  SPRGB/BLRNK G21 ... 84 A4
Balrossie Dr *KLMCLM* PA13 ... 75 J2
Balruddery Pl *BSHPBGS* G64 ... 84 D1
Balshagray Av *SCOT* G14 ... 81 M6
Balshagray Crs *PTCK* G11 ... 81 L7
Balshagray Dr *PTCK* G11 ... 81 M6
Balshagray La *PTCK* G11 ... 81 M6
Balshagray Pl *PTCK* G11 ... 81 M6
Baltersan Gdns *HMLTN* ML3 ... 174 F6
Baltic Ct *DMNK/BRGTN* G40 ... 106 A6
Baltic La *DMNK/BRGTN* G40 ... 12 E9
Baltic Pl *DMNK/BRGTN* G40 ... 12 D7
Baltic St *DMNK/BRGTN* G40 ... 12 F9
  DMNK/BRGTN G40 ... 106 B6
Balure St *DEN/PKHD* G31 ... 13 K2
Balvaird Crs *RUTH* G73 ... 129 G2
Balvaird Dr *RUTH* G73 ... 129 G2
Balvenie St *CTBR* ML5 ... 110 B6
Balveny St *STPS/GTHM/RID* G33 ... 85 K7
Balvicar Dr *GVH/MTFL* G42 ... 104 F8
Balvicar St *GVH/MTFL* G42 ... 104 F7
Balvie Av *DRUM* G15 ... 61 C8
  GIF/THBK G46 ... 127 K7
Balvie Crs *MLNGV* G62 ... 41 M7
Balvie Rd *MLNGV* G62 ... 41 M7
Banavie Rd *PTCK* G11 ... 82 B6
  WISHAW ML2 ... 159 M3
Banchory Av *AIRDRIE* ML6 ... 88 F4
  PLKSW/MSWD G43 ... 127 H4
  RNFRW PA4 ... 79 K2
Banchory Crs *BSDN* G61 ... 62 A7
Banchory Rd *WISHAW* ML2 ... 159 H4
Baneberry Pth *EKILN* G74 ... 153 K5
Banff Av *AIRDRIE* ML6 ... 111 G5
Banff Pl *EKILS* G75 ... 14 A5
  GRNKW/INVK PA16 ... 31 K4
Banff Qd *WISHAW* ML2 ... 159 H4
Banff Rd *GRNKW/INVK* PA16 ... 31 K4
Banff St *STPS/GTHM/RID* G33 ... 85 H7
Bangorshill St *GIF/THBK* G46 ... 126 F6
Bank Av *MLNGV* G62 ... 42 A6
Bankbrae Av *PLK/PH/NH* G53 ... 126 A3
Bank Ct *IRV* KA12 ... 203 L5
Bankend *BRWEIR* PA11 ... 98 E2
Bankend Pl *KLMNKN/STW* KA3 ... 207 J4
Bankend Rd *BRWEIR* PA11 ... 98 F3
  DMBTN G82 ... 36 F5
Bankend St
  STPS/GTHM/RID G33 ... 85 G8

Bankfaulds Av *KBRN* KA25 ... 143 G8
Bankfield Dr *HMLTN* ML3 ... 174 D2
Bankfoot Dr
  CARD/HILL/MSPK G52 ... 103 H4
Bankfoot Pl *NMRNS* G77 ... 151 H5
Bankfoot Rd
  CARD/HILL/MSPK G52 ... 103 H5
  PSLYN/LNWD PA3 ... 8 B2
Bankglen Rd *DRUM* G15 ... 61 H5
Bankhall St *GVH/MTFL* G42 ... 105 H7
Bankhead Av *AIRDRIE* ML6 ... 111 K2
  BLSH ML4 ... 133 H6
  CTBR ML5 ... 109 J5
  IRVSE KA11 ... 205 G7
  KNTSWD G13 ... 81 G3
Bankhead Dr *RUTH* G73 ... 129 G2
Bankhead Pl *AIRDRIE* ML6 ... 111 K2
  CTBR ML5 ... 109 J5
Bankhead Rd
  CRMNK/CLK/EAG G76 ... 152 D2
  KKNTL G66 ... 66 B2
  KLWNG KA13 ... 193 M6
  RUTH G73 ... 128 F2
Bankhead Ter *LNK/LMHG* ML11 ... 199 H7
Bankholm Pl
  CRMNK/CLK/EAG G76 ... 151 M4
Bankhouse Av *LARGS* KA30 ... 115 K7
Bankhouse Crs *LARGS* KA30 ... 115 K7
Banknock St *CAR/SHTL* G32 ... 106 E3
Bank Pk *EKILS* G75 ... 14 D5
Bank Pl *IRV* KA12 ... 203 L5
Bank Rd *CAR/SHTL* G32 ... 130 C3
  SHOTTS ML7 ... 137 M5
Bankside Av *JNSTN* PA5 ... 99 M6
Bankside Gdns *KBRN* KA25 ... 143 G5
Banks Rd *KKNTL* G66 ... 45 L8
Bank St *AIRDRIE* ML6 ... 111 G1
  ALEX/LLW G83 ... 25 L5
  BLTYR/CAMB G72 ... 130 A3
  BRHD/NEIL G78 ... 125 J7
  BRHD/NEIL G78 ... 148 D2
  CTBR ML5 ... 109 M3
  GRNK PA15 ... 2 D6
  IRV KA12 ... 203 J7
  KBRN KA25 ... 143 G7
  KLMNK KA1 ... 16 E4
  KVD/HLHD G12 ... 4 A4
  PSLY PA1 ... 9 K4
  PSTWK KA9 ... 225 H1
  TROON KA10 ... 216 B6
Banktop Pl *JNSTN* PA5 ... 99 M6
Bank Vw *AIRDRIE* ML6 ... 111 K7
Bankview Dr *KKNTL* G66 ... 65 G1
Bannachra Crs *ALEX/LLW* G83 ... 25 J2
Bannachra Dr *HBR/GL* G84 ... 20 B7
Bannatyne Av *DEN/PKHD* G31 ... 13 H1
Bannatyne St *LNK/LMHG* ML11 ... 199 G5
Bannercross Av
  BAIL/MDB/MHD G69 ... 108 A4
Bannercross Dr
  BAIL/MDB/MHD G69 ... 108 A3
Bannercross Gdns
  BAIL/MDB/MHD G69 ... 108 A4
Banner Dr *KNTSWD* G13 ... 61 J8
Bannerman Dr *BLSH* ML4 ... 133 K4
  KLMNKN/STW KA3 ... 207 K7
Bannerman Pl *CLYDBK* G81 ... 60 B7
Banner Rd *BSDN* G61 ... 61 K7
Bannoch Pl *KLWNG* KA13 ... 194 A6
Bannoch Rd *KLWNG* KA13 ... 194 B5
Bannockburn Pl *LRKH* ML9 ... 176 C8
Bannockburn Pl
  KLMNKN/STW KA3 ... 207 H6
  MTHW ML1 ... 134 A7
Bannockburn St
  GRNKW/INVK PA16 ... 32 C6
Bantaskin St *MRYH/FIRH* G20 ... 82 C2
Banton Pl *STPS/GTHM/RID* G33 ... 108 A2
Banyan Crs *UD/BTH/TAN* G71 ... 109 K8
Barassie *EKILN* G74 ... 153 K6
Barassiebank La *TROON* KA10 ... 216 D4
Barassie Ct *UD/BTH/TAN* G71 ... 131 M7
Barassie Dr *BRWEIR* PA11 ... 98 C3
Barassie Pl *KLMNK* KA1 ... 211 L5
Barassie St *TROON* KA10 ... 216 C6
Barbadoes Pl *KLMNK* KA1 ... 16 C9
Barbadoes Rd *KLMNK* KA1 ... 16 D8
Barbados Gn *EKILS* G75 ... 153 G8
Barbae Pl *UD/BTH/TAN* G71 ... 132 A6
Barbana Rd *EKILN* G74 ... 152 E7
Barbegs Crs *KSYTH* G65 ... 47 M5
Barberry Av *PLK/PH/NH* G53 ... 126 B7
Barberry Dr *BEITH* KA15 ... 168 A1
Barberry Gdns
  PLK/PH/NH G53 ... 126 B7
Barberry Pl *PLK/PH/NH* G53 ... 126 B7
Barbeth Gdns *CUMB* G67 ... 68 B4
Barbeth Pl *CUMB* G67 ... 68 A3
Barbeth Rd *CUMB* G67 ... 68 A3
Barbeth Wy *CUMB* G67 ... 68 A3
Barbour's Pk
  KLMNKN/STW KA3 ... 197 L1
Barbreck Rd *GVH/MTFL* G42 ... 104 F7
Barcaldine Av
  BAIL/MDB/MHD G69 ... 86 B1
Barcapel Av *NMRNS* G77 ... 150 E2
Barclaugh Dr *RAYR/DAL* KA6 ... 231 G5
Barclaven Rd *KLMCLM* PA13 ... 75 L1
Barclay Av *JNSTN* PA5 ... 100 B7
Barclay Ct *OLDK* G60 ... 59 H3
Barclay Dr *HBR/GL* G84 ... 20 C6
  KLMNKN/STW KA3 ... 207 J7
Barclay Gdns *IRVSE* KA11 ... 204 D3
Barclay Rd *MTHW* ML1 ... 157 H3
Barclay St *SPRGB/BLRNK* G21 ... 83 M4
Barcraigs Dr *PSLYS* PA2 ... 124 F1
Bard Av *KNTSWD* G13 ... 81 H1
Bardowie St *PPK/MIL* G22 ... 83 J5
Bardrain Av *JNSTN* PA5 ... 100 C7
Bardrainney Av *PGL* PA14 ... 54 F2
Bardrain Rd *PSLYS* PA2 ... 124 C2
Bardrill Dr *BSHPBGS* G64 ... 63 L8
Bardykes Rd *BLTYR/CAMB* G72 ... 155 J1
Barefield St *LRKH* ML9 ... 176 A5
Barend St *GTCI* KA28 ... 138 B6
Barfillan Dr
  CARD/HILL/MSPK G52 ... 103 L4
Bargaran Rd *PLK/PH/NH* G53 ... 103 H5

Bargarron Rd *ERSK* PA8 ... 58 F7
Bargarron Dr *PSLYN/LNWD* PA3 ... 102 A2
Bargeddie St
  STPS/GTHM/RID G33 ... 7 M4
Bar Hill Pl *KSYTH* G65 ... 47 H1
Barholm Sq
  STPS/GTHM/RID G33 ... 85 K8
Barke Rd *CUMB* G67 ... 49 G6
Barkly Ter *EKILS* G75 ... 14 A6
Barlanark Av *CAR/SHTL* G32 ... 107 K2
Barlanark Crs *CAR/SHTL* G32 ... 107 K2
Barlanark Pl
  STPS/GTHM/RID G33 ... 107 L2
Barlanark Rd
  STPS/GTHM/RID G33 ... 107 K2
  CAR/SHTL G32 ... 107 K2
Barlandfauld St *KSYTH* G65 ... 47 K1
Barlia Dr *CSMK* G45 ... 128 E6
Barlia St *CSMK* G45 ... 128 E6
Barlia Ter *CSMK* G45 ... 128 F6
Barloan Crs *DMBTN* G82 ... 37 G4
Barloan Pl *DMBTN* G82 ... 37 G4
Barloch Av *MLNGV* G62 ... 42 A7
Barloch Rd *MLNGV* G62 ... 42 B8
Barloch St *PPK/MIL* G22 ... 83 J5
Barlogan Av
  CARD/HILL/MSPK G52 ... 103 L4
Barlogan Qd
  CARD/HILL/MSPK G52 ... 103 L4
Barmore Av *CARLUKE* ML8 ... 189 G1
Barmouth Av
  GRNKW/INVK PA16 ... 31 M4
Barmulloch Rd
  SPRGB/BLRNK G21 ... 6 F1
Barnbeth Rd *PLK/PH/NH* G53 ... 103 H7
Barncluith Rd *HMLTN* ML3 ... 156 F6
Barnes Rd *MRYH/FIRH* G20 ... 83 G3
Barness Pl
  STPS/GTHM/RID G33 ... 107 G1
Barnes St *BRHD/NEIL* G78 ... 125 H7
Barnett Ct *SALT* KA21 ... 200 F1
Barnett Crs *SALT* KA21 ... 200 F2
Barnflat St *RUTH* G73 ... 106 B8
Barnford Crs *AYRS* KA7 ... 229 G7
Barngore Dr *RAYR/DAL* KA6 ... 231 H5
Barn Gn *KLBCH* PA10 ... 99 G6
Barnhill Dr *HMLTN* ML3 ... 155 K7
  NMRNS G77 ... 150 D6
  SPRGB/BLRNK G21 ... 6 F2
Barnhill Rd *DMBTN* G82 ... 37 K6
Barnhill St *GRNK* PA15 ... 3 J7
Barnkirk Av *DRUM* G15 ... 61 G6
Barns Crs *AYRS* KA7 ... 18 E4
Barnscroft *KLBCH* PA10 ... 99 H5
Barnsford Av *RNFRW* PA4 ... 79 H5
Barnsford Rd *RNFRW* PA4 ... 79 H6
Barns Pk *AYRS* KA7 ... 18 E4
Barns Rd *AYRS* KA7 ... 18 E4
Barns Street La *AYRS* KA7 ... 18 E4
Barns St *AYRS* KA7 ... 18 E5
Barns Terrace La *AYRS* KA7 ... 18 E5
Barnton St *CAR/SHTL* G32 ... 106 E2
Barnweill Dr *KLMNK* KA1 ... 212 E4
Barnweill Rd *KLMNK* KA1 ... 211 L4
Barnwell Av *PSTWK* KA9 ... 225 J3
Barnwell Ter *GOV/IBX* G51 ... 103 L2
Barochan Pl
  PSLYN/LNWD PA3 ... 101 G5
Barochan Rd
  CRG/CRSL/HOU PA6 ... 57 H8
  CRG/CRSL/HOU PA6 ... 77 H5
  CRG/CRSL/HOU PA6 ... 103 G2
  PLK/PH/NH G53 ... 103 H6
Baronald Dr *KVD/HLHD* G12 ... 82 B3
Baronald Ga *KVD/HLHD* G12 ... 82 B3
Baronald St *RUTH* G73 ... 106 B8
Baron Ct *HMLTN* ML3 ... 157 G7
Barone Dr
  CRMNK/CLK/EAG G76 ... 151 J1
Baronhall Dr *BLTYR/CAMB* G72 ... 155 J1
Baronhill *CUMB* G67 ... 49 G4
Baron Rd *PSLYN/LNWD* PA3 ... 102 A3
Baronscourt Dr *PSLY* PA1 ... 100 F5
Baronscourt Gdns
  PSLYN/LNWD PA3 ... 100 F5
Baronscourt Rd *PSLYN/LNWD* PA3 ... 100 F6
Barons Ga *UD/BTH/TAN* G71 ... 131 L5
Barons Rd *MTHW* ML1 ... 158 C7
Barony Ct *ARD* KA22 ... 191 K8
Barony Dr *BAIL/MDB/MHD* G69 ... 108 B3
Barony Gdns
  BAIL/MDB/MHD G69 ... 108 B4
Barony Glebe *WKIL* KA23 ... 181 K4
Barony Pl *BALLOCH* G68 ... 47 L8
Barony Rd *PSTWK* KA9 ... 225 J3
Barony Ter *KBRN* KA25 ... 167 G2
Barony Wynd
  BAIL/MDB/MHD G69 ... 108 B3
Barra Av *RNFRW* PA4 ... 80 C8
  WISHAW ML2 ... 159 L4
Barrachnie Ct
  BAIL/MDB/MHD G69 ... 107 M4
Barrachnie Crs
  BAIL/MDB/MHD G69 ... 107 M4
Barrachnie Rd
  BAIL/MDB/MHD G69 ... 107 M4
Barrack St *COWCAD* G4 ... 12 B3
  HMLTN ML3 ... 156 D4
Barra Crs *IRVSE* KA11 ... 204 C7
Barra Dr *AIRDRIE* ML6 ... 111 L3
Barra Gdns *OLDK* G60 ... 59 J4
Barra La *IRVSE* KA11 ... 204 C7
Barra Pl *IRVSE* KA11 ... 204 C7
Barra Rd *OLDK* G60 ... 59 J4
Barraston Rd *BSHPBGS* G64 ... 44 A6
Barr Av *BRHD/NEIL* G78 ... 148 E1
Barra Wynd *IRVSE* KA11 ... 204 C7
Barr Castle Gdns *GLSTN* KA4 ... 214 C4
Barrcraig Rd *BRWEIR* PA11 ... 98 C1
Barr Crs *CLYDBK* G81 ... 60 B6
Barrhead Rd *NMRNS* G77 ... 150 B4
  PLK/PH/NH G53 ... 125 M2

PSLYS PA2 ... 9 M8
Barrhill Court. *KKNTL* G66 ... 66 A1
Barrhill Crs *KLBCH* PA10 ... 99 H7
Barrhill Rd *GRK* PA19 ... 31 K2
  KKNTL G66 ... 66 A1
Barriedale Av *HMLTN* ML3 ... 156 B6
Barrie Qd *CLYDBK* G81 ... 60 A5
Barrie Rd *CARD/HILL/MSPK* G52 ... 103 G2
  EKILN G74 ... 154 D4
Barrie St *MTHW* ML1 ... 157 L3
Barrie Ter *ARD* KA22 ... 191 K7
Barrington Av *BEITH* KA15 ... 144 B8
Barrington Dr *KVGV* G3 ... 4 C5
Barrisdale Rd *MRYH/FIRH* G20 ... 82 D2
  WISHAW ML2 ... 159 M3
Barrisdale Wy *RUTH* G73 ... 129 H5
Barrland Dr *GIF/THBK* G46 ... 127 J6
Barrland St *PLKSD/SHW* G41 ... 105 G5
Barrmill Rd *BEITH* KA15 ... 168 C2
  BEITH KA15 ... 169 H7
  GLSTN KA4 ... 214 C3
  PLKSW/MSWD G43 ... 127 G4
Barrochan Rd
  CRG/CRSL/HOU PA6 ... 99 L3
  JNSTN PA5 ... 99 L5
Barrowfield St *CTBR* ML5 ... 109 M5
  DMNK/BRGTN G40 ... 12 F6
Barrpath *KSYTH* G65 ... 47 M2
Barr Pl *NMRNS* G77 ... 150 C4
  PSLY PA1 ... 8 F5
Barrs Brae *KLMCLM* PA13 ... 55 K8
  PGL PA14 ... 34 C8
Barrs Brae La *PGL* PA14 ... 34 C8
Barrs Ct *DMBTN* G82 ... 24 A8
Barrs Crs *DMBTN* G82 ... 35 G1
Barrs Rd *DMBTN* G82 ... 35 G1
Barrs Ter *DMBTN* G82 ... 35 G1
Barr St *ARD* KA22 ... 191 J8
  GLSTN KA4 ... 214 C4
  MRYH/FIRH G20 ... 4 C3
  MTHW ML1 ... 157 L1
Barr Ter *EKILN* G74 ... 14 F2
Barrwood Ga *GLSTN* KA4 ... 214 C4
Barrwood Pl *UD/BTH/TAN* G71 ... 132 A1
Barrwood St
  STPS/GTHM/RID G33 ... 84 E7
Barry Gdns *BLTYR/CAMB* G72 ... 155 J3
Barscube Av *PGL* PA14 ... 54 E2
Barscube Ter *PSLYS* PA2 ... 9 M8
Barshaw Dr *PSLY* PA1 ... 9 M1
Barshaw Pl *PSLY* PA1 ... 102 D4
Barshaw Rd
  CARD/HILL/MSPK G52 ... 102 E3
Barskiven Rd *PSLYN/LNWD* PA3 ... 100 F5
Barterholm Rd *PSLYS* PA2 ... 9 H8
Bartholomew St
  DMNK/BRGTN G40 ... 12 E9
Bartiebeith Rd
  STPS/GTHM/RID G33 ... 107 K2
Bartonhall Rd *WISHAW* ML2 ... 159 K8
Barty's Rd *BLSH* ML4 ... 133 J4
Barward Rd *GLSTN* KA4 ... 214 A4
Barwheys Dr *RAYR/DAL* KA6 ... 227 G3
Barwood Hl *DMBTN* G82 ... 37 H3
Bassett Av *KNTSWD* G13 ... 81 H1
Bassett Crs *KNTSWD* G13 ... 81 H1
Bathgate St *DEN/PKHD* G31 ... 12 F3
Bathgo Av *PSLY* PA1 ... 102 E5
Bath La *CGLW* G2 ... 4 E8
Bath Pl *AYRS* KA7 ... 18 C3
Bath Sq *ARD* KA22 ... 200 C1
Bath St *CGLW* G2 ... 4 D8
  GRK PA19 ... 31 L1
  KLMNKN/STW KA3 ... 206 F7
  LARGS KA30 ... 115 J6
Bathurst Dr *AYRS* KA7 ... 229 G8
Bathville Rd *KBRN* KA25 ... 143 G8
Baton Rd *SHOTTS* ML7 ... 137 K3
Batson St *GVH/MTFL* G42 ... 105 H7
Battery Park Dr
  GRNKW/INVK PA16 ... 32 B1
Battismains *LNK/LMHG* ML11 ... 199 J5
Battlefield Av *GVH/MTFL* G42 ... 128 A2
Battlefield Gdns
  GVH/MTFL G42 ... 128 A2
Battlefield Rd *GVH/MTFL* G42 ... 128 A2
Bavelaw St *STPS/GTHM/RID* G33 ... 85 K7
Bawhirley Rd *GRNK* PA15 ... 3 H8
Baxter La *ALEX/LLW* G83 ... 25 L2
  LNK/LMHG ML11 ... 199 G5
Baxter St *GRNK* PA15 ... 3 L8
Bayfield Av *DRUM* G15 ... 61 G6
Bayfield Ter *DRUM* G15 ... 61 G6
Bay St *FAIRLIE* KA29 ... 139 K5
  PGL PA14 ... 34 C8
Bay View Rd *GRK* PA19 ... 31 M2
Beach Dr *IRV* KA12 ... 202 F8
Beach Rd *TROON* KA10 ... 216 C2
Beachway *LARGS* KA30 ... 115 H5
Beaconsfield Rd *KVD/HLHD* G12 ... 82 B4
Beagle Crs *AYRS* KA7 ... 228 C6
Beansburn *KLMNKN/STW* KA3 ... 207 G6
Beanshields Rd *CARLUKE* ML8 ... 188 F4
Beard Crs *BAIL/MDB/MHD* G69 ... 86 F4
Beardmore Pl *CLYDBK* G81 ... 59 K6
Beardmore St *CLYDBK* G81 ... 59 K6
Beardmore Wy *CLYDBK* G81 ... 59 L7
Bearford Dr
  CARD/HILL/MSPK G52 ... 103 H4
Bearhope St *GRNK* PA15 ... 2 C4
Bearsden Rd *BSDN* G61 ... 81 M1
Beatock Pl *GRNKW/INVK* PA16 ... 50 D5
Beaton Rd *ALEX/LLW* G83 ... 25 L1
  PLKSD/SHW G41 ... 104 E7
Beaton St *LRKH* ML9 ... 175 M5
Beaton Ter *IRV* KA12 ... 203 J4
Beatrice Dr *MTHW* ML1 ... 133 M4
Beatrice Gdns
  CRG/CRSL/HOU PA6 ... 99 K1
Beattock St *DEN/PKHD* G31 ... 13 M6
Beattock Wynd *HMLTN* ML3 ... 156 A4
Beatty Pl *HBR/GL* G84 ... 21 G7
Beatty St *CLYDBK* G81 ... 59 L6
Beaufield Gdns
  KLMNKN/STW KA3 ... 206 B2
Beaufort Av *PLKSW/MSWD* G43 ... 127 J4
Beaufort Dr *KKNTL* G66 ... 65 H1
Beaufort Gdns *BSHPBGS* G64 ... 63 L8

Beauly Crs *KLMCLM* PA13 ... 75 K2
  KLMNK KA1 ... 212 A4
Beauly Dr *PSLYS* PA2 ... 100 E8
Beauly Pl *BAIL/MDB/MHD* G69 ... 86 D5
  CTBR ML5 ... 110 B6
  EKILN G74 ... 14 D1
  MRYH/FIRH G20 ... 82 D3
  MTHW ML1 ... 134 A3
Beauly Rd *BAIL/MDB/MHD* G69 ... 108 A6
Beaumont Ga *PTCK* G11 ... 82 C7
Beckford St *HMLTN* ML3 ... 156 C4
Bedale Rd *BAIL/MDB/MHD* G69 ... 107 M5
Bedcow Vw *KKNTL* G66 ... 65 M2
Bedford Av *CLYDBK* G81 ... 60 D7
Bedford La *GBLS* G5 ... 11 H7
  GRNKW/INVK PA16 ... 32 D2
Bedford St *GBLS* G5 ... 11 G6
  GRNKW/INVK PA16 ... 32 D2
Bedlay Ct
  BAIL/MDB/MHD G69 ... 67 G6
Bedlay Pl *CTBR* ML5 ... 67 M8
Bedlay Vw *UD/BTH/TAN* G71 ... 109 H8
Beech Av *BAIL/MDB/MHD* G69 ... 108 A4
  BEITH KA15 ... 144 B7
  BLTYR/CAMB G72 ... 129 K3
  BRWEIR PA11 ... 76 D8
  BSDN G61 ... 62 A2
  GOV/IBX G51 ... 104 B4
  HMLTN ML3 ... 174 F5
  IRV KA12 ... 203 K7
  JNSTN PA5 ... 100 C7
  KLMNK KA1 ... 16 B5
  LRKH ML9 ... 176 D7
  MTHW ML1 ... 134 B6
  NMRNS G77 ... 150 E5
  PLKSD/SHW G41 ... 104 B5
  PSLYS PA2 ... 102 A8
  RUTH G73 ... 129 J5
Beechbank Av *AIRDRIE* ML6 ... 88 F3
Beechburn Crs *LOCHW* PA12 ... 120 D6
Beech Crs *BLTYR/CAMB* G72 ... 130 E5
  MTHW ML1 ... 134 C2
  NMRNS G77 ... 150 E6
Beech Dr *AIRDRIE* ML6 ... 90 F5
  CLYDBK G81 ... 60 A4
Beeches Av *CLYDBK* G81 ... 59 M3
Beeches Rd *CLYDBK* G81 ... 59 M3
The Beeches
  CRG/CRSL/HOU PA6 ... 77 K8
  JNSTN PA5 ... 99 J3
  LNK/LMHG ML11 ... 199 H7
  RAYR/DAL KA6 ... 231 H5
Beechfield Dr *CARLUKE* ML8 ... 189 G1
Beechfield Rd *BEITH* KA15 ... 167 M2
Beech Gdns
  BAIL/MDB/MHD G69 ... 108 A4
Beech Gv *AYR* KA8 ... 19 L4
  BAIL/MDB/MHD G69 ... 87 G4
  CARLUKE ML8 ... 177 M3
  EKILS G75 ... 171 H3
  WISHAW ML2 ... 159 J2
Beechgrove Av
  UD/BTH/TAN G71 ... 132 C2
Beechgrove Pl *HBR/GL* G84 ... 23 G1
Beechgrove Qd *MTHW* ML1 ... 134 A4
Beechgrove St
  DMNK/BRGTN G40 ... 106 B7
Beechlands Av *LNPK/KPK* G44 ... 127 L7
Beechlands Dr
  CRMNK/CLK/EAG G76 ... 151 J3
Beechmount Rd *KKNTL* G66 ... 65 J5
Beech Pl *BLTYR/CAMB* G72 ... 155 L2
  BSHPBGS G64 ... 84 B1
Beech Rd *BSHPBGS* G64 ... 84 B1
  JNSTN PA5 ... 99 K8
  KKNTL G66 ... 65 J3
  MTHW ML1 ... 134 C2
Beech Ter *LRKH* ML9 ... 176 B8
Beechtree Ter *KKNTL* G66 ... 45 J4
Beechwood *KLWNG* KA13 ... 193 M6
  LRKH ML9 ... 176 A4
  WISHAW ML2 ... 158 D8
Beechwood Av
  CRMNK/CLK/EAG G76 ... 151 J3
  HMLTN ML3 ... 174 B1
  PGL PA14 ... 56 C2
  RUTH G73 ... 129 J5
Beechwood Ct *BSDN* G61 ... 61 M6
  CUMB G67 ... 68 F1
Beechwood Crs *WISHAW* ML2 ... 159 J7
Beechwood Dr *CTBR* ML5 ... 110 C4
  PTCK G11 ... 81 M5
  RNFRW PA4 ... 80 B8
Beechwood Gdns *BLSH* ML4 ... 133 J5
Beechwood Gv
  BRHD/NEIL G78 ... 125 J8
Beechwood La
  TROON KA10 ... 217 H5
Beechwood Pl *PTCK* G11 ... 81 M5
Beechworth Dr *MTHW* ML1 ... 134 D7
Beecroft Pl *BLTYR/CAMB* G72 ... 131 L8
Beggs Ter *ARD* KA22 ... 191 K6
Beil Dr *KNTSWD* G13 ... 80 F2
Beith Dr *AIRDRIE* ML6 ... 111 G5
Beithglass Av *SKLM* SA17 ... 70 B5
Beith Rd *DALRY* KA24 ... 184 L1
  GLGNK KA14 ... 167 K3
  GRNK PA15 ... 2 B9
  HWWD PA9 ... 122 B3
  JNSTN PA5 ... 100 A7
Beith St *PTCK* G11 ... 82 A8
Belford Ct *NMRNS* G77 ... 150 D7
Belford Gv *NMRNS* G77 ... 150 D7
Belgrave La *KVD/HLHD* G12 ... 4 A3
Belgrave St *BLSH* ML4 ... 132 F3
Belhaven Pk
  BAIL/MDB/MHD G69 ... 86 C2
Belhaven Rd *HMLTN* ML3 ... 155 L6
  WISHAW ML2 ... 159 G6
Belhaven St *PGL* PA14 ... 34 B7
Belhaven Ter *KVD/HLHD* G12 ... 82 C5
  WISHAW ML2 ... 159 G6
Belhaven Terrace La
  KVD/HLHD G12 ... 82 C5

Belhaven Ter West
 KVD/HLHD G12 .... 82 C5
Belhaven Terrace West La
 KVD/HLHD G12 .... 82 C5
Bellahouston Dr
 CARD/HILL/MSPK G52 .... 103 C6
Bellairs Pl BLTYR/CAMB G72 ... 131 J8
Bellard Rd WKIL KA23 .... 181 J5
Bellas Pl AIRDRIE ML6 .... 90 A7
Bell Crs IRV KA12 .... 203 K4
Bell Dr BLTYR/CAMB G72 ...... 155 G5
Belleaire Dr
 GRNKW/INVK PA16 .... 32 C1
Bellefield Rd LNK/LMHG ML11 . 199 G4
Belleisle Av UD/BTH/TAN G71 . 131 L3
Belleisle Cl KLWNG KA13 ...... 193 L5
Belleisle Crs BALLOCH G68 .... 48 E5
Belleisle Crs BRWEIR PA11 .... 98 C3
Belleisle Gdns BALLOCH G68 ... 48 E5
Belleisle Gv BALLOCH G68 ..... 48 E5
Belleisle Pl GRK PA19 .... 31 G5
 KLMNK KA1 .... 211 L5
Belleisle St GVH/MTFL G42 .... 105 H8
Bellesdale Av LARGS KA30 ..... 115 L6
Bellesleyhill Av AYR KA8 ...... 225 H6
Bellesleyhill Rd AYR KA8 ...... 225 G5
Bellevale Qd AYRS KA7 .... 228 F4
Bellevue Av KKNTL G66 .... 65 H1
Bellevue La AYRS KA7 .... 18 E6
Bellevue Rd AYRS KA7 .... 18 D6
 KKNTL G66 .... 65 H1
 KLMNK KA1 .... 16 B2
 PSTWK KA9 .... 225 J1
Bellevue St AYRS KA7 .... 18 F6
Bellfield Av KLMNK KA1 .... 212 D3
Bellfield Ct KLMNK KA1 .... 212 D3
Bellfield Crs BRHD/NEIL G78 .. 125 H6
Bellfield Dr WISHAW ML2 ...... 159 J7
Bellfield La PSTWK KA9 .... 225 H1
Bellfield Rd KKNTL G66 .... 65 H1
Bellfield St DEN/PKHD G31 .... 12 E3
Bellflower Av PLK/PH/NH G53 .. 126 C6
Bellflower Gv EKILN G74 ...... 153 J6
Bellflower Gdns
 PLK/PH/NH G53 .... 126 C6
Bellflower Gv EKILN G74 ...... 153 J6
Bellflower Pl
 PLK/PH/NH G53 .... 126 C6
Bell Gn East EKILS G75 .... 15 G6
Bell Gn West EKILS G75 .... 14 F5
Bellgrove St DEN/PKHD G31 .... 12 D3
Bellman's Cl BEITH KA15 ...... 144 B8
 LARGS KA30 .... 115 J6
Bellrock Ct
 STPS/GTHM/RID G33 .... 107 H1
Bellrock Crs
 STPS/GTHM/RID G33 .... 107 G1
Bellrock Rd AYR KA8 .... 225 C5
Bellrock St
 STPS/GTHM/RID G33 .... 107 G1
Bellscroft Av RUTH G73 .... 128 F2
Bellsdyke Rd AIRDRIE ML6 ..... 110 F3
Bellshaugh Gdns KVD/HLHD G12 82 C4
Bellshaugh La KVD/HLHD G12 ... 82 C4
Bellshaugh Pl KVD/HLHD G12 .. 82 C4
Bellshaugh Rd KVD/HLHD G12 .. 82 C4
Bellshill Rd BLSH ML4 .... 132 E6
 MTHW ML1 .... 133 J7
 UD/BTH/TAN G71 .... 131 M4
 UD/BTH/TAN G71 .... 132 C8
 UD/BTH/TAN G71 .... 156 C1
Bellside Rd AIRDRIE ML6 ...... 111 M8
 MTHW ML1 .... 135 G1
 MTHW ML1 .... 135 K8
Bellsland Dr KLMNK KA1 .... 16 F7
Bellsland Pl KLMNK KA1 .... 16 F7
Bellsmyre Av DMBTN G82 .... 37 G3
Bell St AIRDRIE ML6 .... 110 F2
 BLSH ML4 .... 133 H2
 CGLE C1 .... 11 L2
 CLYDBK G81 .... 80 D2
 COWCAD G4 .... 12 A3
 GRNK PA15 .... 33 L7
 RNFRW PA4 .... 80 D5
 WISHAW ML2 .... 158 F6
Bells Wynd LNK/LMHG ML11 ... 199 J4
Belltree Av KLMNKN/STW KA3 . 197 K1
Belltrees Crs PSLYN/LNWD PA3 . 101 C5
Bell Trees Rd HWWD PA9 ...... 121 J6
Bellvale Av RNFRW PA4 .... 228 F4
Bell View Ct RNFRW PA4 ...... 80 D5
Bellvue Crs BLSH ML4 .... 132 F5
 PSTWK KA9 .... 225 J2
Bellwood St PLKSD/SHW G41 ... 127 L1
Bellziehill Rd BLSH ML4 ...... 132 E4
Belmont Av AYRS KA7 .... 19 G8
Belmont Crs AYRS KA7 .... 19 H9
 KLMNKN/STW KA3 .... 206 B2
 KVD/HLHD G12 .... 4 B3
Belmont Dr AYRS KA7 .... 229 G4
 BRHD/NEIL G78 .... 125 K8
 EKILS G75 .... 171 H1
 GIF/THBK G46 .... 127 H6
 RUTH G73 .... 129 H2
Belmont La KVD/HLHD G12 ...... 4 B3
Belmont Pl East AYRS KA7 .... 19 G8
Belmont Pl West AYRS KA7 .... 19 G8
Belmont Rd AYRS KA7 .... 229 G4
 BLTYR/CAMB G72 .... 129 L6
 KLMCLM PA13 .... 75 J2
 PSLYN/LNWD PA3 .... 102 A3
Belmont St CLYDBK G81 .... 60 B8
 CTBR ML5 .... 87 J8
 KVD/HLHD G12 .... 4 B3
 WISHAW ML2 .... 177 H3
Belses Dr CARD/HILL/MSPK G52 . 103 J4
Belses Gdns
 CARD/HILL/MSPK G52 ...... 103 J4
Belstane Pk CARLUKE ML8 ..... 178 F6
Belstane Rd UD/BTH/TAN G71 . 132 A6
Belstane Rd CARLUKE ML8 ..... 179 G6
 CUMB G67 .... 68 F4
Belsyde Av DRUM G15 .... 61 G7
Beltane St KVCV G3 .... 4 D8
 WISHAW ML2 .... 159 G7

Beltrees Av PLK/PH/NH G53 .... 103 C8
Beltrees Crs PLK/PH/NH G53 .. 103 C7
Beltrees Rd PLK/PH/NH G53 ... 103 C8
Belvedere Vw GLSTN KA4 ...... 214 C4
Belvidere Crs BLSH ML4 ...... 133 H5
 BSHPBGS G64 .... 64 A7
Belvidere Rd BLSH ML4 .... 133 G5
Belvidere Ter AYR KA8 .... 225 G7
Belville Av GRNK PA15 .... 3 H7
Belville St GRNK PA15 .... 3 H7
Belvoir Pl BLTYR/CAMB G72 ... 155 K1
Bemersyde Av
 PLKSW/MSWD G43 .... 127 H4
Bemersyde Pl LRKH ML9 ...... 176 A8
Bemersyde Rd PSLYS PA2 ..... 123 K1
Ben Alder Dr PSLYS PA2 ...... 102 D8
Benalder St PTCK G11 .... 82 C7
Benbain Pl IRVSE KA11 ...... 204 A3
Benbecula EKILN G74 .... 154 C8
Benbecula Rd
 KLMNKN/STW KA3 .... 207 G3
Ben Bouie Dr HBR/GL G84 .... 21 G8
Benbow Rd CLYDBK G81 ...... 59 M7
Bencleuch Pl IRVSE KA11 ..... 204 B6
Bencloich Crs KKNTL G66 .... 29 L1
Bencloich Rd KKNTL G66 ..... 44 L1
Benclutha PGL PA14 .... 34 E8
Bencroft Dr LNPK/KPK G44 ... 128 C4
Ben Donich Pl GIF/THBK G46 . 126 D4
Ben Edra Pl GIF/THBK G46 ... 126 D5
Benford Av MTHW ML1 .... 134 D5
Benford Knowe MTHW ML1 .... 134 D5
Bengairn Av DEN/PKHD G31 ... 13 K2
Bengal Pl PLKSW/MSWD G43 .. 127 J2
Bengal St PLKSW/MSWD G43 .. 127 J2
Ben Garrisdale Pl
 GIF/THBK G46 .... 126 D5
Benhar Pl
 GIF/THBK G46 .... 126 D5
Benhar Rd SHOTTS ML7 ...... 137 M5
Benholm St CAR/SHTL G32 ... 106 F6
Ben Hope Av PSLYS PA2 ...... 102 D7
Ben Laga Pl GIF/THBK G46 ... 126 D5
Ben Lawers Dr BALLOCH G68 .. 48 B7
 PSLYS 102 D7
Ben Ledi Av PSLYS PA2 ...... 102 D7
Ben Ledi Crs BALLOCH G68 ... 48 B7
Ben Loyal Av PSLYS PA2 ..... 102 D7
Ben Lui Dr PSLYS PA2 .... 102 D8
Ben Lui Pl BALLOCH G68 ..... 48 B7
Ben Macdui Gdns
 GIF/THBK G46 .... 126 D5
Benmore PSTWK KA9 .... 225 J4
Ben More Dr BALLOCH G68 .... 48 A7
 PSLYS 102 D7
Bennan Pl EKILS G75 .... 171 G5
Bennan Sq GVH/MTFL G42 .... 105 J7
Ben Nevis Rd PSLYS PA2 ..... 102 D8
Ben Nevis Wy BALLOCH G68 .. 48 B7
Bennoch Pl PSTWK KA9 ...... 225 K4
Benrig Av KLMNKN/STW KA3 .. 206 B2
Bensley Av IRVSE KA11 ...... 203 M4
Bensley Ri IRVSE KA11 ...... 203 M5
Benson St CTBR ML5 .... 110 A5
Bent Crs UD/BTH/TAN G71 ... 132 C3
Bentfield Av PSTWK KA9 ..... 225 H4
Bentfoot Rd WISHAW ML2 .... 177 J3
Benthall St GBLS C5 .... 11 L8
Bentinck Crs TROON KA10 ... 216 D7
Bentinck Dr TROON KA10 .... 216 D7
Bentinck St GLSTN KA4 ..... 214 C3
 GRNKW/INVK PA16 .... 32 D1
 KLMNK KA1 .... 16 F7
 KVCV G3 .... 4 A7
Bent Rd AIRDRIE ML6 .... 111 K6
 HMLTN ML3 .... 156 C6
Bents Rd BAIL/MDB/MHD G69 . 108 B6
Benty's La CARLUKE ML8 .... 188 F1
Ben Uird Pl GIF/THBK G46 .. 126 D5
Benvue Rd KKNTL G66 ...... 44 E2
Ben Vorlich Dr GIF/THBK G46 126 D5
Benview Rd BALLOCH G68 .... 48 A7
Benview Dr
 CRMNK/CLK/EAG G76 ..... 151 M4
Benview St MRYH/FIRH G20 .. 82 F5
Benview Ter PSLYS PA2 ..... 102 B7
Ben Wyvis Dr PSLYS PA2 .... 102 C8
Berchem Pl SALT KA21 ...... 200 F1
Bereland Av PSTWK KA9 ..... 225 K1
Berelands Crs RUTH G73 .... 128 C2
Berelands Pl RUTH G73 ..... 128 C2
Berelands Rd PSTWK KA9 .... 221 J8
Beresford Av SCOT G14 ..... 81 L5
Beresford Gv IRV KA12 ..... 203 L4
Beresford Av AYRS KA7 ..... 18 F6
Beresford Ter AYRS KA7 .... 18 F6
Berkeley St KVCV G3 .... 4 B8
Berkeley Terrace La KVCV G3 . 4 C8
Berkley Dr BLTYR/CAMB G72 . 131 J8
Berl Av CRG/CRSL/HOU PA6 .. 99 J1
Bernadette Crs MTHW ML1 ... 134 D7
Bernadette St MTHW ML1 .... 134 D6
Bernard St DMNK/BRGTN G40 . 12 F7
Bernard's Wynd
 LNK/LMHG ML11 .... 199 G5
Bernard Ter DMNK/BRGTN G40 12 E7
Berneray St PPK/MIL G22 ... 83 J2
Berridale Av LNPK/KPK G44 . 128 A4
Berridale Rd TROON KA10 ... 216 D7
Berriedale EKILS G75 ...... 170 E1
Berriedale Av
 BAIL/MDB/MHD G69 ...... 108 A5
Berriedale Qd WISHAW ML2 . 159 H4
Berryburn Rd SPRGB/BLRNK G21 . 7 J1
Berry Dr IRV KA12 .... 203 L6
Berryhill Av IRVSE KA11 ... 204 B4
Berryhill Dr GIF/THBK G46 . 127 H7
Berryhill Rd CUMB G67 ..... 48 E8
 GIF/THBK G46 .... 127 H8
Berryknowe Av
 BAIL/MDB/MHD G69 ...... 86 C2

Berryknowes Av
 CARD/HILL/MSPK G52 ..... 103 J4
Berryknowes La
 CARD/HILL/MSPK G52 ..... 103 J4
Berryknowes Rd
 CARD/HILL/MSPK G52 ..... 103 J4
 GOV/IBX G51 .... 103 K3
Berryyards Rd GRNK PA15 ... 2 C7
Bertram Dr SHOTTS ML7 ..... 113 H7
Bertram Pl SHOTTS ML7 ..... 137 K4
Bertram St HMLTN ML3 ...... 156 A4
 LRKH ML9 .... 176 C8
 PLKSD/SHW G41 .... 104 E8
 SHOTTS ML7 .... 137 L4
Bervie St GOV/IBX G51 ..... 103 M3
Berwick Crs AIRDRIE ML6 ... 110 F4
 PSLYN/LNWD PA3 .... 99 M2
Berwick Dr
 CARD/HILL/MSPK G52 ..... 103 H5
 RUTH G73 .... 129 K2
Berwick Pl CTBR ML5 .... 110 B6
 EKILN G74 .... 154 C6
 GRNKW/INVK PA16 .... 31 K5
Berwick Rd
 GRNKW/INVK PA16 .... 31 J5
 PGL PA14 .... 34 C8
Berwick St CTBR ML5 .... 110 B6
 HMLTN ML3 .... 156 B4
Bessemer Dr EKILS G75 ..... 172 A4
Betula Dr CLYDBK G81 ...... 60 A4
Bevan Ct ARD KA22 .... 191 H5
Bevan Gdns KLWNG KA13 .... 193 L5
Bevan Gv JNSTN PA5 .... 99 J7
Beveridge Ter BLSH ML4 .... 133 K5
Beverley Rd PLKSW/MSWD G43 127 J3
Bevin Av CLYDBK G81 .... 60 D8
Bideford Crs CAR/SHTL G32 . 107 K6
The Bield WISHAW ML2 ...... 159 J4
Biggar Rd MTHW ML1 .... 134 F3
Biggar Rd DEN/PKHD G31 ... 13 H4
Biggart Rd PSTWK KA9 ..... 225 J2
Bigholm Rd BEITH KA15 .... 144 C8
Bigton St STPS/GTHM/RID G33 35 H7
Bilby Ter IRV KA12 .... 203 J4
Billings Rd MTHW ML1 ..... 157 H4
Bilsland Ct MRYH/FIRH G20 . 83 H4
Bilsland Dr MRYH/FIRH G20 . 82 F4
Bilsland Pl DMBTN G82 .... 25 K8
Bimson Pl IRV KA12 .... 203 G8
Bimson Rw IRV KA12 .... 203 G8
Binend Rd PLK/PH/NH G53 .. 126 C1
Binniehill Rd BALLOCH G68 . 48 D7
Binnie La GRK PA19 .... 31 L2
Binnie Pl DMNK/BRGTN G40 . 12 A6
Binnie St GRK PA19 .... 31 K1
Binns Rd STPS/GTHM/RID G33 85 J7
Birch Av CRMNK/CLK/EAG G76 151 M3
 JNSTN PA5 .... 100 A8
Birch Dr BLTYR/CAMB G72 .. 130 C3
 KKNTL G66 .... 65 K4
Birchend Dr SPRGB/BLRNK G21 7 G4
Birchend Pl SPRGB/BLRNK G21 7 G4
Birchfield Dr SCOT G14 .... 81 H5
Birchfield Rd HMLTN ML3 ... 156 B6
Birchgrove CRG/CRSL/HOU PA6 77 K7
Birch Gv LRKH ML9 .... 176 C8
 UD/BTH/TAN G71 .... 132 B2
Birchlea Dr GIF/THBK G46 . 127 K5
Birchmount Ct AIRDRIE ML6 111 K1
Birch Pl BLTYR/CAMB G72 .. 130 F5
 BLTYR/CAMB G72 .... 155 K1
 KLMNK KA1 .... 16 B5
Birch Qd AIRDRIE ML6 ..... 111 K2
Birch Rd AYRS KA7 .... 229 J5
 CLYDBK G81 .... 60 A5
 CUMB G67 .... 49 L6
 DMBTN G82 .... 36 F5
Birch St GBLS C5 .... 11 L9
 MTHW ML1 .... 134 B9
Birch Ter ARD KA22 .... 191 J6
Birch Vw BSDN G61 .... 62 A4
Birchview Dr
 CRMNK/CLK/EAG G76 .... 151 M4
Birchwood Av CAR/SHTL G32 107 L5
Birchwood Dr PSLYS PA2 ... 101 H8
Birchwood Pl CAR/SHTL G32 107 L5
Birdsfield Dr BLTYR/CAMB G72 155 K3
Birdsfield St BLTYR/CAMB G72 155 M3
Birdston Rd KKNTL G66 .... 45 J5
 SPRGB/BLRNK G21 .... 84 C3
Birgidale Av CSMK G45 .... 128 D8
Birgidale Rd CSMK G45 .... 128 D7
Birgidale Ter CSMK G45 ... 128 D7
Birkdale EKILN G74 .... 153 J6
Birkdale Cl KLWNG KA13 ... 193 J5
Birkdale Ct
 UD/BTH/TAN G71 .... 131 M7
Birkdale Crs BALLOCH G68 . 48 F3
Birkenburn Rd CUMB G67 ... 49 M3
Birken Rd KKNTL G66 ...... 65 L5
Birkenshaw Rd DEN/PKHD G31 13 H1
Birkenshaw St DEN/PKHD G31 13 H1
Birkfield Loan CARLUKE ML8 179 J8
Birkfield Pl CARLUKE ML8 . 179 J8
Birkhall Av
 CARD/HILL/MSPK G52 .... 102 F5
 RNFRW PA4 .... 79 K2
Birkhall Dr BSDN G61 ..... 61 M7
Birkhill Av BSHPBGS G64 .. 64 B7
Birkhill Gdns BSHPBGS G64 64 B7
Birkhill Rd CARLUKE ML8 .. 188 C7
 HMLTN ML3 .... 174 D2
Birkmyre Av PGL PA14 ..... 34 A7
Birkmyre Rd GOV/IBX G51 .. 103 M3
Birkscairn Wy IRVSE KA11 . 204 C7
Birks Ct CARLUKE ML8 ..... 177 M4
Birkshaw Brae WISHAW ML2 177 G1
Birkshaw Pl WISHAW ML2 .. 177 G1
Birks Hl IRVSE KA11 ...... 204 A5
Birks Pl LNK/LMHG ML11 .. 199 G5
Birks Rd CARLUKE ML8 .... 177 L6
Birkwood Pl NMRNS G77 ... 150 D7
Birkwood St
 DMNK/BRGTN G40 .... 106 B7

Birmingham Rd RNFRW PA4 .. 80 B8
Birnam Av BSHPBGS G64 .... 64 B7
Birnam Crs BSDN G61 ...... 62 B4
Birnam Pl HMLTN ML3 ..... 155 L6
 NMRNS G77 .... 151 H5
Birnam Rd DEN/PKHD G31 .. 13 M9
Birness Dr PLKSW/MSWD G43 127 K2
Birnie Ct SPRGB/BLRNK G21 7 J1
Birniehill Rd MTHW ML1 .. 135 M5
Birnie Rd SPRGB/BLRNK G21 7 K1
Birnock Av RNFRW PA4 .... 80 E8
Birrell Rd MLNGV G62 .... 41 M6
Birrens Rd MTHW ML1 .... 157 J1
Birsay Rd PPK/MIL G22 ... 83 H2
Bishopdale EKILN G74 .... 153 J6
Bishop Gdns BSHPBGS G64 . 63 L7
 HMLTN ML3 .... 174 C2
Bishop La KVGV G3 .... 10 C1
Bishopmill Pl
 SPRGB/BLRNK G21 ...... 84 C5
Bishops Ga EKILN G74 .... 152 C6
Bishopsgate Rd
 SPRGB/BLRNK G21 ...... 83 L2
Bishops Pk EKILN G74 .... 152 B6
Bissett Crs CLYDBK G81 .. 59 L3
Blackadder Pl EKILS G75 . 170 D2
Blackbog Rd CUMB G67 ... 68 F7
Blackbraes Rd EKILN G74 . 154 E8
Blackburn Crs DMBTN G82 . 36 D5
 KKNTL G66 .... 66 A1
Blackburn Dr AYRS KA7 .. 18 B8
Blackburn Rd AYRS KA7 .. 18 C7
Blackburn Rd AYRS KA7 .. 18 C7
Blackburn Sq BRHD/NEIL G78 125 K6
Blackburn St GOV/IBX G51 . 10 A4
Blackbyres Crs BRHD/NEIL G78 125 K5
Blackbyres Rd BRHD/NEIL G78 125 J3
Blackcraig Av DRUM G15 .. 61 G6
Blackcroft Av AIRDRIE ML6 111 L4
Blackcroft Gdns
 CAR/SHTL G32 .... 107 K5
Blackcroft Rd CAR/SHTL G32 107 K5
Blackcroft Ter SHOTTS ML7 113 H7
Blackdales Av LARGS KA30 115 K7
Blackdyke Rd KKNTL G66 .. 65 L1
Blackfarm Rd NMRNS G77 . 150 D5
Blackfaulds Rd RUTH G73 . 128 C1
Blackford Crs PSTWK KA9 . 221 L5
Blackford Rd PSLYS PA2 .. 9 M7
Blackfriars St CGLE C1 ... 11 L2
Blackfriars Wk AYRS KA7 . 18 F3
Blackhall La PSLY PA1 .... 9 K6
Blackhall St PSLY PA1 .... 9 K6
Blackhill Dr HBR/GL G84 . 20 D5
Blackhill Pl STPS/GTHM/RID G33 7 M5
Blackhill Rd SMSTN G23 .. 62 F7
Blackhill St AYRS KA7 .... 19 K9
Blackhill Vw CARLUKE ML8 178 A4
Blackhouse Av NMRNS G77 150 F5
Blackhouse Gdns
 NMRNS G77 .... 150 F5
Blackhouse Rd NMRNS G77 150 F5
Blackie St KVGV G3 ...... 104 D1
Blacklands Av KLWNG KA13 193 L8
Blacklands Crs KLWNG KA13 193 L8
Blacklands Pl KKNTL G66 . 65 M5
Blacklands Rd EKILN G74 . 14 D3
Blacklaw Dr EKILN G74 ... 15 L4
Blacklaw La PSLYN/LNWD PA3 9 H2
Blackmoor Pl MTHW ML1 .. 134 A6
Blackmoss Dr BLSH ML4 .. 132 F5
Blackness St CTBR ML5 ... 110 B6
Blackshaw Dr WKIL KA23 . 181 K3
Blackstone Av PLK/PH/NH G53 126 B2
Blackstone Crs PLK/PH/NH G53 103 J8
Blackstone Rd
 PSLYN/LNWD PA3 ...... 101 G1
Blackstoun Av
 PSLYN/LNWD PA3 ...... 100 B3
Blackstoun Ov PSLYN/LNWD PA3 8 B3
Blackstoun Rd PSLYN/LNWD PA3 8 B3
Black St AIRDRIE ML6 .... 89 H8
 COWCAD G4 .... 5 M7
Blackswell La HMLTN ML3 . 156 F6
Blacksyke Av KLMNK KA1 .. 211 M6
Blackthorn Av BEITH KA15 144 A8
 KKNTL G66 .... 65 H4
Blackthorn Gv KKNTL G66 65 H4
Blackthorn Rd CUMB G67 . 49 L5
 UD/BTH/TAN G71 .... 132 C1
Blackthorn St PPK/MIL G22 83 L4
Blackwood EKILS G75 ..... 171 K4
Blackwood Av KLMNK KA1 . 16 B7
 NMRNS G77 .... 150 F6
 PSLYN/LNWD PA3 .... 100 A4
Blackwood Gdns MTHW ML1 133 J8
Blackwood Rd BALLOCH G68 47 L8
 MLNGV G62 .... 41 M6
Blackwoods Crs BLSH ML4 . 133 J5
Blackwood St BRHD/NEIL G78 125 C7
 KNTSWD G13 .... 81 L2
Blackwood Ter JNSTN PA5 122 D1
Bladda La PSLY PA1 ...... 9 J5
Blades Ct BAIL/MDB/MHD G69 87 G3
Bladnoch Dr DRUM G15 ... 61 J7
Blaeloch Av CSMK G45 ... 128 C8
Blaeloch Dr CSMK G45 ... 128 C8
Blaeloch Ter CSMK G45 .. 128 B8
Blaeshill Rd EKILS G75 . 170 E1
Blairafton Wynd KLWNG KA13 193 J4
Blairatholl Crs NMRNS G77 151 H5
Blairatholl Gdns PTCK G11 82 A6
Blair Atholl Dr LRKH ML9 176 C8
Blair Atholl Gdns NMRNS G77 151 H5
Blair Av KLMNK KA1 ...... 212 E3
Blairbeth Dr LNPK/KPK G44 128 B2
Blairbeth Rd RUTH G73 .. 129 H4
Blairbeth Ter RUTH G73 . 129 J4
Blair Crs
 BAIL/MDB/MHD G69 ..... 108 A6
 GLSTN KA4 .... 214 C3
 KLMNK KA1 .... 212 E3
Blairdardie Rd DRUM G15 . 61 H4
Blairdenan Av
 BAIL/MDB/MHD G69 ..... 66 F6
Blairdenon Dr BALLOCH G68 48 C6

Blairdenon Wy IRVSE KA11 . 204 B3
Blair Dr KKNTL G66 ...... 45 H4
Blair Gdns BSHPBGS G64 .. 44 B8
 GRK PA19 .... 30 F4
 NMRNS G77 .... 150 B4
Blairgowrie Rd
 CARD/HILL/MSPK G52 ... 103 J5
Blairhall Av PLKSD/SHW G41 127 M1
Blairhill Av KKNTL G66 .. 66 A3
Blairhill Pl CTBR ML5 ... 109 L2
Blairhill St CTBR ML5 ... 109 M2
Blairholm Dr BLSH ML4 .. 133 H6
Blairlands Dr DALRY KA24 184 E2
Blairlinn Rd CUMB G67 .. 69 G3
Blairlogie St
 STPS/GTHM/RID G33 .... 85 H8
Blairmore Av PSLY PA1 .. 102 C4
Blairmore Crs GRNK PA15 . 3 J9
Blairmore Av GRNK PA15 . 33 H7
Blairpark Av CTBR ML5 .. 109 L1
Blair Pth MTHW ML1 ..... 157 M4
Blair Rd CARLUKE ML8 ... 188 A8
 CTBR ML5 .... 109 L2
 DALRY KA24 .... 184 E2
 KLMNK KA1 .... 212 E3
 KLWNG KA13 .... 193 M5
 PSLY PA1 .... 102 E3
Blairston Gdns
 UD/BTH/TAN G71 .... 132 B8
Blair St CAR/SHTL G32 .. 106 F4
 GLSTN KA4 .... 214 C3
 KLMNKN/STW KA3 .... 206 F7
Blairtum Dr RUTH G73 ... 129 H4
Blairtummock Rd
 STPS/GTHM/RID G33 .... 107 K1
Blakely Rd SALT KA21 ... 201 H3
Blake Rd CUMB G67 ...... 49 G7
Blane Av CMPFG/LLE G63 . 27 G5
Blane Crs CMPFG/LLE G63 . 27 G5
Blane Dr MLNGV G62 ..... 42 B6
Blanefield Av PSTWK KA9 225 H3
Blane Pl CMPFG/LLE G63 . 27 G5
Blane St CTBR ML5 ...... 110 A1
Blaneview STPS/GTHM/RID G33 85 K5
Blantyre Crs CLYDBK G81 . 59 L2
Blantyre Dr BSHPTN PA7 . 58 A5
Blantyre Farm Rd
 BLTYR/CAMB G72 .... 131 J7
 UD/BTH/TAN G71 .... 131 J7
Blantyre Gdns BALLOCH G68 47 L8
Blantyre Mill Rd
 UD/BTH/TAN G71 .... 132 A7
Blantyre Pl CTBR ML5 ... 109 L3
Blantyre Rd UD/BTH/TAN G71 132 A7
Blantyre St CTBR ML5 ... 109 L3
 KVGV G3 .... 82 D8
Blaven Ct
 BAIL/MDB/MHD G69 ..... 108 A6
Blaven Head IRVSE KA11 . 204 A5
Blawarthill St SCOT G14 . 80 F4
Bleachfield MLNGV G62 .. 41 M6
Bleasdale Ct CLYDBK G81 60 D7
Bleeze Rd DALRY KA24 ... 184 B1
Blenheim Av EKILS G75 .. 14 B8
 STPS/GTHM/RID G33 .... 85 K3
Blenheim Ct PSLY PA1 ... 8 E3
Blenheim Rd CARLUKE ML8 179 G8
Blochairn Rd SPRGB/BLRNK G21 6 F6
Bluebell Gdns CSMK G45 . 129 G3
 MTHW ML1 .... 133 J7
Bluebell Wy AIRDRIE ML6 88 F7
 CARLUKE ML8 .... 188 F1
 KKNTL G66 .... 44 F2
Blueknowes Rd CARLUKE ML8 177 L4
Bluevale St DEN/PKHD G31 12 E4
Blythe Pl
 STPS/GTHM/RID G33 .... 107 K3
Blyth Rd STPS/GTHM/RID G33 107 L3
Blythswood Av RNFRW PA4 80 D5
Blythswood Crs LARGS KA30 115 K7
Blythswood Dr PSLYN/LNWD PA3 8 E1
Blythswood Rd RNFRW PA4 80 D4
Blythswood Sq CGLW G2 . 4 F9
Blythswood St CGLW G2 .. 5 G9
Boathouse Av LARGS KA30 115 H3
Boathouse Rd LARGS KA30 115 H3
Boclair Av BSDN G61 .... 61 M5
Boclair Crs BSDN G61 ... 62 A4
 BSHPBGS G64 .... 64 A5
Boclair Rd BSDN G61 .... 62 A4
 BSHPBGS G64 .... 64 A7
Boclair St KNTSWD G13 .. 81 L1
Bodden Sq MTHW ML1 .... 134 E2
Boden Qd MTHW ML1 ..... 133 J7
Boden St DMNK/BRGTN G40 12 F4
Bodmin Gdns
 BAIL/MDB/MHD G69 ..... 66 F6
Bogany Ter CSMK G45 .... 128 E7
Bogbain Rd ESTRH G34 ... 108 A1
Bogfoot Rd SHOTTS ML7 .. 113 C6
Boggknowe UD/BTH/TAN G71 131 K1
Boghall Rd CARLUKE ML8 . 189 H3
 UD/BTH/TAN G71 .... 108 A6
Boghall St STPS/GTHM/RID G33 85 H8
Boghead BEITH KA15 ..... 168 B1
Boghead Av DMBTN G82 .. 37 H5
Boghead Rd DMBTN G82 .. 37 G5
 KKNTL G66 .... 65 G4
 SPRGB/BLRNK G21 ...... 84 A5
Bogiewood Rd PGL PA14 . 34 B8
Boglemart St SVSTN KA20 201 J1
Bogleshole Rd
 BLTYR/CAMB G72 .... 129 L2
Boglestone Av PGL PA14 . 54 E1
Bogle St GRNK PA15 ..... 2 E5
Bogmoor Pl GOV/IBX G51 . 81 J8
Bogmoor Rd GOV/IBX G51 103 J1
Bogside Rd KSYTH G65 .. 47 K2
 PGL PA14 .... 54 F1
 STPS/GTHM/RID G33 .... 85 G4
Bogside St DMNK/BRGTN G40 13 H8
Bogstonhill Rd
 CRG/CRSL/HOU PA6 ..... 77 H2
Bogston La GRNK PA15 ... 33 M7
Bogs Vw BLSH ML4 ...... 132 F6
Bogton Av LNPK/KPK G44 . 127 M5

Bogton Avenue La
LNPK/KPK G44 127 M5
Boleyn Rd PLKSD/SHW G41 104 E7
Bolingbroke EKILN G74 154 C5
Bolivar Ter GVH/MTFL G42 128 C1
Bolton Dr GVH/MTFL G42 128 A1
Bolton Ter KKNTL G66 44 E1
Bon Accord Crs SHOTTS ML7 137 K4
Bon Accord Rd
CRMNK/CLK/EAG G76 151 M3
Bon Accord Sq CLYDBK G81 80 B1 1
Bonar Crs BRWEIR PA11 98 E2
Bonar La BRWEIR PA11 98 E2
Bonar Law Av HBR/GL G84 20 B7 1
Bonawe St MRYH/FIRH G20 4 D2
Bonds Dr WISHAW ML2 160 B3
Bo'ness Rd AIRDRIE ML6 134 C1
MTHW ML1 134 B3
Boness St DMNK/BRGTN G40 13 H8
Bonhill Rd DMBTN G82 37 G5
Bonhill St PPK/MIL G22 5 G2
Bonkle Gdns WISHAW ML2 160 B4
Bonkle Rd WISHAW ML2 160 B4
Bonnar St DMNK/BRGTN G40 106 A6 3
Bonnaughton Rd BSDN G61 61 H3
Bonnet Ct KLMNKN/STW KA3 197 K1
Bonnet Rd LNK/LMHG ML11 199 G5 2
Bonnington Av
LNK/LMHG ML11 199 G6
Bonnyholm Av PLK/PH/NH G53 103 G6
Bonnyrigg Dr
PLKSW/MSWD G43 127 G4
Bonnyton Pl IRVSE KA11 204 A4
Bonnyton Rd KLMNK KA1 16 A2
Bontine Av DMBTN G82 36 D5
Bonyton Av KNTSWD G13 80 F3
Boon Dr DRUM G15 61 H7
Boquhanran Rd CLYDBK G81 60 A6 1
Borden La KNTSWD G13 81 L4 3
Borden Rd KNTSWD G13 81 L4
Border Av SALT KA21 200 F1
Border Pl SALT KA21 200 F1 2
Border St GRNK PA15 3 J8
Border Wy KKNTL G66 65 L1
Borebrae NMLNS KA16 215 J2
Borebrae Crs NMLNS KA16 215 J2
Boreland Dr HMLTN ML3 155 L7 2
KNTSWD G13 81 H2
Boreland Pl KNTSWD G13 81 H3 1
Bore Rd AIRDRIE ML6 111 H1
Borestone Av KBRN KA25 167 G1 2
Borgie Crs BLTYR/CAMB G72 130 A4
Borland Br KLMNKN/STW KA3 207 J3
Borland Rd BSDN G61 62 A6
Borron St COWCAD G4 5 J3
Borrowdale EKILS G75 170 F4 1
Borthwick Dr EKILS G75 170 D2
Borthwick St
STPS/GTHM/RID G33 85 H8 1
Bosfield Cnr EKILN G74 153 M6 1
Bosfield Pl EKILN G74 153 M6
Bosfield Rd EKILN G74 153 L6
Boston Dr HBR/GL G84 20 F6 1
Boswell Ct PLKSD/SHW G41 127 M2 1
Boswell Dr BLTYR/CAMB G72 155 K2
Boswell Pk AYRS KA7 18 E3
EKILN G74 154 C5
Boswell Sq
CARD/HILL/MSPK G52 102 F2
Bosworth Rd EKILN G74 154 C5
Botanic Crs MRYH/FIRH G20 82 D5
Bothlin Dr STPS/GTHM/RID G33 85 K3
Bothlyn Av KKNTL G66 65 L2
Bothlyn Crs BAIL/MDB/MHD G69 86 E2
Bothlyn Rd BAIL/MDB/MHD G69 86 D1
Bothwellhaugh Qd
BLSH ML4 132 F6 1
Bothwellhaugh Rd BLSH ML4 132 F8
Bothwell La CGLW G2 10 F1
KVD/HLHD G12 4 B4
Bothwellpark Pl
UD/BTH/TAN G71 132 D3 1
Bothwellpark Rd
UD/BTH/TAN G71 132 C5
Bothwell Pl CTBR ML5 109 M2
PSLYS PA2 123 L1
Bothwell Rd CARLUKE ML8 178 E5
HMLTN ML3 156 C2
UD/BTH/TAN G71 131 M5
Bothwellshields Rd MTHW ML1 112 D7
Bothwell St BLTYR/CAMB G72 129 L3
CGLW G2 10 F1
HMLTN ML3 156 C4
The Boulevard KKNTL G66 29 G8
Boundary Rd AYR KA8 225 K5 1
PSTWK KA9 225 K5
Bourne Ct RNFRW PA4 79 K2
Bourne Crs RNFRW PA4 79 K2
Bournemouth Rd
GRNKW/INVK PA16 31 L4
Bourne St HMLTN ML3 156 F6 1
Bourock Sq BRHD/NEIL G78 125 K8
Bourtree Pk AYRS KA7 19 G7
Bourtree Rd HMLTN ML3 155 L8
Bouverie St PGL PA14 34 C8
RUTH G73 128 F1
SCOT G14 80 E3
Bowden Dr
CARD/HILL/MSPK G52 103 H3
Bowden Pk EKILS G75 14 B6
Bowencraig LARGS KA30 115 K8
Bower St KVD/HLHD G12 4 A3
Bowerwalls St BRHD/NEIL G78 125 L5
Bowes Crs BAIL/MDB/MHD G69 107 M5
Bowfield Av
CARD/HILL/MSPK G52 102 F3
Bowfield Crs
CARD/HILL/MSPK G52 102 F3
Bowfield Dr
CARD/HILL/MSPK G52 102 F3
Bowfield Pl
CARD/HILL/MSPK G52 102 F3
Bowfield Rd HWWD PA9 121 M4
WKIL KA23 181 J5
Bowhousebog Rd SHOTTS ML7 137 G7
Bowhousebrae Rd
AIRDRIE ML6 111 L4
Bowhouse Ri IRVSE KA11 204 B4
Bowhouse Rd AIRDRIE ML6 111 M5
Bowie Rd ALEX/LLW G83 25 L3
Bowie St DMBTN G82 36 E6 1
Bowling Green La SCOT G14 81 K6
Bowling Green Rd
BAIL/MDB/MHD G69 86 D1 1
CAR/SHTL G32 107 K5
LNPK/KPK G44 128 A4 2
SCOT G14 81 K6 1
Bowling Green St BLSH ML4 133 H4 3
Bowling Green Vw
BLTYR/CAMB G72 130 F5
Bowling St CTBR ML5 109 M2
Bowman Rd AYRS KA7 18 F7
Bowman St GVH/MTFL G42 105 G7 1
Bowmont Pl EKILS G75 170 D2
Bowmont Ter KVD/HLHD G12 82 C6
Bowmore Ct IRVSE KA11 204 A3 1
Bowmore Gdns RUTH G73 129 L6 1
UD/BTH/TAN G71 131 L1 1
Bowmore Rd
CARD/HILL/MSPK G52 103 L4 2
Bowmount Gdns
KVD/HLHD G12 82 C6 2
Bow Rd GRNKW/INVK PA16 32 B5
Bowyer Vennel BLSH ML4 132 F3 2
Boyd Ct KLMNKN/STW KA3 17 G2
Boyd Dr MTHW ML1 157 H2
Boydfield Av PSTWK KA9 221 K8
Boyd Orr Crs KLMNKN/STW KA3 206 A2
Boyd Orr Rd SALT KA21 192 A7
Boydstone Pl GIF/THBK G46 126 F4
Boydstone Rd GIF/THBK G46 126 F5
PLKSW/MSWD G43 126 E3
Boydston Rd ARD KA22 191 J5
Boydston Wy
KLMNKN/STW KA3 207 J3
Boyd St GLSTN KA4 214 B3
GVH/MTFL G42 105 H8
KLMNKN/STW KA3 16 F2
LARGS KA30 115 J5
PSTWK KA9 225 J1 1
Boylestone Rd BRHD/NEIL G78 125 G5
Boyle St CLYDBK G81 80 D1
Boyndie St ESTRH G34 108 B1 1
Brabloch Crs PSLYN/LNWD PA3 101 M3
Bracadale Dr
BAIL/MDB/MHD G69 108 D5 1
Bracadale Gdns
BAIL/MDB/MHD G69 108 D5 2
Bracadale Gv
BAIL/MDB/MHD G69 108 C5 2
Bracadale Rd
BAIL/MDB/MHD G69 108 C5
Bracco Rd AIRDRIE ML6 113 G1
Brachelston St
GRNKW/INVK PA16 32 D5
Brackenbrae Av BSHPBGS G64 63 L7
Brackenbrae Rd BSHPBGS G64 63 M8
Brackenburn Br
KLMNKN/STW KA3 197 J7
Brackendene
CRG/CRSL/HOU PA6 77 K8
Brackenhill Av
KLMNKN/STW KA3 207 G4
Brackenhill Dr HMLTN ML3 174 B2
Brackenhill Rd CARLUKE ML8 178 A3
Brackenhirst Rd AIRDRIE ML6 88 D3
Brackenhurst St DMBTN G82 37 J3 1
Brackenknowe Rd AIRDRIE ML6 69 K6
Brackenrig Rd GIF/THBK G46 126 E7
Bracken Rd PGL PA14 55 G1 1
Bracken St MTHW ML1 134 A6
PPK/MIL G22 83 H3
Bracken Ter UD/BTH/TAN G71 132 A6
Brackla Av KNTSWD G13 80 E1
Bradan Av KNTSWD G13 80 E1
Bradan Dr AYRS KA7 229 H7
Bradan Rd TROON KA10 216 A7
Bradda Av RUTH G73 129 J5
Bradfield Av KVD/HLHD G12 82 C4
Bradshaw Crs HMLTN ML3 155 L6 1
Bradshaw St SALT KA21 200 F2 1
Brady Crs BAIL/MDB/MHD G69 67 G6
Braedale Av AIRDRIE ML6 111 H2
MTHW ML1 157 H3
Braedale Crs WISHAW ML2 160 B4
Braedale Pl WISHAW ML2 160 C4 1
Braedale Rd LNK/LMHG ML11 199 G4
Braeface Rd CUMB G67 48 E7
Braefield Dr GIF/THBK G46 127 G6
Braefoot IRV KA12 203 M4
RAYR/DAL KA6 227 G7
Braefoot Av MLNGV G62 62 A1
Braefoot Ct CARLUKE ML8 177 M5
Braefoot Crs CARLUKE ML8 177 M5
PSLYS PA2 124 F1
Braefoot La BRHD/NEIL G78 147 G6
Braehead BEITH KA15 168 B1 1
BLTYR/CAMB G72 155 K3 1
DALRY KA24 184 C1
LOCHW PA12 120 C6
Braehead Av BRHD/NEIL G78 148 D2
CLYDBK G81 60 A2
CTBR ML5 109 K6
LOCHW PA12 120 C6
LRKH ML9 175 L7 1
MLNGV G62 41 M8
Braehead Ct KLMNKN/STW KA3 17 G4
Braehead Crs CLYDBK G81 60 A2
Braehead Dr BLSH ML4 132 F5
Braehead Glebe
KLMNKN/STW KA3 197 L1 3
Braehead Pl BLSH ML4 132 F5 2
DALRY KA24 184 C1
SALT KA21 200 F1 2
Braehead Qd
BRHD/NEIL G78 148 D2 1
MTHW ML1 134 D5 1
Braehead Rd AYR KA8 225 J7
CLYDBK G81 60 A2
CUMB G67 49 H6
EKILN G74 152 C6
PGL PA14 54 E1 1
PSLYS PA2 124 D1
Braehead St KKNTL G66 45 J8 1
Braehead Ter
KLMNKN/STW KA3 206 C3 1
Braemar Av CLYDBK G81 59 M5
Braemar Ct GIF/THBK G46 127 L5
Braemar Crs BSDN G61 61 M7
CARLUKE ML8 179 G6
PSLYS PA2 101 M8
Braemar Dr JNSTN PA5 100 B8
Braemar Rd RNFRW PA4 79 K2
RUTH G73 129 K6
Braemar Sq AYR KA8 225 K7
Braemar St GVH/MTFL G42 127 M2 2
HMLTN ML3 156 B3
Braemar Vw CLYDBK G81 59 M4
Braemore Gdns PPK/MIL G22 83 K5 1
Braemount Av PSLYS PA2 124 C3
Braes Av CLYDBK G81 60 D8
Braesburn Pl CUMB G67 49 M3 1
Braesburn Rd CUMB G67 49 M3 2
Braeside IRV KA12 203 M4
KLWNG KA13 193 L4
RAYR/DAL KA6 227 G7
Braeside Av
BAIL/MDB/MHD G69 66 F7
LARGS KA30 115 L5
MLNGV G62 62 A1
RUTH G73 129 J2
Braeside Crs
BAIL/MDB/MHD G69 108 F4
BRHD/NEIL G78 125 L8
Braeside Dr BRHD/NEIL G78 125 K8
DMBTN G82 37 H4
Braeside Gdns HMLTN ML3 174 E1 1
Braeside Pl BLTYR/CAMB G72 130 B5
Braeside Rd AYR KA8 225 K7
GRNKW/INVK PA16 31 K6
MTHW ML1 134 D5
Braeside St KLMNK KA1 17 G4
MRYH/FIRH G20 4 D2
Braes O' Yetts KKNTL G66 66 A1 1
Braes Rd SALT KA21 200 E2
The Brae KLMNKN/STW KA3 206 B2 1
Brae Vw GRNKW/INVK PA16 32 C4 1
Braeview Av PSLYS PA2 124 B2
Braeview Dr PSLYS PA2 124 B2
Braeview Gdns PSLYS PA2 124 B2 1
Braeview Pl EKILN G74 154 A5
Braeview Rd PSLYS PA2 124 B2
Braidbar Farm Rd
GIF/THBK G46 127 K6
Braidbar Rd GIF/THBK G46 127 J6
Braid Ct KLWNG KA13 193 H6 1
Braidcraft Pl
PLK/PH/NH G53 126 C1 1
Braidcraft Rd PLK/PH/NH G53 126 D1
Braidcraft Ter
PLK/PH/NH G53 103 K8 1
Braidfauld Gdns CAR/SHTL G32 106 F6
Braidfauld Pl CAR/SHTL G32 106 F7 1
Braidfauld St CAR/SHTL G32 106 F7
Braidfield Gv CLYDBK G81 60 B4
Braidfield Rd CLYDBK G81 60 C4
Braidfute LNK/LMHG ML11 199 J4 2
Braidholm Crs GIF/THBK G46 127 J5
Braidholm Rd GIF/THBK G46 127 K5
Braidhurst St MTHW ML1 157 L1
Braidley Crs EKILS G75 171 L4
Braidpark Dr GIF/THBK G46 127 K6
Braid Sq COWCAD G4 4 F5
Braid's Rd PSLYS PA2 101 L8
Braid St COWCAD G4 4 F5
Braidwood Pl PSLYN/LNWD PA3 99 M3
Braidwood Rd CARLUKE ML8 188 C7
KLWNG KA13 193 L5
Braidwood St WISHAW ML2 159 J2 1
Bramah Av EKILS G75 15 H7
Bramblehedge Pth
ALEX/LLW G83 25 M2 1
Brambling Ct WISHAW ML2 159 G8 1
Bramley Pl AIRDRIE ML6 111 J3 1
KKNTL G66 65 L5
Brampton EKILS G75 170 F3
Branchalfield Dr WISHAW ML2 159 L5
Branchalmuir Crs WISHAW ML2 159 M3
Branchal Rd WISHAW ML2 159 K4
Branchock Av
BLTYR/CAMB G72 130 D5 1
Branchton Rd
GRNKW/INVK PA16 31 M6
Brancumhall Rd EKILN G74 154 D6
Brandon Dr BSDN G61 61 L2
Brandon Gdns
BLTYR/CAMB G72 129 L4 1
PSTWK KA9 225 H2
Brandon Pl BLSH ML4 132 E6
Brandon St CTBR ML5 109 L5 2
DEN/PKHD G31 12 D3
HMLTN ML3 156 E6
MTHW ML1 157 L3
Brandon Wy CTBR ML5 109 K5
Brand Pl GOV/IBX G51 104 C3
Brand St GOV/IBX G51 104 C3
Brankholm Brae HMLTN ML3 155 K5
Brannock Av MTHW ML1 134 D5
Brannock Pl MTHW ML1 134 D5 2
Brannock Rd MTHW ML1 134 D6
Brassey St MRYH/FIRH G20 82 E3
Braxfield Rd LNK/LMHG ML11 199 G8
Braxfield Ter LNK/LMHG ML11 198 F7
Breadalbane Crs MTHW ML1 133 K8 1
Breadalbane Gdns RUTH G73 129 K5 1
Breadalbane St KVGV G3 4 C9
Breadie Dr MLNGV G62 61 M1
Breamish Pl EKILS G75 170 F3 2
Bream Pl CRG/CRSL/HOU PA6 99 K1
Brechin Rd BSHPBGS G64 64 C8
Brechin St KVGV G3 4 B8
Breck Av PSLYS PA2 123 K2
Brediland Rd PSLYN/LNWD PA3 100 A3
PSLYS PA2 100 F8
Bredin Wy MTHW ML1 157 H1
Bredisholm Crs
UD/BTH/TAN G71 109 J8
Bredisholm Dr
BAIL/MDB/MHD G69 108 C5
Bredisholm Rd
BAIL/MDB/MHD G69 108 C5
Bredisholm Ter
BAIL/MDB/MHD G69 108 C5
Brenfield Av LNPK/KPK G44 127 M5
Brenfield Dr LNPK/KPK G44 127 M5 1
Brenfield Rd LNPK/KPK G44 127 M5
Brent Ct EKILN G74 153 L6 2
Brent Crs CRG/CRSL/HOU PA6 99 J1
Brent Dr GIF/THBK G46 126 F4
Brent Gdns GIF/THBK G46 126 F4
Brent Rd EKILN G74 153 L6
GIF/THBK G46 126 F4
Brent Wy GIF/THBK G46 126 F4 1
Brentwood Av PLK/PH/NH G53 126 A5
Brentwood Dr PLK/PH/NH G53 126 A5
Brentwood Sq
PLK/PH/NH G53 126 B5 1
Brereton St GVH/MTFL G42 105 J8
Bressay EKILN G74 153 L6
Bressay Pl KLMNKN/STW KA3 207 H4
Bressay Rd
STPS/GTHM/RID G33 107 L3
Breval Crs CLYDBK G81 60 A2
Brewery Rd KLMNK KA1 16 F7 1
Brewery St JNSTN PA5 99 M6
Brewlands Crs KLMNK KA1 218 C5
Brewlands Dr KLMNK KA1 218 C5
Brewlands Rd KLMNK KA1 218 C6
Brewland St GLSTN KA4 214 B4
Brewster Av PSLYN/LNWD PA3 102 A2
Brewster Pl IRVSE KA11 208 F2
Briar Bank KKNTL G66 45 H4
Briarcroft Dr
STPS/GTHM/RID G33 84 D2
Briarcroft Pl
STPS/GTHM/RID G33 84 E3 3
Briarcroft Rd
STPS/GTHM/RID G33 84 D3 1
Briar Dr CLYDBK G81 60 B5
Briar Gdns PLKSW/MSWD G43 127 K4
Briar Gv AYRS KA7 229 J5
PLKSW/MSWD G43 127 K4 1
Briarhill Ct PSTWK KA9 225 K1 1
Briarhill Rd PSTWK KA9 225 J1
Briarhill St PSTWK KA9 225 J1 1
Briarlea Dr GIF/THBK G46 127 J5
Briar Neuk BSHPBGS G64 84 B1 1
Briar Pl GRK PA19 31 K3 1
Briar Rd KKNTL G66 65 M1
PLKSW/MSWD G43 127 K4
Briar Wk KKNTL G66 66 A1 1
Briarwell La MLNGV G62 42 B8 1
Briarwell Rd MLNGV G62 42 B8
Briarwood Ct CAR/SHTL G32 107 L7 1
Briarwood Rd WISHAW ML2 158 E5
Brick La PSLYN/LNWD PA3 9 J2 1
Bridgebar St BRHD/NEIL G78 125 L5 1
Bridgeburn Dr
BAIL/MDB/MHD G69 66 E7
Bridgeford Av BLSH ML4 133 J2 1
Bridgegait MLNGV G62 62 C1 2
Bridgegate CGLE G1 11 K4
IRV KA12 203 J7
Bridgehousehill Rd KLMNK KA1 211 M7
Bridgend DALRY KA24 184 D2
KLMNKN/STW KA3 197 L1
NMLNS KA16 215 K2 1
Bridgend Av PGL PA14 54 E1
Bridgend Crs
BAIL/MDB/MHD G69 66 E7
Bridgend La DALRY KA24 184 D2
KLWNG KA13 193 M5
Bridgend Pl
BAIL/MDB/MHD G69 66 E7
Bridgend Rd GRNK PA15 3 K9
KBRN KA25 143 H7
Bridgend Vw CARLUKE ML8 178 F8
Bridge of Weir Rd
CRG/CRSL/HOU PA6 77 G8
JNSTN PA5 99 H4
KLMCLM PA13 75 L3
PSLYN/LNWD PA3 100 B4
Bridgepark ARD KA22 191 K8
Bridge Rd PGL PA14 54 E1 2
Bridge St ALEX/LLW G83 25 L5
BLTYR/CAMB G72 130 A3
CLYDBK G81 59 L6
DMBTN G82 36 E6
GBLS G5 11 H4
HMLTN ML3 156 C7
KBRN KA25 143 H7 1
PSLY PA1 9 H5
PSLYN/LNWD PA3 100 C3
PSTWK KA9 225 H1
WISHAW ML2 158 E6
Bridgeway Ct KKNTL G66 65 M2 1
Bridgeway Rd KKNTL G66 65 M2
Bridgeway Ter KKNTL G66 65 M2 2
Bridie Ter EKILN G74 154 C5
Brierie Av CRG/CRSL/HOU PA6 77 H8 1
Brierie Gdns
CRG/CRSL/HOU PA6 99 H1 1
Brierie Hill Ct
CRG/CRSL/HOU PA6 99 H1
Brierie-Hill Gv
CRG/CRSL/HOU PA6 99 H1 2
Brierie-Hill Rd
CRG/CRSL/HOU PA6 99 G1
Brierie La CRG/CRSL/HOU PA6 99 G1
Brierybank Av LNK/LMHG ML11 199 G6
Brigbrae Av BLSH ML4 133 J6
Brigham Pl SMSTN G23 82 E1 1
Brighton Pl GOV/IBX G51 104 B3 1
Brighton St GOV/IBX G51 104 B3
Brightside Av PGL PA14 55 G1
UD/BTH/TAN G71 131 M4
Brig O'lea Ter BRHD/NEIL G78 148 C3
Brigside Gdns HMLTN ML3 157 G7
Brisbane Ct GIF/THBK G46 127 K6
Brisbane Crs LARGS KA30 115 J4 1
Brisbane Glen Rd LARGS KA30 115 K5
Brisbane Rd BSHPTN PA7 58 B6
LARGS KA30 115 K4
Brisbane St CLYDBK G81 59 K5
GRNKW/INVK PA16 32 D3
LARGS KA30 115 J4
LNPK/KPK G44 128 A2
Brisbane Ter EKILS G75 14 A7
Britannia Pl AYR KA8 225 H7
Broadfield Av PGL PA14 55 G1
Broadford St COWCAD G4 5 K4
Broadholm St PPK/MIL G22 83 J3
Broadleys Av BSHPBGS G64 63 M7
Broadlie Ct BRHD/NEIL G78 148 D2 2
Broadlie Dr DALRY KA24 184 A1
KNTSWD G13 81 G3
Broadlie Rd BRHD/NEIL G78 148 C2
Broadloan RNFRW PA4 80 C7
Broadmoss Av NMRNS G77 151 J5
Broad Sq BLTYR/CAMB G72 155 J1 1
Broadstone Av PGL PA14 34 A8
Broad St DMNK/BRGTN G40 12 D6
Broadway ARD KA22 191 K6 1
The Broad Wy WISHAW ML2 158 E5
Broadwood RAYR/DAL KA6 231 H5
Broadwood Dr LNPK/KPK G44 128 B3
Broadwood Pk AYRS KA7 229 G8
Brockburn Crs PLK/PH/NH G53 126 B1
Brockburn Rd PLK/PH/NH G53 103 H8
Brockburn Ter
PLK/PH/NH G53 126 C1 2
Brocklehill Av RAYR/DAL KA6 227 H6
Brocklehill Dr RAYR/DAL KA6 227 G3
Brocklinn Pk EKILS G75 170 E2 1
Brockly Vw KBRN KA25 143 H5
Brock Ov PLK/PH/NH G53 126 C3
Brock Pl PLK/PH/NH G53 126 C2
Brock Rd PLK/PH/NH G53 126 B3
Brock Ter PLK/PH/NH G53 126 C3
Brockville St CAR/SHTL G32 106 F3 1
Brodick Av KLWNG KA13 193 J5
MTHW ML1 157 H2
Brodick Cl KLWNG KA13 193 J5
Brodick Dr EKILN G74 153 K6
GRK PA19 30 F4 2
HBR/GL G84 20 F6 2
Brodick St SPRGB/BLRNK G21 6 E6
Brodie Av TROON KA10 216 D5
Brodie Park Av PSLYS PA2 9 G9
Brodie Park Crs PSLYS PA2 8 E8
Brodie Park Gdns PSLYS PA2 9 G9
Brodie Pl EKILN G74 153 K6
KLMNKN/STW KA3 207 J6
Brodie Rd SPRGB/BLRNK G21 84 D2
Brogan Crs MTHW ML1 157 H2
Bron Wy CUMB G67 49 G8
Brookbank Ter CARLUKE ML8 179 G8 1
Brookfield Rd PGL PA14 54 F1
Brooklands ALEX/LLW G83 25 K3 2
EKILN G74 153 G8
Brooklands Av
UD/BTH/TAN G71 131 L2
Brooklea Dr GIF/THBK G46 127 J4
PLKSW/MSWD G43 127 J4 1
Brooklime Dr EKILN G74 153 K5 2
Brooklime Gdns EKILN G74 153 J5 1
Brooklyn Pl WISHAW ML2 177 H3
Brookside St DMNK/BRGTN G40 12 E6
Brook St CLYDBK G81 59 M5
DMNK/BRGTN G40 12 D5
Broom Av ERSK PA8 79 H2
Broomberry Dr GRK PA19 31 L2
Broomburn Dr NMRNS G77 150 F5
Broom Crs BRHD/NEIL G78 125 G4
EKILS G75 171 K4
Broomcroft Rd NMRNS G77 151 G3
Broom Dr CLYDBK G81 60 A5
LRKH ML9 176 A4 2
Broomelton Rd HMLTN ML3 175 K8
Broomfield CRG/CRSL/HOU PA6 77 K8
LARGS KA30 115 J7 1
Broomfield Av
BLTYR/CAMB G72 129 K2 1
NMRNS G77 150 F6
Broomfield Crs LARGS KA30 115 J7
Broomfield Gdn AYRS KA7 18 E8
Broomfield La
SPRGB/BLRNK G21 83 M4
Broomfield Pl LARGS KA30 115 J7
SPRGB/BLRNK G21 83 M4 2
Broomfield Rd AYRS KA7 18 E8
NMRNS G77 151 G3 1
SPRGB/BLRNK G21 83 M4
Broomfield St AIRDRIE ML6 111 H2
KLWNG KA13 193 L4
Broomfield Ter
UD/BTH/TAN G71 108 F8 3
Broomfield Wk KKNTL G66 65 K1
Broom Gdns KKNTL G66 65 H3
Broomgate LNK/LMHG ML11 198 F6
Broomhill Av CAR/SHTL G32 130 B1 1
NMRNS G77 150 F5
PTCK G11 81 M7 2
Broomhill Ct LRKH ML9 176 A7 1
Broomhill Crs BLSH ML4 132 F6 1
ERSK PA8 79 H2
Broomhill Dr DMBTN G82 37 H4
PTCK G11 81 M6
RUTH G73 129 H4
Broomhill Farm Ms KKNTL G66 45 L8 1
Broomhill Gdns NMRNS G77 150 F5 3
PTCK G11 81 M6 2
Broomhill Ga LRKH ML9 176 A7 2
Broomhill La PTCK G11 81 M6
Broomhill Pl PTCK G11 81 M7 3
Broomhill Qd KLMNK KA1 212 A5
Broomhill Rd LRKH ML9 176 A7 3
Broomhill Rd East
KLMNK KA1 212 A5 1
Broomhill Rd West
KLMNK KA1 211 M5 1
Broomhill St GRNK PA15 2 B6
Broomhill Ter PTCK G11 81 M7
Broomhill Vw LRKH ML9 175 L7
Broomieknowe Dr
RUTH G73 129 H3 1
Broomieknowe Gdns
RUTH G73 129 G3 1
Broomieknowe Rd RUTH G73 129 H3
Broomielaw KVGV G3 10 E3
Broomknoll St AIRDRIE ML6 111 G2 2
Broomknowe BALLOCH G68 48 D6
Broomknowe Rd KLMCLM PA13 75 J1
Broomknowes Av KKNTL G66 65 L5 1
Broomknowes Rd
SPRGB/BLRNK G21 84 A5
Broomlands Av ERSK PA8 79 K1
Broomlands Busway
IRVSE KA11 203 M7
Broomlands Crs ERSK PA8 79 L1 1

Broomlands Dr *IRV* KA12 .... 203 J7
Broomlands Gdns *ERSK* PA8 ...... 79 K1 🏠
Broomlands Rd *CUMB* G67 .... 69 G1
  IRVSE KA11 .... 204 B8 🏠
Broomlands St *PSLY* PA1 .... 8 C5
Broomlands Wy *ERSK* PA8 .... 79 K1 🏠
Broomlea Crs *RNFRW* PA4 .... 79 J3
Broomlee Rd *CUMB* G67 .... 68 F3
Broomley Crs *ALEX/LLW* G83 ...... 25 J2
  ALEX/LLW G83 .... 25 K2 🏠
Broomley Dr *GIF/THBK* G46 .... 127 J8
Broomley La *GIF/THBK* G46 .... 127 J8
Broomloan Rd *GOV/IBX* G51 ...... 104 A3
Broompark Av
  BLTYR/CAMB G72 .... 155 J3
  PSTWK KA9 .... 225 J1
Broompark Circ *DEN/PKHD* G31 .... 6 D9
Broompark Crs *AIRDRIE* ML6 ...... 89 C7
  PSTWK KA9 .... 225 J1 🏠
Broompark Dr *DEN/PKHD* G31 .... 12 C1
  NMRNS G77 .... 150 F3
  RNFRW PA4 .... 79 K2
Broompark La *DEN/PKHD* G31 .... 12 D1
Broompark Rd
  BLTYR/CAMB G72 .... 155 J2
  WISHAW ML2 .... 158 D5
Broompark St *DEN/PKHD* G31 .. 12 D1 🏠
Broom Pl *BRWEIR* PA11 .... 98 E1
  CTBR ML5 .... 109 M6
  KLMNK KA1 .... 212 B4
  MTHW ML1 .... 134 C5
Broom Rd *CUMB* G67 .... 49 K4
  NMRNS G77 .... 151 G3
  PLKSW/MSWD G43 .... 127 K4
  WMYSB PA18 .... 50 A8 🏠
Broom Rd East *NMRNS* G77 .... 151 H6
Broomside Crs *MTHW* ML1 ...... 157 L5 🏠
Broomside St *MTHW* ML1 .... 157 L5 🏠
Broomstone Av *NMRNS* G77 .... 150 F6
Broom Ter *JNSTN* PA5 .... 99 M8
Bromton Rd
  SPRGB/BLRNK G21 .... 84 C2
Broomvale Dr *NMRNS* G77 ...... 150 F4
Broomward Dr *JNSTN* PA5 ...... 100 B6
Brora Ct *HMLTN* ML3 .... 173 M1
Brora Dr *BSDN* G61 .... 62 B5
  GIF/THBK G46 .... 127 K7
  RNFRW PA4 .... 80 E6
Brora Gdns *BSHPBGS* G64 ...... 64 B8
Brora Rd *BSHPBGS* G64 .... 64 B8
Brora St *STPS/GTHM/RID* G33 ... 7 L7
Brougham St *GRNKW/INVK* PA16.. 32 E2
Broughton *EKILS* G75 .... 171 L4 🏠
Broughton Dr *SMSTN* G23 ...... 82 E1 🏠
Broughton Gdns *SMSTN* G23 ... 62 F8 🏠
Broughton Pl *CTBR* ML5 .... 110 B6
  HMLTN ML3 .... 156 A6
Broughton Rd *SMSTN* G23 ...... 62 E8
Broun Dr *AYRS* KA7 .... 228 E8
Brouster HI *EKILN* G74 .... 14 F3
Brouster Pl *EKILN* G74 .... 14 F3
Brown Av *CLYDBK* G81 .... 80 D1
  DMBTN G82 .... 37 J5 🏠
  TROON KA10 .... 216 D6
Browncarrick Dr *AYRS* KA7 ..... 228 B8
Brownhill Dr *KBRN* KA25 .... 166 F1
Brownhill Rd *GIF/THBK* G46 .... 127 H5
Brownhill Vw *WISHAW* ML2 ..... 160 D3
Brownieside Pl *AIRDRIE* ML6 ... 90 A6 🏠
Brownieside Rd *RNFRW* PA4 .... 79 H4
Brownlee Rd *CARLUKE* ML8 ..... 177 K5
  WISHAW ML2 .... 177 K5
Brownlie St *GVH/MTFL* G42 .... 128 B1 🏠
Brown Pl *BLTYR/CAMB* G72 ..... 130 A3 🏠
Brown Rd *CUMB* G67 .... 48 F7
Brownsburn Rd *AIRDRIE* ML6 ... 111 H5
Brown's Crs *RAYR/DAL* KA6 ..... 227 H6
Brownsdale Rd *RUTH* G73 ...... 128 F2
Brownsfield Crs *RNFRW* PA4 .... 79 H4
Brownsfield Rd *RNFRW* PA4 .... 79 H4
Brownshill Av *CTBR* ML5 .... 109 M5
Brownside Av
  BLTYR/CAMB G72 .... 129 L4 🏠
  BRHD/NEIL G78 .... 125 G4
Brownside Crs
  BRHD/NEIL G78 .... 125 G4 🏠
Brownside Dr *BRHD/NEIL* G78 .. 125 G4
  KNTSWD G13 .... 80 F3
Brownside Gv *BRHD/NEIL* G78 .. 125 G4
Brownside Rd *RUTH* G73 .... 129 K4
Brown's La *PSLY* PA1 .... 9 G5
Brown's Rd *NMLNS* KA16 ...... 215 K2
Brown St *CARLUKE* ML8 .... 178 F6
  CTBR ML5 .... 110 A4
  GRNK PA15 .... 3 L8
  KLMNKN/STW KA3 .... 197 K1 🏠
  KVGV G3 .... 10 F2
  LRKH ML9 .... 176 D5
  MTHW ML1 .... 157 M1
  NMLNS KA16 .... 215 J2
  PGL PA14 .... 34 B7
  PSLY PA1 .... 8 D3
  RNFRW PA4 .... 80 A8
  WISHAW ML2 .... 160 A5 🏠
Brown St *IRV* KA12 .... 203 J4
Browside Av *PSLYS* PA2 .... 124 C2 🏠
Bruce Av *CRH/DND* KA2 .... 209 M7
  JNSTN PA5 .... 122 E1
  MTHW ML1 .... 134 C5
  PSLYN/LNWD PA3 .... 102 A2 🏠
  PSTWK KA9 .... 225 H3
Bruce Crs *AYRS* KA7 .... 18 D3
  KLMNK KA1 .... 211 M5
Brucefield Pl *ESTRH* G34 ...... 108 D1
Brucehill Rd *DMBTN* G82 ...... 36 C5
Bruce La *EKILS* G75 .... 15 H8
Bruce Pl *EKILS* G75 .... 15 H8
Bruce Rd *BSHPTN* PA7 .... 58 A6
  MTHW ML1 .... 134 B7 🏠
  PLKSW/SHW G41 .... 10 A8
  PSLYN/LNWD PA3 .... 102 A3
  RNFRW PA4 .... 80 A8
Bruce St *AIRDRIE* ML6 .... 90 A7
  BLSH ML4 .... 133 H4
  CLYDBK G81 .... 60 B8
  CTBR ML5 .... 110 D1 🏠
  DMBTN G82 .... 37 G7
  GRNK PA15 .... 2 B4

Bruce St (cont.) *KLMNK* KA1 .... 211 M5
  PGL PA14 .... 34 D8
Bruce Ter *BLTYR/CAMB* G72 ... 131 L8
  EKILS G75 .... 15 H8
  IRV KA12 .... 203 K4
Brueacre Rd *WMYSB* PA18 ..... 50 A8
Brunel Wy *EKILS* G75 .... 15 H6
Brunstane Rd *ESTRH* G34 ..... 86 A8
Brunswick La *CGLE* G1 .... 11 K2 🏠
Brunswick St *CGLE* G1 .... 11 K2
Brunton St *LNPK/KPK* G44 .... 128 A4
Brunton Ter *LNPK/KPK* G44 ... 127 M5
Bruntsfield Av *KLWNG* KA13 .. 193 H5
Bruntsfield Gdns
  PLK/PH/NH G53 .... 126 B6
Bryan St *HMLTN* ML3 .... 156 M4
Bryce Gdns *LRKH* ML9 .... 176 A5
Bryce Pl *EKILS* G75 .... 14 B9
Brydson Pl *PSLYN/LNWD* PA3 .. 100 B3 🏠
Brymner St *GRNK* PA15 ...... 2 E4
Bryon Ct *UD/BTH/TAN* G71 ... 132 B7 🏠
Bryson Ct *HMLTN* ML3 .... 174 D2
Bryson St *CLYDBK* G81 ...... 60 E2 🏠
Buccleuch Av
  CARD/HILL/MSPK G52 .... 102 E1
  CRMNK/CLK/EAG G76 ..... 151 K2
Buccleuch Dr *BSDN* G61 ..... 61 L2
Buccleuch La *KVGV* G3 ...... 4 F7
Buccleuch St *KVGV* G3 ...... 4 E7
Buccleuch St *GRNK* PA15 .... 2 C4 🏠
Buchanan Av *BSHPTN* PA7 ... 58 B5
Buchanan Crs *HMLTN* ML3 ... 156 B7
  SPRGB/BLRNK G21 .... 84 C2 🏠
Buchanan Dr *BLTYR/CAMB* G72 . 129 L3
  BSDN G61 .... 62 A5
  BSHPBGS G64 .... 84 C1 🏠
  CARLUKE ML8 .... 178 A3 🏠
  KKNTL G66 .... 65 K5
  NMRNS G77 .... 150 F2
  RUTH G73 .... 129 H3
Buchanan Gv
  BAIL/MDB/MHD G69 ...... 108 A8
Buchanan Pl *BSHPBGS* G64 ... 44 B8
Buchanan Rd *HBR/GL* G84 .... 21 C8 🏠
Buchanan St *AIRDRIE* ML6 ... 111 C2 🏠
  BAIL/MDB/MHD G69 ...... 108 B4 🏠
  CGLE G1 .... 11 H2
  CTBR ML5 .... 109 M3
  DMBTN G82 .... 37 G7
  GRNKW/INVK PA16 .... 32 E2 🏠
  JNSTN PA5 .... 99 L7
  LARGS KA30 .... 115 H3
  MLNGV G62 .... 42 B7 🏠
Buchandyke Rd *EKILN* G74 ... 154 B5
Buchan Gn *EKILN* G74 .... 154 B6
Buchan Rd *MTHW* ML1 .... 134 A7
  TROON KA10 .... 216 F5
Buchan St *HMLTN* ML3 .... 174 C1
  WISHAW ML2 .... 159 J3
Buchan Ter *BLTYR/CAMB* G72 . 129 L6
Buchlyvie Gdns *BSHPBGS* G64 . 83 M1
Buchlyvie Pth *ESTRH* G34 .... 108 B2
Buchlyvie Rd *PSLY* PA1 ...... 102 E4
Buchlyvie St *ESTRH* G34 ..... 108 B2
Buckingham Ct *HMLTN* ML3 .. 155 L5 🏠
Buckingham Dr
  CAR/SHTL G32 .... 107 H8 🏠
  RUTH G73 .... 129 K2
Buckingham St
  KVD/HLHD G12 .... 82 D6 🏠
Buckingham Ter *KVD/HLHD* G12 . 82 D6
Bucklaw Gdns
  CARD/HILL/MSPK G52 ... 103 J5
Bucklaw Pl
  CARD/HILL/MSPK G52 ... 103 J5 🏠
Bucklaw Ter
  CARD/HILL/MSPK G52 ... 103 J5
Buckley St *PPK/MIL* G22 .... 83 K3
Bucksburn Rd
  SPRGB/BLRNK G21 ...... 84 C5 🏠
Buckthorne Pl *PLK/PH/NH* G53 . 126 B6
Buddon St *DMNK/BRGTN* G40 . 13 J8
Budhill Av *CAR/SHTL* G32 ... 107 H4
Budshaw Av *AIRDRIE* ML6 .... 111 J7
Buiston Rd *KLMNKN/STW* KA3 . 197 J6
Bulldale Ct *SCOT* G14 ...... 80 E4
Bulldale St *SCOT* G14 ...... 80 E3
Bullionslaw Dr *RUTH* G73 ... 129 K3
Bulloch Rd *GIF/THBK* G46 ... 127 K7
Bull Rd *CRMNK/CLK/EAG* G76 . 151 M3
Bullwood Av *PLK/PH/NH* G53 . 102 F8
Bullwood Ct *PLK/PH/NH* G53 . 125 M1
Bullwood Dr *PLK/PH/NH* G53 . 102 F8
Bullwood Gdns
  PLK/PH/NH G53 .... 102 F8
Bullwood Pl *PLK/PH/NH* G53 . 102 F8 🏠
Bunessan St
  CARD/HILL/MSPK G52 ... 103 M4
Bunhouse Rd *KVGV* G3 ...... 82 C8
Bunting Pl *KLMNK* KA1 ...... 17 L7
Burghead Dr *GOV/IBX* G51 .. 103 L1
Burghead Pl *GOV/IBX* G51 ... 103 L1 🏠
Burgher St *DEN/PKHD* G31 .. 13 K7
Burgh Hall La *PTCK* G11 .... 82 B7 🏠
Burgh Hall St *PTCK* G11 .... 82 B7 🏠
Burgh La *KVD/HLHD* G12 .... 82 D6 🏠
Burgh Rd *PSTWK* KA9 .... 225 H1
Burgh Wk *GRK* PA19 .... 31 L1 🏠
Burgoyne Dr *RAYR/DAL* KA6 .. 231 H5 🏠
Burleigh Rd *UD/BTH/TAN* G71 . 132 B6
Burleigh St *CTBR* ML5 ...... 110 B6
  GOV/IBX G51 .... 104 A1 🏠
Burley Pl *EKILN* G74 .... 152 F7
Burlington Av *KVD/HLHD* G12 . 82 B3
Burma Rd *HBR/GL* G84 ...... 20 E6 🏠
Burmola St *PPK/MIL* G22 .... 83 H5
Burnacre Gdns
  UD/BTH/TAN G71 .... 131 L2 🏠
Burnawn Pl *GLSTN* KA4 ..... 214 D4
Burnbank Braes
  CARLUKE ML8 .... 178 F8 🏠
Burnbank Centre
  HMLTN ML3 .... 156 A4 🏠
Burnbank Dr *BRHD/NEIL* G78 . 125 J8
Burnbank Gdns *MRYH/FIRH* G20 . 4 D4
Burnbank Pl *AYRS* KA7 ..... 229 H5 🏠
  MRYH/FIRH G20 .... 4 D4

Burnbank Qd *AIRDRIE* ML6 .. 110 F1 🏠
Burnbank Rd *AYRS* KA7 ..... 229 H5
  HMLTN ML3 .... 156 B5
Burnbank St *AIRDRIE* ML6 ... 110 F1
  CTBR ML5 .... 110 B1
  SVSTN KA20 .... 201 K1
Burnbank Ter *COWCAD* G4 ... 4 D5
Burnblea St *HMLTN* ML3 .... 156 D7
Burnbrae *CLYDBK* G81 ...... 60 A3
  KSYTH G65 .... 46 F5
Burnbrae Av
  BAIL/MDB/MHD G69 .... 67 G7
  BSDN G61 .... 62 A2
Burnbrae Crs *IRVSE* KA11 ... 204 C4
Burnbrae Dr *IRVSE* KA11 .... 204 C4
  PSLYN/LNWD PA3 ...... 100 D5
  RUTH G73 .... 129 K4 🏠
Burnbrae Pl *EKILN* G74 .... 14 B2
Burnbrae Rd
  BAIL/MDB/MHD G69 .... 66 B6
  BLTYR/CAMB G72 ...... 155 J2
  JNSTN PA5 .... 100 B5
  KKNTL G66 .... 65 M7
  KKNTL G66 .... 66 B2
  SHOTTS ML7 .... 137 L7
Burnbrae St *CLYDBK* G81 ... 60 D1
  LRKH ML9 .... 175 M6
  SPRGB/BLRNK G21 ..... 6 F1
Burncleuch Av
  BLTYR/CAMB G72 ...... 130 A5
  MTHW ML1 .... 134 A5
Burn Crs *AIRDRIE* ML6 ..... 111 K7
  MTHW ML1 .... 134 A5
Burncrooks Av *BSDN* G61 ... 61 K2
  EKILN G74 .... 14 B2
Burndale La *KLMCLM* PA13 .. 75 K1
Burndyke Ct *GOV/IBX* G51 .. 104 C3
Burndyke Sq *GOV/IBX* G51 .. 104 C2 🏠
Burness Av *AYRS* KA7 ...... 228 D7
Burnet Rose Ct *EKILN* G74 .. 153 J5 🏠
Burnet Rose Gdns *EKILN* G74 . 153 J5 🏠
Burnet Rose Pl *EKILN* G74 .. 153 J5 🏠
Burnett Rd
  STPS/GTHM/RID G33 .... 107 L2 🏠
Burnett Ter *AYR* KA8 ...... 225 H1
Burnfield Av *GIF/THBK* G46 . 127 H5
Burnfield Dr *GIF/THBK* G46 . 127 H5
Burnfield Gdns *GIF/THBK* G46 . 127 J5
Burnfield Rd *GIF/THBK* G46 . 127 G4
Burnfoot *DMBTN* G82 .... 35 H2
Burnfoot Crs *TROON* KA10 ... 216 D4
Burnfoot Crs *PSLYS* PA2 .... 124 C2
  RUTH G73 .... 129 K4
Burnfoot Dr
  CARD/HILL/MSPK G52 ... 103 H4
Burnfoot La *ARD* KA22 ..... 191 H5
Burnfoot Pl *KLMNKN/STW* KA3 . 206 E5
Burnfoot Rd *AIRDRIE* ML6 ... 110 E1
  FAIRLIE KA29 .... 139 K7
  LOCHW PA12 .... 120 B7
Burngreen *KSYTH* G65 ...... 47 L1
Burnhall Pl *WISHAW* ML2 ... 159 J7
Burnhall Rd *WISHAW* ML2 ... 159 J7
Burnhall St *WISHAW* ML2 ... 159 K8
Burnham Rd *SCOT* G14 ..... 81 G5
Burnhaven *ERSK* PA8 ...... 59 G7
Burnhead La *PGL* PA14 ..... 54 C1
Burnhead Rd *AIRDRIE* ML6 .. 89 K8
  BALLOCH G68 .... 48 C7
  LRKH ML9 .... 176 C6
  PGL PA14 .... 54 C1
  PLKSW/MSWD G43 ...... 127 L4
Burnhill Qd *RUTH* G73 ..... 128 F1 🏠
Burnhill St *RUTH* G73 ...... 128 F1
Burnhouse Brae *NMRNS* G77 . 151 G6
Burnhouse Crs *HMLTN* ML3 . 156 B8
Burnhouse Rd *EKILS* G75 ... 171 C7
  HMLTN ML3 .... 156 B8
Burnhouse St *MRYH/FIRH* G20 . 82 D3
Burniebrae *AIRDRIE* ML6 .... 110 F1 🏠
Burniebrae Rd *AIRDRIE* ML6 . 111 L6
Burnlea Crs *CRG/CRSL/HOU* PA6 . 77 G7
Burnlea Pl *SVSTN* KA20 .... 192 E7
Burnlea Rd *LARGS* KA30 ... 115 J6
Burnlip Rd *CTBR* ML5 ...... 88 A5
Burnmouth Ct *BSDN* G61 ... 62 A4
Burnmouth Rd
  STPS/GTHM/RID G33 .... 107 M3
Burnock Pl *EKILS* G75 ..... 170 E2 🏠
Burnpark Av
  UD/BTH/TAN G71 .... 131 K2 🏠
Burnpark Rd *KLMNK* KA1 ... 211 M6
Burn Pl *BLTYR/CAMB* G72 .. 129 L2 🏠
Burn Rd *ARD* KA22 .... 200 D1
  CARLUKE ML8 .... 178 E6
  NMLNS KA16 .... 215 L2 🏠
Burns Av *BSHPTN* PA7 ..... 58 B6 🏠
  KLMNKN/STW KA3 ...... 207 C6
  SALT KA21 .... 191 M6
Burns Ct *KKNTL* G66 ...... 46 A8
Burn's Crs *AIRDRIE* ML6 ... 111 H3
  IRVSE KA11 .... 203 M4
Burns Dr *JNSTN* PA5 ...... 122 E1
  KKNTL G66 .... 46 A7
Burns Gdns *BLTYR/CAMB* G72 . 131 J8 🏠
Burns Gv *GIF/THBK* G46 ... 127 G7
Burnside *BSDN* G61 .... 61 J2
Burnside Av *AIRDRIE* ML6 .. 111 H7
  BLSH ML4 .... 133 J5
  BRHD/NEIL G78 .... 125 H5 🏠
  JNSTN PA5 .... 99 J8
  KKNTL G66 .... 65 H2
  PGL PA14 .... 54 F1
Burnside Ct *BSDN* G61 .... 61 J3 🏠
  RUTH G73 .... 129 J4 🏠
Burnside Crs *ALEX/LLW* G83 . 25 M2 🏠
  BLTYR/CAMB G72 ...... 155 M3
  CLYDBK G81 .... 60 B2
  SHOTTS ML7 .... 137 K3
Burnside Gdns
  CRMNK/CLK/EAG G76 ... 151 K2
  KLBCH PA10 .... 99 H7
  PSTWK KA9 .... 221 J8
Burnside Ga *RUTH* G73 .... 129 J4 🏠
Burnside Gv *JNSTN* PA5 ... 99 L7

Burnside La *HMLTN* ML3 .... 156 E7 🏠
Burnside Pl *DMBTN* G82 .... 37 H7
  IRV KA12 .... 203 H5 🏠
  LRKH ML9 .... 176 B0
  PSLYN/LNWD PA3 ...... 101 G2 🏠
  SVSTN KA20 .... 192 D8 🏠
  TROON KA10 .... 216 C5
Burnside Qd *MTHW* ML1 .... 134 A4 🏠
  GIF/THBK G46 .... 151 H3
  GRK PA19 .... 31 M3
  JNSTN PA5 .... 100 C8
  LARGS KA30 .... 115 K4
  MTHW ML1 .... 134 D5
  PSTWK KA9 .... 221 K5
  RUTH G73 .... 129 J4 🏠
Burnside St *CLGNK* KA14 ... 167 H3
  KLMNK KA1 .... 16 D9
  MTHW ML1 .... 158 B5 🏠
Burnside Vw *CTBR* ML5 .... 109 L4 🏠
Burnside Wk *CTBR* ML5 .... 109 L4
Burnside Wy *LARGS* KA30 .. 115 L4
Burns La *AIRDRIE* ML6 ..... 111 K6 🏠
Burns Pk *EKILN* G74 ...... 15 K1
Burns Pl *KLWNG* KA13 ..... 193 H6
  SHOTTS ML7 .... 137 G3
  SVSTN KA20 .... 192 E8 🏠
Burns Rd *AIRDRIE* ML6 ..... 111 K5 🏠
  CUMB G67 .... 49 G6
  GRNKW/INVK PA16 ..... 31 K5 🏠
  KKNTL G66 .... 45 M8
  TROON KA10 .... 216 F5 🏠
Burns Sq *ARD* KA22 ...... 191 J5 🏠
  GRNKW/INVK PA16 ..... 31 K5 🏠
Burns Statue Sq *AYRS* KA7 . 18 F5
Burns St *ALEX/LLW* G83 .... 25 L1
  CLYDBK G81 .... 59 L6
  COWCAD G4 .... 5 C4
  DMBTN G82 .... 25 L7
  HMLTN ML3 .... 156 D7
  IRV KA12 .... 203 H6
Burns Ter *ARD* KA22 ...... 191 J5
Burn St *ALEX/LLW* G83 .... 25 M5 🏠
Burn Street La *ALEX/LLW* G83 . 25 M5 🏠
Burns' Wicket *AYRS* KA7 .. 228 E8 🏠
Burntbroom Dr
  BAIL/MDB/MHD G69 ... 107 M6
Burntbroom Gdns
  CAR/SHTL G32 .... 107 M6
Burntbroom Rd
  UD/BTH/TAN G71 ..... 107 M7 🏠
Burntbroom St
  STPS/GTHM/RID G33 .. 107 K1 🏠
Burn Ter *BLTYR/CAMB* G72 . 129 L2
Burntshields Rd *KLBCH* PA10 . 98 C3
Burn Vw *CUMB* G67 ...... 49 J6
Burnwood Dr *AIRDRIE* ML6 . 112 A3 🏠
Burra Gdns *BSHPBGS* G64 .. 64 D7
Burrell Ct *PLKSD/SHW* G41 . 104 C7
Burrell's La *COWCAD* G4 .. 12 A1
Burrelton Rd
  PLKSW/MSWD G43 ..... 127 M3
Burton La *GVH/MTFL* G42 .. 105 C8 🏠
Busbiehill Pl *KLMNK* KA1 .. 16 B2
Busbie Vw *CRH/DND* KA2 .. 205 L8
Busby Pl *KLWNG* KA13 .... 193 M5
Busby Rd *BLSH* ML4 ...... 132 F6
  CRMNK/CLK/EAG G76 .. 151 M3
  CRMNK/CLK/EAG G76 .. 152 D2
Bush Crs *WISHAW* ML2 .... 159 J7 🏠
Bushelhead Rd *CARLUKE* ML8 . 188 E4
Bushes Av *PSLYS* PA2 .... 101 K8
Busheyhill St *BLTYR/CAMB* G72 . 130 A4
Bute *EKILN* G74 .... 154 C8
Bute Av *MTHW* ML1 ...... 157 J2
  PGL PA14 .... 55 H1
  RNFRW PA4 .... 80 D8
Bute Dr *BSDN* G61 .... 61 M7
  OLDK G60 .... 59 J4
  PSLYS PA2 .... 124 D2
  SHOTTS ML7 .... 137 K5
Bute Gdns *KVD/HLHD* G12 . 82 D7
  LNPK/KPK G44 .... 127 M6
  OLDK G60 .... 59 J3
Bute La *KVD/HLHD* G12 ... 82 D7
  PSLYN/LNWD PA3 ..... 79 K8
Bute Pl *ARD* KA22 .... 191 H8 🏠
Bute St *CTBR* ML5 .... 110 B5
  GRK PA19 .... 31 K3
  HMLTN ML3 .... 156 B3
Bute Ter *RUTH* G73 ...... 129 C4
  SALT KA21 .... 191 L8
  UD/BTH/TAN G71 ...... 132 B2
Butt La *HBR/GL* G84 ..... 20 E6 🏠
Butterbiggins Rd
  GVH/MTFL G42 .... 105 G6
Butterburnpark St *HMLTN* ML3 . 156 D6
Butterfield Pl *CVH/MTFL* G42 . 105 G6 🏠
Buttermere *EKILS* G75 .... 170 F4
Buttsley Ct *LNK/LMHG* ML11 . 198 E5
Byars Rd *KKNTL* G66 ...... 65 H1
By-pass Rd *BEITH* KA15 ... 168 C1
Byrebush Rd *PLK/PH/NH* G53 . 103 J9 🏠
Byrehill Av *KLWNG* KA13 ... 193 H7
  KLWNG KA13 .... 193 J8
Byrehill Rd *KLWNG* KA13 ... 193 J8
  KLWNG KA13 .... 202 E1
Byres Av *PSLYN/LNWD* PA3 . 9 L1
Byres Crs *PSLYN/LNWD* PA3 . 102 A3
Byresknowe La *MTHW* ML1 . 134 B8 🏠
Byres Rd *JNSTN* PA5 ...... 100 B7
  KLWNG KA13 .... 193 K6
  KVD/HLHD G12 .... 82 D7
  MTHW ML1 .... 134 C5
Byrestone Av *NMRNS* G77 . 151 J5
Byretown Rd *LNK/LMHG* ML11 . 198 E6
Byron Rd *SHOTTS* ML7 .... 137 G3
Byron St *CLYDBK* G81 ..... 60 A5
  PTCK G11 .... 81 M7
Byshot St *PPK/MIL* G22 ... 5 L1

C

Cable Depot Rd *CLYDBK* G81 . 59 M8
Cables Dr *ALEX/LLW* G83 ... 25 M4
Cadder Ct *BSHPBGS* G64 .. 64 B4
Cadder Pl *MRYH/FIRH* G20 . 82 E2
Cadder Rd *BSHPBGS* G64 .. 64 A3
  MRYH/FIRH G20 .... 82 E2
Cadder Wy *BSHPBGS* G64 .. 64 B4
Caddlehill St *GRNKW/INVK* PA16 . 32 D4
Cadell Gdns *EKILN* G74 ... 154 D4
Cadger's Sheuch *KSYTH* G65 . 48 A1
Cadoc St *BLTYR/CAMB* G72 . 130 B3
Cadogan St *CGLW* G2 ..... 10 F1
Cadzow Av *GIF/THBK* G46 . 151 H1
Cadzow Crs *CTBR* ML5 .... 109 K5
Cadzow Dr *BLTYR/CAMB* G72 . 130 A4
Cadzow Gn *EKILN* G74 .... 14 D2
Cadzow Pk *HMLTN* ML3 ... 156 E5 🏠
Cadzow Rd *HMLTN* ML3 ... 174 F6 🏠
  HMLTN ML3 .... 156 D5
  LRKH ML9 .... 176 A5
  MTHW ML1 .... 157 K3
Caerlaverock Av *PSTWK* KA9 . 225 J1
Caerlaverock Rd *PSTWK* KA9 . 225 J1
Caird Av *GRNKW/INVK* PA16 . 32 C2 🏠
Caird Dr *PTCK* G11 .... 82 B7
Caird Gdns *HMLTN* ML3 ... 156 D4 🏠
Caird St *HMLTN* ML3 ...... 156 C4
Cairn Av *RNFRW* PA4 ..... 80 E8
Cairnban St *GOV/IBX* G51 . 103 K3
Cairnbrook Rd *ESTRH* G34 . 86 C8 🏠
Cairn Ct *EKILN* G74 ...... 153 L5
Cairn Crs *AYRS* KA7 ...... 228 D8
Cairncurran Ct *GRNK* PA15 . 2 A7
Cairndhu Av *HBR/GL* G84 . 20 A7
Cairndhu Gdns *HBR/GL* G84 . 20 A7
Cairndow Av *LNPK/KPK* G44 . 127 M5 🏠
Cairndow Avenue La
  LNPK/KPK G44 .... 127 M5 🏠
Cairndow Ct *LNPK/KPK* G44 . 127 M5
Cairn Dr *PSLYN/LNWD* PA3 . 100 B3
Cairndyke Crs *AIRDRIE* ML6 . 111 G3
Cairneymount Rd
  CARLUKE ML8 .... 178 F7
Cairney Pl *WISHAW* ML2 .. 160 D3
Cairnfore Av *TROON* KA10 . 216 F3
Cairngorm Ct *IRVSE* KA11 . 204 B4
Cairngorm Crs *BRHD/NEIL* G78 . 125 J8
  BSDN G61 .... 61 H3
  PSLYS PA2 .... 101 K3
  WISHAW ML2 .... 158 F6
Cairngorm Gdns *BALLOCH* G68 . 48 A8
Cairngorm Rd *KLMNK* KA13 . 212 A6
  PLKSW/MSWD G43 ..... 127 J4
Cairnhill Circ
  CARD/HILL/MSPK G52 .. 102 F6
Cairnhill Ct *CARLUKE* ML8 . 178 F7 🏠
Cairnhill Crs *CTBR* ML5 ... 110 D6
Cairnhill Dr
  CARD/HILL/MSPK G52 .. 102 F6
Cairnhill Pl
  CARD/HILL/MSPK G52 .. 102 F6 🏠
Cairnhill Rd *AIRDRIE* ML6 . 110 F4
  BSDN G61 .... 61 M8
Cairnhope Av *AIRDRIE* ML6 . 110 F4
Cairnlea Dr *GOV/IBX* G51 . 104 B3
Cairnlea Gdns *BLSH* ML4 .. 133 H6
Cairnlea Rd *MLNGV* G62 .. 41 L8 🏠
Cairnmount Rd *IRVSE* KA11 . 203 M2
Cairnmuir Rd *EKILN* G74 .. 153 H4
Cairnoch HI *BALLOCH* G68 . 48 C7 🏠
Cairn Pl *EKILN* G74 ...... 153 L5
  GLSTN KA4 .... 214 D3
Cairnryan *EKILN* G74 ..... 153 K6
Cairns Av *BLTYR/CAMB* G72 . 130 C5
Cairns Dr *MLNGV* G62 .... 42 A7
Cairnsmore Av *AYRS* KA7 . 228 C8
  BSDN G61 .... 61 H2 🏠
Cairnsmore Rd *DRUM* G15 . 60 F7
Cairnsmore Wy *IRVSE* KA11 . 204 B7
Cairns Rd *BLTYR/CAMB* G72 . 130 B5
  BSHPTN PA7 .... 58 A5
Cairns St *MTHW* ML1 ..... 157 L3 🏠
Cairns Ter *KLMNK* KA1 .... 16 C4
Cairn St *SPRGB/BLRNK* G21 . 83 M3 🏠
Cairnswell Av *BLTYR/CAMB* G72 . 130 C5
Cairnswell Pl
  BLTYR/CAMB G72 ..... 130 C5 🏠
Cairn Ter *GLSTN* KA4 ..... 214 D3
Cairntoul Ct *BALLOCH* G68 . 48 B7 🏠
Cairntoul Dr *KNTSWD* G13 . 81 G3
Cairntoul Pl *SCOT* G14 ... 81 G4
Cairn Vw *AIRDRIE* ML6 .... 110 F3
  GLSTN KA4 .... 214 D3
  KKNTL G66 .... 66 A2
Cairnview Rd *KKNTL* G66 .. 45 H4
Cairnwood Dr *AIRDRIE* ML6 . 110 F4
Caithness Rd *EKILN* G74 .. 154 D6 🏠
  GRNKW/INVK PA16 ..... 31 J5
Caithness St *BLTYR/CAMB* G72 . 155 J3
  MRYH/FIRH G20 .... 82 F5
Cala Sona Ct *WISHAW* ML2 . 176 E1
Calcots Pl *ESTRH* G34 .... 86 C8 🏠
Caldarvan St *PPK/MIL* G22 . 5 G2
Caldeen Rd *CTBR* ML5 .... 110 B4
Calder Av *AIRDRIE* ML6 ... 90 F5
  BRHD/NEIL G78 .... 125 J8
  CTBR ML5 .... 110 B5
  WISHAW ML2 .... 160 A3
Calderbank Rd *AIRDRIE* ML6 . 111 C4
Calderbank Ter *MTHW* ML1 . 157 M1 🏠
Calderbank Vw
  BAIL/MDB/MHD G69 ... 108 B6
Calderbraes Av
  UD/BTH/TAN G71 ..... 131 L1
Caldercruix Rd *AIRDRIE* ML6 . 91 K4
Caldercuilt Rd *MRYH/FIRH* G20 . 62 C8
Calder Dr *BLSH* ML4 ..... 133 J5
  BLTYR/CAMB G72 ..... 130 A4
  LOCHW PA12 .... 120 C6
Calder Ga *BSHPBGS* G64 .. 63 M5 🏠

Calderglen Av
BLTYR/CAMB G72................ 131 J6
Calderglen Rd *EKILN* G74 .... 154 C8
Caldergrove *MTHW* ML1 .... 157 L1
Calderhaugh La *LOCHW* PA12... 120 B7
Calderhead Rd *SHOTTS* ML7 .... 137 K2
Calderigg Pl *AIRDRIE* ML6 .... 111 K2
Calderpark Av *LOCHW* PA12 .... 120 C6
UD/BTH/TAN G71 .... 108 B7
Calderpark Crs
UD/BTH/TAN G71 .... 108 B7
Calderpark St *LOCHW* PA12 .... 120 C6
Calder Pl
BAIL/MDB/MHD G69 .... 108 B5
KLMNK KA1 .... 212 A4
Calder Rd *BLSH* ML4 .... 133 J5
PSLYN/LNWD PA3 .... 101 G4
SHOTTS ML7 .... 160 F1
UD/BTH/TAN G71 .... 131 J4
Calderside Gv *EKILN* G74 .... 154 E5
Calderside Rd *EKILN* G74 .... 172 D1
Calder St *AIRDRIE* ML6 .... 111 L5
BLTYR/CAMB G72 .... 155 K1
CTBR ML5 .... 110 B5
GVH/MTFL G42 .... 105 H7
LOCHW PA12....................... 120 B6
Caldervale St *AIRDRIE* ML6 .... 111 L5
Calder Vw *HMLTN* ML3.............. 174 B1
MTHW ML1 .... 157 M2
Calderview Av *CTBR* ML5 .... 110 D6
Calderwood *KLWNG* KA13 .... 193 L4
Calderwood Av
BAIL/MDB/MHD G69 .... 108 A6
Calderwood Dr
BAIL/MDB/MHD G69 .... 108 A6
BLTYR/CAMB G72 .... 155 K3
Calderwood Gdns
BAIL/MDB/MHD G69 .... 108 A6
EKILN G74........................... 154 E5
Calderwood Rd *EKILN* G74 .... 15 L3
PLKSW/MSWD G43 .... 127 K3
RUTH G73............................ 129 J2
Caldon Rd *IRV* KA12 .... 205 K5
Caldwell Av *KNTSWD* G13 .... 81 J6
PSLYN/LNWD PA3 .... 100 A4
Caldwell Gv *BLSH* ML4 .... 133 G1
Caldwell Qd *MTHW* ML1 .... 157 L4
Caldwell Rd *CARLUKE* ML8 .... 189 L1
WKIL KA23 .... 181 L5
Caledonia Av *GBLS* G5 .... 105 J6
RUTH G73............................ 129 H1
Caledonia Ct *KLMNK* KA1........... 16 D3
PSLYN/LNWD PA3 .... 101 G4
GRK PA19 .... 31 M2
Caledonia Dr
BAIL/MDB/MHD G69 .... 108 B6
MTHW ML1 .... 134 E5
Caledonian Av *BLSH* ML4 .... 132 F5
Caledonian Ct *EKILN* G74........... 14 F5
Caledonian Crs *KVD/HLHD* G12 ... 4 B1
Caledonian Pl *GLGNK* KA14 .... 167 H2
LRKH ML9 .... 176 A6
SVSTN KA20 .... 201 K2
WISHAW ML2 .... 159 G7
Caledonia Rd *ARD* KA22............ 191 J2
AYRS KA7.............................. 19 K8
BEITH KA15 .... 144 B8
GBLS G5 .... 11 H7
SALT KA21 .... 191 L8
SHOTTS ML7 .... 137 L4
UD/BTH/TAN G71 .... 108 A6
Caledonia St *CLYDBK* G81.......... 59 L7
GBLS G5 .... 105 K6
PGL PA14............................. 34 D8
PSLYN/LNWD PA3 .... 8 F1
Caledonia Ter *DMBTN* G82 .... 36 C6
Caledonia Wy *PSLYN/LNWD* PA3 .. 79 K8
Caledonia Wy East
PSLYN/LNWD PA3 .... 79 L8
Caledonia Wy West
PSLYN/LNWD PA3 .... 79 K8
Caledon La *KVD/HLHD* G12 .... 82 C7
Caledon St *KVD/HLHD* G12 .... 82 C6
Calfhill Rd *PLK/PH/NH* G53 .... 103 H6
Calfmuir Rd *KKNTL* G66 .... 66 A3
Calgary Pk *EKILS* G75 .... 14 C5
Calgary St *COWCAD* G4 .... 5 K7
Callaghan Wynd
BLTYR/CAMB G72 .... 131 H8
Callander Ct *BALLOCH* G68 .... 48 F5
Callander Rd *AIRDRIE* ML6 .... 111 K8
BALLOCH G68 .... 48 F5
PSTWK KA9 .... 225 K4
Callander St *MRYH/FIRH* G20 ...... 4 F3
Callendar Pl *AYR* KA8 .... 225 H5
Callieburn Rd *BSHPBGS* G64 ...... 84 A1
Callon St *AIRDRIE* ML6 .... 111 G2
Cally Av *DRUM* G15.................. 61 G6
Calside *PSLYS* PA2 .... 9 G7
Calside Av *PSLYS* PA2 .... 8 F7
Calvay Rd *STPS/GTHM/RID* G33.. 107 K2
Calvay Rd *STPS/GTHM/RID* G33 .. 107 L2
Calvinston Rd *PSTWK* KA9......... 225 K3
Cambourne Rd
BAIL/MDB/MHD G69 .... 66 F6
Cambridge Av *CLYDBK* G81 .... 60 C7
GRK PA19 .... 32 A3
Cambridge Rd
GRNKW/INVK PA16 .... 31 K5
RNFRW PA4.......................... 80 C7
Cambridge St *CGLW* G2 .... 5 C8
Camburn St *CAR/SHTL* G32 .... 106 F4
Cambusdoon Dr *AYRS* KA7 .... 228 E2
Cambusdoon Rd *KLWNG* KA13... 193 J6
Cambusdoon Rd
STPS/GTHM/RID G33.............. 85 J7
Cambuskeith Rd *SVSTN* KA20 .... 192 C1
Cambuskenneth Gdns
CAR/SHTL G32 .... 107 K4
Cambuslang Rd
BLTYR/CAMB G72 .... 129 L1
CAR/SHTL G32 .... 129 M1
RUTH G73............................ 106 C8
Cambuslea Rd *AYR* KA8 .... 225 H6
Cambusnethan St
WISHAW ML2 .... 159 L5

Cambus Pl
STPS/GTHM/RID G33.............. 85 J7
Camden St *GBLS* G5 .... 11 H8
Camelon Crs *BLTYR/CAMB* G72... 155 K2
Camelon St *CAR/SHTL* G32 .... 106 F3
Cameron Av *BSHPTN* PA7 .... 58 B6
Cameron Ct *CLYDBK* G81 .... 80 C1
Cameron Crs
CRMNK/CLK/EAG G76 .... 152 E2
HMLTN ML3.......................... 156 B6
Cameron Dr *ALEX/LLW* G83 .... 25 K2
BSDN G61 .... 62 A6
KLMNKN/STW KA3 .... 207 J7
NMRNS G77 .... 150 E2
UD/BTH/TAN G71 .... 132 A1
Cameronian Ct
LNK/LMHG ML11 .... 199 J4
Cameronian Dr
CARLUKE ML8 .... 179 H8
Cameronian Pl *BLSH* ML4 .... 132 F6
Cameron Rd *AIRDRIE* ML6 .... 69 J7
CARLUKE ML8 .... 189 H1
Cameron Sq *CLYDBK* G81 .... 60 C3
Cameron St
CARD/HILL/MSPK G52 .... 102 E2
CTBR ML5 .... 110 B1
MTHW ML1 .... 157 K3
Cameron Wy
BLTYR/CAMB G72 .... 155 K1
Camlachie St *DEN/PKHD* G31 ..... 13 G5
DMNK/BRGTN G40 .... 12 F4
Camp Av *BSHPTN* PA7 .... 58 B6
DMBTN G82 .... 37 J5
MLNGV G62.......................... 42 A8
SALT KA21 .... 200 E1
SVSTN KA20 .... 192 D1
Campbell Ct *AYR* KA8 .... 19 M3
GRNKW/INVK PA16 .... 32 E2
NMLNS KA16........................ 215 L2
Campbell Crs *ALEX/LLW* G83 ...... 25 K2
NMRNS G77 .... 150 E3
UD/BTH/TAN G71 .... 132 A5
Campbell Dr *BRHD/NEIL* G78 ..... 125 J7
BSDN G61 .... 61 K4
DMBTN G82 .... 37 J5
HBR/GL G84 .... 23 G2
TROON KA10......................... 216 D4
Campbell Pl *BSHPBGS* G64 .... 44 B8
EKILS G75 .... 14 E7
IRVSE KA11.......................... 209 L1
Campbell St *ALEX/LLW* G83 .... 25 M5
AYR KA8............................... 225 G6
BLSH ML4 .... 133 H4
GRNKW/INVK PA16 .... 32 D5
HBR/GL G84 .... 20 C7
HMLTN ML3.......................... 156 E6
JNSTN PA5 .... 99 M7
MRYH/FIRH G20 .... 82 D2
NMLNS KA16........................ 215 L2
RNFRW PA4.......................... 80 D5
WISHAW ML2 .... 159 J6
Campbell Ter *DMBTN* G82 .... 37 J5
Campbeltown Dr
KLMNKN/STW KA3 .... 206 F6
Camperdown Ct *HBR/GL* G84...... 21 G7
Camphill *PSLYS* PA2 .... 8 F6
Camphill Av *KKNTL* G66 .... 65 J1
PLKSD/SHW G41 .... 127 M1
Camphill Crs *BSHPTN* PA7 .... 58 C6
Camphill Dr *KBRN* KA25 .... 166 F2
Camphill Gdns *BSHPTN* PA7 ...... 58 C6
Camphill Pl *AYRS* KA7 .... 229 H4
Campion Rd *MTHW* ML1 .... 157 L1
Camp Rd *BAIL/MDB/MHD* G69 ... 108 B4
MTHW ML1 .... 157 L5
RUTH G73............................ 105 M7
Camps Crs *RNFRW* PA4 .... 80 E7
Campsie Av *BRHD/NEIL* G78 ..... 125 J8
IRVSE KA11.......................... 204 B6
Campsie Ct *LRKH* ML9 .... 175 L4
Campsie Crs *AIRDRIE* ML6 .... 110 F1
Campsie Dene Rd
CMPF/LLE G63 .... 27 G5
Campsie Dr *BSDN* G61 .... 61 K2
MLNGV G62.......................... 42 B7
PSLYN/LNWD PA3 .... 79 L8
PSLYS PA2 .... 124 D1
Campsie Gdns
CRMNK/CLK/EAG G76 .... 151 J1
Campsie Pl *BAIL/MDB/MHD* G69 .. 86 C1
Campsie Rd *BSHPBGS* G64 .... 44 B7
EKILS G75 .... 171 G6
KKNTL G66 .... 45 G3
KLMNK KA1 .... 212 A6
PGL PA14............................. 55 G3
WISHAW ML2 .... 158 E5
Campsie Vw *SPRGB/BLRNK* G21 .. 83 M4
Campsie Vw
BAIL/MDB/MHD G69 .... 86 C1
BAIL/MDB/MHD G69 .... 108 A7
BLTYR/CAMB G72 .... 130 E6
CUMB G67............................ 49 H6
HMLTN ML3.......................... 155 M7
KKNTL G66 .... 65 G1
STPS/GTHM/RID G33.............. 85 K5
UD/BTH/TAN G71 .... 132 A1
Campsie View Dr *CMPF/LLE* G63 .. 27 H5
Campsie Wy *IRVSE* KA11........... 204 A7
Campston Pl
STPS/GTHM/RID G33.............. 85 H8
Camp St *MTHW* ML1 .... 157 L4
Camsail Av *HBR/GL* G84 .... 20 B7
Camsbusmore Pl
STPS/GTHM/RID G33.............. 85 J7
Camsdale Av *SHOTTS* ML7 .... 113 H7
Camstradden Dr East *BSDN* G61 .. 61 J5
Camstradden Dr West
BSDN G61 .... 61 J5
Camus Pl *DRUM* G15................. 60 F5
Canal Av *JNSTN* PA5 .... 100 A7
Canal Crs *SVSTN* KA20 .... 201 K2
Canal La *KKNTL* G66 .... 45 K8
Canal Pl *SALT* KA21 .... 201 G2
Canal Rd *JNSTN* PA5 .... 100 A7
Canal St *COWCAD* G4 .... 5 K6
JNSTN PA5 .... 100 A6
JNSTN PA5 .... 100 D6
KKNTL G66 .... 45 K8

Canal Ter *PSLY* PA1 .... 8 E5
RNFRW PA4.......................... 80 D5
SALT KA21 .... 201 G2
Canberra Av *CLYDBK* G81 .... 59 K5
Canberra Dr *EKILS* G75 .... 14 B6
Cander Rigg *BSHPBGS* G64 .... 64 A5
Candleriggs *CGLE* G1 .... 11 L3
Candren Rd *PSLYN/LNWD* PA3 ... 100 D3
PSLYN/LNWD PA3 .... 101 G5
Candren Wy
PSLYN/LNWD PA3 .... 101 G4
Caneluk Av *CARLUKE* ML8 .... 179 H8
Canmore Crs *GRNKW/INVK* PA16.. 32 A5
Canmore Pl *DEN/PKHD* G31 ...... 13 L8
Canmore St *DEN/PKHD* G31 ...... 13 L8
Cannerton Crs *KKNTL* G66.......... 45 H4
Cannerton Pk *KKNTL* G66 .... 45 H4
Cannich Dr *PSLYS* PA2 .... 102 B8
Cannich Pl *WISHAW* ML2 .... 159 M3
Canniesburn Rd *BSDN* G61 .... 61 J7
Canonbie St *ESTRH* G34 .... 86 D8
Canon Ct *MTHW* ML1 .... 134 D7
Canterbury *EKILS* G75 .... 171 H4
Canthill Gdns *SHOTTS* ML7 .... 136 F6
Cantieslaw Dr *EKILN* G74 .... 154 A6
Canting Wy *GOV/IBX* G51 .... 104 C2
Canyon Rd *WISHAW* ML2 .... 158 D7
Capel Av *NMRNS* G77 .... 150 F3
Capel Gv *EKILN* G74 .... 154 B6
Capel Pl *IRVSE* KA11 .... 204 B7
Capelrig Dr *EKILN* G74 .... 154 B6
NMRNS G77 .... 150 E1
Capelrig La *NMRNS* G77 .... 150 D3
Capelrig Rd *NMRNS* G77 .... 150 D1
Capelrig St *GIF/THBK* G46 .... 126 F5
Caplaw Pl *WISHAW* ML2 .... 176 F1
Caplaw Rd *BRHD/NEIL* G78 ...... 123 J7
PSLYS PA2 .... 124 C3
Caplethill Rd *PSLYS* PA2 .... 124 F3
Caponcraig Av *SVSTN* KA20 ...... 192 C8
Capper Vw *PSTWK* KA9 .... 221 J7
Caprington Av *KLMNK* KA1 .... 211 L6
Caprington St
STPS/GTHM/RID G33.............. 85 G8
Captain St *GRNK* PA15.............. 2 B5
Cara Dr *GOV/IBX* G51 .... 103 L1
Carbarns *WISHAW* ML2 .... 158 E8
Carbarns East *WISHAW* ML2 ..... 158 D8
Carbarns Rd *WISHAW* ML2 .... 158 D8
Carbarns West *WISHAW* ML2 ..... 158 D8
Carberry Rd *PLKSD/SHW* G41 ... 104 D7
Carbeth Rd *MLNGV* G62 .... 41 M8
Carbeth St *PPK/MIL* G22 .... 83 H5
Carbieston Av *RAYR/DAL* KA6 ... 231 L5
Carbisdale St *PPK/MIL* G22 .... 83 L4
Carbost St *SMSTN* G23 .... 62 D8
Carbrook St *PSLY* PA1 .... 8 C4
SPRGB/BLRNK G21 .... 6 E7
Carcluie Crs *AYRS* KA7 .... 229 H7
Cardarrach St
SPRGB/BLRNK G21 .... 84 A5
Cardean Rd *BLSH* ML4 .... 133 L3
Cardell Av *PSLYS* PA2 .... 101 G7
Cardell Crs *AIRDRIE* ML6 .... 111 K7
Cardell Dr *PSLYS* PA2 .... 101 G6
Cardell Rd *PSLYS* PA2 .... 101 G6
Cardonald Dr
CARD/HILL/MSPK G52 .... 103 G5
Cardonald Gdns
CARD/HILL/MSPK G52 .... 103 H5
Cardonald Place Rd
CARD/HILL/MSPK G52 .... 103 H5
Cardowan Dr *BALLOCH* G68 ...... 47 K8
STPS/GTHM/RID G33.............. 85 K4
Cardowan Pk *UD/BTH/TAN* G71.. 109 H8
Cardow Crs *IRVSE* KA11 .... 204 A3
Cardow Rd *SPRGB/BLRNK* G21... 7 K1
Cardrona St
STPS/GTHM/RID G33.............. 85 H6
Cardross Av *PGL* PA14 .... 54 E1
Cardross Crs *GRNK* PA15 .... 33 J7
Cardross Pl *GRNK* PA15 .... 33 J7
Cardross Rd *DMBTN* G82 .... 23 L8
DMBTN G82 .... 25 H7
DMBTN G82 .... 36 B5
HBR/GL G84 .... 22 F1
Cardross St *DEN/PKHD* G31 ...... 12 D2
Cardwell Rd *GRK* PA19 .... 31 M2
Cardwell St *PLKSD/SHW* G41 .... 10 F8
Cardyke St *SPRGB/BLRNK* G21 ... 6 F1
Careston Pl *BSHPBGS* G64 .... 64 D8
Carey Gdns *MTHW* ML1 .... 135 J8
Carey Rd *SALT* KA21 .... 191 M6
Carfin Dr *CARLUKE* ML8 .... 188 C7
Carfin Mill Rd *MTHW* ML1 .... 134 D7
Carfin Rd *MTHW* ML1 .... 134 D7
WISHAW ML2 .... 158 C7
Carfin St *MTHW* ML5................ 110 B5
GVH/MTFL G42 .... 105 H7
MTHW ML1 .... 134 A6
Carfrae St *KVGV* G3 .... 104 C1
Cargill Dr *PSTWK* KA9 .... 225 K4
Cargill Sq *BSHPBGS* G64 .... 84 B1
Carham Dr
CARD/HILL/MSPK G52 .... 103 J4
Carillon Rd *GOV/IBX* G51 .... 104 C4
Carisbrooke Crs
BSHPBGS G64 .... 64 B5
Carlaverock Rd
PLKSW/MSWD G43 .... 127 K3
Carleith Av *CLYDBK* G81 .... 59 M3
Carleith Qd *GOV/IBX* G51 .... 103 K2
Carleith Ter *CLYDBK* G81 .... 59 M3
Carleston St *SPRGB/BLRNK* G21.. 83 M5
Carleton Ct *GIF/THBK* G46 .... 127 J5
Carleton Dr *GIF/THBK* G46 .... 127 J5
Carleton Gdns *PSTWK* KA9 .... 225 J2
Carleton Ga *GIF/THBK* G46 .... 127 J5
Carlibar Av *KNTSWD* G13 .... 80 F5
Carlibar Dr *BRHD/NEIL* G78...... 125 J6
Carlibar Gdns
BRHD/NEIL G78 .... 125 J6
Carlibar Rd *BRHD/NEIL* G78 ..... 125 H6
Carlile Pl *PSLYN/LNWD* PA3 ...... 9 H1
Carlisle Rd *AIRDRIE* ML6............ 111 J4

Carlisle St *SPRGB/BLRNK* G21 .... 5 N1
Carlowrie Av *BLTYR/CAMB* G72 .. 131 J7
Carlton Ct *GBLS* G5 .... 11 G4
Carlton Pl *GBLS* G5 .... 11 H4
Carlung Pl *WKIL* KA23 .... 181 J6
Carlyle Av
CARD/HILL/MSPK G52 .... 102 F1
Carlyle Dr *EKILN* G74 .... 15 L1
Carlyle Ter *EKILN* G74 .... 15 L1
Carmaben Rd
STPS/GTHM/RID G33.............. 107 K1
Carman Rd *DMBTN* G82 .... 25 K8
DMBTN G82 .... 35 J1
Carmel Av *KLMNK* KA1 .... 206 C5
Carmel Dr *IRVSE* KA11 .... 205 G8
Carmel Pl *KLMNK* KA1 .... 16 A2
KLMNKN/STW KA3 .... 206 A2
Carmel Ter *KLMNK* KA1 .... 16 A1
Carment Dr *PLKSD/SHW* G41 .... 127 K1
SVSTN KA20 .... 201 L2
Carmen Vw *DMBTN* G82 .... 37 G3
Carmichael Ct
LNK/LMHG ML11 .... 199 J4
Carmichael Pl *GVH/MTFL* G42... 127 M2
Carmichael St *CARLUKE* ML8 ..... 177 M4
GOV/IBX G51........................ 104 B3
GRNKW/INVK PA16 .... 32 D3
Carmichael Wy
CARLUKE ML8 .... 177 M4
Carmunnock By-Pass
CRMNK/CLK/EAG G76 .... 152 C3
CSMK G45 .... 152 B1
Carmunnock Rd
CRMNK/CLK/EAG G76 .... 152 B3
CSMK G45 .... 152 B1
EKILN G74........................... 153 J6
LNPK/KPK G44 .... 128 B1
Carmyle Av *CAR/SHTL* G32 .... 107 H8
CAR/SHTL G32 .... 130 B1
Carmyle Gdns *CTBR* ML5 .... 109 L6
Carmyle Pl *SVSTN* KA20 .... 201 K2
Carna Dr *LNPK/KPK* G44 .... 128 C4
Carnalea St *GLSTN* KA4 .... 214 C4
Carnarvon St *KVGV* G3.............. 4 D6
Carnbroe Rd *BLSH* ML4 .... 133 H1
CTBR ML5 .... 110 D7
Carneddans Rd *MLNGV* G62 ...... 41 J5
Carnegie Hl *EKILS* G75 .... 14 C6
Carnegie Pl *EKILS* G75 .... 14 C6
Carnegie Rd
CARD/HILL/MSPK G52 .... 103 G2
Carnell Crs *PSTWK* KA9 .... 225 K2
Carnell Dr *RAYR/DAL* KA6 .... 231 H5
Carnell Ter *PSTWK* KA9 .... 225 K2
Carnoch St *SMSTN* G23 .... 62 D8
Carnoustie Ct *KLWNG* KA13 ..... 193 H6
UD/BTH/TAN G71 .... 131 M7
Carnoustie Crs *BSHPBGS* G64 ... 64 C8
EKILS G75 .... 171 G3
Carnoustie Pl *BLSH* ML4 .... 133 G2
GBLS G5 .... 10 D6
IRVSE KA11.......................... 208 E2
Carnoustie Wy *BALLOCH* G68 .... 48 F3
Carntyne Pl *CAR/SHTL* G32 ...... 106 F2
Carntyne Rd *CAR/SHTL* G32 ..... 107 H2
DEN/PKHD G31 .... 13 K3
Carnwadric Rd *GIF/THBK* G46 ... 126 C5
Carnwath Av
PLKSW/MSWD G43 .... 128 B2
Carnwath Rd *CARLUKE* ML8 ...... 178 F8
Caroline St *DEN/PKHD* G31 ...... 106 C4
Carolside Av
CRMNK/CLK/EAG G76 .... 151 L2
Carolside Dr *DRUM* G15............. 61 H6
Carousel Crs *WISHAW* ML2 .... 159 J6
Carradale Crs *BALLOCH* G68 ..... 67 M1
Carradale Gdns *CARLUKE* ML8 ... 189 G1
Carradale Pl *PSLYN/LNWD* PA3... 100 A3
Carradale St *CTBR* ML5 .... 109 M2
Carranbuie Rd *CARLUKE* ML8 .... 178 F6
Carrbridge Dr
MRYH/FIRH G20 .... 82 D3
Carresbrook Av *KKNTL* G66........ 66 A3
Carriagehill Av *PSLYS* PA2 .... 9 G9
Carriagehill Dr *PSLYS* PA2 .... 101 L3
Carrickarden Rd *BSDN* G61 .... 61 M6
Carrick Av *AYRS* KA7................. 18 E7
SALT KA21 .... 192 A6
Carrick Ct *KKNTL* G66 .... 46 A7
Carrick Crs *GIF/THBK* G46 .... 127 J8
Carrick Dr *CAR/SHTL* G32 .... 107 L5
CTBR ML5 .... 109 K2
IRV KA12 .... 203 H4
RUTH G73............................ 129 G4
Carrick Gdns *AYRS* KA7 .... 18 F8
BLSH ML4 .... 133 G1
BLTYR/CAMB G72 .... 155 K3
CARLUKE ML8 .... 189 G1
HMLTN ML3.......................... 155 L7
Carrick Gv *CAR/SHTL* G32 .... 107 L5
Carrick Pk *ARD* KA22 .... 191 J6
Carrick Pl *ARD* KA22 .... 191 J6
BLSH ML4 .... 133 H1
CTBR ML5 .... 87 L4
CTBR ML5 .... 109 K2
LRKH ML9 .... 176 B5
PSTWK KA9 .... 225 H2
Carrick Rd *AYRS* KA7................. 18 F7
BSHPBGS G64 .... 64 C8
BSHPTN PA7 .... 58 B7
CUMB G67............................ 49 G5
EKILN G74........................... 153 M6
RUTH G73............................ 128 F4
TROON KA10......................... 216 D2
Carrick Road Ct *AYRS* KA7 .... 18 F7
Carrickstone Rd *BALLOCH* G68 .. 48 E5
Carrickstone Vw
BALLOCH G68 .... 48 F4
Carrick St *AYRS* KA7................. 18 E4

KVGV G3............................... 10 F3
MTHW ML1 .... 176 C7
Carrick Ter *DMBTN* G82 .... 36 B5
GRNKW/INVK PA16 .... 31 K6
Carrick V *MTHW* ML1 .... 135 J8
Carrington St *KVGV* G3.............. 4 D5
RAYR/DAL KA6 .... 231 H4
Carrochan Crs *ALEX/LLW* G83 .... 25 M1
Carrochan Rd *ALEX/LLW* G83 .... 25 L1
Carroglen Gdns *CAR/SHTL* G32... 107 K4
Carroglen Gv *CAR/SHTL* G32 ..... 107 K4
Carroll Crs *MTHW* ML1 .... 134 C7
Carron Av *KLMNK* KA1 .... 212 B4
Carron Ct *HMLTN* ML3.............. 156 B8
Carron Crs *BSDN* G61 .... 61 J6
BSHPBGS G64 .... 64 B8
KKNTL G66 .... 65 L5
SPRGB/BLRNK G21 .... 83 K4
Carron Dr *BSHPTN* PA7 .... 58 C7
Carron Pl *CTBR* ML5 .... 87 K8
EKILS G75 .... 171 M3
IRV KA12 .... 203 J3
PPK/MIL G22 .... 83 L4
Carron Rd *WMYSB* PA18 .... 50 A8
Carron St *PPK/MIL* G22 .... 83 L4
WISHAW ML2 .... 159 H8
Carrour Gdns *BSHPBGS* G64 ...... 63 M7
Carruth Dr *KLMCLM* PA13 .... 75 J1
Carruth Rd *BRWEIR* PA11 .... 98 C1
Carsaig Dr
CARD/HILL/MSPK G52 .... 103 L4
Carscallan Rd *HMLTN* ML3......... 174 D3
Carsegreen Av *PSLYS* PA2 .... 124 C3
Carseloch Rd *AYRS* KA7 .... 228 F8
Carseview Dr *BSDN* G61 .... 62 A3
Carsewood Av *HWWD* PA9 .... 121 M4
Carson Dr *IRV* KA12 .... 208 C1
Carson Rd *ALEX/LLW* G83 .... 25 L1
Carstairs St *DMNK/BRGTN* G40... 106 A7
Carswell Gdns *PLKSD/SHW* G41 .. 104 E7
Carswell Rd *NMRNS* G77 .... 150 B4
Cartcraigs Rd
PLKSW/MSWD G43 .... 127 H3
Carters Pl *IRV* KA12 .... 203 K7
Cartha St *PLKSW/MSWD* G43 .... 127 K2
Cartland Av *CARLUKE* ML8......... 188 F1
Cartland Rd *LNK/LMHG* ML11 .... 198 C1
Cartland Vw *LNK/LMHG* ML11 ... 198 F4
Cart La *PSLYN/LNWD* PA3 .... 9 H1
Cartsbridge Rd
CRMNK/CLK/EAG G76 .... 151 L3
Cartsburn St *GRNK* PA15 .... 2 F7
Cartsdyke Av *GRNK* PA15 .... 3 J5
Cartside Av *JNSTN* PA5 .... 99 K8
RNFRW PA4.......................... 79 H5
Cartside Dr
CRMNK/CLK/EAG G76 .... 152 A3
Cartside Pl
CRMNK/CLK/EAG G76 .... 151 M4
Cartside Qd *PLKSW/MSWD* G43 .. 128 A2
Cartside Rd
CRMNK/CLK/EAG G76 .... 151 M4
Cartside St *GVH/MTFL* G42 .... 127 M2
Cart St *CLYDBK* G81 .... 80 B1
Cartvale La *PSLYN/LNWD* PA3 ... 101 L3
Cartvale Rd *GVH/MTFL* G42 ...... 127 M2
Cartview Ct
CRMNK/CLK/EAG G76 .... 151 M3
Carvale Av *SHOTTS* ML7 .... 113 J7
Carwinshoch Vw *AYRS* KA7 .... 228 D4
Carwood St *GRNK* PA15 .... 3 K7
Caskie Dr *BLTYR/CAMB* G72 ...... 131 L8
SKLM PA17 .... 70 B6
Cassels Gv *MTHW* ML1 .... 133 J8
Cassels St *CARLUKE* ML8 .... 178 F7
MTHW ML1 .... 157 L1
Cassillis St *AYRS* KA7 .... 18 F3
Cassiltoun Gdns *CSMK* G45 ...... 128 D7
Cassley Av *RNFRW* PA4 .... 80 F7
Castburn Rd *CUMB* G67 .... 49 M3
Castle Av *HBR/GL* G84 .... 20 A7
JNSTN PA5 .... 100 B8
MTHW ML1 .... 134 B3
SVSTN KA20 .... 192 E6
UD/BTH/TAN G71 .... 131 L6
Castlebank Ct *KNTSWD* G13 ...... 81 L3
Castlebank Crs *PTCK* G11 .... 82 A8
Castlebank Gdns *KNTSWD* G13 .. 81 L3
Castlebank St *PTCK* G11 .... 81 M8
Castlebank Vls *KNTSWD* G13 ..... 81 L3
Castlebay Dr *PPK/MIL* G22 .... 63 J8
Castlebay Pl *PPK/MIL* G22 .... 83 J1
Castlebay St *PPK/MIL* G22 .... 83 J1
Castlecary Rd *CUMB* G67 .... 49 K2
Castle Chimmins Av
BLTYR/CAMB G72 .... 130 D5
Castle Chimmins Rd
BLTYR/CAMB G72 .... 130 D6
Castle Ct *CUMB* G67 .... 49 M1
KKNTL G66 .... 65 K1
Castle Crs *BSHPTN* PA7 .... 58 B7
Castlecroft Gdns
UD/BTH/TAN G71 .... 131 M4
Castle Dr *KBRN* KA25 .... 143 G8
KLMNKN/STW KA3 .... 207 G5
MTHW ML1 .... 134 B3
RAYR/DAL KA6 .... 231 H3
WKIL KA23 .... 181 K4
Castlefern Rd *RUTH* G73............ 129 G6
Castlefield Gdns *EKILS* G75 .... 171 H4
Castle Gait *PSLY* PA1 .... 9 G6
Castle Gdns
BAIL/MDB/MHD G69 .... 66 F7
PSLYS PA2 .... 101 G6
Castlegate *LNK/LMHG* ML11 ...... 198 F6
Castle Ga *NMRNS* G77 .... 151 G6
UD/BTH/TAN G71.................. 131 L4
Castleglen Rd *EKILN* G74 .... 152 F5
Castlegreen Crs *DMBTN* G82 ..... 37 H7
Castlegreen St *DMBTN* G82 ...... 37 H7
Castle Gv *KBRN* KA25 .... 143 G8
Castlehill Av *PGL* PA14 .... 55 G1
Castlehill Crs *AIRDRIE* ML6 .... 111 M8
AYRS KA7.............................. 19 H8
CARLUKE ML8 .... 178 A5
HMLTN ML3.......................... 157 K8

KLMCLM PA13 ..... 55 H8
RNFRW PA4 ..... 80 D5
Castlehill Dr LARGS KA30 ..... 115 K6
NMRNS G77 ..... 150 F5
Castlehill Gdns HMLTN ML3 ..... 156 F7
Castlehill Gn EKILN G74 ..... 152 F5
Castlehill Qd DMBTN G82 ..... 36 C4
Castlehill Rd AYRS KA7 ..... 19 H7
BSDN G61 ..... 61 H3
CARLUKE ML8 ..... 178 E4
DMBTN G82 ..... 36 C4
KLMCLM PA13 ..... 75 J1
WISHAW ML2 ..... 158 F8
Castle Keep Gdns IRVSE KA11 ..... 203 M5
Castlelaw Gdns
CAR/SHTL G32 ..... 107 H3
Castlelaw St CAR/SHTL G32 ..... 107 H3
Castle Mains Rd MLNGV G62 ..... 41 K7
Castlemilk Crs LNPK/KPK G44 ..... 128 E4
Castlemilk Dr CSMK G45 ..... 128 E6
Castlemilk Rd LNPK/KPK G44 ..... 128 E2
RUTH G73 ..... 128 F4
Castlemount Av NMRNS G77 ..... 150 F6
Castle Park Dr FAIRLIE KA29 ..... 139 L6
Castle Park Gdns FAIRLIE KA29 ..... 139 L6
Castle Qd AIRDRIE ML6 ..... 111 K2
Castle Rd AIRDRIE ML6 ..... 111 K1
ARD KA22 ..... 191 K6
BRWEIR PA11 ..... 76 D3
DMBTN G82 ..... 37 C8
GRNK PA15 ..... 3 J9
JNSTN PA5 ..... 100 C6
NMRNS G77 ..... 150 C5
PGL PA14 ..... 34 D8
WMYSB PA18 ..... 50 A8
Castle St AIRDRIE ML6 ..... 111 J7
BAIL/MDB/MHD G69 ..... 107 M6
CLYDBK G81 ..... 59 L6
COWCAD G4 ..... 6 B7
DMBTN G82 ..... 36 F5
HMLTN ML3 ..... 156 F5
IRV KA12 ..... 203 H6
NMLNS KA16 ..... 215 K2
PSLY PA1 ..... 8 D4
PTCK G11 ..... 82 C8
RUTH G73 ..... 129 G1
Castle Ter CRH/DND KA2 ..... 205 M6
Castleton Av NMRNS G77 ..... 150 F6
SPRGB/BLRNK G21 ..... 83 L2
Castleton Crs NMRNS G77 ..... 150 F6
Castleton Dr NMRNS G77 ..... 150 F6
Castleton Gv NMRNS G77 ..... 150 F6
Castleview BALLOCH G68 ..... 49 L1
CRH/DND KA2 ..... 209 L6
KKNTL G66 ..... 28 F6
Castle Vw KKNTL G66 ..... 29 C8
WISHAW ML2 ..... 160 A3
WKIL KA23 ..... 181 K3
Castleview Av GLSTN KA4 ..... 214 D3
PSLYS PA2 ..... 124 A2
Castleview Dr PSLYS PA2 ..... 124 A2
Castle Wk AYRS KA7 ..... 228 C6
FAIRLIE KA29 ..... 139 L6
Castle Wy CUMB G67 ..... 49 J6
Castle Wynd HMLTN ML3 ..... 174 E6
UD/BTH/TAN G71 ..... 132 B7
Catacol Av SALT KA21 ..... 191 M7
Cathay St PPK/MIL G22 ..... 83 J1
Cathburn Rd WISHAW ML2 ..... 160 C5
Cathcart Crs PSLYS PA2 ..... 9 L7
Cathcart Pl RUTH G73 ..... 128 F2
Cathcart Rd GBLS G5 ..... 11 H7
GVH/MTFL G42 ..... 105 H7
GVH/MTFL G42 ..... 128 B2
LARGS KA30 ..... 115 K7
LNPK/KPK G44 ..... 128 B2
RUTH G73 ..... 128 F2
Cathcart Sq GRNK PA15 ..... 2 E4
Cathcart St AYRS KA7 ..... 18 E2
GRNK PA15 ..... 2 E4
Cathedral Sq COWCAD G4 ..... 12 A1
Cathedral St CGLE G1 ..... 5 K9
Catherine Dr GLSTN KA4 ..... 214 A4
Catherine St MTHW ML1 ..... 157 L5
Catherine Wy MTHW ML1 ..... 133 M6
RUTH G73 ..... 129 J2
Cathkin Av BLTYR/CAMB G72 ..... 129 J3
RUTH G73 ..... 129 J2
Cathkin By-Pass RUTH G73 ..... 129 K6
Cathkin Ct BALLOCH G68 ..... 48 E4
Cathkin Dr
CRMNK/CLK/EAG G76 ..... 151 J1
Cathkin Pl BLTYR/CAMB G72 ..... 129 L3
KLWNG KA13 ..... 193 H5
Cathkin Rd
CRMNK/CLK/EAG G76 ..... 152 E1
GVH/MTFL G42 ..... 127 M2
UD/BTH/TAN G71 ..... 108 E8
Cathkinview Pl
GVH/MTFL G42 ..... 128 B2
Cathkinview Rd GVH/MTFL G42 ..... 128 A2
Catrine EKILN G74 ..... 14 C1
Catrine Av PLK/PH/NH G53 ..... 126 A1
Catrine Crs MTHW ML1 ..... 158 A5
Catrine Gdns PLK/PH/NH G53 ..... 126 A1
Catrine Pl PLK/PH/NH G53 ..... 126 A1
Catrine Rd PLK/PH/NH G53 ..... 126 A1
Catrine St LRKH ML9 ..... 176 C7
Cauldstream Pl MLNGV G62 ..... 41 L8
Causewayside Crs
CAR/SHTL G32 ..... 107 G6
Causewayside St
CAR/SHTL G32 ..... 107 G7
The Causeway FAIRLIE KA29 ..... 139 K6
Causeyfoot Dr KBRN KA25 ..... 143 J3
Causeyside St PSLY PA1 ..... 9 H4
PSLYS PA2 ..... 9 H6
Cavendish Dr NMRNS G77 ..... 150 F3
Cavendish La TROON KA10 ..... 216 D7
Cavendish Pl GBLS G5 ..... 11 C7
TROON KA10 ..... 216 D7
Cavendish St GBLS G5 ..... 11 G7
Cavin Dr CSMK G45 ..... 128 E5
Cavin Rd CSMK G45 ..... 128 E5
Cawder Ct BALLOCH G68 ..... 48 D4
Cawder Pl BALLOCH G68 ..... 48 E4
Cawder Rd BALLOCH G68 ..... 48 E4
Cawder Vw BALLOCH G68 ..... 48 E4
Cawder Wy BALLOCH G68 ..... 48 E4

Cawdor Crs BSHPTN PA7 ..... 58 B7
GRNKW/INVK PA16 ..... 32 A5
Cawdor Pl GRNKW/INVK PA16 ..... 32 A5
Cawdor Wy EKILN G74 ..... 153 K6
Cayton Gdns
BAIL/MDB/MHD G69 ..... 107 M5
Cecil St CRMNK/CLK/EAG G76 ..... 151 L2
CTBR ML5 ..... 110 A4
KVD/HLHD G12 ..... 82 D6
Cedar Av BEITH KA15 ..... 168 A1
CLYDBK G81 ..... 59 K5
JNSTN PA5 ..... 122 F1
UD/BTH/TAN G71 ..... 132 B1
Cedar Ct BLTYR/CAMB G72 ..... 130 E5
EKILS G75 ..... 171 J4
KLBCH PA10 ..... 99 G6
MRYH/FIRH G20 ..... 4 F4
Cedar Crs PA15 ..... 33 L7
HMLTN ML3 ..... 156 E8
Cedar Dr EKILS G75 ..... 171 J4
KKNTL G66 ..... 45 J4
KKNTL G66 ..... 65 J4
UD/BTH/TAN G71 ..... 132 D1
Cedar Gdns CARLUKE ML8 ..... 177 M3
MTHW ML1 ..... 134 C5
RUTH G73 ..... 129 J6
Cedar Gv DMBTN G82 ..... 35 H2
Cedar La MTHW ML1 ..... 134 B4
EKILS G75 ..... 171 J4
GRK PA19 ..... 31 K3
Cedar Rd AYRS KA7 ..... 229 K5
BSHPBGS G64 ..... 84 B1
CUMB G67 ..... 49 K6
IRV KA12 ..... 203 K5
KLMNK KA1 ..... 16 A5
Cedar St MRYH/FIRH G20 ..... 4 F4
Cedarwood Av NMRNS G77 ..... 150 F4
Cedarwood Rd NMRNS G77 ..... 150 F5
Cedric Pl KNTSWD G13 ..... 81 K2
Cedric Rd KNTSWD G13 ..... 81 K2
Celtic St MRYH/FIRH G20 ..... 82 C2
Cemetery Rd BLTYR/CAMB G72 ..... 155 J3
CARD/HILL/MSPK G52 ..... 103 L5
GLSTN KA4 ..... 214 C4
Centenary Av AIRDRIE ML6 ..... 110 D2
Centenary Ct CLYDBK G81 ..... 60 B8
Centenary Gdns CTBR ML5 ..... 110 A4
HMLTN ML3 ..... 156 F7
Centenary Pl ARD KA22 ..... 191 K6
Centenary Qd MTHW ML1 ..... 134 A4
Central Av ARD KA22 ..... 191 K6
BLTYR/CAMB G72 ..... 129 M3
BLTYR/CAMB G72 ..... 155 L4
CAR/SHTL G32 ..... 107 K6
KBRN KA25 ..... 167 G2
KLMNK KA1 ..... 211 M6
MTHW ML1 ..... 133 M4
MTHW ML1 ..... 134 A7
PTCK G11 ..... 81 M7
TROON KA10 ..... 216 F5
UD/BTH/TAN G71 ..... 132 C3
Central Gv MTHW ML1 ..... 134 A7
Central Pth CAR/SHTL G32 ..... 107 L5
Central Qd ARD KA22 ..... 191 J6
Central Rd PSLY PA1 ..... 9 H3
Central Wy CUMB G67 ..... 48 F7
PSLY PA1 ..... 9 H3
Centre St AIRDRIE ML6 ..... 111 J7
CTBR ML5 ..... 87 J3
GBLS G5 ..... 11 G4
Centre Wy BRHD/NEIL G78 ..... 125 H6
Ceres Gdns BSHPBGS G64 ..... 64 D8
Cessnock Dr KLMNK KA1 ..... 212 F4
Cessnock Pl AYRS KA7 ..... 19 L8
GLSTN KA4 ..... 214 C4
Cessnock Rd GLSTN KA4 ..... 214 D4
KLMNK KA1 ..... 212 F3
STPS/GTHM/RID G33 ..... 85 M3
TROON KA10 ..... 216 D6
Cessock Pl KLMNK KA1 ..... 212 F4
Chalmers Av AYRS KA7 ..... 19 G9
Chalmers Crs EKILS G75 ..... 15 G8
Chalmers Dr EKILS G75 ..... 15 H7
Chalmers Ga DMNK/BRGTN G40 ..... 12 B4
Chalmers Rd AYRS KA7 ..... 19 G8
Chalmers St CLYDBK G81 ..... 60 B8
DMNK/BRGTN G40 ..... 12 A5
GRK PA19 ..... 31 M2
Chamberlain La KNTSWD G13 ..... 81 L4
Chamberlain Rd KNTSWD G13 ..... 81 L3
Chancellor St PTCK G11 ..... 82 B7
Chantinghall Rd HMLTN ML3 ..... 156 B6
Chantinghall Ter HMLTN ML3 ..... 156 B6
Chapelacre Gv HBR/GL G84 ..... 20 E6
Chapel Ct RUTH G73 ..... 128 F1
Chapel Crs HMLTN ML3 ..... 174 D3
Chapelcross Av AIRDRIE ML6 ..... 89 G8
Chapelhill Mt ARD KA22 ..... 191 J4
Chapelhill Rd PSLYS PA2 ..... 9 M8
PSLYS PA2 ..... 102 B8
Chapelknowe Rd MTHW ML1 ..... 134 D8
Chapel La GLSTN KA4 ..... 214 B3
Chapelpark Rd AYRS KA7 ..... 228 F4
Chapel Pl BRHD/NEIL G78 ..... 148 D2
Chapel Rd CLYDBK G81 ..... 60 A3
CRG/CRSL/HOU PA6 ..... 77 H6
WISHAW ML2 ..... 160 B8
Chapelside Av AIRDRIE ML6 ..... 111 G1
Chapelside Rd EKILN G74 ..... 154 A3
Chapel St AIRDRIE ML6 ..... 111 G1
CARLUKE ML8 ..... 178 F7
GRK PA19 ..... 31 M2
GRNK PA15 ..... 2 F5
HMLTN ML3 ..... 156 E6
KKNTL G66 ..... 44 D1
MRYH/FIRH G20 ..... 82 E4
MTHW ML1 ..... 135 H8
RUTH G73 ..... 128 F1
Chapelton Av BSDN G61 ..... 61 M5
DMBTN G82 ..... 37 G4
Chapelton Dr LARGS KA30 ..... 115 K3
Chapelton Gdns BSDN G61 ..... 61 M5
DMBTN G82 ..... 37 G4
Chapelton La WKIL KA23 ..... 181 J6
Chapelton Rd CUMB G67 ..... 68 D3

WKIL KA23 ..... 181 K7
Chapelton St PGL PA14 ..... 34 A7
PPK/MIL G22 ..... 83 J3
Chapelton Wy LARGS KA30 ..... 115 K3
Chapeltoun Ter
KLMNKN/STW KA3 ..... 196 F5
Chapelwell St SALT KA21 ..... 200 F2
Chapland Rd LNK/LMHG ML11 ..... 199 G4
Chaplet St KNTSWD G13 ..... 81 J1
Chapman Av CTBR ML5 ..... 87 J3
Chapman St GVH/MTFL G42 ..... 105 G7
Chappell St BRHD/NEIL G78 ..... 125 H6
Charing Cross La KVGV G3 ..... 4 D8
Charles Av PSTWK KA9 ..... 221 K4
RNFRW PA4 ..... 80 D5
Charles Crs CARLUKE ML8 ..... 179 H8
Charles Dr TROON KA10 ..... 216 F6
Charleson Rw KSYTH G65 ..... 47 M6
Charles Pl GRNK PA15 ..... 2 C3
KLMNK KA1 ..... 16 D5
Charles Qd MTHW ML1 ..... 134 A4
Charles St KLMNK KA1 ..... 16 D5
LARGS KA30 ..... 115 J7
SPRGB/BLRNK G21 ..... 6 C6
WISHAW ML2 ..... 158 C5
Charlotte Av BSHPBGS G64 ..... 64 B1
Charlotte Pl PSLYS PA2 ..... 9 G8
Charlotte St AYRS KA7 ..... 18 C3
CGLE G1 ..... 11 M4
DMBTN G82 ..... 36 D5
HBR/GL G84 ..... 20 E7
Charlotte Street La AYRS KA7 ..... 18 C3
Charnwood Av JNSTN PA5 ..... 122 D1
Chassels St CTBR ML5 ..... 110 A1
Chateau Gv HMLTN ML3 ..... 157 G7
Chatelherault Av
BLTYR/CAMB G72 ..... 129 L4
Chatelherault Crs HMLTN ML3 ..... 174 E1
Chatham EKILS G75 ..... 14 A8
Chatton St SMSTN G23 ..... 62 D8
Cheapside St KVGV G3 ..... 10 D2
Chelmsford Dr KVD/HLHD G12 ..... 82 B4
Cherry Bank KKNTL G66 ..... 65 H4
Cherrybank Rd
PLKSW/MSWD G43 ..... 127 M4
Cherrybank Wk CTBR ML5 ..... 110 D1
Cherry Crs CLYDBK G81 ..... 60 A5
Cherry Gdns IRV KA12 ..... 203 L4
Cherry Hill Rd AYRS KA7 ..... 229 H7
Cherryhill Vw LRKH ML9 ..... 175 M7
Cherry Pl BSHPBGS G64 ..... 84 B1
JNSTN PA5 ..... 100 A8
KKNTL G66 ..... 45 H4
MTHW ML1 ..... 134 B4
MTHW ML1 ..... 134 B5
UD/BTH/TAN G71 ..... 132 D1
Cherry Rd KLMNK KA1 ..... 211 J2
Cherrytree Crs LRKH ML9 ..... 176 A4
Cherrytree Dr
BLTYR/CAMB G72 ..... 130 E5
Cherry Wk MTHW ML1 ..... 157 L6
Cherrywood Dr BEITH KA15 ..... 144 C7
Cherrywood Rd JNSTN PA5 ..... 100 C6
Chesterfield Av KVD/HLHD G12 ..... 82 A4
Chester Rd GRNKW/INVK PA16 ..... 31 L5
Chesters Crs MTHW ML1 ..... 157 J1
Chesters Pl RUTH G73 ..... 129 G2
Chester St BSDN G61 ..... 61 J5
Chester St CAR/SHTL G32 ..... 107 G4
Chestnut Av BEITH KA15 ..... 168 A1
BSHPTN PA7 ..... 57 M4
CUMB G67 ..... 49 L4
Chestnut Ct CUMB G67 ..... 49 L4
KKNTL G66 ..... 45 H4
Chestnut Crs EKILS G75 ..... 171 J3
HMLTN ML3 ..... 156 E7
UD/BTH/TAN G71 ..... 132 C2
Chestnut Dr CLYDBK G81 ..... 60 A4
KKNTL G66 ..... 65 H3
Chestnut Gv BLTYR/CAMB G72 ..... 155 J1
CARLUKE ML8 ..... 178 E8
CTBR ML5 ..... 87 J3
LRKH ML9 ..... 176 A4
MTHW ML1 ..... 157 K5
RAYR/DAL KA6 ..... 231 H5
Chestnut La CUMB G62 ..... 41 L8
JNSTN PA5 ..... 123 G1
KLMNK KA1 ..... 16 A5
Chestnut Pl CUMB G67 ..... 49 L4
JNSTN PA5 ..... 123 G1
Chestnut Rd AYRS KA7 ..... 229 K3
Chestnut St PPK/MIL G22 ..... 83 K4
Chestnut Wy HMLTN ML3 ..... 174 F5
Cheviot Av BRHD/NEIL G78 ..... 125 J7
Cheviot Crs EKILS G75 ..... 171 G5
WISHAW ML2 ..... 158 F6
Cheviot Dr NMRNS G77 ..... 150 C6
Cheviot Head IRVSE KA11 ..... 203 M6
Cheviot Pl KLMNK KA1 ..... 212 A6
Cheviot Rd HMLTN ML3 ..... 156 F7
LRKH ML9 ..... 176 C7
PLKSW/MSWD G43 ..... 127 J4
PSLYS PA2 ..... 101 L8
Cheviot St BLTYR/CAMB G72 ..... 155 J2
Cheviot Wy IRVSE KA11 ..... 204 A6
Chillin Pl LRKH ML9 ..... 176 C7
Chirmorie Pl PLK/PH/NH G53 ..... 103 G8
Chirnside Pl
CARD/HILL/MSPK G52 ..... 103 G3
Chirnside Rd
CARD/HILL/MSPK G52 ..... 103 G3
Chisholm Av BSHPTN PA7 ..... 58 C6
Chisholm Dr NMRNS G77 ..... 150 E3
Chisholm Pl MTHW ML1 ..... 158 B7
Chisholm St CTBR ML5 ..... 110 B1
Chisolm St CGLE G1 ..... 11 L3
Chrighton Gn
UD/BTH/TAN G71 ..... 132 A1
Chriss Av HMLTN ML3 ..... 174 D2
Christchurch Pl EKILS G75 ..... 171 H2
Christian St PLKSW/MSWD G43 ..... 127 J1
Christie Gdns SALT KA21 ..... 200 F1
Christie La PSLY PA1 ..... 9 H2
Christie St BLSH ML4 ..... 133 K5
PSLY PA1 ..... 9 K3
Christopher St SPRGB/BLRNK G21 ..... 6 E6
Chromars Pl GRNK PA15 ..... 2 A7

Chryston Rd
BAIL/MDB/MHD G69 ..... 86 D1
KKNTL G66 ..... 66 C3
Chuckie La JNSTN PA5 ..... 99 J3
Church Av DMBTN G82 ..... 35 C1
RUTH G73 ..... 129 J4
STPS/GTHM/RID G33 ..... 85 K3
WISHAW ML2 ..... 159 M5
Church Ct DMBTN G82 ..... 36 F6
Church Crs AIRDRIE ML6 ..... 89 L8
Church Dr RAYR/DAL KA6 ..... 227 H4
Church Hl PSLY PA5 ..... 9 G3
Church Hill St GTCI KA28 ..... 138 A7
Churchill Av EKILN G74 ..... 15 C3
JNSTN PA5 ..... 122 C1
KLWNG KA13 ..... 193 M5
Churchill Crs AYR KA8 ..... 19 M3
UD/BTH/TAN G71 ..... 132 B6
Churchill Dr ARD KA22 ..... 191 J5
BSHPTN PA7 ..... 58 B6
PTCK G11 ..... 82 A6
Churchill Pl KLBCH PA10 ..... 99 G7
Churchill Rd KLMCLM PA13 ..... 75 J2
Churchill Sq HBR/GL G84 ..... 21 C7
Church La CTBR ML5 ..... 110 A2
GLSTN KA4 ..... 214 C3
KLMNK KA1 ..... 211 M6
Church Manse La BRWEIR PA11 ..... 98 D1
Church Pl AIRDRIE ML6 ..... 90 F5
ARD KA22 ..... 191 J4
Church Rd BAIL/MDB/MHD G69 ..... 86 C2
BRWEIR PA11 ..... 75 L6
BRWEIR PA11 ..... 98 E2
CRMNK/CLK/EAG G76 ..... 151 M3
GIF/THBK G46 ..... 127 J7
WISHAW ML2 ..... 160 D3
Church St ALEX/LLW G83 ..... 25 L5
BAIL/MDB/MHD G69 ..... 108 C5
BLTYR/CAMB G72 ..... 155 L2
CLYDBK G81 ..... 60 A6
CTBR ML5 ..... 110 A2
DMBTN G82 ..... 36 F5
GRK PA19 ..... 31 L3
HMLTN ML3 ..... 156 E5
IRV KA12 ..... 203 H7
JNSTN PA5 ..... 99 M6
KLBCH PA10 ..... 99 G6
KLMNKN/STW KA3 ..... 16 F3
KLWNG KA13 ..... 193 L6
KSYTH G65 ..... 47 L1
LARGS KA30 ..... 115 J6
LOCHW PA12 ..... 120 C7
LRKH ML9 ..... 176 A6
MTHW ML1 ..... 134 F1
PGL PA14 ..... 34 C7
PTCK G11 ..... 82 C8
TROON KA10 ..... 216 C6
UD/BTH/TAN G71 ..... 131 L4
Church Vw BLTYR/CAMB G72 ..... 130 A2
CTBR ML5 ..... 110 A2
Church View Gdns BLSH ML4 ..... 133 C4
Circus Dr DEN/PKHD G31 ..... 12 D1
Circus Pl DEN/PKHD G31 ..... 12 D1
Circus Place La DEN/PKHD G31 ..... 6 D9
Citadel Pl AYRS KA7 ..... 18 D2
MTHW ML1 ..... 157 J1
Citizen La CGLE G1 ..... 11 J1
Citrus Crs UD/BTH/TAN G71 ..... 132 C1
Cityford Dr RUTH G73 ..... 128 F3
Civic St COWCAD G4 ..... 5 G6
Civic Wy KKNTL G66 ..... 65 J2
Clachan Dr GOV/IBX G51 ..... 103 L1
The Clachan WISHAW ML2 ..... 159 H6
Claddens Pl KKNTL G66 ..... 65 M5
Claddens Qd PPK/MIL G22 ..... 83 H3
Claddens St PPK/MIL G22 ..... 83 H3
Cladence Gv EKILS G75 ..... 171 M4
Claire St WISHAW ML2 ..... 159 M6
Clairinch Gdns RNFRW PA4 ..... 80 C8
Clairmont Gdns KVGV G3 ..... 4 C7
Clair Rd BSHPBGS G64 ..... 64 D8
Clamp Rd WISHAW ML2 ..... 158 C5
Clamps Gv EKILN G74 ..... 15 G6
Clamps Ter EKILN G74 ..... 15 L6
Clamps Wd EKILS G75 ..... 15 K6
Clanrye Dr CTBR ML5 ..... 110 A5
Clapperhow Rd MTHW ML1 ..... 134 C4
Claremont Av KKNTL G66 ..... 45 H4
Claremont Dr MLNGV G62 ..... 42 A8
Claremont Gdns MLNGV G62 ..... 42 A8
Claremont Pas KVGV G3 ..... 4 C7
Claremont Pl KVGV G3 ..... 4 C7
Claremont St KVGV G3 ..... 4 B8
Claremont Ter KVGV G3 ..... 4 C7
Claremount Av GIF/THBK G46 ..... 127 J7
Claremount Terrace La KVGV G3 ..... 4 B7
Clarence Dr PSLY PA1 ..... 9 M4
PTCK G11 ..... 82 A6
Clarence Gdns PTCK G11 ..... 82 A6
Clarence La PTCK G11 ..... 82 B6
GRNKW/INVK PA16 ..... 2 C1
PSLY PA1 ..... 9 L3
Clarendon Pl AYRS KA7 ..... 19 L9
COWCAD G4 ..... 4 E5
Clarendon Rd WISHAW ML2 ..... 158 E8
Clarendon St MRYH/FIRH G20 ..... 4 E5
Clare St SPRGB/BLRNK G21 ..... 6 E6
Clarinda Crs KKNTL G66 ..... 46 A7
Clarinda Pl MTHW ML1 ..... 134 C6
Clarion Crs KNTSWD G13 ..... 81 G1
Clarion Rd KNTSWD G13 ..... 81 G2
Clark Crs SVSTN KA20 ..... 201 K2
Clark Dr IRV KA12 ..... 203 K7
Clarke Av AYRS KA7 ..... 18 C3
Clark Pl NMRNS G77 ..... 149 L2
SALT KA21 ..... 192 A7
Clarkston Av LNPK/KPK G44 ..... 127 M5
Clarkston Dr AIRDRIE ML6 ..... 111 K2
Clarkston Rd
CRMNK/CLK/EAG G76 ..... 151 L1
LNPK/KPK G44 ..... 127 M4
Clark St AIRDRIE ML6 ..... 111 H1
CLYDBK G81 ..... 59 M5
JNSTN PA5 ..... 99 M6
KLMNK KA1 ..... 16 F5
PSLYN/LNWD PA3 ..... 101 J3

RNFRW PA4 ..... 80 B6
WISHAW ML2 ..... 159 M3
Clarkwell Rd HMLTN ML3 ..... 155 L6
Clarkwell Ter HMLTN ML3 ..... 155 M6
Clathic Av BSDN G61 ..... 62 A6
Claude Av BLTYR/CAMB G72 ..... 130 E6
Claude St LRKH ML9 ..... 176 A6
Claud Rd PSLYN/LNWD PA3 ..... 102 A3
Clavens Rd
CARD/HILL/MSPK G52 ..... 102 E3
Claverhouse Pl PSLYS PA2 ..... 9 M7
Claverhouse Rd
CARD/HILL/MSPK G52 ..... 102 F2
Clavering St East PSLY PA1 ..... 8 D3
Clavering St West PSLY PA1 ..... 8 D4
Clay Crs BLSH ML4 ..... 133 H2
Clayhouse Rd
STPS/GTHM/RID G33 ..... 85 L5
Claymore Dr
CRG/CRSL/HOU PA6 ..... 99 K1
Claypotts Pl
STPS/GTHM/RID G33 ..... 85 G8
Claypotts Rd
STPS/GTHM/RID G33 ..... 85 G8
Clay Rd BLSH ML4 ..... 133 J2
Clayslaps Rd KVGV G3 ..... 82 D8
Clayslaps Vw KLMNK KA1 ..... 212 B5
Claythorn Av DMNK/BRGTN G40 ..... 12 A5
Claythorn Circ
DMNK/BRGTN G40 ..... 12 A5
Claythorn Pk DMNK/BRGTN G40 ..... 12 A5
Claythorn Ter DMNK/BRGTN G40 ..... 12 A5
Clayton Av IRV KA12 ..... 203 J5
Clayton Ter DEN/PKHD G31 ..... 12 D1
Clearfield Av HMLTN ML3 ..... 156 B5
Clearmount Av NMLNS KA16 ..... 215 J2
Cleddans Crs CLYDBK G81 ..... 60 C3
Cleddans Rd CLYDBK G81 ..... 60 C4
KKNTL G66 ..... 45 L8
Cleddans Vw AIRDRIE ML6 ..... 88 E5
Cleddens Ct BSHPBGS G64 ..... 64 A8
Cleeves Qd PLK/PH/NH G53 ..... 126 A4
Cleeves Rd PLK/PH/NH G53 ..... 126 A4
Cleghorn Av LNK/LMHG ML11 ..... 199 H4
Cleghorn Dr MTHW ML1 ..... 134 C8
Cleghorn Rd LNK/LMHG ML11 ..... 199 G3
Cleghorn St PPK/MIL G22 ..... 5 G2
Cleish Av BSDN G61 ..... 61 J1
Cleland La GBLS G5 ..... 11 H6
Cleland Pl EKILN G74 ..... 154 A6
Cleland Rd MTHW ML1 ..... 134 C8
WISHAW ML2 ..... 159 G6
Cleland St GBLS G5 ..... 11 J6
Clelland Av BSHPBGS G64 ..... 84 A1
Clem Attlee Gdns LRKH ML9 ..... 176 B7
Clements Pl SVSTN KA20 ..... 192 E7
Clerwood St CAR/SHTL G32 ..... 13 M3
Cleuch Gdns
CRMNK/CLK/EAG G76 ..... 151 K1
Clevans Rd BRWEIR PA11 ..... 98 B2
Cleveden Crs KVD/HLHD G12 ..... 82 B4
Cleveden Crescent La
KVD/HLHD G12 ..... 82 B4
Cleveden Dr KVD/HLHD G12 ..... 82 B4
RUTH G73 ..... 129 J3
Cleveden Drive La
KVD/HLHD G12 ..... 82 C5
Cleveden Gdns KVD/HLHD G12 ..... 82 C4
Cleveden La KVD/HLHD G12 ..... 82 B3
Cleveden Pl KVD/HLHD G12 ..... 82 B3
Cleveden Rd KVD/HLHD G12 ..... 82 B3
Cleveland La CGLW G2 ..... 4 D8
Cleveland St KVGV G3 ..... 4 D8
Clifford Gdns GOV/IBX G51 ..... 104 B4
Clifford La GOV/IBX G51 ..... 104 D2
Clifford Pl GOV/IBX G51 ..... 104 D2
Clifford St GOV/IBX G51 ..... 104 B4
Cliff Rd KVGV G3 ..... 4 C6
Cliff Terrace Rd WMYSB PA18 ..... 70 A1
Clifton Pl CTBR ML5 ..... 110 C3
KVGV G3 ..... 4 B8
Clifton Rd GIF/THBK G46 ..... 127 H6
Clifton St GTCI KA28 ..... 138 A6
KVGV G3 ..... 4 B7
Clifton Ter BLTYR/CAMB G72 ..... 129 L6
Climie Pl KLMNKN/STW KA3 ..... 17 J4
Clincarthill Rd RUTH G73 ..... 129 G3
RUTH G73 ..... 129 H2
Clincart Rd GVH/MTFL G42 ..... 128 B1
Clinchyard Pl GLSTN KA4 ..... 214 A4
Clippens Rd CRG/CRSL/HOU PA6 ..... 99 L1
PSLYN/LNWD PA3 ..... 100 A4
Clive St SHOTTS ML7 ..... 137 L4
Cloak Rd PGL PA14 ..... 55 H4
Cloan Av DRUM G15 ..... 61 H7
Cloan Crs BSHPBGS G64 ..... 64 B5
Clober Farm La MLNGV G62 ..... 41 L6
Cloberfield MLNGV G62 ..... 41 M5
Cloberfield Gdns MLNGV G62 ..... 41 M6
Cloberhill Rd KNTSWD G13 ..... 61 J8
Clober Rd MLNGV G62 ..... 41 L6
Clochbar Av MLNGV G62 ..... 41 M6
Clochbar St MLNGV G62 ..... 41 M7
Cloch Brae GRK PA19 ..... 31 G3
Clochoderick Av KLBCH PA10 ..... 99 H7
Clochranhill Rd AYRS KA7 ..... 228 F7
Cloch Rd GRK PA19 ..... 30 F3
Cloch St STPS/GTHM/RID G33 ..... 107 G1
Clockerhill Pl MTHW ML1 ..... 134 E5
Clockston Pl GLSTN KA4 ..... 214 D4
Clockston Rd GLSTN KA4 ..... 214 D5
Cloister Av AIRDRIE ML6 ..... 111 J5
Clonbeith St
STPS/GTHM/RID G33 ..... 85 L7
Closeburn St PPK/MIL G22 ..... 83 J4
Cloth St BRHD/NEIL G78 ..... 125 J7
Clouden Rd CUMB G67 ..... 49 H7
Cloudhowe Ter
BLTYR/CAMB G72 ..... 131 J8
Clouston Ct MRYH/FIRH G20 ..... 4 A1
Clouston St MRYH/FIRH G20 ..... 82 D5
Clova Pl UD/BTH/TAN G71 ..... 131 M3
Clova St GIF/THBK G46 ..... 126 F5
Clove Mill Wynd LRKH ML9 ..... 175 L7
Cloverbank St SPRGB/BLRNK G21 ..... 6 F6
Clovergate BSHPBGS G64 ..... 63 M8
Cloverhill AYRS KA7 ..... 229 K3

Cloverhill Pl
 BAIL/MDB/MHD G69 .... 86 C1 🔢
Cloverhill Ter *EKILN* G74 .... 14 E3
Cloverhill Vw *EKILN* G74 .... 14 D3
Clover Leaf Pth *ALEX/LLW* G83 .... 25 L5
Cluanie Av *SHOTTS* ML7 .... 137 L3 🔢
Clune Brae *PGL* PA14 .... 34 E8
Clune Dr *PSTWK* KA9 .... 225 K1
Clune Park St *PGL* PA14 .... 34 E8 🔢
 WISHAW ML2 .... 159 M3
Clunie Pl *CTBR* ML5 .... 110 B6
 WISHAW ML2 .... 159 M3
Clunie Rd
 CARD/HILL/MSPK G52 .... 103 L5
Cluny Av *BSDN* G61 .... 62 A7
 CLYDBK G81 .... 60 C2
Cluny Dr *BSDN* G61 .... 62 A7
 NMRNS G77 .... 150 B4
 PSLYN/LNWD PA3 .... 102 A3
Cluny Gdns
 BAIL/MDB/MHD G69 .... 108 A5
 SCOT G14 .... 81 L5
Clutha Pl *EKILS* G75 .... 171 G2
Clutha St *GOV/IBX* G51 .... 104 D3 🔢
Clyde Av *BRHD/NEIL* G78 .... 125 K8
 BSHPBGS G64 .... 64 B1 🔢
 HMLTN ML3 .... 157 J8
 UD/BTH/TAN G71 .... 131 M8
Clydebrae Dr *UD/BTH/TAN* G71 ... 156 B1
Clydebrae St *GOV/IBX* G51 .... 104 B1
Clyde Crs *LNK/LMHG* ML11 .... 199 H4
Clyde Dr *BLSH* ML4 .... 133 J5
Clydeford Dr *CAR/SHTL* G32 ...... 106 E6
 UD/BTH/TAN G71 .... 131 K2
Clydeford Rd *BLTYR/CAMB* G72 ... 130 B3
 CAR/SHTL G32 .... 130 A1
Clydeholm Rd *SCOT* G14 .... 81 K7 🔢
Clydeholm Ter *CLYDBK* G81 .... 80 D2 🔢
Clydeneuk Dr *UD/BTH/TAN* G71 ... 131 K2
Clyde Pl *ARD* KA22 .... 191 K5 🔢
 BLTYR/CAMB G72 .... 130 D5
 GBLS G5 .... 10 F3
 JNSTN PA5 .... 122 C1 🔢
 KLMNK KA1 .... 212 A4 🔢
 MTHW ML1 .... 134 A5
 TROON KA10 .... 216 F4
Clyde Rd *GRK* PA19 .... 31 M3
 PSLYN/LNWD PA3 .... 102 A2
Clydesdale Av *HMLTN* ML3 .... 174 D3
 PSLYN/LNWD PA3 .... 80 A8
 WISHAW ML2 .... 158 D8 🔢
Clydesdale Pl *HMLTN* ML3 .... 174 D3 🔢
Clydesdale St *BLSH* ML4 .... 133 M5
 HMLTN ML3 .... 156 C5
 LRKH ML9 .... 176 A5 🔢
Clydesholm Ct *LNK/LMHG* ML11 .. 198 D5
Clydeshore Rd *DMBTN* G82 .... 36 E7
Clydeside Rd *RUTH* G73 .... 105 M7
Clydesmill Dr *CAR/SHTL* G32 ..... 130 A2
Clydesmill Gv *CAR/SHTL* G32 ..... 130 A2
Clydesmill Pl *CAR/SHTL* G32 ...... 130 A1
Clydesmill Rd *CAR/SHTL* G32 ..... 130 A1
Clyde St *CARLUKE* ML8 .... 178 E7
 CGLE G1 .... 11 H3
 CLYDBK G81 .... 80 C2
 CTBR ML5 .... 110 C2
 RNFRW PA4 .... 80 D4
Clyde St East *HBR/GL* G84 .... 22 E1
Clyde Ter *ARD* KA22 .... 191 K5
 MTHW ML1 .... 158 C7
 UD/BTH/TAN G71 .... 131 M8
Clydevale *UD/BTH/TAN* G71 ...... 132 B8 🔢
Clyde Valley Av *MTHW* ML1 ...... 157 L5
Clyde Vw *HMLTN* ML3 .... 156 B8
 PSLYS PA2 .... 102 B7
Clydeview *DMBTN* G82 .... 36 E7
 UD/BTH/TAN G71 .... 132 B8
Clyde View Av *SVSTN* KA20 ...... 192 C8
Clyde View Ct *OLDK* G60 .... 58 C1 🔢
Clydeview Gv *GRNK* PA15 .... 3 G9
 PGL PA14 .... 54 E1
Clydeview Ter *CAR/SHTL* G32 .... 130 C1 🔢
Clyde Wynd *GRNK* PA15 .... 2 A7
 GRNK PA15 .... 32 D6 🔢
Clynder Rd *GRNK* PA15 .... 33 J7
Clynder St *GOV/IBX* G51 .... 104 B3
Clyth Dr *GIF/THBK* G46 .... 127 K7
Coach Cl *KSYTH* G65 .... 48 A1
Coach Pl *KSYTH* G65 .... 47 L2
Coach Rd *KSYTH* G65 .... 47 M2
Coalburn Rd *UD/BTH/TAN* G71 ... 132 B4
Coalburn St *AIRDRIE* ML6 .... 69 M7
Coalhall Av *MTHW* ML1 .... 134 A8 🔢
 MTHW ML1 .... 134 B8 🔢
Coatbank St *CTBR* ML5 .... 110 B3 🔢
Coatbank Wy *CTBR* ML5 .... 110 B3
Coatbridge Rd *AIRDRIE* ML6 ...... 88 D6
 BAIL/MDB/MHD G69 .... 86 E7
 BAIL/MDB/MHD G69 .... 108 C4
 CTBR ML5 .... 87 M4
Coathill St *CTBR* ML5 .... 110 A5
Coats Crs *BAIL/MDB/MHD* G69 .... 108 A4
Coats Dr *PSLYS* PA2 .... 8 A7
Coatshill Av *BLTYR/CAMB* G72 ... 131 J8
Coats Pl *CRH/DND* KA2 .... 209 L2
 RAYR/DAL KA6 .... 231 H6 🔢
Coats St *CTBR* ML5 .... 110 B2
Cobbett Rd *MTHW* ML1 .... 157 H4
Cobbleton Rd *MTHW* ML1 .... 133 M7
Cobham St *GRNK* PA15 .... 33 L7
Cobington Pl
 STPS/GTHM/RID G33 .... 85 H8 🔢
Cobinshaw St *CAR/SHTL* G32 ..... 107 G3
Coburg St *GBLS* G5 .... 11 G5
Cochno Rd *CLYDBK* G81 .... 60 A1
Cochno St *CLYDBK* G81 .... 80 C1
Cochrane Av *CRH/DND* KA2 ...... 209 L2
Cochranemill Rd *JNSTN* PA5 ...... 99 J8
Cochrane Pl *HBR/GL* G84 .... 21 G7 🔢
 PSTWK KA9 .... 225 H1
Cochrane Pl East
 LARGS KA30 .... 115 J5 🔢
Cochrane Sq
 PSLYN/LNWD PA3 .... 100 B3 🔢
Cochrane St *BLSH* ML4 .... 132 F3
 BRHD/NEIL G78 .... 125 H7
 CGLE G1 .... 11 K1
 IRV KA12 .... 203 G7

 KBRN KA25 .... 143 G7
Cochran St *PSLY* PA1 .... 9 K4
Cockburn St *CTBR* ML5 .... 109 M5
Cockels Loan *RNFRW* PA4 .... 80 B8
Cockenzie St *CAR/SHTL* G32 ..... 107 G4
Cockhill Wy
 UD/BTH/TAN G71 .... 132 D3 🔢
Cockmuir St *SPRGB/BLRNK* G21 .. 84 A5
Coddington Crs *BLSH* ML4 .... 133 M2
Cogan Pl *BRHD/NEIL* G78 .... 125 H7 🔢
Cogan Rd *PLKSW/MSWD* G43 .... 127 J2 🔢
Cogan St *BRHD/NEIL* G78 .... 125 H7
 PLKSW/MSWD G43 .... 127 J2
Coila Av *PSTWK* KA9 .... 225 J3
Colbert St *DMNK/BRGTN* G40 .... 12 C9
Colbreggan Ct *CLYDBK* G81 ...... 60 C3 🔢
Colbreggan Gdns *CLYDBK* G81 ... 60 C3
Colchester Dr *KVD/HLHD* G12 .... 82 A3
Coldingham Av *KBRN* KA25 .... 143 G8
Coldingham Av *SCOT* G14 .... 80 E3
Coldstream Crs *WISHAW* ML2 .... 159 J4
Coldstream Dr *PSLYS* PA2 .... 101 G3 🔢
 RUTH G73 .... 129 K3
Coldstream Pl *COWCAD* G4 ...... 5 K3
Coldstream Rd *CLYDBK* G81 ...... 60 B8
Coldstream St
 BLTYR/CAMB G72 .... 155 K2 🔢
Colebrooke Pl *KVD/HLHD* G12 .... 4 B3
Colebrooke St
 BLTYR/CAMB G72 .... 130 A3 🔢
 KVD/HLHD G12 .... 4 B3
Colebrooke Ter *KVD/HLHD* G12 ... 4 B3 🔢
Coleburn Ct *IRVSE* KA11 .... 203 M3 🔢
Coleridge *EKILS* G75 .... 171 G2
Coleridge Av *UD/BTH/TAN* G71 ... 132 B7
Colfin St *ESTRH* G34 .... 86 C8
Colgrain St *MRYH/FIRH* G20 ...... 83 G3
Colgrave Crs *CAR/SHTL* G32 ..... 106 F6 🔢
Colinbar Cir *BRHD/NEIL* G78 ...... 125 H8
Colinslee Av *PSLYS* PA2 .... 101 M8
Colinslee Crs *PSLYS* PA2 .... 101 M8
Colinslee Dr *PSLYS* PA2 .... 101 M8
Colinslie Rd *PLK/PH/NH* G53 ..... 126 C1
Colintraive Av
 STPS/GTHM/RID G33 .... 84 E6
Colintraive Crs
 STPS/GTHM/RID G33 .... 84 E6
Coll *EKILN* G74 .... 172 C2
Collace Av *BRWEIR* PA11 .... 98 D2
Colla Gdns *BSHPBGS* G64 .... 64 D7
Coll Av *PGL* PA14 .... 55 H2
 RNFRW PA4 .... 80 D8
College La *CGLE* G1 .... 11 H2
College Pk *IRVSE* KA11 .... 216 E2 🔢
College St *CGLE* G1 .... 11 L2
 DMBTN G82 .... 36 F5 🔢
 GTCI KA28 .... 138 A6
College Wynd *KLMNK* KA1 .... 16 E4
Collenan Av *TROON* KA10 .... 217 G5
Collessie Dr
 STPS/GTHM/RID G33 .... 85 J7
Coll Gdns *IRVSE* KA11 .... 209 L1
Collier St *JNSTN* PA5 .... 99 M6
Colliertree Rd *AIRDRIE* ML6 .... 111 K1
Collina St *MRYH/FIRH* G20 .... 82 C3
Collingwood Pl *HBR/GL* G84 ...... 21 G7 🔢
Collins Dr *TROON* KA10 .... 217 G5
Collins Rd *HBR/GL* G84 .... 23 C1
Collins St *CLYDBK* G81 .... 60 C3
 COWCAD G4 .... 12 A1
Coll Pl *AIRDRIE* ML6 .... 111 J4
 SPRGB/BLRNK G21 .... 7 H4
Coll St *SPRGB/BLRNK* G21 .... 7 H4
 WISHAW ML2 .... 159 M3
Collylinn Rd *BSDN* G61 .... 61 L5
Colmonell Av *KNTSWD* G13 ...... 80 F2 🔢
Colonsay *EKILN* G74 .... 15 M8
Colonsay Av *PGL* PA14 .... 55 H2
 RNFRW PA4 .... 80 C8
Colonsay Dr *NMRNS* G77 .... 150 B4
Colonsay Pl *KLMNKN/STW* KA3 ... 207 H3
Colonsay Rd
 CARD/HILL/MSPK G52 .... 103 L4 🔢
 PSLYS PA2 .... 124 D2
Colquhoun *DMBTN* G82 .... 37 G5
Colquhoun Av
 CARD/HILL/MSPK G52 .... 103 G2
Colquhoun Dr *ALEX/LLW* G83 .... 25 L2
 BSDN G61 .... 61 K4
Colquhoun Rd *DMBTN* G82 ...... 37 L8
 KLMNKN/STW KA3 .... 207 J3
Colquhoun Sq *HBR/GL* G84 ...... 20 C8 🔢
Colquhoun St *DMBTN* G82 .... 37 G5
 HBR/GL G84 .... 20 D7
Colson Pl *BLSH* ML4 .... 133 J6 🔢
Colston Av *SPRGB/BLRNK* G21 ... 83 M2
Colston Dr *BSHPBGS* G64 .... 83 M2
Colston Gdns *BSHPBGS* G64 ..... 83 L2 🔢
Colston Pth
 SPRGB/BLRNK G21 .... 83 L2 🔢
Colston Pl *AIRDRIE* ML6 .... 111 J2 🔢
 SPRGB/BLRNK G21 .... 83 L2 🔢
Colston Rd *AIRDRIE* ML6 .... 111 J2
 PPK/MIL G22 .... 83 L2
 SPRGB/BLRNK G21 .... 83 M2
Colston Ter *AIRDRIE* ML6 .... 111 J2 🔢
Colt Av *CTBR* ML5 .... 87 L8
Coltmuir Crs *BSHPBGS* G64 ...... 83 L1 🔢
Coltmuir Dr *PPK/MIL* G22 .... 83 L1 🔢
Coltmuir Gdns *BSHPBGS* G64 .... 83 L1 🔢
Coltmuir St *PPK/MIL* G22 .... 83 K1
Coltness Av *SHOTTS* ML7 .... 160 F1
Coltness Dr *BLSH* ML4 .... 133 H5
Coltness La
 STPS/GTHM/RID G33 .... 107 J2
Coltness Rd *WISHAW* ML2 .... 159 J5
Coltness St
 STPS/GTHM/RID G33 .... 107 J1
Coltpark Av *BSHPBGS* G64 .... 83 L1
Coltpark La *BSHPBGS* G64 .... 83 M1 🔢
Colt Pl *CTBR* ML5 .... 110 A1
Coltsfoot Dr *PLK/PH/NH* G53 .... 126 B6
Coltswood Rd *CTBR* ML5 .... 88 A8
Colt Ter *CTBR* ML5 .... 110 A2
Columba Pth
 BLTYR/CAMB G72 .... 155 J1 🔢

Columba St *GOV/IBX* G51 .... 104 B2
 GRNKW/INVK PA16 .... 32 D5
 HBR/GL G84 .... 20 D7 🔢
Columbia Pl *EKILS* G75 .... 171 H1 🔢
Columbia Wy *EKILS* G75 .... 171 H1
Columbine Wy *CARLUKE* ML8 .... 188 F1
Colvend Dr *RUTH* G73 .... 129 H6 🔢
Colvend St *DMNK/BRGTN* G40 ... 105 M6
Colville Ct *MTHW* ML1 .... 134 C8 🔢
Colville Dr *RUTH* G73 .... 129 K3
Colvilles Pl *EKILS* G75 .... 15 L9
Colvilles Rd *EKILS* G75 .... 172 A4
Colwood Av
 PLK/PH/NH G53 .... 126 A6 🔢
Colwood Gdns
 PLK/PH/NH G53 .... 126 A6
Colwood Sq *PLK/PH/NH* G53 .... 126 A5 🔢
Colwyn Ct *AIRDRIE* ML6 .... 89 G8
Colzium Vw *KSYTH* G65 .... 47 L1
Combe Qd *BLSH* ML4 .... 132 E6 🔢
Comedie Rd
 STPS/GTHM/RID G33 .... 85 L5
Comely Bank *HMLTN* ML3 .... 155 M6
Comely Park La *DMBTN* G82 ..... 36 D5 🔢
Comelybank Rd *DMBTN* G82 ..... 36 D5 🔢
Comelypark St *DEN/PKHD* G31 ... 12 C4
Commerce St *GBLS* G5 .... 11 G5
Commercial Rd *BRHD/NEIL* G78 .. 125 J6
 GBLS G5 .... 11 K7
Commoncraig Pl
 GRNKW/INVK PA16 .... 50 C5
Common Gn *HMLTN* ML3 .... 156 E5 🔢
Commonhead Av *AIRDRIE* ML6 ... 88 F8
Commonhead La
 AIRDRIE ML6 .... 88 F8 🔢
Commonhead Rd *ESTRH* G34 .... 108 D1 🔢
 KLMNK KA1 .... 211 M6
Commonhead St *AIRDRIE* ML6 ... 88 F8
Commonside St *AIRDRIE* ML6 .... 88 F8
Commore Av *BRHD/NEIL* G78 .... 125 K8
Commore Dr *KNTSWD* G13 .... 81 G2
Community Av *BLSH* ML4 .... 133 G7 🔢
Community Pl *BLSH* ML4 .... 133 H6 🔢
Community Rd *BLSH* ML4 .... 132 F6 🔢
Comrie Crs *HMLTN* ML3 .... 155 K6
Comrie Rd
 STPS/GTHM/RID G33 .... 85 J4 🔢
Comrie St *CAR/SHTL* G32 .... 107 H6
Cona St *GIF/THBK* G46 .... 126 E5 🔢
Condor Gln *BLSH* ML4 .... 133 L2
Condorrat Ring Rd *CUMB* G67 ... 68 B3 🔢
Condorrat Rd *AIRDRIE* ML6 ...... 88 D2
 CUMB G67 .... 68 B4
Congress Rd *KVGV* G3 .... 104 D2
Congress Wy *KVGV* G3 .... 10 A1
Conifer Pl *KKNTL* G66 .... 65 H3
Conisborough Rd *ESTRH* G34 .... 85 M7
Coniston *EKILS* G75 .... 170 F4 🔢
Coniston Crs *HMLTN* ML3 .... 174 C3 🔢
Coniston Dr *BLSH* ML4 .... 133 H6
Conistone Crs
 BAIL/MDB/MHD G69 .... 107 M5
Connal St *DMNK/BRGTN* G40 .... 106 B3 🔢
Connell Crs *MLNGV* G62 .... 42 C8
Conniston St *CAR/SHTL* G32 ..... 106 E2 🔢
Connor Rd *BRHD/NEIL* G78 ...... 125 H6 🔢
Connor St *AIRDRIE* ML6 .... 89 L8
Conon Av *BSDN* G61 .... 61 K6
Conservation Pl
 WISHAW ML2 .... 159 J8 🔢
Consett La
 STPS/GTHM/RID G33 .... 107 J1 🔢
Constarry Rd *BALLOCH* G68 ...... 48 A6
 KSYTH G65 .... 47 L4
Container Wy *GRNK* PA15 .... 2 D5
Content Av *AYR* KA8 .... 19 H4
Content St *AYR* KA8 .... 19 G2
Contin Pl *MRYH/FIRH* G20 .... 82 D4
Coodham Pl *KLWNG* KA13 .... 193 K6 🔢
Cook Rd *ALEX/LLW* G83 .... 25 M1
Cook St *GBLS* G5 .... 10 F5
Coolgardie Pl *EKILS* G75 .... 14 B7
Cooperage Ct *KNTSWD* G13 ..... 80 B3 🔢
Co-operative Ter *JNSTN* PA5 ..... 100 A6 🔢
Cooper Av *CARLUKE* ML8 .... 178 E6 🔢
Copeland Crs *GTCI* KA28 .... 138 B6
Copenhagen Av *EKILS* G75 ...... 171 L3
Copland Pl *GOV/IBX* G51 .... 104 B3
Copland Qd *GOV/IBX* G51 .... 104 B3 🔢
Copland Rd *GOV/IBX* G51 .... 104 B4
Coplaw St *GVH/MTFL* G42 .... 105 G6
Copperfield La
 UD/BTH/TAN G71 .... 132 A2 🔢
Coralmount Gdns *KKNTL* G66 .... 65 L2 🔢
Coranbae Pl *AYRS* KA7 .... 228 B8
Corbett Ct *CAR/SHTL* G32 .... 106 F6 🔢
Corbett St *CAR/SHTL* G32 .... 107 G6
Corbie Pl *MLNGV* G62 .... 41 K7
Cordale Av *DMBTN* G82 .... 25 K7
Cordiner St *GOV/IBX* G51 .... 128 B2 🔢
Cordon Rd *KLMNKN/STW* KA3 ... 206 E1 🔢
Corkerhill Gdns
 CARD/HILL/MSPK G52 .... 103 L5 🔢
Corkerhill Pl
 CARD/HILL/MSPK G52 .... 103 K7
Corkerhill Rd
 CARD/HILL/MSPK G52 .... 103 K6
Corlaich Av *GVH/MTFL* G42 ...... 128 E2
Corlaich Dr *RUTH* G73 .... 128 E2
Corlic St *GRNK* PA15 .... 3 H9
Cormack Av *BSHPBGS* G64 ...... 44 C8
Cormorant Av
 CRG/CRSL/HOU PA6 .... 99 K1
Cornaig Rd *PLK/PH/NH* G53 ..... 126 B1
Cornalee Gdns *PLK/PH/NH* G53 .. 126 B1
Cornalee Pl *PLK/PH/NH* G53 ..... 126 B1
Cornalee Rd *PLK/PH/NH* G53 .... 126 B1
Cornelian Ter *BLSH* ML4 .... 133 G5 🔢
Cornelia St *MTHW* ML1 .... 133 H8
Cornhaddock St *GRNK* PA15 .... 32 D5
Cornhill Dr *CTBR* ML5 .... 109 L1
Cornhill St *SPRGB/BLRNK* G21 ... 84 A1 🔢
Cornock Crs *CLYDBK* G81 .... 60 B6 🔢
Cornock St *CLYDBK* G81 .... 60 B6
Cornsilloch Brae *LRKH* ML9 ...... 176 F6
Corn St *COWCAD* G4 .... 5 G5
Cornwall Av *RUTH* G73 .... 129 K4 🔢
Cornwall St *EKILN* G74 .... 14 E4

 GOV/IBX G51 .... 104 D4
Cornwall St South
 PLKSD/SHW G41 .... 104 D5
Coronation Pl
 BAIL/MDB/MHD G69 .... 86 E2
Coronation Rd *MTHW* ML1 .... 133 M5
Coronation St *PSTWK* KA9 .... 221 K4
 WISHAW ML2 .... 159 K6
Coronation Wy *BSDN* G61 .... 61 M7
Corpach Pl *ESTRH* G34 .... 86 D3 🔢
Corra Linn *HMLTN* ML3 .... 156 A6
Corran St *STPS/GTHM/RID* G33 .. 106 F1
Correen Gdns *BSDN* G61 .... 61 H2
Corrie Ct *HMLTN* ML3 .... 156 A8 🔢
Corrie Crs *KLMNKN/STW* KA3 ... 206 F6 🔢
 SALT KA21 .... 191 M7
Corrie Dr *MTHW* ML1 .... 157 H2 🔢
 PSLY PA1 .... 102 E5
Corrie Gdns *EKILS* G75 .... 171 H5
Corrie Gv *LNPK/KPK* G44 .... 127 M5
Corrie Pl *HBR/GL* G84 .... 20 F6 🔢
 KKNTL G66 .... 65 L5
 TROON KA10 .... 216 E2 🔢
Corrie Vw *BALLOCH* G68 .... 67 M1 🔢
Corrie Wy *LRKH* ML9 .... 176 F7
Corrour Rd *NMRNS* G77 .... 150 C3
 PLKSW/MSWD G43 .... 127 K2
Corsankell Wynd *SALT* KA21 ..... 191 L6
Corse Av *IRVSE* KA11 .... 204 F3 🔢
Corsebar Dr *PSLYS* PA2 .... 8 C9
Corsebar Crs *PSLYS* PA2 .... 101 J8 🔢
Corsebar La *PSLYS* PA2 .... 101 H8 🔢
Corsebar Rd *PSLYS* PA2 .... 101 H8 🔢
Corsebar Wy *PSLYS* PA2 .... 8 D6 🔢
Corse Dr *BRHD/NEIL* G78 .... 125 H5
Corsefield Rd *LOCHW* PA12 ...... 119 L7
Corseford Av *JNSTN* PA5 .... 122 C1
Corsehill Av *RAYR/DAL* KA6 ...... 231 L5
Corsehill Dr *WKIL* KA23 .... 181 J4
Corsehill Mount Rd *IRVSE* KA11 . 203 M8
Corsehill Pk *AYRS* KA7 .... 228 F4
 IRVSE KA11 .... 209 K1 🔢
Corsehill Pl *AYRS* KA7 .... 228 F4
 ESTRH G34 .... 108 C1
Corsehill St *ESTRH* G34 .... 108 C1 🔢
Corselet Rd *PLK/PH/NH* G53 ..... 126 A8
Corse Pl *CRH/DND* KA2 .... 210 F1 🔢
Corserine Bank *IRVSE* KA11 ...... 203 M6 🔢
Corserine Rd *AYRS* KA7 .... 228 F4
Corse Rd *CARD/HILL/MSPK* G52 . 102 E3
Corse St *WKIL* KA23 .... 181 J4
Corsewall Av *CAR/SHTL* G32 .... 107 L6 🔢
Corsewall St *CTBR* ML5 .... 109 L1
Corsford Dr *PLK/PH/NH* G53 ..... 126 C3
Corsliehill Rd
 CRG/CRSL/HOU PA6 .... 76 C2
Corsock Av *HMLTN* ML3 .... 155 L7
Corsock St *DEN/PKHD* G31 ...... 13 J1
Corston St *STPS/GTHM/RID* G33 . 7 L9
Cortachy Pl *BSHPBGS* G64 ...... 64 D8
Coruisk Dr
 CRMNK/CLK/EAG G76 .... 151 K1
Corunna Ct *CARLUKE* ML8 .... 179 H8
Corunna St *KVGV* G3 .... 4 A8
Cosy Neuk *LRKH* ML9 .... 176 C8
Cottar St *MRYH/FIRH* G20 .... 82 E2
Cotter Dr *KLMNKN/STW* KA3 .... 17 M5
Cotton Av *PSLYN/LNWD* PA3 .... 100 B3 🔢
Cotton St *DMNK/BRGTN* G40 ... 105 M7
 PSLY PA1 .... 9 J4
Cotton V *MTHW* ML1 .... 134 E8
Coulin Gdns *PPK/MIL* G22 .... 83 K5 🔢
Coulport Pl *HBR/GL* G84 .... 20 B7
Coulter Av *CTBR* ML5 .... 109 L1
 WISHAW ML2 .... 159 J2
Coulthard Dr *PSTWK* KA9 .... 225 K3
Countess St *SALT* KA21 .... 200 F2 🔢
County Av *BLTYR/CAMB* G72 .... 129 K2
County Dr *LNK/LMHG* ML11 ..... 199 J6 🔢
County Pl *PSLY* PA1 .... 9 H3
County Sq *PSLY* PA1 .... 9 H3
Couper St *COWCAD* G4 .... 5 L7
Coursington Crs *MTHW* ML1 ..... 158 A2 🔢
Coursington Gdns
 MTHW ML1 .... 157 M2 🔢
Coursington Pl *MTHW* ML1 ...... 157 M2 🔢
Coursington Rd *MTHW* ML1 ..... 157 M2 🔢
Courthill *BSDN* G61 .... 61 K3
Courthill Av *LNPK/KPK* G44 ..... 128 B4
Courthill Crs *KSYTH* G65 .... 47 L1
Courthill Pl *DALRY* KA24 .... 184 C1
Courthill St *DALRY* KA24 .... 184 C1
Courtrai Av *HBR/GL* G84 .... 20 B7
Court Rd *PGL* PA14 .... 34 C8
Court St *LARGS* KA30 .... 115 J5
Coustonholm Rd
 PLKSW/MSWD G43 .... 127 K2
Couther Qd *AIRDRIE* ML6 .... 89 G7
Covanburn Av *HMLTN* ML3 .... 156 F8
Cove Crs *SHOTTS* ML7 .... 137 L3
Covenant Crs *LRKH* ML9 .... 176 B7
Covenanters Ct *NMLNS* KA16 ... 215 J2 🔢
Covenant Pl *WISHAW* ML2 .... 158 C7 🔢
Coventry Dr *DEN/PKHD* G31 ..... 7 G8
Cove Pl *HBR/GL* G84 .... 20 B7 🔢
Cove Rd *GRK* PA19 .... 31 M2
Cowal Crs *GRK* PA19 .... 31 H1 🔢
 KKNTL G66 .... 46 B8
Cowal Dr *PSLYN/LNWD* PA3 ..... 100 A4
Cowal St *MRYH/FIRH* G20 .... 82 C2
Cowal Vw *GRK* PA19 .... 31 H1
Cowan Crs *AYR* KA8 .... 225 J6
 BRHD/NEIL G78 .... 125 K7
Cowan La *KVD/HLHD* G12 .... 4 B1
Cowan Rd *BALLOCH* G68 .... 48 B7
Cowan St *KVD/HLHD* G12 .... 4 B1
Cowan Wilson Av
 BLTYR/CAMB G72 .... 155 K1
Cowan Wynd *UD/BTH/TAN* G71 . 132 A1
 WISHAW ML2 .... 177 J2 🔢
Cowcaddens Rd *COWCAD* G4 ... 5 G7
Cowcaddens St *CGLW* G2 .... 5 H8

Cowdenhill Circ *KNTSWD* G13 .... 81 K1
Cowdenhill Pl *KNTSWD* G13 ..... 81 K1 🔢
Cowdenhill Rd *KNTSWD* G13 .... 81 K1
Cowden St *GOV/IBX* G51 .... 103 K2 🔢
Cowdray Crs *RNFRW* PA4 .... 80 D6 🔢
Cowgate *KKNTL* G66 .... 65 J1 🔢
Cowglen Rd *PLK/PH/NH* G53 .... 126 C2
Cowlairs Rd *SPRGB/BLRNK* G21 . 6 A1
Coxdale Av *KKNTL* G66 .... 65 H1
Coxhill St *COWCAD* G4 .... 5 L3
Coxton Pl *STPS/GTHM/RID* G33 . 85 K8
Coylebank *PSTWK* KA9 .... 225 J3
Coyle Pk *TROON* KA10 .... 216 E4
Coylton Crs *HMLTN* ML3 .... 155 L8 🔢
Coylton Rd *PLKSW/MSWD* G43 .. 127 M4
Crabb Qd *MTHW* ML1 .... 133 J8
Cragdale *EKILN* G74 .... 153 J6
Craggan Dr *KNTSWD* G13 .... 80 F3
Crags Av *PSLYS* PA2 .... 101 M8
Crags Crs *PSLYS* PA2 .... 9 K9
Crags Rd *PSLYS* PA2 .... 101 M8
Cragwell Pk
 CRMNK/CLK/EAG G76 .... 152 E2
Craigallian Av
 BLTYR/CAMB G72 .... 130 D6
 MLNGV G62 .... 42 A5
Craiganour La
 PLKSW/MSWD G43 .... 127 J3
Craigard Pl *RUTH* G73 .... 129 K6
Craigash Qd *MLNGV* G62 .... 41 L7
Craigash Rd *MLNGV* G62 .... 41 L7
Craig Av *ALEX/LLW* G83 .... 25 J2 🔢
 DALRY KA24 .... 184 A1
Craigbank Dr *PLK/PH/NH* G53 ... 126 A3
Craigbank St *LRKH* ML9 .... 176 A8
Craigbarnet Av *BSHPBGS* G64 ... 64 A1 🔢
Craigbarnet Crs
 STPS/GTHM/RID G33 .... 85 H5 🔢
Craigbarnet Rd *MLNGV* G62 ..... 41 K7
Craigbet Av *BRWEIR* PA11 .... 75 L7
Craigbet Crs *BRWEIR* PA11 ...... 75 L7 🔢
Craigbet Pl *BRWEIR* PA11 .... 75 L7 🔢
Craigbo Av *SMSTN* G23 .... 62 D8
Craigbog Av *JNSTN* PA5 .... 122 D1 🔢
Craigbo Rd *SMSTN* G23 .... 62 D8
Craigbo St *SMSTN* G23 .... 62 D8 🔢
Craigburn Av
 CRG/CRSL/HOU PA6 .... 99 K2
Craigburn Ct *LRKH* ML9 .... 176 F8 🔢
Craigburn Crs
 CRG/CRSL/HOU PA6 .... 99 K2 🔢
Craigburn Pl
 CRG/CRSL/HOU PA6 .... 99 K2 🔢
Craigburn St *HMLTN* ML3 .... 174 D1 🔢
Craigdene Dr *SVSTN* KA20 .... 192 D8
Craigdhu Av *AIRDRIE* ML6 .... 111 L2
 MLNGV G62 .... 41 M8
Craigdhu Rd *MLNGV* G62 .... 41 M8
 MLNGV G62 .... 42 A8 🔢
Craigdonald Pl *JNSTN* PA5 .... 99 M6 🔢
 JNSTN PA5 .... 99 M7 🔢
Craig Dr *CRH/DND* KA2 .... 205 L8
Craigellan Rd
 PLKSW/MSWD G43 .... 127 K3 🔢
Craigelvan Av *CUMB* G67 .... 67 M3 🔢
Craigelvan Ct *CUMB* G67 .... 67 M3 🔢
Craigelvan Dr *CUMB* G67 .... 67 M3 🔢
Craigelvan Gdns *CUMB* G67 ..... 67 M3 🔢
Craigelvan Gv *CUMB* G67 .... 67 M3 🔢
Craigelvan Pl *CUMB* G67 .... 67 M3 🔢
Craigelvan Vw *CUMB* G67 .... 67 M3 🔢
Craigenbay Crs *KKNTL* G66 ...... 65 L4
Craigenbay Rd *KKNTL* G66 .... 65 K5
Craigenbay St *SPRGB/BLRNK* G21 7 G1
Craigend Crs *MLNGV* G62 .... 41 M7
Craigend Dr *CTBR* ML5 .... 109 J5
Craigend Dr West *MLNGV* G62 .. 41 L7
Craigendmuir Rd
 STPS/GTHM/RID G33 .... 85 L5 🔢
Craigendmuir St
 STPS/GTHM/RID G33 .... 7 L5
Craigendon Ov *PSLYS* PA2 ...... 124 C3 🔢
Craigendon Rd *PSLYS* PA2 .... 124 C3 🔢
Craigendoran Av *HBR/GL* G84 ... 22 F1
Craigend Pl *KNTSWD* G13 .... 81 L3 🔢
Craigend Rd *CUMB* G67 .... 67 M4 🔢
 EKILS G75 .... 170 F8
 TROON KA10 .... 216 F8
Craigends Av *BRWEIR* PA11 ..... 75 L6
Craigends Dr *KLBCH* PA10 .... 99 G6
Craigends Pl *BRWEIR* PA11 ...... 75 L6
Craigends Rd
 CRG/CRSL/HOU PA6 .... 77 L7
 GLGNK KA14 .... 167 H3
Craigend St *KNTSWD* G13 .... 81 L3 🔢
Craigend Vw *CUMB* G67 .... 67 M4
Craigenfeoch Av *JNSTN* PA5 ..... 99 K8 🔢
Craigenlay Av *CMPF/LLE* G63 ... 27 J5
Craig-en-ros Rd *GTCI* KA28 ..... 138 B6
Craigens Rd *AIRDRIE* ML6 .... 112 A4
Craigfaulds Av *PSLYS* PA2 .... 8 B9
Craigfell Ct *HMLTN* ML3 .... 155 L7
Craigfern Dr *CMPF/LLE* G63 ..... 27 J5
Craigfin Ct *PSTWK* KA9 .... 225 K4
Craigflower Gdns
 PLK/PH/NH G53 .... 126 A5 🔢
Craigflower Rd
 PLK/PH/NH G53 .... 126 A5
Craighalbert Rd *BALLOCH* G68 ... 48 C6
Craighalbert Wy *BALLOCH* G68 .. 48 C5
Craighall Pl *AYRS* KA7 .... 229 G7
Craighall Qd *BRHD/NEIL* G78 .... 148 D3 🔢
Craighall Rd *COWCAD* G4 .... 5 H5
Craighaw St *CLYDBK* G81 .... 60 D1
Craighead Av
 STPS/GTHM/RID G33 .... 7 M3
Craighead Dr *MLNGV* G62 .... 41 K7
Craighead Rd *BSHPTN* PA7 ...... 58 B7
Craighead Wy *BRHD/NEIL* G78 .. 125 H7
Craig HI *EKILS* G75 .... 14 B8
Craighill Dr
 CRMNK/CLK/EAG G76 .... 151 K3
Craighill Gv
 CRMNK/CLK/EAG G76 .... 151 K3 🔢
Craighirst Dr *CLYDBK* G81 .... 60 A2

Craighirst Rd *MLNGV* G62 .... 41 K7
Craighlaw Av
   CRMNK/CLK/EAG G76 .... 151 K7
Craighlaw Dr
   CRMNK/CLK/EAG G76 .... 151 K7 🔢
Craigholm Rd *AYRS* KA7 .... 229 K2
Craighouse St
   STPS/GTHM/RID G33 .... 85 G8
Craighton Gdns *KKNTL* G66 .... 44 F1
Craighurst Rd *MLNGV* G62 .... 41 K7 🔢
Craigie Av *AYR* KA8 .... 19 H3
   KLMNK KA1 .... 211 M5
Craigiebar Dr *PSLYS* PA2 .... 124 C1 🔢
Craigieburn Gdns
   MRYH/FIRH G20 .... 82 B1
Craigieburn Rd *CUMB* G67 .... 48 F8
Craigie Dr *NMRNS* G77 .... 150 E6
Craigiehall Av *ERSK* PA8 .... 79 G2
Craigiehall Pl *GOV/IBX* G51 .... 104 D3
Craigiehall Wy *ERSK* PA8 .... 79 G2
Craigieknowes St *GRNK* PA15 .... 3 K8
Craigie Lea *AYR* KA8 .... 19 K4
Craigielea Crs *MLNGV* G62 .... 41 L7
Craigielea Dr *PSLYN/LNWD* PA3 .... 8 C1
Craigielea Rd *CLYDBK* G81 .... 59 M2
   RNFRW PA4 .... 80 C6
Craigielea St *DEN/PKHD* G31 .... 12 F1
Craigielinn Av *PSLYS* PA2 .... 124 B3
Craigie Pk *KKNTL* G66 .... 65 L4
Craigie Pl *CRH/DND* KA2 .... 210 F1
   GLSTN KA4 .... 214 B3 🔢
   KLMNK KA1 .... 211 M4
Craigie Rd *AYR* KA8 .... 19 J3
   KLMNK KA1 .... 211 M8
   KLMNK KA1 .... 212 F4
Craigie St *GVH/MTFL* G42 .... 105 G7
   PSTWK KA9 .... 225 H1
Craigievar Pl *NMRNS* G77 .... 150 B4 🔢
Craigievar St
   STPS/GTHM/RID G33 .... 85 L7 🔢
Craigie Wy *AYR* KA8 .... 19 J3
Craiglea Av *CRH/DND* KA2 .... 205 L8
Craiglea Pl *AIRDRIE* ML6 .... 111 J1 🔢
Craiglea Ter *AIRDRIE* ML6 .... 89 M6
Craiglee *EKILS* G75 .... 171 L5
Craigleith St *CAR/SHTL* G32 .... 106 E3 🔢
Craiglinn Park Rd *BALLOCH* G68 .... 48 A8
Craiglockhart St
   STPS/GTHM/RID G33 .... 85 K7 🔢
   STPS/GTHM/RID G33 .... 85 K8 🔢
Craiglomond Gdns
   ALEX/LLW G83 .... 25 K1 🔢
Craiglynn Gdns
   ALEX/LLW G83 .... 25 M1 🔢
Craigmaddie Gdns
   BSHPBGS G64 .... 64 A1 🔢
Craigmaddie Rd *MLNGV* G62 .... 42 F4
Craigmaddie Terrace La
   KVGV G3 .... 4 A7 🔢
Craigmarloch Av *BSHPBGS* G64 .... 64 B1
Craigmarloch Vw
   CMPF/LLE G63 .... 27 H5 🔢
Craigmillar Av *MLNGV* G62 .... 42 B7
Craigmillar Rd
   GVH/MTFL G42 .... 128 A2 🔢
Craigmochan Av *AIRDRIE* ML6 .... 88 F7 🔢
Craigmont Dr *MRYH/FIRH* G20 .... 82 E4
Craigmont St *MRYH/FIRH* G20 .... 82 E3
Craigmore Rd *BSDN* G61 .... 61 H2
Craigmore St *DEN/PKHD* G31 .... 13 J3
Craigmount Av *PSLYS* PA2 .... 124 C3
Craigmuir Crs
   CARD/HILL/MSPK G52 .... 102 F3
Craigmuir Gdns
   BLTYR/CAMB G72 .... 155 H3 🔢
Craigmuir Pl
   CARD/HILL/MSPK G52 .... 102 E3
Craigmuir Rd *BLTYR/CAMB* G72 ... 155 H3
   CARD/HILL/MSPK G52 .... 102 E3
Craigmuschat Rd *GRK* PA19 .... 31 L2 🔢
Craignaw Pl *IRVSE* KA11 .... 204 B6
Craigneil Dr *PSTWK* KA9 .... 225 J2 🔢
Craigneil St
   STPS/GTHM/RID G33 .... 85 L7 🔢
Craigneith Ct *EKILN* G74 .... 154 E5
Craignethan Rd
   CARLUKE ML8 .... 178 E5 🔢
   GIF/THBK G46 .... 151 G2
   WISHAW ML2 .... 158 C5
Craigneuk Av *AIRDRIE* ML6 .... 111 L2
Craigneuk St *MTHW* ML1 .... 158 B4
   WISHAW ML2 .... 158 C5
Craignure Av *AIRDRIE* ML6 .... 111 J2
Craignure Rd *RUTH* G73 .... 129 H6
Craigpark *DEN/PKHD* G31 .... 12 E1
Craigpark Av *PSTWK* KA9 .... 225 H5
Craigpark Dr *DEN/PKHD* G31 .... 12 E1
Craigpark St *CLYDBK* G81 .... 60 D2
Craigpark Wy
   UD/BTH/TAN G71 .... 132 A2 🔢
Craig Pl *NMRNS* G77 .... 150 B4 🔢
Craig Rd *BRHD/NEIL* G78 .... 148 D5
   LNPK/KPK G44 .... 128 A4
   PSLYN/LNWD PA3 .... 99 M2
   TROON KA10 .... 216 A6
Craigs Av *CLYDBK* G81 .... 60 C2
Craigsheen Av
   CRMNK/CLK/EAG G76 .... 152 D2
Craigshiel Pl *AYRS* KA7 .... 228 D5
Craigside Ct *BALLOCH* G68 .... 67 M2
Craigside Rd *BALLOCH* G68 .... 67 M2
Craigskeen Pl *PSTWK* KA9 .... 225 K4 🔢
Craigson Pl *AIRDRIE* ML6 .... 111 M3
Craigspark *ARD* KA22 .... 191 J6
Craigs Pl *SALT* KA21 .... 201 C1
Craigstewart Crs *AYRS* KA7 .... 228 C8
The Craigs *GRNKW/INVK* PA16 .... 32 C2
Craigston Av *AYRS* KA7 .... 19 M7
Craigstone Vw *KSYTH* G65 .... 47 M1
Craigston Rd *JNSTN* PA5 .... 99 J7
Craig St *AIRDRIE* ML6 .... 110 F2
   BLTYR/CAMB G72 .... 155 L2
   CTBR ML5 .... 109 M5
   GTCI KA28 .... 138 B6 🔢
Craigton Av *BRHD/NEIL* G78 .... 125 L8 🔢

   MLNGV G62 .... 41 M7
Craigton Crs *NMRNS* G77 .... 150 B4
Craigton Dr *BRHD/NEIL* G78 .... 125 L8
   GOV/IBX G51 .... 103 L3
   NMRNS G77 .... 150 C4
Craigton Gdns *MLNGV* G62 .... 41 M6
Craigton Pl *BLTYR/CAMB* G72 ... 131 K8
   GOV/IBX G51 .... 103 L3 🔢
Craigton Rd *GOV/IBX* G51 .... 103 M2
   KBRN KA25 .... 167 H1
   MLNGV G62 .... 41 L6
   NMRNS G77 .... 149 H6
Craigton St *CLYDBK* G81 .... 60 D1
Craigvale Crs *AIRDRIE* ML6 .... 111 J2
Craigvicar Gdns
   CAR/SHTL G32 .... 107 K5 🔢
Craig Vw *IRVSE* KA11 .... 204 F7
Craigview *RAYR/DAL* KA6 .... 231 L5
Craigview Av *JNSTN* PA5 .... 122 C1 🔢
Craigview Rd *MTHW* ML1 .... 157 L1 🔢
   NMLNS KA16 .... 215 K2 🔢
Craigview Ter *JNSTN* PA5 .... 99 K8 🔢
Craigwell Rd *AYRS* KA7 .... 18 C7
Craigwell Av *RUTH* G73 .... 129 K3
Craiksland Pl *TROON* KA10 .... 217 G5
Crail St *DEN/PKHD* G31 .... 13 M6
Crammond Av *CTBR* ML5 .... 109 J5
Cramond Av *RNFRW* PA4 .... 80 E7
Cramond Pl *IRVSE* KA11 .... 203 M7
Cramond St *GBLS* G5 .... 105 K7
Cramond Ter *CAR/SHTL* G32 .... 107 H4 🔢
Cramond Wy *IRVSE* KA11 .... 203 M7
Cranberry Moss Rd
   KLWNG KA13 .... 193 K6
Cranberry Rd *KLWNG* KA13 .... 193 H7
Cranborne Rd *KVD/HLHD* G12 .... 82 A3
Cranbrooke Dr *MRYH/FIRH* G20 ... 82 D2
Crandleyhill Rd *PSTWK* KA9 .... 225 H3
Crannog Rd *DMBTN* G82 .... 37 L8
Crannog Wy *KLWNG* KA13 .... 193 J5
Cranston St *KVGV* G3 .... 10 C1 🔢
Cranworth La *KVD/HLHD* G12 .... 82 D6
Cranworth St *KVD/HLHD* G12 .... 82 D6
Crarae Av *BSDN* G61 .... 61 M7
Crarea Pl *NMRNS* G77 .... 150 B4 🔢
Crathes Av *LNPK/KPK* G44 .... 127 L5 🔢
Crathie Dr *AIRDRIE* ML6 .... 88 F5
   ARD KA22 .... 191 J3
   PTCK C11 .... 82 A7
Crathie Pl *NMRNS* G77 .... 151 H5 🔢
Crathie Qd *WISHAW* ML2 .... 159 H4
Crathie Rd *KLMNKN/STW* KA3 ... 206 E7
Craufurd Av *WKIL* KA23 .... 181 L5
Craufurd Crs *BEITH* KA15 .... 168 C5
Craufurdland Rd
   KLMNKN/STW KA3 .... 207 G4
Craven Gv *IRV* KA12 .... 203 L4
Crawberry Rd *GRNK* PA15 .... 2 F9
Crawford Av *KKNTL* G66 .... 65 L6
   PSTWK KA9 .... 225 J3
Crawford Crs
   BLTYR/CAMB G72 .... 131 K8 🔢
   UD/BTH/TAN G71 .... 131 L2 🔢
Crawford Dr *DRUM* G15 .... 61 G8
   EKILN G74 .... 15 M1
   HBR/GL G84 .... 20 E6
Crawford Gdns *MTHW* ML1 .... 157 J4 🔢
Crawford Hl *EKILN* G74 .... 15 M1 🔢
Crawford Rd
   CRG/CRSL/HOU PA6 .... 77 K8
   MLNGV G62 .... 41 M5
Crawford St *HMLTN* ML3 .... 156 A4 🔢
   LARGS KA30 .... 115 J6
   MTHW ML1 .... 157 K3
   PGL PA14 .... 34 C7 🔢
   PTCK C11 .... 82 A7 🔢
   PTCK C11 .... 82 A8 🔢
Crawfurd Av *RUTH* G73 .... 129 H4
Crawfurd Dr *PSLYN/LNWD* PA3 ... 8 A1
Crawfurd Gdns *RUTH* G73 .... 129 J5
Crawfurdland Rd *CRH/DND* KA2 ... 205 K8
Crawfurd Rd *RUTH* G73 .... 129 H5
Crawfurd St *GRNKW/INVK* PA16 ... 2 C1
Crawfurds Vw *LOCHW* PA12 .... 120 D6
Crawhin Gdns
   GRNKW/INVK PA16 .... 32 D6 🔢
Craw Pl *LOCHW* PA12 .... 120 C7
Crawriggs Av *KKNTL* G66 .... 65 K3
Craw Rd *PSLYS* PA2 .... 8 D6
Creamery Rd *WISHAW* ML2 .... 159 J8
Crebar Dr *BRHD/NEIL* G78 .... 125 J7
Crebar St *GIF/THBK* G46 .... 126 E5
Credon Dr *AIRDRIE* ML6 .... 111 G4
   CRH/DND KA2 .... 210 F1
Credon Gdns *RUTH* G73 .... 129 J5
Cree Av *BSHPBGS* G64 .... 64 D8
Creebank Pl *TROON* KA10 .... 216 E3
Cree Gdns *CAR/SHTL* G32 .... 106 F4
Cree Pl *EKILS* G75 .... 153 H8
Creighton Gv *EKILN* G74 .... 14 F3
Creighton Ct *KLMNKN/STW* KA3 ... 207 G4
Creran Ct *HMLTN* ML3 .... 156 A8
   PSTWK KA9 .... 225 J4 🔢
Creran Dr *RNFRW* PA4 .... 80 B5
Crescent Rd *SCOT* G14 .... 81 H4
Crescent St *GRNK* PA15 .... 3 G6
The Crescent *CLYDBK* G81 .... 59 L6
   CRMNK/CLK/EAG G76 .... 152 A4
   SKLM PA17 .... 70 B5
Cresswell Gv *NMRNS* G77 .... 150 D6
Cresswell La *KVD/HLHD* G12 .... 82 D6 🔢
Cresswell Pl *NMRNS* G77 .... 150 E7
Cresswell St *KVD/HLHD* G12 .... 82 D6 🔢
Cressy St *GOV/IBX* G51 .... 103 L1
Crest Av *KNTSWD* G13 .... 81 H1
Crestlea Av *PSLYS* PA2 .... 124 E1
Creveul Ct *ALEX/LLW* G83 .... 25 L4 🔢
Crichton Av *DALRY* KA24 .... 184 A1
Crichton St *CTBR* ML5 .... 110 A1
   SPRGB/BLRNK G21 .... 6 A1
Cricketfield La
   CRG/CRSL/HOU PA6 .... 77 H6 🔢
Crieff Av *AIRDRIE* ML6 .... 111 K8
Criffell Gdns *CAR/SHTL* G32 ... 107 K6 🔢
Criffell Rd *CAR/SHTL* G32 .... 107 K5
Criffel Pl *KLMNK* KA1 .... 212 A5
Crighton Wynd
   UD/BTH/TAN G71 .... 132 D4 🔢

Crimea St *CGLW* G2 .... 10 E2
Crinan Crs *CTBR* ML5 .... 87 K8
Crinan Gdns *BSHPBGS* G64 .... 64 C8
Crinan Pl *ARD* KA22 .... 191 J4
   BLSH ML4 .... 133 H3 🔢
Crinan St *DEN/PKHD* G31 .... 7 G8
Crindledyke Crs *WISHAW* ML2 ... 160 A3
Cripps Av *CLYDBK* G81 .... 60 D8
Crisswell Cl *GRNKW/INVK* PA16 ... 31 J7 🔢
Croe Pl *KLMNK* KA1 .... 212 A5
Croftbank Av *UD/BTH/TAN* G71 .. 132 B8
Croftbank Crs
   UD/BTH/TAN G71 .... 131 M3
   UD/BTH/TAN G71 .... 132 B8 🔢
Croftbank Ga *UD/BTH/TAN* G71 .. 132 B8
Croftbank St *SPRGB/BLRNK* G21 ... 6 D1
   SPRGB/BLRNK G21 .... 83 M5 🔢
Croftburn Dr *LNPK/KPK* G44 .... 128 A5
Croftcot Av *BLSH* ML4 .... 132 F6
Croftcroighn Rd
   STPS/GTHM/RID G33 .... 85 H8
Croftend Av *LNPK/KPK* G44 .... 128 E3
Croftend La *RUTH* G73 .... 128 F4 🔢
Croftfoot Crs *CSMK* G45 .... 129 G5 🔢
Croftfoot Dr *CSMK* G45 .... 128 F5
Croftfoot Pl
   BAIL/MDB/MHD G69 .... 87 G3 🔢
Croftfoot Qd *CSMK* G45 .... 128 D5
Croftfoot Rd *CSMK* G45 .... 128 D5
   LNPK/KPK G44 .... 128 D5
Croftfoot St *CSMK* G45 .... 129 G5 🔢
Croftfoot Ter *CSMK* G45 .... 128 F5
Crofthead Av
   KLMNKN/STW KA3 .... 207 G4
Crofthead Dr *KKNTL* G66 .... 29 J8 🔢
Crofthead Pl *BLSH* ML4 .... 132 F6 🔢
   NMRNS G77 .... 150 E6
Crofthead Rd *AYRS* KA7 .... 19 M9
   KLMNKN/STW KA3 .... 206 B2
   PSTWK KA9 .... 221 J8
Crofthead St *UD/BTH/TAN* G71 ... 131 M4
Crofthill Av *UD/BTH/TAN* G71 ... 131 M3
Crofthill Rd *LNPK/KPK* G44 .... 128 E5 🔢
Crofthouse Dr
   LNPK/KPK G44 .... 128 E5 🔢
Croftmont Av *LNPK/KPK* G44 ... 128 E5
Croftmoraig Av
   BAIL/MDB/MHD G69 .... 67 G5
Crofton Av *LNPK/KPK* G44 .... 128 D5
Croftpark Av *LNPK/KPK* G44 .... 128 E4
Croftpark Crs *BLTYR/CAMB* G72 ... 155 L3
Croftpark Rd *CLYDBK* G81 .... 60 D2
Croftpark Rd *BLSH* ML4 .... 133 G3
Croft Pl *LRKH* ML9 .... 175 M6
Croft Rd *BLTYR/CAMB* G72 .... 130 B4
   EKILS G75 .... 14 E7
   LRKH ML9 .... 175 M6
Croftside Av *LNPK/KPK* G44 .... 128 E5
Croftspar Av *CAR/SHTL* G32 .... 107 K3
Croftspar Dr *CAR/SHTL* G32 .... 107 J3
Croftspar Gv *CAR/SHTL* G32 .... 107 K3
Croftspar Pl *CAR/SHTL* G32 .... 107 J3
Croft St *ALEX/LLW* G83 .... 25 M6
   KLMNK KA1 .... 16 F3
   MAUCH/CAT KA5 .... 223 M5
Croft Ter *IRVSE* KA11 .... 204 F7
Croft Wy *RNFRW* PA4 .... 80 D8
Croftwood Av *LNPK/KPK* G44 .. 128 D5
Croftwood Rd *HMLTN* ML3 .... 156 D8 🔢
Croft Wynd
   UD/BTH/TAN G71 .... 132 A3 🔢
Crogal Crs *AIRDRIE* ML6 .... 111 K7
Cromalt Av *EKILS* G75 .... 171 K6
Cromalt Crs *BSDN* G61 .... 61 J1
Cromarty Av *BSHPBGS* G64 .... 64 D7
   PLKSW/MSWD G43 .... 127 M2
Cromarty Crs *BSDN* G61 .... 61 M2
Cromarty Gdns
   CRMNK/CLK/EAG G76 .... 128 A8
Cromarty Pl
   BAIL/MDB/MHD G69 .... 66 D8 🔢
   EKILN G74 .... 154 C6 🔢
Cromarty Rd *AIRDRIE* ML6 .... 110 F5
Crombie Gdns
   BAIL/MDB/MHD G69 .... 107 M6 🔢
Cromdale Rd *KLMNK* KA1 .... 212 A5
   PGL PA14 .... 54 F3
Cromdale St *GOV/IBX* G51 .... 103 L3
Cromdale Wy *MTHW* ML1 .... 134 A7 🔢
Cromer St *MRYH/FIRH* G20 .... 82 F4
Crompton Av *LNPK/KPK* G44 ... 128 B4
Crompton Wy *IRV* KA12 .... 203 L5
Cromwell La *COWCAD* G4 .... 4 E5 🔢
Cromwell Rd *AYRS* KA7 .... 18 C2
Cromwell St *COWCAD* G4 .... 4 E5
Crona Dr *HMLTN* ML3 .... 155 L5
Cronberry Qd
   CARD/HILL/MSPK G52 .... 102 F6
Cronberry Ter
   CARD/HILL/MSPK G52 .... 102 F6 🔢
Cronin Pl *BLSH* ML4 .... 133 H2
Cronulla Pl *KSYTH* G65 .... 47 M1
Crookedshields Rd *EKILN* G74 ... 154 D2 🔢
Crookfur Rd *NMRNS* G77 .... 150 D4 🔢
Crookhill Dr *LOCHW* PA12 .... 120 C6 🔢
Crookhill Gdns *LOCHW* PA12 .. 120 C6 🔢
Crookston Av
   CARD/HILL/MSPK G52 .... 103 G5
Crookston Ct
   CARD/HILL/MSPK G52 .... 103 G5 🔢
Crookston Dr
   CARD/HILL/MSPK G52 .... 102 F5
   PSLY PA1 .... 102 F5
Crookston Gdns
   CARD/HILL/MSPK G52 .... 102 F5 🔢
Crookston Gv
   CARD/HILL/MSPK G52 .... 103 G5 🔢
Crookston Pl
   CARD/HILL/MSPK G52 .... 102 F5 🔢
Crookston Qd
   CARD/HILL/MSPK G52 .... 102 F5
Crookston Rd
   CARD/HILL/MSPK G52 .... 102 F7
   PLK/PH/NH G53 .... 102 F7
Crookston Ter
   CARD/HILL/MSPK G52 .... 103 G5 🔢

Crosbie Ct *TROON* KA10 .... 220 D1
Crosbie Dr *PSLYS* PA2 .... 123 L2
   WKIL KA23 .... 181 K5 🔢
Crosbie La *MRYH/FIRH* G20 .... 82 C1
Crosbie Pl *TROON* KA10 .... 220 D2
Crosbie Rd *TROON* KA10 .... 220 D1
Crosbie St *MRYH/FIRH* G20 .... 82 C1
Crosbie Wd *PSLYS* PA2 .... 101 H8
Cross *BEITH* KA15 .... 168 B3 🔢
Cross Arthurlie Stree
   BRHD/NEIL G78 .... 125 H6
Crossbank Av *GVH/MTFL* G42 ... 105 L8
Crossbank Dr *GVH/MTFL* G42 ... 105 K8 🔢
Crossbank Rd
   GVH/MTFL G42 .... 105 K8 🔢
Crossbank Ter *GVH/MTFL* G42 ... 105 K8
Crossburn *AYRS* KA7 .... 228 B8
Crossburn Av *MLNGV* G62 .... 41 M8
Crossburn Ter *TROON* KA10 .... 217 H5
Crossclyde Vw *CARLUKE* ML8 ... 188 C8
Crossdene Rd *CRH/DND* KA2 ... 210 F1
Crossdykes *KKNTL* G66 .... 66 A2
Crossflat Crs *PSLY* PA1 .... 9 L3
Crossford Dr *SMSTN* G23 .... 62 E8 🔢
Cross Gates *BLSH* ML4 .... 133 H5
Crossgates St *LRKH* ML9 .... 175 M5
Crosshill Av *GVH/MTFL* G42 ... 105 H8 🔢
   KKNTL G66 .... 65 K3
Crosshill Dr *MTHW* ML1 .... 135 H6
   RUTH G73 .... 129 H3
Crosshill Pl *PGL* PA14 .... 54 F2 🔢
Crosshill Rd *BSHPBGS* G64 .... 64 C4
   KKNTL G66 .... 65 J6
   PGL PA14 .... 54 F2
Crosshill St *AIRDRIE* ML6 .... 110 F2
   CTBR ML5 .... 109 J5 🔢
   KKNTL G66 .... 29 K8 🔢
   MTHW ML1 .... 157 M3
Crosshill Wynd
   KLMNKN/STW KA3 .... 207 J3 🔢
Crosshouse Rd *EKILS* G75 .... 170 F4
   KKNTL G66 .... 29 G5
   KLMNKN/STW KA3 .... 206 B4
Crosslaw Av *LNK/LMHG* ML11 ... 199 J6
Crosslea Gdns
   CRG/CRSL/HOU PA6 .... 77 H8
Crosslee Crs
   CRG/CRSL/HOU PA6 .... 77 J8 🔢
Crosslee Pk *CRG/CRSL/HOU* PA6 ... 77 J8
Crosslee Rd *BRWEIR* PA11 .... 99 G3
   JNSTN PA5 .... 98 F3
Crosslees Dr *GIF/THBK* G46 .... 126 F6
Crosslees Pk *GIF/THBK* G46 .... 126 F6
Crosslees Rd *GIF/THBK* G46 .... 126 F7
Crosslee St
   CARD/HILL/MSPK G52 .... 103 K4
Crosslet Ct *DMBTN* G82 .... 37 H6 🔢
Crosslet Pl *DMBTN* G82 .... 37 H6
Crosslet Rd *DMBTN* G82 .... 37 G6
Crossloan Rd *GOV/IBX* G51 .... 103 M2
Crossloan Ter *GOV/IBX* G51 .... 103 M2
Crossmill Av *BRHD/NEIL* G78 ... 125 K5
Crosspoint Dr *SMSTN* G23 .... 62 E8 🔢
Cross Rd *PSLYS* PA2 .... 8 B8
Cross Stone Pl *MTHW* ML1 .... 157 M3 🔢
Cross St *CAR/SHTL* G32 .... 107 J8 🔢
   PSLY PA1 .... 8 D4
The Cross *DALRY* KA24 .... 184 C2 🔢
Crosstobs Rd *PLK/PH/NH* G53 ... 103 L8
Crossveggate *MLNGV* G62 .... 42 B8 🔢
Crossview Av
   BAIL/MDB/MHD G69 .... 108 D4 🔢
Crossview Pl
   BAIL/MDB/MHD G69 .... 108 D4
Crossways *CRG/CRSL/HOU* PA6 ... 77 K7
Crovie Rd *PLK/PH/NH* G53 .... 126 A2 🔢
Crow Av *MTHW* ML1 .... 134 B4
Crowflats Rd
   UD/BTH/TAN G71 .... 131 L3 🔢
Crowflat Vw
   UD/BTH/TAN G71 .... 109 J8 🔢
Crowhill Crs *AIRDRIE* ML6 .... 88 F7
Crowhill Rd *BSHPBGS* G64 .... 83 M1
Crowhill St *PPK/MIL* G22 .... 83 J3
Crow La *KNTSWD* G13 .... 81 M4 🔢
Crowlin Crs
   STPS/GTHM/RID G33 .... 107 H1
Crown Av *CLYDBK* G81 .... 60 A6
Crown Circ *KVD/HLHD* G12 .... 82 C6 🔢
Crown Gdns *KVD/HLHD* G12 .. 82 C6 🔢
Crownhall Pl *CAR/SHTL* G32 .... 107 J4
Crownhall Rd *CAR/SHTL* G32 ... 107 J4
Crownpoint Rd
   DMNK/BRGTN G40 .... 12 F5 🔢
Crown Rd North
   KVD/HLHD G12 .... 82 C6 🔢
Crown Rd South *KVD/HLHD* G12 ... 82 C6
Crown St *AIRDRIE* ML6 .... 111 H6
   AYR KA8 .... 224 F7
   BAIL/MDB/MHD G69 .... 107 M6 🔢
   CTBR ML5 .... 110 C2
   GBLS G5 .... 11 J7
   GRNK PA15 .... 2 D4 🔢
Crown Ter *KVD/HLHD* G12 .... 82 B6
Crow-Wood Crs *AIRDRIE* ML6 .. 111 H7
Crowwood Dr *AIRDRIE* ML6 .... 111 K4
Crow-Wood Rd *AIRDRIE* ML6 ... 111 H7
Crow Wood Rd
   BAIL/MDB/MHD G69 .... 86 B2
Crow Wood Ter
   BAIL/MDB/MHD G69 .... 86 B2 🔢
Croy *EKILN* G74 .... 153 K6 🔢
Croy Av *NMRNS* G77 .... 151 G4
Croy Pl *SPRGB/BLRNK* G21 .... 84 C4
Croy Rd *CTBR* ML5 .... 109 L5
   SPRGB/BLRNK G21 .... 84 C4
Cruachan Av *PSLYS* PA2 .... 124 C1
   RNFRW PA4 .... 80 C8
Cruachan Dr *BRHD/NEIL* G78 ... 148 A1
   NMRNS G77 .... 150 F6
Cruachan Pl *KLMNK* KA1 .... 212 B5 🔢
Cruachan Rd *BSDN* G61 .... 61 H2
   RUTH G73 .... 129 K6

Cruachan St *GIF/THBK* G46 .... 126 F5
Cruachan Wy *BRHD/NEIL* G78 ... 125 J8
Crum Av *GIF/THBK* G46 .... 127 G6
Crummock Gdns *BEITH* KA15 ... 144 C8
Crummock St *BEITH* KA15 .... 144 C8
Crusader Av *KNTSWD* G13 .... 61 K8
Crusader Crs *KLMNKN/STW* KA3... 197 J1
Cubie St *DMNK/BRGTN* G40 .... 12 D5
Cubrieshaw Dr *WKIL* KA23 .... 181 K5 🔢
Cubrieshaw St *WKIL* KA23 .... 181 K3
Cuckoo Wy *MTHW* ML1 .... 134 B4
Cuff Crs *BEITH* KA15 .... 168 A2
Cuilhill Rd *BAIL/MDB/MHD* G69 ... 109 G3
   CTBR ML5 .... 108 F1
Cuillin Pl *IRVSE* KA11 .... 204 A5
   KLMNK KA1 .... 212 A6
Cuillins Av *PGL* PA14 .... 54 F3
The Cuillins *BAIL/MDB/MHD* G69 ... 67 C1
   UD/BTH/TAN G71 .... 108 E8
Cuillin Wy *BRHD/NEIL* G78 .... 125 J7
Cuilmuir Ter *KSYTH* G65 .... 47 M4
Cuilmuir Vw *KSYTH* G65 .... 47 L4
Cuilt Pl *CMPF/LLE* G63 .... 27 G5 🔢
Cuilts Rd *CMPF/LLE* G63 .... 26 A5
Culbin Dr *KNTSWD* G13 .... 80 F1
Cullen La *EKILS* G75 .... 14 D7
Cullen Pl *UD/BTH/TAN* G71 ... 132 A1 🔢
Cullen Rd *EKILS* G75 .... 14 D7
   MTHW ML1 .... 157 J4
Cullen St *ALEX/LLW* G83 .... 25 J2 🔢
   CAR/SHTL G32 .... 107 G5
Cullins Rd *RUTH* G73 .... 129 K6
Cullion Wy *MTHW* ML1 .... 134 F4
Cullochrig Rd *AIRDRIE* ML6 .... 68 C7
Culloch Rd *BSDN* G61 .... 61 J1
Culloden Pl *KLMNKN/STW* KA3 ... 207 H6
Culloden St *DEN/PKHD* G31 .... 7 G8
Culrain Gdns *CAR/SHTL* G32 ... 107 G4 🔢
Culrain St *CAR/SHTL* G32 .... 107 G4
Culross Hl *EKILN* G74 .... 14 C3
Culross Pl *CTBR* ML5 .... 109 M2
   EKILN G74 .... 14 C3
Culross St *CAR/SHTL* G32 .... 107 J5
Culross Wy
   BAIL/MDB/MHD G69 .... 67 G6 🔢
Cult Rd *KKNTL* G66 .... 65 L5 🔢
Cults St *GOV/IBX* G51 .... 103 M3
Culvain Av *BSDN* G61 .... 61 H1
Culzean *AIRDRIE* ML6 .... 88 F4
Culzean Av *CTBR* ML5 .... 109 L5
   PSTWK KA9 .... 225 K2
Culzean Crs
   BAIL/MDB/MHD G69 .... 108 A5 🔢
   KLMNKN/STW KA3 .... 17 K4
   NMRNS G77 .... 150 F5
Culzean Dr *CAR/SHTL* G32 .... 107 K5 🔢
   GRK PA19 .... 30 F4 🔢
   MTHW ML1 .... 134 C6
Culzean Pl *EKILN* G74 .... 153 K6
   KLWNG KA13 .... 193 J5
Culzean Rd *AYRS* KA7 .... 228 D6
Cumberland Av *HBR/GL* G84 .. 20 A6
Cumberland Pl *CTBR* ML5 .... 109 J5
   GBLS G5 .... 11 K8 🔢
Cumberland Rd
   GRNKW/INVK PA16 .... 31 L5
Cumberland St *GBLS* G5 .... 11 J7 🔢
Cumbernauld Rd
   BAIL/MDB/MHD G69 .... 67 G7
   BAIL/MDB/MHD G69 .... 86 D1
   CUMB G67 .... 67 K5
   DEN/PKHD G31 .... 13 G2
   DMNK/BRGTN G40 .... 12 E8
   STPS/GTHM/RID G33 .... 7 L9
Cumbrae *EKILN* G74 .... 154 C8
Cumbrae Av *PGL* PA14 .... 55 H2
Cumbrae Ct *CLYDBK* G81 .... 60 B7 🔢
Cumbrae Crs *CTBR* ML5 .... 110 E4
Cumbrae Crs North
   DMBTN G82 .... 36 C4 🔢
Cumbrae Crs South *DMBTN* G82 ... 36 B4
Cumbrae Dr *GTCI* KA28 .... 138 C6
   KLMNKN/STW KA3 .... 207 H3
   MTHW ML1 .... 157 J2
Cumbrae Pl *AIRDRIE* ML6 .... 110 E5 🔢
   GRK PA19 .... 31 K3 🔢
   WKIL KA23 .... 181 J5
Cumbrae Rd *PSLYS* PA2 .... 124 E2
   RNFRW PA4 .... 80 D8 🔢
   SALT KA21 .... 191 M7
Cumbrae St
   STPS/GTHM/RID G33 .... 107 G1
Cumlodden Dr *MRYH/FIRH* G20 ... 82 C1
Cumming Dr *GVH/MTFL* G42 ... 128 B1
Cumnock Dr *AIRDRIE* ML6 .... 111 G5 🔢
   BRHD/NEIL G78 .... 125 J8
   HMLTN ML3 .... 155 K8 🔢
Cumnock Rd
   STPS/GTHM/RID G33 .... 84 C5 🔢
Cumroch Rd *KKNTL* G66 .... 29 J8
Cunard St *CLYDBK* G81 .... 80 B1
Cuningair Dr *MTHW* ML1 .... 157 J1
Cuningham Crs *AYRS* KA7 .... 19 K8
Cuningham Dr *GIF/THBK* G46 .. 127 L6
   LARGS KA30 .... 115 K7
Cuninghame Dr *KLMNK* KA1 .. 211 L5
Cuninghame Rd *EKILN* G74 .... 14 E2
   IRV KA12 .... 203 L5 🔢
   PSTWK KA9 .... 225 J2 🔢
   RUTH G73 .... 129 J1
   SALT KA21 .... 201 C1
Cunningham Rd
   CARD/HILL/MSPK G52 .... 102 F1 🔢
Cunningham St
   MAUCH/CAT KA5 .... 223 M6
   MTHW ML1 .... 157 J3
Cunning Park Dr *AYRS* KA7 .... 228 D6
Cupar Dr *GRNKW/INVK* PA16 .. 31 M6
Cuparhead Av *CTBR* ML5 .... 109 K5
Cuppleton Brae *HWWD* PA9 .... 121 J7 🔢
Curfew Rd *KNTSWD* G13 .... 61 K8
Curle St *SCOT* G14 .... 81 K7
Curlew Crs *GRNKW/INVK* PA16 ... 32 B5

Curlew La GRNKW/INVK PA16 32 B5 2
Curlew Pl JNSTN PA5 122 C2
Curling Crs GVH/MTFL G42 128 C1
Curlinghall LARGS KA30 115 J7
Curlinghaugh Crs WISHAW ML2 155 J6
Curlingmire EKILS G75 14 F9
Curran Av WISHAW ML2 158 E8 1
Currie Ct ARD KA22 191 J8 3
Currieside Av SHOTTS ML7 137 K5
Currieside Pl SHOTTS ML7 137 K5
Currie St MRYH/FIRH G20 82 E3
Curtecan Pl AYRS KA7 18 F8
Curtis Av LNPK/KPK G44 128 D2
Curzon St MRYH/FIRH G20 82 E3
Customhouse Pl GRNK PA15 2 F4 1
Cuthbert Pl KLMNKN/STW KA3 17 G1
Cuthbertson St
PLKSD/SHW G41 105 G6
Cuthbert St
UD/BTH/TAN G71 132 B2 1
Cuthelton Dr DEN/PKHD G31 106 E5 1
Cuthelton St DEN/PKHD G31 13 M8
Cuthelton Ter DEN/PKHD G31 13 M8
Cutsburn Pl KLMNKN/STW KA3 197 M1
Cutsburn Rd KLMNKN/STW KA3 197 M1
Cutstraw Rd KLMNKN/STW KA3 197 L1
Cypress Av BEITH KA15 144 C7
BLTYR/CAMB G72 155 J1
UD/BTH/TAN G71 132 B1
Cypress Ct EKILS G75 171 J4
HMLTN ML3 156 E7 3
KKNTL G66 65 H3 2
Cypress Crs EKILS G75 171 J4
Cypress Gdns IRV KA12 203 L4
Cypress Pl EKILS G75 171 J4 2
Cypress St PPK/MIL G22 83 K4 1
Cyprus Av JNSTN PA5 100 B7
Cyril St PSLY PA1 9 M4

D

Daer Av RNFRW PA4 80 E8
Daer Wy HMLTN ML3 156 A6
Daff Av GRNKW/INVK PA16 50 D4
Daffodil Wy MTHW ML1 157 L1 3
Dairsie Gdns BSHPBGS G64 84 D1
Dairsie St LNPK/KPK G44 127 M5 1
Daisybank GLGNK KA14 167 J3
Daisy St GVH/MTFL G42 105 H7
Dalbeth Rd CAR/SHTL G32 106 F7
Dalblair Rd AYRS KA7 18 E4
Dalcharn Pl ESTRH G34 108 A1 1
Dalcraig Crs BLTYR/CAMB G72 131 J8
Dalcross St PTCK G11 82 C7 2
Dalcruin Gdns
BAIL/MDB/MHD G69 67 G5
Daldowie Av CAR/SHTL G32 107 K6 2
Daldowie Rd UD/BTH/TAN G71 108 A7
Daldowie St CTBR ML5 109 L6
Dale Av EKILS G75 14 B8
Dale Ct WISHAW ML2 158 C7
Dale Crs IRV KA12 203 K5
Dale Dr MTHW ML1 134 A5
Dale St DMNK/BRGTN G40 12 D8
Daleview Av KVD/HLHD G12 82 B3 3
Daleview Dr
CRMNK/CLK/EAG G76 151 K3
Daleview Gv
CRMNK/CLK/EAG G76 151 K3 2
Dale Wy RUTH G73 129 G5
Dalfoil Ct PSLY PA1 102 F5 3
Dalgarroch Av KNTSWD G13 80 E1
Dalgarven Ms
KLMNKN/STW KA3 207 J3 3
Dalgleish Av CLYDBK G81 59 M3
Dalgraig Crs BLTYR/CAMB G72 131 J7
Dalhousie Gdns BSHPBGS G64 63 M7
Dalhousie La KVGV G3 4 F7
Dalhousie Rd KLBCH PA10 99 H7
Dalhousie St CGLW G2 4 F8
COWCAD G4 5 G7 1
Dalilea Dr ESTRH G34 86 D8
Dalilea Pl ESTRH G34 86 D8 4
Dalintober St GBLS G5 10 E4 1
Dalkeith Av BSHPBGS G64 64 B6
PLKSD/SHW G41 104 B5
Dalkeith Rd BSHPBGS G64 64 B5 4
Dallas La TROON KA10 216 C7
Dallas Pl TROON KA10 216 C7
Dallas Rd TROON KA10 216 C7
Dalmacoulter Rd AIRDRIE ML6 89 H6
Dalmahoy Crs BRWEIR PA11 98 C3 2
Dalmahoy St CAR/SHTL G32 106 E2 3
Dalmahoy Wy KLWNG KA13 193 H6 3
Dalmailing Av IRVSE KA11 204 B8
Dalmally St GRNK PA15 33 M7
MRYH/FIRH G20 4 D2
Dalmarnock Rd
DMNK/BRGTN G40 12 D8
Dalmary Dr PSLY PA1 102 B3
Dalmellington Ct HMLTN ML3 155 K8
Dalmellington Dr EKILN G74 14 D1
Dalmellington Rd AYRS KA7 229 J5
PLK/PH/NH G53 126 A1
Dalmeny Av GIF/THBK G46 127 J6
Dalmeny Dr BRHD/NEIL G78 125 G7
Dalmeny Rd HMLTN ML3 156 D7 2
Dalmeny St GBLS G5 105 L7 3
Dalmilling Crs AYR KA8 225 K8
Dalmilling Dr AYR KA8 225 K7
Dalmilling Rd AYR KA8 225 K7
Dalmoak Rd GRNK PA15 33 J8
Dalmonach Rd ALEX/LLW G83 25 M5
Dalmore Crs HBR/GL G84 20 A6
Dalmore Pl IRVSE KA11 203 M3
Dalmore Wy IRVSE KA11 203 M3
Dalnair Pl MLNGV G62 41 K8
Dalnair St KVGV G3 82 C8
Dalness St CAR/SHTL G32 107 G6
Dalnottar Av OLDK G60 59 H3
Dalnottar Dr OLDK G60 59 H4
Dalnottar Gdns OLDK G60 59 H4
Dalnottar Hill Rd OLDK G60 59 H4
Dalreoch Av
BAIL/MDB/MHD G69 108 C4
Dalreoch Ct DMBTN G82 36 D5 4
Dalriada Crs MTHW ML1 133 K8
Dalriada Dr BSHPBGS G64 44 C8
Dalriada Rd GRNKW/INVK PA16 31 K7
Dalriada St DMNK/BRGTN G40 13 J7
Dalry Gdns HMLTN ML3 155 K7
Dalrymple Ct IRV KA12 203 L6
Dalrymple Dr EKILN G74 154 F7
IRV KA12 203 K7
NMRNS G77 151 G5 2
Dalrymple St GRNK PA15 2 D3
Dalrymple Vw RAYR/DAL KA6 231 H6
Dalry Pl AIRDRIE ML6 134 D1
Dalry Rd ARD KA22 191 J5 2
BEITH KA15 168 A2
KBRN KA25 167 G2
KLWNG KA13 193 K4
LARGS KA30 115 L8
SALT KA21 192 A8
UD/BTH/TAN G71 132 B2
Dalry St CAR/SHTL G32 107 H5
Dalserf Crs GIF/THBK G46 127 H8
Dalserf St DEN/PKHD G31 13 G6
Dalsetter Av DRUM G15 60 F7
Dalsetter Pl DRUM G15 61 G7 1
Dalshannon Pl CUMB G67 68 B2 2
Dalshannon Rd CUMB G67 68 B2
Dalshannon Vw CUMB G67 68 B2 3
Dalsholm Rd MRYH/FIRH G20 82 B2
Dalskeith Av PSLYN/LNWD PA3 101 G4
Dalskeith Crs
PSLYN/LNWD PA3 101 G4 3
Dalskeith Rd PSLYN/LNWD PA3 101 G5
Dalswinton Pth ESTRH G34 108 D1 1
Dalswinton St ESTRH G34 108 C1
Dalton Av CLYDBK G81 60 E8
Dalton Hl HMLTN ML3 155 K7
Dalton St DEN/PKHD G31 106 E4
Dalvait Gdns ALEX/LLW G83 25 L1 4
Dalvait Rd ALEX/LLW G83 25 L1
Dalveen Ct BRHD/NEIL G78 125 J8
Dalveen Dr UD/BTH/TAN G71 131 L1
Dalveen Qd CTBR ML5 110 D4
Dalveen St CAR/SHTL G32 106 F4 2
Dalveen Wy RUTH G73 129 J6
Dalwhatswood Rd
NMLNS KA16 215 L1
Dalwhinnie Av
BLTYR/CAMB G72 131 J7
Dalwood Rd PSTWK KA9 225 H1 1
Daly Gdns BLTYR/CAMB G72 131 K8
Dalzell Av MTHW ML1 158 A5
Dalzell Dr MTHW ML1 158 A6
Dalziel Dr PLKSD/SHW G41 104 C6
Dalziel Rd
CARD/HILL/MSPK G52 102 F1
Dalziel St HMLTN ML3 156 B4
MTHW ML1 157 L2
Damhead Rd KLMNK KA1 211 L6
Damshot Crs PLK/PH/NH G53 126 D1
Damshot Rd PLK/PH/NH G53 126 D2
Damside AYR KA8 224 F7
Danby Rd BAIL/MDB/MHD G69 107 M5
Danefield Av LARGS KA30 115 H2
Danes Av SCOT G14 81 J5
Danes Crs SCOT G14 81 H4 1
Danes Dr SCOT G14 81 H4
Danes La North SCOT G14 81 J5
Danes La South SCOT G14 81 J5
Daniel Mclaughlin Pl
KKNTL G66 45 L8 3
Dankeith Dr KLMNK KA1 218 C5
Dankeith Rd KLMNK KA1 218 C5
Dargarvel Av PLKSD/SHW G41 104 B5
Dargavel Av BSHPTN PA7 58 C7
Dargavel Rd ERSK PA8 58 D8
Darg Rd SVSTN KA20 201 K1
Dark Brig Rd CARLUKE ML8 188 B7
Darkwood Ct PSLYN/LNWD PA3 8 A1
Darkwood Crs PSLYN/LNWD PA3 8 A1
Darleith Rd ALEX/LLW G83 25 L3 3
DMBTN G82 24 A8
Darleith St CAR/SHTL G32 106 F4
Darley Crs TROON KA10 216 D8
Darley Pl HMLTN ML3 174 A1
TROON KA10 216 D8
Darley Rd BALLOCH G68 48 E4
Darluith Rd PSLYN/LNWD PA3 99 L3
Darmeid Pl SHOTTS ML7 161 H1
Darmule Dr KLWNG KA13 193 J4
Darnaway Av
STPS/GTHM/RID G33 85 K7
Darnaway Dr
STPS/GTHM/RID G33 85 K7
Darnaway St
STPS/GTHM/RID G33 85 K7
Darndaff Rd GRNK PA15 2 F8
Darngaber Gdns HMLTN ML3 174 E6 1
Darngaber Rd HMLTN ML3 174 E6
Darngavil Rd AIRDRIE ML6 89 L3
Darnick St SPRGB/BLRNK G21 6 F3
Darnley Crs BSHPBGS G64 63 M6
Darnley Dr KLMNK KA1 211 L4
Darnley Gdns PLKSD/SHW G41 104 E7
Darnleyhill Wk NMLNS KA16 215 J2
Darnley Mains Rd
PLK/PH/NH G53 126 C6
Darnley Pl PLKSD/SHW G41 104 E7 1
Darnley Rd BRHD/NEIL G78 125 L6
PLKSD/SHW G41 104 E7
Darnley St PLKSD/SHW G41 104 F6
Darnshaw Cl IRVSE KA11 204 C4
Darragh Gn WISHAW ML2 160 A3
Darroch Av GRK PA19 31 L2 2
Darroch Dr ERSK PA8 58 F6
GRK PA19 31 L2 3
Darroch Wy CUMB G67 49 G6
Dartford St PPK/MIL G22 5 G2
Dartmouth Av
GRNKW/INVK PA16 31 L4
Darvel Crs PSLY PA1 102 D5
Darvel Dr NMRNS G77 151 G4
Darvel Rd NMLNS KA16 215 M2
Darvel St PLK/PH/NH G53 125 M3
Darwin Pl CLYDBK G81 59 K6
Darwin Rd EKILS G75 14 A6
Davaar EKILN G74 154 C8 1
Davaar Dr CTBR ML5 109 K2
KLMNKN/STW KA3 207 H4
MTHW ML1 133 J7
PSLYS PA2 124 E2
Davaar Pl NMRNS G77 150 C3
Davaar Rd GRNKW/INVK PA16 31 J6
RNFRW PA4 80 D8
SALT KA21 191 M7
Davaar St DMNK/BRGTN G40 13 H7
Dava St GOV/IBX G51 104 A2
Daventry Dr KVD/HLHD G12 82 A4 3
Davey St GRNKW/INVK PA16 32 B4
David Dale Av
KLMNKN/STW KA3 197 J2
David Gage St KLWNG KA13 193 L4
David Gray Dr KKNTL G66 46 A8
David Orr St KLMNK KA1 16 C3
David Pl BAIL/MDB/MHD G69 107 M5
David's Crs KLWNG KA13 193 K7
Davidson Av GLGNK KA14 167 K3
Davidson Crs KSYTH G65 46 E6
Davidson Dr GRK PA19 31 L2
Davidson Pl CAR/SHTL G32 107 J3 2
Davidson Qd CLYDBK G81 59 L2 1
Davidson Rd ALEX/LLW G83 25 M2
Davidson St AIRDRIE ML6 110 F1
CLYDBK G81 80 E1
CTBR ML5 110 B5
DMNK/BRGTN G40 106 A7
David St CTBR ML5 110 C2
DMNK/BRGTN G40 12 F5
SHOTTS ML7 113 H7 2
Davieland Rd GIF/THBK G46 127 G8
Davie's Acre EKILN G74 152 F5
Davies Dr ALEX/LLW G83 25 L3
Davies Qd MTHW ML1 133 K7 2
Davington Dr HMLTN ML3 155 K7
Daviot St GOV/IBX G51 103 K3
Dawson Av EKILS G75 153 H8
Dawson Pl COWCAD G4 5 H3
Dawson Rd COWCAD G4 5 H3
Deaconsbank Av GIF/THBK G46 126 D8
Deaconsbank Crs
GIF/THBK G46 126 D8 3
Deacons Rd KSYTH G65 47 K1
Dealston Rd BRHD/NEIL G78 125 H5
Deanbrae St
UD/BTH/TAN G71 131 M3 2
Dean Crs BAIL/MDB/MHD G69 66 D8 2
HMLTN ML3 156 C8
Deanfield Qd
CARD/HILL/MSPK G52 102 F3
Deanfield Quadrant
CARD/HILL/MSPK G52 102 F3
Deanhill La KLMNKN/STW KA3 207 G6
Dean La KLMNKN/STW KA3 17 G1
Dean Park Av
UD/BTH/TAN G71 132 A7 1
Dean Park Dr
BLTYR/CAMB G72 130 D5 2
Dean Park Rd RNFRW PA4 80 D7
Dean Pl CRH/DND KA2 210 F1
Dean Rd KBRN KA25 143 H7
KLMNKN/STW KA3 207 G6
Deans Av BLTYR/CAMB G72 130 D6
Deanside Rd
CARD/HILL/MSPK G52 103 G1
Deanston Av BRHD/NEIL G78 125 H8
Deanston Dr PLKSD/SHW G41 127 L1
Deanstone Pl CTBR ML5 110 D6 1
Deanstone Wk CTBR ML5 110 D7
Deanston Gv CTBR ML5 109 L6 1
Deanston Pk
BRHD/NEIL G78 125 H8 1
Dean St BLSH ML4 133 H4
CLYDBK G81 60 C8
KLMNKN/STW KA3 17 G1
Deanwood Av GIF/THBK G46 127 M6
Deanwood Rd GIF/THBK G46 127 M6
Deas Rd SHOTTS ML7 137 J4
Dechmont EKILS G75 171 K4
Dechmont Av
BLTYR/CAMB G72 130 D6 1
MTHW ML1 157 J2
Dechmont Gdns
BLTYR/CAMB G72 131 J8 7
Dechmont Pl BLTYR/CAMB G72 130 D6
Dechmont Rd
UD/BTH/TAN G71 108 E8 2
Dechmont St DEN/PKHD G31 13 K7
HMLTN ML3 156 C7
Dechmont Vw BLSH ML4 132 F6 4
UD/BTH/TAN G71 132 A2 3
Dee Av KLMNK KA1 212 B5
PSLYS PA2 100 F7
RNFRW PA4 80 E6
Deedes St AIRDRIE ML6 110 D3
Dee Dr PSLYS PA2 100 F8
Deep Dl EKILN G74 153 J6
Deepdene Rd
BAIL/MDB/MHD G69 66 F7 2
BSDN G61 61 K6
Dee Pl EKILS G75 170 E2
JNSTN PA5 122 C1
Deerdykes Ct North
BALLOCH G68 67 L3
Deerdykes Ct South
BALLOCH G68 67 L4 1
Deerdykes Pl BALLOCH G68 67 L3
Deerdykes Rd BALLOCH G68 67 K4
Deerdykes Vw BALLOCH G68 67 K4
Deer Park Av SVSTN KA20 201 L2
Deer Park Ct HMLTN ML3 174 D2 4
Deer Park Pl HMLTN ML3 174 E2 1
Deeside Dr CARLUKE ML8 179 G6
Dee St CTBR ML5 87 J7
GRNKW/INVK PA16 32 B4
SHOTTS ML7 137 K4
STPS/GTHM/RID G33 7 L8
Dee Ter HMLTN ML3 174 B1
Delfie Dr GRNKW/INVK PA16 32 B5 3
Delhi Av CLYDBK G81 59 J5
Dellburn St MTHW ML1 157 M4
Dellingburn St GRNK PA15 2 E6
The Dell BLSH ML4 133 K6
Delny Pl STPS/GTHM/RID G33 107 L2 3
Delves Rd LNK/LMHG ML11 199 G6
Delvin Rd LNPK/KPK G44 128 A3
De Morville Pl BEITH KA15 168 B2 1
Dempsey Rd BLSH ML4 132 F6
Dempster St GRNK PA15 2 A5
Denbak Av HMLTN ML3 156 A7
Denbeck St CAR/SHTL G32 106 F4
Denbrae St CAR/SHTL G32 106 F4
Denewood Av PSLYS PA2 124 D1
Denham St PPK/MIL G22 5 G2
Denholm Crs EKILS G75 14 F5 1
Denholm Dr GIF/THBK G46 151 J1
WISHAW ML2 159 J3
Denholm Gdns
GRNKW/INVK PA16 32 C4
HMLTN ML3 174 E6
Denholm Gn EKILS G75 15 G5
Denholm St GRNKW/INVK PA16 32 D3
Denholm Ter GRNKW/INVK PA16 32 D4
HMLTN ML3 155 L6
Denholm Wy BEITH KA15 168 A2 1
Denmark St PPK/MIL G22 83 J5
Denmilne Rd
BAIL/MDB/MHD G69 108 D2
Denmilne St ESTRH G34 108 C2
Dennistoun Crs HBR/GL G84 22 F2
Dennistoun Rd PGL PA14 56 B2
Dennistoun St BLSH ML4 133 G4
Dennyholm Wynd KBRN KA25 143 H8
Dennystoun Forge DMBTN G82 36 E5
Dentdale EKILN G74 153 J6
Deramore Av GIF/THBK G46 151 G2
Derby St KVGV G3 4 A8
Derby Terrace La KVGV G3 82 D8
Derrywood Rd KKNTL G66 45 J3
Derwent Dr CTBR ML5 87 J7
Derwent St PPK/MIL G22 5 G1
Derwentwater EKILS G75 170 F3
Despard Av CAR/SHTL G32 107 K5
Despard Gdns CAR/SHTL G32 107 L5 3
Deveron Av GIF/THBK G46 127 K7
Deveron Crs HMLTN ML3 155 K5
Deveron Rd BSDN G61 61 J7
EKILN G74 15 L3
KLMNK KA1 212 A4
MTHW ML1 134 B3
TROON KA10 216 E3
Deveron St CTBR ML5 87 J8
STPS/GTHM/RID G33 7 L7
Devilla Ct PSTWK KA9 225 J4 3
Devine Gv WISHAW ML2 160 A2
Devlin Ct BLTYR/CAMB G72 155 L2 1
Devlin Gv BLTYR/CAMB G72 155 L2
Devol Av PGL PA14 34 A8
Devol Crs PLK/PH/NH G53 126 B1
Devol Rd PGL PA14 54 C4
Devondale Av
BLTYR/CAMB G72 131 J8
Devon Dr BSHPTN PA7 58 C6
Devon Gdns BSHPBGS G64 63 M6
CARLUKE ML8 178 E7
Devonhill Av HMLTN ML3 174 D2
Devon Pl GVH/MTFL G42 11 G8
Devonport Pk EKILS G75 171 G2
Devon Rd GRNKW/INVK PA16 31 K5
Devonshire Gardens La
KVD/HLHD G12 82 B5 1
Devonshire Ter KVD/HLHD G12 82 B5
Devonshire Terrace La
KVD/HLHD G12 82 B5 2
Devon St GBLS G5 11 G8
Devonview Pl AIRDRIE ML6 110 F3 1
Devonview St AIRDRIE ML6 110 F2
Devon Wk BALLOCH G68 67 L1
Devon Wy MTHW ML1 157 H3 1
De Walden Ter
KLMNKN/STW KA3 17 H3
Dewar Cl UD/BTH/TAN G71 109 G8
Dhuhill Dr East HBR/GL G84 20 E5
Diamond St BLSH ML4 133 G5
Diana Av KNTSWD G13 81 H1
Diana Qd MTHW ML1 134 A4 5
Diana Vernon Ct HBR/GL G84 22 F1 1
Dick Crs IRV KA12 203 K4
Dickens Av CLYDBK G81 59 M5
Dick Rd KLMNK KA1 17 G5
Dickson Dr IRV KA12 203 J4
Dickson St LRKH ML9 176 C8 4
Dicks Pk EKILS G75 14 D5
Dick St MRYH/FIRH G20 4 D3
Dick Ter IRV KA12 203 K4
Diddup Dr SVSTN KA20 192 B8
Differ Av KSYTH G65 46 F7
Dillichip Cl ALEX/LLW G83 25 M7
Dillichip Gdns ALEX/LLW G83 25 M6 1
Dillichip Loan ALEX/LLW G83 25 L6
Dilwara Av SCOT G14 81 L7
Dimity St JNSTN PA5 99 M7
Dimsdale Crs WISHAW ML2 159 J8 1
Dimsdale Rd WISHAW ML2 159 J8
Dinard Dr GIF/THBK G46 127 J5
Dinart St STPS/GTHM/RID G33 7 L7
Dinduff St ESTRH G34 86 C8
Dingwall Dr
GRNKW/INVK PA16 31 M6 1
Dinmont Av PSLYS PA2 123 M1 1
Dinmont Crs MTHW ML1 133 J7
Dinmont Rd PLKSD/SHW G41 104 D8
Dinmurchie Rd TROON KA10 216 E4
Dinwiddie St SPRGB/BLRNK G21 7 J4
Dinyra Pl CTBR ML5 87 J3
Dippin Pl SALT KA21 191 M7
Dipple Ct KBRN KA25 143 H7
Dipple Pl DRUM G15 61 H7
Dipple Rd KBRN KA25 143 H6
Dipple Vw KBRN KA25 143 H6
Dirleton Dr PLKSD/SHW G41 127 L1
PSLYS PA2 101 G8 2
Dirleton Ga BSDN G61 61 K6
Dirrans Ter KLWNG KA13 193 M7
Ditton Dr KLMNK KA1 211 L5 1
Divernia Wy BRHD/NEIL G78 149 K1
Divert Rd GRK PA19 31 J3
Dixon Av DMBTN G82 36 E6 2
GVH/MTFL G42 105 G7
Dixon Dr DMBTN G82 36 D7
Dixon Pl EKILN G74 153 H6
Dixon Rd GVH/MTFL G42 105 J8
HBR/GL G84 20 E6 2
Dixon St CGLE G1 11 H3
CTBR ML5 110 B5
HMLTN ML3 156 D6
PSLY PA1 9 K4 1
Dickens Gv MTHW ML1 134 D7 2
Dobbies Ct CARLUKE ML8 178 A3
Dobbie's Loan CGLW G2 5 K6
COWCAD G4 5 K7 1
Dobbie's Loan Pl COWCAD G4 5 L8
Dochart Av RNFRW PA4 80 E8
Dochart Dr CTBR ML5 87 J7
Dochart St STPS/GTHM/RID G33 84 E7
Dock Breast GRNK PA15 2 F4
Dockhead Pl SALT KA21 200 E2
Dock Rd ARD KA22 191 H8 2
Dock St CLYDBK G81 80 D2
Dodhill Pl KNTSWD G13 81 H3
Dodside Gdns CAR/SHTL G32 107 J5 1
Dodside Pl CAR/SHTL G32 107 J5 2
Dodside St CAR/SHTL G32 107 J5 3
Dolan St BAIL/MDB/MHD G69 108 B4
Dollar Pk MTHW ML1 158 B6
Dollar Ter MRYH/FIRH G20 82 C1 1
Dolphin Rd PLKSD/SHW G41 104 D7
Dominica Gn EKILS G75 153 G8 4
Donald Crs TROON KA10 216 D5
Donaldfield Rd BRWEIR PA11 98 B2
Donaldson Av KSYTH G65 47 K2
SALT KA21 200 F1
SVSTN KA20 192 E7
Donaldson Crs KKNTL G66 65 J2 1
Donaldson Dr IRV KA12 203 K5
KLMNKN/STW KA3 207 K6
RNFRW PA4 80 D6 2
Donaldson Gn
UD/BTH/TAN G71 132 A1 3
Donaldson Rd LRKH ML9 176 C8
Donaldson St HMLTN ML3 156 A4
KKNTL G66 65 J2
Donaldswood Pk PSLYS PA2 124 C1
Donaldswood Rd PSLYS PA2 124 C1
Donald Ter HMLTN ML3 156 C8
Donald Wy UD/BTH/TAN G71 132 A2
Don Av RNFRW PA4 80 E7
Doncaster St MRYH/FIRH G20 4 E2
Don Ct HMLTN ML3 174 A1
Don Dr PSLYS PA2 100 F8
Dongola Rd AYRS KA7 19 G7
Donnelly Wy WISHAW ML2 158 C5
Donnies Brae BRHD/NEIL G78 124 F8
Don Pl JNSTN PA5 122 C1 3
Don St GRNKW/INVK PA16 32 C4
STPS/GTHM/RID G33 7 L8
Doon Av PSTWK KA9 225 H4
Doon Crs BSDN G61 61 K6
Doonfoot Gdns EKILN G74 14 D1
Doonfoot Rd AYRS KA7 228 D6
PLKSW/MSWD G43 127 J3
Doonholm Pk AYRS KA7 228 F8
Doonholm Pl AYRS KA7 228 F8 1
Doon Pl KKNTL G66 45 M7
KLMNK KA1 212 B5
SALT KA21 192 A6
TROON KA10 216 E4
Doon Rd KKNTL G66 45 M8
Doon Side CUMB G67 49 H7
Doon St CLYDBK G81 60 C6 2
LRKH ML9 176 C7 5
MTHW ML1 158 A5
Doon Wy KKNTL G66 46 A8
Dorain Rd MTHW ML1 134 D6 2
Dora St DMNK/BRGTN G40 106 A6
Dorchester Av KVD/HLHD G12 82 A3
Dorchester Ct KVD/HLHD G12 82 A3
Dorchester Pl KVD/HLHD G12 82 A4
Dorian Dr CRMNK/CLK/EAG G76 151 J1
Dorlin Rd STPS/GTHM/RID G33 85 L4
Dormanside Ct
PLK/PH/NH G53 103 H6 1
Dormanside Ga
PLK/PH/NH G53 103 H6 2
Dormanside Gv
PLK/PH/NH G53 103 H6 3
Dormanside Rd
PLK/PH/NH G53 103 H6
Dornal Av KNTSWD G13 80 E2
Dornal Dr TROON KA10 216 F3 1
Dornford Av CAR/SHTL G32 107 K7
Dornford Rd CAR/SHTL G32 107 K7 1
Dornie Dr CAR/SHTL G32 130 B1 2
Dornoch Av GIF/THBK G46 127 J8
Dornoch Ct BLSH ML4 133 G4
KLWNG KA13 193 H6 3
Dornoch Pk AYRS KA7 18 D7
Dornoch Pl
BAIL/MDB/MHD G69 66 D8 3
EKILN G74 14 C2
Dornoch Rd BSDN G61 61 K7
MTHW ML1 134 B4
Dornoch St DMNK/BRGTN G40 12 C5
Dornoch Wy AIRDRIE ML6 110 F4 1
BALLOCH G68 49 G4
Dorset Rd GRNKW/INVK PA16 31 L5 1
Dorset St KVGV G3 4 C9
Dosk Av KNTSWD G13 80 E1
Dosk Pl KNTSWD G13 80 F1
Double Hedges Rd
BRHD/NEIL G78 148 D3
Dougalston Av MLNGV G62 42 B8
Dougalston Crs MLNGV G62 42 B8 3
Dougalston Gdns North
MLNGV G62 42 B8
Dougalston Gdns South
MLNGV G62 42 B8
Dougalston Rd SMSTN G23 62 E8
Douglas Av CAR/SHTL G32 107 H8 3
DALRY KA24 184 D2
GIF/THBK G46 127 J8
JNSTN PA5 100 B7
KKNTL G66 65 K4
PGL PA14 56 C2
PSTWK KA9 225 H3
RUTH G73 129 J4
Douglas Brown Pl
RAYR/DAL KA6 231 H6 2
Douglas Crs AIRDRIE ML6 111 G3
ERSK PA8 58 F6
HMLTN ML3 174 D3
UD/BTH/TAN G71 132 B1
Douglasdale EKILN G74 14 C1
Douglas Dr
BAIL/MDB/MHD G69 107 M4

BLSH ML4 .... **133** K5
BLTYR/CAMB G72 .... **129** M5
DRUM G15 .... **60** F8
EKILS G75 .... **170** E2
HBR/GL G84 .... **20** D5
NMRNS G77 .... **150** M3
UD/BTH/TAN G71 .... **132** B1
Douglas Dr East *HBR/GL* G84 .... **20** E6
Douglas Gdns *BSDN* G61 .... **61** M5
GIF/THBK G46 .... **127** J8
UD/BTH/TAN G71 .... **131** M4
Douglas Ga *BLTYR/CAMB* **130** A4
Douglas La *AYRS* KA7 .... **18** E3 🔲
CGLW G2 .... **4** F9 🔲
Douglas Muir Dr *MLNGV* G62 ... **41** J6
Douglas Muir Gdns
MLNGV G62 .... **41** J6
Douglas Muir Pl *MLNGV* G62 ...... **41** J6
Douglas Muir Rd *CLYDBK* G81 .... **60** D2
MLNGV G62 .... **41** K7
Douglas Park Crs *BSDN* G61 .... **62** A3
Douglas Park La *HMLTN* ML3 .. **156** C5 🔲
Douglas Pl *BSDN* G61 .... **61** L4 🔲
HMLTN ML3 .... **174** D3 🔲
KKNTL G66 .... **65** K4
LARGS KA30 .... **115** J4
Douglas Rd *DMBTN* G82 .... **37** H6
RAYR/DAL KA6 .... **231** H5 🔲
RNFRW PA4 .... **102** A1
Douglas St *AIRDRIE* ML6 .... **111** G5
AYRS KA7 .... **18** E3
BLTYR/CAMB G72 .... **155** J1
CARLUKE ML8 .... **178** E7
CGLW G2 .... **4** F8
HMLTN ML3 .... **156** C5 🔲
KLMNK KA1 .... **16** E6
LARGS KA30 .... **115** J4
LRKH ML9 .... **176** A5
MTHW ML1 .... **157** K2
PSLY PA1 .... **8** D3
UD/BTH/TAN G71 .... **132** B2
WISHAW ML2 .... **177** J2
Douglas Ter *PLKSD/SHW* G41 ... **104** F7 🔲
Dougliehill Pl *PGL* PA14 .... **54** C1
Dougliehill Rd *PGL* PA14 .... **54** C1
Dougliehill Ter *PGL* PA14 .... **54** C1
Dougray Pl *BRHD/NEIL* G78 ..... **125** J7 🔲
Dougrie Dr *CSMK* G45 .... **128** D6
Dougrie Pl *CSMK* G45 .... **128** E6
Dougrie Rd *CSMK* G45 .... **128** D6
Dougrie St *CSMK* G45 .... **128** D6
Dougrie Ter *CSMK* G45 .... **128** D6
Dougrie Gdns *CSMK* G45 .... **128** D7
Doune *AIRDRIE* ML6 .... **111** K8 🔲
BSHPBGS G64 .... **64** B5
NMRNS G77 .... **150** F4
Doune Gdns *GRK* PA19 .... **30** F4
MRYH/FIRH G20 .... **4** B2
Doune Gardens La
MRYH/FIRH G20 .... **4** B2
Doune Park Wy *CTBR* ML5 ..... **109** M5
Doune Qd *MRYH/FIRH* G20 .... **4** B2
Doune Ter *CTBR* ML5 .... **87** K8
Doura Dr *IRVSE* KA11 .... **203** M4
Dovecote *PLKSW/MSWD* G43 ... **127** J1 🔲
Dovecote Vw *KKNTL* G66 .... **65** M2
Dovecot La *KLWNG* KA13 ..... **193** L6
LNK/LMHG ML11 .... **199** G5 🔲
Doveholm *DMBTN* G82 .... **37** G4 🔲
Doveholm Av *DMBTN* G82 ...... **37** H4
Dove Pl *EKILS* G75 .... **170** F3 🔲
Dover St *CTBR* ML5 .... **87** K7
KVGV G3 .... **4** C9
Dove St *PLK/PH/NH* G53 ...... **126** A4
Dove Wynd *BLSH* ML4 .... **132** F2
Downanfield Rd *CUMB* G67 ..... **48** D8
Downanhill St *PTCK* G11 .... **82** C7
Dowan Rd *MLNGV* G62 .... **42** C7
Downanside La *KVD/HLHD* G12 ... **82** C6
Dowanside Rd *KVD/HLHD* G12 ... **82** C6
Downcraig Dr *CSMK* G45 .... **128** C7
Downcraig Gv *CSMK* G45 ...... **128** C7 🔲
Downcraig Rd *CSMK* G45 ...... **128** C7
Downcraig Ter *CSMK* G45 ..... **128** D7
Downfield Dr *HMLTN* ML3 ...... **174** B2
Downfield Gdns
UD/BTH/TAN G71 .... **131** M7
Downfield St *CAR/SHTL* G32 ... **106** E6
Downhill St *KVD/HLHD* G12 ..... **82** C6
Downiebrae Rd *RUTH* G73 ...... **106** B7
Downie Cl *UD/BTH/TAN* G71 .... **132** B1
Downie St *HMLTN* ML3 .... **156** D8
Downs St *SPRGB/BLRNK* G21 ... **83** M4 🔲
Dowrie Crs *PLK/PH/NH* G53 .... **103** H8
Draffen St *MTHW* ML1 .... **157** M2 🔲
Drakemire Av *CSMK* G45 .... **128** C5
Drakemire Dr *CSMK* G45 .... **128** B7
Drake St *DMNK/BRGTN* G40 .... **12** B5
Dreghorn Rd *IRVSE* KA11 ..... **209** K3
Dreghorn St *DEN/PKHD* G31 ..... **13** J2
Dresling Rd *GRNK* PA15 .... **2** A7
Drimnin Rd *STPS/GTHM/RID* G33.. **85** M4
Drive Rd *GOV/IBX* G51 .... **103** L1
Drochil St *ESTRH* G34 .... **86** A3
Drove Hl *BALLOCH* G68 .... **48** B6
Druid Dr *KLWNG* KA13 .... **193** L5
Drumadoon Dr *HBR/GL* G84 ...... **20** F7
Drumbathie Rd *AIRDRIE* ML6 ... **111** J3
Drumbeg Dr *PLK/PH/NH* G53 ... **126** A3
Drumbeg Ter *MLNGV* G62 .... **41** K7
Drumbottie Rd
SPRGB/BLRNK G21 .... **84** A4 🔲
Drumbreck Pl *KKNTL* G66 .... **65** L5
Drumby Crs
CRMNK/CLK/EAG G76 ..... **127** K8
Drumby Dr
CRMNK/CLK/EAG G76 .... **151** K1 🔲
Drumcarn Dr *MLNGV* G62 .... **41** M8
Drumcavel Rd
BAIL/MDB/MHD G69 .... **86** D2
Drumchapel Gdns *DRUM* G15 ... **61** G7 🔲
Drumchapel Pl *DRUM* G15 .... **61** H7
Drumchapel Rd *DRUM* G15 ...... **61** H7
Drumclair Pl *AIRDRIE* ML6 ...... **111** K2
Drumclog Av *MLNGV* G62 .... **42** A5
Drumclog Gdns
STPS/GTHM/RID G33 ...... **84** F3 🔲

Drumclog Pl
KLMNKN/STW KA3 .... **207** H6 🔲
Drumcoyle Dr
RAYR/DAL KA6 .... **231** H4 🔲
Drumcross Rd *BSHPTN* PA7 ...... **58** D6
PLK/PH/NH G53 .... **103** J8
Drumduff *EKILS* G75 .... **171** K4 🔲
Drumellan Rd *AYRS* KA7 .... **229** G7
Drumfin Av *AIRDRIE* ML6 .... **90** F5
Drumfork Ct *HBR/GL* G84 .... **22** F1 🔲
Drumfork Rd *HBR/GL* G84 .... **23** C1
Drumfrochar Pl *GRNK* PA15 .... **2** C7
Drumfrochar Rd *GRNK* PA15 ...... **2** B6
GRNKW/INVK PA16 .... **32** D6
Drumgelloch St *AIRDRIE* ML6 ... **111** K1
Drumglass Vw *KSYTH* G65 .... **47** M5 🔲
Drumgray Gdns *AIRDRIE* ML6 ... **69** K8
Drumgray La *AIRDRIE* ML6 .... **69** K8
Drumhead Pl *CAR/SHTL* G32 .... **106** F8
Drumhead Rd *CAR/SHTL* G32 ... **106** F8
Drumhill *KKNTL* G66 .... **46** B7
Drumilaw Rd *RUTH* G73 .... **129** G4
Drumilaw Wy *RUTH* G73 .... **106** C8
Drumillan Hl *GRNKW/INVK* PA16 ... **31** J7
Drumkinnon Rd
ALEX/LLW G83 .... **25** K1 🔲
Drumlaken Av
MRYH/FIRH G20 .... **62** C8 🔲
Drumlaken Ct
MRYH/FIRH G20 .... **62** C8 🔲
Drumlaken St *MRYH/FIRH* G20 ... **62** C8 🔲
Drumlanrig Av *ESTRH* G34 ...... **108** D1 🔲
Drumlanrig Pl *ESTRH* G34 .... **108** D1 🔲
Drumley Av *RAYR/DAL* KA6 .... **227** G3
Drumley Dr *RAYR/DAL* KA6 ..... **227** G3
Drumleyhill Dr *KLMNK* KA1 ..... **212** F4
Drumlin Dr *MLNGV* G62 .... **61** M1
Drumloch Gdns *EKILS* G75 ...... **171** L4 🔲
Drumlochy Rd
STPS/GTHM/RID G33 .... **85** G8
Drum Mains Pk *BALLOCH* G68 ... **67** J1
Drummilling Av *WKIL* KA23 .... **181** K3 🔲
Drummilling Dr *WKIL* KA23 .... **181** K3 🔲
Drummilling Rd *WKIL* KA23 ... **181** M1 🔲
Drummond Av *RUTH* G73 .... **128** F1 🔲
Drummond Crs *AYR* KA8 .... **225** L7 🔲
Drummond Dr *PSLY* PA1 .... **102** D5 🔲
WISHAW ML2 .... **159** H7
Drummond Hl *EKILN* G74 .... **154** E7
Drummond Pl *EKILN* G74 .... **154** B6 🔲
KLMNKN/STW KA3 .... **207** J7
Drummond St
GRNKW/INVK PA16 .... **32** C5
Drummond Wy *NMRNS* G77 ..... **150** A4
Drummore Av *CTBR* ML5 .... **110** D7
Drummore Rd *DRUM* G15 .... **61** G4
Drumnessie Ct *BALLOCH* G68 ... **67** M1 🔲
Drumnessie Rd *BALLOCH* G68 ... **67** M2
Drumnessie Vw
BALLOCH G68 .... **67** M1 🔲
Drumore Av *AIRDRIE* ML6 ..... **111** K8 🔲
Drumover Dr *DEN/PKHD* G31 ... **106** C5
Drumoyne Av *GOV/IBX* G51 .... **103** L2 🔲
Drumoyne Circ *GOV/IBX* G51 ... **103** L3
Drumoyne Dr *GOV/IBX* G51 .... **103** L2 🔲
Drumoyne Pl *GOV/IBX* G51 .... **103** L3 🔲
Drumoyne Qd *GOV/IBX* G51 .... **103** L3 🔲
Drumoyne Rd *GOV/IBX* G51 .... **103** L2
Drumoyne Sq *GOV/IBX* G51 .... **103** L2 🔲
Drumpark St *CTBR* ML5 .... **109** H5
GIF/THBK G46 .... **126** F5 🔲
Drumpellier Av
BAIL/MDB/MHD G69 ...... **108** B6
CTBR ML5 .... **109** K2
CUMB G67 .... **68** C2 🔲
Drumpellier Ct *CUMB* G67 .... **68** C2 🔲
Drumpellier Crs *CTBR* ML5 ..... **109** K3
Drumpellier Gdns *CUMB* G67 ... **68** C2 🔲
Drumpellier Gv *CUMB* G67 ...... **68** C2 🔲
Drumpellier Pl
BAIL/MDB/MHD G69 ...... **108** B5 🔲
CUMB G67 .... **68** C2 🔲
Drumpellier Rd
BAIL/MDB/MHD G69 ...... **108** A6
Drumpellier St
STPS/GTHM/RID G33 .... **7** M5
Drumreoch Dr *GVH/MTFL* G42 ... **128** E2
Drumreoch Pl *GVH/MTFL* G42 .. **128** E1
Drumry Rd *CLYDBK* G81 .... **60** C6
Drumry Rd East *DRUM* G15 ...... **60** F7
Drumsack Av
BAIL/MDB/MHD G69 .... **86** A7
Drumsargard Rd *RUTH* G73 ..... **129** K4
Drums Av *PSLYN/LNWD* PA3 .... **8** C2
Drums Crs *PSLYN/LNWD* PA3 ...... **8** C2
Drumshangie Pl *AIRDRIE* ML6 .... **89** G7
Drumshangie St *AIRDRIE* ML6 ... **89** G7 🔲
Drumshantie Rd *GRK* PA19 .... **31** G2 🔲
Drumshaw Dr *CAR/SHTL* G32 ... **130** C1
Drums Rd *PLK/PH/NH* G53 ..... **103** G6
Drums Ter *GRNKW/INVK* PA16 ... **32** B1 🔲
Drumsuy Ct *RAYR/DAL* KA6 .... **231** H6 🔲
Drumtrocher St *KSYTH* G65 ..... **47** K1 🔲
Drury St *CGLW* G2 .... **11** H1
Dryad St *GIF/THBK* G46 .... **126** E4 🔲
Drybridge Rd *CRH/DND* KA2 .... **209** L7
Dryburgh Av *PSLYS* PA2 .... **101** G8
RUTH G73 .... **129** H2
Dryburgh Gdns *MRYH/FIRH* G20 .... **4** C2
Dryburgh Hl *EKILN* G74 .... **14** C3
Dryburgh La *EKILN* G74 .... **14** D3
Dryburgh Pl *CTBR* ML5 .... **109** M2
Dryburgh Rd *BSDN* G61 .... **61** J3 🔲
WISHAW ML2 .... **159** G5
Dryburgh St *HMLTN* ML3 .... **156** B3 🔲
Dryburgh Wk
BAIL/MDB/MHD G69 .... **67** G6 🔲
Dryburn Av
CARD/HILL/MSPK G52 ..... **103** G4
Dryden St *HMLTN* ML3 .... **156** B3 🔲
Drygait *HWWD* PA9 .... **122** A3
Drygate *COWCAD* G4 .... **12** A1
Drygatehead *NMLNS* KA16 .... **215** K1
Drygate St *LRKH* ML9 .... **176** A5
NMLNS KA16 .... **215** K2 🔲
Drygrange Rd
STPS/GTHM/RID G33 .... **85** J7
Drymen Pl *KKNTL* G66 .... **65** K6

Drymen Rd *BSDN* G61 .... **61** L4
Drymen St
CARD/HILL/MSPK G52 ..... **103** L4
Drynoch Pl *PPK/MIL* G22 .... **83** H2
Drysdale St *SCOT* G14 .... **80** F4
Duart Av *PSTWK* KA9 .... **225** J1
Duart Crs *PSTWK* KA9 .... **225** J1 🔲
Duart Dr *EKILN* G74 .... **153** K6 🔲
JNSTN PA5 .... **100** B8
NMRNS G77 .... **151** G4
Duart St *MRYH/FIRH* G20 .... **62** C8
Dubbs Rd *PGL* PA14 .... **54** D1
Dubton St *ESTRH* G34 .... **86** B8
Duchall Pl *SCOT* G14 .... **81** H5 🔲
Duchal Rd *KLMCLM* PA13 .... **75** K1
Duchal St *PGL* PA14 .... **54** D1
Duchess Ct *HMLTN* ML3 .... **157** C7 🔲
Duchess Dr *HBR/GL* G84 .... **20** B5
Duchess Palace *RUTH* G73 ..... **129** J1 🔲
Duchess Pk *HBR/GL* G84 .... **20** B6
Duchess Rd *RUTH* G73 .... **106** C8
Duchray Dr *PSLY* PA1 .... **102** F5
Duchray La *STPS/GTHM/RID* G33... **7** L7
Duchray Pl *RAYR/DAL* KA6 .... **231** L5 🔲
Duchray St *STPS/GTHM/RID* G33... **7** L7
Duddingston Av *KLWNG* KA13 .. **193** H5 🔲
Dudhope St
STPS/GTHM/RID G33 .... **85** K7
Dudley Dr *CTBR* ML5 .... **87** J7
KVD/HLHD G12 .... **82** A6
Dudley La *KVD/HLHD* G12 .... **82** A6
Duffield Dr *LARGS* KA30 .... **115** K7
Duff Pl *KLMNKN/STW* KA3 ..... **207** J6 🔲
SALT KA21 .... **192** A7
Duff St *GRNK* PA15 .... **2** E4
Duffus Pl *CAR/SHTL* G32 .... **130** C1
Duffus St *ESTRH* G34 .... **85** M8
Duffus Ter *CAR/SHTL* G32 ...... **130** C1
Duguid Dr *SALT* KA21 .... **192** A8 🔲
Duich Gdns *SMSTN* G23 .... **62** E8 🔲
Duisdale Rd *CAR/SHTL* G32 .... **130** C1 🔲
Dukes Ga *UD/BTH/TAN* G71 .... **131** L5 🔲
Dukes Pl *HMLTN* ML3 .... **174** D3
Dukes Rd *BAIL/MDB/MHD* G69... **108** F4
RUTH G73 .... **129** K4
TROON KA10 .... **216** B6
Duke St *COWCAD* G4 .... **12** A2
DEN/PKHD G31 .... **13** J3
CLSTN KA4 .... **214** C4
HMLTN ML3 .... **156** E6
LRKH ML9 .... **176** A5
MTHW ML1 .... **157** L1
PSLYS PA2 .... **9** H9
WISHAW ML2 .... **159** M3
Dulnain St *BLTYR/CAMB* G72 ... **130** D4
Dulsie Rd *SPRGB/BLRNK* G21 .... **84** C3 🔲
Dumbarton Rd *CLYDBK* G81 ..... **59** K5
OLDK G60 .... **58** C1
PTCK G11 .... **81** M7
SCOT G14 .... **80** E3
Dumbreck Av
CARD/HILL/MSPK G52 ..... **104** A6
Dumbreck Ct *PLKSD/SHW* G41 .. **104** A6
Dumbreck Pth
PLKSD/SHW G41 .... **104** A6 🔲
Dumbreck Pl
PLKSD/SHW G41 .... **104** B7
Dumbreck Rd *PLKSD/SHW* G41 .. **104** B7
Dumbreck Sq
PLKSD/SHW G41 .... **104** A6 🔲
Dumbrock Crs *CMPF/LLE* G63 ... **27** J6 🔲
Dumbrock Dr *CMPF/LLE* G63 .... **27** H6 🔲
Dumbrock Rd *CMPF/LLE* G63 .... **27** H6 🔲
MLNGV G62 .... **41** K7
Dumbuck Crs *DMBTN* G82 .... **37** J7
Dumbuck Rd *DMBTN* G82 .... **37** H7 🔲
DMBTN G82 .... **37** G4
Dumbuie Av *DMBTN* G82 .... **37** H5
Dumfries Crs *AIRDRIE* ML6 ..... **110** F4
Dumfriespark *RAYR/DAL* KA6 .. **229** D1 🔲
Dumgoyne Av *MLNGV* G62 .... **41** M8
Dumgoyne Dr *BSDN* G61 .... **61** K2
Dumgoyne Pl
CRMNK/CLK/EAG G76 ..... **151** J2 🔲
Dumgoyne Rd *KLMNK* KA1 .... **212** A6 🔲
Dumgoyne St *MRYH/FIRH* G20 ... **82** C1 🔲
Dunagoil Rd *CSMK* G45 .... **128** D7
Dunagoil St *CSMK* G45 .... **128** E7
Dunagoil Ter *CSMK* G45 .... **128** E8 🔲
Dunalastair Dr
STPS/GTHM/RID G33 .... **85** H4
Dunan Pl
STPS/GTHM/RID G33 ..... **107** L2 🔲
Dunard Rd *RUTH* G73 .... **129** H2
Dunard St *MRYH/FIRH* G20 .... **4** D1
Dunaskin St *PTCK* G11 .... **82** C8
Dunavon Pl *CTBR* ML5 .... **110** D5 🔲
Dunbar Av *CTBR* ML5 .... **109** K5
JNSTN PA5 .... **100** B8
RUTH G73 .... **129** J2
Dunbar Dr *MTHW* ML1 .... **158** A5 🔲
Dunbar Hl *EKILN* G74 .... **14** A3
Dunbar La *MTHW* ML1 .... **134** A7
Dunbar Pl *EKILN* G74 .... **14** A3
Dunbar Rd *PSLYS* PA2 .... **101** G8
Dunbar St *HMLTN* ML3 .... **156** B4
Dunbeath Av *NMRNS* G77 ...... **150** F4
Dunbeith Pl *MRYH/FIRH* G20 ..... **82** D4 🔲
Dunbeth Av *CTBR* ML5 .... **110** B2
Dunbeth Rd *CTBR* ML5 .... **110** A1
Dunblane Dr *EKILN* G74 .... **15** H1
Dunblane Pl *CTBR* ML5 .... **110** A1 🔲
Dunblane St *CGLW* G2 .... **5** H6
COWCAD G4 .... **5** H5
Dunbritton Rd *DMBTN* G82 .... **37** J6
Duncan Av *SCOT* G14 .... **81** J6
Duncan Ct *KLMNKN/STW* KA3 .. **207** K5 🔲
MTHW ML1 .... **133** K2 🔲
Duncan Dr *IRV* KA12 .... **203** K7 🔲
Duncan Graham St *LRKH* ML9 .. **176** B5
Duncan La North *SCOT* G14 ...... **81** J5 🔲
Duncan La South *SCOT* G14 ...... **81** J5 🔲
Duncan Mcintosh Rd
BALLOCH G68 .... **49** H2
Duncan Rd *HBR/GL* G84 .... **20** E6

PGL PA14 .... **34** B8 🔲
Duncansby Rd
STPS/GTHM/RID G33 ..... **107** K3 🔲
Duncan St *CLYDBK* G81 .... **60** B6 🔲
GRNK PA15 .... **2** B5
Duncannock Av *BRHD/NEIL* G78.. **148** E2
Duncannock Crs
BRHD/NEIL G78 .... **148** E2
Dunchattan Gv *TROON* KA10 ... **216** F7
Dunchattan Pl *DEN/PKHD* G31 ... **12** C3
Dunchattan St *DEN/PKHD* G31 ... **12** C1
Dunchurch Rd *PSLY* PA1 .... **102** F4
Dunclutha Dr *UD/BTH/TAN* G71.. **132** A8
Dunclutha St
DMNK/BRGTN G40 .... **106** B7
Duncolm Pl *MLNGV* G62 .... **41** K7
Duncombe Av *CLYDBK* G81 .... **60** B2
Duncombe St *MRYH/FIRH* G20 ... **82** D2
Duncraig Crs *JNSTN* PA5 .... **122** C1
Duncrub Dr *BSHPBGS* G64 .... **63** L8
Duncruin St *MRYH/FIRH* G20 ..... **82** C2
Duncruin Ter *MRYH/FIRH* G20 ... **82** D2
Duncryne Av *CAR/SHTL* G32 .... **107** K5
Duncryne Gdns
CAR/SHTL G32 .... **107** L5 🔲
Duncryne Pl *BSHPBGS* G64 ...... **83** L1
Duncryne Rd *ALEX/LLW* G83 ..... **25** L3 🔲
CAR/SHTL G32 .... **107** K5 🔲
Dundaff Hl *BALLOCH* G68 .... **48** C7 🔲
Dundas Av *BSHPBGS* G64 .... **64** B1
Dundashill *COWCAD* G4 .... **5** H5
Dundas Pl *EKILN* G74 .... **14** F1
Dundas St *CGLE* G1 .... **5** J9
Dundee Dr
CARD/HILL/MSPK G52 ..... **103** H6
Dundonald Av *JNSTN* PA5 .... **99** G3 🔲
Dundonald Crs *IRVSE* KA11 .... **208** E8 🔲
NMRNS G77 .... **151** G4
Dundonald Dr *HMLTN* ML3 ..... **174** D2 🔲
Dundonald Pl
BRHD/NEIL G78 .... **148** D2 🔲
Dundonald Rd *IRVSE* KA11 ..... **204** C8
KLMNK KA1 .... **211** J2
KVD/HLHD G12 .... **82** C5
PSLYN/LNWD PA3 .... **102** A2
TROON KA10 .... **216** F6
Dundonald St
BLTYR/CAMB G72 .... **155** J1
Dundrennan Rd *GVH/MTFL* G42... **127** M2
Dundyvan Ga *CTBR* ML5 .... **110** A4 🔲
Dundyvan La *WISHAW* ML2 ..... **158** F6 🔲
Dundyvan Rd *CTBR* ML5 .... **110** A4
Dundyvan St *WISHAW* ML2 ..... **159** J3
Dundyvan Wy *CTBR* ML5 .... **109** M4
Dunearn Pl *PSLYS* PA2 .... **9** L7
Dunearn St *COWCAD* G4 .... **4** D5
Dunedin Ct *EKILS* G75 .... **171** L1 🔲
Dunedin Dr *EKILS* G75 .... **153** G8
Dunedin Rd *LRKH* ML9 .... **176** B8
Dunellan Av
BAIL/MDB/MHD G69 .... **67** G7 🔲
Dunellan Crs
BAIL/MDB/MHD G69 .... **67** G7
Dunellan Dr *CLYDBK* G81 .... **60** B2
Dunellan Gdns
BAIL/MDB/MHD G69 .... **67** G7
Dunellan Rd *MLNGV* G62 .... **41** J7
Dunellan St
CARD/HILL/MSPK G52 ..... **103** L4
Dungavel Gdns *HMLTN* ML3 .... **174** E1
Dungavel Rd *KLMNK* KA1 .... **212** A5
Dungeonhill Rd *ESTRH* G34 ..... **108** D1
Dunglass Av *EKILN* G74 .... **153** M6
SCOT G14 .... **81** J5 🔲
Dunglass La *SCOT* G14 .... **81** J5 🔲
Dunglass La North *SCOT* G14 .... **81** J5 🔲
Dunglass La South *SCOT* G14 .... **81** J5 🔲
Dunglass Pl *MLNGV* G62 .... **41** L6
NMRNS G77 .... **150** A4
Dunglass Rd *BSHPTN* PA7 .... **58** C7
Dunglass Sq *EKILN* G74 .... **153** M6 🔲
Dunglass Vw *CMPF/LLE* G63 ..... **27** K5
Dungoil Av *BALLOCH* G68 .... **48** B6 🔲
Dungoil Rd *KKNTL* G66 .... **65** L5 🔲
Dungourney Dr
GRNKW/INVK PA16 .... **32** C2 🔲
Dungoyne St *MRYH/FIRH* G20 ... **82** C1 🔲
Dunira St *CAR/SHTL* G32 .... **106** F6
Dunivaig St
STPS/GTHM/RID G33 ..... **107** K1
Dunkeld Av *RUTH* G73 .... **129** H2
Dunkeld Dr *BSDN* G61 .... **62** B3
Dunkeld Pl *CTBR* ML5 .... **109** M5
HMLTN ML3 .... **155** H8
NMRNS G77 .... **151** H5
Dunkeld St *DEN/PKHD* G31 .... **13** K7
Dunkenny Rd *DRUM* G15 .... **60** F5
Dunkirk St *AIRDRIE* ML6 .... **91** H4
Dunlin *EKILN* G74 .... **153** L6
RUTH G73 .... **129** J2
Dunlin Crs *CRG/CRSL/HOU* PA6 ... **77** J8
Dunlop Av *RAYR/DAL* KA6 ...... **227** F7
Dunlop Ct *HMLTN* ML3 .... **174** E2 🔲
Dunlop Crs *AYR* KA8 .... **225** K8
IRVSE KA11 .... **204** B8
UD/BTH/TAN G71 .... **132** A8
Dunlop Gv *UD/BTH/TAN* G71 ... **109** G8
Dunlop Pl *MLNGV* G62 .... **41** M6 🔲
Dunlop Rd *BEITH* KA15 .... **169** G6
Dunlop St *BLTYR/CAMB* G72 ... **130** E3
CGLE G1 .... **11** J4
GRNKW/INVK PA16 .... **32** C6
KLMNK KA1 .... **16** E5 🔲
PSLYN/LNWD PA3 .... **100** C3
RNFRW PA4 .... **80** D5 🔲
Dunlop Ter *AYR* KA8 .... **229** K1
Dunmore Dr *MLNGV* G62 .... **62** C1
Dunmore St *CLYDBK* G81 .... **80** C1
Dunnachie Dr *CTBR* ML5 .... **109** H5
Dunnet Av *AIRDRIE* ML6 .... **88** F4
Dunnet Dr
CRG/CRSL/HOU PA6 .... **77** H8 🔲
Dunnett Av *KLMNK* KA1 .... **17** J6
Dunnichen Gdns *BSHPBGS* G64 .. **64** D8
Dunnikier Wk *BALLOCH* G68 ..... **47** L8 🔲
Dunning St *DEN/PKHD* G31 .... **13** M8 🔲
Dunn Ms *KLMNK* KA1 .... **211** J1
Dunnottar Ct *EKILN* G74 .... **153** J6 🔲

Dunnottar Crs *EKILN* G74 .... **153** J6 🔲
Dunnottar St *BSHPBGS* G64 ...... **64** D7
STPS/GTHM/RID G33 .... **85** H7
Dunn St *CLYDBK* G81 .... **59** L6
CLYDBK G81 .... **59** M3
DMNK/BRGTN G40 .... **12** D9
GRNK PA15 .... **2** A6
PSLY PA1 .... **9** L3
Dunns Wood Rd *CUMB* G67 ...... **49** K3
Dunolly Dr *NMRNS* G77 .... **150** F4
Dunolly St *SPRGB/BLRNK* G21 ..... **6** E6
Dunoon Av *KLMNKN/STW* KA3 .. **206** F5
Dunottar Av *CTBR* ML5 .... **110** B7
Dunottar Pl *CTBR* ML5 .... **110** B6 🔲
Dunphail Dr *ESTRH* G34 .... **108** D1
Dunphail Rd *ESTRH* G34 .... **108** D1
Dunragit St *DEN/PKHD* G31 .... **13** J2
Dunrobin Ct *EKILN* G74 .... **153** K6 🔲
Dunrobin Crs *EKILN* G74 .... **153** K6 🔲
Dunrobin Dr *EKILN* G74 .... **153** K5
GRK PA19 .... **31** G3 🔲
Dunrobin Pl *CTBR* ML5 .... **109** M2
Dunrobin Rd *AIRDRIE* ML6 ...... **111** J3
Dunrobin St *DEN/PKHD* G31 ...... **13** H4
Dunrod Hl *EKILN* G74 .... **153** M6
Dunrod Rd *GRNKW/INVK* PA16 ... **51** G2
Dunrod St *CAR/SHTL* G32 .... **107** K5
Dunscore Brae *HMLTN* ML3 .... **155** L7
Duns Crs *WISHAW* ML2 .... **159** J3
Dunside Dr *PLK/PH/NH* G53 .... **126** A3
Dunsiston Rd *AIRDRIE* ML6 ..... **112** B5
Dunskaith Pl *ESTRH* G34 .... **108** D2
Dunskaith St *ESTRH* G34 .... **108** D1
Dunsmore Rd *BSHPTN* PA7 .... **58** A5
Dunsmuir St *GOV/IBX* G51 ..... **104** B2
Duns Pth *CTBR* ML5 .... **110** D6
Dunswin Av *CLYDBK* G81 .... **59** L6
Dunsyre Av *SMSTN* G23 .... **62** E8 🔲
Dunsyre Pl
STPS/GTHM/RID G33 ..... **106** E1 🔲
Duntarvie Av *ESTRH* G34 .... **108** C1
Duntarvie Cl *ESTRH* G34 .... **108** C1
Duntarvie Crs *ESTRH* G34 .... **108** B1 🔲
Duntarvie Dr *ESTRH* G34 .... **108** B1 🔲
Duntarvie Gdns *ESTRH* G34 ..... **108** B1 🔲
Duntarvie Pl *ESTRH* G34 .... **108** B1 🔲
Duntarvie Quandrant
ESTRH G34 .... **108** C1 🔲
Duntarvie Rd *ESTRH* G34 .... **108** B1
Dunterlie Av *KNTSWD* G13 .... **81** G3
Dunterlie Ct *BRHD/NEIL* G78 ... **125** J6 🔲
Duntiblae Rd *KKNTL* G66 .... **66** A2
Duntiglennan Rd *CLYDBK* G81 ... **60** A3 🔲
Duntilland Av *SHOTTS* ML7 ..... **113** H7
Duntilland Rd *AIRDRIE* ML6 .... **112** E1
Duntocher Rd *BSDN* G61 .... **61** K3 🔲
CLYDBK G81 .... **60** A4 🔲
Duntreath Av *DRUM* G15 .... **60** F7
KNTSWD G13 .... **80** E1
Duntreath Dr *DRUM* G15 .... **60** F8
Duntreath Gdns *DRUM* G15 ...... **60** F7
Duntreath Gv *DRUM* G15 .... **60** F8 🔲
Duntreath Ter *KSYTH* G65 .... **47** K1 🔲
Duntroon Av *DEN/PKHD* G31 ...... **7** G8
Dunure Cts *KLWNG* KA13 .... **193** K6
Dunure Dr *HMLTN* ML3 .... **155** F8
KLMNKN/STW KA3 .... **17** K5
NMRNS G77 .... **151** G4
RUTH G73 .... **128** F4
Dunure Pl *CTBR* ML5 .... **109** L6 🔲
NMRNS G77 .... **151** G5
Dunure St *CTBR* ML5 .... **109** L6
MRYH/FIRH G20 .... **82** D2
Dunvegan *AIRDRIE* ML6 .... **88** C5
Dunvegan Av *CTBR* ML5 .... **87** K8
GRK PA19 .... **30** F4
JNSTN PA5 .... **100** B8
Dunvegan Dr *BSHPBGS* G64 ...... **64** A5
NMRNS G77 .... **151** G4
Dunvegan Pl *EKILN* G74 .... **153** K6 🔲
IRV KA12 .... **203** J4
UD/BTH/TAN G71 .... **131** K1 🔲
Dunvegan Qd *RNFRW* PA4 .... **80** B5 🔲
Dunwan Av *KNTSWD* G13 .... **80** F2
Dunwan Pl *KNTSWD* G13 .... **80** F2
Dura Rd *SHOTTS* ML7 .... **161** H1
Durban Av *CLYDBK* G81 .... **59** K5
EKILS G75 .... **171** G5
Durham Rd
GRNKW/INVK PA16 .... **31** L4 🔲
Durham Rd *PLKSD/SHW* G41 ... **104** D4
Durisdeer Dr *HMLTN* ML3 ...... **155** L8
Durness Av *BSDN* G61 .... **62** B4
Duror St *CAR/SHTL* G32 .... **107** G8
Durris Gdns *CAR/SHTL* G32 .... **107** K6 🔲
Durrockstock Crs *PSLYS* PA2 ... **123** M2
Durrockstock Rd *PSLYS* PA2 .... **123** M2
Durward *EKILN* G74 .... **154** E5
Durward Av *PLKSD/SHW* G41 ... **104** D8
Durward Ct *PLKSD/SHW* G41 ... **104** D8
Durward Crs *PSLYS* PA2 .... **100** F8
Duthie Rd *GRK* PA19 .... **32** A3
Duthil St *GOV/IBX* G51 .... **103** K3
Dyce Av *AIRDRIE* ML6 .... **110** E5
Dyce La *PTCK* G11 .... **82** A7
Dyer's Wynd *PSLY* PA1 .... **9** H3
Dyfrig St *BLTYR/CAMB* G72 ... **155** J1 🔲
SHOTTS ML7 .... **137** L5
Dykebar Av *KNTSWD* G13 .... **81** G3
Dykebar Crs *PSLYS* PA2 .... **102** B7
Dykehead Crs *AIRDRIE* ML6 ..... **88** F7 🔲
Dykehead La
STPS/GTHM/RID G33 ..... **107** K2
Dykehead Rd *AIRDRIE* ML6 .... **88** F7
BAIL/MDB/MHD G69 ...... **108** F2
BALLOCH G68 .... **48** C3
Dykehead Sq *HMLTN* ML3 ...... **155** M6
Dykehead St
STPS/GTHM/RID G33 ..... **107** K2
Dykemuir Pl *SPRGB/BLRNK* G21 ... **7** G1
Dykemuir Qd
SPRGB/BLRNK G21 .... **6** E1 🔲
Dykemuir St *SPRGB/BLRNK* G21 ... **6** F1
Dykeneuk Rd *PGL* PA14 .... **54** D2
Dyke Rd *KNTSWD* G13 .... **81** G1
Dykesfield Pl *SALT* KA21 .... **191** L7

Dykesmains Rd *SALT* KA21 .... 191 L7
Dykes Pl *SALT* KA21 .... 191 M7
The Dykes *KBRN* KA25 .... 167 G1 🔲
Dyke St *BAIL/MDB/MHD* G69 ...... 108 C4
    CTBR ML5 .... 109 H5 🔲
Dysart Ct *BALLOCH* G68 .... 47 L8 🔲
Dysart Wy *AIRDRIE* ML6 .... 112 A3

E

Eagle Crs *BSDN* G61 .... 61 H3
Eaglesham Ct *GOV/IBX* G51 ...... 10 A4 🔲
Eaglesham Pl *GOV/IBX* G51 ...... 10 A4 🔲
Eaglesham Rd
    CRMNK/CLK/EAG G76 .... 151 L5
    EKILS G75 .... 152 E8
    NMRNS G77 .... 150 D6
Eagle St *COWCAD* G4 .... 5 J4
Earl Av *AIRDRIE* ML6 .... 91 C4
Earlbank Av *SCOT* G14 .... 81 J5
Earlbank La North *SCOT* G14 .... 81 J5 🔲
Earlbank La South *SCOT* G14 .... 81 J5 🔲
Earl Dr *CRH/DND* KA2 .... 209 M7
Earl Haig Rd
    CARD/HILL/MSPK G52 .... 102 F2
Earl La *SCOT* G14 .... 81 J6
Earl Pl *BRWEIR* PA11 .... 98 D3
    SCOT G14 .... 81 J5 🔲
Earlsburn Rd *KKNTL* G66 .... 65 L5
Earlscourt
    BAIL/MDB/MHD G69 .... 66 F8
Earlsgate *CRG/CRSL/HOU* PA6 .. 77 H8
Earl's Ga *UD/BTH/TAN* G71 ...... 131 L6
Earl's Hl *BALLOCH* G68 .... 48 B6
Earlshill Dr *HWWD* PA9 .... 121 L4
Earlspark Av
    PLKSW/MSWD G43 .... 127 M3
Earlston Av *KLMNK* KA1 .... 211 M6
Earlston Crs *CTBR* ML5 .... 110 D6 🔲
Earlston St *WISHAW* ML2 .... 159 J3 🔲
Earl St *SCOT* G14 .... 81 H5
Earls Wy *AYRS* KA7 .... 228 C7
Earn Av *BSDN* G61 .... 62 B5
    RNFRW PA4 .... 80 E7
Earn Crs *WISHAW* ML2 .... 159 H8
Earnhill Rd *GRK* PA19 .... 31 J5
Earnock Av *MTHW* ML1 .... 157 J2
Earnock Gdns *HMLTN* ML3 .... 156 A7
Earnock Rd *HMLTN* ML3 .... 155 F7
Earnock St *HMLTN* ML3 .... 156 A5
    STPS/GTHM/RID G33 .... 7 L1
Earn Pl *KLMNK* KA1 .... 212 B4
Earn Rd *NMRNS* G77 .... 150 D2 🔲
    TROON KA10 .... 216 F5
Earnside St *CAR/SHTL* G32 ...... 107 H4 🔲
Earn St *STPS/GTHM/RID* G33 .... 84 E8
Earn Ter *SHOTTS* ML7 .... 137 L3
Easdale *EKILN* G74 .... 15 L7
Easdale Dr *CAR/SHTL* G32 ...... 106 F5
Easdale Pl *NMRNS* G77 .... 150 B4 🔲
Easdale Ri *HMLTN* ML3 .... 155 L6
East Academy St *WISHAW* ML2 .. 159 L1 🔲
East Av *AIRDRIE* ML6 .... 90 A6
    BLTYR/CAMB G72 .... 155 K4
    CARLUKE ML8 .... 178 D7
    MTHW ML1 .... 134 A7
    RNFRW PA4 .... 80 D6
    UD/BTH/TAN G71 .... 132 C3
Eastbank Dr *CAR/SHTL* G32 ..... 107 J4 🔲
East Barmoss Av *PGL* PA14 ..... 54 F2
East Barns St *CLYDBK* G81 ...... 80 D1
East Bath La *CGLE* G1 .... 4 C8
East Blackhall St *GRNK* PA15 ... 2 F6
East Bowhouse Head
    IRVSE KA11 .... 204 B4
East Bowhouse Wy *IRVSE* KA11.. 204 B4
East Breast *GRNK* PA15 .... 2 C4
East Buchanan St *PSLY* PA1 ..... 9 J3
Eastburn Crs
    SPRGB/BLRNK G21 .... 84 B3 🔲
Eastburn Rd *SPRGB/BLRNK* G21 .. 84 B4
East Burnside St *KSYTH* G65 .... 47 L3 🔲
East Campbell St *COWCAD* G4 .. 12 A3
East Castle Av *LARGS* KA30 ..... 115 K6 🔲
East Church Ct *NMLNS* KA16 .... 215 K2 🔲
Eastcote Av *SCOT* G14 .... 81 L5
East Crawford St *GRNK* PA15 ... 3 K7
Eastcroft *RUTH* G73 .... 129 H1
Eastcroft Ter *SPRGB/BLRNK* G21 .. 6 E1
East Dean St *BLSH* ML4 .... 133 H4 🔲
Eastend *LOCHW* PA12 .... 120 D6
Eastend Av *MTHW* ML1 .... 134 B8
Easter Craigs *DEN/PKHD* G31 ... 7 H9
Easter Crs *WISHAW* ML2 .... 159 L5
Easter Garngaber Rd *KKNTL* G66.. 65 L4
Easterhill Pl *CAR/SHTL* G32 ..... 106 F6 🔲
Easterhill Rd *HBR/GL* G84 ...... 20 E6
Easterhill St *CAR/SHTL* G32 .... 106 F6
Easterhouse Pl *ESTRH* G34 ..... 108 C1 🔲
Easterhouse Qd *ESTRH* G34 .... 108 C2 🔲
Easterhouse Rd
    BAIL/MDB/MHD G69 .... 108 B4
    ESTRH G34 .... 108 C2
Eastermains *KKNTL* G66 .... 46 B7
Easter Ms *UD/BTH/TAN* G71 .... 131 L4 🔲
Eastern Av *LARGS* KA30 .... 115 L6
Eastern Crs *KBRN* KA25 .... 167 G2
Easter Queenslie Rd
    STPS/GTHM/RID G33 .... 107 L1
Easter Rd *CRMNK/CLK/EAG* G76.. 152 A4
    SHOTTS ML7 .... 137 K4
Easterton Av
    CRMNK/CLK/EAG G76 .... 152 A4
Easter Wood Crs
    UD/BTH/TAN G71 .... 109 G4
East Faulds Rd
    LNK/LMHG ML11 .... 199 L4
Eastfield Av *BLTYR/CAMB* G72 .. 129 L4
Eastfield Crs *DMBTN* G82 .... 37 H7
Eastfield Pl *DMBTN* G82 .... 37 H7
Eastfield Rd *AIRDRIE* ML6 ...... 91 C5
    BALLOCH G68 .... 48 B6
    CARLUKE ML8 .... 189 G1
    FLK FK1 .... 91 M1
    SPRGB/BLRNK G21 .... 83 L5
Eastfield Ter *BLSH* ML4 .... 133 K5 🔲

Eastgate *BAIL/MDB/MHD* G69 ... 87 G4
    WISHAW ML2 .... 159 K6
East George St *CTBR* ML5 .... 110 B1 🔲
East Glebe Ter *HMLTN* ML3 ..... 156 D7
East Greenlees Av
    BLTYR/CAMB G72 .... 130 C6
East Greenlees Crs
    BLTYR/CAMB G72 .... 130 B6
East Greenlees Dr
    BLTYR/CAMB G72 .... 130 B6
East Greenlees Rd
    BLTYR/CAMB G72 .... 130 A6
East Gv *TROON* KA10 .... 216 F5
East Hallhill Rd
    BAIL/MDB/MHD G69 .... 107 M3
Easthall Pl
    STPS/GTHM/RID G33 .... 107 M2 🔲
East Hamilton St *GRNK* PA15 ... 3 K6
East High St *AIRDRIE* ML6 .... 111 L1 🔲
East Kilbride Rd
    BLTYR/CAMB G72 .... 129 M8
    CRMNK/CLK/EAG G76 .... 152 D5
    RUTH G73 .... 129 J4
East Kirkland *DALRY* KA24 ..... 184 D2
East La *PSLY* PA1 .... 102 B4 🔲
Eastlea Pl *AIRDRIE* ML6 .... 111 H3
East Lennox Dr *HBR/GL* G84 ... 20 C6
East Machan St *LRKH* ML9 ...... 176 B8 🔲
East Mains Rd *EKILN* G74 .... 153 M5
East Milton Gv *EKILS* G75 ...... 153 H8
East Montrose St *HBR/GL* G84 .. 20 E7
East Netherton St *KLMNK* KA1 .. 16 F7
Easton Pl *CTBR* ML5 .... 110 B4
East Park Crs
    KLMNKN/STW KA3 .... 206 B1
East Park Dr *KLMNKN/STW* KA3.. 206 B2
East Park Rd *AYR* KA8 .... 225 H6
East Rd *IRV* KA12 .... 203 J7
    KLBCH PA10 .... 99 C5
    MTHW ML1 .... 134 A5
    PSTWK KA9 .... 225 J5
East Rossdhu Dr *HBR/GL* G84 .. 20 E6
East Scott Ter *HMLTN* ML3 ...... 156 D8
East Shaw St *GRNK* PA15 .... 2 C4
    KLMNK KA1 .... 16 F8
Eastside *KKNTL* G66 .... 45 K8
East Springfield Ter
    BSHPBGS G64 .... 84 B1
East Stewart Pl *CTBR* ML5 ...... 110 C2
East Stewart St *CTBR* ML5 ...... 110 C3
    GRNK PA15 .... 3 C6
East Strd *NMLNS* KA16 .... 215 K2 🔲
East Strk *GRNK* PA15 .... 33 M7
East Thomson St *CLYDBK* G81 .. 60 B6 🔲
East Thornlie St *WISHAW* ML2 .. 159 H7
Eastvale Pl *KVGV* G3 .... 104 C1
East Wellbrae Crs *HMLTN* ML3 .. 156 B8
East Wellington St
    DEN/PKHD G31 .... 13 L5
East William St *GRNK* PA15 ..... 3 J7
Eastwood Av *GIF/THBK* G46 .... 127 J7
    IRV KA12 .... 203 K5 🔲
    PLKSD/SHW G41 .... 127 K1
Eastwood Crs *GIF/THBK* G46 ... 126 F5 🔲
Eastwood Dr *WISHAW* ML2 ..... 160 A4
Eastwood La *HBR/GL* G84 ...... 22 F1 🔲
Eastwoodmains Rd
    GIF/THBK G46 .... 127 J8
Eastwood Rd
    BAIL/MDB/MHD G69 .... 66 F7
East Woodside Av *PGL* PA14 ... 54 F3
Eastwood Vw
    BLTYR/CAMB G72 .... 130 E5
Easwald Bank *KLBCH* PA10 .... 99 H3
Ebroch Dr *KSYTH* G65 .... 47 L1
Ebroch Pk *KSYTH* G65 .... 47 L1
Eccles St *PPK/MIL* G22 .... 83 L4 🔲
Eckford St *CAR/SHTL* G32 ...... 107 G5 🔲
Eday St *PPK/MIL* G22 .... 83 K3
Edderton Pl
    STPS/GTHM/RID G33 .... 108 A2 🔲
Eddington Dr *NMRNS* G77 ...... 150 C6
Eddlewood Ct
    STPS/GTHM/RID G33 .... 108 A2 🔲
Eddlewood Pth
    STPS/GTHM/RID G33 .... 107 M2 🔲
Eddlewood Pl
    STPS/GTHM/RID G33 .... 107 M2
Eddlewood Rd
    STPS/GTHM/RID G33 .... 107 M2
Eden Ct *KLWNG* KA13 .... 193 H6 🔲
Eden Dr *EKILS* G75 .... 170 F3
Eden Gdns *EKILS* G75 .... 170 F2 🔲
Eden Gv *EKILS* G75 .... 170 F2
Edenhall Ct *NMRNS* G77 .... 150 D7
Edenhall Gv *NMRNS* G77 .... 150 D7 🔲
Edenhall Rd *AYR* KA8 .... 225 H5 🔲
Edenkill Pl *CMPF/LLE* G63 ..... 27 J6
Eden La *STPS/GTHM/RID* G33 .. 7 L6
Eden Pl *KLMNK* KA1 .... 212 B4 🔲
    RNFRW PA4 .... 80 E7
Edenside *BALLOCH* G68 .... 49 H2
Eden St *STPS/GTHM/RID* G33 .. 7 M6
Edenwood St
    DEN/PKHD G31 .... 106 E4 🔲
Edgam Dr
    CARD/HILL/MSPK G52 .... 103 J4
Edgefauld Av *SPRGB/BLRNK* G21.. 6 D1
Edgefauld Rd *SPRGB/BLRNK* G21.. 6 D1
Edgefauld Pl
    SPRGB/BLRNK G21 .... 83 M4 🔲
Edgefauld Rd
    SPRGB/BLRNK G21 .... 83 M5
Edgehill La *PTCK* G11 .... 82 A5
Edgehill Rd *BSDN* G61 .... 61 L3
    PTCK G11 .... 81 M5 🔲
Edgemont Pk *HMLTN* ML3 ...... 174 C1 🔲
Edgemont St *PLKSD/SHW* G41 .. 127 L1
Edinbeg Av *GVH/MTFL* G42 ..... 128 E1
Edinbeg Pl *GVH/MTFL* G42 ..... 128 E1 🔲
Edinburgh La *GRK* PA19 .... 30 E4 🔲
Edinburgh Rd *CAR/SHTL* G32 ... 107 G2

    MTHW ML1 .... 134 D3
    STPS/GTHM/RID G33 .... 106 E2 🔲
Edington Gdns
    BAIL/MDB/MHD G69 .... 66 F6
Edington St *COWCAD* G4 .... 5 G5
Edison Pl *KLWNG* KA13 .... 193 L8
Edison St *CARD/HILL/MSPK* G52.. 102 E1
Edmiston Av *PSTWK* KA9 .... 225 H2
Edmiston Dr *GOV/IBX* G51 ...... 104 A3
    PSLYN/LNWD PA3 .... 99 M3
Edmonstone Dr *KSYTH* G65 .... 47 K2 🔲
Edmonstone Ter *EKILS* G75 ..... 14 B5
Edmund Kean *EKILN* G74 .... 154 C4 🔲
Edrom Ct *CAR/SHTL* G32 .... 106 F4
Edrom St *CAR/SHTL* G32 .... 106 F5
Edward Av *RNFRW* PA4 .... 80 D5
Edward Dr *HBR/GL* G84 .... 20 C6
Edward St *BAIL/MDB/MHD* G69.. 108 D2
    CLYDBK G81 .... 80 D2
    HMLTN ML3 .... 156 D2
    MTHW ML1 .... 157 M4
Edwin St *GOV/IBX* G51 .... 104 D4
Edzell Ct *SCOT* G14 .... 81 K7
Edzell Dr *JNSTN* PA5 .... 100 D3
    NMRNS G77 .... 150 E5
Edzell Gdns *BSHPBGS* G64 ..... 84 C1
    WISHAW ML2 .... 159 G7 🔲
Edzell Pl *SCOT* G14 .... 81 K6 🔲
Edzell Rw *KLWNG* KA13 .... 193 H6
Edzell St *CTBR* ML5 .... 109 K5
    SCOT G14 .... 81 K7
Egidia Av *GIF/THBK* G46 .... 127 J7 🔲
Egilsay Crs *PPK/MIL* G22 .... 83 J1
Egilsay Pl *PPK/MIL* G22 .... 83 J1
Egilsay St *PPK/MIL* G22 .... 83 J1
Egilsay Ter *PPK/MIL* G22 .... 83 J1 🔲
Eglinton Av *GBLS* G5 .... 11 G6
    SALT KA21 .... 200 D2 🔲
Eglinton Crs *TROON* KA10 ...... 216 D7
Eglinton Dr *GIF/THBK* G46 ...... 127 J7
    SKLM PA17 .... 70 A4
    TROON KA10 .... 216 D7
Eglinton Gdns *SKLM* PA17 ...... 70 A5
Eglinton Pl *AYRS* KA7 .... 18 D2
    KLWNG KA13 .... 193 L6
    SALT KA21 .... 200 D2 🔲
Eglinton Rd *ARD* KA22 .... 191 H5
Eglinton Sq *ARD* KA22 .... 191 H5 🔲
Eglinton Ter *AYRS* KA7 .... 18 D2
    SKLM PA17 .... 70 A8
Egmont Pk *EKILS* G75 .... 171 G2
Eider *EKILS* G75 .... 171 G5
Eider Av *EKILS* G75 .... 171 G4
Eider Gv *EKILS* G75 .... 171 G4
Eider Pl *EKILS* G75 .... 171 G5
Eighth St *UD/BTH/TAN* G71 ..... 108 E8
Eildon Crs *AIRDRIE* ML6 .... 111 M8
Eildon Dr *BRHD/NEIL* G78 ...... 125 J8
Eildon Rd *KKNTL* G66 .... 65 M1
Eileen Gdns *BSHPBGS* G64 ..... 64 B7
Elba St *AYR* KA8 .... 19 G2
Elcho St *DMNK/BRGTN* G40 ... 12 C4
Elder Av *BEITH* KA15 .... 168 A1
Elderbank *BSDN* G61 .... 61 L6
Elder Crs *BLTYR/CAMB* G72 .... 130 E5
Elder Gv *UD/BTH/TAN* G71 ..... 132 B2
Elderpark Gdns
    GOV/IBX G51 .... 103 M2 🔲
Elderpark Gv *GOV/IBX* G51 .... 103 M2 🔲
Elderpark St *GOV/IBX* G51 ..... 103 M2
Elderslea Rd *CARLUKE* ML8 .... 189 G1
Elderslie Crs *KLMNK* KA1 .... 211 L5
Elderslie St *KVGV* G3 .... 4 C8
Elder St *GOV/IBX* G51 .... 103 M2
Eldin Pl *BRWEIR* PA11 .... 98 C3
    JNSTN PA5 .... 100 B7
Eldon Gdns *BSHPBGS* G64 ..... 63 L8
Eldon Pl *GRNKW/INVK* PA16 ... 32 C1 🔲
Eldon St *GRNKW/INVK* PA16 ... 32 C1
    KVGV G3 .... 4 B5
Elgin Av *EKILN* G74 .... 153 M6
Elgin Gdns
    CRMNK/CLK/EAG G76 .... 151 M1
Elgin Pl *AIRDRIE* ML6 .... 110 E4
    CTBR ML5 .... 110 B6
    EKILN G74 .... 153 M6
Elgin Rd *BSDN* G61 .... 61 M2
Elgin Ter *HMLTN* ML3 .... 155 L5
Elgin Wy *BLSH* ML4 .... 133 G3
Elibank St *STPS/GTHM/RID* G33.. 85 G3
Elie St *PTCK* G11 .... 82 C7
Eliot Crs *HMLTN* ML3 .... 156 D8
Eliot Ter *HMLTN* ML3 .... 156 D7
Elizabeth Av *KKNTL* G66 .... 45 H3
Elizabeth Crs *GIF/THBK* G46 ... 127 G7
Elizabeth Qd *MTHW* ML1 .... 133 M4 🔲
Elizabeth St *GOV/IBX* G51 ..... 104 C4
Elizabeth Wynd *HMLTN* ML3 ... 174 C2 🔲
Ella Gdns *BLSH* ML4 .... 133 J5
Ellangowan Rd *MLNGV* G62 .... 42 A8 🔲
    PLKSD/SHW G41 .... 127 J1
Ellergreen Rd *BSDN* G61 .... 61 L5
Ellerslie St *JNSTN* PA5 .... 100 A6
Ellesmere St *PPK/MIL* G22 ..... 4 F1
Elliot Av *GIF/THBK* G46 .... 127 G7
    PSLYS PA2 .... 123 L2
Elliot Dr *MTHW* ML1 .... 133 K8 🔲
Elliot Crs *EKILN* G74 .... 15 L1
Elliot Dr *GIF/THBK* G46 .... 127 G6 🔲
Elliot Pl *KVGV* G3 .... 10 B1
Elliot St *KVGV* G3 .... 10 B2
Ellisland *EKILN* G74 .... 154 D6
    KKNTL G66 .... 46 B7
Ellisland Av *CLYDBK* G81 .... 60 C6
Ellisland Crs *CSMK* G45 .... 128 E4 🔲
Ellisland Dr *BLTYR/CAMB* G72 .. 155 H3
    KKNTL G66 .... 46 A7
    KLMNKN/STW KA3 .... 17 M5
Ellisland Pl *AYRS* KA7 .... 19 J8
    SALT KA21 .... 192 A6 🔲
Ellisland Rd
    CRMNK/CLK/EAG G76 .... 151 L4
    CUMB G67 .... 49 H7
    PLKSW/MSWD G43 .... 127 K3

Ellisland Sq *AYRS* KA7 .... 19 J8
Ellismuir Farm Rd
    BAIL/MDB/MHD G69 .... 108 D5 🔲
Ellismuir Pl
    BAIL/MDB/MHD G69 .... 108 C5 🔲
Ellismuir Rd
    BAIL/MDB/MHD G69 .... 108 C5
Ellismuir St *CTBR* ML5 .... 109 L6
Ellismuir Wy *UD/BTH/TAN* G71.. 109 G8
Ellis St *KLMNK* KA1 .... 110 A3
    KLMNK KA1 .... 16 D5
Elliston Av *PLK/PH/NH* G53 .... 126 C4
Elliston Crs *PLK/PH/NH* G53 ... 126 C4
Elliston Dr *PLK/PH/NH* G53 .... 126 C4
Elliston Pl *HWWD* PA9 .... 121 M4
Elliston Rd *HWWD* PA9 .... 121 M4
Ellis Wy *MTHW* ML1 .... 157 M4
Ellon Dr *PSLYN/LNWD* PA3 ..... 100 A4 🔲
Ellon Gv *PSLYN/LNWD* PA3 .... 102 A2
Ellrig *EKILS* G75 .... 171 K4
Elm Av *KKNTL* G66 .... 65 J3
    RNFRW PA4 .... 80 C5
Elm Bank *BSHPBGS* G64 .... 84 B1
    KKNTL G66 .... 65 K1
Elmbank Av *KLMNK* KA1 .... 17 G4
    UD/BTH/TAN G71 .... 132 B2
    HMLTN ML3 .... 156 M1
Elmbank Crs *CGLW* G2 .... 4 E8
    KLMNK KA1 .... 17 G4
    LRKH ML9 .... 176 C8
Elmbank Dr *ALEX/LLW* G83 .... 25 M4
    KLMNK KA1 .... 17 G4
Elmbank Rd *PGL* PA14 .... 56 C2
Elmbank St *AYR* KA8 .... 224 F6
    BLSH ML4 .... 133 C5 🔲
    CARLUKE ML8 .... 189 G1
    CGLW G2 .... 4 E9
Elmbank Street La *KVGV* G3 ... 4 E9
Elmbank Ter *IRV* KA12 .... 203 K5
Elm Ct *HMLTN* ML3 .... 174 F5
Elm Crs *UD/BTH/TAN* G71 ..... 132 D2
Elm Dr *AIRDRIE* ML6 .... 111 L6
    BLTYR/CAMB G72 .... 130 C4
    CUMB G67 .... 49 M5
    JNSTN PA5 .... 122 F1
Elmfoot St *GBLS* G5 .... 105 K7
Elm Gdns *BSDN* G61 .... 61 L3
    TROON KA10 .... 217 G3
Elm Gv *PGL* PA14 .... 56 C2 🔲
Elmhurst *MTHW* ML1 .... 157 K5
Elmira Rd *BAIL/MDB/MHD* G69.. 86 C2
Elmore Av *LNPK/KPK* G44 ..... 128 B4
Elm Pl *EKILS* G75 .... 171 J3
Elm Qd *AIRDRIE* ML6 .... 111 K3
Elm Rd *BRWEIR* PA11 .... 98 B1 🔲
    CLYDBK G81 .... 60 A4
    DMBTN G82 .... 36 F4
    MTHW ML1 .... 134 A7 🔲
    PSLYS PA2 .... 102 A8
    RUTH G73 .... 129 H5
Elmslie Ct *BAIL/MDB/MHD* G69.. 108 C5
Elms Pl *BEITH* KA15 .... 144 B8
    SVSTN KA20 .... 192 E7
Elm St *BLTYR/CAMB* G72 .... 155 L2
    CRMNK/CLK/EAG G76 .... 151 M3
    CTBR ML5 .... 110 C4 🔲
    KKNTL G66 .... 44 E1
    MTHW ML1 .... 157 K2
    SCOT G14 .... 81 K6 🔲
Elm Ter *GRK* PA19 .... 31 L3 🔲
Elmvale Rw *PPK/MIL* G22 ...... 83 L4 🔲
Elmvale St *PPK/MIL* G22 .... 83 L4
Elm View Ct *BLSH* ML4 .... 133 K5 🔲
Elm Wk *BSDN* G61 .... 61 L3
Elm Wy *BLTYR/CAMB* G72 ..... 130 E5
Elmway *LRKH* ML9 .... 176 A4
Elmwood Av *NMRNS* G77 ...... 150 F3 🔲
    PTCK G11 .... 81 M5 🔲
Elmwood Ct *UD/BTH/TAN* G71.. 132 A7
Elmwood La *PTCK* G11 .... 81 M5 🔲
Elphinstone Crs *EKILS* G75 ..... 15 J9
Elphinstone Pl *GOV/IBX* G51 ... 104 C2
Elphinstone Rd *GIF/THBK* G46 .. 151 G2
Elphin St *SMSTN* G23 .... 62 D8 🔲
Elrig Rd *LNPK/KPK* G44 .... 127 M4
Elspeth Gdns *BSHPBGS* G64 ... 64 C7
Elswick Dr *AIRDRIE* ML6 .... 91 G5
Eltham St *PPK/MIL* G22 .... 5 G2
Elvan Pl *EKILS* G75 .... 170 E2 🔲
Elvan St *CAR/SHTL* G32 .... 106 F4
    MTHW ML1 .... 157 K3
Embo Dr *KNTSWD* G13 .... 81 H3 🔲
Emerald Ter *BLSH* ML4 .... 133 G5
Emerson Rd *BSHPBGS* G64 .... 64 A1
Emerson Rd West *BSHPBGS* G64.. 64 A4
Emerson St *MRYH/FIRH* G20 ... 83 G3
Emily Dr *MTHW* ML1 .... 157 L5
Emma Jay Rd *BLSH* ML4 .... 133 H4
Empire Wy *MTHW* ML1 .... 133 J8 🔲
Empress Ct *GRNK* PA15 .... 3 G6 🔲
Empress Dr *HBR/GL* G84 ...... 20 A6
Endfield Av *KVD/HLHD* G12 .... 82 A6
Endrick Bank *BSHPBGS* G64 ... 64 A5 🔲
Endrick Dr *BSDN* G61 .... 61 M5
    PSLY PA1 .... 102 B3
Endrick St *SPRGB/BLRNK* G21 .. 5 M1
Endrick Wy *ALEX/LLW* G83 .... 25 K3 🔲
Engels St *ALEX/LLW* G83 ...... 25 L2 🔲
Englewood Av *AYR* KA8 .... 225 H4
English Rw *AIRDRIE* ML6 .... 111 J6
English St *WISHAW* ML2 .... 158 D6
Ennerdale *EKILS* G75 .... 170 F3
Ennisfree Rd *BLTYR/CAMB* G72.. 155 K1
Ensay St *PPK/MIL* G22 .... 83 K2 🔲
Enterkin St *CAR/SHTL* G32 ..... 106 F5 🔲
Eribol Pl *SHOTTS* ML7 .... 137 L3
Ericht Rd *PLKSW/MSWD* G43 .. 127 K4
Eriska Av *SCOT* G14 .... 81 C4
Eriskay Av *HMLTN* ML3 .... 155 M7
    NMRNS G77 .... 150 B4
Eriskay Crs *NMRNS* G77 .... 150 B4
Eriskay Dr *OLDK* G60 .... 59 J3 🔲
Ermelo Gdns *EKILS* G75 .... 171 H5
Erradale St *PPK/MIL* G22 .... 83 G2

Errogie St *ESTRH* G34 .... 108 B1
Erskine Av *PLKSD/SHW* G41 .... 104 B5
Erskine Br *ERSK* PA8 .... 59 J4
Erskine Crs *AIRDRIE* ML6 .... 110 F4
Erskinefauld Rd
    PSLYN/LNWD PA3 .... 100 B3
Erskine Ferry Rd *OLDK* G60 ... 59 G4
Erskine Pl *KLMNKN/STW* KA3 .. 207 J7
    SALT KA21 .... 200 F2 🔲
Erskine Rd *GIF/THBK* G46 ...... 151 H3
Erskine Sq
    CARD/HILL/MSPK G52 .... 102 F2
Erskine Wy *SHOTTS* ML7 ...... 137 L5
Ervie St *ESTRH* G34 .... 108 C2 🔲
Escart Rd *CARLUKE* ML8 .... 178 F6
Esdaile Ct *MTHW* ML1 .... 134 A6 🔲
Esk Av *RNFRW* PA4 .... 80 E7
Eskbank St *CAR/SHTL* G32 ..... 107 G3
Esk Dl *EKILN* G74 .... 153 J6 🔲
Eskdale Dr *RUTH* G73 .... 129 K2
Eskdale Rd *BSDN* G61 .... 61 K7
Eskdale St *GVH/MTFL* G42 ..... 105 H8 🔲
Esk Dr *PSLYS* PA2 .... 100 E8
Esk St *KLMNK* KA1 .... 212 B5
    TROON KA10 .... 216 E4
Esk St *SCOT* G14 .... 80 F4
Esmond St *KVGV* G3 .... 82 C8
Espedair St *PSLYS* PA2 .... 9 H6
Esperanto Rd *PSTWK* KA9 ..... 225 L1
Espieside Crs *CTBR* ML5 .... 109 L1
Esplanade *AYRS* KA7 .... 18 C1
    GRNKW/INVK PA16 .... 32 C1
    PSTWK KA9 .... 221 H7
    PSTWK KA9 .... 225 G2
Essenside Av *DRUM* G15 ...... 61 J7
Essex Dr *SCOT* G14 .... 81 L5
Essex La *SCOT* G14 .... 81 L6 🔲
Essex Rd *GRNKW/INVK* PA16 .. 31 L5 🔲
Esslemont Av *SCOT* G14 .... 81 H5
Esson Pl *KLMNKN/STW* KA3 ... 207 G6
Estate Qd *CAR/SHTL* G32 ...... 130 C1 🔲
Estate Rd *CAR/SHTL* G32 ...... 130 C1
Etive Av *BSDN* G61 .... 62 B5
    HMLTN ML3 .... 156 A8
Etive Ct *CLYDBK* G81 .... 60 C4
    CUMB G67 .... 68 B3
Etive Crs *BSHPBGS* G64 .... 64 B8
    CUMB G67 .... 68 B3
    WISHAW ML2 .... 177 H1
Etive Dr *AIRDRIE* ML6 .... 111 J4
    BSHPTN PA7 .... 58 C7
    CUMB G67 .... 68 B3
    GIF/THBK G46 .... 127 K8
Etive Pl *CUMB* G67 .... 68 C3 🔲
    IRV KA12 .... 203 K4
Etive Rd *WMYSB* PA18 .... 50 A8
Etive St *CAR/SHTL* G32 .... 107 G4
    WISHAW ML2 .... 159 H8
Etna St *WISHAW* ML2 .... 158 C5
Eton La *KVD/HLHD* G12 .... 4 A4
Ettrick Av *BLSH* ML4 .... 133 G3 🔲
    RNFRW PA4 .... 80 F7
Ettrick Crs *KLMNKN/STW* KA3.. 206 F5
    RUTH G73 .... 129 J2
Ettrick Dr *BSDN* G61 .... 61 J2
    BSHPTN PA7 .... 58 C7
Ettrick Hl *EKILN* G74 .... 154 A6 🔲
Ettrick Pl *AYR* KA8 .... 225 H5
    PLKSW/MSWD G43 .... 127 K2
Ettrick St *WISHAW* ML2 .... 159 G4
Ettrick Ter *JNSTN* PA5 .... 122 C1
Euchan Pl *TROON* KA10 .... 216 F4
Evan Crs *GIF/THBK* G46 .... 127 K7
Evan Dr *GIF/THBK* G46 .... 127 K8
Evanton Dr *GIF/THBK* G46 ..... 126 E6
Evanton Pl *GIF/THBK* G46 ...... 126 E6
Evelyn Ter *KLWNG* KA13 .... 193 L7
Everard Ct *SPRGB/BLRNK* G21 .. 83 L2
Everard Dr *SPRGB/BLRNK* G21 .. 83 L3
Everard Pl *SPRGB/BLRNK* G21 .. 83 L2 🔲
Everard Qd *SPRGB/BLRNK* G21 .. 83 L2
Eversley St *CAR/SHTL* G32 ..... 107 G6 🔲
Everton Rd *PLK/PH/NH* G53 .... 103 J7 🔲
Ewart Crs *HMLTN* ML3 .... 156 A7
Ewart Ter *HMLTN* ML3 .... 156 B7 🔲
Ewenfield Av *AYRS* KA7 .... 228 F5
Ewenfield Gdns *AYRS* KA7 ..... 228 F5
Ewenfield Pk *AYRS* KA7 .... 228 F5
Ewenfield Rd *AYRS* KA7 .... 228 F5
Ewing Ct *HMLTN* ML3 .... 174 C2
Ewing Pl *DEN/PKHD* G31 ...... 13 K6
Ewing Rd *LOCHW* PA12 .... 120 C6
Ewing St *KLBCH* PA10 .... 99 G6
    RUTH G73 .... 129 G2
Ewing Wk *MLNGV* G62 .... 42 C8
Ewing Wy *KLMNKN/STW* KA3 .. 197 K1
Excelsior St *WISHAW* ML2 ...... 158 D6
Exeter Dr *PTCK* G11 .... 82 A7 🔲
Exeter St *CTBR* ML5 .... 110 A4
Exmouth Pl
    GRNKW/INVK PA16 .... 31 L4 🔲
Eynort St *PPK/MIL* G22 .... 83 G2
Eyrepoint Ct
    STPS/GTHM/RID G33 .... 107 G1 🔲

F

Factory Rd *MTHW* ML1 .... 157 L4 🔲
Fagan Ct *BLTYR/CAMB* G72 ..... 131 L8
Faifley Rd *CLYDBK* G81 .... 60 C2
Failford Pl *KLMNKN/STW* KA3 .. 207 H4
Fairbairn Crs *GIF/THBK* G46 ... 127 J2
Fairburn St *CAR/SHTL* G32 ..... 106 F5
Fairfax Av *LNPK/KPK* G44 ...... 128 C4
Fairfield Ct
    CRMNK/CLK/EAG G76 .... 151 L4
Fairfield Dr
    CRMNK/CLK/EAG G76 .... 151 L4
    RNFRW PA4 .... 80 D8
Fairfield Gdns *GOV/IBX* G51 ... 103 M1 🔲
    GOV/IBX G51 .... 103 M1 🔲
    HMLTN ML3 .... 156 E8
    UD/BTH/TAN G71 .... 132 B7
Fairfield Rd *AYRS* KA7 .... 18 D5 🔲
Fairfield St *GOV/IBX* G51 .... 103 M1

Fairford Dr *CUMB* G67 .... 68 D3
Fairhaven *TROON* KA10 .... 216 E2 🔢
Fairhaven Av *AIRDRIE* ML6 .... 111 L3
Fairhaven St *SMSTN* G23 .... 82 D1
Fairhaven Sq *KLWNG* KA13 .... 193 H5
Fairhill Av *HMLTN* ML3 .... 156 C8
   PLK/PH/NH G53 .... 126 C2
Fairhill Crs *HMLTN* ML3 .... 156 C8
Fairhill Pl *HMLTN* ML3 .... 174 B2
Fairholm Av *HMLTN* ML3 .... 157 K8
Fairholm St *CAR/SHTL* G32 ...... 106 F5 🔢
   LRKH ML9 .... 175 M5
Fairley St *GOV/IBX* G51 .... 104 B3
Fairlie *EKILN* G74 .... 14 D1
Fairlie Av *KLMNK* KA1 .... 16 A7
Fairlieburne Gdns
   FAIRLIE KA29 .... 139 K7 🔢
Fairlie Dr *IRVSE* KA11 .... 204 B3
Fairlie Park Dr *PTCK* G11 .... 82 A7 🔢
Fairlie Vw *CRH/DND* KA2............. 210 D4
Fair Oaks
   CRMNK/CLK/EAG G76 .... 152 E1 🔢
Fairrie St *GRNK* PA15 .... 3 L8
Fair View Dr *LNK/LMHG* ML11 ... 198 B5
Fairway *BSDN* G61 .... 61 H4
Fairway Av *PSLYS* PA2 .... 124 D1
Fairways *KLMNKN/STW* KA3 ...... 197 L1
   LRKH ML9 .... 176 C6 🔢
Fairways Vw *CLYDBK* G81 .... 60 D3
Fairweather Pl *NMRNS* G77 .... 150 C5
Fairyhill Pl *KLMNK* KA1 .... 16 D8
Fairyhill Rd *KLMNK* KA1 .... 16 D8
Fairyknowe Gdns
   UD/BTH/TAN G71 .... 132 B7
Faith Av *BRWEIR* PA11 .... 75 L7
Falconbridge Rd *EKILN* G74 ...... 154 C5 🔢
   PSLYS/LNWD PA3 .... 8 A5
Falconer Ter *PGL* PA14 .... 34 C7 🔢
Falconer Ter *HMLTN* ML3 .... 156 C8
Falcon Rd *JNSTN* PA5 .... 122 D2
Falcon Ter *MRYH/FIRH* G20 .... 82 C1
Falcon Terrace La
   MRYH/FIRH G20 .... 82 C1
Falfield St *GBLS* G5 .... 10 F7
Falkland Av *NMRNS* G77 .... 151 G5
Falkland Crs *BSHPBGS* G64 .... 84 D1
Falklandcrs *BSHPBGS* G64 .... 64 D8
Falkland Dr *EKILN* G74 .... 14 C3
Falkland La *KVD/HLHD* G12 .... 82 B6
Falkland Pk *EKILN* G74 .... 14 C3
Falkland Park Rd *AYR* KA8 .... 225 G6
Falkland Pl *AYR* KA8 .... 225 G6
   CTBR ML5 .... 110 B6 🔢
   EKILN G74 .... 14 D4
Falkland Rd *AYR* KA8 .... 225 G6
Falkland St *KVD/HLHD* G12 .... 82 B6
Falloch Pl *WISHAW* ML2 .... 159 M3
Falloch Rd *BSDN* G61 .... 61 J7
   GVH/MTFL G42 .... 128 A2
   MLNGV G62 .... 41 L6
Fallside Av *UD/BTH/TAN* G71 ..... 132 C3
Fallside Rd *UD/BTH/TAN* G71 ..... 132 A7
   UD/BTH/TAN G71 .... 132 B8
Falmouth Dr *GRNKW/INVK* PA16 ... 31 M4
Falside Av *PSLYS* PA2 .... 101 L8
Falside Rd *CAR/SHTL* G32 .... 107 G7
   PSLYS PA2 .... 101 K8
Falstaff *EKILN* G74 .... 154 C4
Fancy Farm Pl
   GRNKW/INVK PA16 .... 31 M5 🔢
Fancy Farm Rd
   GRNKW/INVK PA16 .... 31 M5
Faraday Av *WISHAW* ML2 .... 159 J5
Faransay Pl
   KLMNKN/STW KA3 .... 207 G4 🔢
Fara St *SMSTN* G23 .... 82 F1
Fardalehill Vw *CRH/DND* KA2.... 205 M8
Farden Pl *PSTWK* KA9 .... 225 K3 🔢
Farie St *RUTH* G73 .... 128 F1
Farlands Vw *WKIL* KA23 .... 181 J5
Farm Ct *UD/BTH/TAN* G71 .... 132 B5
Farm Crs *MTHW* ML1 .... 134 F5
Farmeloan Rd *RUTH* G73 .... 129 H1
Farmfield Ter *WKIL* KA23 .... 181 K4
Farmgate Sq *BLSH* ML4 .... 132 F5
Farmington Av
   CAR/SHTL G32 .... 107 K5 🔢
Farmington Gdns
   CAR/SHTL G32 .... 107 K4 🔢
Farmington Gv
   CAR/SHTL G32 .... 107 K4 🔢
Farm La *BLSH* ML4 .... 132 F6 🔢
Farm Pk *KNTLL* G66 .... 65 K5
Farm Rd *BLTYR/CAMB* G72 .... 131 K8
   CLYDBK G81 .... 59 N6
   CLYDBK G81 .... 60 A2
   HMLTN ML3............................ 155 M5
   KLMNKN/STW KA3 .... 206 E6
   PGL PA14 .... 54 E2 🔢
   PLKSD/SHW G41 .... 104 B4
Farm St *MTHW* ML1 .... 157 K2 🔢
Farndale *EKILN* G74 .... 153 J6
Farne Dr *LNPK/KPK* G44 .... 128 B5
Farnell St *COWCAD* G4 .... 5 G4
Farquhar Rd *PGL* PA14 .... 33 M7
Farrell Pl *AYR* KA8 .... 225 H7
Farrier Ct *JNSTN* PA5 .... 99 M6
Faskally Av *BSHPBGS* G64 .... 63 L6
Faskin Crs *PLK/PH/NH* G53 .... 125 M2
   AIRDRIE ML6 .... 110 F4
Faskine Av *AIRDRIE* ML6 .... 110 F4
Faskine Crs *AIRDRIE* ML6 .... 110 F4
Faskin Pl *PLK/PH/NH* G53 .... 125 M2
Faskin Rd *PLK/PH/NH* G53 .... 125 M2
Fasque Pl *DRUM* G15 .... 60 E4
Fauldhouse St *GBLS* G5 .... 105 K6
Faulds *BAIL/MDB/MHD* G69 ..... 108 C4
Faulds Gdns
   BAIL/MDB/MHD G69 .... 108 C4 🔢
Fauldspark Crs
   BAIL/MDB/MHD G69 .... 108 C3
Faulds Park Rd *GRK* PA19 .... 30 E4
Faulds St *CTBR* ML5 .... 109 L6
Fauldswood Crs *PSLYS* PA2 .... 8 B9

Fauldswood Dr *PSLYS* PA2 .... 8 A9
Faulkner Gv *MTHW* ML1 .... 158 F1
Fearnan Pl *GRNKW/INVK* PA16 ... 32 A5
Fearnmore Rd *MRYH/FIRH* G20 ... 82 D2
Fearnoch *PSTWK* KA9 .... 225 J4 🔢
The Fells *KNTLL* G66 .... 44 E1
Fellsview Av *KKNTL* G66 .... 45 M8
Felton Pl *KNTSWD* G13 .... 80 F2
Fencedyke Wy *IRVSE* KA11 .... 204 A6
Fendoch St *CAR/SHTL* G32 .... 107 G5
Fenella St *CAR/SHTL* G32 .... 107 H4 🔢
Fennsbank Av *RUTH* G73 .... 129 K6
Fenwick Dr *BRHD/NEIL* G78 ...... 125 K8
   HMLTN ML3.............................. 174 C2
Fenwickland Av *AYRS* KA7 .... 229 G5
Fenwickland Pl *AYRS* KA7 .... 229 G5
Fenwick Pl *GIF/THBK* G46 .... 127 H8 🔢
Fenwick Rd *GIF/THBK* G46 .... 127 L6
   KLMNKN/STW KA3 .... 206 C2
Ferclay St *CLYDBK* G81 .... 60 D2
Fereneze Av *BRHD/NEIL* G78 ..... 125 H6
   CRMNK/CLK/EAG G76 .... 151 J1
   RNFRW PA4 .... 102 A1 🔢
Fereneze Crs *HMLTN* ML3 .... 155 M6
   KNTSWD G13 .... 80 F2
Fereneze Dr *PSLYS* PA2 .... 124 B1
Fereneze Rd *BRHD/NEIL* G78 ..... 125 H6
Fereneze Rd *BRHD/NEIL* G78 ..... 147 M2
Fergus Av *PSLYN/LNWD* PA3.... 101 G4
Fergus Dr *GRNKW/INVK* PA16 ... 32 A5 🔢
   MRYH/FIRH G20........................ 4 B1
   PSLYN/LNWD PA3 .... 101 G4
Fergus Gdns *HMLTN* ML3 .... 156 F7
Fergushill Rd *KLWNG* KA13 .... 193 M6
Fergus La *MRYH/FIRH* G20 .... 4 C1
Ferguslie *PSLY* PA1 .... 8 A5
Ferguslie Park Av
   PSLYN/LNWD PA3 .... 101 G5
Ferguslie Park Crs
   PSLYN/LNWD PA3 .... 101 G5
Ferguslie Wk *PSLY* PA1 .... 8 B5
Ferguson Av *MLNGV* G62 .... 42 A8
   PSTWK KA9 .... 225 K1
   RNFRW PA4 .... 80 D6
Ferguson Dr *MTHW* ML1 .... 157 L6
Ferguson St *AYR* KA8 .... 225 J7
   JNSTN PA5 .... 99 L6
   RNFRW PA4 .... 80 D6
Fergus Pl *GRNKW/INVK* PA16 ... 32 A5 🔢
Fergus Rd *GRNKW/INVK* PA16 ... 32 A5 🔢
Fergusson Rd *CUMB* G67 .... 48 F7
Ferguston Rd *BSDN* G61 .... 61 M5
Fergus Wy *RAYR/DAL* KA6 .... 231 G5
Fernan St *CAR/SHTL* G32 .... 106 F4
Fern Av *BSHPBGS* G64 .... 84 B1
   ERSK PA8 .... 79 H2
   KKNTL G66 .... 65 J5
Fernbank *PSTWK* KA9 .... 225 H4
Fernbank Av
   BLTYR/CAMB G72 .... 130 C5 🔢
Fernbank St *PPK/MIL* G22 .... 83 L4 🔢
Fernbrae Av *RUTH* G73 .... 129 H7
Fernbrae Wy *RUTH* G73 .... 129 H6 🔢
Ferncroft Dr *LNPK/KPK* G44 ...... 128 D4
Ferndale Crs *SMSTN* G23 .... 82 D1
Ferndale Dr *MRYH/FIRH* G20 ...... 82 C1
Ferndale Gdns *SMSTN* G23 .... 82 D1
Ferndale Pl *SMSTN* G23 .... 82 D1
Fern Dr *BRHD/NEIL* G78 .... 125 J7 🔢
Ferness Ov *SPRGB/BLRNK* G21 .. 84 C2
Ferness Pl *SPRGB/BLRNK* G21 ... 84 C2 🔢
Ferness Rd *SPRGB/BLRNK* G21 .. 84 C3
Fern Gv *BAIL/MDB/MHD* G69 .... 87 G3
Ferngrove Av *KVD/HLHD* G12 ..... 82 B3 🔢
Fernhill Gra *UD/BTH/TAN* G71 ... 132 A3
Fernhill Rd *RUTH* G73 .... 129 G5
Ferniegair Av *HBR/GL* G84 .... 20 A7
Fernie Gdns *MRYH/FIRH* G20 ..... 82 E2 🔢
Fernieshaw Rd *MTHW* ML1 .... 135 M6
Fern La *KNTSWD* G13 .... 81 M4
Fernlea *BSDN* G61 .... 61 L6
Fernleigh Rd
   PLKSW/MSWD G43 .... 127 K4
Fern Pl *KLMNK* KA1 .... 211 J2
Fernslea Av *BLTYR/CAMB* G72 ... 155 J1
Fern St *MTHW* ML1 .... 158 A5
Ferryden St *SCOT* G14 .... 81 L7
Ferry Loan *ALEX/LLW* G83 .... 25 L4 🔢
Ferry Rd *BSHPTN* PA7 .... 58 A5
   DMBTN G82 .... 35 H3
   GTCI KA28 .... 138 C6 🔢
   KVGV G3 .... 82 C8
   RNFRW PA4 .... 80 D5
   UD/BTH/TAN G71 .... 131 L3
   UD/BTH/TAN G71 .... 132 A7
Fersit St *PLKSW/MSWD* G43 ..... 127 J3 🔢
Fetlar Dr *KLMNKN/STW* KA3 ..... 207 G3 🔢
   LNPK/KPK G44 .... 128 C4
Fetlar Rd *BRWEIR* PA11 .... 98 C1
Fettercairn Av *DRUM* G15 .... 60 B5
Fettes St *STPS/GTHM/RID* G33 .. 106 F1
Fiddison Pl *PSTWK* KA9 .... 225 L4
Fiddoch Ct *WISHAW* ML2 .... 159 M2
Fidra St *STPS/GTHM/RID* G33 .... 106 F1 🔢
Fielden Pl *DMNK/BRGTN* G40 ..... 12 F6
Fielden St *DMNK/BRGTN* G40 .... 12 F6
Field Gv *CRMNK/CLK/EAG* G76 .. 151 M4
Fieldhead Dr
   PLKSW/MSWD G43 .... 127 G4
Fieldhead Sq
   PLKSW/MSWD G43 .... 127 G4 🔢
Field Rd *CLYDBK* G81 .... 60 D1
   CRMNK/CLK/EAG G76 .... 151 M4
   LRKH ML9 .... 176 B7
Fields La *CRG/CRSL/HOU* PA6 .... 77 H6
Field St *HMLTN* ML3 .... 156 D8
Fife Av *AIRDRIE* ML6 .... 111 G4
   CARD/HILL/MSPK G52 .... 103 H5
   FAIRLIE KA29 .... 139 L5
Fife Crs *UD/BTH/TAN* G71 .... 132 A8
Fife Dr *GRNKW/INVK* PA16 .... 31 K4 🔢
   MTHW ML1............................. 133 K7
Fife Pl *FAIRLIE* KA29 .... 139 L6
Fife Rd *GRNKW/INVK* PA16 .... 31 K4
Fife Wy *BSHPBGS* G64 .... 84 D1

Fifth Av *AIRDRIE* ML6 .... 111 J1
   KVD/HLHD G12 .... 81 M4
   RNFRW PA4 .... 80 C7
   STPS/GTHM/RID G33 .... 85 H4 🔢
Fifth Rd *BLTYR/CAMB* G72 .... 155 L4 🔢
Fifty Pitches Pl *GOV/IBX* G51 .... 103 J3
Fifty Pitches Rd *GOV/IBX* G51 .... 103 H3
Finart Dr *PSLYS* PA2 .... 102 B8
Finaven Gdns *BSDN* G61 .... 61 H1
Finch Dr *KNTSWD* G13 .... 80 F1
Finch Pl *JNSTN* PA5 .... 122 D2
   KLMNKN/STW KA3 .... 17 L6
Findhorn Av *PSLYS* PA2 .... 100 F8
   RNFRW PA4 .... 80 E6
Findhorn Ct *EKILS* G75 .... 170 C1
Findhorn Pl *EKILS* G75 .... 170 D1 🔢
   TROON KA10 .... 216 E4
Findhorn St *STPS/GTHM/RID* G33 .. 7 L8
Findlay's Brae *SALT* KA21 .... 200 F2 🔢
Findlay St *KSYTH* G65 .... 47 K1 🔢
   MTHW ML1.............................. 157 M4
Findochty St
   STPS/GTHM/RID G33................ 85 L8
Fingal La *MRYH/FIRH* G20 .... 82 C2 🔢
Fingal St *MRYH/FIRH* G20 .... 82 D2
Fingalton Rd *NMRNS* G77 .... 149 L4
Fingask St *CAR/SHTL* G32 .... 107 J5
Finglas Av *PSLYS* PA2 .... 102 B8
Finglen Pl *PLK/PH/NH* G53 .... 126 B5
Fingleton Av *BRHD/NEIL* G78 .... 125 K8
Finhaven St *CAR/SHTL* G32 .... 106 E6
Finlarig St *ESTRH* G34 .... 108 C2 🔢
Finlas Av *AYRS* KA7 .... 229 H6
Finlas St *PPK/MIL* G22 .... 83 K5
Finlay Dr *DALRY* KA24 .... 184 D2
Finlay Dr *DEN/PKHD* G31 .... 12 F2
   PSLYN/LNWD PA3 .... 99 M4 🔢
Finlay Ri *MLNGV* G62 .... 42 B8
Finlayson Dr *AIRDRIE* ML6 .... 111 L2
   KLMNKN/STW KA3 .... 207 K6
Finlayson Qd *AIRDRIE* ML6 .... 111 L2 🔢
Finlaystone Pl *KLMCLM* PA13 .... 55 K7 🔢
Finlaystone Rd *KLMCLM* PA13 ... 55 K7
   PGL PA14 .... 55 G2 🔢
Finlaystone St *CTBR* ML5 .... 109 L2
Finnart Crs *GRK* PA19 .... 31 J3
Finnart Rd *GRNKW/INVK* PA16 ... 32 D3
Finnart Sq *DMNK/BRGTN* G40 .... 12 D9
Finnart St *DMNK/BRGTN* G40 .... 12 D9
   GRNKW/INVK PA16 .... 32 C2
Finneston St *GRNK* PA15 .... 3 H7
Finnick Gln *AYRS* KA7 .... 229 G6
Finnieston Sq *KVGV* G3 .... 4 B9
Finnieston St *KVGV* G3 .... 10 B2
Finnie Ter *GRK* PA19 .... 31 K3
   IRVSE KA11 .... 204 F7
Finnie Wynd *MTHW* ML1 .... 158 B5 🔢
Finnockbog Dr
   GRNKW/INVK PA16 .... 50 D5 🔢
Finnockbog Rd
   GRNKW/INVK PA16 .... 50 D5
Finsbay St *GOV/IBX* G51 .... 103 K3
Fintaig La *WISHAW* ML2 .... 159 L6 🔢
Fintrie Ter *HMLTN* ML3 .... 155 L5
Fintry Av *PSLYS* PA2 .... 124 C1
Fintry Crs *BRHD/NEIL* G78 .... 125 J8 🔢
   BSHPBGS G64 .... 64 C8 🔢
Fintry Dr *LNPK/KPK* G44 .... 128 C2
Fintry Gdns *BSDN* G61 .... 61 J1
Fintry Pl *EKILS* G75 .... 171 H5
   IRVSE KA11 .... 204 A7
Fintry Rd *GRNK* PA15 .... 33 H8
Fir Bank *AYRS* KA7 .... 229 J4
Firbank Av *BSHPBGS* G64 .... 64 B1
Fir Bank Av *LRKH* ML9 .... 176 B7
Firbank Ter *BRHD/NEIL* G78 ...... 125 L8
Firdon Crs *DRUM* G15 .... 61 G8
Fir Gv *EKILS* G75 .... 171 L4
Fir Gv *MTHW* ML1 .... 134 A7
   UD/BTH/TAN G71 .... 132 C2
Firhill Av *AIRDRIE* ML6 .... 110 F3
Firhill Dr *PSTWK* KA9 .... 221 K4
Firhill Rd *MRYH/FIRH* G20 .... 83 G5
Firhill St *MRYH/FIRH* G20 .... 4 E1
Firlee *EKILS* G75 .... 170 F2
Firpark Rd *BSHPBGS* G64 .... 84 B1
Firpark St *DEN/PKHD* G31 .... 6 E2
Fir Park St *MTHW* ML1 .... 157 M5
Firpark Ter *DEN/PKHD* G31 .... 12 C1
Fir Pl *BAIL/MDB/MHD* G69 ...... 108 A6 🔢
   BLTYR/CAMB G72 .... 130 C4
   JNSTN PA5 .... 100 A7
First Av *ALEX/LLW* G83 .... 25 M4
   BSDN G61 .... 62 A6
   DMBTN G82 .... 37 J7
   IRV KA12 .... 208 C1
   KKNTL G66 .... 65 K8
   LNPK/KPK G44 .... 127 M7
   RNFRW PA4 .... 80 C7
   STPS/GTHM/RID G33 .... 85 H4
First Gdns *PLKSD/SHW* G41 ...... 104 A5 🔢
Fir St *GRNK* PA15 .... 33 L7
First Rd *BLTYR/CAMB* G72 .... 155 L4
First St *UD/BTH/TAN* G71 .... 131 M1
Fir Ter *GRK* PA19 .... 31 K3 🔢
Firth Crs *GRK* PA19 .... 31 H5
Firth Gdns *TROON* KA10 .... 216 D2
Firth Rd *IRVSE* KA11 .... 216 D1
Firth View Ter *ARD* KA22 .... 191 K5
Firthview Ter *DMBTN* G82 .... 36 C6
Fir tree Pl *WISHAW* ML2 .... 160 B3
Fir tree Rd *WISHAW* ML2 .... 160 B3
Fir Vw *AIRDRIE* ML6 .... 111 H7
Firwood Cts *NMRNS* G77 .... 150 E5
Firwood Dr *LNPK/KPK* G44 .... 128 C3
Firwood Rd *NMRNS* G77 .... 150 E4
Fischer Gdns *PSLYN/LNWD* PA3 .. 100 F5
Fisher Av *KSYTH* G65 .... 47 K1
   PSLYN/LNWD PA3 .... 100 F5
Fisher Ct *CRH/DND* KA2............. 205 M6
Fisher Crs *CLYDBK* G81 .... 60 B4
Fisher Dr *PSLYN/LNWD* PA3 ...... 100 F5
Fisher Pl *HBR/GL* G84 .... 21 G7 🔢
Fisher St *LRKH* ML9 .... 176 B8

Fisher Wy *PSLYN/LNWD* PA3..... 100 F5
Fisherwood Rd *ALEX/LLW* G83 ... 25 L1 🔢
Fishescoates Av *RUTH* G73 .... 129 K5 🔢
   RUTH G73 .... 129 K4 🔢
Fishescoates Gdns
   RUTH G73 .... 129 K4 🔢
Fitzalan Rd *PSLYN/LNWD* PA3 .... 80 A8
Fitzroy La *KVGV* G3 .... 4 A8
Five Roads *KLWNG* KA13 .... 194 A6
Flakefield *EKILN* G74 .... 153 H7 🔢
Flanders St *CLYDBK* G81 .... 60 C2
Flatterton Rd
   GRNKW/INVK PA16 .... 31 J7
Flatt Rd *LARGS* KA30 .... 115 K6
Flaxfield Gv *MTHW* ML1 .... 133 K7 🔢
Flaxmill Av *WISHAW* ML2 .... 158 D5
Flax Rd *UD/BTH/TAN* G71 .... 132 A4
Fleck Av *SALT* KA21 .... 192 A7
Fleet Av *RNFRW* PA4 .... 80 E8
Fleet St *CAR/SHTL* G32 .... 107 H5
Fleming Av *BAIL/MDB/MHD* G69 .. 86 C2
   CLYDBK G81 .... 80 D1
Fleming Ct *CARLUKE* ML8 .... 178 E8 🔢
   HMLTN ML3............................ 155 L5
   MTHW ML1............................ 158 A5
Fleming Crs *SALT* KA21 .... 192 A6
   KLMNKN/STW KA3 .... 197 J1
Fleming Dr *BLSH* ML4 .... 133 H3
Fleming Pl *EKILS* G75 .... 14 D5
Fleming Rd *BLSH* ML4 .... 133 H3
   BSHPTN PA7 .... 58 B6
   CRG/CRSL/HOU PA6 .... 77 C7
   CUMB G67 .... 48 F7
Fleming St *DEN/PKHD* G31 .... 13 H3
   KLMNK KA1 .... 211 L4
   PSLYN/LNWD PA3 .... 101 L2 🔢
Fleming Ter *IRV* KA12 .... 203 H4
Flemington St *SPRGB/BLRNK* G21 .. 6 C2
Fleming Wy *HMLTN* ML3 .... 155 K5
Flenders Av
   CRMNK/CLK/EAG G76 .... 151 J3
Flenders Rd
   CRMNK/CLK/EAG G76 .... 151 J3
Fletcher Av *GRK* PA19 .... 31 L3
Fleurs Av *PLKSD/SHW* G41 .... 104 B6
Fleurs Rd *PLKSD/SHW* G41 .... 104 B5 🔢
Flinders Pl *EKILS* G75 .... 171 H1
Flint Mill La *GRNK* PA15 .... 3 G9
Floyd St *CTBR* ML5 .... 109 M2
Floorsburn Crs *JNSTN* PA5 .... 99 L7
Floors Rd *CRMNK/CLK/EAG* G76 .. 151 J8
Floors St *JNSTN* PA5 .... 99 M7
Flora Gdns *BSHPBGS* G64 .... 64 C7
Florence Dr *GIF/THBK* G46 .... 127 J7
   KLMCLM PA13 .... 75 H1
Florence Gdns *RUTH* G73 .... 129 J5
Florence St *GBLS* G5 .... 11 K6
   GRNKW/INVK PA16 .... 32 B5
Florida Av *GVH/MTFL* G42 .... 128 B1
Florida Crs *GVH/MTFL* G42 .... 128 B1
Florida Dr *GVH/MTFL* G42 .... 128 A1 🔢
Florida Gdns
   BAIL/MDB/MHD G69 .... 108 A4 🔢
Florida Sq *GVH/MTFL* G42 .... 128 B1
Florida St *GVH/MTFL* G42 .... 128 A1
Florish Rd *ERSK* PA8 .... 79 K1
Flowerdale Pl
   PLK/PH/NH G53 .... 126 B6 🔢
Flowerhill St *AIRDRIE* ML6 .... 111 H1
Fluchter Rd *MLNGV* G62 .... 43 C8
Flures Av *ERSK* PA8 .... 79 L1
Flures Crs *ERSK* PA8 .... 79 L1
Flures Dr *ERSK* PA8 .... 79 L1
   RNFRW PA4 .... 79 L1
Flures Pl *ERSK* PA8 .... 79 L1
Fochabers Dr
   CARD/HILL/MSPK G52 .... 103 J3
Fogo Pl *MRYH/FIRH* G20 .... 82 D5 🔢
Foinavon Rd *HMLTN* ML3 .... 174 E6
Footfield Rd *BLSH* ML4 .... 132 F6
Foot of Lone Rd
   LNK/LMHG ML11 .... 198 B4
Forbes Dr *DMNK/BRGTN* G40 .... 12 C5 🔢
   MTHW ML1............................. 133 H7
   PSTWK KA9 .... 225 J5
Forbes Pl *KLMNKN/STW* KA3 ... 207 H7
   PSLY PA1 .... 9 H4
Forbes St *DMNK/BRGTN* G40 ..... 12 C4
Ford Av *IRVSE* KA11 .... 204 D8
Forde Crs *SVSTN* KA20 .... 192 F7
Fordneuk St *DMNK/BRGTN* G40 .. 12 E5
Fordoun St *ESTRH* G34 .... 108 D1 🔢
Ford Rd *KVD/HLHD* G12 .... 82 D3
   NMRNS G77 .... 150 D6
Fordyce St *PTCK* G11 .... 82 B7
Forehill Rd *AYRS* KA7 .... 19 K7
Forehouse Rd *KLBCH* PA10 .... 98 C5
Fore Rw *HMLTN* ML3 .... 156 E5 🔢
   HMLTN ML3............................ 174 D3
Forest Av *BLSH* ML4 .... 133 J6
   HMLTN ML3............................ 174 D3
Forest Dr *UD/BTH/TAN* G71 ...... 132 A6
Forestfield Gdns *AIRDRIE* ML6 ... 91 G5 🔢
Forest Gdns *KNTLL* G66 .... 65 G5
Forest Ga *UD/BTH/TAN* G71 ..... 109 H8
Forest Gv *KLMNKN/STW* KA3 ... 207 H5
Foresthall Crs *SPRGB/BLRNK* G21 .. 6 E2
Foresthall Dr *SPRGB/BLRNK* G21 .. 6 E2
Forest Kirk *CARLUKE* ML8 .... 189 H1
Forest La *HMLTN* ML3 .... 174 D3 🔢
Forest Pk *WISHAW* ML2 .... 159 K4
Forest Pl *CARLUKE* ML8 .... 188 B8
   KKNTL G66 .... 65 G5
   PSLYS PA2 .... 9 G3
Fore St *PGL* PA14 .... 34 C7
   SCOT G14 .... 81 J6
Forest Rd *CUMB* G67 .... 49 M4
   LRKH ML9 .... 176 B7
Forest Vw *CUMB* G67 .... 49 J6
Forfar Av
   CARD/HILL/MSPK G52 .... 103 H5
Forfar Crs *BSHPBGS* G64 .... 84 C1
Forfar Rd *GRNKW/INVK* PA16 ..... 31 M4
Forgan Gdns *BSHPBGS* G64 .... 84 D1
Forge Dr *CTBR* ML5 .... 109 M2
Forge Pl *SPRGB/BLRNK* G21 .... 7 H3
Forge Rd *AIRDRIE* ML6 .... 111 M3
   AYR KA8 .... 225 H5
Forge Rw *AIRDRIE* ML6 .... 111 J6

Forge St *KLMNK* KA1 .... 16 D3
   SPRGB/BLRNK G21 .... 7 G5
Forge Vennal *KLWNG* KA13 .... 193 L8
Forgewood Pth *AIRDRIE* ML6..... 111 M3
Forgewood Rd *MTHW* ML1 .... 133 J7
Forglen St *ESTRH* G34 .... 86 B8
Formby Dr *SMSTN* G23 .... 82 D1
Forres Av *GIF/THBK* G46 .... 127 K6
Forres Crs *BLSH* ML4 .... 133 G3
Forres Ga *GIF/THBK* G46 .... 127 K7
Forres Qd *WISHAW* ML2 .... 159 H4 🔢
Forres St *BLTYR/CAMB* G72 ...... 155 J3
   SMSTN G23 .... 62 E8 🔢
Forrest Dr *BSDN* G61 .... 41 H8
Forrester Ct *BSHPBGS* G64 .... 83 M1 🔢
Forrestfield Crs *NMRNS* G77 ..... 150 E4
Forrestfield Gdns
   NMRNS G77 .... 150 E4 🔢
Forrestfield Rd *AIRDRIE* ML6 ...... 91 L2
Forrest Ga *UD/BTH/TAN* G71 .... 156 B8
Forrestlea Rd *CARLUKE* ML8 ..... 189 G3
Forrest Rd *LNK/LMHG* ML11 ..... 199 H4
Forrest St *AIRDRIE* ML6 .... 111 L1
   BLTYR/CAMB G72 .... 155 M2
   DMNK/BRGTN G40 .... 12 E5 🔢
   SHOTTS ML7 .... 137 L4
Forsyth Ct *LNK/LMHG* ML11 ...... 199 J5
Forsyth Gv
   GRNKW/INVK PA16 .... 32 D3 🔢
Forsyth St *AIRDRIE* ML6 .... 111 H1 🔢
   GRNKW/INVK PA16 .... 32 D3
Fortacre Pl *IRVSE* KA11 .... 204 B4
Forteviot Av
   BAIL/MDB/MHD G69 .... 108 C3 🔢
   BAIL/MDB/MHD G69 .... 108 C3 🔢
Forteviot Pl
   BAIL/MDB/MHD G69 .... 108 C4 🔢
Forth Av *PSLYS* PA2 .... 100 E8
Forth Ct *EKILS* G75 .... 170 E2 🔢
Forth Crs *EKILS* G75 .... 170 E1 🔢
Forth Pl *JNSTN* PA5 .... 122 C1
   KLMNK KA1 .... 212 A4 🔢
Forth Rd *BLTYR/CAMB* G72 .... 155 L4
   BSDN G61 .... 61 K7
   BSHPBGS G64 .... 64 B1
Forth St *CLYDBK* G81 .... 80 C1
   GRNKW/INVK PA16 .... 32 B4
Forth Ter *HMLTN* ML3 .... 174 C8
Forties Ct *GIF/THBK* G46 .... 126 F4 🔢
Forties Crs *GIF/THBK* G46 .... 127 G4 🔢
Forties Gdns *GIF/THBK* G46 ...... 127 G4 🔢
Forties Rd *CRG/CRSL/HOU* PA6 ... 99 J1
Forties Wy *GIF/THBK* G46 .... 127 G4 🔢
Fortieth Av *EKILS* G75 .... 171 M4
Fortingall Av *KVD/HLHD* G12 ..... 82 C3 🔢
Fortingall Pl *KVD/HLHD* G12 ...... 82 C3
Fortingall Rd *BLTYR/CAMB* G72 .. 155 M4
Fortissat Av *SHOTTS* ML7 .... 137 K4
Fortissat Rd *SHOTTS* ML7 .... 137 H1
Fort Matilda Pl
   GRNKW/INVK PA16 .... 32 B2
Fortrose St *PTCK* G11 .... 82 B7
Fort St *AYR* KA7 .... 18 E3
   LARGS KA30 .... 115 J6
   MTHW ML1............................. 157 H1
Fossil Gv *KKNTL* G66 .... 46 E8
Fosterland *SKLM* PA17 .... 70 A6 🔢
Foswell Pl *DRUM* G15 .... 60 F4
Fotheringay La
   PLKSD/SHW G41 .... 104 D7
Fotheringay Rd
   PLKSD/SHW G41 .... 104 D7
Fothringham Rd *AYR* KA8 .... 19 H3
Foulburn Rd *MTHW* ML1 .... 136 C7
Foulis La *KNTSWD* G13 .... 81 M3 🔢
Foulis St *KNTSWD* G13 .... 81 M3 🔢
Foulpapple Rd *NMLNS* KA16 ..... 215 M1
Foulsykes Rd *WISHAW* ML2 ...... 159 L4
Foundry La *BRHD/NEIL* G78 ...... 125 J7 🔢
Foundry Rd *MTHW* ML1 .... 135 J7
   SHOTTS ML7 .... 137 L5
Foundry Wynd *KLWNG* KA13 ..... 193 J5
Fountain Av *RNFRW* PA4............. 79 H5
Fountain Crs *RNFRW* PA4 .... 79 H4
Fountain Dr *RNFRW* PA4 .... 79 J5
Fountainwell Av *COWCAD* G4 ...... 5 M4
Fountainwell Dr *COWCAD* G4 ...... 5 M4
Fountainwell Pl *COWCAD* G4 ...... 5 M4
Fountainwell Rd *COWCAD* G4 ...... 5 M4
Fountainwell Sq *COWCAD* G4 ...... 6 A4
Fountainwell Ter
   SPRGB/BLRNK G21 .... 6 A4
Four Acres Dr
   KLMNKN/STW KA3 .... 206 D1
Fourth Av *DMBTN* G82 .... 37 J6
   KKNTL G66 .... 65 K8
   RNFRW PA4 .... 80 C7
   STPS/GTHM/RID G33 .... 85 H4
Fourth Gdns *PLKSD/SHW* G41 ... 104 A5
Fourth St *UD/BTH/TAN* G71 ...... 108 F8
Four Windings
   CRG/CRSL/HOU PA6 .... 77 H7 🔢
Fowlds St *KLMNK* KA1 .... 16 F5
Fowler Pl *EKILS* G75 .... 15 J9
Fowlis Dr *NMRNS* G77 .... 150 C3
Foxbar Crs *PSLYS* PA2 .... 123 L2
Foxbar Dr *KNTSWD* G13 .... 81 H3
   PSLYS PA2 .... 123 L2
Foxbar Rd *PSLYS* PA2 .... 123 L2
Foxes Gv *KKNTL* G66 .... 65 L4
Foxglove Pl *PLK/PH/NH* G53 ..... 126 B6
Fox Gv *MTHW* ML1 .... 157 H2 🔢
Foxhills Pl *SMSTN* G23 .... 62 E8
Foxley St *CAR/SHTL* G32 .... 107 J8 🔢
Fox St *CGLE* G1 .... 11 H3
   GRNKW/INVK PA16 .... 32 D2
Foyers Ter *SPRGB/BLRNK* G21 ..... 6 E1
Francis St *GBLS* G5 .... 10 F7
Frankfield Rd
   STPS/GTHM/RID G33 .... 85 L4
Frankfield St
   STPS/GTHM/RID G33 .... 7 M4
Frankfort St *PLKSD/SHW* G41 .... 104 E8
Franklin Pl *EKILS* G75 .... 153 H6 🔢
Franklin Rd *SALT* KA21 .... 191 L8

Franklin St DMNK/BRGTN G40 ...... 12 C9
Fraser Av BSHPTN PA7 .... 58 A5
  DMBTN G82 .... 37 J5
  JNSTN PA5 .... 100 A7
  NMRNS G77 .... 150 E3
  RUTH G73 .... 129 J2
  TROON KA10 .... 216 D4
Fraser Ct HMLTN ML3 .... 156 B7
  NMLNS KA16 .... 215 G2 ▣
Fraser Gdns KKNTL G66 .... 65 H1
Fraser St BLTYR/CAMB G72 .... 129 L3
  MTHW ML1 .... 135 H7
Frazer Av HBR/GL G84 .... 20 A6
Frazer St DMNK/BRGTN G40 .... 13 C6
  LARGS KA30 .... 115 J6
Frederick St CTBR ML5 .... 109 L1
Freeland Ct PLK/PH/NH G53 .. 126 C3 ▣
Freeland Crs PLK/PH/NH G53 .... 126 B3
Freeland Dr BRWEIR PA11 .... 76 D8 ▢
  ERSK PA8 .... 79 J3
  PLK/PH/NH G53 .... 126 B3
Freeland Pl KKNTL G66 .... 65 K1
Freeland Rd ERSK PA8 .... 79 H2
Freelands Crs OLDK G60 .... 59 H4
Freelands Rd OLDK G60 .... 59 J5
Freesia Ct MTHW ML1 .... 157 L4
French St CLYDBK G81 .... 59 L6
  DMNK/BRGTN G40 .... 105 M6
  RNFRW PA4 .... 80 B7
  WISHAW ML2 .... 159 H6
Freuchie St ESTRH G34 .... 108 B2
Frew St AIRDRIE ML6 .... 111 K4
Frew Ter IRV KA12 .... 203 J4
Friar Av BSHPBGS G64 .... 64 B5
Friarscourt Av KNTSWD G13 .... 61 K8
Friarscourt Rd
  BAIL/MDB/MHD G69 .... 66 B8
Friars Cft IRV KA12 .... 203 H7
  KKNTL G66 .... 65 L1
Friarsdene LNK/LMHG ML11 .... 198 F5 ▢
Friarsfield Rd LNK/LMHG ML11 .... 198 F5
Friar's La LNK/LMHG ML11 .... 198 F6
Friars Pl KNTSWD G13 .... 81 K1 ▢
Friars Wy AIRDRIE ML6 .... 111 L5
Friar's Wynd
  LNK/LMHG ML11 .... 198 F5 ▢
Friarton Rd PLKSW/MSWD G43 .. 127 M4
Frobisher Pl HBR/GL G84 .... 21 G7 ▢
Frood St MTHW ML1 .... 133 J8
Fruin Av NMRNS G77 .... 150 E3
Fruin Dr WISHAW ML2 .... 159 L6
Fruin Ri HMLTN ML3 .... 155 L7
Fruin Rd DRUM G15 .... 60 F8
Fruin St PPK/MIL G22 .... 83 J5
Fudstone Dr KBRN KA25 .... 167 G1
Fulbar Av RNFRW PA4 .... 80 C5
Fulbar Ct RNFRW PA4 .... 80 D5 ▢
Fulbar Crs PSLYS PA2 .... 100 F7
Fulbar Gdns PSLYS PA2 .... 100 F7
Fulbar La RNFRW PA4 .... 80 D5 ▢
Fulbar Rd GOV/IBX G51 .... 103 J2
  PSLYS PA2 .... 100 F7
Fulbar St RNFRW PA4 .... 80 D5
Fullarton Av CAR/SHTL G32 .... 107 G7
  CRH/DND KA2 .... 209 M1
Fullarton Crs TROON KA10 .... 216 E7
Fullarton Dr TROON KA10 .... 216 E8
Fullarton La CAR/SHTL G32 .... 107 G7
Fullarton Pl CTBR ML5 .... 109 K6
Fullarton Rd BALLOCH G68 .... 48 E4
  CAR/SHTL G32 .... 107 G8
  PSTWK KA9 .... 225 J3
Fullarton St AYRS KA7 .... 18 E3
  CTBR ML5 .... 109 L6
  IRV KA12 .... 203 H7
  KLMNK KA1 .... 16 C4
Fullers Ga CLYDBK G81 .... 60 C2
Fullerton Dr WKIL KA23 .... 181 K5
Fullerton La GRNK PA15 .... 33 L6
Fullerton Sq ARD KA22 .... 191 J7 ▢
Fullerton Ter PSLYN/LNWD PA3 ... 101 K2
Fulmar Pk EKILN G74 .... 153 K6 ▢
Fulmar Pl JNSTN PA5 .... 122 C3 ▢
Fulshaw Ct PSTWK KA9 .... 225 K4 ▢
Fulshaw Crs AYR KA8 .... 225 M7
Fulton Crs KLBCH PA10 .... 99 H6
Fulton Dr CRG/CRSL/HOU PA6 ... 99 J1
Fulton Gdns CRG/CRSL/HOU PA6 ... 99 J1
Fulton Rd MLNGV G62 .... 42 B8 ▢
Fulton's La KLMNKN/STW KA3 ... 16 F2
Fulton St KNTSWD G13 .... 81 L2
Fulwood Av KNTSWD G13 .... 80 F2
  PSLYN/LNWD PA3 .... 100 B3
Fulwood Pl KNTSWD G13 .... 80 F2
The Furlongs HMLTN ML3 .... 156 D5
Furnace Ct KLMNK KA1 .... 212 D3
Furnace Rd HMLTN ML3 .... 174 F6
Fyfe Shore Rd PGL PA14 .... 34 E8
Fyffe Park Rd PGL PA14 .... 34 E8
Fyneart St WISHAW ML2 .... 159 L5
Fyne Ct HMLTN ML3 .... 156 A8 ▢
Fyne Crs LRKH ML9 .... 175 M4
Fynloch Pl CLYDBK G81 .... 59 J2
Fyvie Av PLKSW/MSWD G43 ..... 127 G4
Fyvie Crs AIRDRIE ML6 .... 111 L2 ▢

G

Gabriel St GRNK PA15 .... 3 O9
Gadgirth Ct RAYR/DAL KA6 .. 231 H5 ▣
Gadie Av RNFRW PA4 .... 80 E7
Gadie St STPS/GTHM/RID G33 ... 7 L8
Gadloch Av KKNTL G66 .... 65 K7
Gadloch St PPK/MIL G22 .... 83 J3
Gadloch Vw KKNTL G66 .... 65 K7
Gadsburn Ct
  SPRGB/BLRNK G21 .... 84 C3 ▣
Gadshill St SPRGB/BLRNK G21 ... 6 C6
Gael St GRNK PA15 .... 3 J7
Gailes Pk UD/BTH/TAN G71 ..... 131 M7
Gailes Pl KLMNK KA1 .... 211 L5
Gailes Rd BALLOCH G68 .... 48 F4
  IRVSE KA11 .... 208 C5
Gailes St DMNK/BRGTN G40 ..... 13 H8

Gain & Shankburn Rd
  AIRDRIE ML6 .... 68 D7
Gainburn Ct CUMB G67 .... 67 M3 ▣
Gainburn Crs CUMB G67 .... 67 M4
Gainburn Gdns CUMB G67 .... 67 M4
Gainburn Pl CUMB G67 .... 67 M3 ▣
Gainburn Vw CUMB G67 .... 68 A3 ▣
Gainford Pl KLMNKN/STW KA3 .. 206 F5
Gain Rd CTBR ML5 .... 67 M8
Gainside Rd CTBR ML5 .... 87 J3
Gairbraid Av MRYH/FIRH G20 ... 82 C3 ▣
Gairbraid Ct MRYH/FIRH G20 ... 82 C3 ▣
Gairbraid Pl MRYH/FIRH G20 ... 82 D3 ▣
Gairbraid Ter
  BAIL/MDB/MHD G69 .... 109 G4 ▣
  WISHAW ML2 .... 159 H8
Gair Crs CARLUKE ML8 .... 179 G3
  WISHAW ML2 .... 159 H4
Gair Rd CARLUKE ML8 .... 179 H4
Gaitskell Av ALEX/LLW G83 ..... 25 K2
Gala Av RNFRW PA4 .... 80 E7
Gala Crs WISHAW ML2 .... 159 G5
Gala St STPS/GTHM/RID G33 ... 7 M6
Galbraith Av CARLUKE ML8 ..... 178 A3 ▣
Galbraith Dr GOV/IBX G51 ..... 103 L1 ▣
  MLNGV G62 .... 61 M3
Galdenoch St
  STPS/GTHM/RID G33 .... 85 H7
Gallacher Av PSLYS PA2 .... 101 C8
Gallacher Crs ALEX/LLW G83 ... 25 M1
Gallahill Av PGL PA14 .... 55 G2
Gallan Av SMSTN G23 .... 62 E8
Galloway Av AYR KA8 .... 225 J7
  HMLTN ML3 .... 174 C2
Galloway Dr RUTH G73 .... 129 H6
Galloway Pl SALT KA21 .... 200 E1 ▣
Galloway Rd AIRDRIE ML6 ..... 110 F4
  EKILN G74 .... 154 C6
Galloway St SPRGB/BLRNK G21 .. 83 M3
Gallowflat St RUTH G73 .... 129 H1 ▣
Gallowgate CGLE G1 .... 11 M3
  COWCAD G4 .... 12 A4
  DEN/PKHD G31 .... 13 H5
  DMNK/BRGTN G40 .... 12 D4
Gallowgate La LARGS KA30 ..... 115 J5 ▣
Gallowhill La LARGS KA30 ..... 115 J6
Gallowhill Av KKNTL G66 .... 65 J3
Gallowhill Gv KKNTL G66 .... 65 J3
Gallowhill Qd RAYR/DAL KA6 .. 231 H5
Gallowhill Rd
  CRMNK/CLK/EAG G76 .... 152 E1
  KKNTL G66 .... 65 J3
  LNK/LMHG ML11 .... 199 G4
  PSLYN/LNWD PA3 .... 9 K1
Galrigside Rd KLMNK KA1 ..... 16 B7 ▣
Galston Av NMRNS G77 .... 151 G4
Galston Ct HMLTN ML3 .... 174 E2 ▣
Galston Rd KLMNK KA1 .... 212 F3
  KLMNK KA1 .... 213 J3
Galston St PLK/PH/NH G53 ..... 125 M3
Galt Av IRV KA12 .... 203 K6
Galt Pl EKILS G75 .... 14 C8
Galt St GRNK PA15 .... 3 J7
Gameshill Vw
  KLMNKN/STW KA3 .... 197 L1
Gamrie Dr PLK/PH/NH G53 ..... 126 A2
Gamrie Gdns PLK/PH/NH G53 .. 126 A1
Gamrie Rd PLK/PH/NH G53 ..... 126 A1
Gannochy Dr BSHPBGS G64 ..... 64 C8
Gantock Crs
  STPS/GTHM/RID G33 .... 107 H2
Ganton Ct KLWNG KA13 .... 193 H6 ▣
Gardenhall EKILS G75 .... 170 D1 ▣
Gardenhall Ct EKILS G75 .... 170 E1 ▣
Gardenside BLSH ML4 .... 133 G5 ▣
Gardenside Av CAR/SHTL G32 .. 130 B1
  UD/BTH/TAN G71 .... 131 L3
Gardenside Crs CAR/SHTL G32 .. 130 B1
Gardenside Pl CAR/SHTL G32 .. 130 B1 ▣
Gardenside Rd HMLTN ML3 ..... 156 D7 ▣
Gardenside St
  UD/BTH/TAN G71 .... 131 L3
Garden Square Wk
  AIRDRIE ML6 .... 110 D1
Garden St AYR KA8 .... 18 F2
  GLSTN KA4 .... 214 C4
  KLMNKN/STW KA3 .... 16 F2
  MAUCH/CAT KA5 .... 223 M6
Gardiner Pl PSTWK KA9 .... 225 J1
Gardner Gv UD/BTH/TAN G71 .. 132 A1
Gardner St PTCK G11 .... 82 B7
Gardrum Pl KLMNKN/STW KA3 .. 206 F5
Gardyne St ESTRH G34 .... 86 A8 ▣
Garelet Pl IRVSE KA11 .... 204 B7 ▣
Gareloch Av AIRDRIE ML6 .... 88 F7
  PSLYS PA2 .... 101 G7
Gareloch La PGL PA14 .... 54 D1
Gareloch Rd GRNK PA15 .... 33 L7
  PGL PA14 .... 54 D1
Garfield Av BLSH ML4 .... 133 J5
Garfield Dr BLSH ML4 .... 133 J5
Garfield St DEN/PKHD G31 ..... 12 E3
Garforth Rd
  BAIL/MDB/MHD G69 .... 107 M5
Gargrave Av
  BAIL/MDB/MHD G69 .... 107 M5
Garion Dr KNTSWD G13 .... 81 H4 ▣
Garlieston Rd
  STPS/GTHM/RID G33 .... 107 M3
Garmouth Ct GOV/IBX G51 ..... 104 A1 ▣
Garmouth Gdns
  GOV/IBX G51 .... 104 A1 ▣
Garmouth St GOV/IBX G51 ..... 103 M1
Garnethill St KVCV G3 .... 4 F7
Garnet St CGLW G2 .... 4 E7
Garngaber Av KKNTL G66 .... 65 K4
Garngaber Ct KKNTL G66 .... 65 K4 ▣
Garnhall Farm Rd BALLOCH G68 .. 49 L1
Garnie Av ERSK PA8 .... 79 K1
Garnieland Rd ERSK PA8 .... 59 K8
Garnie La ERSK PA8 .... 59 K8
Garnie Ov ERSK PA8 .... 59 K8 ▣
Garnie Pl ERSK PA8 .... 59 K8
Garnkirk La STPS/GTHM/RID G33.. 85 L4
Garnock Ct KBRN KA25 .... 143 G8 ▣
Garnock Pk EKILN G74 .... 15 L3
Garnock Rd KLMNK KA1 .... 212 A4

SVSTN KA20 .... 201 K1
Garnockside GLGNK KA14 ..... 167 H3 ▣
Garnock St DALRY KA24 .... 184 C2
  KBRN KA25 .... 143 H7
  SPRGB/BLRNK G21 .... 6 C5
Garpel Wy LOCHW PA12 .... 120 B6 ▣
Garrawy Rd HBR/GL G84 .... 20 F8
Garrell Pl KSYTH G65 .... 47 J1
Garrell Rd KSYTH G65 .... 47 J1
Garrell Wy CUMB G67 .... 48 E7
  KSYTH G65 .... 47 J1
Garrier Pl KLMNK KA1 .... 16 B1
Garrier Rd IRVSE KA11 .... 204 F7
Garrioch Crs MRYH/FIRH G20 .. 82 D4 ▣
Garrioch Dr MRYH/FIRH G20 .. 82 D4 ▣
Garrioch Ga MRYH/FIRH G20 .. 82 D4 ▣
Garriochmill Rd MRYH/FIRH G20.. 82 D5 ▣
Garrioch Qd MRYH/FIRH G20 .. 82 D4
Garrioch Rd MRYH/FIRH G20 .. 82 D5
Garrion Pl ARDN ML9 .... 176 F8
Garrion St WISHAW ML2 .... 177 J3
Garrowhill Dr
  BAIL/MDB/MHD G69 .... 107 M4
Garry Av BSDN G61 .... 62 A7
Garry Dr PSLYS PA2 .... 101 G7
Garryhorn PSTWK KA9 .... 225 K4
Garry Pl KLMNK KA1 .... 212 A4
  TROON KA10 .... 216 F4
Garry St LNPK/KPK G44 .... 128 A2
Garscadden Rd COWCAD G4 ..... 5 C7
Garscadden Rd South
  DRUM G15 .... 80 F1 ▣
  KNTSWD G13 .... 81 G1
Garscube Rd COWCAD G4 .... 5 C7
Garshake Rd DMBTN G82 .... 37 J4
Garshake Rd DMBTN G82 .... 37 J5
Gartartan Pl PSLY PA1 .... 102 F4 ▣
Gartcloss Rd CTBR ML5 .... 87 J7
Gartconnell Dr BSDN G61 ..... 61 L3
Gartconnell Gdns BSDN G61 ... 61 L3 ▣
Gartconnell Rd BSDN G61 ..... 61 L4 ▣
Gartconner Av KKNTL G66 ..... 66 B1
Gartcosh Rd
  BAIL/MDB/MHD G69 .... 108 F3
  CTBR ML5 .... 109 G1
Gartcosh Wk BLSH ML4 .... 132 F4
Gartcraig Pl
  STPS/GTHM/RID G33 .... 84 F8
Gartcraig Rd
  STPS/GTHM/RID G33 .... 85 G8 ▣
Gartferry Av
  BAIL/MDB/MHD G69 .... 66 C6
Gartferry Rd
  BAIL/MDB/MHD G69 .... 66 C6
Gartferry St
  SPRGB/BLRNK G21 .... 84 A5 ▣
Gartfield St AIRDRIE ML6 ..... 111 H3
Gartgill Rd CTBR ML5 .... 87 L6
Garthamlock Rd
  STPS/GTHM/RID G33 .... 85 L8
Garthland Dr DEN/PKHD G31 .. 12 F2
Garthland La PSLY PA1 .... 9 K2
Garth St CGLE G1 .... 11 K2
Gartlea Av AIRDRIE ML6 .... 111 G2
Gartleahill AIRDRIE ML6 .... 111 H3
Gartlea Rd AIRDRIE ML6 .... 111 G2
Gartliston Rd CTBR ML5 .... 87 M6
Gartliston Ter
  BAIL/MDB/MHD G69 .... 109 G4
Gartloch Rd
  BAIL/MDB/MHD G69 .... 85 M7
  BAIL/MDB/MHD G69 .... 86 E5
  STPS/GTHM/RID G33 .... 85 G6
Gartly St LNPK/KPK G44 .... 127 M5 ▣
Gartmore Gdns
  UD/BTH/TAN G71 .... 131 L1 ▣
Gartmore Rd PSLY PA1 .... 102 C5
Gartmore Ter BLTYR/CAMB G72.. 129 L6
Gartness Dr AIRDRIE ML6 ..... 111 L4
Gartness Rd AIRDRIE ML6 ..... 112 A6
Gartocher Dr CAR/SHTL G32 .. 107 J4
Gartocher Rd CAR/SHTL G32 .. 107 J4
Gartocher Ter CAR/SHTL G32 .. 107 J4
Gartons Rd SPRGB/BLRNK G21.. 84 C4
Gartsherrie Av CTBR ML5 ..... 109 L1
Gartshore Crs KSYTH G65 ..... 46 A1
Gartshore Gdns BALLOCH G68 .. 47 L8 ▣
Garturk St CTBR ML5 .... 110 B5 ▣
  GVH/MTFL G42 .... 105 H7
Garvald St DMNK/BRGTN G40 .. 106 B6
  GRNK PA15 .... 3 J7
Garve Av LNPK/KPK G44 .... 128 A5
Garvel Crs
  STPS/GTHM/RID G33 .... 107 L3 ▣
Garvel Dr GRNK PA15 .... 32 B8
Garvel Pl MLNGV G62 .... 41 K7 ▣
Garvel Rd MLNGV G62 .... 41 K7
  STPS/GTHM/RID G33 .... 107 L3
Garven Rd SVSTN KA20 .... 201 L2
Garvie Av GRK PA19 .... 31 M3
Garvine Rd RAYR/DAL KA6 ..... 231 H5
Garvin Lea BLSH ML4 .... 133 G1 ▣
Garvock Dr GRNKW/INVK PA16.. 32 D6
  PLKSW/MSWD G43 .... 127 H4
Garwhitter Dr MLNGV G62 ..... 42 B7 ▣
Gascoyne EKILS G75 .... 14 A7
Gask Pl KNTSWD G13 .... 80 F1
Gas La GLSTN KA4 .... 214 B4
Gasworks Rd CARLUKE ML8 ..... 178 C6
Gatehead Rd CRH/DND KA2 ..... 205 L8
Gatehouse St CAR/SHTL G32 .. 107 H4
Gateside Pl KLMNK KA1 .... 211 L5 ▣
Gateside Rd BRHD/NEIL G78.. 124 F8

GLSTN KA4 .... 214 A4
WISHAW ML2 .... 158 E5
Gateside St DEN/PKHD G31 ..... 13 G3
  HMLTN ML3 .... 156 E6 ▣
  LARGS KA30 .... 115 J6 ▣
  WKIL KA23 .... 181 K3
Gates Rd LOCHW PA12 .... 120 E6
The Gateway EKILN G74 .... 154 A5
Gauldry Av
  CARD/HILL/MSPK G52 .... 103 J6
Gauze St PSLY PA1 .... 9 H3
Gavell Rd KSYTH G65 .... 46 F2
Gavin Dr DMBTN G82 .... 37 J7
Gavinburn Gdns OLDK G60 ..... 59 G2 ▣
Gavinburn Pl OLDK G60 .... 59 G2
Gavin Hamilton Ct AYRS KA7 .. 19 L8 ▣
Gavin's Mill Rd MLNGV G62 .. 42 A8 ▣
Gavins Rd CLYDBK G81 .... 60 B4
Gavin St MTHW ML1 .... 157 L4
Gavinton St LNPK/KPK G44 ..... 127 M4
Gayne Dr CTBR ML5 .... 87 J3
Gean Ct CUMB G67 .... 49 M5
Gearholm Rd AYRS KA7 .... 228 D6 ▣
Geary St SMSTN G23 .... 62 D8
Geddes Hl EKILN G74 .... 154 B5
Geddes Rd SPRGB/BLRNK G21 .. 84 C2
Geelong Gdns KKNTL G66 .... 29 K8
Geils Av DMBTN G82 .... 37 J7
Geils Qd DMBTN G82 .... 37 J7
Geilsland Rd BEITH KA15 ..... 168 D2
Geilston Pk DMBTN G82 .... 35 G2
Geirston Rd KBRN KA25 .... 142 F7
Gelston St CAR/SHTL G32 ..... 107 H5
Gemmell Crs AYR KA8 .... 19 M1
Gemmel Pl NMRNS G77 .... 150 B5
General Roy Wy
  CARLUKE ML8 .... 189 J1 ▣
Gentle Rw CLYDBK G81 .... 59 M3
George Av CLYDBK G81 .... 60 C6 ▣
George Crs CLYDBK G81 .... 60 C6 ▣
George Gray St RUTH G73 ..... 129 J1
George La PSLY PA1 .... 9 H5
George Mann Ter RUTH G73 .. 129 G5 ▣
George Pl PSLY PA1 .... 9 G5
George Reith Av KVD/HLHD G12.. 81 M4
George Sq CGLE G1 .... 11 J1
George's Av AYR KA8 .... 225 H6
George St AIRDRIE ML6 .... 110 E2
  AIRDRIE ML6 .... 111 K6
  ALEX/LLW G83 .... 25 M6
  AYR KA8 .... 19 G2
  BAIL/MDB/MHD G69 .... 108 B5
  BRHD/NEIL G78 .... 125 H6 ▣
  CGLE G1 .... 11 L1
  GTCI KA28 .... 138 B6
  HBR/GL G84 .... 20 C7
  HMLTN ML3 .... 156 A4
  HWWD PA9 .... 121 M4
  JNSTN PA5 .... 99 M6
  LARGS KA30 .... 115 K5
  MTHW ML1 .... 134 A5
  MTHW ML1 .... 157 L5
  PSLY PA1 .... 8 E5
  SVSTN KA20 .... 201 K2
George Street La
  ALEX/LLW G83 .... 25 M6 ▣
George Ter IRV KA12 .... 203 J2
Gerard Pl BLSH ML4 .... 133 H2 ▣
Gertrude Pl BRHD/NEIL G78 .. 125 C7
Ghillies La MTHW ML1 .... 133 J8
Gibbon Crs EKILN G74 .... 154 C6 ▣
Gibb St AIRDRIE ML6 .... 111 K6
  MTHW ML1 .... 135 H8
Gibshill Rd GRNK PA15 .... 33 L7
Gibson Av DMBTN G82 .... 37 L7
Gibson Crs JNSTN PA5 .... 99 L7
Gibson La KLMCLM PA13 .... 55 K8
Gibson Qd MTHW ML1 .... 133 J8 ▣
Gibson Rd RNFRW PA4 .... 102 B1
Gibson St DMBTN G82 .... 37 G5
  DMNK/BRGTN G40 .... 12 A4
  GRNK PA15 .... 33 L7
  KLMNK KA1 .... 16 A3
  KVD/HLHD G12 .... 4 A4
Giffen Rd SALT KA21 .... 201 C1
Giffnock Park Av GIF/THBK G46.. 127 J5
Gifford Dr
  CARD/HILL/MSPK G52 .... 103 G4
Gifford Wynd JNSTN PA5 ..... 100 F7
Gigha Crs IRVSE KA11 .... 204 B7
Gigha Gdns CARLUKE ML8 ..... 189 C1 ▣
Gigha Pl IRVSE KA11 .... 204 B7
Gigha Qd WISHAW ML2 .... 158 E8 ▣
Gigha Ter IRVSE KA11 .... 204 B7
Gigha Wynd IRVSE KA11 .... 204 B7
Gilbertfield Pl
  STPS/GTHM/RID G33 .... 85 H7 ▣
Gilbertfield Rd
  BLTYR/CAMB G72 .... 130 D6
Gilbertfield St
  STPS/GTHM/RID G33 .... 85 H7
Gilbert St KVCV G3 .... 104 C1
Gilburn Pl SHOTTS ML7 .... 137 M5 ▣
Gilchrist St CTBR ML5 .... 110 B1
Gilchrist Wy WISHAW ML2 ..... 159 J8
Gilderdale EKILS G75 .... 14 B1
Gilfillan Av SALT KA21 .... 192 A7
Gilfillan Pl WISHAW ML2 ..... 177 J2 ▣
Gilfoot NMLNS KA16 .... 215 G2
Gilhill St MRYH/FIRH G20 ..... 82 D2
Gillbank Av CARLUKE ML8 ..... 178 D7 ▣
Gilliburn Rd KLMCLM PA13 ..... 75 K1 ▣
Gilliburn St WISHAW ML2 ..... 177 J3
Gillespie Dr HBR/GL G84 ..... 20 D5
Gillies Crs EKILN G74 .... 154 D4
Gillies La BAIL/MDB/MHD G69.. 108 C3 ▣
Gillies St TROON KA10 .... 216 D6
Gill Rd WISHAW ML2 .... 177 K3
Gilmartin Rd PSLYN/LNWD PA3 .. 99 L2
Gilmerton St CAR/SHTL G32 .. 107 G5
Gilmour Av CLYDBK G81 .... 60 B4
  EKILN G74 .... 152 B7
Gilmour Crs RUTH G73 .... 128 F1 ▣
Gilmour Dr HMLTN ML3 .... 155 M7
Gilmour Pl BLSH ML4 .... 132 F4 ▣

CTBR ML5 .... 109 L1
GBLS G5 .... 11 K8
Gilmour St ALEX/LLW G83 ..... 25 K4
  CLYDBK G81 .... 60 C5
  GRNK PA15 .... 3 K8
  KLMNK KA1 .... 17 G6
  PSLY PA1 .... 9 H3
Gilmourton Crs NMRNS G77 .. 150 D5
Gilroy Cl LNK/LMHG ML11 ..... 199 J4
Gimmerscroft Crs
  AIRDRIE ML6 .... 111 M3 ▣
Girdle Ct IRV KA12 .... 203 M4
Girthon St CAR/SHTL G32 ..... 107 J5
Girvan Crs AIRDRIE ML6 .... 111 K8
  NMLNS KA16 .... 215 G2
Girvan St STPS/GTHM/RID G33.. 7 L7
The Glade LRKH ML9 .... 176 B7
Gladney Av KNTSWD G13 .... 80 E1
Gladsmuir Rd
  CARD/HILL/MSPK G52 .... 103 G3
Gladstone Av BRHD/NEIL G78 .. 125 H7
  JNSTN PA5 .... 122 D2 ▣
Gladstone Ct HMLTN ML3 ..... 156 A4 ▣
Gladstone St BLSH ML4 .... 133 H4 ▣
  CLYDBK G81 .... 59 M7
  COWCAD G4 .... 4 E5
Glaive Rd KNTSWD G13 .... 61 K8
Glamis Av CARLUKE ML8 .... 178 F7
  JNSTN PA5 .... 100 B8
  NMRNS G77 .... 150 F4
Glamis Ct MTHW ML1 .... 134 C6
Glamis Dr EKILN G74 .... 153 M6
  GRNKW/INVK PA16 .... 32 A4
Glamis Pl GRNKW/INVK PA16 .. 32 A4 ▣
Glamis Rd DEN/PKHD G31 ..... 13 L7
Glanderston Av
  BRHD/NEIL G78 .... 125 L7 ▣
  NMRNS G77 .... 150 B3
Glanderston Ct KNTSWD G13 .. 81 G2 ▣
Glanderston Dr KNTSWD G13 .. 81 G2 ▣
Glanderston Ga NMRNS G77 .. 150 B3 ▣
Glanderston Rd NMRNS G77 .. 149 J4
Glasgow & Edinburgh Rd
  BAIL/MDB/MHD G69 .... 108 C4
  MTHW ML1 .... 134 E1
Glasgow Br KKNTL G66 .... 64 F2
Glasgow La ARD KA22 .... 191 J7
Glasgow Rd
  BAIL/MDB/MHD G69 .... 107 M5
  BALLOCH G68 .... 68 B1
  BLTYR/CAMB G72 .... 130 A8
  BLTYR/CAMB G72 .... 155 L2
  BRHD/NEIL G78 .... 125 K5
  CLYDBK G81 .... 60 C3
  CMPF/LLE G63 .... 27 G5
  CRMNK/CLK/EAG G76 .... 151 K7
  CTBR ML5 .... 109 H3
  CUMB G67 .... 49 H5
  DMBTN G82 .... 36 E6
  EKILN G74 .... 154 A4
  HMLTN ML3 .... 156 A4
  KKNTL G66 .... 65 G1
  KLMNKN/STW KA3 .... 207 G5
  KSYTH G65 .... 46 C2
  LNK/LMHG ML11 .... 198 E4
  MLNGV G62 .... 62 B1
  PGL PA14 .... 34 F8
  PLK/PH/NH G53 .... 125 L4
  PSLY PA1 .... 9 J3
  RNFRW PA4 .... 80 E7
  RUTH G73 .... 105 M7
  UD/BTH/TAN G71 .... 108 C8
  WISHAW ML2 .... 158 D5
Glasgow St ARD KA22 .... 191 J8
  GTCI KA28 .... 138 A7
  HBR/GL G84 .... 20 C7
  KBRN KA25 .... 143 G2 ▣
  KVD/HLHD G12 .... 4 A3
Glasgow Vennel IRV KA12 ..... 203 J7
Glassel Rd ESTRH G34 .... 86 D8
Glasserton Pl
  PLKSW/MSWD G43 .... 127 M4 ▣
Glasserton Rd
  PLKSW/MSWD G43 .... 127 M4
Glassford St CGLE G1 .... 11 K2
  MTHW ML1 .... 157 H4
Glassock Rd KLMNKN/STW KA3.. 206 F4
Glaudhall Av
  BAIL/MDB/MHD G69 .... 86 E2 ▣
Glazert Dr KKNTL G66 .... 29 G8
Glazert Meadow KKNTL G66 .. 44 E2
Glazert Park Dr KKNTL G66 .. 44 E2
Glazert Pl KKNTL G66 .... 45 H4
Glebe Av CRMNK/CLK/EAG G76.. 152 C2
  CTBR ML5 .... 109 K6
  KLMNK KA1 .... 17 H5
  UD/BTH/TAN G71 .... 132 B7
Glebe Ct BEITH KA15 .... 168 B1
  COWCAD G4 .... 5 M8
Glebe Crs AIRDRIE ML6 .... 111 K1
  AYR KA8 .... 224 F7
  EKILN G74 .... 15 G3
  HMLTN ML3 .... 156 C7
Glebe Dr LNK/LMHG ML11 ..... 199 G5 ▣
Glebe Gdns ALEX/LLW G83 ..... 25 L5
  CRG/CRSL/HOU PA6 .... 75 H7
Glebe Hollow UD/BTH/TAN G71.. 132 B7 ▣
Glebelands Wy BEITH KA15 .. 168 B2
Glebe La NMRNS G77 .... 150 D5
Glebe Pk DMBTN G82 .... 37 H4
Glebe Pl BLTYR/CAMB G72 ..... 130 B4 ▣
  CTBR ML5 .... 109 K6
  KLMNK KA1 .... 17 H5
  UD/BTH/TAN G71 .... 132 B7
Glebe Rd AYR KA8 .... 224 F7
  BEITH KA15 .... 168 C1 ▣
  GLSTN KA4 .... 214 B3
  GRNKW/INVK PA16 .... 50 E4 ▣
  KLMCLM PA13 .... 75 K1 ▣
  KLMNK KA1 .... 17 H6
  NMRNS G77 .... 150 D5
Glebe St BLSH ML4 .... 132 F4
  COWCAD G4 .... 5 M7
  EKILN G74 .... 15 G3
  HMLTN ML3 .... 156 D7
  KLWNG KA13 .... 193 G5
  RNFRW PA4 .... 80 D6
  SALT KA21 .... 200 F1

SVSTN KA20	192 C8
The Glebe IRVSE KA11	204 C8
LNK/LMHG ML11	198 F5
UD/BTH/TAN G71	132 A7
Glebe Wynd UD/BTH/TAN G71	132 B7
Gleddoch Rd	
CARD/HILL/MSPK G52	102 E3
Gledstane Rd BSHPTN PA7	58 B7
Glenacre Crs UD/BTH/TAN G71	131 L1
Glenacre Dr AIRDRIE ML6	111 K3
CSMK G45	128 D6
LARGS KA30	115 K5
Glenacre Rd CUMB G67	68 F1
Glenacre St CSMK G45	128 D6
Glenacre Ter CSMK G45	128 D6
Glenafeoch Rd CARLUKE ML8	179 G8
Glen Affric EKILN G74	15 M3
Glen Affric Dr AIRDRIE ML6	111 K8
Glen Affric Pl CRH/DND KA2	211 J3
Glen Affric Wy AIRDRIE ML6	111 K8
Glen Afton Ct CRH/DND KA2	211 J3
Glenafton Vw HMLTN ML3	174 B1
Glen Alby Pl GIF/THBK G46	126 C5
Glenalla Crs AYRS KA7	228 C8
Glenallan Ter MTHW ML1	133 K8
Glen Almond EKILN G74	154 C7
Glenalmond St CAR/SHTL G32	107 G5
Glenapp Av PSLYS PA2	102 B8
Glenapp Pl KLWNG KA13	193 J7
Glenapp Qd KLMNK KA1	17 K6
Glenapp Rd PSLYS PA2	102 B8
Glenapp St PLKSD/SHW G41	104 F6
Glenarklet Dr PSLYS PA2	102 A8
Glen Arroch EKILN G74	15 L4
Glenartney	
CRG/CRSL/HOU PA6	77 G7
Glenartney Rd	
BAIL/MDB/MHD G69	66 C8
Glenashdale Wy PSLYS PA2	102 A8
Glen Av BAIL/MDB/MHD G69	66 F7
BRHD/NEIL G78	148 E2
CAR/SHTL G32	107 H3
GRK PA19	31 M3
LARGS KA30	115 K3
LRKH ML9	176 A8
PGL PA14	34 B8
Glenavon Ct HMLTN ML3	156 B8
Glen Avon Dr AIRDRIE ML6	111 K8
Glenavon Rd MRYH/FIRH G20	82 D2
Glenbank Av KKNTL G66	65 K5
Glenbank Dr GIF/THBK G46	126 F7
Glenbank Rd KKNTL G66	65 K5
Glenbarr St SPRGB/BLRNK G21	6 B6
Glen Bervie EKILN G74	15 M2
Glenbervie Dr KLWNG KA13	193 H6
Glenbervie Pl GRK PA19	31 H3
NMRNS G77	150 A4
SMSTN G23	62 D8
Glenbervie Wynd IRVSE KA11	208 D1
Glenboig Farm Rd CTBR ML5	87 L3
Glenboig New Rd CTBR ML5	87 M3
Glenboig Rd CTBR ML5	87 H2
Glen Brae BRWEIR PA11	98 D1
Glenbrae La GRNK PA15	3 G9
Glenbrae Rd GRNK PA15	3 G9
PGL PA14	54 D2
Glenbride Rd WKIL KA23	181 J6
Glenbrittle Dr PSLYS PA2	102 A8
Glenbrittle Wy PSLYS PA2	102 A8
Glenbuck Av	
STPS/GTHM/RID G33	84 F3
Glenbuck Dr	
STPS/GTHM/RID G33	84 F3
Glenburn Av	
BAIL/MDB/MHD G69	66 F6
BAIL/MDB/MHD G69	108 C4
BLTYR/CAMB G72	129 K4
MTHW ML1	134 C5
Glenburn Crs KKNTL G66	45 J4
LARGS KA30	115 J5
PSLYS PA2	124 D2
UD/BTH/TAN G71	132 B1
Glenburn Gdns BSHPBGS G64	63 M7
CTBR ML5	87 J3
Glenburnie Pl	
STPS/GTHM/RID G33	107 M2
Glenburn La KLMCLM PA13	55 K8
MRYH/FIRH G20	82 E2
Glenburn Rd BSDN G61	61 K4
EKILN G74	153 C6
GIF/THBK G46	127 H8
HMLTN ML3	156 B6
KLMCLM PA13	55 K8
PSLYS PA2	124 D1
PSTWK KA9	225 L1
Glenburn St MRYH/FIRH G20	82 E2
PGL PA14	34 A7
Glenburn Ter CARLUKE ML8	188 E1
MTHW ML1	134 B8
Glenburn Wy EKILN G74	152 F6
Glencairn Av WISHAW ML2	158 D5
Glencairn Ct RUTH G73	128 F1
Glencairn Dr	
BAIL/MDB/MHD G69	66 E7
PLKSD/SHW G41	104 E7
RUTH G73	128 F1
Glencairn Gdns	
BLTYR/CAMB G72	130 D4
PLKSD/SHW G41	104 E7
Glencairn La PLKSD/SHW G41	104 E7
Glencairn Rd AYRS KA7	19 K8
CUMB G67	49 J7
DMBTN G82	36 C6
GRNKW/INVK PA16	31 L6
KLMCLM PA13	75 L1
PGL PA14	56 C2
PSLYN/LNWD PA3	102 A2
Glencairn Sq KLMNK KA1	16 F8
Glencairn St MTHW ML1	157 L4
SALT KA21	200 F2
SVSTN KA20	192 D8
Glencairn Ter	
KLMNKN/STW KA3	206 B2
Glencalder Crs BLSH ML4	133 L6
Glen Cally EKILN G74	15 M2
Glencally Av PSLYS PA2	102 B8
Glen Cannich EKILN G74	15 M4
Glen Carron EKILN G74	15 L4
Glencart Gv KLBCH PA10	99 J8
Glen Clova EKILN G74	154 D7
Glen Clova Dr BALLOCH G68	48 C5
Glencloy St MRYH/FIRH G20	82 C2
Glenclune Ct KLMCLM PA13	75 J2
Glen Clunie Av EKILN G74	154 D7
Glen Clunie Dr GIF/THBK G46	126 C5
Glen Clunie Pl GIF/THBK G46	126 C5
Glen Clunie Rd GIF/THBK G46	126 C5
Glencoats Crs PSLYN/LNWD PA3	8 A3
Glencoats Dr PSLYN/LNWD PA3	101 M8
Glencoe Pl HMLTN ML3	174 B1
KNTSWD G13	81 L2
Glencoe Rd CARLUKE ML8	179 G8
Glencoe St KNTSWD G13	81 M2
Glen Cona Dr GIF/THBK G46	126 C4
Glenconner Pl AYRS KA7	19 K8
Glenconner Rd AYRS KA7	19 K8
Glen Conner Dr PSLYS PA2	8 C8
Glencorse St	
STPS/GTHM/RID G33	106 E2
Glen Cova Gdns	
CRH/DND KA2	211 J3
Glencraigs Dr	
KLMNKN/STW KA3	206 F4
Glencraig St AIRDRIE ML6	110 C2
Glen Creran Crs	
BRHD/NEIL G78	148 C3
Glen Crs GRNKW/INVK PA16	50 E4
KNTSWD G13	80 E2
SVSTN KA20	192 C8
Glencroft Av UD/BTH/TAN G71	131 L1
Glencroft Rd LNPK/KPK G44	128 D4
Glencryan Rd CUMB G67	49 H8
Glendale Av AIRDRIE ML6	111 K3
Glendale Crs AYRS KA7	229 H5
BSHPBGS G64	84 C1
Glendale Dr BSHPBGS G64	84 C1
Glendale Gv CTBR ML5	109 L6
Glendale Pl AYRS KA7	229 H5
DEN/PKHD G31	13 G3
SPRGB/BLRNK G21	13 G3
Glendale St DEN/PKHD G31	13 G3
Glendaruel Av BSDN G61	62 B5
Glendaruel Rd	
CRMNK/CLK/EAG G76	129 L7
Glendarvel Gdns PPK/MIL G22	83 K5
Glendee Gdns RNFRW PA4	80 D7
Glendee Rd RNFRW PA4	80 D7
Glendentan Rd BRWEIR PA11	98 C2
Glen Derry EKILN G74	154 D6
Glen Dessary EKILN G74	15 L5
Glen Devon EKILN G74	154 D8
Glendevon Pl CLYDBK G81	59 M6
HMLTN ML3	174 B1
Glendevon Sq	
STPS/GTHM/RID G33	85 H7
Glendinning Rd KNTSWD G13	61 L8
Glendoick Pl NMRNS G77	150 A4
Glen Doll EKILN G74	15 M3
Glen Doll Rd BRHD/NEIL G78	148 B3
Glendorch Av WISHAW ML2	159 J3
Glendore St SCOT G14	81 L7
Glen Douglas Dr BALLOCH G68	48 C5
Glen Douglas Rd	
GRNKW/INVK PA16	32 C6
Glendoune Rd	
CRMNK/CLK/EAG G76	151 L4
Glen Dr HBR/GL G84	20 D5
MTHW ML1	134 B4
Glenduffhill Rd	
BAIL/MDB/MHD G69	107 M4
Glen Dye EKILN G74	15 M2
Glen Eagles EKILN G74	154 C8
Gleneagles Av BALLOCH G68	49 G4
KLWNG KA13	193 J5
Gleneagles Dr GRK PA19	31 G3
NMRNS G77	151 H5
Gleneagles Gdns BSHPBGS G64	63 M6
Gleneagles Ga NMRNS G77	151 H5
Gleneagles La North SCOT G14	81 J5
Gleneagles La South SCOT G14	81 J6
Gleneagles Pk	
UD/BTH/TAN G71	131 M7
Glenelg Crs KKNTL G66	46 A8
Glenelg Qd ESTRH G34	86 D8
Glenelm Pl BLSH ML4	133 G3
Glen Esk EKILN G74	154 D7
Glenesk Crs GIF/THBK G46	126 C5
Glen Esk Dr GIF/THBK G46	126 C5
Glenesk Pl GIF/THBK G46	126 C5
Glen Etive Pl	
CRMNK/CLK/EAG G76	129 L7
Glen Falloch EKILN G74	154 C8
Glen Falloch Crs	
BRHD/NEIL G78	148 C4
Glen Farg EKILN G74	154 C8
Glenfarg Ct HMLTN ML3	174 B1
Glenfarg Crs BSDN G61	62 B5
Glenfarg Rd RUTH G73	129 H5
Glenfarg St MRYH/FIRH G20	4 E5
Glenfarm Rd MTHW ML1	134 E5
Glen Farrar EKILN G74	15 L3
Glen Farrar Wk CRH/DND KA2	211 J3
Glen Feshie EKILN G74	15 M4
Glenfield Av PSLYS PA2	124 D3
Glenfield Crs PSLYS PA2	124 D3
Glenfield Gdns KLMNK KA1	16 F8
PSLYS PA2	124 D3
Glenfield Gv PSLYS PA2	124 D3
Glenfield Pl KLMNK KA1	16 F9
Glenfield Rd EKILS G75	15 K9
PSLYS PA2	124 D2
Glenfinlas St HBR/GL G84	20 E8
Glen Finlet Rd BRHD/NEIL G78	148 B4
Glenfinnan Dr BSDN G61	62 B6
MRYH/FIRH G20	82 D3
Glenfinnan Pl	
MRYH/FIRH G20	82 D3
Glenfinnan Rd MRYH/FIRH G20	82 D4
Glenfruin Crs PSLYS PA2	102 B8
Glen Fruin Dr LRKH ML9	176 D3
Glen Fruin Pl AIRDRIE ML6	111 K7
Glenfruin Rd BLTYR/CAMB G72	155 J2
Glen Fruin Rd	
GRNKW/INVK PA16	32 D6
Glen Fyne Rd BALLOCH G68	48 B5
Glen Gairn EKILN G74	154 D7
Glen Gairn Crs BRHD/NEIL G78	148 C3
Glen Gdns JNSTN PA5	100 C6
Glengarriff Rd BLSH ML4	133 H1
Glen Garry EKILN G74	15 M5
Glengarry Dr	
CARD/HILL/MSPK G52	103 J4
Glengavel Crs	
STPS/GTHM/RID G33	84 F3
Glengavel Gdns WISHAW ML2	159 J2
Glengowan Rd AIRDRIE ML6	91 G5
BRWEIR PA11	98 C1
Glen Gv EKILS G75	14 C7
LARGS KA30	115 K3
Glengyre St ESTRH G34	108 C1
Glenhead Crs CLYDBK G81	60 A2
PPK/MIL G22	83 J5
Glenhead Rd CLYDBK G81	60 A4
KKNTL G66	65 J5
Glenhead St PPK/MIL G22	83 J3
Glenholme Av PSLYS PA2	101 H8
Glenhove Rd CUMB G67	49 G7
Glenhuntly Rd PGL PA14	34 B8
Glenhuntly Ter PGL PA14	34 B8
Gleniffer Av KNTSWD G13	81 G3
Gleniffer Crs JNSTN PA5	100 C8
Gleniffer Dr BRHD/NEIL G78	125 G4
Gleniffer Rd BRHD/NEIL G78	146 B8
BRHD/NEIL G78	146 D6
PSLYS PA2	123 H7
PSLYS PA2	123 L4
RNFRW PA4	102 B1
Gleniffer Vw BRHD/NEIL G78	148 D1
Gleninver Rd GRNKW/INVK PA16	31 M5
Glen Isla EKILN G74	154 C7
Glenisla Av BAIL/MDB/MHD G69	67 G5
Glen Isla Rd BRHD/NEIL G78	148 C4
Glenisla St DEN/PKHD G31	13 M9
Glen Kinglas Av	
GRNKW/INVK PA16	32 D7
Glen Kinglas Rd	
GRNKW/INVK PA16	32 C7
Glenkirk Dr DRUM G15	61 H7
Glen La BRHD/NEIL G78	147 G6
PSLYN/LNWD PA3	9 G2
Glen Lee EKILN G74	154 C7
Glenlee St HMLTN ML3	155 M4
Glenleith Pl IRVSE KA11	204 C7
Glen Lethnot EKILN G74	154 C7
Glen Livet Pl GIF/THBK G46	126 C5
Glenlivet Pl KLMNKN/STW KA3	207 H6
Glenlivet Rd BRHD/NEIL G78	148 C4
Glen Lochay Gdns BALLOCH G68	48 B5
Glenlora Dr PLK/PH/NH G53	126 A3
Glenlora Ter PLK/PH/NH G53	126 B2
Glen Loy Pl GIF/THBK G46	126 C5
Glen Luce Dr CAR/SHTL G32	107 K6
Glenluce Gdns	
BAIL/MDB/MHD G69	67 G6
Glenluce Ter EKILN G74	14 B2
Glenluggie Rd KKNTL G66	66 A2
Glenlui Av RUTH G73	129 H4
Glen Luss Gdns BALLOCH G68	48 B5
Glen Luss Pl CTBR ML5	110 D4
Glen Luss Rd	
GRNKW/INVK PA16	32 D7
Glen Lyon EKILN G74	154 C8
Glen Lyon Ct BALLOCH G68	48 B5
Glenlyon Ct HMLTN ML3	174 B1
Glen Lyon Crs CRH/DND KA2	211 J3
Glenlyon Gv IRV KA12	203 M4
Glenlyon Pl RUTH G73	129 J6
Glen Lyon Rd	
BRHD/NEIL G78	148 C3
Glenmalloch Pl JNSTN PA5	100 C6
Glenmanor Av	
BAIL/MDB/MHD G69	66 E6
Glen Mark EKILN G74	154 C7
Glen Markie Dr GIF/THBK G46	126 C5
Glen Mark Rd	
BRHD/NEIL G78	148 C3
Glenmavis Crs CARLUKE ML8	178 F8
Glenmavis Rd AIRDRIE ML6	88 E6
Glenmavis St COWCAD G4	5 H7
Glen More EKILN G74	15 L4
Glenmore Av ALEX/LLW G83	25 K3
BLSH ML4	133 H6
GVH/MTFL G42	128 E1
Glenmore Rd MTHW ML1	134 C5
Glen Moriston EKILN G74	15 M4
Glen Moriston Rd BALLOCH G68	48 B5
GIF/THBK G46	126 C4
Glenmoss Av ERSK PA8	58 F8
Glenmosston Rd KLMCLM PA13	75 L1
Glenmount Pl AYRS KA7	228 D8
Glen Moy EKILN G74	15 M4
Glenmuir Dr PLK/PH/NH G53	126 B4
Glenmuir Pl AYR KA8	225 K6
Glenmuir Rd AYR KA8	225 K7
Glen Nevis EKILN G74	15 M5
Glen Nevis Pl CRH/DND KA2	211 J3
RUTH G73	129 J7
LOCHW PA12	120 C6
Glenpark St DEN/PKHD G31	13 C3
WISHAW ML2	159 G5
Glenpark Ter	
BLTYR/CAMB G72	129 L2
Glenpath DMBTN G82	37 J6
Glenpatrick Rd JNSTN PA5	100 D8
Glen Pl CRMNK/CLK/EAG G76	151 L2
Glen Prosen EKILN G74	154 C7
Glen Quoich EKILN G74	154 D6
Glenraith Rd	
STPS/GTHM/RID G33	85 H6
Glen Rannoch Dr AIRDRIE ML6	111 K8
Glenriddet Av KBRN KA25	167 H1
Glen Rinnes Dr	
BRHD/NEIL G78	148 D4
AIRDRIE ML6	90 F7
BSHPTN PA7	58 A5
CAR/SHTL G32	107 H2
EKILN G74	152 F5
FAIRLIE KA29	139 K7
KKNTL G66	29 C7
MTHW ML1	134 D2
OLDK G60	59 H3
SHOTTS ML7	137 M5
WISHAW ML2	159 C5
WKIL KA23	181 K4
Glen Rosa Gdns BALLOCH G68	48 B5
Glen Roy Dr BRHD/NEIL G78	148 C3
Glen Sannox Dr BALLOCH G68	48 B5
Glen Sannox Vw BALLOCH G68	48 B5
Glen Sannox Wy BALLOCH G68	48 B5
Glen Sax Dr RNFRW PA4	80 E8
Glen Shee EKILN G74	154 C7
Glen Shee Av BRHD/NEIL G78	148 C3
Glen Shee Crs AIRDRIE ML6	111 K8
Glenshee Gdns DEN/PKHD G31	13 M8
Glenshee St DEN/PKHD G31	13 M8
Glenshee Ter HMLTN ML3	174 B1
Glenshiel Av PSLYS PA2	102 A8
Glen Shiel Crs KLMNK KA1	211 J3
Glenshira Av PSLYS PA2	102 A8
Glen Shirva Rd KSYTH G65	46 F5
Glenside Av PLK/PH/NH G53	103 H7
Glenside Crs WKIL KA23	181 K6
Glenside Dr BLTYR/CAMB G72	129 K3
Glenside Gv WKIL KA23	181 K6
Glenside Rd DMBTN G82	37 J3
PGL PA14	54 D2
Glenspean Pl CTBR ML5	110 C3
Glenspean St	
PLKSW/MSWD G43	127 K3
Glen St BLTYR/CAMB G72	130 D5
BRHD/NEIL G78	125 J6
GRNKW/INVK PA16	32 D2
MTHW ML1	133 L8
MTHW ML1	134 D5
PSLYN/LNWD PA3	9 G2
Glentanar Dr	
BAIL/MDB/MHD G69	67 G7
Glentanar Pl PPK/MIL G22	83 H2
Glentanar Rd PPK/MIL G22	83 H2
Glen Tanner EKILN G74	154 C7
Glen Tarbert Dr BRHD/NEIL G78	148 C3
Glentarbert Rd RUTH G73	129 K6
Glen Tennet EKILN G74	154 C7
Glentore Qd AIRDRIE ML6	89 G7
Glentrool Gdns	
BAIL/MDB/MHD G69	67 G6
PPK/MIL G22	83 K5
Glen Trool Wk CRH/DND KA2	211 J3
Glen Truim Vw CRH/DND KA2	211 J3
Glen Turret EKILN G74	154 C7
Glenturret St CAR/SHTL G32	107 G5
Glentyan Av KLBCH PA10	99 G5
Glentyan Dr PLK/PH/NH G53	126 A3
Glentyan Ter PLK/PH/NH G53	126 A3
Glen Urquhart EKILN G74	15 M3
Glen Vw CUMB G67	25 K7
DMBTN G82	25 K7
HMLTN ML3	174 D3
Glenview AIRDRIE ML6	111 K3
LRKH ML9	175 M5
Glenview Av AIRDRIE ML6	91 G5
Glenview Crs	
BAIL/MDB/MHD G69	66 F6
Glenview Pl	
BLTYR/CAMB G72	131 K8
Glenview St AIRDRIE ML6	88 E5
Glenville Av GIF/THBK G46	127 H6
Glenville Ga	
CRMNK/CLK/EAG G76	152 A4
Glenville Ter	
CRMNK/CLK/EAG G76	152 A4
Glenward Av KNTSWD G13	44 E1
Glenwell St AIRDRIE ML6	88 E6
Glenwood Av AIRDRIE ML6	111 J5
Glenwood Ct KKNTL G66	65 G4
Glenwood Dr GIF/THBK G46	126 F7
Glenwood Gdns KKNTL G66	65 G4
Glenwood Pth CSMK G45	128 E6
Glenwood Pl CSMK G45	128 E6
KKNTL G66	65 G4
Glenwood Rd KKNTL G66	65 G4
Glorat Av KKNTL G66	44 E1
Gloucester Av	
CRMNK/CLK/EAG G76	151 K2
RUTH G73	129 K4
Gloucester St GBLS G5	10 D5
Goatfell Vw TROON KA10	216 E2
Goatfoot Rd GLSTN KA4	214 A3
Gockston Rd PSLYN/LNWD PA3	101 K2
Goddard Pl WISHAW ML2	160 B4
Gogar St STPS/GTHM/RID G33	106 E1
Gogoside Dr LARGS KA30	115 K6
Gogoside Rd LARGS KA30	115 K6
Gogo St LARGS KA30	115 J6
Goldberry Av SCOT G14	81 H4
Goldeneacre Rd AIRDRIE ML6	89 M6
Goldenberry Av WKIL KA23	181 G5
Goldenlee Vw	
CRG/CRSL/HOU PA6	99 G1
Goldie Pl SVSTN KA20	192 C8
Goldie Rd UD/BTH/TAN G71	132 A5
Golf Av BLSH ML4	133 G4
SVSTN KA20	201 M3
Golf Course Rd BRWEIR PA11	98 B1
BSHPBGS G64	63 K1
SKLM KA17	70 B5
Golf Crs TROON KA10	216 D7
Golf Dr DRUM G15	60 F8
PGL PA14	54 D1
PSLY PA1	102 C5
Golffields Rd IRV KA12	203 K8
Golf Gdns LRKH ML9	176 C7
Golfhill Dr ALEX/LLW G83	25 M4
DEN/PKHD G31	6 E9
HBR/GL G84	20 F7
Golfhill Qd AIRDRIE ML6	89 C7
Golfhill Rd WISHAW ML2	158 D5
Golfloan KLMNKN/STW KA3	197 L1
Golf Pl BLSH ML4	133 H6
GRNKW/INVK PA16	32 C2
IRV KA12	203 H4
TROON KA10	216 D7
Golf Rd BSHPTN PA7	58 A5
CRMNK/CLK/EAG G76	151 K1
GRK PA19	31 J3
RUTH G73	129 H5
Golfview BSDN G61	61 G4
Golf Vw CLYDBK G81	59 M5
Golfview Pl CTBR ML5	109 J2
Golfview Pl CTBR ML5	109 J3
Golspie Av AIRDRIE ML6	110 E5
Golspie St GOV/IBX G51	104 A1
Goodview Gdns LRKH ML9	176 C7
Goodwin Dr RAYR/DAL KA6	227 H7
Goosedubbs CGLE G1	11 H1
Gooseholm Crs DMBTN G82	37 G4
Gooseholm Rd DMBTN G82	37 G4
Gopher Av UD/BTH/TAN G71	132 B1
Gorbals St GBLS G5	11 G3
Gordon Av BAIL/MDB/MHD G69	107 M4
BSHPTN PA7	58 A5
CARD/HILL/MSPK G52	102 E2
LNPK/KPK G44	127 L7
GIF/THBK G46	127 L6
Gordon Crs NMRNS G77	150 E3
Gordon Dr EKILN G74	154 B6
GIF/THBK G46	127 L6
Gordon La CGLE G1	11 H1
Gordon Pl BLSH ML4	132 F7
Gordon Rd HMLTN ML3	155 M5
LNPK/KPK G44	127 L7
Gordon St AYR KA8	225 G6
CGLE G1	11 H1
CGLW G2	11 G1
GRNK PA15	2 A6
PSLY PA1	9 H5
Gordon Ter AYR KA8	19 H3
BLTYR/CAMB G72	131 J7
HMLTN ML3	155 M6
Gorebridge St CAR/SHTL G32	106 E2
Goremire Rd CARLUKE ML8	179 J8
Gorget Av KNTSWD G13	61 J8
Gorget Pl KNTSWD G13	61 J8
Gorget Qd DRUM G15	61 H8
Gorse Crs BRWEIR PA11	98 E2
Gorsehall St MTHW ML1	135 H7
Gorse Pl UD/BTH/TAN G71	132 B1
Gorsewood BSHPBGS G64	63 L8
Gorstan Pl MRYH/FIRH G20	82 D1
Gorstan St SMSTN G23	82 D1
Goschen Ter AYR KA8	225 H7
Gosford La SCOT G14	81 G5
Gottries Rd IRV KA12	203 G8
Goudie St PSLYN/LNWD PA3	101 K2
Gough St STPS/GTHM/RID G33	7 L8
Goukscroft Pk AYRS KA7	228 C3
Gould St AYR KA8	225 J7
Gourlay EKILN G74	154 D4
Gourlay Dr WISHAW ML2	177 J3
Gourlay St SPRGB/BLRNK G21	5 M2
Gourock St GBLS G5	10 E8
Govan Dr ALEX/LLW G83	25 K3
Govanhill St GVH/MTFL G42	105 H7
Govan Rd GOV/IBX G51	81 K8
Gowanbank Gdns JNSTN PA5	99 L7
Gowanbank Rd AYRS KA7	229 H7
Gowan Brae AIRDRIE ML6	91 H5
Gowanlea Av DRUM G15	61 G8
Gowanlea Dr GIF/THBK G46	127 K5
Gowanlea Ter	
UD/BTH/TAN G71	132 B2
Gowanside Pl CARLUKE ML8	178 D7
Gower Pl AYRS KA7	229 H6
Gower St PLKSD/SHW G41	104 C4
Gower Ter PLKSD/SHW G41	104 C4
Gowkhall Av MTHW ML1	134 F6
Gowkhouse Rd KLMCLM PA13	75 L1
Goyle Av DRUM G15	61 J6
Grace Av BAIL/MDB/MHD G69	108 F4
Grace St KVGV G3	10 C1
Graeme Pl MTHW ML1	133 K7
Graffham Av GIF/THBK G46	127 K6
Grafton Pl CGLE G1	5 K9
Graham Av BLTYR/CAMB G72	130 D5
CLYDBK G81	60 B6
EKILN G74	14 F1
HMLTN ML3	174 D1
Graham Ct DMBTN G82	35 H2
Grahamfield Pl BEITH KA15	168 A1
Graham Pl HBR/GL G84	21 G7
KLMNKN/STW KA3	17 M1
LRKH ML9	176 F8
Graham Rd CARLUKE ML8	188 E8
DMBTN G82	36 D5
Grahams Av LOCHW PA12	120 C6
Grahamsdyke Rd KKNTL G66	45 L8
Grahamshill Av AIRDRIE ML6	111 J1
Grahamshill St AIRDRIE ML6	111 J1
Graham Sq DMNK/BRGTN G40	12 C4
Grahamston Av GLGNK KA14	167 H3
Grahamston Ct PSLYS PA2	125 J1
Grahamston Crs PSLYS PA2	125 J1
Grahamston Pk	
BRHD/NEIL G78	125 J4
Grahamston Rd PSLYS PA2	125 J3
Graham St AIRDRIE ML6	111 G2
BRHD/NEIL G78	125 H6
GRNKW/INVK PA16	32 C4
HMLTN ML3	156 E6
JNSTN PA5	99 L7

MTHW ML1 ...... 134 A4
WISHAW ML2 ...... 159 H7
Graham Ter *BSHPBGS* G64...... 84 B2
Graignestock Pl
 DMNK/BRGTN G40 ...... 12 B6 ⬛
Graignestock St
 DMNK/BRGTN G40...... 12 B5
Graigside Pl *BALLOCH* G68 ...... 67 M2 ⬛
Grainger Rd *BSHPBGS* G64 ...... 64 D8
Grampian Av *PSLYS* PA2 ...... 124 D1
Grampian Ct *IRVSE* KA11 ...... 204 B5
Grampian Crs *AIRDRIE* ML6 ...... 111 M8 ⬛
 CAR/SHTL G32 ...... 107 H5
Grampian Pl *CAR/SHTL* G32 ...... 107 H5 ⬛
Grampian Rd *KLMNK* KA1 ...... 212 A6
 PGL PA14 ...... 55 G3 ⬛
 WISHAW ML2 ...... 158 F5 ⬛
Grampian St *CAR/SHTL* G32 ...... 107 H5
Grampian Wy *BALLOCH* G68 ...... 48 A7
 BRHD/NEIL G78 ...... 125 J8
 BSDN G61 ...... 61 J1 ⬛
 BSDN G61 ...... 61 K2 ⬛
Granby La *KVD/HLHD* G12 ...... 82 D7
Grandtuly Dr *KVD/HLHD* G12 ...... 82 C3
Grange Av *AYRS* KA7 ...... 229 H7
 MLNGV G62 ...... 42 B7
 WISHAW ML2 ...... 158 E8
Grange Ct *LNK/LMHG* ML11 ...... 198 F4
Grange Gdns
 UD/BTH/TAN G71 ...... 132 B8 ⬛
Grangemuir Rd *PSTWK* KA9 ...... 225 H2
Grangeneuk Gdns
 BALLOCH G68 ...... 48 C8 ⬛
Grange Pl *ALEX/LLW* G83 ...... 25 L4 ⬛
Grange Rd *BSDN* G61 ...... 61 M4
 GVH/MTFL G42 ...... 128 A1
 SVSTN KA20 ...... 192 D8
Granger Rd *ALEX/LLW* G83 ...... 25 M1 ⬛
 KLMNK KA1 ...... 211 L4
Grange St *KLMNK* KA1 ...... 16 D4
 MTHW ML1 ...... 158 A5
Grange Ter *KLMNK* KA1 ...... 16 A4
Gran St *CLYDBK* G81 ...... 80 E1
Grant Ct *HMLTN* ML3 ...... 174 C3
Grant Crs *DMBTN* G82 ...... 25 K8 ⬛
Grantholm Av *MTHW* ML1 ...... 134 B3
Grantlea Gv *CAR/SHTL* G32 ...... 107 K5
Grantlea Ter *CAR/SHTL* G32 ...... 107 K5 ⬛
Grantley Gdns *PLKSD/SHW* G41 ...... 127 K1
Grantley St *PLKSW/MSWD* G43 ...... 127 K1
Grantoften Pth *EKILS* G75 ...... 171 L3 ⬛
Granton St *GBLS* G5 ...... 105 L7 ⬛
Grantown Av *AIRDRIE* ML6 ...... 111 L3
Grantown Gdns *AIRDRIE* ML6 ...... 88 F4
Grant Pl *KLMNKN/STW* KA3 ...... 207 J7
Grants Av *PSLYS* PA2 ...... 101 J8
Grant St *GRNK* PA15 ...... 3 J7
 HBR/GL G84 ...... 20 D8
 KVGV G3 ...... 4 D6
Grants Wy *PSLYS* PA2 ...... 101 J8
Granville St *CLYDBK* G81 ...... 60 B6
 HBR/GL G84 ...... 20 F8
 KVGV G3 ...... 4 D8
Grasmere *EKILS* G75 ...... 170 F4 ⬛
Grasmere Ct *HMLTN* ML3 ...... 174 D3 ⬛
Grassyards Rd
 KLMNKN/STW KA3 ...... 17 J3
Grathellen Ct *MTHW* ML1 ...... 158 A1
Gray Crs *IRV* KA12 ...... 208 C1
Gray Dr *BSDN* G61 ...... 61 M6
Gray's Cl *LNK/LMHG* ML11 ...... 198 C5
Grayshill Rd *BALLOCH* G68 ...... 67 K2
Gray's Rd *UD/BTH/TAN* G71 ...... 132 B4
Graystonelee Rd
 SHOTTS ML7 ...... 137 K3 ⬛
Graystones *KLWNG* KA13 ...... 193 L4
Gray St *ALEX/LLW* G83 ...... 25 L4 ⬛
 GRNK PA15 ...... 3 H8
 KKNTL G66 ...... 66 B2 ⬛
 KVGV G3 ...... 4 A7
 LRKH ML9 ...... 176 A5
 MTHW ML1 ...... 135 H8
 PSTWK KA9 ...... 225 J1
Great Dovehill *COWCAD* G4...... 11 M3
Great George La *KVD/HLHD* G12 .. 82 D7
Great Hamilton St *PSLYS* PA2 ...... 9 G8
Great Kelvin La *KVD/HLHD* G12 ...... 4 A4
Great Western Rd *CLYDBK* G81 ...... 60 C5
 KNTSWD G13 ...... 81 J1
 KVD/HLHD G12 ...... 82 B4 ⬛
 OLDK G60 ...... 58 B1
Great Western Ter
 KVD/HLHD G12 ...... 82 C5
Great Western Terrace La
 KVD/HLHD G12 ...... 82 C5 ⬛
Green *LARGS* KA30 ...... 115 J6 ⬛
Greenacres *ARD* KA22 ...... 191 L6
 MTHW ML1 ...... 157 J4
Greenan Av *LNPK/KPK* G44 ...... 128 C2 ⬛
Greenan Gv *AYRS* KA7 ...... 228 B6 ⬛
Greenan Pl *AYRS* KA7 ...... 228 C6
Greenan Rd *AYRS* KA7 ...... 228 B6
 KLMNKN/STW KA3 ...... 17 L5
Greenan Wy *AYRS* KA7 ...... 228 B6
Green Av *IRV* KA12 ...... 203 J5
Greenbank Av *GIF/THBK* G46 ...... 151 G2
Greenbank Ct *IRV* KA12 ...... 203 J8 ⬛
Greenbank Dr *PSLYS* PA2 ...... 124 D2
Green Bank Rd *BALLOCH* G68 ...... 48 C7 ⬛
Greenbank Rd *IRV* KA12 ...... 203 J8
 WISHAW ML2 ...... 159 J6
Greenbank Ter *CARLUKE* ML8 ...... 178 F7
Greendyke St *CGLE* G1 ...... 11 L4
Greenend Av *PSLYS* PA2 ...... 99 K8
Greenend Pl *CAR/SHTL* G32 ...... 107 J2 ⬛
Greenend Rd *BLSH* ML4 ...... 132 F5
Greenfarm Rd *NMRNS* G77 ...... 150 B4
Green Farm Rd
 PSLYN/LNWD PA3 ...... 100 B3
Greenfaulds Crs *CUMB* G67 ...... 69 G1 ⬛
Greenfaulds Rd *CUMB* G67 ...... 68 D2
Greenfield Av *IRV* KA12 ...... 203 K7
 WISHAW ML2 ...... 159 K5
Greenfield Crs *WISHAW* ML2 ...... 159 K5
Greenfield Qd *MTHW* ML1 ...... 134 F5 ⬛

Greenfield Rd *CAR/SHTL* G32 ...... 107 J3
 CARLUKE ML8 ...... 178 F6
 CRMNK/CLK/EAG G76 ...... 151 L3
 HMLTN ML3...... 156 A3
Greenfield St *GOV/IBX* G51 ...... 103 M1
 WISHAW ML2 ...... 159 K5
Greengairs Av *GOV/IBX* G51 ...... 103 K2
Greengairs Rd *AIRDRIE* ML6 ...... 69 L7
Green Gdns *MTHW* ML1 ...... 135 J7 ⬛
Greenhall Pl *BLTYR/CAMB* G72 ...... 155 J3
Greenhead *NMLNS* KA16 ...... 215 K2
Greenhead Av *SVSTN* KA20 ...... 192 E7
Greenhead Rd *BSDN* G61 ...... 61 M5 ⬛
 DMBTN G82 ...... 37 J6
 RNFRW PA4 ...... 79 J2
 WISHAW ML2 ...... 159 J7
Greenhead St
 DMNK/BRGTN G40 ...... 12 B6 ⬛
Greenhill *BSHPBGS* G64 ...... 64 C8 ⬛
 LARGS KA30 ...... 115 K6 ⬛
Greenhill Av
 BAIL/MDB/MHD G69 ...... 86 E2
 GIF/THBK G46 ...... 127 J8
Greenhill Ct *IRVSE* KA11 ...... 204 B5
 RUTH G73 ...... 129 G1
Greenhill Crs *JNSTN* PA5 ...... 100 D7
 PSLYN/LNWD PA3 ...... 100 B4
Greenhill Dr
 PSLYN/LNWD PA3 ...... 100 C3 ⬛
Greenhill Rd *MTHW* ML1 ...... 135 M5
 PSLYN/LNWD PA3 ...... 101 J3
 RUTH G73 ...... 129 G2
Greenhills Crs *EKILS* G75 ...... 171 H4 ⬛
Greenhills Rd *EKILS* G75 ...... 171 G3
Greenhill St *RUTH* G73 ...... 129 G2 ⬛
Greenhill Ter *CRH/DND* KA2 ...... 205 M7
Greenholm Av
 CRMNK/CLK/EAG G76 ...... 151 L2
 UD/BTH/TAN G71 ...... 131 L2 ⬛
Greenholme St
 LNPK/KPK G44 ...... 128 B3 ⬛
Greenholm St *KLMNK* KA1...... 16 E9
Greenknowe Dr *CARLUKE* ML8 ...... 177 M3
Greenknowe Rd
 PLKSW/MSWD G43 ...... 127 H3 ⬛
Greenknowe St *WISHAW* ML2...... 177 H3
Greenlaw Av *PSLY* PA1...... 9 L2
 WISHAW ML2 ...... 159 J4
Greenlaw Crs *PSLY* PA1...... 9 M1
Greenlaw Dr *PSLY* PA1...... 9 M5
Greenlaw Rd *NMRNS* G77 ...... 150 C4
 SCOT G14 ...... 80 D3
Greenlea Rd
 BAIL/MDB/MHD G69 ...... 86 B1
Greenlea St *KNTSWD* G13 ...... 81 L3 ⬛
Greenlees Ct *DALRY* KA24 ...... 184 B1
Greenlees Gdns
 BLTYR/CAMB G72 ...... 129 M6
Greenlees Gv *CTBR* ML5 ...... 110 D4 ⬛
Greenlees Pk *BLTYR/CAMB* G72 . 130 A6
Greenlees Rd *BLTYR/CAMB* G72 . 129 M7
 BLTYR/CAMB G72 ...... 130 A6
Greenloan Av *GOV/IBX* G51 ...... 103 K1 ⬛
Greenmoss Pl *BLSH* ML4 ...... 133 H4
Greenmount *PPK/MIL* G22 ...... 83 G2 ⬛
Greenock Av *LNPK/KPK* G44 ...... 128 B4
Greenock Rd *BSHPTN* PA7 ...... 57 H3
 GRNK PA15 ...... 33 L6
 LARGS KA30 ...... 115 G2
 PGL PA14...... 34 E8
 PSLYN/LNWD PA3 ...... 101 K2
 RNFRW PA4 ...... 79 H3
Green Pk *AYRS* KA7...... 228 B6
Green Pl *AIRDRIE* ML6 ...... 111 H7
Greenrig *UD/BTH/TAN* G71 ...... 131 M3 ⬛
Greenrig Rd *CUMB* G67 ...... 49 H8
Greenrigg St
 UD/BTH/TAN G71 ...... 131 M3 ⬛
Greenrig St *STPS/GTHM/RID* G33.. 7 M3
Green Rd *PSLYS* PA2 ...... 101 G6
Greens Av *KKNTL* G66 ...... 65 J1
Greens Crs *KKNTL* G66 ...... 65 J2
Greenshields Rd
 BAIL/MDB/MHD G69 ...... 108 B4
Greenside *NMLNS* KA16 ...... 215 K2
Greenside Av *IRVSE* KA11 ...... 204 F8
 KBRN KA25 ...... 167 G1
 PSTWK KA9 ...... 225 K2
Greenside Crs
 STPS/GTHM/RID G33...... 84 E6
Greenside La *LNK/LMHG* ML11 ...... 199 G5
Greenside Pl *BSDN* G61 ...... 61 J1 ⬛
Greenside Rd *CLYDBK* G81 ...... 60 B2
 MTHW ML1 ...... 134 C2
 WISHAW ML2 ...... 159 J7
Greenside St *CTBR* ML5 ...... 88 B8
 MTHW ML1 ...... 134 C2
 STPS/GTHM/RID G33...... 84 E6
Greenside Ter *IRVSE* KA11 ...... 205 G7
Greenside Vw *IRVSE* KA11 ...... 204 A5
Greens Rd *CUMB* G67 ...... 68 F3
Green St *AYR* KA8 ...... 18 E1
 CLYDBK G81 ...... 60 A6
 DMNK/BRGTN G40 ...... 12 B5
 KLMNK KA1...... 16 F3
 SALT KA21 ...... 200 F2
 UD/BTH/TAN G71 ...... 132 B7
Green Street La *AYR* KA8 ...... 18 E1
The Green *DMNK/BRGTN* G40 ...... 12 B7
Greentowers Rd
 LNK/LMHG ML11 ...... 189 K8
Greentree Dr
 BAIL/MDB/MHD G69 ...... 107 M6
Greentree Pk *AYRS* KA7 ...... 229 J4
Greenview St
 PLKSW/MSWD G43 ...... 127 J1 ⬛
Greenways Av *PSLYS* PA2 ...... 101 G7
Greenways Ct *PSLYS* PA2 ...... 101 G7 ⬛
Greenwood Av
 BLTYR/CAMB G72 ...... 130 E3 ⬛
Greenwood Crs *CTBR* ML5 ...... 110 C4
Greenwood Dr *BSDN* G61 ...... 62 A5
 JNSTN PA5 ...... 122 D1
Greenwood Qd *CLYDBK* G81 ...... 60 D8
Greenwood Rd
 CRMNK/CLK/EAG G76 ...... 151 K2
 IRVSE KA11 ...... 204 C3
Greenwood St *SHOTTS* ML7 ...... 137 L5

Greer Qd *CLYDBK* G81 ...... 60 B5
Greeto Falls Av *LARGS* KA30 ...... 115 L5
Grenada Pl *EKILS* G75 ...... 153 G6
Grenadier Gdns *MTHW* ML1 ...... 157 K5 ⬛
Grenville Dr *BLTYR/CAMB* G72 ...... 129 M5
Grenville Rd *GRK* PA19 ...... 31 M3
Gresham Sq *MTHW* ML1...... 158 B7
Gresta St *DMNK/BRGTN* G40 ...... 13 H8
Greta Meek La *KKNTL* G66 ...... 45 J3
Greyfriars Dr *UD/BTH/TAN* G71 .. 131 J1
Greyfriars St *CAR/SHTL* G32 ...... 106 F2
Greystone Av *RUTH* G73 ...... 129 J3
Greywood St *KNTSWD* G13 ...... 81 L2 ⬛
Grier Pl *LRKH* ML9 ...... 175 M7
Grierson La
 STPS/GTHM/RID G33...... 7 L9 ⬛
Grierson St *STPS/GTHM/RID* G33 .... 7 L9
Griers Wk *IRVSE* KA11 ...... 209 K3
Grieve Cft *UD/BTH/TAN* G71 ...... 131 M8
Grieve Rd *CUMB* G67 ...... 49 G6
 GRNKW/INVK PA16 ...... 32 A4
Griffen Av *PSLYN/LNWD* PA3...... 100 E4
Griffin Pl *BLSH* ML4 ...... 133 G1
Griffiths Wy *CARLUKE* ML8 ...... 177 M5
Griqua Ter *UD/BTH/TAN* G71 ...... 132 B7
Grogarry Rd *DRUM* G15 ...... 61 G5
Grosvenor Crs *KVD/HLHD* G12 .. 82 D6 ⬛
Grosvenor Crescent La
 KVD/HLHD G12 ...... 82 D6 ⬛
Grosvenor La *KVD/HLHD* G12 ...... 82 D6
Grosvenor Rd *GRNK* PA15 ...... 3 L8
Grosvenor Ter *KVD/HLHD* G12 .. 82 D6 ⬛
Grougar Rd *KLMNKN/STW* KA3 . 207 H4
Grougar St *KLMNKN/STW* KA3 .. 212 D1
Groveburn Av *GIF/THBK* G46 ...... 127 G5
Grove Crs *LRKH* ML9 ...... 176 C7
Grove Pk *KKNTL* G66 ...... 65 K5
Grovepark Ct *MRYH/FIRH* G20 ...... 4 E4
Grove Park Gdns *MRYH/FIRH* G20... 4 E4
Grovepark St *MRYH/FIRH* G20 ...... 4 E3
The Groves *BRHD/NEIL* G78 ...... 148 C3 ⬛
The Grove *BRHD/NEIL* G78 ...... 148 C3 ⬛
 BRWEIR PA11 ...... 98 E3 ⬛
 BSHPTN PA7 ...... 58 A6
 GIF/THBK G46 ...... 151 H1
 KLBCH PA10 ...... 99 G6 ⬛
Grudie St *ESTRH* G34 ...... 108 A1 ⬛
Gryfebank Av
 CRG/CRSL/HOU PA6 ...... 77 L8
Gryfebank Cl
 CRG/CRSL/HOU PA6 ...... 77 L8 ⬛
Gryfebank Crs
 CRG/CRSL/HOU PA6 ...... 77 K8
Gryfebank Wy
 CRG/CRSL/HOU PA6 ...... 77 L8 ⬛
Gryfe Rd *BRWEIR* PA11 ...... 98 D2
 PGL PA14...... 54 E2
Gryfe St *GRNK* PA15 ...... 3 H9
Gryfewood Crs
 CRG/CRSL/HOU PA6 ...... 77 L8
Gryfewood Wy
 CRG/CRSL/HOU PA6 ...... 77 L8 ⬛
Gryffe Av *BRWEIR* PA11 ...... 76 D8
 RNFRW PA4 ...... 80 B4
Gryffe Crs *PSLYS* PA2 ...... 100 F8 ⬛
Gryffe Gv *BRWEIR* PA11 ...... 98 D1
Gryffe Rd *KLMCLM* PA13 ...... 75 K2
Gryffe St *LNPK/KPK* G44 ...... 128 A3
Guildford St *GTCI* KA28 ...... 138 A7
 STPS/GTHM/RID G33...... 85 J3
Guiltreehill *AYRS* KA7...... 229 G8
Gullane Crs *BALLOCH* G68 ...... 48 F3 ⬛
Gullane Pl *KLWNG* KA13 ...... 193 H6
Gullane St *PTCK* G11 ...... 82 B8 ⬛
Gulliland Av *CRH/DND* KA2 ...... 209 M7
Gullin Dr *PSTWK* KA9 ...... 225 K4 ⬛
Gunn Qd *BLSH* ML4 ...... 132 E6
Guthrie Dr *UD/BTH/TAN* G71 ...... 109 G8
Guthrie Pl *BSHPBGS* G64 ...... 64 C1
 EKILN G74 ...... 15 H1
Guthrie Rd *SALT* KA21 ...... 201 G1
Guthrie St *HMLTN* ML3 ...... 156 D5 ⬛
 MRYH/FIRH G20 ...... 82 D3
Guy Mannering Rd *HBR/GL* G84... 22 F1
Gyle Pl *WISHAW* ML2 ...... 159 L6 ⬛

H

Habbieauld Rd
 KLMNKN/STW KA3 ...... 206 B1
Haberlea Av *PLK/PH/NH* G53 ...... 126 C6
Haberlea Gdns
 PLK/PH/NH G53 ...... 126 C7 ⬛
Haco St *LARGS* KA30 ...... 115 K5
Haddington Gdns *IRVSE* KA11 ...... 204 B3
Haddington Wy *CTBR* ML5 ...... 109 L6
Haddow Gv *UD/BTH/TAN* G71 ...... 132 A1
Haddow St *HMLTN* ML3 ...... 156 E6
Hadrian Ter *MTHW* ML1...... 157 J1 ⬛
Hagart Rd *CRG/CRSL/HOU* PA6 ...... 77 H7
Hagen Dr *MTHW* ML1 ...... 134 E8
Hagg Crs *JNSTN* PA5...... 99 L5
Hagg Pl *JNSTN* PA5...... 99 L6
Hagg Rd *JNSTN* PA5 ...... 99 L7
Haggs La *PLKSD/SHW* G41 ...... 104 C7
Haggs Rd *PLKSD/SHW* G41 ...... 104 C8
Haggswood Av
 PLKSD/SHW G41 ...... 104 C7
Haghill Rd *DEN/PKHD* G31 ...... 13 J3
Hagholm Rd *LNK/LMHG* ML11 ...... 199 M2
Hagmill Crs *CTBR* ML5 ...... 110 C7
Hagmill Rd *CTBR* ML5...... 110 B7
Hagthorn Av *KBRN* KA25 ...... 167 G1
Haig Dr *BAIL/MDB/MHD* G69 ...... 107 M5
Haig St *GRNK* PA15 ...... 2 C7
 SPRGB/BLRNK G21 ...... 6 E1
Hailes Av *CAR/SHTL* G32 ...... 107 K4
Haining Av *KLMNK* KA1 ...... 212 A5
Haining Rd *RNFRW* PA4 ...... 80 D6
The Haining *RNFRW* PA4 ...... 80 D7 ⬛
Hairmyres Dr *EKILS* G75 ...... 170 F1 ⬛
Hairmyres La *EKILS* G75 ...... 170 F1 ⬛
Hairmyres Pk *EKILS* G75 ...... 170 F1 ⬛
Hairmyres St *GVH/MTFL* G42 ...... 105 J8 ⬛

Hairst St *RNFRW* PA4 ...... 80 D5
Halbeath Av *DRUM* G15 ...... 60 F6
Halbert St *PLKSD/SHW* G41 ...... 104 E8
Haldane La *SCOT* G14 ...... 81 K6
Haldane Pl *EKILS* G75 ...... 15 G7
Haldane St *SCOT* G14 ...... 81 K6
Halfmerk North *EKILN* G74 ...... 15 K1
Halfmerk South *EKILN* G74 ...... 15 K1
Halfway St *WKIL* KA23 ...... 181 J4
Halgreen Av *DRUM* G15 ...... 60 E6
Halketburn Rd *SKLM* PA17 ...... 70 A6
Halketburn Ter *SKLM* PA17 ...... 70 B6
Halkett Crs *ALEX/LLW* G83...... 25 L2
Halkshill Dr *LARGS* KA30 ...... 115 L6
Hallbrae St
 STPS/GTHM/RID G33 ...... 84 E7 ⬛
Hallcraig St *AIRDRIE* ML6...... 111 G1
Halley Dr *KNTSWD* G13 ...... 80 E3
Halley Pl *KNTSWD* G13 ...... 80 E3
Halley St *KNTSWD* G13 ...... 80 E2
Hallforest St
 STPS/GTHM/RID G33 ...... 85 H7 ⬛
Hallgraig Pl *CARLUKE* ML8...... 178 D7
Hallhill Crs
 STPS/GTHM/RID G33 ...... 107 L3 ⬛
Hallhill Rd *BAIL/MDB/MHD* G69 .. 108 A3
 CAR/SHTL G32 ...... 107 K3
 JNSTN PA5 ...... 122 C2
Halliburton Crs *ESTRH* G34 ...... 107 M2 ⬛
Halliburton Ter *ESTRH* G34 ...... 108 A2 ⬛
Hallidale Crs *RNFRW* PA4 ...... 80 F7
Hallinan Gdns *WISHAW* ML2 ...... 158 F8
Hall Pl *ALEX/LLW* G83 ...... 188 E5 ⬛
Hall Rd *LNK/LMHG* ML11 ...... 199 G5
Hallrule Dr
 CARD/HILL/MSPK G52 ...... 103 J4
Hallside Av *BLTYR/CAMB* G72 ...... 130 E4 ⬛
Hallside Bvd *BLTYR/CAMB* G72 .. 130 F6
Hallside Crs *WISHAW* ML2...... 159 L5
Hallside Dr *BLTYR/CAMB* G72 ...... 130 E4 ⬛
Hallside Pl *GBLS* G5 ...... 11 K8
Hallside Rd *BLTYR/CAMB* G72 ...... 130 E5
Hallside St *HWWD* PA9 ...... 121 M4 ⬛
Hall St *ALEX/LLW* G83 ...... 25 M5
 CLYDBK G81 ...... 60 B8
 DMBTN G82 ...... 36 D1
 HMLTN ML3 ...... 156 D8
 MTHW ML1 ...... 134 A5
Halls Vennal *AYR* KA8 ...... 224 F7 ⬛
Hallydown Dr *KNTSWD* G13 ...... 81 J4
Halpin Cl *UD/BTH/TAN* G71 ...... 132 D4
Halton Gdns
 BAIL/MDB/MHD G69 ...... 107 M5 ⬛
Hamersley Pl *EKILS* G75 ...... 171 H2
Hamilcomb Rd *BLSH* ML4 ...... 133 G6
Hamill Dr *KSYTH* G65 ...... 47 M1
Hamilton Av *PLKSD/SHW* G41 ...... 104 B6
Hamilton Ct
 KLMNKN/STW KA3 ...... 206 B2 ⬛
 BLTYR/CAMB G72 ...... 130 C5
 BSDN G61 ...... 61 L2
 BSHPTN PA7 ...... 57 M6
 CTBR ML5 ...... 110 A4
 RNFRW PA4 ...... 80 D4
 SVSTN KA20 ...... 192 F7
Hamilton Dr *AIRDRIE* ML6...... 89 H8
 BLTYR/CAMB G72 ...... 130 A4
 BLTYR/CAMB G72 ...... 155 L4
 ERSK PA8 ...... 58 F6
 GIF/THBK G46 ...... 127 K7
 KVD/HLHD G12 ...... 4 A2
 LARGS KA30 ...... 115 K2
 MTHW ML1 ...... 157 M5
 UD/BTH/TAN G71 ...... 132 B8
Hamiltonhill Crs *PPK/MIL* G22 ...... 5 H1 ⬛
Hamiltonhill Rd *PPK/MIL* G22 ...... 5 H2
Hamilton Park Av *KVD/HLHD* G12 .. 4 A2
Hamilton Pl *EKILS* G75 ...... 14 E7
 HMLTN ML3 ...... 174 D3
 MTHW ML1 ...... 134 A1
 RAYR/DAL KA6 ...... 231 H6 ⬛
Hamilton Rd *BLSH* ML4 ...... 132 F5
 BLTYR/CAMB G72 ...... 130 B4 ⬛
 BLTYR/CAMB G72 ...... 155 G3
 CAR/SHTL G32 ...... 107 J7
 EKILN G74 ...... 154 B5
 LRKH ML9 ...... 175 M4
 MTHW ML1 ...... 157 K3
 RUTH G73 ...... 129 H2
 UD/BTH/TAN G71 ...... 107 M7
 UD/BTH/TAN G71 ...... 132 B8
Hamilton St *CARLUKE* ML8 ...... 178 F8 ⬛
 CLYDBK G81 ...... 80 D2
 GVH/MTFL G42 ...... 105 J8
 KLWNG KA13 ...... 193 L6
 LRKH ML9 ...... 175 M5
 PSLYN/LNWD PA3 ...... 9 J2
 SALT KA21 ...... 200 E1
Hamilton Ter *CLYDBK* G81 ...... 80 D2
Hamilton Vw *UD/BTH/TAN* G71 .. 132 A2
Hamilton Wy *PSTWK* KA9 ...... 221 J7 ⬛
Hamlet *EKILN* G74 ...... 154 C4
Hampden Dr *LNPK/KPK* G44 ...... 128 B2
Hampden La *GVH/MTFL* G42 ...... 128 B1
Hampden Ter *GVH/MTFL* G42 ...... 128 B1
Hangingshaw Pl
 GVH/MTFL G42 ...... 128 C1
Hanover Cl *GVH/MTFL* G42 ...... 128 A1 ⬛
Hanover Ct *CGLE* G1 ...... 5 K9
 CGLE G1 ...... 11 J1
 HBR/GL G84 ...... 22 E1 ⬛
Hanover St *CGLE* G1 ...... 11 J1
Hanson St *DEN/PKHD* G31 ...... 12 D1
Hapland Av *PLK/PH/NH* G53 ...... 103 J7 ⬛
Hapland Rd *PLK/PH/NH* G53 ...... 103 J7
Happyhills *WKIL* KA23 ...... 181 J4 ⬛
Harbour La *PSLY* PA1 ...... 9 H2 ⬛
Harbour Pl *ARD* KA22 ...... 191 H8 ⬛
 IRV KA12 ...... 203 G8
 PSLYN/LNWD PA3 ...... 101 L2
Harbour Rd *ARD* KA22 ...... 191 H8
 IRV KA12 ...... 202 F8
 SALT KA21 ...... 200 F2
Harburn Pl *SCOT* G14 ...... 80 F3
Harburn Pl *SCOT* G14 ...... 80 F3
 SMSTN G23 ...... 62 E7

Harcourt Dr *DEN/PKHD* G31 ...... 7 G8
Hardacres *LNK/LMHG* ML11 ...... 199 G4
Hardgate Dr *GOV/IBX* G51 ...... 103 J1
Hardgate Gdns *GOV/IBX* G51 ...... 103 J2
Hardgate Pl *GOV/IBX* G51 ...... 103 J1
Hardgate Rd *GOV/IBX* G51 ...... 103 J1
Hardie Av *RUTH* G73 ...... 129 J1
Hardie St *ALEX/LLW* G83 ...... 25 K2
 BLTYR/CAMB G72 ...... 155 K2
 HMLTN ML3 ...... 156 B7
 MTHW ML1 ...... 157 L1
Hardmuir Gdns *KKNTL* G66 ...... 45 L8 ⬛
Hardridge Av
 CARD/HILL/MSPK G52 ...... 103 L7 ⬛
Hardridge Pl
 CARD/HILL/MSPK G52 ...... 103 L7 ⬛
Hardridge Rd
 CARD/HILL/MSPK G52 ...... 103 K7
Hardy Hl *HBR/GL* G84 ...... 21 G7
Harefield Dr *SCOT* G14 ...... 81 H4
Harelaw Av *BRHD/NEIL* G78 ...... 125 K8
 BRHD/NEIL G78 ...... 148 D3
 LNPK/KPK G44 ...... 127 L5
 PGL PA14 ...... 54 D1 ⬛
Harelaw Crs *PSLYS* PA2 ...... 124 C2
Hareleeshill Rd *LRKH* ML9 ...... 176 C2
Hareshaw Rd *MTHW* ML1 ...... 135 K4
Harestanes Gdns *KKNTL* G66 ...... 46 A8
Harestanes Rd *CARLUKE* ML8 ...... 188 E5 ⬛
Harestone Rd *WISHAW* ML2 ...... 159 J6 ⬛
Harestone Rd *WISHAW* ML2 ...... 159 J7
Harhill St *GOV/IBX* G51 ...... 104 A2
Harkins Av *BLTYR/CAMB* G72 ...... 155 J2
Harkness Av *KKNTL* G66 ...... 45 H4
Harland St *SCOT* G14 ...... 81 J6
Harley St *GOV/IBX* G51 ...... 104 C4
Harling Dr *TROON* KA10 ...... 216 D7
Harmetray St *PPK/MIL* G22 ...... 83 K3
Harmony Pl *GOV/IBX* G51 ...... 104 A3
Harmony Rw *GOV/IBX* G51 ...... 104 A1 ⬛
Harmony Sq *GOV/IBX* G51 ...... 104 A2
Harmsworth St *PTCK* G11 ...... 81 L7 ⬛
Harper Crs *LARGS* KA30 ...... 115 K5
 WISHAW ML2 ...... 159 L5
Harperland Dr *KLMNK* KA1 ...... 16 A7
Harport St *GIF/THBK* G46 ...... 126 E5
Harriet Pl *PLKSW/MSWD* G43 .. 127 H3 ⬛
Harriet Rd *KLMNKN/STW* KA3 ...... 17 G1
Harriet St *RUTH* G73 ...... 129 G1
Harrington Rd *EKILN* G74 ...... 14 E3
Harris Cl *NMRNS* G77 ...... 150 B3
Harris Crs *OLDK* G60 ...... 59 H4 ⬛
Harris Dr *OLDK* G60 ...... 59 H4
Harris Gdns *OLDK* G60 ...... 59 J4
Harrison Dr *GOV/IBX* G51 ...... 104 B3 ⬛
Harris Pl *KLMNKN/STW* KA3 ...... 207 J4 ⬛
Harris Qd *WISHAW* ML2 ...... 159 L4
Harris Rd *OLDK* G60 ...... 59 H4
 PGL PA14 ...... 55 H2 ⬛
 SMSTN G23 ...... 62 D8 ⬛
Harrow Ct *DRUM* G15 ...... 60 F6 ⬛
Harrow Pl *DRUM* G15 ...... 60 F6 ⬛
Hartfield Crs *BRHD/NEIL* G78 ...... 148 E2
Hartfield Rd *AYRS* KA7 ...... 18 F9
Hartfield Ter *PSLYS* PA2 ...... 9 K9
 SHOTTS ML7 ...... 161 H1
Harthall *AYR* KA8 ...... 225 L7
Hartlaw Crs
 CARD/HILL/MSPK G52 ...... 103 G3
Hartree Av *KNTSWD* G13 ...... 80 E1
Hartstone Rd *PLK/PH/NH* G53 ...... 126 D2
Hart St *CLYDBK* G81 ...... 60 D2
 DEN/PKHD G31 ...... 106 E4
 PSLYN/LNWD PA3 ...... 100 B4
Hartwood Gdns *SHOTTS* ML7 ...... 136 F7
Hartwood Rd *SHOTTS* ML7 ...... 136 F8
Harvest Dr *MTHW* ML1 ...... 157 K5
Harvey St *ARD* KA22 ...... 191 H6 ⬛
 COWCAD G4 ...... 5 J4
Harvey Ter *LOCHW* PA12 ...... 120 C7
Harvey Wy *BLSH* ML4 ...... 133 J2
Harvie Av *NMRNS* G77 ...... 150 D3
Harvie St *GOV/IBX* G51 ...... 104 D3
Harwood Gdns
 BAIL/MDB/MHD G69 ...... 67 G6 ⬛
Harwood Rd *SHOTTS* ML7 ...... 137 J4
Harwood St *CAR/SHTL* G32 ...... 106 E2 ⬛
Hastie Av *GTCI* KA28 ...... 138 B6
Hastie St *KVGV* G3 ...... 82 D3 ⬛
Hastings *EKILS* G75 ...... 171 G2
Hatfield Dr *KVD/HLHD* G12 ...... 81 M4
Hathaway Dr *GIF/THBK* G46 ...... 127 H7
Hathaway La *MRYH/FIRH* G20 ...... 82 E4
Hathaway St *MRYH/FIRH* G20 ...... 82 E4
Hathersage Av
 BAIL/MDB/MHD G69 ...... 108 B4
Hathersage Dr
 BAIL/MDB/MHD G69 ...... 108 B4
Hathersage Gdns
 BAIL/MDB/MHD G69 ...... 108 B4 ⬛
Hatton Gdns
 CARD/HILL/MSPK G52 ...... 103 G5
Hatton Pl *MTHW* ML1 ...... 134 C7
Hattonrigg Rd *BLSH* ML4 ...... 133 H2
Hatton Ter *MTHW* ML1 ...... 134 C7
Haughburn Av
 PLK/PH/NH G53 ...... 126 B2 ⬛
Haughburn Rd *PLK/PH/NH* G53.. 126 B2
Haughburn Ter
 PLK/PH/NH G53 ...... 126 B2
Haugh Pl *HMLTN* ML3 ...... 156 F8
Haugh Rd *KSYTH* G65 ...... 47 J1
 KVGV G3 ...... 104 D1
Haughview Av *MTHW* ML1 ...... 157 H3 ⬛
Haupland Rd *ARD* KA22 ...... 191 H4
Havelock La *PTCK* G11 ...... 82 C7 ⬛
Havelock Pk *EKILS* G75 ...... 153 G8
Havelock Pl *HBR/GL* G84 ...... 20 F7
 PTCK G11 ...... 82 C7
Haven Pk *EKILS* G75 ...... 170 F3
Havoc Rd *DMBTN* G82 ...... 36 B6
Hawbank Rd *EKILN* G74 ...... 153 G6
Hawick Av *PSLYS* PA2 ...... 101 H8 ⬛
Hawick Ct *GRNK* PA15 ...... 3 G7

Hawick Crs LRKH ML9 ... 176 A7
Hawick Dr CTBR ML5 ... 110 D6
Hawick St KNTSWD G13 ... 80 E2
  WISHAW ML2 ... 159 J4
Hawkhead Av PSLYS PA2 ... 102 B8
Hawkhead Rd PSLY PA1 ... 102 B5
  PSLYS PA2 ... 102 C7
Hawkhill Av AYR KA8 ... 19 H1
Hawkhill Avenue La AYR KA8 ... 19 H1
Hawkhill Dr SVSTN KA20 ... 192 F8
Hawkhill Pl SVSTN KA20 ... 192 E7
Hawkwood EKILS G75 ... 171 K4
Hawkwood Rd BSHPBGS ML6 ... 88 F5
Hawthorn Av BSDN G61 ... 62 A2
  BSHPBGS G64 ... 84 B1
  DMBTN G82 ... 36 A4
  ERSK PA8 ... 79 L1
  JNSTN PA5 ... 100 A8
  KKNTL G66 ... 65 J4
  PSTWK KA9 ... 225 J2
  WISHAW ML2 ... 160 C3
Hawthorn Ct KLWNG KA13 ... 193 L7
Hawthorn Crs BEITH KA15 ... 168 A1
  ERSK PA8 ... 79 L1
Hawthornden Gdns
  SMSTN G23 ... 62 E7
Hawthorn Dr AIRDRIE ML6 ... 111 K2
  AYRS KA7 ...
  BRHD/NEIL G78 ... 149 K1
  CTBR ML5 ... 110 D4
  MTHW ML1 ... 134 B6
  SVSTN KA20 ... 192 E6
  WISHAW ML2 ... 159 J7
Hawthorne Pl GRK PA19 ... 31 H3
  TROON KA10 ... 216 D5
Hawthorn Gdns BSLK ML4 ... 133 H5
  CRMNK/CLK/EAG G76 ... 151 L3
  LRKH ML9 ... 176 C7
  PSTWK KA9 ... 225 J2
Hawthorn Hl HMLTN ML3 ... 156 E8
Hawthornhill Rd DMBTN G82 ... 36 B4
Hawthorn Pl
  BLTYR/CAMB G72 ... 155 L2
  SHOTTS ML7 ... 160 F1
Hawthorn Qd PPK/MIL G22 ... 83 J4
Hawthorn Rd
  CRMNK/CLK/EAG G76 ... 151 M4
  CUMB G67 ... 49 M5
  ERSK PA8 ... 79 L1
Hawthorn Sq KLMNK KA1 ... 16 A5
Hawthorn St BSHPBGS G64 ... 44 C8
  CLYDBK G81 ... 60 A5
  PPK/MIL G22 ... 83 J4
  SPRGB/BLRNK G21 ... 83 M4
Hawthorn Ter EKILS G75 ... 171 H3
  UD/BTH/TAN G71 ... 132 B2
Hawthorn Wk
  BLTYR/CAMB G72 ... 129 K4
Hawthorn Wy ERSK PA8 ... 79 L1
Hay Av BSHPTN PA7 ... 58 C6
Hayburn Crs PTCK G11 ... 82 A6
Hayburn Ga PTCK G11 ... 82 B7
Hayburn La KVD/HLHD G12 ... 82 A6
  PTCK G11 ... 82 A6
Hayburn St PTCK G11 ... 82 B8
Hay Dr JNSTN PA5 ... 100 B6
Hayes Av ALEX/LLW G83 ... 25 L3
Hayfield St GBLS G5 ... 11 L1
Hay HI AYR KA8 ... 229 K1
Hayhill Rd EKILN G74 ... 170 B2
Hayle Gdns BAIL/MDB/MHD G69 ... 66 F4
Haylie Gdns LARGS KA30 ... 115 K7
Haylie Neuk LARGS KA30 ... 115 K7
Haymarket St CAR/SHTL G32 ... 106 F2
Hayocks Rd SVSTN KA20 ... 192 E8
Haystack Pl KKNTL G66 ... 65 K5
Hayston Crs MRYH/FIRH G20 ... 83 H4
Hayston Rd BALLOCH G68 ... 48 E5
  KKNTL G66 ... 65 G1
Hayston St MRYH/FIRH G20 ... 83 H4
Hay St GRNK PA15 ... 2 D1
Haywood St PPK/MIL G22 ... 83 H3
Hazel Av ARD KA22 ... 191 J5
  BSDN G61 ... 62 A2
  DMBTN G82 ... 36 A4
  JNSTN PA5 ... 100 A8
  KKNTL G66 ... 65 K3
  KLMNK KA1 ... 16 A6
  LNPK/KPK G44 ... 127 M5
Hazel Bank KKNTL G66 ... 45 H5
Hazelbank Wk AIRDRIE ML6 ... 110 D1
Hazeldean Crs WISHAW ML2 ... 159 J4
Hazel Dene BSHPBGS G64 ... 64 B8
Hazel Gdns MTHW ML1 ... 157 L6
Hazel Gv KKNTL G66 ... 65 K3
  KLWNG KA13 ... 193 M5
Hazelhead EKILN G74 ... 15 M1
Hazellea Dr GIF/THBK G46 ... 127 L5
Hazelmere Rd KLMCLM PA13 ... 75 H1
Hazel Pk HMLTN ML3 ... 156 E7
Hazel Rd CUMB G67 ... 49 K6
Hazel Ter GRK PA19 ... 31 J3
  UD/BTH/TAN G71 ... 132 B2
Hazelton MTHW ML1 ... 157 K4
Hazel Wd WISHAW ML2 ... 159 K4
Hazelwood Av NMRNS G77 ... 150 C5
  PSLYS PA2 ... 123 L2
Hazelwood Dr
  BLTYR/CAMB G72 ... 155 J1
Hazelwood Gdns RUTH G73 ... 129 J3
Hazelwood La BRWEIR PA11 ... 98 D2
Hazelwood Rd AYRS KA7 ... 18 F9
  BRWEIR PA11 ... 98 D3
  PLKSD/SHW G41 ... 104 C5
Hazlitt Gdns MRYH/FIRH G20 ... 83 G3
Hazlitt Pl MRYH/FIRH G20 ... 83 G3
Hazlitt St MRYH/FIRH G20 ... 83 H4
Headhouse Ct EKILS G75 ... 14 C6
Headrigg WKIL KA23 ... 181 J4
Headrigg Rd WKIL KA23 ... 181 J4
Headsmuir Av CARLUKE ML8 ... 178 D7
Head St BEITH KA15 ... 144 C8
Heath Av BSHPBGS G64 ... 84 B1
  KKNTL G66 ... 65 J5
Heathcliffe Av
  BLTYR/CAMB G72 ... 131 J8
Heathcot Av DRUM G15 ... 60 D7
Heathcot Pl DRUM G15 ... 60 D7

Heather Av ALEX/LLW G83 ... 25 L3
  BRHD/NEIL G78 ... 125 G4
  BSDN G61 ... 61 K1
  CLYDBK G81 ... 60 A2
  MTHW ML1 ... 134 A4
Heatherbank Wk CTBR ML5 ... 110 D1
Heatherbrae BSHPBGS G64 ... 63 L8
Heather Dr KKNTL G66 ... 65 G5
Heathergardens KKNTL G66 ... 65 G5
Heatherhouse Rd IRV KA12 ... 208 B1
Heather Pl JNSTN PA5 ... 100 A7
  KLMNK KA1 ... 16 A6
Heather Rd LNK/LMHG ML11 ... 198 B3
Heather Rw CARLUKE ML8 ... 178 E6
Heatherstane Bank IRVSE KA11 ... 204 B7
Heatherstane Wy IRVSE KA11 ... 204 C7
Heather St AIRDRIE ML6 ... 91 G4
Heather Vw KKNTL G66 ... 29 L8
Heathery Knowe EKILS G75 ... 14 E7
Heatheryknowe Rd
  BAIL/MDB/MHD G69 ... 108 E1
Heathery Lea Av CTBR ML5 ... 110 D6
Heathery Rd WISHAW ML2 ... 158 F6
Heathfield WISHAW ML2 ... 177 G2
Heathfield Av
  BAIL/MDB/MHD G69 ... 67 G7
Heathfield Dr MLNGV G62 ... 42 B6
Heathfield Rd AYR KA8 ... 225 H5
Heathfield St
  STPS/GTHM/RID G33 ... 107 J1
Heathpark AYR KA8 ... 225 J4
Heath Rd LRKH ML9 ... 176 B6
Heathside Rd GIF/THBK G46 ... 127 K6
Heathwood Dr GIF/THBK G46 ... 127 G6
Hecla Av DRUM G15 ... 60 F6
Hecla Pl DRUM G15 ... 60 F6
Hecla Sq DRUM G15 ... 60 F6
Hector Rd PLKSD/SHW G41 ... 127 K1
Heggies Av PGL PA14 ... 55 G1
Helensburgh Dr KNTSWD G13 ... 81 K3
Helenslea BLTYR/CAMB G72 ... 130 F3
Helenslea Pl BLSH ML4 ... 132 F5
Helenslee Ct DMBTN G82 ... 36 D6
Helenslee Crs DMBTN G82 ... 36 D6
Helenslee Rd DMBTN G82 ... 36 D6
  PGL PA14 ... 56 C2
Helen's Ter KLWNG KA13 ... 193 L7
Helen St CARD/HILL/MSPK G52 ... 103 M4
  GOV/IBX G51 ... 104 A3
Helenvale Ct DEN/PKHD G31 ... 13 L6
Helenvale St DEN/PKHD G31 ... 13 K7
Helen Wy ALEX/LLW G83 ... 25 M7
Helen Wynd LRKH ML9 ... 176 A7
Helmsdale Av
  BLTYR/CAMB G72 ... 131 J6
Helmsdale Dr PSLYS PA2 ... 100 F7
Hemlock St KNTSWD G13 ... 81 M3
Hemmingen Ct
  CARLUKE ML8 ... 178 E6
Hemphill Vw CRH/DND KA2 ... 205 M6
Henderland Dr BSDN G61 ... 61 L7
Henderland Rd BSDN G61 ... 61 L7
Henderson Av
  BLTYR/CAMB G72 ... 130 D3
Henderson Rd TROON KA10 ... 216 D6
Henderson St AIRDRIE ML6 ... 111 H1
  CTBR ML5 ... 109 M3
  KNTSWD G13 ... 80 E1
  MRYH/FIRH G20 ... 4 C3
  PSLY PA1 ... 8 E3
Henderson Ter GRK PA19 ... 31 J3
Henrietta St GLSTN KA4 ... 214 C3
  SCOT G14 ... 81 J6
Henry Bell St HBR/GL G84 ... 20 D5
Henry St BRHD/NEIL G78 ... 125 H6
Hepburn Hl HMLTN ML3 ... 174 D1
Hepburn Rd
  CARD/HILL/MSPK G52 ... 103 G2
Hepburn Wy IRVSE KA11 ... 204 B2
Herald Av KNTSWD G13 ... 61 K8
Herald Gv MTHW ML1 ... 157 K5
Herald St ARD KA22 ... 200 B1
Herbert Rd MRYH/FIRH G20 ... 4 C3
Herbertson Crs IRV KA12 ... 203 K5
Herbertson Gv
  BLTYR/CAMB G72 ... 131 H8
Herbertson St
  BLTYR/CAMB G72 ... 155 L2
Herbert St MRYH/FIRH G20 ... 4 D3
Heriot Av PSLYS PA2 ... 123 M1
Heriot Crs BSHPBGS G64 ... 64 A6
Heriot Rd KKNTL G66 ... 65 J6
Heritage Ct NMRNS G77 ... 150 E4
Heritage Wy CTBR ML5 ... 109 M1
Herma St SMSTN G23 ... 82 E1
Hermes Wy BLSH ML4 ... 133 M4
Hermiston Av CAR/SHTL G32 ... 107 H3
Hermiston Pl CAR/SHTL G32 ... 107 J3
Hermiston Rd CAR/SHTL G32 ... 107 H3
Hermitage Av KNTSWD G13 ... 81 J2
Hermitage Crs CTBR ML5 ... 110 B6
Herndon Ct NMRNS G77 ... 151 G3
Heron Ct CLYDBK G81 ... 60 B4
Heron Pl JNSTN PA5 ... 122 D2
Heron Rd GRNKW/INVK PA16 ... 32 A5
Heronswood KLWNG KA13 ... 193 K4
Herriet St PLKSD/SHW G41 ... 10 C9
Herriot Av KBRN KA25 ... 143 C5
Herriot St CTBR ML5 ... 109 L1
Herschell St KNTSWD G13 ... 81 M3
Hertford Av KVD/HLHD G12 ... 82 B3
Hestan Pl KLMNKN/STW KA3 ... 207 H4
Hewett Crs CRG/CRSL/HOU PA6 ... 77 J8
Hexham Gdns PLKSD/SHW G41 ... 104 C5
Heys St BRHD/NEIL G78 ... 125 J7
Hibernia St
  GRNKW/INVK PA16 ... 32 D5
Hickman St GVH/MTFL G42 ... 105 H8
Hickman Ter GVH/MTFL G42 ... 105 J7
Hickory Crs UD/BTH/TAN G71 ... 109 J8
Hickory St PPK/MIL G22 ... 83 L4
High Avon St LRKH ML9 ... 175 M5
High Barholm KLBCH PA10 ... 99 H6
High Barrwood Rd KSYTH G65 ... 47 M1
High Beeches
  CRMNK/CLK/EAG G76 ... 152 E1
High Blantyre Rd
  BLTYR/CAMB G72 ... 155 M4

HMLTN ML3 ... 156 A4
Highburgh Av LNK/LMHG ML11 ... 199 H5
Highburgh Dr RUTH G73 ... 129 H4
Highburgh Rd KVD/HLHD G12 ... 82 C7
High Burnside Av CTBR ML5 ... 109 L4
High Calside PSLYS PA2 ... 8 F6
High Carnegie Rd PGL PA14 ... 54 F1
High Common Rd EKILN G74 ... 15 M7
  EKILN G74 ... 154 C8
Highcraig Av JNSTN PA5 ... 99 K8
High Craighends KLMNK KA1 ... 47 L1
Highcroft Av LNPK/KPK G44 ... 128 E4
Highcross Av CTBR ML5 ... 109 K5
Highet Gdns IRV KA12 ... 203 H5
Highfield Av KLMNKN/STW KA3 ... 207 G6
  PSLYS PA2 ... 124 C2
  PSTWK KA9 ... 225 K2
Highfield Ct KKNTL G66 ... 65 M1
Highfield Crs MTHW ML1 ... 158 A4
  PSLYS PA2 ... 124 D2
Highfield Dr
  CRMNK/CLK/EAG G76 ... 151 K2
  KVD/HLHD G12 ... 82 B3
  RUTH G73 ... 129 J6
  SVSTN KA20 ... 192 E8
Highfield Pl EKILN G74 ... 153 M6
  KVD/HLHD G12 ... 82 B3
  KKNTL G66 ... 45 L8
  LRKH ML9 ... 176 B6
High Field Rd KLWNG KA13 ... 193 M5
Highfield Ter FAIRLIE KA29 ... 139 L6
High Flender Rd
  CRMNK/CLK/EAG G76 ... 151 K4
High Glencairn St KLMNK KA1 ... 16 F8
High Graighall St COWCAD G4 ... 5 H5
Highholm Av PGL PA14 ... 34 B7
Highholm St PGL PA14 ... 34 B7
High Kirk Vw JNSTN PA5 ... 99 M7
Highland Av BLTYR/CAMB G72 ... 155 J1
Highland La GOV/IBX G51 ... 104 C2
High Mains Av DMBTN G82 ... 37 G6
High Meadow CARLUKE ML8 ... 179 J8
High Mill Rd CARLUKE ML8 ... 179 G7
Highpark Rd RAYR/DAL KA6 ... 231 H6
High Parksail ERSK PA8 ... 79 J1
High Parks Crs HMLTN ML3 ... 174 D3
High Patrick St HMLTN ML3 ... 156 F7
High Pleasance LRKH ML9 ... 176 A6
High Rd AYR KA8 ... 225 L6
  MTHW ML1 ... 157 K2
  PSLYS PA2 ... 8 D6
  SALT KA21 ... 191 M8
  SVSTN KA20 ... 192 B8
Highstonehall Rd HMLTN ML3 ... 156 A8
High St AIRDRIE ML6 ... 110 F1
  AYRS KA7 ... 18 F3
  BRHD/NEIL G78 ... 148 E2
  COWCAD G4 ... 11 M2
  DMBTN G82 ... 36 E6
  GRNK PA15 ... 2 D4
  IRV KA12 ... 203 J7
  JNSTN PA5 ... 99 M6
  KBRN KA25 ... 143 C6
  KLMCLM PA13 ... 55 K8
  KLMNKN/STW KA3 ... 17 G2
  KLMNKN/STW KA3 ... 197 L1
  LNK/LMHG ML11 ... 199 G5
  LOCHW PA12 ... 120 C6
  MTHW ML1 ... 134 E5
  NMLNS KA16 ... 215 K2
  PSLY PA1 ... 8 F4
  RNFRW PA4 ... 80 D6
  RUTH G73 ... 129 G1
  SHOTTS ML7 ... 137 M5
Highthorne Crs WKIL KA23 ... 181 L4
High Whitehills Rd EKILS G75 ... 171 L4
Hilary Crs AYRS KA7 ... 19 G7
Hilary Dr BAIL/MDB/MHD G69 ... 107 M4
Hillary Av RUTH G73 ... 129 K3
Hill Av NMRNS G77 ... 150 C5
Hillbank St ALEX/LLW G83 ... 25 M5
Hill Crs CRMNK/CLK/EAG G76 ... 151 M3
Hillcrest BAIL/MDB/MHD G69 ... 86 D1
  CRMNK/CLK/EAG G76 ... 152 D1
  KLMNKN/STW KA3 ... 197 L1
Hillcrest Av CAR/SHTL G32 ... 130 B1
  CLYDBK G81 ... 60 A2
  CTBR ML5 ... 110 C3
  CUMB G67 ... 68 F1
  LNPK/KPK G44 ... 127 L5
  PSLYS PA2 ... 124 B3
  WISHAW ML2 ... 158 E5
Hillcrest Dr NMRNS G77 ... 151 G4
  SVSTN KA20 ... 201 L1
Hillcrest Pl KLWNG KA13 ... 193 M6
Hillcrest Rd BSDN G61 ... 61 M5
  CAR/SHTL G32 ... 130 C1
  KSYTH G65 ... 46 F1
  UD/BTH/TAN G71 ... 132 A2
Hillcrest St MLNGV G62 ... 42 B7
Hillcrest Ter
  UD/BTH/TAN G71 ... 132 B6
Hillcroft Ter BSHPBGS G64 ... 83 M1
Hillend Crs CLYDBK G81 ... 59 M2
  CRMNK/CLK/EAG G76 ... 151 J3
Hillend Dr GRNK PA15 ... 3 J1
Hillend Pl GRNK PA15 ... 3 J8
Hillend Rd
  CRMNK/CLK/EAG G76 ... 151 K3
  PPK/MIL G22 ... 83 G2
  RUTH G73 ... 129 H5
Hillfoot CRG/CRSL/HOU PA6 ... 99 K1
  DMBTN G82 ... 25 K7
Hillfoot Av DMBTN G82 ... 37 J5
  RUTH G73 ... 129 G2
  WISHAW ML2 ... 159 K2
Hillfoot Crs AYRS KA7 ... 19 J9
  WISHAW ML2 ... 159 K2
Hillfoot Dr BSDN G61 ... 61 M4
  CTBR ML5 ... 109 K3
  HWWD PA9 ... 121 M4

Hillfoot St DEN/PKHD G31 ... 12 E2
Hillfoot Ter CARLUKE ML8 ... 179 G8
Hillhead BAIL/MDB/MHD G69 ... 66 F7
  CARLUKE ML8 ... 179 G7
  MTHW ML1 ... 134 A7
  RUTH G73 ... 129 H5
Hillhead Av AIRDRIE ML6 ... 111 G3
  MTHW ML1 ... 134 A7
Hillhead Crs HMLTN ML3 ... 155 L6
  MTHW ML1 ... 134 A7
Hillhead Dr AIRDRIE ML6 ... 111 G3
  MTHW ML1 ... 134 A7
Hillhead Pl RUTH G73 ... 129 H5
Hillhead Rd KKNTL G66 ... 45 K8
  SPRGB/BLRNK G21 ... 84 D2
  SVSTN KA20 ... 192 E6
Hillhead Sq
  KLMNKN/STW KA3 ... 206 F6
Hillhead St KVD/HLHD G12 ... 82 D7
  MLNGV G62 ... 42 A7
Hillhead Ter HMLTN ML3 ... 155 L6
Hillhouse Crs HMLTN ML3 ... 155 M6
Hillhouse Farm Ga
  LNK/LMHG ML11 ... 198 E4
Hillhouse Gdns TROON KA10 ... 216 D3
Hillhouse Ga CARLUKE ML8 ... 189 J1
Hillhouseridge Rd SHOTTS ML7 ... 137 K4
Hillhouse Rd BLTYR/CAMB G72 ... 155 K5
  HMLTN ML3 ... 155 M6
  TROON KA10 ... 216 D3
Hillhouse St SPRGB/BLRNK G21 ... 84 A5
Hillhouse Ter HMLTN ML3 ... 155 M6
Hillington Gdns
  CARD/HILL/MSPK G52 ... 103 J5
Hillington Park Circ
  CARD/HILL/MSPK G52 ... 103 J4
Hillington Qd
  CARD/HILL/MSPK G52 ... 103 G4
Hillington Rd
  CARD/HILL/MSPK G52 ... 103 G1
Hillington Rd South
  CARD/HILL/MSPK G52 ... 103 G3
Hillington Ter
  CARD/HILL/MSPK G52 ... 103 G4
Hill Int IRV KA12 ... 203 L3
Hillkirk Pl SPRGB/BLRNK G21 ... 83 M5
Hillkirk St SPRGB/BLRNK G21 ... 83 M5
Hill La ARD KA22 ... 191 J7
Hillmoss KLMNKN/STW KA3 ... 206 D3
Hillneuk Av BSDN G61 ... 61 M4
Hillneuk Dr BSDN G61 ... 62 A4
Hillocks Pl TROON KA10 ... 216 E2
Hillpark RAYR/DAL KA6 ... 226 F3
Hillpark Av PSLYS PA2 ... 101 K8
Hillpark Dr KLMNKN/STW KA3 ... 206 F7
  PLKSW/MSWD G43 ... 127 H3
Hillpark Ri KLWNG KA13 ... 193 H6
Hill Pl ARD KA22 ... 191 J8
  BLSH ML4 ... 132 F6
  MTHW ML1 ... 134 C7
  SHOTTS ML7 ... 137 L4
Hillrigg AIRDRIE ML6 ... 69 K8
Hillrigg Av AIRDRIE ML6 ... 111 J1
Hill Rd CUMB G67 ... 68 F7
  GRNKW/INVK PA16 ... 50 D5
  HWWD PA9 ... 121 M4
Hillsborough Rd
  BAIL/MDB/MHD G69 ... 107 M4
Hillshaw Gn IRVSE KA11 ... 204 C7
Hillside CRG/CRSL/HOU PA6 ... 99 K1
  KSYTH G65 ... 47 M4
  WKIL KA23 ... 181 J5
Hillside Av ALEX/LLW G83 ... 25 K6
  BSDN G61 ... 61 M4
  CRMNK/CLK/EAG G76 ... 151 K2
  KLMCLM PA13 ... 55 K8
Hillside Ct GIF/THBK G46 ... 126 F6
Hillside Crs BRHD/NEIL G78 ... 148 D2
  CTBR ML5 ... 109 M5
  HMLTN ML3 ... 156 F7
  MTHW ML1 ... 134 D6
  PSTWK KA9 ... 225 K4
Hillside Dr BRHD/NEIL G78 ... 125 G6
  BSDN G61 ... 62 A4
  BSHPBGS G64 ... 64 A7
  PGL PA14 ... 34 B8
Hillside Gardens La PTCK G11 ... 82 B6
Hillside Gv BRHD/NEIL G78 ... 125 G7
Hillside La HMLTN ML3 ... 156 C7
Hillside Pk CLYDBK G81 ... 60 B3
Hillside Pl MTHW ML1 ... 134 D6
  NMLNS KA16 ... 215 J2
Hillside Qd
  PLKSW/MSWD G43 ... 127 H4
Hillside Rd BRHD/NEIL G78 ... 124 F7
  BRHD/NEIL G78 ... 148 D2
  DMBTN G82 ... 24 B8
  GRK PA19 ... 31 K2
  GRNK PA15 ... 3 H9
  PLKSW/MSWD G43 ... 127 H4
  PSLYS PA2 ... 9 L9
Hillside St SVSTN KA20 ... 201 J1
Hillside Ter HMLTN ML3 ... 156 C7
  KKNTL G66 ... 45 H4
Hill St AIRDRIE ML6 ... 90 F4
  AIRDRIE ML6 ... 111 K7
  ALEX/LLW G83 ... 25 K4
  ARD KA22 ... 191 J8
  DMBTN G82 ... 36 D6
  GRNK PA15 ... 2 E6
  HMLTN ML3 ... 155 M6
  IRV KA12 ... 203 J7
  KLMNKN/STW KA3 ... 16 E1
  KVGV G3 ... 4 F7
  LARGS KA30 ... 115 L5
  LRKH ML9 ... 176 A7
  SALT KA21 ... 200 D1
  WISHAW ML2 ... 159 G7
Hill Vw DMBTN G82 ... 37 M8
  EKILS G75 ... 14 E6
Hillview AIRDRIE ML6 ... 69 M7
  SKLM KA17 ... 70 B5
Hillview Av KKNTL G66 ... 44 E1

KSYTH G65 ... 47 K2
Hillview Crs BLSH ML4 ... 133 G1
  LRKH ML9 ... 176 B8
  UD/BTH/TAN G71 ... 131 L1
Hillview Dr BLTYR/CAMB G72 ... 131 K7
  CRMNK/CLK/EAG G76 ... 151 K2
  HBR/GL G84 ... 20 D5
Hillview Gdns
  SPRGB/BLRNK G21 ... 84 D1
Hillview Pl
  CRMNK/CLK/EAG G76 ... 151 L2
  NMRNS G77 ... 150 D5
Hillview Rd BRWEIR PA11 ... 98 E2
  JNSTN PA5 ... 100 F3
Hill View Rd LNK/LMHG ML11 ... 198 A6
Hillview St CAR/SHTL G32 ... 106 F4
Hilltonbank St HMLTN ML3 ... 156 B5
Hilton Gdns KNTSWD G13 ... 81 M2
Hilton Pk BSHPBGS G64 ... 63 M6
Hilton Rd BSHPBGS G64 ... 63 M6
  MLNGV G62 ... 41 L7
Hilton Ter BLTYR/CAMB G72 ... 129 L6
  BSHPBGS G64 ... 63 M6
  KNTSWD G13 ... 81 L2
Hindsland Rd LRKH ML9 ... 176 B8
Hinshaw St MRYH/FIRH G20 ... 4 E2
Hinshelwood Dr GOV/IBX G51 ... 104 A4
Hinshelwood Pl
  GOV/IBX G51 ... 104 B4
Hirst Gdns SHOTTS ML7 ... 137 K4
Hirst Rd SHOTTS ML7 ... 113 K7
Hobart Crs CLYDBK G81 ... 59 K4
Hobart Qd WISHAW ML2 ... 159 L6
Hobart Rd EKILS G75 ... 14 A6
Hobart St PPK/MIL G22 ... 83 H5
Hobden St SPRGB/BLRNK G21 ... 6 F3
Hoddam Av CSMK G45 ... 128 F6
Hoddam Ter CSMK G45 ... 129 G6
Hoey Dr WISHAW ML2 ... 177 J2
Hogan Wy MTHW ML1 ... 134 E8
Hogarth Av CAR/SHTL G32 ... 13 L1
  SALT KA21 ... 191 L7
Hogarth Ct ALEX/LLW G83 ... 25 L3
Hogarth Gdns CAR/SHTL G32 ... 13 L1
Hogganfield St
  STPS/GTHM/RID G33 ... 7 L4
Hogg Av JNSTN PA5 ... 99 L8
Hogg Rd AIRDRIE ML6 ... 111 K5
Hogg St AIRDRIE ML6 ... 111 G2
Holeburn La
  PLKSW/MSWD G43 ... 127 J3
Holeburn Rd
  PLKSW/MSWD G43 ... 127 J3
Hole Farm Rd
  GRNKW/INVK PA16 ... 32 C6
Holehills Dr AIRDRIE ML6 ... 89 H7
Holehills Pl AIRDRIE ML6 ... 89 H7
Holehouse Brae
  BRHD/NEIL G78 ... 148 C2
Holehouse Ct LARGS KA30 ... 115 L5
Holehouse Dr KBRN KA25 ... 143 F7
  KNTSWD G13 ... 81 G3
Holehouse Rd
  KLMNKN/STW KA3 ... 17 K4
  LARGS KA30 ... 115 L5
Holehouse Ter
  BRHD/NEIL G78 ... 148 C2
Hole Rd RAYR/DAL KA6 ... 231 H6
Hollandbush Gv HMLTN ML3 ... 174 D1
Hollandhurst Rd CTBR ML5 ... 87 M7
Holland St CGLW G2 ... 4 E9
Holliinwell Rd SMSTN G23 ... 82 D1
Hollowglen Rd CAR/SHTL G32 ... 107 H3
Hollow Pk AYRS KA7 ... 229 M7
Hollows Av PSLYS PA2 ... 123 M2
Hollows Crs PSLYS PA2 ... 123 M2
Holly Bank AYRS KA7 ... 228 C5
Hollybank Pl
  BLTYR/CAMB G72 ... 130 B5
Hollybank St SPRGB/BLRNK G21 ... 6 F1
Hollybrook St GVH/MTFL G42 ... 105 H8
Hollybush Av PSLYS PA2 ... 124 B3
Hollybush Pl
  KLMNKN/STW KA3 ... 207 H3
Hollybush Rd
  CARD/HILL/MSPK G52 ... 102 F4
Holly Dr DMBTN G82 ... 36 B4
  SPRGB/BLRNK G21 ... 6 E5
Holly Gv BLSH ML4 ... 133 M4
Hollymount BSDN G61 ... 61 M7
Holly Pl JNSTN PA5 ... 123 G1
  KLMNK KA1 ... 16 A4
Holly St AIRDRIE ML6 ... 111 J2
  CLYDBK G81 ... 60 A5
Hollywood LARGS KA30 ... 115 H2
Holm Av PSLYS PA2 ... 9 J8
  UD/BTH/TAN G71 ... 131 M2
Holmbank Av
  PLKSW/MSWD G43 ... 127 K2
Holmbrae Av UD/BTH/TAN G71 ... 131 M2
Holmbrae Rd UD/BTH/TAN G71 ... 131 M2
Holmbyre Rd CSMK G45 ... 128 B8
Holmbyre Ter CSMK G45 ... 128 C7
Holm Crest CARLUKE ML8 ... 188 B7
Holmes Av RNFRW PA4 ... 80 C8
Holmes Crs KLMNK KA1 ... 16 B8
Holmes Farm Rd KLMNK KA1 ... 16 B8
Holmes Qd BLSH ML4 ... 133 H5
Holmes Rd GLSTN KA4 ... 214 B3
  KLMNK KA1 ... 16 B8
Holmfauldhead Dr
  GOV/IBX G51 ... 103 L1
Holmfauld Pl GOV/IBX G51 ... 81 L8
Holmfauld Rd GOV/IBX G51 ... 103 L1
Holm Gdns BLSH ML4 ... 133 J5
Holmhead KBRN KA25 ... 167 G1
Holmhead Crs LNPK/KPK G44 ... 128 A3
Holmhead Pl LNPK/KPK G44 ... 128 A4
Holmhill Av BLTYR/CAMB G72 ... 130 A3
Holmhills Dr BLTYR/CAMB G72 ... 129 M6
Holmhills Gdns
  BLTYR/CAMB G72 ... 129 M5
Holmhills Gv BLTYR/CAMB G72 ... 129 M5
Holmhills Pl
  BLTYR/CAMB G72 ... 129 M5
Holmhills Rd BLTYR/CAMB G72 ... 129 M6

Holmhills Ter *BLTYR/CAMB* G72 ...... **129** M5
Holmlands Pl *KLMNK* KA1 .... **16** B8
Holm La *EKILN* G74 .... **14** E2
Holmlea Dr *KLMNK* KA1 .... **16** C8
Holmlea Pl *KLMNK* KA1 .... **16** B8
Holmlea Rd *GVH/MTFL* G42 .... **128** A2
Holm Pl *PSLYN/LNWD* PA3 .... **100** B2
Holm Rd *CARLUKE* ML8 .... **188** A6
Holms Av *IRVSE* KA11 .... **204** D8
Holms Crs *ERSK* PA8 .... **58** F7
Holmscroft Av *GRNK* PA15 .... **2** A4
Holmscroft St *GRNK* PA15 .... **2** A4
Holms Rd *GLGNK* KA14 .... **167** H3
Holmston Crs *AYRS* KA7 .... **19** M6
Holmston Dr *AYRS* KA7 .... **19** M7
Holmston Rd *AYRS* KA7 .... **19** H6
AYRS KA7 .... **19** M6
Holm St *CARLUKE* ML8 .... **178** E7
CGLW G2 .... **11** G2
KLMNKN/STW KA3 .... **197** L1
MTHW ML1 .... **134** A6
Holmswood Av
BLTYR/CAMB G72 .... **155** K1
Holmwood Av
UD/BTH/TAN G71 .... **131** M2
Holmwood Ct *LARGS* KA30 .... **115** H2
Holmwood Gdns
UD/BTH/TAN G71 .... **131** M3
Holyknowe Crs *KKNTL* G66 .... **44** E1
Holyknowe Rd *KKNTL* G66 .... **44** E2
Holyoake Ct *KLMNK* KA1 .... **212** F2 ▫
Holyrood Crs *MRYH/FIRH* G20 .... **4** D4
Holyrood Qd *MRYH/FIRH* G20 .... **4** C4
Holyrood St *HMLTN* ML3 .... **156** A4 ▫
Holytown Rd *BLSH* ML4 .... **133** L4
Holywell St *DEN/PKHD* G31 .... **13** H5
Holytown Rd *BLSH* ML4 .... **133** L4
Homer Pl *BLSH* ML4 .... **133** L4
Homeston Dr
UD/BTH/TAN G71 .... **132** A6 ▫
Home St *LNK/LMHG* ML11 .... **199** J4
Honeybank Crs *CARLUKE* ML8 ...... **178** F6
Honeybog Rd
CARD/HILL/MSPK G52 .... **102** E3
Honeyman Crs
LNK/LMHG ML11 .... **199** J5
Honeysuckle La
ALEX/LLW G83 .... **25** M2 ▫
Honeywell Crs *AIRDRIE* ML6 .... **111** L8
Hood St *CLYDBK* G81 .... **60** C7
GRNK PA15 .... **2** C2
Hope Av *BRWEIR* PA11 .... **75** L7 ▫
Hope Crs *LRKH* ML9 .... **176** B6
Hopefield Av *KVD/HLHD* G12 .... **82** C4 ▫
Hopehill Gdns *MRYH/FIRH* G20 ...... **4** E3
Hopehill Rd *MRYH/FIRH* G20 .... **4** E3
Hopeman Av *GIF/THBK* G46 .... **126** E5
Hopeman Dr *GIF/THBK* G46 .... **126** E5
Hopeman Rd *GIF/THBK* G46 .... **126** E5
Hopeman St *GIF/THBK* G46 .... **126** E5
Hope St *BLSH* ML4 .... **133** J4
CARLUKE ML8 .... **179** C7
CGLW G2 .... **11** H1
GRNK PA15 .... **2** D6
HBR/GL G84 .... **22** F1 ▫
HMLTN ML3 .... **156** E6
LNK/LMHG ML11 .... **199** C5
MTHW ML1 .... **157** L2 ▫
WISHAW ML2 .... **160** A5
Hopetoun Bank *IRVSE* KA11 .... **204** C7 ▫
Hopetoun Pl *SMSTN* G23 .... **52** E8 ▫
Hopetoun Ter *SPRGB/BLRNK* G21 .... **6** F2
Horatius St *MTHW* ML1 .... **133** H8
Hornal Rd *UD/BTH/TAN* G71 .... **132** A5
Hornbeam Dr *CLYDBK* G81 .... **59** M5 ▫
Hornbeam Rd *CUMB* G67 .... **49** M4 ▫
UD/BTH/TAN G71 .... **132** B1
Horndean Crs
STPS/GTHM/RID G33 .... **85** K8 ▫
Horne St *PPK/MIL* G22 .... **83** L4 ▫
Hornock Rd *CTBR* ML5 .... **87** M8
Hornshill Dr *MTHW* ML1 .... **135** H7 ▫
Hornshill Farm Rd
STPS/GTHM/RID G33 .... **85** L3
Hornshill St *SPRGB/BLRNK* G21 .... **6** L1
Horsburgh St
STPS/GTHM/RID G33 .... **85** K7 ▫
Horse Shoe Rd *BSDN* G61 .... **61** L5 ▫
Horsewood Rd *BRWEIR* PA11 .... **98** C2 ▫
Horslethill Rd *KVD/HLHD* G12 ...... **82** C5 ▫
Horslet St *CTBR* ML5 .... **109** J5
Horsley Brae *WISHAW* ML2 .... **177** H5
Horton *HBR/GL* G84 .... **21** G6 ▫
Hospital Rd *WISHAW* ML2 .... **159** J8
Hospital St *CTBR* ML5 .... **110** A5
GBLS G5 .... **11** H8
Hospitland Dr *LNK/LMHG* ML11 ... **199** H4
Hotspur St *MRYH/FIRH* G20 .... **82** E5
Houldsworth Crs *SHOTS* ML7 ...... **161** C1
Houldsworth La *KVGV* G3 .... **4** B9
Houldsworth St *KVGV* G3 .... **4** B9
Housel Av *KNTSWD* G13 .... **81** H3
Houston Crs *DALRY* KA24 .... **184** B2
Houstonfld Qd
CRG/CRSL/HOU PA6 .... **77** G7
Houston St *GBLS* G5 .... **10** C4
JNSTN PA5 .... **100** F2
CRG/CRSL/HOU PA6 .... **77** H7 ▫
KLMCLM PA13 .... **75** L2
RNFRW PA4 .... **79** G5
Houston St *GRNKW/INVK* PA16 ...... **2** B1
HMLTN ML3 .... **156** D8
PLKSD/SHW G41 .... **10** C5

RNFRW PA4 .... **80** D5
WISHAW ML2 .... **159** K7
Houston Ter *EKILN* G74 .... **14** D2
Houstoun Sq *JNSTN* PA5 .... **99** M6
Howacre *LNK/LMHG* ML11 .... **198** F4
Howard Av *EKILN* G74 .... **154** A4
Howard Ct *EKILN* G74 .... **154** A4
Howard Park Dr *KLMNK* KA1 .... **16** D7
Howard St *CGLE* G1 .... **11** J3
GTCI KA28 .... **138** A7
KLMNK KA1 .... **16** D5
LRKH ML9 .... **176** C8 ▫
PSLY PA1 .... **9** L3
Howat Crs *IRV* KA12 .... **203** L6
Howatshaws Rd *DMBTN* G82 .... **37** H3
Howat St *GOV/IBX* G51 .... **104** A1
Howden Av *KLWNG* KA13 .... **193** L5
MTHW ML1 .... **134** D1
Howden Dr
PSLYN/LNWD PA3 .... **100** A4 ▫
Howden Pl *MTHW* ML1 .... **134** A4
Howe Gdns
UD/BTH/TAN G71 .... **132** A2 ▫
Howe Rd *KSYTH* G65 .... **47** K2
Howes St *CTBR* ML5 .... **110** B5
Howe St *PSLY* PA1 .... **100** F5 ▫
Howford Rd
CARD/HILL/MSPK G52 .... **103** H5
Howgate *KLWNG* KA13 .... **193** K6 ▫
Howgate Av *DRUM* G15 .... **60** F6
Howgate Rd *HMLTN* ML3 .... **174** C1
Howieshill Av
BLTYR/CAMB G72 .... **130** B4 ▫
Howieshill Rd
BLTYR/CAMB G72 .... **130** B5
Howie St *LRKH* ML9 .... **176** B8 ▫
Howletnest Rd *AIRDRIE* ML6 .... **111** J3 ▫
Howson Lea *MTHW* ML1 .... **158** B5 ▫
Howson Vw *MTHW* ML1 .... **157** H2 ▫
Howth Dr *KNTSWD* G13 .... **81** M1
Howth Ter *KNTSWD* G13 .... **81** M1 ▫
Hoylake Pk *UD/BTH/TAN* G71 .... **131** M7
Hoylake Pl *SMSTN* G23 .... **52** E8
Hoylake Sq *KLWNG* KA13 .... **193** L5 ▫
Hozier Crs *UD/BTH/TAN* G71 .... **131** M1
Hozier St *CARLUKE* ML8 .... **178** E7
CTBR ML5 .... **110** A5
Hudson Ter *EKILS* G75 .... **171** H1
Hudson Wy *EKILS* G75 .... **14** A5 ▫
Huggin Craig Rd *NMLNS* KA16 ..... **215** J1
Hughenden Dr
KVD/HLHD G12 .... **82** B5 ▫
Hughenden Gdns
KVD/HLHD G12 .... **82** A5
Hughenden La
KVD/HLHD G12 .... **82** B5 ▫
Hughenden Rd
KVD/HLHD G12 .... **82** B5 ▫
Hugh Murray Dr
BLTYR/CAMB G72 .... **130** C4 ▫
Hugh Watt Pl
KLMNKN/STW KA3 .... **206** A2
Hugo St *MRYH/FIRH* G20 .... **82** F4
Hulks Rd *AIRDRIE* ML6 .... **69** H6
Humbie Ct *NMRNS* G77 .... **150** E7
Humbie Ga *NMRNS* G77 .... **150** E7 ▫
Humbie Rd *NMRNS* G77 .... **150** E6 ▫
Humbie Lawns *NMRNS* G77 .... **150** E7
Humbie Rd *NMRNS* G77 .... **150** E7
Hume Dr *UD/BTH/TAN* G71 .... **131** L2
Hume Pl *EKILS* G75 .... **14** D6
Hume Rd *CUMB* G67 .... **49** G6
Hume St *CLYDBK* G81 .... **60** B8
Hunter Av *ARD* KA22 .... **191** K7
Hunter Crs *TROON* KA10 .... **217** G6
Hunter Dr *IRV* KA12 .... **203** H3
Hunter Pl *KLBCH* PA10 .... **99** C7 ▫
KLWNG KA13 .... **194** A6
MLNGV G62 .... **41** L8
Hunter Rd *CRH/DND* KA2 .... **210** F1
HMLTN ML3 .... **156** B3
MLNGV G62 .... **41** L8
RUTH G73 .... **106** C8 ▫
Hunter's Av *AYR* KA8 .... **225** J4 ▫
DMBTN G82 .... **37** J6
Huntersfield Rd *JNSTN* PA5 .... **99** J8
Hunters Hill Ct
SPRGB/BLRNK G21 .... **83** M3 ▫
Huntershill Rd *BSHPBGS* G64 .... **84** A1 ▫
Huntershill St
SPRGB/BLRNK G21 .... **83** L3 ▫
Huntershill Wy *BSHPBGS* G64 ...... **83** M2 ▫
Hunters Rd *WKIL* KA23 .... **181** J5
Hunter St *AIRDRIE* ML6 .... **88** F8
BLSH ML4 .... **133** G4
COWCAD G4 .... **12** A3
EKILN G74 .... **15** G2
PSLY PA1 .... **9** G3
PSTWK KA9 .... **225** J1 ▫
SHOTS ML7 .... **137** K4
Hunt HI *BALLOCH* G68 .... **47** J8
Hunthill La *BLTYR/CAMB* G72 ...... **155** H3
Hunthill Pl
CRMNK/CLK/EAG G76 .... **152** A1 ▫
Hunthill Rd *BLTYR/CAMB* G72 ...... **155** H3
Huntingdon Sq
SPRGB/BLRNK G21 .... **6** A1 ▫
Huntingdon Rd *COWCAD* G4 .... **6** A5
Hunting Lodge Gdns
HMLTN ML3 .... **157** G7 ▫
Huntingtower Rd
BAIL/MDB/MHD G69 .... **107** M5
Huntly Av *BLSH* ML4 .... **133** G3
GIF/THBK G46 .... **127** K6
Huntly Dr *BLTYR/CAMB* G72 .... **130** B5
BSDN G61 .... **61** L2
CTBR ML5 .... **109** K5
Huntly Pl *KLMNKN/STW* KA3 ...... **207** J7
PGL PA14 .... **34** B7 ▫

Huntly Qd *WISHAW* ML2 .... **159** H4
Huntly Rd *CARD/HILL/MSPK* G52 ... **102** F1
KVD/HLHD G12 .... **82** C6 ▫
Huntly Ter *PGL* PA14 .... **34** B7
PSLYS PA2 .... **9** K9
Hurlawcrook Rd *EKILS* G75 .... **171** M8
Hurlet Rd *PSLYS* PA2 .... **102** A3
Hurlford Av *KNTSWD* G13 .... **80** F2
Hurlford Rd *KLMNK* KA1 .... **212** A4
Hurly Hawkin *BSHPBGS* G64 .... **84** D1
Hutcheson Dr *LARGS* KA30 .... **115** K8 ▫
Hutcheson Rd *GIF/THBK* G46 .... **127** G7
Hutcheson St *CGLE* G1 .... **11** K3
Hutchison Pl
BLTYR/CAMB G72 .... **130** E6
Hutchison Dr *BSDN* G61 .... **62** A7
Hutchison Pl *CTBR* ML5 .... **109** M3
Hutchison St *HMLTN* ML3 .... **156** D8 ▫
WISHAW ML2 .... **177** J2
Hutchison Pl
CARD/HILL/MSPK G52 .... **103** H4
Hutton *KVD/HLHD* G12 .... **82** C6 ▫
Hutton Av *CRG/CRSL/HOU* PA6 ...... **99** J1
Hutton Dr *GOV/IBX* G51 .... **103** L1
Hutton Park Crs *LARGS* KA30 ...... **115** J4
Huxley St *MRYH/FIRH* G20 .... **82** F3
Hyacinth Wy *CARLUKE* ML8 .... **188** F1 ▫
Hydepark St *KVGV* G3 .... **10** C2
Hyndal Av *PLK/PH/NH* G53 .... **103** J8
Hyndford Pl
LNK/LMHG ML11 .... **199** G5 ▫
Hyndford Rd *LNK/LMHG* ML11 ..... **199** H6
LNK/LMHG ML11 .... **199** M8
Hyndland Av *PTCK* G11 .... **82** B7 ▫
Hyndland Rd *KVD/HLHD* G12 .... **82** C7
Hyndland St *PTCK* G11 .... **82** C7
Hyndlee Dr
CARD/HILL/MSPK G52 .... **103** J4
Hyndman Rd *WKIL* KA23 .... **181** J6
Hyndshaw Rd *CARLUKE* ML8 ...... **178** F6
Hyndshaw Vw *CARLUKE* ML8 ..... **178** A5
Hyslop Pl *CLYDBK* G81 .... **60** A6
Hyslop Rd *SVSTN* KA20 .... **192** E7
Hyslop St *AIRDRIE* ML6 .... **110** E1**

I

Iain Dr *BSDN* G61 .... **61** J3
Iain Rd *BSDN* G61 .... **61** J3
Ian Smith Ct *CLYDBK* G81 .... **80** D1 ▫
Ibroxholm Ov *GOV/IBX* G51 .... **104** B3
Ibroxholm Pl *GOV/IBX* G51 .... **104** B4 ▫
Ibrox St *GOV/IBX* G51 .... **104** C3
Ibrox Ter *GOV/IBX* G51 .... **104** B3
Ida Qd *BLSH* ML4 .... **132** F4 ▫
Iddesleigh Av *MLNGV* G62 .... **42** A7 ▫
Ilay Av *BSDN* G61 .... **82** A1
Ilay Ct *BSDN* G61 .... **82** A1
Ilay Rd *BSDN* G61 .... **82** A1 ▫
Imlach Pl *MTHW* ML1 .... **157** K4
Imperial Dr *AIRDRIE* ML6 .... **110** F4
Inchbrae Rd
CARD/HILL/MSPK G52 .... **103** J5
Inchcolm Pl *EKILN* G74 .... **14** B1
Inches Rd *ARD* KA22 .... **200** B1
Inchfad Dr *DRUM* G15 .... **60** E6
Inchfad Pl *DRUM* G15 .... **60** E6 ▫
Inch Garve *EKILN* G74 .... **154** D8
Inchgotrick Rd *KLMNK* KA1 .... **211** L6
Inchgreen St *GRNK* PA15 .... **33** M7 ▫
Inchholm La *PTCK* G11 .... **81** L7 ▫
Inchholm St *PTCK* G11 .... **81** L7 ▫
Inchinnan Dr *RNFRW* PA4 .... **80** A1
Inchinnan Rd *PSLYN/LNWD* PA3 ... **101** L2
RNFRW PA4 .... **80** A5
Inch Keith *EKILN* G74 .... **154** D8
Inchkeith Pl *CAR/SHTL* G32 .... **107** H2 ▫
Inchlaggan Pl *DRUM* G15 .... **60** E5 ▫
Inchlee St *SCOT* G14 .... **81** L7
Inch Marnock *EKILN* G74 .... **172** C1
Inch Murrin *EKILN* G74 .... **154** D8
Inchmurrin Av *KKNTL* G66 .... **66** B1 ▫
Inchmurrin Dr
CRMNK/CLK/EAG G76 .... **129** K7
KLMNKN/STW KA3 .... **207** G4
Inchmurrin Gdns
CRMNK/CLK/EAG G76 .... **129** K7 ▫
Inchmurrin Pl
CRMNK/CLK/EAG G76 .... **129** K7 ▫
LARGS KA30 .... **115** K7
NMLNS KA16 .... **215** J7
Inchneuk Rd *CTBR* ML5 .... **87** L3
Inchnock Av
BAIL/MDB/MHD G69 .... **87** G3
Inchoch St *STPS/GTHM/RID* G33 ... **85** L7
Incholm Gdns
BAIL/MDB/MHD G69 .... **67** G6 ▫
Inchory Pl *DRUM* G15 .... **60** E5
Inchwood Ct *BALLOCH* G68 .... **68** A2 ▫
Inchwood Pl *BALLOCH* G68 .... **67** M2 ▫
Inchwood Rd *BALLOCH* G68 .... **67** M2
Incle St *PSLY* PA1 .... **9** J3
Indale Av *PSTWK* KA9 .... **225** L2 ▫
India Dr *RNFRW* PA4 .... **79** J4
India St *ALEX/LLW* G83 .... **25** L4 ▫
CGLW G2 .... **4** E8
Industry St *KKNTL* G66 .... **65** K2
Inga St *MRYH/FIRH* G20 .... **82** F2
Ingerbreck Av *RUTH* G73 .... **129** K4 ▫
Ingleby Dr *DEN/PKHD* G31 .... **12** F1 ▫
Inglefield Ct *AIRDRIE* ML6 .... **110** F2
Inglefield St *GVH/MTFL* G42 .... **105** H7 ▫
Ingleneuk Av
STPS/GTHM/RID G33 .... **85** H4
Inglestone Av *GIF/THBK* G46 ...... **127** G7 ▫
Ingleston St *GRNK* PA15 .... **2** F7 ▫
Inglewood Crs *EKILS* G75 .... **171** G1
PSLYS PA2 .... **8** D4
Inglis Pl *EKILS* G75 .... **14** F8
Inglis St *DEN/PKHD* G31 .... **12** F3 ▫
WISHAW ML2 .... **158** D7
Ingliston Dr *BSHPTN* PA7 .... **57** M6
Ingram St *CGLE* G1 .... **11** L2
Ingram St *CGLE* G1 .... **11** L2
Inishail Rd *STPS/GTHM/RID* G33 ... **85** J8
Inkerman Pl *KLMNK* KA1 .... **16** C3
Inkerman Rd
CARD/HILL/MSPK G52 .... **102** F4
Innellan Dr *KLMNKN/STW* KA3 ... **206** F6

Innellan Rd *WMYSB* PA18 .... **50** A8
Innerleithen Dr *WISHAW* ML2 ...... **159** K3
Innermanse Qd *MTHW* ML1 .... **134** F4 ▫
Innerwick Dr
CARD/HILL/MSPK G52 .... **103** H4
Innerwood Rd *KLWNG* KA13 .... **193** L5
Innes Ct *EKILN* G74 .... **153** L5
Innes Park Rd *SKLM* PA17 .... **70** B5
International Av
BLTYR/CAMB G72 .... **155** K5 ▫
Inveraray Gdns *MTHW* ML1 .... **134** C7 ▫
Inverary Dr *BSHPBGS* G64 .... **64** B5
Inveravon Dr *MTHW* ML1 .... **157** H4
Invercanny Dr *DRUM* G15 .... **61** G5
Invercanny Pl *DRUM* G15 .... **61** G5
Invercargill *EKILS* G75 .... **171** G2
Invercloy Pl
KLMNKN/STW KA3 .... **206** F5 ▫
Invercloy Ct *EKILS* G75 .... **171** H5 ▫
Inverclyde Gdns *RUTH* G73 .... **129** K6
Inverclyde Vw *LARGS* KA30 .... **115** K3
Inveresk Pl *CTBR* ML5 .... **110** A1
Inveresk Qd *CAR/SHTL* G32 .... **107** G3
Inveresk St *CAR/SHTL* G32 .... **107** G3
Inverewe Av *GIF/THBK* G46 .... **126** D7
Inverewe Dr *GIF/THBK* G46 .... **126** D7
Inverewe Gdns *GIF/THBK* G46 ..... **126** D7
Inverewe Pl *GIF/THBK* G46 .... **126** D6
Inverewe Wy *NMRNS* G77 .... **150** A4 ▫
Invergarry Av *GIF/THBK* G46 .... **126** D7
Invergarry Ct *GIF/THBK* G46 .... **126** E7 ▫
Invergarry Dr *GIF/THBK* G46 .... **126** D7
Invergarry Gdns *GIF/THBK* G46 ... **126** D8
Invergarry Gv *GIF/THBK* G46 ...... **126** D7
Invergarry Pl *GIF/THBK* G46 ...... **126** E7 ▫
Invergarry Quad *GIF/THBK* G46 ... **126** E7 ▫
Invergarry Vw *GIF/THBK* G46 ..... **126** E7 ▫
Inverglas Av *RNFRW* PA4 .... **80** F8 ▫
Invergordon Av
PLKSW/MSWD G43 .... **127** M2
Invergyle Dr
CARD/HILL/MSPK G52 .... **103** H4
Inverkar Dr *PSLYS* PA2 .... **101** G7 ▫
Inverkar Rd *AYRS* KA7 .... **19** C8
Inverkip Dr *SHOTS* ML7 .... **137** L4
Inverkip Rd *GRNKW/INVK* PA16 ... **31** L6
Inverkip St *GRNK* PA15 .... **2** B4
Inverlair Av *PLKSW/MSWD* G43 ... **127** M2
Inverleith St *CAR/SHTL* G32 .... **13** L3
Inverleven Pl *IRVSE* KA11 .... **203** M2
Inverlochy St
STPS/GTHM/RID G33 .... **85** K8
Inverness St *GOV/IBX* G51 .... **103** K3
Inveroran Dr *BSDN* G61 .... **62** B5
Inver Rd *STPS/GTHM/RID* G33 ..... **107** L2
Invershiel Rd *SMSTN* G23 .... **52** D8
Invershin Dr *MRYH/FIRH* G20 ..... **82** D4 ▫
Inverurie St *SPRGB/BLRNK* G21 ...... **5** M2
Invervale Av *AIRDRIE* ML6 .... **111** M3
Inzievar Ter *CAR/SHTL* G32 .... **107** H8
Iona Av *EKILN* G74 .... **154** A1 ▫
Iona Crs *GRK* PA19 .... **31** J3
OLDK G60 .... **59** J4
Iona Dr *PSLYS* PA2 .... **124** D2
Iona Pl *CTBR* ML5 .... **87** K8
KLMNKN/STW KA3 .... **207** G4
Iona Qd *WISHAW* ML2 .... **159** L4
Iona Rdg *HMLTN* ML3 .... **155** L8
Iona Rd *PGL* PA14 .... **55** G2
RNFRW PA4 .... **79** J4
RUTH G73 .... **129** L6 ▫
Iona St *GOV/IBX* G51 .... **104** B3
GRNKW/INVK PA16 .... **32** C5
MTHW ML1 .... **133** K8
Iona Wy *KKNTL* G66 .... **66** A1
STPS/GTHM/RID G33 .... **85** J8
Iona Wynd *ALEX/LLW* G83 .... **25** M3 ▫
Iris Av *CSMK* G45 .... **129** G6
Irongray St *DEN/PKHD* G31 .... **13** K1
Irvine Crs *CTBR* ML5 .... **110** C2
Irvine Dr *PSLYN/LNWD* PA3 .... **99** M2
Irvine Gdns *KKNTL* G66 .... **45** H4
Irvine Mains Crs *IRV* KA12 .... **203** J3
Irvine Rd *CRH/DND* KA2 .... **205** K8
IRV KA12 .... **203** G1
KLMNK KA1 .... **206** C8
KLMNKN/STW KA3 .... **205** L2
KLWNG KA13 .... **193** M7
LARGS KA30 .... **115** K7
NMLNS KA16 .... **215** J7
Irvine St *AIRDRIE* ML6 .... **88** F5
DMNK/BRGTN G40 .... **13** G9
Irvine Ter *HMLTN* ML3 .... **174** D1
Irving Av *CLYDBK* G81 .... **60** B4
Irving Ct *CLYDBK* G81 .... **60** B3
Irving Qd *CLYDBK* G81 .... **60** B3 ▫
Irwin St *GRNK* PA15 .... **33** L7 ▫
Isabella Gdns *HMLTN* ML3 .... **157** H8
Isla Av *WISHAW* ML2 .... **159** M3
Island Rd *CUMB* G67 .... **68** D1
Island Vw *ARD* KA22 .... **191** K5
Islay Av *PGL* PA14 .... **55** H2
RUTH G73 .... **129** L6
Islay Ct *HMLTN* ML3 .... **156** C6
Islay Crs *OLDK* G60 .... **59** J4 ▫
PSLYS PA2 .... **124** D2
SALT KA21 .... **191** M7
Islay Dr *NMRNS* G77 .... **150** B4
OLDK G60 .... **59** J4
Islay Gdns *CARLUKE* ML8 .... **188** F1 ▫
LRKH ML9 .... **176** B6
Islay Qd *WISHAW* ML2 .... **158** E8 ▫
Islay Rd *KKNTL* G66 .... **66** A1
Islay Wy *CTBR* ML5 .... **109** K5
Isle of Pin Rd *TROON* KA10 .... **216** F8
Isles St *NMLNS* KA16 .... **215** L2 ▫
Ivanhoe *EKILN* G74 .... **154** D5
Ivanhoe Ct *CARLUKE* ML8 .... **178** D6
Ivanhoe Crs *WISHAW* ML2 .... **159** J6
Ivanhoe Dr *KKNTL* G66 .... **65** L1
Ivanhoe Rd *CUMB* G67 .... **68** C1
KNTSWD G13 .... **81** K1
PSLYS PA2 .... **100** E8
Ivybank Av *BLTYR/CAMB* G72 ..... **130** C5

Ivybank Crs *PGL* PA14 .... **34** A8
Ivybank Rd *PGL* PA14 .... **34** B8 ▫
Ivy Crs *GRK* PA19 .... **31** L3 ▫
Ivy Pl *AYRS* KA7 .... **229** K4
BLTYR/CAMB G72 .... **155** J1
Ivy Rd *UD/BTH/TAN* G71 .... **132** C1
Ivy Ter *MTHW* ML1 .... **134** A1
Ivy Wy *AIRDRIE* ML6 .... **111** L6

J

Jackson Pl *CARLUKE* ML8 .... **178** E6
DMBTN G82 .... **25** K7 ▫
Jackson St *CTBR* ML5 .... **110** B2
Jack's Rd *SALT* KA21 .... **200** F1
UD/BTH/TAN G71 .... **132** A5
MTHW ML1 .... **158** B5
Jack St *HMLTN* ML3 .... **174** D1
Jacks Vw *WKIL* KA23 .... **181** J4
Jackton Rd *EKILS* G75 .... **170** D4
Jacobs Dr *GRK* PA19 .... **31** K2
Jacob's Ladder Wy
WISHAW ML2 .... **177** J2 ▫
Jagger Gdns
BAIL/MDB/MHD G69 .... **107** M5
Jamaica Dr *EKILS* G75 .... **153** H8
Jamaica La *GRNK* PA15 .... **2** B2
Jamaica St *CGLE* G1 .... **11** H3
GRNK PA15 .... **2** B2
James Brown Av *AYR* KA8 .... **225** L6
James Campbell Rd *AYR* KA8 .... **19** K3
James Crs *IRV* KA12 .... **203** H5
James Dempsey Ct *CTBR* ML5 ..... **109** M3
James Dempsey Gdns
CTBR ML5 .... **109** M3 ▫
James Dunlop Gdns
BSHPBGS G64 .... **84** B2 ▫
James Gray St
PLKSD/SHW G41 .... **127** L1 ▫
James Hamilton Dr *BLSH* ML4 ..... **133** H4
James Healy Dr *HMLTN* ML3 .... **174** C2
James Leeson Ct *KKNTL* G66 .... **45** H3
James Little St *KLMNK* KA1 .... **16** F7
James Miller Crescen
SALT KA21 .... **201** G2
James Morrison St *CGLE* G1 .... **11** L4 ▫
James Nisbet St
SPRGB/BLRNK G21 .... **6** C8
James St *ALEX/LLW* G83 .... **25** L4 ▫
AYR KA8 .... **19** G2
BLSH ML4 .... **132** C2
CARLUKE ML8 .... **178** F8
DALRY KA24 .... **184** B1
DMNK/BRGTN G40 .... **12** B7
HBR/GL G84 .... **20** D7
MTHW ML1 .... **157** K2
PSTWK KA9 .... **225** H4
James Sym Crs *KLMNK* KA1 .... **16** C8 ▫
James Vw *MTHW* ML1 .... **133** M6 ▫
James Watt Av *EKILS* G75 .... **15** J6
James Watt Pl *EKILN* G74 .... **153** H6
James Watt Rd *MLNGV* G62 .... **41** M6
James Watt St *KVGV* G3 .... **10** F2
James Watt Wy *GRNK* PA15 .... **3** J5
James Wilson Pl
CARLUKE ML8 .... **188** B7 ▫
Jamieson Ct *CLYDBK* G81 .... **60** B2 ▫
CVH/MTFL G42 .... **105** H7 ▫
Jamieson Dr *EKILN* G74 .... **15** K2
Jamieson Gdns *SHOTS* ML7 .... **137** L4 ▫
Jamieson St *CVH/MTFL* G42 .... **105** H7 ▫
Janebank Av *BLTYR/CAMB* G72 .... **130** C5
Janefield Av *JNSTN* PA5 .... **99** L7
Janefield Pl *BEITH* KA15 .... **144** B8
BLTYR/CAMB G72 .... **155** J1
KKNTL G66 .... **29** K8
Janefield St *DEN/PKHD* G31 .... **13** J7
DMNK/BRGTN G40 .... **13** J7
Jane Rae Gdns *CLYDBK* G81 .... **80** D1 ▫
Jane's Brae *CUMB* G67 .... **68** F1 ▫
Janesmith St *WISHAW* ML2 .... **158** C5
Janetta St *CLYDBK* G81 .... **60** A6
Jardine St *MRYH/FIRH* G20 .... **4** C3 ▫
Jardine Ter
BAIL/MDB/MHD G69 .... **86** F4 ▫
Jarvie Av *AIRDRIE* ML6 .... **90** B7
Jarvie Crs *KSYTH* G65 .... **47** K2
Jarvie Wy *PSLYS* PA2 .... **123** L1
Jasmine Pl *CUMB* G67 .... **68** B2
Jasmine Rd *KLMNK* KA1 .... **211** J2
Jasmine Wy *CARLUKE* ML8 .... **188** E1
Java St *MTHW* ML1 .... **133** J8
Jean Armour Dr *CLYDBK* G81 .... **60** C6
Jean Armour Pl *SALT* KA21 .... **192** A7 ▫
Jean Armour Ter
GRNKW/INVK PA16 .... **31** K6
Jeanette Av *HMLTN* ML3 .... **174** D2
Jeanie Deans Dr *HBR/GL* G84 ...... **23** G1 ▫
Jean Maclean Pl
BSHPBGS G64 .... **64** B5 ▫
Jean St *PGL* PA14 .... **34** B7
Jedburgh Av *RUTH* G73 .... **129** H2
Jedburgh Dr *PSLYS* PA2 .... **101** G8
Jedburgh Gdns
MRYH/FIRH G20 .... **4** C2 ▫
Jedburgh Pl *CTBR* ML5 .... **109** M6
EKILN G74 .... **15** G1
Jedburgh St *BLTYR/CAMB* G72 .... **155** K2 ▫
WISHAW ML2 .... **159** J4
Jedworth Av *DRUM* G15 .... **61** H6
Jedworth Rd *DRUM* G15 .... **61** H6 ▫
Jeffrey St *KLMNK* KA1 .... **211** M4
Jellicoe Pl *HBR/GL* G84 .... **21** G7 ▫
Jellicoe St *CLYDBK* G81 .... **59** L6
Jennie Lee Dr *WISHAW* ML2 .... **177** H2 ▫
WISHAW ML2 .... **177** J2 ▫
Jennys Well Ct *PSLYS* PA2 .... **102** B7
Jennys Well Rd *PSLYS* PA2 .... **102** B7
Jermond Dr *IRV* KA12 .... **203** K5
Jervis Pl *HBR/GL* G84 .... **21** G7 ▫
Jervis Ter *EKILS* G75 .... **171** H2
Jerviston Ct *MTHW* ML1 .... **134** A8 ▫
Jerviston Rd *MTHW* ML1 .... **134** A8
STPS/GTHM/RID G33 .... **85** J7

Jerviston St *MTHW* ML1 .... 134 A5
  MTHW ML1 .... 157 M1
Jerviswood *MTHW* ML1 .... 134 A8
Jerviswood Dr
  LNK/LMHG ML11 .... 199 M2
Jerviswood Rd
  LNK/LMHG ML11 .... 199 G5
Jetty Rd *FAIRLIE* KA29 .... 139 K6
Joanna Ter *BLTYR/CAMB* G72 .... 155 K1
Jocelyn Sq *CGLE* G1 .... 11 K4
Jockshorn Ter
  KLMNKN/STW KA3 .... 206 C3
John Bowman Gdns *BLSH* ML4 .... 133 H3
John Brannan Wy
  UD/BTH/TAN G71 .... 132 D3
John Brown Pl
  BAIL/MDB/MHD G69 .... 86 C1
John Burnside Dr *CLYDBK* G81 .... 60 C2
John Campbell St *GRK* PA19 .... 31 M2
John Clark St *LARGS* KA30 .... 115 K5
John Dickie St *KLMNK* KA1 .... 16 E3
John Ewing Gdns *LRKH* ML9 .... 176 A5
John Finnie St *KLMNK* KA1 .... 16 E4
John Gregor Pl *LOCHW* PA12 .... 120 C7
John Hendry Rd
  UD/BTH/TAN G71 .... 132 A5
John Knox St *CLYDBK* G81 .... 80 D2
  COWCAD G4 .... 12 B1
  GLSTN KA4 .... 214 B4
John Lang St *JNSTN* PA5 .... 100 A6
John Marshall Dr *PPK/MIL* G22 .... 83 L1
John Murray Ct *MTHW* ML1 .... 157 L6
Johnsburn Dr
  PLK/PH/NH G53 .... 126 B3
Johnsburn Rd
  PLK/PH/NH G53 .... 126 B3
Johnshaven St
  PLKSW/MSWD G43 .... 127 J2
Johnshill *LOCHW* PA12 .... 120 D5
John Smith Ct *AIRDRIE* ML6 .... 110 F1
John Smith Gdns *CTBR* ML5 .... 110 C3
Johnson Ct *HBR/GL* G84 .... 20 F8
Johnson Dr
  BLTYR/CAMB G72 .... 130 B4
Johnston Av *KSYTH* G65 .... 47 K2
Johnston Dr *TROON* KA10 .... 216 D3
Johnstone Av
  CARD/HILL/MSPK G52 .... 103 H2
  CLYDBK G81 .... 80 D1
Johnstone Dr *LOCHW* PA12 .... 120 C7
  RAYR/DAL KA6 .... 227 H3
  RUTH G73 .... 129 G2
Johnstone Rd *HMLTN* ML3 .... 156 E7
Johnstone St *BLSH* ML4 .... 133 J4
Johnstone Ter *KSYTH* G65 .... 46 F6
Johnston Rd
  BAIL/MDB/MHD G69 .... 86 F3
Johnston St *AIRDRIE* ML6 .... 111 H1
  GRNKW/INVK PA16 .... 32 D2
  PSLY PA1 .... 9 H5
Johnston Ter
  GRNKW/INVK PA16 .... 32 D2
John St *AYR* KA8 .... 19 G2
  BLSH ML4 .... 133 L4
  BLTYR/CAMB G72 .... 155 L2
  BRHD/NEIL G78 .... 125 H6
  CARLUKE ML8 .... 178 F8
  CGLE G1 .... 11 K2
  DMBTN G82 .... 36 D4
  GRK PA19 .... 31 L2
  GRNK PA15 .... 3 G7
  HBR/GL G84 .... 20 C8
  HMLTN ML3 .... 156 E6
  KKNTL G66 .... 45 K8
  LARGS KA30 .... 115 J7
  LRKH ML9 .... 176 A7
  WISHAW ML2 .... 158 C5
John Street La *HBR/GL* G84 .... 20 C7
John Wilson St *GRNK* PA15 .... 3 L8
John Wood St *PGL* PA14 .... 34 C8
Jones Wynd *MTHW* ML1 .... 134 E8
Jonquil Wy *CARLUKE* ML8 .... 188 F1
Joppa *RAYR/DAL* KA6 .... 231 H5
Joppa St
  STPS/GTHM/RID G33 .... 106 E2
Jordanhill Cres *KNTSWD* G13 .... 81 K4
Jordanhill Dr *KNTSWD* G13 .... 81 K4
Jordanhill La *KNTSWD* G13 .... 81 L4
Jordan St *SCOT* G14 .... 81 K7
Jordanvale Av *SCOT* G14 .... 81 K7
Jowitt Av *CLYDBK* G81 .... 60 D8
Jubilee Ct
  CARD/HILL/MSPK G52 .... 102 F2
Jubilee Gdns *BSDN* G61 .... 61 L5
Jubilee Ter *JNSTN* PA5 .... 99 K8
Julian Av *KVD/HLHD* G12 .... 82 C5
Julian La *KVD/HLHD* G12 .... 82 C5
Juniper Av *EKILS* G75 .... 171 K4
Juniper Ct *KKNTL* G66 .... 65 H4
Juniper Dr *KKNTL* G66 .... 45 H5
Juniper Gn *AYRS* KA7 .... 229 K3
Juniper Gv *HMLTN* ML3 .... 156 F7
Juniper Pl *CAR/SHTL* G32 .... 107 M5
  JNSTN PA5 .... 123 L1
  UD/BTH/TAN G71 .... 132 D1
Juniper Rd *UD/BTH/TAN* G71 .... 132 D1
Juniper Ter *CAR/SHTL* G32... .... 107 L5
Juno St *MTHW* ML1 .... 133 L4
Juno Ter *GRNKW/INVK* PA16 .... 31 K6
Jupiter St *MTHW* ML1 .... 133 L4
Jupiter Ter *GRNKW/INVK* PA16 .... 31 K6
Jura *EKILN* G74 .... 15 M7
Jura Av *RNFRW* PA4 .... 80 D8
Jura Dr *BLTYR/CAMB* G72 .... 131 L4
  NMRNS G77 .... 150 B3
  OLDK G60 .... 59 J4
Jura Gdns *CARLUKE* ML8 .... 189 G1
  HMLTN ML3 .... 156 A7
  LRKH ML9 .... 176 C6
Jura Pl *TROON* KA10 .... 216 E2
Jura Qd *WISHAW* ML2 .... 158 E8
Jura Rd *OLDK* G60 .... 59 J4
  PSLYS PA2 .... 124 D2
Jura St *CARD/HILL/MSPK* G52 .... 103 M4
  GRNKW/INVK PA16 .... 32 C5
Jura Wynd *CTBR* ML5 .... 87 J3
Jutland St *HBR/GL* G84 .... 20 A7

K

Kaim Dr *PLK/PH/NH* G53 .... 126 C3
Kaim Vw *FAIRLIE* KA29 .... 139 K7
Kames Bay *GTCI* KA28 .... 138 C6
Kames Ct *IRVSE* KA11 .... 204 B3
Kames Rd *SHOTTS* ML7 .... 137 L3
Kane St *DMBTN* G82 .... 25 K7
Karadale Gdns *LRKH* ML9 .... 176 A7
Katewell Av *DRUM* G15 .... 60 E5
Katewell Pl *DRUM* G15 .... 60 E5
Katherine Pl *DMBTN* G82 .... 25 L7
Katherine St *AIRDRIE* ML6 .... 111 L1
Kathleen Pk *HBR/GL* G84 .... 20 A6
Katrine Av *BSHPBGS* G64 .... 64 B8
Katrine Ct *KLMNK* KA1 .... 212 A4
Katrine Crs *AIRDRIE* ML6 .... 88 F8
Katrine Dr *NMRNS* G77 .... 151 H5
  PSLYS PA2 .... 100 F7
Katrine Pl *BLTYR/CAMB* G72 .... 130 A3
  CTBR ML5 .... 87 K8
  IRV KA12 .... 203 K3
Katrine Rd *GRNK* PA15 .... 2 F8
  SHOTTS ML7 .... 137 L3
  WMYSB PA18 .... 70 A1
Kay Gdns *MTHW* ML1 .... 157 H3
Kay Park Crs *KLMNKN/STW* KA3... .... 17 J3
Kay Park Ter *KLMNKN/STW* KA3... .... 17 J3
Kaystone Rd *DRUM* G15 .... 61 G8
Kay St *SPRGB/BLRNK* G21 .... 83 M5
Keal Av *DRUM* G15 .... 61 H8
Keal Crs *DRUM* G15 .... 61 H8
Keal Dr *DRUM* G15 .... 81 G1
Keal Pl *DRUM* G15 .... 81 G1
Kearn Av *DRUM* G15 .... 61 H8
Kearn Pl *DRUM* G15 .... 61 H8
Keats Pk *UD/BTH/TAN* G71 .... 132 B6
Keil Crs *DMBTN* G82 .... 36 D6
Keir Crs *WISHAW* ML2 .... 159 H5
Keir Dr *BSHPBGS* G64 .... 63 M7
Keir Hardie Av *MTHW* ML1 .... 134 B4
Keir Hardie Dr *ARD* KA22 .... 191 H5
  BLSH ML4 .... 132 F5
  KBRN KA25 .... 143 G8
  KSYTH G65 .... 47 K2
Keir Hardie Pl *SALT* KA21 .... 192 A7
Keir Hardie Rd *LRKH* ML9 .... 176 B8
  SVSTN KA20 .... 192 E8
Keir Hardie St *GRNK* PA15 .... 33 L7
Keir's Wk *BLTYR/CAMB* G72 .... 130 A3
Keith Av *GIF/THBK* G46 .... 127 J6
Keith Ct *PTCK* G11 .... 82 C7
Keith Pl *KLMNKN/STW* KA3 .... 207 J7
Keith Qd *WISHAW* ML2 .... 159 H4
Keith St *BLSH* ML4 .... 133 G3
  HMLTN ML3 .... 156 F5
  PTCK G11 .... 82 C7
Kelbourne Crs *BLSH* ML4 .... 132 F4
Kelbourne St *MRYH/FIRH* G20 .... 82 E5
Kelburn Av *FAIRLIE* KA29 .... 139 L5
Kelburn Br *FAIRLIE* KA29 .... 139 L3
Kelburn Ct *LARGS* KA30 .... 115 J6
Kelburn Crs *KLMNK* KA1 .... 211 L5
Kelburne Dr *PSLY* PA1 .... 102 B4
Kelburne Gdns
  BAIL/MDB/MHD G69 .... 108 A6
  PSLY PA1 .... 9 M2
Kelburn Ov *PSLY* PA1 .... 9 M3
Kelburn St *BRHD/NEIL* G78 .... 125 G8
  GTCI KA28 .... 138 B6
Kelburn Ter *FAIRLIE* KA29 .... 139 K6
  PGL PA14 .... 34 F3
Kelhead Av
  CARD/HILL/MSPK G52 .... 102 F5
Kelhead Dr
  CARD/HILL/MSPK G52 .... 102 F4
Kelhead Pth
  CARD/HILL/MSPK G52 .... 102 F4
Kelhead Pl *PSLY* PA1 .... 102 F4
Kellas St *GOV/IBX* G51 .... 104 A2
Kellie Gv *EKILN* G74 .... 154 A6
Kellock Crs *CTBR* ML5 .... 109 K5
Kells Pl *DRUM* G15 .... 60 E5
Kelly St *GRNK* PA15 .... 2 B2
  GRNKW/INVK PA16 .... 32 D4
Kelso Av *BRWEIR* PA11 .... 98 C2
  PSLYS PA2 .... 101 G8
  RUTH G73 .... 129 H2
Kelso Crs *WISHAW* ML2 .... 159 H3
Kelso Dr *CARLUKE* ML8 .... 179 H8
  EKILN G74 .... 154 A6
Kelso Gdns
  BAIL/MDB/MHD G69 .... 66 F6
Kelso Pl *SCOT* G14 .... 80 F1
Kelso Qd *CTBR* ML5 .... 109 M1
Kelso St *KNTSWD* G13 .... 80 F1
  SCOT G14 .... 80 F1
Kelton St *CAR/SHTL* G32 .... 107 H5
Kelvin Av *CARD/HILL/MSPK* G52... .... 102 F1
  KLWNG KA13 .... 193 K5
Kelvin Ct *KKNTL* G66 .... 45 J8
Kelvin Crs *BSDN* G61 .... 61 M7
Kelvindale Gdns
  MRYH/FIRH G20 .... 82 D3
Kelvindale Pl *MRYH/FIRH* G20 .... 82 D3
Kelvindale Rd *KVD/HLHD* G12 .... 82 C4
Kelvin Dr *AIRDRIE* ML6 .... 89 H8
  BAIL/MDB/MHD G69 .... 66 E7
  BRHD/NEIL G78 .... 125 K8
  BSHPBGS G64 .... 63 M8
  EKILS G75 .... 15 H8
  KKNTL G66 .... 65 G1
  MRYH/FIRH G20 .... 82 D5
Kelvingrove St *KVGV* G3 .... 4 A8
Kelvinhaugh Ga *KVGV* G3 .... 104 D1
Kelvinhaugh Pl *KVCV* G3 .... 104 D1
Kelvinhaugh St *KVGV* G3 .... 104 D1
Kelvin Pk South *EKILS* G75 .... 172 A5
Kelvin Pl *EKILS* G75 .... 15 J8
Kelvin Rd *BLSH* ML4 .... 133 H2
  CUMB G67 .... 49 G1
  EKILS G75 .... 15 H7
  MLNGV G62 .... 41 L6
  UD/BTH/TAN G71 .... 131 L2
Kelvin Rd North *CUMB* G67 .... 69 G1
Kelvinside Av *MRYH/FIRH* G20 .... 4 C2
  MRYH/FIRH G20 .... 82 E5
Kelvinside Dr *MRYH/FIRH* G20 .... 4 B1
Kelvinside Gdns *MRYH/FIRH* G20... .... 4 B1
Kelvinside Gdns East
  MRYH/FIRH G20 .... 4 C2
Kelvinside Gardens La
  MRYH/FIRH G20 .... 4 B1
Kelvinside Ter South
  MRYH/FIRH G20 .... 4 A2
Kelvinside Ter West
  MRYH/FIRH G20 .... 4 A2
Kelvin St *CTBR* ML5 .... 110 C4
  LARGS KA30 .... 115 K5
Kelvinvale *KKNTL* G66 .... 45 K8
Kelvin Vw *BSHPBGS* G64 .... 64 C1
  KSYTH G65 .... 46 F7
Kelvin Wk *LARGS* KA30 .... 115 J3
Kelvin Wy *KKNTL* G66 .... 65 G1
  KVGV G3 .... 82 D8
Kemp Av *PSLYN/LNWD* PA3... .... 80 A8
Kempock Pl *GRK* PA19 .... 31 L1
Kempock St *DMNK/BRGTN* G40 .... 13 J8
  GRK PA19 .... 31 L1
Kempsthorn Cresent
  PLK/PH/NH G53 .... 103 G8
Kempsthorn Rd
  PLK/PH/NH G53 .... 103 G8
Kemp St *HMLTN* ML3 .... 156 D6
  SPRGB/BLRNK G21 .... 6 B1
Kenbank Crs *BRWEIR* PA11 .... 98 D1
Kenbank Rd *BRWEIR* PA11 .... 98 D1
Kendal Av *GIF/THBK* G46 .... 127 J6
  KVD/HLHD G12 .... 82 A3
Kendal Dr *EKILS* G75 .... 170 F3
Kendoon Av *DRUM* G15 .... 60 E6
Kenilburn Av *AIRDRIE* ML6 .... 89 H7
Kenilburn Crs *AIRDRIE* ML6 .... 89 H7
Kenilworth *EKILN* G74 .... 154 D5
Kenilworth Av *HBR/GL* G84 .... 23 G2
  PLKSD/SHW G41 .... 127 K1
  PSLYS PA2 .... 123 M1
  WISHAW ML2 .... 159 H6
Kenilworth Ct *CARLUKE* ML8 .... 178 E8
Kenilworth Crs *BLSH* ML4 .... 133 G3
  BSDN G61 .... 61 J3
  GRNKW/INVK PA16 .... 32 D6
  HMLTN ML3 .... 155 M5
Kenilworth Dr *AIRDRIE* ML6 .... 111 J1
  SALT KA21 .... 192 A7
Kenilworth Rd *KKNTL* G66 .... 65 L1
  LNK/LMHG ML11 .... 199 H5
Kenilworth Wy *CUMB* G67 .... 68 E1
Kenmar Gdns
  UD/BTH/TAN G71 .... 131 L1
Kenmar Rd *HMLTN* ML3 .... 156 B4
Kenmar Ter *HMLTN* ML3 .... 156 B4
Kenmore *TROON* KA10 .... 216 D5
Kenmore Av *PSTWK* KA9 .... 225 J3
Kenmore Dr *GRNKW/INVK* PA16... .... 32 A5
Kenmore Gdns *BSDN* G61 .... 62 B4
Kenmore Pl *GRNKW/INVK* PA16 .... 32 A5
Kenmore Rd *CUMB* G67 .... 49 H7
  KLMCLM PA13 .... 75 J2
Kenmore St *CAR/SHTL* G32 .... 107 G4
Kenmuiraid Pl *BLSH* ML4 .... 132 F6
Kenmuir Av *CAR/SHTL* G32 .... 107 L6
Kenmuirhill Rd *CAR/SHTL* G32 .... 107 K7
Kenmuir St *CTBR* ML5 .... 109 H5
Kenmure Av *BSHPBGS* G64 .... 63 L8
Kenmure Crs *BSHPBGS* G64 .... 63 M8
Kenmure Dr *BSHPBGS* G64 .... 63 M8
Kenmure Gdns *BSHPBGS* G64 .... 63 L8
Kenmure La *BSHPBGS* G64 .... 63 M8
Kenmure Rd *GIF/THBK* G46 .... 151 H3
Kenmure St *PLKSD/SHW* G41 .... 104 F5
Kenmure Vw *HWWD* PA9 .... 121 L4
Kenmure Wy *RUTH* G73 .... 129 H6
Kennedar Dr *GOV/IBX* G51 .... 103 L1
Kennedy Ct
  KLMNKN/STW KA3 .... 207 J6
Kennedy Dr *AIRDRIE* ML6 .... 110 F2
  HBR/GL G84 .... 20 D5
  KLMNKN/STW KA3 .... 207 J6
Kennedy Gdns *WISHAW* ML2... .... 177 H2
Kennedy Rd *SALT* KA21 .... 200 F1
  TROON KA10 .... 216 A7
Kennedy St *COWCAD* G4 .... 5 M7
  KLMNK KA1 .... 16 E8
  WISHAW ML2 .... 159 J6
Kennelburn Rd *AIRDRIE* ML6 .... 111 K8
Kenneth Rd *MTHW* ML1 .... 157 J4
Kennihill *AIRDRIE* ML6 .... 89 G8
Kennihill Qd *AIRDRIE* ML6 .... 89 G8
Kennishead Av *GIF/THBK* G46 .... 126 E4
Kennishead Pl *GIF/THBK* G46 .... 126 E4
Kennishead Rd
  GIF/THBK G46 .... 126 F5
Kennisholm Av *GIF/THBK* G46 .... 126 E4
Kennoway Dr *PTCK* G11 .... 81 M7
Kennyhill Sq *DEN/PKHD* G31 .... 7 H9
Ken Rd *KLMNK* KA1 .... 212 A4
Kensington Ga
  KVD/HLHD G12 .... 82 C5
Kensington Gate La
  KVD/HLHD G12 .... 82 C5
Kensington Rd *KVD/HLHD* G12 .... 82 C5
Kentallen Rd
  STPS/GTHM/RID G33 .... 107 K3
Kent Dr *HBR/GL* G84 .... 21 G6
  RUTH G73 .... 129 K4
Kentigern Ter *BSHPBGS* G64... .... 84 A1
Kentmere Cl *EKILS* G75 .... 171 K3
Kentmere Dr *EKILS* G75 .... 171 K3
Kentmere Pl *EKILS* G75 .... 170 F3
Kent Pl *EKILS* G75 .... 170 F3
Kent Rd *KVGV* G3 .... 4 B8
Kent St *CGLE* G1 .... 12 A4
Keppel Dr *LNPK/KPK* G44 .... 128 E2
Keppenburn Av *FAIRLIE* KA29 .... 139 L5
Keppochhill Dr *COWCAD* G4 .... 5 L3
Keppochhill Rd *COWCAD* G4 .... 5 K3
Keppoch St *SPRGB/BLRNK* G21 .... 5 M2
Kerelaw Av *SVSTN* KA20 .... 192 E7
Kerelaw Rd *SVSTN* KA20 .... 192 D8
Kerfield Pl *DRUM* G15 .... 60 E5
Kerr Av *SALT* KA21 .... 201 G1
Kerr Crs *HMLTN* ML3 .... 156 C8
Kerr Dr *DMNK/BRGTN* G40 .... 12 C6
  IRV KA12 .... 203 K7
  MTHW ML1 .... 157 J3
Kerrera Pl
  STPS/GTHM/RID G33 .... 107 K3
Kerrera Rd
  STPS/GTHM/RID G33 .... 107 K3
  UD/BTH/TAN G71 .... 132 A1
Kerrix Rd *PSTWK* KA9 .... 217 L8
Kerrmuir Av *KLMNK* KA1 .... 212 F4
Kerr Pl *DMNK/BRGTN* G40 .... 12 C6
  IRV KA12 .... 203 K7
Kerrs La *SALT* KA21 .... 200 E1
Kerr St *BLTYR/CAMB* G72 .... 155 L1
  BRHD/NEIL G78 .... 125 G6
  DMNK/BRGTN G40 .... 12 C6
  KKNTL G66 .... 65 J1
  PSLYN/LNWD PA3 .... 8 F2
Kerrycroy Av *GVH/MTFL* G42 .... 128 D1
Kerrycroy Pl *GVH/MTFL* G42 .... 128 D1
Kerrycroy St *GVH/MTFL* G42 .... 128 D1
Kerrydale St *DMNK/BRGTN* G40 .... 13 H7
Kerrylamont Av
  GVH/MTFL G42 .... 128 D2
Kerry Pl *DRUM* G15 .... 60 D6
Kerse Av *DALRY* KA24 .... 184 E2
Kersepark *AYRS* KA7 .... 229 G8
Kershaw St *WISHAW* ML2 .... 177 J3
Kersland Crs *KLMNK* KA1 .... 212 E3
Kersland Dr *MLNGV* G62 .... 42 B7
Kersland Gait
  KLMNKN/STW KA3 .... 197 L1
Kersland La *KVD/HLHD* G12 .... 82 D6
  MLNGV G62 .... 42 B7
Kersland Rd *GLGNK* KA14 .... 167 J3
Kersland St *KVD/HLHD* G12 .... 82 D6
Ker St *GRNK* PA15 .... 2 C1
Kerswinning Av *KBRN* KA25 .... 166 F2
Kessington Dr *BSDN* G61 .... 62 A5
Kessington Rd *BSDN* G61 .... 62 A6
Kessock Dr *PPK/MIL* G22 .... 5 H2
Kessock Pl *PPK/MIL* G22 .... 5 H2
Kestrel Ct *CLYDBK* G81 .... 60 A4
Kestrel Crs *GRNKW/INVK* PA16 .... 32 A4
Kestrel Pl *GRNKW/INVK* PA16 .... 32 A4
  JNSTN PA5 .... 122 D2
Kestrel Rd *KNTSWD* G13 .... 81 J3
Keswick Rd *EKILS* G75 .... 170 F3
Kethers La *MTHW* ML1 .... 157 H5
Kethers St *MTHW* ML1 .... 157 J5
Kevoc Cotts *RAYR/DAL* KA6 .... 226 A4
Kew Gdns *UD/BTH/TAN* G71 .... 132 B2
Kew La *KVD/HLHD* G12 .... 82 D6
Kew Ter *KVD/HLHD* G12 .... 82 D6
Keystone Av *MLNGV* G62 .... 62 A1
Keystone Qd *MLNGV* G62 .... 61 M1
Keystone Rd *MLNGV* G62 .... 62 A1
Kibbleston Rd *KLBCH* PA10 .... 99 G3
Kidsneuk *IRV* KA12 .... 203 G5
Kidsneuk Gdns *IRV* KA12 .... 203 G5
Kidston Dr *HBR/GL* G84 .... 20 A7
Kierhill Rd *BALLOCH* G68 .... 48 C7
Kilallan Av *BRWEIR* PA11 .... 76 D8
Kilallan Rd *CRG/CRSL/HOU* PA6 .... 75 M2
  CRG/CRSL/HOU PA6 .... 77 G5
Kilbarchan Rd *JNSTN* PA5 .... 98 F3
  JNSTN PA5 .... 99 K8
  KLBCH PA10 .... 99 J7
Kilbarchan St *GBLS* G5 .... 11 G6
Kilbeg Ter *GIF/THBK* G46 .... 126 D6
Kilberry St *SPRGB/BLRNK* G21 .... 6 C5
Kilbirnie St *GBLS* G5 .... 10 F7
Kilblain St *GRNK* PA15 .... 2 C3
Kilbowie Pl *AIRDRIE* ML6 .... 111 K4
Kilbowie Rd *CLYDBK* G81 .... 60 B8
  CUMB G67 .... 69 G1
Kilbrandon Crs *AYRS* KA7 .... 228 B7
Kilbrandon Wy *AYRS* KA7 .... 228 B7
Kilbrannan Av *SALT* KA21 .... 191 M7
Kilbrannan Dr
  GRNKW/INVK PA16 .... 32 B6
Kilbreck Gdns *BSDN* G61 .... 61 J1
Kilbrennan Dr *MTHW* ML1 .... 157 G2
Kilbrennan Rd
  PSLYN/LNWD PA3 .... 100 B3
Kilbride Dr *HBR/GL* G84 .... 20 E6
Kilbride St *GBLS* G5 .... 105 K7
Kilbride Vw
  UD/BTH/TAN G71 .... 132 A2
Kilburn Gv *BLTYR/CAMB* G72 .... 131 K8
Kilburn Pl *KNTSWD* G13 .... 81 H3
Kilburn Water *LARGS* KA30 .... 115 L2
Kilchattan Dr *LNPK/KPK* G44 .... 128 C2
Kilchattan Pl *WMYSB* PA18 .... 50 A7
Kilchoan Rd
  STPS/GTHM/RID G33 .... 85 J7
Kilcloy Av *DRUM* G15 .... 61 G5
Kilcreggan Vw *GRNK* PA15 .... 33 J8
Kildale Rd *LOCHW* PA12 .... 120 B7
Kildale Wy *RUTH* G73 .... 128 F1
Kildare Dr *LNK/LMHG* ML11... .... 199 H5
Kildare Rd *LNK/LMHG* ML11 .... 199 H5
Kildary Av *LNPK/KPK* G44 .... 128 A4
Kildary Rd *LNPK/KPK* G44 .... 128 A4
Kildermorie Rd *ESTRH* G34 .... 107 M1
Kildonan Ct *WISHAW* ML2 .... 159 M2
Kildonan Dr *HBR/GL* G84 .... 20 F7
  PTCK G11 .... 82 A7
Kildonan Pl *MTHW* ML1 .... 157 J1
  SALT KA21 .... 191 M7
Kildonan St *CTBR* ML5 .... 110 B2
Kildrostan St
  PLKSD/SHW G41 .... 104 F7
Kildrummy Pl *EKILN* G74 .... 153 K6
Kildrum Rd *CUMB* G67 .... 49 G7
Kilearn Rd *PSLYN/LNWD* PA3 .... 102 B2
Kilearn Wy *PSLYN/LNWD* PA3 .... 102 B2
Kilfinan Rd *SHOTTS* ML7 .... 137 K3
Kilfinan St *PPK/MIL* G22 .... 83 H2
Kilgarth St *CTBR* ML5 .... 109 H5
Kilgraston Rd *BRWEIR* PA11 .... 98 D3
Kilkerran Ct *NMRNS* G77 .... 150 B5
Kilkerran Dr
  STPS/GTHM/RID G33 .... 84 F3
  TROON KA10 .... 216 D2
Kilkerran Pk *NMRNS* G77 .... 150 B5
Kilkerran Wy *NMRNS* G77 .... 150 B5
Killearn Dr *PSLY* PA1 .... 102 F5
Killearn Rd *GRNK* PA15 .... 33 H1
Killearn St *PPK/MIL* G22 .... 5 K1
Killermont Av *BSDN* G61 .... 62 B7
Killermont Mdw
  UD/BTH/TAN G71 .... 131 L7
Killermont Pl *KLWNG* KA13 .... 193 H6
Killermont Rd *BSDN* G61 .... 61 M6
Killermont St *CGLE* G1 .... 5 J8
Killiegrew Rd *PLKSD/SHW* G41 .... 104 D7
Killin Pl *GRNKW/INVK* PA16 .... 32 A5
  TROON KA10 .... 216 D5
Killin St *CAR/SHTL* G32 .... 107 H6
Killoch Av *PSLYN/LNWD* PA3 .... 101 G4
Killoch Dr *BRHD/NEIL* G78 .... 125 K8
  KNTSWD G13 .... 81 G2
Killoch La *PSLYN/LNWD* PA3 .... 101 G4
Killoch Pl *IRVSE* KA11 .... 203 M5
Killoch Rd *IRVSE* KA11 .... 203 M5
Killoch Wy *IRVSE* KA11 .... 203 M5
  PSLYN/LNWD PA3 .... 101 G4
Kilmacolm Pl *GRNK* PA15 .... 33 J8
Kilmacolm Rd *BRWEIR* PA11 .... 76 B7
  CRG/CRSL/HOU PA6 .... 77 H6
  GRNK PA15 .... 3 H9
  PGL PA14 .... 54 F2
Kilmahew Av *DMBTN* G82 .... 24 A8
Kilmahew Ct *DMBTN* G82 .... 24 A8
Kilmahew Dr *DMBTN* G82 .... 24 A8
Kilmahew Gv *DMBTN* G82 .... 24 B8
Kilmahew St *ARD* KA22 .... 191 J8
Kilmailing Rd *LNPK/KPK* G44 .... 128 B4
Kilmair Pl *MRYH/FIRH* G20 .... 82 D4
Kilmaluag Ter *GIF/THBK* G46 .... 126 D6
Kilmany Dr *CAR/SHTL* G32 .... 106 F4
Kilmany Gdns *CAR/SHTL* G32 .... 106 F4
Kilmardinny Av *BSDN* G61 .... 62 A3
Kilmardinny Crs *BSDN* G61 .... 62 A3
Kilmardinny Dr *BSDN* G61 .... 62 A3
Kilmardinny Ga *BSDN* G61 .... 61 M4
Kilmardinny Gv *BSDN* G61 .... 61 M3
Kilmarnock Rd *CRH/DND* KA2 .... 206 A8
  CRH/DND KA2 .... 209 M7
  IRVSE KA11 .... 205 G7
  KLMNK KA1 .... 218 C8
  KLMNKN/STW KA3 .... 206 C2
  PLKSW/MSWD G43 .... 127 K3
  PSTWK KA9 .... 221 L4
  TROON KA10 .... 216 D3
Kilmartin Pl *GIF/THBK* G46 .... 126 E5
  UD/BTH/TAN G71 .... 109 G8
Kilmaurs Dr *GIF/THBK* G46 .... 127 L6
Kilmaurs Rd *CRH/DND* KA2 .... 205 L8
  KLMNKN/STW KA3 .... 206 F6
Kilmaurs St *GOV/IBX* G51 .... 103 M3
Kilmeny Crs *WISHAW* ML2 .... 159 J4
Kilmeny Ter *ARD* KA22 .... 191 K8
Kilmichael Av *WISHAW* ML2 .... 160 A3
Kilmorie Dr *RUTH* G73 .... 128 E2
Kilmory Av *UD/BTH/TAN* G71 .... 132 A2
Kilmory Ct *EKILS* G75 .... 171 H5
Kilmory Dr *NMRNS* G77 .... 150 E3
Kilmory Gdns *CARLUKE* ML8 .... 178 F6
Kilmory Rd *KLMNKN/STW* KA3 .... 206 E5
  TROON KA10 .... 216 F4
Kilmory Rd *CARLUKE* ML8 .... 189 H1
  SALT KA21 .... 191 M7
Kilmuir Crs *GIF/THBK* G46 .... 126 D5
Kilmuir Dr *GIF/THBK* G46 .... 126 E5
Kilmuir Rd *GIF/THBK* G46 .... 126 F5
  UD/BTH/TAN G71 .... 108 D8
Kilmun Rd *GRNK* PA15 .... 33 H1
Kilmun St *MRYH/FIRH* G20 .... 82 D2
Kilnbank Crs *AYRS* KA7 .... 229 K2
Kilnburn Rd *MTHW* ML1 .... 157 J2
Kilncadzow Rd *CARLUKE* ML8... .... 179 H8
Kilnford Crs *CRH/DND* KA2 .... 209 K7
Kilnford Dr *CRH/DND* KA2 .... 209 K7
Kilnholm St *NMLNS* KA16 .... 215 J2
Kilnside Rd *PSLY* PA1 .... 9 K3
Kilnwell Qd *MTHW* ML1 .... 157 K5
Kiloran Gv *NMRNS* G77 .... 150 A5
Kiloran Pl *NMRNS* G77 .... 150 A5
Kiloran St *GIF/THBK* G46 .... 126 F5
Kilpatrick Av *PSLYS* PA2 .... 8 B8
Kilpatrick Crs *PSLYS* PA2 .... 101 K8
Kilpatrick Dr *BSDN* G61 .... 61 J1
  EKILS G75 .... 171 H6
  ERSK PA8 .... 59 H7
  RNFRW PA4 .... 102 B1
Kilpatrick Gdns
  CRMNK/CLK/EAG G76 .... 151 K2
Kilpatrick Pl *IRVSE* KA11 .... 204 F3
Kilpatrick Vw *DMBTN* G82 .... 37 H5
Kilpatrick Wy
  UD/BTH/TAN G71 .... 132 A1
Kilrig Av *KLWNG* KA13 .... 193 L5
Kilruskin Dr *WKIL* KA23 .... 181 J6
Kilsyth Crs *IRVSE* KA11 .... 204 A6
Kilsyth Rd *KKNTL* G66 .... 45 K8
  KSYTH G65 .... 46 E2
Kiltarie Crs *AIRDRIE* ML6 .... 111 M3
Kiltearn Rd
  STPS/GTHM/RID G33 .... 107 M2
Kilvaxter Dr *GIF/THBK* G46 .... 126 E6
Kilwinning Crs *HMLTN* ML3 .... 155 L8
Kilwinning Rd *DALRY* KA24 .... 184 B3
  IRV KA12 .... 203 H5
  KLMNKN/STW KA3 .... 197 J1
  SVSTN KA20 .... 192 E8
Kimberley Gdns *EKILS* G75 .... 14 A6
Kimberley St *CLYDBK* G81 .... 59 K4
  WISHAW ML2 .... 159 L1
Kinalty Rd *PLKSW/MSWD* G43 .... 128 A4
Kinarvie Crs *PLK/PH/NH* G53 .... 125 M2
Kinarvie Pl *PLK/PH/NH* G53 .... 125 M2
Kinarvie Rd *PLK/PH/NH* G53 .... 125 M2

Kinarvie Ter PLK/PH/NH G53 ..... 125 M2
Kinbuck St PPK/MIL G22 ..... 5 L1
Kincaid Ct KKNTL G66 ..... 29 J8
Kincaid Fld KKNTL G66 ..... 45 J4
Kincaid Gdns BLTYR/CAMB G72 ..... 130 A3
Kincaidston Dr AYRS KA7 ..... 229 J7
Kincaid St GRNKW/INVK PA16 ..... 32 B1
Kincaid Wy KKNTL G66 ..... 45 H4
Kincardine Dr BSHPBGS G64 ..... 84 B1
Kincardine Pl EKILN G74 ..... 154 C6
  SPRGB/BLRNK G21 ..... 84 C2
Kincardine Sq
  STPS/GTHM/RID G33 ..... 85 K8
Kincath Av RUTH G73 ..... 129 J6
Kinclaven Av DRUM G15 ..... 61 G6
Kincraig St GOV/IBX G51 ..... 103 K3
Kinellan Rd BSDN G61 ..... 61 M8
Kinellar Dr SCOT G14 ..... 81 H4
Kinfauns Dr DRUM G15 ..... 60 F6
  DRUM G15 ..... 61 J6
  NMRNS G77 ..... 150 F4
Kingarth La GVH/MTFL G42 ..... 105 G7
Kingarth St HMLTN ML3 ..... 174 D1
  PLKSD/SHW G41 ..... 105 G7
Kingcase Av PSTWK KA9 ..... 225 H3
King Edward La KNTSWD G13 ..... 81 L4
King Edward Rd
  KNTSWD G13 ..... 81 M4
King Edward St ALEX/LLW G83 ..... 25 L3
Kingfisher Dr KNTSWD G13 ..... 80 F2
King George Dr RNFRW PA4 ..... 80 E8
King George Gdns
  RNFRW PA4 ..... 80 E7
King George Park Av
  RNFRW PA4 ..... 80 E8
King George Pl RNFRW PA4 ..... 80 E8
King George Wy RNFRW PA4 ..... 80 E8
Kinghorn Dr LNPK/KPK G44 ..... 128 C3
Kinglas Rd BSDN G61 ..... 61 J7
King Pl BAIL/MDB/MHD G69 ..... 109 G4
Kingsacre Rd LNPK/KPK G44 ..... 128 C2
  RUTH G73 ..... 128 C2
Kingsbarns Dr LNPK/KPK G44 ..... 128 B2
Kingsborough Gdns
  KVD/HLHD G12 ..... 82 B5
Kingsborough Ga
  KVD/HLHD G12 ..... 82 B6
Kingsborough La
  KVD/HLHD G12 ..... 82 B6
Kingsborough La East
  KVD/HLHD G12 ..... 82 B6
Kingsbrae Av LNPK/KPK G44 ..... 128 C2
Kingsbridge Crs LNPK/KPK G44 ..... 128 D3
Kingsbridge Dr
  LNPK/KPK G44 ..... 128 C3
  RUTH G73 ..... 128 C3
Kingsburgh Dr PSLY PA1 ..... 102 B4
Kingsburn Dr RUTH G73 ..... 129 G3
Kingsburn Gv RUTH G73 ..... 129 G3
Kingscliffe Av LNPK/KPK G44 ..... 128 C2
Kings Ct AYR KA8 ..... 19 G1
  BEITH KA15 ..... 144 B8
Kingscourt Av
  LNPK/KPK G44 ..... 128 C3
King's Crs BLTYR/CAMB G72 ..... 130 B4
  CARLUKE ML8 ..... 179 G7
  HBR/GL 20 E8
  JNSTN PA5 ..... 100 C6
  NMLNS KA16 ..... 215 K2
Kingscroft Rd PSTWK KA9 ..... 225 H2
Kingsdale Av LNPK/KPK G44 ..... 128 C2
King's Dr BALLOCH G68 ..... 48 F3
  DMNK/BRGTN G40 ..... 12 A8
  MTHW ML1 ..... 133 M4
  NMRNS G77 ..... 150 F6
Kingsdyke Av LNPK/KPK G44 ..... 128 D2
Kingsford Av LNPK/KPK G44 ..... 127 L5
Kingsford Ct NMRNS G77 ..... 150 B3
King's Gdns NMRNS G77 ..... 151 G6
Kingsheath Av RUTH G73 ..... 128 C3
Kingshill Av BALLOCH G68 ..... 47 L8
Kingshill Dr LNPK/KPK G44 ..... 128 C3
Kingshill Rd SHOTTS ML7 ..... 161 G1
Kingshill Vw CARLUKE ML8 ..... 178 A5
Kingshouse Av LNPK/KPK G44 ..... 128 C3
Kingshurst Av LNPK/KPK G44 ..... 128 C3
King's Inch Rd RNFRW PA4 ..... 80 F5
Kingsknowe Dr RUTH G73 ..... 128 E3
Kingsland Dr
  CARD/HILL/MSPK G52 ..... 103 H3
Kingslea Rd CRG/CRSL/HOU PA6 ..... 77 H7
Kingsley Av GVH/MTFL G42 ..... 105 H8
Kingsley Ct UD/BTH/TAN G71 ..... 132 A2
Kingslynn Dr LNPK/KPK G44 ..... 128 D3
Kings Myre LNK/LMHG ML11 ..... 199 H5
Kings Pk BSHPBGS G64 ..... 44 C8
King's Park Av LNPK/KPK G44 ..... 128 B3
  RUTH G73 ..... 128 C3
King's Park Rd LNPK/KPK G44 ..... 128 B3
King's Pl PPK/MIL G22 ..... 83 H3
King's Rd BEITH KA15 ..... 144 B8
  JNSTN PA5 ..... 100 B7
Kingston Av AIRDRIE ML6 ..... 111 J2
  BRHD/NEIL PA 148 D3
  UD/BTH/TAN G71 ..... 132 A1
Kingston Gv BSHPTN PA7 ..... 58 B6
Kingston Pl CLYDBK G81 ..... 59 J5
Kingston Rd BRHD/NEIL PA 148 C4
  BSHPTN PA7 ..... 58 C5
King St AYR KA8 ..... 19 G1
  CGLE 11 K4
  CLYDBK G81 ..... 80 D1
  CTBR ML5 ..... 109 L3
  DMBTN G82 ..... 25 K8
  CRK PA19 ..... 31 L2
  GRNK PA15 ..... 2 D4
  HMLTN ML3 ..... 155 M5
  KLMNK KA1 ..... 16 F1
  KLWNG KA13 ..... 193 L5
  KSYTH G65 ..... 47 K1
  LRKH ML9 ..... 176 A6
  NMLNS KA16 ..... 215 K2
  PGL PA14 ..... 34 C7
  PSLY PA1 ..... 8 C3
  RUTH G73 ..... 129 G1
  SHOTTS ML7 ..... 137 L4
  WISHAW ML2 ..... 159 H7

WISHAW ML2 ..... 159 M4
King St East HBR/GL G84 ..... 20 D8
King Street La RUTH G73 ..... 129 G1
King's Vw BALLOCH G68 ..... 48 F3
King's Wy DMBTN G82 ..... 36 C4
Kingsway DALRY KA24 ..... 184 A1
  EKILN G74 ..... 15 K5
  CRK PA19 ..... 31 K3
  KKNTL G66 ..... 46 B7
  SCOT G14 ..... 81 H4
Kingsway Ct SCOT G14 ..... 81 H4
Kingswell Av KLMNKN/STW KA3.. 207 G4
Kingswood Dr LNPK/KPK G44 ..... 128 C3
Kingswood Rd BSHPTN PA7 ..... 57 M5
Kingussie Dr LNPK/KPK G44 ..... 128 C3
Kiniver Dr DRUM G15 ..... 61 G8
Kinkell Gdns KKNTL G66 ..... 46 B7
Kinloch Av BLTYR/CAMB G72 ..... 130 B5
  PSLYN/LNWD PA3 ..... 100 A4
Kinloch Dr MTHW ML1 ..... 133 K7
Kinloch Rd KLMNK KA1 ..... 212 A4
  NMRNS G77 ..... 150 C3
  RNFRW PA4 ..... 80 B8
Kinloch St DMNK/BRGTN G40 ..... 13 J7
Kinloch Ter GRNKW/INVK PA16 ..... 31 L6
Kinloss Pl EKILN G74 ..... 15 H1
Kinmount Av LNPK/KPK G44 ..... 128 B2
Kinnaird Av NMRNS G77 ..... 151 G4
Kinnaird Crs BSDN G61 ..... 62 B4
Kinnaird Dr PSLYN/LNWD PA3 ..... 100 A3
Kinnaird Pl BSHPBGS G64 ..... 84 B1
Kinnear Rd DMNK/BRGTN G40 ..... 13 G9
Kinneil Pl HMLTN ML3 ..... 155 M7
Kinnell Av
  CARD/HILL/MSPK G52 ..... 103 J6
Kinnell Crs
  CARD/HILL/MSPK G52 ..... 103 J6
Kinnell Pl CARD/HILL/MSPK G52 .. 103 K6
Kinnier Rd SALT KA21 ..... 201 G1
Kinning St GBLS G5 ..... 10 D5
Kinnis Vennel KLWNG KA13 ..... 193 J4
Kinnoul La KVD/HLHD G12 ..... 82 C6
Kinnoull Pl BLTYR/CAMB G72 ..... 155 K2
Kinnoull Rd KLMNK KA1 ..... 212 A6
Kinpurnie Rd PSLY PA1 ..... 102 D4
Kinross Av
  CARD/HILL/MSPK G52 ..... 103 H5
  PGL PA14 ..... 34 C8
Kinross Pk EKILN G74 ..... 154 D6
Kinsail Dr
  CARD/HILL/MSPK G52 ..... 102 F3
Kinstone Av SCOT G14 ..... 81 G4
Kintessack Pl BSHPBGS G64 ..... 64 D7
Kintillo Dr KNTSWD G13 ..... 81 H3
Kintore Pk HMLTN ML3 ..... 174 B2
Kintore Rd PLKSW/MSWD G43 ..... 127 M3
Kintra St GOV/IBX G51 ..... 104 B2
Kintyre Av PSLYN/LNWD PA3 ..... 100 A5
Kintyre Crs AIRDRIE ML6 ..... 89 M6
  NMRNS G77 ..... 150 C3
Kintyre Gdns KKNTL G66 ..... 46 B7
Kintyre Rd BLTYR/CAMB G72 ..... 155 J1
Kintyre St SPRGB/BLRNK G21 ..... 6 E7
Kintyre Ter GRNKW/INVK PA16 ..... 31 K6
Kip Av GRNKW/INVK PA16 ..... 50 D5
Kipland Wk CTBR ML5 ..... 110 D4
Kippen Dr
  CRMNK/CLK/EAG G76 ..... 152 B4
Kippen St AIRDRIE ML6 ..... 110 D3
  PPK/MIL G22 ..... 83 K3
Kipperoch Rd DMBTN G82 ..... 36 A2
Kippford Pl AIRDRIE ML6 ..... 111 M8
Kippford St CAR/SHTL G32 ..... 107 J5
Kipps Av AIRDRIE ML6 ..... 110 E1
Kirkaig Av RNFRW PA4 ..... 80 F7
Kirkbean Av RUTH G73 ..... 129 G5
Kirkbriggs Gdns RUTH G73 ..... 129 H4
Kirkburn Av BLTYR/CAMB G72 ..... 130 A5
Kirkburn Dr CMPF/LLE G63 ..... 27 J6
Kirkcaldy Rd PLKSD/SHW G41 ..... 104 D7
Kirkconnel Av BALLOCH G68 ..... 47 L8
  KNTSWD G13 ..... 80 F3
Kirkconnel Dr RUTH G73 ..... 128 F4
Kirk Crs OLDK G60 ..... 59 G2
Kirkcudbright Pl EKILN G74 ..... 154 D5
Kirkdale Dr
  CARD/HILL/MSPK G52 ..... 103 L5
Kirkdene Av NMRNS G77 ..... 151 H4
Kirkdene Bank NMRNS G77 ..... 151 H4
Kirkdene Crs NMRNS G77 ..... 151 H4
Kirkdene Gv NMRNS G77 ..... 151 H4
Kirkdene Pl NMRNS G77 ..... 151 H4
Kirkfieldbank Brae
  LNK/LMHG ML11 ..... 198 D5
Kirkfield Bank Wy
  HMLTN ML3 ..... 156 A6
Kirkfield Rd LNK/LMHG ML11 ..... 198 D6
  UD/BTH/TAN G71 ..... 132 A6
Kirkfield Wynd HWWD PA9 ..... 121 L4
Kirkford Rd
  BAIL/MDB/MHD G69 ..... 66 E7
Kirkgate IRV KA12 ..... 203 J7
  SALT KA21 ..... 200 F2
  WISHAW ML2 ..... 159 M5
Kirk Glebe KLMNKN/STW KA3 ..... 197 K1
Kirkhall Gdns ARD KA22 ..... 191 K7
Kirkhall Rd MTHW ML1 ..... 134 D5
Kirkhill Av BLTYR/CAMB G72 ..... 130 A6
Kirkhill Crs BRHD/NEIL G78 ..... 148 E1
  PSTWK KA9 ..... 225 H3
Kirkhill Dr MRYH/FIRH G20 ..... 82 D4
Kirkhill Gdns BLTYR/CAMB G72 ... 130 A6
Kirkhill Ga NMRNS G77 ..... 151 H5
Kirkhill Pl BLTYR/CAMB G72 ..... 130 A6
  MRYH/FIRH G20 ..... 82 D4
  WISHAW ML2 ..... 158 C7
Kirkhill Rd BAIL/MDB/MHD G69 .. 86 F4
  NMRNS G77 ..... 151 H4
  UD/BTH/TAN G71 ..... 131 L1
  WISHAW ML2 ..... 158 C8
Kirkhill St WISHAW ML2 ..... 158 D8
Kirkholm Av AYR KA8 ..... 225 G5
Kirkhope Dr DRUM G15 ..... 61 H7
Kirkhouse Av CMPF/LLE G63 ..... 27 H5
Kirkhouse Crs CMPF/LLE G63 ..... 27 J5
Kirkhouse Rd CMPF/LLE G63 ..... 27 H5

Kirkinner Rd CAR/SHTL G32 ..... 107 K6
Kirkintilloch Rd BSHPBGS G64 ..... 83 M1
  KKNTL G66 ..... 45 G7
  KKNTL G66 ..... 65 K2
  KKNTL G66 ..... 66 B1
Kirkland Av CMPF/LLE G63 ..... 27 J5
Kirkland Ct DALRY KA24 ..... 184 A2
Kirkland Gdns
  KLMNKN/STW KA3 ..... 206 C3
Kirkland Gv JNSTN PA5 ..... 99 M6
Kirklandhom PSTWK KA9 ..... 225 J3
Kirkland La ALEX/LLW G83 ..... 25 M6
Kirklandneuk Rd RNFRW PA4 ..... 80 A5
Kirkland Rd GLGNK KA14 ..... 167 H2
Kirklands Crs KSYTH G65 ..... 47 K2
  UD/BTH/TAN G71 ..... 132 A6
Kirklands Pl NMRNS G77 ..... 150 D7
Kirkland St MRYH/FIRH G20 ..... 4 D2
  MTHW ML1 ..... 157 K2
Kirkland Ter IRVSE KA11 ..... 204 F7
Kirk La BLSH ML4 ..... 61 L4
  PLKSW/MSWD G43 ..... 127 J2
Kirklea Gdns
  PSLYN/LNWD PA3 ..... 101 G4
Kirkle Dr NMRNS G77 ..... 151 G4
Kirklee Circ KVD/HLHD G12 ..... 82 C5
  KVD/HLHD G12 ..... 82 D5
Kirklee Gdns KVD/HLHD G12 ..... 82 C5
Kirklee Gardens La
  KVD/HLHD G12 ..... 82 C5
Kirklee Pl KVD/HLHD G12 ..... 82 D5
Kirklee Qd KVD/HLHD G12 ..... 82 D5
Kirklee Quadrant La
  KVD/HLHD G12 ..... 82 D5
Kirklee Rd BLSH ML4 ..... 133 K5
  KVD/HLHD G12 ..... 82 C5
  MTHW ML1 ..... 133 L8
Kirklee Ter KVD/HLHD G12 ..... 82 C5
Kirklee Terrace La
  KVD/HLHD G12 ..... 82 C5
Kirklee Terrace Rd
  KVD/HLHD G12 ..... 82 C5
Kirkliston St CAR/SHTL G32 ..... 106 F3
Kirkmichael Gdns PTCK G11 ..... 82 A6
Kirkmichael Rd HBR/GL G84 ..... 20 F8
Kirkmuir Dr RUTH G73 ..... 129 H6
Kirkness St AIRDRIE ML6 ..... 111 G1
Kirknethan WISHAW ML2 ..... 158 C8
Kirknewton St
  CAR/SHTL G32 ..... 107 H3
Kirkoswald EKILN G74 ..... 154 D6
Kirkoswald Dr CLYDBK G81 ..... 60 D6
Kirkoswald Rd MTHW ML1 ..... 134 C5
  PLKSW/MSWD G43 ..... 127 K3
Kirkpatrick St
  DMNK/BRGTN G40 ..... 12 E7
Kirk Pl BSDN G61 ..... 61 L4
  CUMB G67 ..... 68 A2
Kirk Port AYR KA7 ..... 18 F3
Kirkport MAUCH/CAT KA5 ..... 223 M6
Kirkriggs Av RUTH G73 ..... 129 H4
Kirk Rd BEITH KA15 ..... 168 C1
  BSDN G61 ..... 61 L4
  CARLUKE ML8 ..... 178 E7
  CRG/CRSL/HOU PA6 ..... 77 H6
  CRMNK/CLK/EAG G76 ..... 152 D2
  LRKH ML9 ..... 177 H7
  MTHW ML1 ..... 134 D2
  SHOTTS ML7 ..... 137 M5
  WISHAW ML2 ..... 159 K6
Kirkshaws Av CTBR ML5 ..... 109 L6
Kirkshaws Pl CTBR ML5 ..... 109 M6
Kirkshaws Rd CTBR ML5 ..... 109 L6
Kirkstall Gdns BSHPBGS G64 ..... 64 B5
Kirkstone Cl EKILS G75 ..... 170 F3
Kirk St CARLUKE ML8 ..... 178 E8
  CTBR ML5 ..... 109 M3
  MLNGV G62 ..... 41 L7
  MTHW ML1 ..... 157 L2
  PSTWK KA9 ..... 221 J7
Kirkstyle Av CARLUKE ML8 ..... 178 E8
Kirkstyle Crs AIRDRIE ML6 ..... 89 M1
  BRHD/NEIL G78 ..... 148 D2
Kirkstyle La BRHD/NEIL G78 ..... 148 E2
Kirkstyle Pl AIRDRIE ML6 ..... 88 D5
Kirksyde Av KKNTL G66 ..... 65 K2
Kirkton ERSK PA8 ..... 59 G6
Kirkton Av BLTYR/CAMB G72 ..... 155 J4
  BRHD/NEIL G78 ..... 148 E3
  CARLUKE ML8 ..... 178 E8
  KNTSWD G13 ..... 80 F3
  WKIL KA23 ..... 181 K5
Kirkton Ct CARLUKE ML8 ..... 178 E8
Kirkton Crs CTBR ML5 ..... 110 C5
  DMBTN G82 ..... 24 A8
  KKNTL G66 ..... 45 J4
  KNTSWD G13 ..... 81 G3
Kirktonfield Rd BRHD/NEIL G78.. 148 E2
Kirkton Ga IRV KA12 ..... 14 F2
Kirkton Ga EKILN G74 ..... 14 D2
Kirktonholme Crs EKILN G74 ..... 14 A2
Kirktonholme Rd EKILN G74 ..... 14 A3
  EKILN G74 ..... 153 H7
Kirkton Pk EKILN G74 ..... 15 H2
Kirkton Pl CTBR ML5 ..... 110 C5
  EKILN G74 ..... 15 H2
Kirkton Rd BLTYR/CAMB G72 ..... 130 B4
  BRHD/NEIL G78 ..... 148 E3
  DMBTN G82 ..... 35 G1
  DMBTN G82 ..... 36 D7
  KLMNKN/STW KA3 ..... 206 C3
  KLMNKN/STW KA3 ..... 206 F4
Kirktonside BRHD/NEIL G78 ..... 125 H8
Kirkton St CARLUKE ML8 ..... 178 F8
Kirkvale Ct NMRNS G77 ..... 151 H4
Kirkvale Crs NMRNS G77 ..... 151 H4
Kirkvale Dr NMRNS G77 ..... 151 H4
Kirkvale Vennel IRV KA12 ..... 203 J7
Kirk Vw BEITH KA15 ..... 144 B8
Kirkview CUMB G67 ..... 68 A3
Kirkview Av SHOTTS ML7 ..... 113 J7
Kirkview Crs NMRNS G77 ..... 150 E6

Kirkview Gdns
  UD/BTH/TAN G71 ..... 131 L1
Kirkville Pl DRUM G15 ..... 61 H8
Kirkwall CUMB G67 ..... 49 H4
Kirkwall Av BLTYR/CAMB G72 ..... 131 J6
Kirkwall Rd GRNKW/INVK PA16 ... 31 M6
Kirkwell Rd LNPK/KPK G44 ..... 128 B4
Kirkwood Av CLYDBK G81 ..... 60 E8
Kirkwood Pl CTBR ML5 ..... 109 L5
  GOV/IBX G51 ..... 104 C1
  RUTH G73 ..... 129 G1
Kirn Dr GRK PA19 ..... 31 J3
Kirn Rd KLMNKN/STW KA3 ..... 206 C3
Kirn St MRYH/FIRH G20 ..... 82 C1
Kirriemuir EKILN G74 ..... 154 D4
Kirriemuir Av
  CARD/HILL/MSPK G52 ..... 103 J6
Kirriemuir Gdns BSHPBGS G64 ... 64 C7
Kirriemuir Pl
  CARD/HILL/MSPK G52 ..... 103 J5
Kirriemuir Rd BSHPBGS G64 ..... 64 C8
Kirstie Pl ALEX/LLW G83 ..... 25 M7
Kirtle Dr RNFRW PA4 ..... 80 E7
Kirtle Pl EKILS G75 ..... 170 E2
Kishorn Pl STPS/GTHM/RID G33... 85 J8
Kishorn Rd WMYSB PA18 ..... 70 A1
Kitchener St WISHAW ML2 ..... 159 H5
Kittoch Pl EKILN G74 ..... 15 G2
Kittochside Rd
  CRMNK/CLK/EAG G76 ..... 152 E2
Kittoch St EKILN G74 ..... 14 F2
Kittyhaw Rd DALRY KA24 ..... 184 A2
Klondike Ct MTHW ML1 ..... 134 B6
Knapdale St PPK/MIL G22 ..... 83 G2
Knightsbridge St KNTSWD G13 ... 81 K3
Knightscliffe Av KNTSWD G13 .... 81 K2
Knights Ga UD/BTH/TAN G71 ..... 131 L4
Knightswood Rd KNTSWD G13 ... 81 K1
Knightswood Ter
  BLTYR/CAMB G72 ..... 131 L8
Knivysbridge Pl BLSH ML4 ..... 132 F6
Knockbuckle Av
  KLMCLM PA13 ..... 55 H8
Knockbuckle Rd KLMCLM PA13 .. 75 H1
Knockburnie Rd
  UD/BTH/TAN G71 ..... 132 A5
Knockhall St
  STPS/GTHM/RID G33 ..... 85 K7
Knockhill Dr LNPK/KPK G44 ..... 128 B2
Knockhill Rd RNFRW PA4 ..... 80 B8
Knockinlaw Rd
  KLMNKN/STW KA3 ..... 206 E5
Knockmarloch Dr KLMNK KA1 ... 211 M6
Knocknair St PGL PA14 ..... 54 E1
Knockrivoch Gdns ARD KA22 ..... 191 L5
Knockrivoch Pl ARD KA22 ..... 191 L5
Knockrivoch Wynd ARD KA22 .... 191 L5
Knockside Av PSLYS PA2 ..... 124 C2
Knoll Pk AYRS KA7 ..... 228 F6
Knollpark Dr
  CRMNK/CLK/EAG G76 ..... 151 K2
Knowe Crs MTHW ML1 ..... 134 D5
Knowehead Dr
  UD/BTH/TAN G71 ..... 131 L3
Knowehead Gdns
  PLKSD/SHW G41 ..... 10 C9
  UD/BTH/TAN G71 ..... 131 L3
Knowehead Rd KKNTL G66 ..... 28 F5
  KLMNK KA1 ..... 211 M5
  KLMNK KA1 ..... 212 F4
  KLMNK KA1 ..... 213 G4
  WISHAW ML2 ..... 159 J7
Knowehead Ter
  PLKSD/SHW G41 ..... 10 B9
Knoweholm AYRS KA7 ..... 228 C7
Knowenoble St MTHW ML1 ..... 135 H7
Knowe Rd BAIL/MDB/MHD G69 ... 86 C1
  GRNK PA15 ..... 3 H6
  PSLYN/LNWD PA3 ..... 102 B2
Knowes Av NMRNS G77 ..... 150 E4
Knowes Rd NMRNS G77 ..... 150 F4
Knowe St MLNGV G62 ..... 41 M7
Knowetap St MRYH/FIRH G20 ..... 82 E2
The Knowe TROON KA10 ..... 216 F2
Knowetop Av MTHW ML1 ..... 157 M4
Knowetop Crs DMBTN G82 ..... 36 C4
Knox Av BRWEIR PA11 ..... 98 C2
Knoxland Sq DMBTN G82 ..... 37 G6
Knox Pl NMRNS G77 ..... 150 B5
  SALT KA21 ..... 192 A8
Knoxville Rd KBRN KA25 ..... 143 H8
Kronborg Wy EKILS G75 ..... 171 L4
Kyleakin Dr
  BLTYR/CAMB G72 ..... 131 L7
Kyleakin Rd GIF/THBK G46 ..... 126 D6
Kyleakin Ter GIF/THBK G46 ..... 126 D6
Kyle Av IRVSE KA11 ..... 204 F7
Kyle Crs RAYR/DAL KA6 ..... 231 H4
  TROON KA10 ..... 217 G5
Kyle Dr GIF/THBK G46 ..... 127 L6
  TROON KA10 ..... 216 D4
Kyle Gv MTHW ML1 ..... 134 A6
Kylemore Crs MTHW ML1 ..... 133 K7
  MTHW ML1 ..... 133 K8
Kylemore Ter GRNKW/INVK PA16. 31 K6
Kylepark Av UD/BTH/TAN G71 .... 131 K3
Kylepark Crs UD/BTH/TAN G71 ... 131 K2
Kylepark Dr UD/BTH/TAN G71 .... 131 K2
Kyle Qd WISHAW ML2 ..... 158 E8
Kylerhea Rd GIF/THBK G46 ..... 126 D6
Kyle Rd CUMB G67 ..... 49 H7
  IRV KA12 ..... 208 B1
Kyleshill SALT KA21 ..... 200 F2
Kyle Sq CSMK G45 ..... 128 E4
The Kyles WMYSB PA18 ..... 70 A1
Kyle St AYRS KA7 ..... 18 F4
  COWCAD G4 ..... 5 L7
  MTHW ML1 ..... 157 H2
  PSTWK KA9 ..... 225 J1
Kyles Vw LARGS KA30 ..... 115 L5
Kyle Ter DMBTN G82 ..... 36 B5

L

La Belle Allee KVGV G3 ..... 4 B7
La Belle Pl KVGV G3 ..... 4 B7
Laberge Gdns MTHW ML1 ..... 134 B6
Laburnum Av BEITH KA15 ..... 168 A1
  EKILS G75 ..... 171 J3
Laburnum Ct EKILS G75 ..... 14 B9
Laburnum Crs WISHAW ML2 ..... 159 H4
Laburnum Dr KKNTL G66 ..... 45 H4
Laburnum Gdns KKNTL G66 ..... 65 H4
Laburnum Gv CTBR ML5 ..... 110 B3
Laburnum Lea HMLTN ML3 ..... 156 E8
Laburnum Pl JNSTN PA5 ..... 123 G1
Laburnum Rd AYRS KA7 ..... 19 K7
  CUMB G67 ..... 49 K7
  KLMNK KA1 ..... 211 J2
  PLKSD/SHW G41 ..... 104 C5
  UD/BTH/TAN G71 ..... 109 J8
Laburnum St GRNK PA15 ..... 33 M7
Lachlan Crs ERSK PA8 ..... 58 E8
Lacy St PSLY PA1 ..... 9 M3
Ladder Ct EKILS G75 ..... 171 H5
Lade Ct LOCHW PA12 ..... 120 C7
Ladeside KLMNKN/STW KA3 ..... 206 C2
  NMLNS KA16 ..... 215 L2
Ladeside Cl NMRNS G77 ..... 150 C3
Ladeside Ct KBRN KA25 ..... 143 G8
Ladeside Dr JNSTN PA5 ..... 99 K7
Ladeside Rd KLMNKN/STW KA3 .. 206 C3
Lade Ter CARD/HILL/MSPK G52 ... 103 G5
The Lade ALEX/LLW G83 ..... 25 M4
Ladhope Pl KNTSWD G13 ..... 80 E1
Ladyacre KLWNG KA13 ..... 193 L5
Ladyacre Rd LNK/LMHG ML11 ..... 199 H5
Ladyacres RNFRW PA4 ..... 79 K3
Ladyacres Wy RNFRW PA4 ..... 79 K3
Lady Ann Crs AIRDRIE ML6 ..... 111 J5
Lady Anne St SCOT G14 ..... 80 F4
Ladybank BALLOCH G68 ..... 48 F3
Ladybank Ct EKILN G74 ..... 14 F2
Ladybank Dr
  CARD/HILL/MSPK G52 ..... 103 L5
Ladybank Gdns EKILN G74 ..... 14 F2
Ladybank Pl EKILN G74 ..... 14 F2
Ladyburn Ct IRVSE KA11 ..... 203 M3
Ladyburn St GRNK PA15 ..... 3 M9
  PSLY PA1 ..... 9 L4
Ladyford Av KLWNG KA13 ..... 193 L6
Ladyhill Dr
  BAIL/MDB/MHD G69 ..... 108 A5
Lady Isle Crs UD/BTH/TAN G71 ... 131 L3
Lady Jane Ga UD/BTH/TAN G71 ... 131 L5
Ladykirk Crs
  CARD/HILL/MSPK G52 ..... 103 H3
  PSLYS PA2 ..... 9 K7
Ladykirk Dr
  CARD/HILL/MSPK G52 ..... 103 H3
Ladyland Dr KBRN KA25 ..... 143 H6
Lady La PSLY PA1 ..... 8 F5
Ladyloan Av DRUM G15 ..... 60 F5
Ladyloan Ct DRUM G15 ..... 60 F5
Ladyloan Gdns DRUM G15 ..... 60 F5
Lady Margaret Dr TROON KA10 .. 217 G7
Ladymuir Cir ERSK PA8 ..... 58 F8
Ladymuir Crs PLK/PH/NH G53 .... 103 J7
Lady's Ga ALEX/LLW G83 ..... 25 M8
Ladysmith Av KLBCH PA10 ..... 99 J7
Ladysmith Rd KBRN KA25 ..... 143 G8
Ladysmith St WISHAW ML2 ..... 158 C6
Ladyton ALEX/LLW G83 ..... 25 M6
Ladyton Dr GLSTN KA4 ..... 214 B3
Lady Watson Gdns
  HMLTN ML3 ..... 156 A7
Ladywell St COWCAD G4 ..... 12 B1
Ladywell Rd MTHW ML1 ..... 157 H3
Lady Wilson St AIRDRIE ML6 ..... 111 K3
Ladywood MLNGV G62 ..... 42 B7
Lagan Rd CARLUKE ML8 ..... 178 F8
Laggan Qd AIRDRIE ML6 ..... 88 E8
Laggan Rd AIRDRIE ML6 ..... 88 E8
  BSHPBGS G64 ..... 64 B8
  NMRNS G77 ..... 150 D2
  PLKSW/MSWD G43 ..... 127 L4
Laggan Ter RNFRW PA4 ..... 80 B5
Laidlaw Av MTHW ML1 ..... 133 M6
Laidlaw Gdns
  UD/BTH/TAN G71 ..... 108 F8
Laidlaw St GBLS G5 ..... 10 E6
Laidon Rd AIRDRIE ML6 ..... 88 E8
Laighcartside St JNSTN PA5 ..... 100 A6
Laigh Ct BEITH KA15 ..... 144 B8
Laighdykes Rd SALT KA21 ..... 191 L8
Laighland PSTWK KA9 ..... 225 J4
Laighlands Rd
  UD/BTH/TAN G71 ..... 132 B2
Laigh Mt AYRS KA7 ..... 229 G8
Laighstonehall Rd HMLTN ML3 .. 156 B7
Laightoun Ct CUMB G67 ..... 68 A3
Laightoun Dr CUMB G67 ..... 68 A3
Laightoun Gdns CUMB G67 ..... 68 A3
Lainshaw Av KLMNK KA1 ..... 211 M5
Lainshaw Dr CSMK G45 ..... 128 B7
  LNPK/KPK G44 ..... 128 A7
Lainshaw St KLMNKN/STW KA3 .. 197 K1
Laird Gv UD/BTH/TAN G71 ..... 132 A1
Laird Pl DMNK/BRGTN G40 ..... 12 C8
Lairds Ga UD/BTH/TAN G71 ..... 131 K4
Lairds Hl CUMB G67 ..... 48 E7
Laird's Hill Ct KSYTH G65 ..... 47 G1
Laird's Hill Pl KSYTH G65 ..... 47 G1
Laird St CTBR ML5 ..... 110 B2
  GRNK PA15 ..... 2 D2
Laird Weir ARD KA22 ..... 191 K6
Lairg Dr BLTYR/CAMB G72 ..... 131 J7

Lairhills Rd EKILS G75 .... 14 F7
Lake Av LNK/LMHG ML11 ...... 199 K6 ▢
Lamberton Dr
  CARD/HILL/MSPK G52........ 103 H3
Lamberton Gdns IRVSE KA11 .. 204 C5
Lambhill St PLKSD/SHW G41 .... 104 D4
Lambie Crs NMRNS G77 .... 150 C4 ▢
Lamb St HMLTN ML3 .... 156 E6 ▢
  PPK/MIL G22 .... 83 H3
Lamerton Rd CUMB G67 .... 49 J7
Lamford Dr AYRS KA7 .... 228 C8
Lamington Rd
  CARD/HILL/MSPK G52........ 103 H5
Lamlash Crs
  STPS/GTHM/RID G33.......... 107 H1
Lamlash Pl EKILS G75 .... 171 H5
  HBR/GL G84 .... 20 F7 ▢
  MTHW ML1 .... 157 J2
  STPS/GTHM/RID G33.......... 107 H1 ▢
Lammermoor Av
  CARD/HILL/MSPK G52........ 103 J6
Lammermoor Crs KKNTL G66 .... 65 M1
Lammermoor Dr CUMB G67 ...... 68 E2
Lammermoor Rd KKNTL G66 .... 65 M2
Lammermoor Ter WISHAW ML2 .. 159 H6
Lammermuir Dr PSLYS PA2 ...... 124 C1 ▢
Lammermuir Gdns BSDN G61 .... 61 J2
Lammermuir Rd KLMNK KA1 .... 212 A6
Lammermuir Wy AIRDRIE ML6 .. 111 M8
Lammermuir Wynd
  LRKH ML9 .... 175 M4 ▢
Lamont Av BSHPTN PA7 .... 58 C6 ▢
Lamont Crs DMBTN G82 .... 25 K7
Lamont Dr IRV KA12 .... 208 C1
Lamont Pl IRV KA12 .... 208 C1
Lamont Rd SPRGB/BLRNK G21 .. 84 B3
Lanark Av AIRDRIE ML6 .... 110 F5
Lanark Rd CARLUKE ML8 .... 178 F4
  LRKH ML9 .... 175 L2
  LRKH ML9 .... 176 C3
Lancaster Av AIRDRIE ML6 ...... 110 F5
  BEITH KA15 .... 168 B2 ▢
Lancaster Crs KVD/HLHD G12 .. 82 C5
Lancaster Crescent La
  KVD/HLHD G12 .... 82 C5 ▢
Lancaster Rd BSHPBGS G64 .... 64 B5
Lancefield Quay KVGV G3 ...... 10 A2
Lancefield St KVGV G3 .... 10 C2
Landemer Dr RUTH G73 .... 128 F3
Landressy Pl DMNK/BRGTN G40 .. 12 B7
Landressy St DMNK/BRGTN G40 .. 12 C7
Landsborough Dr
  KLMNK/STW KA3 .... 207 G6
Landsborough Pl
  SVSTN KA20 .... 192 F7 ▢
Landsdowne Gdns
  HMLTN ML3 .... 156 F6 ▢
Landsdowne Rd LRKH ML9 ...... 176 C7 ▢
The Lane BALLOCH G68 .... 48 D3
  SKLM PA17 .... 70 B5
Lanfine Rd PSLY PA1 .... 102 C5
Lanfine Ter IRVSE KA11 .... 203 M3
Lanfine Wy IRVSE KA11 .... 203 M3
Langa St MRYH/FIRH G20 .... 82 E1
  RNFRW PA4 .... 80 D8
Langbank Dr KLMCLM PA13 .... 55 L8
Langbank Ri KLMCLM PA13 ...... 55 L8
Langbar Crs
  STPS/GTHM/RID G33.......... 107 M2 ▢
Langbyres Rd MTHW ML1 .... 135 K8 ▢
Langcraigs Ct PSLYS PA2 .... 124 C1 ▢
Langcraigs Dr PSLYS PA2 .... 124 C3 ▢
Langcraigs Ter PSLYS PA2 ...... 124 C3 ▢
Langcroft Av PSTWK KA9 .... 221 L8
Langcroft Dr BLTYR/CAMB G72 .. 130 C5
Langcroft Pl GOV/IBX G51 ...... 103 J2 ▢
Langcroft Rd GOV/IBX G51 ...... 103 K2
Langcroft Ter GOV/IBX G51 .... 103 K2 ▢
Langdale EKILN G74 .... 153 L2
Langdale Av
  STPS/GTHM/RID G33.......... 84 E6
Langdales Av BALLOCH G68 ...... 48 C7
Langdale St
  STPS/GTHM/RID G33.......... 84 E6
Langfaulds Crs CLYDBK G81 .... 60 E3 ▢
Langford Dr PLK/PH/NH G53 .... 126 A6
Langford Pl PLK/PH/NH G53 .... 126 B6 ▢
Langhill Dr BALLOCH G68........ 48 D6
Langholm EKILS G75 .... 170 F3
Langholm Crs WISHAW ML2 .... 159 H3
Langholm Dr PSLYN/LNWD PA3 .. 100 B4
Langhouse Av
  GRNKW/INVK PA16 .... 50 E4
Langhouse Pl
  GRNKW/INVK PA16 .... 50 E4 ▢
Langhouse Rd
  GRNKW/INVK PA16 .... 50 E4
Langlands Av EKILS G75 .... 171 M5
  GOV/IBX G51 .... 103 K2 ▢
Langlands Ct EKILS G75 .... 172 A5
  GOV/IBX G51 .... 103 M2 ▢
Langlands Dr EKILS G75 .... 171 M5
  GOV/IBX G51 .... 103 J1
  MAUCH/CAT KA5 .... 223 M7
Langlands Pl EKILS G75 .... 171 M5
Langlands Rd EKILS G75 .... 171 L7
  GOV/IBX G51 .... 103 K2
Langlands Sq EKILS G75 .... 171 M6
Langlands St KLMNK KA1 ...... 16 E3
Langlands Ter DMBTN G82 ...... 37 H3
Langlea Av BLTYR/CAMB G72 .. 129 J3
Langlea Ct BLTYR/CAMB G72 .. 129 L5
Langlea Dr BLTYR/CAMB G72 .. 129 L4
Langlea Gdns
  BLTYR/CAMB G72 .... 129 L4 ▢
Langlea Gv BLTYR/CAMB G72 .. 129 L5
Langlea Rd BLTYR/CAMB G72 .. 129 L4
Langlees Av NMRNS G77 .... 151 H4
Langley Av KNTSWD G13 .... 81 H2
Langloan Crs CTBR ML5 .... 109 L3 ▢
Langloan Pl CTBR ML5 .... 109 L3
Langloan St CTBR ML5 .... 109 L4
Langmuir Av IRVSE KA11 .... 204 C4
  KKNTL G66 .... 45 L8

Langmuirhead Rd KKNTL G66 .. 85 G1
Langmuir Rd
  BAIL/MDB/MHD G69 .... 109 G4
  KKNTL G66 .... 45 M8
Langmuir Wy CTBR ML5 .... 109 G4
Langness Rd
  STPS/GTHM/RID G33.......... 107 H1
Langoreth Av HMLTN ML3........ 155 M1
Lang Pl JNSTN PA5 .... 99 L6
Langrig Rd NMRNS G77 .... 150 C6
  SPRGB/BLRNK G21 .... 84 A5
Lang Rd TROON KA10 .... 216 E2 ▢
Langshaw Crs CARLUKE ML8 .... 178 F7
Langshot St GOV/IBX G51 ...... 104 D4 ▢
Langside Av KLMNK KA1 .... 211 M6
  PLKSD/SHW G41 .... 104 E8
  UD/BTH/TAN G71 .... 132 C3
Langside Ct
  UD/BTH/TAN G71 .... 132 B8 ▢
Langside Dr KLBCH PA10 .... 99 G7
  PLKSW/MSWD G43 .... 127 L5
Langside Gdns
  GVH/MTFL G42 .... 128 A2 ▢
Langside La GVH/MTFL G42 .... 105 G8
Langside Pk KLBCH PA10 .... 99 G7
Langside Pl KBRN KA25 .... 143 G8
  PLKSD/SHW G41 .... 127 M1
Langside Rd GVH/MTFL G42 .... 105 G8
  UD/BTH/TAN G71 .... 132 B8
Langside St CLYDBK G81 .... 60 D3
Langside Ter PGL PA14 .... 54 D1
Langstile Rd
  CARD/HILL/MSPK G52........ 102 F4
Lang St PSLY PA1 .... 9 L4
Langton Crs BRHD/NEIL G78 .... 125 K8
  PLK/PH/NH G53 .... 103 J8
Langton Gdns
  BAIL/MDB/MHD G69 .... 107 M5 ▢
Langton Ga NMRNS G77 .... 150 C4
Langton Pl NMRNS G77 .... 150 C4
Langton Rd PLK/PH/NH G53 .... 126 C1
Langtree Av GIF/THBK G46 .... 127 G8
Lanrig Pl BAIL/MDB/MHD G69 .. 86 B1
Lanrig Rd BAIL/MDB/MHD G69 .. 66 C8
Lansbury Gdns
  PSLYN/LNWD PA3 .... 101 K2 ▢
Lansbury St ALEX/LLW G83 ...... 25 K1 ▢
  GRNK PA15 .... 33 M7
Lansbury Ter LRKH ML9 .... 176 C8
Lansdowne Crs MRYH/FIRH G20 .. 4 C4
Lansdowne Crescent La
  COWCAD C4 .... 4 C4
Lansdowne Dr BALLOCH G68 .... 48 F5
Lansdowne Rd AYR KA8 .... 225 G5
Lantana Gv MTHW ML1 .... 157 K1 ▢
Lanton Dr
  CARD/HILL/MSPK G52........ 103 H4
Lanton Rd PLKSW/MSWD G43 .. 127 L4
Lappin St CLYDBK G81 .... 80 D1
Laputa Pl KLMNK KA1 .... 211 L6
Larch Av BSHPBGS G64 .... 84 B1
  KKNTL G66 .... 65 J4
Larch Ct BLTYR/CAMB G72 ...... 155 J1
  CUMB G67 .... 49 L5
  EKILS G75 .... 171 H4 ▢
Larch Crs KKNTL G66 .... 65 J3
Larch Dr EKILS G75 .... 171 H4
The Larches
  BAIL/MDB/MHD G69 .... 67 G5
  SCOT G14 .... 81 H5
  WISHAW ML2 .... 159 H3
Larchfield Ct NMRNS G77 ...... 150 D5 ▢
Larchfield Crs WISHAW ML2 .... 159 J3 ▢
Larchfield Dr RUTH G73 .... 129 J5
Larchfield Gdns
  WISHAW ML2 .... 159 K3 ▢
Larchfield Gv WISHAW ML2 .... 159 K2 ▢
Larchfield Pl SCOT G14 .... 81 H5 ▢
Larchfield Rd BSDN G61 .... 61 M8
Larch Gv CUMB G67 .... 49 K5
  HMLTN ML3 .... 156 E7
Larchgrove Av CAR/SHTL G32 .. 107 J5 ▢
Larchgrove Pl CAR/SHTL G32 .. 107 J2 ▢
Larchgrove Rd CAR/SHTL G32 .. 107 J2
Larch Pl EKILS G75 .... 171 H4 ▢
  JNSTN PA5 .... 122 F1
  KLMNK KA1 .... 16 B5
  UD/BTH/TAN G71 .... 132 D1
Larch Rd CUMB G67 .... 49 K5
  PLKSD/SHW G41 .... 104 B5
Larch Ter BEITH KA15 .... 168 C1
Larchwood Rd AYRS KA7 .... 229 J5
Larchwood Ter
  BRHD/NEIL G78 .... 149 K1 ▢
Larghill La AYRS KA7 .... 19 K9
Largie Rd LNPK/KPK G44 .... 127 M4
Largo Pl GOV/IBX G51 .... 103 L2 ▢
Largs Av KLMNKN/STW KA3 .... 207 H6
  WKIL KA23 .... 163 H5
Largs Rd KBRN KA25 .... 142 B8
Larkfield Ct BLTYR/CAMB G72 .. 155 J3
Larkfield Dr BLTYR/CAMB G72 .. 155 K3
Larkfield Gv
  GRNKW/INVK PA16 .... 31 M5 ▢
Larkfield Rd GRK PA19 .... 31 L3 ▢
  GRNKW/INVK PA16 .... 31 M4
  KKNTL G66 .... 65 L4
Larkfield St GVH/MTFL G42 .... 105 H6 ▢
Larkin Gdns
  PSLYN/LNWD PA3 .... 101 K2 ▢
Larkins Dr CARLUKE ML8 ...... 189 C1 ▢
Larkspur Dr EKILS G74 .... 153 J5
Larkspur Wy CARLUKE ML8 .... 188 F1 ▢
Lashley Gv WISHAW ML2 ...... 159 M3
Lasswade St SCOT G14 .... 80 E3 ▢
Latherton Dr MRYH/FIRH G20 .. 82 D4 ▢
Latimer Gdns
  CARD/HILL/MSPK G52........ 103 G5 ▢
Latta St DMBTN G82 .... 37 G5
Lauchope Rd MTHW ML1 ...... 134 C8
Lauchope St AIRDRIE ML6 ...... 111 L7
Lauder Ct KLMNKN/STW KA3 .. 207 H5 ▢
Lauder Crs WISHAW ML2 ...... 159 H3 ▢

Lauderdale Gdns PTCK G11 .... 82 B6
Lauderdale La KVD/HLHD G12 .. 82 B6
Lauder Dr PSLYN/LNWD PA3 .. 100 B4
  RUTH G73 .... 129 K2 ▢
  RUTH G73 .... 129 K3 ▢
  CTBR ML5 .... 110 D6
Lauder Gn EKILS G74 .... 154 B5 ▢
Lauder St GBLS G5 .... 10 F8 ▢
Laudervale Gdns
  ALEX/LLW G83 .... 25 K1 ▢
Laughland Dr MTHW ML1 ...... 134 D6
Laughlanglen Rd AYRS KA7 .... 229 G7
Laundry La STPS/GTHM/RID G33 .. 85 J4
Lauranne Pl BLSH ML4 .... 132 E4 ▢
Laurel Av CLYDBK G81 .... 59 K5
  KKNTL G66 .... 65 K3
Laurel Bank CTBR ML5 .... 110 A1
Laurelbank HMLTN ML3 .... 174 C1
Laurel Bank HMLTN ML3 .... 174 C1
Laurelbank Rd
  BAIL/MDB/MHD G69 .... 86 B2 ▢
  CAR/SHTL G32 .... 130 C1 ▢
Laurel Ct EKILS G75 .... 171 K4
Laurel Dr EKILS G75 .... 171 K4
  LRKH ML9 .... 176 C7
  WISHAW ML2 .... 158 D5
Laurel Gdns AIRDRIE ML6 ...... 111 J7
  UD/BTH/TAN G71 .... 131 M1
Laurel Gv AIRDRIE ML6 .... 69 M7
Laurel Park Gdns
  KNTSWD G13 .... 81 J4 ▢
Laurel Pl EKILS G75 .... 171 K4 ▢
  KLMNK KA1 .... 16 A6
  PTCK G11 .... 82 A7
The Laurels NMRNS G77 .... 150 D4 ▢
Laurel St PTCK G11 .... 82 A7
Laurel Wy BRHD/NEIL G78 .... 125 H6
Laurence Dr BSDN G61 .... 61 K3
Laurie Ct UD/BTH/TAN G71 .... 132 B1 ▢
Lauren Vw AIRDRIE ML6 .... 110 F2
Lauren Wy PSLYS PA2 .... 100 F8 ▢
Laurieland Av CRH/DND KA2 .. 205 L8 ▢
Laurieston Rd GBLS G5 .... 11 H7
Laurieston Wy RUTH G73 ...... 129 G5 ▢
Lauriston Gv NMRNS G77 ...... 150 B4
Lavelle Dr CTBR ML5 .... 110 C2
Lavender Dr EKILS G75 .... 171 K4
Lavender La CARLUKE ML8 .... 188 C1 ▢
Laverock Av
  GRNKW/INVK PA16 .... 32 D6 ▢
  HMLTN ML3 .... 157 G2
Laverock Dr LARGS KA30 ...... 115 K4
Laverockhall St
  SPRGB/BLRNK G21 .... 6 C3
Laverock Rd AIRDRIE ML6 ...... 89 H7
Laverock Ter
  BAIL/MDB/MHD G69 .... 66 F8 ▢
Law Brae WKIL KA23 .... 181 K4
Law Dr MTHW ML1 .... 134 C5
Lawer Pl IRVSE KA11 .... 204 A5
Lawers Crs KLMNK KA1 .... 212 A5 ▢
Lawers Dr BSDN G61 .... 61 H2
Lawers Pl GRNKW/INVK PA16 .. 32 A5 ▢
Lawers Rd KLMNK KA1 .... 212 A5 ▢
  PLKSW/MSWD G43 .... 127 H4
  RNFRW PA4 .... 80 E8
Lawfield Av NMRNS G77 ...... 151 H4
  WKIL KA23 .... 181 K4
Lawhill Av CSMK G45 .... 128 D5 ▢
Lawhill Rd CARLUKE ML8 ...... 177 M4
  KLMNK KA1 .... 218 C5 ▢
Lawhope Mill Rd AIRDRIE ML6 .. 111 M6
Lawmarnock Crs
  BRWEIR PA11 .... 98 C2 ▢
Lawmarnock Rd BRWEIR PA11 .. 98 B3
Lawmoor Av GBLS G5 .... 105 J6
Lawmoor Pl GBLS G5 .... 105 J7 ▢
Lawmoor St GBLS G5 .... 11 J7
Lawmuir Crs CLYDBK G81 ...... 60 E2 ▢
Lawmuir Pl BLSH ML4 .... 133 G6 ▢
Lawmuir Rd BLSH ML4 .... 133 G6
  WISHAW ML2 .... 177 M3
Lawnmoor Rd GBLS G5 .... 105 J6
Lawn Pk MLNGV G62 .... 42 C8
Lawn St PSLY PA1 .... 9 J3
Law Pl EKILN G74 .... 153 M5 ▢
Lawrence Av GIF/THBK G46 .... 127 J8
  HBR/GL G84 .... 23 G2
Lawrence St PTCK G11 .... 82 C7
Lawrie St NMLNS KA16 .... 215 H2 ▢
  PTCK G11 .... 82 B7
  WISHAW ML2 .... 159 M4
Lawson Av MTHW ML1 .... 157 L6
Lawson Dr ARD KA22 .... 191 K5
Lawson St AYR KA8 .... 225 J1
  KLMNK KA1 .... 17 G7
Law St DEN/PKHD G31 .... 12 F6
Lawthorn Rd IRVSE KA11 ...... 204 B4
Law Vw WISHAW ML2.......... 177 J3
Laxford Av LNPK/KPK G44 .... 128 A5
Laxford Pl CTBR ML5 .... 110 D4
Laxford Rd ERSK PA8 .... 58 E8
Laxton Dr KKNTL G66 .... 65 L5
Lea Av BRHD/NEIL G78 .... 148 D2
Leabank Av PSLYS PA2.......... 124 E1
Leadburn Rd SPRGB/BLRNK G21 .. 7 J1
Leadburn St CAR/SHTL G32 .. 106 E2 ▢
Leader St STPS/GTHM/RID G33 .. 7 M6
Leadhills Rd KLMNK KA1 ...... 212 A6
Leaend Rd AIRDRIE ML6 .... 88 E8
Leander Crs BLSH ML4 .... 133 L4
  RNFRW PA4 .... 80 E7
Learigg Rd AIRDRIE ML6 .... 90 B6
Learmont Pl MLNGV G62 ...... 41 M7
Leathem Pl WISHAW ML2 ...... 158 C8 ▢
Leathen Pl ERSK PA8 .... 58 E8
Leckethill Av BALLOCH G68 .... 67 M2 ▢
Leckethill Ct BALLOCH G68 .... 67 M2 ▢
Leckethill Pl BALLOCH G68 .... 67 M2 ▢
Leckethill Vw BALLOCH G68 .... 67 M2 ▢
Leckie Dr HMLTN ML3 .... 156 C6
Leckie Pl ALEX/LLW G83 .... 25 L3
Leckie St PLKSW/MSWD G43 .. 127 J1 ▢
Ledaig St DEN/PKHD G31 ...... 13 K1
Ledard Rd GVH/MTFL G42 .... 127 M2
Ledcameroch Crs BSDN G61 .... 61 K5
Ledcameroch Pk BSDN G61 .... 61 K5 ▢

Ledcameroch Rd BSDN G61 .... 61 K5
Ledgate KKNTL G66 .... 45 K8
Ledgowan Pl MRYH/FIRH G20 .. 82 D1
Ledi Dr BSDN G61 .... 61 H2
Ledi Rd PLKSW/MSWD G43 .... 127 J4
Ledmore Dr DRUM G15 .... 60 F5
Lednock Rd
  CARD/HILL/MSPK G52........ 103 G4
  STPS/GTHM/RID G33.......... 85 J4
Lee Av STPS/GTHM/RID G33 .... 84 E8
Leebank Dr LNPK/KPK G44 .... 127 M8
Leeburn Av CRG/CRSL/HOU PA6 .. 77 J8
Leechford LNK/LMHG ML11 .... 199 H4 ▢
Leechlee Rd HMLTN ML3 ...... 156 E6
Lee Crs BSHPBGS G64 .... 83 M1
Leefield Dr LNPK/KPK G44 .... 127 M7 ▢
Leehill Rd SPRGB/BLRNK G21 .. 83 L2
Lee Pl BLSH ML4 .... 133 K5
Leesburn Pl EKILN G74 .... 153 M5
Leesland UD/BTH/TAN G71 .... 132 A1
Leeward Cir EKILS G75 .... 153 C8
Leeward Pk AYRS KA7 .... 229 C6
Leewood Dr LNPK/KPK G44 .... 128 A7 ▢
Le Froy Gdns EKILS G75 .... 14 A5
Le Froy La EKILS G75 .... 14 B5
Lefroy St CTBR ML5 .... 109 L2
Legbrannock Av MTHW ML1 .. 134 D3
Legbrannock Crs MTHW ML1 .. 134 D4
Legbrannock Rd MTHW ML1 .. 134 E3
Leggate Wy BSHPBGS G64 .... 64 A8
Leglen Wood Rd
  STPS/GTHM/RID G33.......... 84 D3
Leicester Av KVD/HLHD G12 .. 82 B4
Leighton St MRYH/FIRH G20 .. 82 E3
  WISHAW ML2 .... 159 H7
Leitchland Rd PSLYS PA2........ 123 K1
Leitch St GRNK PA15 .... 3 M8
Leithland Av
  PLK/PH/NH G53 .... 103 H8 ▢
Leithland Rd PLK/PH/NH G53 .. 103 H8
Leith St STPS/GTHM/RID G33 .. 7 M9
Leman Dr CRG/CRSL/HOU PA6 .. 99 K1
Leman Gv CRG/CRSL/HOU PA6 .. 99 K1 ▢
Lembert Dr
  CRMNK/CLK/EAG G76 ...... 151 K1
Lemmon St GRNKW/INVK PA16 .. 32 D6
Lendale La BSHPBGS G64 ...... 64 A6
Lendalfoot Gdns HMLTN ML3 .. 155 K7 ▢
Lendal Pl EKILS G75 .... 170 E3
Lendel Pl GOV/IBX G51 .... 104 D3 ▢
Lenihall Dr CSMK G45 .... 128 E7
Lenihall Ter CSMK G45 .... 128 E7 ▢
Lennox Av BSHPTN PA7 .... 58 B6
  CTBR ML5 .... 109 L2 ▢
  MLNGV G62 .... 42 A8
  SCOT G14 .... 81 J6
Lennox Crs BSHPBGS G64 .... 83 M1
  KLMNK KA1 .... 206 C8
Lennox Dr BSDN G61 .... 61 M3 ▢
  CLYDBK G81 .... 60 D2
  PSTWK KA9 .... 225 J4
Lennox Gdns DMBTN G82 .... 36 A5
  SCOT G14 .... 81 K5 ▢
Lennox La East SCOT G14 ...... 81 K6
Lennox La West SCOT G14 .... 81 K5 ▢
Lennox Rd CUMB G67 .... 48 F7
  DMBTN G82 .... 37 H6
  DMBTN G82 .... 37 M8
  KKNTL G66 .... 29 J8
Lennox St ALEX/LLW G83 ...... 25 L4 ▢
  DMBTN G82 .... 36 D1
  DMBTN G82 .... 37 G2 ▢
  MRYH/FIRH G20 .... 82 C2 ▢
  WISHAW ML2 .... 159 L5
Lennox Ter PSLYN/LNWD PA3 .. 102 A1
Lentran St ESTRH G34 .... 108 D2
Lenwood Gdns
  ALEX/LLW G83 .... 25 M6 ▢
Leny St MRYH/FIRH G20 .... 82 F5
Lenziemill Rd CUMB G67 ...... 68 F2
Lenzie Rd KKNTL G66 .... 65 K2
  KKNTL G66 .... 85 L1
  STPS/GTHM/RID G33.......... 85 L1
Lenzie St SPRGB/BLRNK G21 .. 83 M4 ▢
Lenzie Wy SPRGB/BLRNK G21 .. 83 L3
Leperstone Av KLMCLM PA13 .. 55 K7
  PGL PA14 .... 54 E2
Lerwick St KLMNKN/STW KA3 .. 207 G6 ▢
Lesley Pl SVSTN KA20 .... 192 E8 ▢
Lesley Qd BLSH ML4 .... 132 F7 ▢
Leslie Av BSHPTN PA7 .... 58 B6
  NMRNS G77 .... 150 E2
Leslie Crs AYRS KA7 .... 19 H7
Leslie Pl KLMNKN/STW KA3 .. 17 J1
Leslie Rd KLMNKN/STW KA3 .. 17 J1
  PLKSD/SHW G41 .... 104 E7
Leslie St MTHW ML1 .... 157 M2
  PLKSD/SHW G41 .... 104 F6
Leslie Ter PSTWK KA9 .... 225 J1
Lesmahagow Rd
  LNK/LMHG ML11 .... 198 A5 ▢
Lesmuir Dr SCOT G14 .... 81 G4
Lesmuir Pl SCOT G14 .... 80 F4
Letham Ct
  PLKSW/MSWD G43 .... 127 L4 ▢
Letham Dr BSHPBGS G64 ...... 84 C1
  PLKSW/MSWD G43 .... 127 L4
Letham Gra BALLOCH G68 ...... 48 F5
Letham Ov BSHPBGS G64 ...... 84 D1 ▢
Lethbridge Pl EKILS G75 ...... 14 B5 ▢
Letherby Dr LNPK/KPK G44 .... 128 B2
Letheron Dr WISHAW ML2 .... 159 H4
Lethington Av PLKSD/SHW G41 .. 127 L1
Lethington Pl PLKSD/SHW G41 .. 127 L1
Lethington Rd GIF/THBK G46 .. 151 G2
Letterfearn Rd SMSTN G23 .. 62 D7 ▢
Letterickhills Crs
  BLTYR/CAMB G72.......... 130 E6
Lettoch St GOV/IBX G51 ...... 104 A2
Levanne Gdns GRK PA19 ...... 30 F3 ▢
Levanne Pl GRK PA19 .... 30 F3
Leven Av BSHPBGS G64 .... 64 B8
Leven Ct BRHD/NEIL G78 ...... 125 H4 ▢

  KLMNK KA1 .... 212 F3
Levencroft Ms ALEX/LLW G83 .. 25 M5 ▢
Leven Dr BSDN G61 .... 61 M5
  HMLTN ML3 .... 174 B1 ▢
  KLMNK KA1 .... 212 F3
Levenford Ter DMBTN G82 .... 36 E6 ▢
Levenhowe Pl ALEX/LLW G83 .. 25 L2 ▢
Levenhowe Rd ALEX/LLW G83 .. 25 L2 ▢
Leven Pl ERSK PA8 .... 58 E8
  GRNK PA15 .... 33 J8 ▢
  IRV KA12 .... 203 K3
  KLMNKN/STW KA3 .... 207 G6
  SHOTTS ML7 .... 137 L3
Leven Qd AIRDRIE ML6 .... 88 F7
Leven Rd CTBR ML5 .... 87 J8
  GRNK PA15 .... 33 H7
  PGL PA14 .... 56 C2 ▢
  TROON KA10 .... 216 F4
  WMYSB PA18 .... 70 A1
Leven St ALEX/LLW G83 .... 25 L5
  DMBTN G82 .... 36 D1
  DMBTN G82 .... 37 G1 ▢
  MTHW ML1 .... 157 L4
  PLKSD/SHW G41 .... 104 F6
Leven Ter MTHW ML1 .... 134 C7
Leven Vw EKILS G75 .... 170 F3
Levern Crs BRHD/NEIL G78 .... 125 H8
Levern Gdns BRHD/NEIL G78 .. 125 H6 ▢
Levernside Av BRHD/NEIL G78 ..
  PLK/PH/NH G53 .... 126 C1 ▢
Levernside Crs PLK/PH/NH G53 .. 103 H8
Levernside Rd PLK/PH/NH G53 .. 103 H8
Lever Rd HBR/GL G84 .... 20 F6
Lewis Av RNFRW PA4 .... 80 D8
  WISHAW ML2 .... 159 L4
Lewis Crs IRVSE KA11 .... 203 M7
  KLBCH PA10 .... 99 J7
  OLDK G60 .... 59 H4
Lewis Dr KLMNKN/STW KA3 .. 207 H4
  OLDK G60 .... 59 H4
Lewis Gdns BSDN G61 .... 61 H3 ▢
  OLDK G60 .... 59 J4
Lewis Gv OLDK G60 .... 59 J4
Lewis Pl AIRDRIE ML6 .... 111 K3
  NMRNS G77 .... 150 B3
  OLDK G60 .... 59 J4
Lewis Ri IRVSE KA11 .... 204 A7 ▢
Lewis Rd GRNKW/INVK PA16 .. 32 C5
  PGL PA14 .... 55 H2 ▢
Lewis Ter IRVSE KA11 .... 204 A7
Lewiston Dr SMSTN G23 ...... 62 D8 ▢
Lewiston Pl SMSTN G23 ...... 62 D8 ▢
Lewiston Rd SMSTN G23 ...... 62 D8 ▢
Lewis Wynd IRVSE KA11 ...... 204 A7 ▢
Lexwell Av JNSTN PA5 .... 100 D6
Leyden Gdns MRYH/FIRH G20 .. 82 E4 ▢
Leyden St MRYH/FIRH G20 .... 82 E4
Leys Pk HMLTN ML3 .... 156 A5
The Leys BSHPBGS G64 .... 64 A8
Libberton Wy HMLTN ML3 .... 156 A6
Liberator Dr AYR KA8 .... 225 L5
Liberton St STPS/GTHM/RID G33 .. 7 M9
Liberty Av BAIL/MDB/MHD G69 .. 108 F4
Liberty Rd AIRDRIE ML6 .... 91 G4
  BLSH ML4 .... 133 G6
Libo Av BRHD/NEIL G78 .... 147 G6
  PLK/PH/NH G53 .... 103 K8
Libo Pl ERSK PA8 .... 58 E7
Library Gdns
  BLTYR/CAMB G72 .... 129 M3 ▢
Library La GIF/THBK G46 ...... 126 F6
Library Rd WISHAW ML2 ...... 159 H6 ▢
Lichtenfels Gdns PSTWK KA9 .. 225 L1
Lickprivick Rd EKILS G75 ...... 171 H2
Liddell St EKILS G75 .... 14 D8
Liddells Ct BSHPBGS G64 ...... 84 A2 ▢
Liddell St CAR/SHTL G32 ...... 107 J8
Liddel Rd CUMB G67 .... 48 E8
Liddesdale Pl PPK/MIL G22 .... 83 L2 ▢
Liddesdale Rd PPK/MIL G22 .. 83 J2
Liddesdale Sq PPK/MIL G22 .. 83 L2 ▢
Liddesdale Ter PPK/MIL G22 .. 83 L2 ▢
Liddoch Wy RUTH G73 .... 128 F1
Liff Gdns BSHPBGS G64 .... 84 D1 ▢
Liff Pl ESTRH G34 .... 86 D3
Lifnock Av KLMNK KA1 .... 212 F3
Lightburn Pl CAR/SHTL G32 .. 107 H2 ▢
Lightburn Rd BLTYR/CAMB G72 .. 130 D5
  DEN/PKHD G31 .... 13 K4
Lilac Av CLYDBK G81 .... 59 K4
  CUMB G67 .... 49 L4
Lilac Crs UD/BTH/TAN G71 .... 132 B1
Lilac Gdns BSHPBGS G64 ...... 84 B1 ▢
Lilac HI CUMB G67 .... 49 M4
  HMLTN ML3 .... 156 F7
Lilac Pl CUMB G67 .... 49 M4
  KLMNK KA1 .... 16 B4
Lilac Wynd BLTYR/CAMB G72 .. 130 F6
Lillyburn Pl DRUM G15 .... 60 E5
Lilybank Av AIRDRIE ML6 ...... 89 H7
  BAIL/MDB/MHD G69 .... 86 C2
  BLTYR/CAMB G72 .... 130 B5
Lilybank Gdns KVD/HLHD G12 .. 82 D7
Lilybank Gardens La
  KVD/HLHD G12 .... 82 D7 ▢
Lilybank La FAIRLIE KA29 .... 139 K7 ▢
  KVD/HLHD G12 .... 82 D7
Lilybank Rd PGL PA14 .... 33 M7
  PSTWK KA9 .... 225 H4
Lilybank St HMLTN ML3 ...... 156 C5
Lilybank Ter KVD/HLHD G12 .. 82 D7 ▢
Lilybank Terrace La
  KVD/HLHD G12 .... 82 D7 ▢
Lily St DMNK/BRGTN G40 ...... 13 G9
Limecraigs Av PSLYS PA2 ...... 124 C2 ▢
Limecraigs Crs PSLYS PA2 .... 124 C2
Limecraigs Rd PSLYS PA2 .... 124 C2
Lime Crs AIRDRIE ML6 .... 111 J2
  CUMB G67 .... 49 L6
Lime Gv BLTYR/CAMB G72...... 131 J8
  KKNTL G66 .... 65 K4
  MTHW ML1 .... 157 L5
Limegrove St BLSH ML4 .... 133 G2 ▢
Limekilnburn Rd HMLTN ML3 .. 174 B7
Limekiln Rd AYR KA8 .... 224 F6
  SVSTN KA20 .... 201 L2
Limekilns Rd CUMB G67 ...... 68 F3

Limekilns St *CLYDBK* G81 .... 60 D3
Limelands Qd *AIRDRIE* ML6 .... 90 F5
Lime Loan *MTHW* ML1 .... 134 B5
Lime Pl *KLMNK* KA1 .... 16 B5
Lime Rd *DMBTN* G82 .... 36 F5
Limeside Av *RUTH* G73 .... 129 J2
Limeside Gdns *RUTH* G73 .... 129 J2
Lime St *GRNK* PA15 .... 2 A6
　SCOT G14 .... 81 K6
Limetree Av *UD/BTH/TAN* G71 .... 132 B1
Limetree Ct *HMLTN* ML3 .... 156 A4
Limetree Crs *NMRNS* G77 .... 150 D5
Limetree Dr *CLYDBK* G81 .... 60 A5
Limetree Qd
　UD/BTH/TAN G71 .... 132 C1
Limetree Wk *KKNTL* G66 .... 45 H5
Limeview Av *PSLYS* PA2 .... 124 B2
Limeview Crs *PSLYS* PA2 .... 124 B2
Limeview Wy *PSLYS* PA2 .... 124 B2
Limonds Wynd *AYR* KA8 .... 19 C1
Limpetlaw *LNK/LMHG* ML11 ...... 199 H4
Linacre Dr *CAR/SHTL* G32 .... 107 J4
Linacre Gdns *CAR/SHTL* G32 ...... 107 K4
Linburn Pl
　CARD/HILL/MSPK G52 .... 103 C3
Linburn Rd
　CARD/HILL/MSPK G52 .... 102 F2
　ERSK PA8 .... 58 E8
Lincoln Av *KNTSWD* G13 .... 81 H3
　UD/BTH/TAN G71 .... 108 F8
Lincoln Rd *GRNKW/INVK* PA16 ... 31 K5
Lincuan Av *GIF/THBK* G46 .... 151 J1
Lindams *UD/BTH/TAN* G71 .... 131 M4
Linden Av *WISHAW* ML2 .... 159 J3
Linden Dr *CLYDBK* G81 .... 60 A3
Linden Lea *HMLTN* ML3 .... 156 B5
　KKNTL G66 .... 45 H4
Linden Pl *KNTSWD* G13 .... 81 M2
Linden St *KNTSWD* G13 .... 81 M2
Lindon Aisle *LARGS* KA30 .... 115 J6
Lindon Ct *LARGS* KA30 .... 115 J6
Lindores Av *RUTH* G73 .... 129 H2
Lindores Dr *EKILN* G74 .... 153 H8
Lindores Pl *EKILN* G74 .... 14 A3
Lindores St *GVH/MTFL* G42 .... 128 B1
Lindrick Dr *SMSTN* G23 .... 62 D8
Lindsay Av *KBRN* KA25 .... 143 H6
　SALT KA21 .... 191 M8
Lindsaybeg Ct
　BAIL/MDB/MHD G69 .... 86 C1
Lindsaybeg Rd
　BAIL/MDB/MHD G69 .... 86 C1
　KKNTL G66 .... 65 L5
Lindsay Crs *LARGS* KA30 .... 115 K5
Lindsay Dr *KLMNKN/STW* KA3 .... 207 J6
　KVD/HLHD G12 .... 82 B3
Lindsayfield Av *EKILS* G75 .... 171 J5
Lindsayfield Rd *EKILS* G75 .... 171 H5
Lindsay Gdns *ALEX/LLW* G83 ...... 25 L3
Lindsay Gv *EKILN* G74 .... 15 H2
Lindsay Pl *EKILN* G74 .... 15 J3
　KVD/HLHD G12 .... 82 B3
Lindsay Rd *EKILN* G74 .... 15 H3
Lindsay Rd *AYR* KA8 .... 225 J7
　KLMNK KA1 .... 16 D4
Lindsay Ter *KKNTL* G66 .... 44 E1
Lindston Pl *AYRS* KA7 .... 229 C7
Lindum Crs *MTHW* ML1 .... 157 H1
Lindum St *MTHW* ML1 .... 157 H1
Linfern Av East *KLMNK* KA1 .... 17 L6
Linfern Av West *KLMNK* KA1 .... 17 L6
Linfern Pl *AYRS* KA7 .... 229 H6
Linfern Rd *KVD/HLHD* G12 .... 82 C6
Linghope Pl *WISHAW* ML2 .... 176 F1
Lingley Av *AIRDRIE* ML6 .... 111 G3
Linhope Pl *EKILS* G75 .... 170 E2
Linhead Dr *PLK/PH/NH* G53 .... 126 C3
Linister Crs *TROON* KA10 .... 216 E3
Links Rd *CAR/SHTL* G32 .... 107 K6
　LNPK/KPK G44 .... 128 B5
　PSTWK KA9 .... 221 H8
　SALT KA21 .... 191 M7
The Links *BALLOCH* G68 .... 49 H3
Links Vw *LRKH* ML9 .... 176 C2
Linksview Rd *MTHW* ML1 .... 134 B8
Linkwood Av *DRUM* G15 .... 60 F6
Linkwood Ct *IRVSE* KA11 .... 204 A3
Linkwood Crs *DRUM* G15 .... 61 G6
Linkwood Dr *DRUM* G15 .... 60 F6
Linkwood Gdns *DRUM* G15 .... 61 H6
Linkwood Pl *DRUM* G15 .... 60 F6
Linlithgow Gdns
　CAR/SHTL G32 .... 107 K4
Linn Av *LARGS* KA30 .... 115 L6
Linnburn Ter *ARD* KA22 .... 191 H5
Linn Crs *LNK/LMHG* ML11 .... 198 A5
　PSLYS PA2 .... 124 C2
Linn Dr *LNPK/KPK* G44 .... 127 M6
Linnet Av *JNSTN* PA5 .... 122 C2
Linnet Pl *KNTSWD* G13 .... 80 F2
Linnet Rd *BLSH* ML4 .... 133 H5
　GRNKW/INVK PA16 .... 32 B5
Linnet Wy *BLSH* ML4 .... 132 F1
Linn Gdns *BALLOCH* G68 .... 47 M7
Linn Glen *KKNTL* G66 .... 44 F1
Linnhead Dr *PLK/PH/NH* G53 ..... 126 B4
Linnhead Pl *SCOT* G14 .... 81 H5
Linnhe Av *BSHPBGS* G64 .... 64 B8
　HMLTN ML3 .... 156 A8
　LNPK/KPK G44 .... 127 M7
Linnhe Ct *LRKH* ML9 .... 175 M4
Linnhe Crs *WISHAW* ML2 .... 177 H1
Linnhe Dr *BRHD/NEIL* G78 .... 125 H4
Linnhe Pl *BLTYR/CAMB* G72 ...... 131 J7
　ERSK PA8 .... 58 E8
Linnhe Rd *WMYSB* PA18 .... 50 A8
Linnpark Av *LNPK/KPK* G44 .... 127 M7
Linn Park Gdns *JNSTN* PA5 .... 100 A7
Linn Rd *ARD* KA22 .... 191 J5
Linnwell Crs *PSLYS* PA2 .... 124 D2
Linrigg Rd *MTHW* ML1 .... 135 J1
Linthaugh Ter
　PLK/PH/NH G53 .... 103 K8
Linthill *LNK/LMHG* ML11 .... 199 H3
Linthouse Buildings
　GOV/IBX G51 .... 103 L1
Linthouse Rd *GOV/IBX* G51 .... 81 K8

Linthouse Vennel *IRV* KA12 .... 203 G8
Lintie Rd *MTHW* ML1 .... 101 G7
Lintlaw *BLTYR/CAMB* G72 .... 131 K7
Lintlaw Dr
　CARD/HILL/MSPK G52 .... 103 H3
Lintmill Ter *BRHD/NEIL* G78 ...... 148 C3
Linton St *STPS/GTHM/RID* G33 ... 106 E1
Lintwhite Crs *BRWEIR* PA11 .... 98 E2
Linwood Av
　CRMNK/CLK/EAG G76 .... 151 M2
　EKILN G74 .... 152 F7
Linwood Rd *PSLYN/LNWD* PA3 ... 100 D4
Linwood Ter *HMLTN* ML3 .... 156 B8
Lion Bank *KKNTL* G66 .... 45 J8
Lisburn Rd *AYR* KA8 .... 225 G5
Lismore *EKILN* G74 .... 172 C1
Lismore Av *MTHW* ML1 .... 157 H1
　PGL PA14 .... 55 H2
　RNFRW PA4 .... 80 D8
Lismore Dr *IRVSE* KA11 .... 209 H1
　PSLYN/LNWD PA3 .... 99 M4
　PSLYS PA2 .... 124 D2
Lismore Gdns *KLBCH* PA10 .... 99 J7
Lismore Hl *HMLTN* ML3 .... 155 K6
Lismore Pl
　BAIL/MDB/MHD G69 .... 67 G6
　NMRNS G77 .... 150 B4
Lismore Rd *KVD/HLHD* G12 .... 82 B4
Lissens Wk *KLWNG* KA13 .... 193 J4
Lister Gdns
　CRMNK/CLK/EAG G76 .... 152 A4
Lister Pl *CARD/HILL/MSPK* G52 ... 103 G2
Lister Rd *CARD/HILL/MSPK* G52 .. 102 F2
Lister St *COWCAD* G4 .... 5 M7
　CRH/DND KA2 .... 206 A8
Lithgow Av *PGL* PA14 .... 56 B2
Lithgow Crs *PSLYS* PA2 .... 9 L9
Lithgow Dr *MTHW* ML1 .... 135 H8
Lithgow Pl *EKILN* G74 .... 153 H7
Little Bellsland Rd *KLMNK* KA1 ... 16 F9
Little Dovehill *COWCAD* G4 .... 11 M3
Littlehill St *SPRGB/BLRNK* G21 ..... 6 E1
Littleholm Pl *CLYDBK* G81 .... 59 L5
Little John Gdns *WISHAW* ML2 ... 159 M5
Littlemill Av *BALLOCH* G68 .... 47 L8
Littlemill La *OLDK* G60 .... 58 C7
Littlesdale Av *PSLYS* PA2 .... 123 K2
Littlestane Ri *IRVSE* KA11 .... 204 A3
Littlestane Rd *IRVSE* KA11 .... 203 M3
Littleston Gdns *ERSK* PA8 .... 58 F8
Little St *KVGV* G3 .... 10 C1
Littleton St *MRYH/FIRH* G20 .... 62 D8
Livingstone Av
　CARD/HILL/MSPK G52 .... 103 G1
Livingstone Bvd
　BLTYR/CAMB G72 .... 155 J4
Livingstone Ct
　KLMNKN/STW KA3 .... 207 J6
Livingstone Crs
　BLTYR/CAMB G72 .... 131 K8
　EKILS G75 .... 14 D7
Livingstone Dr *EKILS* G75 .... 14 D5
Livingstone Gdns *LRKH* ML9 ...... 176 B6
Livingstone Pl *AIRDRIE* ML6 ...... 111 H3
Livingstone St *CLYDBK* G81 .... 60 D8
　HMLTN ML3 .... 155 M5
Livingstone Ter *IRV* KA12 .... 203 K5
Lloyd Av *CAR/SHTL* G32 .... 107 G7
Lloyd Dr *MTHW* ML1 .... 134 A8
Lloyds St *CTBR* ML5 .... 110 A4
Lloyd St *DEN/PKHD* G31 .... 6 E9
　MTHW ML1 .... 134 A8
　RUTH G73 .... 106 B8
Lloyd Wk *KLMNKN/STW* KA3 ...... 197 J1
Loach Av *IRV* KA12 .... 203 K8
Loadingbank *KBRN* KA25 .... 167 G2
Loanbank Pl *GOV/IBX* G51 .... 104 A2
Loanbank Qd *GOV/IBX* G51 .... 104 A2
Loancroft Av
　BAIL/MDB/MHD G69 .... 108 C6
Loancroft Gdns
　UD/BTH/TAN G71 .... 131 M4
Loancroft Ga *UD/BTH/TAN* G71 . 131 L4
Loancroft Pl
　BAIL/MDB/MHD G69 .... 108 B6
Loanfoot Av *BRHD/NEIL* G78 ...... 148 D3
　KLMNK KA1 .... 16 A3
　KNTSWD G13 .... 81 G2
Loanfoot Rd
　BLTYR/CAMB G72 .... 155 K4
Loanhead Av *MTHW* ML1 .... 134 D6
　PSLYN/LNWD PA3 .... 100 A3
　RNFRW PA4 .... 80 D6
Loanhead Crs *MTHW* ML1 .... 134 D6
Loanhead Rd *ARD* KA22 .... 191 K7
　MTHW ML1 .... 134 C6
　PSLYN/LNWD PA3 .... 100 A3
Loanhead St *CAR/SHTL* G32 .... 106 F2
　CTBR ML5 .... 109 K6
Loaninghead Dr *DMBTN* G82 .... 37 H3
The Loaning *AYRS* KA7 .... 228 F8
Loanhead Av *MTHW* ML1 .... 134 D6
Loch Awe *EKILN* G74 .... 15 L5
Loch Awe Pl *CTBR* ML5 .... 109 M3

Lochbroom Dr *NMRNS* G77 .... 150 F3
　PSLYS PA2 .... 101 G7
Loch Brora Crs *CTBR* ML5 .... 109 L3
Lochburn Crs *MRYH/FIRH* G20 .... 82 E2
Lochburn Pas
　MRYH/FIRH G20 .... 82 E2
Lochburn Rd *MRYH/FIRH* G20 ..... 82 E2
Lochdochart Rd *ESTRH* G34 .... 108 D1
Loch Dr *HBR/GL* G84 .... 20 A7
Lochearn Crs *AIRDRIE* ML6 .... 88 F7
　PSLYS PA2 .... 101 G7
Lochend Av
　BAIL/MDB/MHD G69 .... 86 E3
Lochend Crs *BSDN* G61 .... 61 K6
Lochend Dr *BSDN* G61 .... 61 K6
Lochend Rd
　BAIL/MDB/MHD G69 .... 86 F3
　BSDN G61 .... 61 L6
　ESTRH G34 .... 86 B8
　GLGNK KA14 .... 167 J2
　TROON KA10 .... 216 D8
Lochend St *MTHW* ML1 .... 157 M3
Locher Av *CRG/CRSL/HOU* PA6 ... 77 L8
Locher Br *KLMCLM* PA13 .... 97 J4
Locherburn Av
　CRG/CRSL/HOU PA6 .... 99 K1
Locherburn Pl
　CRG/CRSL/HOU PA6 .... 99 L1
Locher Crs
　CRG/CRSL/HOU PA6 .... 99 L1
Locher Gait
　CRG/CRSL/HOU PA6 .... 99 L1
Locher Gdns
　CRG/CRSL/HOU PA6 .... 99 L1
Locher Rd *KLBCH* PA10 .... 98 F4
Locher Wy *CRG/CRSL/HOU* PA6 .. 99 L1
Lochfauld Rd *SMSTN* G23 .... 63 G7
Lochfield Crs *PSLYS* PA2 .... 101 M8
Lochfield Dr *PSLYS* PA2 .... 102 A8
Lochfield Rd *PSLYS* PA2 .... 101 M8
Lochgarry Wy *CTBR* ML5 .... 109 K5
Lochgilp St *MRYH/FIRH* G20 .... 82 E2
Loch Goil *EKILN* G74 .... 15 K4
Lochgoin Av *DRUM* G15 .... 60 E5
Lochgreen Av *CTBR* ML5 .... 87 J7
　HMLTN ML3 .... 174 B1
　KLMNK KA1 .... 211 L5
Lochgreen St
　STPS/GTHM/RID G33 .... 7 M3
Lochhead Av *PSLYN/LNWD* PA3 . 100 B4
Lochiel Dr *KKNTL* G66 .... 45 J3
Lochiel Rd *GIF/THBK* G46 .... 126 F5
Lochinch Pl *NMRNS* G77 .... 150 A4
Lochinvar Rd *CUMB* G67 .... 68 D2
Lochinver Crs *PSLYS* PA2 .... 101 G7
Lochinver Dr *LNPK/KPK* G44 ...... 128 A4
Lochinver Gv
　BLTYR/CAMB G72 .... 130 B4
Lochknowe St *CARLUKE* ML8 ..... 188 F4
Loch Laidon St *CAR/SHTL* G32 ... 107 K5
Lochlands Gv *BEITH* KA15 .... 168 C1
Loch Laxford *EKILN* G74 .... 15 L6
Lochlea Av *CLYDBK* G81 .... 60 C6
Loch Lea *KKNTL* G66 .... 45 M7
Lochlea Av *CLYDBK* G81 .... 60 C6
Lochlea Rd *AYRS* KA7 .... 19 J8
Lochlea Rd
　CRMNK/CLK/EAG G76 .... 151 L4
　CUMB G67 .... 49 H6
　PLKSW/MSWD G43 .... 127 K3
　RUTH G73 .... 128 F4
　SALT KA21 .... 192 A6
Lochlea Wy *MTHW* ML1 .... 134 E5
Lochleven La *GVH/MTFL* G42 ..... 128 A2
Lochleven Rd *GVH/MTFL* G42 .... 128 A2
Lochlibo Av *KNTSWD* G13 .... 80 F3
Lochlibo Ct *IRVSE* KA11 .... 204 A3
Lochlibo Crs *BRHD/NEIL* G78 ..... 125 G8
Lochlibo Rd *BEITH* KA15 .... 169 L6
　BEITH KA15 .... 187 G4
　BRHD/NEIL G78 .... 147 G6
　IRVSE KA11 .... 195 H7
　IRVSE KA11 .... 204 A3
Lochlibo Ter *BRHD/NEIL* G78 ..... 125 G8
Lochlie Pl *SVSTN* KA20 .... 192 E8
Lochlip Rd *LOCHW* PA12 .... 120 D7
Loch Long *EKILN* G74 .... 15 L5
Loch Loyal *EKILN* G74 .... 15 M6
Lochmaben Dr
　CARD/HILL/MSPK G52 .... 102 F5
Lochmaddy Av *LNPK/KPK* G44 ... 128 A5
Loch Maree *EKILN* G74 .... 15 L5
Loch Meadie *EKILN* G74 .... 15 L5
Lochnagar Dr *BSDN* G61 .... 61 H2
Lochnagar Rd *KLMNK* KA1 .... 212 A5
Loch Naver *EKILN* G74 .... 15 M6
Lochore Av *PSLYN/LNWD* PA3 .... 100 A2
Lochpark *AYRS* KA7 .... 228 C6
Loch Pk *WISHAW* ML2 .... 159 J6
Loch Park Av *CARLUKE* ML8 .... 188 E1
Loch Park Pl *LRKH* ML9 .... 176 A8
Loch Pl *BRWEIR* PA11 .... 98 D1
Lochranza Dr *EKILS* G75 .... 171 H5
　HBR/GL G84 .... 20 F7
Lochranza La *EKILS* G75 .... 171 J5
Lochranza Pl *SALT* KA21 .... 192 A7
Loch Rd *AIRDRIE* ML6 .... 111 K7
　BRWEIR PA11 .... 98 D1
　KKNTL G66 .... 65 L2
　MLNGV G62 .... 42 B6
　STPS/GTHM/RID G33 .... 85 K4
Loch Shin *EKILN* G74 .... 15 M6
Lochside *BAIL/MDB/MHD* G69 ..... 86 F3
　BSDN G61 .... 61 M6
Lochside Rd *AYR* KA8 .... 225 J5
Lochside St *PLKSD/SHW* G41 ..... 104 E8
Loch St *AIRDRIE* ML6 .... 111 H7
Loch Striven *EKILN* G74 .... 15 L6
Loch Torridon *EKILN* G74 .... 15 L6
Loch Vw *AIRDRIE* ML6 .... 111 H7
　AIRDRIE ML6 .... 111 H7
Lochview Av *GRK* PA19 .... 32 A2
Lochview Crs
　STPS/GTHM/RID G33 .... 84 F6

Lochview Dr
　STPS/GTHM/RID G33 .... 84 F6
Lochview Gdns
　STPS/GTHM/RID G33 .... 84 F6
Lochview Pl
　STPS/GTHM/RID G33 .... 84 F6
Lochview Rd *BEITH* KA15 .... 167 M2
　BSDN G61 .... 61 L6
　CTBR ML5 .... 87 J8
　PGL PA14 .... 34 B8
Loch Voil St *CAR/SHTL* G32 .... 107 K5
Lochwinnoch Rd *KLMCLM* PA13 .. 75 H2
Lochwood Loan
　BAIL/MDB/MHD G69 .... 67 G6
Lochwood St
　STPS/GTHM/RID G33 .... 84 E7
Lochy Av *RNFRW* PA4 .... 80 F8
Lochy Pl *ERSK* PA8 .... 58 E7
Lochy St *WISHAW* ML2 .... 159 G8
Lockerbie Av
　PLKSW/MSWD G43 .... 127 M3
Locket Yett Vw *BLSH* ML4 .... 132 E4
Lockhart Av *BLTYR/CAMB* G72 ... 130 D3
Lockhart Dr
　BLTYR/CAMB G72 .... 130 D3
　LNK/LMHG ML11 .... 198 E4
Lockhart Pl
　UD/BTH/TAN G71 .... 108 B7
　WISHAW ML2 .... 159 L5
Lockhart St *CARLUKE* ML8 .... 178 F7
　HMLTN ML3 .... 174 C3
　SPRGB/BLRNK G21 .... 7 H4
Lockhart Ter *EKILN* G74 .... 15 L1
Locksley Av *CUMB* G67 .... 68 E3
　KNTSWD G13 .... 81 J1
Locksley Crs *CUMB* G67 .... 68 E3
Locksley Pl *CUMB* G67 .... 68 E3
Locksley Rd *CUMB* G67 .... 68 E3
　PSLYS PA2 .... 100 F8
Locks St *CTBR* ML5 .... 110 D3
Lodge Crs *KLMCLM* PA13 .... 75 L2
Lodge Gdns *KLMCLM* PA13 .... 55 L8
Lodge Gv *KLMCLM* PA13 .... 55 L8
Lodge Pk *KLMCLM* PA13 .... 55 L8
Logan Av *NMRNS* G77 .... 150 A3
Logandale Av *WISHAW* ML2 .... 159 M3
Logan Dr *BALLOCH* G68 .... 48 D6
　PSLYN/LNWD PA3 .... 8 C1
　TROON KA10 .... 216 D6
Logan Gdns *BLTYR/CAMB* G72 ... 155 L2
　HMLTN ML3 .... 174 B1
　KLMNK KA1 .... 211 L5
Lochgreen St
　STPS/GTHM/RID G33 .... 84 E3
Logans Rd *MTHW* ML1 .... 157 H1
Logan St *BLTYR/CAMB* G72 .... 155 L2
　GBLS G5 .... 105 K7
Loganswell Dr *GIF/THBK* G46 .... 126 E7
Loganswell Gdns *GIF/THBK* G46 . 126 E7
Loganswell Pl *GIF/THBK* G46 ..... 126 E7
Loganswell Rd *GIF/THBK* G46 .... 126 E7
Logie Pk *EKILN* G74 .... 154 A4
Logie Sq *EKILN* G74 .... 154 A6
Lomax St *STPS/GTHM/RID* G33 ..... 7 L8
Lomond *EKILS* G75 .... 171 L4
Lomond Av *KLMNK* KA1 .... 212 F3
　PGL PA14 .... 54 D1
　RNFRW PA4 .... 80 B8
Lomond Ct *BRHD/NEIL* G78 .... 125 J7
　CUMB G67 .... 68 C2
Lomond Crs *ALEX/LLW* G83 .... 25 K2
　BEITH KA15 .... 144 B7
　BRWEIR PA11 .... 98 C1
　CUMB G67 .... 68 C2
　PSLYS PA2 .... 124 D1
Lomond Dr *AIRDRIE* ML6 .... 88 C8
　ALEX/LLW G83 .... 25 K2
　BRHD/NEIL G78 .... 125 H5
　BSHPBGS G64 .... 63 M6
　CUMB G67 .... 68 B2
　DMBTN G82 .... 37 H3
　NMRNS G77 .... 150 D2
　UD/BTH/TAN G71 .... 132 B6
　WISHAW ML2 .... 159 G8
Lomond Gdns *JNSTN* PA5 .... 100 C7
Lomond Gv *CUMB* G67 .... 68 C2
　HMLTN ML3 .... 155 M7
　KLMNK KA1 .... 218 C5
Lomond Pl *CTBR* ML5 .... 87 L2
　CUMB G67 .... 68 B2
　ERSK PA8 .... 58 E8
　IRV KA12 .... 203 K3
　STPS/GTHM/RID G33 .... 85 K5
Lomondside Av
　CRMNK/CLK/EAG G76 .... 151 J2
Lomond St *HBR/GL* G84 .... 20 C8
　PPK/MIL G22 .... 83 H4
Lomond Vw *CUMB* G67 .... 68 C2
　HMLTN ML3 .... 155 M7
　KLMNK KA1 .... 218 C5
Lomond Wy *IRVSE* KA11 .... 204 A5
London Rd *CAR/SHTL* G32 .... 107 F7
　DEN/PKHD G31 .... 13 L8
　DMNK/BRGTN G40 .... 12 A4
　KLMNKN/STW KA3 .... 17 H4
London St *LRKH* ML9 .... 176 A5
　RNFRW PA4 .... 80 D4
Lonend *PSLY* PA1 .... 9 J6
Longay Pl *PPK/MIL* G22 .... 83 J3
Longay St *PPK/MIL* G22 .... 83 J1
Longbank Dr *AYRS* KA7 .... 229 J5
Longbank Rd *AYRS* KA7 .... 228 F5
Longbar Av *GLGNK* KA14 .... 167 K3
Long Craigs Vw *DMBTN* G82 .... 37 J3
Longcrofts Rd *SALT* KA21 .... 191 J4
Longden St *CLYDBK* G81 .... 80 D1
Long Dr *EKILS* G75 .... 15 J8
　IRV KA12 .... 203 M3
　IRVSE KA11 .... 203 M3
　IRVSE KA11 .... 209 G3
Longfield Av *SALT* KA21 .... 191 J4
Longfield Pl *SALT* KA21 .... 191 J4
Longford Av *KLWNG* KA13 .... 193 L8

Longford St *STPS/GTHM/RID* G33 .. 7 M8
Long Hl *SKLM* PA17 .... 70 A5
Longhill Av *AYRS* KA7 .... 228 F5
Longhill Pk *AYRS* KA7 .... 228 F5
Longlee *BAIL/MDB/MHD* G69 ..... 108 B5
Longmeadow *JNSTN* PA5 .... 99 J8
Longpark Av *KLMNKN/STW* KA3 . 206 F2
Long Rw *BAIL/MDB/MHD* G69 .... 108 C3
Longrow Gdns *IRVSE* KA11 .... 203 M2
Longstone Rd
　STPS/GTHM/RID G33 .... 107 H1
Longwill Ter *CUMB* G67 .... 49 H5
Lonmay Rd
　STPS/GTHM/RID G33 .... 107 K1
Lonsdale Av *GIF/THBK* G46 .... 127 J6
Loom Wk *KLBCH* PA10 .... 99 G6
Lora Dr
　CARD/HILL/MSPK G52 .... 103 L5
Loreny Dr *KLMNK* KA1 .... 211 L7
Loretto Pl
　STPS/GTHM/RID G33 .... 106 F1
Loretto St *STPS/GTHM/RID* G33 . 106 F1
Lorimer Crs *EKILS* G75 .... 14 C8
Lorn Av *BAIL/MDB/MHD* G69 ...... 86 D1
Lorne Crs *BSHPBGS* G64 .... 64 D7
Lorne Dr *MTHW* ML1 .... 133 K7
　PSLYN/LNWD PA3 .... 100 A4
Lorne Gdns *SHOTTS* ML7 .... 113 G7
Lorne Pl *CTBR* ML5 .... 110 D4
Lorne Rd *CARD/HILL/MSPK* G52 . 102 F1
Lorne St *GOV/IBX* G51 .... 104 D3
　HBR/GL G84 .... 20 D7
　HMLTN ML3 .... 156 C5
Lorne Ter *BLTYR/CAMB* G72 ...... 129 M6
　RAYR/DAL KA6 .... 231 K5
Lorn Pl *KKNTL* G66 .... 46 C8
Lorraine Gdns
　KVD/HLHD G12 .... 82 C5
Lorraine Gardens La
　KVD/HLHD G12 .... 82 C5
Lorraine Rd *KVD/HLHD* G12 .... 82 C5
Lorraine Wy *ALEX/LLW* G83 .... 25 M8
Loskin Dr *PPK/MIL* G22 .... 83 H2
Lossie Crs *RNFRW* PA4 .... 80 F7
Lossie St *STPS/GTHM/RID* G33 ...... 7 M6
Lothian Crs *PSLYS* PA2 .... 101 K8
Lothian Dr
　CRMNK/CLK/EAG G76 .... 151 K1
Lothian Gdns *MRYH/FIRH* G20 ..... 4 B2
Lothian Rd *AYRS* KA7 .... 19 H7
　GRNKW/INVK PA16 .... 31 K5
　KLMNKN/STW KA3 .... 197 L1
Lothian St
　CARD/HILL/MSPK G52 .... 102 E1
　BLTYR/CAMB G72 .... 154 C6
Loudon Av *GLSTN* KA4 .... 214 A4
　KLMNK KA1 .... 212 A5
Loudon Crs *KLWNG* KA13 .... 193 H5
　NMLNS KA16 .... 215 J2
Loudon Pl *CRH/DND* KA2 .... 210 F1
Loudon Rd *NMLNS* KA16 .... 215 G2
Loudon Rd West *NMLNS* KA16 .... 215 G2
Loudoun Av *KLMNKN/STW* KA3 .. 197 L2
Loudoun Ter *PSTWK* KA9 .... 225 K2
Louise Gdns *BLSH* ML4 .... 133 M4
Louisville Av *WISHAW* ML2 .... 159 K4
Lounsdale Av *PSLYS* PA2 .... 8 A7
Lounsdale Crs *PSLYS* PA2 .... 101 G7
Lounsdale Dr *PSLYS* PA2 .... 8 A8
Lounsdale Pl *SCOT* G14 .... 81 H5
Lounsdale Rd *PSLYS* PA2 .... 8 A8
Lourdes Av
　CARD/HILL/MSPK G52 .... 103 K5
Lovat Av *BSDN* G61 .... 61 J2
Lovat Dr *KKNTL* G66 .... 65 H1
Lovat Pl *CARD/HILL/MSPK* G52 . 102 E2
　RUTH G73 .... 129 K5
Lovat St *LARGS* KA30 .... 115 K6
Love Av *BRWEIR* PA11 .... 75 L7
Love St *KLWNG* KA13 .... 194 A6
　PSLYN/LNWD PA3 .... 101 L3
Low Barholm *KLBCH* PA10 .... 99 H7
Low Broadlie Rd
　BRHD/NEIL G78 .... 148 D2
Low Craigends *KSYTH* G65 .... 47 L1
Low Crs *CLYDBK* G81 .... 80 E1
Lower Auchingramont Rd
　HMLTN ML3 .... 156 E5
Lower Bourtree Dr *RUTH* G73 .... 129 J3
Lower Bouverie St *PGL* PA14 .... 34 D8
Lower Millgate
　UD/BTH/TAN G71 .... 131 M3
Lower Mill Rd
　CRMNK/CLK/EAG G76 .... 151 M3
Lower Stoneymollan Rd
　ALEX/LLW G83 .... 25 J1
Lower Sutherland Crs
　HBR/GL G84 .... 20 B6
Low Flender Rd
　CRMNK/CLK/EAG G76 .... 151 K4
Low Glencairn St *KLMNK* KA1 ...... 16 F9
Low Green Rd *IRV* KA12 .... 203 H6
Lowndes St *BRHD/NEIL* G78 .... 125 J7
Low Parksail *ERSK* PA8 .... 79 J2
Low Patrick St *HMLTN* ML3 .... 156 F6
Low Pleasance *LRKH* ML9 .... 176 B6
Low Rd *AYR* KA8 .... 225 L6
　PSLYS PA2 .... 8 D6
Lowther Av *BSDN* G61 .... 61 J2
Lowther Bank *IRVSE* KA11 .... 204 C3
Lowther Pl *KLMNK* KA1 .... 212 A5
Lowther Ter *KVD/HLHD* G12 .... 82 C5
Loyal Av *ERSK* PA8 .... 58 F8
Loyal Gdns *BSDN* G61 .... 61 H1
Loyal Pl *ERSK* PA8 .... 58 F8
Loyne Dr *RNFRW* PA4 .... 80 F7

Luath St *GOV/IBX* G51 .... **104** A1
Lubas Av *CVH/MTFL* G42 .... **128** D2
Lubas Pl *CVH/MTFL* G42 .... **128** D2
Lubnaig Dr *ERSK* PA8 .... **58** E8
Lubnaig Gdns *BSDN* G61 .... **61** J2
Lubnaig Pl *AIRDRIE* ML6 .... **88** E7
Lubnaig Rd *PLKSW/MSWD* G43 .... **127** L4
Luce Av *KLMNK* KA1 .... **212** A4
Luckiesfauld *BRHD/NEIL* G78 .... **148** D3 ⚅
Luckingsford Av *RNFRW* PA4 .... **79** K2
Luckingsford Dr *RNFRW* PA4 .... **79** K3 ⚅
Luckingsford Rd *RNFRW* PA4 .... **79** J2
Lucy Brae *UD/BTH/TAN* G71 .... **131** L1
Luffness Gdns *CAR/SHTL* G32 .... **107** H7
Lugar Crs *PSTWK* KA9 .... **225** J1
Lugar Dr *CARD/HILL/MSPK* G52 .... **103** L5
Lugar Pl *LNPK/KPK* G44 .... **128** E4 ⚅
   TROON KA10 .... **216** F4
Lugar St *CTBR* ML5 .... **110** B1
Luggiebank Pl
   BAIL/MDB/MHD G69 .... **109** G5 ⚅
Luggiebank Rd *KKNTL* G66 .... **65** K1 ⚅
Luggie Rd *CARLUKE* ML8 .... **178** D7
Luggie Vw *CUMB* G67 .... **68** A2 ⚅
Luing
   CARD/HILL/MSPK G52 .... **103** L4 ⚅
Luma Gdns *GOV/IBX* G51 .... **103** J2
Lumloch St
   SPRGB/BLRNK G21 .... **84** A5 ⚅⚅
Lumsden La *KVGV* G3 .... **82** D8 ⚅
Lumsden Pl *SVSTN* KA20 .... **192** E8 ⚅
Lumsden St *KVGV* G3 .... **104** D1 ⚅
Lunan Dr *BSHPBGS* G64 .... **84** C1
Lunan Pl *GOV/IBX* G51 .... **103** L2 ⚅
Luncarty Pl *CAR/SHTL* G32 .... **107** G6 ⚅
Luncarty St *CAR/SHTL* G32 .... **107** G6 ⚅
Lunderston Dr *PLK/PH/NH* G53 .... **126** A3
Lundie Gdns *BSHPBGS* G64 .... **84** D1 ⚅
Lundie St *CAR/SHTL* G32 .... **106** E6 ⚅
Lurg St *PGL* PA14 .... **54** D1 ⚅
Luss Av *GRNK* PA15 .... **33** H8
Luss Brae *HMLTN* ML3 .... **155** L7
Lusset Gln *OLDK* G60 .... **59** H3
Lusset Rd *OLDK* G60 .... **59** H3
Lusshill Ter *UD/BTH/TAN* G71 .... **108** B7
Luss Pl *GRNK* PA15 .... **33** J8
Luss Rd *ALEX/LLW* G83 .... **25** K2
   GOV/IBX G51 .... **103** M2
   HBR/GL G84 .... **21** G4
Lye Brae *CUMB* G67 .... **49** C7
Lyell Gv *EKILN* G74 .... **153** L6
Lyell Pl *EKILN* G74 .... **153** L6
Lyle Crs *BSHPTN* PA7 .... **57** M5
Lylefoot Crs
   GRNKW/INVK PA16 .... **32** B1 ⚅
Lylefoot Pl *GRNKW/INVK* PA16 .... **32** B2 ⚅
Lyle Gv *GRNKW/INVK* PA16 .... **32** B2
Lyle Pl *GRNKW/INVK* PA16 .... **32** A2 ⚅
   PSLYS PA2 .... **9** K9
Lyle St *AIRDRIE* ML6 .... **111** M2
   GRNKW/INVK PA16 .... **32** A1 ⚅
   KLMCLM PA13 .... **75** K1 ⚅
Lylesland Ct *PSLYS* PA2 .... **9** H8
Lyle Sq *MLNGV* G62 .... **41** L7
Lyle St *GRNK* PA15 .... **2** D5
Lyman Dr *WISHAW* ML2 .... **159** J2
Lymburn Pl *AYR* KA8 .... **19** J3
Lymburn Av *KVGV* G3 .... **82** D8
Lymekilns Rd *EKILN* G74 .... **14** C1
Lyndale Pl *MRYH/FIRH* G20 .... **82** E1 ⚅
Lyndale Rd *MRYH/FIRH* G20 .... **82** D1 ⚅
Lyndhurst Gdns *MRYH/FIRH* G20 .... **4** D2
Lyndhurst Gardens La
   MRYH/FIRH G20 .... **4** B2
Lyne Cft *BSHPBGS* G64 .... **64** A5
Lynedoch Crs *KVGV* G3 .... **4** C6
Lynedoch Crescent La *KVGV* G3 .... **4** C6
Lynedoch Pl *KVGV* G3 .... **4** C7
Lynedoch St *GRNK* PA15 .... **2** D6
   KVGV G3 .... **4** C7
Lynedoch Ter *KVGV* G3 .... **4** C7 ⚅
Lyne St *WISHAW* ML2 .... **159** L3
Lynmouth Pl
   GRNKW/INVK PA16 .... **31** L4 ⚅
Lynn Av *DALRY* KA24 .... **184** C2
Lynnburn Av *BLSH* ML4 .... **133** C4
Lynn Ct *LRKH* ML9 .... **176** A7 ⚅
Lynn Dr *KBRN* KA25 .... **143** H6
   MLNGV G62 .... **42** C7 ⚅
Lynne Dr *SMSTN* G23 .... **62** E8 ⚅
Lynnhurst *UD/BTH/TAN* G71 .... **131** M3
Lynnwood Rd *WISHAW* ML2 .... **160** C3 ⚅
Lynton Av *GIF/THBK* G46 .... **127** G4
Lyoncross Av *BRHD/NEIL* G78 .... **125** K7
Lyoncross Crs
   BRHD/NEIL G78 .... **125** K6 ⚅
Lyoncross Rd *PLK/PH/NH* G53 .... **103** H7
Lyon Rd *ERSK* PA8 .... **58** E7
   PSLYN/LNWD PA3 .... **100** B5
   PSLYS PA2 .... **100** B5
Lysa Vale Pl *BLSH* ML4 .... **132** E4 ⚅
Lytham Dr *SMSTN* G23 .... **62** E8 ⚅
Lytham Mdw
   UD/BTH/TAN G71 .... **131** L7 ⚅
Lythgow Wy *LNK/LMHG* ML11 .... **199** J4
Lyttelton *EKILS* G75 .... **171** H2

M

Mabel St *MTHW* ML1 .... **157** L4
Macadam Gdns *BLSH* ML4 .... **133** G3 ⚅
Macadam Pl *AYR* KA8 .... **19** G2
   EKILS G75 .... **14** F6
   KLMNKN/STW KA3 .... **17** L2
Macallan Pl *IRVSE* KA11 .... **203** M2
Macallister Pl
   KLMNKN/STW KA3 .... **17** L3 ⚅
Macalpine Pl *KLMNKN/STW* KA3 .... **17** L1
Macandrew Pl
   KLMNKN/STW KA3 .... **17** M3 ⚅
Macara Dr *IRV* KA12 .... **203** L6
Macarthur Av *AIRDRIE* ML6 .... **88** D6
Macarthur Ct *EKILN* G74 .... **153** J6 ⚅
Macarthur Crs *EKILN* G74 .... **153** J5 ⚅
Macarthur Dr *EKILN* G74 .... **153** J6

Macarthur Gdns *EKILN* G74 .... **153** J6 ⚅
Macarthur Wynd
   BLTYR/CAMB G72 .... **130** C4
Macaulay Pl *HBR/GL* G84 .... **20** A7 ⚅
Macauley Pl *KLMNKN/STW* KA3 .... **17** L2
Macbeth Dr *KLMNKN/STW* KA3 .... **17** M3
Macbeth Pl *DEN/PKHD* G31 .... **13** L7
Macbeth Rd *GRNKW/INVK* PA16 .... **32** A4
Macbeth St *DEN/PKHD* G31 .... **13** L8
Mac Callum Dr
   BLTYR/CAMB G72 .... **130** C4
Maccrimmon Pk *EKILN* G74 .... **153** H5 ⚅
Macdairmid Dr *HMLTN* ML3 .... **174** B2 ⚅
Macdonald Av *EKILN* G74 .... **153** G5
Macdonald Ct *BEITH* KA15 .... **168** A2 ⚅
Macdonald Crs *KSYTH* G65 .... **46** F6
Macdonald Dr
   KLMNKN/STW KA3 .... **17** M3
Macdonald Gv *BLSH* ML4 .... **132** F7 ⚅
Macdonald Pl
   KLMNKN/STW KA3 .... **17** M3
Macdonald St *MTHW* ML1 .... **157** M4 ⚅
   RUTH G73 .... **129** G2 ⚅
Macdougall Pl
   KLMNKN/STW KA3 .... **17** L3
Macdougall St *GRNK* PA15 .... **3** L7
   PLKSW/MSWD G43 .... **127** J2 ⚅
Macdougall Qd *BLSH* ML4 .... **132** F7 ⚅
Macdowall St *JNSTN* PA5 .... **99** M6
   PSLYN/LNWD PA3 .... **8** E1
Macduff *DEN/PKHD* G31 .... **13** L8
Macduff St *DEN/PKHD* G31 .... **13** L8
Macedonian Gv *MTHW* ML1 .... **134** C5
Mace Rd *KNTSWD* G13 .... **61** J8
Macewan Pl *KLMNKN/STW* KA3 .... **17** L4
Macfarlane Crs
   BLTYR/CAMB G72 .... **130** C4 ⚅
Macfarlane Dr
   KLMNKN/STW KA3 .... **17** L2
Macfarlane Rd *BSDN* G61 .... **61** M6
Macfie Pl *EKILN* G74 .... **153** H5 ⚅
Macgregor Dr
   KLMNKN/STW KA3 .... **17** K4
Machan Av *LRKH* ML9 .... **176** A6
Machanhill *LRKH* ML9 .... **176** B7
Machanhill Vw *LRKH* ML9 .... **176** B7
Machan Rd *LRKH* ML9 .... **176** A7
Machrie Dr *CSMK* G45 .... **128** F5
   HBR/GL G84 .... **20** F6
   NMRNS G77 .... **150** E3
Machrie Gn *EKILS* G75 .... **171** H5 ⚅
Machrie Pl *KLWNG* KA13 .... **193** J6
Machrie Rd *CSMK* G45 .... **128** F5
   KLMNKN/STW KA3 .... **206** E5
Machrie St *CSMK* G45 .... **128** F6 ⚅
   MTHW ML1 .... **157** H2
Macinnes Pl *KLMNKN/STW* KA3 .... **17** L2
Macintosh Pl *EKILS* G75 .... **14** B8
Macintyre Pl *KLMNKN/STW* KA3 .... **17** L2
Macintyre Rd *PSTWK* KA9 .... **221** J7
Macintyre St *KVGV* G3 .... **10** D1
Macivor Crs *EKILN* G74 .... **153** G5
Macivor Pl *KLMNKN/STW* KA3 .... **17** L3
Mackean St *PSLYN/LNWD* PA3 .... **101** J3
Mackeith St *DMNK/BRGTN* G40 .... **12** C7
Mackellar Pl *KLMNKN/STW* KA3 .... **17** L1
Mackenzie Dr *KLBCH* PA10 .... **99** H8
   KLMNKN/STW KA3 .... **17** L4
Mackenzie Gdns *EKILN* G74 .... **153** G5 ⚅
Mackenzie St *GRNK* PA15 .... **3** L7
Mackenzie Ter *BLSH* ML4 .... **133** G2 ⚅
Mackerston Pl *LARGS* KA30 .... **115** J6
Mackie Av *PGL* PA14 .... **34** A8
Mackie Pl *KLMNKN/STW* KA3 .... **17** L2
Mackie's Mill Rd *JNSTN* PA5 .... **123** K1
Mackinlay Pl *KLMNK* KA1 .... **17** H6
Mackinlay St *GBLS* G5 .... **11** G8
Mackinnon Dr
   KLMNKN/STW KA3 .... **17** L4
Mackinnon Ter *IRV* KA12 .... **203** L5
Mackintosh Pl *IRVSE* KA11 .... **203** L8
Mack St *AIRDRIE* ML6 .... **111** G1
Maclachlan Pl *HBR/GL* G84 .... **20** E6 ⚅
Maclachlan Rd *HBR/GL* G84 .... **20** E6
Maclaren Pl *KLMNKN/STW* KA3 .... **17** L4
Maclay Av *KLBCH* PA10 .... **99** G7
Maclean Ct *EKILN* G74 .... **153** H5 ⚅
Maclean Dr *KLMNKN/STW* KA3 .... **17** K3
Maclean Gv *EKILN* G74 .... **153** H5
Maclean Pl *EKILN* G74 .... **153** H5
Maclean Sq *GOV/IBX* G51 .... **10** A3
Maclean St *CLYDBK* G81 .... **80** E1 ⚅
   GOV/IBX G51 .... **104** D3
Maclehose Rd *CUMB* G67 .... **49** J6
Maclellan Rd *BRHD/NEIL* G78 .... **148** D3
Macleod Crs *HBR/GL* G84 .... **20** B5
Macleod Dr *HBR/GL* G84 .... **20** C5
   KLMNKN/STW KA3 .... **17** L4
Macleod Pl *EKILN* G74 .... **154** B6
Macleod St *COWCAD* G4 .... **12** A1
Macmillan Gdns
   UD/BTH/TAN G71 .... **109** G8 ⚅
Macmillan Pl *KLMNKN/STW* KA3 .... **17** L3
Macmillan St *LRKH* ML9 .... **175** M7
Macnab Pl *KLMNKN/STW* KA3 .... **17** K3
Macnaughton Dr
   KLMNKN/STW KA3 .... **17** L3
Macneill Dr *EKILN* G74 .... **153** H5
Macneill Gdns *EKILN* G74 .... **153** G5
Macneil Pl *KLMNKN/STW* KA3 .... **17** K3
Macneil St *LRKH* ML9 .... **175** M6
Macneish Wy *EKILN* G74 .... **153** J6
Macnicol Ct *EKILN* G74 .... **153** C5 ⚅
Macnicol Pk *EKILN* G74 .... **153** C5 ⚅
Macnicol Pl *KLMNKN/STW* KA3 .... **17** L3
Macphail Dr *KLMNKN/STW* KA3 .... **17** K3
Macpherson Pk *EKILN* G74 .... **153** J6 ⚅
Macpherson Pl
   KLMNKN/STW KA3 .... **17** M3
Macphie Rd *DMBTN* G82 .... **37** J4
Macrae Pl *PSTWK* KA9 .... **221** J7
Macrae Gdns *EKILN* G74 .... **153** J6
Macreadie Pl *IRVSE* KA11 .... **204** D3

Macrimmon Pl *EKILS* G75 .... **14** E5
Macrobert Av *IRVSE* KA11 .... **204** B8 ⚅
Mactaggart Rd *CUMB* G67 .... **68** E1
Madeira La *GRNKW/INVK* PA16 .... **32** D2
Madeira St *GRNKW/INVK* PA16 .... **32** D2
Madison Av *LNPK/KPK* G44 .... **128** B4
Madras Pl *BRHD/NEIL* G78 .... **148** C2
Madras St *DMNK/BRGTN* G40 .... **12** C9
Mafeking St *GOV/IBX* G51 .... **104** B3 ⚅
   WISHAW ML2 .... **158** D5 ⚅
Mafeking Ter *BRHD/NEIL* G78 .... **148** C2
Magna St *MTHW* ML1 .... **157** H1
Magnolia Dr *BLTYR/CAMB* G72 .... **130** F6
Magnolia Gdns *MTHW* ML1 .... **134** C6 ⚅
Magnolia Pl
   UD/BTH/TAN G71 .... **132** C1 ⚅
Magnolia St *WISHAW* ML2 .... **159** H4
Magnus Crs *LNPK/KPK* G44 .... **128** B5
Magnus Rd *CRG/CRSL/HOU* PA6 .... **99** J1
Magpie Crs *GRNKW/INVK* PA16 .... **50** E4
Mahon Ct *BAIL/MDB/MHD* G69 .... **66** F8
Maidens *EKILN* G74 .... **153** K6
Maidens Av *NMRNS* G77 .... **151** G4
Maidland Rd *PLK/PH/NH* G53 .... **126** C2
Maid Morville Av *IRVSE* KA11 .... **209** J1
Mailerbeg Gdns
   BAIL/MDB/MHD G69 .... **66** F6
Mailing Av *BSHPBGS* G64 .... **64** D7
Maimhor Rd *WKIL* KA23 .... **181** H5
Mainhill Av
   BAIL/MDB/MHD G69 .... **108** D4 ⚅
Mainhill Dr
   BAIL/MDB/MHD G69 .... **108** C4
Mainhill Pl *BAIL/MDB/MHD* G69 .... **108** C4
Mainhill Rd
   BAIL/MDB/MHD G69 .... **108** F4
Mainholm Crs *AYR* KA8 .... **225** K8
Mainholm Rd *AYR* KA8 .... **225** K7
   RAYR/DAL KA6 .... **225** K7
Main Rd *AYR* KA8 .... **225** L7 ⚅
   CRH/DND KA2 .... **210** E4
   CUMB G67 .... **67** G5
   DMBTN G82 .... **35** H1
   FAIRLIE KA29 .... **139** K2
   IRVSE KA11 .... **204** F7
   JNSTN PA5 .... **100** C6
   KBRN KA25 .... **143** H8
   KLMNKN/STW KA3 .... **212** D2
   PGL PA14 .... **56** B2 ⚅
   PGL PA14 .... **56** E3
   PSLYS PA2 .... **8** E6
Mains Av *BEITH* KA15 .... **144** A8
   GIF/THBK G46 .... **127** H8
   HBR/GL G84 .... **20** A6
Mains Ct *LNK/LMHG* ML11 .... **199** J3
Mainscroft *ERSK* PA8 .... **59** J3
Mains Dr *ERSK* PA8 .... **59** J3
Mains Hl *ERSK* PA8 .... **59** H8
Mainshill Av *ERSK* PA8 .... **59** H8
Mainshill Gdns *ERSK* PA8 .... **59** H8
Mains Pl *BLSH* ML4 .... **133** G6
Mains River *ERSK* PA8 .... **59** J3
Mains Rd *BEITH* KA15 .... **144** A8
   EKILN G74 .... **153** L4
Main St *AIRDRIE* ML6 .... **90** A7
   AIRDRIE ML6 .... **91** A7
   AIRDRIE ML6 .... **91** G5
   AIRDRIE ML6 .... **111** J6
   AIRDRIE ML6 .... **111** L6
   ALEX/LLW G83 .... **25** L4 ⚅
   ALEX/LLW G83 .... **25** M5
   AYR KA8 .... **18** F1
   BAIL/MDB/MHD G69 .... **86** C1
   BAIL/MDB/MHD G69 .... **108** C5
   BEITH KA15 .... **144** B8 ⚅
   BEITH KA15 .... **168** C1
   BLSH ML4 .... **132** F4
   BLTYR/CAMB G72 .... **129** M3
   BLTYR/CAMB G72 .... **155** J3
   BRHD/NEIL G78 .... **125** H7
   BRHD/NEIL G78 .... **148** D2
   BRWEIR PA11 .... **98** D1
   BSDN G61 .... **62** A2
   BSHPBGS G64 .... **64** B1
   CAR/SHTL G32 .... **107** K5
   CRG/CRSL/HOU PA6 .... **77** G6
   CRH/DND KA2 .... **209** M8
   CRMNK/CLK/EAG G76 .... **151** K3
   CTBR ML5 .... **87** K4
   CTBR ML5 .... **110** A3
   CUMB G67 .... **49** H4
   DALRY KA24 .... **184** C2
   DMBTN G82 .... **25** K7
   DMNK/BRGTN G40 .... **12** C9
   EKILN G74 .... **15** G1
   GIF/THBK G46 .... **126** F6
   GLGNK KA14 .... **167** H3
   GRNK PA15 .... **3** H6
   GRNKW/INVK PA16 .... **50** D4
   HWWD PA9 .... **121** M4
   IRVSE KA11 .... **204** A8
   IRVSE KA11 .... **209** K3
   KKNTL G66 .... **44** D1
   KLMNK KA1 .... **218** C5
   KKNTL G66 .... **65** M1
   KLMNKN/STW KA3 .... **197** K1
   KLMNKN/STW KA3 .... **206** C2
   KLWNG KA13 .... **193** L6
   KSYTH G65 .... **46** F5
   KSYTH G65 .... **47** K1
   LARGS KA30 .... **115** J6
   LOCHW PA12 .... **120** C7
   MLNGV G62 .... **42** A8
   MTHW ML1 .... **134** A4
   MTHW ML1 .... **135** J8
   NMLNS KA16 .... **215** J2
   PSTWK KA9 .... **221** K5
   PSTWK KA9 .... **225** J1
   RUTH G73 .... **129** G1
   SVSTN KA20 .... **201** K1
   TROON KA10 .... **217** H6
   UD/BTH/TAN G71 .... **131** L3
   UD/BTH/TAN G71 .... **132** A7
   WISHAW ML2 .... **159** G6
   WISHAW ML2 .... **160** A5
   WISHAW ML2 .... **177** J2
   WKIL KA23 .... **181** J4
Mains Wd *ERSK* PA8 .... **59** K8
Mair Av *DALRY* KA24 .... **184** D2
Mair St *GOV/IBX* G51 .... **10** A4

Maitland Bank *LRKH* ML9 .... **176** C6
Maitland Dr *BSHPBGS* G64 .... **44** B8
Maitland Pl *RNFRW* PA4 .... **80** B7
Maitland St *COWCAD* G4 .... **5** H6
   HBR/GL G84 .... **20** D8 ⚅
Malborough La North
   PTCK G11 .... **81** M6 ⚅
Malborough La South *PTCK* G11 .... **81** M6
Malcolm Gdns *EKILN* G74 .... **14** A2
Malcolm Pl *HBR/GL* G84 .... **20** D5
Malcolm St *MTHW* ML1 .... **157** J3
Malin Pl *STPS/GTHM/RID* G33 .... **106** F3
Mallaig Pl *GOV/IBX* G51 .... **103** K2 ⚅
Mallaig Rd *GOV/IBX* G51 .... **103** K2
   PGL PA14 .... **54** F2
Mallard Crs *EKILS* G75 .... **171** G4 ⚅
   GRNKW/INVK PA16 .... **32** A3
Mallard Pl *EKILS* G75 .... **171** G4 ⚅
Mallard Rd *CLYDBK* G81 .... **60** B4
Mallard Ter *EKILS* G75 .... **171** G4 ⚅
Mallard Wy *BLSH* ML4 .... **109** M8
Malleable Gdns *MTHW* ML1 .... **133** J7
Malletsheugh Rd *NMRNS* G77 .... **150** B6
Malloch Crs *JNSTN* PA5 .... **100** B7
Malloch Pl *EKILN* G74 .... **15** L2
Malloch St *MRYH/FIRH* G20 .... **82** E4
Malov Ct *EKILS* G75 .... **171** L4
Malplaquet Ct *CARLUKE* ML8 .... **179** H8
Maltbarns St *MRYH/FIRH* G20 .... **4** E2
Mambeg Dr *GOV/IBX* G51 .... **103** L1 ⚅
Mamore Pl *PLKSW/MSWD* G43 .... **127** J3
Mamore St *PLKSW/MSWD* G43 .... **127** J3
Manchester Dr *KVD/HLHD* G12 .... **82** A5
Mandora Ct *CARLUKE* ML8 .... **179** H8 ⚅
Manitoba Crs *EKILS* G75 .... **153** H8
Mannering Av *EKILN* G74 .... **154** D5
Mannering Ct
   PLKSD/SHW G41 .... **127** J1 ⚅
Mannering Rd *PLKSD/SHW* G41 .... **127** J1
   PSLYS PA2 .... **123** L1
Mannofield *BSDN* G61 .... **61** K5 ⚅
Manor Av *KLMNKN/STW* KA3 .... **207** G5
Manor Crs *GRK* PA19 .... **31** M2
Manor Dr *AIRDRIE* ML6 .... **110** E1
Manor Ga *NMRNS* G77 .... **150** F6
Manor Rd *BAIL/MDB/MHD* G69 .... **86** F4
   DRUM G15 .... **60** F8
   PSLYS PA2 .... **100** F8
   SCOT G14 .... **81** L5
Manor Vw *AIRDRIE* ML6 .... **111** H7
   LRKH ML9 .... **176** C7
Manor Wy *RUTH* G73 .... **129** J5
Manresa Pl *COWCAD* G4 .... **5** C5
Manse Av *BSDN* G61 .... **61** M4
   CTBR ML5 .... **109** K5
   UD/BTH/TAN G71 .... **132** A7
Manse Brae *LNPK/KPK* G44 .... **128** B3
   LRKH ML9 .... **177** J8
Manse Ct *BRHD/NEIL* G78 .... **125** K6
   CARLUKE ML8 .... **178** A5 ⚅
   KSYTH G65 .... **47** K2
   LARGS KA30 .... **115** J6 ⚅
Manse Crs
   CRG/CRSL/HOU PA6 .... **77** H7 ⚅
Mansfield Av
   BLTYR/CAMB G72 .... **130** A5
Mansfield Crs *LARGS* KA30 .... **115** J4
   OLDK G60 .... **59** G2 ⚅
Manse Garden's
   ALEX/LLW G83 .... **25** M1 ⚅
Manse La *EKILN* G74 .... **153** M6 ⚅
Mansel St *SPRGB/BLRNK* G21 .... **83** M4
Manse Pl *AIRDRIE* ML6 .... **110** F2
Manse Rd *BAIL/MDB/MHD* G69 .... **108** E3
   BRHD/NEIL G78 .... **148** D2
   BSDN G61 .... **61** M4
   CAR/SHTL G32 .... **107** K5
   CRMNK/CLK/EAG G76 .... **152** D2
   KSYTH G65 .... **47** K2
   LNK/LMHG ML11 .... **198** F5
   MTHW ML1 .... **157** M5
   OLDK G60 .... **58** D1
   RAYR/DAL KA6 .... **231** L5
   SHOTTS ML7 .... **113** K7
   WISHAW ML2 .... **159** M5
   WKIL KA23 .... **181** K4 ⚅
Manse St *CTBR* ML5 .... **109** M3
   KLMNK KA1 .... **17** L5
   RNFRW PA4 .... **80** D5
   SALT KA21 .... **200** E1
Manseview *LRKH* ML9 .... **176** B7 ⚅
Mansel St *PTCK* G11 .... **81** M6
Manse Vw *MTHW* ML1 .... **134** B5
Mansewell Rd *PSTWK* KA9 .... **221** J8
Mansewood Dr *DMBTN* G82 .... **37** H4
Mansewood Rd *GIF/THBK* G46 .... **127** H5
   PLKSW/MSWD G43 .... **127** H4
Mansfield Crs
   CRMNK/CLK/EAG G76 .... **151** K3
Mansfield Rd *BLSH* ML4 .... **132** F5 ⚅
   CARD/HILL/MSPK G52 .... **102** F2
   CRMNK/CLK/EAG G76 .... **151** L3
   HMLTN ML3 .... **174** D2
   LOCHW PA12 .... **120** D6 ⚅
   PSTWK KA9 .... **225** H3
Mansfield St *PTCK* G11 .... **82** C7 ⚅
Mansfield Wy *IRVSE* KA11 .... **204** A4 ⚅
Mansion Av *PGL* PA14 .... **55** H1 ⚅
Mansion Ct *BLTYR/CAMB* G72 .... **130** A3 ⚅
Mansionhouse Av
   CAR/SHTL G32 .... **130** C1
Mansionhouse Dr
   CAR/SHTL G32 .... **107** J3
Mansionhouse Gdns
   PLKSD/SHW G41 .... **127** L2
Mansionhouse Gv
   CAR/SHTL G32 .... **107** L6 ⚅
Mansionhouse Rd
   CAR/SHTL G32 .... **107** L5
   PLKSD/SHW G41 .... **127** L2
   PSLY PA1 .... **9** L3
Mansion St *BLTYR/CAMB* G72 .... **130** A3
   PPK/MIL G22 .... **83** J4
Manson Av *PSTWK* KA9 .... **221** K8
Manson Pl *EKILS* G75 .... **172** A4
Manson Rd *IRV* KA12 .... **203** L3
Manuel Av *BEITH* KA15 .... **168** A2
Manuel Ct *KBRN* KA25 .... **167** G1

Maple Av *DMBTN* G82 .... **36** A4
   KKNTL G66 .... **45** M4
   NMRNS G77 .... **150** D5
Maple Bank *HMLTN* ML3 .... **156** F7
Maple Ct *CUMB* G67 .... **49** M4
Maple Crs *BLTYR/CAMB* G72 .... **130** F6
   BEITH KA15 .... **144** B7
Maple Dr *AYRS* KA7 .... **229** K4
   BRHD/NEIL G78 .... **149** K1
   CLYDBK G81 .... **59** M4
   JNSTN PA5 .... **122** F1
   KKNTL G66 .... **65** G4
   LRKH ML9 .... **176** A4
Maple Pl *EKILS* G75 .... **171** H3
   KLMNK KA1 .... **16** A5
   UD/BTH/TAN G71 .... **132** D1
Maple Qd *AIRDRIE* ML6 .... **111** K3
Maple Rd *CUMB* G67 .... **49** M4
   GRNKW/INVK PA16 .... **32** B6
   MTHW ML1 .... **134** B4
   PLKSD/SHW G41 .... **104** B5
Maple Ter *EKILS* G75 .... **171** H3
Maplewood *WISHAW* ML2 .... **158** D8 ⚅
Mar Av *BSHPTN* PA7 .... **58** B6
Marble Av *IRVSE* KA11 .... **209** K1
Marchbank Gdns *PSLY* PA1 .... **102** D5
Marchburn Av *PSTWK* KA9 .... **225** L1
Marchdyke Crs *KLMNK* KA1 .... **211** L6
The Marches *LNK/LMHG* ML11 .... **199** H4
Marchfield Av
   PSLYN/LNWD PA3 .... **101** K1
Marchfield Qd *PSLY* PA1 .... **225** G4
Marchfield Rd *AYR* KA8 .... **225** G4
Marchglen Pl *GOV/IBX* G51 .... **103** K2 ⚅
Marchmont Ct *KLMNK* KA1 .... **17** G6
Marchmont Gdns *BSHPBGS* G64 .... **63** M6
Marchmont Rd *AYRS* KA7 .... **18** E7
Marchmont Road La *AYRS* KA7 .... **18** D6
Marchmont Ter
   KVD/HLHD G12 .... **82** C6 ⚅
March St *PLKSD/SHW* G41 .... **104** F7
Mardale *EKILN* G74 .... **153** J6
Mar Dr *BSDN* G61 .... **61** M2
Maree Dr
   CARD/HILL/MSPK G52 .... **103** L5 ⚅
   CUMB G67 .... **68** B2
Maree Gdns *BSHPBGS* G64 .... **64** B3 ⚅
Maree Pl *IRV* KA12 .... **203** K2
Maree Rd *PSLYS* PA2 .... **101** G7
Marfield St *CAR/SHTL* G32 .... **106** E2
Mar Gdns *RUTH* G73 .... **129** K5 ⚅
Margaret Av *GLSTN* KA4 .... **214** A4
   SHOTTS ML7 .... **113** H7
Margaret Dr *ALEX/LLW* G83 .... **25** K4
Margaret Pl *BLSH* ML4 .... **132** E4 ⚅
Margaret Rd *HMLTN* ML3 .... **156** B3
Margaret's Pl *LRKH* ML9 .... **176** A6
Margaret St *CTBR* ML5 .... **110** A5
   GRK PA19 .... **31** M2 ⚅
   GRNKW/INVK PA16 .... **32** D2
Margaretvale Dr *LRKH* ML9 .... **176** A7
Marguerite Av *KKNTL* G66 .... **65** J3
Marguerite Gdns
   UD/BTH/TAN G71 .... **132** B7
Marian Dr *MTHW* ML1 .... **134** C7 ⚅
Marigold Av *MTHW* ML1 .... **157** L1
Marigold Wy *CARLUKE* ML8 .... **188** F1 ⚅
Marina Pl *BLSH* ML4 .... **132** E6
Marina Rd *PSTWK* KA9 .... **225** H1
Marine Ct *FAIRLIE* KA29 .... **139** K5 ⚅
Marine Crs *GOV/IBX* G51 .... **10** B4 ⚅
Marine Dr *IRV* KA12 .... **208** A1
Marine Gdns *GOV/IBX* G51 .... **10** B4
Mariner Ct *CLYDBK* G81 .... **60** A7
Marion St *BLSH* ML4 .... **133** K4
Mariscat Rd *PLKSD/SHW* G41 .... **104** F7 ⚅
Marjory Dr *PSLYN/LNWD* PA3 .... **102** A2
Marjory Rd *RNFRW* PA4 .... **80** A8
Market End *LNK/LMHG* ML11 .... **199** G5 ⚅
Markethill Rd *EKILN* G74 .... **153** L5
Market Pl *CARLUKE* ML8 .... **178** F7 ⚅
   KKNTL G66 .... **66** A2
   UD/BTH/TAN G71 .... **132** C2
Market St *AIRDRIE* ML6 .... **111** G2
   KSYTH G65 .... **47** K1
   UD/BTH/TAN G71 .... **132** C2
Markinch Rd *PGL* PA14 .... **54** F3 ⚅
Marlborough Av *PTCK* G11 .... **81** M6
Marlborough Pk *EKILS* G75 .... **171** G2
Marldon La *PTCK* G11 .... **81** M6
Marlepark *AYRS* KA7 .... **229** G6
Marley Wy *KKNTL* G66 .... **45** G3
Marlfield Gdns *BLSH* ML4 .... **133** G2 ⚅
Marloch Av *PGL* PA14 .... **55** J2 ⚅
Marlow St *PLKSD/SHW* G41 .... **10** B7
Marmion Av *HBR/GL* G84 .... **23** G2
Marmion Crs *MTHW* ML1 .... **133** K7
Marmion Dr *KKNTL* G66 .... **65** M1
Marmion Pl *CUMB* G67 .... **68** E2
Marmion Rd *CUMB* G67 .... **68** E2
   PSLYS PA2 .... **123** L1
Marne St *DEN/PKHD* G31 .... **13** G1
Marnoch Dr *CTBR* ML5 .... **87** K3
Marnock Ter *PSLYS* PA2 .... **9** L8
Marr Dr *TROON* KA10 .... **216** D5
Marress Rd *IRV* KA12 .... **203** H6
Marrswood Gn *HMLTN* ML3 .... **156** B5
Marrs Wynd *LNK/LMHG* ML11 .... **199** J4 ⚅
Marrwood Av *KKNTL* G66 .... **66** B3
Marshall Gv *HMLTN* ML3 .... **156** B6
Marshall La *WISHAW* ML2 .... **159** G6
Marshall's La *PSLY* PA1 .... **9** H4 ⚅
Marshall St *CTBR* ML5 .... **109** K5
   LRKH ML9 .... **176** A6
   WISHAW ML2 .... **159** G6
Marsmount Rd *PSTWK* KA9 .... **221** L7
Mars Rd *GRNKW/INVK* PA16 .... **31** J6
Martha St *CGLE* G1 .... **5** K9
Martin Av *IRV* KA12 .... **203** K4
   RAYR/DAL KA6 .... **227** H3
Martin Ct *HMLTN* ML3 .... **156** C6
Martin Crs *BAIL/MDB/MHD* G69 .... **108** C4
Martin Pl *MTHW* ML1 .... **157** K7
Martinside *EKILS* G75 .... **171** L4
Martin Sq *SALT* KA21 .... **192** A7
Martin St *CTBR* ML5 .... **110** D2 ⚅

DMNK/BRGTN G40 .... 105 M6
Martlet Dr JNSTN PA5............. 99 K8
Martnaham Dr RAYR/DAL KA6...... 231 H5
Mart St CGLE G1 .... 11 K4
Martyn St AIRDRIE ML6 .... 110 E2
Martyrs Pl BSHPBGS G64.......... 84 A1
Marwick St DEN/PKHD G31 .... 13 H1
Maryborough Av PSTWK KA9....... 225 H5
Maryborough Rd PSTWK KA9....... 225 G5
Mary Dr BLSH ML4 .... 132 E6
Maryfield Pl AYR KA8 .... 225 H5
Maryfield Rd AYR KA8 .... 225 H5
Mary Gln WISHAW ML2........... 159 K4
Maryhill Rd BSDN G61 .... 62 A7
  COWCAD G4 .... 4 E6
  MRYH/FIRH G20 .... 4 D2
Maryknowe Rd MTHW ML1 .... 134 C8
Maryland Dr
  CARD/HILL/MSPK G52 .... 103 L4
Maryland Gdns
  CARD/HILL/MSPK G52 .... 103 L4
Maryland Rd DMBTN G82 .... 37 J5
Mary Love Pl SVSTN KA20 ...... 192 M8
Marypark Rd PGL PA14 .... 56 B2
Mary Rae Rd BLSH ML4 .... 132 E6
Maryston St STPS/GTHM/RID G33.. 7 M4
Mary St GRNKW/INVK PA16 ...... 32 C5
  HMLTN ML3................... 156 D7
  JNSTN PA5 .... 100 A6
  PGL PA14 .... 34 A7
  PSLYS PA2 .... 9 H9
Maryville Av GIF/THBK G46 ... 127 J7
Maryville Gdns GIF/THBK G46 . 127 J7
Maryville Vw UD/BTH/TAN G71.. 108 D8
Marywood Sq
  PLKSD/SHW G41 .... 104 F7
Mary Young Pl
  CRMNK/CLK/EAG G76 .... 151 M3
Masonfield Av BALLOCH G68 ... 48 D7
Masonhill Pl AYRS KA7 .... 19 M9
Mason La MTHW ML1 .... 157 L3
Mason St LRKH ML9 .... 176 C8
Masterton St COWCAD G4 ...... 5 K3
Masterton Wy
  UD/BTH/TAN G71............. 109 H8
Matherton Av NMRNS G77 ...... 151 K4
Mathew Smith Av KLMNK KA1 ... 16 B6
Mathie Crs GRK PA19 .... 31 L3
Mathieson Rd RUTH G73 .... 106 C8
Mathieson St PSLY PA1 .... 102 B2
Matilda Rd PLKSD/SHW G41 .... 10 A8
Matthew Mcwhirter Pl
  LRKH ML9 .... 176 B5
Matthew St KLWNG KA13 .... 193 L4
Mauchline Av KKNTL G66 ...... 46 A7
Mauchline Ct HMLTN ML3 ...... 155 K7
Mauchline Rd KLMNK KA1 ...... 212 F3
  RAYR/DAL KA6 .... 227 G3
Mauchline Ter
  GRNKW/INVK PA16 .... 31 L6
Maukinfauld Ct
  DEN/PKHD G31 .... 13 M9
Maukinfauld Rd CAR/SHTL G32 . 106 E6
Mauldslie Dr CARLUKE ML8 .... 177 M3
Mauldslie Rd CARLUKE ML8 .... 177 K6
Mauldslie St BLSH ML4 .... 133 G5
  CTBR ML5 .... 110 A4
  DMNK/BRGTN G40 .... 13 G7
Maule Dr PTCK G11 .... 82 A7
Mausoleum Dr HMLTN ML3....... 156 E4
Mavis Bank BSHPBGS G64 ...... 83 M1
Mavisbank Gdns BLSH ML4 ..... 133 G5
  GOV/IBX G51................ 10 A3
Mavisbank Rd GOV/IBX G51 .... 104 D3
Mavisbank St AIRDRIE ML6 .... 110 E1
  WISHAW ML2 .... 160 C3
Mavisbank Ter JNSTN PA5 ..... 99 M7
  PSLY PA1 .... 9 K6
Mavis Rd GRNKW/INVK PA16..... 32 A4
Mavor Av EKILN G74........... 153 M5
Maxholm Rd KLMNK KA1 .... 211 L4
Maxton Av BRHD/NEIL G78 ..... 125 G6
Maxton Crs WISHAW ML2 .... 159 J3
Maxton Gv BRHD/NEIL G78...... 125 G7
Maxton Ter BLTYR/CAMB G72... 129 M6
Maxwell Av
  BAIL/MDB/MHD G69 .... 108 A5
  BSDN G61 .... 61 L7
  PLKSD/SHW G41 .... 10 B8
Maxwell Ct BEITH KA15 .... 168 A2
  KLMNK/STW KA3 .... 207 K6
Maxwell Crs BLTYR/CAMB G72.. 155 K3
Maxwell Dr
  BAIL/MDB/MHD G69 .... 107 M4
  EKILN G74 .... 15 H2
  ERSK PA8 .... 58 F6
  PLKSD/SHW G41 .... 104 C5
Maxwell Gdns KLMNK KA1 ...... 212 E3
  PLKSD/SHW G41 .... 104 C5
Maxwell Gn IRVSE KA11........ 204 A5
Maxwell Gv PLKSD/SHW G41 .... 104 D5
Maxwell La PLKSD/SHW G41 .... 10 B8
Maxwell Ov PLKSD/SHW G41 .... 10 C8
Maxwell Pl BRWEIR PA11 ...... 98 D1
  PLKSD/SHW G41 .... 10 F9
  SVSTN KA20 .... 192 E7
  UD/BTH/TAN G71 .... 132 A3
Maxwell Rd BSHPTN PA7........ 58 B6
  PLKSD/SHW G41 .... 10 C8
Maxwell St
  BAIL/MDB/MHD G69 .... 108 B5
  CGLE G1 .... 11 J3
  CLYDBK G81 .... 59 M5
  PGL PA14 .... 34 E8
  PSLY PA1 .... 9 H2
Maxwellton Av EKILN G74...... 15 K1
Maxwellton Pl EKILN G74 ..... 154 B6
Maxwellton Rd EKILN G74 ..... 154 C5
  PGL PA14 .... 54 F3
  PSLY PA1 .... 8 C6
Maxwellton St PSLY PA1 ...... 8 C6
Maxwelton Rd
  STPS/GTHM/RID G33........... 7 L5
Maxwood Rd GLSTN KA4 .... 214 D3
Maybank La GVH/MTFL G42 ..... 105 G8
Maybank St GVH/MTFL G42 ..... 105 G8
Mayberry Crs CAR/SHTL G32 ... 107 J4

Mayberry Gdns CAR/SHTL G32 ... 107 K4
Mayberry Pl BLTYR/CAMB G72... 155 K1
Maybole Crs NMRNS G77 .... 151 G5
Maybole Dr AIRDRIE ML6....... 111 G5
Maybole Gdns HMLTN ML3 ...... 155 K7
Maybole Gv NMRNS G77 .... 151 G5
Maybole Pl CTBR ML5 .... 110 D6
Maybole Rd AYRS KA7 .... 229 G5
  PGL PA14................... 54 F3
Maybole St PLK/PH/NH G53 .... 125 M3
Mayfield Av
  CRMNK/CLK/EAG G76 .... 151 L2
  KLMNK KA1 .... 212 F4
Mayfield Ct HWWD PA9 .... 121 M3
Mayfield Crs HWWD PA9 .... 121 M3
  SVSTN KA20 .... 192 C8
Mayfield Dr HWWD PA9 .... 121 M3
Mayfield Gdns CARLUKE ML8 ... 189 G2
Mayfield Gv SVSTN KA20 ...... 192 C8
Mayfield Pl CTBR ML5 .... 110 A6
  SALT KA21 .... 201 G1
Mayfield Rd HMLTN ML3 .... 155 M5
  SALT KA21 .... 192 A8
  SVSTN KA20 .... 192 C8
Mayfield St MRYH/FIRH G20 ... 82 F3
May Rd PSLYS PA2 .... 124 E2
May St HMLTN ML3 .... 156 D4
  LARGS KA30 .... 115 K7
Mayter GIF/THBK G46 .... 127 J6
  GVH/MTFL G42 .... 128 B1
Mayville St SVSTN KA20 ...... 192 C8
Mcadam Ct PSTWK KA9 .... 225 L4
Mc Alister Rd ALEX/LLW G83 .. 25 L4
Mcallister Av AIRDRIE ML6 ... 111 K1
Mcalpine St KVGV G3 .... 10 E3
  WISHAW ML2 .... 159 H7
Mcardle Av MTHW ML1 .... 157 H2
Mcarthur Pk KKNTL G66 .... 65 H7
Mcarthur St
  PLKSW/MSWD G43 .... 127 J2
Mcaslin Ct COWCAD G4 .... 5 M8
Mcaslin St COWCAD G4 .... 6 A8
Mcauslan Pl HBR/GL G84 ...... 20 F7
Mccall's Av AYR KA8 .... 225 G6
Mccallum Ct EKILN G74 .... 153 H5
Mccallum Crs GRK PA19 .... 31 L2
Mccallum Gv EKILN G74....... 153 G5
Mccallum Pl EKILN G74 .... 153 H5
Mccallum Rd LRKH ML9 .... 176 B8
Mccardel Wy
  KLMNKN/STW KA3 .... 197 L1
Mccarrison Rd WISHAW ML2 .... 160 A3
Mccash Pl KKNTL G66 .... 65 J2
Mcclue Av RNFRW PA4 .... 80 B5
Mcclue Rd RNFRW PA4 .... 80 B5
Mccolgan Pl AYR KA8 .... 225 J6
Mccoll Pl ALEX/LLW G83 ...... 25 J5
Mcconnell St LOCHW PA12 ..... 120 B7
Mccormack Gdns
  MTHW ML1 .... 134 E5
Mccracken Av RNFRW PA4 ...... 80 B7
Mccracken Dr
  UD/BTH/TAN G71............. 132 C3
Mccreery St CLYDBK G81 ...... 80 D1
Mc Culloch Av
  UD/BTH/TAN G71............. 132 C3
Mcculloch St PLKSD/SHW G41 .. 10 C8
Mcdonald Av JNSTN PA5 .... 99 L8
Mcdonald Crs CLYDBK G81 ..... 80 D1
Mcdonald Dr IRV KA12 .... 203 K5
Mcdonald Pl BRHD/NEIL G78 ... 148 E2
  MTHW ML1................... 134 A7
Mcdowall Av ARD KA22 .... 191 K7
Mcdowall Pl ARD KA22 .... 191 K6
Mcewan Crs RAYR/DAL KA6 ..... 227 H3
Mcewan Dr HBR/GL G84 .... 20 F6
Mcewan Gdns EKILN G74 .... 153 G5
Mcfarlane St COWCAD G4 ...... 12 A4
  PSLYN/LNWD PA3 .... 101 J2
Mcgavin Av KLWNG KA13 .... 194 A6
Mcgavin Wy KLWNG KA13 .... 193 K5
Mc Ghee St CLYDBK G81 .... 60 B6
Mcgibney Dr IRV KA12 .... 203 K8
Mcgillivray Av SALT KA21..... 191 M8
Mcgowan Pl HMLTN ML3 .... 156 A4
Mcgown Pl PSLYN/LNWD PA3 .... 101 K3
Mcgregor Av AIRDRIE ML6 ..... 111 K1
  RNFRW PA4 .... 80 B7
  SVSTN KA20 .... 192 D8
Mcgregor Dr DMBTN G82 .... 37 J5
Mcgregor Rd CUMB G67 .... 48 E8
Mcgregor St CLYDBK G81 ...... 80 D1
  GOV/IBX G51................ 103 M3
  WISHAW ML2 .... 158 D5
Mcgrigor Rd MLNGV G62 .... 41 M6
Mchardy Crs BEITH KA15 ...... 168 F6
Mcinnes Ct WISHAW ML2 .... 159 H7
Mcinnes Pl WISHAW ML2 .... 177 H2
Mcintosh Od AIRDRIE ML6 ..... 132 F7
Mcintosh St DEN/PKHD G31 .... 12 C2
Mcintosh Wy MTHW ML1 .... 157 J4
Mcintyre Ter
  BLTYR/CAMB G72 .... 130 A3
Mcisaac Rd SALT KA21 .... 201 G1
Mciver St BLTYR/CAMB G72 .... 130 D3
Mckay Crs JNSTN PA5 .... 100 A7
Mckay Gv BLSH ML4 .... 132 F3
Mckay Pl EKILN G74 .... 153 G5
  NMRNS G77 .... 150 C5
Mckechnie St GOV/IBX G51 .... 104 A1
Mckellar Av ARD KA22 .... 191 K7
Mckenna Dr AIRDRIE ML6 ...... 110 E1
Mckenzie Av CLYDBK G81 ...... 60 B5
Mckenzie St PSLYN/LNWD PA3... 8 C1
Mckerrell St PSLY PA1 .... 9 L3
Mckillop Pl SALT KA21 .... 191 L7
Mckinlay Crs IRV KA12 .... 203 H8
Mckinnon St SALT KA21 .... 192 A7
Mclaren Av RNFRW PA4 .... 80 C8
Mclaren Ct GIF/THBK G46 ..... 127 H8
Mclaren Crs MRYH/FIRH G20 ... 82 E2
Mclaren Gdns
  MRYH/FIRH G20 .... 82 E2
Mclaren Gv EKILN G74 .... 153 G5

Mc Laurin Crs JNSTN PA5...... 99 K8
Mclean Dr BLSH ML4 .... 132 F7
Mclean Pl PSLYN/LNWD PA3 .... 101 K2
Mclean St CLYDBK G81 .... 80 C2
Mclean St BLSH ML4 .... 225 J7
Mclees La MTHW ML1 .... 157 H2
Mc Lelland Dr AIRDRIE ML6 ... 90 B7
Mclelland Dr KLMNK KA1 ...... 16 C7
Mclennan St GVH/MTFL G42 .... 128 B1
Mcleod Rd DMBTN G82 .... 37 J5
Mcleod St GRNK PA15 .... 3 M8
Mcluckie Dr KLWNG KA13 ...... 193 J5
Mcluckie Pk KLWNG KA13 ...... 193 J5
Mcmahon Dr WISHAW ML2 .... 160 A3
Mcmahon Gv BLSH ML4......... 133 H3
Mcmillan Crs BEITH KA15 ..... 168 A2
Mcmillan Dr ARD KA22 .... 191 G5
Mcmillan Rd WISHAW ML2 ...... 158 D7
Mcmillan Wy CARLUKE ML8 ..... 177 M4
Mcnair St CAR/SHTL G32 ...... 107 G4
Mcnaught Pl
  KLMNKN/STW KA3 .... 206 A2
Mcnay Crs SALT KA21 .... 191 M8
Mcnay Rd PSTWK KA9 .... 221 J6
Mcneil Av CLYDBK G81 .... 60 E8
Mcneil Dr BLSH ML4 .... 133 L2
  MTHW ML1 .... 134 B2
Mcneil Gdns GBLS G5 .... 11 M7
Mcneil Pl KLWNG KA13 .... 221 K8
Mc Neil Pl WISHAW ML2 .... 177 J2
Mcneil St GBLS G5............ 11 M7
Mcphail Av MTHW ML1 .... 134 F6
Mcphail St DMNK/BRGTN G40 ... 12 B7
Mc Phail St GRNK PA15 .... 3 L8
Mcphater St CGLW G2 .... 5 H7
Mcpherson Cr AIRDRIE ML6 .... 111 L8
Mcpherson Dr GRK PA19 .... 31 K2
  UD/BTH/TAN G71 .... 132 B6
Mcpherson St BLSH ML4 .... 133 K4
Mcshannon Gv BLSH ML4 .... 133 G6
Meadow Av BLTYR/CAMB G72 .... 155 K3
  IRV KA12 .... 203 J5
Meadowbank La PSTWK KA9 ..... 225 H2
Meadowbank Pl NMRNS G77 ..... 150 D4
Meadowbank Rd LARGS KA30 .... 115 K3
Meadowbank St DMBTN G82 ..... 36 E5
  DMBTN G82 .... 36 F5
Meadowburn BSHPBGS G64 ...... 64 A5
Meadowburn Av KKNTL G66 ..... 65 L4
  NMRNS G77 .... 150 D4
Meadowburn Rd WISHAW ML2 .... 159 J6
Meadow Ct CARLUKE ML8 .... 179 J8
  DMBTN G82 .... 36 F4
Meadowfield Pl WISHAW ML2 ... 160 C3
Meadowfoot Rd WKIL KA23 ..... 181 K4
Meadowhead Av IRVSE KA11 .... 208 E5
  IRVSE KA11 .... 208 F5
Meadowhill St LRKH ML9 ...... 176 B6
Meadow La RNFRW PA4 .... 80 D4
Meadow Pk AYRS KA7 .... 19 H9
  RAYR/DAL KA6 .... 231 H5
Meadowpark Dr AYRS KA7 ...... 19 H9
Meadowpark St DEN/PKHD G31 .. 7 G9
Meadow Rd CARLUKE ML8 .... 189 G5
  DMBTN G82 .... 37 G5
  MTHW ML1 .... 158 A4
  PTCK G11 .... 82 A8
Meadows Av LRKH ML9 .... 176 B6
Meadowside BEITH KA15 .... 168 A1
  HMLTN ML3 .... 174 D3
  KLMNKN/STW KA3 .... 212 D1
  WKIL KA23 .... 181 K4
Meadowside Av JNSTN PA5 ..... 100 D7
Meadowside Gdns
  AIRDRIE ML6 .... 111 K2
Meadowside Pl AIRDRIE ML6 ... 111 K2
Meadowside Rd GLSTN KA4 ..... 214 B3
  KSYTH G65 .... 46 E1
Meadowside St PTCK G11 ...... 82 A8
  RNFRW PA4 .... 80 D4
The Meadows
  CRG/CRSL/HOU PA6 .... 77 K8
  KLWNG KA13 .... 193 K5
Meadow St CTBR ML5 .... 110 B5
Meadow Vw AIRDRIE ML6 .... 90 A6
  CUMB G67 .... 49 J6
Meadow Wk CTBR ML5 .... 110 B4
Meadow Wy NMRNS G77 .... 150 D4
Meadowwell St
  CAR/SHTL G32 .... 107 H4
Meadside Av KLBCH PA10 ...... 99 G5
Meadside Rd KLBCH PA10 ...... 99 G5
Mealkirk St CLYDBK G81 ...... 60 C2
Mearns Ct HMLTN ML3 .... 174 E2
Mearnscroft Gdns NMRNS G77 . 150 F6
Mearnscroft Rd NMRNS G77 ... 150 F6
Mearnskirk Rd NMRNS G77 ..... 150 D7
Mearns Rd MTHW ML1 .... 157 J1
  NMRNS G77 .... 150 F7
Mearns St GRNK PA15 .... 2 C6
Medine Av BEITH KA15 .... 144 B8
Medine Ct BEITH KA15 .... 144 B8
Medlar Rd CUMB G67 .... 49 K7
Medrox Gdns CUMB G67 .... 67 M4
Medwin Ct EKILS G75 .... 170 E2
Medwin Gdns EKILS G75 .... 170 E2
Medwin St BLTYR/CAMB G72 .... 130 D4
Medwyn St SCOT G14 .... 81 K6
Meek Pl BLTYR/CAMB G72 ...... 130 B4
Meetinghouse La PSLY PA1 .... 9 G3
Megan Ga DMNK/BRGTN G40 ..... 12 C7
Megan St DMNK/BRGTN G40 ..... 12 C7
Meikle Av RNFRW PA4 .... 80 C7
Meikle Bin Brae KNNTL G66 ... 44 B3
Meikle Crs AIRDRIE ML6 ...... 89 K1
  HMLTN ML3 .... 174 C1
Meikle Drumgray Rd
  AIRDRIE ML6 .... 89 K1
Meikle Earnock Rd HMLTN ML3. 173 M3
Meiklehill Ct KKNTL G66 ..... 45 L8
Meiklehill Rd KKNTL G66 ..... 45 L8
Meiklerig Crs PLK/PH/NH G53 . 103 J7
Meikleriggs Dr PSLYS PA2 .... 101 G8
Meikle Rd PLK/PH/NH G53 ..... 126 C1
Meiklewood Av PSTWK KA9 ..... 221 J8
Meiklewood Rd GOV/IBX G51.... 103 K3

Melbourne Av CLYDBK G81 ..... 59 K4
  EKILS G75 .... 14 A6
Melbourne Ct GIF/THBK G46... 127 K6
Melbourne Gn EKILS G75 ...... 14 A6
Melbourne Rd SALT KA21 ...... 200 E2
Melbourne St DEN/PKHD G31 ... 12 C3
Melbourne Ter SALT KA21 ..... 200 F2
Meldon Pl GOV/IBX G51 .... 103 K2
Meldrum Gdns
  PLKSD/SHW G41 .... 104 D7
Meldrum Mains AIRDRIE ML6 ... 88 E5
Meldrum St CLYDBK G81 .... 80 D1
Melford Av GIF/THBK G46 ..... 127 K7
  KKNTL G66 .... 65 H1
Melford Rd BLSH ML4 .... 132 E3
Melfort Av CLYDBK G81 .... 60 C6
  PLKSD/SHW G41 .... 104 B5
Melfort Gdns KLBCH PA10 ..... 99 J8
Melfort Rd HMLTN ML3 .... 155 L7
  WMYSB PA18 .... 70 A1
Mellerstain Dr SCOT G14 ..... 80 E3
Melness Pl GOV/IBX G51 ...... 103 K2
Melrose Av AIRDRIE ML6 ...... 111 K7
  BAIL/MDB/MHD G69 .... 108 F4
  MTHW ML1 .... 134 B5
  PSLYN/LNWD PA3 .... 100 B4
  PSLYS PA2 .... 101 G8
  RUTH G73 .... 129 H2
Melrose Crs WISHAW ML2 ...... 159 G4
Melrose Gdns MRYH/FIRH G20.. 4 C2
Melrose Pl BLTYR/CAMB G72 ... 131 J8
  CTBR ML5 .... 109 M2
  LRKH ML9 .... 176 A8
Melrose Rd CUMB G67 .... 68 C2
  PGL PA14 .... 54 F2
Melrose St COWCAD G4 .... 4 D6
  HMLTN ML3 .... 156 B4
Melrose Ter EKILN G74 .... 15 G1
  HMLTN ML3 .... 156 B3
Melvaig Pl MRYH/FIRH G20 .... 82 D3
Melvick Pl GOV/IBX G51 ...... 103 K2
Melville Ct CGLE G1 .... 11 K3
Melville Dr MTHW ML1 .... 157 M3
Melville Gdns BSHPBGS G64 ... 64 A7
Melville Pk EKILN G74 .... 154 B6
Melville Pl CARLUKE ML8 ..... 178 E7
Melville St KLMNKN/STW KA3 .. 17 J5
  PLKSD/SHW G41 .... 104 F6
Melvinhall Rd LNK/LMHG ML11 . 199 G4
Memel St PPK/MIL G22 .... 83 L4
Memus Av
  CARD/HILL/MSPK G52 .... 103 J5
Mennock Ct HMLTN ML3 .... 155 L7
Mennock Dr BSHPBGS G64 ...... 64 A5
Mennock St MTHW ML1 .... 135 J7
Menock Rd LNPK/KPK G44 ...... 128 C3
Menteith Av BSHPBGS G64 ..... 64 B8
Menteith Dr RUTH G73 .... 129 K7
Menteith Gdns BSDN G61 ...... 61 J1
Menteith Pl RUTH G73 .... 129 K7
Menteith Rd MTHW ML1 .... 157 L2
Menzies Dr SPRGB/BLRNK G21 . 84 A4
Menzies Pl SPRGB/BLRNK G21 . 84 A4
Menzies Rd SPRGB/BLRNK G21 . 84 A4
Merchant La CGLE G1 .... 11 K4
Merchants Cl KLBCH PA10 ..... 99 G6
Merchiston Av PSLYN/LNWD PA3. 99 K4
Merchiston Dr JNSTN PA5 ..... 99 K4
Merchiston St CAR/SHTL G32 .. 106 E2
Merino Rd GRNK PA15 .... 2 A7
Merkins Av DMBTN G82 .... 37 H3
Merkland Dr KKNTL G66 .... 46 A8
Merkland Pl KKNTL G66 .... 45 M8
Merkland Rd AYRS KA7 .... 229 G2
  CTBR ML5 .... 87 J7
Merkland St PTCK G11 .... 82 B7
Merkland Wy EKILS G75 .... 171 J5
Merksworth Av DALRY KA24.... 184 C2
Merlewood Av
  UD/BTH/TAN G71............. 132 B5
Merlewood Rd WKIL KA23 ...... 181 H5
Merlin Av BLSH ML4 .... 133 G4
  GRNKW/INVK PA16 .... 32 A3
Merlinford Av RNFRW PA4 ..... 80 E6
Merlinford Crs RNFRW PA4 .... 80 E6
Merlinford Dr RNFRW PA4 ..... 80 E6
Merlinford Wy RNFRW PA4 ..... 80 E6
Merlin La GRNKW/INVK PA16 ... 32 A3
Merlin Wy PSLYN/LNWD PA3.... 102 B2
Merrick Av PSTWK KA9 .... 221 K8
  TROON KA10 .... 216 F5
Merrick Gdns BSDN G61 .... 61 J2
  GOV/IBX G51 .... 104 B3
  HMLTN ML3 .... 174 C1
Merrick Rd KLMNK KA1 .... 212 B5
Merrick Ter UD/BTH/TAN G71.. 132 B2
Merrick Wy RUTH G73 .... 129 H6
Merryburn Av
  PLKSW/MSWD G43 .... 127 K5
Merrycrest Av GIF/THBK G46 . 127 K5
Merrycroft Av GIF/THBK G46 . 127 K5
Merryflats KSYTH G65 .... 46 F5
Merryland Pl GOV/IBX G51 .... 104 B3
Merryland St GOV/IBX G51 .... 104 B2
Merrylee Av PGL PA14 .... 54 D2
Merrylee Crs
  PLKSW/MSWD G43 .... 127 J4
Merrylee Pk GIF/THBK G46 ... 127 J4
Merrylee Park Av
  GIF/THBK G46 .... 127 K5
Merrylees Rd BLTYR/CAMB G72. 155 J2
Merrystone St CTBR ML5 ...... 109 M2
Merry St MTHW ML1 .... 157 L2
Merryton Av DRUM G15 .... 61 H9
  GIF/THBK G46 .... 127 J5
Merryton Pl DRUM G15 .... 61 H9
Merryton Rd LRKH ML9 .... 175 M3
  MTHW ML1 .... 158 B7
Merryton St LRKH ML9 .... 175 M4
Merryvale Av
  PLKSW/MSWD G43 .... 127 K5
Merryvale Pl
  PLKSW/MSWD G43 .... 127 K4
Merryvale Rd IRV KA12 .... 203 J8
Merton Dr CARD/HILL/MSPK G52 103 G4
Meryon Gdns CAR/SHTL G32.... 107 K7

Meryon Rd CAR/SHTL G32 ...... 107 K6
Methil Rd PGL PA14 .... 54 F3
Methil St SCOT G14 .... 81 J6
Methlan Pk DMBTN G82 .... 36 D7
Methlick Av AIRDRIE ML6 ..... 110 E5
Methuen Rd PSLYN/LNWD PA3 .. 101 M1
Methven Av BSDN G61 .... 62 B4
  KLMNK KA1 .... 211 M5
Methven Pl EKILN G74 .... 14 B2
  KLMNK KA1 .... 211 M5
Methven Rd GIF/THBK G46 ..... 151 G3
Methven St CLYDBK G81 .... 59 M5
  DEN/PKHD G31 .... 13 M9
Mews La AYRS KA7 .... 18 D3
  GRNKW/INVK PA16 .... 32 C1
  KLMNK KA1 .... 16 C7
  PSLYN/LNWD PA3 .... 101 M2
Mey Ct NMRNS G77 .... 150 A5
Mey Pl NMRNS G77 .... 150 A5
Mharie Pl ALEX/LLW G83 ...... 25 M7
Michael Mcparland Dr
  BSHPBGS G64 .... 44 B8
Michael Ter AIRDRIE ML6 ..... 111 K8
Micklehouse Ov
  BAIL/MDB/MHD G69 .... 108 B3
Micklehouse Pl
  BAIL/MDB/MHD G69 .... 108 B3
Micklehouse Rd
  BAIL/MDB/MHD G69 .... 108 B3
Micklehouse Wynd
  BAIL/MDB/MHD G69 .... 108 B3
Midas Pl BLSH ML4 .... 133 L4
Mid Av PGL PA14 .... 54 F1
Mid Barrwood Rd KSYTH G65 ... 47 M2
Mid Barwood Rd KSYTH G65 .... 48 A1
Mid Carbarns WISHAW ML2 ..... 158 D8
Midcroft Av LNPK/KPK G44 .... 128 E4
Middlefield EKILS G75 .... 171 L4
Middlehouse Ct CARLUKE ML8 . 178 D7
Middlemass Dr
  KLMNKN/STW KA3 .... 17 J5
Middlemuir Rd KKNTL G66 ..... 65 K3
Middlepart SVSTN KA20 .... 192 A7
Middlepenny Pl PGL PA14 ..... 56 B2
Middlepenny Rd PGL PA14 ..... 56 B2
Middlerigg Rd BALLOCH G68 ... 48 D7
Middlesex Gdns
  PLKSD/SHW G41 .... 10 A5
Middlesex St PLKSD/SHW G41 .. 10 A5
Middleton Crs
  PSLYN/LNWD PA3 .... 101 H3
Middleton Dr HBR/GL G84 ..... 22 F1
  LARGS KA30 .... 115 K5
  MLNGV G62 .... 42 B7
Middleton La IRVSE KA11 ..... 204 A5
Middleton Rd IRVSE KA11 ..... 204 A4
  PSLYN/LNWD PA3 .... 100 C2
  PSLYN/LNWD PA3 .... 101 H3
Middleton St ALEX/LLW G83 .. 25 K4
  GOV/IBX G51 .... 104 C4
Middle Ward St CLYDBK G81 ... 60 D2
Mid Dykes Rd SALT KA21 ...... 191 L7
Midfaulds Av RNFRW PA4 ...... 80 E7
Midland St CGLE G1 .... 11 G2
Midlem Dr
  CARD/HILL/MSPK G52 .... 103 J4
Midlem Ov
  CARD/HILL/MSPK G52 .... 103 J4
Mid-loan St CARLUKE ML8 ..... 188 E5
Midlock St GOV/IBX G51 ...... 104 C4
Midlothian Dr
  PLKSD/SHW G41 .... 104 D8
Mid Pk EKILS G75 .... 14 E5
Mid Rd BEITH KA15 .... 144 A8
  CUMB G67 .... 68 F3
Midton Av PSTWK KA9 .... 225 H1
Midton Rd AYRS KA7 .... 18 E9
  HWWD PA9 .... 122 A3
  KLMNK KA1 .... 211 M7
  PSTWK KA9 .... 225 J1
Midton St SPRGB/BLRNK G21 .. 6 C3
Mid-wharf St COWCAD G4....... 5 K5
Migvie Pl MRYH/FIRH G20 ..... 82 C4
Milford EKILS G75 .... 171 L2
Milford St STPS/GTHM/RID G33. 107 G1
Milgarholm Av IRV KA12 ...... 203 K8
Millands Av BLTYR/CAMB G72.. 131 J8
Millands Rd GLSTN KA4 .... 213 M4
Millarbank St SPRGB/BLRNK G21. 6 B1
Millar Gv HMLTN ML3 .... 156 B6
Millar Rd SALT KA21 .... 201 G1
Millars Pl KKNTL G66 .... 65 K5
Millarston Av PSLY PA1 ...... 101 G5
Millarston Dr PSLY PA1 ...... 101 G5
Millar St GRNK PA15 .... 3 H9
  PSLY PA1 .... 9 K3
Mill Av KLMNKN/STW KA3 ...... 206 C2
Millbank Av BLSH ML4 .... 133 H6
Millbank Rd PGL PA14 .... 54 C1
  WISHAW ML2 .... 158 F7
Millbeg Crs
  STPS/GTHM/RID G33 .... 107 M4
Millbeg Pl STPS/GTHM/RID G33. 107 L4
Mill Brae AYRS KA7 .... 19 G5
  BRWEIR PA11 .... 98 D1
Millbrae Rd BAIL/MDB/MHD G69. 86 D1
Millbrae Crs GVH/MTFL G42 ... 127 L2
  WISHAW G13 .... 80 D2
Millbrae Gdns
  PLKSD/SHW G41 .... 127 M2
Millbrae Rd GVH/MTFL G42 .... 127 M2
Millbrix Av SCOT G14 .... 81 G4
Millbrook EKILN G74 .... 153 G8
Millburn Av KNTSWD G13 ...... 80 F1
  RNFRW PA4 .... 80 D6
  RUTH G73 .... 129 G3
Millburn Ct EKILS G75 .... 170 E2
Millburn Crs DMBTN G82 ...... 37 H6
Millburn Dr KLMCLM PA13...... 75 H1
  RNFRW PA4 .... 80 E6
Millburn Gdns EKILS G75 ..... 170 E2
  LARGS KA30 .... 115 K6
Millburn La ALEX/LLW G83 .... 25 K6
  DMBTN G82 .... 37 H6
  LRKH ML9 .... 176 F8

PGL PA14 .... 54 C1 🔢
RNFRW PA4 .... 80 D6
Millburn St KKNTL G66 .... 44 D1
MTHW ML1 .... 157 L2
SPRGB/BLRNK G21 .... 6 E7
Millburn Wy EKILS G75 .... 170 A2
RNFRW PA4 .... 80 E6
Mill Ct HMLTN ML3 .... 156 C7
RUTH G73 .... 129 G3 🔢
Mill Crs BSHPBGS G64 .... 44 C8
DMNK/BRGTN G40 .... 12 C9
IRV KA12 .... 203 L1
NMLNS KA16 .... 215 L2
Millcroft Rd CUMB G67 .... 49 H8
CUMB G67 .... 68 C5
CUMB G67 .... 69 C5
RUTH G73 .... 105 M7
Mildam Rd CLYDBK G81 .... 60 C2
Miller Av FAIRLIE KA29 .... 139 K8
Miller Ct DMNK/BRGTN G40 .. 106 B6
Millerfield Rd DMNK/BRGTN G40 .. 106 B6
Miller Field Pl HMLTN ML3 .. 156 F6 🔢
Millerfield Rd
DMNK/BRGTN G40 .... 106 B6
Miller Pl ARD KA22 .... 191 C5
RAYR/DAL KA6 .... 227 C3
Miller Rd ALEX/LLW G83 .... 25 M1
AYRS KA7 .... 18 E5
Millerslea Gdns HBR/GL G84 .... 20 F8 🔢
Millersneuk Av KKNTL G66 .... 65 K5
Millersneuk Ct KKNTL G66 .... 65 K5 🔢
Millersneuk Crs
STPS/GTHM/RID G33 .... 85 C4
Millersneuk Rd KKNTL G66 .... 65 K5
Millersneuk Dr KKNTL G66 .... 65 K5 🔢
Miller's Pl AIRDRIE ML6 .... 111 C1
Millerston St DEN/PKHD G31 .... 12 F4
Miller St BAIL/MDB/MHD G69 .. 108 B5
CARLUKE ML8 .... 179 C7
CGLE G1 .... 11 J2
CLYDBK G81 .... 60 B8
CTBR ML5 .... 110 B4
DMBTN G82 .... 37 H5
HMLTN ML3 .... 156 F6
JNSTN PA5 .... 100 B8
LRKH ML9 .... 176 A6
WISHAW ML2 .... 159 C6
Millfield Av ERSK PA8 .... 58 F8
MTHW ML1 .... 157 M1
Millfield Crs ERSK PA8 .... 59 C8
Millfield Dr ERSK PA8 .... 59 C8
RNFRW PA4 .... 79 C1
Millfield Gdns ERSK PA8 .... 59 C8
Millfield Hl ERSK PA8 .... 58 F8
Millfield Mdw ERSK PA8 .... 58 F8
Millfield Pl ERSK PA8 .... 58 F8
Millfield Vw ERSK PA8 .... 58 F8
Millfield Wk RNFRW PA4 .... 79 C1 🔢
Millfield Wynd ERSK PA8 .... 58 F8
Milford St PSLYN/LNWD G53 .... 100 B4
Millgate Av UD/BTH/TAN G71 .. 131 M1
Millgate Ct UD/BTH/TAN G71 .. 131 M1
Millgate Rd HMLTN ML3 .... 156 C7
Millglen Rd ARD KA22 .... 191 K5
Mill Gv HMLTN ML3 .... 156 C7
Millhall Rd
CRMNK/CLK/EAG G76 .... 170 A6
Millheugh Brae LRKH ML9 .... 175 L7
Millheugh Pl BLTYR/CAMB G72 .. 155 J3
Millheugh Rd LRKH ML9 .... 175 L8
Millhill Av KLMNKN/STW KA3 .. 206 C4
Millhill Ter KLMNKN/STW KA3 .. 206 E4
Millholm Rd LNPK/KPK G44 .... 128 B5
Millhouse Crs MRYH/FIRH G20 .. 82 C2 🔢
Millhouse Dr MRYH/FIRH G20 .. 82 B2
Millhouse Rd GRNKW/INVK PA16 .. 50 E4
Millichen Rd SMSTN G23 .... 62 D5
Millig St HBR/GL G84 .... 20 C6
Milliken Dr KLBCH PA10 .... 99 J7
Milliken Park Rd KLBCH PA10 .. 99 J8
Milliken Rd KLBCH PA10 .... 99 J7
Mill Loan AIRDRIE ML6 .... 111 C1
Mill of Gryffe Rd BRWEIR PA11 .. 98 D1
Mill Pk DALRY KA24 .... 184 D2
Mill Pl PSLYN/LNWD PA3 .... 100 A3
Millport Av LNPK/KPK G44 .... 128 C2
Millport Rd PGL PA14 .... 54 F3
Mill Rig EKILS G75 .... 171 K4
Mill Ri KKNTL G66 .... 65 K5
Mill Rd AIRDRIE ML6 .... 69 C8
AIRDRIE ML6 .... 89 C8
BLTYR/CAMB G72 .... 130 D5
CARLUKE ML8 .... 178 E8
DMBTN G82 .... 24 A8
HMLTN ML3 .... 156 C7
IRV KA12 .... 203 K7
KBRN KA25 .... 143 H8
KNTSWD G13 .... 80 D2
KSYTH G65 .... 46 E2
MTHW ML1 .... 157 M1
NMLNS KA16 .... 215 L2
RAYR/DAL KA6 .... 227 C7
SHOTTS ML7 .... 160 F1
UD/BTH/TAN G71 .... 132 A8
WISHAW ML2 .... 160 C5
Millroad Dr DMNK/BRGTN G40 .. 12 B4
Millroad St DMNK/BRGTN G40 .. 12 A4
Millstream Ct PSLY PA1 .... 9 K5
Millstream Crs AIRDRIE ML6 .... 90 F4
Mill St AIRDRIE ML6 .... 90 F4
AYRS KA7 .... 19 C4
DMNK/BRGTN G40 .... 12 C9
GRNK PA15 .... 2 B6
KLMNK KA1 .... 16 E7
PSLY PA1 .... 9 J4
RUTH G73 .... 129 C1
Millview BRHD/NEIL G78 .... 125 K6
Millview Mdw
BRHD/NEIL G78 .... 148 C2 🔢
Millview Pl PLK/PH/NH G53 .... 126 B5 🔢
Millview Ter BRHD/NEIL G78 .. 148 C2 🔢
Mill Wy KKNTL G66 .... 66 A2
Millwood St PLKSD/SHW G41 .. 127 L1
Mill Wynd AYRS KA7 .... 18 F3
Milnbank St DEN/PKHD G31 .... 6 F3
Milncroft Pl
STPS/GTHM/RID G33 .... 85 C8 🔢

Milncroft Rd
STPS/GTHM/RID G33 .... 85 C8
Milndavie Crs CMPF/LLE G63 .... 27 J6
Milndavie Rd CMPF/LLE G63 .... 27 H7
Milner La KNTSWD G13 .... 81 L4 🔢
Milner Rd KNTSWD G13 .... 81 L4 🔢
Milngavie Rd BSDN G61 .... 61 M6
CMPF/LLE G63 .... 27 J7
Milnpark Gdns GOV/IBX G51 .. 104 D4
Milnpark St PLKSD/SHW G41 .. 10 A5
MTHW ML1 .... 133 J7 🔢
Milnwood Dr BLSH ML4 .... 133 K5
Milovaig Av SMSTN G23 .... 62 D8 🔢
Milovaig St SMSTN G23 .... 62 D8
Milrig Rd RUTH G73 .... 128 F2
Milroy Gdns BLSH ML4 .... 133 C1
Milton Av BLTYR/CAMB G72 .... 129 L4
KLMNKN/STW KA3 .... 17 M3
Milton Brae DMBTN G82 .... 37 K6
Milton Ct DMBTN G82 .... 37 M7
IRVSE KA11 .... 204 C8
Milton Crs CARLUKE ML8 .... 178 E8
IRVSE KA11 .... 204 C8
TROON KA10 .... 216 F5
Milton Douglas Rd CLYDBK G81 .. 60 A3
Milton Dr BSHPBGS G64 .... 83 M2 🔢
KLMNKN/STW KA3 .... 17 M3
Milton Gdns UD/BTH/TAN G71 .. 131 L1
Milton Hl DMBTN G82 .... 37 M8
Milton Mains Rd CLYDBK G81 .. 60 A4
Milton Pk AYRS KA7 .... 229 H6
KBRN KA25 .... 143 H7 🔢
RAYR/DAL KA6 .... 231 H5 🔢
Milton Qd KBRN KA25 .... 143 C6
Milton Rd EKILN G74 .... 153 C7
GLSTN KA4 .... 214 B3 🔢
IRVSE KA11 .... 204 C8
KBRN KA25 .... 143 C6
KKNTL G66 .... 44 E2
KKNTL G66 .... 45 J7
KLMNKN/STW KA3 .... 17 M4
KLMNKN/STW KA3 .... 207 L8
PGL PA14 .... 54 E3
Milton St AIRDRIE ML6 .... 111 C1
CARLUKE ML8 .... 178 E7
CGLW G2 .... 5 J7
HMLTN ML3 .... 156 A4
MTHW ML1 .... 157 L1
Milton Vw CRH/DND KA2 .... 210 E4
Milverton Av BSDN G61 .... 61 J3
Milverton Rd GIF/THBK G46 .... 127 C8
Mimosa Rd BRWEIR PA11 .... 98 D1
Minard Rd PGL PA14 .... 54 E2
PLKSD/SHW G41 .... 104 E8
SHOTTS ML7 .... 137 K3
Minard Wy UD/BTH/TAN G71 .. 132 A2 🔢
Mincher Crs MTHW ML1 .... 157 L5 🔢
Minch Wy AIRDRIE ML6 .... 111 K4
Minella Gdns BLSH ML4 .... 133 C1
Minerva St KVGV G3 .... 4 A4
Minerva Ter GRNKW/INVK PA16 .. 31 K6
Minerva Wy KVGV G3 .... 104 D1
Mingarry La MRYH/FIRH G20 .. 4 A1
Mingarry St MRYH/FIRH G20 .. 4 A1
Mingulay Crs PPK/MIL G22 ...... 83 L1
Mingulay Pl PPK/MIL G22 .... 83 L1
Mingulay St PPK/MIL G22 .... 83 K1
Minishant St PPK/MIL G22 .... 83 H4
Ministers Pk EKILN G74 .... 152 F5 🔢
Minmoir Rd PLK/PH/NH G53 .... 125 M2
Minstrel Rd KNTSWD G13 .... 61 K8
Minto Av RUTH G73 .... 129 K5 🔢
Minto Crs
CARD/HILL/MSPK G52 .... 103 M4
Minto Pk WISHAW ML2 .... 159 J3
Minto St CARD/HILL/MSPK G52 .. 103 M4
Mireton St PPK/MIL G22 .... 83 H4
Mirren Dr CLYDBK G81 .... 59 M2
Mirren's Shore PGL PA14 .... 34 C7 🔢
Mirrlees Dr KVD/HLHD G12 ...... 82 C5
Mirrlees La KVD/HLHD G12 ...... 82 C5
Misk Knowes SVSTN KA20 .... 201 L3
Mitchell Av BLTYR/CAMB G72 .. 130 C2
RNFRW PA4 .... 80 B7
Mitchell Ct EKILN G74 .... 14 A2
Mitchell Dr DMBTN G82 .... 35 H3 🔢
MLNGV G62 .... 42 C8
RUTH G73 .... 129 H3 🔢
Mitchell Gv EKILN G74 .... 14 A1
Mitchell Hill Rd CSMK G45 ...... 128 F7
Mitchell La CGLE G1 .... 11 H1
Mitchell Pl SALT KA21 .... 191 L8
Mitchell Rd CUMB G67 .... 48 F7
Mitchell St AIRDRIE ML6 .... 110 F1
BEITH KA15 .... 144 C8 🔢
CGLE G1 .... 11 H2
CTBR ML5 .... 109 H4
GRNK PA15 .... 33 M7
Mitchell Wy ALEX/LLW G83 ..... 25 L4
Mitchison Rd CUMB G67 .... 49 C6
Mitre Ct PTCK G11 .... 81 M6
Mitre La SCOT G14 .... 81 L5 🔢
Mitre La West SCOT G14 .... 81 K5 🔢
Mitre Rd PTCK G11 .... 81 M5
SCOT G14 .... 81 L5
Moat Av KNTSWD G13 .... 81 J2
Mochrum Ct PSTWK KA9 .... 225 K3 🔢
Mochrum Rd
PLKSW/MSWD G43 .... 127 L3
Moffat Ct EKILS G75 .... 170 E2
Moffathill AIRDRIE ML6 .... 111 L4
Moffat Pl BLTYR/CAMB G72 .... 131 K8 🔢
CTBR ML5 .... 110 D5
EKILS G75 .... 170 D2
Moffat Rd AIRDRIE ML6 .... 111 M2
PSTWK KA9 .... 221 J6
Moffat Vw AIRDRIE ML6 .... 90 A7
Mogarth Av PSLYS PA2 .... 123 M1
Moidart Av RNFRW PA4 .... 80 B5 🔢
Moidart Ct BRHD/NEIL G78 ..... 125 H5 🔢
Moidart Crs
CARD/HILL/MSPK G52 .... 103 M4 🔢
Moidart Gdns KKNTL G66 .... 46 B8
NMRNS G77 .... 150 E3

Moidart Pl
CARD/HILL/MSPK G52 .... 103 M4 🔢
Moidart Rd
CARD/HILL/MSPK G52 .... 103 L4
PGL PA14 .... 54 E2
Moir St CGLE G1 .... 11 M4
Molendinar St CGLE G1 .... 11 M3
Molendinar Ter
BRHD/NEIL G78 .... 148 C3 🔢
Mollinsburn Rd AIRDRIE ML6 .. 88 C3 🔢
CTBR ML5 .... 87 M1
CUMB G67 .... 67 L6
Mollinsburn St SPRGB/BLRNK G21 .. 6 B2
Mollins Ct BALLOCH G68 .... 67 K4 🔢
Mollins Rd BALLOCH G68 .... 47 H8
BALLOCH G68 .... 67 J4
Monach Gdns IRVSE KA11 .... 209 H1
Monach Rd PGL PA14 .... 55 C2 🔢
STPS/GTHM/RID G33 .... 107 J1
Monaebrook Pl HBR/GL G84 .... 22 F1 🔢
Monar Dr PPK/MIL G22 .... 5 H2
Monar St PPK/MIL G22 .... 5 H2
Monart Pl MRYH/FIRH G20 ...... 82 F5
Moncrieff Av KKNTL G66 .... 65 K4
Moncrieff St PSLY PA1 .... 9 C2
Moncur Rd KLWNG KA13 .... 194 A6
Moncur St DMNK/BRGTN G40 .. 12 A4
Moness Dr
CARD/HILL/MSPK G52 .... 103 L5
Money Gv MTHW ML1 .... 158 B5 🔢
Monifieth Av
CARD/HILL/MSPK G52 .... 103 K6
Monikie Gdns BSHPBGS G64 .. 64 D8 🔢
Monkcastle Dr
BLTYR/CAMB G72 .... 130 A3
Monkland Av KKNTL G66 .... 65 K3
Monklands TROON KA10 .... 216 F2 🔢
Monkland St AIRDRIE ML6 .... 111 H2
Monkland Ter CTBR ML5 .... 87 K3
Monkland Vw UD/BTH/TAN G71 .. 109 G8
Monkland View Crs
BAIL/MDB/MHD G69 .... 109 G4
Monkreddan Crs
KLWNG KA13 .... 193 J4 🔢
Monksbridge Av KNTSWD G13 .. 81 K1 🔢
Monkscourt Av AIRDRIE ML6 .. 110 E1
Monkscroft Av PTCK G11 .... 82 A6 🔢
Monkscroft Ct PTCK G11 .... 82 A7 🔢
Monkscroft Gdns PTCK G11 .... 82 A7 🔢
Monks La CARLUKE ML8 .... 188 E5
Monks Rd AIRDRIE ML6 .... 111 J5
Monkton Ct PSTWK KA9 .... 221 K7
Monkton Dr DRUM G15 .... 61 H8
Monkton Gdns NMRNS G77 .... 151 C5 🔢
TROON KA10 .... 216 F8
Monkton Rd PSTWK KA9 .... 221 K7
Monkwood Pl AYRS KA7 .... 229 C7
Monmouth Av KVD/HLHD G12 .. 82 A4 🔢
Monreith Av BSDN G61 .... 61 K7
Monreith Rd
PLKSW/MSWD G43 .... 127 K3
Monreith Rd East
LNPK/KPK G44 .... 128 A4
Monroe Dr UD/BTH/TAN G71 .. 108 F8
Monroe Pl UD/BTH/TAN G71 .. 108 F8 🔢
Montague La KVD/HLHD G12 .. 82 B5
Montague St KVGV G3 .... 4 C5
Montalto Av MTHW ML1 .... 134 A8
Montclair Pl
PSLYN/LNWD PA3 .... 100 A3 🔢
Montego Gn EKILS G75 .... 153 C6
Monteith Dr
CRMNK/CLK/EAG G76 .... 152 A1
Monteith Gdns
CRMNK/CLK/EAG G76 .... 151 M1
Monteith Pl
DMNK/BRGTN G40 .... 12 A5 🔢
DMNK/BRGTN G40 .... 12 A5
Monteith Rw CGLE G1 .... 11 M4
DMNK/BRGTN G40 .... 12 A5
Montfode Ct ARD KA22 .... 191 H5
Montfode Dr ARD KA22 .... 191 H5
Montford Av LNPK/KPK G44 .. 128 D2
RUTH G73 .... 128 E2
Montgomerie Av
FAIRLIE KA29 .... 139 K8
Montgomerie Crs
FAIRLIE KA29 .... 139 K7 🔢
SALT KA21 .... 200 E1
Montgomerie Dr
FAIRLIE KA29 .... 139 K7
SKLM PA17 .... 70 B4
Montgomerie Pier Rd
ARD KA22 .... 191 H8
Montgomerie Rd PSTWK KA9 .. 225 H1
SALT KA21 .... 200 E1
Montgomerieston Plac
KBRN KA25 .... 143 C8 🔢
Montgomerieston Stre
KBRN KA25 .... 143 H8 🔢
Montgomerie St ARD KA22 ..... 191 H8
PGL PA14 .... 34 D8 🔢
Montgomerie Ter AYRS KA7 ..... 18 D2
KLWNG KA13 .... 194 A6
SKLM PA17 .... 70 A5
Montgomery Av BEITH KA15 .. 168 C1
CTBR ML5 .... 109 M1
PSLYN/LNWD PA3 .... 102 B1
Montgomery Crs WISHAW ML2 .. 158 E8
Montgomery Dr
GIF/THBK G46 .... 127 J8 🔢
KLBCH PA10 .... 99 C5 🔢
Montgomery Pl EKILN G74 .... 15 C2 🔢
LRKH ML9 .... 176 B3 🔢
Montgomery Rd
PSLYN/LNWD PA3 .... 102 A1
Montgomery St
BLTYR/CAMB G72 .... 130 E4 🔢
DMNK/BRGTN G40 .... 12 C2
EKILN G74 .... 15 C2 🔢
IRV KA12 .... 203 C8
KLMNKN/STW KA3 .... 206 F7 🔢
LRKH ML9 .... 176 A5
Montgomery Ter KKNTL G66 .... 45 H4
Montgreenan Vw KLWNG KA13 .. 193 M6
Montraive St RUTH G73 .... 106 C8 🔢

Montrave St
CARD/HILL/MSPK G52 .... 103 K5
Montreal Pk EKILS G75 .... 14 A5
Montrose Av CAR/SHTL G32 .... 107 H8
CARD/HILL/MSPK G52 .... 102 F1
PGL PA14 .... 54 E2
Montrose Crs HMLTN ML3 .... 156 D5
Montrose Dr BSDN G61 .... 61 L2
Montrose Gdns
BLTYR/CAMB G72 .... 131 J7 🔢
MLNGV G62 .... 42 A6
Montrose Pl
PSLYN/LNWD PA3 .... 100 A3 🔢
Montrose Rd PSLYS PA2 .... 123 M1
Montrose St CGLE G1 .... 11 L2
CLYDBK G81 .... 60 B7
MTHW ML1 .... 133 K8 🔢
Montrose Ter BRWEIR PA11 .... 98 D2
SPRGB/BLRNK G21 .... 84 C2
Monument Crs PSTWK KA9 ..... 221 L8
Monument Rd AYRS KA7 .... 228 F4
Monymusk Gdns BSHPBGS G64 .. 64 D7
Monymusk Pl CLYDBK G81 ...... 60 C4
Moodiesburn St
STPS/GTHM/RID G33 .... 7 M5
Moorburn Av GIF/THBK G46 .... 127 H6
Moorburn Pl PSLYN/LNWD PA3 .. 99 M3
Moorburn Rd LARGS KA30 ...... 115 K6
Moorcroft Dr AIRDRIE ML6 ...... 111 L2
Moorcroft Rd NMRNS G77 .... 150 C6
Moore Dr BSDN G61 .... 61 M6
HBR/GL G84 .... 23 C2 🔢
Moore Gdns HMLTN ML3 .... 174 E2
Moore St DMNK/BRGTN G40 .. 12 C3
MTHW ML1 .... 134 A6
Moorfield Av KLMNK KA1 .... 16 A7
KLMNK KA1 .... 211 J2
PGL PA14 .... 54 D2
Moorfield Crs AIRDRIE ML6 ..... 111 M2 🔢
Moorfield La GRK PA19 .... 31 J3 🔢
Moorfield Pl CRH/DND KA2 .... 210 D4
Moorfield Rd BLTYR/CAMB G72 .. 155 J3
GRK PA19 .... 31 J3
PSTWK KA9 .... 225 J2
Moorfoot EKILS G75 .... 171 H6 🔢
PSLYS PA2 .... 101 K8
WISHAW ML2 .... 158 F6
Moorfoot Av GIF/THBK G46 .... 127 C6
PSLYS PA2 .... 124 D1
Moorfoot Dr GRK PA19 .... 31 J3
WISHAW ML2 .... 158 F6
Moorfoot Gdns EKILS G75 .... 171 H6 🔢
Moorfoot St CAR/SHTL G32 .... 106 E3
Moorfoot Wy BSDN G61 .... 61 J1
IRVSE KA11 .... 204 A4
Moorhill Crs NMRNS G77 .... 150 C6
Moorhill Rd NMRNS G77 .... 150 C6
Moorhouse Av KNTSWD G13 .. 80 F3
PSLYS PA2 .... 8 A9
Moorhouse St BRHD/NEIL G78 .. 125 J7
The Moorings PSLY PA1 .... 8 B6
Moorland Dr AIRDRIE ML6 ...... 111 L1
Moorpark Av AIRDRIE ML6 ...... 111 L2 🔢
BAIL/MDB/MHD G69 .... 86 C2 🔢
CARD/HILL/MSPK G52 .... 102 F3
Moor Park Crs PSTWK KA9 ..... 225 J4
Moorpark Dr
CARD/HILL/MSPK G52 .... 103 C5
Moor Park Pl PSTWK KA9 .... 225 J4
Moorpark Rd East SVSTN KA20 .. 201 K2
Moorpark Rd West SVSTN KA20 .. 201 J2
Moorpark Sq RNFRW PA4 .... 80 B7
Moor Pl AYR KA8 .... 225 J5 🔢
CMPF/LLE G63 .... 27 J8
MLNGV G62 .... 42 B7
Moor Rd AYR KA8 .... 225 J5
CMPF/LLE G63 .... 27 J8
MLNGV G62 .... 42 B7
Moorside St CARLUKE ML8 ...... 179 C7
Morag Av BLTYR/CAMB G72 .... 131 J8
Moraine Av DRUM G15 .... 61 C8
Moraine Circ DRUM G15 .... 61 C8
Moraine Dr
CRMNK/CLK/EAG G76 .... 151 K1 🔢
DRUM G15 .... 61 C8
Moraine Pl DRUM G15 .... 61 H8 🔢
Morar Av CLYDBK G81 .... 60 B5
Morar Ct CUMB G67 .... 68 B1
HMLTN ML3 .... 156 A8 🔢
Morar Crs AIRDRIE ML6 .... 88 E8
BSHPBGS G64 .... 63 M7
BSHPTN PA7 .... 58 B5
CLYDBK G81 .... 60 B5
CTBR ML5 .... 87 K8
Morar Dr BSDN G61 .... 62 B6
CLYDBK G81 .... 60 B5
CUMB G67 .... 68 B1
PSLYN/LNWD PA3 .... 100 A4
PSLYS PA2 .... 100 F7
RUTH G73 .... 128 E3
Morar Pl CLYDBK G81 .... 60 B5
EKILN G74 .... 153 M6
IRV KA12 .... 203 J2
NMRNS G77 .... 150 D2
RNFRW PA4 .... 80 B5
Morar Rd CARD/HILL/MSPK G52 .. 103 L4
CLYDBK G81 .... 60 B5
PGL PA14 .... 54 E2
WMYSB PA18 .... 70 A1 🔢
Morar St WISHAW ML2 .... 159 G8
Morar Ter RUTH G73 .... 129 K5 🔢
UD/BTH/TAN G71 .... 132 B2
Moravia Av UD/BTH/TAN G71 .. 132 A6
Moray Av AIRDRIE ML6 .... 111 C4
Moray Dr BSHPBGS G64 .... 44 B8
CRMNK/CLK/EAG G76 .... 151 M2
Moray Gdns BALLOCH G68 ...... 48 F4 🔢
CRMNK/CLK/EAG G76 .... 151 M1
UD/BTH/TAN G71 .... 131 M5
Moray Ga UD/BTH/TAN G71 .. 131 M5
Moray Pl BLTYR/CAMB G72 .... 155 J3
BSHPBGS G64 .... 64 C8
KKNTL G66 .... 46 A8
PLKSD/SHW G41 .... 104 E7
PSLYN/LNWD PA3 .... 100 A3
Moray Qd BLSH ML4 .... 133 C4
Morays Rd PGL PA14 .... 34 C2
Mordaunt St DMNK/BRGTN G40 .. 12 C4
Moredun Crs CAR/SHTL G32 .. 107 J2
Moredun Dr PSLYS PA2 .... 101 H8

Moredun Rd PSLYS PA2 .... 101 H8
Moredun St CAR/SHTL G32 .... 107 J2
Morefield Rd GOV/IBX G51 .... 103 K2
Morgan Ms GVH/MTFL G42 .... 105 H6
Morgan St HMLTN ML3 .... 156 D7
LRKH ML9 .... 175 M6
Morina Gdns PLK/PH/NH G53 .. 126 C6
Morion Rd KNTSWD G13 .... 81 K1
Moriston Ct WISHAW ML2 .... 159 M3
Morland EKILN G74 .... 154 D4
Morley St LNPK/KPK G44 .... 128 A2
Morna La SCOT G14 .... 81 L7 🔢
Morningside Rd WISHAW ML2 .. 160 C6
Morningside St
STPS/GTHM/RID G33 .... 7 L9
Morrin St SPRGB/BLRNK G21 .. 6 A2 🔢
Morris Crs BLTYR/CAMB G72 .. 155 K2
KLMNK KA1 .... 212 E3
MTHW ML1 .... 134 E8
Morrishall Rd EKILN G74 .... 154 C5
Morrishill Dr BEITH KA15 .... 168 A3
Morris La KLMNKN/STW KA3 .. 16 F2 🔢
Morris Moodie Av SVSTN KA20 .. 201 L2
Morrison Av SVSTN KA20 .... 192 E8
Morrison Ct SVSTN KA20 .... 192 E8
Morrison Dr KKNTL G66 .... 44 E2
Morrison Gdns AYR KA8 .... 19 K3
Morrison Pl KLMNKN/STW KA3 .. 17 G4
Morrison Qd CLYDBK G81 .... 60 E8
Morrison St CLYDBK G81 .... 59 M3
GBLS G5 .... 10 E4
Morris Rd PSTWK KA9 .... 221 J8
Morris St GRNK PA15 .... 3 K8
HMLTN ML3 .... 156 D8
LARGS KA30 .... 115 J6 🔢
LRKH ML9 .... 176 D3
Morriston Crs RNFRW PA4 ...... 80 E8
Morriston Park Dr
BLTYR/CAMB G72 .... 130 A2
Morriston St BLTYR/CAMB G72 .. 130 A3
Morton Av AYRS KA7 .... 19 H9
Morton Gdns PLKSD/SHW G41 .. 104 C8
Morton Pl KLMNK KA1 .... 16 C4
Morton Rd AYRS KA7 .... 19 C9
KLMNKN/STW KA3 .... 197 J1
Morton St MTHW ML1 .... 157 L1
Morven Av BLTYR/CAMB G72 .. 131 J8
BSHPBGS G64 .... 64 C8
KLMNKN/STW KA3 .... 206 F6
PSLYS PA2 .... 124 D1
Morven Crs TROON KA10 .... 216 D7
Morven Dr
CRMNK/CLK/EAG G76 .... 151 K1
PSLYN/LNWD PA3 .... 100 A4
TROON KA10 .... 216 D6
Morven Gait ERSK PA8 .... 79 L1 🔢
Morven Gdns
UD/BTH/TAN G71 .... 131 M1 🔢
Morven Rd
BLTYR/CAMB G72 .... 129 M6
BSDN G61 .... 61 L3
Morven St
CARD/HILL/MSPK G52 .... 103 L4
CTBR ML5 .... 110 A1
Morville St KLWNG KA13 .... 193 L4
Mosesfield St SPRGB/BLRNK G21 .. 83 M4
Mosque Av GBLS G5 .... 11 J5
Mossacre Rd WISHAW ML2 ...... 159 J5
Moss Av AIRDRIE ML6 .... 90 F4
PSLYN/LNWD PA3 .... 100 B3
Mossband La SHOTTS ML7 ...... 137 L3 🔢
Mossbank BLTYR/CAMB G72 .. 155 K3 🔢
EKILS G75 .... 170 F1
Mossbank Av STPS/GTHM/RID G33 .. 84 F5
Mossbank Crs MTHW ML1 .... 134 F5
Mossbank Dr STPS/GTHM/RID G33 .. 84 F5
Mossbank Pl RAYR/DAL KA6 .. 227 H3 🔢
Mossbank Rd WISHAW ML2 ..... 159 J5
Mossblown St LRKH ML9 .... 175 M6 🔢
Mossburn Rd WISHAW ML2 ..... 159 K6
Mossburn Rd WISHAW ML2 ..... 159 K8 🔢
Mosscastle Rd
STPS/GTHM/RID G33 .... 85 J7 🔢
Mossdale EKILN G74 .... 153 J6
Mossdale Gdns HMLTN ML3 .... 155 K7
Moss Dr BRHD/NEIL G78 .... 125 C4
ERSK PA8 .... 79 H2
IRVSE KA11 .... 208 E4
Mossend Av HBR/GL G84 .... 20 F8 🔢
KBRN KA25 .... 167 C5
Mossend La
STPS/GTHM/RID G33 .... 107 K1
Mossend St
STPS/GTHM/RID G33 .... 107 K2 🔢
Mossgiel EKILS G75 .... 171 H2
Mossgiel Av KLMNKN/STW KA3 .. 17 M5
RUTH G73 .... 129 C4
TROON KA10 .... 216 F5
Mossgiel Crs
CRMNK/CLK/EAG G76 .... 151 M4
Mossgiel Dr CLYDBK G81 .... 60 C6
IRV KA12 .... 203 K6 🔢
Mossgiel Gdns KKNTL G66 ...... 45 M8
UD/BTH/TAN G71 .... 131 L1
Mossgiel Pl AYRS KA7 .... 19 H7 🔢
RUTH G73 .... 129 C4 🔢
SVSTN KA20 .... 192 E8
Mossgiel Rd ARD KA22 .... 191 K5
AYRS KA7 .... 19 H8
CUMB G67 .... 49 H6
PLKSW/MSWD G43 .... 127 K2
SALT KA21 .... 192 A6
Mossgiel St BLTYR/CAMB G72 .. 155 K2
Mosshall Gv MTHW ML1 .... 134 F5
Mosshall Rd MTHW ML1 .... 134 D2
Mosshall St MTHW ML1 .... 134 F6
Mosshead Rd BSDN G61 .... 61 M2
KLMNK KA1 .... 211 M6
Moss Heights Av
CARD/HILL/MSPK G52 .... 103 K4
Mosshill Rd BLSH ML4 .... 133 H2
Mosside Pl KLMNKN/STW KA3 .. 206 F5
Mosside Rd AYR KA8 .... 225 J5
Moss Knowe CUMB G67 .... 49 H7
Mossland Dr WISHAW ML2 ...... 159 J5
Mossland Rd
CARD/HILL/MSPK G52 .... 102 D1

Mosslands Rd PSLYN/LNWD PA3 ... 101 K2
Mosslingal EKILS G75 ... 171 L4
Mossmulloch EKILS G75 ... 171 K4
Mossneuk Av EKILS G75 ... 170 A5
Mossneuk Crs WISHAW ML2 ... 159 J5
Mossneuk Dr EKILS G75 ... 170 F2
PSLYS PA2 ... 124 C1
WISHAW ML2 ... 159 J5
Mossneuk Pk WISHAW ML2 ... 159 J5
Mossneuk Rd EKILS G75 ... 171 G1
Mossneuk St CTBR ML5 ... 109 M6
Mosspark Av CARD/HILL/MSPK G52 ... 103 M6
MLNCV G62 ... 42 A6
Mosspark Bvd CARD/HILL/MSPK G52 ... 103 M6
Mosspark Dr CARD/HILL/MSPK G52 ... 103 L7
Mosspark Ov CARD/HILL/MSPK G52 ... 103 L6
Mosspark Rd CTBR ML5 ... 109 K1
MLNCV G62 ... 42 A6
Mosspark Sq CARD/HILL/MSPK G52 ... 103 L6
Moss Rd AIRDRIE ML6 ... 111 G3
BAIL/MDB/MHD G69 ... 86 C2
BRWEIR PA11 ... 98 E2
CRG/CRSL/HOU PA6 ... 78 B6
CUMB G67 ... 49 L5
DMBTN G82 ... 23 J5
EKILS G75 ... 171 J5
GOV/IBX G51 ... 103 K1
KKNTL G66 ... 65 H3
KLMCLM PA13 ... 75 K1
PGL PA14 ... 54 F2
PSLYN/LNWD PA3 ... 100 C3
WISHAW ML2 ... 159 L6
Moss-Side Av AIRDRIE ML6 ... 110 L1
Moss-Side Av CARLUKE ML8 ... 178 D7
Moss-Side Rd PLKSD/SHW G41 ... 104 E8
Moss St PSLY PA1 ... 9 G3
Mossvale La PSLYN/LNWD PA3 ... 101 K3
Mossvale Rd STPS/GTHM/RID G33 ... 85 H7
STPS/GTHM/RID G33 ... 85 J7
Mossvale Sq STPS/GTHM/RID G33 ... 85 H7
Mossvale St PSLYN/LNWD PA3 ... 101 K2
Mossvale Ter BAIL/MDB/MHD G69 ... 67 G6
Mossview Crs AIRDRIE ML6 ... 111 G3
Mossview La CARD/HILL/MSPK G52 ... 103 J4
Mossview Qd CARD/HILL/MSPK G52 ... 103 K4
Mossview Rd STPS/GTHM/RID G33 ... 85 L5
Mosswell Rd MLNCV G62 ... 42 B6
Mossywood Av PGL PA14 ... 54 F2
Mossywood Ct BALLOCH G68 ... 67 G3
Mossywood Pl BALLOCH G68 ... 67 M2
Mossywood Rd BALLOCH G68 ... 67 L2
Mote Hl HMLTN ML3 ... 156 E5
Mote Hill Rd PSLYN/LNWD PA3 ... 102 A3
Motehill Rd PSLYN/LNWD PA3 ... 102 B2
Motherwell Rd BLSH ML4 ... 133 G5
HMLTN ML3 ... 156 F6
MTHW ML1 ... 134 B8
MTHW ML1 ... 135 J3
Motherwell St AIRDRIE ML6 ... 89 J8
Moulin Circ CARD/HILL/MSPK G52 ... 103 H5
Moulin Pl CARD/HILL/MSPK G52 ... 103 C5
Moulin Rd CARD/HILL/MSPK G52 ... 103 C5
Moulin Ter CARD/HILL/MSPK G52 ... 103 G6
Mountainblue St DMNK/BRGTN G40 ... 12 F5
Mount Annan Dr LNPK/KPK G44 ... 128 B2
Mount Av KLMNK KA1 ... 16 A7
KLMNK KA1 ... 218 C3
Mountblow Rd CLYDBK G81 ... 59 K3
Mount Cameron Dr North EKILN G74 ... 15 K5
Mount Cameron Dr South EKILN G74 ... 15 K6
Mount Charles Crs AYRS KA7 ... 228 D7
Mountgarrie Rd GOV/IBX G51 ... 103 K2
Mount Harriet Av STPS/GTHM/RID G33 ... 85 L3
Mount Harriet Dr STPS/GTHM/RID G33 ... 85 K3
Mountherrick EKILS G75 ... 171 L4
Mount Lockhart UD/BTH/TAN G71 ... 108 B7
Mount Oliphant Crs AYRS KA7 ... 19 J7
Mount Oliphant Pl AYRS KA7 ... 19 J7
Mount Pl KLMNK KA1 ... 16 A8
Mount Pleasant Crs KKNTL G66 ... 45 H3
Mount Pleasant Dr OLDK G60 ... 59 H2
Mount Pleasant St GRNK PA15 ... 2 A5
Mount Stewart St CARLUKE ML8 ... 178 E7
Mount St MRYH/FIRH G20 ... 4 D3
Mount Stuart St LARGS KA30 ... 115 J3
Mountstuart St GTCI KA28 ... 138 B6
Mount Stuart St PLKSD/SHW G41 ... 127 L1
The Mount AYRS KA7 ... 229 H5
Mount Vernon Av CAR/SHTL G32 ... 107 L6
CTBR ML5 ... 109 L2
Mount Vw IRVSE KA11 ... 204 C8
Mount Village KLMNK KA1 ... 211 J2
Mournian Wy HMLTN ML3 ... 156 D8
Mousebank Rd LNK/LMHG ML11 ... 198 F5
Mousemill Rd LNK/LMHG ML11 ... 198 D4
Mowbray EKILN G74 ... 154 C5
Mowbray Av BAIL/MDB/MHD G69 ... 86 F4
Moyne Rd PLK/PH/NH G53 ... 103 G7
Moy St PTCK G11 ... 82 C7

Muckcroft Rd BAIL/MDB/MHD G69 ... 66 B5
Mugdock Rd MLNGV G62 ... 42 A7
Muirbank Av RUTH G73 ... 128 F2
Muirbank Gdns RUTH G73 ... 128 F2
Muirbrae Rd RUTH G73 ... 129 H5
Muirbrae Wy RUTH G73 ... 129 H5
Muirburn Rd BEITH KA15 ... 144 A6
Muircroft Dr MTHW ML1 ... 135 H7
Muir Dr IRV KA12 ... 203 K6
SVSTN KA20 ... 201 J1
TROON KA10 ... 216 D3
Muirdrum Av CARD/HILL/MSPK G52 ... 103 K6
Muirdyke Rd CTBR ML5 ... 88 A4
CTBR ML5 ... 109 K1
Muirdykes Av CARD/HILL/MSPK G52 ... 103 G4
PGL PA14 ... 54 D2
Muirdykes Crs PSLYN/LNWD PA3 ... 101 H3
Muirdykes Rd CARD/HILL/MSPK G52 ... 103 G4
PSLYN/LNWD PA3 ... 101 H3
Muiredge And Jersy Rd MTHW ML1 ... 136 B6
SHOTTS ML7 ... 136 C2
SHOTTS ML7 ... 136 F1
Muiredge Ct UD/BTH/TAN G71 ... 131 M3
Muiredge Ter BAIL/MDB/MHD G69 ... 108 B5
Muirend Av LNPK/KPK G44 ... 127 M4
KLMNKN/STW KA3 ... 206 F4
LNPK/KPK G44 ... 127 L5
Muirend St KBRN KA25 ... 143 J6
Muirfield Ct LNPK/KPK G44 ... 127 M5
Muirfield Crs SMSTN G23 ... 62 E8
Muirfield Mdw UD/BTH/TAN G71 ... 131 L7
Muirfield Pl KLWNG KA13 ... 193 J5
Muirfield Rd BALLOCH G68 ... 49 G4
Muirhall Ter SHOTTS ML7 ... 113 H7
Muirhead Dr MTHW ML1 ... 134 F5
PSLYN/LNWD PA3 ... 100 A4
Muirhead Gdns BAIL/MDB/MHD G69 ... 108 C5
SHOTTS ML7 ... 113 H7
Muirhead Ga UD/BTH/TAN G71 ... 132 B1
Muirhead Gv BAIL/MDB/MHD G69 ... 108 C5
Muirhead Rd BAIL/MDB/MHD G69 ... 108 B6
Muirhead St LOCHW PA12 ... 120 D7
Muirhead Ter MTHW ML1 ... 157 L5
Muirhead Wy BSHPBGS G64 ... 64 D8
Muirhill Av LNPK/KPK G44 ... 127 L5
Muirhill Crs KNTSWD G13 ... 80 F2
Muirhouse Av MTHW ML1 ... 158 B6
WISHAW ML2 ... 160 B3
Muirhouse Dr MTHW ML1 ... 158 C7
Muirhouse La EKILS G75 ... 15 G6
Muirhouse Pk BSDN G61 ... 61 K1
Muirhouse Rd MTHW ML1 ... 158 B8
Muirhouse St PLKSD/SHW G41 ... 10 F9
Muirkirk Dr HMLTN ML3 ... 155 K7
KNTSWD G13 ... 81 M2
Muirlee Rd CARLUKE ML8 ... 179 H8
Muirlees Crs MLNGV G62 ... 41 J7
Muirmadkin Rd BLSH ML4 ... 133 H4
Muirmaillen Av MTHW ML1 ... 135 J8
Muirpark Av RNFRW PA4 ... 80 C7
Muirpark Dr BSHPBGS G64 ... 84 A1
Muirpark Rd BEITH KA15 ... 144 B8
Muirpark St PTCK G11 ... 82 B7
Muirpark Ter BSHPBGS G64 ... 84 A1
Muir Rd DMBTN G82 ... 37 J3
Muirshiel Crs PLK/PH/NH G53 ... 126 C3
Muirshiel La PGL PA14 ... 54 D1
Muirshiel Pl PGL PA14 ... 54 D1
Muirshiel Rd PGL PA14 ... 54 D1
Muirshot Rd LRKH ML9 ... 176 B5
Muirside Av CAR/SHTL G32 ... 107 L6
KKNTL G66 ... 66 A1
Muirside Pl WISHAW ML2 ... 159 M3
Muirside Rd BAIL/MDB/MHD G69 ... 108 B5
KLWNG KA13 ... 193 H7
Muirside St BAIL/MDB/MHD G69 ... 108 B5
Muirskeith Crs PLKSW/MSWD G43 ... 128 A3
Muirskeith Pl PLKSW/MSWD G43 ... 127 M3
Muirskeith Rd PLKSW/MSWD G43 ... 127 M3
Muir St ALEX/LLW G83 ... 25 K2
BLTYR/CAMB G72 ... 155 K3
BSHPBGS G64 ... 64 A1
CARLUKE ML8 ... 177 M3
CTBR ML5 ... 109 L2
HMLTN ML3 ... 156 E5
LRKH ML9 ... 176 A4
MTHW ML1 ... 157 K1
RNFRW PA4 ... 80 D5
Muir Ter PSLYN/LNWD PA3 ... 102 A2
Muirton Dr BSHPBGS G64 ... 63 M6
Muiryfauld Dr CAR/SHTL G32 ... 106 E5
Muiryhall St CTBR ML5 ... 110 A2
Muiryhall St East CTBR ML5 ... 110 C2
Mulben Crs PLK/PH/NH G53 ... 125 M2
Mulben Pl PLK/PH/NH G53 ... 125 M2
Mulben Ter PLK/PH/NH G53 ... 125 M2
Mulberry Dr EKILS G75 ... 171 J4
Mulberry Rd PLKSW/MSWD G43 ... 127 K3
UD/BTH/TAN G71 ... 109 J8
Mulberry Wy EKILS G75 ... 171 J4
Mulberry Wynd BLTYR/CAMB G72 ... 130 F6
Mulgrew Av SVSTN KA20 ... 192 A4
Mull EKILN G74 ... 172 C2
Mullardoch St SMSTN G23 ... 62 D8
Mull Av PGL PA14 ... 55 G2
PSLYS PA2 ... 124 C2
RNFRW PA4 ... 80 C8
Mull Crs IRVSE KA11 ... 204 A7

Mull Pl IRVSE KA11 ... 204 A7
Mull Qd WISHAW ML2 ... 159 L4
Mull St SPRGB/BLRNK G21 ... 7 G4
Mull Ter IRVSE KA11 ... 204 A6
Mulvey Crs AIRDRIE ML6 ... 110 C2
Mungo Pk EKILS G75 ... 171 L4
Munlochy Rd GOV/IBX G51 ... 103 H2
Munnoch Crs ARD KA22 ... 191 H5
Munro Av KLMNK KA1 ... 16 A3
Munro Ct Dr KBRN KA25 ... 167 H1
KKNTL G66 ... 45 H4
Munro Dr East HBR/GL G84 ... 20 E6
Munro Dr West HBR/GL G84 ... 20 D6
Munro La KNTSWD G13 ... 81 L1
Munro La East KNTSWD G13 ... 81 L1
Munro Pl EKILN G74 ... 154 B6
KLMNK KA1 ... 16 B1
KNTSWD G13 ... 81 L2
SALT KA21 ... 192 A7
Munro Rd KNTSWD G13 ... 81 L1
Munro St ALEX/LLW G83 ... 25 L4
GRNKW/INVK PA16 ... 32 A5
Murano St MRYH/FIRH G20 ... 82 F5
Murchie Dr PSTWK KA9 ... 225 K4
Murchison Dr EKILS G75 ... 171 H2
Murchison Rd CRG/CRSL/HOU PA6 ... 77 J8
Murchland Wy IRV KA12 ... 203 J6
Murdieston St GRNK PA15 ... 32 D5
Murdoch Crs SVSTN KA20 ... 201 K2
Murdoch Dr MLNGV G62 ... 62 D1
Murdoch Pl IRVSE KA11 ... 208 F3
MTHW ML1 ... 133 M6
Murdoch Rd EKILS G75 ... 14 F6
Murdoch's Lone AYRS KA7 ... 228 E8
Murdoch Sq BLSH ML4 ... 133 J2
Murdostoun Gdns WISHAW ML2 ... 159 H4
Murdostoun Ter MTHW ML1 ... 135 L8
Murdostoun Vw WISHAW ML2 ... 159 M3
Mure Av KLMNKN/STW KA3 ... 207 G5
Mure Pl BRHD/NEIL G78 ... 147 C6
NMLNS KA16 ... 215 H2
Murial Blue Ct GRK PA19 ... 31 M2
Muriel La BRHD/NEIL G78 ... 125 J6
Muriel St BRHD/NEIL G78 ... 125 J6
Murray Av KSYTH G65 ... 47 K1
SALT KA21 ... 191 L7
Murray Crs WISHAW ML2 ... 160 A2
Murrayfield Dr BSDN G61 ... 61 L8
Murrayfield St CAR/SHTL G32 ... 106 E2
Murrayhill EKILS G75 ... 14 C5
Murray Pl AYR KA8 ... 225 J6
BLSH ML4 ... 132 E2
BRHD/NEIL G78 ... 125 K5
DMBTN G82 ... 37 J5
GRK PA19 ... 31 L3
KLMNKN/STW KA3 ... 207 J7
Murray Rd CARLUKE ML8 ... 177 M5
UD/BTH/TAN G71 ... 132 A2
The Murray Rd EKILS G75 ... 14 C7
Murray St AYR KA8 ... 225 J7
GRNKW/INVK PA16 ... 32 C4
PSLYN/LNWD PA3 ... 8 C1
RNFRW PA4 ... 80 C6
Murray Ter MTHW ML1 ... 157 H2
Murrin Av BSHPBGS G64 ... 64 D8
Murroch Av DMBTN G82 ... 37 H3
Murroes Rd GOV/IBX G51 ... 103 G2
Musgrove Pl EKILS G75 ... 14 A6
Muslin St DMNK/BRGTN G40 ... 12 B3
Muttonhole Rd HMLTN ML3 ... 173 H1
Mybster Pl GOV/IBX G51 ... 103 K2
Myers Crs UD/BTH/TAN G71 ... 132 A4
Myreside Pl CAR/SHTL G32 ... 13 M3
Myreside Rd CAR/SHTL G32 ... 106 E3
Myres Rd PLK/PH/NH G53 ... 126 D1
Myreton Av KLMCLM PA13 ... 75 J2
Myrie Gdns BSHPBGS G64 ... 64 B8
Myrtle Av KKNTL G66 ... 65 J4
Myrtle Bank BEITH KA15 ... 168 A1
Myrtle Dr MTHW ML1 ... 134 B4
WISHAW ML2 ... 158 D5
Myrtle Hill La GVH/MTFL G42 ... 128 C1
Myrtle La LRKH ML9 ... 176 B8
Myrtle Pk GVH/MTFL G42 ... 105 H8
Myrtle Pl GVH/MTFL G42 ... 128 C1
Myrtle Rd CLYDBK G81 ... 59 K5
UD/BTH/TAN G71 ... 132 B1
Myrtle Sq BSHPBGS G64 ... 84 A1
Myrtle St BLTYR/CAMB G72 ... 131 K8
Myrtle View Rd GVH/MTFL G42 ... 128 C1
Myrtle Wk BLTYR/CAMB G72 ... 129 M3
Myvot Av CUMB G67 ... 68 B3
Myvot Rd CUMB G67 ... 68 B3

N

Nairn Av BLSH ML4 ... 133 G3
Nairn Ct KLWNG KA13 ... 193 H6
Nairn Crs AIRDRIE ML6 ... 111 G4
Nairn Dr GRNKW/INVK PA16 ... 31 K4
Nairn Pl CLYDBK G81 ... 59 M6
EKILN G74 ... 154 C6
Nairn Qd WISHAW ML2 ... 159 H4
Nairn Rd GRNKW/INVK PA16 ... 31 K5
Nairnside Rd SPRGB/BLRNK G21 ... 84 C2
Nairn St BLTYR/CAMB G72 ... 155 J3
CLYDBK G81 ... 59 M6
KVGV G3 ... 82 D8
LRKH ML9 ... 175 M7
Nairn Wy BALLOCH G68 ... 49 G4
Naismith St CAR/SHTL G32 ... 130 C1
Naismith Wk BLSH ML4 ... 133 J2
Nansen St MRYH/FIRH G20 ... 4 E3
Napier Dr DMBTN G82 ... 35 H1
Napier Ct BALLOCH G68 ... 49 K1
DMBTN G82 ... 35 H1
OLDK G60 ... 59 J4
Napier Dr GOV/IBX G51 ... 104 B1
Napier Gdns PSLYN/LNWD PA3 ... 100 C3

Napier Hl EKILS G75 ... 14 F6
Napier La EKILS G75 ... 14 F6
Napier Pk BALLOCH G68 ... 49 J3
Napier Pl BALLOCH G68 ... 49 J1
GOV/IBX G51 ... 104 B1
OLDK G60 ... 59 J4
Napier Rd BALLOCH G68 ... 49 J2
CARD/HILL/MSPK G52 ... 80 F3
GOV/IBX G51 ... 104 B1
Napiershall La COWCAD G4 ... 4 D4
Napiershall Pl MRYH/FIRH G20 ... 4 D4
Napiershall St COWCAD G4 ... 4 D4
MRYH/FIRH G20 ... 4 D3
Napier Sq BLSH ML4 ... 133 J2
Napierston Rd ALEX/LLW G83 ... 25 M4
Napier St CLYDBK G81 ... 80 C2
GOV/IBX G51 ... 104 B1
JNSTN PA5 ... 99 L6
PSLYN/LNWD PA3 ... 100 C3
Napier Ter GOV/IBX G51 ... 104 B1
Napier Wy BALLOCH G68 ... 49 J2
Naproch Pl NMRNS G77 ... 151 J4
Naseby Av PTCK G11 ... 81 M6
Naseby La PTCK G11 ... 81 M6
Nasmyth Av BSDN G61 ... 61 H1
EKILS G75 ... 15 H7
Nasmyth Pl EKILS G75 ... 15 H7
Nasmyth Rd CARD/HILL/MSPK G52 ... 103 G2
Nasmyth Rd North CARD/HILL/MSPK G52 ... 103 G2
Nasmyth Rd South CARD/HILL/MSPK G52 ... 103 G2
Nassau Pl EKILS G75 ... 153 C8
National Bank La CGLE G1 ... 11 H1
Navar Pl PSLYS PA2 ... 9 L9
Naver St STPS/GTHM/RID G33 ... 84 E8
Naylor La AIRDRIE ML6 ... 111 H1
Naysmyth Bank EKILS G75 ... 15 G6
Needle Gn CARLUKE ML8 ... 178 F7
Neidpath Av CTBR ML5 ... 110 A6
Neidpath Dr CTBR ML5 ... 110 A6
Neidpath Pl CTBR ML5 ... 110 A6
Neidpath Rd CARLUKE ML8 ... 178 E6
Neidpath East NMRNS G77 ... 151 G3
Neidpath West NMRNS G77 ... 151 G2
Neil Av IRV KA12 ... 203 K4
Neilsland Dr HMLTN ML3 ... 174 B2
MTHW ML1 ... 157 H3
Neilsland Ov PLK/PH/NH G53 ... 126 D1
Neilsland Rd HMLTN ML3 ... 156 B7
PLK/PH/NH G53 ... 103 K8
Neilsland Sq HMLTN ML3 ... 156 C8
PLK/PH/NH G53 ... 126 C8
Neilsland Sq HMLTN ML3 ... 156 C8
Neilson Ct HMLTN ML3 ... 156 E7
Neilson St BLSH ML4 ... 133 G4
Neilston Av PLK/PH/NH G53 ... 126 C4
Neilston Rd BRHD/NEIL G78 ... 147 C6
BRHD/NEIL G78 ... 148 E2
PSLYS PA2 ... 9 H8
Neil St GRNKW/INVK PA16 ... 32 A5
RNFRW PA4 ... 80 D4
Neilvaig Dr RUTH G73 ... 129 J6
Neistpoint Dr STPS/GTHM/RID G33 ... 107 G2
Nelson Av CTBR ML5 ... 109 L5
Nelson Crs MTHW ML1 ... 158 B5
Nelson Mandela Pl CCLW G2 ... 5 J9
Nelson Pl BAIL/MDB/MHD G69 ... 108 B5
HBR/GL G84 ... 21 G7
Nelson Rd GRK PA19 ... 31 M3
SALT KA21 ... 201 H1
Nelson St BAIL/MDB/MHD G69 ... 108 B5
GBLS G5 ... 10 F4
GRNK PA15 ... 2 B3
KLMNK KA1 ... 16 E4
LARGS KA30 ... 115 J5
NMLNS KA16 ... 215 J2
Nelson Ter EKILN G74 ... 15 K6
Nelville Dr GLSTN KA4 ... 214 A4
Nemphlar Moor Rd CARLUKE ML8 ... 188 D8
Nemphlat Hl LNK/LMHG ML11 ... 198 F4
Neptune St GOV/IBX G51 ... 104 B2
Neptune Wy BLSH ML4 ... 133 L4
Nerston Rd EKILN G74 ... 153 K3
Ness Av JNSTN PA5 ... 122 C1
Ness Dr BLTYR/CAMB G72 ... 131 L8
EKILN G74 ... 15 L3
Ness Gdns BSHPBGS G64 ... 64 B8
Ness Pl TROON KA10 ... 216 F4
Ness Rd GRNKW/INVK PA16 ... 32 C4
RNFRW PA4 ... 80 C6
Ness St STPS/GTHM/RID G33 ... 84 E8
WISHAW ML2 ... 177 H1
Ness Ter HMLTN ML3 ... 156 A8
Nethan Av WISHAW ML2 ... 158 C7
Nethanfoot Rd CARLUKE ML8 ... 188 B7
Nethan Ga HMLTN ML3 ... 156 C6
Nethan Gln CARLUKE ML8 ... 188 A7
Nethan Pl HMLTN ML3 ... 174 D3
Nethan St MTHW ML1 ... 133 J7
Nether Auldhouse Rd PLKSW/MSWD G43 ... 127 J3
Netherbank Rd WISHAW ML2 ... 158 D7
Netherbog Rd DMBTN G82 ... 37 H5
Netherburn Av CRG/CRSL/HOU PA6 ... 99 L2
LNPK/KPK G44 ... 127 M8
Netherburn Gdns CRG/CRSL/HOU PA6 ... 99 L1
Netherby Dr PLKSD/SHW G41 ... 104 D5
Nethercairn Pl NMRNS G77 ... 151 J4
Nethercairn Rd GIF/THBK G46 ... 127 J5
Nethercliffe Av LNPK/KPK G44 ... 127 M7
Nethercraigs Dr PSLYS PA2 ... 124 B2
Nethercraigs Rd PSLYS PA2 ... 124 B2
Nethercroy Rd KSYTH G65 ... 47 L4
Netherdale Crs WISHAW ML2 ... 158 C7
Netherdale Dr PSLY PA1 ... 102 F6
Netherdale Rd WISHAW ML2 ... 158 E7
Netherfield St DEN/PKHD G31 ... 13 J3
Nethergreen Crs RNFRW PA4 ... 80 B6
Nethergreen Wynd RNFRW PA4 ... 80 B6
Netherhall Rd WISHAW ML2 ... 158 E7
Netherhill Av LNPK/KPK G44 ... 127 M8
Netherhill Crs PSLYN/LNWD PA3 ... 102 A3

Netherhill Rd BAIL/MDB/MHD G69 ... 66 F8
PSLYN/LNWD PA3 ... 9 K1
Netherhouse Av CTBR ML5 ... 109 M6
KKNTL G66 ... 65 L5
Netherhouse Pl BAIL/MDB/MHD G69 ... 108 E1
Netherhouse Rd BAIL/MDB/MHD G69 ... 108 E2
Netherland Rd KLMNKN/STW KA3 ... 197 L1
Netherlee Crs DALRY KA24 ... 166 B8
Netherlee Pl LNPK/KPK G44 ... 128 A5
Netherlee Rd LNPK/KPK G44 ... 128 A5
Nethermains Rd KLWNG KA13 ... 193 L8
MLNGV G62 ... 62 A1
Nethermiln Rd WKIL KA23 ... 181 K5
Netherpark Av LNPK/KPK G44 ... 127 M8
Netherpark Crs LARGS KA30 ... 115 J3
Netherplace Crs NMRNS G77 ... 150 C5
PLK/PH/NH G53 ... 126 F3
Netherplace Rd NMRNS G77 ... 149 M5
PLK/PH/NH G53 ... 126 B1
Netherton Av PGL PA14 ... 55 G2
Netherton Ct NMRNS G77 ... 150 F3
Netherton Dr BRHD/NEIL G78 ... 125 K7
Netherton Hl KKNTL G66 ... 29 G8
Netherton Ov KKNTL G66 ... 44 B1
Netherton Rd EKILS G75 ... 14 A9
EKILS G75 ... 170 F5
KNTSWD G13 ... 81 L1
NMRNS G77 ... 150 F3
WISHAW ML2 ... 158 C7
Netherton St KNTSWD G13 ... 81 M2
WISHAW ML2 ... 158 F7
Nethervale Av LNPK/KPK G44 ... 127 M8
Netherview Rd LNPK/KPK G44 ... 128 A8
Netherway LNPK/KPK G44 ... 127 M8
Netherwood Av BALLOCH G68 ... 68 A1
Netherwood Ct BALLOCH G68 ... 68 A1
Netherwood Gv BALLOCH G68 ... 68 A1
Netherwood Rd BALLOCH G68 ... 67 M1
MTHW ML1 ... 158 C6
Netherwood Wy BALLOCH G68 ... 68 A1
Neuk Av BAIL/MDB/MHD G69 ... 86 C2
CRG/CRSL/HOU PA6 ... 77 J8
Neuk Crs CRG/CRSL/HOU PA6 ... 77 J7
The Neuk WISHAW ML2 ... 158 E6
Neukfoot La BRHD/NEIL G78 ... 146 F6
Nevis Av HMLTN ML3 ... 156 A8
Nevis Ct BRHD/NEIL G78 ... 125 J8
Nevis Dr BSHPBGS G64 ... 44 B8
Nevis St LRKH ML9 ... 176 B7
Nevis Pl KLMNK KA1 ... 212 A5
Nevis Rd BSDN G61 ... 61 H2
PLKSW/MSWD G43 ... 127 H4
RNFRW PA4 ... 80 B8
Nevis Wy IRVSE KA11 ... 204 A5
PSLYN/LNWD PA3 ... 79 L8
Neward Crs PSTWK KA9 ... 225 K3
Newark Av GRNKW/INVK PA16 ... 32 C2
Newark Crs AYRS KA7 ... 228 B8
Newark Dr PLKSD/SHW G41 ... 104 E6
PSLYS PA2 ... 124 C1
WISHAW ML2 ... 159 J3
Newark Pl PGL PA14 ... 34 D8
WISHAW ML2 ... 159 K3
Newark St GRNKW/INVK PA16 ... 32 B1
Newarthill Rd MTHW ML1 ... 134 C7
New Ashtree St WISHAW ML2 ... 158 E6
New Av HWWD PA9 ... 121 M3
Newbarns St CARLUKE ML8 ... 178 F6
Newbattle Av AIRDRIE ML6 ... 111 K4
Newbattle Ct CAR/SHTL G32 ... 107 H7
Newbattle Gdns CAR/SHTL G32 ... 107 H7
Newbattle Pl CAR/SHTL G32 ... 107 H7
Newbattle Rd CAR/SHTL G32 ... 107 G8
Newbold Av SPRGB/BLRNK G21 ... 83 M2
New Bridge St AYRS KA7 ... 18 C2
Newburgh St PLKSW/MSWD G43 ... 127 K2
Newcastleton Dr SMSTN G23 ... 62 E8
New City Rd COWCAD G4 ... 4 F6
New Cordale Rd DMBTN G82 ... 25 K7
Newcraigs Drive CRMNK/CLK/EAG G76 ... 152 D2
Newcroft Dr LNPK/KPK G44 ... 128 D4
New Dock La GRNK PA15 ... 2 F4
Newdyke Rd KKNTL G66 ... 65 L1
Newdykes Farm Rd PSTWK KA9 ... 221 K8
Newdykes Rd PSTWK KA9 ... 221 K8
New Edinburgh Rd UD/BTH/TAN G71 ... 131 L2
UD/BTH/TAN G71 ... 132 D3
New England Rd SALT KA21 ... 192 C7
Newfield Crs HMLTN ML3 ... 156 B5
Newfield Dr CRH/DND KA2 ... 209 M7
Newfield Pl GIF/THBK G46 ... 126 F7
IRVSE KA11 ... 204 A4
RUTH G73 ... 128 C2
Newfield Sq PLK/PH/NH G53 ... 126 A3
Newford Gv CRMNK/CLK/EAG G76 ... 151 L4
Newhall St DMNK/BRGTN G40 ... 12 B9
Newhaven Gv LARGS KA30 ... 115 J3
Newhaven Rd STPS/GTHM/RID G33 ... 107 H1
Newhouse Dr CAR/SHTL G32 ... 107 G2
Newhills Rd STPS/GTHM/RID G33 ... 107 L2
Newhouse Dr KBRN KA25 ... 166 F4
Newhousemill Rd EKILN G74 ... 172 C2
Newhouse Wy IRVSE KA11 ... 204 A4
Newhut Rd MTHW ML1 ... 157 K1
New Inchinnan Rd PSLYN/LNWD PA3 ... 101 L2
Newington St CAR/SHTL G32 ... 106 F3
New Kirk Rd BSDN G61 ... 61 L4
New Lairdsland Rd KKNTL G66 ... 65 K1
New Lanark Rd LNK/LMHG ML11 ... 198 F7
Newlands Dr HMLTN ML3 ... 174 D1
KLMNKN/STW KA3 ... 206 E4

Newlandsfield Rd
PLKSW/MSWD G43 127 K2
Newlands Gdns JNSTN PA5 100 C8 1
Newlandsmuir Rd EKILS G75 170 F3
Newlands Pl EKILN G74 14 F4
Newlands Rd EKILS G75 170 E5
PLKSW/MSWD G43 127 L3
UD/BTH/TAN G71 131 M1
Newlands St CTBR ML5 110 A5
LNK/LMHG ML11 199 J6
Newlands Ter CARLUKE ML8 178 F7 6
New La AIRDRIE ML6 111 H7
New Luce Dr CAR/SHTL G32 107 K6
Newmains Av RNFRW PA4 79 G4
Newmains Rd RNFRW PA4 80 C8
Newmarket St AYRS KA7 18 E3
Newmill & Canthill Rd
SHOTTS ML7 113 M7
SHOTTS ML7 137 G5
Newmill Gdns SHOTTS ML7 136 F7
New Mill Rd KLMNK KA1 17 H6
Newmill Rd
SPRGB/BLRNK G21 84 C4 1
Newnham Rd PSLY PA1 102 D5
Newpark Crs
BLTYR/CAMB G72 130 A2 2
New Park St HMLTN ML3 156 C4
New Plymouth EKILS G75 171 G2
New Rd AYR KA8 224 F7
BLTYR/CAMB G72 130 E5
GLSTN KA4 214 B3 3
Newrose Av BLSH ML4 133 H2
Newshot Dr ERSK PA8 79 K1
RNFRW PA4 79 K2
New Sneddon St
PSLYN/LNWD PA3 101 L3
Newstead Gdns SMSTN G23 62 F8 2
New Stevenston Rd
MTHW ML1 134 B7
New St BEITH KA15 168 B1
BLTYR/CAMB G72 155 J2
CLYDBK G81 60 A3
DALRY KA24 184 C2 2
IRV KA12 203 H7
KLBCH PA10 99 G6
KLMNK KA1 211 M4
LARGS KA30 115 K6
LOCHW PA12 120 C7
PSLY PA1 9 H4
SVSTN KA20 201 K1
Newton Av BLTYR/CAMB G72 130 D3
BRHD/NEIL G78 149 K1
JNSTN PA5 100 E6
Newton Brae BLTYR/CAMB G72 130 F4
Newton Ct NMRNS G77 150 D6
Newton Dr JNSTN PA5 100 E6
UD/BTH/TAN G71 132 A2
WISHAW ML2 160 A4
Newton Farm Rd
BLTYR/CAMB G72 130 F2
Newtongrange Av
CAR/SHTL G32 107 H7
Newtongrange Gdns
CAR/SHTL G32 107 H7 4
Newton Gv NMRNS G77 150 D6
Newtonlea Av NMRNS G77 150 F5
Newton of Barr LOCHW PA12 120 B7
Newton Park Ct AYR KA8 225 H6 1
Newton Pl KVGV G3 4 C7
NMRNS G77 150 E6
Newton Rd BSHPTN PA7 57 M6
KKNTL G66 65 L5
Newton Station Rd
BLTYR/CAMB G72 130 E4
Newton St CTBR ML5 109 L5
GRNK PA15 2 A4
GRNKW/INVK PA16 32 D3
KBRN KA25 143 H8
PSLY PA1 8 C5
Newton Ter PSLYS PA2 100 F6
Newton Terrace La KVGV G3 4 C8
Newtown St KSYTH G65 47 K1
Newtyle Pl BSHPBGS G64 64 D8 3
Newtyle Rd PSLY PA1 102 C5
New View Dr BLSH ML4 133 G6
New View Pl BLSH ML4 133 G6 4
New Wynd CGLE G1 11 K3 2
Nicholas St CGLE G1 11 M1
Nicholson St GBLS G5 11 H4
Nicklaus Wy MTHW ML1 134 E2
Nicol Dr GRNKW/INVK PA16 32 B4
Nicolson Ct STPS/GTHM/RID G33 85 K4
Nicolson St GRNK PA15 2 B3
Nicol St AIRDRIE ML6 89 J8
GRNKW/INVK PA16 32 B5
Niddrie Rd GVH/MTFL G42 104 F7
Niddrie Sq GVH/MTFL G42 104 F8 1
Niddry St PSLYN/LNWD PA3 9 H2
Nigel Gdns PLKSD/SHW G41 104 D8
Nigel St MTHW ML1 157 K3
Nigg Pl ESTRH G34 108 A1
Nightingale Pl JNSTN PA5 122 D2 2
Nile Ct AYRS KA7 18 F3
Nile St GRNK PA15 2 C6
Nimmo Dr GOV/IBX G51 103 L2
Nimmo Pl CARLUKE ML8 178 E6 4
WISHAW ML2 159 J6 4
Nimmo St GRNKW/INVK PA16 32 C5
Nineyard St SALT KA21 200 F2 2
Ninian Av CRG/CRSL/HOU PA6 99 J1
Ninian Rd AIRDRIE ML6 111 H4
Ninian's Ri KKNTL G66 65 M2
Ninian's Ter KLWNG KA13 193 M7
Ninian St GTCI KA28 138 C6
Nisbet Dr PSTWK KA9 225 K4 2
Nisbet St DEN/PKHD G31 13 M6
Nisbett Pl AIRDRIE ML6 111 L6
Nisbett St AIRDRIE ML6 111 L7
Nith Av PSLYS PA2 100 F8
Nith Dr HMLTN ML3 174 A1
RNFRW PA4 80 E7
Nith Pl KLMNK KA1 17 H9
Nith Qd MTHW ML1 134 C6
Nithsdale EKILN G74 154 D6 4
Nithsdale Crs BSDN G61 61 J3
Nithsdale Dr PLKSD/SHW G41 104 F7
Nithsdale Pl PLKSD/SHW G41 104 F6 2
Nithsdale Rd ARD KA22 191 K4
PLKSD/SHW G41 104 C5
PLKSD/SHW G41 104 F7
PLKSD/SHW G41 104 F7 5
Nithsdale St PLKSD/SHW G41 104 F7 6
SHOTTS ML7 137 K4
Nith St STPS/GTHM/RID G33 7 L6
Nitshill Rd GIF/THBK G46 126 E7 4
PLK/PH/NH G53 125 M3
PLK/PH/NH G53 126 C6 2
Niven Ct KLMNKN/STW KA3 207 K5
Niven St MRYH/FIRH G20 82 C3
Noble Rd BLSH ML4 133 G4
Nobles Pl BLSH ML4 132 F5
Nobleston ALEX/LLW G83 25 M7
Nobles Vw BLSH ML4 132 F5
Noddleburn Rd LARGS KA30 115 J4
Noldrum Av CAR/SHTL G32 130 C1
Noldrum Gdns
CAR/SHTL G32 130 C1 5
Noltmire Rd AYR KA8 225 J5
Noran Crs TROON KA10 216 F4
Norbreck Dr GIF/THBK G46 127 J5
Norby Rd PTCK G11 81 M6 5
Norfield Dr LNPK/KPK G44 128 B2
Norfolk Ct GBLS G5 11 H5
Norfolk Crs BSHPBGS G64 63 L6
Norfolk Rd GRNKW/INVK PA16 31 L5
Norfolk St GBLS G5 11 H5
Norham St PLKSD/SHW G41 104 E8
Norman Crs IRV KA12 203 H4
Norman St DMNK/BRGTN G40 105 M6
Norse La North SCOT G14 81 J5
Norse La South SCOT G14 81 J5 9
Norse Pl SCOT G14 81 J5 10
Norse Rd SCOT G14 81 J5
Northacre KLWNG KA13 193 L4
Northacre Gv KLWNG KA13 193 L4
Northall Qd MTHW ML1 134 A8
Northampton Dr KVD/HLHD G12 82 B3
North And South Rd
MTHW ML1 135 L8
North Av BLTYR/CAMB G72 129 M3 5
CARLUKE ML8 178 D7
CLYDBK G81 60 A7
MTHW ML1 134 A7 5
Northbank Av
BLTYR/CAMB G72 130 D3
North Bank Pl CLYDBK G81 80 C1
Northbank Rd KKNTL G66 65 J1
Northbank St
BLTYR/CAMB G72 130 D3 2
North Bank St CLYDBK G81 80 C1 2
North Barr Av ERSK PA8 59 G6
North Berwick Av
BALLOCH G68 48 F4 5
North Berwick Crs EKILS G75 171 G3
North Biggar Rd AIRDRIE ML6 111 H1
North Birbiston Rd KKNTL G66 44 D1
Northbrae Pl KNTSWD G13 81 H3 3
North Bridge St AIRDRIE ML6 110 F1
North British Rd
UD/BTH/TAN G71 131 M3
Northburn Av AIRDRIE ML6 89 H8
Northburn Pl AIRDRIE ML6 89 H7
Northburn Rd CTBR ML5 88 C8
Northburn St AIRDRIE ML6 90 B7 2
North Bute St CTBR ML5 110 B5
North Caldeen Rd CTBR ML5 110 C4
North Calder Dr AIRDRIE ML6 111 K5
North Calder Gv
UD/BTH/TAN G71 108 B7 3
North Calder Rd
UD/BTH/TAN G71 109 J8
North Campbell Av MLNGV G62 41 M8
North Canal Bank COWCAD G4 5 K5
North Canal Bank St COWCAD G4 5 J5
North Carbrain Rd CUMB G67 49 G7
North Claremont La
MLNGV G62 42 A7 2
North Claremont St KVGV G3 4 B7
North Corsebar Rd PSLYS PA2 8 C9
North Ct CGLE G1 11 J1
North Court La CGLE G1 11 J1
Northcraig Rd
KLMNKN/STW KA3 206 F7
North Crescent Av ARD KA22 191 H6
North Crescent Rd ARD KA22 191 H6
Northcroft Rd
BAIL/MDB/MHD G69 66 E7
North Croft St PSLYN/LNWD PA3 9 H2
North Dean Park Av
UD/BTH/TAN G71 132 A7 2
Northdoon Pl AYRS KA7 228 D6
North Douglas St CLYDBK G81 80 C1 3
North Dr KBRN KA25 167 G1
PSLYN/LNWD PA3 100 B3
TROON KA10 216 F5
North Dryburgh Rd
WISHAW ML2 159 J3
North Dumgoyne Av
MLNGV G62 41 M7
North Elgin Pl CLYDBK G81 80 C2
North Elgin St CLYDBK G81 80 D1
North Erskine Pk BSDN G61 61 K4
North Faulds Rd
LNK/LMHG ML11 199 L4
Northfield EKILS G75 170 F2
Northfield Av AYR KA8 225 G6
PGL PA14 54 F1
Northfield Dr ALEX/LLW G83 25 M4
Northfield Pk LARGS KA30 115 H3 5
Northfield Pl AYR KA8 225 G6 2
Northfield Rd ALEX/LLW G83 25 M5 5
Northfield St MTHW ML1 157 L1
Northflat Pl CARLUKE ML8 189 J1
North Frederick St CGLE G1 5 K9 1
North Gardner St PTCK G11 82 B7
North Gargieston Rd
KLMNK KA1 211 J3 5
Northgate Qd
SPRGB/BLRNK G21 84 C3
Northgate Rd
SPRGB/BLRNK G21 84 C2
North Gower St
GOV/IBX G51 104 C4 1
North Grange Rd BSDN G61 61 L3
North Hamilton Pl
KLMNK KA1 16 D3 1
North Hamilton St KLMNK KA1 16 D4
North Hanover St CGLE G1 5 K9
Northinch St SCOT G14 81 K7
North Iverton Park Rd
JNSTN PA5 100 A6
North Kilmeny Crs
WISHAW ML2 159 J3
Northland Av SCOT G14 81 J4 2
Northland Dr SCOT G14 81 J5 11
Northland Gdns SCOT G14 81 J4 3
Northland La SCOT G14 81 J5
North La PSLYN/LNWD PA3 100 C3
North Lodge Av MTHW ML1 157 L5
North Lodge Rd RNFRW PA4 80 C5
North Main St ALEX/LLW G83 25 K3
North Middleton Driv
LARGS KA30 115 K5
Northmuir Dr WISHAW ML2 159 K5
Northmuir Rd DRUM G15 61 H5
North Neuk IRVSE KA11 216 E2 6
North Orchard St MTHW ML1 157 K2
North Park Av AYR KA8 225 H6
BRHD/NEIL G78 125 H6
GIF/THBK G46 126 F5 4
Northpark St MRYH/FIRH G20 4 D1
North Portland St CGLE G1 11 L1
North Rd BALLOCH G68 68 A4
BLSH ML4 110 A8
BLSH ML4 133 G4
JNSTN PA5 99 L7
PGL PA14 54 E1
WKIL KA23 181 J4
North Shore Rd TROON KA10 216 D4
North St ALEX/LLW G83 25 L4
CGLW G2 4 D9
CRG/CRSL/HOU PA6 77 H6
DALRY KA24 184 C1
GRNKW/INVK PA16 32 C1 2
MTHW ML1 157 M1
PSLYN/LNWD PA3 9 G1
Northumberland St
MRYH/FIRH G20 82 E5 4
North Vennel LNK/LMHG ML11 199 G5
North Vw BSDN G61 61 K7
North View Rd JNSTN PA5 98 F3 2
North Wallace St COWCAD G4 5 L7
Northway BLTYR/CAMB G72 131 J8
Northwood Dr WISHAW ML2 160 A3
North Woodside Rd COWCAD G4 4 C4
MRYH/FIRH G20 4 D3
Norval St PTCK G11 82 A7
Norwich Dr KVD/HLHD G12 82 B4 3
Norwood Av KKNTL G66 45 H8
Norwood Dr GIF/THBK G46 127 G8
Norwood Pk BSDN G61 61 M6
Norwood Ter UD/BTH/TAN G71 132 A2
Nottingham Av
KVD/HLHD G12 82 B3 3
Nottingham La
KVD/HLHD G12 82 B3 3
Novar Dr KVD/HLHD G12 82 A5
Novar Gdns BSHPBGS G64 63 L8
Novar St HMLTN ML3 156 D7
Nuneaton St DMNK/BRGTN G40 12 F9
Nurseries Rd
BAIL/MDB/MHD G69 107 M3
Nursery Av BSHPTN PA7 58 E5
KLMNK KA1 17 H6
PSTWK KA9 225 H3
Nursery Ct CARLUKE ML8 178 E6
Nursery Gv KLMCLM PA13 55 J8
Nursery La KLMCLM PA13 55 J8
PLKSD/SHW G41 104 F7
Nursery Pk CARLUKE ML8 178 E7 2
Nursery Pl BLTYR/CAMB G72 155 K3
Nursery Rd AYRS KA7 229 H4
Nursery St HBR/GL G84 22 F1 7
KLMNK KA1 16 E7
PLKSD/SHW G41 105 G6 3
Nutberry Ct GVH/MTFL G42 105 H8

O

Oak Av BSDN G61 61 M2
EKILS G75 171 H3
Oakbank Av WISHAW ML2 158 E8 5
Oakbank Dr BRHD/NEIL G78 149 L1
Oakbank Rd PGL PA14 54 F1 2
Oakbank St AIRDRIE ML6 111 K2
Oakburn Av MLNGV G62 41 M8
Oakburn Crs MLNGV G62 41 M8
Oak Crs BAIL/MDB/MHD G69 108 A5 2
Oakdene Av BLSH ML4 133 G2
UD/BTH/TAN G71 132 B2 3
Oakdene Crs MTHW ML1 134 C5
Oak Dr BLTYR/CAMB G72 130 C5 3
KKNTL G66 65 H4
Oak Fern Dr EKILN G74 153 K5
Oak Fern Gv EKILN G74 153 K5 3
Oakfield Av KVD/HLHD G12 4 A3 1
Oakfield Dr MTHW ML1 157 M3 4
Oakfield La KVD/HLHD G12 4 A5
Oakfield Rd MTHW ML1 157 L4
Oakhill Av CAR/SHTL G32 107 M6
Oakland Dr SVSTN KA20 192 E7 6
Oaklands Av IRV KA12 203 J5
Oak Lea HMLTN ML3 156 F7
Oaklea Crs BLTYR/CAMB G72 155 J1 5
Oakleigh Dr
GRNKW/INVK PA16 32 D1 2
Oakley Dr LNPK/KPK G44 127 M6
Oakley Ter DEN/PKHD G31 12 D2
Oak Pk BSHPBGS G64 84 B1
MTHW ML1 157 K5
Oak Pl CTBR ML5 110 C4
EKILS G75 171 H3
KLMNK KA1 16 B5
UD/BTH/TAN G71 132 C2
Oak Rd ARD KA22 191 J5
CLYDBK G81 59 M4
CUMB G67 49 L5
PSLYS PA2 102 A8
Oakshaw Brae PSLY PA1 8 E3
Oakshawhead PSLY PA1 8 E3
Oakshaw St East PSLY PA1 8 F3
Oakshaw St West PSLY PA1 8 F3
The Oaks JNSTN PA5 99 K7
Oak St KVGV G3 10 E1
Oaktree Gdns CSMK G45 128 F5
DMBTN G82 37 J7
Oakview Qd BLSH ML4 132 F6 5
Oakwood Av AYR KA8 225 L7
PSLYS PA2 101 H8
Oakwood Dr BEITH KA15 168 A1
CTBR ML5 109 K4 1
NMRNS G77 150 F5
Oak Wynd BLTYR/CAMB G72 130 F6
Oates Gdns MTHW ML1 158 B5
Oatfield St SPRGB/BLRNK G21 7 G1
Oban Dr MRYH/FIRH G20 4 B1
Oban La MRYH/FIRH G20 4 B1
Obiston Gdns CAR/SHTL G32 107 G4 6
Obree Av PSTWK KA9 225 K4
Observatory Rd
KVD/HLHD G12 82 D6 5
Ochil Ct EKILS G75 171 H5
IRVSE KA11 204 A4
Ochil Dr BRHD/NEIL G78 125 J8
PSLYS PA2 124 D1
Ochil Pl CAR/SHTL G32 107 G5
KLMNK KA1 212 B6
Ochil Rd BSDN G61 61 H2
BSHPBGS G64 64 C8
RNFRW PA4 80 B8
Ochil St CAR/SHTL G32 107 G5
WISHAW ML2 158 F5
Ochiltree Av KNTSWD G13 81 M2
Ochiltree Dr HMLTN ML3 155 L8
Ochiltree Pl
KLMNKN/STW KA3 207 H3 2
Ochil Vw UD/BTH/TAN G71 132 A1 7
Octavia Ter GRNKW/INVK PA16 32 B1
Odense Ct EKILS G75 171 L3 5
Ogilvie Pl DEN/PKHD G31 13 M7 1
Ogilvie St DEN/PKHD G31 13 M7
O'hare ALEX/LLW G83 25 M5
Old Aisle Rd KKNTL G66 65 M2
Old Auchans Vw CRH/DND KA2 209 K7
Old Avon Rd HMLTN ML3 157 G7
Old Biggar Rd AIRDRIE ML6 89 H1
Old Bore Rd AIRDRIE ML6 111 K1
Old Bothwell Rd
UD/BTH/TAN G71 132 B8
Old Bridgend CARLUKE ML8 178 F8 4
Old Bridge of Weir Rd
CRG/CRSL/HOU PA6 77 G7
Old Bridge Rd AYR KA8 225 L6
Old Bridge St AYRS KA7 18 F2
Old Caley Rd IRV KA12 203 J5
Old Castle Rd LNPK/KPK G44 128 A3 3
Old Church Gdns
BAIL/MDB/MHD G69 109 G4 3
Old Coach Rd EKILN G74 153 M6
Old Dalmarnock Rd
DMNK/BRGTN G40 12 E9 1
Old Dalnottar Rd OLDK G60 59 H4
Old Dullatur Rd BALLOCH G68 48 C1
Old Dumbarton Rd KVGV G3 82 D8 5
Old Edinburgh Rd
UD/BTH/TAN G71 132 B2
Old Farm Rd AYR KA8 225 K6
Old Gartloch Rd
BAIL/MDB/MHD G69 86 F5
Old Glasgow Rd CUMB G67 49 G5
UD/BTH/TAN G71 131 K1
Old Govan Rd RNFRW PA4 80 F6
Old Greenock Rd BSHPTN PA7 58 A6
ERSK PA8 78 F1
ERSK PA8 79 J2
PGL PA14 55 L2
Oldhall Dr KLMCLM PA13 55 K8
Oldhall Rd PSLY PA1 102 D4
Old Hillfoot Rd AYRS KA7 19 K9
Old Humbie Rd NMRNS G77 150 E7
Old Inverkip Rd
GRNKW/INVK PA16 32 C5
Old Irvine Rd KLMNK KA1 16 D4
Old Lanark Rd CARLUKE ML8 178 F8
CARLUKE ML8 188 F1
LNK/LMHG ML11 198 E1
Old Largs Rd GRNK PA15 2 A9
GRNK PA15 52 D4
Old Loans Rd TROON KA10 217 G5
Old Luss Rd ALEX/LLW G83 25 J1
HBR/GL G84 22 F1
Old Manse Gdns CTBR ML5 110 A2 2
Old Manse Rd CAR/SHTL G32 107 K5
WISHAW ML2 176 E1
Old Mill Rd BLTYR/CAMB G72 130 D4
CLYDBK G81 60 A3
EKILN G74 15 G1
KLMNK KA1 17 G5
PSLY PA1 8 A6
SHOTTS ML7 137 G8
UD/BTH/TAN G71 131 M2
Old Mill Vw KSYTH G65 47 M6
Old Monkland Rd CTBR ML5 109 K6
Old Mugdock Rd MLNGV G62 42 C2
Old Playfield Rd
CRMNK/CLK/EAG G76 152 D1 1
Old Quarry Rd BALLOCH G68 67 K4
SVSTN KA20 201 K1
Old Raise Rd SALT KA21 201 G1
Old Renfrew Rd RNFRW PA4 81 G7
Old Rd JNSTN PA5 100 C6
Old Rome Wy CRH/DND KA2 210 E3
Old Rutherglen Rd GBLS G5 11 J6 1
GBLS G5 11 L8 1
Old Schoolhouse La
CRG/CRSL/HOU PA6 77 H6 2
Old Shettleston Rd
CAR/SHTL G32 107 G4
Old Sneddon St PSLY PA1 9 G2
Old Stable Rw CTBR ML5 110 B2 1
Old St CLYDBK G81 59 M3
KLMNK KA1 211 M4
Old Union St AIRDRIE ML6 111 H2
Old Willowyard Rd BEITH KA15 168 A2
Old Wishaw Rd CARLUKE ML8 178 E6
Old Wood Rd
BAIL/MDB/MHD G69 108 A6
Old Woodwynd Rd
KLWNG KA13 193 L5
Old Wynd CGLE G1 11 K3 5
Olifard Av UD/BTH/TAN G71 132 B6
Oliphant Crs
CRMNK/CLK/EAG G76 151 L4
PSLYS PA2 123 L1
Oliphant Dr KLMNKN/STW KA3 17 M4
Olive Bank UD/BTH/TAN G71 109 J8
Olive Rd KLMNK KA1 16 A4
Olive St STPS/GTHM/RID G33 7 M1
Olympia Ct EKILN G74 15 G5
Olympia St DMNK/BRGTN G40 12 C6
Omoa Rd MTHW ML1 135 G8
O'Neill Av BSHPBGS G64 84 B1
O'Neil Ter ALEX/LLW G83 25 L5 5
Onslow EKILS G75 14 A7
Onslow Dr DEN/PKHD G31 12 F1
Onslow Rd CLYDBK G81 60 C7
Onslow Sq DEN/PKHD G31 12 E1
Ontario Pk EKILS G75 153 H8
Ontario Pl EKILS G75 153 H8 1
Onthank Dr KLMNKN/STW KA3 206 F5
Onyx St BLSH ML4 133 G5
Open Shore GRNK PA15 2 F4 5
Oran Gdns MRYH/FIRH G20 82 E4 5
Oran Ga MRYH/FIRH G20 82 E4
Orangefield Dr PSTWK KA9 221 K8
Orangefield La GRNK PA15 2 A4 1
Oran Pl MRYH/FIRH G20 82 E5 5
Oran St MRYH/FIRH G20 82 E5
Orbiston Dr BLSH ML4 133 H6
CLYDBK G81 60 D2 2
Orbiston Pl CLYDBK G81 60 D2 3
Orbiston Rd BLSH ML4 132 F5
Orbiston Sq BLSH ML4 132 F6 5
Orbiston St MTHW ML1 157 M4
Orcades Dr LNPK/KPK G44 128 B5
Orchard Av AYRS KA7 19 J8
UD/BTH/TAN G71 132 B8
Orchard Ct CAR/SHTL G32 130 B1 5
GIF/THBK G46 127 G6 1
Orchard Dr BLTYR/CAMB G72 155 J1
GIF/THBK G46 127 H6
RUTH G73 128 F2 5
Orchard Fld KKNTL G66 65 K5
Orchard Ga LRKH ML9 176 A7
Orchard Gn EKILN G74 154 B5
Orchard Gv CTBR ML5 110 B3
GIF/THBK G46 127 H5
KLMCLM PA13 75 J1 2
KLWNG KA13 193 L5
Orchard Pk GIF/THBK G46 127 J6 5
Orchard Park Av GIF/THBK G46 127 G5
Orchard Pl AYRS KA7 19 J7 2
BLSH ML4 132 F6
HMLTN ML3 156 D6
KKNTL G66 65 M2
KLWNG KA13 193 L5
Orchard St
BAIL/MDB/MHD G69 107 M6 5
CARLUKE ML8 178 F8
GLSTN KA4 214 B4
GRNK PA15 3 G7
HMLTN ML3 156 D6
KLMNKN/STW KA3 16 F1
MTHW ML1 157 K2
PSLY PA1 9 H4
RNFRW PA4 80 D5
WISHAW ML2 177 H3
WKIL KA23 181 J4
Orchardton Rd BALLOCH G68 67 K2
Orchard View Dr
LNK/LMHG ML11 198 A6
Orchy Av CRMNK/CLK/EAG G76 151 M1
Orchy Ct CLYDBK G81 60 C4
Orchy Crs AIRDRIE ML6 111 J4
BSDN G61 61 K8
PSLYS PA2 100 F8
Orchy Dr CRMNK/CLK/EAG G76 127 M8
Orchy Gdns
CRMNK/CLK/EAG G76 127 M8
Orchy St LNPK/KPK G44 128 A3
Orefield Pl EKILN G74 153 L6 5
Oregon Pl GBLS G5 11 K8 2
Orion Pl BLSH ML4 133 L4
Orion Wy BLTYR/CAMB G72 130 A3 7
CARLUKE ML8 178 D7
Orkney Dr KLMNKN/STW KA3 207 G4
Orkney Pl GOV/IBX G51 104 B2 1
Orkney Qd WISHAW ML2 159 K5
Orkney St GOV/IBX G51 104 B2
Orlando EKILN G74 154 C4 2
Orleans Av SCOT G14 81 L6
Orleans La SCOT G14 81 L6 2
Ormiston Av SCOT G14 81 J5
Ormiston Dr HMLTN ML3 174 C1
Ormiston La SCOT G14 81 J5 12
Ormiston La North SCOT G14 81 J5 13
Ormiston La South SCOT G14 81 J5 14
Ormiston Pl IRVSE KA11 204 B2 1
Ormonde Av LNPK/KPK G44 127 M6
Ormonde Ct LNPK/KPK G44 127 L6
Ormonde Crs LNPK/KPK G44 127 M6
Ormonde Dr LNPK/KPK G44 127 M6
Ornsay St PPK/MIL G22 83 K2
Oronsay Av PGL PA14 55 G3
Oronsay Crs BSDN G61 62 B6
OLDK G60 59 J3
Oronsay Gdns OLDK G60 59 J3
Oronsay Pl OLDK G60 59 J3
Orr Sq PSLY PA1 9 G3
Orr St DMNK/BRGTN G40 12 C6
PSLY PA1 8 F3
PSLYS PA2 9 H7
Orr Ter BRHD/NEIL G78 148 C3 5
Orton Pl GOV/IBX G51 104 A3
Osborne Crs EKILN G74 152 B6
Osborne St CGLE G1 11 J3
CLYDBK G81 60 A6
Osbourne Av RAYR/DAL KA6 227 H3
Osprey Dr KLMNK KA1 17 L6
UD/BTH/TAN G71 132 A2
Osprey Rd GRNKW/INVK PA16 32 A5
Ossian Av PSLY PA1 102 F4
Ossian Rd PLKSW/MSWD G43 127 L3
Oswald Dr PSTWK KA9 221 J8
Oswald La AYR KA8 224 E7
Oswald Pl AYR KA8 225 G4
Oswald Rd AYR KA8 225 G5
Oswald's Br RAYR/DAL KA6 226 D6

Oswald St CGLE G1 11 G3
Oswald Wk MLNGV G62 62 C1 3
Otago La KVD/HLHD G12 4 B4
Otago La North KVD/HLHD G12 4 B4 2
Otago Pk EKILS G75 153 G8
Otago St KVD/HLHD G12 4 B4
Othello EKILN G74 154 B4
Ottawa Crs CLYDBK G81 59 K5
Otterburn Av
KLMNKN/STW KA3 207 H6
Otterburn Dr GIF/THBK G46 127 J7
Otterswick Pl
STPS/GTHM/RID G33 85 J7
Ottoline Dr TROON KA10 216 F7
Oudenarde Ct CARLUKE ML8 179 H8 2
Outdale Av PSTWK KA9 225 K2
The Oval CRMNK/CLK/EAG G76 127 M8
CTBR ML5 87 J3
Overbrae Pl DRUM G15 60 F4
Overburn Av DMBTN G82 36 F5
Overburn Crs DMBTN G82 36 F4
Overdale Av GVH/MTFL G42 127 M1 2
Overdale Crs PSTWK KA9 225 J3
Overdale Gdns
GVH/MTFL G42 127 M1 3
Overdale Pl WISHAW ML2 177 J3
Overdale St GVH/MTFL G42 127 M1
Overjohnstone Dr
WISHAW ML2 158 C5 1
Overlea Av RUTH G73 129 K3
Overlee Rd
CRMNK/CLK/EAG G76 151 L2
Overmills Crs AYRS KA7 229 K2
Overmills Rd AYRS KA7 229 L2
Overnewton Pl KVGV G3 104 D1 4
Overnewton Sq KVGV G3 104 D1 5
Overnewton St KVGV G3 82 D8
Overton Crs GRNK PA15 32 D6 5
JNSTN PA5 100 B7
WKIL KA23 181 J4
Overton Dr WKIL KA23 181 H4
Overton Gdns KLMCLM PA13 55 L8 2
Overton Gv KLMCLM PA13 55 L8
Overton Rd ALEX/LLW G83 25 K5
BLTYR/CAMB G72 130 D5
JNSTN PA5 100 A7
Overton St ALEX/LLW G83 25 K5
BLTYR/CAMB G72 130 D5
Overtoun Av DMBTN G82 37 H7
Overtoun Dr CLYDBK G81 59 M5
RUTH G73 129 G2
Overtoun Rd CLYDBK G81 59 M5 1
IRVSE KA11 204 F6
Overtown Av PLK/PH/NH G53 126 A3
Overtown Rd WISHAW ML2 159 M8
Overtown St DEN/PKHD G31 12 F6
Overwood Dr DMBTN G82 37 H5
LNPK/KPK G44 128 C3
Owen Av EKILS G75 14 A8
Owendale Av BLSH ML4 133 H2
Owen Pk EKILS G75 14 C8
Owen St MTHW ML1 157 L1
O'wood Av MTHW ML1 134 B3
Oxford Av GRK PA19 32 A3
Oxford Dr PSLYN/LNWD PA3 100 B3
Oxford La GBLS G5 11 H5
RNFRW PA4 80 C6 3
Oxford Rd GRNKW/INVK PA16 31 K5
RNFRW PA4 80 C6
Oxford St CTBR ML5 109 M3
GBLS G5 11 G4
KKNTL G66 65 J1 3
Oxgang Pl KKNTL G66 65 L2
Oxhill Pl DMBTN G82 36 D6
Oxhill Rd DMBTN G82 36 D6
Oxton Dr CARD/HILL/MSPK G52 103 H4

P

Pacemuir Rd KLMCLM PA13 75 J1
Paddockdyke SKLM PA17 70 B6 2
Paddockholm Rd KBRN KA25 143 H8
Paddock St CTBR ML5 110 D5
The Paddock
CRMNK/CLK/EAG G76 152 A4
Paduff Pl KBRN KA25 143 G7 3
Paidmyre Crs NMRNS G77 150 D6
Paidmyre Gdns NMRNS G77 150 D6
Paidmyre Rd NMRNS G77 150 D6
Paisley Rd BRHD/NEIL G78 125 H5
GBLS G5 10 D4
PLKSD/SHW G41 10 C4
RNFRW PA4 80 B8
Paisley Rd West
CARD/HILL/MSPK G52 103 K5
GOV/IBX G51 104 C4
Paisley St ARD KA22 191 J7
Palacecraig St CTBR ML5 110 A6
Palace Grounds Rd HMLTN ML3 156 F5
Paladin Av KNTSWD G13 81 H1
Palermo St SPRGB/BLRNK G21 6 B1
Palladium Pl SCOT G14 81 K6 4
Palmer Av KNTSWD G13 61 K8
Palmerston EKILS G75 171 G2
Palmerston Pl JNSTN PA5 122 C2
KVGV G3 104 D1 6
Palm Pl UD/BTH/TAN G71 109 H8
Pandora Wy
UD/BTH/TAN G71 132 A2 9
Pankhurst Pl EKILN G74 15 G2
Panmure St MRYH/FIRH G20 83 G5
Pantonville Rd WKIL KA23 181 J6
Papermill Rd GRNKW/INVK PA16 32 D7
Parkandarroch Crs
CARLUKE ML8 179 G8
Park Av BEITH KA15 144 B8
BRHD/NEIL G78 125 H8
BSHPBGS G64 64 A6
CARLUKE ML8 178 F6
DMBTN G82 37 H6
GRK PA19 32 A2
JNSTN PA5 100 C7
KKNTL G66 65 J1
KLWNG KA13 193 L6
KSYTH G65 46 F5
KVGV G3 4 C5
MLNGV G62 42 A8
MTHW ML1 134 A4
PSLYS PA2 101 J8
PSTWK KA9 225 H1
Park Bank ERSK PA8 59 H8 1
Park Brae ERSK PA8 79 J1
Parkbrae Gdns
MRYH/FIRH G20 83 G3 3
Parkbrae Pl MRYH/FIRH G20 83 G3 4
Parkburn Av KKNTL G66 65 J3
Park Burn Ct HMLTN ML3 156 A3
Park Circ AYRS KA7 18 E5
CARLUKE ML8 178 F6 1
KVGV G3 4 B6
Park Circus La AYRS KA7 18 E5
KVGV G3 4 B6
Park Circus Pl KVGV G3 4 C6
Park Ct BEITH KA15 168 C1 4
BSHPBGS G64 64 B6
GIF/THBK G46 127 H6
Park Crs BLTYR/CAMB G72 155 J3
BSDN G61 61 J4
BSHPBGS G64 44 C8
BSHPBGS G64 64 A6
DMBTN G82 36 F4
KLMNKN/STW KA3 197 K1
RNFRW PA4 79 J2
Park Dr BLSH ML4 133 G5
EKILN G74 152 C6
ERSK PA8 79 J1
HMLTN ML3 157 J8
LNK/LMHG ML11 198 E5
RUTH G73 129 G2
WISHAW ML2 160 A4
Parkend Av SALT KA21 201 G2 2
Parkend Gdns SALT KA21 201 G2 3
Parkend Rd SALT KA21 200 F2
Parker Pl KSYTH G65 47 K1
LRKH ML9 176 B6 2
Parkfield EKILS G75 171 L4
Park Gdns KLBCH PA10 99 H5
KVGV G3 4 B7
Park Gardens La KVGV G3 4 B7
Park Ga ERSK PA8 79 H1
KVGV G3 4 B6
Park Gate Pl BLSH ML4 132 F4
Park Gld ERSK PA8 79 J1
Park Gn ERSK PA8 79 H1
Park Gv DMBTN G82 35 H1 2
ERSK PA8 79 J1
Parkgrove Av GIF/THBK G46 127 K6
Parkgrove Ter KVGV G3 4 A7
Parkgrove Terrace La KVGV G3 4 A7
Parkhall Rd CLYDBK G81 59 M5
Parkhall St EKILN G74 14 F1
Parkhall Ter CLYDBK G81 59 M4
Parkhead Av KLWNG KA13 193 M6
Parkhead St AIRDRIE ML6 111 G1
MTHW ML1 157 M4
Park Hl ERSK PA8 59 H8
Parkhill Av CRH/DND KA2 210 E1
PGL PA14 55 G1
Parkhill Dr DALRY KA24 184 C2
LOCHW PA12 120 D6
RUTH G73 129 G2
Parkhill Rd PLKSW/MSWD G43 127 J1
Parkholm La GBLS G5 10 C4
Parkhouse Dr KBRN KA25 143 G8
Parkhouse Rd ARD KA22 191 K7
PLK/PH/NH G53 125 M5
Parkhouse St AYRS KA7 18 F6
Parkinch ERSK PA8 79 J2
Parklands Rd LNPK/KPK G44 127 M6
Park La ARD KA22 191 J6
BLTYR/CAMB G72 155 K1
CARLUKE ML8 178 E8
DMNK/BRGTN G40 12 D6
KLWNG KA13 193 K4
KSYTH G65 47 K1
Park Lea AIRDRIE ML6 90 F5
Parklee Dr
CRMNK/CLK/EAG G76 152 E2
Park Moor ERSK PA8 79 H1
Parkneuk Rd BLTYR/CAMB G72 155 G7
PLKSW/MSWD G43 127 H5
Parkneuk St MTHW ML1 157 K1
Park Pl BLSH ML4 132 E6 3
CMPF/LLE G63 27 H6
EKILN G74 152 C6 1
IRV KA12 203 H4
LNK/LMHG ML11 198 F5
Park Qd KVGV G3 4 B6
WISHAW ML2 158 E8 6
Park Rd AIRDRIE ML6 111 H7
ARD KA22 191 J7
BAIL/MDB/MHD G69 86 C1
BAIL/MDB/MHD G69 108 F4
BAIL/MDB/MHD G69 109 G4
BLSH ML4 133 G5
BRWEIR PA11 76 D8
BSHPBGS G64 64 A7
CAR/SHTL G32 130 C1
CLYDBK G81 59 M6
GIF/THBK G46 127 J7
GLSTN KA4 214 B3
HMLTN ML3 156 D6
JNSTN PA5 99 M8
KLMCLM PA13 75 J1 3
KVGV G3 4 B5
MLNGV G62 42 A8
MTHW ML1 134 B7
PSLYS PA2 124 D1
RNFRW PA4 79 K2
SALT KA21 200 E2
SHOTTS ML7 137 K4 2
Parksail ERSK PA8 79 J2
Parksail Dr ERSK PA8 79 J1
Parkside IRVSE KA11 204 A6
Parkside Gdns MRYH/FIRH G20 83 G3
Parkside Pl MRYH/FIRH G20 83 G3 5
Parkside Rd MTHW ML1 157 H3
SHOTTS ML7 137 K5
Park St AIRDRIE ML6 110 E1
ALEX/LLW G83 25 K4
CARLUKE ML8 178 F8
CTBR ML5 110 B2
DMBTN G82 37 G6
KKNTL G66 66 B2
KLMNK KA1 16 D3
MTHW ML1 133 M6
MTHW ML1 135 H6
MTHW ML1 157 L2
Park St South KVGV G3 4 B6
Parks Vw HMLTN ML3 174 D3
Park Ter AYRS KA7 18 D4
DMBTN G82 35 G1 1
EKILN G74 14 E3
GRK PA19 31 L2 6
KVGV G3 4 B6
Park Terrace East La KVGV G3 4 B6
Park Terrace La KVGV G3 4 B6
Parkthorn Vw CRH/DND KA2 209 L7
Park Top ERSK PA8 79 J1 1
Parkvale Av ERSK PA8 79 K1
Parkvale Crs ERSK PA8 79 K1
Parkvale Dr ERSK PA8 79 K1 2
Parkvale Gdns ERSK PA8 79 K1 3
Parkvale Wy ERSK PA8 79 K1 4
Parkview AYRS KA7 228 F8
Park Vw AIRDRIE ML6 91 G4
ARD KA22 191 K7
KBRN KA25 143 G8
KLBCH PA10 99 G5
LARGS KA30 115 K6 4
LRKH ML9 176 B7
PSLYS PA2 8 F9
Parkview Av KKNTL G66 65 K2
Parkview Ct KKNTL G66 65 K2
Parkview Crs WISHAW ML2 160 A5 2
Parkview Dr CTBR ML5 109 L2
STPS/GTHM/RID G33 85 L3
Parkville Dr BLTYR/CAMB G72 155 L3
Parkville Rd BLSH ML4 133 J2
Park Wy CUMB G67 49 H5
Parkway ERSK PA8 79 H1
Parkway Ct CTBR ML5 109 L3
Parkway Pl CTBR ML5 109 L4
Park Winding ERSK PA8 79 J1
Park Wd ERSK PA8 59 J8
Parnell St AIRDRIE ML6 110 F4
Parnie St CGLE G1 11 L3 2
Parry Ter EKILS G75 153 H8
Parsonage Rw COWCAD G4 11 M2
Parsonage Sq COWCAD G4 11 M2
Parterre IRV KA12 203 J7
Partick Bridge St PTCK G11 82 C8 1
Partickhill Av PTCK G11 82 B7
Partickhill Rd PTCK G11 82 B7
Partridge Rd
GRNKW/INVK PA16 32 A3 2
Paterson Av IRV KA12 203 K5
Paterson Crs IRV KA12 203 K4
Paterson Dr HBR/GL G84 20 B5
Paterson Pl BSDN G61 61 J1
Paterson St AYR KA8 225 H5
GBLS G5 10 E6
MTHW ML1 157 L2 2
Paterson Ter EKILS G75 14 C7
Pather St WISHAW ML2 159 H7
Pathfoot KLWNG KA13 193 M6
Pathhead Gdns
STPS/GTHM/RID G33 84 F3 4
Pathhead Rd
CRMNK/CLK/EAG G76 152 D2
Patna Ct HMLTN ML3 155 L8
Patna St DMNK/BRGTN G40 13 G9
Paton Qd LARGS KA30 115 L5 1
Paton St DEN/PKHD G31 13 G2
GRNKW/INVK PA16 32 C5
Patrick Av SVSTN KA20 192 C8
Patrick St GRNKW/INVK PA16 2 A3
PSLYS PA2 9 J6
Patterson Dr CARLUKE ML8 178 A3
Patterton Dr BRHD/NEIL G78 125 K8
Pattison St CLYDBK G81 59 L6
Pattle Pl AYRS KA7 228 F8
Pavilion Pl ARD KA22 191 J8 7
Pavilion Rd AYRS KA7 18 C4
Payne St COWCAD G4 5 J6
Peace Av BRWEIR PA11 75 M7
KLMNK KA1 16 B3
Peacock Av PSLYS PA2 100 F7
Peacock Dr HMLTN ML3 156 C5 3
PSLYS PA2 100 F7
Pearce La GOV/IBX G51 104 A1 6
Pearce St GOV/IBX G51 104 A1 7
Pearl St BLSH ML4 133 H6 2
Pearson Dr RNFRW PA4 80 D7
Pearson Pl PSLYN/LNWD PA3 100 B4 2
Peathill Av BAIL/MDB/MHD G69 66 B8
Peathill St PPK/MIL G22 5 K3
Peatland Qd KLMNK KA1 212 A6
Peatland Rd KLMNK KA1 212 A6 3
Peat Rd BRWEIR PA11 98 E2
GRNKW/INVK PA16 32 D6
PLK/PH/NH G53 126 A3
Peden Av DALRY KA24 184 B2
Pedmyre La
CRMNK/CLK/EAG G76 152 C2
Peebles Dr RUTH G73 129 K2
Peebles Pth CTBR ML5 110 D6
Peebles St AYR KA8 224 F7
Peel Glen Gdns DRUM G15 61 G4
Peel Glen Rd BSDN G61 61 G3
Peel La PTCK G11 82 A7
Peel Park Pl EKILN G74 152 F7
Peel Pl CTBR ML5 109 K4
UD/BTH/TAN G71 132 A6
Peel Rd EKILN G74 152 C5
Peel St DMBTN G82 35 H2
PTCK G11 82 B7
Pegasus Av CARLUKE ML8 178 E7
PSLYN/LNWD PA3 100 D4
Pegasus Rd BLSH ML4 133 L4
Peggieshill Rd AYRS KA7 229 G5
Peile St GRNKW/INVK PA16 32 C3
Pemberton Va AYRS KA7 229 G7
Pembroke EKILN G74 154 C5
Pembroke Rd
GRNKW/INVK PA16 31 K5 4
Pembroke St KVGV G3 4 C9 1
Pencaitland Dr CAR/SHTL G32 107 G6
Pencaitland Gv
CAR/SHTL G32 107 G6 5
Pencaitland Pl SMSTN G23 62 E8 3
Pencil Vw LARGS KA30 139 K1
Pendeen Crs
STPS/GTHM/RID G33 107 L4
Pendeen Pl
STPS/GTHM/RID G33 107 M3 1
Pendeen Rd
STPS/GTHM/RID G33 107 M4
Pendicle Crs BSDN G61 61 K6
Pendicle Rd BSDN G61 61 K6
Penfold Crs EKILS G75 14 C5
Penicuik St CAR/SHTL G32 13 L3
Penilee Rd PSLYN/LNWD PA3 102 D1
Penilee Ter
CARD/HILL/MSPK G52 102 E2
Peninver Dr GOV/IBX G51 103 K1
Penman Av RUTH G73 128 F1
Pennan Pl SCOT G14 81 G4
Penneld Rd
CARD/HILL/MSPK G52 102 F4
Penniecroft Av DMBTN G82 37 J4
Pennyburn Rd KLWNG KA13 193 K6
Pennyfern Dr
GRNKW/INVK PA16 32 B6 2
Pennyfern Rd
GRNKW/INVK PA16 32 B6
Pennyroyal Ct EKILN G74 153 K6 10
Pennyvenie Wy IRVSE KA11 204 A4
Penrioch Dr EKILS G75 171 J5 3
Penrith Av GIF/THBK G46 127 J7
Penrith Dr KVD/HLHD G12 82 A3
Penrith Pl EKILS G75 170 F3 4
Penryn Gdns CAR/SHTL G32 107 K6 6
Penston Rd
STPS/GTHM/RID G33 107 K1
Pentland Av PGL PA14 54 F3
PSLYN/LNWD PA3 100 A3
Pentland Crs LRKH ML9 175 M4
PSLYS PA2 124 D1
Pentland Dr BRHD/NEIL G78 125 J8
BSHPBGS G64 64 D7
PSTWK KA9 225 K4
RNFRW PA4 102 B1 2
Pentland Pl BSDN G61 61 H2
IRVSE KA11 204 A6 2
Pentland Road.
BAIL/MDB/MHD G69 66 D8
Pentland Rd
BAIL/MDB/MHD G69 86 D1
EKILS G75 171 G6
KLMNK KA1 212 A6
PLKSW/MSWD G43 127 J4
WISHAW ML2 158 E5
Penzance Wy
BAIL/MDB/MHD G69 66 F7
Peockland Gdns JNSTN PA5 100 A6 2
Peockland Pl JNSTN PA5 100 A6 3
Peploe Dr EKILN G74 154 D4
Perchy Vw WISHAW ML2 159 J8 3
Percy Dr GIF/THBK G46 127 J8
Percy Rd PSLYN/LNWD PA3 102 A1
Percy St GOV/IBX G51 104 C4 2
LRKH ML9 176 A5
Perran Gdns
BAIL/MDB/MHD G69 66 E7
Perray Av DMBTN G82 36 B4
Perrays Crs DMBTN G82 36 A4 1
Perrays Dr DMBTN G82 36 A4
Perrays Wy DMBTN G82 36 A4
Perth Av AIRDRIE ML6 111 G4
Perth Crs CLYDBK G81 59 K4
Perth St KVGV G3 10 D1 1
Peter D Stirling Rd KKNTL G66 45 K8 1
Petersburn Pl AIRDRIE ML6 111 K3 2
Petersburn Rd AIRDRIE ML6 111 K3
Petershill Dr SPRGB/BLRNK G21 7 H1
Petershill Pl SPRGB/BLRNK G21 7 H1
Petershill Rd SPRGB/BLRNK G21 6 C3
Peterson Dr KNTSWD G13 80 E1
Peterson Gdns KNTSWD G13 80 E1 3
Peter St IRV KA12 203 G8
Petition Pl UD/BTH/TAN G71 132 A4
Pettigrew St CAR/SHTL G32 107 G4 7
Peveril Av PLKSD/SHW G41 104 D8
RUTH G73 129 J4
Philip Murry Rd
UD/BTH/TAN G71 132 D3
Philipshill Ga EKILN G74 152 E6
Philipshill Rd EKILN G74 152 E6
Philip Sq AYR KA8 19 G1 2
Phillips Av LARGS KA30 115 L5
Phoenix Crs BLSH ML4 132 F1 1
Phoenix Pl JNSTN PA5 100 D6
MTHW ML1 134 A6 4
Phoenix Rd BLSH ML4 133 L4
Piccadilly St KVGV G3 10 D2
Picken St KLMNK KA1 211 M4
Pickerstonhill MTHW ML1 134 E5 4
Picketlaw Dr
CRMNK/CLK/EAG G76 152 D2
Picketlaw Farm Rd
CRMNK/CLK/EAG G76 152 C2
Pier Rd FAIRLIE KA29 139 K5
Piershill St CAR/SHTL G32 106 F2 4
Piersland Pl IRVSE KA11 204 A4
Pikeman Rd KNTSWD G13 81 J2
Pillans Ct HMLTN ML3 156 A3
Pilmuir Av LNPK/KPK G44 127 M5
Pilrig St CAR/SHTL G32 106 E2
Pilton Rd DRUM G15 61 G6
Pine Av BLTYR/CAMB G72 130 F6
Pine Brae AYRS KA7 19 L9
Pine Cl CUMB G67 49 L5
Pine Ct CUMB G67 49 L5
EKILS G75 171 H4 5
Pine Crs CUMB G67 49 L5
EKILS G75 171 H4
JNSTN PA5 100 A8
Pine Gv AIRDRIE ML6 111 H7
CUMB G67 49 L5
UD/BTH/TAN G71 132 B1
Pine Lawn WISHAW ML2 159 K4
Pine Pk HMLTN ML3 156 E8
Pine Pl CUMB G67 49 L5
GBLS G5 11 K7
Pine Rd CLYDBK G81 59 K5
CUMB G67 49 L5
DMBTN G82 36 F5
KLMNK KA1 16 A6
Pine St AIRDRIE ML6 111 K2 4
GRNK PA15 2 A6
KKNTL G66 44 E1
PSLYS PA2 9 M9
Pinewood Av KKNTL G66 65 G4
Pinewood Ct DMBTN G82 37 H4
KKNTL G66 65 G4
Pinewood Pl KKNTL G66 65 G4
Pinkerton Av RUTH G73 128 F1
Pinkerton La RNFRW PA4 80 D8 3
Pinkston Dr COWCAD G4 6 A5
Pinkston Rd COWCAD G4 5 L4
Pinmore Pl PLK/PH/NH G53 125 M4
Pinmore St PLK/PH/NH G53 125 M4
Pinwherry Dr
STPS/GTHM/RID G33 84 F3 5
Pinwherry Pl
UD/BTH/TAN G71 132 A6 4
Piper Av CRG/CRSL/HOU PA6 99 J1
Piperhill AYRS KA7 229 G7
Piper Rd AIRDRIE ML6 111 J4
CRG/CRSL/HOU PA6 99 J1
Pirnie Pl KSYTH G65 47 K1 3
Pirnmill Av EKILS G75 171 H5 3
MTHW ML1 157 H2
Pirnmill Pl HBR/GL G84 20 F7 3
Pirnmill Rd SALT KA21 191 M7
Pitcairn Crs EKILS G75 170 F1
Pitcairn Gv EKILS G75 171 G1
Pitcairn Pl EKILS G75 170 F1
Pitcairn St DEN/PKHD G31 106 E5 2
Pitcairn Ter HMLTN ML3 156 A5
Pitcaple Dr
PLKSW/MSWD G43 127 H3 5
Pitlochry Dr
CARD/HILL/MSPK G52 103 H5
LRKH ML9 176 C8 7
Pitmedden Rd BSHPBGS G64 64 D7
Pitmilly Rd DRUM G15 61 J5
Pitreavie Ct HMLTN ML3 174 B1
Pitreavie Pl
STPS/GTHM/RID G33 85 J7
Pit Rd BLSH ML4 132 F3
KKNTL G66 66 B2
Pitt St CGLW G2 4 F9
Place of Bonhill ALEX/LLW G83 25 K6
Place Vw KBRN KA25 142 F8
Pladda Av IRVSE KA11 204 A7
PGL PA14 55 H2
Pladda Ct IRVSE KA11 204 B7
Pladda Crs IRVSE KA11 204 A7
Pladda Dr PSTWK KA9 225 J3
Pladda Rd RNFRW PA4 80 D8 4
SALT KA21 191 M7
Pladda St MTHW ML1 157 H2 5
Pladda Ter IRVSE KA11 204 B7
Pladda Wy HBR/GL G84 20 F7
Pladda Wynd IRVSE KA11 204 A7
Plaintrees Ct PSLYS PA2 101 L8 2
Plane Pl UD/BTH/TAN G71 109 H8
Planetree Pl JNSTN PA5 100 A8
Planetree Rd CLYDBK G81 60 A5
Plantation Av MTHW ML1 134 B3
Plantation Park Gdns
GOV/IBX G51 104 D4 4
Plantation Sq GOV/IBX G51 10 A4
Plant St DEN/PKHD G31 13 J3
Plan Vw KBRN KA25 143 H6
Plateau Dr TROON KA10 216 F2 4
Platthorn Dr EKILN G74 15 J3
Platthorn Rd EKILN G74 15 H4
Playfair St DMNK/BRGTN G40 12 E9
Playingfield Rd CRH/DND KA2 205 L8
Pleaknowe Crs
BAIL/MDB/MHD G69 66 E7
Pleamuir Pl BALLOCH G68 48 C7
Plean St SCOT G14 81 G4
Pleasance St
PLKSW/MSWD G43 127 J1
Pleasantfield Rd PSTWK KA9 225 H4
Pleasantside Av PGL PA14 55 G1
Plover Dr EKILS G75 171 G4
Plover Pl JNSTN PA5 122 C2
Plymouth Av GRNKW/INVK PA16 31 L4
Pochard Wy BLSH ML4 132 F1
Poet's Vw KKNTL G66 65 M2
Poindfauld Ter DMBTN G82 37 G5
Pointhouse Rd KVGV G3 104 C1
Pollick Av BRHD/NEIL G78 147 H6 1
Pollick Farm La BRHD/NEIL G78 147 G7
Pollock Av HMLTN ML3 156 A5
Pollock Crs KLWNG KA13 193 L7
Pollock Rd BSDN G61 62 A6
NMRNS G77 150 C5
Pollock St BLSH ML4 133 J4
MTHW ML1 157 L2
Pollok Dr BSHPBGS G64 63 L8
Pollok La EKILN G74 154 B6
Pollok Pl EKILN G74 154 B6 6
Pollokshaws Rd
PLKSD/SHW G41 11 G8
PLKSW/MSWD G43 127 H2
Pollokshields Sq
PLKSD/SHW G41 104 E7 3
Polmadie Rd GBLS G5 105 L6
GVH/MTFL G42 105 K8
Polmadie St GVH/MTFL G42 105 J8
Polnoon Av KNTSWD G13 81 G3
Polo Av TROON KA10 216 E7
Polo Gdns TROON KA10 216 E7
Polquhap Ct PLK/PH/NH G53 126 A1 3
Polquhap Gdns
PLK/PH/NH G53 126 A1
Polquhap Pl PLK/PH/NH G53 126 A1
Polquhap Rd PLK/PH/NH G53 126 A1
Polson Dr JNSTN PA5 99 L7
Polsons Crs PSLYS PA2 8 F8
Polwarth La KVD/HLHD G12 82 B6
Polwarth St GLSTN KA4 214 C3
KVD/HLHD G12 82 B6
Pomona Pl HMLTN ML3 155 M7
Poplar Av BSHPTN PA7 58 B7
JNSTN PA5 100 A8
NMRNS G77 150 E6
PTCK G11 81 M5 4
Poplar Crs BSHPTN PA7 58 B7
Poplar Dr CLYDBK G81 59 M4
KKNTL G66 45 J4
KKNTL G66 65 G4

Poplar Gdns *EKILS* G75 .... 171 J4
Poplar Pl *BLTYR/CAMB* G72..... 131 J8
GRK PA19 .... 31 J5 🔢
MTHW ML1 .... 134 B5
UD/BTH/TAN G71 .... 132 D1
Poplar St *DMBTN* G82.................. 36 F5
The Poplars *BSDN* G61 .... 61 K1 🔢
Poplar Wy *AYRS* KA7 .... 229 K4
BLTYR/CAMB G72...................... 130 F6 🔢
Poplin St *DMNK/BRGTN* G40 ...... 12 D9
DMNK/BRGTN G40...................... 105 M6 🔢
Porchester St
STPS/GTHM/RID G33............... 85 K7
Portal Rd *KNTSWD* G13 .... 81 J1
Port Dundas Pl *CGLW* C2................ 5 J8
Port Dundas Rd *COWCAD* C4 .... 5 H6
Portencross Rd *WKIL* KA23 .... 181 L4
Porterfield Rd *KLMCLM* PA13 .... 75 K2 🔢
RNFRW PA4 .... 80 B6
Porter St *GOV/IBX* G51 .... 104 C4 🔢
Porters Well *UD/BTH/TAN* G71 .. 131 L4
Portessie *ERSK* PA8 .... 59 C7
Port Glasgow Rd *GRNK* PA15 ...... 33 M7
PGL PA14...................................... 55 H5
Portland Av *IRV* KA12............... 208 B1
Portland Brae
KLMNKN/STW KA3............... 212 E2
Portland Pk *HMLTN* ML3.......... 156 E7 🔢
Portland Pl *HMLTN* ML3........... 156 E7
IRV KA12..................................... 208 B1
KLMNK KA1.................................. 16 C5
LNK/LMHG ML11.................... 199 H5 🔢
SVSTN KA20............................... 201 K2
Portland Rd *BALLOCH* G68 .... 48 F4
GLSTN KA4.................................. 214 B4
IRV KA12..................................... 208 A1
KLMNK KA1.................................. 16 C4
PSLYS PA2.................................. 102 B6
Portland Sq *HMLTN* ML3.......... 156 E7 🔢
Portland St *CTBR* ML5................ 110 B1
KLMNK KA1.................................. 16 F5
KLMNKN/STW KA3.................... 16 F5
TROON KA10............................... 216 C6
Portland Ter *TROON* KA10......... 216 C6
Portman St *PLKSD/SHW* G41 ..... 10 B5
Portmark Av *AYRS* KA7 .... 228 C8
Portmarnock Dr *SMSTN* G23 ..... 82 L1 🔢
Portpatrick Rd *OLDK* G60 .... 58 F2
Portreath Rd
GRNKW/INVK PA16................... 31 L4 🔢
Portsoy Av *KNTSWD* G13 .... 80 F1 🔢
Portsoy Pl *KNTSWD* G13 .... 80 F1
Port St *KVGV* G3 .... 10 C1
Portugal St *GBLS* G5 .... 11 H6
Portwell *HMLTN* ML3 .... 156 E5 🔢
Possil Rd *COWCAD* G4 .... 5 G4
Postgate *HMLTN* ML3 .... 156 E5
Potassels Rd
BAIL/MDB/MHD G69................ 86 C2
Potrail Pl *HMLTN* ML3 .... 156 A6
Potter Cl *CAR/SHTL* G32 .... 106 E6 🔢
Potter Gv *CAR/SHTL* G32 .... 106 E6 🔢
Potterhill Av *PSLYS* PA2............. 124 C1
Potterhill Rd *PLK/PH/NH* G53 ... 103 C7
Potter St *CAR/SHTL* G32 .... 106 E6 🔢
Potters Wynd *LNK/LMHG* ML11 .. 199 J4
Pottery Pl *KLMNKN/STW* KA3 ... 206 F7
Pottery St *GRNK* PA15 .... 33 L6
Potts Wy *MTHW* ML1 .... 133 J8
Powbrone *EKILS* G75 .... 171 L4 🔢
Powburn Crs *UD/BTH/TAN* G71 .. 131 K2
Powfoot Cl *DEN/PKHD* G31 .... 13 M6
Powforth Cl *LRKH* ML9 .... 175 L6
Powgree Crs *BEITH* KA15......... 168 C4 🔢
Powmill Gdns *PSTWK* KA9........ 221 K7
Powmill Pl *PSTWK* KA9............. 221 K7
Powmill Rd *PSTWK* KA9............ 221 K7
Powrie St *STPS/GTHM/RID* G33 ... 85 J6
Prentice La
UD/BTH/TAN G71 .... 132 A1 🔢
Prentice Rd *HMLTN* ML3 .... 157 H4
Prestonfield *MLNGV* G62.............. 41 L8
Prestonfield Av *KLWNG* KA13 ... 193 H5
Preston Pl *GRK* PA19.................. 31 K2 🔢
GVH/MTFL G42......................... 105 H7
Preston St *GVH/MTFL* G42 .... 105 H7
Prestwick Rd *BALLOCH* G68 ...... 48 F5 🔢
Prestwick Pl *NMRNS* G77........ 151 G5 🔢
Prestwick Rd *AYR* KA8............. 225 G6
Prestwick St *PLK/PH/NH* G53... 126 A3
Priesthill Av *PLK/PH/NH* G53 .. 126 C3 🔢
Priesthill Crs *PLK/PH/NH* G53.. 126 C3
Priesthill Rd *PLK/PH/NH* G53 .. 126 B3
Prieston Rd *BRWEIR* PA11........ 98 D2
Primrose Av *BLSH* ML4 .... 133 G2
GRNKW/INVK PA16 .... 50 E4
MTHW ML1 .... 157 H4
Primrose Crs *GRNKW/INVK* PA16 .. 50 E4
MTHW ML1 .... 157 H4
Primrose Pl *CUMB* G67 .... 68 B2
GRNKW/INVK PA16 .... 50 E4 🔢
SALT KA21 .... 192 A7
UD/BTH/TAN G71 .... 132 C1 🔢
Primrose St *SCOT* G14 .... 81 J6
Primrose Wy *CARLUKE* ML8 ..... 188 E1
Prince Albert Rd *KVD/HLHD* G12 .. 82 B6
Prince Edward St
GVH/MTFL G42....................... 105 G7
Prince of Wales Gdns
MRYH/FIRH G20 .... 82 C1
Prince Pl *WISHAW* ML2............. 160 A3
Princes Ct *AYR* KA8................... 225 G7
Prince's Gdns *KVD/HLHD* G12 ... 82 B7
UD/BTH/TAN G71 .... 131 L5
Princes Pk *BSHPTN* PA7.............. 58 C5
Princes Pl *ARD* KA22................ 191 H8 🔢
KVD/HLHD G12 .... 82 C6
Princess Ct *KLMNK* KA1 .... 212 B5 🔢
Princess Crs *PSLY* PA1.............. 102 B3
Princess Dr
BAIL/MDB/MHD G69............... 109 G4
Princes Sq *BRHD/NEIL* G78..... 125 K6 🔢

Princess Rd *MTHW* ML1............ 133 M5
Princes St *AIRDRIE* ML6............. 91 G4
ARD KA22.................................. 191 H8
PA15 .... 2 B3
GRNK PA15 .... 16 F5
KLMNK KA1.................................. 16 F5
MTHW ML1 .... 157 L1 🔢
PGL PA14...................................... 34 B7 🔢
Princes St East *HBR/GL* G84 ...... 20 D8
Prince's Ter *KVD/HLHD* G12 ...... 82 C6
Princes Terrace La
KVD/HLHD G12 .... 82 C6 🔢
Priorwood Rd *NMRNS* G77....... 150 A5
Priory Av *PSLYN/LNWD* PA3 .... 102 A2
Priory Dr *UD/BTH/TAN* G71....... 131 K2
Priory Ga *WISHAW* ML2 .... 177 H2
Priory Pl *BALLOCH* G68 .... 47 L8 🔢
KNTSWD G13 .... 81 K2 🔢
Priory Rd *KNTSWD* G13 .... 81 K2
BLTYR/CAMB G72.................... 155 K2 🔢
Priory Ter *WISHAW* ML2........... 158 C7
Procession Rd *PSLYS* PA2.......... 124 D3
Progress Dr *AIRDRIE* ML6 .... 90 F4
Promenade *AYR* KA8................ 224 F6
Prosen St *CAR/SHTL* G32......... 106 E6
Prospect Av *BLTYR/CAMB* G72.. 129 M3
UD/BTH/TAN G71 .... 131 M2 🔢
Prospect Ct *BLTYR/CAMB* G72.. 155 K4
Prospecthill Circ
GVH/MTFL G42....................... 105 K8
Prospecthill Crs *GVH/MTFL* G42.. 128 E1
Prospecthill Dr
GVH/MTFL G42....................... 128 C1 🔢
RUTH G73 .... 128 D1
Prospecthill Rd *GVH/MTFL* G42 .. 128 B1
SALT KA21 .... 192 A8
Prospecthill Sq
GVH/MTFL G42....................... 128 D1 🔢
Prospecthill St *GRNK* PA15 .... 2 A6
Prospect Rd *BALLOCH* G68 .... 48 C3
PLKSW/MSWD G43.................. 127 K1 🔢
Provand Hall Crs
BAIL/MDB/MHD G69............... 108 B6
Provanhill St
SPRGB/BLRNK G21 .... 6 C6
Provanmill Rd
STPS/GTHM/RID G33................ 7 M3
Provan Rd *DEN/PKHD* G31 .... 7 K7
Provost Driver Ct *RNFRW* PA4.... 80 E7 🔢
Provost Ga *WISHAW* ML2.......... 175 M6
Provost's Loan *GTCI* KA28 .... 138 C6 🔢
Pundeavon Av *KBRN* KA25 .... 143 G6
Purdie *EKILN* G74 .... 154 D4 🔢
Purdie St *HMLTN* ML3 .... 156 A4
Purdon St *PTCK* G11................... 82 B7
Putyan Av *DALRY* KA24............ 184 B2
Pyatshaw Rd *LRKH* ML9 .... 176 B8

Q

Quadrant Rd
PLKSW/MSWD G43.................. 127 L4
The Quadrant
CRMNK/CLK/EAG G76 .... 151 M1
Quail Rd *AYR* KA8..................... 225 G5
Quarrelton Gv *JNSTN* PA5 .... 99 M8 🔢
Quarrelton Rd *JNSTN* PA5 .... 99 L7
Quarrier St *GRNK* PA15 .... 3 M8
Quarry Dr *KNTSWD* G13 .... 81 L2
Quarrybank *KLBCH* PA10............. 99 J7
Quarrybrae Av
CRMNK/CLK/EAG G76 .... 151 K2
Quarrybrae Gdns
UD/BTH/TAN G71 .... 132 C3 🔢
Quarrybrae St *DEN/PKHD* G31.... 13 M6
DEN/PKHD G31 .... 106 E4
KLMCLM PA13............................ 55 K7
Quarry Knowe *DMBTN* G82........ 36 D4
Quarryknowe *LNK/LMHG* ML11 .. 199 G5
RUTH G73 .... 128 F2
Quarryknowe Gdns
DEN/PKHD G31 .... 106 E4 🔢
Quarry Knowe Pl *BLSH* ML4 ..... 132 F6 🔢
Quarryknowe St *CLYDBK* G81 .... 60 E2 🔢
DEN/PKHD G31 .... 106 E4
Quarry La *KKNTL* G66 .... 29 K8
Quarry Pk *EKILS* G75 .... 14 E6
Quarry Pl *BLTYR/CAMB* G72 ..... 129 L3
DMBTN G82 .... 36 D4
SHOTTS ML7 .... 137 K4
Quarry Rd *AIRDRIE* ML6............. 88 D5
BRHD/NEIL ML8..................... 125 H5 🔢
CARLUKE ML8.......................... 177 M7
EKILS G75 .... 171 K4
IRV KA12................................... 203 J6
LRKH ML9 .... 176 A7
PGL PA14...................................... 54 F2
PSLYS PA2............................... 101 M8 🔢
SHOTTS ML7 .... 137 K4
Quarryside St *AIRDRIE* ML6........ 88 D5
Quarry St *CTBR* ML5.................. 110 D3
HMLTN ML3............................. 156 E6
JNSTN PA5 .... 99 M6
LRKH ML9 .... 176 B8
MTHW ML1 .... 134 A5
SHOTTS ML7 .... 137 K4
WISHAW ML2........................... 159 G6
Quarrywood Av
SPRGB/BLRNK G21 .... 84 C5 🔢
Quarrywood Rd
SPRGB/BLRNK G21 .... 84 D5
STPS/GTHM/RID G33................ 7 L1
Quayhead St *GTCI* KA28 .... 138 A7 🔢
Quay Pend *DMBTN* G82.............. 36 E6 🔢
Quay Rd *RUTH* G73 .... 129 G1
Quay Rd North *RUTH* G73 .... 106 A8
Quay St *DMBTN* G82................... 36 F6 🔢
SALT KA21 .... 200 F2
Quebec Dr *EKILS* G75 .... 14 A4
Quebec Wynd
CAR/SHTL G32 .... 130 C1 🔢
Queen Elizabeth Av
CARD/HILL/MSPK G52............ 102 E2

Queen Margaret Dr
KVD/HLHD G12.......................... 4 A2
Queen Margaret Rd
MRYH/FIRH G20 .... 4 A1
Queen Mary Av *CLYDBK* G81..... 60 D7
GVH/MTFL G42......................... 105 H8
Queen Mary St
DMNK/BRGTN G40.................... 12 D8
Queen Rd *IRV* KA12.................. 203 J1
Queen's Av *BLTYR/CAMB* G72.. 130 B3
LARGS KA30............................. 115 K5
Queensbank Av
BAIL/MDB/MHD G69................ 86 E2
Queensberry Av *BSDN* G61......... 61 L2
CRMNK/CLK/EAG G76 .... 151 L2
Queensborough Gdns
KVD/HLHD G12.......................... 82 A5
Queensby Av
BAIL/MDB/MHD G69................ 108 B4 🔢
Queensby Pl
BAIL/MDB/MHD G69................ 108 C3 🔢
Queensby Rd
BAIL/MDB/MHD G69................ 108 B3
Queen's Ct *MLNGV* G62.............. 62 A1
Queen's Crs *AIRDRIE* ML6.......... 111 K6
BAIL/MDB/MHD G69................ 132 F5 🔢
BLSH ML4 .... 132 F5 🔢
CARLUKE ML8.......................... 179 C7
COWCAD C4 .... 4 D5
MTHW ML1 .... 133 M6 🔢
NMLNS KA16............................. 215 H2
Queen's Dr *ALEX/LLW* G83 .... 25 K6
ARD KA22.................................. 191 J6
BALLOCH G68............................ 48 F3
BSHPTN PA7.............................. 58 C5
GVH/MTFL G42......................... 104 F7
HMLTN ML3.............................. 174 D3
KLMNK KA1.................................. 17 G7
PSTWK KA9............................... 221 K4
TROON KA10............................. 216 D3
Queensferry St *GBLS* G5 .... 105 L7 🔢
Queen's Gdns *KVD/HLHD* G12.... 82 C6
Queen's Ga
CRMNK/CLK/EAG G76 .... 151 L1 🔢
Queenside Crs *ERSK* PA8 .... 58 F8
Queensland Ct
CARD/HILL/MSPK G52............ 103 J3 🔢
Queensland Dr
CARD/HILL/MSPK G52............ 103 J3
Queensland Gdns
CARD/HILL/MSPK G52............ 103 J3
Queensland La East
CARD/HILL/MSPK G52............ 103 J3 🔢
Queensland La West
CARD/HILL/MSPK G52............ 103 J3
Queenslie St
STPS/GTHM/RID G33................ 7 M4
Queen's Park Av
GVH/MTFL G42......................... 105 H8
Queen's Qd *AYR* KA8................. 19 H1
Queen Sq *PLKSD/SHW* G41 ..... 104 F7
Queen's Rd *JNSTN* PA5 .... 100 C7
Queen's St *MTHW* ML1............. 135 H7
Queen's Ter *AYRS* KA7............... 18 C3
PSTWK KA9............................... 221 H8
Queen's Terrace La *AYRS* KA7... 18 C5 🔢
Queen St *ALEX/LLW* G83 .... 25 K5
AYR KA8.................................... 19 H1
CGLE G1..................................... 11 J2
HBR/GL G84 .... 20 D6
HMLTN ML3 .... 156 A4 🔢
KKNTL G66 .... 65 J1 🔢
KLMNK KA1.................................. 16 F5
KLWNG KA13............................. 194 A6
MTHW ML1 .... 157 L2
PGL PA14...................................... 34 C7 🔢
PSLY PA1.................................. 8 D4
RNFRW PA4 .... 80 C5
RUTH G73 .... 129 G1
WISHAW ML2........................... 159 M3 🔢
Queens Vw *BSHPBGS* G64 .... 64 B1
Queens Wy *ALEX/LLW* G83 .... 25 K5
Queensway *EKILS* G75 .... 15 H5
GRK PA19 .... 31 J5 🔢
Queen Victoria Dr *SCOT* G14 ..... 81 J5
Queen Victoria Ga *SCOT* G14 .... 81 J4 🔢
Queen Victoria St *AIRDRIE* ML6 .. 110 F2
Quendale Dr *CAR/SHTL* G32 ..... 106 E6
Quentin St *PLKSD/SHW* G41 ..... 104 E8
Quinton Gdns
BAIL/MDB/MHD G69 .... 108 A4 🔢

R

Raasay Crs *AIRDRIE* ML6 .... 111 L3
Raasay Dr *PSLYS* PA2............... 124 D2
Raasay Gdns *NMRNS* G77........ 150 B4 🔢
Raasay Pl *PPK/MIL* G22 .... 83 J1 🔢
Raasay St *PPK/MIL* G22 .... 83 J1
Racecourse Rd *AYRS* KA7 .... 18 D7
Racecourse Vw *HMLTN* ML3..... 156 E4
Rachan St *ESTRH* G34................ 86 D8 🔢
Radnor St *CLYDBK* G81.............. 60 A6 🔢
Raeberry St *MRYH/FIRH* G20 .... 4 C3
Raebog Crs *AIRDRIE* ML6 .... 88 F7 🔢
Raebog Rd *AIRDRIE* ML6 .... 88 F5
Raeburn Av *EKILN* G74............. 154 B5
Raeburn Crs *HMLTN* ML3.......... 155 L6
Raeburn Pl *EKILN* G74.............. 154 B5
Raeside Av *NMRNS* G77........... 150 D6
Raes Rd *CARLUKE* ML8.............. 188 B1
Raeswood Dr *PLK/PH/NH* G53 .. 125 M1
Raeswood Rd *PLK/PH/NH* G53 .. 125 M1
Raewell Crs *BLSH* ML4 .... 132 F6 🔢
Rafford St *GOV/IBX* G51 .... 104 A3 🔢
Raggithill Av *RAYR/DAL* KA6 .... 226 F3 🔢
Raglan St *ALEX/LLW* G83 .... 25 M6
COWCAD C4 .... 5 G4
Raglan Street La
ALEX/LLW G83 .... 25 M6 🔢
Raillies Av *LARGS* KA30............ 115 K3
Raillies Rd *LARGS* KA30............ 115 K3
Railway Rd *AIRDRIE* ML6........... 110 D2
Raise St *SALT* KA21 .... 200 F1
Raith Av *CSMK* G45................... 128 D5 🔢

PSTWK KA9............................... 225 L2
Raithburn Av *CSMK* G45........... 128 C5
KLMNKN/STW KA3................... 206 F5
Raithburn Rd *CSMK* G45........... 128 C6
GVH/MTFL G42......................... 105 H8
Raith Dr *BALLOCH* G68 .... 47 K8
BLSH ML4 .... 133 H5
Raithhill *AYRS* KA7 .... 229 H8
Raith Ter *PSTWK* KA9............... 225 L2
Ralston Av
CARD/HILL/MSPK G52............ 102 F5
PSLY PA1.................................. 102 F5
Ralston Ct
CARD/HILL/MSPK G52............ 102 F5
Ralston Dr
CARD/HILL/MSPK G52............ 102 F5
KLMNKN/STW KA3................... 212 D1
Ralston Pl
CARD/HILL/MSPK G52............ 102 F5
Ralston Rd *BRHD/NEIL* G78...... 125 J7
BSDN G61 .... 61 L4
Ralston St *AIRDRIE* ML6............ 110 E2
PSLY PA1.................................. 9 L5
Ralstonyards Rd
KLMNKN/STW KA3................... 206 F5
Ramage Rd *CARLUKE* ML8........ 179 H8
Ramillies Ct *CARLUKE* ML8....... 179 G8
Ramoth *LNK/LMHG* ML11 .... 198 D5
Rampart Av *KNTSWD* G13 .... 81 G1
Ramsay Av *JNSTN* PA5............... 99 L8
Ramsay Ct *NMRNS* G77............ 150 E6
Ramsay Crs *KLBCH* PA10 .... 99 H7
Ramsay Hl *EKILN* G74 .... 154 A6 🔢
Ramsay Pl *CTBR* ML5................ 109 J4
JNSTN PA5 .... 99 L8 🔢
Ramsay St *CLYDBK* G81............. 59 M6
Ramseyston Dr
RAYR/DAL KA6 .... 231 H5 🔢
Ramstone Pl *IRVSE* KA11.......... 204 C4
Ram St *CAR/SHTL* G32.............. 106 F4 🔢
Ranald Gdns *RUTH* G73............ 129 K6
Randolph Av
CRMNK/CLK/EAG G76 .... 128 A8 🔢
Randolph Dr
CRMNK/CLK/EAG G76 .... 127 M8
Randolph Gdns
CRMNK/CLK/EAG G76 .... 127 M8 🔢
Randolph La *PTCK* G11............... 81 M5
Randolph Rd *PTCK* G11.............. 81 M5
Ranfurly Dr *BALLOCH* G68 .... 48 E5
Ranfurly Pl *BRWEIR* PA11......... 98 E3
Ranfurly Rd *BRWEIR* PA11......... 98 E3
Range Av *MTHW* ML1............... 158 C6
Range Pl *HMLTN* ML3 .... 156 E8
Rangerhouse Rd *EKILS* G75 ...... 171 M4
Range Rd *MTHW* ML1 .... 158 B5
Ranken Crs *IRV* KA12............... 203 K6
Ranken Dr *IRV* KA12................. 203 K6
Rankin Ct *KLMNKN/STW* KA3 ... 207 J6
Rankin Crs *AIRDRIE* ML6............ 69 M7
Rankin Dr *LARGS* KA30............. 115 K4
NMRNS G77............................. 150 C3
Rankine Av *EKILS* G75 .... 15 K7
Rankine Pl *JNSTN* PA5.............. 99 M6
Rankine St *JNSTN* PA5.............. 99 M6
Rankin Rd *WISHAW* ML2........... 159 L5
Rankin St *CARLUKE* ML8........... 178 F7
GRNKW/INVK PA16................... 32 C5
Rannoch Av *BSHPBGS* G64 .... 64 B8
CTBR ML5 .... 87 K8
HMLTN ML3.............................. 156 A4 🔢
KKNTL G66 .... 65 J1 🔢
KLWNG KA13............................. 194 A6
MTHW ML1 .... 157 L2
PGL PA14...................................... 34 C7 🔢
PSLY PA1.................................. 80 D6
RNFRW PA4 .... 80 C5
RUTH G73 .... 129 G1
WISHAW ML2........................... 159 M3 🔢
Rannoch Ct *CUMB* G67 .... 68 B3
Rannoch Dr *BSDN* G61................ 62 A7
CUMB G67 .... 68 B3
KKNTL G66 .... 46 A8
RNFRW PA4 .... 80 C5
WISHAW ML2........................... 177 H1
Rannoch Gn *EKILN* G74............ 153 M6 🔢
Rannoch Pl *IRV* KA12................ 203 J3
PSLYS PA2.................................... 9 L7
SHOTTS ML7 .... 137 L3 🔢
Rannoch Rd *AIRDRIE* ML6........... 88 F8
JNSTN PA5 .... 99 M8
KLMCLM PA13............................ 75 J2 🔢
UD/BTH/TAN G71 .... 108 E8
WMYSB PA18 .... 70 A1 🔢
Rannoch St *LNPK/KPK* G44...... 128 A3
Rannoch Ter *LRKH* ML9 .... 176 C8 🔢
Raploch Av *SCOT* G14............... 81 H5
Raploch Crs *CLYDBK* G81 .... 60 D2 🔢
Raploch La *SCOT* G14................ 81 H5
Raploch Rd *LRKH* ML9 .... 175 M7
Raploch St *LRKH* ML9 .... 175 M7
Rashielee *ERSK* PA8 .... 59 G7
Rashielee Av *ERSK* PA8............. 59 H7
Rashielee Rd *ERSK* PA8............. 59 G7
Rashley Sq *ARD* KA22............... 191 K5
Rathlin Av *KLMNK* KA1............. 211 M5
Rathlin St *GOV/IBX* G51 .... 104 A1
Rathlin Ter *DMBTN* G82............. 36 C4
Ratho Dr *BALLOCH* G68 .... 48 E4
SPRGB/BLRNK G21 .... 83 L5
Ratho Pk *HMLTN* ML3 .... 174 D3
Ratho St *GRNK* PA15 .... 3 K6
Rattray Rw *DEN/PKHD* G31 ...... 13 L6
Ravel Rw *DEN/PKHD* G31 .... 13 L6
Ravelston Rd *BSDN* G61 .... 61 L7
Ravelston St *CAR/SHTL* G32 ..... 13 M3
Ravel Wynd *UD/BTH/TAN* G71 .. 132 A1
Raven Rd *GRNKW/INVK* PA16 ... 32 K4 🔢
Ravenscliffe Dr *GIF/THBK* G46 .. 127 H6
Ravenscourt *EKILN* G74............ 152 C6
Ravenscraig Av *PSLYS* PA2 .... 101 J8 🔢
PSLYS PA2................................ 101 J8 🔢
Ravenscraig Ct *BLSH* ML4 .... 133 H4
Ravenscraig Dr
PLK/PH/NH G53 .... 126 B3
Ravenscraig Rd
KLMNKN/STW KA3................... 197 K1
Ravenscraig Ter
PLK/PH/NH G53 .... 126 C4 🔢
Ravenshall Rd *PLKSD/SHW* G41.. 127 J1
Ravenshill Dr *MTHW* ML1.......... 135 J8
Ravenstone Dr *GIF/THBK* G46 .. 127 J4
Ravenswood Av *PSLYS* PA2 ...... 123 L2 🔢

Ravenswood Dr
PLKSD/SHW G41..................... 104 D8
Ravenswood Rd
BAIL/MDB/MHD G69................ 108 C5
Raven Wynd *WISHAW* ML2........ 159 H6
Rawyards Av *AIRDRIE* ML6......... 89 H7
Raymond Pl *EKILS* G75 .... 14 B4
Rayne Pl *DRUM* G15.................... 61 H5
Ream Av *AIRDRIE* ML6.............. 111 M3
Reay Av *DMBTN* G82................... 35 G1
EKILN G74 .... 153 H7
Reay Gdns *EKILN* G74 .... 153 H7 🔢
Recawr Pk *AYRS* KA7 .... 229 K6
Redan St *DMNK/BRGTN* G40 ..... 12 D5
Redbrae Rd *KNTL* G66 .... 45 K8
Redburn Av *GIF/THBK* G46 .... 151 H1
Redburn Ct *CUMB* G67 .... 49 M3 🔢
Redburn Pl *CUMB* G67 .... 49 M3
IRV KA12................................... 203 H4
Redburn Rd *CUMB* G67 .... 49 M3
Redcastle Sq
STPS/GTHM/RID G33............... 85 K8 🔢
Redcliffe Dr *EKILS* G75 .... 171 H1 🔢
Redclyffe Gdns *HBR/GL* G84 ..... 20 D5
Reddance Ter *DALRY* KA24 .... 184 A3
Red Deer Rd *EKILS* G75 .... 14 A8
Redding Av *KLMNKN/STW* KA3 .. 206 F5
Rederech Crs *HMLTN* ML3......... 155 L8
Redford St *STPS/GTHM/RID* G33 ... 7 L8
Red Fox Dr *ALEX/LLW* G83........ 25 L1
Red Gables Sq *ARD* KA22.......... 191 H6
Redgate Pl *SCOT* G14................. 81 H5 🔢
Redgauntlet Rd *HBR/GL* G84 ..... 22 F1
Redgrave *EKILN* G74 .... 154 C4
Redhill Rd *BALLOCH* G68 .... 48 D6
Redhills Vw *KNTL* G66 .... 44 E2
Redhurst Crs *PSLYS* PA2 .... 124 C2 🔢
Redhurst La *PSLYS* PA2 .... 124 C2 🔢
Redhurst Wy *PSLYS* PA2 .... 124 C2 🔢
Redlands La *KVD/HLHD* G12 ..... 82 C5 🔢
Redlands Rd *KVD/HLHD* G12..... 82 C5
Redlands Ter *KVD/HLHD* G12 .. 82 C5 🔢
Redlands Terrace La
KVD/HLHD G12 .... 82 C5 🔢
Redlawood Pl
BLTYR/CAMB G72.................... 131 G3
Redlawood Rd
BLTYR/CAMB G72.................... 131 G3
Redmire Crs *SHOTTS* ML7 .... 161 H1
Redmoss Rd *CLYDBK* G81 .... 59 M3
KKNTL G66 .... 45 H4
Redmoss St *PPK/MIL* G22 .... 83 H4 🔢
Rednock St *PPK/MIL* G22 .... 5 K1
Redpath Dr
CARD/HILL/MSPK G52............ 103 H3
SPRGB/BLRNK G21 .... 7 H1
Red Rd *DMBTN* G82.................. 23 M5
SPRGB/BLRNK G21 .... 7 H2
Red Road Ct *SPRGB/BLRNK* G21.. 7 H2
Red Rw *DMBTN* G82.................. 25 K7
Redstone Av *KLWNG* KA13....... 193 M5
Redwing Gdns *WISHAW* ML2 .... 159 G8 🔢
Redwood Av *EKILN* G74............ 152 E8
Redwood Ct *EKILN* G74............ 152 E8
Redwood Crs *BLTYR/CAMB* G72.. 130 F5
BSHPTN PA7.............................. 58 C6
EKILN G74 .... 152 E7
UD/BTH/TAN G71 .... 132 C1
Redwood Dr *EKILN* G74............ 152 E6
SPRGB/BLRNK G21 .... 6 E2 🔢
Redwood Gv *CTBR* ML5............. 110 B3
Redwood Pl *EKILN* G74............. 152 F7
UD/BTH/TAN G71 .... 132 C1
Redwood Rd *CUMB* G67 .... 49 K7
MTHW ML1 .... 134 B4
Reedloch Dr *TROON* KA10........ 216 F2
Reek St *BEITH* KA15................. 168 E2
Reelick Av *KNTSWD* G13 .... 80 E1 🔢
Reelick Qd *KNTSWD* G13 .... 80 E1
Reema Rd *BLSH* ML4 .... 133 J3
Reen Pl *UD/BTH/TAN* G71 .... 132 B5
Reform St *BEITH* KA15.............. 144 B8
Regal Gv *SHOTTS* ML7 .... 137 L5
Regency Wy *HMLTN* ML3 .... 157 G7 🔢
MTHW ML1 .... 133 M5 🔢
Regent Dr *RUTH* G73 .... 129 G1 🔢
Regent Moray St *KVGV* G3........ 82 D7
Regent Park Sq
PLKSD/SHW G41..................... 104 F7
Regent Pl *CLYDBK* G81.............. 59 L5
Regents Ct *NMLNS* KA16 .... 215 J2 🔢
Regents Ga *UD/BTH/TAN* G71 .. 131 L5 🔢
Regent Sq *KKNTL* G66 .... 65 J5
Regent St *CLYDBK* G81.............. 59 L5
GRNK PA15 .... 2 D5
KKNTL G66 .... 65 J1 🔢
PSLY PA1.................................. 102 B4
Register Av *BLSH* ML4 .... 133 G6
Register Rd *KSYTH* G65............. 47 K1
Regwood St *PLKSD/SHW* G41... 127 K1
Reid Av *BSDN* G61..................... 62 A3
DALRY KA24............................. 184 B3
PSLYN/LNWD PA3 .... 100 B4
Reid Gv *MTHW* ML1................. 158 B5
Reid Pl *DMNK/BRGTN* G40 .... 12 D8
Reid's Av *SVSTN* KA20.............. 192 D7
Reid St *AIRDRIE* ML6................. 89 H8
CTBR ML5 .... 110 A1
DMNK/BRGTN G40.................... 12 D9
DMNK/BRGTN G40.................. 105 M6
GTCI KA28 .... 138 A7
HMLTN ML3............................. 155 M4
RUTH G73 .... 129 H1
SHOTTS ML7 .... 113 G7
Reid Ter *SALT* KA21 .... 201 G2
Reidvale St *DEN/PKHD* G31 ...... 12 D3
Reilly Rd *CRG/CRSL/HOU* PA6... 77 J1
Reith Dr *EKILS* G75 .... 14 C8
Remus Pl *BLSH* ML4 .... 133 L4
Renfield La *CGLW* G2................. 11 H1
Renfield St *CGLW* G2................... 5 H8
RNFRW PA4 .... 80 D5
Renfrew Ct *CGLW* G2................. 5 J8 🔢
Renfrew Rd *GOV/IBX* G51 .... 81 J8 🔢
PSLYN/LNWD PA3 .... 9 J1
PSLYN/LNWD PA3 .... 101 M2
RNFRW PA4 .... 81 G8
Renfrew St *CGLW* G2................... 4 F7
CTBR ML5 .... 109 J5

Rennie Pl *EKILN* G74 .... 153 G6
  SALT KA21 .... 200 F1 🔲
Rennie St *KLMNK* KA1 .... 16 F5
Renshaw Pl
  CARD/HILL/MSPK G52 .... 103 H3
Renshaw Rd *BSHPTN* PA7 .... 58 B6
  JNSTN PA5 .... 100 D4
Renton Pk *IRVSE* KA11 .... 204 C2
Renton Rd *DMBTN* G82 .... 36 D1
  GRNK PA15 .... 33 J8
Renton St *COWCAD* G4 .... 5 J6
Renwick Wy *PSTWK* KA9 .... 225 K4
Reservoir Rd *GRK* PA19 .... 31 M3
Resipol Rd
  STPS/GTHM/RID G33 .... 85 L4 🔲
Reston Dr
  CARD/HILL/MSPK G52 .... 103 H3
Reuther Av *RUTH* G73 .... 129 H2 🔲
Revoch Dr *KNTSWD* G13 .... 81 G2
Reynolds Av *EKILS* G75 .... 15 K7
Reynolds Pth *WISHAW* ML2 .... 159 K8 🔲
Rhannan Rd *LNPK/KPK* G44 .... 128 A4
Rhannan Ter *LNPK/KPK* G44 .... 128 A4 🔲
Rhindhouse Pl
  BAIL/MDB/MHD G69 .... 108 D4 🔲
Rhindhouse Rd
  BAIL/MDB/MHD G69 .... 108 D4 🔲
Rhindmuir Av
  BAIL/MDB/MHD G69 .... 108 C4
Rhindmuir Ct
  BAIL/MDB/MHD G69 .... 108 C3 🔲
Rhindmuir Crs
  BAIL/MDB/MHD G69 .... 108 D3 🔲
Rhindmuir Dr
  BAIL/MDB/MHD G69 .... 108 C4
Rhindmuir Gdns
  BAIL/MDB/MHD G69 .... 108 C3 🔲
Rhindmuir Pth
  BAIL/MDB/MHD G69 .... 108 D3 🔲
Rhindmuir Pl
  BAIL/MDB/MHD G69 .... 108 D3 🔲
Rhindmuir Rd
  BAIL/MDB/MHD G69 .... 108 C3
Rhindmuir Wynd
  BAIL/MDB/MHD G69 .... 108 D3 🔲
Rhindsdale Crs
  BAIL/MDB/MHD G69 .... 108 C4
Rhinds St *CTBR* ML5 .... 109 H5
Rhu Road Higher *HBR/GL* G84 .... 20 A4
Rhu Road Lower *HBR/GL* G84 .... 20 A7
Rhyber Av *LNK/LMHG* ML11 .... 199 H4
Rhymer St *SPRGB/BLRNK* G21 .... 6 B7
Rhymie Rd *CAR/SHTL* G52 .... 107 K6 🔲
Riach Gdns *MTHW* ML1 .... 133 J8
Ribblesdale *EKILN* G74 .... 153 J6
Riccarton *EKILS* G75 .... 171 H2
Riccarton Rd *KLMNK* KA1 .... 17 M9
  KLMNK KA1 .... 212 E3
Riccarton St *GVH/MTFL* G42 .... 105 J7
Riccartsbar Av *PSLYS* PA2 .... 8 D7
Rice Wy *MTHW* ML1 .... 158 B5 🔲
Richardland Pl *KLMNK* KA1 .... 17 G6 🔲
Richardson Av *KLMNK* KA1 .... 213 G4
Richie Av *DMBTN* G82 .... 35 G1
Richmond Av
  CRMNK/CLK/EAG G76 .... 151 L2
Richmond Ct *RUTH* G73 .... 129 J1 🔲
Richmond Dr *BLTYR/CAMB* G72 ... 129 L4
  PSLYN/LNWD PA3 .... 100 A4
  RUTH G73 .... 129 K2
Richmond Gdns
  BAIL/MDB/MHD G69 .... 66 B8
Richmond Gv *RUTH* G73 .... 129 J2
Richmond Pl *GLSTN* KA4 .... 214 C4 🔲
  RUTH G73 .... 129 J1
Richmond Rd *RUTH* G73 .... 129 K2 🔲
Richmond St *CGLE* G1 .... 11 L1
  CLYDBK G81 .... 60 C8
Riddell St *CLYDBK* G81 .... 60 C6
  CTBR ML5 .... 110 C2
Riddon Av *KNTSWD* G13 .... 80 E1
Riddon Pl *KNTSWD* G13 .... 80 E1
Riddrie Crs
  STPS/GTHM/RID G33 .... 106 E1
Riddrie Knowes
  STPS/GTHM/RID G33 .... 106 E1
Riddrievale Ct
  STPS/GTHM/RID G33 .... 84 E8
Riddrievale St
  STPS/GTHM/RID G33 .... 84 E8 🔲
Ridgepark Dr *LNK/LMHG* ML11 ... 198 F4
Ried Ct *KLMNKN/STW* KA3 .... 212 E2
Rigby St *CAR/SHTL* G32 .... 13 M3
Rigfoot *IRVSE* KA11 .... 204 B4
Rigghead *KLMNKN/STW* KA3 .... 197 J1
Rigghead Av *CUMB* G67 .... 49 H4
Riggside Rd
  STPS/GTHM/RID G33 .... 85 J7
The Riggs *MLNGV* G62 .... 42 A6 🔲
  PSTWK KA9 .... 221 J8
Riglaw Pl *KNTSWD* G13 .... 80 F4
Rigmuir Rd *GOV/IBX* G51 .... 103 J3 🔲
Rigwoodie Pl *AYRS* KA7 .... 228 E8
Rimmon Crs *SHOTTS* ML7 .... 137 L3 🔲
Rimsdale St *DMNK/BRGTN* G40 ... 12 E4
Ringford St *SPRGB/BLRNK* G21 .... 6 C2
Ripon Dr *KVD/HLHD* G12 .... 82 A3
Risk St *CLYDBK* G81 .... 59 M5
  DMBTN G82 .... 36 E6 🔲
Ritchie Ct *KLMNKN/STW* KA3 .... 207 J6
Ritchie Crs *JNSTN* PA5 .... 100 C6
Ritchie Pk *JNSTN* PA5 .... 100 B8
Ritchie Pl *NMRNS* G77 .... 150 C5 🔲
Ritchie St *GBLS* G5 .... 10 F7
  GTCI KA28 .... 138 A7 🔲
  WISHAW ML2 .... 158 D6 🔲
  WKIL KA23 .... 181 J4
Riverbank Dr *BLSH* ML4 .... 133 K6 🔲
Riverbank Pl *KLMNK* KA1 .... 17 G2
Riverbank St *NMLNS* KA16 .... 215 J2
  PLKSW/MSWD G43 .... 127 J2
River Ct *CRMNK/CLK/EAG* G76 ... 151 M3
Riverdale Gdns *HMLTN* ML3 .... 156 E3 🔲
River Dr *RNFRW* PA4 .... 79 J4
Riverford Rd
  PLKSW/MSWD G43 .... 127 J2
  RUTH G73 .... 106 C8 🔲

River Rd *CAR/SHTL* G32 .... 130 B2
Riversdale La *SCOT* G14 .... 81 G5 🔲
Riverside *ALEX/LLW* G83 .... 25 L1 🔲
  CRG/CRSL/HOU PA6 .... 77 L8
  KKNTL G66 .... 29 H7
  MLNGV G62 .... 42 A7 🔲
Riverside Ct *LNPK/KPK* G44 .... 127 M7
Riverside Gdns
  CRMNK/CLK/EAG G76 .... 151 M4 🔲
Riverside La *DMBTN* G82 .... 36 E6 🔲
Riverside Pl *AYR* KA8 .... 19 G3
  BLTYR/CAMB G72 .... 130 E3 🔲
Riverside Rd *GLSTN* KA4 .... 214 B3
  GRNK PA15 .... 2 F8
  IRVSE KA11 .... 204 D8
  KBRN KA25 .... 143 H8
  KLMNKN/STW KA3 .... 197 L1
  LNK/LMHG ML11 .... 198 B5
  PLKSW/MSWD G43 .... 127 L2
Riverside Ter
  CRMNK/CLK/EAG G76 .... 151 M3 🔲
Riverside Wk *MTHW* ML1 .... 157 M1
Riverside Wy *IRVSE* KA11 .... 208 F1
River St *AYR* KA8 .... 18 F2
River Ter *AYR* KA8 .... 18 F2
Riverton Dr *EKILS* G75 .... 171 H1 🔲
Riverview Dr *GBLS* G5 .... 10 E3
Riverview Gdns *KVGV* G3 .... 10 F3
Riverview Pl *GBLS* G5 .... 10 E3
River Wk *KLWNG* KA13 .... 193 L4
Roaden Av *PSLYS* PA2 .... 123 M2
Roaden Rd *PSLYS* PA2 .... 123 M2
Roadside *CUMB* G67 .... 49 G4
Roadside Pl *AIRDRIE* ML6 .... 89 K1
Robert Burns Av *CLYDBK* G81 .... 60 C6
  MTHW ML1 .... 134 E5
Robert Burns Ct *BEITH* KA15 .... 144 B8
Robert Burns Qd *BLSH* ML4 .... 132 F4
Robert Creighton Pl
  KLMNKN/STW KA3 .... 16 F2
Robert Gilson Gdns
  CTBR ML5 .... 110 B4 🔲
Robertland Rigg
  KLMNKN/STW KA3 .... 197 L1
Robert Noble Pl *KLMNK* KA1 .... 16 B1
Roberton Av
  PLKSD/SHW G41 .... 104 C7 🔲
Roberton St *AIRDRIE* ML6 .... 111 K6
Robert Smillie Crs *LRKH* ML9 .... 176 A8 🔲
Robertson Crs *AYR* KA8 .... 229 K1
  SALT KA21 .... 201 G2 🔲
Robertson Dr *BLSH* ML4 .... 133 G5 🔲
  EKILN G74 .... 15 M1
Robertson La *CGLW* G2 .... 10 F2
Robertson Pl *KLMNK* KA1 .... 16 F5
Robertson St *AIRDRIE* ML6 .... 110 E1
  BRHD/NEIL G78 .... 125 H6
  GRNKW/INVK PA16 .... 32 D3
  HMLTN ML3 .... 155 M4
  KVGV G3 .... 11 G3
Roberts Qd *BLSH* ML4 .... 133 H6 🔲
Roberts St *WISHAW* ML2 .... 159 G6
Robert Stewart Pl
  KLMNK KA1 .... 16 C3 🔲
Robert St *GOV/IBX* G51 .... 104 A2
  PGL PA14 .... 34 E8
  SHOTTS ML7 .... 137 L5
Robert Templeton Dr
  BLTYR/CAMB G72 .... 130 B4
Robert Wynd *WISHAW* ML2 .... 160 A3 🔲
Robin Pl *WISHAW* ML2 .... 159 H6 🔲
Robin Rd *GRNKW/INVK* PA16 .... 32 B4
Robroyston Av
  STPS/GTHM/RID G33 .... 84 E6
Robroyston Rd *BSHPBGS* G64 .... 64 F8
  STPS/GTHM/RID G33 .... 7 M2
  STPS/GTHM/RID G33 .... 84 F2
Robsland Av *AYRS* KA7 .... 18 F9
Roblees Crs *GIF/THBK* G46 .... 127 G6 🔲
Roblee Dr *GIF/THBK* G46 .... 127 H6
Roblee Rd *GIF/THBK* G46 .... 127 G6
Robson Gv *GVH/MTFL* G42 .... 105 H6 🔲
Roche Wy *DALRY* KA24 .... 184 C2
Rochsoles Crs *AIRDRIE* ML6 .... 89 G7 🔲
Rochsoles Dr *AIRDRIE* ML6 .... 88 F7
Rochsolloch Rd *AIRDRIE* ML6 .... 110 D3
Rockall Dr *LNPK/KPK* G44 .... 128 B5
Rockbank Pl *DMNK/BRGTN* G40 ... 12 E5
Rockbank St *DMNK/BRGTN* G40 ... 12 E5
Rockburn Crs *BLSH* ML4 .... 133 G2
Rockburn Dr
  CRMNK/CLK/EAG G76 .... 151 J1
Rockcliffe Pth *AIRDRIE* ML6 .... 111 M8 🔲
Rockcliffe St
  DMNK/BRGTN G40 .... 105 M6 🔲
Rock Dr *KLBCH* PA10 .... 99 H7
Rockfield Pl
  SPRGB/BLRNK G21 .... 84 C4 🔲
Rockfield Rd *SPRGB/BLRNK* G21 ... 84 C4
Rockhampton Av *EKILS* G75 .... 171 H2
Rockland Pk *LARGS* KA30 .... 139 K1
Rockmount Av *BRHD/NEIL* G78 ... 125 K8
  GIF/THBK G46 .... 127 G6
Rockpark Ct *SALT* KA21 .... 201 G2 🔲
Rock St *PPK/MIL* G22 .... 5 J3
Rockwell Av *PSLYS* PA2 .... 124 C1 🔲
Roddinghead Rd *NMRNS* G77 ... 151 G3
The Rodding *LNK/LMHG* ML11 ... 199 H4
Rodger Av *NMRNS* G77 .... 150 C4
Rodger Dr *RUTH* G73 .... 129 G3
Rodger Pl *RUTH* G73 .... 129 G3 🔲
Rodil Av *LNPK/KPK* G44 .... 128 C5
Rodney St *GRNK* PA15 .... 2 C2
  SP COWCAD G4 .... 5 G4
Roebank Dr *BRHD/NEIL* G78 .... 125 J8
Roebank Rd *BEITH* KA15 .... 144 C8
Roebank St *DEN/PKHD* G31 .... 7 G9
Roffey Park Rd *PSLY* PA1 .... 102 D4
Rogart St *DMNK/BRGTN* G40 ... 12 D6
Rogerfield Rd
  BAIL/MDB/MHD G69 .... 108 C2
Rokeby La *KVD/HLHD* G12 .... 4 A8
Roland Crs *NMRNS* G77 .... 150 F6
Roman Av *BSDN* G61 .... 61 M4 🔲
  DRUM G15 .... 61 G8

Roman Ct *BSDN* G61 .... 61 L4
  LNK/LMHG ML11 .... 199 M4
Roman Dr *BLSH* ML4 .... 133 H5
  BSDN G61 .... 61 M4
Roman Gdns *BSDN* G61 .... 61 M4 🔲
Roman Hill Rd *CLYDBK* G81 .... 60 A2
  PL BLSH ML4 .... 132 E6
Roman Rd *AYRS* KA7 .... 229 J5
  BSDN G61 .... 61 M4 🔲
  CLYDBK G81 .... 60 A3
  KKNTL G66 .... 65 H1
  MTHW ML1 .... 157 L2 🔲
Roman Wy *GLSTN* KA4 .... 214 C4
Romney Av *LNPK/KPK* G44 .... 128 C4 🔲
Rona Av *PGL* PA14 .... 55 H2
Ronaldsay Dr *BSHPBGS* G64 .... 64 D7
Ronaldsay Pl *CUMB* G67 .... 68 D1
Ronaldsay St *PPK/MIL* G22 .... 83 J2
Ronaldshaw Pk *AYRS* KA7 .... 18 D7
Rona Pl *KLMNKN/STW* KA3 .... 207 H4
Rona St *SPRGB/BLRNK* G21 .... 7 C4
Rona Ter *BLTYR/CAMB* G72 .... 129 M6
Ronay St *PPK/MIL* G22 .... 83 K2
  WISHAW ML2 .... 159 J4
Rook Rd *GRNKW/INVK* PA16 .... 32 A4 🔲
Rooksdell Av *PSLYS* PA2 .... 101 J8 🔲
Ropework La *CGLE* G1 .... 11 J4
Rorison Pl *LRKH* ML9 .... 176 F8 🔲
Rosa Burn Av *EKILS* G75 .... 171 H5
Rosa Pl *SALT* KA21 .... 191 M7
Rosebank Av *BLTYR/CAMB* G72 ... 131 L8
  KKNTL G66 .... 45 L8
Rosebank Crs *AYRS* KA7 .... 18 E9
Rosebank Dr *BLTYR/CAMB* G72 ... 130 C5
  UD/BTH/TAN G71 .... 132 C2
Rosebank Gdns *IRVSE* KA11 .... 203 M2
Rosebank Pl *HMLTN* ML3 .... 156 A6 🔲
  KLMNKN/STW KA3 .... 206 F1
  UD/BTH/TAN G71 .... 108 B7 🔲
Rosebank Rd *BLSH* ML4 .... 133 H1
  WISHAW ML2 .... 177 J3
Rosebank Ter
  BAIL/MDB/MHD G69 .... 108 F5
  KLMCLM PA13 .... 55 K8
Roseberry La *HMLTN* ML3 .... 156 A5
Roseberry Pl *HMLTN* ML3 .... 156 A5
Roseberry Rd *AIRDRIE* ML6 .... 111 K3
Roseberry St *GBLS* G5 .... 105 L7
Roseburn Ct *CUMB* G67 .... 49 M4
Rose Crs *GRK* PA19 .... 31 K3 🔲
  HMLTN ML3 .... 155 M5
Rose Dl *BSHPBGS* G64 .... 84 B1 🔲
Rosedale *EKILN* G74 .... 153 J6
Rosedale Av *PSLYS* PA2 .... 123 K3
Rosedale Dr
  BAIL/MDB/MHD G69 .... 108 A5
Rosedale Gdns *HBR/GL* G84 .... 20 F8 🔲
  MRYH/FIRH G20 .... 82 C1 🔲
Rosedale St *LNK/LMHG* ML11 ... 198 F7
Rosedene Ter *BLSH* ML4 .... 133 G3 🔲
Rosefield Gdns
  UD/BTH/TAN G71 .... 131 L2
Rosegreen Crs *BLSH* ML4 .... 133 C1
Rosehall Av *CTBR* ML5 .... 110 B5
Rosehall Rd *SHOTTS* ML7 .... 137 K6
Rosehall Ter *WISHAW* ML2 .... 158 E8 🔲
Rosehill Dr *CUMB* G67 .... 68 A2
Rosehill Rd *BSHPBGS* G64 .... 64 C1
Roseholm Av *IRV* KA12 .... 203 L4
Rose Knowe Rd *GVH/MTFL* G42 ... 128 D1
Roselea Gdns *KNTSWD* G13 .... 81 M2
Roselea Pl *BLTYR/CAMB* G72 .... 131 J8
Roselea Rd *UD/BTH/TAN* G71 ... 131 L1 🔲
Roselea St *LRKH* ML9 .... 176 B5
Rosemary Crs *EKILN* G74 .... 153 K5 🔲
Rosemary Pl *EKILN* G74 .... 153 K5 🔲
Rosemount *BALLOCH* G68 .... 48 F4
Rosemount Av *NMRNS* G77 .... 150 D7
Rose Mount Ct *AIRDRIE* ML6 .... 111 J1
Rosemount Dr *IRVSE* KA11 .... 216 D1 🔲
Rosemount La *BRWEIR* PA11 .... 98 B3
Rosemount Mdw
  UD/BTH/TAN G71 .... 131 L7
Rosemount Pl *GRK* PA19 .... 31 G3 🔲
Rosemount St *SPRGB/BLRNK* G21 ... 6 D7
Rosendale Wy
  BLTYR/CAMB G72 .... 155 L2 🔲
Roseneath Dr *HBR/GL* G84 .... 20 B7 🔲
Roseneath St
  GRNKW/INVK PA16 .... 32 C1 🔲
Roseness Pl
  STPS/GTHM/RID G33 .... 107 G3 🔲
Rosenheath Ga *EKILN* G74 .... 14 B1 🔲
Rosepark Av *UD/BTH/TAN* G71 ... 132 C3
Rose St *CGLW* G2 .... 5 C8
  CUMB G67 .... 68 B3
  GRNKW/INVK PA16 .... 32 C5
  KKNTL G66 .... 65 K1 🔲
  MTHW ML1 .... 158 A4
Rosevale Crs *BLSH* ML4 .... 133 J5
  HMLTN ML3 .... 156 B7 🔲
Rosevale Rd *BSDN* G61 .... 61 L5
Rosevale St *PTCK* G11 .... 82 A7
Rosewood Av *BLSH* ML4 .... 133 H2 🔲
  PSLYS PA2 .... 101 H8
Rosewood Pth *BLSH* ML4 .... 132 E4 🔲
Rosewood St *KNTSWD* G13 .... 81 L2 🔲
Roseyard St *PGL* PA14 .... 34 C8 🔲
Roslea Dr *DEN/PKHD* G31 .... 12 F2
Roslin Ct *KLMCLM* PA13 .... 75 J2 🔲
Roslin St *GRNK* PA15 .... 2 C2
Roslyn Dr *BAIL/MDB/MHD* G69 ... 108 F4
Rosneath Rd *PGL* PA14 .... 54 D1 🔲
Rosneath St *GOV/IBX* G51 .... 104 A1 🔲
Ross Av *KKNTL* G66 .... 65 M1
  RNFRW PA4 .... 80 A8
Rossbank Rd *PGL* PA14 .... 34 A7
Ross Crs *MTHW* ML1 .... 157 J4
Ross Dr *AIRDRIE* ML6 .... 110 E5
  MTHW ML1 .... 157 J4 🔲
  UD/BTH/TAN G71 .... 109 J8
Rossendale Ct
  PLKSW/MSWD G43 .... 127 J1 🔲

Rossendale Rd
  PLKSW/MSWD G43 .... 127 J1 🔲
Ross Gdns *MTHW* ML1 .... 157 J4
Rosshall Av *PSLY* PA1 .... 102 C5
Ross Hall Pl *RNFRW* PA4 .... 80 D6
Rosshill Av
  CARD/HILL/MSPK G52 .... 102 F4
Rosshill Rd
  CARD/HILL/MSPK G52 .... 102 F4
Rossie Crs *BSHPBGS* G64 .... 84 C1
Rossie Gv *NMRNS* G77 .... 150 B4 🔲
Rossland Crs *BSHPTN* PA7 .... 58 A6
Rosslea *GIF/THBK* G46 .... 127 J7
Rosslyn Av *EKILN* G74 .... 129 J2
  RUTH G73 .... 156 A5 🔲
Rosslyn Ct *HMLTN* ML3 .... 155 A5
Rosslyn Pl *AYR* KA8 .... 225 H6
Rosslyn Rd *BSDN* G61 .... 61 H3
Rosslyn Ter *KVD/HLHD* G12 .... 82 C5
Ross Pl *RUTH* G73 .... 129 K5
Ross Rd *SALT* KA21 .... 191 M7
Ross St *AYR* KA8 .... 225 H7
  CGLE G1 .... 11 M4
  CTBR ML5 .... 110 A2 🔲
  PSLY PA1 .... 9 L6
Ross Ter *HMLTN* ML3 .... 157 J8
Rostan Rd *PLKSW/MSWD* G43 ... 127 J4
Rosyth Rd *GBLS* G5 .... 105 L7
Rosyth St *GBLS* G5 .... 105 L7
Rotherwick Dr *PSLY* PA1 .... 102 E5
Rotherwood Av *KNTSWD* G13 ... 61 K3
  PSLYS PA2 .... 123 M1 🔲
Rotherwood La *KNTSWD* G13 ... 61 J7 🔲
Rotherwood Pl *KNTSWD* G13 ... 81 K1 🔲
Rothesay Crs *CTBR* ML5 .... 110 B6
Rothesay Pl *CTBR* ML5 .... 110 B5 🔲
  EKILN G74 .... 14 E5
  KLMKNKN/STW KA3 .... 206 F6
Rothesay Rd *GRNKW/INVK* PA16 ... 31 M4
Rothesay St *EKILS* G75 .... 14 E5
Rothes Dr *SMSTN* G23 .... 82 D1
Rothes Pl *MRYH/FIRH* G20 .... 62 C8
Rottenburn Br
  GRNKW/INVK PA16 .... 71 M3
Rottenrow *CGLE* G1 .... 5 L9
  COWCAD G4 .... 12 A1
Rottenrow East *COWCAD* G4 ... 11 M1
Roughcraig St *AIRDRIE* ML6 .... 89 C7
Roughlea Pl *TROON* KA10 .... 216 F3 🔲
Roughrigg Rd *AIRDRIE* ML6 .... 112 A3
Roukenburn St *GIF/THBK* G46 ... 126 E5
Rouken Glen Rd *GIF/THBK* G46 ... 126 E5
The Roundel *LARGS* KA30 .... 115 L5
  WISHAW ML2 .... 159 J2
Roundhill Dr *JNSTN* PA5 .... 100 E6
Roundknowe Rd
  UD/BTH/TAN G71 .... 108 C8
Round Riding Rd *DMBTN* G82 ... 37 C5
Routenburn Rd *LARGS* KA30 ... 115 H1
Rowallan Crs *PSTWK* KA9 .... 225 K2
Rowallan Dr *KLMNKN/STW* KA3 ... 207 C5
Rowallan Gdns
  KLMNKN/STW KA3 .... 207 H3 🔲
  PTCK G11 .... 81 M6
Rowallan La
  CRMNK/CLK/EAG G76 .... 151 L2 🔲
  PTCK G11 .... 81 M6
Rowallan La East *PTCK* G11 .... 82 A6
Rowallan Rd *GIF/THBK* G46 .... 126 F7
Rowallan St *HBR/GL* G84 .... 20 B6 🔲
Rowallan Ter
  STPS/GTHM/RID G33 .... 85 H5 🔲
Rowan Av *KKNTL* G66 .... 45 H4
  RNFRW PA4 .... 80 C5
Rowanbank Pl *CTBR* ML5 .... 110 B1 🔲
Rowanbank Rd *PSTWK* KA9 .... 225 L2
Rowan Ct *BLTYR/CAMB* G72 ... 130 F5 🔲
Rowan Crs *AYRS* KA7 .... 19 L9
  KKNTL G66 .... 65 J4
Rowandale Av
  BAIL/MDB/MHD G69 .... 108 A5
Rowand Av *GIF/THBK* G46 .... 127 J7
Rowanden Av *BLSH* ML4 .... 133 G3
Rowan Dr *BSDN* G61 .... 61 M2
  CLYDBK G81 .... 59 M5
  DMBTN G82 .... 36 A5
Rowan Gdns *PLKSD/SHW* G41 ... 104 B5
Rowan Ga *PSLYS* PA2 .... 9 J9
Rowan Gv *HMLTN* ML3 .... 174 F6
Rowanhill Pl *KLMNK* KA1 .... 16 B6
Rowanlea Av *PSLYS* PA2 .... 123 K2
Rowanlea Dr *GIF/THBK* G46 .... 127 K5
Rowanpark Dr *BRHD/NEIL* G78 ... 125 G4
Rowan Pl *BLTYR/CAMB* G72 ... 130 C3 🔲
  BLTYR/CAMB G72 .... 155 K1
  CTBR ML5 .... 109 L5 🔲
  KLMNK KA1 .... 16 A6
Rowan Ri *HMLTN* ML3 .... 156 F7 🔲
Rowan Rd *CUMB* G67 .... 49 K6
  PLKSD/SHW G41 .... 104 B5
  PSLYN/LNWD PA3 .... 99 M2
Rowans Gdns *UD/BTH/TAN* G71 ... 132 B5
Rowanside Ter *ARD* KA22 .... 191 J6
The Rowans *BSHPBGS* G64 .... 63 M7 🔲
Rowan St *BEITH* KA15 .... 168 C1
  GRNKW/INVK PA16 .... 32 C4
  PSLYS PA2 .... 9 J9
  WISHAW ML2 .... 159 H4
Rowan Ter *IRV* KA12 .... 203 K5 🔲
Rowantree Av *MTHW* ML1 .... 134 D2
  RUTH G73 .... 129 H4 🔲
  UD/BTH/TAN G71 .... 132 C2
Rowantree Av *ALEX/LLW* G83 ... 25 L1 🔲
Rowantreehill Rd *KLMCLM* PA13 ... 75 K1
Rowantree Pl *JNSTN* PA5 .... 99 M8 🔲
  KKNTL G66 .... 44 E2
  LRKH ML9 .... 176 D7 🔲
Rowantree Rd *JNSTN* PA5 .... 99 M8
Rowantree Ter *KKNTL* G66 .... 44 E2
  MTHW ML1 .... 134 D4
Rowanwood Crs *CTBR* ML5 .... 109 K4
Rowena Av *KNTSWD* G13 .... 61 K3
Roxburgh Av *GRNK* PA15 .... 2 B5
Roxburgh Dr *BSDN* G61 .... 61 L2
  CTBR ML5 .... 110 D5 🔲
Roxburgh Pk *EKILN* G74 .... 15 H4
Roxburgh Rd *KLMNK* KA1 .... 212 E3
  PSLYS PA2 .... 123 K2

Roxburgh St *GRNK* PA15 .... 2 B4
  KVD/HLHD G12 .... 82 D6
Royal Av *LARGS* KA30 .... 115 K5
Royal Crs *KVGV* G3 .... 4 A8
Royal Dr *HMLTN* ML3 .... 157 G7
Royal Exchange Ct *CGLE* G1 .... 11 J1
Royal Exchange Sq *CGLE* G1 .... 11 J1
Royal Inch Ter *RNFRW* PA4 .... 80 D4 🔲
Royal St *GRK* PA19 .... 31 L1
Royal Ter *KVGV* G3 .... 4 A7
  WISHAW ML2 .... 159 J2
Royal Terrace La *KVGV* G3 .... 4 A7
Royellen Av *HMLTN* ML3 .... 155 M7
Roystonhill *SPRGB/BLRNK* G21 ... 6 C7
Royston Rd *COWCAD* G4 .... 6 B7
  SPRGB/BLRNK G21 .... 6 D6
  STPS/GTHM/RID G33 .... 7 L3
Royston Sq *SPRGB/BLRNK* G21 ... 6 B6
Roy St *SPRGB/BLRNK* G21 .... 5 L3
Rozelle Av *DRUM* G15 .... 61 H6 🔲
  NMRNS G77 .... 150 B5
Rozelle Dr *NMRNS* G77 .... 150 B5 🔲
Rozelle Pl *NMRNS* G77 .... 150 B5 🔲
Rozelle Ter *AYRS* KA7 .... 229 H8
Rubie Crs *IRV* KA12 .... 208 C1
Rubislaw Dr *BSDN* G61 .... 61 L6
Ruby St *DMNK/BRGTN* G40 .... 12 E8
Ruchazie Pl
  STPS/GTHM/RID G33 .... 106 F1 🔲
Ruchazie Rd
  STPS/GTHM/RID G33 .... 106 F1
Ruchill Pl *MRYH/FIRH* G20 .... 82 F4 🔲
Ruchill St *MRYH/FIRH* G20 .... 82 E4
Rue End St *GRNK* PA15 .... 2 F5
Ruel St *LNPK/KPK* G44 .... 128 A2
Rufflees Av *BRHD/NEIL* G78 .... 125 K6
Rugby Av *KNTSWD* G13 .... 81 H1
Rugby Crs *KLMNK* KA1 .... 16 B6
Rugby Rd *KLMNK* KA1 .... 16 B6
Rullion Pl
  STPS/GTHM/RID G33 .... 106 F1 🔲
Rumford St *DMNK/BRGTN* G40 ... 12 C9
Runciman Pl *EKILN* G74 .... 154 B5
Rupert St *COWCAD* G4 .... 4 D5
Rushyhill St
  SPRGB/BLRNK G21 .... 84 A5 🔲
Ruskin La *KVD/HLHD* G12 .... 4 A2
Ruskin Pl *KSYTH* G65 .... 47 K1 🔲
Ruskin Ter *KVD/HLHD* G12 .... 4 A3
Russell Colt St *CTBR* ML5 .... 110 A1
Russell Ct *KLMNKN/STW* KA3 ... 207 J6
Russell Dr *ALEX/LLW* G83 .... 25 J2 🔲
  AYR KA8 .... 19 G1
  BSDN G61 .... 61 L3
  DALRY KA24 .... 184 D1
Russell Gdns
  UD/BTH/TAN G71 .... 132 A3 🔲
Russell La *WISHAW* ML2 .... 159 G7 🔲
Russell Pl *CRMNK/CLK/EAG* G76 ... 152 A4
  EKILS G75 .... 14 A8
  PSLYN/LNWD PA3 .... 99 M3
  LNK/LMHG ML11 .... 199 H4
Russell St *AIRDRIE* ML6 .... 111 L7
  AYR KA8 .... 19 H1
  BLSH ML4 .... 133 K4
  HMLTN ML3 .... 155 M4
  JNSTN PA5 .... 100 A6 🔲
  PSLYN/LNWD PA3 .... 101 K2
  WISHAW ML2 .... 159 G7
Rutherford Av *BSDN* G61 .... 61 H1
Rutherford Ct *CLYDBK* G81 .... 60 A7
Rutherford La *EKILS* G75 .... 15 G7
Rutherford Sq *EKILS* G75 .... 15 G6 🔲
Ruthven Av *GIF/THBK* G46 .... 127 K8
Ruthven La *KVD/HLHD* G12 .... 82 C6
Ruthven Pl *BSHPBGS* G64 .... 84 C1 🔲
Ruthven St *KVD/HLHD* G12 .... 82 C6
Rutland Crs *GOV/IBX* G51 .... 10 B4
Rutland Pl *GOV/IBX* G51 .... 10 A4
Ryan Rd *BSHPBGS* G64 .... 64 B8 🔲
  WMYSB PA18 .... 70 A1
Ryan Wy *RUTH* G73 .... 129 J6
Ryat Dr *NMRNS* G77 .... 150 C3
Ryat Gn *NMRNS* G77 .... 150 C4 🔲
Ryatt Linn *ERSK* PA8 .... 58 F8
Rydal Gv *EKILS* G75 .... 170 F3
Rydal Pl *EKILS* G75 .... 170 F3
Ryden Mains Rd *AIRDRIE* ML6 ... 88 D5
Ryde Rd *WISHAW* ML2 .... 159 J6
Rye Crs *SPRGB/BLRNK* G21 .... 84 B4
Ryecroft Dr
  BAIL/MDB/MHD G69 .... 108 B4
Ryedale Pl *DRUM* G15 .... 61 G5
Ryefield Av *CTBR* ML5 .... 109 K2
  JNSTN PA5 .... 99 K8
Ryefield Pl *JNSTN* PA5 .... 99 K8 🔲
Ryefield Rd
  SPRGB/BLRNK G21 .... 84 B4
Ryehill Pl *SPRGB/BLRNK* G21 ... 84 C4 🔲
Ryehill Rd *SPRGB/BLRNK* G21 ... 7 J1
  SPRGB/BLRNK G21 .... 84 C4
Ryemount Rd
  SPRGB/BLRNK G21 .... 84 C4
Rye Rd *SPRGB/BLRNK* G21 .... 84 B4
Ryeside Rd *DALRY* KA24 .... 166 C8 🔲
Ryeside Rd *SPRGB/BLRNK* G21 ... 84 B5
Ryewraes Rd
  PSLYN/LNWD PA3 .... 100 B3 🔲
Rylands Dr *CAR/SHTL* G32 .... 107 K5
Rylands Gdns *CAR/SHTL* G32 ... 107 L5 🔲
Rylees Crs
  CARD/HILL/MSPK G52 .... 102 E2
Rylees Pl
  CARD/HILL/MSPK G52 .... 102 E3
Rylees Rd
  CARD/HILL/MSPK G52 .... 102 E3
Rysland Av *NMRNS* G77 .... 150 E4
Rysland Crs *NMRNS* G77 .... 150 E4 🔲
Ryvra Rd *KNTSWD* G13 .... 81 K3

S

Sachelcourt Av *BSHPTN* PA7 .... 58 B7
Sackville Av *KNTSWD* G13 .... 81 M4
Sackville La *KNTSWD* G13 .... 81 M4 🔲
Saddell Rd *DRUM* G15 .... 61 H5

Saffron Crs *WISHAW* ML2 .... 158 D8
Saffronhall Av *HMLTN* ML3 ...... 156 D5
Saffronhall La *HMLTN* ML3 ...... 156 D5
St Abb's Dr *PSLYS* PA2 .... 101 G8
St Aidan's Pth *WISHAW* ML2 ...... 159 J3
St Andrew's Av *BSHPBGS* G64 ...... 63 L7
   PSTWK KA9 .... 225 J3
   UD/BTH/TAN G71 .... 132 A8
St Andrew's Brae *DMBTN* G82 .... 37 H3
St Andrews Ct *EKILS* G75 .... 171 J3
St Andrew's Crs *DMBTN* G82 ...... 37 H4
   PLKSD/SHW G41 .... 10 B7
   PSLYN/LNWD PA3 .... 79 J8
St Andrews Dr *BALLOCH* G68 .... 49 H3
   BRWEIR PA11 .... 98 B3
   BSDN G61 .... 61 K2
   GRK PA19 .... 31 G3
   HMLTN ML3 .... 155 K5
   PLKSD/SHW G41 .... 104 C7
   PSLYN/LNWD PA3 .... 101 K1
St Andrew's Dr West
   PSLYN/LNWD PA3 .... 101 J1
St Andrew's Gdns *AIRDRIE* ML6 .. 111 H1
   DALRY KA24 .... 184 B3
St Andrew's La *CGLE* G1 .... 11 L3
   GRK PA19 .... 31 G3
St Andrews Pl *ARD* KA22 .... 191 K5
   PLKSD/SHW G41 .... 10 C8
   RNFRW PA4 .... 80 C6
St Andrew's Sq *CGLE* G1 .... 11 L4
   CGLE G1 .... 11 L3
   KLMNK KA1 .... 16 F7
   MTHW ML1 .... 134 A4
St Andrew St *GRNK* PA15 .... 3 C6
St Andrews Wy *IRVSE* KA11 ...... 208 D1
   WISHAW ML2 .... 159 J3
St Andrews Wynd *HBR/GL* G84 .. 20 E6
St Annes Av *ERSK* PA8 .... 79 K1
St Annes Wynd *ERSK* PA8 .... 79 J1
St Ann's Dr *GIF/THBK* G46 .... 127 J7
St Barchan's Rd *KLBCH* PA10 .... 99 H7
St Blane's Dr *RUTH* G73 .... 128 E3
St Boswell's Crs *PSLYS* PA2 ...... 101 G8
St Boswells Dr *CTBR* ML5 .... 110 D5
St Bride's Av *UD/BTH/TAN* G71 .. 132 C2
St Bride's Dr *WKIL* KA23 .... 181 K4
St Bride's Rd
   PLKSW/MSWD G43 .... 127 K4
   WKIL KA23 .... 181 J3
St Brides Wy *UD/BTH/TAN* G71 .. 132 A5
St Bryde St *EKILN* G74 .... 15 G2
St Catherines Crs *SHOTTS* ML7 .. 137 K3
St Catherines Rd *AYR* KA8 ...... 225 M7
   GIF/THBK G46 .... 127 J7
St Clair Av *GIF/THBK* G46 .... 127 J6
St Clair St *MRYH/FIRH* G20 ...... 4 D4
St Clair Ter *TROON* KA10 .... 216 A7
St Columba Dr *KKNTL* G66 .... 65 L2
St Cuthbert's Rd *PSTWK* KA9 .... 225 J3
St Cyrus Gdns *BSHPBGS* G64 .... 64 C8
St Cyrus Rd *BSHPBGS* G64 .... 64 C8
St Davids Dr *AIRDRIE* ML6 .... 111 H1
St David's Pl *LRKH* ML9 .... 176 A6
St Denis Wy *CTBR* ML5 .... 109 M1
St Edmunds Gv *MLNGV* G62 ...... 42 A6
St Enoch Av *UD/BTH/TAN* G71 .. 132 C1
St Enoch Pl *CGLE* G1 .... 11 H3
St Fillans Dr *CRG/CRSL/HOU* PA6 .. 77 C7
St Fillans Rd
   STPS/GTHM/RID G33 .... 85 J4
St Flanan Rd *KKNTL* G66 .... 46 D7
St George's Rd *AYR* KA8 .... 225 H6
   CGLW G2 .... 4 D8
   COWCAD G4 .... 4 E5
   KVGV G3 .... 4 D7
St Germains *BSDN* G61 .... 61 L5
St Giles Pk *HMLTN* ML3 .... 156 B7
St Giles Wy *HMLTN* ML3 .... 156 B7
St Helena Crs *CLYDBK* G81 ...... 60 C3
St Inan Av *IRV* KA14 .... 203 K6
St Inan's Dr *BEITH* KA15 .... 144 C8
St Ives Rd *BAIL/MDB/MHD* G69 .. 66 F6
St James Av *PSLYN/LNWD* PA3 .. 101 H1
St James Ct *CTBR* ML5 .... 109 L6
St James St *COWCAD* G4 .... 5 M9
St James' St *PSLYN/LNWD* PA3 .. 8 F2
St James Wy *CTBR* ML5 .... 109 L6
St Joan's Crs *KLWNG* KA13 ...... 193 L7
St John's Ct *PLKSD/SHW* G41 .... 10 A8
St John's Qd *PLKSD/SHW* G41 .. 10 B8
St John's Rd *GRK* PA19 .... 31 L1
   PLKSD/SHW G41 .... 104 D6
St John St *AYRS* KA7 .... 18 E2
   CTBR ML5 .... 110 A2
   PSTWK KA9 .... 225 J1
St Joseph's Ct *SPRGB/BLRNK* G21 .. 6 D7
St Joseph's Vw
   SPRGB/BLRNK G21 .... 6 D8
St Kenneth Dr *GOV/IBX* G51 .... 103 K1
St Kentigerns Rd
   LNK/LMHG ML11 .... 199 H4
St Kilda Bank *IRVSE* KA11 .... 203 M7
St Kilda Dr *SCOT* G14 .... 81 L5
St Kilda Pl *IRVSE* KA11 .... 204 A7
St Kilda Wy *WISHAW* ML2 .... 159 L4
St Lawrence Pk *EKILS* G75 .... 14 B4
St Lawrence Pl *SALT* KA21 .... 192 A8
St Lawrence Wk *GRNK* PA15 ...... 3 H6
St Leonard's Ct *AYRS* KA7 .... 19 G9
St Leonard's Dr
   GIF/THBK G46 .... 127 J6
   EKILN G74 .... 15 G4
   LNK/LMHG ML11 .... 199 H5
St Leonard St *LNK/LMHG* ML11 .. 199 H5
St Leonards Wk *CTBR* ML5 .... 110 C6
St Luke's Av *CARLUKE* ML8 ...... 188 C1
St Machan's Wy *KKNTL* G66 ...... 29 K8
St Machars Rd *BRWEIR* PA11 .... 98 E2
St Margaret Av *DALRY* KA24 .... 184 A2
St Margaret's Dr
   WISHAW ML2 .... 158 E8
St Margaret's Pl *CGLE* G1 .... 11 K4
St Margaret's Rd *ARD* KA22 .... 191 K6
St Mark Gdns *CAR/SHTL* G32 .. 106 F4
St Mark's Ct *WISHAW* ML2 ...... 159 J3

St Mark St
   DMNK/BRGTN G40 .... 12 E5
   KLMNK KA1 .... 16 E5
St Marnock St
   CAR/SHTL G32 .... 106 E4
St Martins Ga *CTBR* ML5 .... 110 A5
St Mary's Ga *BRHD/NEIL* G78 .. 125 J7
St Marys Gdns
   BRHD/NEIL G78 .... 125 K7
St Mary's La *CGLW* G2 .... 11 H1
St Mary's Pl *SALT* KA21 .... 191 L8
St Mary's Rd *BLSH* ML4 .... 132 E4
   BSHPBGS G64 .... 63 L7
St Mary's Wy *DMBTN* G82 .... 36 F6
St Maur's Crs
   KLMNKN/STW KA3 .... 206 E5
St Maur's Pl *KLMNKN/STW* KA3 .. 206 E6
St Medan's Pl *SALT* KA21 .... 191 M8
St Meddans Crs *TROON* KA10 .. 216 D6
St Meddans St *TROON* KA10 .... 216 C7
St Michael Dr *HBR/GL* G84 .... 20 E7
St Michael Rd *WISHAW* ML2 .... 158 B8
St Mirren's Rd *KSYTH* G65 .... 47 L1
St Mirren St *PSLY* PA1 .... 9 H4
St Monance St
   SPRGB/BLRNK G21 .... 83 M4
St Mungo Av *CGLE* G1 .... 5 K8
   COWCAD G4 .... 5 M8
Saint Mungo Ct *BRWEIR* PA11 .. 98 E1
St Mungo Pl *COWCAD* G4 .... 5 M8
   HMLTN ML3 .... 155 K5
St Mungo's *LNK/LMHG* ML11 .... 199 G6
St Mungo's Rd *CUMB* G67 .... 48 F8
St Mungo St *BSHPBGS* G64 ...... 83 M1
St Nicholas Rd *LNK/LMHG* ML11 .. 199 H4
   PSTWK KA9 .... 225 H2
St Ninian's *LNK/LMHG* ML11 .... 199 H4
St Ninian's Crs *PSLYS* PA2 .... 9 K9
St Ninian's Dr *ARD* KA22 .... 191 K5
St Ninian's Pl *HMLTN* ML3 ...... 155 M6
St Ninian's Rd *HMLTN* ML3 ...... 155 M6
   PSLYS PA2 .... 9 J9
   PSTWK KA9 .... 225 H3
St Ninian Ter *GBLS* G5 .... 11 J6
St Palladius Ter *DALRY* KA24 .... 184 D1
St Patrick's Ct *LNK/LMHG* ML11 .. 198 F5
St Patrick's Rd
   LNK/LMHG ML11 .... 198 E5
St Peter's La *CGLW* G2 .... 10 F1
St Phillans Av *AYR* KA8 .... 19 H7
St Quivox Rd *PSTWK* KA9 .... 225 J1
St Ronan's Dr *HMLTN* ML3 ...... 174 C1
   PLKSD/SHW G41 .... 104 D8
   RUTH G73 .... 129 J3
St Stephens Av *RUTH* G73 .... 129 K6
St Stephen's Crs *RUTH* G73 ...... 129 K6
St Stephen's Pl *SVSTN* KA20 .... 192 F7
St Teiling *LNK/LMHG* ML11 ...... 199 H3
St Vigeans Av *NMRNS* G77 ...... 150 B5
St Vincent Crs *AYRS* KA7 .... 228 F7
   KVGV G3 .... 104 D1
St Vincent Crescent La *KVGV* G3 .. 4 A8
St Vincent La *CGLW* G2 .... 4 F9
St Vincent Pl *CGLE* G1 .... 11 J1
   EKILS G75 .... 171 G1
   LNK/LMHG ML11 .... 199 H5
   MTHW ML1 .... 157 L2
St Vincent St *CGLW* G2 .... 4 F9
   KVGV G3 .... 4 C9
St Vincent Ter *KVGV* G3 .... 4 D9
St Winifred's Wy
   WISHAW ML2 .... 159 G5
St Winning's La *KLWNG* KA13 .. 193 K6
St Winning's Rd *KLWNG* KA13 .. 193 K6
St Winning's Well
   KLWNG KA13 .... 193 K6
St Winnoc Rd *LOCHW* PA12 .... 120 D6
Salamanca St *DEN/PKHD* G31 .. 13 M5
Salasaig Ct
   STPS/GTHM/RID G33 .... 107 G2
Salen St *CARD/HILL/MSPK* G52 .. 103 M4
Saline St *AIRDRIE* ML6 .... 110 D3
Salisbury *EKILN* G74 .... 154 D5
Salisbury Av *KLMNK* KA1 .... 212 F2
Salisbury Crs *MTHW* ML1 .... 133 H8
Salisbury Pl *CLYDBK* G81 .... 59 K4
   PSTWK KA9 .... 225 J1
Salisbury St *GBLS* G5 .... 11 H7
Salkeld St *GBLS* G5 .... 11 G7
Salmona St *PPK/MIL* G22 .... 5 G1
Salmon St *GRNK* PA15 .... 2 E4
Saltaire Av *UD/BTH/TAN* G71 .. 132 B4
Saltcoats Rd *SVSTN* KA20 .... 201 J1
Salterland Rd *BRHD/NEIL* G78 .. 125 L4
Saltfield La *AYR* KA8 .... 224 F7
Saltire Crs *LRKH* ML9 .... 176 C7
Saltmarket *CGLE* G1 .... 11 K4
Saltmarket Pl *CGLE* G1 .... 11 K4
Saltoun La *KVD/HLHD* G12 ...... 82 D6
Saltoun St *KVD/HLHD* G12 ...... 82 D6
Saltpans Rd *AYR* KA8 .... 224 F6
Salvia St *BLTYR/CAMB* G72 ...... 129 L3
Samson St *KLMNK* KA1 .... 17 J6
Sandaig Rd
   STPS/GTHM/RID G33 .... 107 L4
Sandalwood Av *EKILN* G74 ...... 153 K5
Sandalwood Ct *EKILN* G74 ...... 153 K5
Sanda Pl *KLMNKN/STW* KA3 .... 207 G4
   SALT KA21 .... 191 M7
Sanda St *MRYH/FIRH* G20 .... 4 A1
Sandbank Av *MRYH/FIRH* G20 .. 82 D2
Sandbank Crs *ALEX/LLW* G83 .. 25 M4
   MRYH/FIRH G20 .... 82 D3
Sandbank Dr *MRYH/FIRH* G20 .. 82 D2
Sandbank St *MRYH/FIRH* G20 .. 82 D2
Sandbank Ter *MRYH/FIRH* G20 .. 82 D2
Sandbed St *KLMNK* KA1 .... 16 F4
Sandend *PLK/PH/NH* G53 .... 126 A2
Sanderling Rd *JNSTN* PA5 .... 122 D3
Sanderling Rd
   PSLYN/LNWD PA3 .... 101 K1
Sanderson Av *IRV* KA12 .... 203 H8
   UD/BTH/TAN G71 .... 132 D3
Sandfield Av *MLNGV* G62 .... 42 A6
Sandfield Rd *PSTWK* KA9 .... 225 J1
Sandfield St *MRYH/FIRH* G20 .. 82 E4
Sandgate *AYRS* KA7 .... 18 E3
Sandgate *CAR/SHTL* G32 .... 107 K6

Sandhaven Pl
   PLK/PH/NH G53 .... 126 A2
Sandhaven Rd *PLK/PH/NH* G53 .. 126 A2
Sandhead Crs *AIRDRIE* ML6 .... 111 L8
Sandhill Gdns *TROON* KA10 .... 216 F6
Sandholes Rd *JNSTN* PA5 .... 99 J4
Sandholes St *PSLY* PA1 .... 8 D4
Sandholm Pl *SCOT* G14 .... 80 F4
Sandholm Ter *SCOT* G14 .... 80 F4
Sandiefield Rd *GBLS* G5 .... 11 J7
Sandielands Av *ERSK* PA8 .... 79 K2
Sandilands Crs *MTHW* ML1 .... 157 H4
Sandilands St *CAR/SHTL* G32 .. 107 H4
Sandmill St *SPRGB/BLRNK* G21 .. 6 E6
Sandpiper Dr *EKILS* G75 .... 171 G4
Sandpiper Pl *EKILS* G75 .... 171 G4
Sandpiper Rd *LOCHW* PA12 .... 120 C7
Sandra Rd *BSHPBGS* G64 .... 64 C7
Sandray Av *PGL* PA14 .... 55 H3
Sandringham Av *NMRNS* G77 .. 151 G3
Sandringham Dr *JNSTN* PA5 .... 100 B8
Sandringham La
   KVD/HLHD G12 .... 82 D6
Sandwood Rd
   CARD/HILL/MSPK G52 .... 103 G3
Sandybrae Rd *SKLM* PA17 .... 70 B5
Sandy Ct *WKIL* KA23 .... 181 J6
Sandyfaulds Sq *GBLS* G5 .... 11 K7
Sandyfaulds St *GBLS* G5 .... 11 L8
Sandyford Av *MTHW* ML1 .... 134 C1
Sandyford Pl *MTHW* ML1 .... 134 D2
Sandyford Place La *KVGV* G3 ...... 4 B8
Sandyford Rd *MTHW* ML1 .... 134 D2
   PSLYN/LNWD PA3 .... 101 M1
   PSTWK KA9 .... 222 B8
   RAYR/DAL KA6 .... 226 F3
Sandyford St *KVGV* G3 .... 104 C1
Sandyhills Crs *CAR/SHTL* G32 .. 107 H6
Sandyhills Dr *CAR/SHTL* G32 .. 107 H6
Sandyhills Gv *CAR/SHTL* G32 .. 107 J7
Sandyhills Pl *CAR/SHTL* G32 .. 107 H6
Sandyhills Rd *CAR/SHTL* G32 .. 107 H6
Sandyknowes Rd *CUMB* G67 .... 68 F1
Sandylands Prom *SALT* KA21 .. 200 F2
Sandy Rd *CARLUKE* ML8 .... 178 F2
   IRV KA12 .... 203 G4
   PTCK G11 .... 82 A3
   RNFRW PA4 .... 80 C8
   WKIL KA23 .... 181 J6
Sannox Dr *MTHW* ML1 .... 157 H2
Sannox Pl *HBR/GL* G84 .... 20 E7
Sannox Vw *AYR* KA8 .... 225 L7
Sanquhar Av *PSTWK* KA9 .... 225 K2
Sanquhar Dr *PLK/PH/NH* G53 .. 126 A1
Sanquhar Farm Rd *AYR* KA8 .... 225 K5
Sanquhar Gdns
   BLTYR/CAMB G72 .... 131 H7
   PLK/PH/NH G53 .... 126 A1
Sapphire Rd *BLSH* ML4 .... 133 G6
Saracen Head Rd *COWCAD* G4 .. 12 A3
Saracen St *PPK/MIL* G22 .... 83 J4
Sarazen Ct *MTHW* ML1 .... 158 E1
Sarazen Dr *TROON* KA10 .... 216 E8
Sardinia La *KVD/HLHD* G12 ...... 82 D6
Sark Dr *TROON* KA10 .... 216 F4
Saskatoon Pl *EKILS* G75 .... 14 F3
Saturn Av *PSLYN/LNWD* PA3 .... 100 E5
Saucel Hill Ter *PSLYS* PA2 .... 9 H5
Saucel St *PSLY* PA1 .... 9 H5
Sauchiehall La *CGLW* G2 .... 4 E8
Sauchiehall St *CGLW* G2 .... 5 G8
   KVGV G3 .... 82 D8
Sauchiesmoor Rd
   CARLUKE ML8 .... 189 C1
Saughs Av *STPS/GTHM/RID* G33 .. 84 F3
Saughs Dr *STPS/GTHM/RID* G33 .. 84 F3
Saughs Ga *STPS/GTHM/RID* G33 .. 84 F3
Saughs Pl
   STPS/GTHM/RID G33 .... 84 F3
Saughs Rd *STPS/GTHM/RID* G33 .. 84 F3
Saughton Av *CAR/SHTL* G32 .. 106 E2
Saughtree Av *SALT* KA21 .... 191 M7
Saunterne Rd *PSTWK* KA9 ...... 221 J8
Savoy Pk *AYRS* KA7 .... 18 C6
Savoy St *DMNK/BRGTN* G40 .... 12 C8
Sawmillfield St *COWCAD* G4 ...... 5 G4
Saxon Rd *KNTSWD* G13 .... 81 K2
Scadlock Rd *PSLYN/LNWD* PA3 .. 8 A1
Scalpay *EKILN* G74 .... 154 C8
Scalpay Pl *KLMNKN/STW* KA3 .. 207 G4
   PPK/MIL G22 .... 83 K2
Scalpay St *PPK/MIL* G22 .... 83 K2
Scapa St *SMSTN* G23 .... 82 E1
Scaraway Dr *PPK/MIL* G22 ...... 83 K1
Scaraway Pl *PPK/MIL* G22 ...... 83 K1
Scaraway St *PPK/MIL* G22 ...... 83 J1
Scaraway Ter *PPK/MIL* G22 ...... 83 K1
Scarba Dr *PLKSW/MSWD* G43 .. 127 H3
Scarba Qd *WISHAW* ML2 .... 158 E8
Scarffe Av *PSLYN/LNWD* PA3 .. 99 M4
Scargie Rd *KLMNK* KA1 .... 211 L5
Scarhill Av *AIRDRIE* ML6 .... 110 F4
Scarhill La *AIRDRIE* ML6 .... 111 G4
Scarhill St *CTBR* ML5 .... 109 M6
   MTHW ML1 .... 135 H7
Scarletmuir *LNK/LMHG* ML11 .. 198 F4
Scarlow St *PGL* PA14 .... 34 C7
Scarrel Dr *CSMK* G45 .... 129 G5
Scarrel Rd *CSMK* G45 .... 129 G5
Scarrel Ter *CSMK* G45 .... 129 G5
Scaur O' Doon Rd *AYRS* KA7 .. 228 C6
Schaw Dr *BSDN* G61 .... 61 L3
   CLYDBK G81 .... 60 D3
Schaw Rd *PSLYN/LNWD* PA3 .. 102 A3
Scholar's Ga *EKILS* G75 .... 171 K3
School Av *BLTYR/CAMB* G72 .. 130 B4
School Brae *FAIRLIE* KA29 .... 139 L6
Schoolhouse La
   BLTYR/CAMB G72 .... 155 L3
School La *CARLUKE* ML8 .... 178 E7
   DMBTN G82 .... 36 D5
   IRV KA12 .... 203 J3
   KKNTL G66 .... 44 D1
School Pl *ARD* KA22 .... 191 J7

School Qd *AIRDRIE* ML6 .... 88 F7
School Rd *BSHPBGS* G64 .... 44 C8
   KBRN KA25 .... 143 G7
   NMRNS G77 .... 150 D5
   PSLY PA1 .... 102 E4
   SHOTTS ML7 .... 113 K6
   STPS/GTHM/RID G33 .... 85 J3
   WISHAW ML2 .... 160 A5
School St *AIRDRIE* ML6 .... 111 K7
   CTBR ML5 .... 110 A5
   HMLTN ML3 .... 156 D8
   LARGS KA30 .... 115 J3
   SHOTTS ML7 .... 137 M5
Schoolwell St *SVSTN* KA20 ...... 192 C8
School Wynd *KBRN* KA25 .... 143 G7
   PSLY PA1 .... 9 G3
Scioncroft Av *RUTH* G73 .... 129 J2
Scone Pl *EKILN* G74 .... 153 K6
   NMRNS G77 .... 151 H5
Scone St *PPK/MIL* G22 .... 5 K3
Sconser St *SMSTN* G23 .... 62 E8
Scorton Gdns *CAR/SHTL* G32 .. 107 M5
Scotia Crs *LRKH* ML9 .... 176 A8
Scotia Gdns *HMLTN* ML3 .... 174 C2
Scotia St *MTHW* ML1 .... 157 J1
Scotland St *GBLS* G5 .... 10 D6
Scotland St West
   GOV/IBX G51 .... 104 D4
   PLKSD/SHW G41 .... 10 A5
   PLKSD/SHW G41 .... 104 D4
Scotlaw Dr *LARGS* KA30 .... 115 K5
Scotsblair Av *KKNTL* G66 .... 65 J2
Scotsburn Rd
   SPRGB/BLRNK G21 .... 84 C5
Scotstoun St *SCOT* G14 .... 81 J6
Scott Av *JNSTN* PA5 .... 122 E1
   KKNTL G66 .... 45 J3
   OLDK G60 .... 58 D1
Scott Ct *HBR/GL* G84 .... 20 C8
Scott Crs *CUMB* G67 .... 68 D2
   KLMNK KA1 .... 16 C7
   LARGS KA30 .... 115 L7
   TROON KA10 .... 216 E5
Scott Dr *BSDN* G61 .... 61 J3
   CUMB G67 .... 68 D2
   LARGS KA30 .... 115 L7
Scott Hl *EKILN* G74 .... 154 A6
Scott Pl *BLSH* ML4 .... 133 H2
Scott Rd *CARD/HILL/MSPK* G52 .. 102 F1
   IRV KA12 .... 203 J3
   KLMNK KA1 .... 16 C7
Scott's Pl *AIRDRIE* ML6 .... 111 H1
Scott's Rd *PSLYS* PA2 .... 102 C6
Scott St *ALEX/LLW* G83 .... 25 M4
   ALEX/LLW G83 .... 25 M5
   BAIL/MDB/MHD G69 .... 108 B5
   CLYDBK G81 .... 59 L5
   GRNK PA15 .... 2 E5
   HMLTN ML3 .... 156 D8
   KVGV G3 .... 4 F7
   LARGS KA30 .... 115 K7
   LRKH ML9 .... 176 B7
   MTHW ML1 .... 157 L2
Seabank Av *LARGS* KA30 .... 115 K8
Seabank Rd *AYRS* KA7 .... 18 C2
   PSTWK KA9 .... 221 H8
Seabank St *SALT* KA21 .... 201 G2
Seafar Rd *CUMB* G67 .... 48 F7
Seafield Av *BSDN* G61 .... 61 M2
Seafield Cottage La
   GRNKW/INVK PA16 .... 32 D3
Seafield Ct *ARD* KA22 .... 191 H6
   PSTWK KA9 .... 221 H8
Seafield Dr *ARD* KA22 .... 191 J6
   AYRS KA7 .... 228 F4
   RUTH G73 .... 129 K6
Seafield Rd *KLMNK* KA1 .... 16 C5
Seaford St *KLMNK* KA1 .... 16 D5
Seaforth Crs *AYR* KA8 .... 225 H5
   BRHD/NEIL G78 .... 125 H4
Seaforth Pl *BLSH* ML4 .... 132 F7
Seaforth Rd *AYR* KA8 .... 225 H5
   CARD/HILL/MSPK G52 .... 103 G3
   CLYDBK G81 .... 60 B8
Seaforth Rd North
   CARD/HILL/MSPK G52 .... 103 G3
Seaforth Rd South
   CARD/HILL/MSPK G52 .... 103 G3
Seagate *IRV* KA12 .... 203 H6
   PSTWK KA9 .... 221 J7
Seagrove St *CAR/SHTL* G32 .... 13 M3
   CAR/SHTL G32 .... 106 E3
Seamill Gdns *EKILS* G75 .... 14 D1
Seamill Pl *PLK/PH/NH* G53 .... 125 M4
Seamore St *LARGS* KA30 .... 115 J5
   MRYH/FIRH G20 .... 4 D4
Seath Av *AIRDRIE* ML6 .... 110 E1
   PGL PA14 .... 56 C3
Seath Rd *RUTH* G73 .... 106 A8
Seath St *GVH/MTFL* G42 .... 105 J7
Seaton Ter *HMLTN* ML3 .... 156 A5
   IRV KA14 .... 203 J4
Seaview Rd *SALT* KA21 .... 200 F2
Seaview Ter *TROON* KA10 .... 217 G5
Seaward La *PLKSD/SHW* G41 .. 10 B6
Seaward Pl *PLKSD/SHW* G41 .. 10 B6
Seaward St *GOV/IBX* G51 .... 10 C5
   PLKSD/SHW G41 .... 10 C5
Second Av *ALEX/LLW* G83 .... 25 M4
   BSDN G61 .... 62 A6
   CLYDBK G81 .... 59 M6
   DMBTN G82 .... 37 J7
   IRV KA12 .... 208 C1
   KKNTL G66 .... 65 J8
   LNPK/KPK G44 .... 128 B3
   RNFRW PA4 .... 80 C5
   STPS/GTHM/RID G33 .... 85 H4
   UD/BTH/TAN G71 .... 108 E8
Second Gdns
   PLKSD/SHW G41 .... 104 A5
Second Rd *BLTYR/CAMB* G72 .. 155 L4
Second St *UD/BTH/TAN* G71 .. 131 M1
Seedhill *PSLY* PA1 .... 9 J3
Seedhill Rd *PSLY* PA1 .... 9 K4
Seggielea La *KNTSWD* G13 ...... 81 K3

Seggielea Rd *KNTSWD* G13 ...... 81 K3
Segton Av *KLWNG* KA13 .... 193 J6
Seil Dr *LNPK/KPK* G44 .... 128 B5
Selborne Pl *KNTSWD* G13 .... 81 L4
Selborne Place La
   KNTSWD G13 .... 81 L4
Selborne Rd *KNTSWD* G13 ...... 81 L4
Selby Gdns *CAR/SHTL* G32 .... 107 K5
Selby Pl *CTBR* ML5 .... 87 K7
Selby St *CTBR* ML5 .... 87 K7
Selkirk Av
   CARD/HILL/MSPK G52 .... 103 G3
   PSLYS PA2 .... 101 G8
Selkirk Dr *RUTH* G73 .... 129 J2
Selkirk Pl *EKILN* G74 .... 154 D6
   HMLTN ML3 .... 156 E7
Selkirk Rd *PGL* PA14 .... 54 D1
Selkirk St *BLTYR/CAMB* G72 .... 155 K2
   HMLTN ML3 .... 156 E7
   WISHAW ML2 .... 159 J4
Selkirk Wy *CTBR* ML5 .... 110 E6
Sella Rd *BSHPBGS* G64 .... 64 D7
Selvieland Rd
   CARD/HILL/MSPK G52 .... 102 E4
Semphill Gdns *EKILN* G74 .... 15 L2
Sempie St *HMLTN* ML3 .... 155 M5
Sempill Av *ERSK* PA8 .... 58 F7
Semple Av *BSHPTN* PA7 .... 58 B6
   LOCHW PA12 .... 120 C6
Semple Crs *FAIRLIE* KA29 .... 139 K8
Semple Pl *PSLYN/LNWD* PA3 .. 100 B2
Semple Rd *PSTWK* KA9 .... 225 K4
Semple Vw *HWWD* PA9 .... 121 M4
Senga Crs *BLSH* ML4 .... 133 G2
Seres Rd *CRMNK/CLK/EAG* G76 .. 151 K1
Sergeant Law Rd
   BRHD/NEIL G78 .... 147 J1
   PSLYS PA2 .... 123 M4
Seright Crs
   KLMNKN/STW KA3 .... 212 D2
Seright Sq *KLMNKN/STW* KA3 .. 212 D1
Serpentine Wk *GRNK* PA15 .... 3 H7
Sersley Dr *KBRN* KA25 .... 142 F8
Service St *KKNTL* G66 .... 29 J8
Seton La *ARD* KA22 .... 191 J7
Seton St *ARD* KA22 .... 191 J7
Seton Ter *DEN/PKHD* G31 .... 12 B2
   SKLM PA17 .... 70 B5
Settle Gdns *CAR/SHTL* G32 .... 107 M5
Seven Sisters *KKNTL* G66 .... 65 L4
Seventh Av
   UD/BTH/TAN G71 .... 131 M1
Seventh Rd
   BLTYR/CAMB G72 .... 155 L4
Severn Rd *EKILS* G75 .... 170 E2
Seymour Av *KLWNG* KA13 ...... 193 M7
Seymour Gn *EKILS* G75 .... 171 H1
Seyton La *EKILN* G74 .... 153 L6
Shaftesbury St *CLYDBK* G81 .... 59 M7
   KVGV G3 .... 4 D8
Shafton Pl *KNTSWD* G13 .... 81 L1
Shafton Rd *KNTSWD* G13 .... 81 L1
Shakespeare Av *CLYDBK* G81 .. 59 M5
Shakespeare St
   MRYH/FIRH G20 .... 82 E4
Shalloch Pk *AYRS* KA7 .... 228 B7
Shalloch Pl *IRVSE* KA11 .... 204 B7
Shamrock St *COWCAD* G4 .... 4 F6
   KKNTL G66 .... 65 K1
Shandon Brae *ALEX/LLW* G83 .. 25 M1
Shandon Crs *ALEX/LLW* G83 .... 25 M1
   BLSH ML4 .... 133 G2
Shandon Pl *GRNK* PA15 .... 33 J7
Shandon Ter *HMLTN* ML3 ...... 155 M6
Shand St *WISHAW* ML2 .... 159 H6
Shandwick St *ESTRH* G34 .... 108 A1
Shankland La *GRNK* PA15 .... 33 M7
Shankland Rd *GRNK* PA15 .... 33 M7
Shanks Av *BRHD/NEIL* G78 .... 125 J7
Shanks Crs *JNSTN* PA5 .... 99 L7
Shanks St *AIRDRIE* ML6 .... 89 G8
   MRYH/FIRH G20 .... 82 E4
Shanks Wy *BRHD/NEIL* G78 .... 125 J4
Shannon St *MRYH/FIRH* G20 .... 82 F4
Shanter Pl *KLMNKN/STW* KA3 .. 17 M4
Shanter Wy *AYRS* KA7 .... 228 E8
Shantron Rd *ALEX/LLW* G83 .... 25 L3
Shapinsay St *PPK/MIL* G22 ...... 83 K1
Sharon St *DALRY* KA24 .... 184 B2
Sharp Av *CTBR* ML5 .... 109 J5
Sharpe Av *IRVSE* KA11 .... 209 K1
Sharphill Rd *SALT* KA21 .... 200 F1
Sharp St *GRK* PA19 .... 31 M2
Shavian Ter *KLWNG* KA13 ...... 193 J6
Shavin Brae *AYRS* KA7 .... 229 K3
Shaw Av *BSHPTN* PA7 .... 58 C5
Shawbank Pl *KLMNK* KA1 .... 17 G6
Shaw Br *KLMNKN/STW* KA3 .. 206 E1
Shawbridge St
   PLKSW/MSWD G43 .... 127 J2
Shawburn St *HMLTN* ML3 ...... 156 A5
Shaw Ct *ERSK* PA8 .... 58 F6
Shawfarm Ct *PSTWK* KA9 ...... 221 K8
Shawfarm Pl *PSTWK* KA9 ...... 221 K8
Shawfarm Rd *PSTWK* KA9 ...... 221 K8
Shawfield Av *AYRS* KA7 .... 229 G5
Shawfield Crs *CARLUKE* ML8 .. 177 M4
Shawfield Dr *GBLS* G5 .... 105 L2
Shawfield St *CARLUKE* ML8 .... 177 M5
Shawhead Av *CTBR* ML5 .... 110 B5
Shawhead Dr *PLKSD/SHW* G41 .. 127 K1
Shawhill Crs *NMRNS* G77 ...... 150 E6
Shawhill Rd *PLKSW/MSWD* G43 .. 127 J3
Shawholm Crs
   PLKSW/MSWD G43 .... 127 H2
Shawmoss Rd *PLKSD/SHW* G41 .. 104 C8
Shawpark St *MRYH/FIRH* G20 .. 82 E3
Shaw Pl *DALRY* KA24 .... 184 B2
   GRNK PA15 .... 2 D4
   PSLYN/LNWD PA3 .... 100 B4
   SALT KA21 .... 192 A7
Shawrigg Rd *LRKH* ML9 .... 176 C7
Shaw Rd *MLNGV* G62 .... 62 A1
   NMRNS G77 .... 150 E5

PSTWK KA9 .... 221 K8
Shaws Rd LRKH ML9 .... 176 D8
Shawstonfoot Rd MTHW ML1 .. 136 A8
Shaw St GOV/IBX G51 .... 104 A1
Shawwood Crs NMRNS G77 .... 150 E6
Shearer Dr HMLTN ML3 .... 174 C2
Sheddens Pl CAR/SHTL G32 .. 106 F3
Sheena Dr ALEX/LLW G83 ...... 25 M7
Sheepburn Rd
UD/BTH/TAN G71 .... 131 L2
Sheila St STPS/GTHM/RID G33 .... 84 E5
Sheiling Hl HMLTN ML3 .... 156 E5
Sheldaig Rd PPK/MIL G22 ...... 83 J1
Sheldrake Pl JNSTN PA5 .... 122 D3
Shellbridge Wy ARD KA22 ..... 191 J7
Shelley Dr CLYDBK G81 .... 60 A5
UD/BTH/TAN G71 .... 132 B7
Shelley Rd KVD/HLHD G12 ..... 81 M4
Shells Rd KKNTL G66 .... 45 L8
Sherbrooke Av
PLKSD/SHW G41 .... 104 C6
Sherbrooke Dr
PLKSD/SHW G41 .... 104 C5
Sherbrooke Gdns
PLKSD/SHW G41 .... 104 C6
Sherbrooke Pl EKILS G75 ...... 14 B4
Sherburn Gdns CAR/SHTL G32 .. 107 M5
Sherdale Av AIRDRIE ML6 ...... 111 K7
Sheriff Park Av RUTH G73 ..... 129 G2
Sherry Av MTHW ML1 .... 133 M4
Sherry Dr HMLTN ML3 .... 156 A8
Sherwood Av PSLY PA1 .... 9 M1
UD/BTH/TAN G71 .... 132 A4
Sherwood Dr GIF/THBK G46 ... 127 G6
Sherwood Pl DRUM G15 .... 61 H6
Sherwood Rd KLMNK KA1 ...... 212 F3
PSTWK KA9 .... 225 L1
Shetland Dr KLMNKN/STW KA3 .. 207 G3
LNPK/KPK G44 .... 128 B5
Shettleston Rd DEN/PKHD G31 .. 13 M5
DEN/PKHD G31 .... 106 C4
Shewalton Rd IRVSE KA11 ..... 208 E3
Shiel Av EKILN G74 .... 153 M6
Shielbridge Gdns SMSTN G23 .. 62 E8
Shiel Ct BRHD/NEIL G78 .... 125 H4
Shieldaig Dr RUTH G73 .... 129 H5
Shieldburn Rd GOV/IBX G51 .. 103 J3
Shieldhall Gdns GOV/IBX G51 .. 103 J2
Shieldhall Rd GOV/IBX G51 ... 103 H1
Shieldhill Rd CARLUKE ML8 .... 188 F1
Shieldmuir St WISHAW ML2 .... 158 C5
Shiel Dr LRKH ML9 .... 175 M4
Shield Rd GLSTN KA4 .... 214 A4
Shields Ct MTHW ML1 .... 158 B6
Shields Dr MTHW ML1 .... 158 B6
Shields Loan
LNK/LMHG ML11 .... 198 F4
Shields Rd EKILS G75 .... 170 E7
MTHW ML1 .... 158 A5
NMLNS KA16 .... 215 J2
PLKSD/SHW G41 .... 10 C6
Shield Ter GLSTN KA4 .... 214 A3
Shiel Hl AYRS KA7 .... 229 H7
Shiel Pl CTBR ML5 .... 110 D4
EKILN G74 .... 153 M6
IRV KA12 .... 203 J3
Shiel Rd BSHPBGS G64 .... 64 B8
Shiel Ter WISHAW ML2 .... 159 M3
Shilford Av KNTSWD G13 ...... 81 G2
Shilford Rd BRHD/NEIL G78 ... 123 H8
Shillay St PPK/MIL G22 .... 83 L1
Shilliaw Dr PSTWK KA9 .... 225 K4
Shilliaw Pl PSTWK KA9 .... 225 K4
Shillingworth Pl BRWEIR PA11 .. 98 D3
Shilton Dr PLK/PH/NH G53 .... 126 C4
Shilton La BSHPTN PA7 .... 58 E5
Shinwell Av CLYDBK G81 ...... 60 D8
Shira Ter EKILN G74 .... 15 L3
Shirley Qd MTHW ML1 .... 157 K6
Shirrel Av BLSH ML4 .... 133 G2
Shirrel Rd MTHW ML1 .... 134 A5
Shirva Lea KSYTH G65 .... 46 F5
Shiskine Dr
KLMNKN/STW KA3 .... 206 E5
MRYH/FIRH G20 .... 82 C1
Shiskine Pl HBR/GL G84 .... 20 F7
MRYH/FIRH G20 .... 82 C1
Shiskine St MRYH/FIRH G20 .. 82 C1
Shore Rd SKLM PA17 .... 70 A6
SVSTN KA20 .... 201 K2
TROON KA10 .... 216 B7
Shore St DMNK/BRGTN G40 ... 105 M7
GRK PA19 .... 31 L1
PGL PA14 .... 34 B7
Shortlees Crs KLMNK KA1 ..... 211 M6
Shortlees Rd KLMNK KA1 ...... 211 M7
Shortridge St MRYH/FIRH G20 .. 82 E4
Shortroods Av
PSLYN/LNWD PA3 .... 101 K2
Shortroods Crs
PSLYN/LNWD PA3 .... 101 K2
Shortroods Rd
PSLYN/LNWD PA3 .... 101 K2
Shottskirk Rd SHOTTS ML7 ... 137 K4
Shotts St STPS/GTHM/RID G33 .. 107 K1
NMRNS G77 .... 150 B3
Shuna Pl MRYH/FIRH G20 ..... 82 E4
NMRNS G77 .... 150 B3
Shuna St MRYH/FIRH G20 ..... 82 E3
Shuttle St CGLE G1 .... 11 M1
KLBCH PA10 .... 99 C5
KSYTH G65 .... 47 K1
PSLY PA1 .... 9 G4
Sidland Rd SPRGB/BLRNK G21 .. 84 C4
Sidlaw Av BRHD/NEIL G78 .... 125 J8
HMLTN ML3 .... 155 M7
PGL PA14 .... 54 F7
Sidlaw Dr WISHAW ML2 .... 159 M7
Sidlaw Foot IRVSE KA11 .... 204 C7
Sidlaw Pl KLMNK KA1 .... 212 A6
RAYR/DAL KA6 .... 227 H3
Sidlaw Rd BSDN G61 .... 61 H3
Sidlaw Wy LRKH ML9 .... 175 M4
Sidney St SALT KA21 .... 200 E2
Sielga Pl ESTRH G34 .... 108 A1
Siemens Pl SPRGB/BLRNK G21 .. 7 G5
Siemens St SPRGB/BLRNK G21 .. 7 G5
WISHAW ML2 .... 159 G8
Sievewright St RUTH G73 ..... 106 C8
Sighthill Ter SHOTTS ML7 ...... 113 H7
Sikeside Pl CTBR ML5 .... 110 D4

Sikeside St CTBR ML5 .... 110 D4
Silkin Av CLYDBK G81 .... 60 D8
Silk St PSLY PA1 .... 9 J5
Sillars Meadow IRV KA12 ...... 203 K7
Silvan Pl
CRMNK/CLK/EAG G76 .... 152 A4
Silverae Ct LARGS KA30 .... 115 K7
Silverburn Crs MTHW ML1 .... 134 D6
Silverburn St
STPS/GTHM/RID G33 .... 106 E1
Silverdale EKILN G74 .... 153 J6
Silverdale Crs LNK/LMHG ML11 .. 198 F5
Silverdale St KSYTH G65 .... 47 L4
Silverdale St DEN/PKHD G31 .. 13 K8
Silverdale Ter AIRDRIE ML6 ... 89 M6
Silverfir St GBLS G5 .... 11 L9
Silvergrove St
DMNK/BRGTN G40 .... 12 B7
Silvermuir Av
LNK/LMHG ML11 .... 199 M2
Silverton Av DMBTN G82 ...... 37 H6
Silvertonhill Av HMLTN ML3 .. 174 B1
Silvertonhill La DMBTN G82 .. 37 H6
Silvertonhill Pl HMLTN ML3 .. 174 D2
Silverwells UD/BTH/TAN G71 .. 132 A8
Silverwood Rd
KLMNKN/STW KA3 .... 212 D1
Simonsburn Rd KLMNK KA1 .. 211 L6
Simons Crs KLMNK KA1 .... 211 L5
RNFRW PA4 .... 80 D4
Simpson Ct CLYDBK G81 ...... 60 A7
UD/BTH/TAN G71 .... 131 M3
Simpson Dr EKILS G75 .... 14 C7
SALT KA21 .... 191 M6
Simpson Pl KLWNG KA13 ..... 193 M8
Simpson St CRH/DND KA2 .... 206 A8
MRYH/FIRH G20 .... 4 D3
Simpson Wy BLSH ML4 .... 133 J2
Simshill Rd LNPK/KPK G44 ... 128 B6
Simson Av WKIL KA23 .... 181 L5
Sim St KLMNKN/STW KA3 ..... 197 J1
Sinclair Av BSDN G61 .... 61 L3
Sinclair Ct KLMNKN/STW KA3 .. 207 J6
Sinclair Dr CTBR ML5 .... 109 K2
GVH/MTFL G42 .... 127 M2
HBR/GL G84 .... 20 E6
LARGS KA30 .... 115 K4
Sinclair Gdns BSHPBGS G64 .. 84 B1
Sinclair Gv BLSH ML4 .... 132 F7
Sinclair La HBR/GL G84 .... 20 E5
Sinclair Pk EKILS G75 .... 15 G5
Sinclair Pl EKILS G75 .... 15 G5
Sinclair St CLYDBK G81 .... 80 D1
GRNK PA15 .... 3 L9
HBR/GL G84 .... 20 D7
MLNGV G62 .... 42 A7
SVSTN KA20 .... 192 C8
Sinclair Ter LARGS KA30 ...... 115 K4
Singer Rd CLYDBK G81 .... 59 M6
EKILS G75 .... 171 M3
Singer St CLYDBK G81 .... 60 B6
Sir Michael Pl GRNK PA15 .... 2 C4
PSLY PA1 .... 8 F5
Sir Michael St GRNK PA15 .... 2 C4
Sixth Av RNFRW PA4 .... 80 C8
Sixth St UD/BTH/TAN G71 .... 108 E8
Skaethorn Rd MRYH/FIRH G20 .. 82 B2
Skaterigg La KNTSWD G13 .... 81 L4
Skelbo Pl ESTRH G34 .... 86 D8
Skellyton Crs LRKH ML9 .... 176 B7
Skelmorlie Castle Rd SKLM PA17 .. 70 A4
Skelmorlie Cross SKLM PA17 .. 70 B5
Skelmorlie Pl KLWNG KA13 ... 193 K6
Skene Rd GOV/IBX G51 .... 104 A4
KLMNKN/STW KA3 .... 207 J7
Skerne Gv EKILS G75 .... 170 F5
Skerray Qd PPK/MIL G22 ...... 83 J1
Skerray St PPK/MIL G22 .... 83 J1
Skerryvore Pl
STPS/GTHM/RID G33 .... 107 H1
Skerryvore Rd
STPS/GTHM/RID G33 .... 107 H1
Skipness Av CARLUKE ML8 .... 189 G1
Skipness Dr GOV/IBX G51 .... 103 K1
Skirsa Ct SMSTN G23 .... 83 G1
Skirsa Pl SMSTN G23 .... 82 F2
Skirsa Sq SMSTN G23 .... 83 G2
Skirsa St SMSTN G23 .... 82 F1
Skirving St PLKSD/SHW G41 .. 127 L1
Skovlunde Wy EKILS G75 ...... 171 L3
Skye EKILN G74 .... 154 C8
Skye Av RNFRW PA4 .... 80 C8
Skye Ct CUMB G67 .... 68 D1
Skye Crs GRK PA19 .... 31 K3
OLDK G60 .... 59 J4
PSLYS PA2 .... 124 D2
Skye Dr CUMB G67 .... 68 D1
OLDK G60 .... 59 J4
Skye Gdns BSDN G61 .... 61 H3
Skye Pl CUMB G67 .... 68 D1
SVSTN KA20 .... 192 F1
Skye Qd WISHAW ML2 .... 159 L4
Skye Rd CUMB G67 .... 68 D1
PGL PA14 .... 55 H3
PSTWK KA9 .... 221 L8
RUTH G73 .... 129 K6
Skye St GRNKW/INVK PA16 .. 32 C5
Slaemuir Av PGL PA14 .... 54 F3
Slakiewood Av
BAIL/MDB/MHD G69 .... 86 E2
Slatefield KKNTL G66 .... 44 D1
Slatefield St DEN/PKHD G31 .. 12 E4
Sleaford Av MTHW ML1 .... 157 K5
Slenavon Av RUTH G73 .... 129 K6
Slessor Dr EKILS G75 .... 14 F8
Sloan Av IRV KA12 .... 203 K7
RAYR/DAL KA6 .... 227 H3
Sloan Pl AYR KA8 .... 225 K7
Sloan St AYR KA8 .... 225 K7
Sloy St PPK/MIL G22 .... 83 K5
WISHAW ML2 .... 159 G8
Small Crs BLTYR/CAMB G72 .. 155 K2
Smeaton Av BSHPBGS G64 ... 64 B1
Smeaton St MRYH/FIRH G20 .. 82 F3
Smiddy Ct LNK/LMHG ML11 .. 199 G5

Smillie Pl CRH/DND KA2 .... 211 J3
Smillie St GRNK PA15 .... 33 L7
Smith Av GLGNK KA14 .... 167 K3
WISHAW ML2 .... 177 G2
Smith Crs CLYDBK G81 .... 60 B4
Smith Dr SALT KA21 .... 201 G1
Smithhills St PSLY PA1 .... 9 H3
Smith Od CTBR ML5 .... 110 C2
Smith's La PSLYN/LNWD PA3 .. 9 H1
Smithstone Ct IRV KA12 .... 203 M4
Smithstone Crs KSYTH G65 .. 47 L4
Smithstone Rd BALLOCH G68 .. 47 M7
Smithycroft HMLTN ML3 .... 157 G7
Smithycroft Rd
STPS/GTHM/RID G33 .... 84 E8
Smithyends CUMB G67 .... 49 H4
Smithy Rd DMBTN G82 .... 35 G1
Smollett Rd DMBTN G82 .... 37 H6
Smollett St ALEX/LLW G83 .... 25 K4
Smugglers Brig Rd
CARLUKE ML8 .... 188 B7
Smyllum Pk LNK/LMHG ML11 .. 199 J5
Smyllum Rd LNK/LMHG ML11 .. 199 J5
Snaefell Av RUTH G73 .... 129 J4
RUTH G73 .... 129 J5
Snaefell Crs RUTH G73 .... 129 J4
Sneddon Av WISHAW ML2 .... 159 J8
Sneddon St HMLTN ML3 .... 156 A3
Sneddon Ter HMLTN ML3 ..... 155 M8
Snowdon St GBLS G5 .... 11 L8
Snowdon Ter WKIL KA23 ...... 181 H4
Snuff Mill Rd LNPK/KPK G44 .. 128 A4
LNPK/KPK G44 .... 128 B4
Society St DEN/PKHD G31 ..... 13 H5
Sollas Pl KNTSWD G13 .... 80 E1
Solway Ct HMLTN ML3 .... 174 B1
Solway Pl BAIL/MDB/MHD G69 .. 66 D8
KLMNK KA1 .... 212 B5
TROON KA10 .... 216 E4
Solway Rd BSHPBGS G64 ..... 64 D7
Solway St DMNK/BRGTN G40 .. 105 M7
Somerford Rd BSDN G61 ...... 61 M8
Somerled Av PSLYN/LNWD PA3 .. 79 M8
Somerset Av HMLTN ML3 ..... 156 B5
Somerset Pl KVGV G3 .... 4 C7
Somerset Place Ms KVGV G3 .. 4 C7
Somerset Rd AYR KA8 .... 225 H7
Somervell St BLTYR/CAMB G72 .. 129 K3
Somerville Dr EKILS G75 .... 15 G8
GVH/MTFL G42 .... 128 B1
Somerville La EKILS G75 ...... 15 G8
Somerville Pl HBR/GL G84 .... 22 E1
Somerville Wy IRVSE KA11 .... 204 B2
Sommerville Dr SVSTN KA20 .. 201 L3
Sophia Crs IRV KA12 .... 203 H3
Sorbie Rd ARD KA22 .... 191 L7
Sorby St DEN/PKHD G31 ...... 13 L6
Sorley St PTCK G11 .... 81 M7
Sorn Pl GLSTN KA4 .... 214 C4
Sorn St DMNK/BRGTN G40 ... 13 G9
Sorrel Dr AYRS KA7 .... 229 J6
Soulis St KLMNKN/STW KA3 .. 16 F3
Sourlie Ter IRVSE KA11 .... 203 M4
Souter Dr KLMNKN/STW KA3 .. 17 M5
Souterhouse Pth CTBR ML5 .. 109 M4
Souterhouse Rd CTBR ML5 ... 109 M4
Souter Pl AYRS KA7 .... 19 J9
Southampton Dr KVD/HLHD G12 .. 82 B3
Southampton La KVD/HLHD G12 .. 82 B3
South Annandale St
GVH/MTFL G42 .... 105 H7
Southannan Rd FAIRLIE KA29 .. 139 K8
South Av BLTYR/CAMB G72 ... 155 K4
CARLUKE ML8 .... 178 E8
CLYDBK G81 .... 60 A7
PSLYS PA2 .... 124 F1
RNFRW PA4 .... 80 D6
Southbank Dr KKNTL G66 ..... 65 J1
Southbank Rd KKNTL G66 .... 65 H2
South Bank Dr CLYDBK G81 .. 80 C2
South Bank St DEN/PKHD G31 .. 13 L6
Southbar Av KNTSWD G13 .... 81 G2
Southbar Rd ERSK PA8 .... 79 G2
South Barrwood Rd KSYTH G65 .. 47 L2
South Beach TROON KA10 .... 216 C1
South Beach Esp TROON KA10 .. 216 C8
South Beach La TROON KA10 .. 216 C8
South Beach Rd ARD KA22 ... 191 K8
AYRS KA7 .... 18 C1
South Biggar Rd AIRDRIE ML6 .. 111 H2
South Brae KKNTL G66 .... 44 C2
Southbrae Av BRWEIR PA11 .. 98 B2
Southbrae Dr KNTSWD G13 .. 81 K5
Southbrae La KNTSWD G13 .. 81 L4
South Bridge St AIRDRIE ML6 .. 111 G1
South Burn Rd AIRDRIE ML6 .. 110 D2
South Caldeen Rd CTBR ML5 .. 110 B4
South Campbell St PSLYS PA2 .. 9 H7
South Carbrain Rd CUMB G67 .. 69 G1
South Chester St
CAR/SHTL G32 .... 107 G4
South Church Pl
ALEX/LLW G83 .... 25 M6
South Circular Rd CTBR ML5 .. 110 A2
South Claremont La
MLNGV G62 .... 42 A8
South Commonhead Av
AIRDRIE ML6 .... 88 F8
South Crescent Rd ARD KA22 .. 191 K8
Southcroft Rd RUTH G73 ...... 105 L8
Southcroft St GOV/IBX G51 .. 104 B2
Spey Av KLMNK KA1 .... 212 A4
PSLYS PA2 .... 100 E8
Speyburn Pl IRVSE KA11 ...... 203 M3
Spey Ct AIRDRIE ML6 .... 111 J4
Spey Dr RNFRW PA4 .... 80 E7
Spey Gdns HMLTN ML3 .... 174 D3
Spey Gv EKILS G75 .... 170 F2
Spey Pl JNSTN PA5 .... 122 C1
Spey Rd BSDN G61 .... 61 J7

PSLYN/LNWD PA3 .... 100 B3
TROON KA10 .... 216 F5
South Dumbreck Rd KSYTH G65 .. 47 H1
South Elgin Pl CLYDBK G81 .. 80 C2
South Elgin St CLYDBK G81 .. 80 C2
Southend Pl BLSH ML4 .... 132 F5
Southend Rd CLYDBK G81 .... 60 B4
Southern Av RUTH G73 .... 129 H4
Southerness Dr BALLOCH G68 .. 49 G4
South Erskine Pk BSDN G61 .. 61 K4
Southesk Av BSHPBGS G64 .. 63 M6
South Exchange Ct CGLE G1 .. 11 J2
Southfield CTBR ML5 .... 110 C4
Southfield Av PGL PA14 .... 54 F1
PSLYS PA2 .... 124 F1
Southfield Crs CTBR ML5 ...... 110 C4
PLK/PH/NH G53 .... 126 C1
Southfield Pk AYRS KA7 .... 19 G9
Southfield Rd BALLOCH G68 .. 48 C8
South Frederick St CGLE G1 .. 11 K2
South Gargieston Dr
CRH/DND KA2 .... 211 J5
Southgate MLNGV G62 .... 42 B8
South Glassford St MLNGV G62 .. 42 B8
South Hamilton Pl KLMNK KA1 .. 16 C6
South Hamilton St KLMNK KA1 .. 16 C6
South Harbour St AYRS KA7 .. 18 F1
Southhook Rd KLMNK KA1 .... 16 A1
Southinch Av KNTSWD G13 .. 80 E3
Southinch La SCOT G14 .... 80 E3
South Isle Rd ARD KA22 ...... 191 J4
South King St HBR/GL G84 .. 20 F8
Southlea Av GIF/THBK G46 ... 127 G6
Southloch Gdns
SPRGB/BLRNK G21 .... 6 D3
Southloch St SPRGB/BLRNK G21 .. 6 D3
South Lodge Ct AYRS KA7 .... 18 D7
South Mains Rd MLNGV G62 .. 41 M8
South Medrox St CTBR ML5 .. 87 J2
South Mound
CRG/CRSL/HOU PA6 .... 77 G7
South Muirhead Rd CUMB G67 .. 49 G7
Southmuir Pl MRYH/FIRH G20 .. 82 D4
South Neuk KBRN KA25 .... 167 G2
South Newmoor Av
IRVSE KA11 .... 203 L8
South Nimmo St
AIRDRIE ML6 .... 111 H2
South Park Av
BRHD/NEIL G78 .... 125 H6
BRHD/NEIL G78 .... 125 K6
Southpark Av KVD/HLHD G12 .. 4 A4
South Park Dr PSLYS PA2 ..... 9 G9
South Park Gv HMLTN ML3 ... 156 D6
Southpark Rd AYRS KA7 ...... 18 D8
South Park Rd HMLTN ML3 ... 156 D7
South Pl BLSH ML4 .... 132 F5
South Portland St GBLS G5 .. 11 H5
South Rd CRMNK/CLK/EAG G76 .. 152 A4
PGL PA14 .... 54 E1
WKIL KA23 .... 181 J5
South Robertson Pl
AIRDRIE ML6 .... 110 E2
South Scott St
BAIL/MDB/MHD G69 .... 108 B5
Southside Av RAYR/DAL KA6 .. 227 G3
South St CRG/CRSL/HOU PA6 .. 77 H7
GRNKW/INVK PA16 .... 32 C3
RNFRW PA4 .... 79 H5
SCOT G14 .... 81 G5
South Vennel LNK/LMHG ML11 .. 199 G5
South Vesalius St
CAR/SHTL G32 .... 107 G4
South Vw BLSH ML4 .... 132 E5
BLTYR/CAMB G72 .... 131 J8
CLYDBK G81 .... 59 M6
Southview BSDN G61 .... 61 J4
Southview Av
CRMNK/CLK/EAG G76 .... 151 L4
Southview Ct
SPRGB/BLRNK G21 .... 83 M2
Southview Crs BRWEIR PA11 .. 76 D8
Southview Dr CMPF/LLE G63 .. 27 H6
Southview Pl
BAIL/MDB/MHD G69 .... 86 E3
Southview Rd CMPF/LLE G63 .. 27 H6
Southview Ter
SPRGB/BLRNK G21 .... 83 M2
Southward Wy TROON KA10 .. 216 F2
South William St JNSTN PA5 .. 99 M7
Southwold Rd PSLY PA1 .... 102 E4
Southwood Dr LNPK/KPK G44 .. 128 C4
Southwood Rd TROON KA10 .. 220 F1
South Woodside Rd COWCAD G4 .. 4 B4
Soutra Pl STPS/GTHM/RID G33 .. 107 H1
Spairdrum Rd CUMB G67 ...... 69 C5
Spalding Dr LARGS KA30 ...... 115 K4
Spalehall Dr MTHW ML1 .... 134 F6
Spallander Rd TROON KA10 .. 216 F3
Sparrow Gdns KLMNK KA1 ... 17 L6
Spateston Rd HWWD PA9 ..... 122 C3
JNSTN PA5 .... 122 D2
Spean Av EKILN G74 .... 15 L3
Spean St LNPK/KPK G44 ...... 128 A2
Speirsfield Gdns PSLYS PA2 .. 8 F6
Speirshall Cl SCOT G14 .... 80 E4
Speirshall Ter SCOT G14 ...... 80 E3
Speirs Pl PSLYN/LNWD PA3 .. 100 C2
Speirs Rd BSDN G61 .... 62 A6
Spencer Dr PSLYS PA2 .... 123 K2
Spencer Field Gdns
HMLTN ML3 .... 156 F6
Spencer St CLYDBK G81 ...... 60 A6
KNTSWD G13 .... 81 M2
Spence St MRYH/FIRH G20 .. 82 C1
Spey Ct AIRDRIE ML6 .... 111 J4

PSTWK KA9 .... 221 K7
TROON KA10 .... 216 F5
Spey St STPS/GTHM/RID G33 .. 106 F1
Spey Ter EKILS G75 .... 170 F2
Spiersbridge Av
GIF/THBK G46 .... 126 E6
Spiersbridge La GIF/THBK G46 .. 126 E6
Spiersbridge Rd GIF/THBK G46 .. 126 F7
Spiersbridge Ter GIF/THBK G46 .. 126 E6
Spiers Gv GIF/THBK G46 .... 126 E6
Spiersland Wy BEITH KA15 ... 168 C2
Spiers Rd CRG/CRSL/HOU PA6 .. 77 H7
JNSTN PA5 .... 100 B6
LOCHW PA12 .... 120 B6
Spindlehowe Rd
UD/BTH/TAN G71 .... 131 M4
Spindleside Rd MTHW ML1 ... 135 K8
Spinners La CLYDBK G81 ..... 60 B2
Spittal Rd CSMK G45 .... 128 F5
Spoolers Rd PSLY PA1 .... 8 B6
Spoutmouth CGLE G1 .... 11 M3
Springbank Gdns IRVSE KA11 .. 204 D2
Springbank Rd AYR KA8 .... 225 H5
PSLYN/LNWD PA3 .... 101 K2
SHOTTS ML7 .... 137 J3
Springbank St MRYH/FIRH G20 .. 4 D1
Springbank Ter
PSLYN/LNWD PA3 .... 101 K2
Springboig Av CAR/SHTL G32 .. 107 J3
Springboig Rd CAR/SHTL G32 .. 107 J3
Springburn Pl EKILN G74 ...... 153 G6
Springburn Rd COWCAD G4 .. 6 A8
SPRGB/BLRNK G21 .... 6 B2
Springburn Wy
SPRGB/BLRNK G21 .... 6 C1
Springcroft Av
BAIL/MDB/MHD G69 .... 108 B3
Springcroft Crs
BAIL/MDB/MHD G69 .... 108 B3
Springcroft Dr
BAIL/MDB/MHD G69 .... 108 A3
Springcroft Gdns
BAIL/MDB/MHD G69 .... 108 C3
Springcroft Gv ALEX/LLW G83 .. 25 M6
BAIL/MDB/MHD G69 .... 108 B3
Springcroft Rd
BAIL/MDB/MHD G69 .... 108 B3
Springfield Av BSHPBGS G64 .. 84 A1
PSLY PA1 .... 102 B5
PSTWK KA9 .... 225 K2
UD/BTH/TAN G71 .... 131 M4
Springfield Ct CGLE G1 .... 11 J2
Springfield Crs
BLTYR/CAMB G72 .... 155 J2
BSHPBGS G64 .... 84 A1
CARLUKE ML8 .... 188 F1
UD/BTH/TAN G71 .... 131 M4
Springfield Dr BRHD/NEIL G78 .. 125 L8
Springfield Gdns
LNK/LMHG ML11 .... 198 F4
Springfield Pk JNSTN PA5 .... 100 A7
Springfield Park Rd RUTH G73 .. 129 J3
Springfield Quay GOV/IBX G51 .. 10 D3
Springfield Rd AIRDRIE ML6 .. 111 J1
BRHD/NEIL G78 .... 148 F2
BRHD/NEIL G78 .... 149 J1
BSHPBGS G64 .... 64 A8
CUMB G67 .... 49 G5
DEN/PKHD G31 .... 13 K7
MAUCH/CAT KA5 .... 223 M6
SHOTTS ML7 .... 113 G7
Springfields Gdns LARGS KA30 .. 115 K8
Springfield Sq BSHPBGS G64 .. 84 A1
Springfield Woods
JNSTN PA5 .... 100 A7
Springhead Rd SHOTTS ML7 .. 161 G1
Springhill Av AIRDRIE ML6 .... 111 H1
CRH/DND KA2 .... 210 E1
CTBR ML5 .... 109 J5
Springhill Dr South
BAIL/MDB/MHD G69 .... 108 A3
Springhill Gdns
PLKSD/SHW G41 .... 104 E8
Springhill Pkwy
BAIL/MDB/MHD G69 .... 108 B2
Springhill Pl CTBR ML5 .... 109 J5
KLMNK KA1 .... 16 C5
Springhill Rd
BAIL/MDB/MHD G69 .... 107 M4
BRHD/NEIL G78 .... 149 J4
CRMNK/CLK/EAG G76 .... 151 M2
PGL PA14 .... 34 C3
Springhill Ter IRVSE KA11 .... 204 F7
Springholm Dr AIRDRIE ML6 .. 88 F7
Springkell Av
PLKSD/SHW G41 .... 104 D8
Springkell Dr PLKSD/SHW G41 .. 104 B7
Springkell Gdns
PLKSD/SHW G41 .... 104 C7
Springkell Ga
PLKSD/SHW G41 .... 104 D7
Springkell St GRNK PA15 ..... 2 F6
Springside Dr DRUM G15 ..... 61 G5
Springs Pk RAYR/DAL KA6 .... 231 J6
Springvale Dr PSLYS PA2 ..... 100 F7
Springvale Pk AYRS KA7 ...... 18 E7
Springvale Rd SALT KA21 .... 200 F1
Springvale Ter AYRS KA7 ..... 18 E7
SALT KA21 .... 200 F2
Springwell Crs
BLTYR/CAMB G72 .... 155 M2
Springwell Pl
KLMNKN/STW KA3 .... 197 L1
Springwells Av AIRDRIE ML6 .. 111 J1
Springwells Crs AIRDRIE ML6 .. 111 J1
Springwood Dr KLMCLM PA13 .. 55 K7
Spruce Av BLTYR/CAMB G72 .. 155 J1
HMLTN ML3 .... 156 E8
JNSTN PA5 .... 100 A8
Spruce Ct HMLTN ML3 .... 156 E8
Spruce Dr BLTYR/CAMB G72 .. 130 F5
KKNTL G66 .... 65 G4
Spruce Pk AYRS KA7 .... 229 K4
Spruce Rd CUMB G67 .... 49 K5
UD/BTH/TAN G71 .... 109 J8
Spruce St PPK/MIL G22 .... 83 K4

Squire St *SCOT* G14 .... 81 K7
Stable Gv *PSLY* PA1 .... 8 A5
Stable Pl *MLNGV* G62 .... 41 M6
Stable Rd *MLNGV* G62 .... 41 M6
Stable Wynd *TROON* KA10 .... 217 H5
Staffa *EKILN* G74 .... 172 C1
Staffa Av *PGL* PA14 .... 55 C2
  RNFRW PA4 .... 80 C8
Staffa Dr *AIRDRIE* ML6 .... 111 M2
  KKNTL G66 .... 66 B1
  PSLYS PA2 .... 124 E2
Staffa Rd *BLTYR/CAMB* G72 ... 129 M6
Staffa St *DEN/PKHD* G31 .... 7 G3
  GRK PA19 .... 31 K3
Staffin Dr *SMSTN* G23 .... 62 D8
Staffin Rd *TROON* KA10 ...... 216 F4
Staffin St *SMSTN* G23 .... 62 E8
Stafflar Dr *KLMNK* KA1 .... 211 L6
Stafford Crs
  GRNKW/INVK PA16 .... 31 M5
Stafford Rd *GRNKW/INVK* PA16 ... 31 M5
Stafford St *BLSH* ML4 .... 132 F5
  COWCAD G4 .... 5 L7
  HBR/GL G84 .... 20 D7
  KLMNKN/STW KA3 .... 206 F7
Stafford St West *HBR/GL* G84 ... 20 C6
Staffordway South
  GRNKW/INVK PA16 .... 31 L5
Stag St *GOV/IBX* G51 .... 104 B2
Staig Wynd *MTHW* ML1 ...... 158 A5
Staikhill *LNK/LMHG* ML11 .... 198 F4
Staineybraes Pl *AIRDRIE* ML6 ... 88 F7
Stairlie Crs *WKIL* KA23 .... 181 K4
Stakehill *LARGS* KA30 .... 115 K6
Stalker St *WISHAW* ML2 ...... 158 C5
Stamford St *DEN/PKHD* G31 .... 13 G6
Stamperland Av
  CRMNK/CLK/EAG G76 ...... 151 M1
Stamperland Dr
  CRMNK/CLK/EAG G76 .... 151 M2
Stamperland Gdns
  CRMNK/CLK/EAG G76 .... 151 M2
Stamperland Hl
  CRMNK/CLK/EAG G76 ...... 127 M8
Stanalane St *GIF/THBK* G46 .... 126 F5
Standalane *KLMNK/STW* KA3 ... 197 K1
  KLMNKN/STW KA3 .... 206 M1
Standburn Rd
  SPRGB/BLRNK G21 .... 84 C3
Staneacre Pk *HMLTN* ML3 .... 156 F6
Stanecastle Dr *IRV* KA12 ..... 203 L4
Stanecastle Rd *IRVSE* KA11 ... 203 M5
Stanecraigs Pl *MTHW* ML1 .... 159 M3
Stanefield Dr *MTHW* ML1 .... 134 E5
Stanely Av *PSLYS* PA2 .... 101 H8
Stanely Ct *PSLYS* PA2 .... 124 B1
Stanely Crs *PSLYS* PA2 .... 124 B1
Stanely Dr *PSLYS* PA2 .... 101 J8
Stanely Rd *PSLYS* PA2 .... 101 J8
Stane Rd *PGL* PA14 .... 54 C1
Stanford St *CLYDBK* G81 ...... 60 C8
Stanhope Dr *RUTH* G73 ...... 129 K4
Stanhope Pl *WISHAW* ML2 ... 177 L1
Stanistone Rd *CARLUKE* ML8 ... 179 G4
Stanlane *LARGS* KA30 .... 115 J6
Stanley Av *ARD* KA22 .... 191 J4
Stanley Dr *ARD* KA22 .... 191 J6
  BLSH ML4 .... 133 C3
  BSHPBGS G64 .... 64 B7
  JNSTN PA5 .... 99 J4
Stanley La *JNSTN* PA5 .... 99 J4
Stanley Pl *BLTYR/CAMB* G72 ... 131 K8
  SALT KA21 .... 191 L8
Stanley Rd *ARD* KA22 .... 191 K6
  SALT KA21 .... 200 E1
Stanley St *HMLTN* ML3 .... 155 M5
  PLKSD/SHW G41 .... 10 B5
Stanley Street La
  PLKSD/SHW G41 .... 10 B5
Stanmore Av *LNK/LMHG* ML11 ... 199 H5
Stanmore Crs *LNK/LMHG* ML11 ... 199 J4
Stanmore Rd *GVH/MTFL* G42 ... 128 B1
  LNK/LMHG 199 K4
Stanners La *GRNK* PA15 .... 3 G6
Stanrigg St *AIRDRIE* ML6 ...... 90 A7
Stark Av *CLYDBK* G81 .... 59 L3
Starling Wy *UD/BTH/TAN* G71 ... 132 E1
Starryshaw Rd *SHOTTS* ML7 ... 137 L3
Startpoint St
  STPS/GTHM/RID G33 .... 107 G1
Station Av *GRNK* PA15 .... 2 E5
  GRNKW/INVK PA16 .... 50 D5
  HWWD PA9 .... 121 M4
Station Brae *BRHD/NEIL* G78 ... 148 C1
  IRVSE KA11 .... 204 C8
Station Br *AYRS* KA7 .... 18 F5
Station Crs *RNFRW* PA4 .... 80 C5
Station Dr *IRVSE* KA11 ...... 204 F6
  KLMNK KA1 .... 212 D3
  PSTWK KA9 .... 221 J8
Station Pl *CARLUKE* ML8 ..... 178 A3
Station Ri *LOCHW* PA12 ...... 120 C7
Station Rd *AIRDRIE* ML6 .... 90 B7
  AIRDRIE ML6 .... 90 F5
  AIRDRIE ML6 .... 111 L1
  AYRS KA7 .... 19 G5
  BAIL/MDB/MHD G69 .... 86 C2
  BAIL/MDB/MHD G69 .... 108 C5
  BLTYR/CAMB G72 .... 155 L1
  BRHD/NEIL G78 .... 148 D2
  BSDN G61 .... 61 K5
  BSHPTN PA7 .... 58 B7
  CARLUKE ML8 .... 178 A3
  CARLUKE ML8 .... 178 C8
  CMPF/LLE G53 .... 26 F5
  CRMNK/CLK/EAG G76 ...... 152 A4
  DMBTN G82 .... 35 G2
  DMBTN G82 .... 36 F5
  FAIRLIE KA29 .... 187 G8
  GIF/THBK G46 .... 127 J6
  GLSTN KA4 .... 214 C3
  GRK PA19 .... 31 L1
  GRNKW/INVK PA16 .... 50 D4
  HBR/GL G84 .... 22 F1
  IRVSE KA11 .... 204 F7
  KKNTL G66 .... 44 D1
  KLBCH PA10 .... 99 G7
  KLBCH PA10 .... 121 L3
  LRKH ML9 .... 176 B5
  MLNGV G62 .... 42 B8
  MLNGV G62 .... 63 G2
  MRYH/FIRH G20 .... 82 C1
  MTHW ML1 .... 134 B6
  MTHW ML1 .... 135 H8
  OLDK G60 .... 59 H3
  PGL PA14 .... 34 C8
  PGL PA14 .... 56 D2
  PSLY PA1 .... 8 A6
  PSTWK KA9 .... 221 J5
  RAYR/DAL KA6 .... 227 C3
  RNFRW PA4 .... 80 D5
  SHOTTS ML7 .... 137 M5
  SKLM PA17 .... 70 A4
  STPS/GTHM/RID G33 .... 85 G4
  SVSTN KA20 .... 201 K2
  UD/BTH/TAN G71 .... 131 L3
  UD/BTH/TAN G71 .... 132 A7
  WISHAW ML2 .... 159 G7
Station Rw *CARLUKE* ML8 .... 178 A3
  IRVSE KA11 .... 209 L3
Station St *DMBTN* G82 .... 25 K8
Station Wynd *KLBCH* PA10 .... 99 H1
Steading Dr *ALEX/LLW* G83 ... 25 M3
The Steading *WISHAW* ML2 ... 159 H4
Steel St *CGLE* G1 .... 11 L4
  GRK PA19 .... 31 M2
  WISHAW ML2 .... 159 H7
Steeple St *KLBCH* PA10 .... 99 G6
Steeples Vw *TROON* KA10 .... 216 E2
Stenhouse Av
  BAIL/MDB/MHD G69 .... 86 C2
Stenton Crs *WISHAW* ML2 ... 158 D7
Stenton Pl *WISHAW* ML2 ..... 158 D8
Stenton St *CAR/SHTL* G32 .... 106 E2
Stepends Rd *AIRDRIE* ML6 ..... 90 D6
  AIRDRIE ML6 .... 112 B3
Stepford Pl
  STPS/GTHM/RID G33 .... 107 M2
Stepford Rd
  STPS/GTHM/RID G33 .... 107 M2
Stephen Crs
  BAIL/MDB/MHD G69 .... 107 M4
Stephen Pl *EKILS* G75 .... 14 C6
Stephenson St
  CARD/HILL/MSPK G52 ..... 102 E1
Stephenson Ter *EKILS* G75 .... 14 C6
Stepps Rd *KKNTL* G66 .... 65 L7
  STPS/GTHM/RID G33 .... 85 J8
  STPS/GTHM/RID G33 .... 107 J1
Steps Rd *IRV* KA12 .... 203 J4
Stevenson Pl *BLSH* ML4 ...... 133 H2
Stevenson St *CARLUKE* ML8 ... 178 E2
  CLYDBK G81 .... 59 M5
  DMNK/BRGTN G40 .... 12 A4
  KLMNK KA1 .... 16 B3
  PSLYS PA2 .... 124 B2
Stevens Pl *GRK* PA19 .... 31 L3
Stevenston Rd *MTHW* ML1 ... 134 A5
Stevenston Rd *KLWNG* KA13 ... 193 L6
Stevenston St *MTHW* ML1 .... 134 A5
Steven St *ALEX/LLW* G83 ...... 25 L4
Stewart Av *BLTYR/CAMB* G72 ... 155 J2
  NMRNS G77 .... 150 E3
  RNFRW PA4 .... 80 A8
Stewart Ct *BRHD/NEIL* G78 ... 125 K5
Stewart Crs *BRHD/NEIL* G78 ... 125 K5
  WISHAW ML2 .... 160 A3
Stewart Dr *CLYDBK* G81 ...... 60 B3
  CRMNK/CLK/EAG G76 ..... 151 K1
  CTBR ML5 .... 109 H3
  IRV KA12 .... 203 K5
Stewartfield Crs *EKILN* G74 .. 153 J6
Stewartfield Dr *EKILN* G74 .. 153 K5
Stewartfield Rd *EKILN* G74 .. 153 J6
Stewartfield Wy *EKILN* G74 .. 152 F5
  EKILN G74 .... 153 J5
Stewartgill Pl *LRKH* ML9 ..... 176 F8
Stewarton Cr
  KLMNKN/STW KA3 .... 207 H3
Stewarton Dr
  BLTYR/CAMB G72 .... 129 L4
Stewarton Rd *NMRNS* G77 ... 150 C2
Stewarton St *WISHAW* ML2 ... 159 J7
Stewart Pl *BRHD/NEIL* G78 ... 125 K5
  CARLUKE ML8 .... 178 F7
Stewart Qd *MTHW* ML1 ...... 134 B3
Stewart Rd *AYR* KA8 .... 225 J5
  PSLYS PA2 .... 124 F1
Stewarts La *WISHAW* ML2 .... 159 J6
Stewart St *BLSH* ML4 .... 133 J4
  BRHD/NEIL G78 .... 125 K5
  CARLUKE ML8 .... 178 F7
  CLYDBK G81 .... 59 L6
  COWCAD G4 .... 5 H6
  CTBR ML5 .... 110 A1
  HMLTN ML3 .... 156 A4
  MLNGV G62 .... 42 A8
Stewartville St *PTCK* G11 ..... 82 B7
Stinchar Pl *PSTWK* KA9 ...... 221 K7
Stirling Av *BSDN* G61 .... 61 L7
  EKILN G74 .... 154 A6
Stirling Crs *KLMNK* KA1 ..... 206 C8
Stirling Dr *BSDN* G61 .... 61 J3
  BSHPBGS G64 .... 63 L6
  GRK PA19 .... 30 F4
  HMLTN ML3 .... 155 L5
  JNSTN PA5 .... 99 K7
  PSLYN/LNWD PA3 .... 99 M4
  RUTH G73 .... 129 H4
Stirlingfauld Pl *GBLS* G5 ...... 11 H4
Stirling Gdns *BSHPBGS* G64 ... 63 L6
Stirling Pl *KKNTL* G66 .... 44 E1
Stirling Rd *AIRDRIE* ML6 ...... 69 G7
  AIRDRIE ML6 .... 89 H5
  AIRDRIE ML6 .... 111 K5
  COWCAD G4 .... 5 M9
  CUMB G67 .... 69 G3
  DMBTN G82 .... 36 F6
Stirling St *AIRDRIE* ML6 ..... 110 F2
  CTBR ML5 .... 87 J8
  CUMB G67 .... 49 H5
  DMBTN G82 .... 25 K8
  MTHW ML1 .... 158 B5
Stirrat St *MRYH/FIRH* G20 ... 82 C3

Stobbs Crs *KLWNG* KA13 ..... 193 L7
Stobbs Ter *KLWNG* KA13 ..... 193 L7
Stobcross Rd *KVCV* G3 .... 10 A1
  KVCV G3 .... 104 C1
Stobcross St *CTBR* ML5 ...... 110 A3
Stobcross Wynd *KVCV* G3 ... 104 D1
Stobhill Crs *AYRS* KA7 .... 229 J4
Stobhill Rd *SPRGB/BLRNK* G21 ... 83 M2
Stobo *EKILN* G74 .... 154 C5
Stobo Ct *EKILN* G74 .... 154 C5
Stobo St *WISHAW* ML2 ...... 159 J4
Stobs Dr *BRHD/NEIL* G78 .... 125 H5
Stock Av *PSLYS* PA2 .... 9 H8
Stockbridge Crs *KBRN* KA25 ... 143 G5
Stockiemuir Av *BSDN* G61 .... 61 L2
Stockiemuir Rd *BSDN* G61 .... 41 M8
  BSDN G61 .... 61 K2
Stocks Rd *MTHW* ML1 .... 135 M8
Stock St *PSLYS* PA2 .... 9 G8
Stockwell Pl *CGLE* G1 .... 11 J3
Stockwell St *CGLE* G1 .... 11 K4
Stonebyres Ct *HMLTN* ML3 ... 156 A6
Stonecraig Rd *WISHAW* ML2 ... 159 J7
Stonedyke Crs *CARLUKE* ML8 ... 179 G6
Stonedyke Gv *DRUM* G15 ..... 61 H7
Stonedyke Rd *CARLUKE* ML8 ... 179 G6
Stonefield Av *KVD/HLHD* G12 ... 82 C3
  PSLYS PA2 .... 101 M8
Stonefield Crs
  BLTYR/CAMB G72 .... 155 J3
  CRMNK/CLK/EAG G76 ...... 151 J1
  PSLYS PA2 .... 101 M8
Stonefield Dr *PSLYS* PA2 .... 101 M8
Stonefield Gdns *PSLYS* PA2 ... 101 L8
Stonefield Pk *AYRS* KA7 ..... 228 C3
Stonefield Park Gdns
  BLTYR/CAMB G72 .... 155 L1
Stonefield Pl *BLTYR/CAMB* G72 ... 155 H2
Stonefield Rd
  BLTYR/CAMB G72 .... 155 J2
Stonehall Av *AIRDRIE* ML6 .... 89 G8
Stonehall Av *HMLTN* ML3 ... 156 B7
Stonehaven Crs *AIRDRIE* ML6 ... 110 E4
Stonehaven Rd
  GRNKW/INVK PA16 .... 31 M6
Stonelaw Dr *RUTH* G73 ...... 129 H2
Stonelaw Rd *RUTH* G73 ...... 129 H2
Stoneleigh Rd
  GRNKW/INVK PA16 .... 32 C2
Stoneside Dr
  PLKSW/MSWD G43 .... 127 H3
Stoneside Sq
  PLKSW/MSWD G43 .... 127 G3
Stoney Brae *PSLY* PA1 .... 9 G5
  PSLYS PA2 .... 124 E1
Stoneyetts Rd
  BAIL/MDB/MHD G69 .... 66 F7
Stoneygate Rd *NMLNS* KA16 ... 215 H3
Stoneyholm Rd *KBRN* KA25 ... 143 H7
Stoneymeadow Rd
  BLTYR/CAMB G72 .... 154 F4
  EKILN G74 .... 154 B4
Stoneymollan Rd *DMBTN* G82 ... 24 A4
Stonyflatt Av *DMBTN* G82 .... 37 H4
Stonyflatt Rd *DMBTN* G82 .... 37 H4
Stonyhill Av *KLMNK* KA1 .... 211 L5
Stonyhurst St *PPK/MIL* G22 .... 5 G1
Stonylee Rd *CUMB* G67 .... 49 G6
Stoopshill Crs *DALRY* KA24 ... 184 E2
Storie St *PSLY* PA1 .... 9 G4
Stormyland Wy
  BRHD/NEIL G78 .... 125 J7
Stornoway Crs *WISHAW* ML2 ... 159 L5
Stornoway St *PPK/MIL* G22 .... 83 J1
Stow Brae *PSLY* PA1 .... 9 G4
Stow St *PSLY* PA1 .... 9 G5
Strachan St *BLSH* ML4 .... 133 G5
Strachur St *PPK/MIL* G22 ..... 83 G2
Strain Crs *AIRDRIE* ML6 ..... 111 H3
Straiton Dr *HMLTN* ML3 ..... 155 K7
Straiton St *CAR/SHTL* G32 ... 106 E2
Strandhead *KLMNKN/STW* KA3 ... 197 J1
Strand St *KLMNK* KA1 .... 16 E3
Strang Pl *PSTWK* KA9 .... 225 K4
Stranka Av *PSLYS* PA2 .... 8 C7
Stranraer Dr *DRUM* G15 .... 61 J7
Stratford *EKILN* G74 .... 154 D4
Stratford St *MRYH/FIRH* G20 ... 82 D4
Strathallan Crs *AIRDRIE* ML6 .. 89 G6
Strathallon Pl *RUTH* G73 .... 129 K5
Strathaven Rd *HMLTN* ML3 ... 174 B6
Strathavon Crs *AIRDRIE* ML6 ... 89 G7
Strathayr Pl *AYR* KA8 .... 18 F2
Strathblane Crs *AIRDRIE* ML6 ... 89 G6
Strathblane Dr *EKILS* G75 ... 170 E1
Strathblane Rd *CMPF/LLE* G63 ... 27 K6
  KKNTL G66 .... 28 E7
  MLNGV G62 .... 42 B7
Strathbran St *DEN/PKHD* G31 ... 13 L8
Strathcairn Crs *AIRDRIE* ML6 ... 89 G6
Strath Carron *CARLUKE* ML8 ... 178 A3
Strathcarron Dr *PSLYS* PA2 ... 102 B3
Strathcarron Pl
  MRYH/FIRH G20 .... 82 C3
Strathcarron Rd *PSLYS* PA2 ... 125 H1
Strathcarron Wy *PSLYS* PA2 ... 102 B3
Strathclyde Av *ARD* KA22 .... 191 G4
Strathclyde Dr *RUTH* G73 ... 129 G2
Strathclyde Pl *HBR/GL* G84 .. 20 A7
Strathclyde Rd *DMBTN* G82 ... 37 G4
  MTHW ML1 .... 157 H3
Strathclyde St
  DMNK/BRGTN G40 .... 106 A7
Strathclyde Vw
  UD/BTH/TAN G71 .... 132 B8
Strathclyde Wy *BLSH* ML4 ... 133 J2
Strathcona Dr *KNTSWD* G13 ... 81 M2
Strathcona Gdns
  MRYH/FIRH G20 .... 82 A2
Strathcona La *EKILS* G75 ..... 14 E8
Strathcona Pl *EKILS* G75 ...... 14 E8
  RUTH G73 .... 129 K5
Strathcona St *KNTSWD* G13 ... 81 M3
Strathconon Gdns *EKILS* G75 ... 170 E1
Strath Crs *NMLNS* KA16 ..... 215 H3

Strath Dearn *CARLUKE* ML8 .. 178 A4
Strathdearn Gv *EKILS* G75 .... 170 C1
Strathdee Av *CLYDBK* G81 .... 60 B4
Strathdee Rd *LNPK/KPK* G44 ... 127 L7
Strathdon Av *LNPK/KPK* G44 ... 127 L7
  PSLYS PA2 .... 8 C8
Strathdon Dr *LNPK/KPK* G44 ... 127 M7
Strathdoon Pl *AYRS* KA7 ..... 228 D7
Strathearn Gv *KKNTL* G66 ..... 46 B7
Strathearn Rd
  CRMNK/CLK/EAG G76 ...... 151 L3
Strath Elgin *CARLUKE* ML8 ... 177 M4
Strathendrick Dr
  PLKSW/MSWD G43 .... 127 L5
Strathfillan Rd *EKILN* G74 ..... 14 D2
Strathgoil Crs *AIRDRIE* ML6 .. 89 G6
Strathgryffe Crs *BRWEIR* PA11 ... 76 C3
Strath Halladale
  CARLUKE ML8 .... 178 A4
Strathkelvin Av
  SPRGB/BLRNK G21 .... 83 M2
Strathlachlan Av
  CARLUKE ML8 .... 179 G8
Strathleven Dr *ALEX/LLW* G83 ... 25 M7
  DMBTN G82 .... 25 M8
Strathmore Av
  BLTYR/CAMB G72 .... 131 J8
  PSLY PA1 .... 102 D5
Strathmore Crs *AIRDRIE* ML6 .. 89 G7
Strathmore Gdns *RUTH* G73 ... 129 K5
Strathmore Gv *EKILS* G75 ... 170 C1
Strathmore Pk *IRVSE* KA11 ... 204 B5
Strathmore Pl *CTBR* ML5 .... 110 D4
  PPK/MIL G22 .... 83 H2
Strathmore Wk *CTBR* ML5 ... 110 D4
Strathmungo Crs
  AIRDRIE ML6 .... 88 F7
Strath Nairn *CARLUKE* ML8 .. 178 A4
Strathnairn Av *EKILS* G75 .... 170 E1
Strathnairn Ct *EKILS* G75 .... 170 E1
Strathnairn Dr *EKILS* G75 .... 170 E1
Strathnairn Wy *EKILS* G75 ... 170 E1
Strath Naver *CARLUKE* ML8 ... 178 A4
Strathnaver Crs *AIRDRIE* ML6 .. 89 G6
Strathnaver Gdns *EKILS* G75 ... 170 F1
Stratholm Ter *NMLNS* KA16 ... 215 C3
Strathord Pl
  BAIL/MDB/MHD G69 .... 67 G5
Strathord St *CAR/SHTL* G32 ... 107 G6
Strath Peffer *CARLUKE* ML8 ... 177 M4
Strathpeffer Crs *AIRDRIE* ML6 .. 89 G7
Strathspey Crs *AIRDRIE* ML6 .. 89 G6
Strathtay Av *EKILS* G75 ...... 170 E1
  LNPK/KPK G44 .... 127 L7
Strathtummel Crs
  AIRDRIE ML6 .... 89 G6
Strathview Gv
  LNPK/KPK G44 .... 127 L7
Strathview Pk *LNPK/KPK* G44 ... 127 L7
Strathview Rd *BLSH* ML4 ..... 132 E7
Strathy Pl *KLMNK* KA1 .... 212 B4
  MRYH/FIRH G20 .... 82 C3
Strathyre Gdns *AIRDRIE* ML6 .. 88 F4
  BSDN G61 .... 62 B4
Strathyre Rd *BLTYR/CAMB* G72 ... 155 M3
Strathyre St *PLKSD/SHW* G41 ... 127 L1
Stratton Dr *GIF/THBK* G46 ... 127 H7
Strauss Av *CLYDBK* G81 ...... 60 E8
Stravaig Pth *PSLYS* PA2 ..... 124 A2
Stravaig Wk *PSLYS* PA2 ..... 124 A2
Stravanan Ct *CSMK* G45 .... 128 E7
Stravanan Rd *CSMK* G45 .... 128 D7
Stravanan St *CSMK* G45 .... 128 D7
Stravanan Ter *CSMK* G45 .... 128 D7
Stravenhouse Rd
  CARLUKE ML8 .... 177 L5
Strawberrybank Rd
  KLMNKN/STW KA3 .... 17 H1
Strawberry Field Rd
  CRG/CRSL/HOU PA6 .... 77 H8
Strawhill Rd
  CRMNK/CLK/EAG G76 ...... 151 L2
Strenabey Av *RUTH* G73 ..... 129 K5
Striven Crs *WISHAW* ML2 .... 159 G8
Striven Gdns *MRYH/FIRH* G20 ... 4 C2
Striven Rd *WMYSB* PA18 ...... 70 A1
Striven Ter *HMLTN* ML3 ..... 156 A8
Stroma *EKILN* G74 .... 154 D4
Stroma St *SPRGB/BLRNK* G21 ... 7 H4
Stromness St *GBLS* G5 .... 10 F7
Strone Crs *GRNK* PA15 .... 3 G8
Strone Gdns *KSYTH* G65 ...... 47 H3
Stronend St *PPK/MIL* G22 ..... 83 H4
Strone Rd *ALEX/LLW* G83 ..... 25 L2
  STPS/GTHM/RID G33 .... 107 H2
Stronsay Pl
  KLMNKN/STW KA3 .... 207 G4
Stronsay St *SPRGB/BLRNK* G21 .. 7 H4
Stronsay Wy *IRVSE* KA11 .... 204 A7
Stronvar Dr *SCOT* G14 .... 81 H5
Stroud Rd *EKILS* G75 .... 15 K9
Strowan Crs *CAR/SHTL* G32 ... 107 H5
Strowan Rd *DMBTN* G82 ...... 37 G6
Strowan St *CAR/SHTL* G32 ... 107 H5
Strowan's Rd *DMBTN* G82 .... 37 G6
Strowan's Well Rd *DMBTN* G82 ... 37 J6
Struan Av *GIF/THBK* G46 .... 127 J6
Struan Gdns *LNPK/KPK* G44 ... 128 A3
Struan Rd *LNPK/KPK* G44 ... 128 A4
Struie St *ESTRH* G34 .... 108 A1
Struma Dr
  CRMNK/CLK/EAG G76 ...... 151 J2
Struthers Av *KLMNKN/STW* KA3 ... 212 D1
Struthers Crs *EKILN* G74 .... 154 B5
Struthers Pl *TROON* KA10 ... 216 F1
Stuart Av *OLDK* G60 .... 59 H4
  RUTH G73 .... 129 H4
Stuart Dr *BSHPBGS* G64 .... 83 L1
  LNK/LMHG ML11 .... 199 H4
  LNK/LMHG 176 C5
Stuart Mount Dr *WMYSB* PA18 ... 50 A8
Stuarton Pk *EKILN* G74 .... 14 F1
Stuart Qd *WISHAW* ML2 ..... 158 D8
Stuart Rd *BSHPTN* PA7 .... 58 B5
  CRMNK/CLK/EAG G76 ...... 152 D1
  DMBTN G82 .... 37 J5

Stuart St *EKILN* G74 .... 15 G2
  GTCI KA28 .... 138 A7
  OLDK G60 .... 59 H4
Stuckleckie Rd *HBR/GL* G84 ... 20 F8
Sturrock St *KLMNK* KA1 ...... 16 F5
Succoth St *KNTSWD* G13 ...... 81 M2
Sudbury Crs *EKILS* G75 ...... 153 H8
Suffolk Rd *GRNKW/INVK* PA16 ... 31 L5
Suffolk St *CGLE* G1 .... 11 M4
  HBR/GL G84 .... 20 B7
Sugworth Av
  BAIL/MDB/MHD G69 .... 108 B4
Sumburgh St
  STPS/GTHM/RID G33 .... 106 F2
Summerfield Rd *CUMB* G67 ... 68 A3
Summerfield St
  DMNK/BRGTN G40 .... 106 A7
Summerhill & Garngibbock Rd
  CUMB G67 .... 68 C6
Summerhill Av *LRKH* ML9 ... 176 A7
Summerhill Dr *DRUM* G15 .... 61 H5
Summerhill Gdns *DRUM* G15 ... 61 H5
Summerhill Pl *DRUM* G15 .... 61 H5
Summerhill Rd
  CRMNK/CLK/EAG G76 ...... 151 M2
  DRUM G15 .... 61 H5
Summerlea Rd *GIF/THBK* G46 ... 126 F5
  WKIL KA23 .... 181 H5
Summerlee Rd *LRKH* ML9 ... 175 M4
  WISHAW ML2 .... 158 C5
Summerlee St *CTBR* ML5 ..... 109 M2
  STPS/GTHM/RID G33 .... 107 J2
Summer St *DMNK/BRGTN* G40 ... 12 D6
Summertown Rd *GOV/IBX* G51 ... 104 C2
Sunart Av *RNFRW* PA4 .... 80 B5
Sunart Gdns *BSHPBGS* G64 ... 64 C8
Sunart Rd *BSHPBGS* G64 ...... 64 C8
  CARD/HILL/MSPK G52 ..... 103 L4
  WMYSB PA18 .... 50 A8
Sunart St *WISHAW* ML2 ..... 159 G8
Sunbury Av
  CRMNK/CLK/EAG G76 ...... 151 J2
Sundale Av
  CRMNK/CLK/EAG G76 ...... 151 K3
Sunderland Av *DMBTN* G82 ... 36 C5
Sundrum Pk *RAYR/DAL* KA6 ... 231 H4
Sundrum Pl *KLWNG* KA13 ... 193 K7
Sunflower Gdns *MTHW* ML1 ... 157 K1
Sunningdale Av *AYRS* KA7 ... 229 G6
  NMRNS G77 .... 150 C7
Sunningdale Dr *BRWEIR* PA11 ... 98 C3
Sunningdale Rd *SMSTN* G23 ... 82 D1
Sunningdale Sq *KLWNG* KA13 ... 193 J5
Sunningdale Wynd
  UD/BTH/TAN G71 .... 131 L6
Sunnybank Dr
  CRMNK/CLK/EAG G76 ...... 151 K3
Sunnybank Gv
  CRMNK/CLK/EAG G76 ...... 151 K3
Sunnyhill *KSYTH* G65 .... 46 F5
Sunnylaw Dr *PSLYS* PA2 .... 8 A9
Sunnylaw St *PPK/MIL* G22 .... 83 H5
Sunnyside *KLMNKN/STW* KA3 ... 206 B2
Sunnyside Av *MTHW* ML1 ... 134 B4
  PGL PA14 .... 55 G1
  UD/BTH/TAN G71 .... 131 M4
Sunnyside Crs *MTHW* ML1 ... 134 A4
Sunnyside Dr
  BAIL/MDB/MHD G69 .... 108 F4
  CRMNK/CLK/EAG G76 ...... 151 K1
  DRUM G15 .... 61 G2
Sunnyside Ov *PSLYS* PA2 .... 101 L8
Sunnyside Pl
  BRHD/NEIL G78 .... 125 H7
  DRUM G15 .... 61 G2
  MTHW ML1 .... 134 A4
Sunnyside Rd *CTBR* ML5 ..... 110 A2
  HMLTN ML3 .... 175 G5
  KLMNK KA1 .... 211 M7
  LNK/LMHG ML11 .... 198 D4
  MTHW ML1 .... 159 H1
  PSLYS PA2 .... 101 K8
Sunnyside Sq East *KLMNK* KA1 ... 211 M7
Sunnyside Sq West *KLMNK* KA1 ... 211 M7
Sunnyside Ter *MTHW* ML1 ... 134 A4
Surrey La *GBLS* G5 .... 11 H7
Surrey St *GBLS* G5 .... 11 H7
Susannah St *ALEX/LLW* G83 ... 25 L4
Sussex St *PLKSD/SHW* G41 .... 10 A5
Sutcliffe Ct *KNTSWD* G13 ..... 81 L2
Sutcliffe Rd *KNTSWD* G13 .... 81 M2
Sutherland Av *BSDN* G61 ...... 61 L2
  PLKSD/SHW G41 .... 104 C6
Sutherland Crs *HMLTN* ML3 ... 156 A5
Sutherland Dr *AIRDRIE* ML6 ... 110 F4
  GIF/THBK G46 .... 127 K8
  KLMNKN/STW KA3 .... 207 K8
Sutherland La
  BLTYR/CAMB G72 .... 155 J4
  HBR/GL G84 .... 20 B7
  PSLY PA1 .... 8 E3
Sutherland Pl *BLSH* ML4 ..... 132 F7
Sutherland Rd *CLYDBK* G81 ... 60 B7
  GRNKW/INVK PA16 .... 32 A3
Sutherland St
  BLTYR/CAMB G72 .... 155 J4
  HBR/GL G84 .... 20 B7
  PSLY PA1 .... 8 E3
Sutherland Ter *GLSTN* KA4 ... 214 D3
Sutherland Wy *EKILN* G74 ... 154 C6
Sutherness Dr
  STPS/GTHM/RID G33 .... 107 G2
Sutton St *KLWNG* KA13 ...... 193 H6
Swaledale *EKILN* G74 .... 153 J6
Swallow Brae
  GRNKW/INVK PA16 .... 50 E4
Swallow Gdns *KNTSWD* G13 ... 80 F2
Swallow Rd *CLYDBK* G81 ...... 60 C7
  WISHAW ML2 .... 159 H6
Swan Pl *JNSTN* PA5 .... 122 C2
Swanson Rd *ALEX/LLW* G83 ... 25 K2
Swanston St
  DMNK/BRGTN G40 .... 106 A7
Swan St *CLYDBK* G81 .... 59 M6
  COWCAD G4 .... 5 K6
Swan Wy *CARLUKE* ML8 ..... 177 M5
Sween Av *LNPK/KPK* G44 .... 128 A5
Sween Dr *HMLTN* ML3 .... 156 A8
Sweethope Gdns
  UD/BTH/TAN G71 .... 132 B7

Sweethope Pl
 UD/BTH/TAN G71 .... 132 A6 ☑
Swift Av GRNKW/INVK PA16 ...... 50 F4
Swift Bank HMLTN ML3 .... 155 L8
Swift Cl WISHAW ML2 .... 159 H6
Swift Crs KNTSWD G13 .... 80 F2
Swift Pl EKILS G75 .... 170 E3
 JNSTN PA5 .... 122 D2 ☑
Swindon St CLYDBK G81 .... 59 L6
Swinstie Rd MTHW ML1 .... 159 J1
Swinstie Vw MTHW ML1 .... 135 J8
Swinton Av
 BAIL/MDB/MHD G69 .... 108 D4
Swinton Crs
 BAIL/MDB/MHD G69 .... 108 C4
 CTBR ML5 .... 109 H5
Swinton Dr
 CARD/HILL/MSPK G52 .... 103 H4
Swinton Gdns
 WISHAW ML2 .... 159 G8
 WKIL KA23 .... 181 L4
Swinton Pth
 BAIL/MDB/MHD G69 .... 108 D4 ☑
Swinton Pl
 CARD/HILL/MSPK G52 .... 103 H4
Swinton Rd
 BAIL/MDB/MHD G69 .... 108 C3 ☑
Swinton Vw
 BAIL/MDB/MHD G69 .... 108 C4 ☑
Swisscot Av HMLTN ML3 .... 174 B1
Swisscot Wk HMLTN ML3 .... 174 B1 ☑
Switchback Rd BSDN G61 .... 61 M7
Swordale Pl ESTRH G34 .... 108 A1 ☑
Sword St AIRDRIE ML6 .... 110 F2
 DEN/PKHD G31 .... 12 D3
Sycamore Av BEITH KA15 .... 144 B7
 JNSTN PA5 .... 100 A1
 KKNTL G66 .... 65 K4
 UD/BTH/TAN G71 .... 132 C2
Sycamore Ct EKILS G75 .... 171 K3 ☑
Sycamore Crs AIRDRIE ML6 ...... 111 K3
 AYRS KA7 .... 229 K3
 EKILS G75 .... 171 K3
Sycamore Dr AIRDRIE ML6 ...... 111 K3
 CLYDBK G81 .... 59 M5
 HMLTN ML3 .... 156 F7
Sycamore Gv
 BLTYR/CAMB G72 .... 155 J1 ☑
Sycamore Pl EKILS G75 .... 171 K3
 GRK PA19 .... 31 J3
 MTHW ML1 .... 134 C6
Sycamore Wy
 BLTYR/CAMB G72 .... 130 F5
 KKNTL G66 .... 45 H4
Sydenham Rd KVD/HLHD G12 .... 82 C6
Sydes Brae BLTYR/CAMB G72 .... 155 G6
Sydney Dr EKILS G75 .... 14 B7
Sydney Pl EKILS G75 .... 14 B6
Sydney St CLYDBK G81 .... 59 J2
 DEN/PKHD G31 .... 12 B3
Sykehead Av BLSH ML4 .... 133 H4 ☑
Sykeside Rd AIRDRIE ML6 .... 110 E5
Symington Pl IRVSE KA11 .... 208 F3
Symington Rd North
 KLMNK KA1 .... 218 C6
Symington Rd South
 KLMNK KA1 .... 218 C7
Syms La AYR KA8 .... 19 G2
Syriam Pl SPRGB/BLRNK G21 .... 83 M5 ☑
Syriam St SPRGB/BLRNK G21 .... 83 M4

T

Tabard Pl KNTSWD G13 .... 81 J1 ☑
Tabard Rd KNTSWD G13 .... 81 J1
Tabernacle La
 BLTYR/CAMB G72 .... 130 A4
Tabernacle St BLTYR/CAMB G72.. 130 A4
Taggart Rd KSYTH G65 .... 47 M6
Taig Rd KKNTL G66 .... 66 B2
Tait Av BRHD/NEIL G78 .... 125 K5
Tait Wk CARLUKE ML8 .... 188 B8
Talbot EKILN G74 .... 154 C5
Talbot Ct SCOT G14 .... 81 H4 ☑
Talbot Dr KNTSWD G13 .... 81 H4
Talbot Pl SCOT G14 .... 81 H4 ☑
Talbot Ter SCOT G14 .... 81 H4
 UD/BTH/TAN G71 .... 131 L1
Talisman Av DMBTN G82 .... 36 C5
Talisman Crs HBR/CL G84 .... 22 F1
 MTHW ML1 .... 133 K7
Talisman Rd KNTSWD G13 .... 81 J3
 PSLYS PA2 .... 123 L2
Tallant Av DRUM G15 .... 61 H6
Tallant Ter DRUM G15 .... 61 J6
Talla Rd CARD/HILL/MSPK G52 .. 103 H4
Tamar Dr EKILS G75 .... 170 F3
Tamarack Crs UD/BTH/TAN G71.. 109 J8
Tambowie Av MLNGV G62 .... 41 M7
Tambowie Crs MLNGV G62 ...... 41 M7
Tambowie St KNTSWD G13 ...... 81 L2
Tamshill St MRYH/FIRH G20 .... 82 F3
Tanar Av RNFRW PA4 .... 80 F8
Tandlehill Rd KLBCH PA10 .... 99 G8
Tanera Av LNPK/KPK G44 .... 128 C4
Tanfield Pl CAR/SHTL G32 .... 107 J2 ☑
Tanfield St CAR/SHTL G32 .... 107 J2
Tankerland Rd
 PLKSW/MSWD G43 .... 128 A3
Tannadice Av
 CARD/HILL/MSPK G52 .... 103 J6
Tanna Dr CARD/HILL/MSPK G52 .. 103 M6
Tannahill Crs JNSTN PA5 .... 122 C1
Tannahill Dr EKILN G74 .... 154 C6
Tannahill Rd
 PLKSW/MSWD G43 .... 127 M3 ☑
 PSLYN/LNWD PA3 .... 8 B1
Tannahill Ter PSLYN/LNWD PA3 .. 8 B1
Tannoch Dr CUMB G67 .... 68 F2
 MLNGV G62 .... 42 B6
Tannoch Pl CUMB G67 .... 68 F2
Tannoch Rd BRHD/NEIL G78 .... 147 H6
Tannochside Dr
 UD/BTH/TAN G71 .... 109 G8
Tannock St KLMNK KA1 .... 16 E8
 PPK/MIL G22 .... 5 H1
Tantallon Av GRK PA19 .... 30 C4

Tantallon Ct CARLUKE ML8 ...... 178 E6 ☑
Tantallon Dr CTBR ML5 .... 87 J8
 PSLYS PA2 .... 101 G8
Tantallon Pk EKILN G74 .... 14 C2
Tantallon Rd
 BAIL/MDB/MHD G69 .... 108 A6
 PLKSD/SHW G41 .... 127 L2
Tanzieknowe Av
 BLTYR/CAMB G72 .... 130 B6 ☑
Tanzieknowe Dr
 BLTYR/CAMB G72 .... 130 B6 ☑
Tanzieknowe Pl
 BLTYR/CAMB G72 .... 130 B6 ☑
Tanzieknowe Rd
 BLTYR/CAMB G72 .... 130 B6
Taransay St GOV/IBX G51 .... 103 M1
Tarbert Av BLTYR/CAMB G72 .... 131 J7
 WISHAW ML2 .... 159 G8
 WKIL KA23 .... 181 L4
Tarbert Ct HMLTN ML3 .... 156 A8 ☑
Tarbert Pl GRK PA19 .... 31 M2
Tarbet St EKILN G74 .... 154 D6
Tarbolton Crs AIRDRIE ML6 ...... 134 D1
Tarbolton Dr CLYDBK G81 .... 60 C6 ☑
Tarbolton Pth LRKH ML9 .... 175 M8 ☑
Tarbolton Pl
 KLMNK/STW KA3 .... 207 J3 ☑
 CUMB G67 .... 49 H7
 KLMNK KA1 .... 218 F4
 PLKSW/MSWD G43 .... 127 K3 ☑
 PSTWK KA9 .... 221 K5
Tarbrax Wy HMLTN ML3 .... 156 A6
Tarfside Av
 CARD/HILL/MSPK G52 .... 103 K5
Tarfside Gdns
 CARD/HILL/MSPK G52 .... 103 K5
Tarfside Ov
 CARD/HILL/MSPK G52 .... 103 K5
Target Rd AIRDRIE ML6 .... 111 H3
Tarland St GOV/IBX G51 .... 103 M3 ☑
Tarras Dr RNFRW PA4 .... 80 E8
Tarryholme Dr IRV KA12 .... 203 J7
Tasker St GRNKW/INVK PA16 .... 32 B4
Tasman Dr EKILS G75 .... 171 H2
Tasmania Qd WISHAW ML2 ...... 159 L6 ☑
Tassie Pl EKILN G74 .... 15 K2
Tassie St PLKSW/MSWD G43 .... 127 L5
Tattershall Rd
 STPS/GTHM/RID G33 .... 85 J7
Tavistock Dr
 PLKSW/MSWD G43 .... 127 K4
Tay Av PSLYS PA2 .... 100 F8
 RNFRW PA4 .... 80 E6 ☑
Taybank Dr AYRS KA7 .... 229 G6
Tay Ct EKILS G75 .... 170 E1
Tay Crs BSHPBGS G64 .... 64 B8
 STPS/GTHM/RID G33 .... 84 E8
Tay Gv EKILS G75 .... 170 E2
Tayinloan Dr CARLUKE ML8 .... 189 H1 ☑
Taylor Av KLBCH PA10 .... 98 F6
Taylor Brown Cl
 KLMNKN/STW KA3 .... 197 M1 ☑
Taylor Pl COWCAD C4 .... 5 M9
Taylor St ALEX/LLW G83 .... 25 J2 ☑
 AYR KA8 .... 224 F7
 CLYDBK G81 .... 80 C1
 COWCAD C4 .... 11 M1
Taymouth Dr GRK PA19 .... 30 F7
Taymouth St CAR/SHTL G32 .... 107 H6
Taynish Dr LNPK/KPK G44 .... 128 B5
Tay Pl DMBTN G82 .... 37 H2
 EKILS G75 .... 170 E2
 JNSTN PA5 .... 122 C1
 KLMNK KA1 .... 212 A4
 SHOTTS ML7 .... 137 L3
Tay Rd BSDN G61 .... 61 K7 ☑
 BSHPBGS G64 .... 64 B8
 PSTWK KA9 .... 221 J6
 TROON KA10 .... 216 C1
Tayside AIRDRIE ML6 .... 88 F8 ☑
Tay St CTBR ML5 .... 87 J8
 GRNKW/INVK PA16 .... 32 B4
Tay Ter EKILS G75 .... 170 E1
Teak Pl UD/BTH/TAN G71 .... 109 K8
Teal Dr KNTSWD G13 .... 81 G2
Teal Crs EKILS G75 .... 170 F4
Tealing Av
 CARD/HILL/MSPK G52 .... 103 J5
Tealing Crs
 CARD/HILL/MSPK G52 .... 103 J5 ☑
Teasel Av PLK/PH/NH G53 ...... 126 B6
Teawell Rd NMRNS G77 .... 150 D4 ☑
Technology Av
 BLTYR/CAMB G72 .... 155 J4
Teesdale EKILN G74 .... 153 J6
Teign Gv EKILS G75 .... 170 E2
Teith Av RNFRW PA4 .... 80 F7
Teith Dr BSDN G61 .... 61 J6
Teith St STPS/GTHM/RID G33 .... 84 E8
Telegraph Rd AIRDRIE ML6 ...... 91 H1
Telephone La KVD/HLHD G12 .... 82 C7 ☑
Telford Pl CUMB G67 .... 69 G2
 IRVSE KA11 .... 203 M8
Telford Rd CUMB G67 .... 69 G1
 EKILS G75 .... 14 D5
Telford St BLSH ML4 .... 133 G3
Teme Pl EKILS G75 .... 170 E2
Templand Crs DALRY KA24 ...... 184 C1
Templand Rd DALRY KA24 ...... 184 B1
Templar Av KNTSWD G13 .... 81 K1
Temple Gdns KNTSWD G13 ...... 81 M2 ☑
Templehill TROON KA10 .... 216 B8
Templeland Rd PLK/PH/NH G53.. 103 K7
Temple Locks Ct
 KNTSWD G13 .... 81 M2 ☑
Temple Locks Pl KNTSWD G13 .. 81 M2 ☑
Templerigg Ct PSTWK KA9 ...... 221 J8 ☑
Templerigg St PSTWK KA9 ...... 221 J8
Temple Rd MRYH/FIRH G20 ...... 82 A2
Templeton Crs PSTWK KA9 ...... 225 K1
Templeton St DMNK/BRGTN G40.. 12 B6
Tennant Av EKILN G74 .... 153 G2
Tennant St RNFRW PA4 .... 80 D5 ☑

Tennent St CTBR ML5 .... 110 B4
Tennyson Dr DEN/PKHD G31 .... 106 E5
Tenters Wy PSLY PA1 .... 8 B6
Tern Pl JNSTN PA5 .... 122 D2
Terrace Rd GRNK PA15 .... 2 E4
Terregles Av PLKSD/SHW G41 .. 104 C7
Terregles Crs PLKSD/SHW G41 .. 104 C7
Terregles Dr PLKSD/SHW G41 .. 104 C7
Teviot Av BSHPBGS G64 .... 64 A6
 PSLYS PA2 .... 123 L1
Teviot Crs BSDN G61 .... 61 K7
Teviot Dr BSHPTN PA7 .... 58 C7
Teviot Pl TROON KA10 .... 216 C5
Teviot St PGL PA14 .... 54 F3
 AYR KA8 .... 225 H6
 CTBR ML5 .... 87 K7
 KVGV G3 .... 104 C1
Teviot Ter JNSTN PA5 .... 122 C1
Tewkesbury Rd EKILN G74 ...... 154 D4
Thane Rd KNTSWD G13 .... 81 J3
Thanes Ga UD/BTH/TAN G71 .... 131 L4
Thankerton Av BLSH ML4 .... 133 M4 ☑
Thankerton Rd LRKH ML9 .... 176 B8
Tharsis St SPRGB/BLRNK G21 .... 6 D7
The Loaning KKNTL G66 .... 65 J2
Thimble St DMBTN G82 .... 25 K7
Third Av ALEX/LLW G83 .... 25 M4
 DMBTN G82 .... 37 J7
 IRV KA12 .... 208 B1
 KKNTL G66 .... 65 K8
 LNPK/KPK G44 .... 128 B2
 RNFRW PA4 .... 80 C7
 STPS/GTHM/RID G33 .... 85 H4
Third Gdns PLKSD/SHW G41 .... 104 A5
Thirdpart Crs KNTSWD G13 ...... 80 E2 ☑
Thirdpart Pl KLMNK KA1 .... 16 B6
Third Rd BLTYR/CAMB G72 ...... 155 L4
Third St UD/BTH/TAN G71 ...... 131 M1 ☑
Thirlmere EKILS G75 .... 170 F4
Thistle Bank KKNTL G66 .... 65 K5
Thistle Crs LRKH ML9 .... 176 B7
Thistledown Gv STPS/GTHM/RID G33.. 110 C3
Thistle Gdns MTHW ML1 .... 134 A5 ☑
Thistle Pl EKILN G74 .... 153 K6 ☑
Thistle Qd AIRDRIE ML6 .... 89 H8 ☑
Thistle Rd MTHW ML1 .... 134 A5
Thistle St AIRDRIE ML6 .... 89 H8 ☑
 GBLS G5 .... 11 J6
 KKNTL G66 .... 65 K2 ☑
 MTHW ML1 .... 135 J8 ☑
 PSLYS PA2 .... 8 C8
Thistle Ter GBLS G5 .... 11 H7
Thomas Campbell St
 SALT KA21 .... 201 G1 ☑
Thomas Muir Av
 BSHPBGS G64 .... 84 A1 ☑
Thomas Muir La GRNK PA15 .... 33 M7 ☑
Thomas Muir St GRNK PA15 .... 33 M7 ☑
Thomas Rd
 PSLY PA1 .... 8 B5
Thompson Av KKNTL G66 .... 65 L1
Thompson Pl CLYDBK G81 .... 60 C2 ☑
Thompson St DEN/PKHD G31 .... 12 E3
Thomson Av JNSTN PA5 .... 99 L6 ☑
 WISHAW ML2 .... 158 D8
Thomson Dr AIRDRIE ML6 .... 110 F3
 BSDN G61 .... 61 M3
 UD/BTH/TAN G71 .... 132 D4
Thomson Gv
 BLTYR/CAMB G72 .... 130 A2 ☑
Thomson St AYR KA8 .... 225 J7
 CARLUKE ML8 .... 178 F8
 JNSTN PA5 .... 99 L7 ☑
 KLMNKN/STW KA3 .... 16 F1
 RNFRW PA4 .... 80 C7
Thomson Ter
 KLMNKN/STW KA3 .... 197 J1
 SHOTTS ML7 .... 137 K4
Thom St GRNKW/INVK PA16 .... 32 C5
Thorn Av EKILN G74 .... 152 C6
 RAYR/DAL KA6 .... 231 H5
Thornbank St KVGV G3 .... 104 C1 ☑
Thorn Brae JNSTN PA5 .... 100 A6
Thornbridge Av
 BAIL/MDB/MHD G69 .... 108 B4 ☑
 KVD/HLHD G12 .... 82 C4 ☑
Thornbridge Gdns
 BAIL/MDB/MHD G69 .... 108 A4 ☑
Thornbridge Rd
 BAIL/MDB/MHD G69 .... 108 A4
Thorncliffe Gdns
 PLKSD/SHW G41 .... 104 E7
Thorncroft Dr LNPK/KPK G44 .. 128 E5
Thorndean Av BLSH ML4 .... 133 H5
Thorndean Crs BLSH ML4 .... 133 H5 ☑
Thorndene Av JNSTN PA5 .... 100 B6
Thorndene JNSTN PA5 .... 100 B6
Thornden La SCOT G14 .... 81 C5 ☑
Thorn Dr BSDN G61 .... 61 K4
 RUTH G73 .... 129 J5
Thorndyke EKILN G74 .... 154 C4
Thornhill JNSTN PA5 .... 100 A7
Thornhill Av BLTYR/CAMB G72.. 155 K1
 JNSTN PA5 .... 100 B7
Thornhill Ct KLWNG KA13 ...... 193 H6 ☑
Thornhill Dr JNSTN PA5 .... 100 B7
Thornhill Gdns JNSTN PA5 ...... 100 A6 ☑
 NMRNS G77 .... 150 D7
Thornhill Rd HMLTN ML3 .... 155 L5
Thornhill Wy CTBR ML5 .... 110 D5
Thornhouse Av IRV KA12 .... 203 K6 ☑
Thorniecroft Dr CUMB G67 ...... 68 C3
Thorniecroft Pl CUMB G67 ...... 68 C4 ☑
Thorniewood Gdns
 UD/BTH/TAN G71 .... 132 A3
Thorniewood Rd
 UD/BTH/TAN G71 .... 131 M1 ☑
Thornkip Pl CTBR ML5 .... 110 D4
Thornlea Dr GIF/THBK G46 ...... 127 J4
Thornlea St LNK/LMHG ML11 .. 199 M2
Thornlea St CARLUKE ML8 ...... 189 G1
Thornley Av KNTSWD G13 .... 81 H3
Thornliebank Rd GIF/THBK G46.. 127 G4
 PLKSW/MSWD G43 .... 127 G4
Thornlie Gill WISHAW ML2 ...... 159 H7
Thornly Park Av PSLYS PA2 ...... 124 F1
Thornly Park Dr PSLYS PA2 ...... 124 F1

Thornly Park Gdns
 PSLYS PA2 .... 101 L8 ☑
Thornly Park Rd PSLYS PA2 ...... 101 M8
Thorn Pl BLSH ML4 .... 133 H4
 BSDN G61 .... 61 K4
Thornside Rd JNSTN PA5 .... 100 A6 ☑
Thorn St KLMNKN/STW KA3 .... 207 G5
 PTCK G11 .... 82 A7
Thornton Av CRH/DND KA2 .... 205 L6
Thornton Pl HMLTN ML3 .... 174 D3 ☑
Thornton St CTBR ML5 .... 87 K7
 MRYH/FIRH G20 .... 82 D2
Thorntree Av BEITH KA15 .... 144 B7
 BLTYR/CAMB G72 .... 155 M4
 HMLTN ML3 .... 155 M4
Thorntree Wy
 UD/BTH/TAN G71 .... 132 B6
Thornwood Av PTCK G11 .... 81 M6
 KKNTL G66 .... 65 G4
 PTCK G11 .... 82 A7
Thornwood Crs PTCK G11 .... 81 M6
 IRV KA12 .... 208 A2
 PTCK G11 .... 81 M6 ☑
Thornwood Dr BRWEIR PA11 .... 98 B2
 IRV KA12 .... 208 A2
 PTCK G11 .... 81 M7
Thornwood Gdns PTCK G11 ...... 82 A7 ☑
Thornwood Pl PTCK G11 .... 81 M6
Thornwood Qd PTCK G11 .... 81 M6 ☑
Thornwood Rd PTCK G11 .... 81 M7
Thornwood Ter PTCK G11 .... 81 M7
Thornyburn Dr
 BAIL/MDB/MHD G69 .... 108 D5
Thornyburn Pl
 BAIL/MDB/MHD G69 .... 108 C5 ☑
Thornyflat Crs AYR KA8 .... 225 M7 ☑
Thornyflat Pl AYR KA8 .... 225 M7
Thornyflat Rd AYR KA8 .... 225 M7
Thornyflat St AYR KA8 .... 225 L7
Thrashbush Av WISHAW ML2 .. 159 K5
Thrashbush Crs WISHAW ML2 .. 159 K5
Thrashbush Rd WISHAW ML2 .. 159 K5
Threave Ct CARLUKE ML8 .... 178 E5 ☑
Threave Pl NMRNS G77 .... 150 B4 ☑
Threepwood Rd BEITH KA15 .... 144 D8
Threestonehill Av
 CAR/SHTL G32 .... 107 H3
Threshold EKILN G74 .... 15 J2
Threshold Pk EKILN G74 .... 15 J2
Thriplee Rd BRWEIR PA11 .... 98 C1
Thrums EKILN G74 .... 154 D4 ☑
Thrums Av BSHPBGS G64 .... 64 C8
Thrushbush La AIRDRIE ML6 .... 89 H7 ☑
Thrushbush Qd AIRDRIE ML6 .... 89 G7
Thrushbush Rd AIRDRIE ML6 .... 89 G7
Thrushcraig Crs PSLYS PA2 .... 9 J9
Thrush Pl JNSTN PA5 .... 122 D2
Thurso St PTCK G11 .... 82 C8 ☑
Thurston Rd
 CARD/HILL/MSPK G52 .... 103 G4
Thyme Sq MTHW ML1 .... 157 L1
Tibbermore Rd PTCK G11 .... 82 A6 ☑
Tig Rd AYR KA8 .... 225 G6
Tillanburn Rd MTHW ML1 ...... 134 F6
Tillet Ov PSLYN/LNWD PA3 ...... 101 K2
Tillie St MRYH/FIRH G20 .... 4 C3
Till St WISHAW ML2 .... 159 H3
Tillycairn Dr
 STPS/GTHM/RID G33 .... 85 K7 ☑
Tillycairn Rd
 STPS/GTHM/RID G33 .... 85 K7
Tillycairn St
 STPS/GTHM/RID G33 .... 85 L7
Tilt Rd WISHAW ML2 .... 159 M3
Tilt St STPS/GTHM/RID G33 ...... 84 E7
Timmons Gv BLSH ML4 .... 133 K4
Timmons Ter AIRDRIE ML6 ...... 111 K8
Tinker's La MTHW ML1 .... 157 J5
Tintagel Gdns
 BAIL/MDB/MHD G69 .... 66 F6
Tinto Av KLMNK KA1 .... 212 A5
Tintock Rd KKNTL G66 .... 46 B7
Tinto Crs WISHAW ML2 .... 159 J7
Tinto Dr BRHD/NEIL G78 .... 149 J1
Tinto Rd AIRDRIE ML6 .... 111 K3
 BSDN G61 .... 61 H3
 PLKSW/MSWD G43 .... 127 J4
Tinto St WISHAW ML2 .... 159 J7
Tinto Vw HMLTN ML3 .... 174 E1
Tinto Wy EKILS G75 .... 171 H4
Tinwald Pth
 CARD/HILL/MSPK G52 .... 103 G4
Tiree EKILN G74 .... 172 C2
Tiree Av PGL PA14 .... 55 G2
 RNFRW PA4 .... 102 C1
Tiree Ct CUMB G67 .... 68 D1
Tiree Crs WISHAW ML2 .... 159 M2
Tiree Dr CUMB G67 .... 68 D1
Tiree Gdns AIRDRIE ML6 .... 88 F4
 BSDN G61 .... 61 H3 ☑
 OLDK G60 .... 59 J3
Tiree Gra HMLTN ML3 .... 173 M8
Tiree Pl CTBR ML5 .... 109 L5 ☑
 NMRNS G77 .... 150 B3
 OLDK G60 .... 59 J3
 SVSTN KA20 .... 192 F8
Tiree Rd CUMB G67 .... 68 D1
Tiree St SPRGB/BLRNK G21 .... 7 J4
Tirry Av RNFRW PA4 .... 80 F7
Titchfield Rd TROON KA10 ...... 216 A7
Titchfield St GLSTN KA4 .... 214 B3
 KLMNK KA1 .... 16 F1
Titchfield Wy IRVSE KA11 ...... 204 A4
Titwood Dr KLMNKN/STW KA3.. 206 F5
Titwood Rd NMRNS G77 .... 150 D8
 PLKSD/SHW G41 .... 104 C7
Tiverton Av CAR/SHTL G32 ...... 107 K6
Tivoli Ct EKILS G75 .... 14 F9 ☑
 EKILS G75 .... 171 L3
Tobago Pl DMNK/BRGTN G40 .. 12 C5
 EKILS G75 .... 153 L6
Tobago St DMNK/BRGTN G40 .. 12 B5
 GRNK PA15 .... 2 C4
Tobermory Rd RUTH G73 .... 129 K6
Todburn Dr PSLYS PA2 .... 124 F2
Todd St DEN/PKHD G31 .... 13 K1
Todhill Av KLMNKN/STW KA3 .. 206 F5
Todhills North EKILS G75 .... 15 G6
Todhills South EKILS G75 .... 15 G6

Todholm Crs PSLYS PA2 .... 102 B7 ☑
Todholm Rd PSLYS PA2 .... 102 B7
Todholm Ter PSLYS PA2 .... 9 M8
 PSLYS PA2 .... 102 B7
Todrig Dr KLMNK KA1 .... 211 K5
Tofthill Av BSHPBGS G64 .... 63 M7
Tofthill Gdns BSHPBGS G64 ...... 63 L7
Tofts DALRY KA24 .... 184 D2
Togo Pl GRNK PA15 .... 2 B6
Tollbrae Av AIRDRIE ML6 .... 111 H2
Tollcross Park Gdns
 CAR/SHTL G32 .... 106 E6
Tollcross Park Gv
 CAR/SHTL G32 .... 106 F6 ☑
Tollcross Park Vw
 CAR/SHTL G32 .... 106 F6 ☑
Tollcross Rd CAR/SHTL G32 ...... 107 H6
 DEN/PKHD G31 .... 13 L6
Tollerton Dr IRV KA12 .... 203 K5
Tollpark Crs WISHAW ML2 ...... 160 A4 ☑
Tollpark Pl BALLOCH G68 .... 49 L1
Tollpark Rd BALLOCH G68 .... 49 L1
Toll St MTHW ML1 .... 157 M4
Toll Wynd HMLTN ML3 .... 174 C2 ☑
Tolsta St SMSTN G23 .... 62 E8
Tomtain Brae BALLOCH G68 .... 67 M2 ☑
Tomtain Ct BALLOCH G68 .... 67 M2 ☑
Toner Gdns WISHAW ML2 ...... 177 H2 ☑
Tontine Crs DMBTN G82 .... 36 D1
Tontine La CGLE G1 .... 11 L3
Tontine Pl RUTH G73 .... 129 L5
Topaz Ter BLSH ML4 .... 133 G6
Toponthank La
 KLMNK/STW KA3 .... 207 G3 ☑
Toppersfield KLBCH PA10 .... 99 J7 ☑
Torbeg Gdns EKILS G75 .... 171 H5 ☑
Torbracken HWWD PA9 .... 122 A3
Torbreck St
 CARD/HILL/MSPK G52 .... 103 M4
Torbrex Rd CUMB G67 .... 49 G8
Torburn Av GIF/THBK G46 ...... 127 H5
Tordene Pth BALLOCH G68 .... 48 D6
Torgyle St SMSTN G23 .... 62 D8
Tormeadow Rd NMRNS G77 .... 150 D4
Tormore St GOV/IBX G51 .... 103 K3
Tormusk Dr CSMK G45 .... 129 G5
Tormusk Gdns CSMK G45 .... 129 G5
Tormusk Gv CSMK G45 .... 129 G5
Tormusk Rd CSMK G45 .... 129 G5
Torness St PTCK G11 .... 82 C7 ☑
Torogay Pl PPK/MIL G22 .... 83 L1 ☑
Torogay St PPK/MIL G22 .... 83 J2
Torogay Ter PPK/MIL G22 .... 83 J1 ☑
Torphin Crs CAR/SHTL G32 ...... 107 G2
Torphin Wk CAR/SHTL G32 ...... 107 H2 ☑
Torrance Av AIRDRIE ML6 .... 111 K2
Torrance Rd BSHPBGS G64 .... 64 C2
 EKILN G74 .... 14 E2
 GRNK PA15 .... 33 H8
Torrance St
 SPRGB/BLRNK G21 .... 83 M5 ☑
Torran Dr RNFRW PA4 .... 79 L2
Torran Rd STPS/GTHM/RID G33.. 107 M2
Torranyard Ter HMLTN ML3 .... 155 L8
Torr Av BRWEIR PA11 .... 75 L7 ☑
Torriden Pl CTBR ML5 .... 109 L4
Torriden St CTBR ML5 .... 109 K4
Torridon Av MTHW ML1 .... 134 D6
 PLKSD/SHW G41 .... 104 B6
Torridon Gdns NMRNS G77 .... 151 H5
Torrington Av GIF/THBK G46 .... 151 G1
Torrington Crs CAR/SHTL G32 .. 107 K6
Torrin Rd SMSTN G23 .... 62 D8
Torrisdale Pl CTBR ML5 .... 109 L2 ☑
Torrisdale St CTBR ML5 .... 109 L2
 GVH/MTFL G42 .... 104 F7 ☑
 PLKSD/SHW G41 .... 104 F7
Torr La BRWEIR PA11 .... 75 L7 ☑
Torr Rd BRWEIR PA11 .... 98 C1
 BSHPBGS G64 .... 64 D8
Torr St PPK/MIL G22 .... 83 K5
Torryburn Rd SPRGB/BLRNK G21.. 7 J1
 SPRGB/BLRNK G21 .... 84 C5 ☑
Torwood Brae HMLTN ML3 ...... 155 M7
Toryglen Rd RUTH G73 .... 128 L1
Toryglen St GBLS G5 .... 105 L7
Tourhill Rd KLMNKN/STW KA3 .. 206 F4
Toward Ct BLTYR/CAMB G72 .... 131 L8 ☑
Toward Rd
 STPS/GTHM/RID G33 .... 107 J2
 WMYSB PA18 .... 50 A8
Toward Vw SKLM PA17 .... 70 B5 ☑
Tower Av BRHD/NEIL G78 .... 125 K5
Tower Crs RNFRW PA4 .... 80 B7
Tower Dr GRK PA19 .... 31 K3
 RNFRW PA4 .... 80 B7
Tower Pl MRYH/FIRH G20 .... 82 D4 ☑
 UD/BTH/TAN G71 .... 131 M3 ☑
Tower Rd BSHPBGS G64 .... 43 J6
 CUMB G67 .... 69 G3
 JNSTN PA5 .... 99 M8
Towerside Crs PLK/PH/NH G53 .. 103 G7
Towerside Rd PLK/PH/NH G53.. 103 G7
Towers Pl AIRDRIE ML6 .... 111 L1
Towers Rd AIRDRIE ML6 .... 111 L1
Tower St PLKSD/SHW G41 .... 10 A5
Tower Ter PSLY PA1 .... 8 E5
Towie Pl MRYH/FIRH G20 .... 82 D4 ☑
 UD/BTH/TAN G71 .... 131 M3 ☑
Townend KLMNKN/STW KA3 .. 206 C2
Townend La DALRY KA24 .... 184 C2
Townend Rd DMBTN G82 .... 37 G4
 KLMNK KA1 .... 211 L6
Townend St DALRY KA24 .... 184 C2
Townend Ter KLMNK KA1 .... 218 C5
Townfoot IRVSE KA11 .... 209 H1
Townhead IRV KA12 .... 203 K7
 KBRN KA25 .... 143 H7 ☑
 KLMNKN/STW KA3 .... 206 C2
 KLWNG KA13 .... 193 K5

Townhead Av BLSH ML4 .... 133 L1
Townhead Cl LARGS KA30 ...... 115 J6 10
Townhead Dr MTHW ML1 .... 134 F6
Townhead Pl
  UD/BTH/TAN G71 .... 132 A1 10
Townhead Rd CTBR ML5 .... 87 G8
  NMRNS G77 .... 150 D5 8
  SALT KA21 .... 201 G1
Townhead St BEITH KA15 ...... 168 B1 8
  HMLTN ML3 .... 156 F6 8
  KSYTH G65 .... 47 K2
  SVSTN KA20 .... 192 D8
Townhead Ter PSLY PA1 .... 8 F4
Townhill Rd HMLTN ML3 .... 155 L6
Townhill Ter HMLTN ML3 .... 155 L6 8
Townmill Rd DEN/PKHD G31 .... 6 E8
Townsend Rd COWCAD C4 .... 5 J6
Tradeston St GBLS C5 .... 10 F4
Trafalgar St CLYDBK G81 .... 59 M6
  DMNK/BRGTN G40 .... 105 M6 8
  GRNK PA15 .... 2 C1
Trainard Av CAR/SHTL G32 ...... 106 F5
Tramore Crs PSTWK KA9 .... 225 J1 8
Tranent Pl MTHW ML1 .... 135 J7
  STPS/GTHM/RID G33 .... 106 E1 8
Traquair Av WISHAW ML2 .... 159 J4
Traquair Dr
  CARD/HILL/MSPK G52 .... 103 H5
Treebank Crs AYRS KA7 .... 19 M5
Treeburn Av GIF/THBK G46 ...... 127 H6
Treemain Rd GIF/THBK G46 ..... 151 L4
Treesbank Rd KLMNK KA1 .... 211 M6 8
Trees Park Av BRHD/NEIL G78 .. 125 H5
Treeswoodhead Rd
  KLMNK KA1 .... 212 A5
Trefoil Av PLKSD/SHW G41 ...... 127 K1 8
Trelawney Ter SVSTN KA20 ...... 201 L3
Trent Pl EKILS G75 .... 170 E3
Trent St CTBR ML5 .... 87 K7
Tresta Rd SMSTN G23 .... 82 F1
Tribboch St LRKH ML9 .... 175 M6 8
Trigoni Ct LARGS KA30 .... 115 K8 8
Trinidad Gn EKILS G75 .... 153 G8 8
Trinity Av
  CARD/HILL/MSPK G52 .... 103 J5
Trinity Av BEITH KA15 .... 144 C8 8
Trinity Dr BLTYR/CAMB G72 .... 130 C6 8
  DALRY KA24 .... 184 B3
Trinley Rd KNTSWD G13 .... 61 K8
Triton Pl BLSH ML4 .... 133 M4
Trondra Pl ESTRH G34 .... 107 M1 8
Trondra Pl ESTRH G34 .... 107 M1 8
Trongate CGLE G1 .... 11 L3
Tron Pl LARGS KA30 .... 115 J6 11
Troon Av EKILS G75 .... 171 G3
Troon Ct EKILS G75 .... 171 H3
Troon Dr BRWEIR PA11 .... 98 C2
Troon Gdns BALLOCH G68 .... 48 F3
Troon Pl NMRNS G77 .... 151 G5
Troon Rd TROON KA10 .... 217 G6
Troon St DMNK/BRGTN G40 .... 13 G9
Trossachs Av MTHW ML1 .... 134 A4 8
Trossachs Ct MRYH/FIRH G20 .. 4 E3
Trossachs Rd RUTH G73 .... 129 K7
Trossachs St MRYH/FIRH G20 .. 4 E3
Troubridge Av KLBCH PA10 ...... 99 J8 8
Troubridge Crs KLBCH PA10 .... 99 H7
Trows Rd WISHAW ML2 .... 177 H3
Truce Rd KNTSWD G13 .... 81 H1
Truro Av BAIL/MDB/MHD G69 .. 66 F6
Tryfield Pl AYR KA8 .... 225 G7
Tryst Rd CUMB G67 .... 48 F8
Tudor La South SCOT G14 .... 81 L6 8
Tudor Rd SCOT G14 .... 81 L6 8
Tudor St
  BAIL/MDB/MHD G69 .... 107 M6 8
Tulley Wynd MTHW ML1 .... 133 K7 8
Tullichewan Crs
  ALEX/LLW G83 .... 25 K2 8
Tullichewan Dr ALEX/LLW G83 . 25 K2 8
Tullichewan Rd ALEX/LLW G83 . 25 K1 8
Tullis St DMNK/BRGTN G40 ..... 12 B8
Tulloch-ard Pl RUTH G73 .... 129 K6 8
Tulloch Gdns MTHW ML1 .... 158 B5
Tulloch St LNPK/KPK G44 .... 128 A3 8
Tullymet Rd HMLTN ML3 .... 174 D1
Tummel Av AIRDRIE ML6 .... 88 F7
Tummel Gn EKILN G74 .... 153 L6 8
Tummel Rd WMYSB PA18 .... 70 A1 8
Tummel St STPS/GTHM/RID G33 84 D3
Tummel Wy CUMB G67 .... 49 G7
Tunnel St KVGV G3 .... 10 A2
Tuphall Rd HMLTN ML3 .... 156 D7
Turnberry Av GRK PA19 .... 31 H3
  PTCK G11 .... 82 B6 8
Turnberry Ct KLWNG KA13 ...... 193 H6 8
Turnberry Crs CTBR ML5 .... 109 L5
Turnberry Dr BRWEIR PA11 ...... 98 C3 8
  HMLTN ML3 .... 155 K7
  KLMNK KA1 .... 211 M6 8
  NMRNS G77 .... 151 G5
  RUTH G73 .... 128 F5
Turnberry Gdns AIRDRIE ML6 .. 111 J8 8
  BALLOCH G68 .... 49 G4 8
Turnberry Pl CSMK G45 .... 128 F5 8
  EKILS G75 .... 171 H5
Turnberry Rd PTCK G11 .... 82 A6 8
Turnberry Wynd IRVSE KA11 .... 208 D1 8
  UD/BTH/TAN G71 .... 131 L6
Turnbull Av ALEX/LLW G83 ...... 25 K6
Turnbull Crs ALEX/LLW G83 ..... 25 K6 8
Turnbull St CGLE G1 .... 11 L4
Turner Pl KLMNKN/STW KA3 ... 207 L6
Turner Rd PSLYN/LNWD PA3 .... 101 M1
Turners Av PSLY PA1 .... 8 A6
Turner St CTBR ML5 .... 109 M3
Turnhill Av ERSK PA8 .... 79 H2 8
Turnhill Crs ERSK PA8 .... 79 H2 8
Turnhill Dr ERSK PA8 .... 79 H2
Turnhill Gdns ERSK PA8 .... 79 H2 8
Turningshaw Rd
  CRG/CRSL/HOU PA6 .... 77 L3
Turnlaw EKILS G75 .... 171 K4
Turnlaw Rd BLTYR/CAMB G72 .. 130 A7
Turnlaw St GBLS C5 .... 11 M8
Turnyland Mdw ERSK PA8 .... 79 H2

Turnyland Wy ERSK PA8 .... 79 H2 8
Turquoise Ter BLSH ML4 .... 133 C6 8
Turret Crs KNTSWD G13 .... 81 J1
Turret Rd KNTSWD G13 .... 81 J1
Turriff St GBLS C5 .... 11 G8
Tweed Av PSLYS PA2 .... 100 F7
Tweed Ct AIRDRIE ML6 .... 111 J4 8
Tweed Crs KLMNK KA1 .... 212 A4 8
  RNFRW PA4 .... 80 E7
  WISHAW ML2 .... 159 J4
Tweed Dr BSDN G61 .... 61 K6
Tweedmuir Pl CTBR ML5 .... 110 C6
Tweedsmuir BSHPBGS G64 ...... 64 C7
Tweedsmuir Crs BSDN G61 ...... 61 C7
Tweedsmuir Pk HMLTN ML3 ..... 174 C1 8
Tweedsmuir Rd
  CARD/HILL/MSPK G52 .... 103 H5
Tweed St AYR KA8 .... 225 H5
  CTBR ML5 .... 110 A6
  EKILS G75 .... 170 E2
  GRNKW/INVK PA16 .... 32 B4
  LRKH ML9 .... 176 A8
Tweedvale Av SCOT G14 .... 80 E3
Tweedvale Pl SCOT G14 .... 80 E3 8
Twinlaw St ESTRH G34 .... 86 D8
Tylney Rd PSLY PA1 .... 102 D4 8
Tyndrum Rd BSDN G61 .... 62 B4 8
Tyndrum St COWCAD C4 .... 5 J6
Tynecastle Crs CAR/SHTL G32 .. 107 H2 8
Tynecastle Pl CAR/SHTL G32 ... 107 H2 8
Tyne Pl EKILS G75 .... 170 E3
Tynron Ct HMLTN ML3 .... 155 K8
Tynwald Av RUTH G73 .... 129 J5

U

Udston Rd HMLTN ML3 .... 155 L5
Udston Ter HMLTN ML3 .... 155 M4 8
Uig Pl STPS/GTHM/RID G33 .... 107 L4 8
Uist Av PGL PA14 .... 55 G2
Uist Crs STPS/GTHM/RID G33 .. 85 L5
Uist Dr KKNTL G66 .... 66 A1
Uist Pl AIRDRIE ML6 .... 111 K3
Uist St GOV/IBX G51 .... 103 M2
Uist Wy WISHAW ML2 .... 159 L4
Ullswater EKILS G75 .... 170 F4 8
Ulundi Rd JNSTN PA5 .... 99 L7
Ulva St CARD/HILL/MSPK G52 .. 103 M4
Ulverston Ter HMLTN ML3 .... 174 C3
Umberly Rd KLMNK KA1 .... 211 L6
Underbank LARGS KA30 .... 115 H2
Underwood La PSLY PA1 .... 8 E3
Underwood Pl KLMNK KA1 .... 212 A6
Underwood Rd PSLY PA1 .... 8 E2
  PSTWK KA9 .... 225 K2
  RUTH G73 .... 129 J3
Underwood St
  PLKSD/SHW G41 .... 127 L1 8
Union Ar AYRS KA7 .... 18 F5
Union Av AYR KA8 .... 225 G6
Union Pl CGLE G1 .... 11 H1
Union St ALEX/LLW G83 .... 25 M5
  CARLUKE ML8 .... 178 F8
  CGLE G1 .... 11 H2
  HMLTN ML3 .... 156 D6
  KKNTL G66 .... 65 J1 8
  KLMNKN/STW KA3 .... 16 F2
  LARGS KA30 .... 115 J6
  LRKH ML9 .... 176 A6
  MTHW ML1 .... 134 A3
  NMLNS KA16 .... 215 L2
Union Street La
  ALEX/LLW G83 .... 25 M5 8
Unitas Crs CARLUKE ML8 .... 188 E1
Unitas Rd BLSH ML4 .... 133 J4
Unity Pk SHOTTS ML7 .... 137 K5
Unity Pl COWCAD C4 .... 4 F5
University Av KVD/HLHD G12 ... 82 D7
University Gdns KVD/HLHD G12 82 D7
University Pl KVD/HLHD G12 .... 82 D7
  PTCK G11 .... 82 C7 11
Unsted Pl PSLY PA1 .... 9 L4
Unthank Rd BLSH ML4 .... 133 J4
Uphall Pl
  STPS/GTHM/RID G33 .... 106 E2 13
Upland La SCOT G14 .... 81 J5 15
Upland Rd SCOT G14 .... 81 J5 16
U P La KSYTH G65 .... 47 H1
Uplawmoor Rd BRHD/NEIL G78 147 J5
Upper Adelaide St
  HBR/GL G84 .... 20 F8 8
Upper Arthur St
  ALEX/LLW G83 .... 25 K5 8
Upper Bourtree Ct RUTH G73 .. 129 J5 8
Upper Bourtree Dr RUTH G73 .. 129 H5 8
Upper Bridge St ALEX/LLW G83 25 K5
Upper Cartsburn St GRNK PA15 2 F8
Upper Colquhoun St
  HBR/GL G84 .... 20 D6
Upper Crofts AYRS KA7 .... 228 F8
Upper Glenburn Rd BSDN G61 . 61 K4
Upper Glenfinlas St HBR/GL G84 20 E7
Upper Loaning AYRS KA7 .... 228 F8
Upper Mill St AIRDRIE ML6 ..... 111 G1
Upper Smollett St
  ALEX/LLW G83 .... 25 K5
Upper Stoneymollan Rd
  ALEX/LLW G83 .... 25 G1
Upper Sutherland Crs
  HBR/GL G84 .... 20 B6
Upper Sutherland St
  HBR/GL G84 .... 20 B6 8
U P Rd KSYTH G65 .... 47 H1 8
Urquhart Crs RNFRW PA4 .... 80 C7
Urquhart Dr EKILN G74 .... 154 A6 8
  GRK PA19 .... 30 F4 8
Urquhart Rd
  KLMNKN/STW KA3 .... 207 K7 8

Urrdale Rd PLKSD/SHW G41 ... 104 B4
Usmore Pl
  STPS/GTHM/RID G33 .... 107 L4 8

V

Vaila St SMSTN G23 .... 82 F2
Valerio Ct BLTYR/CAMB G72 .... 155 K1 8
Valetta Pl CLYDBK G81 .... 59 K6
Valeview Ter DMBTN G82 .... 37 G3
  GVH/MTFL G42 .... 128 A1 8
Vallantine Crs
  UD/BTH/TAN G71 .... 132 A1 8
Vallay St PPK/MIL G22 .... 83 K1
Vallay Ct HMLTN ML3 .... 156 C7
Valleyfield EKILS G75 .... 14 C4
  KKNTL G66 .... 45 G3
Valleyfield Dr BALLOCH G68 .... 47 L8 8
Valleyfield St SPRGB/BLRNK G21 6 B2 8
Valley Vw BLTYR/CAMB G72 .... 130 C3 8
  MTHW ML1 .... 158 B6
Vancouver Dr EKILS G75 .... 153 H8
Vancouver La SCOT G14 .... 81 J5 7
  SCOT G14 .... 81 K5 8
Vancouver Pl CLYDBK G81 .... 59 K5 8
Vancouver Rd SCOT G14 .... 81 J6
Vanguard St CLYDBK G81 .... 60 D7
Vardar Av CRMNK/CLK/EAG 151 J1
Vardon Lea MTHW ML1 .... 134 E2
Varna La SCOT G14 .... 81 L6
Varna Rd SCOT G14 .... 81 L5
Varnsdorf Wy AIRDRIE ML6 ..... 111 K3
Vassart Pl MRYH/FIRH G20 ..... 82 F4 8
Vaults La KLWNG KA13 .... 193 L4
Veir Ter DMBTN G82 .... 36 E6
Veitches Ct CLYDBK G81 .... 60 A3 8
Veitch Pl KKNTL G66 .... 44 D1
Vennacher Rd SHOTTS ML7 ..... 137 L3
Vennacher Rd RNFRW PA4 ...... 80 A5
Vennal St DALRY KA24 .... 184 B2
Vennel La BSHPBGS/STW KA3 . 197 L1
Vennel St KLMNKN/STW KA3 .. 197 L1
Vermont Av RUTH G73 .... 129 G2 8
Vermont St PLKSD/SHW G41 ... 104 D4
Vernon Bank EKILN G74 .... 153 L6
Vernon Dr PSLYN/LNWD PA3 ... 100 A3
Vernon Pl CRH/DND KA2 .... 209 L7
Vernon St SALT KA21 .... 200 F2
Verona Av SCOT G14 .... 81 J5
Verona Gdns SCOT G14 .... 81 J5 8
Verona La SCOT G14 .... 81 J5
Vesalius St CAR/SHTL G32 ...... 107 G4 8
Viaduct Cir KLWNG KA13 .... 193 L4
Viaduct Rd
  CRMNK/CLK/EAG G76 .... 151 M3
Vicarfield St GOV/IBX G51 ...... 104 B2
Vicarland Rd BLTYR/CAMB G72 130 A4
Vicars Wk BLTYR/CAMB G72 ... 130 B4
Vickers St MTHW ML1 .... 157 H1
Victoria Av CARLUKE ML8 .... 178 E8
Victoria Circ KVD/HLHD G12 ... 82 C6 10
Victoria Crs AIRDRIE ML6 .... 110 E3
  CRMNK/CLK/EAG G76 .... 151 M2
  IRV KA12 .... 203 H8
  KSYTH G65 .... 47 J1
  WISHAW ML2 .... 158 D5 8
Victoria Crescent La
  KVD/HLHD G12 .... 82 C6 8
Victoria Crescent Pl
  KVD/HLHD G12 .... 82 C6 9
Victoria Crescent Rd
  KVD/HLHD G12 .... 82 C6 8
Victoria Dr BRHD/NEIL G78 .... 125 H5 8
  TROON KA10 .... 216 C7
Victoria Dr East RNFRW PA4 ... 80 C7 8
Victoria Dr West RNFRW PA4 .. 80 B6
Victoria Gdns
  BRHD/NEIL G78 .... 125 H5 8
  KLMCLM PA13 .... 55 J8
Victoria La NMRNS G77 .... 150 D7
Victoria Pk AYRS KA7 .... 18 D8
  KSYTH G65 .... 47 H1
Victoria Park Cnr SCOT G14 .... 81 K5
Victoria Park Dr North
  SCOT G14 .... 81 K6
Victoria Park Dr South
  SCOT G14 .... 81 K6 8
Victoria Park Gdns North
  PTCK G11 .... 81 M6
Victoria Park Gdns South
  PTCK G11 .... 81 M6
Victoria Park La South
  SCOT G14 .... 81 K6 8
Victoria Park St SCOT G14 ...... 81 K6 8
Victoria Pl AIRDRIE ML6 .... 110 F3
  BLSH ML4 .... 132 F5 8
  BRHD/NEIL G78 .... 125 J5
  KSYTH G65 .... 47 J1
  MLNGV G62 .... 42 B8 8
Victoria Qd MTHW ML1 .... 133 M4
Victoria Rd BALLOCH G68 .... 48 D3
  BRHD/NEIL G78 .... 125 H5 8
  GRK PA19 .... 31 J2
  JNSTN PA5 .... 99 K4
  KKNTL G66 .... 65 J4 8
  PSLYS PA2 .... 8 D9
  RUTH G73 .... 129 H3
  SALT KA21 .... 200 F1
  STPS/GTHM/RID G33 .... 85 K4
Victoria St ALEX/LLW G83 .... 25 L5 8
  AYR KA8 .... 19 H2
  BLTYR/CAMB G72 .... 155 K3
  DMBTN G82 .... 37 G3
  HMLTN ML3 .... 156 B3
  KKNTL G66 .... 65 J1
  LRKH ML9 .... 176 A6
  RUTH G73 .... 129 G1
  WISHAW ML2 .... 160 A5
Victor St AIRDRIE ML6 .... 90 A7
Victory Dr KLBCH PA10 .... 99 G5 8
Viewbank Av AIRDRIE ML6 ...... 111 H7
Viewbank St CTBR ML5 .... 87 M4
Viewfield AIRDRIE ML6 .... 110 F3

Viewfield Av
  BAIL/MDB/MHD G69 .... 107 M4
  BLTYR/CAMB G72 .... 131 L8
  BSHPBGS G64 .... 83 L1 8
  KKNTL G66 .... 45 H4
  KKNTL G66 .... 65 J4
  LOCHW PA12 .... 120 D7 8
Viewfield Dr
  BAIL/MDB/MHD G69 .... 107 L4
Viewfield La KVD/HLHD G12 .... 4 E3
Viewfield Rd AYR KA8 .... 225 C7
  BLSH ML4 .... 132 F6
  BSHPBGS G64 .... 83 L1 8
  CTBR ML5 .... 109 J5
Viewglen Ct CSMK G45 .... 128 D8
Viewmount Dr MRYH/FIRH G20 82 D2
Viewpark Av DEN/PKHD G31 ... 7 G8
Viewpark Dr RUTH G73 .... 129 H3
Viewpark Gdns RNFRW PA4 ..... 80 B7
Viewpark Pl MTHW ML1 .... 157 J3
Viewpark Rd MTHW ML1 .... 157 J3
Viewpoint Rd
  SPRGB/BLRNK G21 .... 83 M1
Viking Crs CRG/CRSL/HOU PA6 99 K1
Viking Rd AIRDRIE ML6 .... 111 K4
Viking Ter EKILS G75 .... 171 L3
Viking Wy GIF/THBK G46 .... 126 F4
  LARGS KA30 .... 115 L6
Villafield Av BSHPBGS G64 ...... 64 A6
Villafield Dr BSHPBGS G64 ...... 64 A6
Village Gdns
  BLTYR/CAMB G72 .... 131 L8 8
Village Rd BLTYR/CAMB G72 ... 130 E4
Vineburgh Av IRV KA12 .... 203 H5
Vineburgh Ct IRV KA12 .... 203 H5
Vine Park Av KLMNKN/STW KA3 206 B2
Vine Park Dr
  KLMNKN/STW KA3 .... 206 B2 8
Vine St PTCK G11 .... 82 B7 8
Vinicombe La
  KVD/HLHD G12 .... 82 D6 8
Vinicombe St KVD/HLHD G12 .. 82 D6
Vintner St COWCAD C4 .... 5 J4
Viola Pl BSHPBGS G64 .... 64 C1
Violet Gdns CARLUKE ML8 ...... 188 E1 8
Violet Pl MTHW ML1 .... 134 B3
Violet St PSLY PA1 .... 9 L4
Virginia Ct CCLE G1 .... 11 J2
Virginia Gdns AYR KA8 .... 225 C7
  MLNGV G62 .... 62 C1 8
Virginia Pl CCLE G1 .... 11 J2
Virginia St CGLE G1 .... 11 J2
  GRNK PA15 .... 2 F5
Viscount Av RNFRW PA4 .... 80 C8
Viscount Ga UD/BTH/TAN G71 . 131 L4
Vivian Av MLNGV G62 .... 41 M8
Voil Dr LNPK/KPK G44 .... 128 A5
Vorlich Ct BRHD/NEIL G78 ...... 125 J8 8
Vorlich Gdns BSDN G61 .... 61 J2
Vorlich Pl KLMNK KA1 .... 212 A5
Vrackie Pl KLMNK KA1 .... 212 A5
Vulcan St MTHW ML1 .... 157 L2
  SPRGB/BLRNK G21 .... 6 B1 8

W

Waddell Av AIRDRIE ML6 .... 88 D5
Waddell Ct KLMNKN/STW KA3 . 206 F5
Waddell St AIRDRIE ML6 .... 89 C8
  GBLS C5 .... 11 L7
Waggon Rd AYR KA8 .... 224 F7
Waid Av NMRNS G77 .... 150 C3
Waldemar Rd KNTSWD G13 ..... 81 J2
Walden St KLMNK KA1 .... 212 E3
Waldo St KNTSWD G13 .... 81 M2 8
Walker Av KLMNKN/STW KA3 .. 17 J5
  TROON KA10 .... 216 D4
Walkerburn Dr WISHAW ML2 ... 159 J3
Walkerburn Rd
  CARD/HILL/MSPK G52 .... 103 H5
Walker Ct PTCK G11 .... 82 B8 8
Walker Dr JNSTN PA5 .... 100 B7
Walker Pth
  UD/BTH/TAN G71 .... 132 A1 11
Walker Rd AYR KA8 .... 225 H7
Walkerston Av LARGS KA30 .... 115 K8 8
  KBRN KA25 .... 143 G8
  PSLY PA1 .... 8 E4
  PTCK G11 .... 82 B8
Walkinshaw Crs
  PSLYN/LNWD PA3 .... 101 H3
Walkinshaw Rd
  PSLYN/LNWD PA3 .... 79 H6
Walkinshaw St
  DMNK/BRGTN G40 .... 12 E7
  JNSTN PA5 .... 99 M6
Wallace Av BSHPTN PA7 .... 58 B5
  CRH/DND KA2 .... 209 M7
  JNSTN PA5 .... 99 M6
  SVSTN KA20 .... 192 D8
  TROON KA10 .... 216 D3
Wallace Ct KLMNK KA1 .... 212 E3 8
Wallace Dr LRKH ML9 .... 176 C7 8
Wallacefield Rd TROON KA10 .. 216 D6
Wallacehill Rd KLMNK KA1 ...... 211 M5
Wallace Pl BLTYR/CAMB G72 ... 131 L8 8
  GRNK PA15 .... 2 D4
  HMLTN ML3 .... 157 G7
Wallace Rd IRV KA12 .... 203 J5
  MTHW ML1 .... 134 B7 8
  PSLYN/LNWD PA3 .... 80 A8
  WMYSB PA18 .... 70 A1
Wallace St AIRDRIE ML6 .... 90 A7
  CLYDBK G81 .... 80 B1
  CTBR ML5 .... 110 A4
  DMBTN G82 .... 37 G7
  GBLS C5 .... 11 G5 8
  GLSTN KA4 .... 214 C3
  GRNKW/INVK PA16 .... 32 C5
  KLMNK KA1 .... 16 D7
  MTHW ML1 .... 157 K2
  PGL PA14 .... 34 B8
  PSLYN/LNWD PA3 .... 9 G1
  RUTH G73 .... 129 G2 8

Viewfield Av
Viewfield Av
Waterside Gdns
  CRMNK/CLK/EAG G76 .... 152 D2
  HMLTN ML3 .... 156 E8 8
Waterside Rd CRMNK/CLK/EAG G76 152
  D1 8
  KKNTL G66 .... 65 L2

Wallacetown Av
  KLMNKN/STW KA3 .... 207 H3 8
Wallace Vw KLMNK KA1 .... 211 M4
Wallace Wy LNK/LMHG ML11 .. 199 J5
Wallacewell Crs
  SPRGB/BLRNK G21 .... 84 B4
Wallacewell Pl
  SPRGB/BLRNK G21 .... 84 B4 8
Wallacewell Qd
  SPRGB/BLRNK G21 .... 84 C3
Wallacewell Rd
  SPRGB/BLRNK G21 .... 84 B4
Wallbrae Rd CUMB G67 .... 68 F1 8
Wallneuk PSLY PA1 .... 9 J2
Wallneuk Rd PSLYN/LNWD PA3 9 K2
Walls St CGLE G1 .... 11 L2
Walmer Crs GOV/IBX G51 .... 104 C4
Walnut Crs JNSTN PA5 .... 123 H1
  PPK/MIL G22 .... 83 K4
Walnut Dr KKNTL G66 .... 65 H3 8
Walnut Pl PPK/MIL G22 .... 83 K4 8
  UD/BTH/TAN G71 .... 109 J8 8
Walnut Rd KLMNK KA1 .... 211 J2
  PPK/MIL G22 .... 83 J4
Walpole Pl JNSTN PA5 .... 122 C2
Walter St DEN/PKHD G31 .... 13 H1
  WISHAW ML2 .... 159 K6
Walton Av NMRNS G77 .... 150 C3
Walton St BRHD/NEIL G78 ...... 125 J6
  PLKSD/SHW G41 .... 127 L1 8
Wamba Av KNTSWD G13 .... 81 L1
Wamphray Pl EKILS G75 .... 170 D2
Wandilla Av CLYDBK G81 .... 60 D7 8
Wanlock St GOV/IBX G51 .... 82 A8
Ward Ct AYR KA8 .... 225 H5
Wardend Rd BSHPBGS G64 ..... 44 B8
Warden Rd KNTSWD G13 .... 81 K2
Wardhill Rd SPRGB/BLRNK G21 84 B4
Wardhouse Rd PSLYS PA2 .... 124 C2
Wardie Pl
  STPS/GTHM/RID G33 .... 107 M2 8
Wardie Rd BAIL/MDB/MHD G69 108 A2 8
Wardlaw Av RUTH G73 .... 129 H2
Wardlaw Crs EKILS G75 .... 15 H9
  TROON KA10 .... 217 G5
Wardlaw Dr RUTH G73 .... 129 H2 8
Wardlaw Gdns IRVSE KA11 ..... 204 B2
Wardlaw Rd BSDN G61 .... 61 M8
  KLMNKN/STW KA3 .... 207 L4
Wardneuk PSTWK KA9 .... 225 J3 8
Wardneuk Dr
  KLMNKN/STW KA3 .... 207 L5
Wardpark Ct CUMB G67 .... 49 K3
Wardpark Pl CUMB G67 .... 49 K3
Wardpark Rd CUMB G67 .... 49 J3
Ward Rd AYR KA8 .... 225 H5
Wardrop Pl EKILN G74 .... 153 M6 8
Wardrop St BEITH KA15 .... 168 C1
  GOV/IBX G51 .... 104 A1 8
  PSLY PA1 .... 9 G5
Wards Crs CTBR ML5 .... 109 L4
Wards Pl KLMNK KA1 .... 16 E6
Ware Rd STPS/GTHM/RID G33 . 107 M2
Warilda Av CLYDBK G81 .... 60 C7 8
Warlock Dr BRWEIR PA11 .... 76 D8 8
Warlock Rd BRWEIR PA11 .... 76 D7
Warly Dr CRH/DND KA2 .... 209 M8
Warly Pl CRH/DND KA2 .... 209 M8
Warner St SVSTN KA20 .... 201 K2
Warnock Crs BLSH ML4 .... 133 H5
Warnock Rd NMRNS G77 .... 150 C3
Warnock St COWCAD C4 .... 6 B9
Warren Park Ms LARGS KA30 .. 115 K8
Warrenpark Rd LARGS KA30 .... 115 K8
Warren Rd HMLTN ML3 .... 174 D1
Warren St GVH/MTFL G42 .... 105 H8
Warren Wk KKNTL G66 .... 44 E2
Warriston Crs
  STPS/GTHM/RID G33 .... 7 M9
Warriston Pl CAR/SHTL G32 .... 107 H2 8
Warriston St
  STPS/GTHM/RID G33 .... 7 L9
Warrix Av IRV KA12 .... 203 K7
Warrix Gdns TROON KA10 .... 220 E1
Warroch St KVGV G3 .... 10 D2
Warwick EKILN G74 .... 154 C5
Warwick Gv
  BLTYR/CAMB G72 .... 155 L4 8
Warwickhill Rd KLMNK KA1 ..... 16 B2
Warwick Rd GRNKW/INVK PA16 31 L5
Washington Rd KKNTL G66 ..... 45 H8
  PSLYN/LNWD PA3 .... 101 M1
Washington St KVGV G3 .... 10 E3
Watchmeal Crs CLYDBK G81 .... 60 C2
Waterbank Rd
  CRMNK/CLK/EAG G76 .... 152 D3
Watercut Rd IRV KA12 .... 202 F1
Waterfoot Av PLK/PH/NH G53 . 126 C1
Waterfoot Rd NMRNS G77 .... 150 F6
Waterfoot Rw
  CRMNK/CLK/EAG G76 .... 151 L6
Waterfoot Ter
  PLK/PH/NH G53 .... 126 C1 8
Waterford Rd GIF/THBK G46 ... 127 H6
Waterlands Gdns
  CARLUKE ML8 .... 179 G6 8
Waterlands Pl CARLUKE ML8 ... 178 A5 8
Waterlands Rd CARLUKE ML8 .. 178 B3
Waterloo Dr
  LNK/LMHG ML11 .... 199 G4 8
Waterloo La CGLW G2 .... 10 F1
Waterloo Rd LNK/LMHG ML11 . 198 F3
  PSTWK KA9 .... 225 H4
Waterloo St CGLW G2 .... 10 F1
Watermill Av KKNTL G66 .... 65 K5
Water Rd BRHD/NEIL G78 .... 125 J6
Water Rw GOV/IBX G51 .... 104 A1
Watersaugh Dr MTHW ML1 ..... 135 H7
Waterside IRV KA12 .... 203 H6
Waterside Av NMRNS G77 .... 150 C5
Waterside Ct KLMNK KA1 .... 16 E5
Waterside Dr NMRNS G77 .... 150 C5
Waterside Gdns
  CRMNK/CLK/EAG G76 .... 152 D2
  HMLTN ML3 .... 156 E8 8
Waterside Rd CRMNK/CLK/EAG G76 152
  D1 8
  KKNTL G66 .... 65 L2

KLWNG KA13 .... 193 L5
Waterside St GBLS G5 .... 11 L8
KLMNK KA1 .... 16 E5
LARGS KA30 .... 115 K6
Waterston Wy LOCHW PA12 .... 120 C6
Water St PGL PA14 .... 34 C7 [7]
Wateryetts Dr KLMCLM PA13 .... 55 K8 [3]
Watling Pl EKILS G75 .... 153 G8 [7]
Watling St MTHW ML1 .... 133 H8
UD/BTH/TAN G71 .... 108 E8
Watson Av PSLYN/LNWD PA3 .... 100 B4
RUTH G73 .... 128 F2
Watson Crs KSYTH G65 .... 47 L1 [6]
Watson Rd BLTYR/CAMB G72 .... 155 H2 [2]
Watson St BLTYR/CAMB G72 .... 155 J2
CGLE G5 .... 11 L3
KLMNKN/STW KA3 .... 17 J5
LRKH ML9 .... 175 M6
MTHW ML1 .... 157 L4
UD/BTH/TAN G71 .... 131 M4
Watson Ter IRV KA12 .... 203 K7
Watsonville Pk MTHW ML1 .... 157 L3 [4]
Watt Crs BLSH ML4 .... 133 H2
Wattfield Rd AYRS KA7 .... 18 D8
Watt La BRWEIR PA11 .... 98 E2
Watt Low Av RUTH G73 .... 128 F3 [5]
RUTH G73 .... 129 G3
Watt Pl GRNK PA15 .... 2 E4
MLNGV G62 .... 41 M6 [8]
Watt Rd BRWEIR PA11 .... 98 D2
CARD/HILL/MSPK G52 .... 102 F2
Watt St AIRDRIE ML6 .... 89 J8
GBLS G5 .... 10 C5
GRNKW/INVK PA16 .... 2 B2
Waukglen Av PLK/PH/NH G53 .... 126 C6
Waukglen Crs PLK/PH/NH G53 .... 126 C6
Waukglen Dr PLK/PH/NH G53 .... 126 B6
Waukglen Gdns
PLK/PH/NH G53 .... 126 B6
Waukglen Pth
PLK/PH/NH G53 .... 126 B6 [5]
Waukglen Pl PLK/PH/NH G53 .... 126 B6
Waukglen Rd PLK/PH/NH G53 .... 126 B6
Waulking Mill Rd CLYDBK G81 .... 60 C2
Waulkmill Av BRHD/NEIL G78 .... 125 J5
Waulkmill Rd KLMNK KA1 .... 17 G6 [6]
Waulkmill St GIF/THBK G46 .... 126 E5
Waulkmill Wy
BRHD/NEIL G78 .... 125 K5 [2]
Waverley EKILN G74 .... 154 D5
Waverley Av HBR/GL G84 .... 23 G1
KLMNK KA1 .... 206 C8
Waverley Ct UD/BTH/TAN G71 .... 132 A7
Waverley Crs CUMB G67 .... 68 D2
HMLTN ML3 .... 155 M5
KKNTL G66 .... 65 K1
LNK/LMHG ML11 .... 199 J4
Waverley Dr AIRDRIE ML6 .... 89 H8
RUTH G73 .... 129 J2 [2]
WISHAW ML2 .... 159 H5
Waverley Gdns JNSTN PA5 .... 100 D7 [7]
PLKSD/SHW G41 .... 104 E8
Waverley Pl SALT KA21 .... 191 L8
Waverley Rd PSLYS PA2 .... 123 M1
Waverley St CTBR ML5 .... 88 B8
GRNKW/INVK PA16 .... 32 C6
HMLTN ML3 .... 155 M5
PLKSD/SHW G41 .... 104 E8
Waverley Ter BLTYR/CAMB G72 .... 155 J4
DMBTN G82 .... 36 B5
Weardale La
STPS/GTHM/RID G33 .... 107 J1
Weardale St
STPS/GTHM/RID G33 .... 107 J1
Weaver Av NMRNS G77 .... 150 D3
Weaver Crs AIRDRIE ML6 .... 111 G4
Weaver La KLBCH PA10 .... 99 G5
Weaver Pl EKILS G75 .... 170 E2
Weavers Av PSLY PA1 .... 8 B7
Weavers Pl NMLNS KA16 .... 215 L2 [3]
Weavers Rd PSLY PA1 .... 8 B7
Weaver St AYR KA8 .... 224 F7
COWCAD G4 .... 11 M1
Weavers Wk LNK/LMHG ML11 .... 199 G6
Weaver Ter PSLYS PA2 .... 9 L7
Webster Groves WISHAW ML2 .... 159 K4
Webster St
DMNK/BRGTN G40 .... 106 A6 [3]
KNTSWD G13 .... 80 E1 [4]
Wedderlea Dr
CARD/HILL/MSPK G52 .... 103 H4
Wee Cl BEITH KA15 .... 144 B8 [10]
Weensmoor Rd
PLK/PH/NH G53 .... 125 M5 [1]
Weeple Dr PSLYN/LNWD PA3 .... 100 B3
Wee Sunnyside Rd HMLTN ML3 .... 175 H7
Weighhouse Cl PSLY PA1 .... 9 G5 [9]
Weighhouse Rd CARLUKE ML8 .... 178 E6
Weir Av BRHD/NEIL G78 .... 125 J7
PSTWK KA9 .... 221 K8
Weir Pl CARLUKE ML8 .... 177 M5
GRNK PA15 .... 3 M9
Weir Rd ARD KA22 .... 191 K5
AYR KA8 .... 224 F7
Weirston Rd KLWNG KA13 .... 194 A6
Weir St CTBR ML5 .... 110 A2
GRNK PA15 .... 33 L7
PSLY PA1 .... 9 J3
Weirwood Av
BAIL/MDB/MHD G69 .... 107 M5
Weirwood Gdns
BAIL/MDB/MHD G69 .... 107 M5 [3]
Welbeck Crs TROON KA10 .... 216 A7
Welbeck Rd GLSTN KA4 .... 214 B4 [4]
PLK/PH/NH G53 .... 126 B4
Welbeck St
GRNKW/INVK PA16 .... 32 C1 [3]
KLMNK KA1 .... 17 H7
Weldon Pl KSYTH G65 .... 47 M6
Welfare Av BLTYR/CAMB G72 .... 130 D3
Welland Pl EKILS G75 .... 170 E2 [7]
Wellbank Av WKIL KA23 .... 181 M7
Wellbank Pl
UD/BTH/TAN G71 .... 131 M4 [3]
Wellbrae LRKH ML9 .... 176 A7 [3]
Wellbrae Rd HMLTN ML3 .... 156 B8
Wellcroft Pl GBLS G5 .... 11 G7
Wellcroft Rd HMLTN ML3 .... 155 L6

Wellcroft Ter HMLTN ML3 .... 155 L6
Well Dr LNK/LMHG ML11 .... 198 E6
Wellesley Crs BALLOCH G68 .... 47 L8 [2]
EKILS G75 .... 170 F2
Wellesley Dr BALLOCH G68 .... 47 K8
EKILS G75 .... 170 F1
Wellfield Av GIF/THBK G46 .... 127 H6
Wellgatehead LNK/LMHG ML11 .... 199 G6
Wellgate St LRKH ML9 .... 176 A5
Well Gn PLKSW/MSWD G43 .... 127 J1 [1]
Wellhall Ct HMLTN ML3 .... 156 B5 [5]
Wellhall Rd HMLTN ML3 .... 155 M7
Wellhead Ct
LNK/LMHG ML11 .... 199 H5 [4]
Wellhouse Crs
STPS/GTHM/RID G33 .... 107 L2
Wellhouse Rd
STPS/GTHM/RID G33 .... 107 M1
Wellington EKILS G75 .... 171 H2
Wellington Av
KLMNKN/STW KA3 .... 212 D1
Wellington La AYRS KA7 .... 18 D4 [1]
CGLW G2 .... 10 F1
Wellington Pl CLYDBK G81 .... 59 K6 [6]
CTBR ML5 .... 109 J4
KLMNKN/STW KA3 .... 16 F1
WISHAW ML2 .... 177 K1 [1]
Wellington Rd BSHPBGS G64 .... 64 B5
Wellington Sq AYRS KA7 .... 18 D3
Wellington St AIRDRIE ML6 .... 89 G8
CGLW G2 .... 11 G1
GRNK PA15 .... 2 B5
KLMNKN/STW KA3 .... 16 F2
PSLYN/LNWD PA3 .... 8 F2
PSTWK KA9 .... 225 H4
WISHAW ML2 .... 158 C4
Wellington Ter
LNK/LMHG ML11 .... 198 F4
Wellknowe Av EKILN G74 .... 152 C6
Wellknowe Pl EKILN G74 .... 152 B6
Wellknowe Rd EKILN G74 .... 152 C6
Well La KKNTL G66 .... 44 D1
Wellmeadow Cl NMRNS G77 .... 150 D4 [1]
Wellmeadow Gn
NMRNS G77 .... 150 D4 [4]
Wellmeadow Rd
PLKSW/MSWD G43 .... 127 G3
Wellmeadow St PSLY PA1 .... 8 E4
Wellmeadow Wy NMRNS G77 .... 150 D4
Wellpark AYRS KA7 .... 228 F8
Wellpark Av KLMNKN/STW KA3 .... 17 L5
Wellpark Gv KLMNKN/STW KA3 .... 17 L4
Wellpark La SALT KA21 .... 200 F1 [1]
Wellpark Pl KLMNKN/STW KA3 .... 17 L5
Wellpark Rd MTHW ML1 .... 157 J3 [3]
SALT KA21 .... 200 F2
Wellpark St COWCAD G4 .... 12 B2
Wellpark Ter BRHD/NEIL G78 .... 148 D3 [3]
LNK/LMHG ML11 .... 199 G6
Wellshot Dr BLTYR/CAMB G72 .... 129 M4
Wellshot Rd CAR/SHTL G32 .... 106 F5
Wellside Av AIRDRIE ML6 .... 89 G8
Wellside Dr BLTYR/CAMB G72 .... 130 C5
Wellside La AIRDRIE ML6 .... 89 G8 [2]
Wellside Qd AIRDRIE ML6 .... 89 G7 [2]
Wellsquarry Rd EKILN G74 .... 153 J5
Wells St CLYDBK G81 .... 59 M6
Well St PSLY PA1 .... 8 C2
WKIL KA23 .... 181 J4
Wellview Dr MTHW ML1 .... 157 K2 [2]
Wellwood Av
LNK/LMHG ML11 .... 199 H4 [4]
Wellwynd AIRDRIE ML6 .... 110 F1
Wellyard La
GRNKW/INVK PA16 .... 31 J6 [6]
Wellyard Wy GRNKW/INVK PA16 .... 31 J7 [7]
Wellyard Wynd
GRNKW/INVK PA16 .... 31 J7 [7]
Welsh Dr BLTYR/CAMB G72 .... 155 K3
HMLTN ML3 .... 174 C2
Wemyss Av NMRNS G77 .... 150 C2
Wemyss Bay Rd WMYSB PA18 .... 70 A1
Wemyss Bay St GRNK PA15 .... 2 A7 [2]
Wemyss Dr BALLOCH G68 .... 47 L8
Wemyss Gdns
BAIL/MDB/MHD G69 .... 108 A6 [4]
Wenlock Rd PSLYS PA2 .... 9 K8
Wensleydale EKILN G74 .... 153 J6 [10]
Wentworth Dr SMSTN G23 .... 62 E8 [11]
Wentworth Sq KLWNG KA13 .... 193 J5 [2]
Wesley St AIRDRIE ML6 .... 110 F2
West Abercromby St
HBR/GL G84 .... 20 D6 [5]
West Academy St WISHAW ML2 .... 158 E6 [1]
Westacres Rd NMRNS G77 .... 150 B5
West Av AIRDRIE ML6 .... 90 A6
BLTYR/CAMB G72 .... 155 L4
CARLUKE ML8 .... 178 D8
MTHW ML1 .... 134 A7
RNFRW PA4 .... 80 C6
STPS/GTHM/RID G33 .... 85 K4
UD/BTH/TAN G71 .... 132 B3
West Balgrochan Rd
BSHPBGS G64 .... 44 B8
Westbank La KVD/HLHD G12 .... 4 A5
Westbank Qd KVD/HLHD G12 .... 4 A5
West Barmoss Av PGL PA14 .... 54 F2
West Blackhall St GRNK PA15 .... 2 C2
GRNKW/INVK PA16 .... 2 C1
Westbourne Av PSTWK KA9 .... 225 K1 [3]
Westbourne Crs BSDN G61 .... 61 J4
Westbourne Dr BSDN G61 .... 61 J4
Westbourne Gdns
PSTWK KA9 .... 225 K1 [1]
Westbourne Gardens La
KVD/HLHD G12 .... 82 C5 [17]
Westbourne Gdns South
KVD/HLHD G12 .... 82 C5
Westbourne Gdns West
KVD/HLHD G12 .... 82 C5
Westbourne Rd
KVD/HLHD G12 .... 82 B5 [5]
Westbourne Terrace La North
KVD/HLHD G12 .... 82 C5 [15]
Westbourne Terrace La South
KVD/HLHD G12 .... 82 B5 [5]
West Bowhouse Gdn IRVSE KA11 204 A4

West Bowhouse Wy IRVSE KA11 204 A4
West Brae PSLY PA1 .... 8 E4
Westbrae Dr SCOT G14 .... 81 L5 [5]
Westbrae Rd NMRNS G77 .... 150 F3
West Bridgend DMBTN G82 .... 36 E5
Westburn Av
BLTYR/CAMB G72 .... 130 D3 [3]
PSLYN/LNWD PA3 .... 101 G4
Westburn Crs CLYDBK G81 .... 60 B2
RUTH G73 .... 128 F2
Westburn Farm Rd
BLTYR/CAMB G72 .... 130 B3
Westburn Rd BLTYR/CAMB G72 .. 130 B3
West Burnside St KSYTH G65 .... 47 K1 [12]
West Campbell St CGLW G2 .... 10 F2
NMLNS KA16 .... 215 L2 [3]
PSLY PA1 .... 8 B5
West Canal St CTBR ML5 .... 109 M3
Westcastle Crs CSMK G45 .... 128 D6
Westcastle Gdns CSMK G45 .... 128 D6
Westcastle Gv CSMK G45 .... 128 D6 [2]
West Chapelton Av BSDN G61 .... 61 M5
West Chapelton Crs BSDN G61 .. 61 M5
West Chapelton Dr BSDN G61 .. 61 M5
West Church St NMLNS KA16 .... 215 K2 [2]
Westcliff DMBTN G82 .... 36 B5
West Clyde St HBR/GL G84 .... 20 B8
LRKH ML9 .... 176 B7
Westclyffe St
PLKSD/SHW G41 .... 104 E8 [4]
West Coats Rd
BLTYR/CAMB G72 .... 129 M5
West Crs TROON KA10 .... 216 F5
West Dhuhill Dr HBR/GL G84 .... 20 D5
West Doura Av SALT KA21 .... 191 M8
West Doura Wy
KLWNG KA13 .... 193 H6 [1]
West Dr AIRDRIE ML6 .... 111 J4
West End DALRY KA24 .... 184 B2
Westend Ct CARLUKE ML8 .... 177 M5 [5]
Westend Dr BLSH ML4 .... 132 F5
Westend Park St KVGV G3 .... 4 C6
West End Dr BLSH ML4 .... 132 F5
Westerburn St CAR/SHTL G32 .... 106 F3
Wester Carriagehill PSLYS PA2 .. 9 G9 [2]
Wester Cleddens Rd
BSHPBGS G64 .... 64 A7
Wester Common Dr
PPK/MIL G22 .... 83 G5 [1]
Wester Common Rd
PPK/MIL G22 .... 83 G5 [2]
Westercraigs DEN/PKHD G31 .... 12 D2
Westerdale EKILN G74 .... 153 J6
Westerfield Rd
CRMNK/CLK/EAG G76 .... 152 D5
Westergill Av AIRDRIE ML6 .... 111 L3
Westergreens Av KKNTL G66 .... 65 J3
Westerhill Rd BSHPBGS G64 .... 64 A5
Westerhouse Ct
CARLUKE ML8 .... 178 D7 [2]
Westerhouse Rd ESTRH G34 .... 108 A1
Westerkirk Dr SMSTN G23 .... 62 E8
Westerlands KVD/HLHD G12 .... 82 A3 [2]
Westerlands Dr NMRNS G77 .... 150 B5
Westerlands Gv NMRNS G77 .... 150 B5 [5]
Wester Leddriegreen Rd
CMPF/LLE G63 .... 27 H5 [5]
Westermains Av KKNTL G66 .... 65 H2
Wester Mavisbank Av
AIRDRIE 110 E1
Wester Moffat Av AIRDRIE ML6 .. 111 L1
Wester Moffat Crs
AIRDRIE .... 111 L2 [4]
Wester Myvot Rd CUMB G67 .... 68 A5
Western Av RUTH G73 .... 129 G3 [1]
Western Crs KBRN KA25 .... 167 G2
Western Isles Rd OLDK G60 .... 59 K2
Western Rd BLTYR/CAMB G72 .... 129 M6
GLSTN KA4 .... 214 A3
KLMNKN/STW KA3 .... 206 F6
Western Rd CAR/SHTL G32 .... 107 K6
Westerton AIRDRIE .... 111 J5 [1]
Westerton Av
CRMNK/CLK/EAG G76 .... 152 A4
KNTSWD G13 .... 81 M1
MTHW 176 A8
Westerton La
CRMNK/CLK/EAG G76 .... 152 A4 [1]
West Fairholm St LRKH ML9 .... 175 M4
West Faulds Rd
LNK/LMHG ML11 .... 199 L4
Westfield DMBTN G82 .... 36 C5
GLGNK KA14 .... 167 H1
Westfield Av RUTH G73 .... 128 F2
Westfield Crs BSDN G61 .... 61 L7 [2]
Westfield Dr BALLOCH G68 .... 67 M2
BSDN G61 .... 61 L7
CARD/HILL/MSPK G52 .... 103 G4
GRNKW/INVK PA16 .... 32 C1 [1]
KLMCLM PA13 .... 75 H1 [1]
Westfield Pl BALLOCH G68 .... 67 K3
Westfield Rd AYRS KA7 .... 18 C8
BALLOCH G68 .... 67 M1
GIF/THBK G46 .... 127 G7
MTHW ML1 .... 134 C2
PGL PA14 .... 54 F1
Westfields BSHPBGS G64 .... 63 L6
West Fullarton St KLMNK KA1 .... 16 C8
Westgarth Pl EKILN G74 .... 153 G6
West Ga WISHAW ML2 .... 159 K6
West George La CGLW G2 .... 11 H1 [3]
West George St CGLE G1 .... 11 J1
CGLW G2 .... 4 E9
CTBR ML5 .... 110 A1
West Glebe Ter HMLTN ML3 .... 156 C7 [3]
West Glen Rd KLMCLM PA13 .... 55 L8
West Graham St KVGV G3 .... 4 D6
West Greenhill Pl KVGV G3 .... 4 A9
West Gv TROON KA10 .... 216 F6
West Highland Wy
CMPF/LLE G63 .... 26 C7
West High St KKNTL G66 .... 45 J8 [1]
Westhouse Av RUTH G73 .... 128 E2
Westhouse Gdns RUTH G73 .... 128 E2 [1]
West Kilbride Rd DALRY KA24... .... 184 B2

West King St HBR/GL G84 .... 20 B7
West Kirklands Pl DALRY KA24.. .... 184 B2
West Kirk St AIRDRIE ML6 .... 110 F2
Westland Dr SCOT G14 .... 81 K6
Westlands Gdns PSLYS PA2... .... 8 F8
West La PSLY PA1 .... 8 A5
West Langlands St KLMNK KA1 .. 16 D3
Westlea Pl AIRDRIE ML6 .... 111 G3
West Lennox Dr HBR/GL G84 .... 20 D6
West Lodge Rd RNFRW PA4 .... 80 B5
West Mains Rd EKILN G74 .... 14 F2
EKILN G74 .... 153 H7
West Montrose St HBR/GL G84 .. 20 C7
Westmoor Crs KLMNK KA1 .... 16 B7
Westmoreland St
GVH/MTFL G42 .... 105 G7
Westmorland Rd
GRNKW/INVK PA16 .... 31 L5
Westmuir Pl RUTH G73 .... 128 E1
Westmuir St DEN/PKHD G31 .... 13 L6
West Nemphlar Rd
LNK/LMHG ML11 .... 198 C3
West Netherton St KLMNK KA1 .. 16 E7
West Nile St CGLE G1 .... 11 H1
Weston Av RAYR/DAL KA6 .... 227 H7
Weston Brae RAYR/DAL KA6 .... 227 H6
Weston Pl PSTWK KA9 .... 225 J3 [1]
Weston Ter WKIL KA23 .... 181 J4
Westpark Crs
KLMNKN/STW KA3 .... 206 B1
West Park Dr
KLMNKN/STW KA3 .... 206 B1
Westpark Dr PSLYN/LNWD PA3 .. 8 A2
West Pl WISHAW ML2 .... 160 A4
Westport EKILS G75 .... 152 F8
West Port LNK/LMHG ML11 .... 198 F5
Westport MAUCH/CAT KA5 .... 223 L6
Westport St KSYTH G65 .... 47 K1 [13]
West Prince's La COWCAD G4 .... 4 B4 [4]
West Prince's St COWCAD G4 .... 4 C4
HBR/GL G84 .... 20 B7
KVGV G3 .... 4 D6
West Quay PGL PA14 .... 34 C7 [4]
Westray Av NMRNS G77 .... 150 C2
PGL PA14 .... 55 H3
Westray Circ PPK/MIL G22 .... 83 K3 [3]
Westray Ct CUMB G67 .... 68 D1
Westray Pl PPK/MIL G22 .... 83 K2 [2]
BSHPBGS G64 .... 64 A7
Westray Rd CUMB G67 .... 68 D1
Westray Sq PPK/MIL G22 .... 83 J2
Westray St PPK/MIL G22 .... 83 J2
West Regent La CGLW G2 .... 5 G9
West Regent St CGLW G2 .... 4 E8
West Rd BSHPBGS G64 .... 44 B8
IRV KA12 .... 203 H6
KLBCH PA10 .... 99 G5
PGL PA14 .... 54 E1
West Rossdhu Dr HBR/GL G84 .. 20 D6
West Sanquhar Rd AYR KA8 .... 225 H7
West Scott Ter HMLTN ML3 .... 156 D8
West Shaw St GRNK PA15 .... 2 B5
KLMNK KA1 .... 16 E8
West Stewart St GRNK PA15... .... 2 C2
HMLTN ML3 .... 156 C5 [4]
West St CLYDBK G81 .... 80 E1
GBLS G5 .... 10 C6
PSLY PA1 .... 8 A5
West Thomson St CLYDBK G81... 60 A6
West Thornlie St WISHAW ML2 ... 159 G7
Westward Wy TROON KA10 .... 216 E2
West Wellbrae Crs HMLTN ML3 .. 155 J3
West Whitby St DEN/PKHD G31... 13 K7
Westwood Av AYR KA8 .... 225 L8
GIF/THBK G46 .... 127 H6
Westwood Crs AYR KA8 .... 225 L8
HMLTN ML3 .... 156 C7
Westwood Dr MTHW ML1 .... 135 L8 [1]
Westwood Gdns
PSLYN/LNWD PA3 .... 8 A2
Westwood HI EKILS G75 .... 171 H2
Westwood Qd CLYDBK G81 .... 60 D8
Westwood Rd EKILS G75 .... 153 H8
PLKSW/MSWD G43 .... 127 H3
WISHAW ML2 .... 159 M2
West Woodside Av PGL PA14 .. 54 F3 [4]
West Woodstock St KLMNK KA1 .. 16 C4
Weymouth Crs
GRNKW/INVK PA16 .... 31 L4
Weymouth Dr KVD/HLHD G12 .... 82 A3
Whamflet Av
BAIL/MDB/MHD G69 .... 108 C2 [4]
Wheatfield Rd AYRS KA7 .... 18 C6
BSDN G61 .... 61 K7
Wheatholm St AIRDRIE ML6 .... 89 H8
Wheating Br KLMNKN/STW KA3.. 197 H8
Wheatland Av
BLTYR/CAMB G72 .... 155 J3
Wheatland Dr LNK/LMHG ML11 .. 198 F5 [7]
Wheatlandhead Ct
BLTYR/CAMB G72 .... 155 J3 [7]
Wheatlands Dr KLBCH PA10 .... 99 G5
Wheatlands Farm Rd
KLBCH PA10 .... 99 G5
Wheatlandside
LNK/LMHG ML11 .... 198 F4
Wheatley Crs KSYTH G65 .... 47 K3 [3]
Wheatley Loan BSHPBGS G64 .. 84 C1
Wheatley Rd SALT KA21 .... 192 A7
SVSTN KA20 .... 192 E8
Wheatpark Rd
LNK/LMHG ML11 .... 198 F5 [5]
Whifflet St CTBR ML5 .... 110 A6
Whin Av BRHD/NEIL G78 .... 125 G5
Whinfell Dr EKILS G75 .... 171 G3
Whinfell Gdns EKILS G75 .... 171 G3
Whinfield Av PSTWK KA9 .... 225 H3
Whinfield Rd
PLK/PH/NH G53 .... 126 A5 [1]
PSTWK KA9 .... 225 H3
Whinhall Av AIRDRIE ML6 .... 88 E8
Whinhall Rd AIRDRIE ML6 .... 88 E8
Whin HI EKILN G74 .... 154 B4
Whinhill Av LARGS KA30 .... 115 K6
Whinhill Crs GRNK PA15 .... 2 F9
Whinhill Rd AYRS KA7 .... 229 G7
Whinhill Rd GRNK PA15 .... 2 F8
PLK/PH/NH G53 .... 103 G6

PSLYS PA2 .... 102 B7 [5]
Whin Loan KSYTH G65 .... 46 D1
Whinney Gv WISHAW ML2 .... 159 L5 [2]
Whinnie Knowe LRKH ML9 .... 175 M8
Whinpark Av BLSH ML4 .... 132 F6 [1]
Whin Pl EKILS G75 .... 154 B4
Whins Rd PLKSD/SHW G41 .... 104 C8
TROON KA10 .... 216 E2
Whirlie Dr
CRG/CRSL/HOU PA6 .... 99 H1 [3]
Whirlie Rd CRG/CRSL/HOU PA6 .. 77 H8
Whirlow Gdns
BAIL/MDB/MHD G69 .... 108 A4
Whirlow Rd
BAIL/MDB/MHD G69 .... 108 A4
Whiskeyhall RAYR/DAL KA6 .... 227 G3
Whistleberry Crs HMLTN ML3 .... 156 B3
Whistleberry Dr HMLTN ML3 .... 156 B3
Whistleberry Pk HMLTN ML3 .... 156 A2
Whistleberry Rd HMLTN ML3 .... 156 A2
Whistlefield Ct BSDN G61 .... 61 L6
Whitacres Rd PLK/PH/NH G53 .... 125 M5
Whitburn St CAR/SHTL G32 .... 106 F2
Whiteadder Pl EKILS G75 .... 170 D2
White Av DMBTN G82 .... 37 H6
White Cart Rd
PSLYN/LNWD PA3 .... 101 L1 [1]
White Craig Rd ARD KA22 .... 191 K5
Whitecraigs Pl SMSTN G23 .... 82 E1 [1]
Whitecrook Sreet CLYDBK G81 .. 80 C1
Whitecrook St CLYDBK G81 .... 80 B1
Whitefield Av BLTYR/CAMB G72 .. 130 A5
Whitefield Rd GOV/IBX G51 .... 104 C3
Whitefield Ter KKNTL G66 .... 29 J8
Whiteford Ct HMLTN ML3 .... 174 C3
Whiteford Crs DMBTN G82 .... 37 J4
Whiteford Pl DMBTN G82 .... 37 J4
Whiteford Rd PSLYS PA2 .... 9 M8
Whiteford Vw AYRS KA7 .... 229 K2
Whitehall Av PSTWK KA9 .... 225 K1
Whitehall St KVGV G3 .... 10 D2
Whitehaugh Av PSLY PA1 .... 102 B4 [2]
Whitehaugh Crs
PLK/PH/NH G53 .... 126 A5
Whitehaugh Dr PSLY PA1 .... 102 B4
Whitehaugh Rd
PLK/PH/NH G53 .... 126 A5
Whitehill Av AIRDRIE ML6 .... 89 G7
BALLOCH G68 .... 48 D7
KKNTL G66 .... 45 L8
STPS/GTHM/RID G33 .... 85 K3
Whitehill Crs CARLUKE ML8 .... 178 F6
CLYDBK G81 .... 60 E2
KKNTL G66 .... 45 M8
LNK/LMHG ML11 .... 198 F5
RAYR/DAL KA6 .... 227 G7
Whitehill Dr RAYR/DAL KA6 .... 227 H7 [7]
Whitehill Farm Rd
STPS/GTHM/RID G33 .... 85 K3
Whitehill Gdns DEN/PKHD G31 .. 12 F2
Whitehill Gv NMRNS G77 .... 150 F7
Whitehill Rd BSDN G61 .... 61 K5
HMLTN 156 B4
Whitehills EKILS G75 .... 14 E8
Whitehills Pl EKILS G75 .... 14 E8
Whitehills Ter EKILS G75 .... 14 E9
Whitehill St DEN/PKHD G31 .... 6 E7
Whitehill Street La
DEN/PKHD G31 .... 12 E2
Whitehill Ter LNK/LMHG ML11 .. 198 F5
Whitehill Wy
RAYR/DAL KA6 .... 231 H5 [11]
Whitehirst Park Rd
KLWNG KA13 .... 193 H6
Whitehurst BSDN G61 .... 61 J3
Whitekirk Pl DRUM G15 .... 61 G2 [1]
Whitelaw Av CTBR ML5 .... 87 M4
Whitelaw Crs BLSH ML4 .... 133 K5
Whitelaw St MRYH/FIRH G20 .... 82 C2
Whitelaw Ter KSYTH G65 .... 46 F5 [5]
Whitelea Av KLMNKN/STW KA3 .. 75 J1
Whitelea Crs KLMNKN/STW KA3.. 75 J1
Whitelea Rd KLMCLM PA13 .... 75 J1
Whitelee EKILS G75 .... 171 K4
Whitelee Crs NMRNS G77 .... 150 B3
Whitelee Ga NMRNS G77 .... 150 B3
Whitelees Rd CUMB G67 .... 49 M3
GRNK PA15 .... 33 M7
LNK/LMHG ML11 .... 199 K6
Whiteloans UD/BTH/TAN G71 .... 132 B6
Whitemoss Av EKILN G74 .... 15 H3
LNPK/KPK G44 .... 127 M5 [1]
Whitemoss Gv EKILN G74 .... 15 J2
Whitemoss Rd EKILN G74 .... 15 H3
Whitepond Av BLSH ML4 .... 132 F6 [1]
Whites Bridge Av PSLY PA1 .... 100 F5
PSLYN/LNWD PA3 .... 100 F4 [5]
PSLYN/LNWD PA3 .... 100 F5 [5]
Whiteshaw Av CARLUKE ML8 .... 178 D8
Whiteshaw Dr CARLUKE ML8 .... 178 D7
Whiteshaw Rd CARLUKE ML8 .... 178 D7
Whiteside Rd PSTWK KA9 .... 225 K2 [2]
Whiteside Ter PSTWK KA9 .... 225 K2 [2]
White St AYR KA8 .... 225 H5
CLYDBK G81 .... 80 D2
PTCK G11 .... 82 B7
Whitevale St DEN/PKHD G31 .... 12 C4
Whitewisp Ct IRVSE KA11 .... 204 A5
Whitfield Dr AYR KA8 .... 225 K6
Whitfield Rd PLK/PH/NH G53 .... 125 M5
Whithorn Crs
BAIL/MDB/MHD G69 .... 66 F3 [3]
Whiting Rd WMYSB PA18 .... 50 A8
Whitlawburn Av
BLTYR/CAMB G72 .... 129 L5
Whitlawburn Rd
BLTYR/CAMB G72 .... 129 L5
Whitlawburn Ter
BLTYR/CAMB G72 .... 129 L5 [2]
Whitletts Crs ARD KA22 .... 191 K7
Whitletts Ct AYR KA8 .... 225 L7 [2]
Whitletts Rd AYR KA8 .... 19 J1
Whittriggs Rd PLK/PH/NH G53 .. 125 M5
Whitslade Pl ESTRH G34 .... 86 A8 [2]
Whitslade St ESTRH G34 .... 86 A8 [3]
Whitsun Dl EKILN G74 .... 153 J6

Whittagreen Av *MTHW* ML1 .... 134 D6
Whittagreen Crs *MTHW* ML1 ...... 134 D6
Whittingehame Dr
  KVD/HLHD G12 .... 81 M4
Whittingehame La
  KNTSWD G13 .... 81 M4 ⁴
Whittington St *CTBR* ML5 .... 110 A3 ⁴
Whittlemuir Av *LNPK/KPK* G44.... 127 M5
Whittle Pl *IRVSE* KA11 .... 203 M7
Whittle Rd *AYR* KA8 .... 225 J6
Whitton Dr *GIF/THBK* G46 .... 127 K5
Whitton St *MRYH/FIRH* G20 .... 82 C1
Whitworth St
  MRYH/FIRH G20 .... 83 G3 ⁴
Whyte Av *BLTYR/CAMB* G72 .... 129 L3
  IRV KA12 .... 203 K8
Wick Av *AIRDRIE* ML6 .... 110 E5
The Wickets *PSLY* PA1 .... 9 M6
Wickham Av *NMRNS* G77 .... 150 D3
Wigton Av *NMRNS* G77 .... 150 C2
Wigtoun Pl *CUMB* G67 .... 49 H5
Wildcat Rd *WKIL* KA23 .... 181 H5
Wildman Rd *CARLUKE* ML8 .... 178 B2
Wilfred Av *KNTSWD* G13 .... 81 K2
Wilkie Crs *LRKH* ML9 .... 176 B7
Wilkie Rd *UD/BTH/TAN* G71 ...... 132 A4
William Dr *HMLTN* ML3 .... 174 D2
Williamfield Gv *IRV* KA12 .... 203 H5 ⁵
Williamfield Pk *IRV* KA12 .... 203 H5 ⁶
William Mann Dr *NMRNS* G77 .... 150 B5
Williamsburgh Ter *PSLY* PA1 ...... 9 M5 ⁴
Williamson Av *DMBTN* G82 .... 37 G5
Williamson Dr *HBR/GL* G84 ...... 20 F8
Williamson Pl *JNSTN* PA5 .... 100 B7
Williamson St *CLYDBK* G81 .... 60 B5
  DMNK/BRGTN G40 .... 13 J8
William Spiers Pl *LRKH* ML9 ...... 176 B8
William St *CLYDBK* G81 .... 60 A3
  CTBR ML5 .... 110 B5
  HBR/GL G84 .... 20 C8
  HMLTN ML3 .... 156 A4 ⁴
  JNSTN PA5 .... 99 M7 ⁴
  KLMNKN/STW KA3 .... 16 F1
  KSYTH G65 .... 47 K1
  KVGV G3 .... 4 D9
  PGL PA14 .... 34 B8
  PSLY PA1 .... 8 C4
William Ure Pl *BSHPBGS* G64 ...... 64 B4
Williamwood Dr *LNPK/KPK* G44.... 127 L7
Williamwood Pk
  LNPK/KPK G44 .... 127 M7 ⁴
Williamwood Pk West
  LNPK/KPK G44 .... 127 M7 ⁵
Willie Ross Pl
  KLMNKN/STW KA3 .... 207 K5
Willison's La *PGL* PA14 .... 34 C8 ⁶
Willock Pl *MRYH/FIRH* G20 .... 82 E2
Willockston Rd *TROON* KA10 ...... 216 E7
Willoughby Dr *KNTSWD* G13 ...... 81 M3 ⁵
Willoughby La *KNTSWD* G13 ...... 81 M3 ⁶
Willow Av *BSHPBGS* G64 .... 84 A1 ⁴
  JNSTN PA5 .... 100 C7 ⁷
  KKNTL G66 .... 65 J4
  MTHW ML1 .... 134 A7
Willowbank Crs *KVGV* G3 .... 4 C5 ⁴
Willowbank Gdns *KKNTL* G66 ...... 65 K1
Willowbank St *KVGV* G3 .... 4 C6
Willowburn Rd *BEITH* KA15 ...... 167 M2
Willow Ct *EKILS* G75 .... 14 A9
Willow Crs *CTBR* ML5 .... 109 M5
Willowdale Crs
  BAIL/MDB/MHD G69 .... 108 A5
Willowdale Gdns
  BAIL/MDB/MHD G69 .... 108 A5 ⁵
Willow Dr *AIRDRIE* ML6 .... 111 K4
  BLTYR/CAMB G72 .... 155 J1
  JNSTN PA5 .... 99 M8
  KKNTL G66 .... 45 J4
Willowford Rd *PLK/PH/NH* G53 .. 125 M5
Willow Gv *MTHW* ML1 .... 134 B4
Willow La *CAR/SHTL* G32 .... 107 H7
Willow Pk *AYRS* KA7 .... 229 J5
Willow Pl *GRNKW/INVK* PA16 .... 50 D5 ⁴
  JNSTN PA5 .... 100 A7 ⁸
  UD/BTH/TAN G71 .... 132 D1 ⁶
Willow Rd *KLMNK* KA1 .... 16 A5
The Willows
  CRMNK/CLK/EAG G76 .... 152 E1 ⁶
Willow St *KNTSWD* G13 .... 81 M2
Willow Wy *HMLTN* ML3 .... 156 B8
Willowyard Rd *BEITH* KA15 ...... 167 M1
Wills Rd *AYR* KA8 .... 225 J7
Willwood Dr *WISHAW* ML2 ...... 159 J2 ⁶
Wilmot Rd *KNTSWD* G13 .... 81 K3 ⁵
Wilsgait St *MTHW* ML1 .... 135 J7
Wilson Av *IRV* KA12 .... 203 J5
  KLMNKN/STW KA3 .... 17 H4
  PSLYN/LNWD PA3 .... 100 A3
  TROON KA10 .... 216 F7
Wilson Ct *BLSH* ML4 .... 132 F4 ⁴
Wilson Pl *CRH/DND* KA2 .... 209 L7
  EKILN G74 .... 154 A5
  NMRNS G77 .... 150 C5
Wilson Rd *SHOTTS* ML7 .... 160 F1
Wilsons Rd *MTHW* ML1 .... 135 L2
Wilson St *AIRDRIE* ML6 .... 110 F1
  ALEX/LLW G83 .... 25 K4
  AYR KA8 .... 225 H7
  BEITH KA15 .... 144 B8 ¹¹
  CGLE G1 .... 11 K2
  CTBR ML5 .... 110 C2
  HMLTN ML3 .... 156 A4 ⁴
  LARGS KA30 .... 115 K6
  LRKH ML9 .... 176 B8
  MTHW ML1 .... 157 M2
  PGL PA14 .... 34 D8

  RNFRW PA4 .... 80 D5
Wiltonburn Rd *PLK/PH/NH* G53 .. 126 A5
Wilton Crescent La
  MRYH/FIRH G20 .... 4 C2
Wilton Dr *MRYH/FIRH* G20 .... 4 D2
Wilton Rd *CARLUKE* ML8 .... 179 H8
Wilton St *CTBR* ML5 .... 87 K7
  MRYH/FIRH G20 .... 4 C2
Wilverton Rd *KNTSWD* G13 .... 81 L1
Winburne Crs *HMLTN* ML3 .... 156 B5 ⁵
Winchester Dr *KVD/HLHD* G12 .... 82 B3
Windemere Gdns
  HMLTN ML3 .... 174 C3 ⁵
Windermere St *BLSH* ML4 .... 132 F5 ⁵
Windermere *EKILS* G75 .... 170 F4
Windhill Crs *PLKSW/MSWD* G43 .. 127 H4
Windhill Rd *PLKSW/MSWD* G43 .. 127 H4
Windlaw Gdns *LNPK/KPK* G44 .... 127 M5
Windlaw Park Gdns
  LNPK/KPK G44 .... 127 M5 ⁶
Windlaw Rd *CSMK* G45 .... 128 D8
Windmill Ct *MTHW* ML1 .... 157 M4 ⁴
Windmillhill St *MTHW* ML1 ...... 157 M4
Windmill Rd *HMLTN* ML3 .... 156 D5
Windmill St *SALT* KA21 .... 200 E2
Windrow Ter *WISHAW* ML2 .... 159 J2
Windsor Av *NMRNS* G77 .... 150 F4
Windsor Ct *CARLUKE* ML8 .... 178 F7 ⁷
Windsor Crs *CLYDBK* G81 .... 60 A6
  JNSTN PA5 .... 100 B8
  PSLY PA1 .... 9 M1
Windsor Dr *AIRDRIE* ML6 .... 88 F5
Windsor Gdns *HMLTN* ML3 ...... 156 A4 ¹⁰
  LARGS KA30 .... 115 K3
Windsor Qd *CARLUKE* ML8 .... 178 F7 ⁷
Windsor Rd *MTHW* ML1 .... 134 A4
  RNFRW PA4 .... 80 C7
Windsor St *CAR/SHTL* G32 .... 107 J3 ⁵
  CTBR ML5 .... 109 L6
  MRYH/FIRH G20 .... 4 E4
  SHOTTS ML7 .... 137 L4
Windsor Ter *MRYH/FIRH* G20 ...... 4 E4
Windward Pk *AYRS* KA7 .... 229 G8
Windward Rd *EKILS* G75 .... 153 G8
Windyedge Crs *KNTSWD* G13 ...... 81 J4 ⁵
Windyedge Pl *KNTSWD* G13 ...... 81 J4 ⁶
Windyedge Rd *MTHW* ML1 .... 135 J6
Windyhill Pk
  CRMNK/CLK/EAG G76 .... 151 K7
Windyridge Pl
  BLTYR/CAMB G72 .... 155 J2 ⁵
Windy Yetts *KSYTH* G65 .... 46 F6
Winehouse Yett *CRH/DND* KA2 .... 209 H7
Winfield Av *BLTYR/CAMB* G72 .. 129 L2 ⁶
Wingate Av *DALRY* KA24 .... 184 B2
Wingate Crs *EKILN* G74 .... 154 C5
Wingate Dr *EKILN* G74 .... 154 C5
Wingate Pk *EKILN* G74 .... 154 C5 ⁷
Wingate St *WISHAW* ML2 .... 158 D1
Wingfaulds Av *DALRY* KA24 ...... 184 A1
Wingfield Gdns
  UD/BTH/TAN G71 .... 132 B8 ⁷
Winifred St *STPS/GTHM/RID* G33 .... 7 L1
Winning Ct *BLTYR/CAMB* G72 .... 131 L8
Winning Rw *DEN/PKHD* G31 ...... 13 M5
Winnipeg Dr *EKILS* G75 .... 171 H1
Winstanley Wynd *KLWNG* KA13 .. 193 J4
Winston Av *PSTWK* KA9 .... 225 K2
Winston Crs *KKNTL* G66 .... 29 J8
Winston Rd *HBR/GL* G84 .... 21 C7
Winton Av *GIF/THBK* G46 .... 127 J7
  KLWNC KA13 .... 193 J6
Winton Circ *SALT* KA21 .... 200 E2
Winton Ct *ARD* KA22 .... 191 J8
Winton Crs *BLTYR/CAMB* G72 .... 155 K2
Winton Dr *KVD/HLHD* G12 .... 82 C4
  SKLM PA17 .... 70 A4
Winton Gdns
  UD/BTH/TAN G71 .... 131 M2 ⁴
Winton La *ARD* KA22 .... 191 J7 ⁶
  KVD/HLHD G12 .... 82 C4
Winton Pk *EKILS* G75 .... 152 F8
Winton Pl *ARD* KA22 .... 191 J7 ⁷
Winton St *ARD* KA22 .... 191 J7
  SALT KA21 .... 200 E1
Wirran Pl *KNTSWD* G13 .... 80 E1
Wishart Av *CLYDBK* G81 .... 60 C2
Wishart Dr *GLSTN* KA4 .... 214 B4
Wishart Dr *DEN/PKHD* G31 .... 6 B9
Wishaw High Rd *MTHW* ML1 ...... 159 J1
Wishawhill St *WISHAW* ML2 ...... 158 F5 ⁵
Wishaw Low Rd *MTHW* ML1 ...... 159 H2
Wishaw Rd *WISHAW* ML2 .... 177 M1
Wisner Ct *GIF/THBK* G46 .... 126 F6 ⁵
Wisteria La *CARLUKE* ML8 .... 188 F1 ⁷
Witch St *BLTYR/CAMB* G72 ...... 130 D4
Witches Linn *ARD* KA22 .... 191 H5
Witchill Pl *KLMNKN/STW* KA3 .... 16 E1
Witchknowe Ct *KLMNK* KA1 ...... 212 A5 ⁴
Witchknowe Rd *KLMNK* KA1 ...... 211 M5
Witch Rd *KLMNKN/STW* KA3 ...... 16 E1
Woddrop St *DMNK/BRGTN* G40 .. 106 B7
Wolcott Dr *BLTYR/CAMB* G72 .. 155 K1 ⁶
Wolfe Av *NMRNS* G77 .... 150 C2
Wolseley St *GBLS* G5 .... 11 L9
Wood Aven Dr *EKILN* G74 .... 153 K5
Woodbank Crs
  CRMNK/CLK/EAG G76 .... 151 L3
  JNSTN PA5 .... 99 M7 ⁴
Woodbank Gdns
  ALEX/LLW G83 .... 25 J2 ⁶
  LARGS KA30 .... 115 H3 ⁶
Woodbank Rd *CRH/DND* KA2 ...... 205 M8
Woodburn Av *AIRDRIE* ML6 .... 110 F3

  BLTYR/CAMB G72 .... 155 L1
  CRMNK/CLK/EAG G76 .... 151 L3
  KLWNG KA13 .... 193 L5
Woodburn Pl
  CRG/CRSL/HOU PA6 .... 99 L2
Woodburn Rd *BEITH* KA15 .... 168 C1 ⁶
  MTHW ML1 .... 134 D2
  PLKSW/MSWD G43 .... 127 K4
Woodburn St *MTHW* ML1 .... 157 L1
Woodburn Ter *LRKH* ML9 .... 176 C7 ⁶
Woodburn Wy *BALLOCH* G68 ...... 48 C7
  MLNGV G62 .... 42 A8
Wood Crs *KLWNG* KA13 .... 193 L5
  MTHW ML1 .... 157 L1
Woodcroft Av *LARGS* KA30 .... 115 L6
  PTCK G11 .... 81 M5
Wooddale *MTHW* ML1 .... 157 K5
Woodend Ct *CAR/SHTL* G32 ...... 107 L7 ⁶
Woodend Dr *AIRDRIE* ML6 .... 89 J8
  KNTSWD G13 .... 81 L4
  PSLY PA1 .... 102 D5
Woodend Gdns
  CAR/SHTL G32 .... 107 K7 ⁶
Woodend La *KNTSWD* G13 .... 81 L4
Woodend Ov *RAYR/DAL* KA6 ...... 229 L7
Woodend Pl *JNSTN* PA5 .... 100 B7 ⁶
Woodend Rd *AYRS* KA7 .... 228 F8
  CAR/SHTL G32 .... 107 K7
  CARLUKE ML8 .... 179 G7
  RUTH G73 .... 129 H5
Woodend St *HBR/GL* G84 .... 20 B7
Wood Farm Rd *GIF/THBK* G46 .... 127 G8
Woodfield *UD/BTH/TAN* G71 .... 132 C3 ⁵
Woodfield Av *AYR* KA8 .... 225 G4
Woodfield Crs *AYR* KA8 .... 225 G5
Woodfield Rd *AYR* KA8 .... 225 G5
Woodfoot Pl
  PLK/PH/NH G53 .... 126 A5 ⁴
Woodfoot Qd *PLK/PH/NH* G53 .. 126 B5
Woodfoot Rd *HMLTN* ML3.......... 156 A7
  PLK/PH/NH G53 .... 126 A5
Woodford Pl
  PSLYN/LNWD PA3 .... 100 A3 ⁵
Woodford St
  PLKSW/MSWD G43 .... 127 K2
Woodgreen Av *LNPK/KPK* G44 .. 128 B3
Woodgreen Wynd
  KLWNG KA13 .... 193 J4
Wood Gv *UD/BTH/TAN* G71 ...... 109 J8
Woodhall *MTHW* ML1 .... 134 A1 ⁵
Woodhall Av *AIRDRIE* ML6 .... 111 H7
  CTBR ML5 .... 109 M6
  HMLTN ML3 .... 156 B5
  MTHW ML1 .... 133 M4
Woodhall Cottage Rd
  AIRDRIE ML6 .... 111 J8
Woodhall Mill Rd *AIRDRIE* ML6 .. 134 C1
Woodhall Pl *CTBR* ML5............ 109 M6
Woodhall Rd *AIRDRIE* ML6 .... 111 H7
  CARLUKE ML8 .... 188 D6
  WISHAW ML2 .... 159 M6
Woodhall St *AIRDRIE* ML6 .... 111 K8
  DMNK/BRGTN G40 .... 106 B7 ⁴
Woodhall Ter *PGL* PA14 .... 55 H1
Woodhead Av *BALLOCH* G68 ...... 67 M2
  KKNTL G66 .... 46 A1
  UD/BTH/TAN G71 .... 132 B8 ⁷
Woodhead Crs *BALLOCH* G68 ...... 67 M2
Woodhead Crs *HMLTN* ML3 .... 174 A1
  UD/BTH/TAN G71 .... 131 M1
Woodhead Gdns
  UD/BTH/TAN G71 .... 131 M1
Woodhead Gv *BALLOCH* G68 ...... 67 M2 ¹⁰
Woodhead Pl *BALLOCH* G68 ...... 67 M2 ¹¹
Woodhead Rd
  BAIL/MDB/MHD G69 .... 86 B3
  BALLOCH G68 .... 67 M2 ¹²
  PLK/PH/NH G53 .... 125 M4
  RAYR/DAL KA6 .... 231 H4
Woodhead Ter
  BAIL/MDB/MHD G69 .... 86 B2 ³
Woodhead Vw
  BALLOCH G68 .... 67 M2 ¹³
Woodhill Crs *IRVSE* KA11 .... 204 B3
Woodhill Pl
  KLMNKN/STW KA3 .... 206 B3 ⁵
Woodhill Rd *BSHPBGS* G64 .... 64 C8
  KLMNKN/STW KA3 .... 206 E6
  SPRGB/BLRNK G21 .... 84 B3 ²
Woodholm Av *LNPK/KPK* G44.... 128 C3
Woodhouse St *KNTSWD* G13 ...... 81 L2
Woodilee Rd *KKNTL* G66 .... 65 L3
  MTHW ML1 .... 134 E5
Woodland Av *AIRDRIE* ML6 .... 111 J5
  KKNTL G66 .... 65 H1
  PSLYS PA2 .... 124 E1
Woodland Crs
  BLTYR/CAMB G72 .... 130 B5
Woodland Gdns
  CRMNK/CLK/EAG G76 .... 152 D2
  HMLTN ML3 .... 156 K7
Woodland Pl *ARD* KA22 .... 191 J6 ⁸
Woodlands Av
  BAIL/MDB/MHD G69 .... 86 E2
  CARLUKE ML8 .... 177 M3
  IRV KA12 .... 203 J5
  UD/BTH/TAN G71 .... 132 A6 ⁶
Woodlands Ct *ALEX/LLW* G83 .... 25 J2 ⁶
  GIF/THBK G46 .... 126 F7 ⁷
Woodlands Crs *AYRS* KA7 .... 229 H5
  GIF/THBK G46 .... 126 F6
  JNSTN PA5 .... 99 K8
  UD/BTH/TAN G71 .... 132 A6
Woodlands Dr *COWCAD* G4......... 4 C5
  CTBR ML5 .... 109 K2
  KVGV G3 .... 4 C5
  MTHW ML1 .... 133 M4

Woodlands Gdns
  UD/BTH/TAN G71 .... 131 M6
Woodlands Ga *GIF/THBK* G46 .... 126 F6
  KVGV G3 .... 4 C6
Woodlands Gv
  KLMNKN/STW KA3 .... 207 H5
  MLNGV G62 .... 42 A6
Woodlands Pk *GIF/THBK* G46 .... 126 F7
Woodlands Pl *CTBR* ML5 .... 109 K2
  KLMNKN/STW KA3 .... 207 H5 ⁴
Woodlands Rd *GIF/THBK* G46 .... 126 F7
  KVGV G3 .... 4 C6
  MTHW ML1 .... 134 D2
  MTHW ML1 .... 157 M6
Woodlands St *GTCI* KA28 .... 138 B6 ⁵
  MLNGV G62 .... 42 A7
  MTHW ML1 .... 157 M5
  PSTWK KA9 .... 225 H1
Woodlands Ter *KVGV* G3 .... 4 B7
The Woodlands *BLSH* ML4 .... 133 K6 ⁸
Woodland Ter *LRKH* ML9 .... 176 C8
Woodland Wy *CUMB* G67 .... 49 H6
Woodlea Av *AIRDRIE* ML6 .... 111 J5
Woodlea Ct *CRH/DND* KA2 .... 205 M7
Woodlea Crs *CRH/DND* KA2 ...... 205 M7
Woodlea Dr *GIF/THBK* G46 ...... 127 K5
  HMLTN ML3 .... 174 D1
Woodlea La *GRK* PA19 .... 32 A3 ²
Woodlea Pl *AIRDRIE* ML6 .... 89 J8
  AYRS KA7 .... 229 H7
Woodlinn Av *LNPK/KPK* G44 ...... 128 B4
Woodmill *KLWNG* KA13 .... 193 M5
Woodmill Dr *BSHPBGS* G64 .... 44 C8
Woodmill Gdns *CUMB* G67 .... 67 M3 ⁵
Woodneuk Rd
  BAIL/MDB/MHD G69 .... 86 F4 ²
  PLK/PH/NH G53 .... 126 B5
Woodneuk St *AIRDRIE* ML6 .... 111 K8
Woodneuk Ter
  BAIL/MDB/MHD G69 .... 86 F4
Wood Pk *AYRS* KA7.................. 229 H5
Wood Qd *CLYDBK* G81 .... 80 E1
Wood Rd *TROON* KA10 .... 216 A7
Woodrow *MTHW* ML1 .... 134 B1
Woodrow Av *KLMCLM* PA13 ...... 55 K8
  MTHW ML1 .... 134 B1
Woodrow Circ *PLKSD/SHW* G41 .. 104 D5
Woodrow Pl *PLKSD/SHW* G41 .... 104 C5
Woodrow Rd *PLKSD/SHW* G41 .... 104 D5
Woodside Av *BRWEIR* PA11 ...... 76 D8 ²
  BRWEIR PA11 .... 98 D1 ³
  GIF/THBK G46 .... 127 G6
  HMLTN ML3 .... 156 F7 ⁵
  KNTL G66 .... 65 K4
  KSYTH G65 .... 47 M1
  RUTH G73 .... 129 K5
Woodside Crs *BRHD/NEIL* G78 .. 125 K7
  KVGV G3 .... 4 B7
  PSLY PA1 .... 8 C4
  WISHAW ML2 .... 160 B3
Woodside Dr *AIRDRIE* ML6 .... 111 C7
  CRMNK/CLK/EAG G76 .... 151 K7
Woodside Gdns
  CRMNK/CLK/EAG G76 .... 151 J2 ⁵
  CRMNK/CLK/EAG G76 .... 152 D2
  CTBR ML5 .... 109 K5 ²
Woodside La *JNSTN* PA5 .... 99 J3
Woodside Pl *KVGV* G3 .... 4 C7
  UD/BTH/TAN G71 .... 132 C1 ⁵
Woodside Place La *KVGV* G3........ 4 C7
Woodside Rd *BEITH* KA15 .... 144 B8 ¹⁰
  CRMNK/CLK/EAG G76 .... 152 D2
  JNSTN PA5 .... 99 K3
  KLWNG KA13 .... 193 J5
Woodside St *AIRDRIE* ML6 .... 111 K7 ⁸
  CTBR ML5 .... 109 K6
  MTHW ML1 .... 134 A6
  MTHW ML1 .... 158 B5
Woodside Ter *KVGV* G3 .... 4 C7
Woodside Terrace La *KVGV* G3.... 4 C7
Woodside Wk *HMLTN* ML3 .... 156 E7
Woodside Gv *RUTH* G73 .... 129 J2 ⁵
Woodstock Av *KKNTL* G66.......... 65 M1
  LNK/LMHG ML11 .... 199 H5 ⁶
  PLKSD/SHW G41 .... 127 K1
  PSLYS PA2 .... 123 L1
Woodstock Dr *WISHAW* ML2 ...... 159 J6 ⁶
Woodstock St *KLMNK* KA1 .... 16 C4
Woodstock Rd
  GRNKW/INVK PA16 .... 32 C6
  LNK/LMHG ML11 .... 199 H5
  KLMNK KA1 .... 16 D4
Wood St *AIRDRIE* ML6 .... 89 H8
  CTBR ML5 .... 109 L2
  DEN/PKHD G31 .... 7 G9
  GRNKW/INVK PA16 .... 32 B1
  KLWNG KA13 .... 193 L5
  MTHW ML1 .... 133 M8
  PSLYS PA2 .... 102 B6
Woodvale Av *AIRDRIE* ML6 .... 111 J5
  BSDN G61 .... 62 B7
  GIF/THBK G46 .... 151 H1
Woodvale Dr *PSLYN/LNWD* PA3 .. 101 G4
Woodview *UD/BTH/TAN* G71 ...... 132 D1
Woodview Dr *AIRDRIE* ML6 .... 111 G4
  BLSH ML4 .... 133 J2 ⁶
Woodview Ter *HMLTN* ML3 .... 156 B5 ⁴
Woodville Pk *GOV/IBX* G51 ...... 104 B3
Woodville St *GOV/IBX* G51 ...... 104 B3
Woodwynd *KLWNG* KA13 .... 193 L5
Woodyard Rd *DMBTN* G82 .... 36 E6
Woodyett Pk
  CRMNK/CLK/EAG G76 .... 151 M4

Woodyett Rd
  CRMNK/CLK/EAG G76 .... 151 M4
Wordsworth Wy
  UD/BTH/TAN G71 .... 132 B6
Worsley Crs *NMRNS* G77 .... 150 C3
Wotherspoon Dr *BEITH* KA15 .... 144 B7 ⁹
Wraes Av *BRHD/NEIL* G78 .... 125 K5
Wraes Vw *BRHD/NEIL* G78 .... 124 F8
Wraisland Crs *BSHPTN* PA7 .... 57 M5 ²
Wrangholm Crs *MTHW* ML1 ...... 134 B6 ⁴
Wrangholm Dr *MTHW* ML1 ...... 134 A6
Wren Ct *BLSH* ML4 .... 132 E1
Wren Pl *JNSTN* PA5 .... 122 D2
Wren Rd *GRNKW/INVK* PA16 ...... 32 A4
Wright Av *BRHD/NEIL* G78 .... 125 G7
Wrightfield Pl *AYRS* KA7 .... 228 E7
Wrightlands Crs *ERSK* PA8 .... 79 L1
Wright St *RNFRW* PA4 .... 79 M8
Wyburn Pl *AYR* KA8 .... 225 G6 ⁵
Wye Crs *CTBR* ML5 .... 87 K8
Wykeham Pl *KNTSWD* G13 .... 81 J3
Wykeham Rd *KNTSWD* G13 .... 81 J3
Wylie *EKILN* G74 .... 154 D4
Wylie Av *ALEX/LLW* G83 .... 25 K6 ²
  NMRNS G77 .... 150 D2
Wylie Pl *DMBTN* G82 .... 25 L7 ²
Wylie St *HMLTN* ML3 .... 156 D7
Wyllie Rd *SALT* KA21 .... 201 G1 ⁵
Wynd Beatson
  UD/BTH/TAN G71 .... 109 C8 ⁵
Wyndford Dr *MRYH/FIRH* G20 .... 82 D4
Wyndford Pl
  MRYH/FIRH G20 .... 82 D4 ¹¹
Wyndford Rd *MRYH/FIRH* G20 .... 82 D4
Wyndford Ter
  UD/BTH/TAN G71 .... 132 B2
Wyndham Ct *KVD/HLHD* G12 .... 82 D5 ⁸
Wyndham St *KVD/HLHD* G12 ...... 82 D5
The Wynd *CUMB* G67 .... 49 H4
Wynyard Gn *EKILS* G75 .... 171 H1
Wyper Pl *DMNK/BRGTN* G40 ...... 12 E4
Wyvil Av *BSDN* G61 .... 61 J2
Wyvis Av *BSDN* G61 .... 61 J2
  KNTSWD G13 .... 80 E1
Wyvis Pl *IRVSE* KA11 .... 204 A5
  KNTSWD G13 .... 80 F1
Wyvis Qd *CLYDBK* G81 .... 80 F1 ⁵
Wyvis Rd *KLMNK* KA1 .... 212 A6 ⁶

Y

Yair Dr *CARD/HILL/MSPK* G52 .... 103 G3
Yardside Rd *KLMNKN/STW* KA3 .. 206 B2
Yarrow Crs *BSHPTN* PA7 .... 58 C7
  WISHAW ML2 .... 159 H5
Yarrow Gdns *MRYH/FIRH* G20 ...... 4 C2
Yarrow Gardens La
  MRYH/FIRH G20 .... 4 C2
Yarrow Pk *EKILN* G74 .... 15 K4
Yarrow Rd *BSHPBGS* G64 .... 64 A5
Yate St *DEN/PKHD* G31 .... 13 G6
Yerton Brae *WKIL* KA23 .... 181 J5
Yetholm St *SCOT* G14 .... 80 E3 ⁵
Yetholm Ter *HMLTN* ML3 .... 155 L6
Yett Rd *MTHW* ML1 .... 134 D6
Yetts Av *KLMNK* KA13 .... 55 K8
Yetts Crs *KKNTL* G66 .... 65 M1
Yetts Hole Rd *AIRDRIE* ML6 .... 88 C1
Yew Dr *SPRGB/BLRNK* G21 .... 6 F2
Yew Pl *JNSTN* PA5................ 99 M8
Yews Crs *HMLTN* ML3 .... 156 B4
Yieldshields Rd *CARLUKE* ML8 .... 179 L7
  CARLUKE ML8 .... 189 K1
Yokerburn Pl *KNTSWD* G13 ...... 80 E2 ²
Yokerburn Ter *CLYDBK* G81 ...... 80 D2 ⁵
Yoker Ferry Rd *RNFRW* PA4 ...... 80 E4
Yoker Mill Gdns *KNTSWD* G13 .... 80 E2 ⁷
Yoker Mill Rd *KNTSWD* G13 ...... 80 E2
Yonderton Pl *WKIL* KA23 .... 181 K5 ⁵
York Dr *RUTH* G73 .... 129 K4
Yorke Pl *KLMNK* KA1 .... 16 B2
Yorke Rd *TROON* KA10 .... 216 D8
Yorkhill Pde *KVGV* G3 .... 82 C8
Yorkhill St *KVGV* G3 .... 104 D1
York Rd *GRNKW/INVK* PA16........ 31 L4
York St *CLYDBK* G81 .... 60 D7
  KVGV G3 .... 10 F2
  WISHAW ML2 .... 159 H7
York Street La *AYR* KA8 .... 18 E1
Young Av *TROON* KA10 .... 216 D3
Younger Dr *PSTWK* KA9 .... 221 J6 ⁵
Young Pl *EKILS* G75 .... 172 A4
  UD/BTH/TAN G71 .... 132 A1 ⁵
  WISHAW ML2 .... 160 B4 ⁸
Young Rd *LNK/LMHG* ML11 ...... 199 L4
Young St *ARD* KA22 .... 191 J7
  AYR KA8 .... 225 H4
  CLYDBK G81 .... 60 B5
  WISHAW ML2 .... 159 H6
Young Ter *SPRGB/BLRNK* G21...... 6 E1
Young Wynd *BLSH* ML4 .... 133 G1
Yukon Ter *EKILS* G75 .... 171 H1
Yvetot Av *LNK/LMHG* ML11 ...... 199 H5 ⁷
Yvetot Ct *CARLUKE* ML8 .... 178 E6 ⁵

Z

Zambesi Dr
  BLTYR/CAMB G72 .... 131 J8 ¹⁰
Zena Crs *STPS/GTHM/RID* G33...... 7 L1
Zena Pl *STPS/GTHM/RID* G33...... 7 L1
Zena St *STPS/GTHM/RID* G33...... 7 L1
Zetland Rd
  CARD/HILL/MSPK G52 .... 102 F1

Abbey Medical Centre
PSLY PA1 .... **9** J5

Abbey Primary School
KLWNG KA13 .... **193** K5

Abercorn Industrial Estate
PSLYN/LNWD PA3 .... **9** H2

Abercorn Secondary School
COWCAD G4 .... **5** G5

Abronhill Health Centre
CUMB G67 .... **49** L5

Abronhill High School
CUMB G67 .... **49** L5

Abronhill Primary School
CUMB G67 .... **49** K6

Acredyke School
SPRGB/BLRNK G21 .... **84** C4

Agricultural Museum
CRMNK/CLK/EAG G76 .... **152** F4

Ailsa Hospital
RAYR/DAL KA6 .... **229** L7

Airdrie Acadamy
AIRDRIE ML6 .... **88** F8

Airdrie Health Centre
AIRDRIE ML6 .... **110** E2

Airdrieonians Football Club
AIRDRIE ML6 .... **111** J3

Air Link Industrial Estate
PSLYN/LNWD PA3 .... **101** L1

Aitkenbar Primary School
DMBTN G82 .... **37** J4

Aitkenhead Primary School
UD/BTH/TAN G71 .... **108** F8

Aiton Primary School
BLTYR/CAMB G72 .... **130** A3

Albert Primary School
AIRDRIE ML6 .... **111** H1

Albert Primary School
SPRGB/BLRNK G21 .... **83** M4

Albion Rovers Football Club
CTBR ML5 .... **110** C3

Alexander Hospital
CTBR ML5 .... **109** L1

The Alexander Kerr Practice
WISHAW ML2 .... **159** H7

Alexandra Parade Primary School
DEN/PKHD G31 .... **6** F9

Alexandra Primary School
AIRDRIE ML6 .... **111** G2

Alexandria Medical Centre
ALEX/LLW G83 .... **25** L4

Alexandria Swimming Pool
ALEX/LLW G83 .... **25** K3

Alison Lea Medical Centre
EKILN G74 .... **154** C6

Allanshaw Industrial Estate
HMLTN ML3 .... **156** D4

Allanton Primary School
SHOTTS ML7 .... **161** H1

Alloway Primary School
AYRS KA7 .... **228** E4

All Saints RC Secondary School
SPRGB/BLRNK G21 .... **84** C4

AMF Bowling
KVGV G3 .... **10** C1

The Anderson Doe Podiatry Clinic
PTCK G11 .... **81** M5

Anderston Medical Centre
KVGV G3 .... **4** B8

Anderston Primary School
KVGV G3 .... **10** C1

Annanhill Primary School
KLMNK KA1 .... **16** B4

Annette Street Primary School
GVH/MTFL G42 .... **105** G7

Annfield Medical Centre
DEN/PKHD G31 .... **12** D2

Annick Primary School
IRVSE KA11 .... **203** M4

Anniesland College
CLYDBK G81 .... **80** C1

Anniesland College of Further Education
PTCK G11 .... **81** M7

Anniesland Industrial Estate
KNTSWD G13 .... **81** L1

The Antonine Sports Centre
CLYDBK G81 .... **60** A3

Aquatec Leisure Centre
MTHW ML1 .... **157** L2

Arcadia Business Centre
CLYDBK G81 .... **60** A8

Arches Theatre
CGLE G1 .... **11** G3

Ardeer Golf Club
SVSTN KA20 .... **192** E5

Ardeer Primary School
SVSTN KA20 .... **201** K2

Arden Primary School
GIF/THBK G46 .... **126** D5

Ardgowan Bowling & Tennis Club
GRNKW/INVK PA16 .... **2** A2

Ardgowan Medical Practice
GRNKW/INVK PA16 .... **2** B3

Ardgowan Primary School
GRNKW/INVK PA16 .... **32** U3

Ardoch Medical Centre
BLTYR/CAMB G72 .... **129** M3

Ardrossan Rugby Football Club
ARD KA22 .... **191** L2

Argo Sports Centre
DRUM G15 .... **60** E6

Argyle Indoor Market
CGLE G1 .... **11** J2

Arkleston Primary School
RNFRW PA4 .... **80** D4

Arran Surgery
PLKSD/SHW G41 .... **10** L3

Art Exposure Gallery
CGLE G1 .... **11** K3

Arts Guild Theatre
GRNKW/INVK PA16 .... **2** A1

Ashcraig School
STPS/GTHM/RID G33 .... **85** H1

Ashfield Greyhound Racing Co
PPK/MIL G22 .... **83** K4

Ashfield Medical Practicett
MLNGV G62 .... **42** A8

Ashley Street School
KVGV G3 .... **4** D6

Atholl Preparatory School
MLNGV G62 .... **42** A6

Auchenback Primary School
BRHD/NEIL G78 .... **125** K8

Auchenlodment Primary School
JNSTN PA5 .... **100** A8

Auchenraith Primary School
BLTYR/CAMB G72 .... **155** L2

Auchinairn Primary School
BSHPBGS G64 .... **84** B1

Auchincruive Agricultural College
RAYR/DAL KA6 .... **226** C6

Auchinloch School
KKNTL G66 .... **65** K7

Auldhouse Primary School
EKILS G75 .... **171** J8

Auldhouse Retail Park
PLKSW/MSWD G43 .... **127** J2

Auld Kirk Museum
KKNTL G66 .... **45** J8

Ayr Acadamie
AYRS KA7 .... **18** D2

Ayr College
AYR KA8 .... **19** H4

Ayr Grammar School
AYRS KA7 .... **18** F6

Ayr Hospital
RAYR/DAL KA6 .... **229** K8

Ayr Ice Rink
AYR KA8 .... **225** G6

Ayrshire Central Hospital
IRV KA12 .... **203** H3

Ayr United Football Club
AYR KA8 .... **225** H7

Baillieston Football Club
BAIL/MDB/MHD G69 .... **108** C5

Baillieston Health Centre
BAIL/MDB/MHD G69 .... **108** B5

Baird Memorial Primary School
CUMB G67 .... **68** C2

Baldernock School
BSHPBGS G64 .... **43** H7

Baljaffray School
BSDN G61 .... **61** J1

Baljaffray Shopping Centre
BSDN G61 .... **61** J2

Ballerup High School
EKILS G75 .... **171** H4

Balmore Surgery
PPK/MIL G22 .... **83** H4

Balmuildy Primary School
BSHPBGS G64 .... **63** M6

Balornock Primary School
SPRGB/BLRNK G21 .... **84** A5

Balrossie School
KLMCLM PA13 .... **75** G2

Bankhead School
RUTH G73 .... **128** F2

Bannerman High School
BAIL/MDB/MHD G69 .... **108** A5

Baras Market
DMNK/BRGTN G40 .... **12** A4

Barassie Primary School
TROON KA10 .... **216** D4

Bargarran Primary School
ERSK PA8 .... **58** F6

Bargeddie Primary School
CTBR ML5 .... **109** G3

Barmulloch Primary School
SPRGB/BLRNK G21 .... **7** K1

Barncluith Business Centre
HMLTN ML3 .... **156** F6

Barras Market
DMNK/BRGTN G40 .... **12** A4

Barratt Trading Estate
COWCAD G4 .... **5** G5

Barrhead Bowling Club
BRHD/NEIL G78 .... **125** J6

Barrhead High School
BRHD/NEIL G78 .... **125** K6

Barrhead Sports Centre
BRHD/NEIL G78 .... **125** J6

Barrowfield School
DMNK/BRGTN G40 .... **13** G7

Barr Thomson Business Park
KLMNK KA1 .... **17** G9

Battlefield Primary School
GVH/MTFL G42 .... **127** M2

Bearsden Primary School
BSDN G61 .... **61** L4

Beckford Street Business Centre
HMLTN ML3 .... **156** D4

The Beechwood Gallery
MLNGV G62 .... **42** A7

Beith Golf Club
BEITH KA15 .... **144** F6

Beith Health Centre
BEITH KA15 .... **144** B8

Bell College of Technology
HMLTN ML3 .... **156** D4

Bellfield Primary School
KLMNK KA1 .... **212** A5

The Bell Leisure Centre
DMBTN G82 .... **36** E6

Belmont House School
NMRNS G77 .... **150** F3

Belvidere Primary School
BLSH ML4 .... **133** G5

Benburb Football Club
GOV/IBX G51 .... **103** L3

Berryhill Primary School
WISHAW ML2 .... **158** E6

Biggart Hospital
PSTWK KA9 .... **225** K2

Bishopbriggs High School
BSHPBGS G64 .... **64** A8

Bishoploch School
ESTRH G34 .... **86** D8

Bishopton Health Centre
BSHPTN PA7 .... **58** B7

Bishoptown Primary School
BSHPTN PA7 .... **58** B6

Blackfriars Primary School
GBLS G5 .... **11** K7

Blacklands Primary School
KLWNG KA13 .... **193** K7

Blacklaw Primary School
EKILN G74 .... **15** M4

Blackwoods Medical Centre
BAIL/MDB/MHD G69 .... **66** F6

Blairtummock Primary School
ESTRH G34 .... **108** B1

Blantyre High School
BLTYR/CAMB G72 .... **155** K2

Blantyre Victoria Football Club
BLTYR/CAMB G72 .... **155** M2

Blawarthill Hospital
KNTSWD G13 .... **81** G3

Blood Transfusion Service
CARLUKE ML8 .... **178** D2

Bluebird Gallery
LOCHW PA12 .... **120** C7

Blythswood Estate
RNFRW PA4 .... **80** B5

Bobbys Leisure Centre
CUMB G67 .... **48** F7

Boglestone Primary School
PGL PA14 .... **54** F1

Bonhill Primary School
ALEX/LLW G83 .... **25** L6

Bonnyholm Primary School
PLK/PH/NH G53 .... **103** G6

Bonnyton Industrial Estate
KLMNK KA1 .... **16** C2

Borderline Theatre Co
AYR KA8 .... **18** E1

Bothwell Castle
UD/BTH/TAN G71 .... **131** K5

Bothwell Medical Centre
UD/BTH/TAN G71 .... **132** A7

Bothwell Primary School
UD/BTH/TAN G71 .... **131** M7

Bourtreehill Health Centre
IRVSE KA11 .... **204** A6

Bowfield Hotel & Country Club
HWWD PA9 .... **121** K7

Boyd Street Health Centre
PSTWK KA9 .... **225** J1

Braehead Industrial Estate
RNFRW PA4 .... **80** F6

Braehead Primary School
AYR KA8 .... **225** J7

Brae Head Primary School
DMBTN G82 .... **37** G4

Braeside School
CSMK G45 .... **128** F5

Braidbar School
GIF/THBK G46 .... **127** K6

Braidcraft Medical Centre
PLK/PH/NH G53 .... **103** K8

Braidfield High School
CLYDBK G81 .... **60** C7

Braidhurst Business Centre
MTHW ML1 .... **133** J6

Braidhurst High School
MTHW ML1 .... **133** K8

Braidwood Primary School
CARLUKE ML8 .... **188** F5

Branch Surgery
CARLUKE ML8 .... **177** M4

Brannock High School
MTHW ML1 .... **134** C6

Brediland Primary School
PSLYS PA2 .... **101** G8

Brenda Temple
CGLE G1 .... **11** K3

Bridge of Weir Primary School
BRWEIR PA11 .... **76** D8

Bridge of Weir Surgery
BRWEIR PA11 .... **98** D2

Bridgeton Business Centre
DMNK/BRGTN G40 .... **12** C5

Bridgeton Health Centre
DMNK/BRGTN G40 .... **12** C5

Brisbane Primary School
LARGS KA30 .... **115** L4

Broadway Leisure Centre
PSTWK KA9 .... **225** J1

Broomhill Industrial Estate
KKNTL G66 .... **45** M7

Broomhill Primary School
PTCK G11 .... **81** M5

Broomlands Primary School
IRVSE KA11 .... **204** A7

Bruce Medical Centre
BLSH ML4 .... **133** H4

Buchanan Business Park
STPS/GTHM/RID G33 .... **85** M3

Buchanan Galleries
CGLE G1 .... **5** J9

Buckingham Clinic
KVD/HLHD G12 .... **82** D6

Budhill Medical Practice
CAR/SHTL G32 .... **107** H4

Burmah Doctors Surgeryt
PTCK G11 .... **82** B7

Burnbank Medical Centre
HMLTN ML3 .... **156** A4

Burnbrae School
PLK/PH/NH G53 .... **126** D4

Burnhead Primary School
UD/BTH/TAN G71 .... **132** D1

Burnhill Sports Centre
RUTH G73 .... **128** F1

Burns Cottage
AYRS KA7 .... **228** E7

Burnside Clinic
IRV KA12 .... **203** H5

Burnside Primary School
RUTH G73 .... **129** H4

Busby District Primary School
CRMNK/CLK/EAG G76 .... **151** M3

Bushes Primary School
PSLYS PA2 .... **124** D1

Butterbiggins Medical Centre
GVH/MTFL G42 .... **105** H6

The Byre Gallery
KVD/HLHD G12 .... **82** D6

Byres Road Market
PTCK G11 .... **82** C7

Cadder Primary School
SMSTN G23 .... **82** F2

Cadzow Business Centre
HMLTN ML3 .... **156** D5

Cadzow Health Centre
HMLTN ML3 .... **174** D1

Cairnbrook Industrial Estate
ESTRH G34 .... **108** C1

Cairnhill Industrial Estate
AIRDRIE ML6 .... **111** G3

Cairnhill Trading Estate
AIRDRIE ML6 .... **111** G3

The Cairns Primary School
BLTYR/CAMB G72 .... **130** C5

Calderbank Primary School
AIRDRIE ML6 .... **111** J3

Caldercuilt Primary School
SMSTN G23 .... **62** D8

Calderhead High School
SHOTTS ML7 .... **137** L4

Calder Primary School
MTHW ML1 .... **157** M2

Caldervale High School
AIRDRIE ML6 .... **111** M2

Calderwood Lodge Primary School
PLKSW/MSWD G43 .... **127** K4

Calderwood Primary School
RUTH G73 .... **129** J3

Caldwell Golf Club
BRHD/NEIL G78 .... **146** F6

Caldwell House Hospital
BRHD/NEIL G78 .... **146** D8

Caledonian University
CGLW G2 .... **5** H8

Caledonian University
COWCAD G4 .... **5** K7

Caledonia Primary School
BAIL/MDB/MHD G69 .... **108** B6

Callander Street Clinic
MRYH/FIRH G20 .... **4** F3

Cambuslang Avory Club
BLTYR/CAMB G72 .... **130** A5

Cambuslang Clinic
BLTYR/CAMB G72 .... **130** B4

Cambuslang College
BLTYR/CAMB G72 .... **130** B4

Cambuslang College
EKILN G74 .... **15** G1

Cambuslang Rangers FC
BLTYR/CAMB G72 .... **129** M3

Cambuslang Recreation Centre
BLTYR/CAMB G72 .... **130** D4

Cambuslang Rugby Club
BLTYR/CAMB G72 .... **129** K4

Cambusnethan Primary School
WISHAW ML2 .... **159** K6

Campsie Black Watch Football Club
KKNTL G66 .... **44** C1

Campsie Recreation Centre
KKNTL G66 .... **44** D1

Campsie View School
KKNTL G66 .... **65** G4

Canberra Primary School
EKILS G75 .... **171** H1

Canniesburn Hospital
BSDN G61 .... **61** L7

Caprington Golf Course
KLMNK KA1 .... **211** K6

Carbrain Primary School
CUMB G67 .... **49** H7

Cardinal Newman High School
BLSH ML4 .... **132** F4

Cardonald Clinic
CARD/HILL/MSPK G52 .... **103** J4

Cardonald Primary School
CARD/HILL/MSPK G52 .... **103** H5

Cardross Golf Club
DMBTN G82 .... **35** H2

Cardross Primary School
DMBTN G82 .... **24** A8

Carleith Primary School
CLYDBK G81 .... **59** L3

Carlibar Primary School
BRHD/NEIL G78 .... **125** J6

Carluke Health Centre
CARLUKE ML8 .... **178** E7

Carluke High School
CARLUKE ML8 .... **179** H7

Carluke Primary School
CARLUKE ML8 .... **179** G6

Carman Leisure Centre
DMBTN G82 .... **25** K7

Carmunnock Primary School
CRMNK/CLK/EAG G76 .... **152** D2

Carmyle Medical Centre
CAR/SHTL G32 .... **130** B1

Carmyle Primary School
CAR/SHTL G32 .... **107** J8

Carnbooth School
CRMNK/CLK/EAG G76 .... **152** B2

Carnbroe Primary School
CTBR ML5 .... **110** D5

Carntyne Primary School
STPS/GTHM/RID G33 .... **7** M9

Carntyne Surgery
STPS/GTHM/RID G33 .... **106** F1

Carnwadric Primary School
GIF/THBK G46 .... **126** F5

Caroleside Primary School
CRMNK/CLK/EAG G76 .... **151** L2

Caroleside Primary School
CRMNK/CLK/EAG G76 .... **151** L3

Carsemeadow School
BRWEIR PA11 .... **75** M7

Carsemeadow School
BRWEIR PA11 .... **75** K7

Castlebank Industrial Estate
PTCK G11 .... **82** A8

Castlefield Primary School
EKILS G75 .... **171** H4

Castlehead High School
PSLYS PA2 .... **8** E6

Castlehill Primary School
BSDN G61 .... **61** H3

Castlehill Primary School
WISHAW ML2 .... **177** G1

Castlemilk Health Centre
CSMK G45 .... **128** E6

Castlemilk High School
CSMK G45 .... **128** E7

Castlepark Primary School
IRV KA12 .... **203** J3

Castle (Remains of)
WKIL KA23 .... **180** D3

Castle Semple Sailing Club
LOCHW PA12 .... **120** D6

Castleton Primary School
CSMK G45 .... **128** D6

Cathcart Street Surgery
AYRS KA7 .... **18** D2

Cathedral RC Primary School
MTHW ML1 .... **157** L2

Cathkin High School
BLTYR/CAMB G72 .... **129** L5

Cathkin Primary School
RUTH G73 .... **129** K6

Celtic Football Club
DEN/PKHD G31 .... **13** J6

Centenary Surgery
CTBR ML5 .... **110** A4

Central College of Commerce
CGLE G1 .... **5** K9

Central Health Centre
CUMB G67 .... **48** F8

Central Mosque
GBLS G5 .... **11** J5

Centre Gallery
CGLW G2 .... **4** E8

Chapel Green Primary School
KSYTH G65 .... **46** E2

Chapelhall Industrial Estate
AIRDRIE ML6 .... **111** K6

Chapelhall Secondary School
AIRDRIE ML6 .... **111** K6

Chapelside Primary School
AIRDRIE ML6 .... **89** G8

Charing Cross Clinic
KVGV G3 .... **4** D7

The Charleston Surgery
PSLYS PA2 .... **9** H6

Chatelherault Primary School
HMLTN ML3 .... **156** E8

Child Health Clinic
PLKSW/MSWD G43 .... **127** J1

Chinese Medical Centre
KVD/HLHD G12 .... **4** A3

Chirnsyde Primary School
PPK/MIL G22 .... **83** K3

Christie Park School
ALEX/LLW G83 .... **25** K4

Christ the King Primary School
MTHW ML1 .... **134** B3

Chryston Primary School
BAIL/MDB/MHD G69 .... **86** C1

Chryston Secondary School
BAIL/MDB/MHD G69 .... **86** C1

Chryston Valley Business Centre
BAIL/MDB/MHD G69 .... **86** C1

Citadel Leisure Centre
AYRS KA7 .... **18** C1

City Chambers
CGLE G1 .... **11** K1

City Council
CGLW G2 .... **5** G9

City Halls & Ticket Office
CGLE G1 .... **11** K2

City of Glasgow Council
CGLE G1 .... **5** J9

City of Glasgow Council
CGLE G1 .... **11** M4

City of Glasgow Council
CSMK G45 .... **128** F6

City of Glasgow Council
GBLS G5 .... **11** K6

Civic Centre
EKILN G74 .... **15** G3

Civic Centre
HMLTN ML3 .... **155** M6

Civic Centre
MTHW ML1 .... **158** A5

Civic Theatre
AYR KA8 .... **19** H4

Claremont High School
EKILN G74 .... **172** C1

Clarkston Primary School
AIRDRIE ML6 .... **111** K1

Cleland Hospital
MTHW ML1 .... **135** J8

Cleland Primary School
MTHW ML1 .... **135** J8

Clevenden Secondary School
KVD/HLHD G12 .... **82** B4

Clevenden Secondary School
MRYH/FIRH G20 .... **4** B1

Clober Golf Club House
MLNGV G62 .... **41** M6

Clober Primary School
MLNGV G62 .... **41** L7

Clune Park Primary School
PGL PA14 .... **34** D8

Clydebank Business Centre
CLYDBK G81 .... **80** C1

Clydebank College
CLYDBK G81 .... **60** B6

Clydebank College
DMBTN G82 .... **36** D5

Clydebank Health Centre
CLYDBK G81 .... **60** B5

Clydebank High School
CLYDBK G81 .... **60** A5

Clydebank Town Hall
CLYDBK G81 .... **60** A8

Clyde Football Club
BALLOCH G68 .... **47** M8

Clyde Industrial Estate
RUTH G73 .... **129** G3

Clydemuir Primary School
CLYDBK G81 .... **59** K5

Clydesdale Business Centre
LNK/LMHG ML11 .... **199** J6

Clyde Valley High School
WISHAW ML2 .... **177** H2

Clydeview School
MTHW ML1 .... **157** J2
Clydeway Business Centre
KVGV G3 .... **10** B1
Coatbridge Business Centre
CTBR ML5 .... **110** C3
Coatbridge College
CTBR ML5 .... **110** C2
Coatbridge Health Centre
CTBR ML5 .... **110** A3
Coatbridge High School
CTBR ML5 .... **110** A2
Coathill Hospital
CTBR ML5 .... **110** A5
Cochrane Castle
Primary School
JNSTN PA5 .... **122** D1
Colgrain Primary School
HBR/GL G84 .... **21** G8
The College &
Cathedral College
GTCI KA28 .... **138** B6
College of Art
CGLW G2 .... **4** F8
College of Building & Printing
CGLE G1 .... **5** K9
College of Food & Technology
CGLE G1 .... **5** K9
Colquhoun Park Primary School
BSDN G61 .... **61** J6
Coltness High School
WISHAW ML2 .... **159** K5
Coltness Primary School
WISHAW ML2 .... **159** J3
Columba High School
CTBR ML5 .... **110** A5
Compass Gallery
CGLW G2 .... **4** F9
Condorrat Health Centre
CUMB G67 .... **68** A3
Condorrat Primary School
CUMB G67 .... **68** B2
Corpus Christi RC School
AIRDRIE ML6 .... **111** H7
Corsehill Primary School
KLWNG KA13 .... **193** M5
Cotton Street Business Park
DMNK/BRGTN G40 .... **106** A7
Council Chambers
GLSTN KA4 .... **214** C3
Country Club Hotel
CMPF/LLE G63 .... **27** J7
The Country Estate Gallery
CARLUKE ML8 .... **188** C8
Courthill Clinic
BSDN G61 .... **61** J3
Cowglen Golf Club
BEITH KA15 .... **168** B1
Cowglen Hospital
PLK/PH/NH G53 .... **126** D2
Coylton Health Clinic
RAYR/DAL KA6 .... **231** H6
Coylton Primary School
RAYR/DAL KA6 .... **231** J6
Craigbank Secondary School
PLK/PH/NH G53 .... **126** C1
Craigdhu Primary School
MLNGV G62 .... **61** M1
Craighead Primary School
KKNTL G66 .... **45** H3
Craighead School
HMLTN ML3 .... **156** B2
Craigholme School
PLKSD/SHW G41 .... **104** D6
Craigie College of Education
AYR KA8 .... **19** M5
Craigilea Primary School
PSLYN/LNWD PA3 .... **101** G3
Craigpark Park
AYR KA8 .... **225** K8
Crawforddyke Primary School
CARLUKE ML8 .... **189** G1
Croftcroighn School
STPS/GTHM/RID G33 ...... **85** L8
Crofthead Industrial Estate
BRHD/NEIL G78 .... **148** C2
Crookfur Primary School
NMRNS G77 .... **150** D2
Crookston (NT)
PLK/PH/NH G53 .... **103** H7
Cross Arthurlie Primary School
BRHD/NEIL G78 .... **125** G5
Crosshouse Hospital
CRH/DND KA2 .... **206** A7
Crosshouse Primary School
CRH/DND KA2 .... **205** L8
Crosslee Primary School
EKILS G75 .... **171** G4
Crowngate Business Centre
DMNK/BRGTN G40 .... **12** D6
Cumbernauld Airport
BALLOCH G68 .... **49** J1
Cumbernauld College
CUMB G67 .... **48** F8
Cumbernauld High School
CUMB G67 .... **49** J8
Cumbernauld Primary School
CUMB G67 .... **49** H5
Cumbernauld Theatre
CUMB G67 .... **49** H5
Cumbrae Primary School
GTCI KA28 .... **138** A6
Cuthbertson Primary School
PLKSD/SHW G41 .... **105** G6
The Cutting Gallery
SHOTTS ML7 .... **137** K4
Cyril Gerber Gallery
CGLW G2 .... **5** G9
Daily Record & Sunday
Mail Offices
KVGV G3 .... **10** C2
Dalgarven Mill Museum
KLWNG KA13 .... **193** K1
Dalmarnock Primary School
DMNK/BRGTN G40 .... **12** E8
Dalmarnock Trading Estate
RUTH G73 .... **106** B8

Dalmilling Golf Club
AYR KA8 .... **225** L8
Dalmilling Primary School
AYR KA8 .... **225** L7
Dalreoch Primary School
DMBTN G82 .... **36** C4
Dalry Primary School
DALRY KA24 .... **184** B2
Dalsholm Industrial Estate
MRYH/FIRH G20 .... **82** B2
Dalziel Business Centre
MTHW ML1 .... **157** L3
Dalziel High School
MTHW ML1 .... **157** K3
Darrows Estate
UD/BTH/TAN G71 .... **132** D3
David Dale College
DMNK/BRGTN G40 .... **12** D5
David Livingstone Centre
BLTYR/CAMB G72 .... **131** L7
David Livingstone
Memorial Primary School
BLTYR/CAMB G72 .... **131** K8
Dental Hospital & School
CGLW G2 .... **4** F8
Department of General Practice
KVD/HLHD G12 .... **82** C5
Devol Industrial Estate
PGL PA14 .... **54** D1
Dinmont Doctors Surgery
PLKSD/SHW G41 .... **104** D8
Doonfoot Primary School
AYRS KA7 .... **228** B6
Douglas Inch Clinic
KVGV G3 .... **4** D7
Dowanhill Primary School
PTCK G11 .... **82** C7
Dr D'silva & Partners
UD/BTH/TAN G71 .... **132** C2
Dreghorn Primary School
IRVSE KA11 .... **204** D8
Dr Huq
CTBR ML5 .... **109** M3
Drs M Agnew & P Mckillop
CTBR ML5 .... **109** M3
Drumchapel Health Centre
DRUM G15 .... **60** F6
Drumchapel High School
DRUM G15 .... **61** G5
Drummore School
DRUM G15 .... **61** J5
Drumoyne Industrial Estate
GOV/IBX G51 .... **103** L3
Drumoyne Primary School
GOV/IBX G51 .... **103** L3
Drumpark Special School
CTBR ML5 .... **109** G3
Drumpellier Cricket Club
CTBR ML5 .... **109** K3
Duchess Industrial Estate
RUTH G73 .... **106** C7
Dumbarton Football Club
DMBTN G82 .... **37** H5
Dumbarton Health Centre
DMBTN G82 .... **36** E5
Dumbarton Joint Hospital
DMBTN G82 .... **36** C5
Dumbarton Peoples Theatre
DMBTN G82 .... **37** H6
Dunard Primary School
MRYH/FIRH G20 .... **4** C1
Dunbartonshire &
Lomond Council
BSHPBGS G64 .... **63** M7
Duncanrig Secondary School
EKILS G75 .... **153** H8
Duncanrig Sports Centre
EKILS G75 .... **171** H1
Dundas Business Centre
COWCAD G4 .... **5** G6
Dundonald Castle
CRH/DND KA2 .... **209** L7
Dundonald Health Centre
CRH/DND KA2 .... **209** M7
Dundonald Medical Practice
CRH/DND KA2 .... **209** M7
Dundonald Primary School
CRH/DND KA2 .... **209** M7
Dunrobin Primary School
AIRDRIE ML6 .... **111** L2
Duntreath Castle
CMPF/LLE G63 .... **26** D2
Dykehead Primary School
SHOTTS ML7 .... **137** K4
Dykesmains Primary School
SALT KA21 .... **191** M6
Earnock Secondary School
HMLTN ML3 .... **156** H4
East Bank Primary School
CAR/SHTL G32 .... **107** J4
East Dunbartonshire Council
BAIL/MDB/MHD G69 ...... **86** C1
East Dunbartonshire Council
BAIL/MDB/MHD G69 ...... **108** A4
East Dunbartonshire Council
BSDN G61 .... **61** K3
East Dunbartonshire Council
BSDN G61 .... **62** A5
East Dunbartonshire Council
BSHPBGS G64 .... **63** L5
East Dunbartonshire Council
BSHPBGS G64 .... **83** M1
East Dunbartonshire Council
KKNTL G66 .... **44** D1
East Dunbartonshire Council
KKNTL G66 .... **65** J2
East Dunbartonshire Council
KSYTH G65 .... **46** F5
East Dunbartonshire Council
MLNGV G62 .... **42** A7
Easter Moffat Golf Club
AIRDRIE ML6 .... **90** B8
Eastfield Primary School
BALLOCH G68 .... **48** B8
East Fulton Primary School
PSLYN/LNWD PA3 .... **99** M3
East Kilbride Ice Rink
EKILN G74 .... **14** F4

East Kilbride Sports Club
EKILN G74 .... **172** C3
East Milton Primary School
EKILS G75 .... **14** A4
Eastmuir Surgery
CAR/SHTL G32 .... **107** J4
East Renfrewshire Council
BRHD/NEIL G78 .... **125** H6
East Renfrewshire Council
CRMNK/CLK/EAG G76 .... **151** L2
East Renfrewshire Council
GIF/THBK G46 .... **127** J8
Eastside Industrial Estate
KKNTL G66 .... **45** K8
Eastwood High School
NMRNS G77 .... **150** E2
Edenkiln Surgery
CMPF/LLE G63 .... **27** J6
Edinbarnet Primary School
CLYDBK G81 .... **60** C1
Eglinton Castle
KLWNG KA13 .... **194** C8
Elderpark Clinic
GOV/IBX G51 .... **103** M2
Elder Park Primary School
GOV/IBX G51 .... **103** L1
Elderslie Cottage Hospital
JNSTN PA5 .... **100** C7
Elise Hospital
BRWEIR PA11 .... **75** K7
Elmvale Primary School
PPK/MIL G22 .... **83** L4
Elmwood Medical Centre
NMRNS G77 .... **150** E3
Elmwood Special School
DMBTN G82 .... **37** G5
Empire Theatre
LRKH ML9 .... **175** M6
Erskine Health Centre
ERSK PA8 .... **59** G6
Erskine Hospital
BSHPTN PA7 .... **58** E3
Erskine Swimming Pool
ERSK PA8 .... **59** J7
Erskine View Clinic
OLDK G60 .... **59** G3
Fallside Secondary School
UD/BTH/TAN G71 .... **132** D3
Family Planning Clinic
KVGV G3 .... **4** C7
Farm Castle Industrial Estate
RUTH G73 .... **129** J1
Farmeloan Industrial Estate
RUTH G73 .... **129** H1
Fencedyke Primary School
IRVSE KA11 .... **204** A6
Ferguslie Cricket Club
PSLYS PA2 .... **8** D7
Ferguslie Primary School
PSLYN/LNWD PA3 .... **8** A1
Ferry Terminal
GRK PA19 .... **31** L1
Ferry Terminal
GRK PA19 .... **31** G3
Ferry Terminal
TROON KA10 .... **216** B6
Festival Business Centre
GOV/IBX G51 .... **104** C3
Fiddle Gallery
MRYH/FIRH G20 .... **4** B1
Film Theatre
CGLE G1 .... **5** G8
The Fireplace & Furnisher Gallery
KVGV G3 .... **82** D8
Fire Service Training Station
COWCAD G4 .... **5** H6
Fire Station
CGLW G2 .... **5** H7
Fire Station
COWCAD G4 .... **12** A3
Firhill Business Centre
MRYH/FIRH G20 .... **4** E1
Flemington Industrial Estate
BLTYR/CAMB G72 .... **130** E5
Florence Street Clinic
GBLS G5 .... **11** K5
The Flower Gallery
DEN/PKHD G31 .... **12** E2
The Flower Gallery
PSLY PA1 .... **9** M3
The Food Gallery
KVGV G3 .... **4** C7
Fordbank Primary School
JNSTN PA5 .... **122** C1
Forehill Primary School
AYRS KA7 .... **19** L8
Forge Industrial Estate
KLMNK KA1 .... **16** C2
Fort Matilda Industrial Estate
GRNKW/INVK PA16 .... **32** A1
The Fort Theatre
BSHPBGS G64 .... **63** M8
Fountain Business Centre
CTBR ML5 .... **110** A2
The Framework Gallery
TROON KA10 .... **216** C6
French Street Industrial Estate
RNFRW PA4 .... **80** B7
Fullwood Health Centre
MTHW ML1 .... **134** A5
Fullwood Industrial Estate
HMLTN ML3 .... **156** B4
Gadburn School
SPRGB/BLRNK G21 .... **84** C4
Gaiety Theatre
AYRS KA7 .... **18** E2
Galleon Leisure Centre
KLMNK KA1 .... **16** E6
The Gallery at Home Creations
RUTH G73 .... **129** J3
Gallery of Modern Art
CGLE G1 .... **11** J1
The Gallery
DEN/PKHD G31 .... **13** L6
The Gallery
WKIL KA23 .... **181** J4
Gallowgate Market
CGLE G1 .... **11** L3

Gallowhill Primary School
PSLYN/LNWD PA3 .... **102** B2
Galston Clinic
GLSTN KA4 .... **214** C3
Galston Primary School
GLSTN KA4 .... **214** C3
Gargieston Primary School
KLMNK KA1 .... **211** J3
Garnetbank Primary School
KVGV G3 .... **4** E7
Garnock Business Park
SVSTN KA20 .... **201** K1
Garrell Business Centre
KSYTH G65 .... **47** J1
Garrowhill Primary School
BAIL/MDB/MHD G69 ...... **108** A4
Gartconner Primary School
KKNTL G66 .... **66** C1
Gartcosh Primary School
BAIL/MDB/MHD G69 ...... **86** F4
Gartcosh Works Sports Club
BAIL/MDB/MHD G69 ...... **87** G4
Garthamlock Secondary School
STPS/GTHM/RID G33 ...... **85** L7
Gartnavel General Hospital
KVD/HLHD G12 .... **82** B5
Gartnavel Royal Hospital
KVD/HLHD G12 .... **82** A5
Gartsherrie Industrial Estate
CTBR ML5 .... **87** M8
Gartsherrie Primary School
CTBR ML5 .... **109** L1
Gask House School
BSHPBGS G64 .... **83** M2
The Gatehouse Gallery
GIF/THBK G46 .... **126** F7
Gavinburn School
OLDK G60 .... **58** F2
GHK Rugby Football Club
KNTSWD G13 .... **81** M3
Giffnock Primary School
GIF/THBK G46 .... **127** J6
Giffnock Synagogue
GIF/THBK G46 .... **127** J7
Giffnock Theatre Player
GIF/THBK G46 .... **127** J7
Glasgow Airport
PSLYN/LNWD PA3 .... **79** L8
Glasgow Art Gallery & Museum
KVGV G3 .... **82** D8
Glasgow Caledonian University
KVD/HLHD G12 .... **82** A3
Glasgow Caledonian University
KVGV G3 .... **4** B5
Glasgow Cathedral
COWCAD G4 .... **6** A9
Glasgow City Council
BAIL/MDB/MHD G69 ...... **108** B5
Glasgow City Council
CAR/SHTL G32 .... **13** L1
Glasgow City Council
CAR/SHTL G32 .... **106** F4
Glasgow City Council
CAR/SHTL G32 .... **107** H4
Glasgow City Council
CARD/HILL/MSPK G52 .... **102** F4
Glasgow City Council
CARD/HILL/MSPK G52 .... **103** K5
Glasgow City Council
CGLE G1 .... **5** J9
Glasgow City Council
CGLE G1 .... **11** L2
Glasgow City Council
CGLE G1 .... **11** J2
Glasgow City Council
CGLW G2 .... **4** E8
Glasgow City Council
CGLW G2 .... **5** G8
Glasgow City Council
COWCAD G4 .... **10** E1
Glasgow City Council
COWCAD G4 .... **5** L8
Glasgow City Council
COWCAD G4 .... **5** J3
Glasgow City Council
COWCAD G4 .... **5** K4
Glasgow City Council
CSMK G45 .... **128** D6
Glasgow City Council
DEN/PKHD G31 .... **7** H8
Glasgow City Council
DEN/PKHD G31 .... **13** L6
Glasgow City Council
DMBTN G82 .... **36** E6
Glasgow City Council
DMNK/BRGTN G40 .... **12** E6
Glasgow City Council
DMNK/BRGTN G40 .... **13** G6
Glasgow City Council
DMNK/BRGTN G40 .... **106** A6
Glasgow City Council
DRUM G15 .... **60** F5
Glasgow City Council
ESTRH G34 .... **108** A1
Glasgow City Council
GBLS G5 .... **10** E4
Glasgow City Council
GBLS G5 .... **10** F5
Glasgow City Council
GBLS G5 .... **11** H5
Glasgow City Council
GBLS G5 .... **11** L7
Glasgow City Council
GIF/THBK G46 .... **126** C5
Glasgow City Council
GOV/IBX G51 .... **103** L3
Glasgow City Council
GOV/IBX G51 .... **104** A1
Glasgow City Council
GOV/IBX G51 .... **104** C3
Glasgow City Council
GVH/MTFL G42 .... **105** H7
Glasgow City Council
GVH/MTFL G42 .... **128** D1
Glasgow City Council
KNTSWD G13 .... **81** M3
Glasgow City Council
KNTSWD G13 .... **81** H3

Glasgow City Council
KVD/HLHD G12 .... **82** C3
Glasgow City Council
KVGV G3 .... **4** A8
Glasgow City Council
LNPK/KPK G44 .... **128** B3
Glasgow City Council
MRYH/FIRH G20 .... **4** E4
Glasgow City Council
MRYH/FIRH G20 .... **4** E2
Glasgow City Council
MRYH/FIRH G20 .... **82** A2
Glasgow City Council
MRYH/FIRH G20 .... **82** D2
Glasgow City Council
MRYH/FIRH G20 .... **82** E4
Glasgow City Council
PLK/PH/NH G53 .... **103** H8
Glasgow City Council
PLK/PH/NH G53 .... **125** M5
Glasgow City Council
PLK/PH/NH G53 .... **126** B2
Glasgow City Council
PLKSD/SHW G41 .... **10** D7
Glasgow City Council
PLKSD/SHW G41 .... **104** D6
Glasgow City Council
PLKSW/MSWD G43 .... **127** J1
Glasgow City Council
PPK/MIL G22 .... **83** L2
Glasgow City Council
PPK/MIL G22 .... **83** H5
Glasgow City Council
PTCK G11 .... **82** B8
Glasgow City Council
SPRGB/BLRNK G21 .... **6** A3
Glasgow City Council
SPRGB/BLRNK G21 .... **6** C3
Glasgow City Council
SPRGB/BLRNK G21 .... **6** C7
Glasgow City Council
SPRGB/BLRNK G21 .... **6** A1
Glasgow City Council
SPRGB/BLRNK G21 .... **7** G3
Glasgow City Council
SPRGB/BLRNK G21 .... **83** M3
Glasgow City Council
SPRGB/BLRNK G21 .... **84** C3
Glasgow City Council
STPS/GTHM/RID G33 ...... **106** F1
Glasgow City Council
STPS/GTHM/RID G33 ...... **107** K3
Glasgow City Council
STPS/GTHM/RID G33 ...... **107** M3
Glasgow City Council
STPS/GTHM/RID G33 ...... **107** H1
Glasgow City Council
STPS/GTHM/RID G33 ...... **107** J1
Glasgow Cricket Club
PLKSD/SHW G41 .... **104** D7
Glasgow Golf Club
IRVSE KA11 .... **208** C4
Glasgow Nuffield Hospital
KVD/HLHD G12 .... **82** B4
Glasgow Royal Infirmary
DEN/PKHD G31 .... **6** C8
Glasgow School of Art
KVGV G3 .... **5** G7
Glasgow Steiner School
KVGV G3 .... **104** D1
Glasgow Western Post Graduate
Medical Centre
KVD/HLHD G12 .... **82** D4
Glasgow Zoo
UD/BTH/TAN G71 .... **108** B7
Glebe Primary School
IRV KA12 .... **203** J7
Glenboig Primary School
CTBR ML5 .... **87** M4
Glenburn Clinic
PSLYS PA2 .... **124** D1
Glenburn Primary School
PSTWK KA9 .... **221** L8
Glenburn School
GRNKW/INVK PA16 .... **31** L7
Glencairn Industrial Estate
KLMNK KA1 .... **16** F8
Glencairn Primary School
MTHW ML1 .... **157** L4
Glencairn Primary School
SVSTN KA20 .... **201** K1
Glencryan School
CUMB G67 .... **68** E2
Glendale Primary School
PLKSD/SHW G41 .... **10** D8
Glengarnock Primary School
GLGNK KA14 .... **167** H2
Glengowan Primary School
AIRDRIE ML6 .... **91** G5
Glenhead Primary School
CUMB G67 .... **49** L4
Gleniffer High School
PSLYS PA2 .... **124** A1
Glenlee Primary School
HMLTN ML3 .... **156** A4
Glenmanor Primary School
BAIL/MDB/MHD G69 ...... **66** F7
Glenmill Surgery
STPS/GTHM/RID G33 ...... **7** M2
Glenpark Industrial Estate
DEN/PKHD G31 .... **13** G3
Glenvale Football Club
PSLY PA1 .... **8** D4
Glenwood Business Centre
CSMK G45 .... **128** E6
Glenwood Business Park
CSMK G45 .... **128** E6
Golden Hill Primary School
CLYDBK G81 .... **60** B1
Golfhill Primary School
AIRDRIE ML6 .... **88** E7
Golfhill Primary School
DEN/PKHD G31 .... **6** C9
Gorbals Health Centre
GBLS G5 .... **11** K7
Gourock Central Junior School
GRK PA19 .... **31** K1

Gourock Golf Club
GRK PA19 .... **31** H3
Gourock Health Centre
GRK PA19 .... **31** L1
Gourock High School
GRK PA19 .... **31** K2
Govan Health Centre
GOV/IBX G51 .... **103** L1
Govan High Secondary School
GOV/IBX G51 .... **103** L2
Govanhill Health Centre
CVH/MTFL G42 .... **105** H7
Greater Glasgow Health Board
DEN/PKHD G31 .... **13** L5
Greenan Gallery
AYRS KA7 .... **18** D3
Greenfaulds High School
CUMB G67 .... **68** D2
Greenfield Street School
GOV/IBX G51 .... **103** M2
Greengairs Primary School
AIRDRIE ML6 .... **69** L7
Greenhill Primary School
CTBR ML5 .... **110** A1
Greenhills Health Centre
EKILS G75 .... **171** G3
Greenhills Primary School
EKILS G75 .... **171** J3
Greenock Cricket Club
GRNKW/INVK PA16 .... **32** D2
Greenock Golf Club House
GRNKW/INVK PA16 .... **32** C5
Greenock Health Centre
GRNK PA15 .... **2** B4
Greenock High School
GRNKW/INVK PA16 .... **31** K7
Greenock Wanderers
Rugby Football Club
GRNKW/INVK PA16 .... **32** B1
Greenwood Acadamy
IRVSE KA11 .... **204** A8
Grovewood Business Centre
BLSH ML4 .... **132** E1
Gryffe High School
CRG/CRSL/HOU PA6 .... **77** G8
Haghill Primary School
DEN/PKHD G31 .... **13** H1
Hairmyres &
Stonehouse Hospitals
NHS Trust
EKILS G75 .... **152** F8
Haldane Primary School
ALEX/LLW G83 .... **25** M1
Halfmerke Primary School
EKILN G74 .... **154** A6
Hallside Primary School
BLTYR/CAMB G72 .... **130** E5
Hamilton Academical
Football Club Ltd
HMLTN ML3 .... **156** C4
Hamilton Business Park
HMLTN ML3 .... **156** D4
Hamilton College
HMLTN ML3 .... **156** D4
Hamilton District Council
LRKH ML9 .... **176** A6
Hamilton Grammar School
HMLTN ML3 .... **156** D6
Hamiltonhill Industrial Estate
PPK/MIL G22 .... **5** J2
Hamilton Race Course
HMLTN ML3 .... **156** D2
Hampden School
CVH/MTFL G42 .... **128** E2
Harbour Industrial Estate
ARD KA22 .... **191** J7
Hareleeshill Primary School
LRKH ML9 .... **176** C7
Harestanes Primary School
KKNTL G66 .... **46** A8
Hartfield Clinic
DMBTN G82 .... **37** G5
Hartwood Hospital
MTHW ML1 .... **136** E7
Hartwood Hospital
SHOTTS ML7 .... **136** F7
The Harvest Clinic
COWCAD G4 .... **4** E6
Haughney Doctors Surgery
NMRNS G77 .... **150** F4
Hawkhead Hospital
PSLYS PA2 .... **102** C7
Haycocks Primary School
SVSTN KA20 .... **192** E7
Haysholm School
IRV KA12 .... **203** L5
Healthcare International (HCI)
CLYDBK G81 .... **59** M7
Health & Welfare Clinic
BAIL/MDB/MHD G69 .... **86** D1
Heatherbank Museum of
Social Work Trust
KVD/HLHD G12 .... **4** B5
Heathery Knowe
Primary School
EKILS G75 .... **14** D8
Heathfield Primary School
AYR KA8 .... **225** H4
Helensburgh Golf Club
HBR/GL G84 .... **20** F6
Helensburgh Medical Centre
HBR/GL G84 .... **20** D8
Helensburgh Swimming Pool
HBR/GL G84 .... **20** D8
The Henderson Theatre
SHOTTS ML7 .... **137** M5
Heriot Primary School
PSLYS PA2 .... **123** M1
Hermitage School
HBR/GL G84 .... **20** D7
High Blantyre Primary School
BLTYR/CAMB G72 .... **155** H2
High Court & Court of Justiciary
CGLE G1 .... **11** K4
Highholm Primary School
PGL PA14 .... **34** B8

Highlanders Academy
Primary School
GRNKW/INVK PA16 .... **32** D5
High School of Glasgow
KNTSWD G13 .... **81** L3
High Street Industrial Estate
KKNTL G66 .... **45** J8
Hillhead High School
KVD/HLHD G12 .... **4** A4
Hillhead Primary School
KKNTL G66 .... **65** L1
Hillhead Primary School
KLMNKN/STW KA3 .... **206** E6
Hillhead Rugby Club
KVD/HLHD G12 .... **82** B5
Hillington Industrial Estate
CARD/HILL/MSPK G52 .... **102** F2
Hillington Primary School
CARD/HILL/MSPK G52 .... **103** G3
Hillpark Secondary School
PLKSW/MSWD G43 .... **127** J4
Hill Street Industrial Estate
ARD KA22 .... **191** J8
Hillstrust Primary School
GOV/IBX G51 .... **104** A1
Hindu Temple
KVD/HLHD G12 .... **4** A4
Hollybrook School
CVH/MTFL G42 .... **105** H7
Hollywood Bowl
BAIL/MDB/MHD G69 .... **109** J6
Holm Industrial Estate
PSLYS PA2 .... **9** J8
Holmlea Primary School
LNPK/KPK G44 .... **128** A3
Holy Cross High School
HMLTN ML3 .... **156** E5
Holycross RC Primary School
GRNKW/INVK PA16 .... **32** B3
Holy Cross School
KSYTH G65 .... **47** M5
Holy Family Primary School
BLSH ML4 .... **133** J4
Holy Family Primary School
KKNTL G66 .... **65** H3
Holy Family RC Primary School
PGL PA14 .... **55** G1
Holy Reedemer RC School
CLYDBK G81 .... **80** D2
Holyrood Secondary School
CVH/MTFL G42 .... **105** J8
Holytown Primary School
MTHW ML1 .... **134** B4
Homoeopaths Surgery
KVGV G3 .... **4** D8
Househillmuir Road School
PLK/PH/NH G53 .... **126** B4
Houston Primary School
CRG/CRSL/HOU PA6 .... **77** H8
Houston Surgery
CRG/CRSL/HOU PA6 .... **77** H6
Howford School
PLK/PH/NH G53 .... **103** G7
Howwood Primary School
HWWD PA9 .... **121** M4
The Hui Chun Clinic
KVGV G3 .... **4** F7
The Hunter Health Centre
EKILN G74 .... **15** G3
Hunter High School
EKILN G74 .... **154** C7
Hunter House Museum
EKILN G74 .... **154** C5
Hunter Primary School
EKILN G74 .... **154** C6
Hunter Sport Centre
KLMNKN/STW KA3 .... **206** F6
Hunterston Castle
WKIL KA23 .... **163** G6
Hurford Primary School
KLMNK KA1 .... **212** E3
Hurlford Primary School
KLMNKN/STW KA3 .... **207** K5
Hutchesons Grammar
Junior School
PLKSD/SHW G41 .... **105** G7
Hutchesons Grammar School
PLKSD/SHW G41 .... **104** D7
Hutchesons St Aloysians
Rugby Club
GIF/THBK G46 .... **127** G4
Hyndland Primary School
PTCK G11 .... **82** B7
Hyndland Senior
Secondary School
KVD/HLHD G12 .... **82** A6
Ian Kenny Gallery
LRKH ML9 .... **175** M5
Ibh Carrick Glen Hospital
RAYR/DAL KA6 .... **229** M8
Ibrox Industrial Estate
GOV/IBX G51 .... **104** B3
Ibrox Primary School
GOV/IBX G51 .... **104** A4
Inchinnan Primary School
RNFRW PA4 .... **79** K2
Indoor Market
DRUM G15 .... **60** F6
Insomnia Gallery
KVGV G3 .... **4** D7
International Christian College
COWCAD G4 .... **5** M9
Inverclyde Royal Hospital
GRNKW/INVK PA16 .... **31** M5
Inverkip Primary School
GRNKW/INVK PA16 .... **50** D4
Irvine Sports Club
IRV KA12 .... **203** H7
Islamic Mosque
KVGV G3 .... **4** D7
Isobel Mair School
CRMNK/CLK/EAG G76 .... **127** K8
Jackton Business Centre
EKILS G75 .... **170** C2
James Mcfarlane School
ARD KA22 .... **191** J6
James Reid School
SVSTN KA20 .... **192** B7

Jamestown Primary School
ALEX/LLW G83 .... **25** M2
James Watt College
GRNK PA15 .... **2** F3
James Watt College
GRNKW/INVK PA16 .... **2** A3
John Galt Primary School
IRV KA12 .... **203** J5
John Hillhouse
Industrial Estate
BLTYR/CAMB G72 .... **129** K1
John Logie Baird
Primary School
HBR/GL G84 .... **20** F7
John Ogilvie High School
HMLTN ML3 .... **155** M5
Johnstone Health Centre
JNSTN PA5 .... **99** M7
Johnstone High School
JNSTN PA5 .... **122** D1
Johnstone Hospital
JNSTN PA5 .... **100** A3
Johnstone Swimming Pool
JNSTN PA5 .... **99** M6
John Street Clinic
DMBTN G82 .... **36** D1
John Wheatley College
ESTRH G34 .... **108** B1
The John Wright Sports Centre
EKILN G74 .... **15** K2
Jordanhill College School
KNTSWD G13 .... **81** K4
Junior High School of Glasgow
BSDN G61 .... **61** K5
Junior Secondary School
MTHW ML1 .... **133** M5
Keil School
DMBTN G82 .... **36** D6
Keir Hardie Memorial
Primary School
MTHW ML1 .... **134** C6
Keir Hardie Sports Centre
MTHW ML1 .... **134** A3
Kelburne Cricket Club
PSLY PA1 .... **9** M2
Kelburn Primary School
LARGS KA30 .... **115** K6
The Kelly Gallery
CGLW G2 .... **4** F8
Kelvindale Primary School
KVD/HLHD G12 .... **82** A4
Kelvin Gallery
CGLW G2 .... **5** G8
Kendon Business Centre
AYRS KA7 .... **18** D5
Kenilworth Medical Centre
CUMB G67 .... **68** E1
Kennyhill School
DEN/PKHD G31 .... **7** J9
Kerelaw School
SVSTN KA20 .... **192** D7
Kerr Practice
DMNK/BRGTN G40 .... **12** D6
The Kibble School
PSLYN/LNWD PA3 .... **101** K1
Kilbarchan Primary School
KLBCH PA10 .... **99** C5
Kilbirnie Golf Club
KBRN KA25 .... **142** F8
Kilbowie Primary School
CLYDBK G81 .... **60** B6
Kildrum Primary School
CUMB G67 .... **49** J6
Kilmacolm Primary School
KLMCLM PA13 .... **75** J7
Kilmarnock (Barassie) Golf Club
TROON KA10 .... **216** D2
Kilmarnock College
IRV KA12 .... **203** J6
Kilmarnock College
KLMNKN/STW KA3 .... **17** H3
Kilmarnock Football Club
KLMNK KA1 .... **16** C6
Kilmarnock Indoor Market
KLMNK KA1 .... **16** F6
Kilmarnock Tennis Club
KLMNKN/STW KA3 .... **17** G3
Kilmaurs Clinic
KLMNKN/STW KA3 .... **206** B2
Kilmaurs Primary School
KLMNKN/STW KA3 .... **206** B2
Kilpatrick Primary School
CLYDBK G81 .... **59** L3
Kilsyth Health Centre
KSYTH G65 .... **47** L1
Kilsyth Primary School
KSYTH G65 .... **47** K1
Kilwinning Clinic
KLWNG KA13 .... **193** M6
Kilwinning Medical Practice
KLWNG KA13 .... **193** L6
Kincaidston Primary School
AYRS KA7 .... **229** G4
Kincase Primary School
PSTWK KA9 .... **225** H3
Kingsgate Retail Park
EKILN G74 .... **154** A3
Kings Glen Primary School
GRNK PA15 .... **33** K8
Kings Park Secondary School
LNPK/KPK G44 .... **128** C4
Kings Theatre
CGLW G2 .... **4** E8
Kingston Business Park
PGL PA14 .... **34** A7
Kingston Industrial Estate
PGL PA14 .... **34** A7
Kinning Park Medical Centre
GOV/IBX G51 .... **10** B4
Kirkfield Primary School
LNK/LMHG ML11 .... **198** D5
Kirkhall Surgery
PSTWK KA9 .... **221** J8
Kirkhill Primary School
NMRNS G77 .... **151** H4
Kirkintilloch Foot Clinic
KKNTL G66 .... **65** J1

Kirkintilloch High School
KKNTL G66 .... **65** M1
Kirkintilloch Industrial Estate
KKNTL G66 .... **45** K7
Kirklandeuk Primary School
RNFRW PA4 .... **80** C5
Kirklandside Hospital
KLMNK KA1 .... **212** C4
Kirkriggs School
CSMK G45 .... **129** G4
Kirkshaws Primary School
CTBR ML5 .... **109** L5
Kirkstyle Primary School
KLMNK KA1 .... **17** H9
Kirktonholme Primary School
EKILN G74 .... **14** C2
Kirkton Primary School
CARLUKE ML8 .... **178** E8
Kirkwood Health Clinic
CTBR ML5 .... **109** J5
Kittoch School
EKILS G75 .... **14** D7
Knock Castle
LARGS KA30 .... **92** A6
Knowetop Primary School
MTHW ML1 .... **158** A5
Knoxland Primary School
DMBTN G82 .... **37** G7
Kylie Acad
AYRS KA7 .... **229** K2
Lady Alice Primary School
GRNKW/INVK PA16 .... **32** C5
Ladybank Business Park
GRNK PA15 .... **33** L6
Lady Margaret Hospital
GTCI KA28 .... **138** A6
Lady Octavia Recreation Centre
GRNK PA15 .... **3** K9
Ladywell Primary School
MTHW ML1 .... **157** G4
Lagoon Leisure Centre
PSLY PA1 .... **9** K3
Laigh Bent Sports Club
HMLTN ML3 .... **156** E6
Lainshaw Primary School
KLMNKN/STW KA3 .... **197** K1
Laird Business Park
DMNK/BRGTN G40 .... **106** A7
Lairdsland Primary School
KKNTL G66 .... **65** J1
Lamlash Primary School
STPS/GTHM/RID G33 .... **107** H1
Lammermoor Primary School
WISHAW ML2 .... **159** H5
Lanark Gallery
LNK/LMHG ML11 .... **199** G5
Lanark Golf Club
LNK/LMHG ML11 .... **199** K6
Lanark Grammar School
LNK/LMHG ML11 .... **199** G6
Lanark Primary School
LNK/LMHG ML11 .... **199** H4
Lanarkshire County Council
LRKH ML9 .... **176** A4
Lanarkshire Health Board
AIRDRIE ML6 .... **111** M1
Lanarkshire Health Board
CARLUKE ML8 .... **178** D2
Lanarkshire Health Board
HMLTN ML3 .... **155** M5
Lanarkshire Health Board
UD/BTH/TAN G71 .... **132** B6
Lanarkshire Health Board
WISHAW ML2 .... **160** A5
Lanark Tennis Club
LNK/LMHG ML11 .... **199** G4
Lanfauld School
DRUM G15 .... **60** F5
Langbank Primary School
PGL PA14 .... **56** B2
Langbrae School
KKNTL G66 .... **65** G4
Langcraigs Primary School
PSLYS PA2 .... **124** C2
Langlands Primary School
CUMB G67 .... **68** F1
Langlands School
GOV/IBX G51 .... **103** L2
Langloan Primary School
CTBR ML5 .... **109** L3
Langside College
CSMK G45 .... **128** F6
Langside College
GVH/MTFL G42 .... **128** A1
Langside Galleries
CVH/MTFL G42 .... **127** M1
Lansdowne Clinic
KVD/HLHD G12 .... **82** A4
Largs Golf Club
LARGS KA30 .... **115** L8
Largs Medical Practice
LARGS KA30 .... **115** J7
Larkfield Primary School
GRNKW/INVK PA16 .... **31** L5
Larkhall Leisure Centre &
Baths
LRKH ML9 .... **175** M7
Lawmuir Primary School
BLSH ML4 .... **133** G6
Law Primary School
CARLUKE ML8 .... **178** A4
Leisure Centre
PSTWK KA9 .... **221** H8
Leithland Road Primary School
PLK/PH/NH G53 .... **103** H8
Lennox Castle Hospital
KKNTL G66 .... **28** F8
Lennoxtown Primary School
KKNTL G66 .... **44** D1
Lenzie Hospital
KKNTL G66 .... **65** L6
Lenzie Moss Primary School
KKNTL G66 .... **65** H4
Lenzie Primary School
KKNTL G66 .... **65** J4
Levenvale Primary School
ALEX/LLW G83 .... **25** J4

Leverndale Hospital
PLK/PH/NH G53 .... **102** F7
Lightburn Hospital
CAR/SHTL G32 .... **107** H2
Lille Art Gallery
MLNGV G62 .... **42** B7
Lillie Art Gallery
BSDN G61 .... **61** L4
Lilybank School
PGL PA14 .... **33** M7
Linburn School
CARD/HILL/MSPK G52 .... **102** F3
Linnvale Primary School
CLYDBK G81 .... **60** D8
Linwood Health Centre
PSLYN/LNWD PA3 .... **100** C4
Linwood High School
PSLYN/LNWD PA3 .... **99** M3
Linwood Moss Sports Centre
PSLYN/LNWD PA3 .... **100** A2
Littlehill Primary School
STPS/GTHM/RID G33 .... **7** L3
Loanhead Primary School
KLMNK KA1 .... **17** G5
Lochend Secondary School
ESTRH G34 .... **86** C8
Lochfield Primary School
PSLYS PA2 .... **101** M8
Lochgoin Primary School
DRUM G15 .... **60** F5
Lochinch Playing Fields &
Sports Club
PLKSW/MSWD G43 .... **103** M8
Lochpark Stadium
CARLUKE ML8 .... **188** F1
Loch Primary School
RUTH G73 .... **129** K5
Lochshore Industrial Estate
GLGNK KA14 .... **167** J2
Lochwinnoch
Community Museum
LOCHW PA12 .... **120** C6
Lochwinnoch Golf Club
LOCHW PA12 .... **120** B7
Lochwinnoch Junior Secondary
School
LOCHW PA12 .... **120** C6
Lockhart Hospital
LNK/LMHG ML11 .... **199** J6
Logans Primary School
MTHW ML1 .... **157** H1
Lomond Healthcare NHS Trust
ALEX/LLW G83 .... **25** K3
Lomond School
HBR/GL G84 .... **20** D6
London Road Primary School
DMNK/BRGTN G40 .... **13** H7
Long Calderwood
Primary School
EKILN G74 .... **154** C4
Loudoun Golf Club
GLSTN KA4 .... **214** E2
Loudoun Montgomery
Primary School
IRV KA12 .... **203** J8
Loudoun Sports Centre
GLSTN KA4 .... **214** D2
Lourdes Primary School
CARD/HILL/MSPK G52 .... **103** J5
Low Waters Medical Centre
HMLTN ML3 .... **174** C1
M8 Trading Estate 81-83
PLKSD/SHW G41 .... **10** B6
Machanhill Primary School
LRKH ML9 .... **176** B6
The Macines Practice
AIRDRIE ML6 .... **111** K6
Madhok Medical Centre
CVH/MTFL G42 .... **128** A2
Manse Road Medical Centre
WISHAW ML2 .... **160** A4
Markets
SPRGB/BLRNK G21 .... **7** G7
Marr College
TROON KA10 .... **216** E5
Marr Rugby Football Club
TROON KA10 .... **217** G8
Maryhill Football Club
MRYH/FIRH G20 .... **82** D3
Maryhill Health Centre
MRYH/FIRH G20 .... **82** E3
The Mary Russell School
PSLYS PA2 .... **102** C7
Masonic Temple
BRHD/NEIL G78 .... **125** H7
Mavisbank School
AIRDRIE ML6 .... **110** F1
Maxwellton Primary School
EKILN G74 .... **15** L1
Mayfield Industrial Estate
KLMNK KA1 .... **213** G3
Mayfield Primary School
SVSTN KA20 .... **192** B7
Mcdougall House
BLSH ML4 .... **133** G1
Mcgill Primary School
PLK/PH/NH G53 .... **103** J7
Mcinnes Doctors Surgery
MTHW ML1 .... **134** E5
Mclean Museum & Art Gallery
GRNKW/INVK PA16 .... **2** B2
Mclellan Galleries
CGLW G2 .... **5** G8
Meadowburn Primary School
BSHPBGS G64 .... **64** A6
Meadowhead Industrial Estate
IRVSE KA11 .... **208** E5
Meadowside Industrial Estate
RNFRW PA4 .... **80** D3
Mearns Castle High School
NMRNS G77 .... **151** G4
Megabowl
CLYDBK G81 .... **60** C8
Melrose Primary School
CUMB G67 .... **68** E2
Merchiston Hospital
JNSTN PA5 .... **99** L4

Merkland School
KKNTL G66 .... **45** M8
Merksworth High School
PSLYN/LNWD PA3 .... **101** K2
Merrylee Primary School
PLKSW/MSWD G43 .... **127** M4
Middlefield School
PTCK G11 .... **82** B7
Middlemuir School
CLYDBK G81 .... **59** M6
Midlock Medical Centre
COV/IBX G51 .... **104** B4
Millersneuk Primary School
KKNTL G66 .... **65** L5
Milngavie & Bearsden
Sports Club
MLNGV G62 .... **62** D2
Milngavie Business Centre
MLNGV G62 .... **42** A8
Milngavie Golf Club
MLNGV G62 .... **41** L4
Miltonbank Primary School
PPK/MIL G22 .... **83** J1
Milton Clinic
PPK/MIL G22 .... **83** J2
Milton Primary School
DMBTN G82 .... **37** M8
Milton School
PPK/MIL G22 .... **83** L2
Mitchell Theatre & Library
KVGV G3 .... **4** D8
Modryvale Medical Centre
MTHW ML1 .... **157** M4
Monklands & Bellshill Hospitals
NHS Trust
BLSH ML4 .... **133** L1
Monklands District General
Hospital
CTBR ML5 .... **110** D2
Monklands Industrial Estate
CTBR ML5 .... **109** M7
Monkton Primary School
PSTWK KA9 .... **221** K5
Moore & Dalziel
Doctors Surgery
PTCK G11 .... **82** B7
Moorfoot Primary School
GRK PA19 .... **31** J3
Moorpark Industrial Estate
SVSTN KA20 .... **201** K2
Moorpark Primary School
RNFRW PA4 .... **80** B7
Morningside Primary School
WISHAW ML2 .... **160** B5
Mosque
GVH/MTFL G42 .... **105** C8
Mossblown Health Centre
RAYR/DAL KA6 .... **227** G3
Mossedge Industrial Estate
PSLYN/LNWD PA3 .... **100** C3
Mossend Primary School
BLSH ML4 .... **133** J5
Mossend Surgery
BLSH ML4 .... **133** J4
Mosshead Primary School
BSDN G61 .... **61** L2
Mossneuk Primary School
EKILS G75 .... **170** F2
Motherwell Business Centre
MTHW ML1 .... **157** M2
Motherwell College
MTHW ML1 .... **157** M5
Motherwell Cricket Club
MTHW ML1 .... **158** A6
Motherwell Football Club
MTHW ML1 .... **157** M5
Mount Cameron Primary School
EKILN G74 .... **15** M7
Mount Florida Medical Centre
GVH/MTFL G42 .... **128** A1
Mount Florida School
LNPK/KPK G44 .... **128** B2
Mount Manor Business Park
KVGV G3 .... **4** A9
Mount Vernon Primary School
CAR/SHTL G32 .... **107** K6
Mugdock Castle
MLNGV G62 .... **41** M2
Muiredge Primary School
UD/BTH/TAN G71 .... **132** A3
Muirhead Primary School
TROON KA10 .... **216** E5
Muirhouse Primary School
MTHW ML1 .... **158** C7
Muir Street Primary School
MTHW ML1 .... **157** K1
Munro Business Centre
KNTSWD G13 .... **81** L3
Murano Medical Centre
MRYH/FIRH G20 .... **82** F5
Murray Primary School
EKILS G75 .... **14** F6
The Murray Surgery
EKILS G75 .... **14** D8
Museum
LNK/LMHG ML11 .... **198** F5
Museum
RNFRW PA4 .... **80** D5
Museum of Royal
Highland Fusiliers
CGLW C2 .... **4** D8
Museum of the Cumbraes
GTCI KA28 .... **138** A6
Museum of Transport
KVGV G3 .... **82** C8
Napiers Dispensary & Clinic
PTCK G11 .... **82** C7
Natural Therapy Clinic
CGLW C2 .... **4** F8
Neilshand Primary School
HMLTN ML3 .... **156** A8
Neilston Primary School
BRHD/NEIL G78 .... **148** E2
Neilston Swimming Pool
BRHD/NEIL G78 .... **148** E2
Nerston Residential School
EKILN G74 .... **154** A2

Nethercommon
Industrial Estate
PSLYN/LNWD PA3 .... **101** L2
Nethercraigs Sports Centre
PLK/PH/NH G53 .... **103** K7
Netherlee Primary School
LNPK/KPK G44 .... **127** M7
Netherton Business Centre
KLMNK KA1 .... **16** E7
Netherton Primary School
WISHAW ML2 .... **158** E8
Netherton School
CSMK G45 .... **128** C7
New Albion Industrial Estate
KNTSWD G13 .... **80** E2
Newark Castle
PGL PA14 .... **34** D7
Newarthill Primary School
MTHW ML1 .... **134** E6
Newmains Primary School
RNFRW PA4 .... **80** C8
Newmains Primary School
WISHAW ML2 .... **159** M5
Newmilns Primary School
NMLNS KA16 .... **215** G2
New Monkland Primary School
AIRDRIE ML6 .... **88** E5
Newspaper Offices
CGLE G1 .... **11** L1
New Stage Theatre
PLKSD/SHW G41 .... **104** F7
Newton Mearns Primary School
NMRNS G77 .... **150** D5
Newton Primary School
AYR KA8 .... **19** G1
The Nicholas Geraghty Clinic
MTHW ML1 .... **157** M2
Nitshill Primary School
PLK/PH/NH G53 .... **126** A5
Noble Primary School
BLSH ML4 .... **133** G2
North Ayrshire Council
GTCI KA28 .... **138** A7
Northcote Surgery
KVD/HLHD G12 .... **82** C6
North Glasgow College
SPRGB/BLRNK G21 .... **6** B2
North Glasgow University
Hospital NHS Trust
SPRGB/BLRNK G21 .... **83** M2
North Lanarkshire Council
AIRDRIE ML6 .... **110** F2
North Lanarkshire Council
BAIL/MDB/MHD G69 .... **66** E7
North Lanarkshire Council
BLSH ML4 .... **132** F4
North Lanarkshire Council
BLSH ML4 .... **133** H4
North Lanarkshire Council
BLSH ML4 .... **133** G3
North Lanarkshire Council
CTBR ML5 .... **109** M4
North Lanarkshire Council
CTBR ML5 .... **110** B2
North Lanarkshire Council
CUMB G67 .... **48** F3
North Lanarkshire Council
CUMB G67 .... **49** H6
North Lanarkshire Council
CUMB G67 .... **49** K3
North Lanarkshire Council
CUMB G67 .... **68** F3
North Lanarkshire Council
CUMB G67 .... **69** G1
North Lanarkshire Council
KSYTH G65 .... **47** J1
North Lanarkshire Council
MTHW ML1 .... **157** L2
North Lanarkshire Council
MTHW ML1 .... **158** B5
North Lanarkshire Council
STPS/GTHM/RID G33 .... **85** L3
North Lanarkshire Council
UD/BTH/TAN G71 .... **132** D3
North Lanarkshire Council
UD/BTH/TAN G71 .... **132** C1
North Lanarkshire Council
WISHAW ML2 .... **158** D6
North Lanarkshire Council
WISHAW ML2 .... **176** C1
North Woodside Swimming Pool
COWCAD G4 .... **4** F5
Notre Dame High School
GRNKW/INVK PA16 .... **32** D6
Notre Dame High School
KVD/HLHD G12 .... **82** C6
Notre Dame Primary School
KVD/HLHD G12 .... **82** C6
Nuneaton Industrial Estate
DMNK/BRGTN G40 .... **12** G4
Oakbank Industrial Estate
MRYH/FIRH G20 .... **4** F3
Oakfield Primary School
GRNK PA15 .... **3** K8
Oakgrove Primary School
COWCAD G4 .... **4** F5
Odeon Cinema
AYRS KA7 .... **18** F5
Odeon Cinema
CGLW G2 .... **5** H9
Odeon Cinema
GOV/IBX G51 .... **10** C4
Old Monkland Primary School
CTBR ML5 .... **109** J5
Onthank Primary School
KLMNKN/STW KA3 .... **206** F4
Open Air Market Stall
CGLE G1 .... **11** K4
Optimax Laser Eye Clinic
CGLW G2 .... **4** E7
Orbiston Business Centre
BLSH ML4 .... **133** G6
Our Lady of Assumption Primary
School
MRYH/FIRH G20 .... **83** G3
Our Lady of Lourdes RC School
EKILS G75 .... **14** B1

Our Lady of Peace RC
Primary School
PSLYN/LNWD PA3 .... **100** A4
Our Lady of the
Annunciation Primary School
PLKSW/MSWD G43 .... **127** L4
Our Lady of the Missions Primary
School
GIF/THBK G46 .... **127** H6
Our Lady & St Francis
Primary School
MTHW ML1 .... **134** C7
Our Lady & St Patricks
High School
DMBTN G82 .... **36** C5
Our Ladys High School
CUMB G67 .... **48** D8
Our Ladys High School
MTHW ML1 .... **158** A5
Outdoor Recreation Centre
BSHPBGS G64 .... **84** A1
Overton Primary School
GRNKW/INVK PA16 .... **32** D6
Overtown Primary School
WISHAW ML2 .... **177** J2
Oxgang Primary School
KKNTL G66 .... **65** M1
Paisley Abbey
PSLY PA1 .... **9** J4
Paisley Golf Club
PSLYS PA2 .... **124** B4
Paisley Grammar School
PSLY PA1 .... **9** L3
Paisley Maternity Hospital
PSLYS PA2 .... **8** D8
Paisley Museum & Art Galleries
PSLY PA1 .... **8** F3
Paisley Picture Framers & Gallery
PSLY PA1 .... **9** H5
Palace Theatre
KLMNKN/STW KA3 .... **17** G4
Parkhead Hospital
DEN/PKHD G31 .... **13** L5
Parkhouse School
PPK/MIL G22 .... **83** K3
Parklands School
HBR/GL G84 .... **20** E7
Park Lodge School
HBR/GL G84 .... **20** E8
Park Mains School
ERSK PA8 .... **59** H8
Park School
KLMNKN/STW KA3 .... **17** J2
Parkview Business Centre
KVGV G3 .... **4** D7
Partick Market
PTCK G11 .... **82** C7
Partick Thistle Football Club
MRYH/FIRH G20 .... **4** E1
The Pavilion Theatre
CGLW G2 .... **5** H8
Penilee Secondary School
CARD/HILL/MSPK G52 ...... **102** F3
Pennyburn Primary School
KLWNG KA13 .... **193** J7
Pentagon Business Centre
KVGV G3 .... **10** E2
Peoples Palace Museum
DMNK/BRGTN G40 .... **12** A5
Peterburn Primary School
AIRDRIE ML6 .... **111** K4
Petershill Football Club
SPRGB/BLRNK G21 .... **6** D2
Petershill Recreation Centre
SPRGB/BLRNK G21 .... **7** H3
Phoenix Industrial Estate
PSLYN/LNWD PA3 .... **101** L1
Pierhead Clinic
GRK PA19 .... **31** L1
Pinewood Primary School
DRUM G15 .... **61** J5
Plains Primary School
AIRDRIE ML6 .... **90** A7
Pollokshields Primary School
PLKSD/SHW G41 .... **10** C9
Port Glasgow Baths
PGL PA14 .... **34** C8
Port Glasgow Golf Club
PGL PA14 .... **54** D2
Port Glasgow Health Centre
PGL PA14 .... **34** C7
Port Glasgow High School
PGL PA14 .... **55** G3
Port Glasgow Juniors
Football Club
PGL PA14 .... **35** G8
Port Glasgow Protestant
Athletic Club
PGL PA14 .... **34** A7
Portland Industrial Estate
SVSTN KA20 .... **201** K2
Portland Park Medical Centre
HMLTN ML3 .... **156** E7
Portland Surgery
TROON KA10 .... **216** B6
Possilpark Health Centre
PPK/MIL G22 .... **83** J5
Prestwick Acad
PSTWK KA9 .... **221** K8
Prestwick Golf Club
PSTWK KA9 .... **221** H8
Prestwick St Cuthbert
Golf Club
PSTWK KA9 .... **225** K3
Prestwick St Nicholas
Golf Club
PSTWK KA9 .... **225** H2
Primary School
RNFRW PA4 .... **80** D7
Primary School Wemyss Bay
WMYSB PA18 .... **50** A8
Pro Bowl
KKNTL G66 .... **45** J7
Pro Lane Bowl
EKILS G75 .... **15** J9
Provand's Lordship
COWCAD G4 .... **6** A9

Public Baths
HMLTN ML3 .... **156** D5
Public Baths
LNK/LMHG ML11 .... **199** G5
Quadrant Shopping Centre
CTBR ML5 .... **110** B2
Quarry Brae Primary School
DEN/PKHD G31 .... **13** M7
Queens Drive Retail Park
KLMNK KA1 .... **17** G7
Queen's Park FC
GVH/MTFL G42 .... **128** B2
Ralston Golf Club
PSLY PA1 .... **102** D5
Ralston Primary School
PSLY PA1 .... **102** E4
Ramgarhia Association
Sikh Temple
KVD/HLHD G12 .... **4** B4
Ramoy Business Centre
PSLY PA1 .... **8** D4
Ramshorn Theatre
CGLE G1 .... **11** L1
Rangers Football Club
GOV/IBX G51 .... **104** B3
Rangers Football Club Plc
GOV/IBX G51 .... **104** B3
Rank Leisure Odeon Cinema
KLMNK KA1 .... **17** G7
Rashielee Primary School
ERSK PA8 .... **59** H4
Ravenscraig Hospital
GRNKW/INVK PA16 .... **32** A4
Ravenscraig Primary School
GRNKW/INVK PA16 .... **31** L6
Ravenscraig Recreation Centre
GRNKW/INVK PA16 .... **31** L6
Ravenspark Golf Club
IRV KA12 .... **203** G3
Ravenspark Hospital
IRV KA12 .... **202** F3
Ravenswood Doctors Surgery
JNSTN PA5 .... **99** L1
Ravenswood Primary School
CUMB G67 .... **68** E1
Redburn Industrial Estate
IRV KA12 .... **203** H1
Redburn School
CUMB G67 .... **49** J7
Red Deer Day Hospital
EKILS G75 .... **14** A5
Regency Medical Clinic
KVGV G3 .... **4** C7
Reid Kerr College
PSLYN/LNWD PA3 .... **101** M3
Renfrew Council
PSLYS PA2 .... **124** E3
Renfrew Council
RNFRW PA4 .... **80** D5
Renfrew Council
RNFRW PA4 .... **80** B7
Renfrew District Welfare Clinic
PSLYS PA2 .... **100** F8
Renfrew Health Centre
RNFRW PA4 .... **80** C7
Renfrew High School
RNFRW PA4 .... **80** D7
Renfrewshire Council
JNSTN PA5 .... **99** L6
Renfrewshire Council
PSLY PA1 .... **9** K5
Renfrewshire Council
PSLY PA1 .... **9** G2
Renfrewshire Council
PSLY PA1 .... **9** J3
Renfrewshire Council
PSLYN/LNWD PA3 .... **8** E2
Renfrewshire Council
PSLYN/LNWD PA3 .... **8** B2
Renfrewshire Council
PSLYS PA2 .... **9** H8
Renfrewshire Healthcare
NHS Trust
PSLYS PA2 .... **125** H1
Renfrewshire & Inverclyde
Primary Care NHS Trust
PSLY PA1 .... **9** H3
Renton Primary School
DMBTN G82 .... **25** K8
Richmond Doctors Surgery
PTCK G11 .... **82** A7
Richmond Park School
GBLS G5 .... **105** K6
Ridge Park School
LNK/LMHG ML11 .... **198** F3
Riverbank Business Centre
KLMNK KA1 .... **17** H6
Riverview Medical Practice
JNSTN PA5 .... **99** M6
Riverway Retail Park
IRV KA12 .... **203** H8
Roadmeetings Hospital
CARLUKE ML8 .... **189** J1
Robert Smillie
Memorial Primary School
LRKH ML9 .... **175** M8
Robertsons Sports Centre
PSLYS PA2 .... **124** F2
Rob Roy Football Club
KKNTL G66 .... **65** G1
Robslee Primary School
GIF/THBK G46 .... **127** H7
Rocholloch Primary School
AIRDRIE ML6 .... **110** E3
Rosebank School
AYRS KA7 .... **19** G8
Rosehall High School
CTBR ML5 .... **109** M6
Rosevale School
PPK/MIL G22 .... **83** K2
Ross Clinic
KVD/HLHD G12 .... **82** B6
Ross Hall Hospital
CARD/HILL/MSPK G52 ...... **103** G6
Routenburn Golf Club
LARGS KA30 .... **115** J3
Rowallan Business Park
KLMNKN/STW KA3 .... **207** J2

Royal Alexandra Hospital
NHS Trust
PSLYS PA2 .... **8** D8
Royal College of Nursing
KVGV G3 .... **4** C7
Royal Concert Hall
CGLE G1 .... **5** J8
Royal Gourock Yacht Club
GRK PA19 .... **31** J2
Royal Hospital for Sick Children
DRUM G15 .... **61** G7
Royal Infirmary
COWCAD G4 .... **5** L9
Royal Infirmary
COWCAD G4 .... **6** B8
Royal Maternity Hospital
CGLE G1 .... **11** L1
Royal Troon Golf Club
TROON KA10 .... **220** D1
Royston Primary School
SPRGB/BLRNK G21 .... **6** C7
RSAMD
CGLW G2 .... **5** H8
Rutherglen Health Centre
RUTH G73 .... **129** H2
Rutherglen High School
RUTH G73 .... **129** H1
Rutherglen Swimming Pool
RUTH G73 .... **129** G2
Sacred Heart Primary School
BLSH ML4 .... **133** G6
Sacred Heart Primary School
CUMB G67 .... **49** H7
Sacred Heart Primary School
DMNK/BRGTN G40 .... **12** D8
Sacred Heart Primary School
GRNKW/INVK PA16 .... **31** L5
SAE Technology College
PLKSD/SHW G41 .... **10** B5
Sailing Club
PSTWK KA9 .... **225** H2
St Agathas Primary School
KKNTL G66 .... **66** B1
St Agnes Primary School
SMSTN G23 .... **82** E1
St Aidans High School
WISHAW ML2 .... **159** H5
St Aidans RC Primary School
WISHAW ML2 .... **159** J4
St Aidans School
CAR/SHTL G32 .... **13** M3
St Alberts Primary School
PLKSD/SHW G41 .... **10** A7
St Alloyisious Primary School
SPRGB/BLRNK G21 .... **83** L4
St Aloysius College
KVGV G3 .... **4** F7
St Aloysius College Junior School
KVGV G3 .... **4** F7
St Aloysius Preparatory School
KVGV G3 .... **4** F7
St Aloysius RC School
AIRDRIE ML6 .... **111** L7
St Ambrose RC School
CTBR ML5 .... **109** L1
St Andrews Cathedral
CGLE G1 .... **11** H3
St Andrews Business Centre
KLMNK KA1 .... **16** F7
St Andrews Clinics for Children
KVD/HLHD G12 .... **82** D6
St Andrews High School
CLYDBK G81 .... **80** C1
St Andrews High School
EKILS G75 .... **14** D9
St Andrews RC Primary School
AIRDRIE ML6 .... **88** E8
St Andrews RC School
BSDN G61 .... **61** J3
St Andrews Secondary RC
School
CAR/SHTL G32 .... **107** G2
St Angelas Primary School
GIF/THBK G46 .... **126** D6
St Angustines RC Primary
School
CTBR ML5 .... **109** M5
St Annes Primary School
DMNK/BRGTN G40 .... **12** A7
St Annes Primary School
ERSK PA8 .... **79** F1
St Annes Primary School
HMLTN ML3 .... **174** D1
St Anns Primary School
RAYR/DAL KA6 .... **227** G3
St Anthonys Football Club
GOV/IBX G51 .... **104** C4
St Anthonys RC Primary School
JNSTN PA5 .... **122** C2
St Anthonys RC School
RUTH G73 .... **129** K5
St Anthonys School
GOV/IBX G51 .... **103** M1
St Athanasuis Primary School
CARLUKE ML8 .... **178** F8
St Augustines Primary School
PPK/MIL G22 .... **83** J2
St Barbaras RC
Secondary School
BAIL/MDB/MHD G69 .... **86** B3
St Bartholomews RC
Primary School
CTBR ML5 .... **87** K8
St Batholmews
Primary School
CSMK G45 .... **128** F5
St Benedicts RC School
ESTRH G34 .... **86** A4
St Bernadette Primary School
MTHW ML1 .... **157** H1
St Bernards RC Primary School
CTBR ML5 .... **110** B6
St Blanes Primary School
BLTYR/CAMB G72 .... **155** J1
St Blanes Primary School
SMSTN G23 .... **62** G3
St Brendans High School
PSLYN/LNWD PA3 .... **100** C3

St Brendans Primary School
MTHW ML1 .... 158 B7
St Brides Primary School
BLTYR/CAMB G72 .... 130 A4
St Brides Primary School
GVH/MTFL G42 .... 105 G7
St Brides RC Primary School
UD/BTH/TAN G71 .... 132 A5
St Brides RC School
EKILN G74 .... 15 J4
St Bridgets Primary School
BAIL/MDB/MHD G69 .... 108 B4
St Bridgets Primary School
KBRN KA25 .... 166 F1
St Bridgets School
GVH/MTFL G42 .... 128 E1
St Brigids Primary School
WISHAW ML2 .... 159 M4
St Cadocs Primary School
NMRNS G77 .... 150 C4
St Cadocs School
BLTYR/CAMB G72 .... 130 C5
St Catherines Primary School
PSLYN/LNWD PA3 .... 101 M3
St Catherines School
SPRGB/BLRNK G21 .... 84 C4
St Charles RC Primary School
PSLYS PA2 .... 9 J9
St Charles RC School
BLTYR/CAMB G72 .... 130 F3
St Clares Primary School
ESTRH G34 .... 108 D1
St Columbas High School
CLYDBK G81 .... 60 C5
St Columbas Primary School
KLMCLM PA13 .... 75 J1
St Columbas Primary School
UD/BTH/TAN G71 .... 132 C2
St Columbas RC High School
GRK PA19 .... 32 A3
St Columbas RC Primary School
KLMNK KA1 .... 17 G5
St Columbas School
KLMCLM PA13 .... 75 K1
St Columbkilles RC School
RUTH G73 .... 129 H2
St Convals Primary School
PLKSW/MSWD G43 .... 127 K1
St Cuthberts Primary School
PPK/MIL G22 .... 83 G5
St Cuthberts RC School
JNSTN PA5 .... 122 C2
St Davids RC Primary School
JNSTN PA5 .... 99 K8
St Davids RC School
AIRDRIE ML6 .... 89 M7
St Denis's Primary School
DEN/PKHD G31 .... 13 G3
St Dominics Primary School
CSMK G45 .... 128 F7
St Dominnics RC Primary School
AIRDRIE ML6 .... 111 J3
St Edwards Primary School
AIRDRIE ML6 .... 111 J2
St Elizabeth RC Primary School
HMLTN ML3 .... 174 D2
St Enoch Business Centre
CGLE G1 .... 11 H3
St Enoch Shopping Centre
CGLE G1 .... 11 J3
St Fergus RC Primary School
PSLYN/LNWD PA3 .... 8 B2
St Fillans RC Primary School
CRG/CRSL/HOU PA6 .... 77 G7
St Flannans RC Primary School
KKNTL G66 .... 45 M8
St Francis of Assisi
Primary School
BAIL/MDB/MHD G69 .... 107 M6
St Francis Primary School
GBLS G5 .... 11 L8
St Francis Primary School
PGL PA14 .... 54 F2
St Francis RC Primary School
BALLOCH G68 .... 68 A2
St Gabriels Primary School
UD/BTH/TAN G71 .... 132 D1
St Gabriels RC Primary School
GRNKW/INVK PA16 .... 31 K6
St Georges Medical Centre
KVGV G3 .... 4 E6
St Georges School
CARD/HILL/MSPK G52 .... 103 G4
St Gerards Primary School
BLSH ML4 .... 133 H2
St Gerards Secondary School
GOV/IBX G51 .... 104 B2
St Gilberts Primary School
SPRGB/BLRNK G21 .... 7 J3
St Helens Primary School
BSHPBGS G64 .... 64 C7
St Helens School
CUMB G67 .... 68 B2
St Hilarys RC Primary School
EKILN G74 .... 15 M5
St Ignatius Primary School
WISHAW ML2 .... 159 H6
St James Primary School
DMNK/BRGTN G40 .... 12 A5
St James Primary School
RNFRW PA4 .... 80 C6
St James RC School
CTBR ML5 .... 109 L5
St James Street Health Centre
PSLY PA1 .... 8 F2
St Joachins RC Primary School
CAR/SHTL G32 .... 107 J8
St Joan of Arc School
PPK/MIL G22 .... 83 H2
St John Bosco Primary School
ERSK PA8 .... 58 F7
St John Ogilvie Primary School
IRVSE KA11 .... 204 B6
St John Ogilvie School
PSLY PA1 .... 102 B5
St Johns Approved
School Springboig
CAR/SHTL G32 .... 107 K2

St Johns Primary School
AYR KA8 .... 19 H1
St Johns Primary School
BRHD/NEIL G78 .... 125 J5
St Johns Primary School
HMLTN ML3 .... 156 D6
St Johns Primary School
SVSTN KA20 .... 192 F8
St Johns RC Primary School
GBLS G5 .... 11 H5
St Johns RC Primary School
PGL PA14 .... 34 A7
St John the Baptist
Primary School
UD/BTH/TAN G71 .... 132 A3
St Josephs Primary School
BLTYR/CAMB G72 .... 155 K1
St Josephs Primary School
CRMNK/CLK/EAG G76 .... 151 L4
St Josephs Primary School
STPS/GTHM/RID G33 .... 85 L4
St Josephs RC Primary School
COWCAD G4 .... 4 F5
St Josephs RC Primary School
GRNKW/INVK PA16 .... 32 A5
St Josephs RC School
CLYDBK G81 .... 60 D2
St Josephs School
CUMB G67 .... 68 F1
St Josephs School
CTBR ML5 .... 87 J2
St Josephs School
HBR/GL G84 .... 20 F7
St Josephs School
MLNGV G62 .... 41 M8
St Judes Primary School
STPS/GTHM/RID G33 .... 107 L3
St Julies Primary School
CSMK G45 .... 128 D5
St Kenneth RC Primary School
EKILN G74 .... 14 E1
St Kenneths RC Primary School
GRNK PA15 .... 33 J7
St Kessogs RC School
ALEX/LLW G83 .... 25 M1
St Kevins Primary School
BAIL/MDB/MHD G69 .... 109 G4
St Lawrence Primary School
GRNK PA15 .... 3 G7
St Leonards Primary School
EKILN G74 .... 154 D6
St Louises Primary School
EKILS G75 .... 14 D8
St Lucys Primary School
CUMB G67 .... 49 M5
St Lukes High School
BRHD/NEIL G78 .... 149 J1
St Lukes Primary School
KLWNG KA13 .... 193 H7
St Machans RC Primary School
KKNTL G66 .... 29 K8
St Margaret Marys
Primary School
CSMK G45 .... 128 C7
St Margaret Marys
Secondary School
CSMK G45 .... 128 D6
St Margarets High School
AIRDRIE ML6 .... 111 H1
St Margarets Primary School
JNSTN PA5 .... 99 L7
St Marks Primary School
CAR/SHTL G32 .... 106 E4
St Marks Primary School
IRV KA12 .... 203 L5
St Marks RC Primary School
BRHD/NEIL G78 .... 125 J8
St Marks RC Primary School
RUTH G73 .... 129 H4
St Marnocks Primary School
PLK/PH/NH G53 .... 103 J8
St Marthas School
SPRGB/BLRNK G21 .... 84 B4
St Martins Primary School
CSMK G45 .... 128 F7
St Martins RC Primary School
ALEX/LLW G83 .... 25 L6
St Marys Cathedral
COWCAD G4 .... 4 C4
St Marys Hospital
LNK/LMHG ML11 .... 199 K4
St Marys Primary School
ALEX/LLW G83 .... 25 L5
St Marys Primary School
KKNTL G66 .... 65 G1
St Marys Primary School
LARGS KA30 .... 115 K5
St Marys Primary School
LRKH ML9 .... 175 M7
St Marys Primary School
MRYH/FIRH G20 .... 82 C2
St Marys Primary School
MTHW ML1 .... 135 H8
St Marys Primary School
PSLY PA1 .... 8 C6
St Marys RC Primary School
AIRDRIE ML6 .... 90 F4
St Marys RC Primary School
CUMB G67 .... 48 E8
St Marys RC Primary School
HMLTN ML3 .... 156 D5
St Marys RC School
CLYDBK G81 .... 59 M3
St Marys RC School
LNK/LMHG ML11 .... 199 J5
St Marys RC Secondary School
GRNKW/INVK PA16 .... 2 B2
St Marys School
CTBR ML5 .... 110 A4
St Matthews Primary School
BSHPBGS G64 .... 64 B7
St Matthews Primary School
KLMNKN/STW KA3 .... 17 M3
St Matthews RC Primary School
WISHAW ML2 .... 158 E5
St Maurices Secondary School
BALLOCH G68 .... 68 A1

St Michaels Primary School
BAIL/MDB/MHD G69 .... 67 G7
St Michaels Primary School
DEN/PKHD G31 .... 13 K6
St Michael's Primary School
DMBTN G82 .... 36 D5
St Mirins High School
PSLY PA1 .... 8 A5
St Mirins Primary School
LNPK/KPK G44 .... 128 C4
St Modans School
STPS/GTHM/RID G33 .... 107 G1
St Monicas RC School
CTBR ML5 .... 109 J5
St Monicas School
PLK/PH/NH G53 .... 103 H8
The St Mungo Museum of
Religious Life & Art
COWCAD G4 .... 6 A9
St Mungo's Primary School
COWCAD G4 .... 5 M8
St Mungos Primary School
GRNK PA15 .... 3 L8
St Ninians High School
GIF/THBK G46 .... 126 F7
St Ninians High School
KKNTL G66 .... 65 H1
St Ninians Primary School
KNTSWD G13 .... 61 J8
St Ninians Primary School
PSTWK KA9 .... 225 K1
St Ninians RC Primary School
GRK PA19 .... 31 K3
St Ninians RC Primary School
HMLTN ML3 .... 155 L5
St Oswalds School
LNPK/KPK G44 .... 127 M4
St Patricks High School
CTBR ML5 .... 110 B2
St Patricks Primary School
DMBTN G82 .... 37 G5
St Patricks Primary School
GRNK PA15 .... 2 A6
St Patricks Primary School
MTHW ML1 .... 133 M6
St Patricks Primary School
SHOTTS ML7 .... 137 M5
St Patricks Primary School
TROON KA10 .... 216 C7
St Patricks RC Primary School
CTBR ML5 .... 110 B2
St Patricks RC School
KSYTH G65 .... 47 K2
St Patricks School RC
Primary School
KVGV G3 .... 10 D1
St Pauls Primary School
CAR/SHTL G32 .... 107 G6
St Pauls Primary School
SCOT G14 .... 81 J6
St Pauls RC Primary School
HMLTN ML3 .... 156 B3
St Peters RC Primary School
DMBTN G82 .... 37 H3
St Peters RC Primary School
PSLYS PA2 .... 124 D1
St Peters School
PTCK G11 .... 82 C7
St Philips School
AIRDRIE ML6 .... 89 M8
St Philomenas Primary School
STPS/GTHM/RID G33 .... 7 M2
St Pius Primary School
DRUM G15 .... 61 G5
St Raymonds School
LNPK/KPK G44 .... 128 B7
St Rochs Secondary School
SPRGB/BLRNK G21 .... 6 B7
St Rose of Lima Primary School
STPS/GTHM/RID G33 .... 85 J7
St Saviours School
GOV/IBX G51 .... 104 B2
St Serfs RC Primary School
AIRDRIE ML6 .... 89 H7
St Sophias Primary School
GLSTN KA4 .... 214 A3
St Stephens High School
PGL PA14 .... 54 F2
St Stephens Primary School
COWCAD G4 .... 6 A5
St Stephens RC Primary School
CTBR ML5 .... 110 E4
St Stephens School
CLYDBK G81 .... 59 M6
St Teresas Primary School
PPK/MIL G22 .... 5 K2
St Theresa RC Primary School
MTHW ML1 .... 134 D6
St Thomas Aquinas RC
Secondary School
SCOT G14 .... 81 K5
St Thomas RC Primary School
BRHD/NEIL G78 .... 148 D2
St Thomas RC Primary School
WISHAW ML2 .... 159 G7
St Timothys Primary School
CAR/SHTL G32 .... 107 G3
St Timothys RC School
CTBR ML5 .... 109 M5
St Vincents Primary School
EKILS G75 .... 171 H4
St Winnings Primary School
KLWNG KA13 .... 193 K6
Saltcoats Health Centre
SALT KA21 .... 200 F2
Sandaig Primary School
STPS/GTHM/RID G33 .... 107 M3
Sanderson High School
EKILS G75 .... 172 C1
Sandwood School
CARD/HILL/MSPK G52 .... 103 G4
Saracen Health Centre
PPK/MIL G22 .... 83 H5
Saracen Primary School
PPK/MIL G22 .... 5 G1
Sauchiehall Shopping Centre
CGLW G2 .... 5 H8

School & Leisure Wear
TROON KA10 .... 216 C6
School of Art
KVGV G3 .... 4 F7
Scotland Street School Museum
GBLS G5 .... 10 D6
Scottish Exhibition and
Conference Centre
KVGV G3 .... 104 D2
Scottish Maritime Museum
DMBTN G82 .... 37 G6
Scottish Maritime Museum
IRV KA12 .... 203 G8
Scottish Youth Theatre
CGLE G1 .... 11 H1
Scott Practice
ALEX/LLW G83 .... 25 L4
Scotus College
BSDN G61 .... 61 J5
Seafiled School
ARD KA22 .... 191 M5
Shaftesbury Medical Practice
SCOT G14 .... 81 K6
Sharmanka Gallery & Workshop
CGLE G1 .... 11 K3
Shawbridge Industrial Estate
PLKSW/MSWD G43 .... 127 H2
Shawhead Primary School
CTBR ML5 .... 110 B6
Shawlands Primary School
PLKSD/SHW G41 .... 104 D8
Shawlands Surgery
PLKSD/SHW G41 .... 127 K1
Sheriff Court
GBLS G5 .... 11 J4
Shettleston Day Hospital
CAR/SHTL G32 .... 106 F5
Shettleston Health Centre
CAR/SHTL G32 .... 107 G4
Shortlees Primary School
KLMNK KA1 .... 211 M6
Shotts Bon Accord
Football & Social Club
SHOTTS ML7 .... 137 K3
Showcase Cinema
BAIL/MDB/MHD G69 .... 109 H5
Showcase Cinemas
PSLYN/LNWD PA3 .... 100 E4
Sighthill Primary School
SPRGB/BLRNK G21 .... 5 M3
Sikeside Primary School
CTBR ML5 .... 110 D4
Simshill Primary School
LNPK/KPK G44 .... 128 B5
Sir John Maxwell School
PLKSW/MSWD G43 .... 127 J2
Skelmorlie Castle
SKLM PA17 .... 92 A1
Skelmorlie Golf Club
SKLM PA17 .... 70 C6
Skelmorlie Primary School
SKLM PA17 .... 70 B4
Slamuir Primary School
PGL PA14 .... 55 G3
Smithycroft Secondary School
STPS/GTHM/RID G33 .... 84 E8
Somerset Eye Clinic
KVGV G3 .... 4 B7
Southbank Surgery
KKNTL G66 .... 65 J1
South Beach Practice
ARD KA22 .... 191 K8
Southern General Hospital
NHS Trust
GOV/IBX G51 .... 103 K1
South Lanarkshire Council
BLTYR/CAMB G72 .... 130 E5
South Lanarkshire Council
BLTYR/CAMB G72 .... 130 A3
South Lanarkshire Council
BLTYR/CAMB G72 .... 155 L4
South Lanarkshire Council
BLTYR/CAMB G72 .... 155 K2
South Lanarkshire Council
CARLUKE ML8 .... 178 E7
South Lanarkshire Council
EKILN G74 .... 14 F4
South Lanarkshire Council
EKILN G74 .... 14 F2
South Lanarkshire Council
EKILN G74 .... 15 G1
South Lanarkshire Council
EKILN G74 .... 15 H3
South Lanarkshire Council
EKILS G75 .... 152 F8
South Lanarkshire Council
EKILS G75 .... 153 G6
South Lanarkshire Council
EKILS G75 .... 15 K9
South Lanarkshire Council
EKILS G75 .... 171 L4
South Lanarkshire Council
HMLTN ML3 .... 155 M6
South Lanarkshire Council
HMLTN ML3 .... 156 B5
South Lanarkshire Council
HMLTN ML3 .... 156 C2
South Lanarkshire Council
HMLTN ML3 .... 156 C5
South Lanarkshire Council
HMLTN ML3 .... 156 E6
South Lanarkshire Council
LRKH ML9 .... 176 A6
South Lanarkshire Council
LRKH ML9 .... 176 A3
South Lanarkshire Council
RUTH G73 .... 129 H1
Southpark Primary School
EKILS G75 .... 14 A9
South Park School
AYRS KA7 .... 19 G9
South Primary School
PSLYS PA2 .... 9 H9
Spectrum Business Centre
RUTH G73 .... 129 H1
Spiersbridge Business Park
GIF/THBK G46 .... 126 E6

Spittal School
RUTH G73 .... 128 F4
Sports Centre
BSDN G61 .... 62 B2
Springburn Museum
SPRGB/BLRNK G21 .... 6 C1
Springburn Sports Centre
SPRGB/BLRNK G21 .... 83 M5
Springfield Primary School
DMNK/BRGTN G40 .... 106 B7
Springfield Primary School
GRK PA19 .... 31 J5
Springhill Primary School
BRHD/NEIL G78 .... 125 H8
Springside Primary School
IRVSE KA11 .... 204 F7
Stakis Glasgow Airport
RNFRW PA4 .... 80 A5
Stanecastle School
IRVSE KA11 .... 204 A4
Stanley Primary School
ARD KA22 .... 191 J6
Strathclyde Regional Council
SPRGB/BLRNK G21 .... 7 H1
Stepps Primary School
STPS/GTHM/RID G33 .... 85 L3
Steunans Primary School
CLYDBK G81 .... 60 C7
Stirling's Library
CGLE G1 .... 11 J2
Stobcross Street
Industrial Estate
CTBR ML5 .... 110 A3
Stobhill General Hospital
SPRGB/BLRNK G21 .... 84 A3
Stock Exchange
CGLE G1 .... 11 H1
Stonedyke Primary School
DRUM G15 .... 61 H7
Stonelaw High School
RUTH G73 .... 129 H2
Stow College
KVGV G3 .... 4 F6
Strathblane Primary School
CMPF/LLE G63 .... 27 H6
Strathclyde Art Centre
KVGV G3 .... 10 E2
Strathclyde Business Centre
GOV/IBX G51 .... 104 D3
Strathclyde Business Centre
GRNK PA15 .... 33 L6
Strathclyde Business Centre
MTHW ML1 .... 133 M5
Strathclyde Business Centre
PLKSD/SHW G41 .... 10 A5
Strathclyde Hospital
MTHW ML1 .... 157 J4
Strathclyde Regional Council
HMLTN ML3 .... 156 C5
Strathclyde Regional Council
LRKH ML9 .... 176 A5
Strathclyde Regional Council
PSLY PA1 .... 9 M4
Strathmore Surgery
EKILN G74 .... 14 F4
Street Level Gallery
CGLE G1 .... 11 K3
Struthers Primary School
TROON KA10 .... 216 F4
Summerhill School
DRUM G15 .... 61 H5
Sunnyside School
STPS/GTHM/RID G33 .... 85 J6
Swinton Primary School
BAIL/MDB/MHD G69 .... 108 D3
Symington Health Centre
KLMNK KA1 .... 218 C5
Symington Primary School
KLMNK KA1 .... 218 D5
Synagogue
GVH/MTFL G42 .... 104 F7
Tam O'shanter Experience
AYRS KA7 .... 228 F8
Tams Brig Surgery
AYR KA8 .... 224 F7
Tannochside Primary School
UD/BTH/TAN G71 .... 132 B2
Taylor High School
MTHW ML1 .... 134 A6
Templehill Surgery
TROON KA10 .... 216 B6
Temple School
KNTSWD G13 .... 81 M2
Templeton Business Centre
DMNK/BRGTN G40 .... 12 A6
Thames Open College
CGLW G2 .... 11 G1
Thomas Muir High School
BSHPBGS G64 .... 64 C7
Thorniewood Football Club
UD/BTH/TAN G71 .... 132 B2
Thornliebank Health Centre
GIF/THBK G46 .... 126 F5
Thornliebank Industrial Estate
GIF/THBK G46 .... 126 E7
Thornlie Primary School
WISHAW ML2 .... 159 G7
Thorntree Primary School
CAR/SHTL G32 .... 107 G3
Thornwood School
PTCK G11 .... 81 M7
Tinto Primary School
PLKSW/MSWD G43 .... 127 J3
Todholm Infants School
PSLYS PA2 .... 102 B7
Tollbrae Primary School
AIRDRIE ML6 .... 111 H2
Tollcross Industrial Estate
CAR/SHTL G32 .... 107 G6
The Toonspeak Young Peoples
Theatre
SPRGB/BLRNK G21 .... 6 D5
Tormusk Primary School
CSMK G45 .... 129 G6
Torrance Primary School
BSHPBGS G64 .... 44 B8
Toryglen School
RUTH G73 .... 128 E1

Toss Theatre
  BLSH ML4 .... 133 J4
Tourhill Industrial Estate
  KLMNKN/STW KA3.................. 206 B3
Towerlands Primary School
  IRVSE KA11 .... 204 C7
Town Hall Business Centre
  MTHW ML1 .... 157 K3
Townhead Clinic
  CTBR ML5 .... 109 L1
Townhead Clinic
  KKNTL G66 .... 65 K2
Townhead Health Centre
  COWCAD G4 .... 6 B8
Townhead Primary School
  CTBR ML5 .... 87 K7
Townhead Surgery
  IRV KA12 .... 203 J7
Townhill Primary School
  HMLTN ML3 .... 155 L7
Transmission Gallery
  CGLE G1 .... 11 K3
Trees Riding School
  RAYR/DAL KA6 .... 230 D7
Treeswoodhead Clinic
  KLMNK KA1............................ 212 A5
Triangle Shopping Mall
  KLWNG KA13 .... 193 L6
Trinity High School
  BLTYR/CAMB G72 .... 129 L2
Trinity High School
  RNFRW PA4 .... 80 D5
Tron Theatre
  CGLE G1 .... 11 L3
Turnbull High School
  BSHPBGS G64.......................... 63 L7
The Turret Surgery
  KKNTL G66 .... 65 J1
Turret Theatre
  KKNTL G66 .... 45 J8
Twechar Primary School
  KSYTH G65 .... 46 F6
UCI Cinema
  CLYDBK G81 .... 60 B7
UCI Cinema
  EKILN G74 .... 15 G4
Uddingston Cricket &
  Sports Club
  UD/BTH/TAN G71 .... 131 L4
Uddingston Grammar School
  UD/BTH/TAN G71 .... 131 L3
Udston Primary School
  HMLTN ML3 .... 155 L5

Underground Gallery
  KVD/HLHD G12 .... 82 D6
University of Glasgow
  BSDN G61 .... 61 K2
University of Glasgow
  BSDN G61 .... 82 A1
University of Glasgow
  KVD/HLHD G12 .... 82 C4
University of Glasgow
  KVD/HLHD G12 .... 82 D7
University of Glasgow
  KVGV G3 .... 4 B6
University of Glasgow
  PTCK G11 .... 82 C8
University of Paisley
  PSLY PA1................................ 8 F4
University of Paisley
  PSLYS PA2.............................. 8 F6
University of Strathclyde
  CGLE G1 .... 5 K9
University of Strathclyde
  CGLE G1 .... 11 M1
University of Strathclyde
  COWCAD G4 .... 5 L9
University of Strathclyde
  KNTSWD G13 .... 81 K4
University of Strathclyde
  STPS/GTHM/RID G33 .... 85 H5
Victoria Buildings
  Business Centre
  PSLY PA1................................ 9 M4
Victoria Industrial Estate
  PSLY PA1................................ 9 M4
Victoria Infirmary
  HBR/GL G84 .... 20 F8
Victoria Infirmary
  PLKSD/SHW G41 .... 127 M1
Victoria Memorial Cottage
  Hospital
  KSYTH G65 .... 47 H1
Victoria Park School
  CARLUKE ML8.......................... 178 F7
Victory Baths
  RNFRW PA4 .... 80 D5
Viewfield Business Centre
  EKILN G74 .... 225 G7
Village Theatre
  EKILN G74 .... 15 H2
Virgin Cinema
  DEN/PKHD G31 .... 13 K5
Walker Clinic
  KVGV G3 .... 4 C8

Wallace Primary School
  JNSTN PA5 .... 100 D7
The Waverley Gallery
  PSTWK KA9............................ 225 J1
Waverley Park Day Hospital
  KKNTL G66 .... 45 K8
Welbeck Golf Club
  TROON KA10........................... 216 D7
Welfare Clinic
  CUMB G67 .... 49 H6
Welhouse Primary School
  STPS/GTHM/RID G33 .... 107 L2
Wellgreen Health Centre
  PLKSW/MSWD G43 .... 127 J1
Wellhall Medical Centre
  HMLTN ML3 .... 156 A6
Wellpark Clinic
  GRNK PA15 .... 2 D5
Wellshot Primary School
  CAR/SHTL G32 .... 106 F5
West Coats Primary School
  BLTYR/CAMB G72 .... 129 M4
West Dunbartonshire Council
  ALEX/LLW G83 .... 25 K4
West Dunbartonshire Council
  CLYDBK G81 .... 59 M7
West Dunbartonshire Council
  CLYDBK G81 .... 60 C8
West Dunbartonshire Council
  DMBTN G82 .... 36 F6
West Dunbartonshire Council
  OLDK G60 .... 59 G2
Wester Cleddens
  Primary School
  BSHPBGS G64.......................... 64 A7
Western Gailes Golf Club
  IRVSE KA11 .... 208 C6
Western Infirmary, A&E
  PTCK G11 .... 82 C7
Westerton Primary School
  BSDN G61 .... 61 L7
Westfield Health Clinic
  CARD/HILL/MSPK G52............. 103 G4
Westfield Primary School
  BALLOCH G68 .... 67 M2
Westfield Surgery
  JNSTN PA5 .... 99 L6
West Kilbride Golf Club
  WKIL KA23 .... 181 H5
West Kilbride Primary School
  WKIL KA23 .... 181 J4

Westmuir Medical Centre
  DEN/PKHD G31 .... 13 M6
West of Scotland Cricket Club
  PTCK G11 .... 82 B7
West Park School
  CRH/DND KA2 .... 205 M8
West Primary School
  PSLY PA1................................ 8 C5
Westwood Business Centre
  ESTRH G34 .... 108 B1
Whinhill Golf Club
  GRNK PA15 .... 2 C9
Whitecraigs Rugby Club
  NMRNS G77 .... 150 A4
Whitecrook Business Centre
  CLYDBK G81 .... 60 C8
Whitecrook Primary School
  CLYDBK G81 .... 60 C8
Whitehill School
  DEN/PKHD G31 .... 13 C1
Whitehill Swimming Pool
  DEN/PKHD G31 .... 12 F1
Whitehirst Park Primary School
  KLWNG KA13........................... 193 J6
Whiteinch Business Park
  SCOT G14 .... 81 K7
Whiteinch Indoor
  Bowling Stadium
  SCOT G14 .... 81 L7
Whiteinch Medical Practice
  SCOT G14 .... 81 K6
Whiteinch Primary School
  SCOT G14 .... 81 L6
Whitlawburn Shopping Centre
  BLTYR/CAMB G72 .... 129 L6
Whitletts Clinic
  AYR KA8 .... 225 K6
Whitletts Primary School
  AYR KA8 .... 225 L6
Williamsburgh Primary School
  PSLY PA1................................ 9 M4
William Street Clinic
  KVGV G3 .... 4 D9
William Temple Chemist
  GOV/IBX G51 .... 104 D4
Williamwood High School
  CRMNK/CLK/EAG G76 .... 151 K1
Williamwood Medical Centre
  CRMNK/CLK/EAG G76 .... 151 K1
Willowbank Primary School
  KVGV G3 .... 4 C5

Willowbank School
  CTBR ML5 .... 109 L3
Windlaw Primary School
  CSMK G45 .... 128 E8
Windyhill Golf Clubhouse
  BSDN G61 .... 61 G1
Winton Primary School
  ARD KA22 .... 191 J7
Wishaw Business Centre
  WISHAW ML2 .... 159 H6
Wishaw Health Centre
  WISHAW ML2 .... 159 H6
Wishaw Sports Centre
  WISHAW ML2 .... 158 F7
Witchhill School
  KLMNKN/STW KA3.................. 16 E1
Woodfarm Secondary School
  GIF/THBK G46 .... 127 G6
Woodhill Primary School
  BSHPBGS G64.......................... 64 C8
Woodilee Industrial Estate
  KKNTL G66 .... 65 L3
Woodlands Primary School
  IRV KA12 .... 203 K6
Woodside Place
  Business Centre
  KVGV G3 .... 4 D7
Woodside Primary School
  HMLTN ML3 .... 156 E7
Woodside Secondary School
  KVGV G3 .... 4 B8
Woodstock Primary School
  KLMNK KA1............................ 16 C4
Woodville Park
  Industrial Estate
  GOV/IBX G51 .... 104 B3
The Wool Gallery
  MLNGV G62 .... 42 A7
Wyndford Recreation Centre
  KVD/HLHD G12 .... 82 D4
Wynd Gallery
  LNK/LMHG ML11 .... 199 G5
XS Superbowl
  PSLYN/LNWD PA3 .... 9 K1
Yoker Primary School
  SCOT G14 .... 80 F3
Yoker Sports Centre
  SCOT G14 .... 80 F3
York Place Surgery
  KKNTL G66 .... 65 J1

Page 21
G7
1 Beatty Pl
2 Churchill Sq
3 Cochrane Pl
4 Collingwood Pl
5 Fisher Pl
6 Frotisher Pl
7 Graham Pl
8 Jellicoe Pl
9 Jervis Pl
10 Nelson Pl
11 Rodney Pl

Page 25
J3
1 Mccoil St
K1
1 Craiglomond Gdns
2 Drumkinnon Rd
3 Laudervale Gdns
4 Tullichewan Rd
K2
1 Broomley Crs
2 Cameron Dr
3 Campbell Crs
4 Kirkpatrick Crs
5 Swanson Rd
6 Tullichewan Crs
K6
1 Turnbull Crs
2 Wylie Av
K7
1 Glen Vw
2 Harrison Pl
3 Jackson Pl
4 Kane St
L1
1 Beaton Rd
2 Carrochan Rd
3 Carson Rd
4 Dalvait Gdns
5 Fisherwood Rd
6 Riverside
L3
1 Darleith Rd
2 Duncryne Rd
3 Hayes Gv
4 Hogarth Ct
5 King Edward St
6 Lindsay Gdns
7 Shantron Rd
L4
1 Creveul Ct
2 Ferry Loan
3 Grange Pl
4 Gray St
5 India St
6 James St
7 Lennox St
8 Mc Alister St
9 Munro St
10 Steven St
11 Susannah St
L5
1 Albert St
2 Arthur St
3 O'neil Ter
4 Rowanree Gv
5 Victoria St
M1
1 Carrochan Crs
2 Craiglynn Gdns
3 Granger Rd
4 Manse Garden's
5 Shandon Crs
M2
1 Bramblehedge Pth
2 Burnside Crs
3 Honeysuckle La
M4
1 Sandbank Crs
2 Scott St
3 Second Av
M5
1 Burn Street La
2 Levencroft Ms
3 Northfield Rd
4 Scott St
5 Union Street La
M6
1 Dillichip Gdns
2 George Street La
3 Kirkland La
4 Lenwood Gdns
5 Raglan Street La
6 South Church St
7 Springcroft Pl
M7
1 Helen Wy
2 Strathleven Pl
M8
1 Iona Wynd

Page 31
J3
1 Beech Pl
2 Hazel Ter
3 Moorfield La
4 Poplar Pl
5 Queensway
K2
1 Hillside Rd
2 Mcpherson Dr
3 Preston Pl
K3
1 Briar Pl
2 Cedar Pl
3 Cumbrae Pl
4 Fir Ter
5 Kingsway
6 Rose Crs
K5
1 Berwick Pl
2 Burns Rd
3 Burns Sq
4 Pembroke Pl
L1
1 Adelaide St
2 Burgh Wk
3 Church St
4 Kempock Pl
5 Station Rd
L3
1 Elm Ter
2 Henderson Ter
3 Ivy Crs
4 Larkfield Rd
5 Murray Pl
6 Stevens Pl
L4
1 Durham Rd
2 Exmouth Pl
3 Lynmouth Pl
4 Portsmouth Pl
L5
1 Dorset Pl
2 Essex Rd
3 Staffordway South
4 Suffolk Pl
M5
1 Mauchline Ter

M2
1 Adam St
2 Bay View Rd
3 Chalmers St
4 Chapel St
5 John Campbell St
6 Margaret St
7 Murial Blue Ct
8 Sharp St
9 Steel St
M4
1 Avonmouth Pl
2 Barmouth Av
M5
1 Fancy Farm Pl
2 Larkfield Gv
3 Stafford Crs
M6
1 Dingwall Dr
2 Huntly Dr
3 Stonehaven Rd

Page 32
A5
1 Cawdor Crs
2 Cawdor Pl
3 Fergus Dr
4 Fergus Pl
5 Killin Pl
6 Lawers Pl
B4
1 Auchneagh Farm Rd
2 Raven Rd
B5
1 Kilbrannan Dr
2 Pennyfern Dr
C1
1 Belleaire Dr
2 Caird Dr
3 Daldourney Dr
4 Golf Pl
5 Newark Av
6 Stoneleigh Rd
C5
1 Mary St
D1
1 Bentinck St
2 Oakleigh Dr
3 Seafield Cottage La
D5
1 Hibernia St
D6
1 Clyde Wynd
2 Crawhin Gdns
3 Glen Fruin Rd
4 Laverock Av
5 Overton Crs
D7
1 Glen Kinglas Av
E2
1 Campbell Ct
E3
1 Houston St
2 Jamaica La
3 Kelly St
E4
1 Bruce St
2 Inverkip St
3 Nelson St
4 Newton St
5 Orangefield La
6 Salmon St
7 West Shaw St
E5
1 Broomhill St
2 Togo Pl
3 Wellington St
4 Wemyss Bay St
F3
1 Ardmore Pl
2 Chromars Pl
3 Dresling Rd
4 Carvel Dr
F5
1 Argyle St
2 Crawford St
3 Grey Pl
4 Haig St
5 Hood St
6 Ker St
7 Laird St
8 Roslin St
9 West Blackhall St
F4
1 Buccleuch St
2 Charles Pl
3 Crown St
4 East Shaw St
5 Hunters Pl
6 Kilblain St
7 Mearns St
8 Nicolson St
9 Shaw Pl
10 Sir Michael Pl
11 Smith St
12 Wallace Pl
13 West Burn St
F6
1 Berryyards Rd
2 Lynedoch St

Page 33
G4
1 Brymner St
2 Cathcart Sq
3 Cathcart St
4 Cross Shore St
5 Customhouse Pl
6 Duff St
7 East Breast
8 East India Breast
9 New Dock La
10 Open Shore
11 Watt Pl
H1
1 Cartsburn St
2 Garelock Rd
3 Whinhill Rd
H5
1 Cartsburn St
2 East Blackhall St
3 Empress Ct
4 Knowe Rd
5 St Andrew St
6 Springkell St
7 Stanners La
J6
1 Auchendarroch St
2 Craigieknowes St
3 East William St
4 Galt St
5 Serpentine Wk

Page 47
M3
1 Barony Pl
2 Blantyre Gdns
3 Dunnikier Wk
4 Dysart Ct
5 Gartshore Gdns
6 Priory Pl
7 Seafield Crs
8 Valleyfield Dr
9 Wellesley Crs

B7
1 Ben Lawers Dr
2 Ben Ledi Crs
3 Ben Lui Pl
4 Ben Nevis Wy
5 Burnhouse Av
6 Cairntoul Ct
C8
1 Grangeneuk Gdns

Page 48
C6
1 Alloway Dr
2 Doon St
3 George Av
4 George Crs
5 Lochlea Av
6 Tarbolton Dr
E2
1 Abercorn St
2 Bryson St
3 Lawmuir Crs
4 Quarryknowe St
E6
1 Inchfad Pl
F1
1 Harrow Ct
2 Harrow Pl
3 Linkwood Av
4 Linkwood Crs
F8
1 Duntreath Gv

Page 61
G7
1 Dalsetter Av
2 Drumchapel Gdns
3 Whitekirk Pl
J1
1 Grampian Wy
2 Greenside Pl
K3
1 Duntocher Rd
D1
1 Ledcameroch Pk
2 Mannofield
K7
1 Banner Pl
2 Tay Rd
E8
1 Gartconnell Gdns
2 Gartconnell Rd
L5
1 Douglas Pl
2 Gartconnell Rd
L7
1 Horse Shoe Rd
D8
1 Lochview Rd
M3
1 Lennox Dr
M4
1 Kilmardinny Ga
2 Roman Av
3 Roman Gdns
4 Roman Rd
M5
1 Greenhead Rd
M6
1 Beechwood Ct
2 Beechwood La
3 Lochside

Page 62
D8
1 Ardessie St
2 Balmartin Rd
3 Carbost St
4 Carnoch St
5 Craigbo Av
6 Craigbo Pl
7 Elphin St
8 Glenbervie Pl
9 Harris Rd
10 Lewiston Dr
11 Lewiston Pl
12 Lewiston Rd
13 Milovaig Av
14 Mullardoch St
15 Staffin Dr
F4
1 Crossford Dr
2 Crosspoint Dr
3 Dungavel Dr
4 Forres St
5 Hopetoun Pl
6 Lymham Dr
7 Newcastleton Dr
8 Pencaitland Pl
9 Scorrier St
10 Wentworth Dr

Page 65
J2
1 Donaldson Crs
2 Mcarthur Pk
3 Scotsblair Av
K1
1 Castle Ct
2 Luggiebank Rd
3 Rose St
L1
1 Thistle St
L1
1 Blackdyke Rd

Page 67
M2
1 Graigside Pl
2 Inchwood Pl
3 Leckethill Ct
4 Leckethill Pl
5 Leckethill Vw
6 Mossywood Ct
7 Mossywood Pl
8 Tomtain Brae
9 Tomtain Ct
10 Woodhead Av
11 Woodhead Ct
12 Woodhead Gv
13 Woodhead Vw
M3
1 Craigelvan Ct
2 Craigelvan Dr
3 Craigelvan Gdns
4 Craigelvan Gv
5 Craigelvan Pl
6 Craigelvan Vw
7 Gairburn Ct
8 Gairburn Pl
J6
1 Henrietta St
K1
1 Cowdenhill Pl
2 Friars Pl
3 Monksbridge Av
4 Rotherwood Pl
K2
1 Cedric Pl
2 Priory Av
K3
1 Seggielea La
2 Seggielea Rd
3 Wilmot Rd
K4
1 Jordanhill Crs
K5
1 Lennox Gdns
2 Lennox La West
3 Mitre La West
4 Vancouver La
K6
1 Bowling Green Rd
2 Edzell Pl
3 Elm St
4 Palladium Pl
5 Victoria Park Gdns South
6 Victoria Park St
K7
1 Clydeholm Rd

D2
1 Clydeholm Ter
2 Millbrae Crs
3 Yokerburn Ter
D4
1 Royal Inch Ter
D5
1 Anderson Dr
2 Dunlop St
3 Fulbar Ct
4 Fulbar La
5 Houston St
6 Muir St
7 Station Rd
8 Tennant St
D6
1 Cowdray Crs
2 Donaldson Dr
3 Loanhead Av
4 Millburn Av
D7
1 The Haining
D8
1 Allen Wy
2 Cumbrae Rd
3 Pinkerton La
4 Pladda Rd
E1
1 Ladhope Pl
2 Maclean St
3 Peterson Gdns
4 Reelick Av
5 Sollas Pl
6 Webster St
E2
1 Thirdpart Crs
2 Yokerburn Pl
3 Yoker Mill Gdns
E5
1 Lasswade St
2 Tweedvale Pl
3 Yetholm St
E6
1 Merlinford Av
2 Merlinford Dr
3 Millburn Dr
4 Millburn Wy
5 Tay Av
E7
1 Ancaster La
2 Foulis St
3 Herschell St
4 Strathcona St
5 Willoughby Dr
6 Willoughby La
M1
1 Howth Ter
M1
1 Linden St
2 Muirkirk Dr
3 Netherton St
4 Sutcliffe Rd
5 Temple Gdns
6 Temple Locks Ct
7 Temple Locks Pl
8 Waldo St
M4
1 Crow La
2 King Edward Rd
3 Sackville La
4 Whittingehame La
M5
1 Beechwood Pl
2 Edgehill Rd
3 Elmwood Av
4 Poplar Av
M6
1 Baishagray Pl
2 Broomhill Gdns
3 Malborough La North
4 Naseby Av
5 Norby Rd
6 Thornwood Dr
7 Thornwood Quadrant
M7
1 Auchentorlie St
2 Dunbeith Pl
3 Broomhill Av
4 Broomhill Rd
5 Central Av
6 Thornwood Gdns
F1
1 Garscadden Rd South
2 Portsoy Av
3 Wyvis Quadrant
F2
1 Colmonell Av
F3
1 Carlibar Av
F4
1 Blawarthill St
2 Lady Anne St
F8
1 Inverglas Av

Page 81
G2
1 Glanderston Ct
2 Glanderston Dr
3 Southbar Av
G4
1 Anniesland Rd
G5
1 Gosford La
2 Riversdale La
3 Thornden La
H3
1 Boreland Pl
2 Embo Dr
3 Northbrae Pl
H4
1 Danes Crs
2 Garion Dr
3 Kingsway Ct
4 Talbot Ct
5 Talbot Pl
H5
1 Duchall Pl
2 Larchfield Pl
3 Linnhead Pl
4 Lounsdale Pl
5 Redgate Pl
J1
1 Tabard Rd
J4
1 Laurel Park Gdns
2 Northland Av
3 Northland Gdns
4 Queen Victoria Ga
5 Windyedge Crs
6 Windyedge Pl
J5
1 Duncan La North
2 Duncan La South
3 Dunglass Av
4 Dunglass La
5 Dunglass La North
6 Dunglass La South
7 Earlbank La North
8 Earl Pl
9 Norse La South
10 Norse Pl
11 Northland Dr
12 Ormiston La
13 Ormiston La South
14 Ormiston La South
15 Upland La
16 Upland Rd
17 Vancouver La
18 Verona Gdns
J6
1 Great Western Rd
B4
1 Great Western Rd
2 Lismore Rd
3 Norwich Dr
E4
1 Amisfield St
2 Leyden Gdns
3 Oran Gdns
4 Sandfield St
5 Shakespeare St
6 Shortridge St
E5
1 Clouston La
2 Kelvinside La
3 Kelvinside Gardens La
4 Northumberland La
5 Oran Pl
E6
1 Alfred La
2 Belmont St
3 Bower St
4 Colebrooke Pl
5 Colebrooke St
6 Hamilton Park Av
7 Kelvinside Ter West
8 Lothian Gdns
9 Southpark Av
E7
1 Bothwell La
2 Caledonian Crs
3 Cecil St
4 Eton La
5 Great George St
6 Oakfield La
7 Otago La North
8 Otago La South
9 South Woodside Rd
10 West Prince's La

L2
1 Greywood St
2 Sutcliffe Rd
L3
1 Castlebank St
2 Castlebank Gdns
3 Castlebank Vls
4 Chamberlain Rd
5 Craigend Pl
6 Craigend St
7 Greenlea St
L4
1 Austen La
2 Austen Rd
3 Borden La
4 Chamberlain La
5 Jordanhill La
6 King Edward La
7 Milner La
8 Milner Rd
9 Selborne Pl
10 Selborne Place La
L5
1 Airthrey La
2 Glendore St
3 Harmsworth St
4 Inchholm La
5 Inchholm St
6 Westbrae Dr
L6
1 Essex La
2 Orleans La
3 Tudor La South
4 Tudor Rd
L7
1 Balshagray Crs
2 Glendore St
3 Harmsworth St
4 Inchholm La
5 Inchholm St
6 Morna La
7 Smith St
C6
1 Athole Gdns
2 Bowmount Gdns
3 Crown Circ
4 Crown Gdns
5 Crown Rd North
6 Downside La
7 Huntly Rd
8 Marchmont Ter
9 Princes Terrace La
10 Victoria Circ
11 Victoria Crescent Pl
12 Victoria Crescent Rd
C7
1 Benalder St
2 Caledon La
3 Dalcross St
4 Havelock La
5 Keith St
6 Mansfield St
7 Moy St
8 Sutherland La
9 Telephone La
10 Torness St
11 University Pl
C8
1 Partick Bridge St
2 Thurso St
D1
1 Arrochar Ct
2 Lyndale Pl
D3
1 Beauly Pl
2 Cartbridge Dr
3 Fogo Pl
4 Gairbraid Pl
5 Glenfinnan Pl
6 Kelvindale Pl
7 Strathcarron Pl
8 Strathy Pl
D4
1 Ardressie Pl
2 Dunbeith Pl
3 Garrioch Crs
4 Garrioch Ga
5 Invershin Dr
6 Kirkhill Dr
7 Kirkhill Pl
8 Latherton Dr
9 Melvaig Pl
10 Towie Pl
11 Wyndford Pl

Page 82
A1
1 Ilay Av
A3
1 Kendal La
2 Westerlands
A4
1 Arnwood Dr
2 Cranborne Rd
3 Daventry Dr
4 Monmouth Av
A6
1 Blairatholl Av
2 Blairatholl Gdns
3 Kirkmichael Gdns
4 Monkscroft Av
5 Tibbermore Rd
A7
1 Apsley La
2 Ardery St
3 Crawford St
4 Exeter Dr
5 Fairlie Park Dr
6 Monkscroft Ct
7 Monkscroft Gdns
8 Thornwood Gdns
A8
1 Crawford St
B3
1 Baronald Ga
2 Cleveden La
3 Daleview Av
4 Ferngrove Av
5 Hertford Av
6 Highfield Pl
7 Lindsay Dr
8 Nottingham Av
9 Nottingham La
D5
1 Kirklee Circ
2 Kirklee Gdns
3 Kirklee Quadrant
4 Kirklee Terrace La
5 Wyndham St
D6
1 Buckingham St
2 Burgh La
3 Cresswell La
4 Cresswell St
5 Grosvenor La
6 Grosvenor Crescent La
7 Kersland La
8 Observatory Rd
9 Saltoun La
10 Sandringham La
11 Vincombe La
D7
1 Ashton La
2 Ashton La North
3 Hillhead St
4 Lilybank Gardens La
5 Lilybank La
6 Lilybank Ter
7 Lilybank Terrace La
D8
1 Arthur St
2 Clayslaps Rd
3 Hastie St
4 Lumsden La
5 Old Dumbarton Rd
E1
1 Brigham Pl
2 Broughton Dr
3 Portmarnock Dr
4 Whitecraigs Pl
E3
1 Fernie Gdns
2 Lochburn Gv
3 Lochburn Pas
4 Mclaren Gdns

C2
1 Fingal La
2 Glencloy St
3 Lennox St
4 Millhouse St
C3
1 Fortingall Av
2 Gairbraid Ct
3 Stonefield Av
C4
1 Bellshaugh Pl
2 Hopefield Av
3 Thornbridge Av
C5
1 Belhaven Ter West
2 Belhaven Terrace West La
3 Great Western Terrace La
4 Kensington Ga
5 Kensington Gate La
6 Kirklee Circ
7 Kirklee Gdns
8 Kirklee Rd
9 Lancaster Crescent La
10 Lorraine Gdns
11 Lorraine Gardens La
12 Lorraine Rd
13 Redlands La
14 Redlands Rd
15 Redlands Terrace La
16 Westbourne Gardens La
17 Westbourne Terrace La North
18 Westbourne Terrace La South

Page 83
E8
1 Claremont Ter
2 Claremont Terrace La
3 Clifton St
4 Craigmaddie Terrace La
5 La Belle Allee
6 La Belle Pl
7 North Claremont St
8 Park Gardens La
9 Parkgrove Terrace La
F4
1 Ruchill Pl
F5
1 Dunard St
2 Kelvindale Av
3 Kelvinside Gardens East
F6
1 Belmont St
2 Bonawe St
3 Drybrugh Gdns
4 Dunard St
5 Henderson St
6 Herbert St
7 Jardine St
8 Jedburgh St
9 North Woodside Rd
10 Yarrow Gdns
F7
1 Barrington Dr
2 Herbert St
3 Holyrood Crs
4 Holyrood Quadrant
5 Lansdowne Crs
6 Montague St
7 Napiershall Pl
8 Queen's Crs
9 St Clair St
10 Westend Park St
11 Willowbank Crs
12 Willowbank St
13 Woodlands Dr
F8
1 Baliol La
2 Clairmont Gdns
3 Claremont Pas
4 Claremont Pl
5 Lynedoch Crs
6 Lynedoch Crescent La
7 Lynedoch St
8 Somerset Pl
9 Somerset Place Ms
10 Woodlands Ga
11 Woodside Pl
12 Woodside La
G2
1 Greenmount
G3
1 Hazlitt Gdns
2 Hazlitt St
3 Parkbrae Gdns
4 Parkbrae Pl
5 Parkside Pl
6 Whitworth St
G5
1 Wester Common Dr
2 Wester Common Rd
G6
1 Barr St
2 Grovepark St
3 Maitlands La
4 Nansen St
G7
1 Braid St
2 Burnbank Pl
3 Cedar Ct
4 Cedar St
5 Clarendon Pl
6 Cromwell St
7 Gladstone St
8 Grovepark Ct
9 Grove Park Gdns
10 St Peter's St
11 Unity Pl
12 Windsor St
G8
1 Hill St
H2
1 Kilfinan St
H4
1 Balmore Pl
H5
1 Ardoch St
2 Carbeth St
M6
1 Appleby St
2 Cleghorn St
3 Eltham St
4 Hornshill St
5 Littlehill St
6 Lumloch St
7 Rushyhill St
H7
1 Dundashill
2 Edington St
3 Mansea Pl
4 Possil Rd
H8
1 Cambridge St
2 Dalhousie St
3 Dunblane St
4 Mcaslin St
5 Larbert St
6 Shamrock St
7 Stewart St
J1
1 Castlebay Pl
2 Egilsay Ter
3 Longay Pl
4 Raasay Pl
5 Skerray Quadrant
6 Torogay Ter
J3
1 Glenhead Crs
J4
1 Hawthorn Quadrant
J5
1 Allander St
2 Bardowie St
3 Stonyhurst St
J6
1 Coldstream St
J8
1 Dobbie's Loan
2 Port Dundas Rd
K2
1 Ensay St
2 Westray Pl
K3
1 Westray Circ
C1
1 Cypress St
2 Spruce St
3 Walnut St

K6
1 Endrick St
2 Inverurie St
3 Keppochhill Dr
4 Keppoch St
K8
1 Kyle St
2 North Wallace St
3 Stafford St
L1
1 Coltmuir Crs
2 Coltmuir Gdns
3 Shillay St
4 Torogay Pl
5 Viewfield St
L2
1 Castleton Av
2 Coliston Pth
3 Coltmuir Dr
4 Everard Pl
5 Liddesdale Pl
6 Liddesdale Pl
7 Liddesdale Sq
L3
1 Huntershill St
L5
1 Gourlay St
2 Millarbank St
3 Springburn Wy
4 Springvale Ter
L6
1 Morrin St
2 Valleyfield St
L7
1 Fountainwell Sq
2 Huntingdon Rd
3 Huntingdon Sq
L6
1 Charles St
L8
1 Coltpark La
2 Forrester Ct
3 Hillcroft Ter
M3
1 Huntershill Wy
2 Milton Dr
3 Newbold Av
4 Southview Ct
5 Strathkelvin Av
M4
1 Barclay St
2 Broomfield Rd
3 Downs St
4 Edgefauld Pl
5 Lenzie St
6 St Monance St
M6
1 Auchinloch St
2 Edgefauld Av
3 Romulus Ct
4 Southloch Gdns
5 Southloch St
M8
1 Gadshill St
2 Glenbarr St

Page 84
A1
1 Huntershill Rd
2 Muirpark Ter
3 Thomas Muir Av
4 Willow Av
A2
1 Liddells Ct
A4
1 Cornhill St
A5
1 Boghead Rd
2 Cardarrach St
3 Cardyke St
4 Dykemuir Quadrant
5 Eastcroft Ter
6 Foyers Ter
7 Gartferry St
8 Hornshill St
9 Lilybank Rd
10 Lumloch St
11 Rushyhill St
A6
1 Aspen Dr
2 Barnhill Dr
3 Forestfield Gdns
4 Holly Dr
5 Redwood Dr
6 Yew Dr
A8
1 Blochairn Pl
2 Brodick St
3 Cartcraig Pl
4 Christopher St
5 Clare St
6 Cloverbank St
7 Dunolly St
8 Forrestfield St
9 Kintyre St
10 Sandmill St
B1
1 Briar Neuk
2 Cargill Sq
3 Heath Av
4 Lilac Gdns
5 Rose Dr
6 Sinclair Gdns
B2
1 James Dunlop Gdns
B3
1 Eastburn Pl
2 Woodhill Rd
B5
1 Dykemuir Pl
2 Petershill Pl

C3
1 Acredyke Rd
2 Birdston Rd
3 Dulsie Rd
4 Gadsburn Ct
C4
1 Newmill Rd
2 Rockfield Pl
3 Ryehill Pl
4 Sidland Rd
C5
1 Bishopmill Pl
2 Bucksburn Rd
3 Leadburn Rd
4 Quarrywood Av
5 Torryburn Rd
D1
1 Hillview Gdns
2 Letham Gv
3 Lundie Gdns
D3
1 Briarcroft Dr
D5
1 Zena Pl
D6
1 Lochgreen St
D7
1 Blackhill Pl
2 Moodiesburn St
D8
1 Duchray La
2 Leader St
3 Nith St
E3
1 Auchinleck Av
2 Auchinleck Gdns
3 Briarcroft Pl
4 Louden Hill Pl
E7
1 Barnwood Ct
2 Hallbrae St
3 Lochwood St
E8
1 Lethamhill Pl
2 Naver St
3 Riddrievale St
4 Teith St
F3
1 Drumcog Gdns
2 Glenbank Dr
3 Glengavel Crs
4 Pathhead Gdns
5 Pinkerry Dr
6 Saughs Pl
F6
1 Lochview Pl

Page 85
H7
1 Banff Pl
2 Gilbertfield Pl
3 Clendenon Sq
4 Hallforest St
5 Lenzie St
6 Maxwell St
7 Meetinghouse La
8 Moncrieff St
9 Mossvale Rd
10 New Sneddon St
11 Orr Sq
12 School Wynd
13 Stoney Brae
H8
1 Borthwick St
2 Campston Pl
3 Coblington Pl

Page 86
D1
1 Bowling Green Rd
2 Hillcrest
L6
1 Auchingill Pl
2 Canonbie St
3 Cordach Pl
4 Dalilea Pl
5 Glenelg Quadrant
6 Rachan St

H6
1 Arkwrights Wy
2 Coats St
3 Spookers Rd
4 Weavers Rd
5 West La
H8
1 Glenholme Av
2 Hawick Av
J4
1 Clavering St East
2 Douglas St
J5
1 Carbrook St
2 Clavering St West
3 Woodside Crs
J7
1 Strathdon Av
2 Thistle St
J8
1 Ravenscraig Av
2 Rooksdell Av
K2
1 Lansbury Gdns
2 Larkin Gdns
3 Mclean Pl
4 Shortroods Crs
K3
1 Caledonia St
2 Mossvale La
K4
1 Henderson St
2 Galshaw Brae
3 Gilmartin Rd
K5
1 Barr Pl
2 Sir Michael Pl
3 Tower Ter
4 Townhead Ter
K7
1 Polsons Crs
L1
1 White Cart Rd
L2
1 Fleming St
2 Laighpark Vw
L3
1 Back Sneddon St
2 Carlile Pl
3 Gilmour St
4 Smith's La
L4
1 Back Sneddon St
2 Blacklaw La
3 Cart La
4 Central Rd
5 Central Wy
6 Christie La
7 County Pl
8 County Sq
9 Dyers' Wynd
10 Harbour La
11 Hunter St
12 Maxwell St
13 Meetinghouse La
14 Moncrieff St
15 New Sneddon St
16 Orr Sq
17 School Wynd
18 Stoney Brae
L5
1 Brown's La
2 Causeyside St
3 Forbes Pl
4 George La
5 George Pl
6 Johnston St
7 Marshall's La
8 New St
9 St Mirren St
L6
1 South Campbell St
2 Speirsfield Gdns
3 Stow St
L7
1 Carriagehill Av
2 Charlotte St
3 Forest Pl
4 Lylesland Ct
5 Mcintyre Pl
6 Union St
7 Wester Carriagehill
L8
1 Cheviot Rd
2 Plaintrees Ct
3 Sunnyside Gv
4 Thornly Park Gdns
M4
1 Bank St
2 Brick La
3 Christie St
4 East Buchanan St
5 Glasgow Rd
6 Millar St
7 Renfrew Rd
8 Walkinreuk
M5
1 Bladda La
2 Dixon St
M6
1 Hunterhill Rd
A6
1 St Ninian's Crs
A8
1 Aboyne Dr
2 Quarry Rd
3 Stonefield Rd

Page 99
L1
1 Locherburn Pl
2 Locher Gait
3 Locher Gdns
4 Netherburn Av
M8
1 Quarrelton Gv
2 Rowantree Rd

Page 100
A4
1 Blackwood Av
2 Caldwell Av
3 Ellon Dr
4 Howden Dr
5 Kinloch Av
6 Lorne Dr
A6
1 Co-operative Ter
2 Peockland Gdns
3 Peockland Pl
A8
1 Cotton Av
2 Pearson Pl
3 Ryewraes Rd

Page 101
G4
1 Calder Rd
2 Candren Wy
3 Dalskeith Crs
4 Fergus Dr
5 Killoch La
6 Killoch Wy
G5
1 Crookston Gdns
2 Crookston Pl
3 Dalfoil Ct
4 Kelhead Av
F6
1 Cairnhill Pl
2 Cronberry Ter
F8
1 Bullwood Dr

H5
1 Ladykirk Crs
H4
1 Bankfoot Dr
H5
1 Angus Pl
2 Cardonald Gdns
3 Moulin Circ
H6
1 Dormanside Pl
2 Dormanside La
3 Dormanside Gv
H8
1 Leithland Av
J1
1 Hardgate Pl
J2
1 Langcroft La
2 Shieldhall Gdns
K1
1 Queensland Ct
2 Queensland La East
3 Queensland La West
4 Rigmuir Rd
K3
1 Berryknowes La
2 Glengarry Dr
3 Hillington Park Circ
4 Midlem Gv
5 Mossview La
J5
1 Blairgowrie Rd
2 Bucklaw Pl
3 Kirriemuir Pl
4 Tealing Crs
J7
1 Everton Rd
2 Hapland Av
J8
1 Byrebush Rd
K1
1 Greenloan Av
K2
1 Cowden St
2 Langcroft Ter
3 Langlands Av
4 Mallaig Pl
5 Marchglen Pl
6 Meldon Pl
7 Melness Pl
8 Melvick Pl
9 Mybster Pl
K4
1 Mossview Quadrant
K8
1 Braidcraft Ter
2 Linthaugh Ter
3 Neilsland Sq
L2
1 Ardnish St
2 Drumoyne Av
3 Drumoyne Sq
4 Largo Pl
5 Lunan Pl
L3
1 Craigton Pl
2 Drumoyne Rd
3 Drumoyne Quadrant
L4
1 Barlogan Quadrant
2 Bowmore Rd
3 Colonsay Rd
4 Luing Rd
L5
1 Cemetery Rd
2 Corkerhill Gdns
3 Lora Dr
4 Maree Dr
L6
1 Alyth Gdns
2 Arnholm Pl
L7
1 Hardridge Av
2 Hardridge Rd
L8
1 Cheviot Rd
M1
1 Fairfield Gdns
2 Fairfield Pl
M2
1 Elderpark Gdns
2 Elderpark Gv
3 Langlands Ct
M3
1 Cruden St
2 Tarland St
M4
1 Moldart Crs
2 Moldart Pl
M6
1 Airth La
2 Balloch Gdns
M7
1 Balblair Rd

Page 102
D4
1 Tylney Rd
D5
1 Drummond Dr
E1
1 Cunningham Dr
F4
1 Gartartan Rd
G4
1 Crookston Ct
2 Crookston Dr
3 Dalfoil Ct
4 Kelhead Av
G7
1 Greenways Ct
2 Inverkar Dr
3 Lochbroom Dr
4 Lochearn Crs
G8
1 Coldstream Dr
2 Delston Dr
3 Kelso Av
4 St Abb's Dr
H3
1 Darkwood Dr
2 Muirdykes Av
H4
1 Westwood Gdns
C5
1 Crookston Ct
2 Crookston Gv
3 Crookston Pl
4 Latimer Gdns
H2
1 Ainslie Rd

Page 103
G1
1 Hillington Gdns
G2
1 Carnegie Rd
2 Nasmyth Rd
3 Seaforth Rd
C1
1 Buchanan St
2 Glendale Gdns
3 Ruthven St
C2
1 Auchinairn Rd
2 Buchanan St
3 Ferness Pl
4 Glendale Pl
5 The Groves
6 Thomas St
H4
1 Westwood Gdns
C5
1 Fergusslie Wk
2 Knox St
3 Thomas St

Page 104
A1
1 Burleigh St
2 Garmouth Ct
3 Garmouth Gdns
4 Harmony Rw
5 Mckechnie St
6 Pearce La
7 Pearce St
8 Rosneath St
9 Wardrop St
A2
1 Harmony Pl
2 Harmony Sq
3 Rafford St
A4
1 Ardo Gdns
A5
1 Dumbreck Sq
2 First Gdns
3 Terregles Av
A6
1 Dumbreck Pth
2 Dumbreck Rd
B2
1 Orkney Pl
B3
1 Brighton Pl
2 Copland Quadrant
3 Harrison Dr
4 Mafeking St
B4
1 Hinshelwood Pl
2 Ibroxholm Pl
3 Merrick Gdns
B5
1 Fleurs Rd
C1
1 Thornbank St
C2
1 Burndyke Sq

M4
1 Albany Crs
2 Central Av
3 Elizabeth Quadrant
4 Thankerton Av

M5
1 Regency Wy

M6
1 James Vw
2 Laidlaw Av
3 Murdoch Pl
4 Queens Crs

Page 134

A4
1 Alexandria Quadrant
2 Beechgrove Quadrant
3 Burnside Quadrant
4 Centenary Quadrant
5 Diana Quadrant
6 Mcdonald Pl
7 St Andrews St
8 Trossachs Av

A6
1 Blackmoor Pl
2 Esdaile Ct
3 Ivy Pl
4 Phoenix Pl

A7
1 Bannockburn Pl
2 Cromdale Wy
3 Elm Rd
4 Hillhead Crs
5 North Av

B8
1 Byresknowe La
2 Coalhall Av
3 Eastend Av
4 Motherwell Rd

E5
1 Caledonia Dr
2 Clockerhill Pl
3 Mccormack Gdns
4 Pickerstonhill

E8
1 Jones Wynd

F4
1 Allandale Av
2 Innermanse Quadrant

F5
1 Church St
2 Greenfield Quadrant
3 Greenside St

Page 144

B8
1 Bellman's Cl
2 Caledonia Rd
3 King's Ct
4 Kirk Vw
5 Laigh Ct
6 Main St
7 Medine Ct
8 Muirpark Rd
9 Somerville Ct
10 Wee Cl
11 Wilson St
12 Woodside Rd

Page 150

B4
1 Blair Gdns
2 Craigievar Pl
3 Craig Pl
4 Crarea Pl
5 Easdale Pl
6 Raasay Gdns
7 Rossie Gv
8 Threave Pl
9 Westerlands Pl

B5
1 Kilkerran Ct
2 Kilkerran Pk
3 Kilkerran Wy
4 Rozelle Dr
5 Rozelle Pl
6 Westerlands Gv

F4
1 Cedarwood Av

F5
1 Blackhouse Gdns
2 Blackhouse Rd
3 Broomhill Gdns

F6
1 Castlemount Av

Page 151

H5
1 Abernethy Pl
2 Bankfoot Pl
3 Birnam Pl
4 Blairatholl Crs
5 Crathie Pl
6 Gleneagles Ga
7 Scone Pl

Page 153

G8
1 Antigua Wy
2 Bahamas Wy
3 Barbados Gn
4 Dominica Gn
5 Tobago Pl
6 Trinidad Gn
7 Watling Pl

J5
1 Brooklime Gdns
2 Burnet Rose Ct
3 Burnet Rose Gdns
4 Burnet Rose Pl
5 Macarthur Crs

J6
1 Bellflower Ct
2 Carmunnock Rd
3 Dunnottar Ct
4 Dunnottar Crs
5 Esk Dl
6 Macarthur Pl
7 Macarthur Gdns
8 Macpherson Pk
9 Silverdale
10 Wensleydale

J7
1 Methven Pl
2 Mitchell Ct
3 Mitchell Gv
4 Rosenheath Ga
5 West Ga

K6
1 Barassie
2 Cawdor Wy
3 Croy
4 Duart Dr
5 Dunrobin Ct
6 Dunrobin Crs
7 Dunvegan Pl
8 Fulmar Pk
9 Kildrummy Pl
10 Pennyroyal Ct
11 Scone Pl
12 Thistle Pl

K7
1 Cadzow Gn
2 Dalmellington Ct
3 Dalmellington Dr
4 Doonfoot Gdns

K8
1 Falkland Pl
2 Valleyfield

L7
1 Ashton Gn
2 Kirkton Ga
3 Ladybank Ct
4 Ladybank Gdns
5 Stuarton Pk

L8
1 Brouster Pl
2 Cloverhill Ter
3 Creighton Gv
4 Cunninghame Rd
5 Holm La
6 Newlands Pl

M6
1 Bosfield Cnr
2 Dunglass Sq
3 Lochaber Pl
4 Manse La
5 Rannoch Gn
6 Wardrop Pl

M7
1 Dunblane Pl
2 Guthrie Pl
3 Jedburgh Pl
4 Kittoch Pl
5 Ladybank Pl
6 Lindsay Gv
7 Montgomery Pl
8 Montgomery St
9 Pankhurst Pl
10 St Bryde St

Page 154

B5
1 Lauder Gn

B6
1 Abercromby Pl
2 Ayton Pk South
3 Drummond Pl
4 Maxwellton Pl
5 Munro Pl
6 Pollok Pl

B8
1 Garnock Pk
2 Glen Urquhart

C8
1 Davaar

Page 155

J1
1 Broad Sq
2 Columba Pth
3 Dyfrig St
4 Kintyre Rd
5 Oaklea Crs
6 Sycamore Gv
7 Wheatlandhead Ct

J2
1 Windyridge Pl

K1
1 Birch Pl
2 Cameron Wy
3 Valerio Ct
4 Wolcott Dr

K2
1 Coldstream St
2 Selkirk St

K3
1 Braehead
2 Carrick Gdns
3 Mossbank

K4
1 Loanfoot Rd

M4
1 Udston Ter

M5
1 Stanley St

M6
1 Hillhouse Ter
2 St Ninian's Pl
3 St Ninian's Rd
4 Shandon Ter

M7
1 Campsie Vw

Page 156

A4
1 Burnbank Centre
2 Crawford St
3 Gladstone Ct
4 Holyrood St
5 Limetree Ct
6 Mcgowan Pl
7 Queen St
8 Stewart St
9 Wilson St
10 Windsor Gdns

B3
1 Abbotsford Crs
2 Atholl St
3 Backmuir St
4 Dryburgh St

B6
1 Cameron Crs
2 Chantinghall Ter

C5
1 Douglas Park La
2 Douglas St
3 Peacock Dr
4 West Stewart St

C7
1 Arden Ter
2 Hillside La
3 West Glebe Ter

D5
1 Almada La
2 Guthrie St
3 Saffronhall Crs
4 Saffronhall La

D7
1 Alness Ter
2 Dalmeny Rd
3 Gardenside Rd
4 Wylie St

D8
1 Alexander Balfour Gdns
2 Arden Ter
3 Croftwood Rd
4 Hutchison St

E5
1 Back O' Barns
2 Cadzow Pk
3 Common Gn
4 Fore Rw
5 Lower Auchingramont Rd
6 Portwell
7 Sheiling Hl

E6
1 Avon St
2 Gateside St
3 Lamb St
4 Strathmore Rd

E7
1 Burnside La
2 Centenary Gdns
3 Cypress Ct
4 Johnstone Rd
5 Neilson Ct
6 Portland Pk
7 Portland Sq
8 Rowan Ri
9 Selkirk Pl
10 Selkirk Pl
11 Woodside Av

E8
1 Allanton Pl
2 Riverdale Gdns
3 Waterside Gdns

F5
1 Back O'barns

F6
1 Bourne St
2 Landsdowne Gdns
3 Miller Field Pl
4 Spencer Field Gdns
5 Staneacre Pk
6 Townhead St

F7
1 Castlehill Gdns
2 Juniper Gv

Page 157

H1
1 Lismore Av

H3
1 Devon Wy
2 Haughview Rd
3 Kay Gdns

J3
1 Wellpark Rd

J6
1 Crawford Gdns
2 Kenneth Rd
3 Ross Dr

K1
1 Lantana Gv
2 Sunflower Gdns

K5
1 Grenadier Gdns

L2
1 Hope St
2 Menteith Rd
3 Paterson St
4 Roman Rd
5 St Vincent Pl
6 Scott St

L4
1 Aster Gdns
2 Factory Rd
3 Glencairn St

M1
1 Calderbank Ter

M2
1 Albert St
2 Calder Vw
3 Coursington Gdns
4 Coursington Pl
5 Coursington Rd
6 Draffen St

M4
1 Blair Pth
2 Macdonald St
3 Toll St
4 Windmill St

M5
1 Woodlands St

Page 158

B5
1 Burnside St
2 Finnie Wynd
3 Howson Lea
4 Money Gv
5 Rice Wy

E6
1 New Ashtree St

Page 159

H4
1 Applecross Quadrant
2 Berriedale Quadrant
3 Forres Quadrant
4 Laburnum Crs
5 Nairn Quadrant
6 The Steading

H6
1 The Clachan
2 Library Rd
3 Robin Pl
4 Shand St
5 Swallow Rd

H7
1 Mcalpine Pl
2 McInnes Ct

J4
1 Stobo St

J7
1 Bush Crs
2 Knowehead Rd
3 The Roundel

J8
1 Conservation Pl
2 Dimsdale Crs
3 Perchy Vw
4 Sneddon Av

K2
1 Larchfield Gv

M3
1 Barrisdale Rd
2 Muirside Pl
3 Queen St
4 Shiel Ter
5 Stanecraigs Pl

Page 171

H1
1 Algoma Pl
2 Columbia Pl
3 Reddiffe Dr
4 Riverton Dr

H5
1 Inverclov Ct
2 Machrie Gn
3 Pirnmill Av
4 Torbeg Gdns

H6
1 Moorfoot Gdns

J1
1 Alberta Crs
2 Barkly Ter
3 Bunbury Ter
4 Hudson Wy
5 Le Froy La
6 Lethbridge Pl
7 Melbourne Gn
8 Sydney Pl

J3
1 St Andrews Ct

K2
1 Armstrong Gv
2 Livingstone Crs
3 Simpson Pl

K3
1 Sycamore Ct

K4
1 Drumduff
2 Laurel Pl
3 Whitelee

L1
1 Bell Gn West
2 Caledonian St
3 Denholm Crs
4 Fleming St
5 Hill Vw
6 Macadam Pl
7 Muirhouse La
8 Rutherford Sq

L2
1 Cullen La
2 Heathery Knowe
3 Lairshill Rd
4 The Murray Sq
5 Strathcona La

L3
1 Andersen Ct
2 Grantoften Pth
3 Odense Ct
4 Tivoli Ct

L4
1 Anderside
2 Broughton
3 Drumloch Gdns
4 Mosslingal
5 Mountherrick
6 Powbrone

M1
1 Denholm Gn
2 Sinclair Pk
3 Todhills North
4 Todhills South

M2
1 Somerville La

Page 176

A8
1 Bemersyde Av
2 Loch Park Pl
3 Robert Smillie Crs

C7
1 Afton St
2 Catrine St
3 Cheviot Rd
4 Chillin Pl
5 Doon St
6 Hareleeshill Rd
7 Landsdowne Rd
8 Wallace Dr
9 Woodburn Ter

C8
1 Bannockburn Dr
2 Bertram St
3 Blair Atholl Dr
4 Dickson St
5 Glen Fruin Dr
6 Howard St
7 Pitlochry Dr
8 Rannoch Ter

Page 178

E6
1 Cooper Av
2 Hemmingen Ct
3 Neidpath Rd
4 Nimmo Pl
5 Tantallion Ct
6 Yvetot Ct

Page 191

J5
1 Armour Pl
2 Dalry Rd
3 Carthland Dr
4 Hazel Av

J6
1 Birch Ter
2 Central Quadrant
3 Cuninghame Rd
4 Eglinton Sq
5 Harvey St
6 Woodland Pl

J7
1 Anderson Ter
2 Fullerton Sq
3 School Pl
4 Seton La
5 Seton St
6 Winton La
7 Winton Pl

Page 193

H6
1 Braid Ct
2 Carnoustie Ct
3 Dalmahoy Wy
4 Dornoch Ct
5 Eden Ct
6 Ganton Ct
7 Nairn Ct
8 Sutton Ct
9 Thornhill Ct
10 Turnberry Ct
11 West Doura Wy

Page 199

G6
1 St Mungo's

Page 206

E8
1 David Orr St
2 Inkerman Pl
3 North Hamilton St
4 Robert Stewart Pl
5 Warwickhill Rd
6 West Fullarton St

Page 207

G8
1 Boyd Ct
2 Morris La
3 Union St

J8
1 Macallister Pl
2 Macauley Pl
3 Macbeth Gdns
4 Macdonald Pl
5 Macdougall Pl
6 Macinnes Pl
7 Macintosh Pl
8 Mackie Pl
9 Macnicol Pl

Page 211

K2
1 Fir Pl
2 Galrigside Rd
3 Heather Pl
4 Laurel Pl
5 Thirdpart Pl

K3
1 East Cargleston Av
2 Holmes Crs

Page 212

A5
1 Broomhill Rd East
2 Lawers Crs
3 Lawers Rd
4 Witchknowe Ct

A6
1 Cheviot Av
2 Dumgoyne Rd
3 Peatland Rd
4 Wyvis Rd

Page 225

G8
1 Content St
2 Limonds Wynd
3 Phillip Sq
4 Queen's Quadrant
5 Russell St

J1
1 Boyd St
2 Briarhill St
3 Broompark Crs
4 Duart Crs
5 Hunter St
6 Salisbury Pl
7 Tramore Crs

J2
1 Craigneil Dr
2 Cunninghame Rd
3 Hawthorn Av
4 Hawthorn Gdns

J4
1 Benmore
2 Creran Ct
3 Devilla Ct
4 Fearnoch
5 Laighland

K5
1 Boundary Rd

L7
1 Drummond Crs
2 Main Rd
3 Sannox Vw
4 Whitletts Ct

M7
1 Thornyflat Crs

Page 231

H5
1 Arthurston Ter
2 Barngore Dr
3 Burgoyne Dr
4 Carnell Dr
5 Chestnut Gv
6 Douglas Rd
7 Gadgirth Ct
8 Meadow Pk
9 Milton Pk
10 Ramseyston Dr
11 Whitehill Wy

Notes

Notes

Notes

Notes